Collins Student Atl

C000224738

MAP SKILLS

- iii Map symbols and Map types
- iv Graphs and Statistics
- 1 Latitude and Longitude
- 2 Scale
- 3 Projections
- 4 Aerial photographs
- 5 Introducing GIS
- 6–7 Satellite images

UNITED KINGDOM

- 8–9 Southeast England
- 10–11 Wales and Southwest England
- 12–13 Northern England
- 14–15 Northern Ireland and Southern Scotland
- 16–17 Northern Scotland
- 18 Ireland
- 19 Satellite Image
- 20–21 Political
- 22 Relief
- 23 Geology
- 24–25 Climate
- 26 Agriculture and Forestry
- 27 Agriculture and Fishing
- 28 Industry
- 29 Energy
- 30–31 Population and Migration
- 32 Transport
- 33 Tourism

EUROPE

- 34 Relief
- 35 Political
- 36 Climate
- 37 Tourism
- 38 Economic Activity
- 39 European Union
- 40 Population
- 41 Cities
- 42 Netherlands, Belgium and Luxembourg
- 43 Scandinavia
- 44 France
- 45 Spain and Portugal
- 46–47 Central Europe
- 48–49 Mediterranean Basin
- 50–51 Southeast Europe
- 52–53 Eastern Europe
- 54–55 Russia

NORTH AMERICA

- 56 Relief
- 57 Political
- 58 Climate
- 59 Natural Hazards
- 60–61 Canada
- 62–63 United States of America
- 64 USA: Population
- 65 USA: Economy
- 66–67 Mexico and the Caribbean

SOUTH AMERICA

- 68 Relief
- 69 Political
- 70 Climate
- 71 Economy and Population
- 72–73 South America
- 74 Brazil: Population
- 75 Brazil: Migration, Economy and Trade
- 76–77 Brazil: Deforestation

AFRICA

- 78 Relief
- 79 Political
- 80 Climate
- 81 Land Use
- 82 Population and Wealth
- 83 Southern Africa
- 84–85 Northern Africa

ASIA

- 86 Relief
- 87 Political
- 88–89 Climate
- 90–91 Population and Cities
- 92 Land Use
- 93 Middle East: Oil and Gas
- 94–95 Middle East
- 96 Pakistan, India, Bangladesh and Myanmar
- 97 India and Bangladesh: Population
- 98–99 China
- 100 China: Population
- 101 China: Land Use and Trade
- 102–103 Southeast Asia
- 104 Japan: Relief and Land Use
- 105 Japan: Economic Activity, Population and Tectonics

OCEANIA

- 106 Relief and Climate
- 107 Political and Climate
- 108–109 Australia and New Zealand
- 110 Australia: Land Use, People and Natural Hazards
- 111 Australia: Minerals and Manufacturing
- 112 The Arctic Ocean and Antarctica

WORLD

- 113 International Organizations
- 114–115 Political
- 116–117 Relief
- 118–119 Tectonics
- 120–121 Climatic Systems
- 122–123 Climatic Regions
- 124–125 Climate Statistics
- 126–127 Biomes, Soils and Soil Erosion
- 128 Agriculture
- 129 Inequalities
- 130–131 Population
- 132 Urbanization
- 133 Migration
- 134 Birth and Death Rate, Infant Mortality Rate
- 135 Life Expectancy, Literacy and Doctors
- 136 HDI, Access to Safe Water and Nutrition
- 137 HIV, Poverty and Aid
- 138–139 Environmental Issues
- 140–141 Climate Change
- 142 Fuel Production and Energy
- 143 GNI, Employment and Trade
- 144–145 Ecological Footprint
- 146–147 Tourism
- 148 Communications
- 149 Air Transport

WORLD STATISTICS

- 150–157 Country Statistics
- 158–163 Regional Indicators
- 164–179 Dictionary of Geographical terms

- 180–204 Index

Published by Collins
An imprint of HarperCollins Publishers
Westerhill Road
Bishopbriggs
Glasgow G64 2QT
www.harpercollins.co.uk

Sixth edition 2018

© HarperCollins Publishers 2018
Maps © Collins Bartholomew Ltd 2018

A catalogue record for this book is available from the British Library.

ISBN 978-0-00-825914-3 (HB)   10 9 8 7 6 5 4 3 2
ISBN 978-0-00-825915-0 (PB)   10 9 8 7 6 5 4 3 2

Printed in Slovenia

MIX
Paper from
responsible sources
FSC™ C007454

This book is produced from independently certified
FSC™ paper to ensure responsible forest management.

For more information visit: www.harpercollins.co.uk/green

All mapping in this atlas is generated from Collins Bartholomew digital databases.
Collins Bartholomew, the UK's leading independent geographical information supplier,
can provide a digital, custom, and premium mapping service to a variety of markets.
For further information:
Tel: +44 (0) 208 307 4515
e-mail: collinsbartholomew@harpercollins.co.uk
or visit our website at: www.collinsbartholomew.com

If you would like to comment on any aspect of this book,
please contact us at the above address or online.

www.collins.co.uk
e-mail: collinsmaps@harpercollins.co.uk

Acknowledgements

Agriculture and Horticulture Development Board, UK
Airports Council International
Australian Government
Bathymetric data: The GEBCO Digital Atlas, published by the British Oceanographic Data Centre
  on behalf of IOC and IHO, 1994
BP Statistical Review of World Energy
Brazilian Institute of Geography and Statistics
British Geological Survey
Dartmouth Flood Observatory, USA
Global Footprint Network National Footprint Accounts, 2017 (http://data.footprintnetwork.org)
Intergovernmental Panel on Climate Change
International Telecommunication Union
IUCN Red List of Threatened Species™
Met Office, UK
NI Forest Service Copyright
Office for National Statistics, UK
UK Government (gov.uk) – public sector information licensed under the Open Government Licence v3.0
UN Commodity Trade Statistics
UN Department of Economic and Social Affairs, Population Division
UN Development Programme
UNESCO World Heritage Centre
UN Food and Agriculture Organization
UNHCR (UN Refugee Agency)
US Bureau of Labor Statistics
US Census Bureau
US Energy Information Administration
USGS Earthquake Hazards Program
USGS Mineral Resources Program
World Bank Group
World Resources Institute
World Tourism Organization

Image credits

p4 Richard Cooke/Alamy Stock Photo (vertical), A.P.S. (UK)/Alamy Stock Photo (oblique); **p5** MODIS Rapid Respose
Team, NASA/GSFC (Alps satellite image); **p6** NASA Earth Observatory (Hurricane Sandy), NOAA Remote Sensing Division
(New Jersey); **p7** NASA Earth Observatory (World at night), NASA/USGS (Manila), NASA/Science Photo Library (Lake
Chad); **p19** Planet Observer/Science Photo Library; **p25** daulon/Shutterstock (Greenhouse gases diagram); **p41** Data
courtesy Marc Imhoff of NASA GSFC and Christopher Elvidge of NOAA NGDC. Image by Craig Mayhew and Robert
Simmon, NASA GSFC; **p59** NASA/NOAA GOES Project; **p76-77** NASA/Earth Observatory; **p91** NASA/Ron Beck, USGS
Eros Data Center Satellite Systems Branch; **p132** NASA Landsat Science Team; **p149** NASA Johnson Space Center

Map symbols

Symbols are used, in the form of points, lines or areas, on maps to show the location of and information about specific features. The colour and size of a symbol can give an indication of the type of feature and its relative size.

The meaning of map symbols is explained in a key shown on each page. Symbols used on reference maps are shown here.

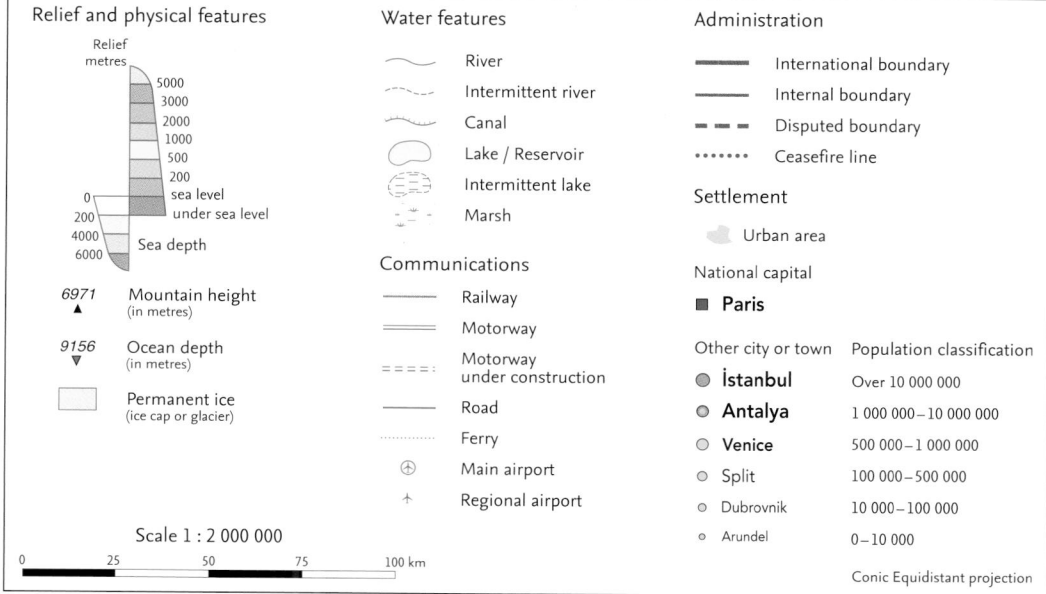

Map types

Many types of map are included in the atlas to show different information. The type of map, its symbols and colours are carefully selected to show the theme of each map and to make them easy to understand. The main types of map used are explained below.

Political maps provide an overview of the size, location and boundaries of countries in a specific area, such as a continent. Coloured squares indicate national capitals. Coloured circles represent other cities or towns.

Physical or relief maps use colour to show oceans, seas, rivers, lakes and the height of the land. The names and heights of major landforms are also indicated.

Reference maps bring together the information provided in the two types of map described on the left. They show relief and physical features as well as country borders, major cities and towns, roads, railways and airports.

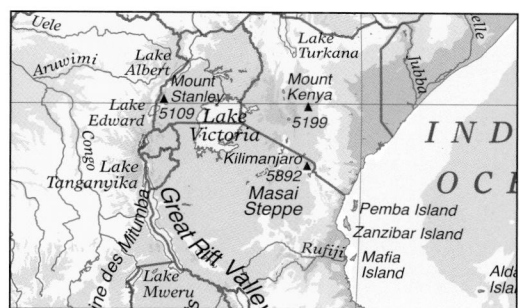

Extract from page 69

Extract from page 78

Extract from page 98

Distribution maps use different colours, symbols, or shading to show the location and distribution of natural or man-made features. In this map, symbols indicate the distribution of the world's largest cities.

Graduated colour maps use colours or shading to show a topic or theme and a measure of its intensity. Generally, the highest values are shaded with the darkest colours. In this map, colours are used to show the number of internet users per 100 people.

Isoline maps use thin lines to show the distribution of a feature. An isoline passes through places of the same value. Isolines may show features such as temperature (isotherm), air pressure (isobar) or height of land (contour). The value of the line is usually written on it. On either side of the line the value will be higher or lower.

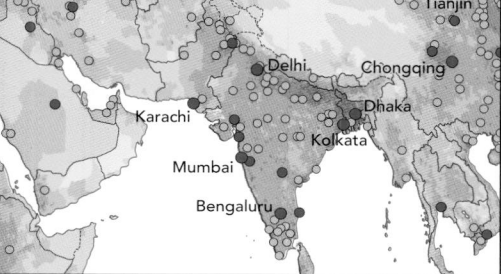

Extract from page 131

Extract from page 148

Extract from page 36

Graphs and Statistics

Graphs are a visual way of presenting statistical information.
There are different kinds of graphs in this atlas.
Some graphs are designed to present a particular
kind of information.

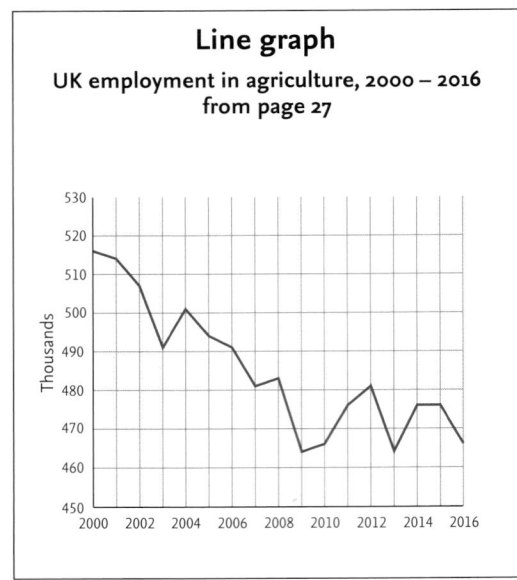

Line graph

UK employment in agriculture, 2000 – 2016
from page 27

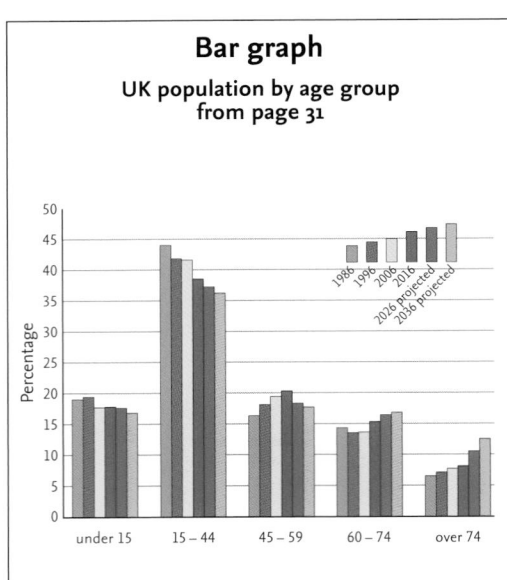

Bar graph

UK population by age group
from page 31

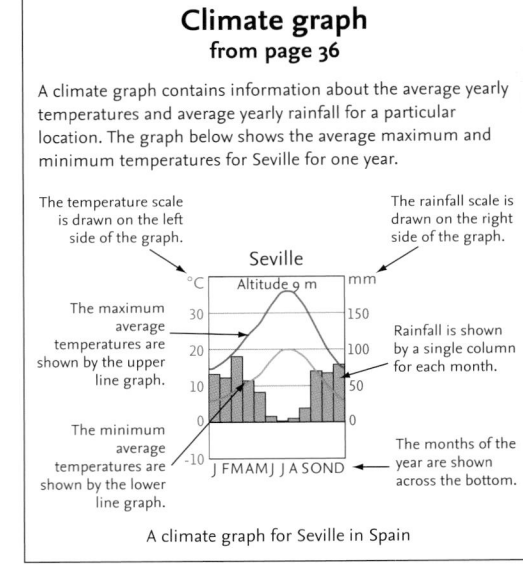

Climate graph
from page 36

A climate graph contains information about the average yearly
temperatures and average yearly rainfall for a particular
location. The graph below shows the average maximum and
minimum temperatures for Seville for one year.

The temperature scale
is drawn on the left
side of the graph.

The rainfall scale is
drawn on the right
side of the graph.

The maximum
average
temperatures are
shown by the upper
line graph.

Rainfall is shown
by a single column
for each month.

The minimum
average
temperatures are
shown by the lower
line graph.

The months of the
year are shown
across the bottom.

A climate graph for Seville in Spain

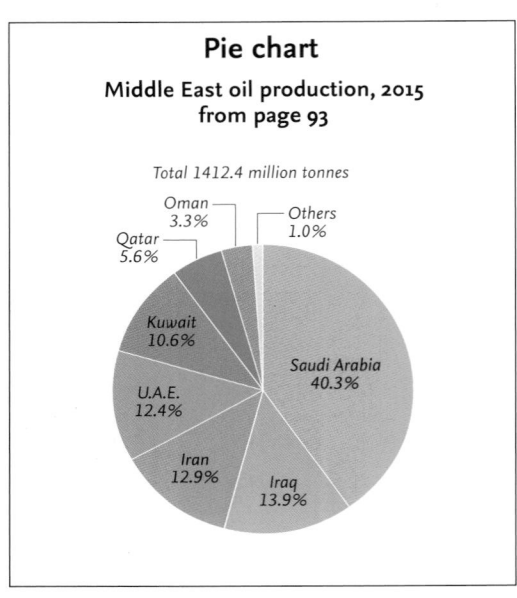

Pie chart

Middle East oil production, 2015
from page 93

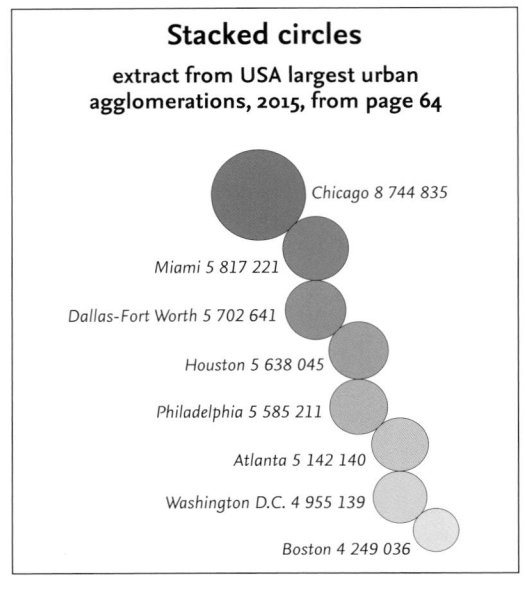

Stacked circles

extract from USA largest urban
agglomerations, 2015, from page 64

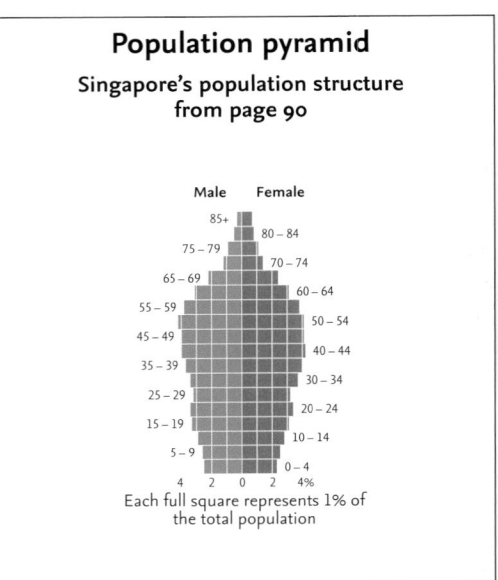

Population pyramid

Singapore's population structure
from page 90

Each full square represents 1% of
the total population

Throughout this atlas there are sets of
statistics presented as tables showing values
or indicators related to the themes covered
on a map spread.

Climate statistics, population statistics,
country indicators, trade values etc are just
some of the tables found throughout the atlas.

Population by country, 2016

Country	Population (thousands)	Density (persons per sq. km)
England	55 268	424
Wales	3113	150
Scotland	5405	69
Northern Ireland	1862	137
United Kingdom	65 648	271

Top 5 largest urban agglomerations, 2015

Urban agglomeration	Population
Tōkyō (Japan)	38 001 018
Delhi (India)	25 703 168
Shanghai (China)	23 740 778
Mumbai (India)	21 042 538
Beijing (China)	20 383 994

Vancouver	Jan	Feb	Mar	Apr	May	Jun	Jul	Aug	Sep	Oct	Nov	Dec
Temperature - max. (°C)	5	7	10	14	18	21	23	23	18	14	9	6
Temperature - min. (°C)	0	1	3	4	8	11	12	12	9	7	4	2
Rainfall - (mm)	218	147	127	84	71	64	31	43	91	147	211	224

Flag	Country	Capital city	Population total 2015	Density persons per sq km 2015	Birth rate per 1000 population 2015
	Samoa	Apia	193 000	68	25
	San Marino	San Marino	32 000	525	8
	São Tomé and Príncipe	São Tomé	190 000	197	34
	Saudi Arabia	Riyadh	31 540 000	14	20

Latitude

Latitude is distance, measured in degrees, north and south of the Equator. Lines of latitude circle the globe in an east-west direction. The distance between lines of latitude is always the same. They are also known as parallels of latitude. Because the circumference of Earth gets smaller toward the poles, the lines of latitude are shorter nearer the poles.

Longitude

Longitude is distance, measured in degrees, east and west of the Greenwich Meridian (prime meridian). Lines of longitude join the poles in a north-south direction. Because the lines join the poles, they are always the same length, but are farthest apart at the Equator and closest together at the poles. These lines are also called meridians of longitude.

Finding places

When lines of latitude and longitude are drawn on a map, they form a grid, which looks like a pattern of squares. This pattern is used to find places on a map. Latitude is always stated before longitude (e.g. 42°N 78°W).

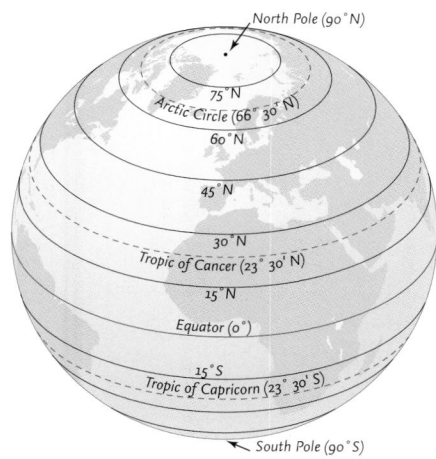

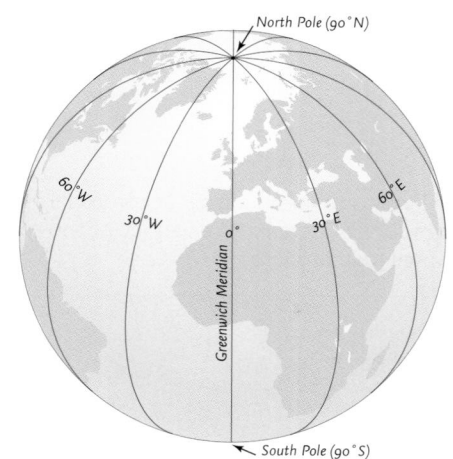

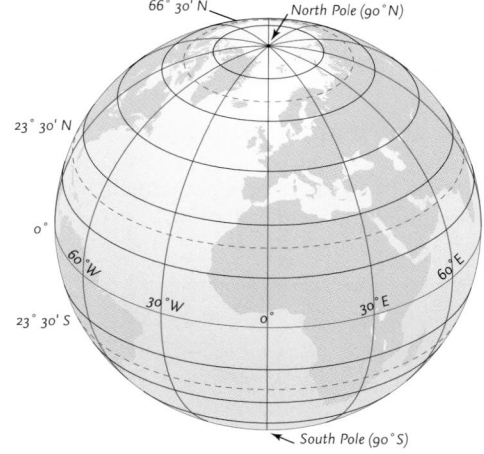

All lines of latitude have numbers between 0° and 90° and a direction, either north or south of the Equator. The Equator is at 0° latitude. The North Pole is at 90° north and the South Pole is at 90° south. The 'tilt' of Earth has given particular importance to some lines of latitude. They include:

- the Arctic Circle at 66° 30' north
- the Antarctic Circle at 66° 30' south
- the Tropic of Cancer at 23° 30' north
- the Tropic of Capricorn at 23° 30' south

The Equator also divides the Earth into two halves. The northern half, north of the Equator, is the **Northern Hemisphere**. The southern half, south of the Equator, is the **Southern Hemisphere**.

Longitude begins along the Greenwich Meridian (prime meridian), at 0°, in London, England. On the opposite side of Earth is the 180° meridian, which is the International Date Line. To the west of the prime meridian are Canada, the United States, and Brazil; to the east of the prime meridian are Germany, India and China. All lines of longitude have numbers between 0° and 180° and a direction, either east or west of the prime meridian.

The Greenwich Meridian and the International Date Line can also be used to divide the world into two halves. The half to the west of the Greenwich Meridian is the **Western Hemisphere**. The half to the east of the Greenwich Meridian is the **Eastern Hemisphere**.

By stating latitude and then longitude of a place, it becomes much easier to find. On the map (below) point A is easy to find as it is exactly latitude 58° north of the Equator and longitude 4° west of the Greenwich Meridian (58°N 4°W).

To be even more accurate in locating a place, each degree of latitude and longitude can also be divided into smaller units called **minutes** ('). There are 60 minutes in each degree. On the map (below) Halkirk is one half (or 30/60ths) of the way past latitude 58°N, and one-half (or 30/60ths) of the way past longitude 3°W. Its latitude is therefore 58 degrees 30 minutes north and its longitude is 3 degrees 30 minutes west. This can be shortened to 58°30'N 3°30'W. Latitude and longitude for all the places and features named on the maps are included in the index.

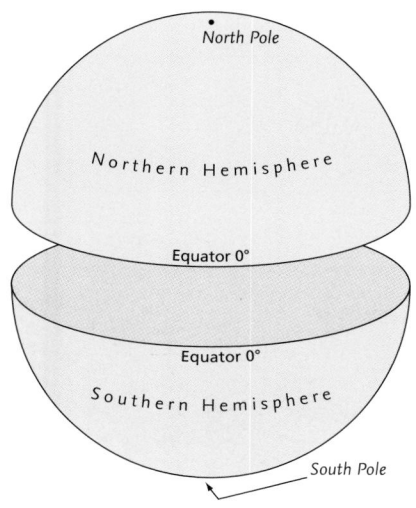

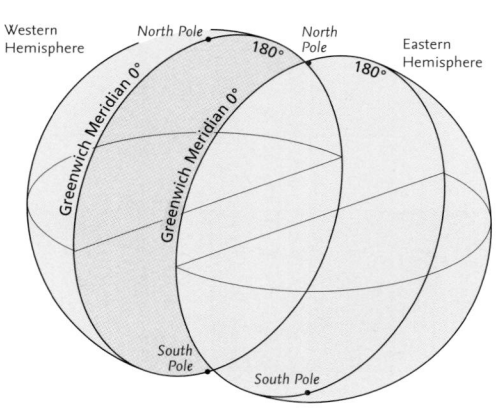

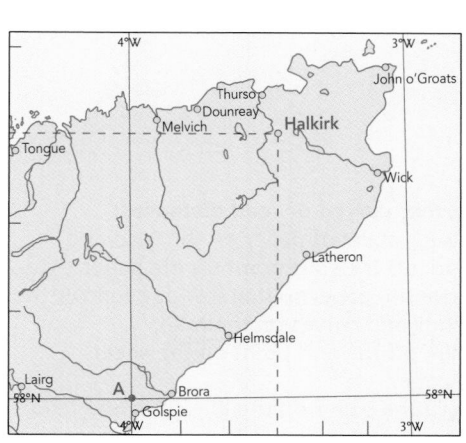

Scale

Scale

To draw a map of any part of the world, the area must be reduced, or 'scaled down,' to the size of a page in this atlas, a foldable road map, or a topographic map. The scale of the map indicates the amount by which an area has been reduced.

The scale of a map can also be used to determine the actual distance between two or more places or the actual size of an area on a map. The scale indicates the relationship between distances on the map and distances on the ground.

Ways of describing scale

Word scale: You can describe the scale in words e.g. one centimetre on the map represents 100 kilometres on the ground.

Line scale: A line with the scale marked on it is an easy way to compare distances on the map with distances on the ground.

Ratio scale: This method uses numbers to compare distances on the map with distances on the ground, e.g. 1:40 000 000. This means that one centimetre on the map represents 40 million centimetres on the ground. This number is too large to mean much to most people, so we convert centimetres to kilometres by dividing by 100 000 which equals 400 kilometres.

Scale and map information

The scale of a map affects how much information the map can show.

As the area shown on a map becomes larger, the amount of detail and accuracy of the map becomes less and less.

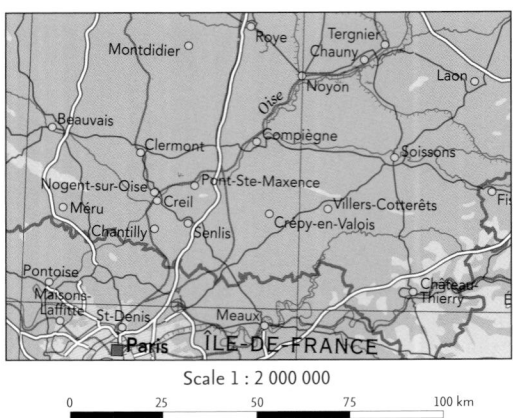

Scale 1 : 2 000 000

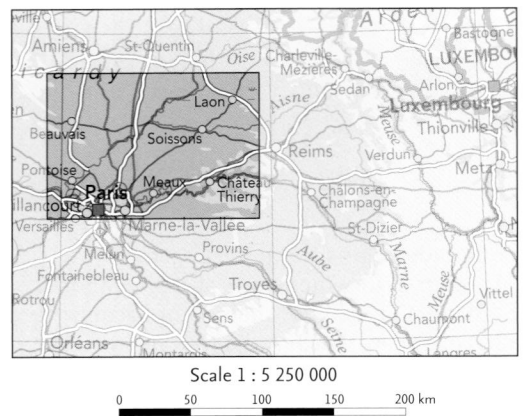

Scale 1 : 5 250 000

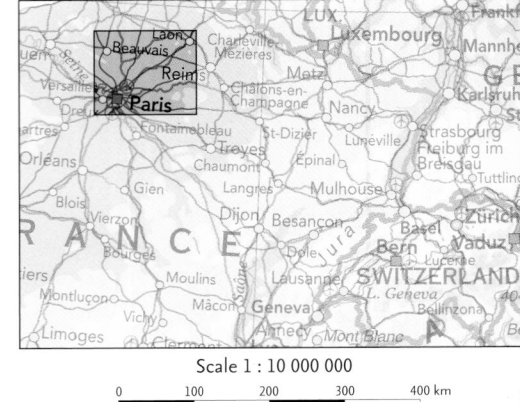

Scale 1 : 10 000 000

Measuring distance

The instructions below show you how to determine how far apart places are on a map, then using the line scale, to determine the actual distance on the ground.

Measuring straight-line distances:
1. place the edge of a sheet of paper on the two places on a map,
2. on the paper, place a mark at each of the two places,
3. place the paper on the line scale,
4. measure the distance on the ground using the scale.

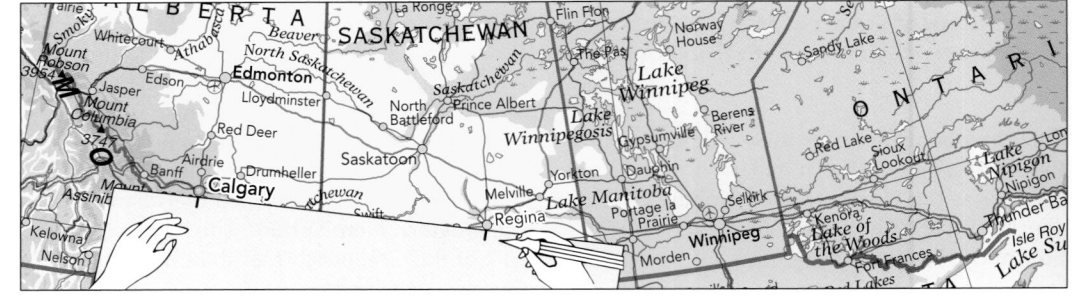

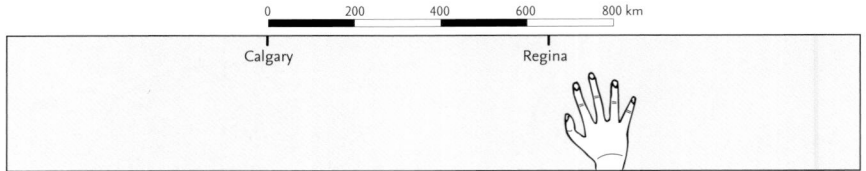

Measuring curved or road distances:
1. place a sheet of paper on the map and mark off the start point on the paper,
2. move the paper so that its edge follows the bends and curves on the map,
3. mark off the end point on the sheet of paper,
4. place the paper on the line scale and read the actual distance following a road or railroad.

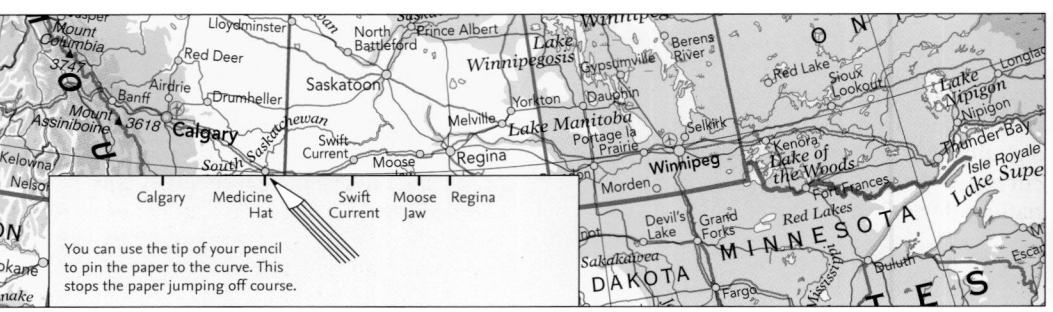

You can use the tip of your pencil to pin the paper to the curve. This stops the paper jumping off course.

Representing a spherical Earth as a flat map has presented a number of challenges for map makers. A map projection is a way of showing the Earth's surface on a flat piece of paper. There are many types of map projections. None of them shows the Earth with perfect accuracy. All map projections distort either: area, direction, shape or distance.

Cylindrical projections

Cylindrical projections are constructed by projecting the surface of the globe or sphere (Earth) onto a cylinder that just touches the outside edges of that globe. Two examples of cylindrical projections are Mercator and Times.

Mercator Projection (see pages 102–103 for an example of this projection)

The Mercator cylindrical projection is useful for areas near the equator and to about 15 degrees north or south of the equator, where distortion of shape is minimal. The projection is useful for navigation, since directions are plotted as straight lines.

Eckert IV (see pages 116–117 for an example of this projection)

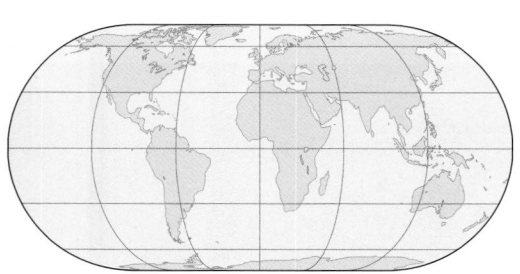

Eckert IV is an equal area projection. Equal area projections are useful for world thematic maps where it is important to show the correct relative sizes of continental areas. Eckert IV has a straight central meridian but all others are curved, which helps suggest the spherical nature of the Earth.

Conic projections

Conic projections are constructed by projecting the surface of a globe or sphere (Earth) onto a cone that just touches the outside edges of that globe. Examples of conic projections are Conic Equidistant and Albers Equal Area Conic.

Conic Equidistant Projection (see pages 54–55 for an example of this projection)

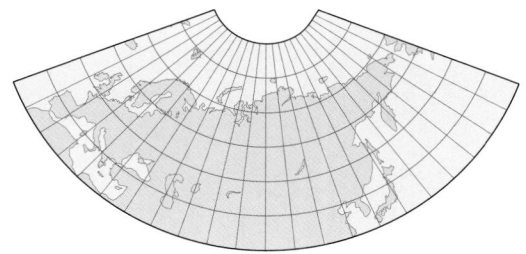

Conic projections are best suited for areas between 30° and 60° north and south of the equator when the east–west distance is greater than the north–south distance (such as Canada and Europe). The meridians are straight and spaced at equal intervals.

Lambert Conformal (see pages 60–61 for an example of this projection)

Lambert's Conformal Conic projection maintains an exact scale along one or two standard parallels (lines of latitude). Angles between locations on the surface of the Earth are correctly shown. Therefore, it is used for aeronautical charts and large scale topographic maps in many countries. It is also used to map areas with a greater east–west than north–south extent.

Azimuthal projections

Azimuthal projections are constructed by projecting the surface of the globe or sphere (Earth) onto a flat surface that touches the globe at one point only. Some examples of azimuthal projections are Lambert Azimuthal Equal Area and Polar Stereographic.

Polar Stereographic Projection (see page 112 for an example of this projection)

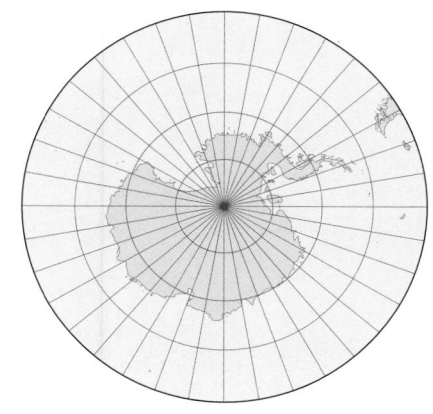

Azimuthal projections are useful for areas that have similar east–west and north–south dimensions such as Antarctica and Australia.

Lambert Azimuthal Equal Area (see pages 108–109 for an example of this projection)

This projection is useful for areas that have similar east–west and north–south dimensions such as Australia.

Aerial photographs

Aerial photographs are images of the land usually taken from an aeroplane. There are two kinds of aerial photographs, vertical aerial photographs and oblique aerial photographs.

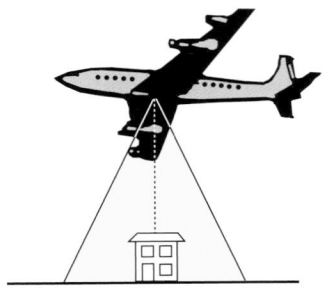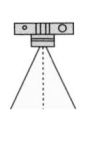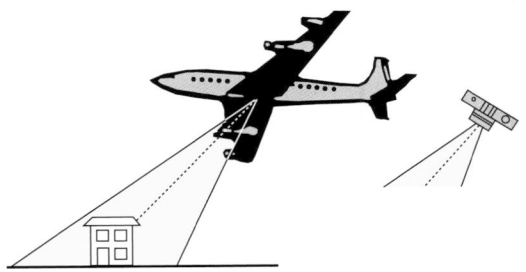

Camera position for a vertical aerial photograph

Camera position for an oblique aerial photograph

Vertical aerial photographs are taken from a digital camera fixed under an aeroplane. The camera points straight down at the ground. Objects are shown from above and may be difficult to identify.

Vertical aerial photographs show the same view of the land as a large scale map. Cartographers use vertical aerial photographs to help them make 1 : 50 000 topographic maps.

A vertical aerial photograph of Whitby, North Yorkshire

Oblique aerial photographs are taken from a camera that is positioned at an angle to the ground. Objects are more easily recognised in oblique aerial photographs. There are two kinds of oblique aerial photographs: high angle and low angle oblique aerial photographs. A high angle aerial photograph shows a large area of land. The horizon is usually visible. In low angle aerial photographs the horizon is not visible. The area of land shown is usually much smaller.

A low angle oblique aerial photograph of the same area of Whitby, North Yorkshire

GIS concepts

A GIS is a set of tools that can be used to collect, store, retrieve, modify and display spatial data. Spatial data can come from a variety of sources including existing maps, satellite imagery, aerial photographs or data collected from GPS (Global Positioning System) surveys.

GIS links this information to its real world location and can display this in a series of layers which you can then choose to turn off and on or to combine using a computer.

A GIS can work with spatial information in three ways.
1 A map made up of a collection of layers containing symbols. The illustration on the right shows a number of GIS layers.
2 As geographic information called a database, stored on a computer.
3 As a set of tools that create new datasets using existing stored geographic data.

Uses of GIS

A GIS can be used in many ways to help solve problems, identify patterns, make decisions and plan development. A local government for example might want to build a new business area in a settlement. A GIS would be able to provide information on: the numbers of people who live in the area, transport routes, the average income of the population, and the kinds of goods people buy. A GIS could also be used to identify the number of houses built on a flood plain. This information could inform emergency planning or the relocation of the houses.

GIS terms

Spatial data: Spatial data describes the location and shape of features. You can see these features on a map or on a computer screen.

Attribute data: Attribute data describes or adds information about a feature, such as: population numbers, names of places, climate statistics. Attribute data may be stored in tables or as text within a GIS. Attribute data is made up of both raster and vector data.

Vector data: Represents map features as points, lines and area, e.g. mountain peaks, rivers, settlements.

  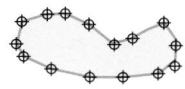

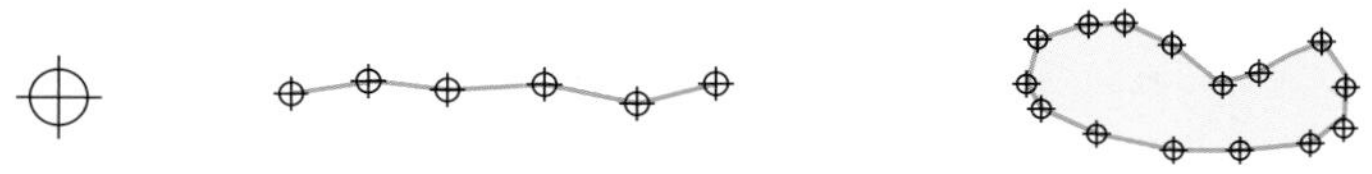

Raster data: Represents map features as cells in a grid. Points, lines and areas can also be stored as cells of a grid. A satellite image is an example of raster data.

GIS layers

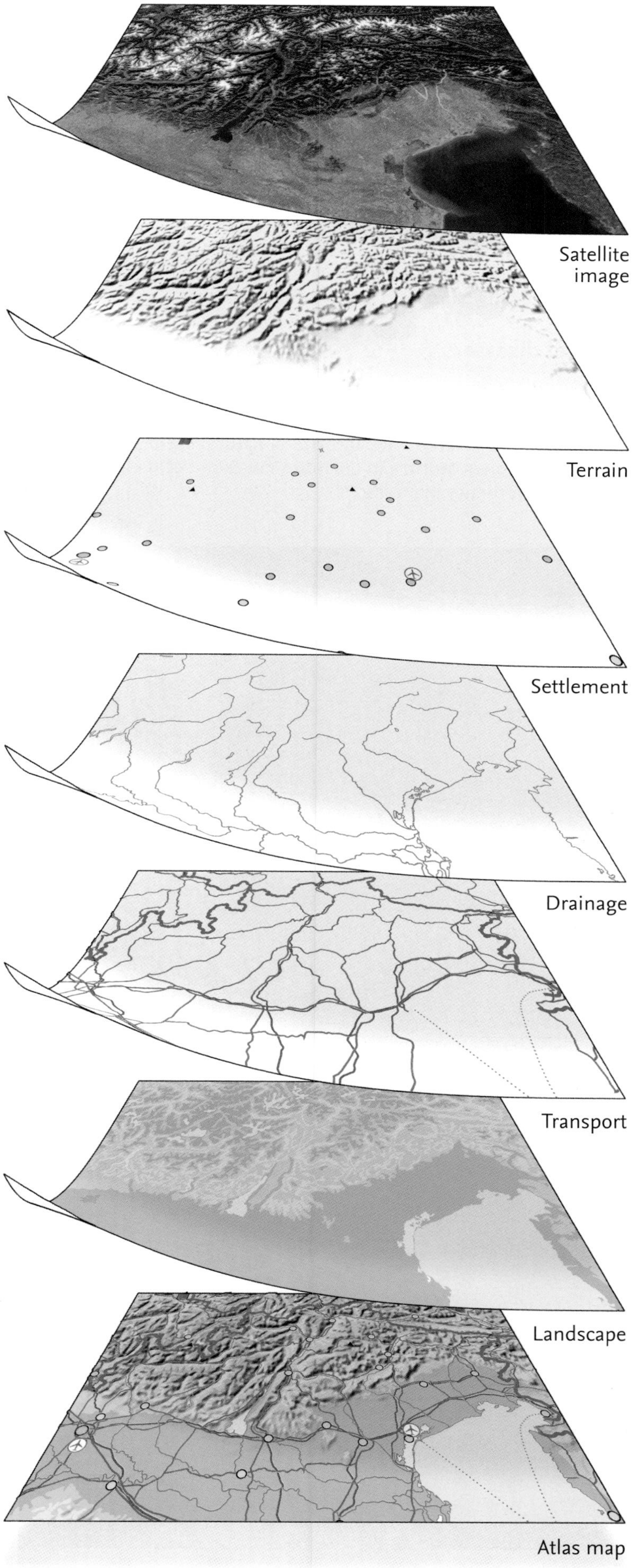

Satellite image

Terrain

Settlement

Drainage

Transport

Landscape

Atlas map

An example of different layers that can be stored and used in a GIS.

Satellite images

Satellite images

Images captured by a large number of Earth-observing satellites provide unique views of the Earth. The science of gathering and interpreting such images is known as remote sensing. Geographers use images taken from high above the Earth to determine patterns, trends and basic characteristics of the Earth's surface. Satellites are fitted with different kinds of scanners or sensors to gather information about the Earth. The most well known satellites are Landsat and SPOT.

Satellite sensors detect electromagnetic radiation – X-rays, ultraviolet light, visible colours and microwave signals. This data can be processed to provide information on soils, land use, geology, pollution and weather patterns.

Natural disasters

Satellite images have many uses. One use is comparing two images to examine how conditions have changed over time. Satellite images taken before and after a natural event such as a flood or a violent storm can illustrate the extent of damage and help emergency planning.

A satellite image showing Hurricane Sandy over northeastern USA, in 2012. Satellite images help people to prepare for approaching natural disasters such as cyclones and floods. Weather scientists use satellite images to help them forecast the weather.

In October 2012, the effects of Hurricane Sandy caused extensive damage and loss of life in the Caribbean and eastern USA. The two satellite images above show part of the town of Mantoloking on the New Jersey coast before (left image) and after (right image) the storm struck.

The world at night

The image on the right was constructed using a collection of satellite images that recorded the amount of light given off by human settlements. Cities and lines of transport stand out as patches of bright light. Deserts, forests, lakes and high mountains are poorly lit or are completely dark. This satellite image highlights urban clusters, which may be seen as an indicator of development.

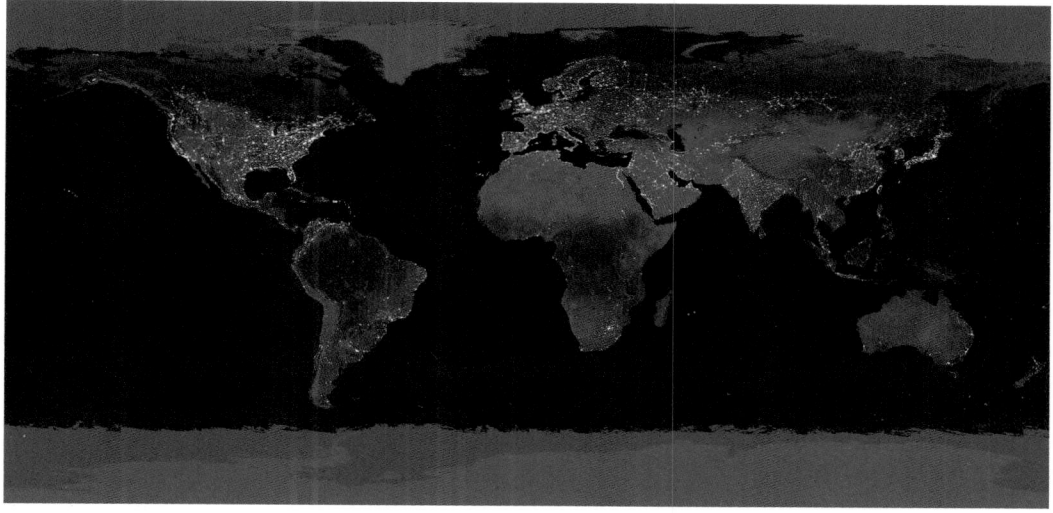

The world at night

City growth

The two satellite images on the right show how the city of Manila, the capital of the Philippines, has grown. The images show the extent of the urban area in 1989 and 2012. Manila is the world's most densely populated city.

Manila, 1989

Manila, 2012

Climate change

Satellite images taken over time can be used to identify the effects of climate change. For example, a series of satellite images can show how far ice sheets have retreated, or how the shorelines of lakes and seas have changed in a certain time period.

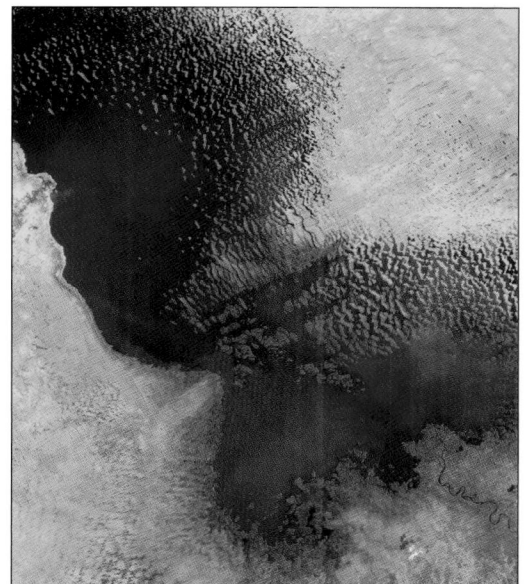

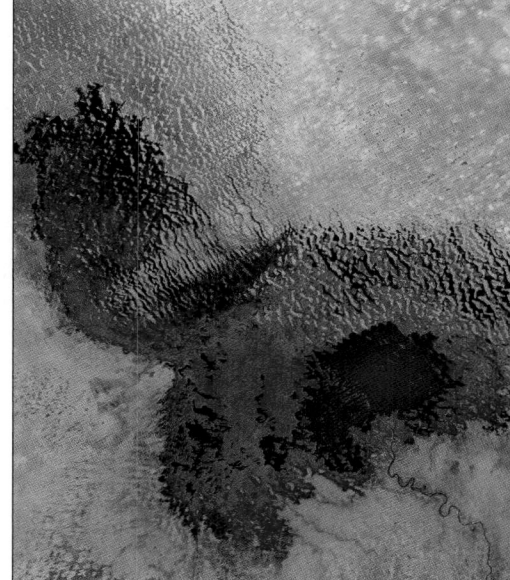

Satellite imagery showing the reduction in size of Lake Chad between 1973 (left) and 2007 (right).

B 3° **C** 2° **D** 1°

4

A 4°

3

2

1

Cardigan Bay

WALES

ENGL...

Bristol Channel

Cambrian Mountains

Brecon Beacons

Black Mountains

Wenlock Edge

Malvern Hills

Cotswold Hills

Chiltern Hills

Hampshire Downs

Salisbury Plain

Marlborough Downs

Berkshire Downs

Mendip Hills

Quantock Hills

Exmoor

Dartmoor

Lyme Bay

Poole Bay

Bigbury Bay

Start Bay

Tor Bay

Babbacombe Bay

Morte Bay

Swansea Bay

Burry Inlet

Gower

Worms Head

Birmingham · Nottingham · Leicester · Coventry · Derby · Stoke-on-Trent · Wolverhampton · Walsall · Dudley · West Bromwich · Sutton Coldfield · Solihull · Warwick · Oxford · Reading · Swindon · Bristol · Cardiff (Caerdydd) · Newport (Casnewydd) · Swansea (Abertawe) · Gloucester · Cheltenham · Worcester · Hereford · Bath · Taunton · Exeter · Plymouth · Bournemouth · Poole · Southampton · Portsmouth · Salisbury · Winchester · Weymouth · Isle of Wight · Isle of Purbeck · Isle of Portland · Bill of Portland · Chesil Beach · The Needles · The Solent · St Catherine's Point · St Aldhelm's Head · Foreland Point · Bolt Head · Start Point · Berry Head

Milton Keynes · Banbury · Buckingham · Leighton Buzzard · Aylesbury · Abingdon · Newbury · Basingstoke · Farnborough · Fleet · Aldershot · Andover · Amesbury

Nottingham · Mansfield · Sutton in Ashfield · Kirkby in Ashfield · Hucknall · Ilkeston · Long Eaton · Loughborough · Melton Mowbray · Oakham · Rutland Water · Uppingham · Market Harborough · Lutterworth · Rugby · Daventry · Northampton · Wellingborough · Kettering

Roscoff · Santander · Cherbourg, Guernsey, Jersey, St-Malo · Bilbao, Santander · St Malo, Guernsey, Jersey · Caen, Le Havre

Relief and physical features

Relief
metres
1000
500
200
100
0   sea level
50
200   under sea level

▲ 1085   Mountain height
(in metres)

Water features

~~~ River

~~~ Canal

Lake / Reservoir

Communications

Railway

Motorway

Road

Car ferry

⊕ Main airport

✈ Regional airport

Administration

Boundaries

International

Internal

Settlement

Urban area

Cities and towns in order of size

National capital   Other city or town

■ London   ◉ Birmingham

◉ Bristol

○ Oxford

○ Colchester

○ Wantage

Scale 1 : 1 200 000

0   10   20   30   40 km

Conic Equidistant projection

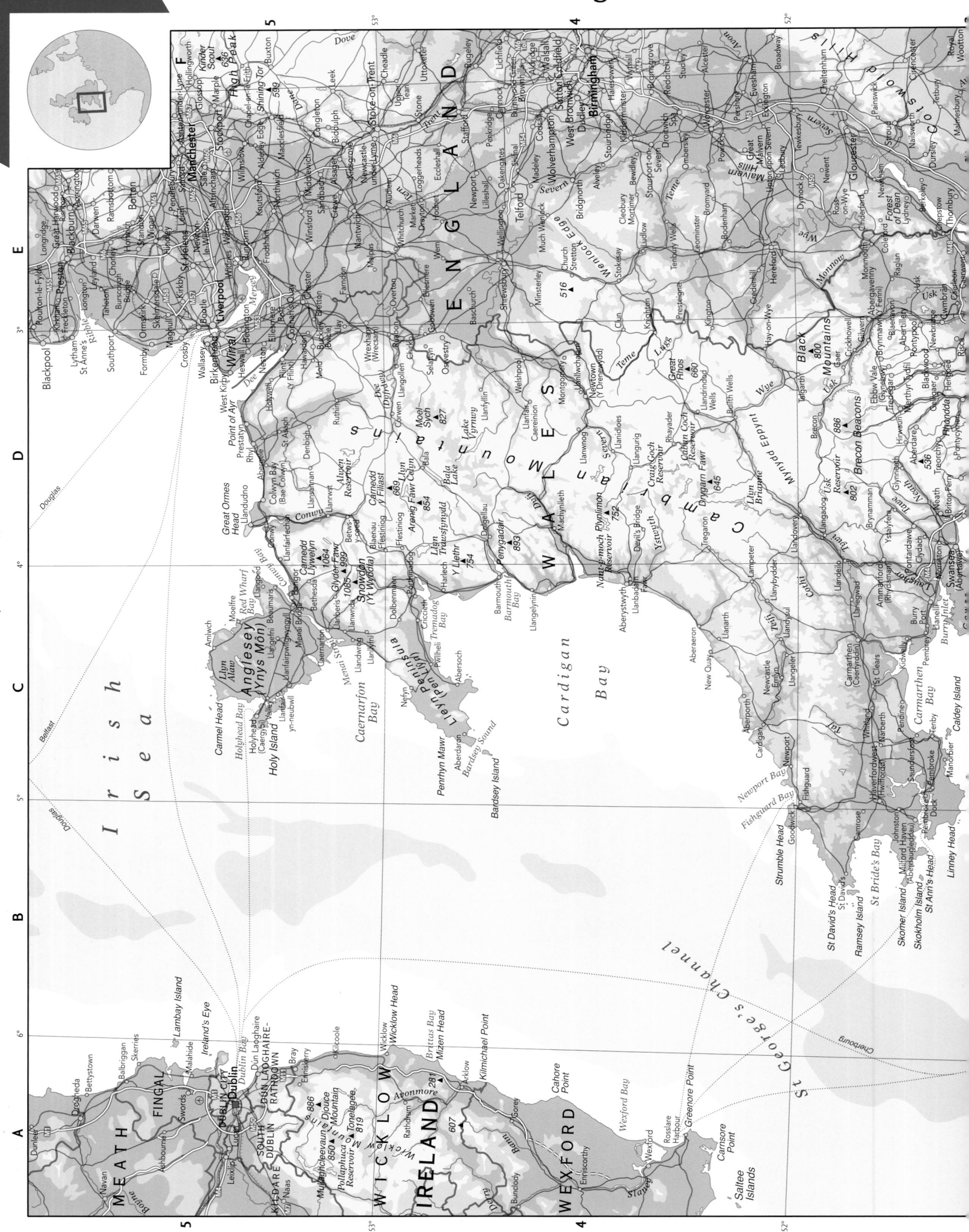

FRANCE

Cap de la Hague
Équeurdreville-Hainneville
Les Pieux
Carteret
Cap de Carteret
Beaumont

Channel Islands

Alderney
St Anne

Guernsey
(British Crown
Dependency)
Sampson
Herm
St Peter Port
St Martin
Sark

Jersey
(British Crown
Dependency)
St John
St Ouen
St Martin
St Helier
St-Malo
St Brelade

Poole
Portsmouth

Relief and physical features

Relief
metres
1000
500
200
100
50
sea level
under sea level

1085 ▲ Mountain height
(in metres)

Scale 1 : 1 200 000

0 10 20 30 40 km

Water features

River
Canal
Lake / Reservoir

Communications

Railway
Motorway
Motorway under
construction
Road
⊕ Car ferry
✈ Main airport
Regional airport

Administration

Boundaries
International
Internal

Settlement

Urban area

Cities and towns in order of size
■ Dublin National capital
● Birmingham Other city or town
● Liverpool
○ Plymouth
○ Exeter
○ Llandeilo

Conic Equidistant projection

Celtic Sea

Bristol Channel

English Channel

Lyme Bay

Bristol

Isles of Scilly
Bryher
Tresco
St Martin's
St Agnes
St Mary's

Land's End
Cape Cornwall
St Just
Penzance
Marazion
Hayle
St Ives
St Ives Bay
Mount's Bay
Porthleven
Helston
Lizard
Lizard Point
Black Head
St Keverne
Camborne
Penryn
Redruth
Falmouth
Falmouth Bay
Truro
Probus
St Mawes
St Agnes
Perranporth
Newquay
Watergate Bay
St Austell
St Austell Bay
Mevagissey
Dodman Point
St Columb Major
Par
Fowey
Lanivet
Lostwithiel
Bodmin
Wadebridge
Polperro
Padstow
Camelford
Tintagel
Bude
Bude Bay
Stratton
Holsworthy
Launceston
Callington
Saltash
St Germans
East Looe
Whitsand Bay
Rame Head
Torpoint
Gunnislake
Tavistock
Lydford
Okehampton
Hatherleigh
Great Torrington
Bideford
Appledore
Westward Ho!
Barnstaple or Bideford Bay
Baggy Point
Morte Bay
Morthoe
Croyde
Braunton
Combe Martin
Ilfracombe
Hartland
Hartland Point
Lundy
Foreland Point
Lynton
Minehead
Porlock
Watchet
Williton
Dunkery Beacon 519
Five Barrows Hill 493
South Molton
Winkleigh
Chulmleigh
Crediton
Tiverton
Silverton
Bampton
Wiveliscombe
Dulverton
Wellington
Bishops Lydeard
Quantock Hills
Bridgwater
Burnham-on-Sea
Highbridge
Bridgwater Bay
Steep Holm
Flat Holm
Weston-super-Mare
Clevedon
Portishead
Long Ashton
Yatton
Congresbury
Blagdon
Chew Valley Lake
Chew Magna
Keynsham
Bath
Kingswood
Corsham
Bradford-on-Avon
Radstock
Midsomer Norton
Shepton Mallet
Wells
Cheddar
Wedmore
Glastonbury
Street
Brue
Langport
Martock
Ilminster
Chard
Crewkerne
Ilchester
Somerton
Castle Cary
Bruton
Yeovil
Sherborne
Wincanton
Mere
Gillingham
Shaftesbury
Stalbridge
Sturminster Newton
Blandford Forum
Stour
Sturminster Marshall
Wimborne Minster
Ferndown
Poole
Isle of Purbeck
Corfe Castle
Swanage
St Aldhelm's Head
Wareham
Bere Regis
Dorchester
Broadmayne
Broadwindsor
Beaminster
Bridport
Lyme Regis
Seaton
Sidmouth
Axminster
Colyton
Honiton
Cullompton
Feniton
Exmouth
Dawlish
Teignmouth
Newton Abbot
Torquay
Tor Bay
Paignton
Brixham
Berry Head
Dartmouth
Start Bay
Start Point
Prawle Point
Salcombe
Bolt Head
Kingsbridge
Modbury
Yealmpton
Plympton
Plymouth
Plymstock
The Sound
Bigbury Bay
Ashburton
Buckfastleigh
Totnes
Dart
Bovey Tracey
Moretonhampstead
Widecombe in the Moor
Yes Tor 619
Dartmoor
Lee Moor
Lydford
Horrabridge
Roadford Reservoir
Exeter
Exminster
Crediton
St Cyres
Newton St Cyres
Topsham
Exe
Culm
Otter
Axe
Parrett
Tone
Barnstaple
South Molton
Taw
Torridge
Okehampton
Bodmin Moor
Liskeard
Looe

Mendip Hills
Salisbury Plain
Wylye
Devizes
Calne
Melksham
Trowbridge
Westbury
Warminster
Mere
Lavington
West Lavington
Frome
Wilton

South Dorset Downs
North Dorset Downs
Chesil Beach
Fortuneswell
Easton
Bill of Portland
Isle of Portland
Weymouth
Preston

Llandeilo
Cowbridge
Llantwit Major
Barry
Sully
Penarth
Caerdydd
Porthcawl

Roscoff
Cherbourg
Roscoff
Santander

North Dorset Downs

Relief and physical features

Relief
metres
1000
500
200
100
sea level
0
50
100
under sea level
200

1085 ▲ Mountain height
(in metres)

Water features
~~~ River
≈≈≈ Canal
⬭ Lake / Reservoir

Communications
——— Railway
═══ Motorway
= = = = Motorway
under construction
——— Road
.... Car ferry
⊕ Main airport
✈ Regional airport

Administration
Boundaries
━━━ International
——— Internal

Settlement
Urban area

Cities and towns in order of size
National capital   Other city or town
■ Dublin   ◉ Manchester
                     ◎ Liverpool
                     ◉ Bradford
                     ○ Carlisle
                     ∘ Keswick

Scale 1 : 1 200 000
0 10 20 30 40 km

Conic Equidistant projection

14

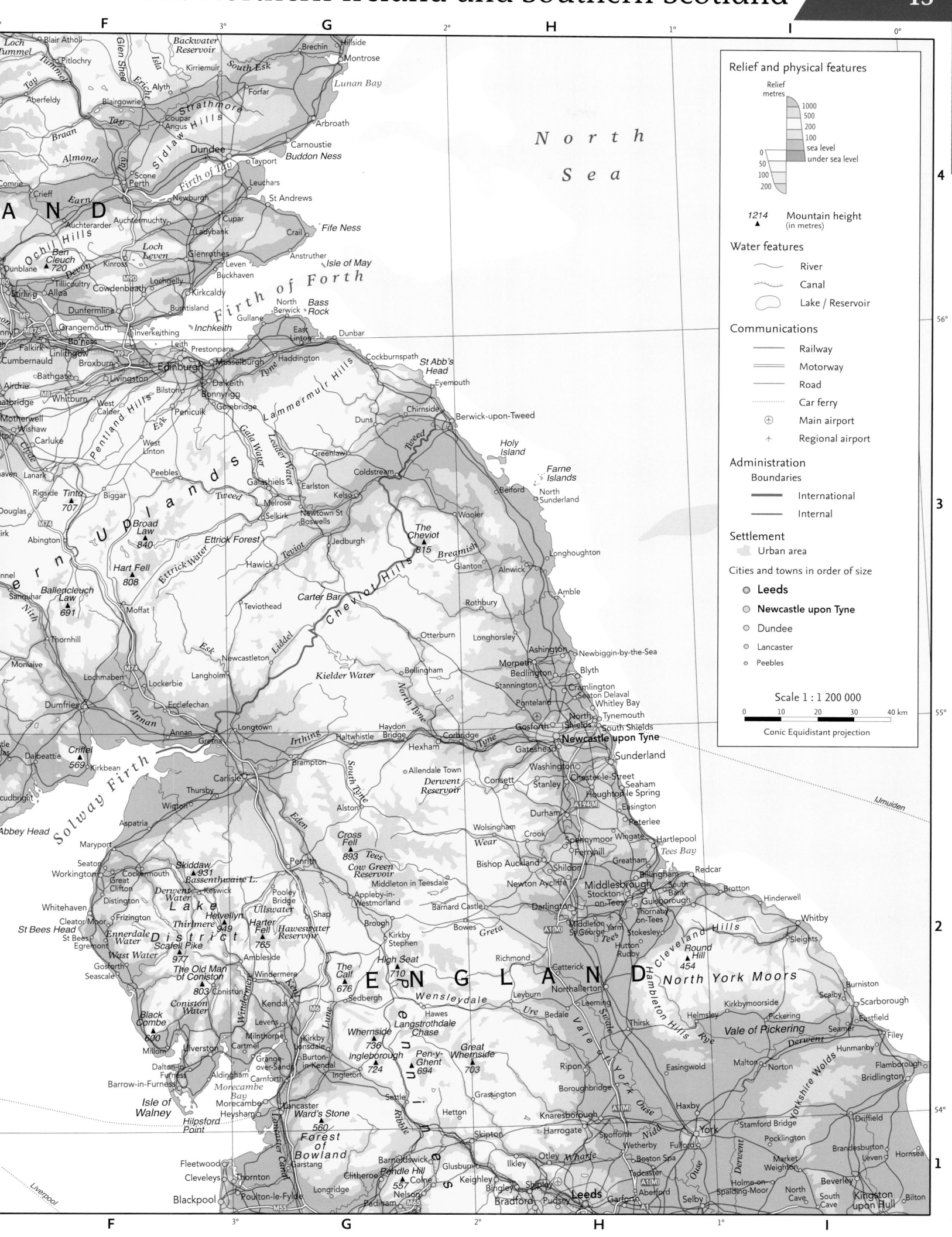

Relief and physical features

Relief
metres

1000
500
200
100
sea level
under sea level
50
100
200

1214 ▲ Mountain height
(in metres)

Water features

River
Canal
Lake / Reservoir

Communications

Railway
Motorway
Road
Car ferry
⊕ Main airport
✈ Regional airport

Administration

Boundaries
International
Internal

Settlement

Urban area

Cities and towns in order of size

◉ Leeds
◉ Newcastle upon Tyne
◎ Dundee
○ Lancaster
∘ Peebles

Scale 1 : 1 200 000

0   10   20   30   40 km

Conic Equidistant projection

North Sea

Relief and physical features

Relief metres
- 1000
- 500
- 200
- 100
- 0 sea level
- under sea level
- 50
- 100
- 200

▲ 1345 Mountain height (in metres)

Scale 1 : 1 200 000

0 10 20 30 40 km

Water features

- ∿ River
- ∿ Canal
- ⬯ Lake / Reservoir

Communications

- —— Railway
- —— Road
- ······ Car ferry
- ⊕ Main airport
- ✈ Regional airport

Settlement

- Urban area

Cities and towns in order of size
- ● Aberdeen
- ◉ Inverness
- ○ Kirkwall

Conic Equidistant projection

ATLANTIC OCEAN

Rona

Cape Wrath

Butt of Lewis
Port of Ness

Flannan Isles

West Loch Roag
Great Bernera
Callanish

Muirneag ▲ 248
Tolsta Head

Isle of Lewis
Stornoway
Broad Bay
Eye Peninsula

Kinlochbervie
Loch Inchard
Loch Laxford
Handa Island
Scourie
Foinaven ▲ 915

Point of Stoer
Loch Assynt
Lochinver
Ben More Assynt ▲ 998
Canisp ▲ 846
Cul Mòr ▲ 849

O u t e r   H e b r i d e s

Mealasta Island
Loch Langavat

North Harris
Kebock Head

Rubha Coigeach
Summer Isles
Loch Lurgainn

Scarp
Tirga Mòr ▲ 679
Clisham ▲ 799

T h e   M i n c h

Ullapool
Loch Broom

Taransay

Tarbert
Greenstone Point
Rubha Reidh
Gruinard Bay

An Teallach ▲ 1062
Beinn Dearg ▲ 1084

St Kilda

South Harris
Loch Langavat
Rodel
Scalpay
Loch Tarbert

Shiant Islands

Gairloch
Gair Loch
Loch Maree

Fionn Loch
W E S T E R
Sgurr Mòr ▲ 1110
Loch Fannich

Pabbay
Berneray
Boreray

Sound of Harris

Rubha Hunish

Loch Ewe
Loch Torridon
Torridon
R O S S
Loch Luic

North Uist
Lochmaddy

L i t t l e   M i n c h

Uig
Loch Snizort
Rona
Sound of Raasay
Inner Sound
Shieldaig

Sound of Monach
Monach Islands

L. Dunvegan
The Storr ▲ 719
Raasay

Loch Monar

Benbecula
Balivanich

L. Bracadale
Portree
Skye

Scalpay
Kyle of Lochalsh

Carn Eighe ▲ 1183

South Uist
Lochboisdale

The Cuillin
Sgurr Alasdair ▲ 993
Blaven ▲ 928

A'Chraig ▲ 1120
Loch Cluanie
Glen Morist

Sound of Barra
Eriskay

Canna
Soay
Cuillin Sound
Loch Eishort
Ardvasar
Sound of Sleat
Ladhar Bheinn ▲ 1020
Loch Hourn
Loch Quoich
Glen Garry
Loch Loyne
Garry

Barra
Castlebay
Vatersay
Sandray
Pabbay
Mingulay
Berneray

Rum
Eigg
Muck

Mallaig
Loch Nevis
Arisaig
Loch Morar
Loch Beoraid
Sound of Arisaig
Eilean Shona
Point of Ardnamurchan

Loch Arkaig

Loch Shiel
Sgurr Dhomhnuill ▲ 888
Fort William

Stob Choir Claurigh ▲ 1177
Ben Nevis ▲ 1345
Kinlochleven
Loch Leven
Loch Lochy
Loch Linnhe

Coll
Tiree
Tobermory
Mull
Loch Arienas
Morvern
Loch Sunart

Glen Coe
Bidean nam Bian ▲ 1150
Meall a' Bhuiridh ▲ 1108
Rannoch Moor

E   4°   F   3°   G   2°   H   1°   I

Mull Head
Papa Westray
Noup Head   North Ronaldsay
Westray   The North
              Sound   North Ronaldsay
              Eday   Sanday
Westray Firth
Brough Head   Rousay
Birsay   Egilsay   Stronsay
Orkney Islands   Loch of   Loth   Sanday
                  Harray   Stronsay   Sound
                  Finstown Firth
Loch of Stenness   Wide Firth   Shapinsay
Stromness   Mainland   Kirkwall   Auskerry
Ward Hill   Gritley
479   Scapa   Copinsay
Hoy   Flow
     Flotta   Burray
South   St Margaret's Hope
Walls   South
         Ronaldsay
         Burwick
Pentland Firth   Brough Ness
Dunnet Head   Island of   Pentland Skerries
Thurso   Stroma
Bay   Dunnet   John o'Groats
Strathy   Dunnet   Duncansby Head
Point   Bay
Dounreay   Loch
         Heilen
Melvich   Thurso
Ben   Halkirk   Loch   Sinclair's Bay
Loyal   Watten   Wick
764   CAITHNESS   Wick
Loch   Wick
Loyal
Loch
Naver   Loch
Ben Klibreck Rimsdale
961   Latheron
UTHERLAND
och Shin   Helmsdale
Loch Shin   Helmsdale
Brora
Lairg
Bonar Bridge   Golspie
Balintore
Dornoch Firth   Tarbat Ness
Tain
Loch Glass   Nigg
Wyvis   Bay   Cromarty
ngwall   Black Isle
       Fortrose
Conon   Moray Firth
Bridge   Moray   Burghead   Lossiemouth   Portknockie   Troup
Beauly Firth Firth   Nairn   Kinloss   Buckie   Portsoy   Head
auly   Inverness   Forres   Fochabers   Cullen   Banff   Macduff   Fraserburgh
Glen More   Nairn   Lossie   Elgin   Deveron   Loch of
Ness   Rothes   Isla   Knock   Aberchirder   Strathbeg
                         Keith   Hill   Turriff   New   Crimond
                              430   Pitsligo   Rattray Head
Findhorn   Dufftown   Deveron   Huntly   North Ugie   Peterhead
Spey   (Charlestown   Bogie   Mintlaw
        of Aberlour)   STRATHBOGIE   Urie   Boddam
Grantown-   Hills of   Insch   Ythan   Cruden Bay
on-Spey   Cromdale   Oldmeldrum
Strathspey   Carn Mòr   Ellon
Aviemore   804   Inverurie
Cairn   Kemnay   Don
Gorm   Geal   Kintore   Dyce
Cairn   Charn   Don   Westhill
nadhliath Mountains   821   Avon   Aberdeen
Carn Dearg   Ben Macdui   Dee   Portlethen
945   Kingussie   Cairn Toul 1309   Aboyne   Newtonhill
Newtonmore   Spey   1291   Ballater   Banchory
Spey   Cairngorm Mts   Mount   Stonehaven
jaidh   Lochnagar   Keen
Ben   Loch   1155   939
Alder   E17icht   Grampian   Mayar
1148   Loch   Beinn   928   Water of Saughs   Inverbervie
Loch   Garry   Dearg   Carn nan   North   Laurencekirk
        1008   Gábhar   Esk
Loch   Forest of Atholl 1121   Backwater   Hillside
Tummel   Blair Atholl   Reservoir   South Esk   Brechin
Schiehallion   Pitlochry   Isla   Kirriemuir   Montrose
1083   Alyth
Loch   Forfar   Lunan Bay
Rannoch   Tay   Aberfeldy   Strathmore
Lyon   Blairgowrie   Arbroath

North Sea

Shetland inset

H   1°   I
2°
Herma Ness
Unst
Baltasound
Point of   Yell Sound
Fethaland   Yell   Fetlar
Isbister   Ronas
Esha Ness   Hill
Hillswick   450   Toft   Out Skerries
St Magnus   Lerwick   Voe   Whalsay
Bay   Muckle
Papa   Roe   Melby
Stour   Walls
Shetland
Islands   Scalloway   Lerwick   Bressay
                    Isle of Noss
Foula   Burra
Mousa
60°   Sumburgh
       Sumburgh Head
Fair Isle

G   2°   H   Kirkwall   I
               Aberdeen

58°
59°
60°

Lerwick

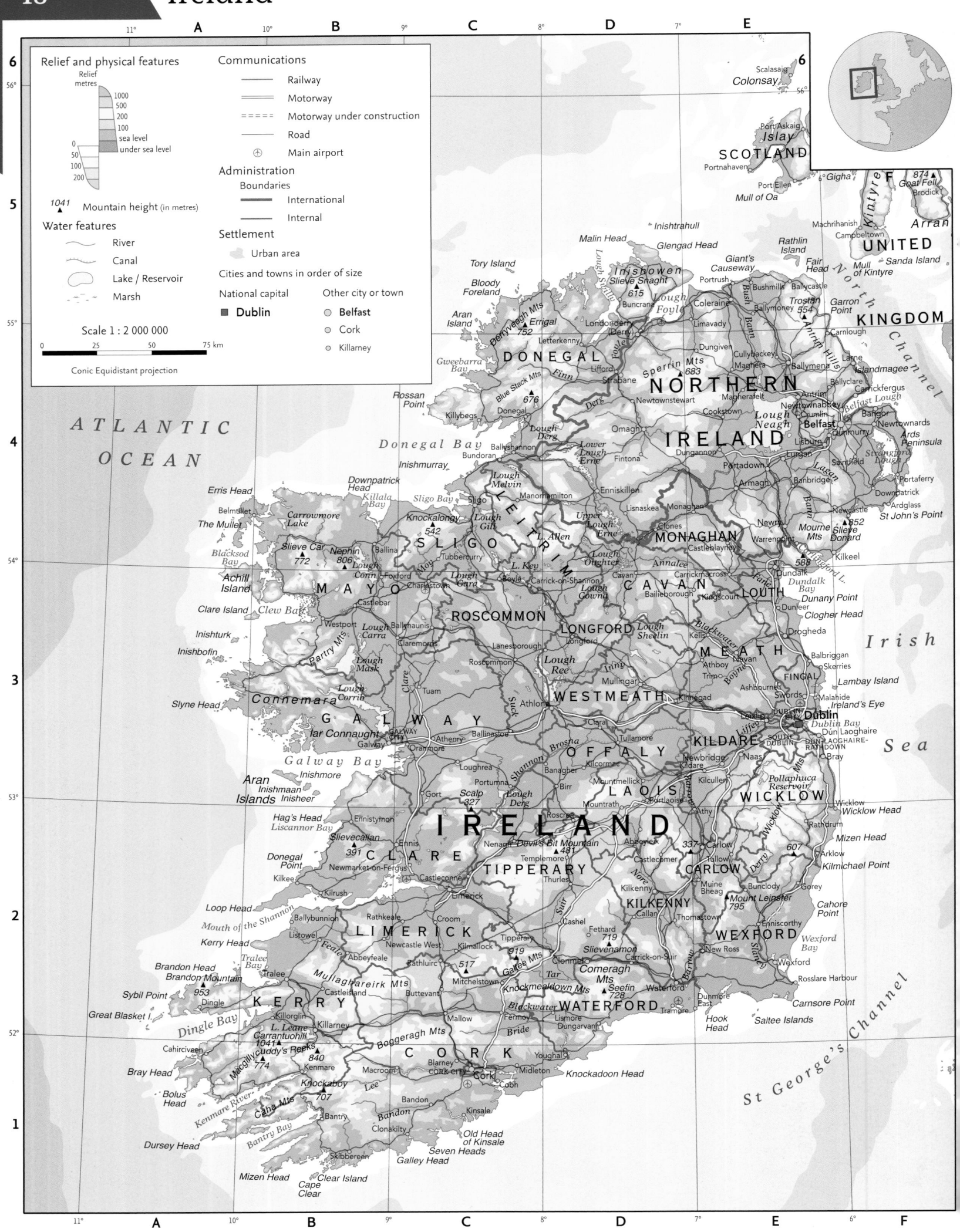

1. Snow-covered mountains in Scotland.

2. The dark green areas are coniferous forests.

3. Mountains covered with heather and poor grass.

4. Large parts of Ireland are covered in rich grassland, shown in green.

5. Much of the land in the UK is used for agriculture. This is why so much of the image shows greens and browns.

6. Areas of grey represent built-up areas.

United Kingdom

SCOTLAND
Edinburgh
ENGLAND
London
NORTHERN IRELAND
Belfast
IRELAND
WALES
Cardiff

West Central Scotland

NORTH LANARKSHIRE
Motherwell
Kirkintilloch
EAST DUNBARTON-SHIRE
GLASGOW CITY
Glasgow
Dumbarton
WEST DUNBARTON-SHIRE
Giffnock
EAST RENFREW-SHIRE
Paisley
RENFREWSHIRE
Greenock
INVERCLYDE

East Central Scotland

Haddington
EAST LOTHIAN
Dalkeith
MIDLOTHIAN
Edinburgh
CITY OF EDINBURGH
Livingston
WEST LOTHIAN
CLACKMANNAN-SHIRE
Alloa
FALKIRK
Falkirk

SHETLAND ISLANDS
Lerwick

ORKNEY ISLANDS
Kirkwall

HIGHLAND
Inverness

MORAY
Elgin

ABERDEEN-SHIRE
ABERDEEN CITY
Aberdeen

ANGUS
Forfar

DUNDEE CITY
Dundee

PERTH & KINROSS
Perth

FIFE
Glenrothes

SCOTLAND

STIRLING
Stirling

ARGYLL AND BUTE
Lochgilphead

Dumbarton
Greenock
RENFREWSHIRE
Paisley
Glasgow
Kirkintilloch
Alloa
Falkirk
Hamilton
Motherwell
SOUTH LANARKSHIRE
EAST AYRSHIRE
Kilmarnock
Irvine
NORTH AYRSHIRE
Ayr
SOUTH AYRSHIRE

Livingston
Edinburgh
Dalkeith
MIDLOTHIAN
EAST LOTHIAN
Haddington

SCOTTISH BORDERS
Newtown St Boswells

DUMFRIES
Dumfries

NA H-EILEANAN SIAR (WESTERN ISLES)
Stornoway

NORTHUMBERLAND
Morpeth
NEWCASTLE UPON TYNE
NORTH TYNESIDE
Wallsend

CAUSEWAY COAST AND GLENS

Key

Administration
Boundaries
International
National
Administrative

Settlement
Capital city
Administrative centre

Scale 1 : 3 000 000
0   25   50   75   100 km

Conic Equidistant projection

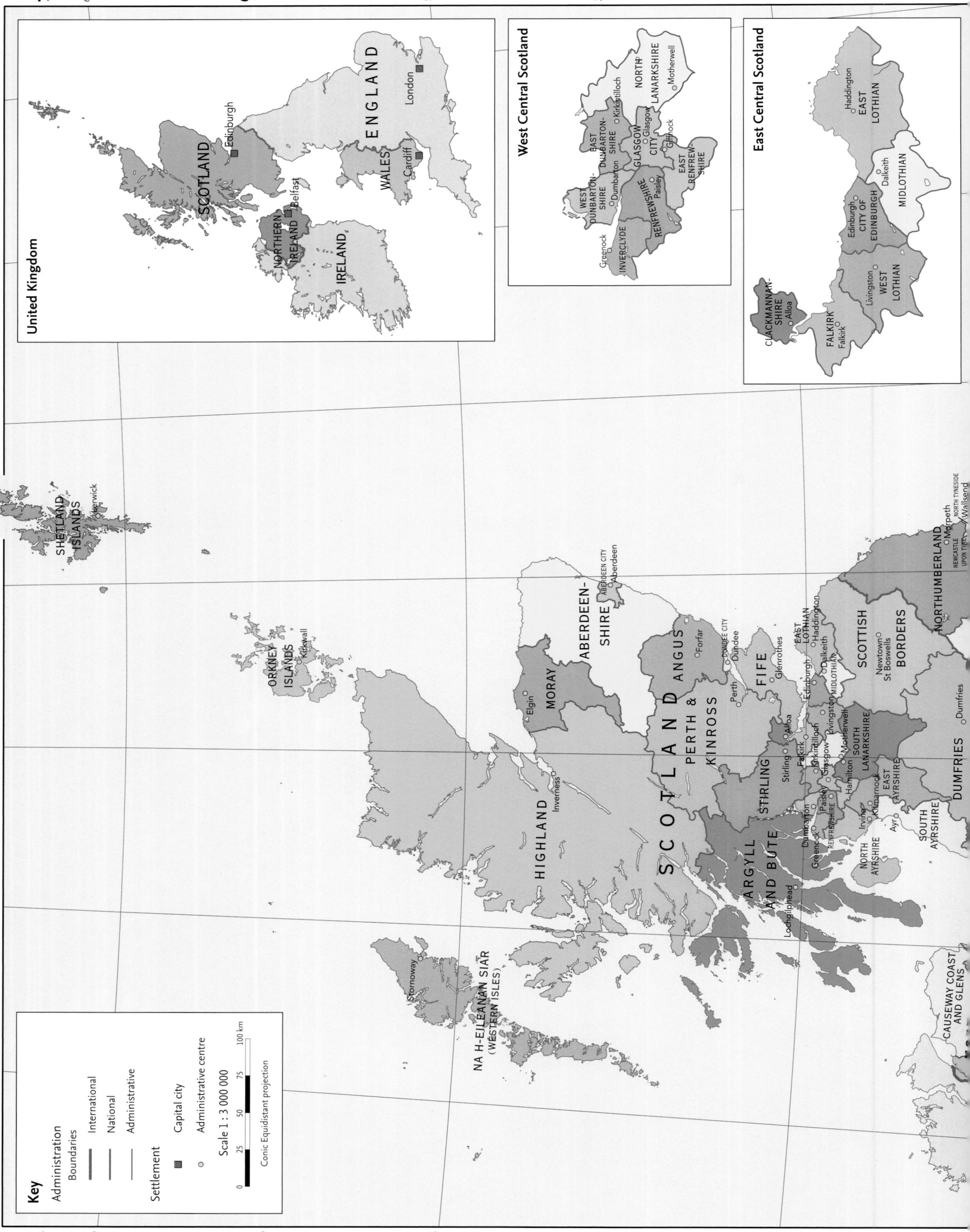

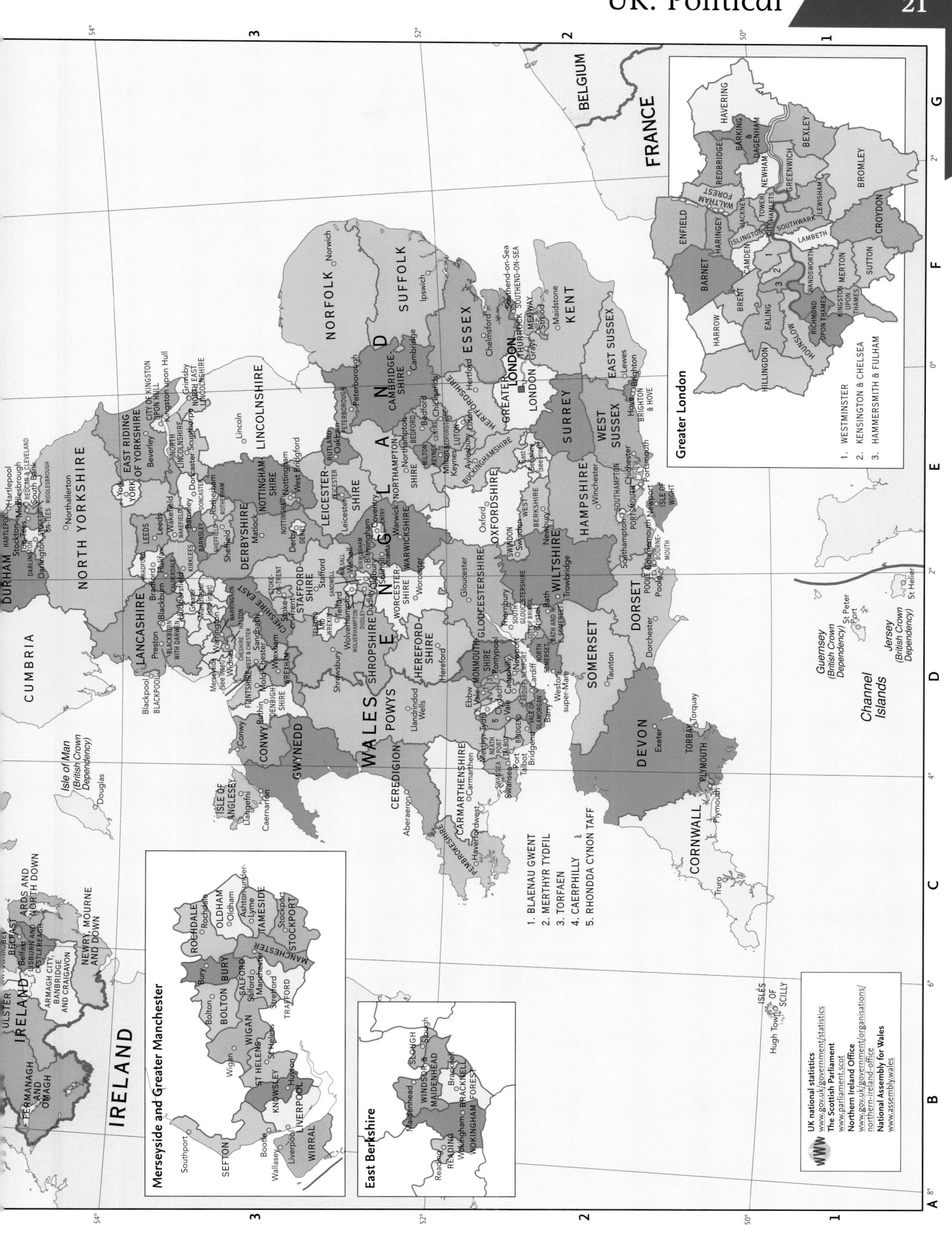

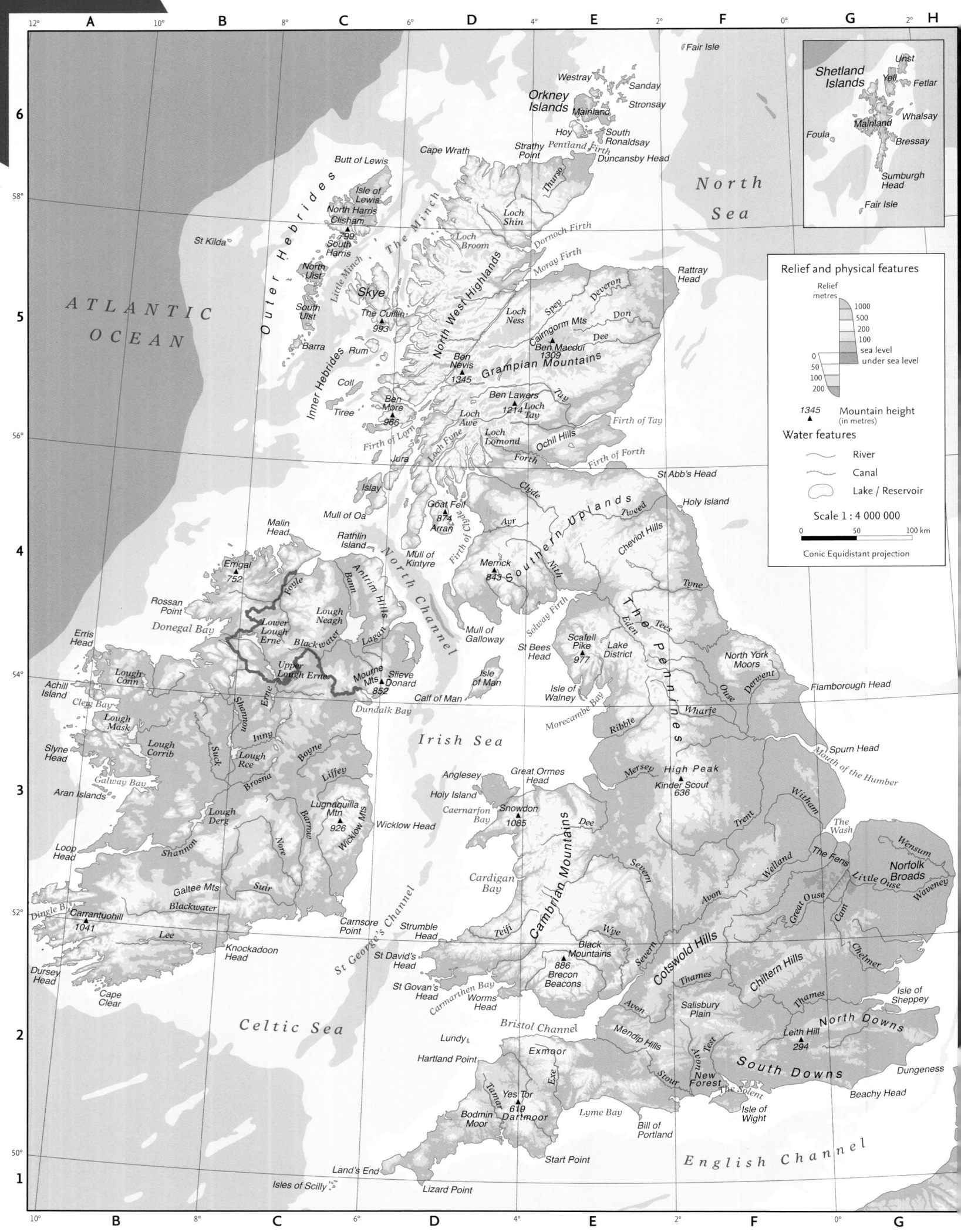

Relief and physical features

Relief metres
1000
500
200
100
0 sea level
50 under sea level
100
200

1345 ▲ Mountain height (in metres)

Water features
~~~ River
~~~ Canal
◯ Lake / Reservoir

Scale 1 : 4 000 000

0   50   100 km

Conic Equidistant projection

Great Britain and Ireland: Geology

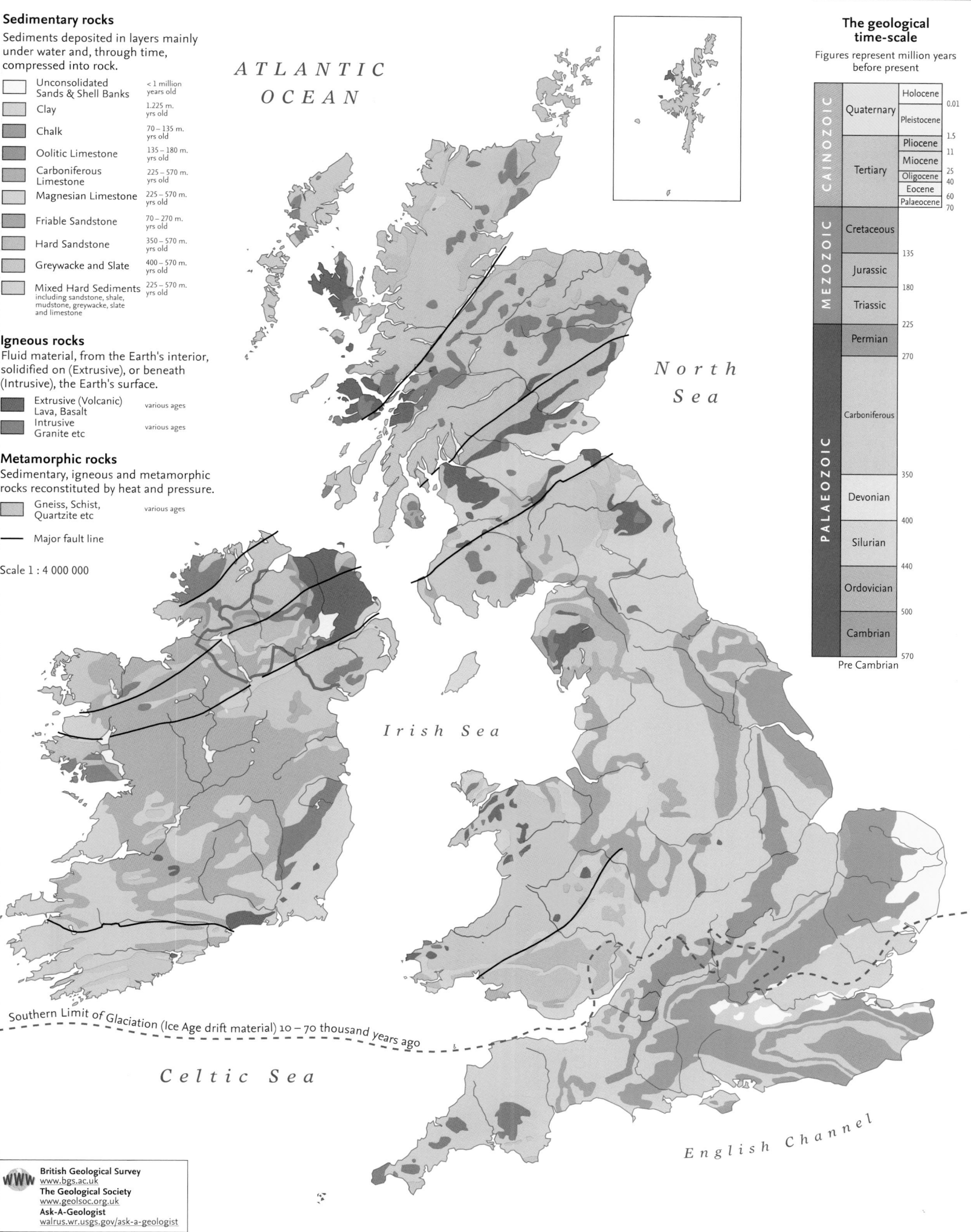

Sedimentary rocks

Sediments deposited in layers mainly under water and, through time, compressed into rock.

	Unconsolidated Sands & Shell Banks	< 1 million years old
	Clay	1.225 m. yrs old
	Chalk	70 – 135 m. yrs old
	Oolitic Limestone	135 – 180 m. yrs old
	Carboniferous Limestone	225 – 570 m. yrs old
	Magnesian Limestone	225 – 570 m. yrs old
	Friable Sandstone	70 – 270 m. yrs old
	Hard Sandstone	350 – 570 m. yrs old
	Greywacke and Slate	400 – 570 m. yrs old
	Mixed Hard Sediments including sandstone, shale, mudstone, greywacke, slate and limestone	225 – 570 m. yrs old

Igneous rocks

Fluid material, from the Earth's interior, solidified on (Extrusive), or beneath (Intrusive), the Earth's surface.

	Extrusive (Volcanic) Lava, Basalt	various ages
	Intrusive Granite etc	various ages

Metamorphic rocks

Sedimentary, igneous and metamorphic rocks reconstituted by heat and pressure.

	Gneiss, Schist, Quartzite etc	various ages
——	Major fault line	

Scale 1 : 4 000 000

ATLANTIC OCEAN

North Sea

Irish Sea

Celtic Sea

English Channel

Southern Limit of Glaciation (Ice Age drift material) 10 – 70 thousand years ago

The geological time-scale

Figures represent million years before present

Era	Period	Epoch	
CAINOZOIC	Quaternary	Holocene	0.01
		Pleistocene	1.5
	Tertiary	Pliocene	11
		Miocene	25
		Oligocene	40
		Eocene	60
		Palaeocene	70
MEZOZOIC	Cretaceous		135
	Jurassic		180
	Triassic		225
PALAEOZOIC	Permian		270
	Carboniferous		350
	Devonian		400
	Silurian		440
	Ordovician		500
	Cambrian		570
	Pre Cambrian		

WWW British Geological Survey
www.bgs.ac.uk
The Geological Society
www.geolsoc.org.uk
Ask-A-Geologist
walrus.wr.usgs.gov/ask-a-geologist

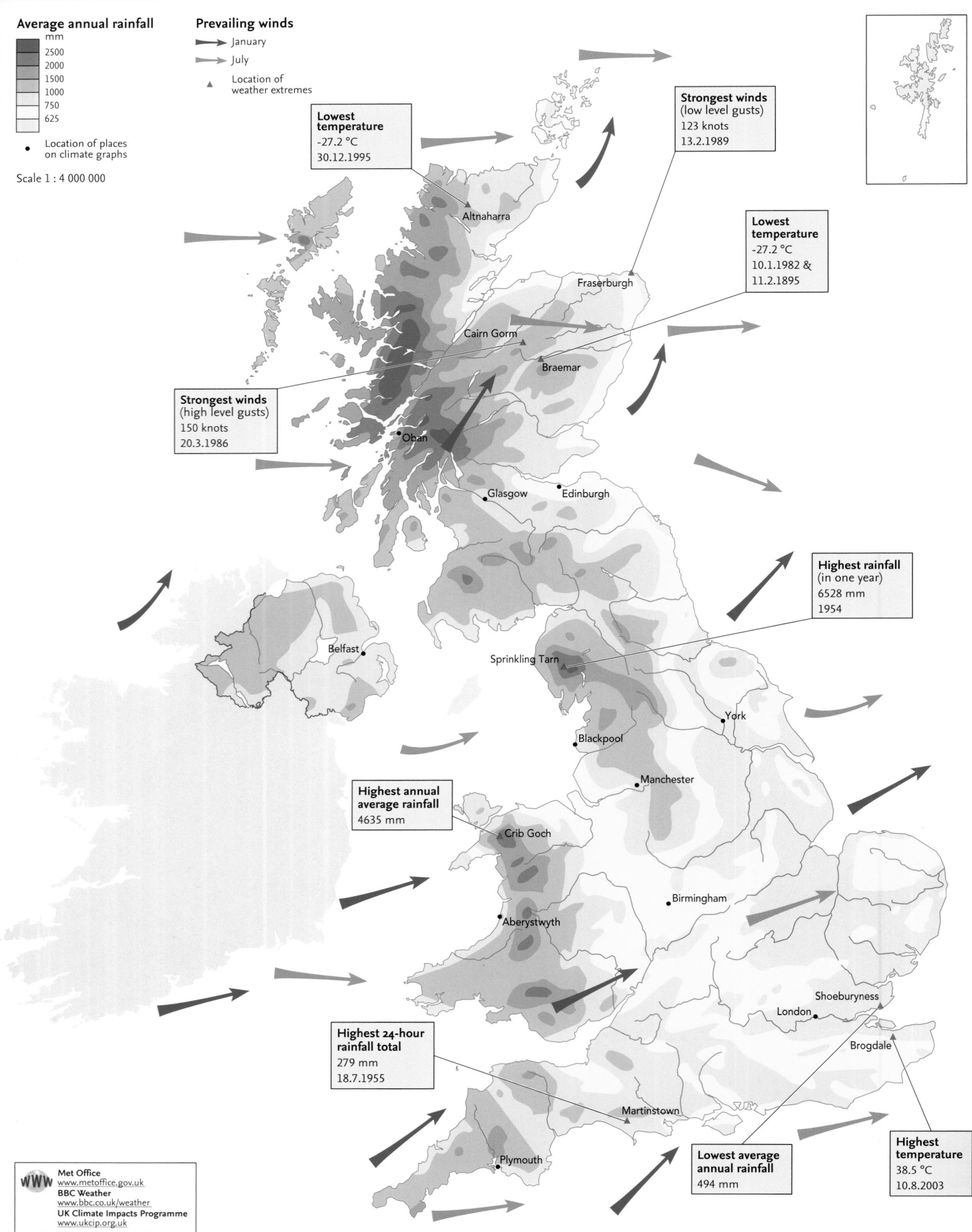

Average annual rainfall
mm
2500
2000
1500
1000
750
625

• Location of places
on climate graphs

Scale 1 : 4 000 000

Prevailing winds
→ January
→ July
▲ Location of
weather extremes

Lowest temperature
-27.2 °C
30.12.1995

Altnaharra

Strongest winds
(low level gusts)
123 knots
13.2.1989

Fraserburgh

Lowest temperature
-27.2 °C
10.1.1982 &
11.2.1895

Cairn Gorm

Braemar

Strongest winds
(high level gusts)
150 knots
20.3.1986

•Oban

Glasgow •Edinburgh

Highest rainfall
(in one year)
6528 mm
1954

Belfast•

Sprinkling Tarn

York

Blackpool•

Manchester•

Highest annual average rainfall
4635 mm

Crib Goch

Birmingham•

Aberystwyth•

Shoeburyness

London•

Brogdale

Highest 24-hour rainfall total
279 mm
18.7.1955

Martinstown

Lowest average annual rainfall
494 mm

Highest temperature
38.5 °C
10.8.2003

Plymouth•

www **Met Office**
www.metoffice.gov.uk
BBC Weather
www.bbc.co.uk/weather
UK Climate Impacts Programme
www.ukcip.org.uk

January temperature

°C
6
4
2
0

Currents

→ Warm
→ Cold

Scale 1 : 12 000 000

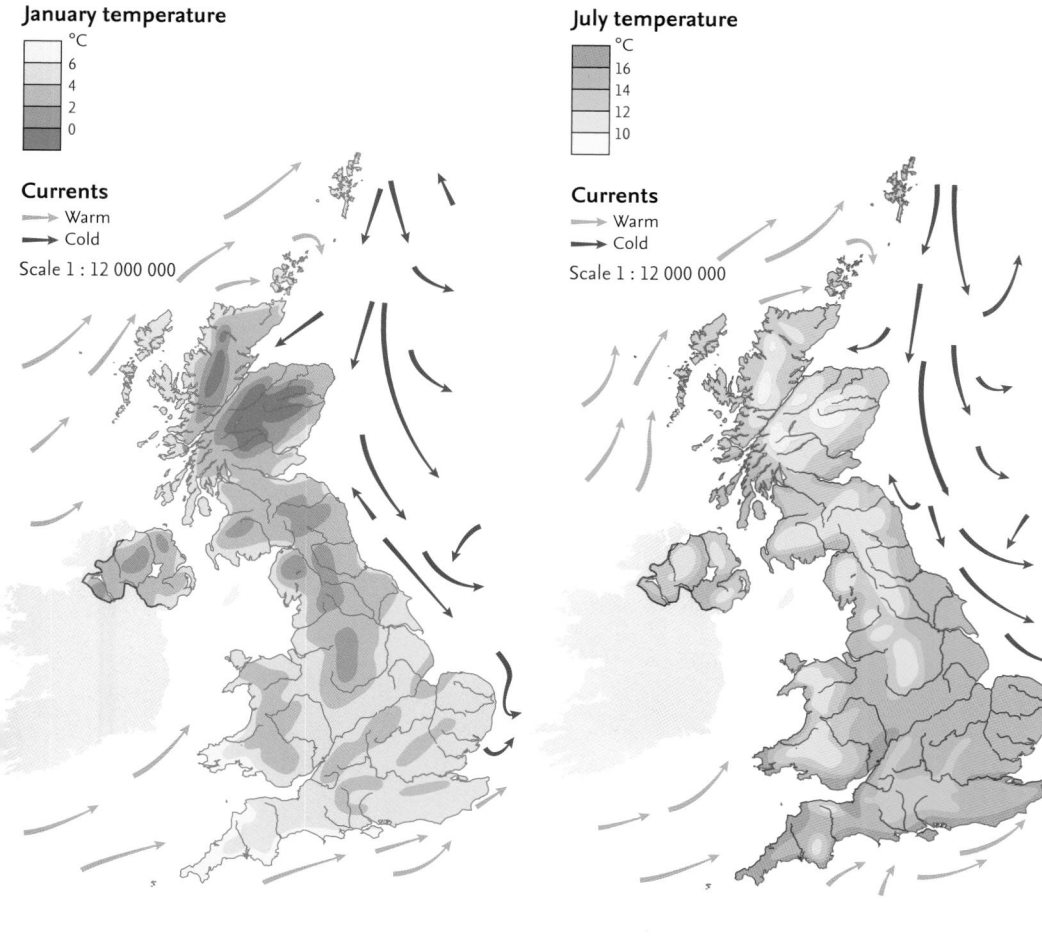

July temperature

°C
16
14
12
10

Currents

→ Warm
→ Cold

Scale 1 : 12 000 000

Climate graphs

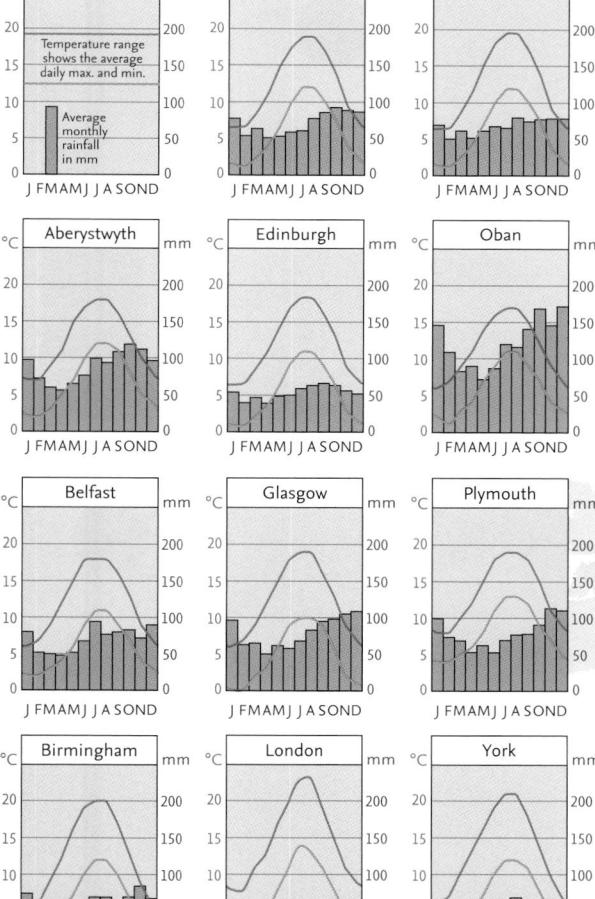

Town — Temperature range shows the average daily max. and min. — Average monthly rainfall in mm

Blackpool

Manchester

Aberystwyth

Edinburgh

Oban

Belfast

Glasgow

Plymouth

Birmingham

London

York

Rainfall change

Percentage change 1916 – 2016

over 20
10 – 20
2.5 – 10
0 – 2.5
-5 – 0

Scale 1 : 12 000 000

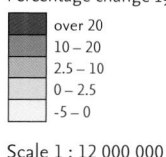

SCOTLAND N

SCOTLAND E

SCOTLAND W

NORTHERN IRELAND

ENGLAND E & NE

ENGLAND NW/ WALES N

MIDLANDS

EAST ANGLIA

ENGLAND SW/ WALES S

ENGLAND SE/ CENTRAL S

Climate change

The Earth's climate has changed on many timescales in response to natural factors.

The Sun drives our climate

1. Most sunlight passes through the atmosphere and warms the Earth.

2. Infrared radiation is given off by the Earth. Most IR escapes through outer space and cools the Earth.

3. But some IR is trapped by gases in the air and this reduces the cooling effect.

This is known as the greenhouse effect.

The gases responsible for this are called greenhouse gases. These include:

Carbon Dioxide / Methane / Ozone / Water vapour / Nitrus Oxide

Greenhouse gases are so effective at keeping the Earth warm that any changes will affect the Earth's temperature.

A changing climate

In the last century our climate has started to change rapidly. How can we tell if these changes are natural or down to us?

What factors cause a warming of our climate?

 More energy from the sun.

Large natural events e.g. El Nino.

Increased greenhouse gases.

There is evidence that the majority of warming seen over the last 100 years is due to increased amounts of greenhouse gases in the atmosphere

Greenhouse gases occur naturally but human activities have increased the amount of carbon dioxide, methane and some others.

Burning of fossil fuels such as coal, gas and oil.

Changes in land use such as clearing forests for crop production.

Carbon dioxide concentrations have increased by around 40% since 1750.

There is a natural carbon cycle in our climate. The increase in CO2 in the atmosphere cannot be explained by this alone.

UK: Agriculture and Forestry

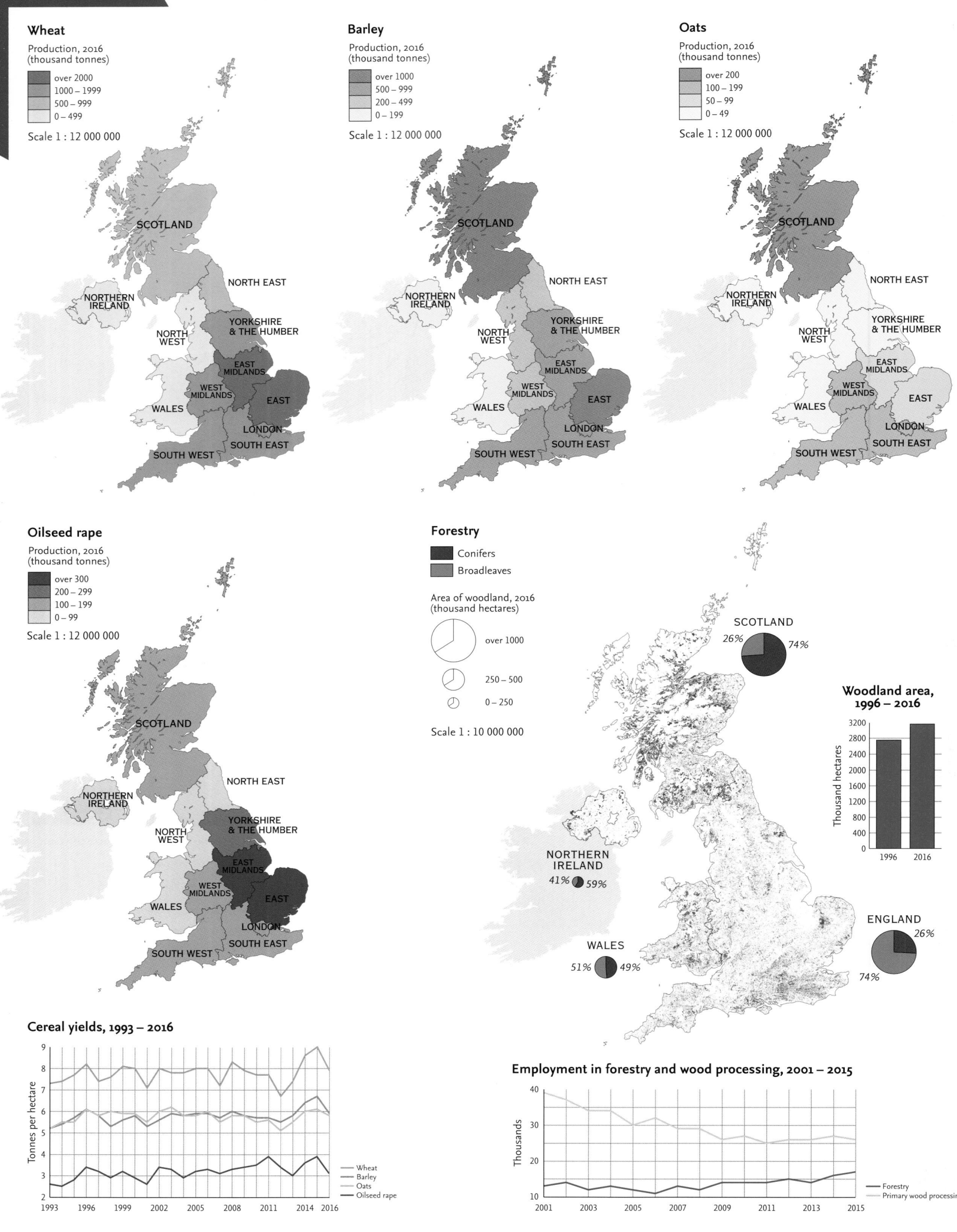

Wheat

Production, 2016
(thousand tonnes)

- over 2000
- 1000 – 1999
- 500 – 999
- 0 – 499

Scale 1 : 12 000 000

SCOTLAND
NORTHERN IRELAND
NORTH EAST
NORTH WEST
YORKSHIRE & THE HUMBER
EAST MIDLANDS
WEST MIDLANDS
WALES
EAST
LONDON
SOUTH EAST
SOUTH WEST

Barley

Production, 2016
(thousand tonnes)

- over 1000
- 500 – 999
- 200 – 499
- 0 – 199

Scale 1 : 12 000 000

SCOTLAND
NORTHERN IRELAND
NORTH EAST
NORTH WEST
YORKSHIRE & THE HUMBER
EAST MIDLANDS
WEST MIDLANDS
WALES
EAST
LONDON
SOUTH EAST
SOUTH WEST

Oats

Production, 2016
(thousand tonnes)

- over 200
- 100 – 199
- 50 – 99
- 0 – 49

Scale 1 : 12 000 000

SCOTLAND
NORTHERN IRELAND
NORTH EAST
NORTH WEST
YORKSHIRE & THE HUMBER
EAST MIDLANDS
WEST MIDLANDS
WALES
EAST
LONDON
SOUTH EAST
SOUTH WEST

Oilseed rape

Production, 2016
(thousand tonnes)

- over 300
- 200 – 299
- 100 – 199
- 0 – 99

Scale 1 : 12 000 000

SCOTLAND
NORTHERN IRELAND
NORTH EAST
NORTH WEST
YORKSHIRE & THE HUMBER
EAST MIDLANDS
WEST MIDLANDS
WALES
EAST
LONDON
SOUTH EAST
SOUTH WEST

Forestry

- Conifers
- Broadleaves

Area of woodland, 2016
(thousand hectares)

- over 1000
- 250 – 500
- 0 – 250

Scale 1 : 10 000 000

SCOTLAND
26% 74%

NORTHERN IRELAND
41% 59%

WALES
51% 49%

ENGLAND
26%
74%

Woodland area, 1996 – 2016

Thousand hectares

3200
2800
2400
2000
1600
1200
800
400
0

1996   2016

Cereal yields, 1993 – 2016

Tonnes per hectare

9
8
7
6
5
4
3
2

1993 1996 1999 2002 2005 2008 2011 2014 2016

- Wheat
- Barley
- Oats
- Oilseed rape

Employment in forestry and wood processing, 2001 – 2015

Thousands

40
30
20
10

2001 2003 2005 2007 2009 2011 2013 2015

- Forestry
- Primary wood processing

Livestock farming

Population by region, 2015

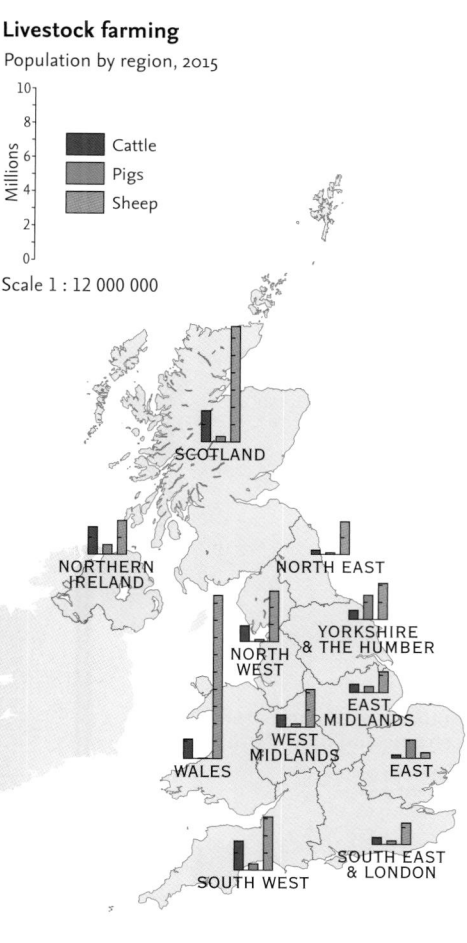

Millions
10
8
6
4
2
0
Cattle
Pigs
Sheep
Scale 1 : 12 000 000
SCOTLAND
NORTHERN IRELAND
NORTH EAST
YORKSHIRE & THE HUMBER
NORTH WEST
EAST MIDLANDS
WEST MIDLANDS
WALES
EAST
SOUTH EAST & LONDON
SOUTH WEST

Dairy farming

Milk production, 2016 (million litres)

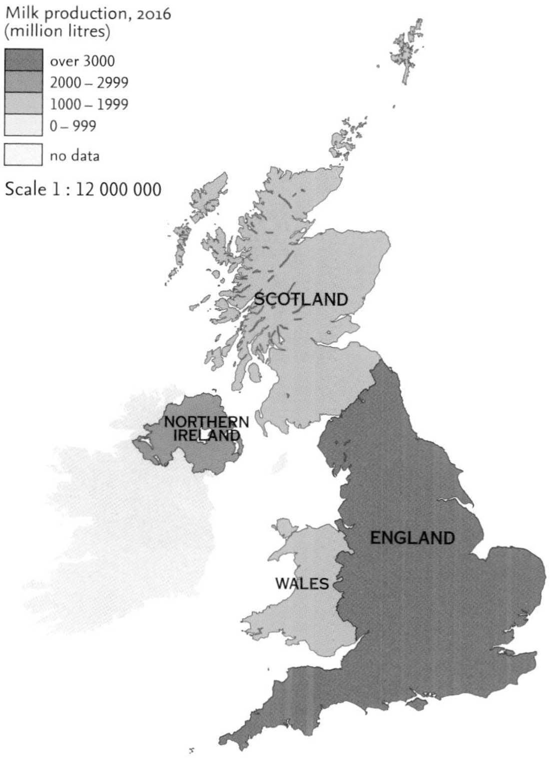

over 3000
2000 – 2999
1000 – 1999
0 – 999
no data
Scale 1 : 12 000 000
SCOTLAND
NORTHERN IRELAND
ENGLAND
WALES

Dairy cows, 1996 – 2016

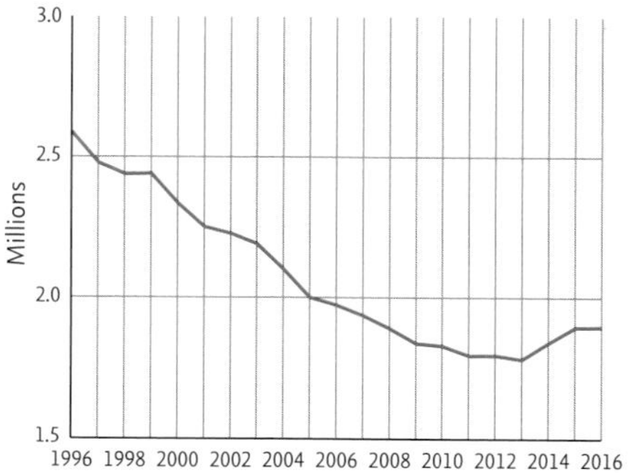

Millions
3.0
2.5
2.0
1.5
1996 1998 2000 2002 2004 2006 2008 2010 2012 2014 2016

UK milk usage, 2014

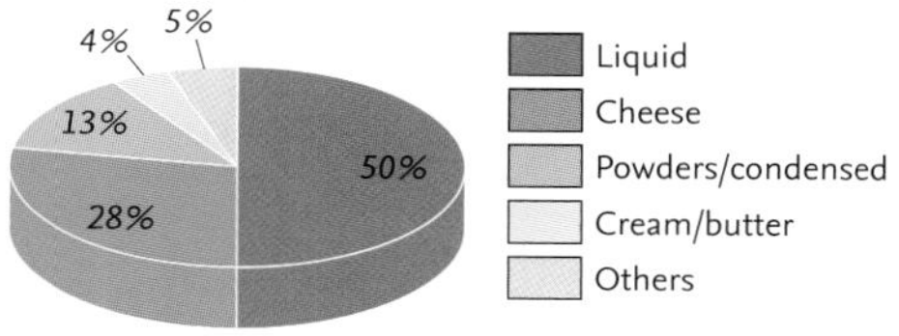

50%
28%
13%
4%
5%
Liquid
Cheese
Powders/condensed
Cream/butter
Others

Employment in agriculture, 2000 – 2016

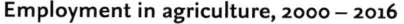

Thousands
530
520
510
500
490
480
470
460
450
2000 2002 2004 2006 2008 2010 2012 2014 2016

Agricultural workforce by country, 2016

Total agricultural workforce = 466 000

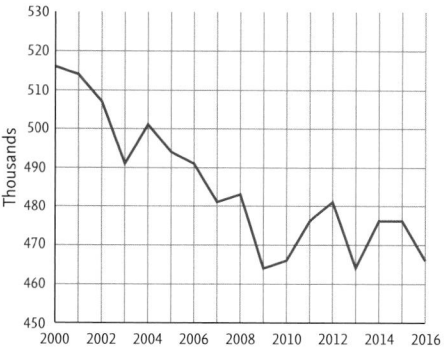

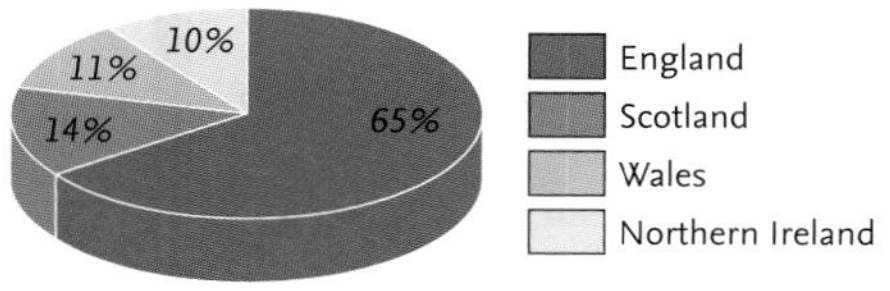

65%
14%
11%
10%
England
Scotland
Wales
Northern Ireland

Fishing workforce by country, 2015

Total fishing workforce = 12 107

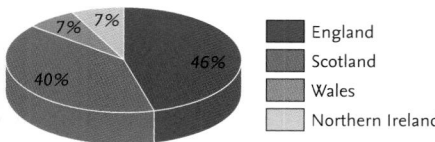

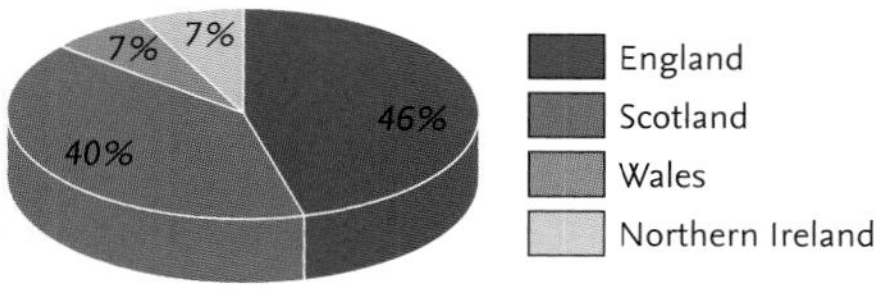

46%
40%
7%
7%
England
Scotland
Wales
Northern Ireland

Major fishing ports

by catch value (£ million), 2015

- over 30
- 20 – 30
- 10 – 20
- 5 – 10
- Other ports less than 5

Type of fish caught

by port

- ■ Demersal
- ▲ Pelagic
- ● Shellfish

Fishing grounds

Most-fished areas

Scale 1 : 10 000 000

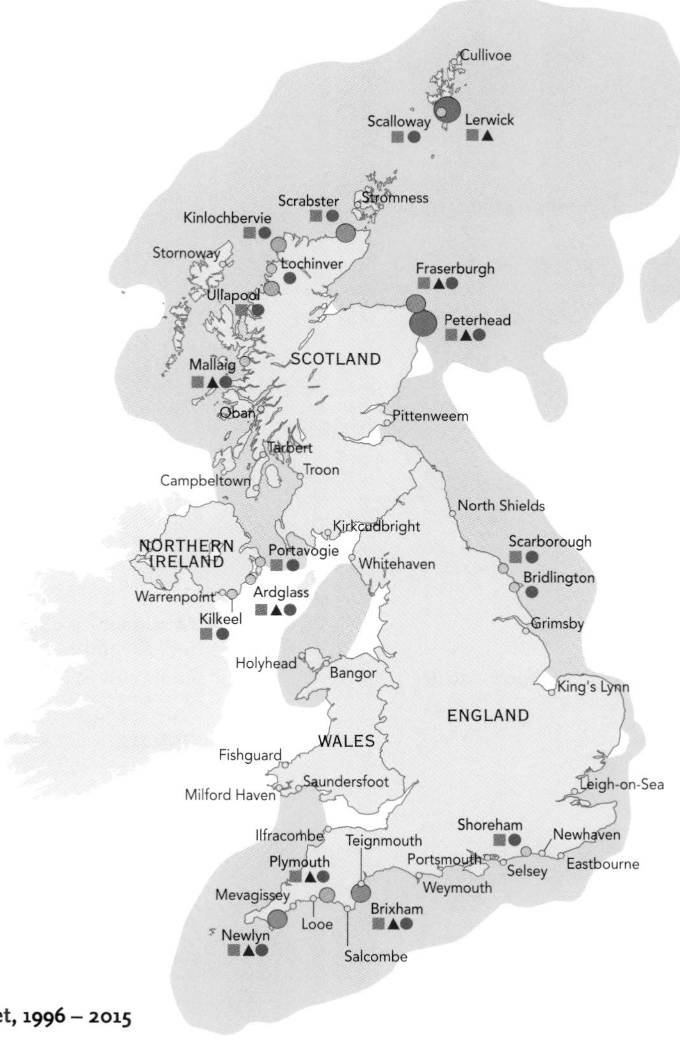

Cullivoe
Scalloway
Lerwick
Scrabster
Stromness
Kinlochbervie
Stornoway
Lochinver
Fraserburgh
Ullapool
Peterhead
Mallaig
SCOTLAND
Oban
Pittenweem
Tarbert
Troon
Campbeltown
North Shields
Kirkcudbright
NORTHERN IRELAND
Portavogie
Whitehaven
Scarborough
Bridlington
Warrenpoint
Ardglass
Kilkeel
Grimsby
Holyhead
Bangor
King's Lynn
ENGLAND
WALES
Fishguard
Saundersfoot
Milford Haven
Leigh-on-Sea
Ilfracombe
Teignmouth
Shoreham
Newhaven
Plymouth
Portsmouth
Selsey
Eastbourne
Weymouth
Mevagissey
Brixham
Looe
Newlyn
Salcombe

Size of the UK fishing fleet, 1996 – 2015

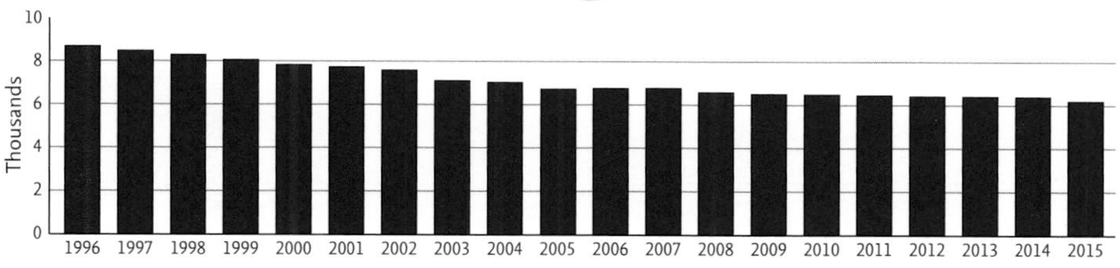

Thousands
10
8
6
4
2
0
1996 1997 1998 1999 2000 2001 2002 2003 2004 2005 2006 2007 2008 2009 2010 2011 2012 2013 2014 2015

Employment by economic sector, 2017

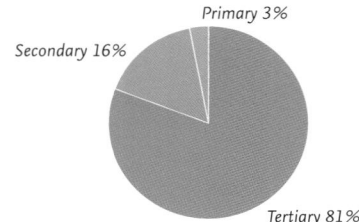

Primary 3%
Secondary 16%
Tertiary 81%

Primary employment by industry sector, 2017

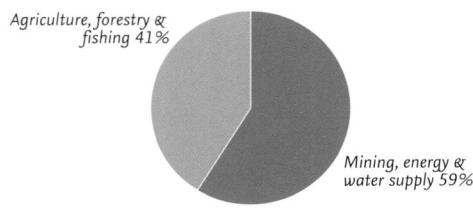

Agriculture, forestry & fishing 41%
Mining, energy & water supply 59%

Secondary employment by industry sector, 2017

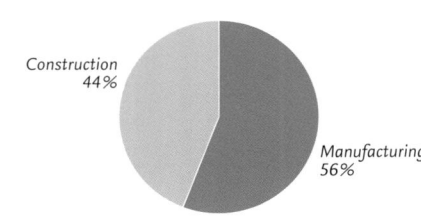

Construction 44%
Manufacturing 56%

Tertiary employment by industry sector, 2017

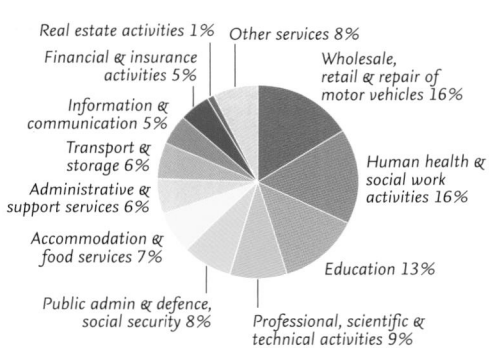

Real estate activities 1%
Other services 8%
Financial & insurance activities 5%
Information & communication 5%
Transport & storage 6%
Administrative & support services 6%
Accommodation & food services 7%
Public admin & defence, social security 8%
Professional, scientific & technical activities 9%
Education 13%
Human health & social work activities 16%
Wholesale, retail & repair of motor vehicles 16%

UK unemployment, 2002 – 2016

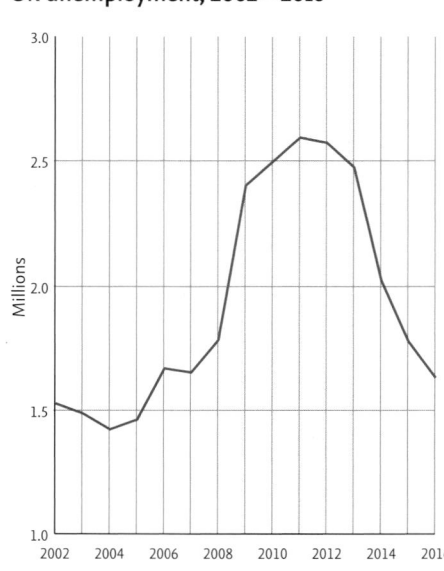

Agriculture, forestry and fishing

Employment compared to national average (index value 1.0), 2015

- over 1.5
- 1.0 – 1.5
- 0.5 – 1.0
- less than 0.5
- no data

Scale 1 : 14 000 000

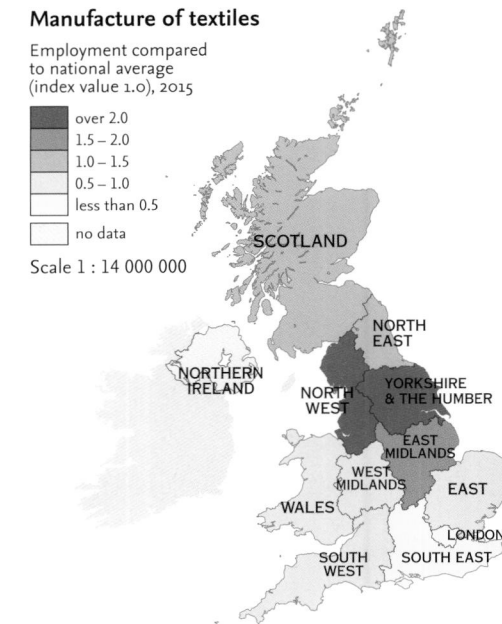

Manufacture of chemicals and chemical products

Employment compared to national average (index value 1.0), 2015

- over 2.0
- 1.5 – 2.0
- 1.0 – 1.5
- 0.5 – 1.0
- less than 0.5
- no data

Scale 1 : 14 000 000

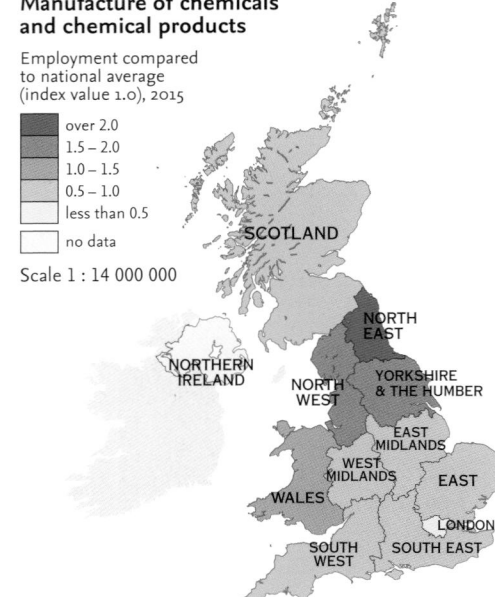

Manufacture of motor vehicles, trailers and semi-trailers

Employment compared to national average (index value 1.0), 2015

- over 2.0
- 1.5 – 2.0
- 1.0 – 1.5
- 0.5 – 1.0
- less than 0.5
- no data

Scale 1 : 14 000 000

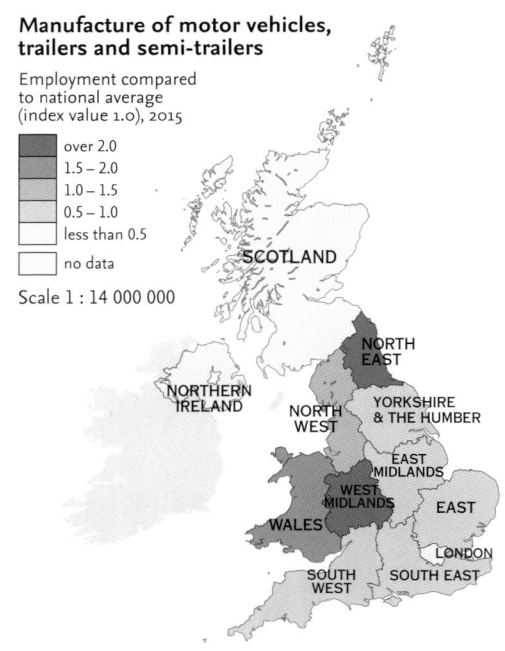

Manufacture of textiles

Employment compared to national average (index value 1.0), 2015

- over 2.0
- 1.5 – 2.0
- 1.0 – 1.5
- 0.5 – 1.0
- less than 0.5
- no data

Scale 1 : 14 000 000

Manufacture of computer, electronic and optical products

Employment compared to national average (index value 1.0), 2015

- over 1.5
- 1.0 – 1.5
- 0.5 – 1.0
- less than 0.5
- no data

Scale 1 : 14 000 000

Financial service activities, except insurance and pension funding

Employment compared to national average (index value 1.0), 2015

- over 2.0
- 1.5 – 2.0
- 1.0 – 1.5
- 0.5 – 1.0
- less than 0.5
- no data

Scale 1 : 14 000 000

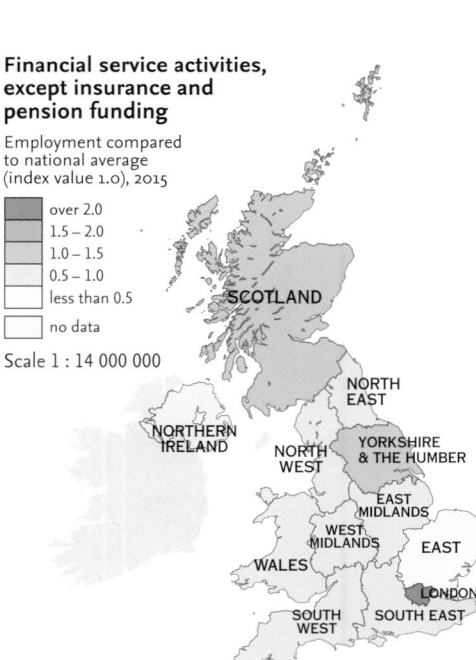

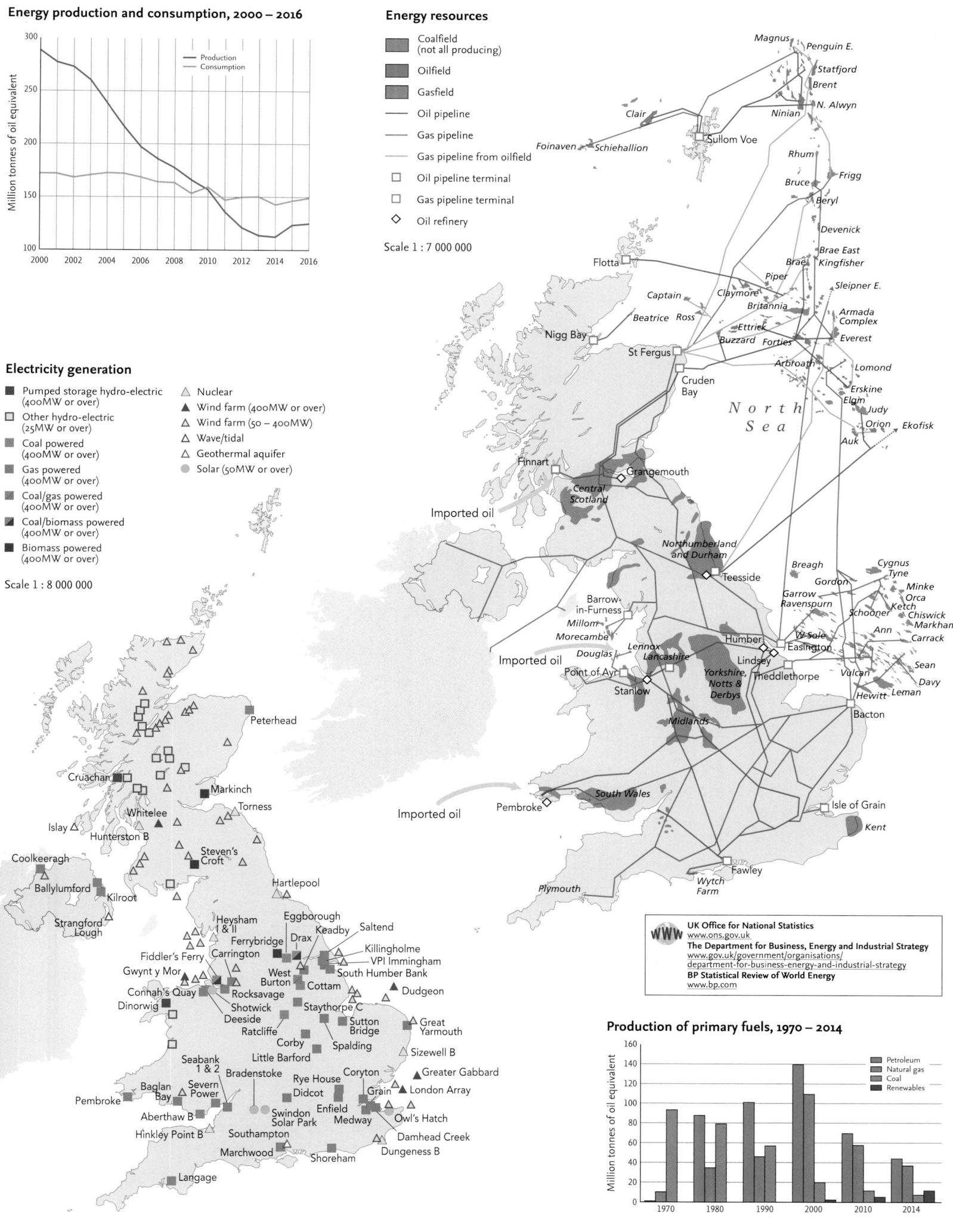

Energy production and consumption, 2000 – 2016

Million tonnes of oil equivalent

Production
Consumption

Energy resources

Coalfield (not all producing)

Oilfield

Gasfield

— Oil pipeline

— Gas pipeline

— Gas pipeline from oilfield

□ Oil pipeline terminal

□ Gas pipeline terminal

◇ Oil refinery

Scale 1 : 7 000 000

Electricity generation

■ Pumped storage hydro-electric (400MW or over)

□ Other hydro-electric (25MW or over)

■ Coal powered (400MW or over)

■ Gas powered (400MW or over)

■ Coal/gas powered (400MW or over)

◪ Coal/biomass powered (400MW or over)

■ Biomass powered (400MW or over)

△ Nuclear

▲ Wind farm (400MW or over)

△ Wind farm (50 – 400MW)

△ Wave/tidal

△ Geothermal aquifer

● Solar (50MW or over)

Scale 1 : 8 000 000

North Sea

Magnus
Penguin E.
Statfjord
Brent
Clair
N. Alwyn
Ninian
Foinaven
Schiehallion
Sullom Voe
Rhum
Bruce
Frigg
Beryl
Devenick
Brae East
Kingfisher
Brae
Flotta
Captain
Claymore
Piper
Sleipner E.
Beatrice
Ross
Britannia
Armada Complex
Nigg Bay
Ettrick
Buzzard
Forties
Everest
St Fergus
Arbroath
Lomond
Cruden Bay
Erskine
Elgin
Judy
Orion
Ekofisk
Auk

Finnart
Grangemouth
Central Scotland
Imported oil
Northumberland and Durham
Breagh
Cygnus
Tyne
Teesside
Gordon
Minke
Orca
Barrow-in-Furness
Garrow
Ravenspurn
Schooner
Ketch
Chiswick
Millom
Markham
Morecambe
Humber
Ann
Carrack
Douglas
Lennox
Lancashire
Easington
Imported oil
Lindsey
Sean
Point of Ayr
Yorkshire, Notts & Derbys
Theddlethorpe
Vulcan
Davy
Stanlow
Leman
Hewitt
Midlands
Bacton
South Wales
Isle of Grain
Pembroke
Kent
Imported oil
Fawley
Plymouth
Wytch Farm

Peterhead
Cruachan
Markinch
Whitelee
Torness
Islay
Hunterston B
Steven's Croft
Coolkeeragh
Hartlepool
Ballylumford
Kilroot
Heysham I & II
Eggborough
Strangford Lough
Keadby
Saltend
Ferrybridge
Drax
Fiddler's Ferry
Carrington
Killingholme
VPI Immingham
Gwynt y Mor
West Burton
South Humber Bank
Connah's Quay
Cottam
Rocksavage
Dudgeon
Dinorwig
Shotwick
Staythorpe C
Deeside
Great Yarmouth
Ratcliffe
Sutton Bridge
Corby
Spalding
Sizewell B
Little Barford
Seabank 1 & 2
Coryton
Greater Gabbard
Bradenstoke
Rye House
Pembroke
Baglan Bay
Grain
London Array
Severn Power
Didcot
Aberthaw B
Enfield
Swindon Solar Park
Medway
Owl's Hatch
Hinkley Point B
Southampton
Damhead Creek
Marchwood
Dungeness B
Langage
Shoreham

WWW UK Office for National Statistics
www.ons.gov.uk
The Department for Business, Energy and Industrial Strategy
www.gov.uk/government/organisations/
department-for-business-energy-and-industrial-strategy
BP Statistical Review of World Energy
www.bp.com

Production of primary fuels, 1970 – 2014

Million tonnes of oil equivalent

Petroleum
Natural gas
Coal
Renewables

1970   1980   1990   2000   2010   2014

UK: Population and Migration

Population density

Persons per sq. km

- over 150
- 10 – 150
- under 10

Cities

- over 5 000 000
- 1 000 000 – 5 000 000
- 500 000 – 1 000 000
- 100 000 – 500 000
- 20 000 – 100 000

Scale 1 : 5 000 000

Population change

Percentage change, 2006 – 2016

- 15.0 and over
- 10.0 – 14.9
- 5.0 – 9.9
- 0.1 – 4.9
- 0 and under

Scale 1 : 10 000 000

SCOTLAND

NORTHERN IRELAND

Glasgow

Manchester

Leeds

Birmingham

WALES

ENGLAND

London

Population statistics

Life expectancy	Birth rate	Death rate	Infant mortality	Unemployment rate	Not in education or employment
82 years	**1.2%** 11.9 per 1000 people	**0.9%** 9.3 per 1000 people	**0.4%** 3.9 per 1000 live births	**4.9%** of workforce	**11.1%** of 16-24 year olds

Population under 16

Percentage, 2016

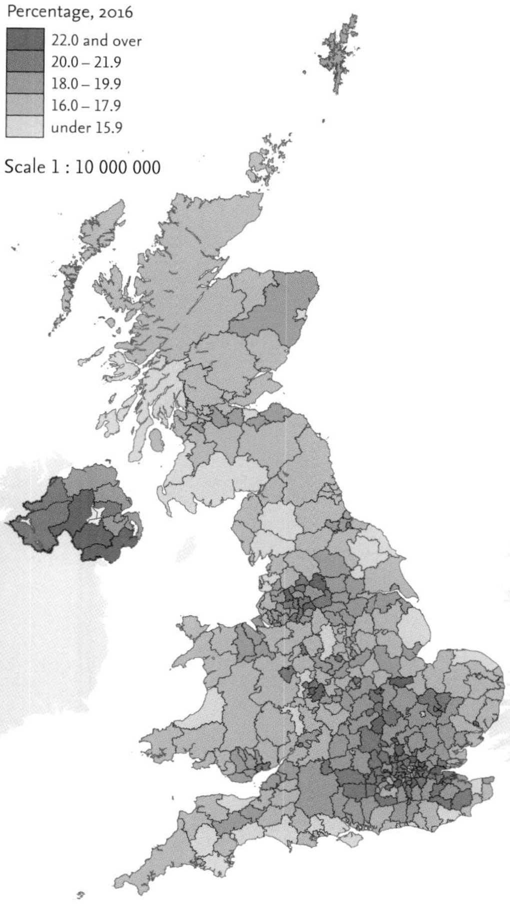

22.0 and over
20.0 – 21.9
18.0 – 19.9
16.0 – 17.9
under 15.9

Scale 1 : 10 000 000

Population over 65

Percentage, 2016

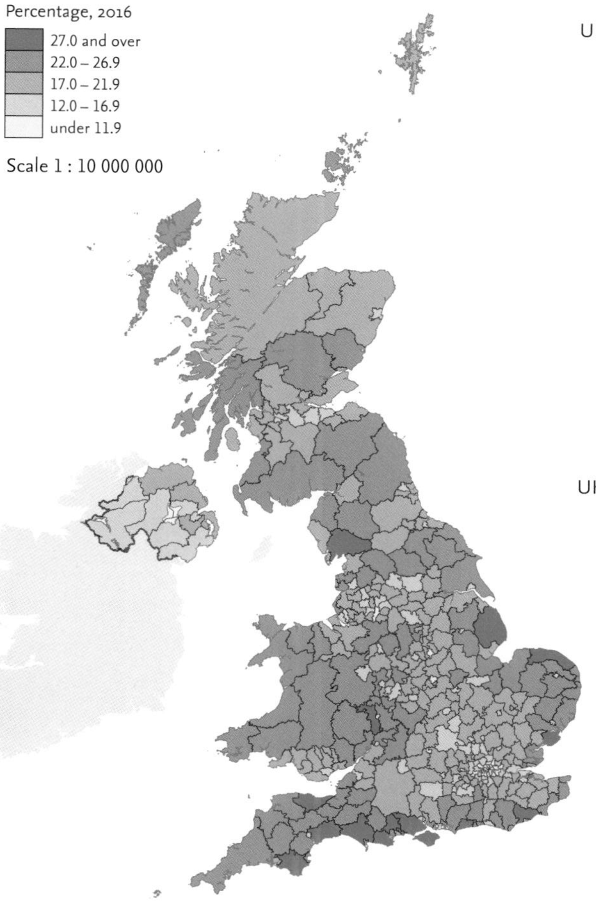

27.0 and over
22.0 – 26.9
17.0 – 21.9
12.0 – 16.9
under 11.9

Scale 1 : 10 000 000

Population structure

UK, 2015

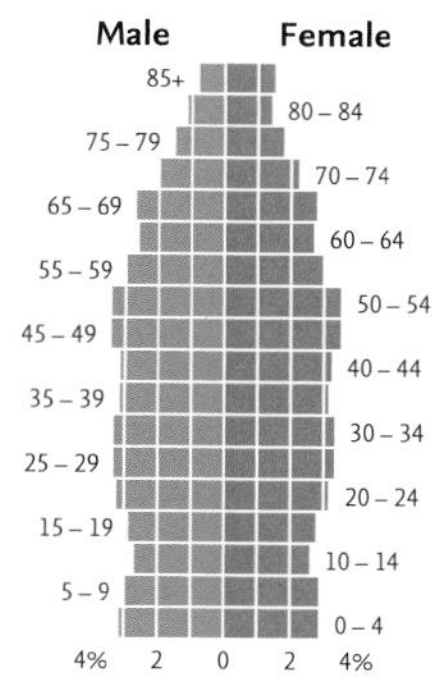

Male
Female
85+
80 – 84
75 – 79
70 – 74
65 – 69
60 – 64
55 – 59
50 – 54
45 – 49
40 – 44
35 – 39
30 – 34
25 – 29
20 – 24
15 – 19
10 – 14
5 – 9
0 – 4
4% 2 0 2 4%

Each full square represents 1% of the total population

UK, 2050

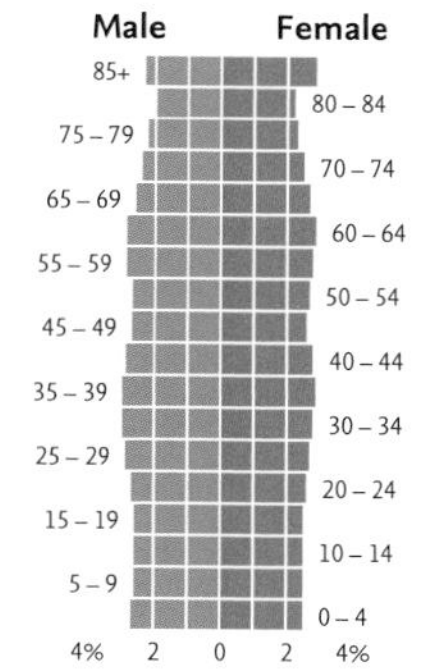

Male
Female
85+
80 – 84
75 – 79
70 – 74
65 – 69
60 – 64
55 – 59
50 – 54
45 – 49
40 – 44
35 – 39
30 – 34
25 – 29
20 – 24
15 – 19
10 – 14
5 – 9
0 – 4
4% 2 0 2 4%

Each full square represents 1% of the total population

Internal migration

Number of people moving, 2016

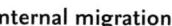

300
250
200
150
100
50
0
Thousands
Moving into area
Moving out of area
SCOTLAND
NORTHERN IRELAND
NORTH EAST
YORKSHIRE & THE HUMBER
NORTH WEST
EAST MIDLANDS
WEST MIDLANDS
WALES
EAST
SOUTH WEST
SOUTH EAST
LONDON

Scale 1 : 10 000 000

Reasons for immigration, 2007 – 2016

350
300
250
200
150
100
50
Thousands
Work related
Formal study
Accompany/join
2007
2008
2009
2010
2011
2012
2013
2014
2015
2016

International migration, 2007 – 2016

700
600
500
400
300
200
100
0
Thousands
Immigration
Emigration
Net migration
2007
2008
2009
2010
2011
2012
2013
2014
2015
2016

Population by ethnic group, 2016

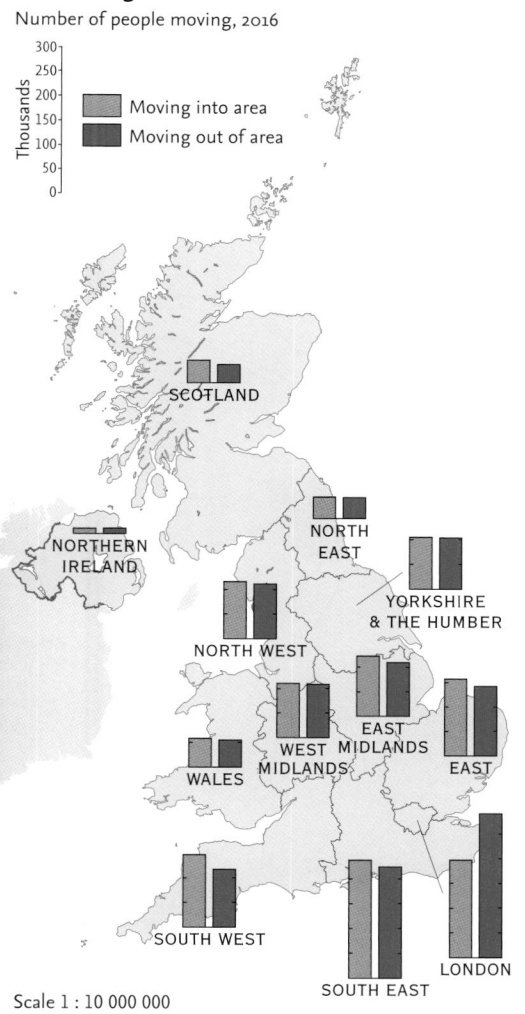

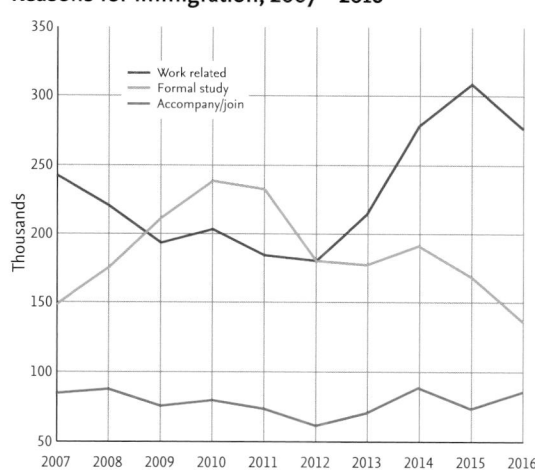

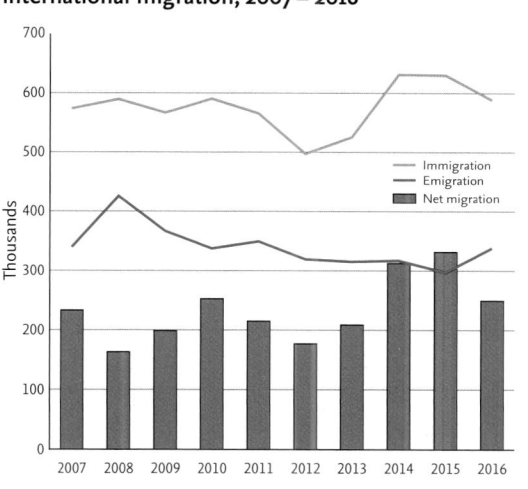

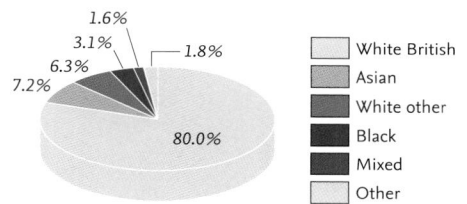

1.6%
3.1%
1.8%
6.3%
7.2%
80.0%
White British
Asian
White other
Black
Mixed
Other

Population by country, 2016

Country	Population (thousands)	Density (persons per sq. km)
England	55 268	424
Wales	3113	150
Scotland	5405	69
Northern Ireland	1862	137
United Kingdom	**65 648**	**271**

Population by age group

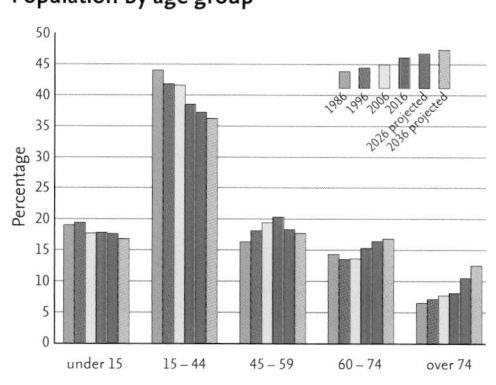

50
45
40
35
30
25
20
15
10
5
0
Percentage
1986
1996
2006
2016
2026 projected
2036 projected
under 15
15 – 44
45 – 59
60 – 74
over 74

UK: Transport

Road network

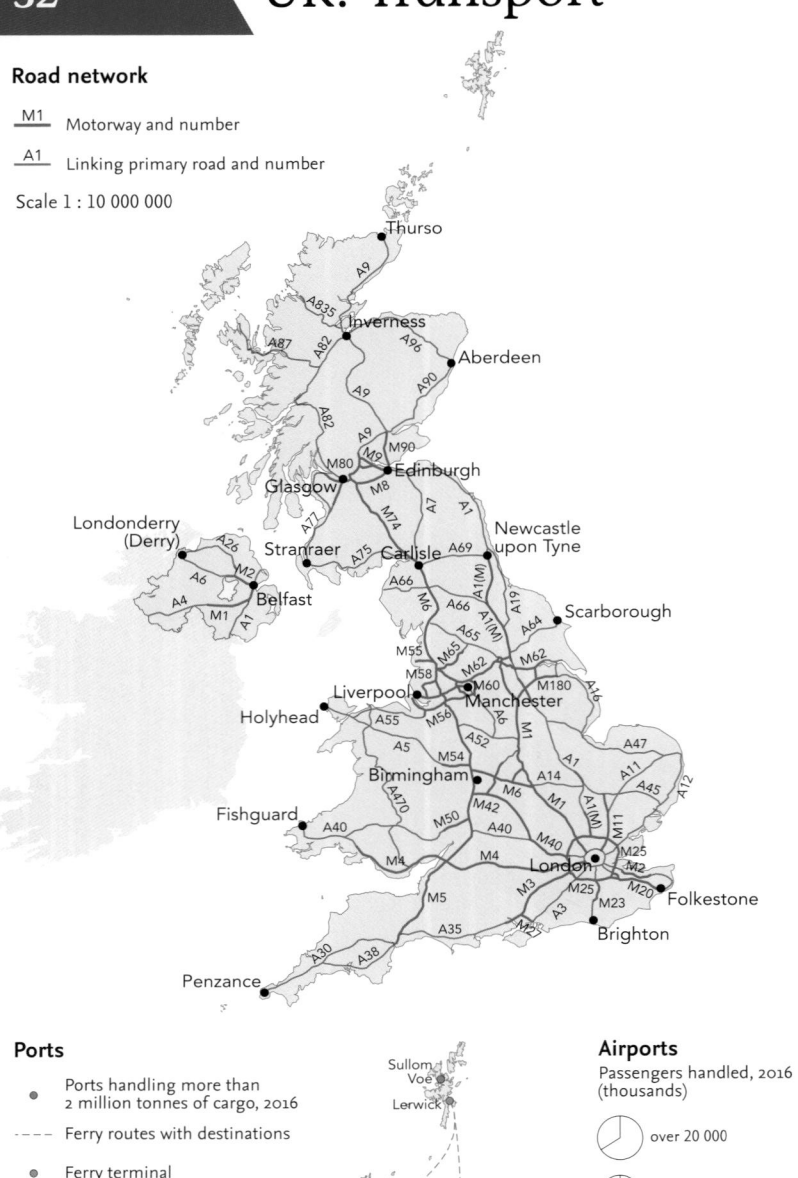

—M1— Motorway and number

—A1— Linking primary road and number

Scale 1 : 10 000 000

Rail network

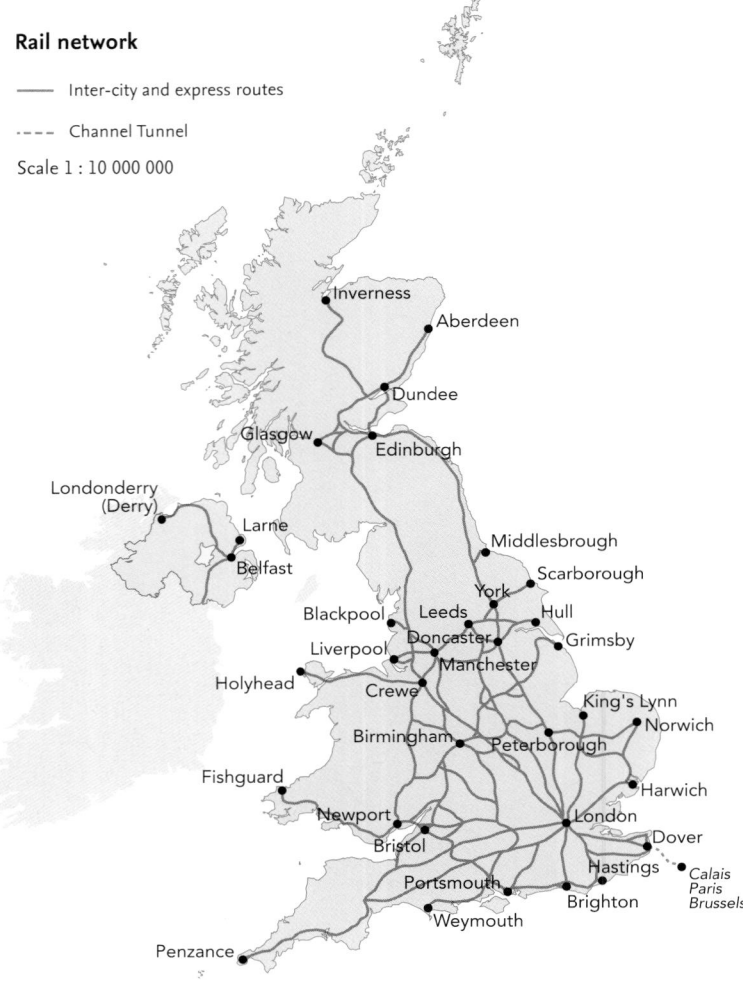

——— Inter-city and express routes

- - - - Channel Tunnel

Scale 1 : 10 000 000

Ports

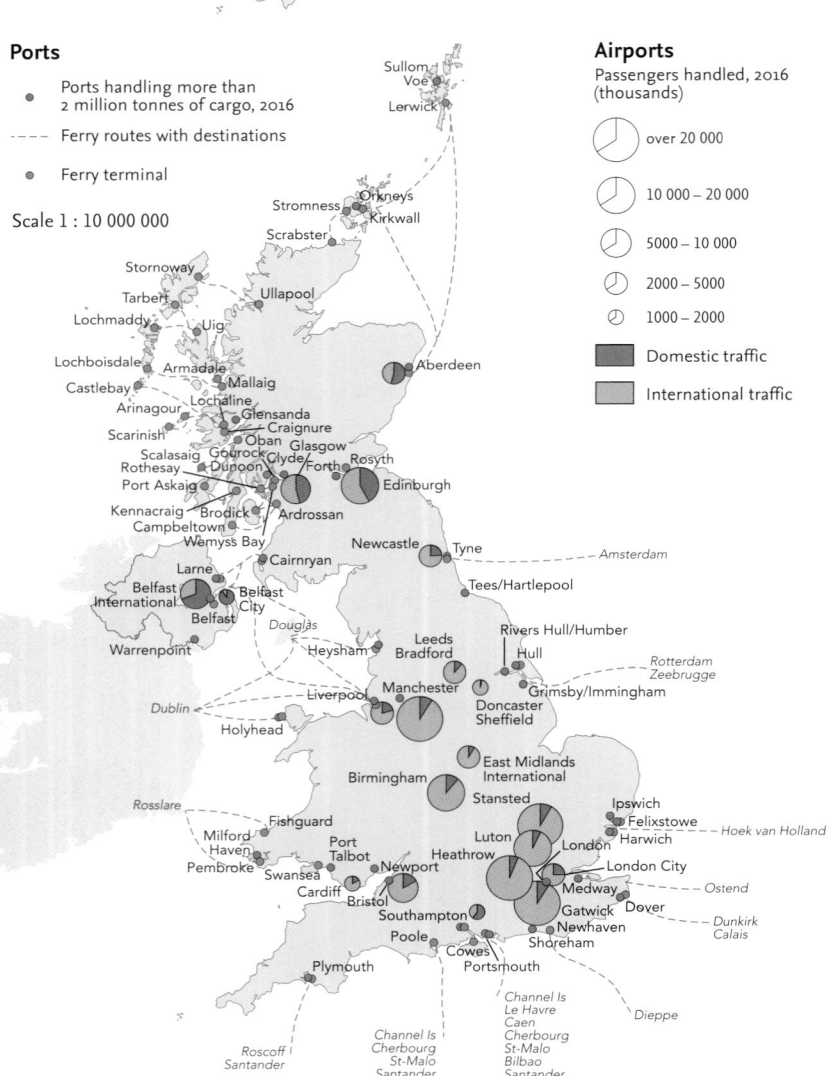

- Ports handling more than 2 million tonnes of cargo, 2016

- - - - Ferry routes with destinations

- Ferry terminal

Scale 1 : 10 000 000

Airports

Passengers handled, 2016 (thousands)

- over 20 000
- 10 000 – 20 000
- 5000 – 10 000
- 2000 – 5000
- 1000 – 2000

Domestic traffic

International traffic

Main trading partners, 2015

Imports
% of total UK imports

Germany 13.0%

USA 11.0%

China 7.1%

Netherlands 6.8%

France 6.7%

Spain 4.6%

Belgium 4.3%

Italy 3.8%

Ireland 3.5%

Norway 2.6%

Exports
% of total UK exports

USA 19.0%

Germany 9.6%

France 6.5%

Netherlands 6.3%

Ireland 5.1%

Switzerland 4.1%

Italy 3.5%

China 3.3%

Belgium 3.0%

Spain 2.9%

Office for National Statistics
www.ons.gov.uk
Department for Transport
www.gov.uk/government/organisations/
department-for-transport
Highways England
www.gov.uk/government/organisations/
highways-england

Transport Scotland
www.transport.gov.scot
Welsh Government Transport
www.gov.wales/topics/transport
**Northern Ireland
Department for Infrastructure**
www.infrastructure-ni.gov.uk

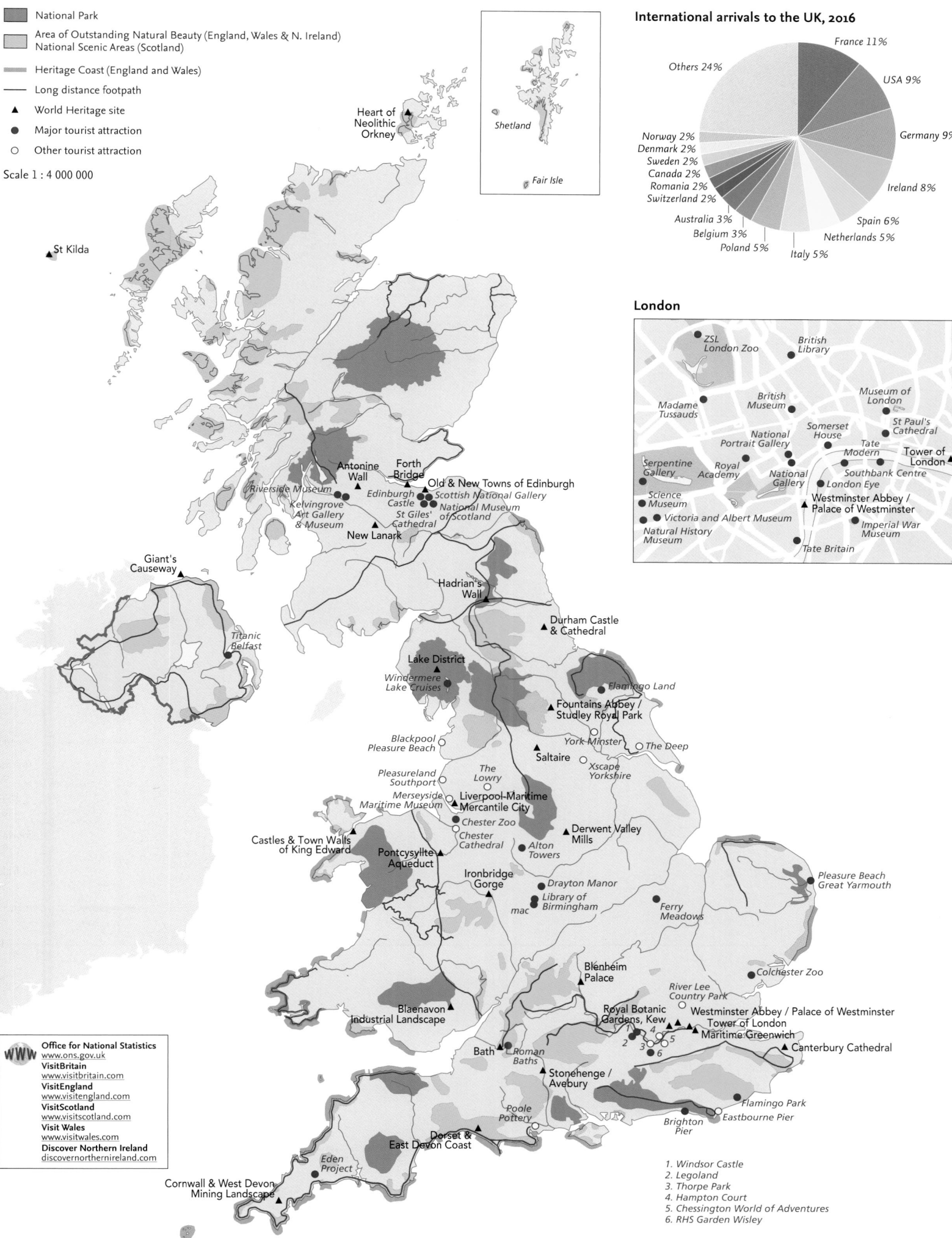

Legend

- National Park
- Area of Outstanding Natural Beauty (England, Wales & N. Ireland)
  National Scenic Areas (Scotland)
- Heritage Coast (England and Wales)
- Long distance footpath
- ▲ World Heritage site
- ● Major tourist attraction
- ○ Other tourist attraction

Scale 1 : 4 000 000

International arrivals to the UK, 2016

- France 11%
- USA 9%
- Germany 9%
- Ireland 8%
- Spain 6%
- Netherlands 5%
- Italy 5%
- Poland 5%
- Belgium 3%
- Australia 3%
- Switzerland 2%
- Romania 2%
- Canada 2%
- Sweden 2%
- Denmark 2%
- Norway 2%
- Others 24%

London

- ZSL London Zoo
- British Library
- Madame Tussauds
- British Museum
- Museum of London
- St Paul's Cathedral
- National Portrait Gallery
- Somerset House
- Tate Modern
- Tower of London
- Serpentine Gallery
- Royal Academy
- National Gallery
- Southbank Centre
- London Eye
- Science Museum
- Westminster Abbey / Palace of Westminster
- Victoria and Albert Museum
- Natural History Museum
- Imperial War Museum
- Tate Britain

Map labels

- Shetland
- Fair Isle
- Heart of Neolithic Orkney
- St Kilda
- Antonine Wall
- Forth Bridge
- Old & New Towns of Edinburgh
- Riverside Museum
- Edinburgh Castle
- Scottish National Gallery
- Kelvingrove Art Gallery & Museum
- National Museum of Scotland
- St Giles' Cathedral
- New Lanark
- Giant's Causeway
- Titanic Belfast
- Hadrian's Wall
- Durham Castle & Cathedral
- Lake District
- Flamingo Land
- Windermere Lake Cruises
- Fountains Abbey / Studley Royal Park
- Blackpool Pleasure Beach
- York Minster
- The Deep
- Saltaire
- Pleasureland Southport
- The Lowry
- Xscape Yorkshire
- Merseyside Maritime Museum
- Liverpool-Maritime Mercantile City
- Chester Zoo
- Castles & Town Walls of King Edward
- Chester Cathedral
- Derwent Valley Mills
- Pontcysyllte Aqueduct
- Alton Towers
- Ironbridge Gorge
- Drayton Manor
- Pleasure Beach Great Yarmouth
- Library of Birmingham
- mac
- Ferry Meadows
- Blenheim Palace
- Colchester Zoo
- River Lee Country Park
- Blaenavon Industrial Landscape
- Royal Botanic Gardens, Kew
- Westminster Abbey / Palace of Westminster
- Tower of London
- Maritime Greenwich
- Bath
- Roman Baths
- Canterbury Cathedral
- Stonehenge / Avebury
- Flamingo Park
- Poole Pottery
- Brighton Pier
- Eastbourne Pier
- Dorset & East Devon Coast
- Eden Project
- Cornwall & West Devon Mining Landscape

1. Windsor Castle
2. Legoland
3. Thorpe Park
4. Hampton Court
5. Chessington World of Adventures
6. RHS Garden Wisley

Sources

WWW
Office for National Statistics
www.ons.gov.uk
VisitBritain
www.visitbritain.com
VisitEngland
www.visitengland.com
VisitScotland
www.visitscotland.com
Visit Wales
www.visitwales.com
Discover Northern Ireland
discovernorthernireland.com

Jan Mayen

Denmark Strait

Húnaflói
Iceland
Faxaflói
Snaefell 1833
Vatnajökull
Fontur

North Cape
Søroya
Inarijärvi
Lappland
Kola Peninsula
Barents Sea
Ostrov Kolguyev
Poluostrov Kanin
Chëshskaya Guba
Mezen
Arctic Circle
Usa
Gora Narodnaya 1895

Norwegian Sea

Lofoten
Vesterålen
Vestfjorden
Scandinavia
Luleälven
Kemijoki
Umeälven
Indalsälven
White Sea
Northern Dvina
Vychegda
Pechora
Ural Mountains

Faroe Islands

Shetland

Gulf of Bothnia
Åland Islands
Lake Onega
Lake Ladoga
Rybinskoye Vodokhranilishche
Valdai Hills
Volga
Kupbyshevskoye Vodokhranilishche
Kama

ATLANTIC OCEAN

Rockall
Outer Hebrides
Orkney
Ben Nevis 1345
Malin Head
Donegal Bay
Galway Bay
Ireland
Cape Clear
Shannon
Irish Sea
Great Britain
Snowdon 1085
Pennines
The Wash
Land's End
Isles of Scilly
Channel Islands
St George's Channel

North Sea

Mälaren
Vänern
Vättern
Hiiumaa
Saaremaa
Gotland
Öland
Bornholm
Jutland
Zealand
Fyn
Skagerrak
Kattegat
Baltic Sea
Gulf of Finland
Gulf of Riga
Lake Peipus
North European Plain
Central Russian Upland
Volga Upland
Ural

Frisian Islands
Ijsselmeer
Weser
Elbe
Ems
Rhine
Maas
Seine
Brittany
Loire
English Channel
Strait of Dover
Thames
Marne
Ardennes
Moselle
Taunus
Bohemian Forest
Erzgebirge
Sudeten
Oder
Vistula
Warta
Vistula
Bug
Pripet Marshes
Kyyivs'ke Vodoskhovyshche
Dnieper
Dniester
Don
Tsimlyanskoye Vodokhranilishche
Don

Bay of Biscay
Cape Finisterre
Vienne
Puy de Sancy 1895
Allier
Gironde
Massif Central
Seine
Saône
Jura
Vosges
Rhône
Rhine
Danube
Lake Constance
Inn
ALPS
Mont Blanc 4810
Matterhorn 4478
Großglockner 3798
Po
Danube
Lake Balaton
Hungarian Plain
Tisza
Mures
Sava
Transylvanian Alps
Morava
Danube
Carpathian Mts
Dniester
Dnieper
Sea of Azov
Crimea
Stavropol'skaya Vozvyshennost'
Caspian Sea
Caucasus
El'brus 5642

Cantabrian Mts
Douro
Duero
Ebro
Pyrenees
Aneto 3404
Tagus
Gulf of Gascony
Gulf of Lions
Côte d'Azur
Gulf of Genoa
Ligurian Sea
Apennines
Adriatic Sea
Dinaric Alps
Balkan Mts
Rhodope Mts
Black Sea
ASIA

Cabo de São Vicente
Sierra Morena
Guadalquivir
Sierra Nevada
Strait of Gibraltar
Golfo de Valencia
Balearic Is
Minorca
Ibiza
Majorca
Sardinia
Corsica
Strait of Bonifacio
Tyrrhenian Sea
Vesuvius 1281
G. of Taranto
Corfu
Pindus Mts
Mt Olympus 2911
Sea of Marmara
Aegean Sea
Evvoia
Dodecanese
Naxos
Rhodes

Mediterranean Sea
Sicily
Mount Etna 3323
C. Passero
Ionian Sea
Zakynthos Sea
Kythira
Crete

AFRICA

Relief and physical features

Relief metres
5000
3000
2000
1000
500
200
0
sea level
200
under sea level
4000
6000

5642 ▲ Mountain height (in metres)

Permanent ice (ice cap or glacier)

Scale 1 : 25 000 000

0   250   500 km

Conic Equidistant projection

Cross-section

line of cross-section

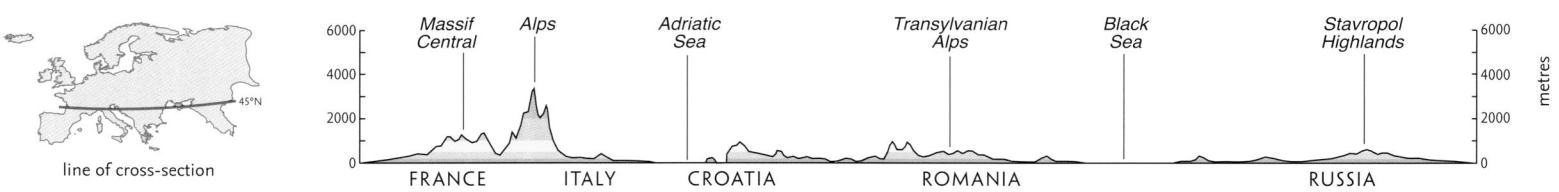

Massif Central — Alps — Adriatic Sea — Transylvanian Alps — Black Sea — Stavropol Highlands

6000 / 4000 / 2000 / 0   metres

FRANCE   ITALY   CROATIA   ROMANIA   RUSSIA

Facts about Europe

Total land area	**9 908 599 sq. km**
Highest peak	**El'brus, 5642 m**
Longest river	**Volga, 3688 km**
Largest country	**Ukraine, 603 700 sq. km** (excluding Russia)
Most populous country	**Germany, 80 689 000** (excluding Russia)

Population by country, 2015 top ten countries

Netherlands 16 925
Belgium 11 299
Romania 19 511
Poland 38 612
Germany 80 689
Ukraine 44 824
UK 64 716
Spain 46 122
France 64 395
Italy 59 798

Population in thousands

GNI by country, 2015 top ten countries

Sweden 504 407
Poland 459 434
Switzerland 686 145
Netherlands 747 565
Germany 3 436 657
Spain 1 192 036
Russia 1 328 996
UK 2 821 761
Italy 1 811 388
France 2 458 117

Gross National Income in US $ millions

Europe: Climate

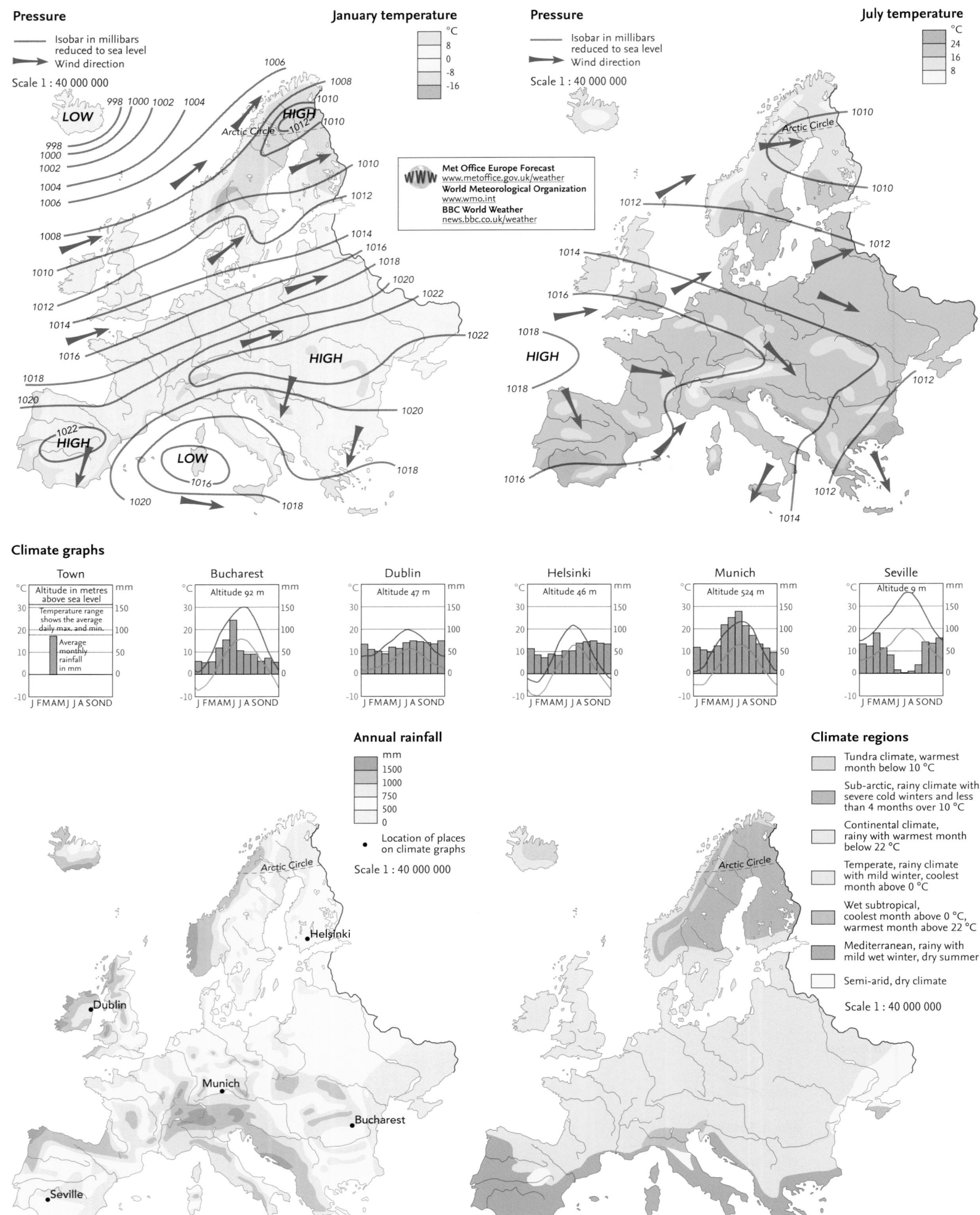

Pressure

Isobar in millibars reduced to sea level

➤ Wind direction

Scale 1 : 40 000 000

January temperature

°C
8
0
-8
-16

Met Office Europe Forecast
www.metoffice.gov.uk/weather
World Meteorological Organization
www.wmo.int
BBC World Weather
news.bbc.co.uk/weather

Pressure

Isobar in millibars reduced to sea level

➤ Wind direction

Scale 1 : 40 000 000

July temperature

°C
24
16
8

Climate graphs

Town

°C / mm

Altitude in metres above sea level

Temperature range shows the average daily max. and min.

Average monthly rainfall in mm

Bucharest

Altitude 92 m

Dublin

Altitude 47 m

Helsinki

Altitude 46 m

Munich

Altitude 524 m

Seville

Altitude 9 m

Annual rainfall

mm
1500
1000
750
500
0

● Location of places on climate graphs

Scale 1 : 40 000 000

Helsinki

Dublin

Munich

Bucharest

Seville

Climate regions

Tundra climate, warmest month below 10 °C

Sub-arctic, rainy climate with severe cold winters and less than 4 months over 10 °C

Continental climate, rainy with warmest month below 22 °C

Temperate, rainy climate with mild winter, coolest month above 0 °C

Wet subtropical, coolest month above 0 °C, warmest month above 22 °C

Mediterranean, rainy with mild wet winter, dry summer

Semi-arid, dry climate

Scale 1 : 40 000 000

Tourist resorts
- Mountain/lake resort
- Coastal resort
- Cultural resort

Scale 1 : 20 000 000

ICELAND

NORWAY

SWEDEN

FINLAND

Fjords

Oslo

Stockholm

Helsinki

Tallinn
ESTONIA

St Petersburg

RUSSIA

Moscow

LATVIA

Riga

LITHUANIA

RUSSIA

Vilnius

BELARUS

DENMARK

Copenhagen

Masurian Lakes

Warsaw

Edinburgh

IRELAND

Dublin
UNITED
KINGDOM
York

Stratford

Oxford

London
Bath

NETH.
Amsterdam
Brugge
Brussels
BELGIUM
LUX.
Cologne
Heidelberg

Berlin

GERMANY

Rhine

Dresden

Prague
CZECHIA

POLAND

Kraków

L'viv

Kiev

UKRAINE

Paris

Brittany

Loire

Strasbourg

FRANCE

Munich

Danube

Vienna

Salzburg

SWITZ.
Geneva

A L P S

Perigord

Rhone

Italian Lakes

Venice

AUSTRIA

SLOVAKIA

Budapest

HUNGARY

SLOVENIA

CROATIA

ROMANIA

MOLDOVA

Caucasus

Santiago de
Compostela

Pyrenees

Nîmes

Avignon
Provence

Carcassonne

ANDORRA

Barcelona

Riviera
Florence
Siena
Côte d'Azur

Corsica

ITALY

Rome

Adriatic Riviera

Dubrovnik

BOSNIA &
HERZ.

MONT.

SERBIA

KOS.

Black Sea

Oporto

Salamanca

Madrid

PORTUGAL

SPAIN

Córdoba

Seville

Granada

Lisbon

Algarve

Costa Brava

Ibiza

Minorca

Majorca

Sardinia

Naples

Costa Blanca

Costa del Sol

MACEDONIA

BULGARIA

ALBANIA

Corfu

Delphi

Athens

GREECE

Greek Islands

Rhodes

TURKEY

Istanbul

Sicily

MALTA

Crete

Tourist arrivals, 2015

Countries with more than 2.5 million international arrivals
(not including Russia and Turkey)

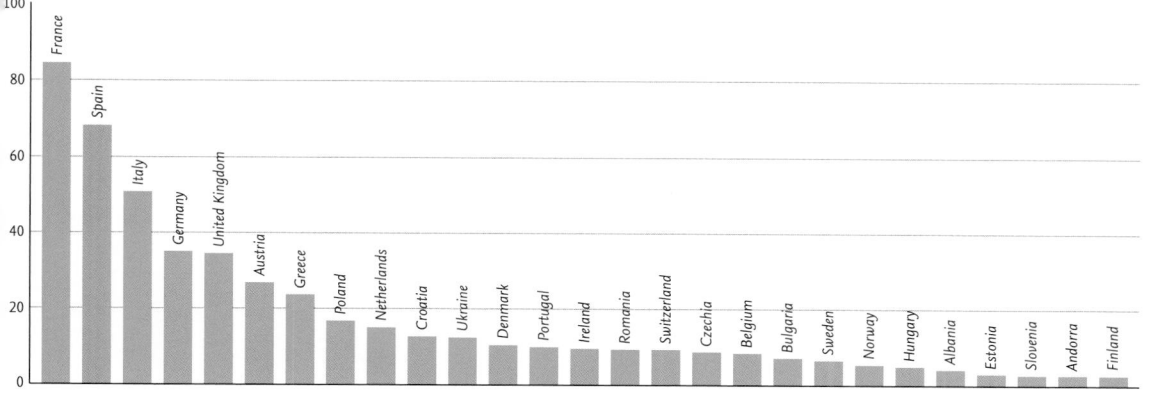

France, Spain, Italy, Germany, United Kingdom, Austria, Greece, Poland, Netherlands, Croatia, Ukraine, Denmark, Portugal, Ireland, Romania, Switzerland, Czechia, Belgium, Bulgaria, Sweden, Norway, Hungary, Albania, Estonia, Slovenia, Andorra, Finland

www World Tourism Organization
www2.unwto.org
UNESCO World Heritage Sites
whc.unesco.org
VisitEurope
www.visiteurope.com

Europe: Economic Activity

Land use

- Industrial and urban area
- Cropland
- Cropland, grassland and woodland
- Grassland and grazing
- Grassland and woodland
- Temperate forest
- Coniferous forest
- Scrubland or desert
- Tundra

● Urban centre

Extractive industry

- Oil
- Gas
- Coal

Scale 1 : 25 000 000

Glasgow
Manchester
Birmingham
London
Le Havre
Paris
Bordeaux
Lyon
Grenoble
Toulouse
Oviedo
Bilbao
Madrid
Lisbon
Seville
Valencia
Cartagena
Barcelona
Marseille
Milan
Bologna
Rome
Naples
Bari
Strasbourg
Metz
Saarbrücken
Rotterdam
Essen-Dortmund
Bremen
Hamburg
Berlin
Dresden
Zwickau
Prague
Linz
Vienna
Graz
Ljubljana
Zagreb
Łódź
Wrocław
Katowice
Warsaw
Gdansk
Bratislava
Budapest
Belgrade
Sofia
Thessaloniki
Istanbul
Piraeus
Bucharest
Odesa
L'viv
Kiev
Donets'k
Rostov-na-Donu
Volgograd
Oslo
Stockholm
Gothenburg
Copenhagen
Helsinki
Tallinn
St Petersburg
Riga
Vilnius
Minsk
Moscow
Nizhniy Novgorod
Kazan'
Samara
Perm

Oil production, 2015

Romania 2.5%
Italy 3.5%
Denmark 4.8%
United Kingdom 28.3%
Norway 55.0%
Others 5.9%

Total: 159.9 million tonnes

Natural gas production, 2015

Denmark 1.8%
Italy 2.4%
Germany 2.8%
Romania 4.1%
Ukraine 6.9%
United Kingdom 15.7%
Netherlands 17.0%
Poland 1.6%
Others 1.2%
Norway 46.4%

Total: 227.4 million tonnes oil equivalent

Coal production, 2015

Hungary 0.9%
Romania 2.8%
United Kingdom 3.2%
Bulgaria 3.5%
Greece 3.5%
Serbia 4.3%
Ukraine 9.7%
Czechia 9.7%
Spain 0.7%
Others 4.5%
Poland 31.8%
Germany 25.4%

Total: 169 million tonnes oil equivalent

Energy consumption by fuel, 2015

Hydro electric 6.8%
Renewables 7.5%
Nuclear energy 12.0%
Oil 34.8%
Coal 16.4%
Natural gas 22.5%

Agricultural production by weight, 2014

- Oats
- Triticale
- Chicken
- Apples
- Tomatoes
- Grapes
- Pig meat
- Rapeseed
- Sunflower seed
- Barley
- Potatoes
- Maize
- Sugar beet
- Milk
- Wheat

0   50   100   150   200   250
Million tonnes

by value, 2013

- Apples
- Rapeseed
- Sunflower seed
- Olives
- Tomatoes
- Eggs
- Barley
- Chicken
- Maize
- Grapes
- Potatoes
- Beef
- Pig meat
- Wheat
- Milk

0   20   40   60   80   100   120
Billion dollars

Employment in industry, 2015

Percentage of total employment

- 30.0 – 39.9
- 20.0 – 29.9
- 10.0 – 19.9
- 5.0 – 9.9
- No data

Scale 1 : 50 000 000

ICELAND
NORWAY
SWEDEN
FINLAND
ESTONIA
LATVIA
LITHUANIA
RUSSIA
RUS.
BELARUS
IRELAND
UNITED KINGDOM
DENMARK
NETHERLANDS
BELGIUM
LUX.
GERMANY
POLAND
UKRAINE
CZECHIA
SLOVAKIA
FRANCE
SWITZ.
AUSTRIA
HUNGARY
SL.
CROATIA
ROMANIA
MOL.
B.H.
SERBIA
PORTUGAL
ANDORRA
ITALY
MON.
KOS.
BULGARIA
ALBANIA
MAC.
SPAIN
GREECE
TURKEY
MALTA

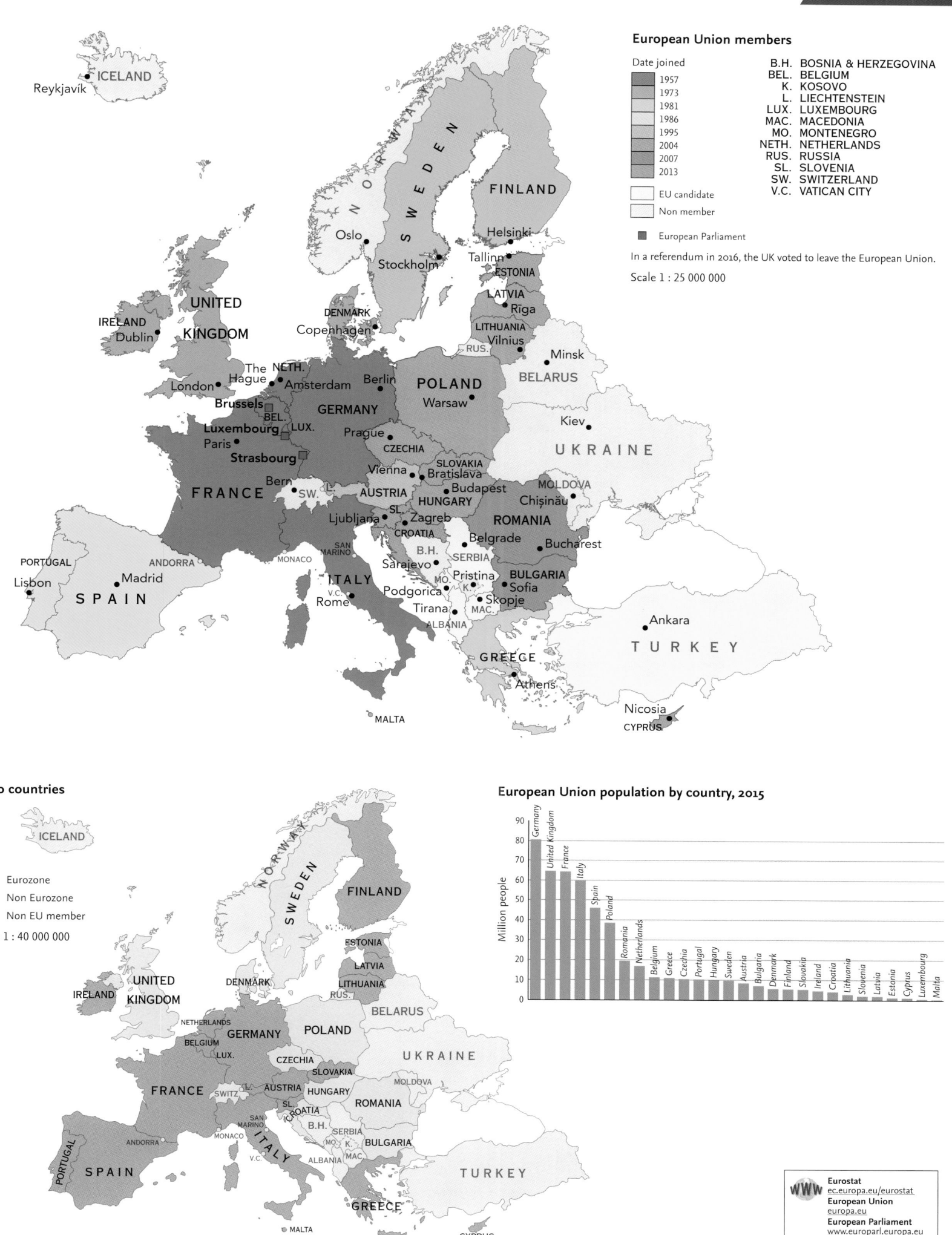

European Union members

Date joined

- 1957
- 1973
- 1981
- 1986
- 1995
- 2004
- 2007
- 2013

- EU candidate
- Non member

- European Parliament

In a referendum in 2016, the UK voted to leave the European Union.

Scale 1 : 25 000 000

B.H. BOSNIA & HERZEGOVINA
BEL. BELGIUM
K. KOSOVO
L. LIECHTENSTEIN
LUX. LUXEMBOURG
MAC. MACEDONIA
MO. MONTENEGRO
NETH. NETHERLANDS
RUS. RUSSIA
SL. SLOVENIA
SW. SWITZERLAND
V.C. VATICAN CITY

Euro countries

- Eurozone
- Non Eurozone
- Non EU member

Scale 1 : 40 000 000

European Union population by country, 2015

Million people

90
80
70
60
50
40
30
20
10
0

Germany, United Kingdom, France, Italy, Spain, Poland, Romania, Netherlands, Belgium, Greece, Czechia, Portugal, Hungary, Sweden, Austria, Bulgaria, Denmark, Finland, Slovakia, Ireland, Croatia, Lithuania, Slovenia, Latvia, Estonia, Cyprus, Luxembourg, Malta

WWW **Eurostat**
ec.europa.eu/eurostat
European Union
europa.eu
European Parliament
www.europarl.europa.eu

Europe: Population

Population per sq. km

- over 500
- 251 – 500
- 101 – 250
- 26 – 100
- 1 – 25
- less than 1

Scale 1 : 25 000 000

EUROSTAT
epp.eurostat.ec.europa.eu
United Nations Population Information Network
www.un.org/popin

ICELAND

NORWAY

SWEDEN

FINLAND

ESTONIA

RUSSIA

LATVIA

LITHUANIA

RUS.

BELARUS

DENMARK

IRELAND

UNITED KINGDOM

NETHERLANDS

POLAND

GERMANY

UKRAINE

BELGIUM

LUX.

CZECHIA

FRANCE

SWITZ.

AUSTRIA

SLOVAKIA

HUNGARY

MOL.

ROMANIA

SL.

CROATIA

B.H.

SERBIA

BULGARIA

ANDORRA

ITALY

MON.

KOS.

MAC.

TURKEY

PORTUGAL

SPAIN

ALBANIA

GREECE

MALTA

Population under 15, 2015

Percentage of total population

- over 20
- 17.5 – 20
- 15 – 17.4
- 12.5 – 14.9
- No data

Scale 1 : 45 000 000

ICELAND

NORWAY

SWEDEN

FINLAND

IRELAND

UNITED KINGDOM

DENMARK

ESTONIA

LATVIA

LITHUANIA

RUS.

BELARUS

NETHERLANDS

BELGIUM

GERMANY

POLAND

LUX.

CZECHIA

UKRAINE

SLOVAKIA

FRANCE

SWITZ.

AUSTRIA

HUNGARY

MOL.

SL.

CROATIA

ROMANIA

B.H.

SERBIA

ANDORRA

MON.

KOS.

BULGARIA

ITALY

MAC.

TURKEY

SPAIN

ALBANIA

PORTUGAL

GREECE

MALTA

Population 65 and over, 2015

Percentage of total population

- over 20
- 15 – 20
- 10 – 14.9
- 5 – 9.9
- No data

Scale 1 : 45 000 000

ICELAND

NORWAY

SWEDEN

FINLAND

IRELAND

UNITED KINGDOM

DENMARK

ESTONIA

LATVIA

LITHUANIA

RUS.

BELARUS

NETHERLANDS

BELGIUM

GERMANY

POLAND

LUX.

CZECHIA

UKRAINE

SLOVAKIA

FRANCE

SWITZ.

AUSTRIA

HUNGARY

MOL.

SL.

CROATIA

ROMANIA

B.H.

SERBIA

ANDORRA

MON.

KOS.

BULGARIA

ITALY

MAC.

TURKEY

SPAIN

ALBANIA

PORTUGAL

GREECE

MALTA

City lights across Europe at night

Largest urban agglomerations, 2015

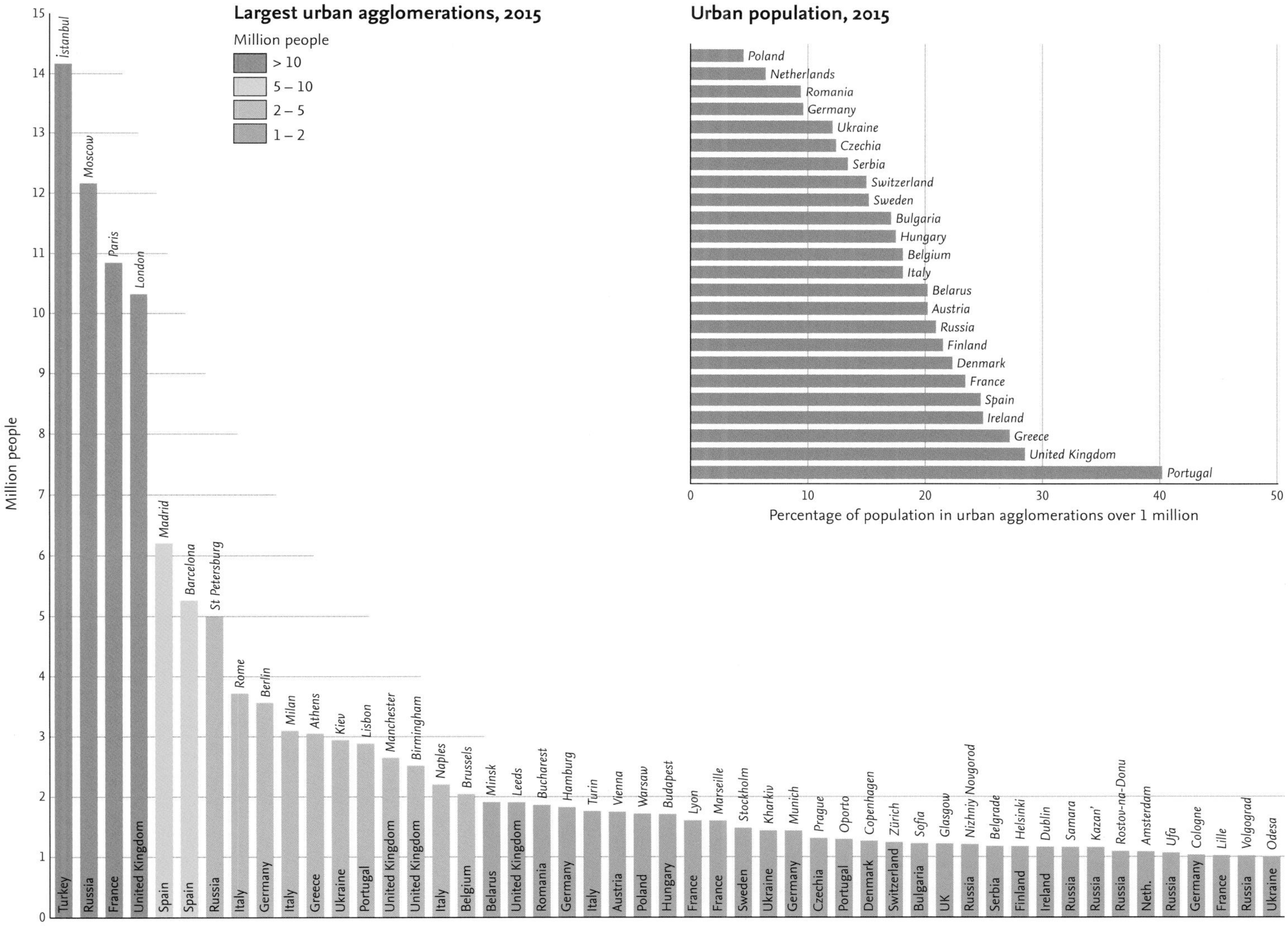

Million people
- > 10
- 5 – 10
- 2 – 5
- 1 – 2

Urban population, 2015

Percentage of population in urban agglomerations over 1 million

Netherlands, Belgium and Luxembourg

Relief and physical features

Relief
metres

5000
3000
2000
1000
500
200
sea level
under sea level
0
200
4000
6000

▲ 818 Mountain height (in metres)

Water features

~~~ River
~~~ Canal
Lake / Reservoir
Marsh

Communications

Railway
Motorway
Road
⊕ Main airport

Administration

Boundaries
International
Internal

Conic Equidistant projection

Settlement

Urban area

Cities and towns in order of size

National capital
■ Brussels

Other city or town
● Lille
● Saarbrücken
○ Antwerp
○ Leuven

Scale 1 : 2 000 000

0   25   50   75   100 km

East Frisian Islands
Langeoog
Juist
Norderney
Borkum
Norden
Wittmund
Wiesmoor
Emden
Leer
Weener
Papenburg

West Frisian Islands
Schiermonnikoog
Ameland
Terschelling
West-Terschelling
Vlieland
Dokkum
Delfzijl
Texel
Den Burg
Waddenzee
Harlingen
Leeuwarden
Groningen
GRONINGEN
Veendam
Stadskanaal
Den Helder
Sneek
FRIESLAND
Drachten
Assen
Klazienaveen
Schagen
IJsselmeer
Heerenveen
DRENTHE
Emmen
Haren
Meppen
Alkmaar
Hoorn
Wolvega
Steenwijk
Hoogeveen
NOORD-HOLLAND
Markermeer
Emmeloord
Meppel
Vechte
NIEDERSACHSEN
Purmerend
Kampen
Ommen
IJmuiden
Lelystad
Zwolle
FLEVOLAND
OVERIJSSEL
Nordhorn
Lingen
Zaandam
Haarlem
Amsterdam
Harderwijk
Raalte
Almelo
Oldenzaal
Amstelveen
NETHERLANDS
Apeldoorn
Deventer
Hengelo
Rheine
Leiden
Hilversum
Amersfoort
107▲
Zutphen
Enschede
Steinfurt
Greven
The Hague
UTRECHT
Arnhem
Doetinchem
Ahaus
Münster
Delft
Utrecht
GELDERLAND
Winterswijk
Velen
ZUID-HOLLAND
Gouda
Lek
Tiel
Nijmegen
Kleve
Rhine
Bocholt
Borken
Hoek van Holland
Vlaardingen
Rotterdam
Oss
's-Hertogenbosch
Goch
Wesel
Lippe
Hamm
Spijkenisse
Dordrecht
Wijchen
NORTH
Oosterschelde
NOORD-BRABANT
Venray
Maas
Niers
Gelsenkirchen
Herne
Dortmund
SEA
Breda
Tilburg
Boxtel
NORDRHEIN-WESTFALEN
Essen
ZEELAND
Roosendaal
Eindhoven
Helmond
Duisburg
Ruhr
Hagen
Goes
Krefeld
Wuppertal
Vlissingen
Turnhout
Valkenswaard
LIMBURG
Roermond
Mönchengladbach
Düsseldorf
663▲
Westerschelde
Terneuzen
Lille
Weert
GERMANY
Zeebrugge
Brugge
Antwerp
Geel
Lommel
Maaseik
Bergisch Gladbach
Ostend
Lokeren
ANTWERPEN
LIMBURG
Genk
Sittard
Leverkusen
Nieuwpoort
St-Niklaas
Willebroek
Mechelen
Heerlen
Cologne
Veurne
Ghent
Scheldt
Diest
Hasselt
Maastricht
Eschweiler
Dunkirk (Dunkerque)
Diksmuide
Tielt
WEST-VLAANDEREN
Dendermonde
Aalst
VLAAMS-BRABANT
Tongeren
Aachen
Düren
Bonn
Calais
Roeselare
OOST-VLAANDEREN
Brussels
Leuven
Maastricht
Coquelles
Ieper
Kortrijk
BELGIUM
Anderlecht
Tienen
Dupeye
Zülpich
Troisdorf
Guînes
Mouscron
Oudenaarde
Vilvoorde
Waremme
Liège
Meckenheim
Hennef
St-Omer
Hazebrouck
Roubaix
Ronse
Halle
BRABANT WALLON
Verviers
Bad Neuenahr-Ahrweiler
Neuwied
Lille
Tournai
Ath
Soignies
Ottignies
LIÈGE
Malmedy
623▲
Mayen
Béthune
Mons
Nivelles
Namur
Marche-en-Famenne
St-Vith
698▲
Prüm
Koblenz
Bruay-la-Buissière
Carvin
Lens
St-Amand-les-Eaux
La Louvière
HAINAUT
Ciney
Houffalize
Moselle
Liévin
Douai
Charleroi
NAMUR
Bastogne
RHEINLAND-PFALZ
HAUTS-DE-FRANCE
Valenciennes
Thuin
Dinant
Rochefort
Wiltz
Bitburg
Wittlich
Arras
Cambrai
Maubeuge
Philippeville
589▲
Ettelbrück
Idar-Oberstein
Nohfelden
FRANCE
Caudry
Aulnoye-Aymeries
Furnay
LUXEMBOURG
Nonnweiler
Glan
Doullens
Bohain-en-Vermandois
Guise
Oise
Hirson
Charleville-Mézières
Bouillon
Neufchâteau
LUXEMBOURG
Morbach
818▲
Amiens
Corbie
Péronne
Sedan
Semois
Mersch
Trier
St Wendel
Albert
Rethel
Mouzon
Arlon
Luxembourg
Merzig
SAARLAND
Aisne
Vouziers
Virton
Esch-sur-Alzette
Völklingen
Homburg
Longuyon
Mosel
Thionville
Saarlouis
Neunkirchen
GRAND EST
Rombas
Freyming-Merlebach
Saarbrücken
Verdun
Metz
Faulquemont
Sarreguemines
Châlons-en-Champagne
Meuse
Pont-à-Mousson

Paris
ÎLE-DE-FRANCE

France

UNITED KINGDOM

NETHERLANDS

BELGIUM

LUXEMBOURG

GERMANY

English Channel

Baie de Seine

Channel Islands

Guernsey (British Crown Dependency)

Jersey (British Crown Dependency)

Golfe de St-Malo

Normandy

Picardy

Brittany

FRANCE

Bay of Biscay

Touraine

Limousin

Massif Central

Gulf of Gascony

Landes

Languedoc

Dauphiné

Maritime Alps

SWITZERLAND

ALPS

Jura

ITALY

Gulf of Genoa

Ligurian Sea

Côte d'Azur

MONACO

SPAIN

Pyrenees

ANDORRA

Andorra La Vella

Gulf of Lions

Corsica (France)

Sardinia (Italy)

Minorca

Relief and physical features

Relief metres
5000
3000
2000
1000
500
200
sea level
0
200
under sea level
4000
6000

4810 ▲ Mountain height (in metres)

Permanent ice (ice cap or glacier)

Water features

〜 River

〜 Intermittent river

〜 Canal

Lake / Reservoir

Marsh

Communications

Railway

Motorway

Road

⊕ Main airport

Administration

Boundaries

International

Settlement

Urban area

Cities and towns in order of size

National capital

■ Paris

Other city or town

● Marseille

● Genoa

○ St-Étienne

○ Roscoff

Scale 1 : 5 250 000

0   50   100   150   200 km

Lambert Conformal Conic projection

AUS. AUSTRIA
LIECH. LIECHTENSTEIN

Relief and physical features

Relief
metres

5000
3000
2000
1000
500
200
sea level
0
under sea level
200
4000
6000

▲ 3482 Mountain height
(in metres)

Lambert Conformal Conic projection

Water features

～～ River
～～ Intermittent river
━ Canal
◯ Lake / Reservoir
❀ Marsh

Communications

━━ Railway
━━ Motorway
━ Road
⊕ Main airport

Administration

Boundaries
━━ International

Settlement

Cities and towns in order of size

National capital
■ Madrid

Other city or town
● Barcelona
● Seville
○ Pamplona
○ Benidorm

Scale 1 : 5 250 000

0   50   100   150   200 km

LATVIA
LITHUANIA
BELARUS
RUSSIA
UKRAINE
ROMANIA
MOLDOVA

Riga · Jūrmala · Jelgava · Bauska · Birżai · Madona · Kārsava
Vilnius · Kaunas · Marijampolė · Alytus · Panevėžys · Utena
Minsk · Hrodna · Baranavichy · Slutsk · Salihorsk · Babruysk
Homyel · Mazyr · Pinsk · Brest · Chernihiv · Kiev · Zhytomyr
Lviv · Ternopil · Rivne · Luts'k · Vinnytsya · Kropyvnyts'kyy
Cherkasy · Kremenchuk · Dnipro · Kryvyy Rih · Zaporizhzhya
Poltava · Kharkiv · Sumy · Belgorod · Kursk
Moscow · Smolensk · Bryansk · Orël · Tula · Kaluga

Dnieper · Pripet · Dniester · Desna · Bug · Pripet Marshes
Carpathian Mountains · Transylvanian Alps

Central Russian Upland

Relief and physical features

Relief metres

| 5000 |
| 3000 |
| 2000 |
| 1000 |
| 500 |
| 200 |
| sea level |
| under sea level |
| 200 |
| 4000 |
| 6000 |

▲ 4635 Mountain height (in metres)

Permanent ice (ice cap or glacier)

Water features
~ River
Canal
Lake / Reservoir
Intermittent lake
Marsh

Communications
— Railway
═ Motorway
— Road
⊕ Main airport

Administration
Boundaries
— International
--- International disputed

Settlement
Cities and towns in order of size
National capital — Other city or town
■ Moscow
○ Poznań
○ Gdańsk
○ Brest
○ Jihlava

Scale 1 : 5 000 000
0 50 100 150 200 km

Conic Equidistant projection

Mediterranean Basin

LIECH. LIECHTENSTEIN
LUX. LUXEMBOURG
Bay of Biscay
FRANCE
SPAIN
PORTUGAL
ANDORRA
SWITZERLAND
GERMANY
ITALY
MONACO
SAN MARINO
VATICAN CITY
MOROCCO
ALGERIA
TUNISIA
MEDITER
Paris
Madrid
Lisbon
Rome
Algiers
Tunis
Rabat
Tripoli
Valletta
Bern
Andorra la Vella
Luxembourg
Vaduz
Prague
Barcelona
Marseille
Lyon
Toulouse
Bordeaux
Nantes
Milan
Turin
Genoa
Naples
Florence
Venice
Bologna
Munich
Zürich
Geneva
Valencia
Seville
Málaga
Zaragoza
Bilbao
Oporto
Casablanca
Fez (Fès)
Marrakech
Oran
Constantine
Sfax
Palermo
Gulf of Lions
Balearic Sea
Balearic Islands
Majorca
Minorca
Ibiza
Formentera
Corsica (France)
Sardinia (Italy)
Sicily
Ligurian Sea
Tyrrhenian Sea
Strait of Gibraltar
Strait of Bonifacio
Gulf of Gabès
Golfe de Hammamet
Pyrenees
Massif Central
Alps
Apennines
Cantabrian Mountains
Sierra Morena
Sierra Nevada
Moyen Atlas
Haut Atlas
Atlas Saharien
Hauts Plateaux
Chott Melrhir
Chott el Jerid
Hammada du Drâa
Tripolitania
Al Hamādah al Hamrā'
Idhān Awbārī
Mont Blanc 4810
Relief and physical features
Relief metres
5000
3000
2000
1000
500
200
sea level
under sea level
0
200
4000
6000
4810 Mountain height (in metres)
Water features
River
Intermittent river
Canal
Lake / Reservoir
Intermittent lake
Marsh
Communications
Railway
Road
Main airport
Administration
Boundaries
International
Disputed
Ceasefire line
Settlement
Cities and towns in order of size
National capital
Cairo
Other city or town
İstanbul
Naples
Valencia
Avignon
Faro
Scale 1 : 10 000 000
0 100 200 300 400 km
Conic Equidistant projection

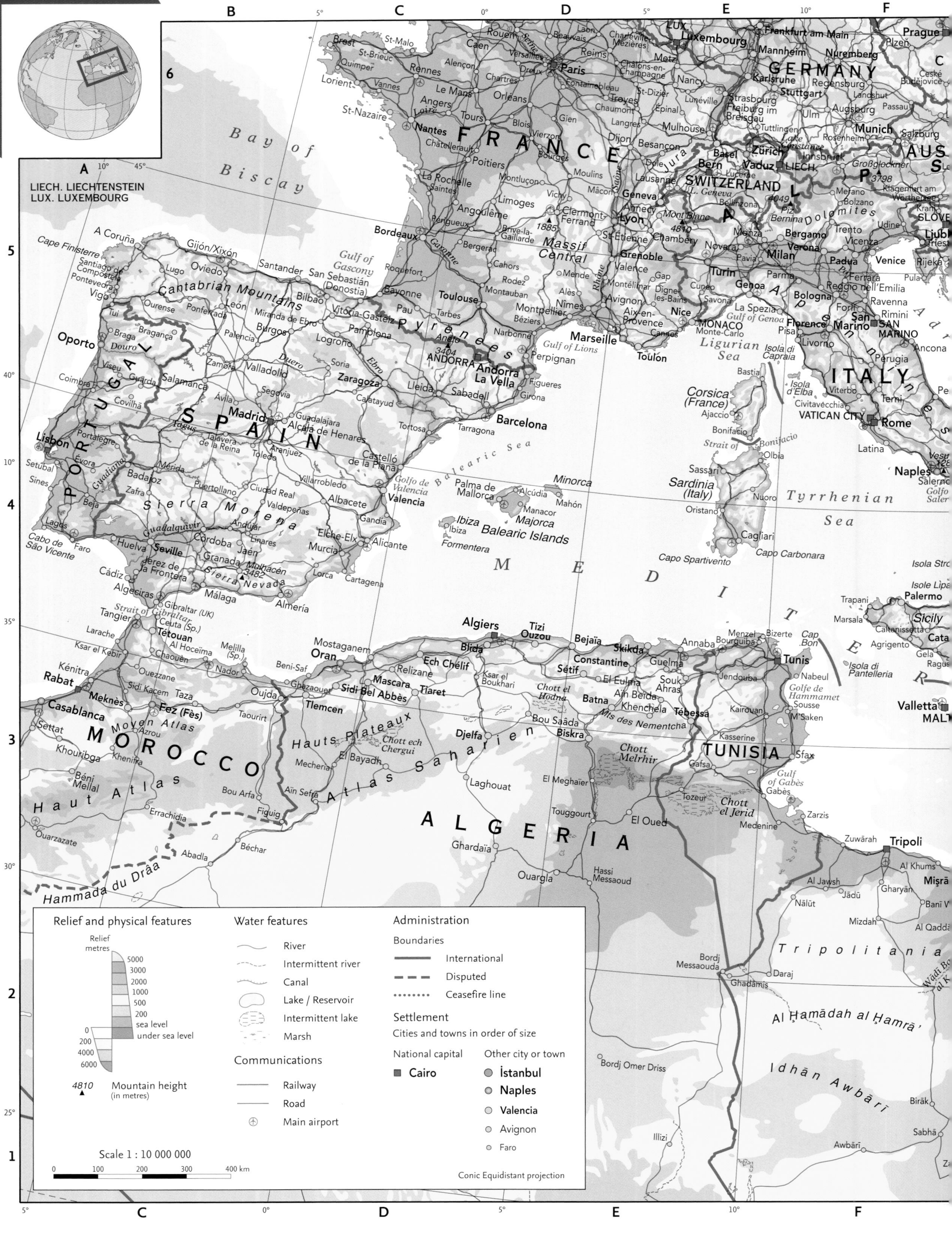

Grid references: G H I J K L (top) · 20° 25° 30° 35° 40° · rows 6 5 4 3 2 1

Countries: SLOVAKIA · HUNGARY · ROMANIA · MOLDOVA · UKRAINE · RUSSIA · GEORGIA · CROATIA · BOSNIA AND HERZEGOVINA · SERBIA · MONTENEGRO · KOSOVO · ALBANIA · MACEDONIA (F.Y.R.O.M.) · BULGARIA · GREECE · TURKEY · CYPRUS · SYRIA · LEBANON · ISRAEL · JORDAN · SAUDI ARABIA · EGYPT · LIBYA · CRIMEA (Administered by Russia)

Seas/water: Black Sea · Sea of Azov · Gulf of Taganrog · Karkinits'ka Zatoka · Sea of Marmara · Aegean Sea · Ionian Sea · Gulf of Taranto · Krytiko Pelagos · Antalya Körfezi · MEDITERRANEAN SEA · Sea of Galilee · Dead Sea · Gulf of Suez · Gulf of Aqaba · Red Sea · Suez Canal · Gulf of Sirte · Qattara Depression

Selected cities and features:

Rybnik · Kraków · Tarnów · L'viv · Ternopil' · Vinnytsya · Zhmerynka · Uman' · Oleksandriya · Dnipro · Pokrovs'k · Shakhty · Taganrog · Rostov-na-Donu · Ostrava · Olomouc · Bielsko-Biała · Przemyśl · Stryy · Ivano-Frankivs'k · Khmel'nyts'kyy · Mohyliv-Podil's'kyy · Kropyvnyts'kyy · Kryvyy Rih · Nikopol' · Zaporizhzhya · Donets'k · Mariupol' · Sal'sk · Divnoye · Brno · Žilina · Poprad · Uzhhorod · Kolomyya · Chernivtsi · Botoşani · Soroca · Bălţi · Suceava · Iaşi · Voznesens'k · Berdyans'k · Yeysk · Pavlovskaya · Tikhoretsk · Svetlograd · Wiener Neustadt · Bratislava · Lučenec · Košice · Satu Mare · Baia Mare · Dej · Chişinău · Tiraspol · Berezivka · Kherson · Melitopol · Heniches'k · Timashevsk · Armavir · Nevinnomyssk · Cherkessk · Kislovodsk · Danube · Győr · Miskolc · Nyíregyháza · Debrecen · Oradea · Cluj-Napoca · Tecuci · Bender · Odesa · Bilhorod-Dnistrovs'kyy · Dzhankoy · Kerch · Krasnodar · Maykop · Sochi · Tuapse · Budapest · Székesfehérvár · Kecskemét · Szeged · Arad · Timişoara · Deva · Târgu Mureş · Sibiu · Braşov · Buzău · Brăila · Izmayil · CRIMEA · Feodosiya · Novorossiysk · Zugdidi · Szombathely · Zagreb · Lake Balaton · Nagykanizsa · Pécs · Subotica · Sombor · Zrenjanin · Lugoj · Râmnicu Vâlcea · Ploieşti · Constanţa · Yevpatoriya · Simferopol · Sudak · GEORGIA · Varaždin · Osijek · Novi Sad · Vršac · Târgu Jiu · Piteşti · Bucharest · Sevastopol · Poti · Batumi · Banja Luka · Tuzla · Belgrade · Drobeta-Turnu Severin · Craiova · Danube · Ruse · Pleven · Varna · Sukhumi · SARAJEVO · Zenica · Mostar · Užice · Kragujevac · Zaječar · Veliko Tarnovo · Shumen · Burgas · Rize · Trabzon · Metković · Dubrovnik · MONTENEGRO · Podgorica · Cetinje · Shkodër · Peć · Pristina · Pernik · Sofia · Stara Zagora · Sliven · İnebolu · Sinop · Bafra · Samsun · Ordu · Giresun · Anadolu Dağları · Split · Kosovska Mitrovica · KOSOVO · Prizren · Kumanovo · Vranje · Niš · Kruševac · Balkan Mountains · Dimitrovgrad · Plovdiv · Edirne · Zonguldak · Karabük · Çankırı · Amasya · Çorum · Turhal · Erzincan · Tirana · Durrës · Lushnjë · Skopje · Veles · Bitola · Serres · Drama · Xanthi · Komotini · Tekirdağ · İstanbul · Kadıköy · Bolu · Merzifon · Yozgat · Sivas · Elazığ · Diyarbakır · ALBANIA · MACEDONIA (F.Y.R.O.M.) · Korçë · Kozani · Thessaloniki · Kavala · Thasos · Samothraki · Gallipoli · Alexandroupoli · Sea of Marmara · İzmit · Adapazarı · Ankara · Kırıkkale · Kayseri · Erciyes Dağı 3917 · Malatya · Kahramanmaraş · Şanlıurfa · Vlorë · Pindus Mts · Ioannina · Trikala · Larisa · Mount Olympus 2911 · Evvoia · Skyros · Limnos · Gökçeada · Çanakkale · Edremit · Balıkesir · Bursa · Eskişehir · Kütahya · Afyonkarahisar · Akşehir · Lake Tuz · Niğde · Taurus Mountains · Birecik · Corfu · Kerkyra · Igoumenitsa · Lefkada · Cephalonia · GREECE · Karditsa · Volos · Lesbos · Chios · İzmir · Manisa · Akhisar · Alaşehir · Uşak · Dinar · Eğirdir Gölü · Konya · Ereğli · Adana · Gaziantep · Aleppo · Ar Raqqah · Zakynthos · Mesolongi · Chalkida · Athens · Piraeus · Patras · Andros · Samos · Ikaria · Aydın · Söke · Yatağan · Isparta · Beyşehir Gölü · Karaman · Mersin · Tarsus · İskenderun · Antakya · SYRIA · Reggio di Calabria · Catanzaro · Crotone · Tripoli · Corinth · Tinos · Paros · Naxos · Dodecanese · Kos · Marmaris · Fethiye · Antalya · Antalya Körfezi · Latakia · Hamāh · Homs · Tadmur · Cosenza · Sparti · Kalamata · Kyparissia · Milos · Amorgos · Ios · Thira · Rhodes · Karpathos · CYPRUS · Kyrenia · Famagusta · Nicosia · Olympos 1951 · Limassol · Tripoli · LEBANON · Beirut · Damascus · Kythira · Iraklion · Chania · Crete · Sidon · Zahlé · Tyre · Haifa · Nazareth · Al Mafraq · Az Zarqā · Ra's al Hilāl · Darnah · Al Baydā' · Al Marj · Tubruq · Marsá Matrūh · Alexandria · Al Mansūrah · Al Ismā'īlīyah · ISRAEL · WEST BANK · 'Amman · Tel Aviv-Yafo · Rehovot · Jerusalem · GAZA · Hebron · Beersheba · JORDAN · Ma'ān · Al Karak · Benghazi · Al Jabal al Akhdar · Umm Sa'ad · Dumyāt · Port Said · Ma'ān · Sirte · An Nawfalīyah · Ajdābiyā · Al 'Uqaylah · Wādī al Hamīm · Al Jaghbūb · Siwah · Az Zaqāzīq · Cairo · Giza · Hulwān · Suez · Eilat · Al 'Aqabah · SAUDI ARABIA · As Sidrah · Marsa al Burayqah · Libyan Plateau · Al Fayyūm · Sinai · Jabal Kātrīna 2637 · Jabal al Lawz 2579 · Tabūk · Waddān · Marādah · Wāhāt Jālū · Jālū · Banī Suwayf · Al Ghardaqah · Dubā · Zillah · Calanscio Sand Sea · Great Sand Sea · Al Minyā · Banī Mazār · Mallawī · Al Bawīti · EGYPT · Bur Safājah · LIBYA · AS SARĪR · CYRENAICA · Asyūt · Tīmā · Sawhāj · Western Desert · Eastern Desert · Nile · Luxor · Armant · Qinā · Marsá al 'Alam · Zīghan · Mūt · Isnā · Idfū · Aswān · Kawm Umbū · Baranis · Tropic of Cancer

A 14° 16° B 18° C 20° D 22° E 24° F 26° G

CROATIA

Nova Mesto
Snežnik
1796
Metlika
Kupa
Zagreb
Karlovac
Sisak
Virovitica
Pécs
Baja
Szeged
Subotica
Arad
Lipova
Brad
Alba Iulia
Miercurea Ciuc
Onești
Rijeka
Ogulin
Sava
Nova Gradiška
Osijek
Sombor
Kikinda
Timișoara
Deva
Mureșul
Sebeș
Sibiu
Sighișoara
Medias
Fāgāraš
Brașov
Târgu Secuiesc
Tecuci
Krk
Cres
Pag
Gospić
Vaganski Vrh
1758
Bihać
Prijedor
Bosanska Dubica
Banja Luka
Doboj
Drava
Novi Sad
Zrenjanin
Vršac
Reșița
Lugoj
Caransebeș
Petroșani
Transylvanian Alps
Vârful Moldoveanu
2544
ROMANIA
Focșani
Buzău
Šibenik
Zadar
Knin
738
Dinaric Alps
BOSNIA AND HERZEGOVINA
Jajce
Travnik
Zenica
Bosna
Tuzla
Loznica
Zvornik
Srebrenica
Ruma
Sabac
Belgrade
Pančevo
Požarevac
Velika Morava
Orșova
Drobeta-Turnu Severin
Negotin
Târgu Jiu
Vârful Parângul Mare
2519
Râmnicu Vâlcea
Pitești
Târgoviște
Ploiești
Urziceni
Slobozia
Dugi Otok
Vis
Split
Brač
Makarska
Hvar
Korčula
Mljet
Dubrovnik
Metković
Mostar
Foča
Gorni Vakuf
Vrbas
Una
Sarajevo
Pločno
2228
Prijepolje
Užice
Kragujevac
Kruševac
Niš
Pirot
SERBIA
Zaječar
Lom
Danube
Montana
Vratsa
Iskur
Calafat
Corabia
Turnu Măgurele
Zimnicea
Giurgiu
Ruse
Craiova
Slatina
Caracal
Alexandria
Bucharest
Danube
Silistra
Razgrad
Shumen
Termoli
San Severo
Vieste
Manfredonia
Adriatic Sea
Durmitor Tara
2522
Novi Pazar
Bijelo Polje
Nikšić
MONTENEGRO
Podgorica
Cetinje
Bar
Maja Jezercë
2694
Lake Scutari
Shkodër
Ibar
Kosovska Mitrovica
Peć
Priština
KOSOVO
Kuršumlija
Leskovac
Vranje
Prizren
Bistra
2660
Tetovo
Kumanovo
Kyustendil
Pernik
Sofia
Botevgrad
Panagyurishte
Plovdiv
Pazardzhik
Musala
2925
Karlovo
Balkan Mountains
Pleven
Osum
Lovech
Gabrovo
Veliko Tarnovo
Sliven
Stara Zagora
Yambol
Burgas
Karnob
Lezhë
Peshkopi
Debar
Kičevo
Gostivar
Skopje
MACEDONIA (F.Y.R.O.M.)
Veles
Štip
Kočani
Strumica
Blagoevgrad
Struma
Sandanski
Petrich
Mesta
Smolyan
Rhodope Mountains
Kardzhali
Dimitrovgrad
Haskovo
Edirne
Elhovo
Tundža
Lüleb
Babaeski
Uzunköprü
Ergene
Maritsa
Durrës
Tirana
Elbasan
Lushnjë
Ohrid
Lake Ohrid
Prilep
Bitola
Lake Prespa
Gevgelija
Vardar
Polykastro
Kilkis
Serres
Strymonas
Drama
Xanthi
Komotini
Keşan
Şarköy
Tekird
ALBANIA
Berat
Vlorë
Patos
Korçë
Florina
Kastoria
Edessa
Veroia
Thessaloniki
Kavala
Alexandroupoli
Thasos
Thrakiko Pelagos
Saros Körfezi
Gallipoli
Brindisi
Lecce
Otranto
Gallipoli
Capo Santa Maria di Leuca
Strait of Otranto
Gjirokastër
Sarandë
Pindus Mountains
Smolikas
2637
Grevena
Kozani
Veroia
Katerini
Thermaïkos Kolpos
Mt Olympus
2911
Ossa
1978
Polygyros
Akra Arapis
Athos
2033
Gökçeada
İmroz
Çanakkale
Samothraki
Limnos
Dardanelles
Çan
Kerkyra
Corfu
Ioannina
Igoumenitsa
Larisa
Trikala
Karditsa
Pineios
Volos
Voreioi Sporades
Skyros
Agios Efstratios
Lesbos
Mytilini
Ayvalık
Edrem
Ezine
Preveza
Arta
Achelöos
Lefkada
Cephalonia
GREECE
Karpenisi
Oiti
2152
Lamia
Parnassos
2457
Amfissa
Levadeia
Chalkida
Agios Konstantinos
Evvoia
Aegean
Marathonas
Psara
Chios
Chios
Bornova
Karşıyaka
Buca
Manis
İz
İzmir Körfezi
Aliaga
Ionian Islands
Zakynthos
Zakynthos
Pyrgos
Mesolongi
Patraïkos Kolpos
Patras
Gulf of Corinth
Megara
Nea Liosia
Kyllini
2376
Corinth
Piraeus
Athens
Akra Kafireas
Andros
Tinos
Ikaria
Samos
Kuşac
Ionian Sea
Kyparissia
Tripoli
Nafplio
Sparti
Aigina
Agios Dimitrios
Kea
Kythnos
Syros
Ermoupoli
Paros
Naxos
Cyclades
Milos
Ios
Amorgos
Kos
Dodecanese
Pylos
Kalamata
Messiniakos Kolpos
Lakonikos Kolpos
Akra Tainaro
Neapoli
Akra Maleas
Kythira
Thira
Antikythira
Akra Spatha
Krytiko Pelagos
Karpathos
Kasos
Kastelli
Chania
Rethymno
Idi
2456
Crete
Iraklion
Agios Nikolaos
Sitela

MEDITERRANEAN

Relief and physical features

Relief metres
5000
3000
2000
1000
500
200
sea level
under sea level
200
4000
6000

3917 ▲ Mountain height (in metres)

Water features

River
Intermittent river
Canal
Lake / Reservoir
Intermittent lake
Marsh

Communications

Railway
Motorway
Road
⊕ Main airport

Administration

Boundaries
International
Disputed
Ceasefire line

Settlement

Cities and towns in order of size

National capital
■ Athens

Other city or town
● İstanbul
● Bursa
● Krasnodar
● Split
○ Dubrovnik

Scale 1 : 5 000 000

0 50 100 150 km

Conic Equidistant projection

H 30° I 32° J 34° K 36° L 38° M

MOLDOVA
Comrat
Cahul
Artsyz
Reni
İzmayil
Bolhrad
Tatarbunary
Bihorod-Dnistrovs'kyy
Odesa
UKRAINE
Skadovs'k
Armyans'k
Novooleksiyivka
Heniches'k
Primorsko-Akhtarsk
Timashëvsk
ăila
rşova
ernovodă
rich
na
Tulcea
Sulina
Babadag
Danube Delta
Constanţa
Mangalia
Kavarna
Nos Kaliakra
Chornomors'ke
Krasnoperekops'k
Dzhankoy
Karkinits'ka Zatoka
CRIMEA
Administered by Russia
Sea of Azov
Nyzhn'ohirs'kyy
Kerch
Temryuk
Anapa
Krymsk
Slavyansk-na-Kubani
Kuban'
Krasnodar
Tshchikskoye Vodokhranilishche
RUSSIA 7
Khadyzhensk
Psebay
Yevpatoriya
Simferopol'
Feodosiya
Sudak
Novorossiysk
Sevastopol'
Yalta
Caucasus
Tuapse
Sochi
Gagra
GEORGIA
Sokhumi
40° N
44° 6

B l a c k   S e a
42°

ğneada Burnu
Sinop
İnebolu
Bafra
Samsun
Terme
Rize
5
ay
Zonguldak
Bartın
Boyabat
Vezirköprü
Anadolu Dağları
Ordu
Giresun
Trabzon
Ereğli
Kastamonu
Devrez
Karabük
Tosya
Merzifon
Amasya
Niksar
Gümüşhane
Şebinkarahisar
Bayburt
İstanbul
Sarıyer
Beykoz
Kadıköy
Kandıra
İzmit
Adapazarı
Düzce
Bolu
Köroğlu Tepesi 2400
Gerede
Çankırı
Kızılırmak
Osmancık
Çorum
Turhal
Yeşilırmak
Tokat
Suşehri
Kızıl Dağı 3025
Erzincan
Bakırköy
Kartal
Yalova
Gölcük
Körfez
Geyve
Göynük
Mudurnu
Beypazarı
Etimesgut
Keçiören
Kalecik
Sungurlu
Yıldızeli
Zara
Sivas
Divriği
Tunceli
Sea of Marmara
Gemlik
Bursa
Bilecik
İnegöl
Uludağ 2493
Sakarya
Bozüyük
Porsuk
Eskişehir
Polatlı
Ankara **Çankaya**
Kırıkkale
Yozgat
Delice
Akdağmadeni
Kızılırmak
Şarkışla
Kangal
Arapgir
Keban Barajı
Elazığ
andırma
tafakemalpaşa
Susurluk
alıkesir
Tavşanlı
Kütahya
Sivrihisar
Sakarya
Kaman
Kırşehir
Boğazlıyan
Kızılırmak
Pınarbaşı
Malatya
Ergani
4 38°
isar
Simav
Eski Gediz
Emirdağ
Yunak
Şereflikoçhisar
Avanos
Nevşehir
Kayseri
Erciyes Dağı 3917
Elbistan
Göksun
Adıyaman
Siverek
T U R K E Y
Demirci
Uşak
Banaz
Afyonkarahisar
Sandıklı
Cihanbeyli
Lake Tuz
Aksaray
Bor
Niğde
Demirkazık Tepe 3756
Kahramanmaraş
Atatürk Barajı
Viranşehir
demiş
Alaşehir
Gediz
A n a t o l i a
Çivril
Gelincik Dağı 2799
Akşehir
Nevşehir
in Nazilli
ükmenderes
Denizli
Dinar
Eğirdir Gölü
Eğirdir
Beyşehir Gölü
Konya
Karapınar
Ereğli
Medetsiz Tepe 3524
Kadirli
Gaziantep
Nizip
Birecik
Euphrates
Şanlıurfa
Akçakale
3
Yatağan
Burdur
Isparta
Beyşehir
Seydişehir
Kozan
Ceyhan
Osmaniye
Kilis
Balıkh
Muğla
Korkuteli
Geyik Dağ 2877
Karaman
Tarsus
Ceyhan
Adana
İskenderun
Antakya
Kırıkhan
Aleppo
Buhayrat al Asad
Ar Raqqah
Marmaris
Dalaman
Elmalı 3073
Serik
Manavgat
Ermenek
Mut
Erdemli
Mersin
İskenderun Körfezi
Samandağ
İdlib
Ma'arrat an Nu'mān
Madīnat ath Thawrah
36°
Fethiye
Antalya
Antalya Körfezi
Alanya
Silifke
J. an Nuşayrīyah
Rhodes
Kaş
Anamur
Cape Apostolos Andreas
Latakia
Jablah
Bāniyās
Ḩamāh
S Y R I A
Rhodes
Lindos
Aigialousa
Kyrenia
Administered as Northern Cyprus
Famagusta
S 2
SEA
Polis
Kyrenia
Nicosia
Olympos 1951
CYPRUS
Larnaca
Ţarţūs
Homs
Tadmur
Cape Arnauti
Paphos
Limassol
Tripoli
Qornet es Saouda 3088
Al Qaryatayn
34°
LEBANON
Zahlé
Sab' Ābār
An Nabk
Beirut
1

H 30° I 32° J 34° K 36° L 38° M

N of globe inset

Yamal Peninsula

O. Belyy

Obskaya Guba

Tazovskaya Guba

Yamburg
Yaptiksale
Pangody
Nadym
Novyy Port

Baydaratskaya Guba

Ust'-Kara
Kara
Amderma

Khrebet Pay-Khoy

Guba Dolgaya
Ostrov Vaygach
Ostrov Dolgaya

Proliv Karskiye Vorota

Kara Sea

Ostrov Yuzhnyy

Krasino

Ostrov Mezhdusharskiy

Novaya Zemlya

Barents Sea

Pechorskoye More

Ostrov Kolguyev

Mezhdusharskaya Guba

Cheshskaya Guba

Mys Kanin Nos

Poluostrov Kanin

Malozemel'skaya Tundra

Belush'ye

Bol'shezemel'skaya Tundra

Tundra

Severnyy
Vorkuta
Inta
Usinsk

Gora Narodnaya ▲ 1895

Gora Telpoziz ▲ 1617

Kyrta
Vuktyl
Ust'-Ilych

Nyrob

Ust'-Tsil'ma
Pechora
Charkayuvom
Usa

Nar'yan-Mar
Novaya

Pechora

Ust'-Tsil'ma
Izhma
Kadzherom
Sosnogorsk
Ukhta

Myla

Timanskiy Kryazh

Sindor

Mikun'

Ob"yachevo

Ezhva
Syktyvkar
Koryazhma

Vychegda

Usogorsk

Vel'sk

Karpogory

Krasnoborsk

Kotlas

Oktyabr'skiy
Velikiy Ustyug

Luza

Murashi

Nikol'sk

Kirs

Kirov

Kotel'nich

Luza

Shakhun'ya

Tot'ma

Konosha

Buy

Galich

Kostroma

Kineshma

Ivanovo

Vel'sk

Myla
Safonovo
Azopol'ye
Mezen'

Mezen'

Pinega

Shilega

Northern
Dvina

Berezník

Onega

Archangel
Novodvinsk

Onega

Obozerskiy
Plesetsk

Savinskiy

Nadvoitsy
Segezha

Maslozero

Medvezh'yegorsk

Vodla

Povenets

Petrozavodsk

Ozero Vygozero

Ozero Beloye
Belozersk

Vologda

Rybinskoye
Vodokhranilishche
Rybinsk

Cherepovets

Volgo
Volga

Yaroslavl'

Sergiyev
Posad

Klin

Aleksandrov

Vladimir

Moscow

Tver'

Vyshniy
Volochek

Torzhok

Pudozh

Vytegra

Kodeynoye Pole

Lake Onega

Lake Ladoga

Kem'

White Sea

Sosnovka

Umba

Kandalaksha

Apatity

Kola Peninsula

Murmanskiy Bereg

Poluostrov Rybachiy

North Cape

Varangerfjorden

NORWAY

Vadsø

Kirkenes

Nikel'

Murmansk

Monchegorsk

Ozero
Lovozero

Loukhi

Ozero Topozero

Kalevala
Kostomuksha

Belomorsk

Suoyarvi

Olonets

Tikhvin

Borovichi

Staraya
Russa

Velikiy
Novgorod

St Petersburg

Vyborg

Lappeenranta

Kingisepp

Kotka

Lovat'

Pskov

Ostrov

Velikiye
Luki

Lake Peipus

Lake Pskov

Nevel'

Vitsyebsk

Hammerfest

Alta

Kautokeino

Karasjok

Inari

Ivalo

Kittilä

Sodankylä

Kemijärvi

Rovaniemi

Tornio

Kemi

Oulu

FINLAND

Kajaani

Iisalmi

Suomussalmi

Kuopio

Nurmes

Joensuu

Savonlinna

Mikkeli

LATVIA

Gulf of Riga

Riga

Jūrmala

Jelgava

Daugavpils

Šiauliai

LITHUANIA

Kaunas

Vilnius

Yekaterinburg

Chelyabinsk

Tyumen'

Kurgan

Shadrinsk

Kamensk-Ural'skiy

Kamyshlov

Tavda

Tavda

Turinsk

Tura

Nizhniy
Tagil

Krasnoufimsk

Perm'

Kungur

Solikamsk
Berezniki

Gora
Konzhakovskiy
Kamen' ▲ 1569

Ivdel'

Krasnoturinsk

Serov

Zlatoust

U r a l   M o u n t a i n s

Kizel
Chusovoy

Ocher

Kama

Glazov

Nefteyugansk

Naberezhnyye Chelny

Kazan'

Zelenodol'sk

Cheboksary

Yoshkar-Ola

Nolinsk

Votkinsk

Sarapul

Izhevsk

Nizhniy Novgorod

Dzerzhinsk

Kovrov

R U S S I A

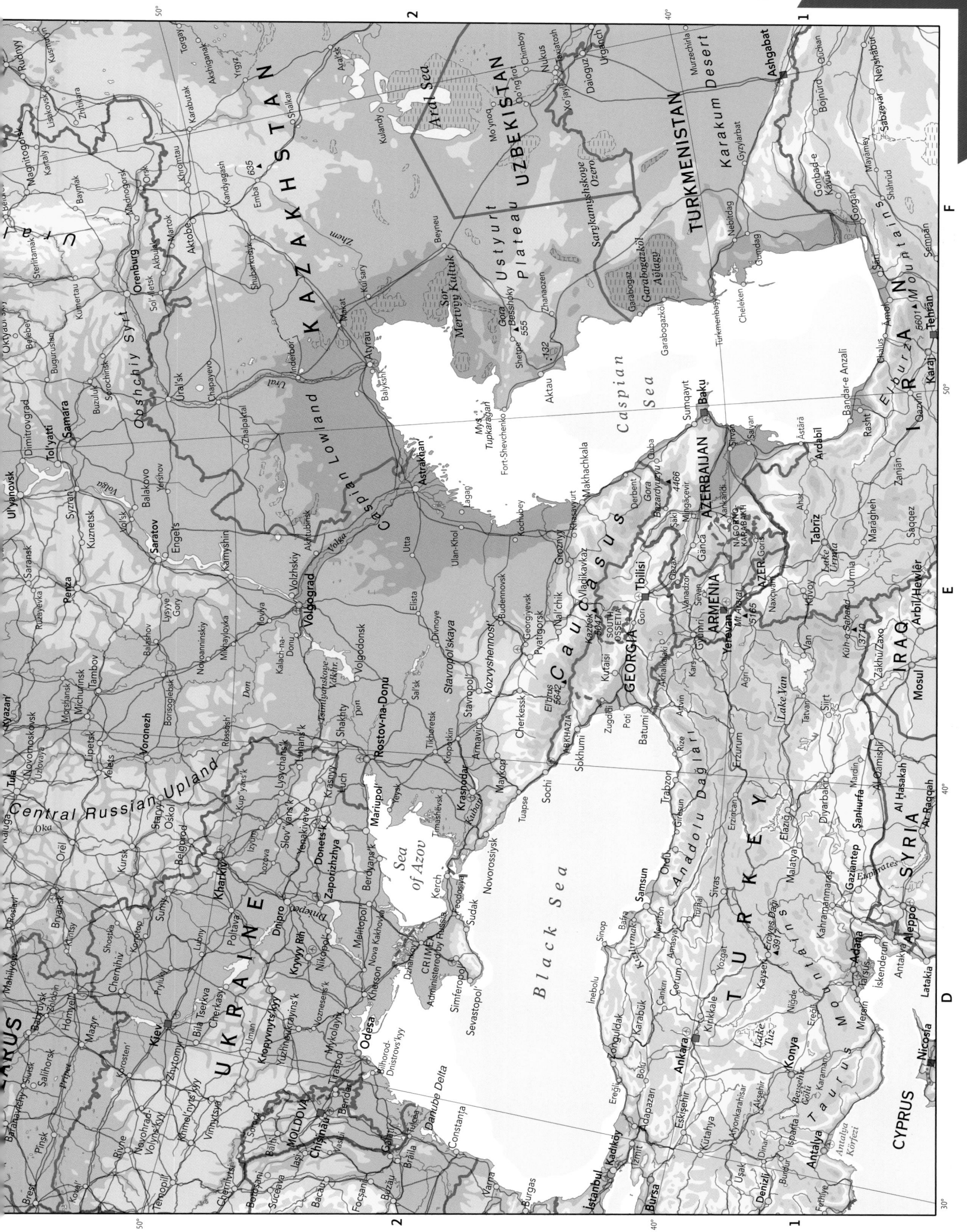

Relief and physical features

Relief
metres

5000
3000
2000
1000
500
200
0 sea level
200 under sea level
4000
6000

5642 ▲ Mountain height
(in metres)

Permanent ice
(ice cap or glacier)

Water features

~~~ River
~~~ Intermittent river
Canal
Lake / Reservoir
Intermittent lake
Marsh

Communications

Railway
Road
⊕ Main airport

Administration

Boundaries

International
Disputed
Ceasefire line

Settlement

Cities and towns in order of size

National capital   Other city or town

■ **Moscow**   ● Ōsaka

● **St Petersburg**

● **Tula**

● Abakan

○ Kyzyl

Scale 1 : 20 000 000

0   200   400   600 km

Conic Equidistant projection

3 60° 4 70° 5 80° 6

A
B
C
D
E
F
G
H

Jan Mayen
(Norway)

Arctic Circle

Faroe Islands
(Denmark)

Torshavn

Shetland

N o r w e g i a n   S e a

Svalbard
(Norway)

Barentsburg
Spitsbergen
Longyearbyen

Nordaustlandet

Magnuspynt

Zemlya Frantsa-Iosifa

Bjørnøya

Edgeøya

B a r e n t s   S e a

Ostrov
Severnyy

Ostrov
Yuzhnyy

N o v a y a   Z e m l y a

Krasino

K a r a   S e a

Bergen

Trondheim

N O R W A Y

Oslo

Östersund
Lillehammer

S W E D E N

Uppsala

Stockholm

Norrköping

Gulf of Bothnia

Turku

Tampere

F I N L A N D

Helsinki

Gulf of Finland

Tallinn

ESTONIA

LATVIA

Riga

LITHUANIA

Vilnius

Kaliningrad

Daugavpils

Minsk

BELARUS

Mahilyow

Homyel'

Tromsø

Narvik

Lapp l and

Kiruna

Luleå

Tornio

North Cape

Murmansk

Kola
Peninsula

Kem'

W h i t e   S e a

Medvezh'yegorsk

Petrozavodsk

Lake
Onega

Lake
Ladoga

St Petersburg

Velikiy Novgorod

Cherepovets

Rybinsk
Rybinskoye

Tver'

Yaroslavl'

Kostroma

Ivanovo

Arkhangel'sk

Severodvinsk

Pinega

Mezen'

Poluostrov
Kanin

Northern Dvina

Vel'sk

Kotlas

Syktyvkar

Kirov

Kama

Solikamsk

Berezniki

Perm'

Izhevsk

Cheboksary

Kazan'

U r a l   M o u n t a i n s

Gora
Narodnaya
1895 ▲

Ob'

Pechora

Ukhta

Pechora

Naryan-Mar

Vorkuta

Salekhard

Ob'

Nadym

Novyy Port

Yamal
Peninsula

Baydaratskaya Guba

Obskaya Guba

Gydan
Peninsula

Urengoy

Taz

Tazovskiy

Noyabr'sk

Surgut

Khanty-
Mansiysk

Nizhnevartovsk

W e s t

S i b e r i a n

P l a i n

R

Serov

Nizhniy
Tagil

Yekaterinburg

Chelyabinsk

Tobol'sk

Irtysh

Tyumen'

Tomsk

Anzhero-Sudzhensk

Omsk

Kemerovo

Novosibirsk

Tatarsk

Barabinsk

Novokuznetsk

Barnaul

Biysk

Rubtsovsk

Pskov

Velikiye Luki

Vitsyebsk

Smolensk

Moscow

Sergiyev

Serpukhov

Kaluga

Bryansk

Orël

Kursk

Belgorod

Staryy Oskol

Kharkiv

UKRAINE

Tula

Lipetsk

Voronezh

Tambov

Michurinsk

Ryazan'

Vladimir

Dzerzhinsk

Arzamas

Nizhniy
Novgorod

Novomoskovsk

Ul'yanovsk

Saransk

Penza

Syzran'

Kuznetsk

Saratov

Kamyshin

Volga

Engel's

Volga

Tol'yatti

Samara

Naberezhnyye
Chelny

Sterlitamak

Ufa

Magnitogorsk

Kumertau

Orenburg

Kurgan

Kamensk-Ural'skiy

Miass

Tobol

Kostanay

Rudnyy

Petropavlovsk

Ishim

Irtysh

Kokshetau

Astana

Karaganda

Temirtau

Pavlodar

Semipalatinsk

Ust'-Kamenogorsk

Gora
1506 ▲

Ust'-
Ishim

Sea of
Azov

Kerch

Mariupol'

Rostov-na-Donu

Taganrog

Novocherkassk

Don

Volgograd

Volga

Volzhskiy

Astrakhan'

Krasnodar

Stavropol'skaya
Vozvyshennost'

Stavropol'

Novorossiysk

Sochi

C a u c a s u s

El'brus
5642 ▲

Groznyy

Makhachkala

Caspian Lowland

Atyrau

Ural'sk

Ural

Aktobe

Kandyagash

Karabutak

Shalkar

Zhezkazgan

K A Z A K H S T A N

Ozero
Kupshak

Yrgyz

Karasuk

Pavlodar

Atasu

Ayagoz

Aktogay

Lake
Zaysan

Tacheng

Karabük

Black Sea

Samsun

Ordu

Sokhumi

Batumi

T U R K E Y

Kayseri

Malatya

Gaziantep

Erzurum

Diyarbakır

GEORGIA

Tbilisi

Rustavi

ARMENIA

Yerevan

Mt Ararat
5165 ▲

Lake Van

Van

AZERBAIJAN

Gäncä

Baku

C a s p i a n

S e a

Şevçenko

Aktau

Ustyurt
Plateau

Garabogazköl
Aylagy

Türkmenbaşy

Makat

Beyneü

A r a l

S e a

Aral'sk

Aral'

Syr Darya

Kyzylorda

Shymkent

U Z B E K I S T A N

Nukus

Urganch

Amu Darya

Karakum
Desert

T U R K M E N I S T A N

Ashgabat

Türkmenabat

Buxoro

Aydarko'l
Ko'li

Tashkent

KYRGYZSTAN

Bishkek

Almaty

Balkhash

Lake Balkhash

Aktogay

Taldykorgan

Chiganak

C H I N A

Yining

Shihezi

Ü

Ar Raqqah

SYRIA

IRAQ

Mosul

Arbil/Hewlêr

Baghdad

Euphrates

Abu Kamal

Tigris

Kirkuk

I R A N

Tabriz

Lake
Urmia

Qazvin

Karaj

Tehran

Qom

Arak

Esfahan

Ahvaz

Hamadan

Kermanshah

Gorgan

Gyzylarbat

30°
50°
F
G 60° H 40° 70° I 80° J

50° 60° 70° 80° 90°
10° 0° 50° 10° 20° 30° 40° 30°

ARCTIC OCEAN

Severnaya Zemlya
Ostrov Komsomolets
Ostrov Oktyabr'skoy Revolyutsii
Ostrov Bol'shevik
Proliv Vil'kitskogo

Taymyr Peninsula
Gory Byrranga
Ozero Taymyr
North Siberian Lowland
Pyasina
Kheta
Khatanga
Kotuy

New Siberia Islands
Ostrov Kotel'nyy
Ostrov Bol'shoy Lyakhovskiy
Ostrov Novaya Sibir'
Laptev Sea
Chaunskaya Zaliv
Olenekskiy Zaliv
Yanskiy Zaliv

East Siberian Sea
Proliv Longa
Wrangel Island
Chukchi Sea
Bering Strait
U.S.A.
Kotzebue
Arctic Circle
Seward Peninsula
Point Hope
St Lawrence Island
St Matthew I.
Chukotskiy Poluostrov
Anadyrskiy Zaliv

Bering Sea

Kamchatka Peninsula
Koryakskiy Khrebet
Khrebet Kolymskiy
Bol'shoy Anyuy
Malyy Anyuy
Omolon
Kolyma
Gizhiga
Zaliv Shelikhova
Petropavlovsk-Kamchatskiy
 Klyuchevskaya 4750
Ozernovskiy
Severo-Kuril'sk

Sea of Okhotsk
Kuril Islands
Kuril'sk
Administered by Russia
Claimed by Japan

Central Siberian Plateau
RUSSIA
SIBERIA
Noril'sk
Gory Kamen' 1678
Ozero Khantayskoye
Podkamennaya Tunguska
Nizhnyaya Tunguska
Yenisey
Angara
Tembenchi
Tura
Chunya
Taymura
Vilyuy
Markha
Olenek
Muna
Lena
Verkhoyanskiy Khrebet
Verkhoyansk
Yana
Adycha
Khrebet Cherskogo
Gora Pobeda 3003
Mama
Indigirka
El'ginskiy
Srednekolymsk
Seymchan
Susuman
Omsukchan
Magadan
Palatka

Krasnoyarsk
Achinsk
Kansk
Bratsk
Ust'-Ilimsk
Ust'-Kut
Lena
Vitim
Olekma
Olekminsk
Lensk
Mirnyy
Chernyshevskiy
Nyurba
Verkhnevilyuysk
Yakutsk
Ust'-Maya
Aldan
Maya
Uchur
Allakh-Yun'
Okhotsk
Khrebet Dzhugdzhur
Ayan
Shantarskiye Ostrova
Nizhneudinsk
Abakan
Kyzyl
Vostochnyy Sayan
Zapadnyy Sayan
Lake Baikal
Kachug
Usol'ye-Sibirskoye
Irkutsk
Ulan-Ude
Kyakhta
Hövsgöl Nuur
Uvs Nuur

Stanovoy Khrebet
Tynda
Zeya
Skovorodino
Svobodnyy
Blagoveshchensk
Amur
Komsomol'sk-na-Amure
Khabarovsk
Sakhalin
Aleksandrovsk-Sakhalinskiy
Nikolayevsk
Okha
Poronaysk
Uglegorsk
Yuzhno-Sakhalinsk
Korsakov
Tatarskiy Proliv
Sikhote-Alin'
Chita
Sretensk
Karymskoye
Borzya
Argun
Hulun Buir
Hulun Nur
Da Hinggan Ling
Yablonovyy Khrebet

MONGOLIA
Ulan Bator
Arvayheer
Bayanhongor
Altay
Bayan-Uul
Choybalsan
Ulanhot
Xilinhot
Gobi
Chifeng

CHINA
MANCHURIA
Qiqihar
Daqing
Harbin
Mudanjiang
Jixi
Jiamusi
Yichun
Bei'an
Fuyu
Jilin
Changchun
Yanji
Shenyang
Fushun
Ahshan
Tonghua
Dandong

NORTH KOREA
P'yŏngyang
Ch'ŏngjin
Kimch'aek
Vladivostok
Nakhodka
Ussuriysk
Lake Khanka

Sea of Japan (East Sea)
JAPAN
Hokkaidō
Sapporo
Asahikawa
Asahi-dake 2290
Wakkanai
Kushiro
Hakodate
Aomori
Akita
Niigata
Sendai
Tokyo
Yokohama
Nagoya
Kyōto
Osaka
Hachinohe

ASIA

Bering Strait

Arctic Circle

60°

80°

80°

C

D

E

F

G

H

5

6

5

ARCTIC OCEAN

Ellesmere Island

Point Barrow

Beaufort Sea

Banks Island

Queen Elizabeth Islands

Parry Islands

Victoria Island

Greenland

Denmark Strait

Arctic Circle

Bering Sea

St Lawrence Island

Nunivak I.

Yukon

Brooks Range

Baffin Bay

Baffin Island

Davis Strait

Cape Farewell

Andreanof Islands

Alaska Range

Denali (Mt McKinley) 6190

Mt Logan 5959

Foxe Basin

Labrador Sea

Bristol Bay

Alaska Pen.

Gulf of Alaska

Kodiak Island

Yukon

Mackenzie Mts

Mackenzie

Great Bear Lake

Southampton Island

Hudson Strait

Labrador

40°

Haida Gwaii

Alexander Archipelago

Coast Mountains

Great Slave Lake

Lake Athabasca

Peace

Churchill

Hudson Bay

Belcher Islands

Churchill

Gulf of Newfoundland
St Lawrence

Cape Breton Island

Mt Waddington 4042

Vancouver Island

Fraser

R o c k y

Saskatchewan

Nelson

Severn

Albany

C a n a d i a n S h i e l d

Cape Sable

PACIFIC OCEAN

Mt Rainier 4392

Cascade Range

Columbia

Snake

Yellowstone

G r e a t   P l a i n s

M o u n t a i n s

Lake Winnipeg

Lake Superior

Lake Huron

St Lawrence

Hudson

Lake Ontario

Lake Michigan

Lake Erie

Cape Cod

Long Island

Chesapeake Bay

ATLANTIC OCEAN

Bermuda

3

Great Salt Lake

Gannett Peak 4202

Missouri

Ohio

Appalachian Mountains

Cape Hatteras

Sierra Nevada

Great Basin

Mt Whitney 4418

Colorado

Colorado Plateau

Grand Canyon

Platte

Arkansas

Mississippi

Tennessee

Alabama

Ozark Plateau

Cape Fear

Red

Brazos

Cape Canaveral

Tropic of Cancer

20°

Guadalupe

Rio Grande

Edwards Plateau

Bahamas

Gulf of California

Sierra Madre Occidental

Altiplano Mexicano

Sierra Madre Oriental

Gulf of Mexico

Straits of Florida

C u b a

Greater Antilles

Hispaniola

Puerto Rico

Lesser Antilles

Cabo Falso

Yucatan Channel

Jamaica

2

Volcán Popocatépetl 5452

Bahía de Campeche

Yucatán

G. of Honduras

Caribbean Sea

Sierra Madre del Sur

Sierra Madre

Golfo del Darién

Île Clipperton

Lake Nicaragua

Isthmus of Panama

Gulf of Panama

SOUTH AMERICA

Equator

0°

1

D

E

F

G

120°

100°

80°

Relief and physical features

Relief metres

5000
3000
2000
1000
500
200
0 sea level
under sea level
200
4000
6000

6190 ▲ Mountain height (in metres)

Permanent ice (ice cap or glacier)

Scale 1 : 45 000 000

0   500   1000 km

Lambert Azimuthal Equal Area projection

Cross-section

line of cross-section

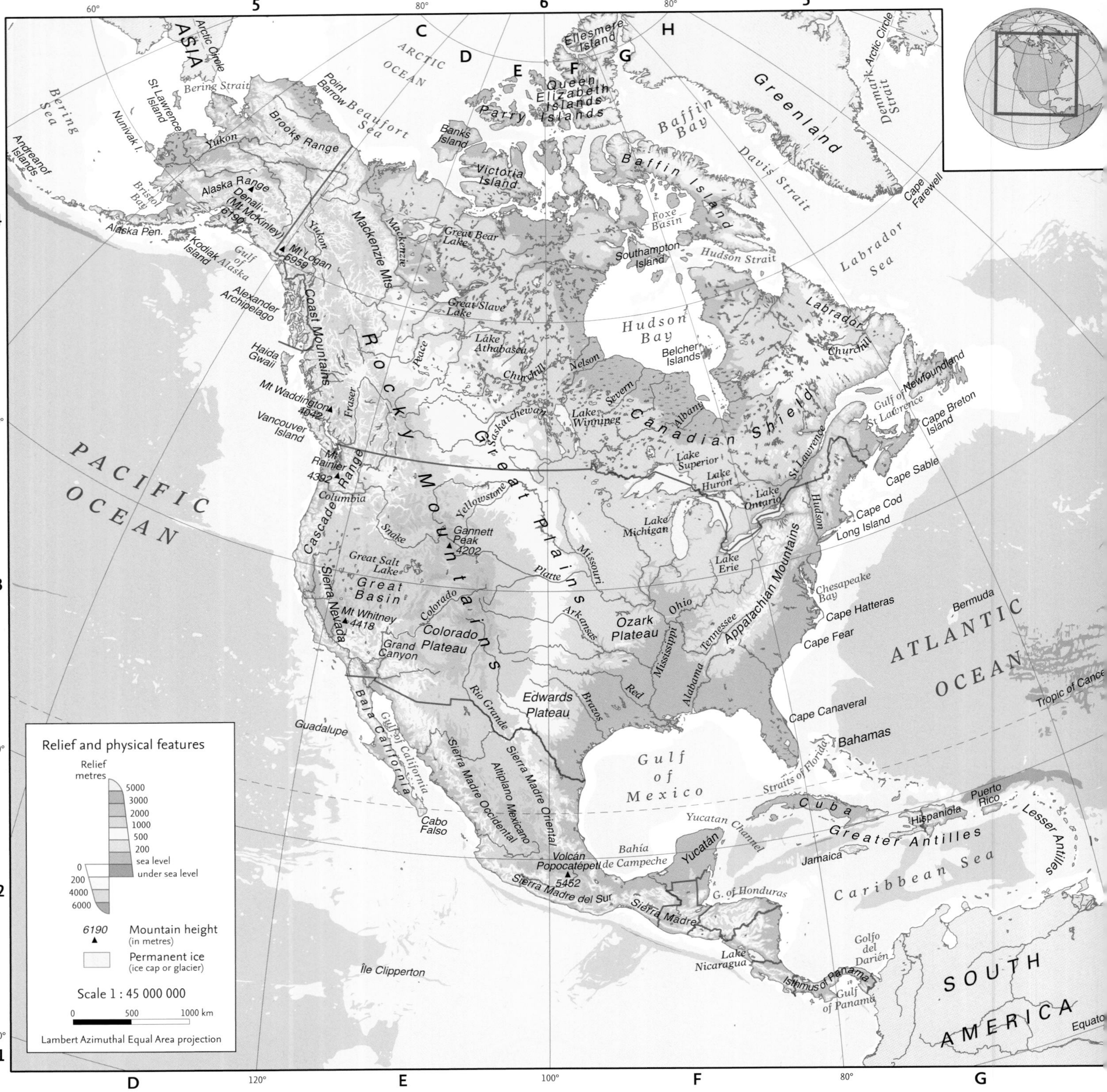

37° 30' N

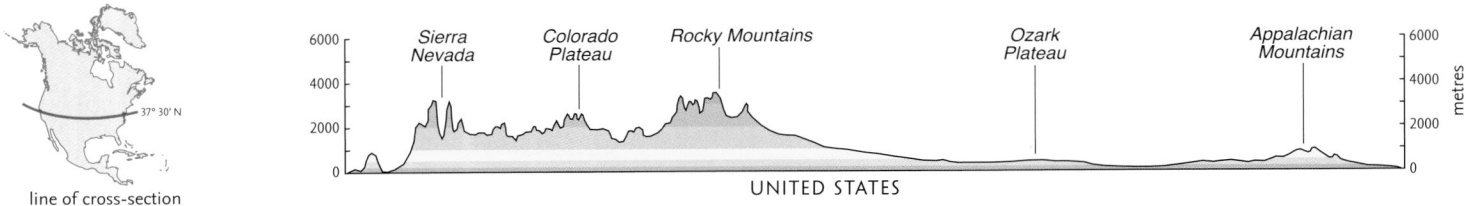

UNITED STATES

60° 5 80° 6 80° 5 60°

ASIA

Arctic Circle

Bering Sea

ARCTIC OCEAN

C D E F G H

Baffin Bay

GREENLAND (Denmark)

Arctic Circle

EUROPE

4

ALASKA
USA

○ Anchorage

Great Bear Lake

Great Slave Lake

○ Nuuk (Godthåb)

○ Iqaluit

Lake Athabasca

Hudson Bay

C A N A D A

○ Edmonton

○ Calgary

Lake Winnipeg

○ St John's

40°

○ Vancouver

○ Winnipeg

○ Quebec

○ Halifax

○ Seattle

○ Portland

Lake Superior

Lake Huron

○ Ottawa ○ Montreal

○ Boston

PACIFIC OCEAN

○ Minneapolis

○ Sacramento

Great Salt Lake ○ Salt Lake City

○ Denver

○ San Francisco

○ Los Angeles

Lake Michigan

○ Chicago

○ Detroit

Lake Ontario

Lake Erie

○ Toronto

○ Pittsburg

○ New York

■ Washington D.C.

ATLANTIC OCEAN

3

U N I T E D   S T A T E S

O F   A M E R I C A

○ Kansas City

○ St Louis

○ Atlanta

○ Phoenix

○ San Diego

○ Dallas

Bermuda (UK)

Tropic of Cancer

○ El Paso

○ Houston

○ New Orleans

○ Miami

Gulf of Mexico

Tropic of Cancer

20°

○ Monterrey

■ Nassau

THE BAHAMAS

■ Havana

CUBA

DOMINICAN REPUBLIC

■ San Juan

ANTIGUA AND BARBUDA

○ Guadalajara

M E X I C O

HAITI ■ ■ Santo Domingo

PUERTO RICO (USA)

DOMINICA

■ Mexico City

○ Puebla

■ Kingston

JAMAICA

Port-au-Prince

Caribbean Sea

ST LUCIA 2

GRENADA

3

2

■ Belmopan

BELIZE

GUATEMALA

HONDURAS

■ Tegucigalpa

■ Guatemala City

■ San Salvador

EL SALVADOR

NICARAGUA

■ Managua

■ San José

COSTA RICA

Panama City

PANAMA

SOUTH AMERICA

Equator 0°

1

120° E 100° F 80° G

Legend

——	International boundary
■	Capital city
○	Important city

1 ST KITTS AND NEVIS
2 ST VINCENT & THE GRENADINES
3 BARBADOS

Scale 1 : 45 000 000

0   500   1000 km

Lambert Azimuthal Equal Area projection

Facts about North America

Total land area	**24 680 331 sq. km**
Highest peak	**Denali (Mt McKinley), 6190 m**
Longest river	**Mississippi-Missouri, 5969 km**
Largest country	**Canada, 9 984 670 sq. km**
Most populous country	**United States, 321 774 000**

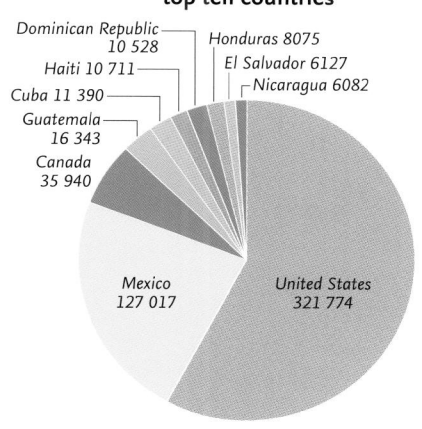

**Population by country, 2015
top ten countries**

Dominican Republic 10 528

Honduras 8075

Haiti 10 711

El Salvador 6127

Cuba 11 390

Nicaragua 6082

Guatemala 16 343

Canada 35 940

Mexico 127 017

United States 321 774

Population in thousands

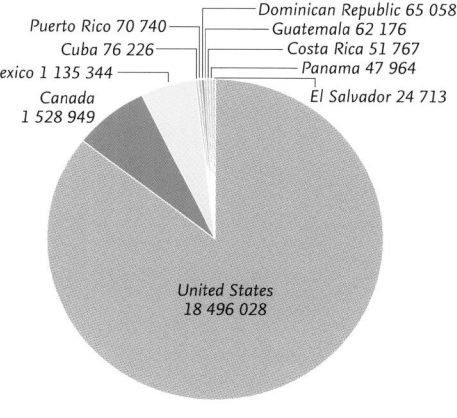

**GNI by country, 2015
top ten countries**

Puerto Rico 70 740

Dominican Republic 65 058

Cuba 76 226

Guatemala 62 176

Mexico 1 135 344

Costa Rica 51 767

Canada 1 528 949

Panama 47 964

El Salvador 24 713

United States 18 496 028

Gross National Income in US $ millions

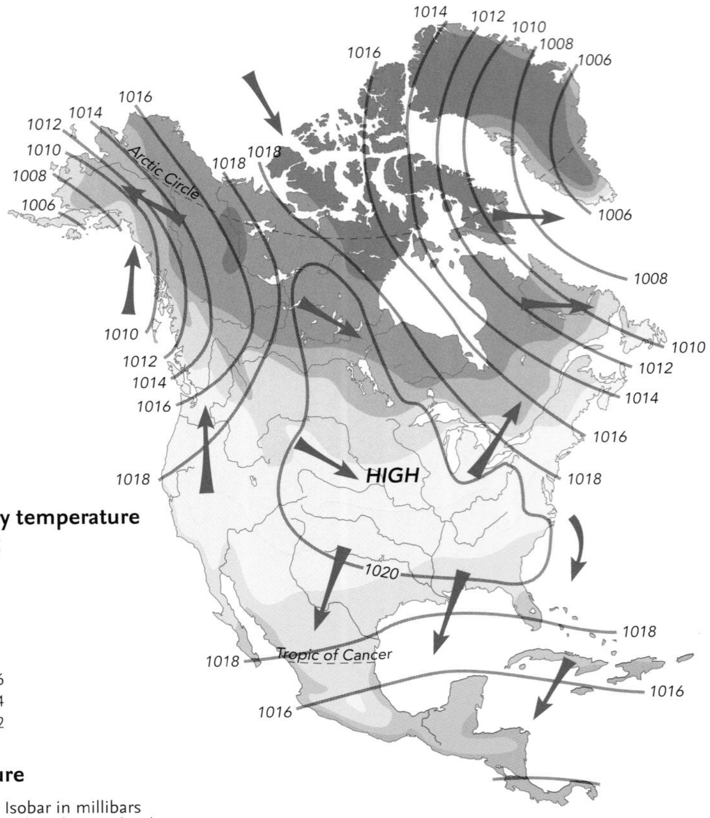

January temperature

°C
24
16
8
0
-8
-16
-24
-32

Pressure

— Isobar in millibars reduced to sea level

➤ Wind direction

Scale 1 : 80 000 000

1014 1012 1010 1008 1006
1016
1016
1012 1014
1010
1008
1006
1018 1018
1006
1008
1010
1012
1010
1012
1014
1014
1016
1016
1016
HIGH
1018
1018
1018
1020
Tropic of Cancer
1018
1016
1016

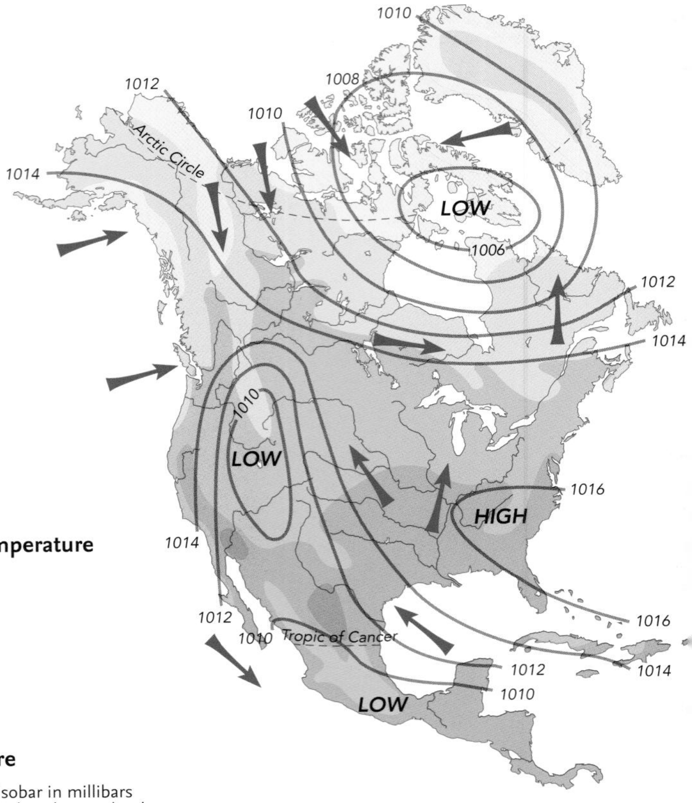

July temperature

°C
32
24
16
8
0
-8

Pressure

— Isobar in millibars reduced to sea level

➤ Wind direction

Scale 1 : 80 000 000

1010
1012
1008
1010
LOW
1006
1014
1012
1014
1010
LOW
1016
HIGH
1014
1016
1012
1010 *Tropic of Cancer*
1012
1010
LOW
1014
1016

Annual rainfall

mm
3000
2000
1000
500
250
0

Scale 1 : 80 000 000

Arctic Circle

Tropic of Cancer

www National Oceanic and Atmospheric Administration
www.noaa.gov
Met Office North America Forecast
www.metoffice.gov.uk/weather
World Meteorological Organization
www.wmo.int
BBC World Weather
news.bbc.co.uk/weather

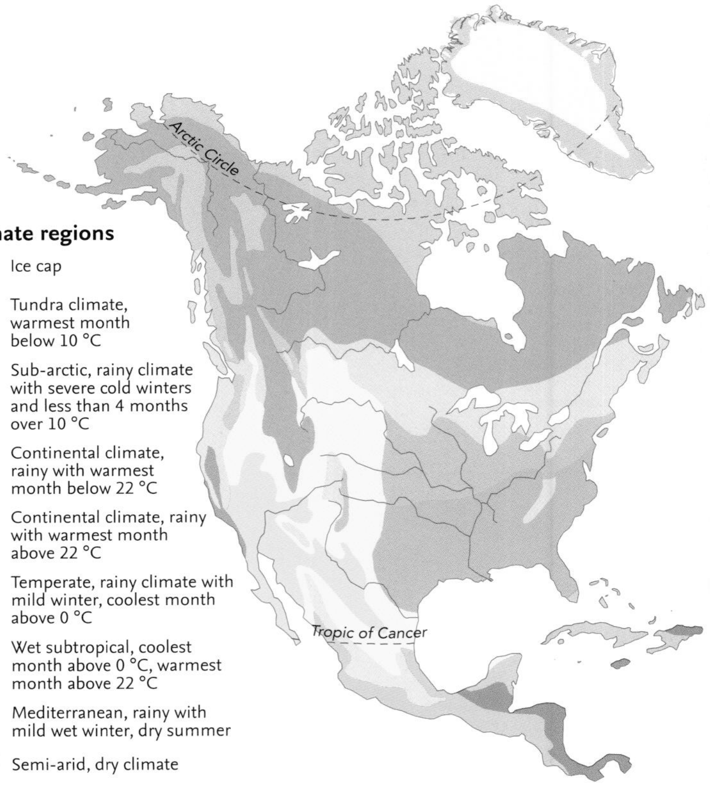

Climate regions

☐ Ice cap

Tundra climate, warmest month below 10 °C

Sub-arctic, rainy climate with severe cold winters and less than 4 months over 10 °C

Continental climate, rainy with warmest month below 22 °C

Continental climate, rainy with warmest month above 22 °C

Temperate, rainy climate with mild winter, coolest month above 0 °C

Wet subtropical, coolest month above 0 °C, warmest month above 22 °C

Mediterranean, rainy with mild wet winter, dry summer

Semi-arid, dry climate

Desert climate

Rainy tropical climate with no winter, coolest month above 18 °C

Rainy tropical climate, constantly wet throughout the year

Scale 1 : 80 000 000

Arctic Circle

Tropic of Cancer

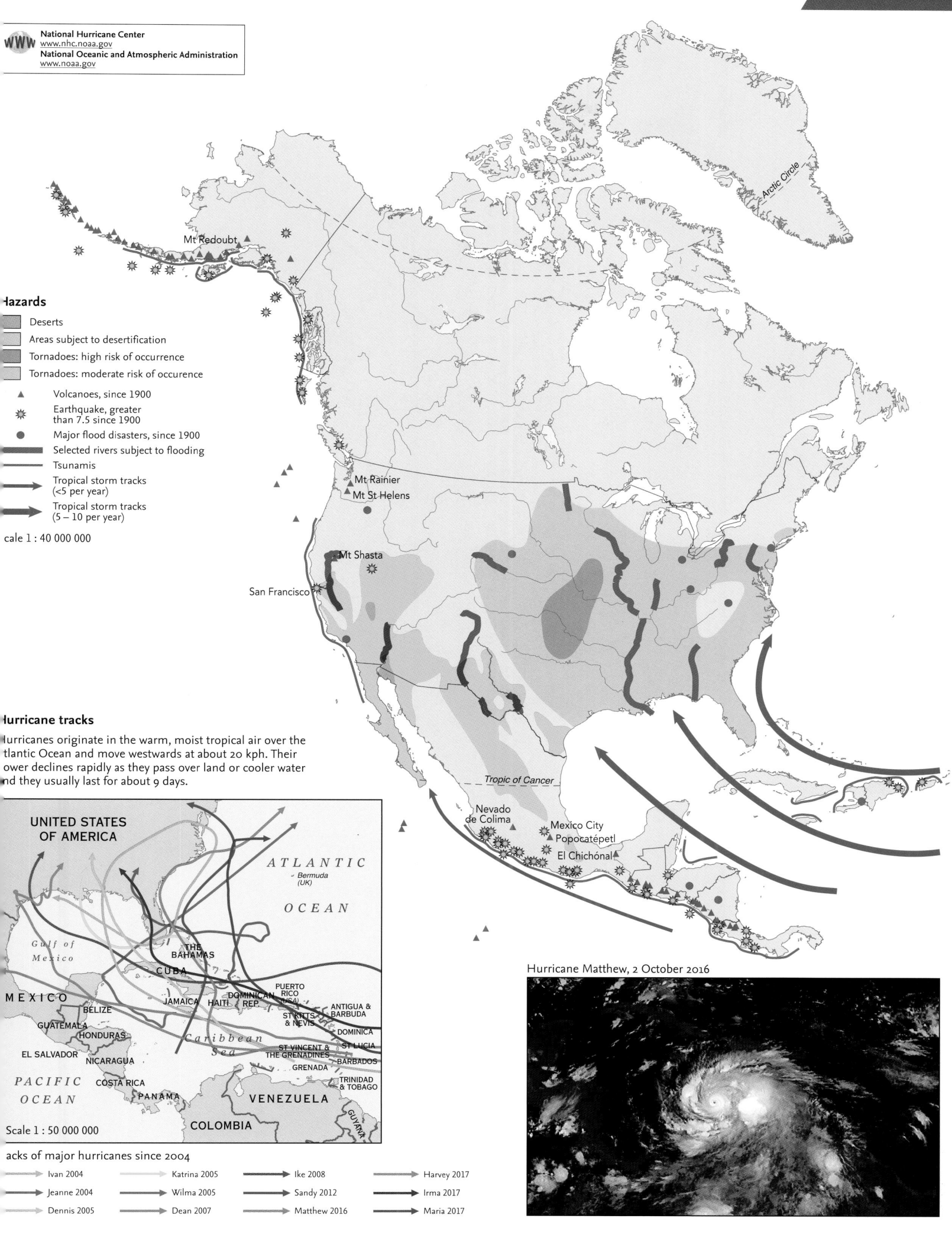

WWW National Hurricane Center
www.nhc.noaa.gov
National Oceanic and Atmospheric Administration
www.noaa.gov

Hazards

	Deserts
	Areas subject to desertification
	Tornadoes: high risk of occurrence
	Tornadoes: moderate risk of occurence
▲	Volcanoes, since 1900
✸	Earthquake, greater than 7.5 since 1900
●	Major flood disasters, since 1900
	Selected rivers subject to flooding
	Tsunamis
→	Tropical storm tracks (<5 per year)
➜	Tropical storm tracks (5 – 10 per year)

Scale 1 : 40 000 000

Hurricane tracks

Hurricanes originate in the warm, moist tropical air over the Atlantic Ocean and move westwards at about 20 kph. Their power declines rapidly as they pass over land or cooler water and they usually last for about 9 days.

Arctic Circle

Mt Redoubt

Mt Rainier
Mt St Helens

Mt Shasta

San Francisco

Tropic of Cancer

Nevado de Colima

Mexico City
Popocatépetl
El Chichónal

UNITED STATES OF AMERICA

ATLANTIC OCEAN

Bermuda (UK)

Gulf of Mexico

THE BAHAMAS

CUBA

MEXICO

BELIZE

JAMAICA HAITI DOMINICAN REP. PUERTO RICO (USA)

ANTIGUA & BARBUDA

ST KITTS & NEVIS

DOMINICA

GUATEMALA
HONDURAS

Caribbean Sea

ST VINCENT & THE GRENADINES ST LUCIA

EL SALVADOR
NICARAGUA

BARBADOS

GRENADA

TRINIDAD & TOBAGO

PACIFIC OCEAN

COSTA RICA

PANAMA

VENEZUELA

COLOMBIA

Scale 1 : 50 000 000

Hurricane Matthew, 2 October 2016

Tracks of major hurricanes since 2004

→ Ivan 2004	→ Katrina 2005	→ Ike 2008	→ Harvey 2017
→ Jeanne 2004	→ Wilma 2005	→ Sandy 2012	→ Irma 2017
→ Dennis 2005	→ Dean 2007	→ Matthew 2016	→ Maria 2017

Relief and physical features

Relief
metres
5000
3000
2000
1000
500
200
0   sea level
       under sea level
200
4000
6000

6194 ▲ Mountain height
         (in metres)

         Permanent ice
         (ice cap or glacier)

Water features

~~~ River
     Canal
     Lake / Reservoir
     Intermittent lake
     Marsh

Communications

     Railway
     Road
  ⊕ Main airport

Administration
Boundaries
     International
     Internal

Settlement
Cities and towns in order of size

National capital   Other city or town
■ Ottawa   ● New York
                        ● Montréal
                        ● Winnipeg
                        ● Saskatoon
                        ○ Churchill

Scale 1 : 17 000 000

0   200   400   600 km

Lambert Conformal Conic projection

H 100° I 90° J 80° K 70° L 60° M 50° N 40° O 80° 30° P 5 20° Q 70° 10° 4 R 60°

10°

British Empire Range
Ellesmere Island
North Geomagnetic Pole (2017)
Nares Strait
Axel Heiberg Island
Amund Ringnes Island
Queen Elizabeth Islands
lands

GREENLAND
(Denmark)

ICELAND
Ísafjörður · Akureyri · Seyðisfjörður · Höfn
Faxaflói · Reykjavík
Keflavík

Cape Parry
Thule
Cape York
Melville Bay
Devon Island
Jones Sound
Cornwallis Island
Resolute
Somerset Island
Lancaster Sound

Baffin Bay

20°

3700 Gunnbjørn Fjeld

Denmark Strait

Kong Christian IX Land

Arctic Circle

3

Broder Peninsula
Arctic Bay
Bylot Island
Mittimatalik
Borden Peninsula
Gulf of Boothia
Boothia Peninsula

Baffin Island

Upernavik
Disko I.
Qasigiannguit
Clyde River
Home Bay

Sisimiut

Kong Frederick VI Kyst

Tasiilaq

Taloyoak
Melville Peninsula
Hall Beach
Prince Charles Island
Penny Icecap
Pangnirtung
Cape Dyer

Cumberland Sound

Maniitsoq

Nuuk (Godthåb)

Cape Farewell

30°

Repulse Bay
Foxe Basin
Nettilling Lake
Amadjuak Lake
Foxe Channel
Foxe Peninsula
Iqaluit
Frobisher Bay

Manittuaq
Southampton Island
Coral Harbour
Coats Island
Fisher Strait
Mansel Island

Salluit
Péninsule d'Ungava
Kangiqsujuaq
Akpatok Island
Cape Chidley

Resolution Island

Labrador Sea

Paamiut
Nanortalik

ATLANTIC OCEAN

A U T

Hudson Strait
Ungava Bay
Kangirsuk
Kangiqsualujjuaq
Nain

NEWFOUNDLAND AND LABRADOR

50°

40°

Arviat
Cape Churchill
Churchill

Hudson Bay

Belcher Islands

Ottawa Islands

Puvirnituq
George
Kuujjuaq
Rivière aux Feuilles
Rivière à la Baleine
Caniapiscau

Hopedale

Cape Harrison

Inukjuak

A N A D A

Fort Severn
Cape Henrietta Maria

James Bay

Lac à l'Eau Claire

Réservoir La Grande 2
Chisasibi
Réservoir La Grande 3
Réservoir La Grande 4

Lac Caniapiscau

Schefferville
Smallwood Reservoir
Churchill
Labrador City
Wabush

Happy Valley-Goose Bay

Port Hope Simpson

St Anthony

2

Winisk
Severn
Big Trout Lake
Sandy Lake
Akimiski Island
Fort Albany

Eastmain
Waskaganish

Eastmain
Lac Mistassini
Mistissini

Gagnon

Petit Mécatina
Strait of Belle Isle

Grand Falls
Windsor
Gander
Bonavista
St John's

O N T A R I O

Albany
Moosonee
Moose
Missinaibi

Lac Evans
Réservoir Gouin

Chibougamau
Roberval

Q U E B E C

Réservoir Manicouagan

Sept-Îles
Baie-Comeau

Île d'Anticosti

Gulf of St Lawrence

Corner Brook
Newfoundland

Channel-Port-aux-Basques
St Pierre and Miquelon (France)

Cape Race

40°

50°

Sioux Lookout
Lake Nipigon
Nipigon
Longlac
Kapuskasing
Timmins

Chibougamau
Amos
Val-d'Or

Chicoutimi
Jonquière
Rivière-du-Loup

Pén. de Gaspé
Gaspé

Rimouski
Edmundston

NEW BRUNSWICK

Bathurst

P.E.I.
Charlottetown

Sydney
Cape Breton Island

Sable Island

Thunder Bay
Isle Royale
Lake Superior
Chapleau
Sault Sainte Marie
Kirkland Lake
Harricana

Val-d'Or

Trois-Rivières

Québec
Montréal

Sherbrooke
Mount Washington 1918

MAINE
Augusta
Fredericton

Moncton
Truro
NOVA SCOTIA
Halifax

Bay of Fundy
Yarmouth
Cape Sable

40°

50°

SOTA
Duluth
Marquette
Escanaba
Sudbury
Georgian Bay
North Bay
Ottawa
Peterborough
Kingston
Burlington
VER.
N.H.
Concord
Portland

Boston

Cape Cod

1

Minneapolis
St Paul
Eau Claire
Green Bay
WISCONSIN
La Crosse

Lake Michigan
MICHIGAN
Traverse City
Bay City
Grand Rapids
Flint
Lansing

Lake Huron
Toronto
Hamilton
Lake Ontario

Rochester
Syracuse
Albany
MASS.
Springfield
Hartford
CO.
Providence

R.I.

A
Milwaukee
Cedar Rapids
Rockford
Iowa City
Des Moines
Chicago
Gary

Lake Michigan
Grand Rapids
Detroit
South Bend
Toledo
Lake Erie
Cleveland
Akron
Erie
London
Buffalo
NEW YORK
Scranton
Allentown
PENN.
Trenton
New York
Long Island

CO.	CONNECTICUT
MASS.	MASSACHUSETTS
N.H.	NEW HAMPSHIRE
P.E.I.	PRINCE EDWARD ISLAND
PENN.	PENNSYLVANIA
R.I.	RHODE ISLAND
VER.	VERMONT

H 90° I J 80° K L 70° M 60° N

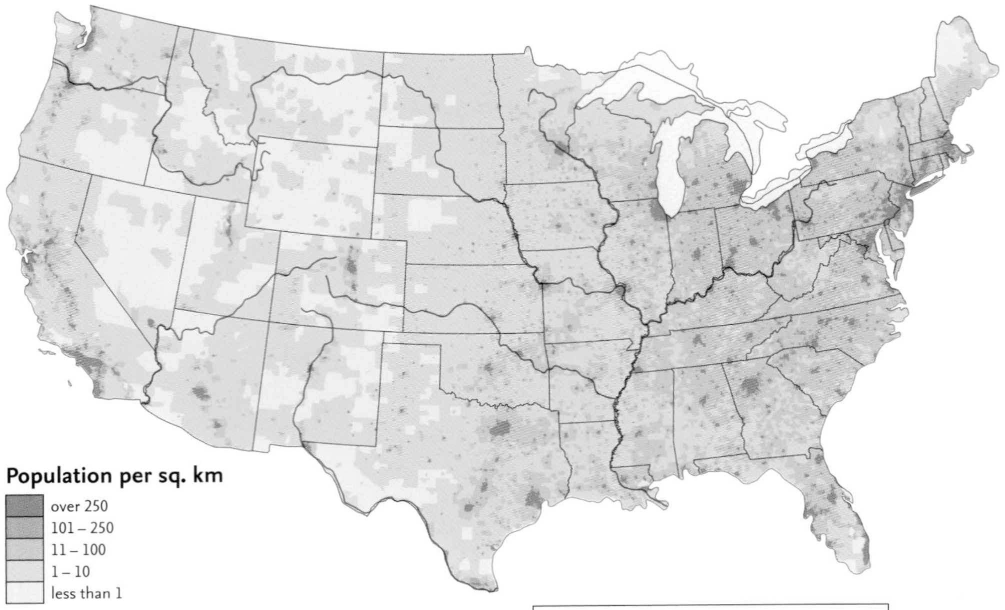

United States of America: Population

Population per sq. km
over 250
101 – 250
11 – 100
1 – 10
less than 1

Scale 1 : 35 000 000

WWW
US Census Bureau
www.census.gov
Population Reference Bureau - AmeriStat
www.prb.org

Seattle
Portland
Minneapolis
Milwaukee
Boston
Providence
Rochester
Hartford
New York
Philadelphia
Baltimore
Washington D.C.
Norfolk
Detroit
Cleveland
Chicago
Columbus
Pittsburgh
Indianapolis
Cincinnati
Richmond
St Louis
Louisville
Raleigh
Nashville
Charlotte
Atlanta
San Francisco
Sacramento
San Jose
Salt Lake City
Denver
Las Vegas
Los Angeles
Riverside
San Diego
Phoenix
Dallas
Austin
San Antonio
Houston
New Orleans
Jacksonville
Orlando
Tampa
West Palm Beach
Fort Lauderdale
Miami
Urban agglomerations
over 10 000 000
5 000 000 – 10 000 000
1 000 000 – 5 000 000
500 000 – 1 000 000
250 000 – 500 000

Scale 1 : 35 000 000

WASHINGTON
OREGON
IDAHO
MONTANA
WYOMING
NORTH DAKOTA
SOUTH DAKOTA
NEBRASKA
MINNESOTA
WISCONSIN
MICHIGAN
IOWA
ILLINOIS
INDIANA
OHIO
NEVADA
UTAH
COLORADO
KANSAS
MISSOURI
KENTUCKY
CALIFORNIA
ARIZONA
NEW MEXICO
OKLAHOMA
ARKANSAS
TENNESSEE
TEXAS
LOUISIANA
MISSISSIPPI
ALABAMA
GEORGIA
FLORIDA
SOUTH CAROLINA
NORTH CAROLINA
VIRGINIA
WEST VIRGINIA
VERMONT
MAINE
NEW HAMPSHIRE
NEW YORK
MASSACHUSETTS
RHODE ISLAND
CONNECTICUT
PENN-SYLVANIA
NEW JERSEY
DELAWARE
MARYLAND
DISTRICT OF COLUMBIA
Population change, 2010 – 2016
Percentage
over 9
6 – 8.9
3 – 5.9
0 – 2.9
-1.2 – 0

Scale 1 : 35 000 000

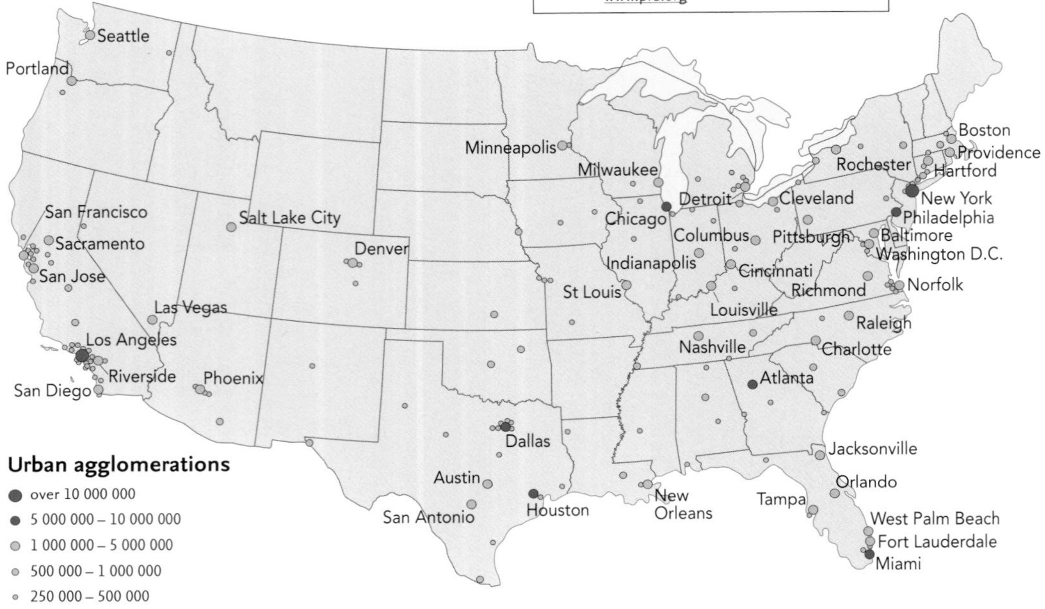

State comparisons

Highest population density

Population per sq. km
4500
500
400
300
200
100
0
District of Columbia 4308
New Jersey
Rhode Island
Massachusetts
Connecticut

Lowest population density

Population per sq. km
5
4
3
2
1
0
South Dakota
North Dakota
Montana
Wyoming
Alaska

Largest urban agglomerations, 2015

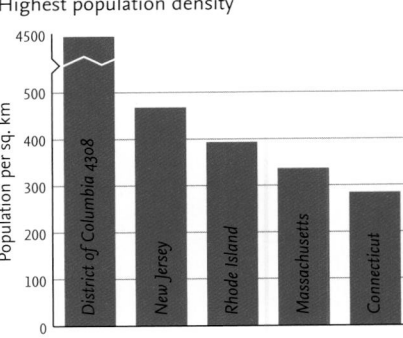

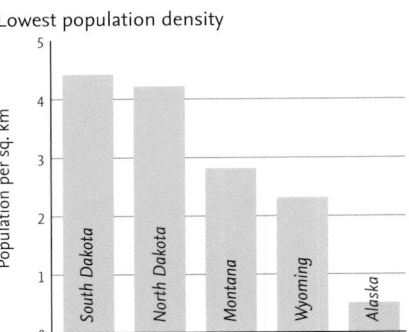

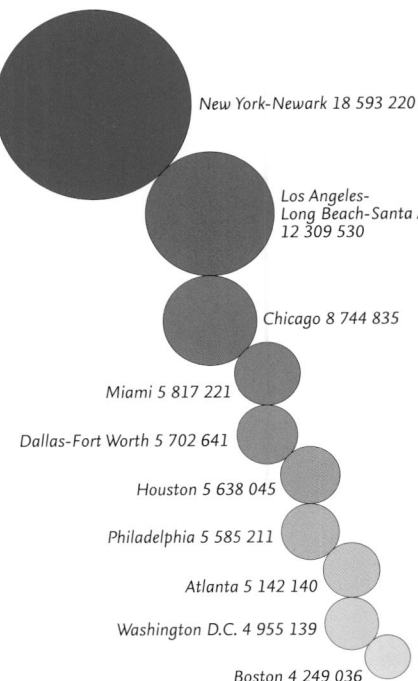

New York-Newark 18 593 220
Los Angeles-Long Beach-Santa A
12 309 530
Chicago 8 744 835
Miami 5 817 221
Dallas-Fort Worth 5 702 641
Houston 5 638 045
Philadelphia 5 585 211
Atlanta 5 142 140
Washington D.C. 4 955 139
Boston 4 249 036

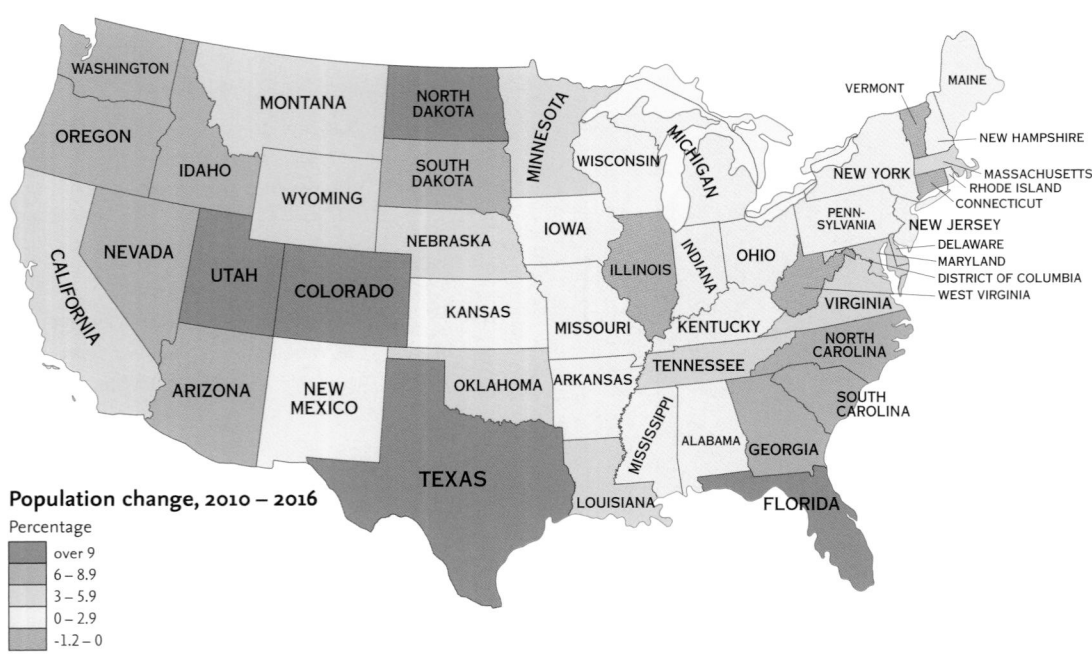

Population by ethnic group, 2015

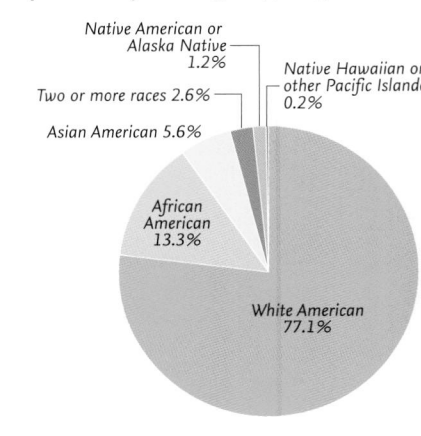

Native American or Alaska Native 1.2%
Native Hawaiian or other Pacific Islande 0.2%
Two or more races 2.6%
Asian American 5.6%
African American 13.3%
White American 77.1%

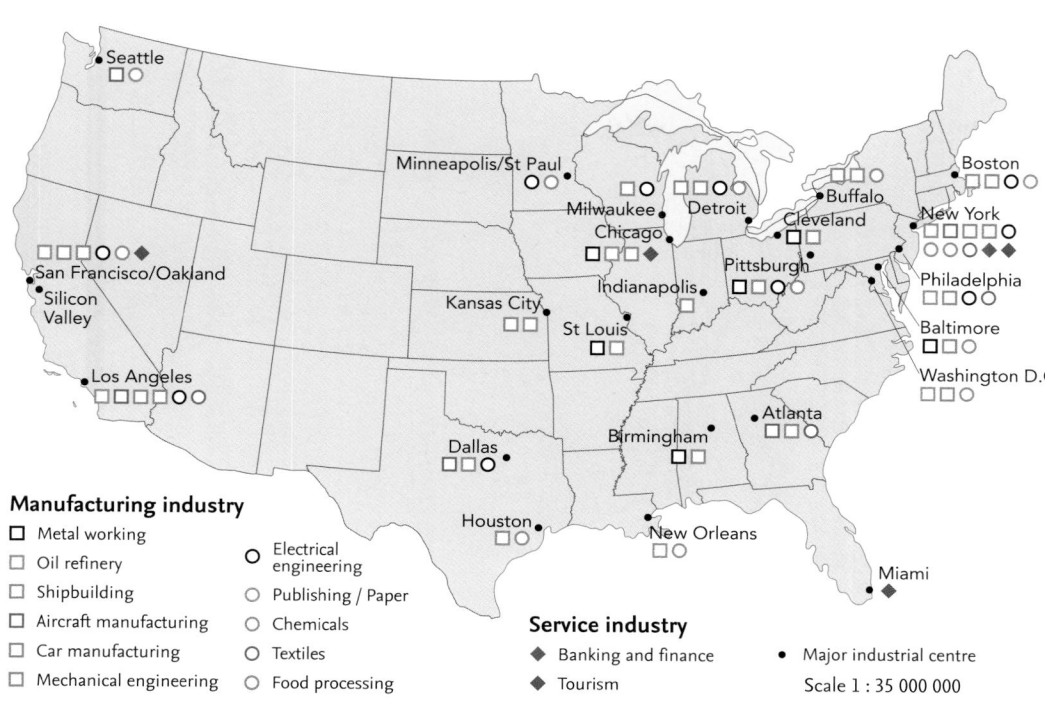

Manufacturing industry

- ☐ Metal working
- ☐ Oil refinery
- ☐ Shipbuilding
- ☐ Aircraft manufacturing
- ☐ Car manufacturing
- ☐ Mechanical engineering
- ○ Electrical engineering
- ○ Publishing / Paper
- ○ Chemicals
- ○ Textiles
- ○ Food processing

Service industry

- ◆ Banking and finance
- ◆ Tourism
- • Major industrial centre

Scale 1 : 35 000 000

Manufacturing sales, 2003 – 2014

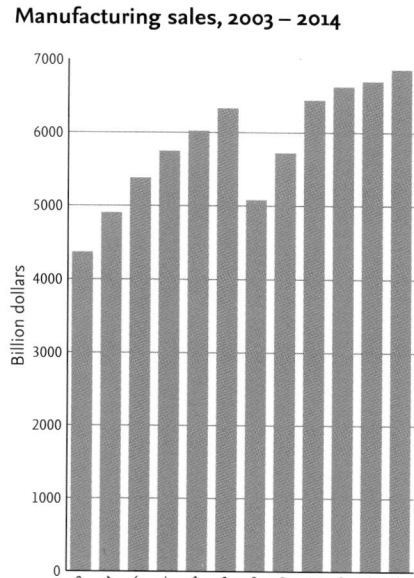

Unemployment, 2017

Percentage

- 6.0 – 6.9
- 5.0 – 5.9
- 4.0 – 4.9
- 3.0 – 3.9
- 2.0 – 2.9

Scale 1 : 35 000 000

Unemployment, 2004 – 2017

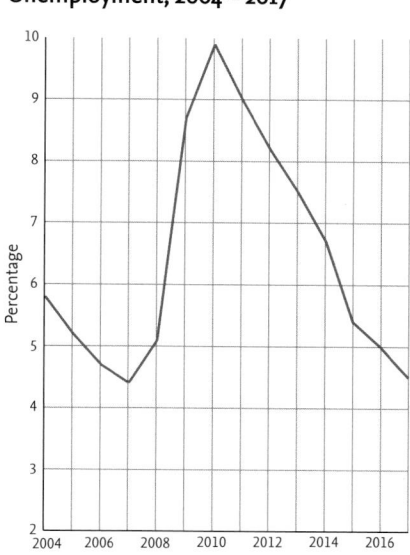

Main trading partners, 2016

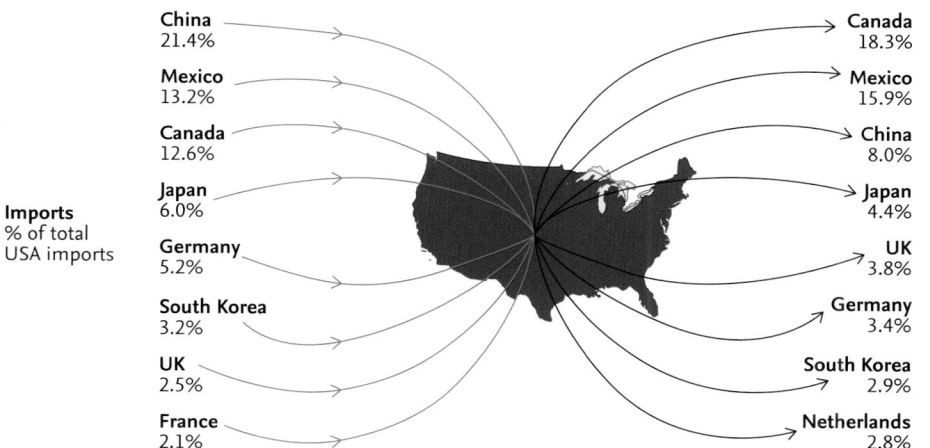

Imports
% of total
USA imports

China	21.4%
Mexico	13.2%
Canada	12.6%
Japan	6.0%
Germany	5.2%
South Korea	3.2%
UK	2.5%
France	2.1%

Exports
% of total
USA exports

Canada	18.3%
Mexico	15.9%
China	8.0%
Japan	4.4%
UK	3.8%
Germany	3.4%
South Korea	2.9%
Netherlands	2.8%

Trade, 2016

Imports

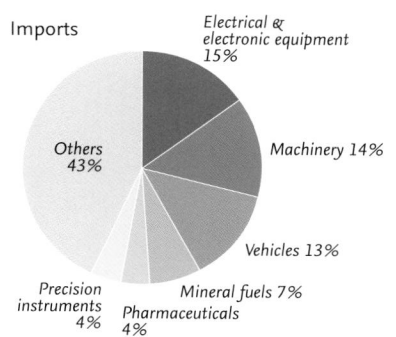

Electrical & electronic equipment 15%
Machinery 14%
Vehicles 13%
Mineral fuels 7%
Pharmaceuticals 4%
Precision instruments 4%
Others 43%

Exports

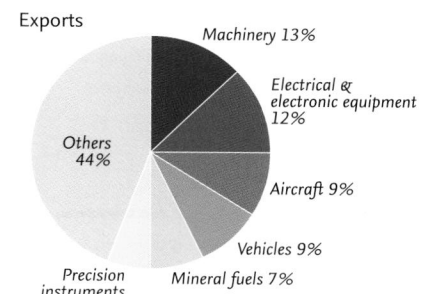

Machinery 13%
Electrical & electronic equipment 12%
Aircraft 9%
Vehicles 9%
Mineral fuels 7%
Precision instruments 6%
Others 44%

A 115° B 110° C 105° D 100° E 95° F 90°

UNITED STATES OF AMERICA

San Diego
Tijuana Mexicali
Ensenada
Yuma
Gila
Phoenix
Casa Grande
ARIZONA
Tucson
Nogales
Douglas
Picacho del Diablo 3096
San Felipe
Puerto Peñasco
Caborca
Lázaro Cárdenas
BAJA CALIFORNIA
Gulf of California

Silver City
NEW MEXICO
Deming
Las Cruces
El Paso
Ciudad Juárez
Roswell
Artesia
Pecos
Big Spring
Midland
Odessa
San Angelo
Alpine
Del Rio
Edwards Plateau
TEXAS
Lubbock
Abilene
Fort Worth
Dallas
Waco
Austin
San Marcos
Houston
Wichita Falls
Lawton
Denton
San Antonio
Victoria
Beeville
Bay City
Galveston
Galveston Bay

Lake Texoma
Red
Arkadelphia
Texarkana
El Dorado
Longview
Shreveport
Tyler
Monroe
Lufkin
Huntsville
Toledo Bend Reservoir
Beaumont
Port Arthur
Morgan City

ARKANSAS
Little Rock
Pine Bluff
Greenville
MISSISSIPPI
Meridian
Jackson
Natchez
Hattiesburg
Baton Rouge
LOUISIANA
Lafayette
Alexandria
New Orleans
Mississippi Delta
Birmingham
Tuscaloosa
AL
Mobile
Biloxi

SONORA
Magdalena
Hermosillo
Guaymas
Santa Rosalía
Isla Tiburón
Isla Ángel de la Guarda
Bahía Sebastián Vizcaíno
Punta Eugenia
BAJA CALIFORNIA SUR
Villa Insurgentes
La Paz
Isla Carmen
Isla San José
Isla Cerralvo
Cabo Falso
San José del Cabo

Caborca
Ciudad Obregón
Navojoa
Sonora
Yaqui
Sierra Madre Occidental
CHIHUAHUA
Cuauhtémoc
Chihuahua
Ciudad Delicias
Conchos
Madera
Nuevo Casas Grandes
Ojinaga
Emory Peak 2668
Serranías del Burro
Hidalgo del Parral
Jiménez
COAHUILA
Sabinas
Monclova
Piedras Negras
Rio Grande
Saltillo
Saltillo

Los Mochis
Guasave
SINALOA
Culiacán
Gómez Palacio
Nazas
DURANGO
Durango
Torreón
Mazatlán
Acaponeta
Mezquital
ZACATECAS
Zacatecas
NAYARIT
Tepic

MEXICO

SAN LUIS POTOSÍ
Cerro Peña Nevada 3664
Ciudad Victoria
TAMAULIPAS
San Luis Potosí
AGUASCALIENTES
León
GUANAJUATO
Guanajuato
Irapuato
QUERÉTARO
Querétaro
HIDALGO
Pachuca
Poza Rica
Tuxpan
Ciudad Madero
Tampico
Laguna de Tamiahua
Ciudad de Valles

Nuevo Laredo
Laredo
Falcon Lake
Reynosa
Matamoros
NUEVO LEÓN
Monterrey
Montemorelos
Saltillo
Corpus Christi
Kingsville
Padre Island
Laguna Madre

Puerto Vallarta
Cabo Corrientes
Guadalajara
JALISCO
Laguna de Chapala
Colima 3339
COLIMA
Nevado de Colima
Uruapan
MICHOACÁN
Morelia
Presa Infiernillo
Lázaro Cárdenas
Balsas
Toluca
Mexico City
Cuernavaca
MÉXICO
MORELOS
Popocatépetl 5452
Puebla
Tlaxcala
PUEBLA
Orizaba
Córdoba
Coatzacoalcos
VERACRUZ
Veracruz
Ciudad del Carmen

Bahía de Campeche
Campeche
Cabo Catoche
Mérida
YUCATÁN
Yucatán
QUINTANA ROO
Laguna de Términos
Escárcega
CAMPECHE
Belmopan
BELIZE

GUERRERO
Chilpancingo
Acapulco
Sierra Madre del Sur
OAXACA
Oaxaca
Ciudad Ixtepec
Juchitán
Arriaga
TABASCO
Villahermosa
Minatitlán
CHIAPAS
Tuxtla Gutiérrez
Puerto Ángel
Gulf of Tehuantepec
Pijijiapan
Lago de Izabal
Gulf of Honduras

Tapachula
Quetzaltenango
GUATEMALA
Guatemala City
Sipacate
Santa Ana
San Salvador
EL SALVADOR
San Miguel
Golfo de Fonseca
San Pedro
HON
Tegucigalpa

Gulf of Mexico

PACIFIC OCEAN

Mexican States numbered on map
1. AGUASCALIENTES
2. DISTRITO FEDERAL
3. TLAXCALA

Relief and physical features
Relief metres
5000
3000
2000
1000
500
200
sea level
0
under sea level
200
4000
6000

5493 Mountain height (in metres)

Water features
River
Intermittent river
Canal
Lake / Reservoir
Intermittent lake
Marsh

Communications
Railway
Road
Main airport

Administration
Boundaries
International
Internal

Settlement
Cities and towns in order of size
National capital
■ Mexico City
Other city or town
● Monterrey
● Chihuahua
● Oaxaca
● Zacatecas

Scale 1 : 13 500 000
0   200   400   600 km
Lambert Conformal Conic projection

Montego Bay
Lucea
Grange Hill
Negril
Savanna-la-Mar
Black River
Montego Bay
Cambridge
Mt Denham 986
Mandeville
955
Santa Cruz
May Pen
Old Harbour
Lionel Town
Rocky Point
Falmouth
Ocho Rios
Mt Diablo 838
Ewarton
St Ann's Bay
Oracabessa
Galina Point
Port Maria
Annotto Bay
Buff Bay
Blue Mts
Blue Mt Peak 2256
Port Antonio
Kingston
Portland Bight
Yallahs
Morant Bay
Port Morant
Morant Point
Portland Point
JAMAICA
Scale 1 : 3 500 000
78°   77°

Punta Borinquen
Aguadilla
Quebradillas
Arecibo
San Juan
Carolina
San Sebastián
Utuado
Cerro de Punta 1338
Cordillera Central
Bayamón
Guaynabo
Caguas
Aibonito
Cayey
Guayama
Coamo
Ponce
Yauco
Sabana Grande
Hormigueros
Mayagüez
Añasco
Cabo Rojo
Isla Caja de Muertos
San Pedro
Guánica
Guayanilla
Salinas
Arroyo
Patillas
Maunabo
Humacao
Juncos
Naguabo
Fajardo
Luquillo
Isla de Culebra
Vieques
PUERTO RICO (USA)
Scale 1 : 3 500 000
67°   66°

B 110° C 105° D 100° E 95° F 90°

Inset maps:

ST LUCIA — Castries
Pointe du Cap, Gros Islet, Cap Marquis, Anse-la-Raye, Canaries, Dennery, Soufrière, Micoud, Choiseul, Laborie, Vieux Fort
Scale 1 : 2 000 000

BARBADOS — Bridgetown
North Point, Speightstown, Holetown, Six Cross Roads, Carlisle Bay, Oistins, South Point, The Crane
Scale 1 : 2 000 000

TRINIDAD AND TOBAGO — Port of Spain
Scale 1 : 2 500 000
VENEZUELA, Diego Martin, Chupara Point, Matelot, Galera Point, Northern Range, Tunapuna, San Juan, Arouca, Arima, Omphe, Matura Bay, Chaguanas, Caroni, Sangre Grande, Gulf of Paria, Couva, Tabaquite, Manzanilla Point, California, Cocos Bay, San Fernando, La Brea, Princes Town, Guataro Point, Pierreville, Point Fortin, Penal, Rio Claro, Ortoire, Mayaro Bay, Bonasse, Siparia, Galeota Point, Icacos Pt, Trinidad

Main map labels:

ATLANTIC OCEAN
Bermuda (UK), Hamilton

SOUTH CAROLINA, Greenville, Florence, Lumberton, Wilmington, Cape Fear, Myrtle Beach, Columbia, Augusta, Macon, Charleston, Cape Romain, Savannah, GEORGIA, Jesup, Brunswick, Bainbridge, Valdosta, Tallahassee, Jacksonville, Lake City, Gainesville, Daytona Beach, Apalachee Bay, FLORIDA, Orlando, Lakeland, Melbourne, Tampa, St Petersburg, Sarasota, Fort Pierce, Lake Okeechobee, West Palm Beach, Fort Lauderdale, Miami, Cape Sable, Florida Keys, Straits of Florida

Grand Bahama, Freeport, Great Abaco, Bimini Islands, Eleuthera, THE BAHAMAS, New Providence, Nassau, Andros, Cat Island, San Salvador, Exuma Cays, Rum Cay, Great Exuma, Tropic of Cancer

Havana, Matanzas, CUBA, Pinar del Río, Guane, Golfo de Batabanó, Santa Clara, Sancti Spíritus, Ciego de Ávila, Cienfuegos, Archipiélago de Sabana, Archipiélago de Camagüey, Crooked I. Pass., Crooked Island, Acklins Island, Little Inagua Island, Turks and Caicos Islands (UK), Cabo Antonio, Isla de la Juventud, Archipiélago de los Canarreos, Archipiélago de los Jardines de la Reina, Golfo de Guacanayabo, Las Tunas, Camagüey, Holguín, Bayamo, Great Inagua, Grand Turk, Turks Islands

Little Cayman, Grand Cayman, Cayman Brac, Cayman Islands (UK), Sa Maestra, 1994, Cabo Cruz, Pico Turquino, Santiago de Cuba, Guantánamo, Baracoa, Cap Haïtien, Port-de-Paix, Hispaniola, San Juan, Virgin Is (UK), Anegada, Leeward Islands

Montego Bay, JAMAICA, Kingston, Jamaica Channel, Jérémie, Gonaïves, HAITI, Port-au-Prince, Pico Duarte 3175, Santiago, Santo Domingo, DOMINICAN REPUBLIC, Mayagüez, Ponce, PUERTO RICO (USA), Virgin Is (USA), St-Martin (Fr.), Anguilla (UK), St-Barthélemy (Fr.), Sint Maarten (Neth.), ANTIGUA AND BARBUDA, St John's

Les Cayes, Jacmel, Isla Beata, Cabo Beata, Isla Mona, Mona Passage, Greater Antilles, Windward Passage, ST KITTS AND NEVIS, Montserrat (UK), Basse-Terre, Guadeloupe (Fr.), Marie-Galante, DOMINICA, Roseau, Martinique (Fr.), Fort-de-France, Lesser Antilles, Castries, ST LUCIA, Kingstown, ST VINCENT AND THE GRENADINES, Bridgetown, BARBADOS, Windward Is

Caribbean Sea, Laguna de Caratasca, Cayos Miskitos, Isla de Providencia (Colombia), Isla de San Andrés (Colombia), Aruba (Neth.), Curaçao (Neth.), Bonaire (Neth.), Isla Orchila (Ven.), Isla Blanquilla (Ven.), Lesser Antilles, GRENADA, St George's, Tobago, TRINIDAD & TOBAGO, Port of Spain

Coco, Costa de Mosquitos, Río Grande, Managua, NICARAGUA, Punta de Perlas, Punta Gorda, Lake Nicaragua, San Juan, COSTA RICA, San José, Chirripó 3819, Bahía de Coronado, Península de Osa, Golfo de Nicoya, Golfo de Chiriquí, David, Aguadulce, PANAMA, Panama Canal, Colón, Panama City, La Palma, Punta Mala, Gulf of Panama, Golfo del Darién, Golfo de Morrosquillo, Turbo, Punta Gallinas, Riohacha, Maicao, Golfo de Venezuela, Punto Fijo, Coro, Cumaná, Barcelona, Pen. de Paria, Güiria, Maiquetía, Isla La Tortuga

Barranquilla, Santa Marta, Cartagena, Valledupar, Sincelejo, Montería, COLOMBIA, Quibdó, Cordillera Occidental, Medellín, Manizales, Pereira, Armenia, Ibagué, Cali, Palmira, Neiva, Buenaventura, Tumaco, Florencia, Bucaramanga, Cúcuta, San Cristóbal, Sierra de Perijá, Cabimas, Maracaibo, Lake Maracaibo, Mérida, Valera, Barinas, Pico Bolívar 5007, Sierra Nevada del Cocuy 5493, Tunja, Bogotá, Villavicencio, Cordillera Central, Cordillera Oriental, Magdalena, Cauca

Maracaibo, Barquisimeto, Valencia, Maracay, Caracas, VENEZUELA, Acarigua, Guanare, San Fernando de Apure, Valle de la Pascua, Zaraza, El Tigre, Ciudad Bolívar, Ciudad Guayana, El Callao, Embalse de Guri, Orinoco, Meta, Guaviare, Llanos, Cerro Yaví 2285, Guiana Highlands, La Gran Sabana, Pakaraima Mountains, Sa Parima, Pico da Neblina 3014, Maturín, Tigre, Guanipa, La Paragua, BRAZIL, Equator

B   80°   C   60°   D   40°   E

Caribbean Sea

ATLANTIC OCEAN

Punta Gallinas   Curaçao   Windward Is

4   Golfo del Darién   Trinidad
    Isthmus of Panamá   L. Maracaibo   Orinoco Delta
    I. de Coco   Orinoco
    Llanos
    Meta   Mt Roraima 2810
    Cordillera Occidental   Guaviare   Guiana Highlands   Essequibo
    Cordillera Central
    Cordillera Oriental   Caquetá   Pico de Neblina 3014   Mouths of the Amazon
    I. de Malpelo
    Volcán Cotopaxi 5896   Japurá   Amazon   Ilha de Marajó
    6310 Chimborazo   Amazon   Negro
    Equator   Marañón   Juruá   Madeira   Tapajós   Xingu   Fernando de Noronha   Equator
    0°   Islas Galápagos   Puns   Selvas   C. de São Roque
    G. de Guayaquil   Araguaia   Tocantins   Parnaíba
    Pta Negra   Brazilian
    Cordillera Central   Nevado de Huascarán 6768
    Cordillera Oriental   São Francisco   Highlands
3   Cordillera Occidental   L. Titicaca
    Andes   Altiplano   Lago de Poopó
    PACIFIC   Atacama Desert   Paraná   2797 Agulhas Negras
    OCEAN   Gran Chaco   I. da Trindade   Is Martín Vaz
    20°   Paraguay   Tropic of Capricorn
    Tropic of Capricorn   6908 Nevado Ojos del Salado
    Islas Desventuradas   Paraná
    Pampas   Uruguay
    6961 Cerro Aconcagua   ATLANTIC
2   Archipiélago Juan Fernández   Río de la Plata   OCEAN

    Golfo San Matías
    Isla de Chiloé   Golfo de San Jorge
    40°   Patagonia
    Bahía Grande   Falkland Is
    Str. of Magellan
    Isla Grande de Tierra del Fuego   South Georgia
1   Cape Horn
    South Sandwich Is

120°   A   100°   B   80°   C   60°   D   40°   E   20°   F

Relief and physical features

Relief metres

5000
3000
2000
1000
500
200
0 sea level
200 under sea level
4000
6000

▲ 6961 Mountain height (in metres)

Permanent ice (ice cap or glacier)

Scale 1 : 40 000 000

0   400   800   1200 km

Lambert Azimuthal Equal Area projection

Cross-section

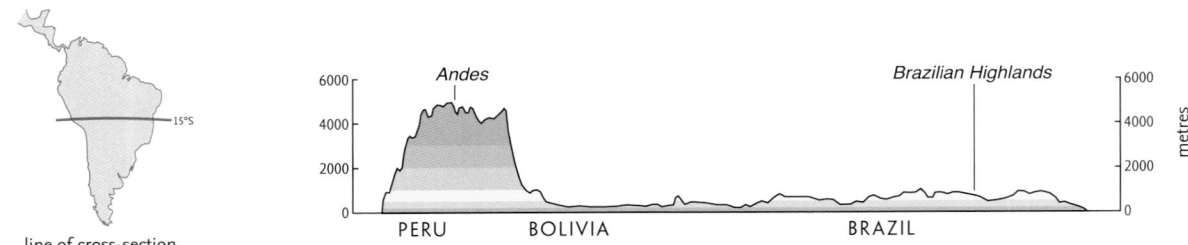

line of cross-section

6000
4000
2000

Andes

Brazilian Highlands

6000
4000
2000
metres

PERU   BOLIVIA   BRAZIL

15°S

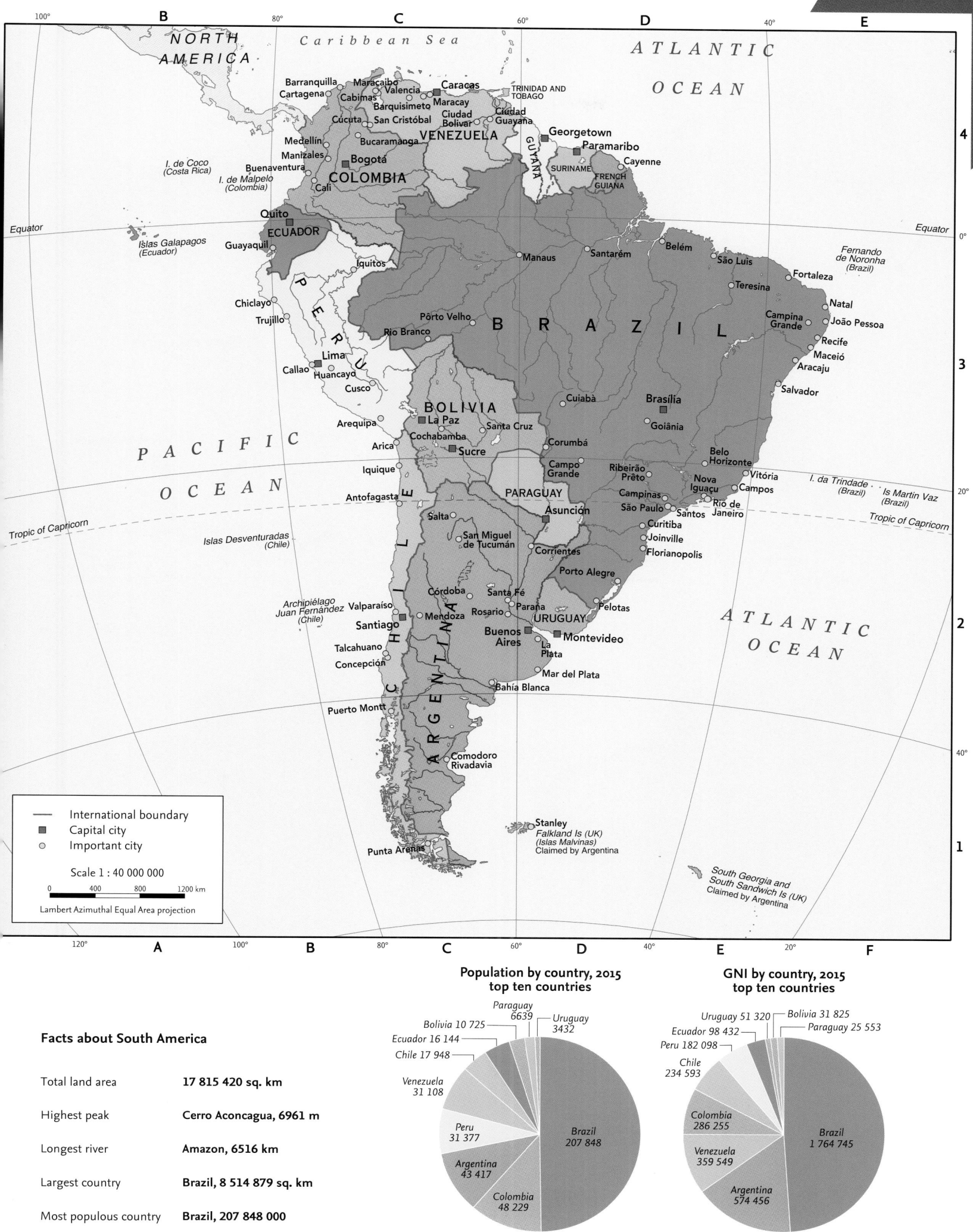

Facts about South America

Total land area	**17 815 420 sq. km**
Highest peak	**Cerro Aconcagua, 6961 m**
Longest river	**Amazon, 6516 km**
Largest country	**Brazil, 8 514 879 sq. km**
Most populous country	**Brazil, 207 848 000**

Population by country, 2015 top ten countries

Paraguay 6639
Uruguay 3432
Bolivia 10 725
Ecuador 16 144
Chile 17 948
Venezuela 31 108
Peru 31 377
Argentina 43 417
Colombia 48 229
Brazil 207 848

Population in thousands

GNI by country, 2015 top ten countries

Uruguay 51 320
Bolivia 31 825
Ecuador 98 432
Paraguay 25 553
Peru 182 098
Chile 234 593
Colombia 286 255
Venezuela 359 549
Argentina 574 456
Brazil 1 764 745

Gross National Income in US $ millions

South America: Climate

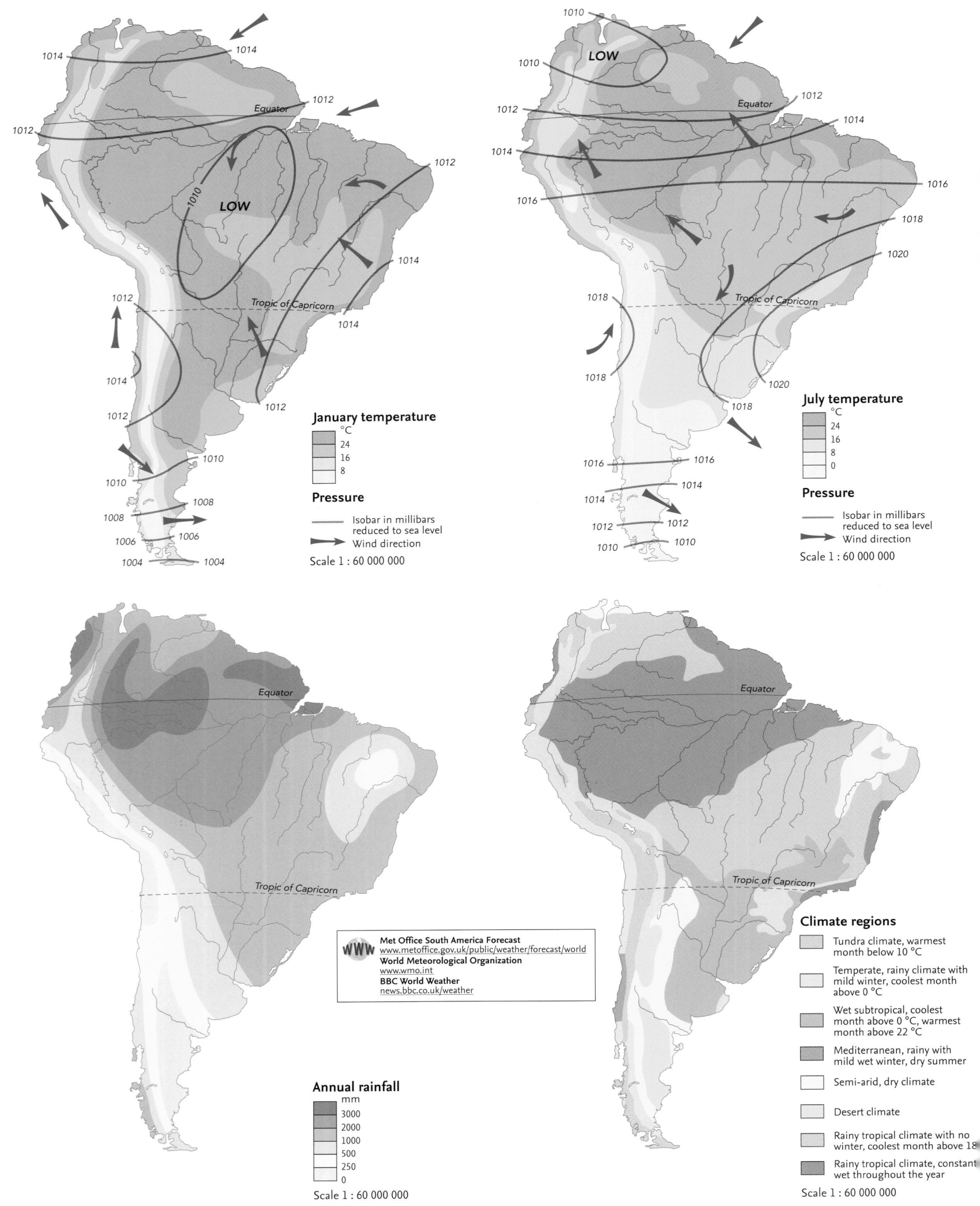

January temperature
°C
24
16
8

Pressure

—— Isobar in millibars
reduced to sea level

➤ Wind direction

Scale 1 : 60 000 000

July temperature
°C
24
16
8
0

Pressure

—— Isobar in millibars
reduced to sea level

➤ Wind direction

Scale 1 : 60 000 000

Annual rainfall
mm
3000
2000
1000
500
250
0

Scale 1 : 60 000 000

WWW Met Office South America Forecast
www.metoffice.gov.uk/public/weather/forecast/world
World Meteorological Organization
www.wmo.int
BBC World Weather
news.bbc.co.uk/weather

Climate regions

Tundra climate, warmest month below 10 °C

Temperate, rainy climate with mild winter, coolest month above 0 °C

Wet subtropical, coolest month above 0 °C, warmest month above 22 °C

Mediterranean, rainy with mild wet winter, dry summer

Semi-arid, dry climate

Desert climate

Rainy tropical climate with no winter, coolest month above 18

Rainy tropical climate, constant wet throughout the year

Scale 1 : 60 000 000

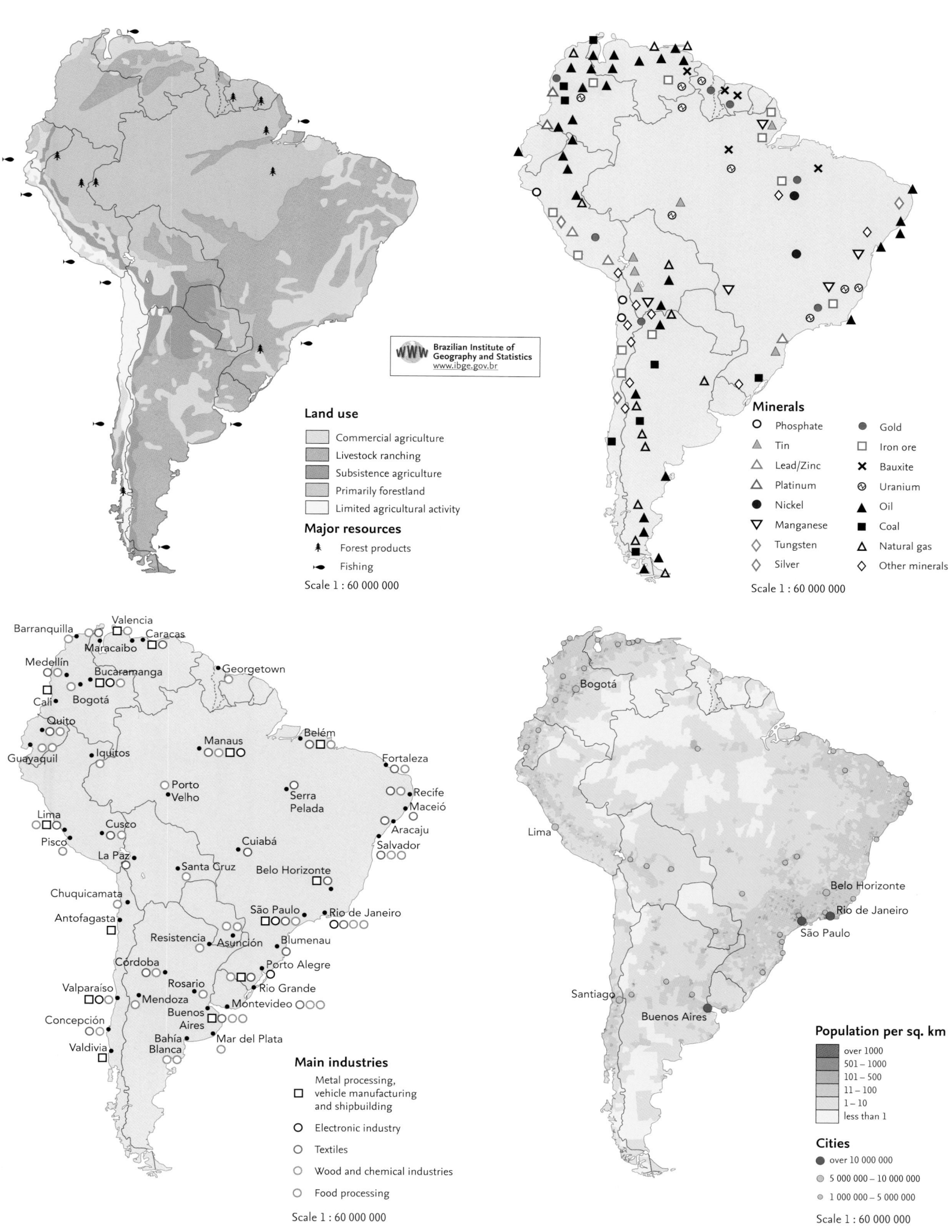

Land use

- Commercial agriculture
- Livestock ranching
- Subsistence agriculture
- Primarily forestland
- Limited agricultural activity

Major resources

- 🌲 Forest products
- 🐟 Fishing

Scale 1 : 60 000 000

Brazilian Institute of
Geography and Statistics
www.ibge.gov.br

Minerals

- ○ Phosphate
- ▲ Tin
- △ Lead/Zinc
- △ Platinum
- ● Nickel
- ▽ Manganese
- ◇ Tungsten
- ◇ Silver
- ● Gold
- □ Iron ore
- ✕ Bauxite
- ⊗ Uranium
- ▲ Oil
- ■ Coal
- △ Natural gas
- ◇ Other minerals

Scale 1 : 60 000 000

Barranquilla, Valencia, Caracas, Maracaibo, Medellín, Bucaramanga, Cali, Bogotá, Georgetown, Quito, Guayaquil, Iquitos, Belém, Manaus, Fortaleza, Porto Velho, Serra Pelada, Recife, Maceió, Aracaju, Salvador, Lima, Cusco, Pisco, La Paz, Cuiabá, Belo Horizonte, Santa Cruz, Chuquicamata, São Paulo, Rio de Janeiro, Antofagasta, Resistencia, Asunción, Blumenau, Córdoba, Porto Alegre, Valparaíso, Rosario, Rio Grande, Mendoza, Montevideo, Concepción, Buenos Aires, Bahía Blanca, Mar del Plata, Valdivia

Main industries

- □ Metal processing, vehicle manufacturing and shipbuilding
- ○ Electronic industry
- ○ Textiles
- ○ Wood and chemical industries
- ○ Food processing

Scale 1 : 60 000 000

Bogotá, Lima, Belo Horizonte, Rio de Janeiro, São Paulo, Santiago, Buenos Aires

Population per sq. km

- over 1000
- 501 – 1000
- 101 – 500
- 11 – 100
- 1 – 10
- less than 1

Cities

- ● over 10 000 000
- ● 5 000 000 – 10 000 000
- ● 1 000 000 – 5 000 000

Scale 1 : 60 000 000

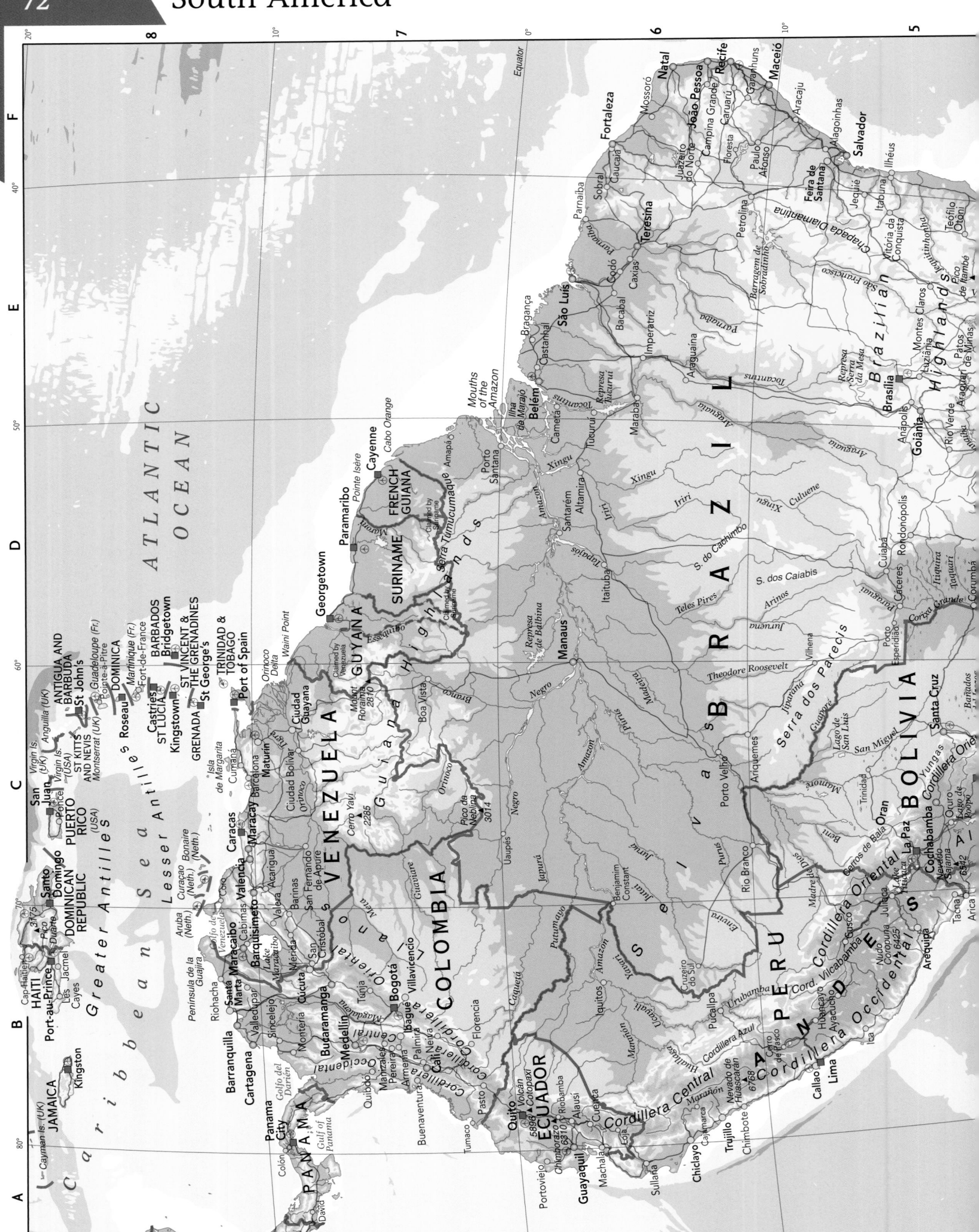

ATLANTIC OCEAN

Caribbean Sea

Greater Antilles

Lesser Antilles

Cayman Is. (UK)
JAMAICA
Kingston

HAITI
Cap-Haïtien
Port-au-Prince
Les Cayes
Jacmel

DOMINICAN REPUBLIC
Santo Domingo
Pico Duarte 3175

PUERTO RICO (USA)
San Juan
Ponce

Virgin Is. (UK)
Virgin Is. (USA)
Anguilla (UK)
ANTIGUA AND BARBUDA
St John's
ST KITTS AND NEVIS
Montserrat (UK)
Guadeloupe (Fr.)
Pointe-à-Pitre
DOMINICA
Roseau
Martinique (Fr.)
Fort-de-France
ST LUCIA
Castries
BARBADOS
Bridgetown
ST VINCENT & THE GRENADINES
Kingstown
GRENADA
St George's
TRINIDAD & TOBAGO
Port of Spain

Aruba (Neth.)
Curaçao (Neth.)
Bonaire (Neth.)
Isla de Margarita
Península de la Guajira

PANAMA
Panama City
Colón
David
Gulf of Panama

COLOMBIA
Cartagena
Barranquilla
Santa Marta
Riohacha
Valledupar
Sincelejo
Montería
Quibdó
Medellín
Manizales
Pereira
Armenia
Ibagué
Bogotá
Tunja
Bucaramanga
Cúcuta
Neiva
Cali
Palmira
Buenaventura
Popayán
Pasto
Tumaco
Florencia
Villavicencio
Golfo del Darién
Cordillera Occidental
Cordillera Central
Cordillera Oriental
Magdalena
Llanos

VENEZUELA
Caracas
Maracay
Valencia
Barquisimeto
Maracaibo
Coro
Barcelona
Cumaná
Maturín
Ciudad Bolívar
Ciudad Guayana
San Fernando de Apure
Barinas
Acarigua
Mérida
San Cristóbal
Lake Maracaibo
Golfo de Venezuela
Orinoco
Orinoco Delta
Cerro Yaví 2286
Pico da Neblina 3014
Mount Roraima 2810
Guaviare
Meta

GUYANA
Georgetown
Essequibo
Waini Point

SURINAME
Paramaribo
Nickerie

FRENCH GUIANA
Cayenne
Pointe Isère
Cabo Orange

Guiana Highlands
Guiana Highlands
Claimed by Venezuela
Claimed by Suriname
Serra Tumucumaque

ECUADOR
Quito
Volcán Cotopaxi 5896
Chimborazo 6310
Guayaquil
Machala
Cuenca
Loja
Riobamba
Alausí
Ambato
Portoviejo
Equator

PERU
Lima
Callao
Trujillo
Chiclayo
Chimbote
Piura
Sullana
Iquitos
Pucallpa
Cusco
Arequipa
Tacna
Puno
Ayacucho
Huancayo
Cerro de Pasco
Cajamarca
Huánuco
Nudo Coropuna 6425
Nevado de Huascarán 6768
Cordillera Occidental
Cordillera Central
Cordillera Oriental
Marañón
Ucayali
Urubamba
Huallaga
Cordillera Azul
Cord. Vilcabamba
Juliaca
Lago de Poopó
Lake Titicaca

BRAZIL
Natal
Recife
João Pessoa
Campina Grande
Maceió
Aracaju
Salvador
Fortaleza
Teresina
São Luís
Belém
Santarém
Manaus
Brasília
Goiânia
Anápolis
Feira de Santana
Ilhéus
Vitória da Conquista
Jequié
Itabuna
Montes Claros
Teófilo Otoni
Patos de Minas
Mossoró
Sobral
Parnaíba
Caxias
Bragança
Castanhal
Cametá
Tucuruí
Marabá
Imperatriz
Araguaína
Palmas
Rio Verde
Rondonópolis
Cuiabá
Cáceres
Porto Velho
Ariquemes
Vilhena
Rio Branco
Cruzeiro do Sul
Benjamin Constant
Boa Vista
Caruaru
Garanhuns
Petrolina
Juazeiro do Norte
Floresta
Paulo Afonso
Barragem de Sobradinho
Caucaia
Codó
Bacabal
Alagoinhas
Jeremoabo
Pico da Bandeira
Brazilian Highlands
Chapada Diamantina
Serra da Mesa
Represa Serra da Mesa
Represa Tucuruí
Represa de Balbina
Serra dos Parecis
S. do Cachimbo
S. dos Caiabis
Mouths of the Amazon
Ilha de Marajó
Porto Santana
Amapá
Marowijne
Amazon
Negro
Branco
Xingu
Xingu
Tapajós
Teles Pires
Arinos
Iriri
Iriri
Juruena
Culuene
Madeira
Purus
Juruá
Jari
Uaupés
Japurá
Theodore Roosevelt
Corixa Grande
Rio São Francisco
Araguaia
Tocantins
Tocantins
Araguaia
Paranaíba
Parnaíba
Jequitinhonha
Tietê

BOLIVIA
La Paz
Cochabamba
Santa Cruz
Oruro
Sucre
Trinidad
Yungas
Cordillera Oriental
Cordillera Occidental
Sajama 6542
Lago de San Luis
Lago Rogaguado
San Miguel
Beni
Mamoré
Guaporé
Madre de Dios
Cerros de Bala
Bañados
Juliaca

Orán
Tarija

ARGENTINA

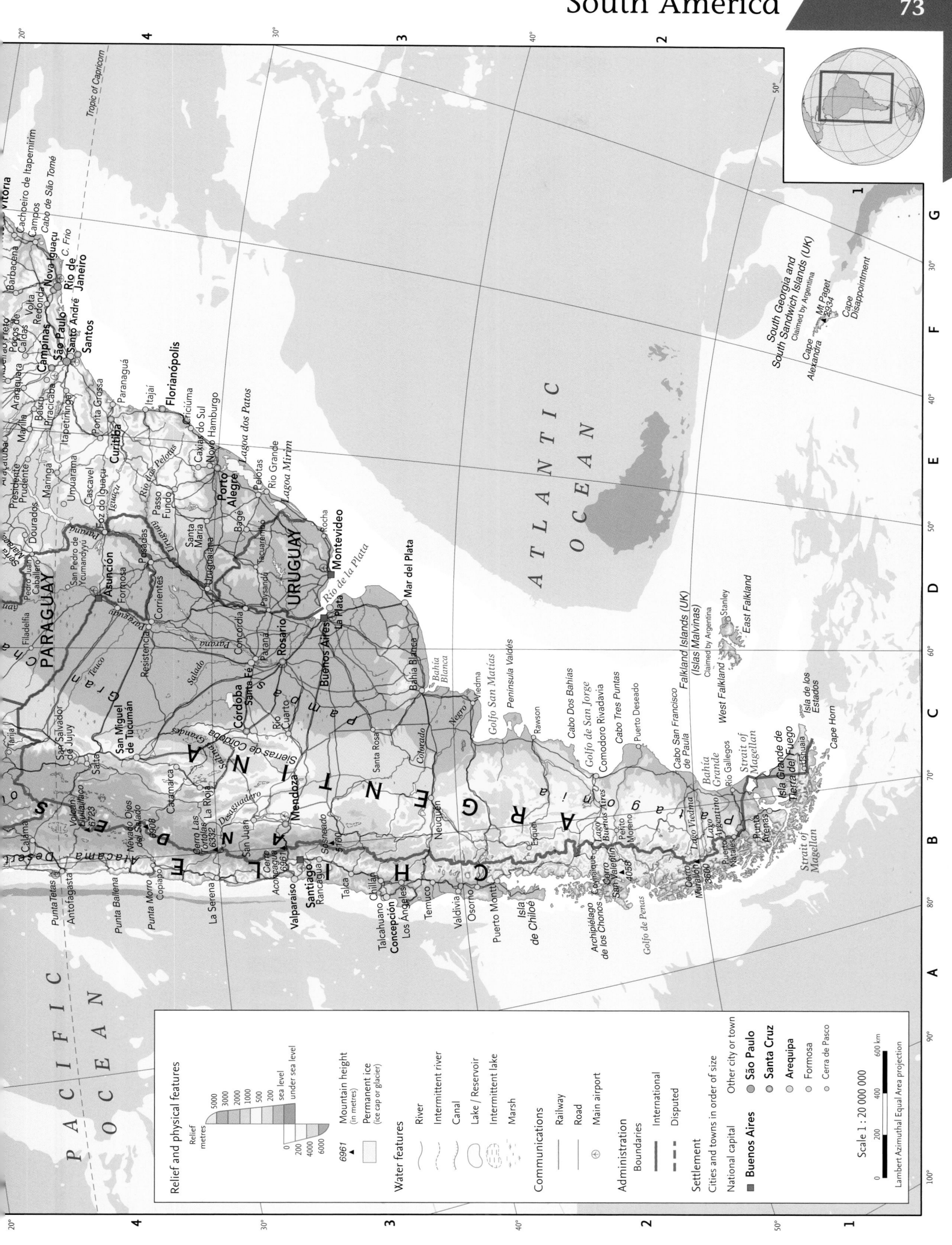

PACIFIC OCEAN

ATLANTIC OCEAN

Tropic of Capricorn

PARAGUAY

ARGENTINA

CHILE

URUGUAY

Vitória
Cachoeiro de Itapemirim
Campos
Cabo de São Tomé
Barbacena
Volta Redonda
Poços de Caldas
Nova Iguaçu
Rio de Janeiro
Rio de C. Frio
Campinas
São Paulo
Santo André
Santos
Araraquara
Bauru
Piracicaba
Marília
Presidente Prudente
Maringá
Umuarama
Cascavel
Foz do Iguaçu
Paranaguá
Ponta Grossa
Curitiba
Itajaí
Florianópolis
Criciúma
Caxias do Sul
Lagoa dos Patos
Novo Hamburgo
Porto Alegre
Passo Fundo
Rio Grande
Pelotas
Lagoa Mirim
Santa Maria
Bagé
Rocha
Dourados
Pedro Juan Caballero
San Pedro de Ycuamandyyú
Asunción
Formosa
Posadas
Uruguaiana
Tacuarembó
Montevideo
Filadelfia
Concordia
Paysandú
La Plata
Mar del Plata
Tarija
Corrientes
Resistencia
Paraná
Rosario
Buenos Aires
San Salvador de Jujuy
Salta
Santa Fé
Córdoba
Río Cuarto
Bahía Blanca
San Miguel de Tucumán
Catamarca
La Rioja
San Juan
Villa María
Santa Rosa
Negro
Calama
Antofagasta
Punta Tetas
Punta Ballena
Punta Morro
Copiapó
La Serena
Valparaíso
Santiago
Rancagua
Talca
Chillán
Talcahuano
Concepción
Los Ángeles
Temuco
Valdivia
Osorno
Puerto Montt
Isla de Chiloé
Archipiélago de los Chonos
Golfo de Penas
Mendoza
San Rafael
Neuquén
Viedma
Rawson
Golfo San Matías
Península Valdés
Golfo San Jorge
Comodoro Rivadavia
Cabo Dos Bahías
Puerto Deseado
Cabo Tres Puntas
Cabo San Francisco de Paula
Río Gallegos
Strait of Magellan
Isla Grande de Tierra del Fuego
Isla de los Estados
Cape Horn
Ushuaia
Punta Arenas
Puerto Madryn
Lago Viedma
Lago Argentino
Esquel
Colorado

Nevado Ojos del Salado 6908
Cerro Las Tórtolas 6332
Cerro Aconcagua 6961
Volcán Llullaillaco 6723
Cerro Murallón 3600
San Valentín 4058

Desierto de Atacama

Falkland Islands (UK) (Islas Malvinas) Claimed by Argentina
Stanley
West Falkland
East Falkland

South Georgia and South Sandwich Islands (UK) Claimed by Argentina
Cape Alexandra
Mt Paget 2934
Cape Disappointment

Scale 1 : 20 000 000

Relief and physical features
Relief
metres
5000
3000
2000
1000
500
200
sea level
under sea level
0
200
4000
6000
6961 ▲ Mountain height (in metres)
Permanent ice (ice cap or glacier)

Water features
River
Intermittent river
Canal
Lake / Reservoir
Intermittent lake
Marsh

Communications
Railway
Road
⊕ Main airport

Administration
Boundaries
International
Disputed

Settlement
Cities and towns in order of size
National capital
■ **Buenos Aires**
● **São Paulo**
● **Santa Cruz**
○ **Arequipa**
○ Formosa
○ Cerra de Pasco
Other city or town

Brazilian Institute of Geography and Statistics
www.ibge.gov.br

Population per sq. km

- over 50
- 11 – 50
- 1 – 10
- less than 1

Cities

- over 10 000 000
- 5 000 000 – 10 000 000
- 1 000 000 – 5 000 000
- 500 000 – 1 000 000
- 100 000 – 500 000

Scale 1 : 35 000 000

Population growth, 2000 – 2060

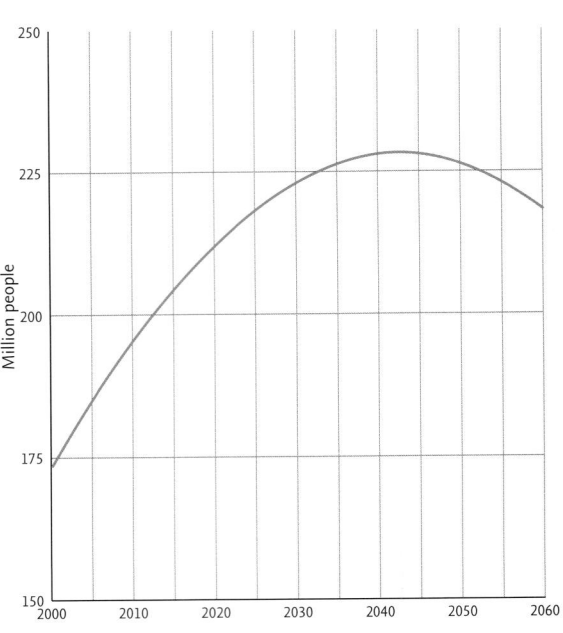

Urban and rural population, 1940 – 2015

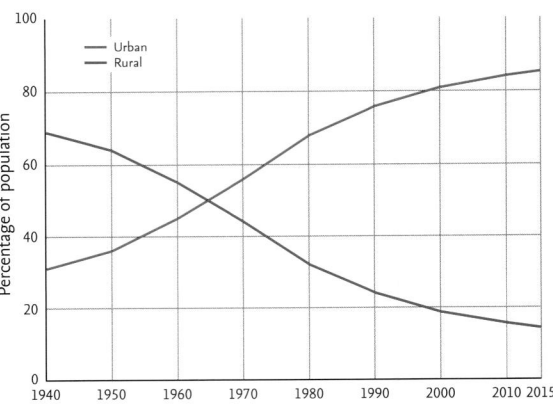

— Urban
— Rural

Largest urban agglomerations, 2015

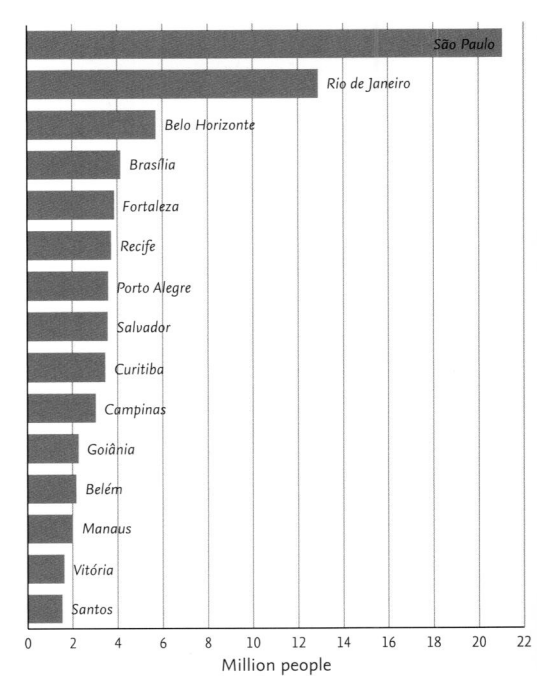

São Paulo
Rio de Janeiro
Belo Horizonte
Brasília
Fortaleza
Recife
Porto Alegre
Salvador
Curitiba
Campinas
Goiânia
Belém
Manaus
Vitória
Santos

Million people

Metropolitan region density

Population per sq. km

- over 5000
- 2000 – 5000
- 1000 – 2500
- less than 1000

- Future area of metropolitan expansion

Scale 1 : 35 000 000

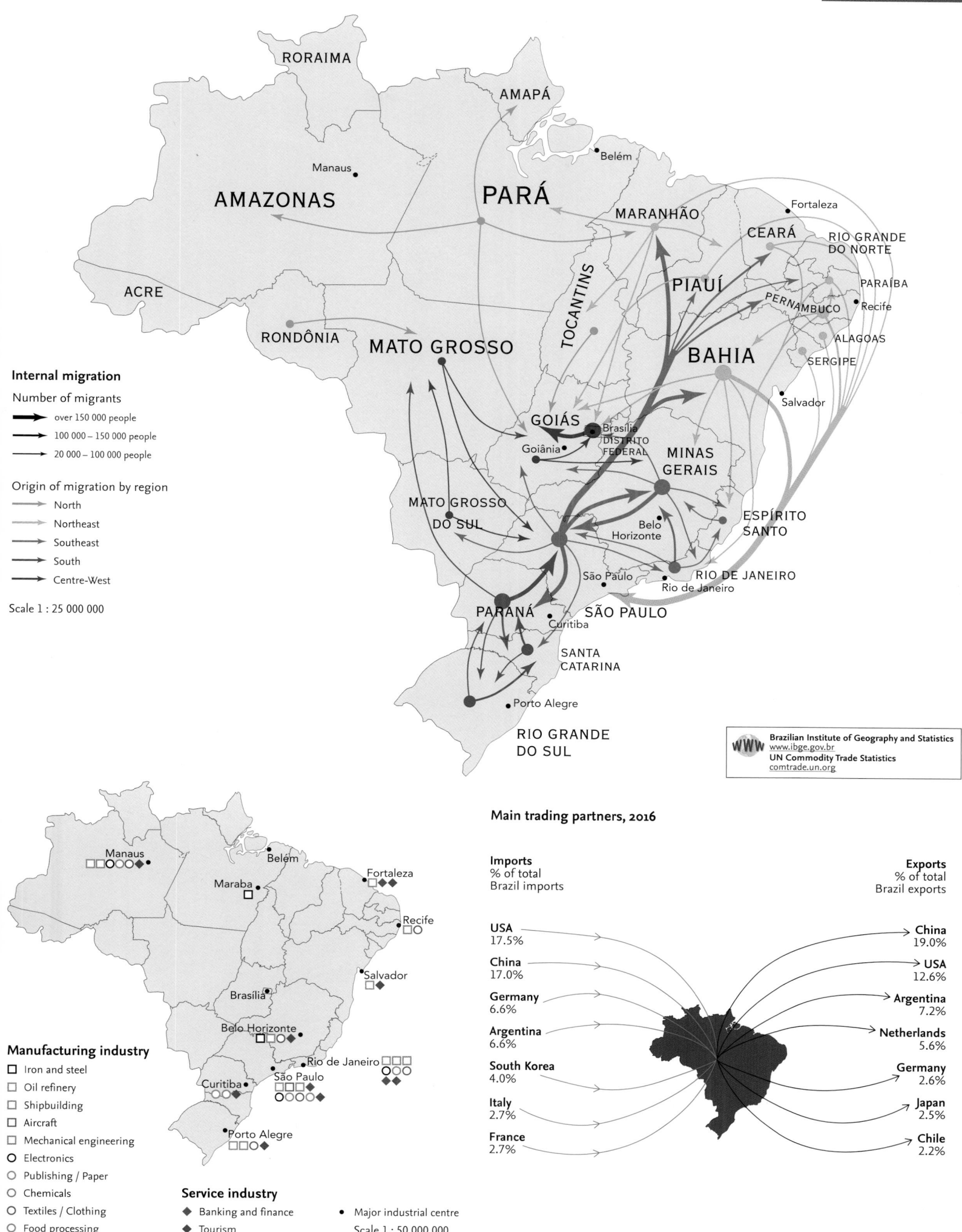

 RORAIMA

AMAPÁ

Manaus

Belém

AMAZONAS

PARÁ

Fortaleza

MARANHÃO

CEARÁ

RIO GRANDE
DO NORTE

ACRE

PIAUÍ

PARAÍBA

PERNAMBUCO

Recife

RONDÔNIA

MATO GROSSO

BAHIA

ALAGOAS

SERGIPE

Salvador

Internal migration

Number of migrants

→ over 150 000 people

→ 100 000 – 150 000 people

→ 20 000 – 100 000 people

Origin of migration by region

→ North

→ Northeast

→ Southeast

→ South

→ Centre-West

Scale 1 : 25 000 000

GOIÁS

Brasília
DISTRITO
FEDERAL

Goiânia

MINAS
GERAIS

MATO GROSSO
DO SUL

Belo
Horizonte

ESPÍRITO
SANTO

São Paulo

RIO DE JANEIRO

Rio de Janeiro

PARANÁ

SÃO PAULO

Curitiba

SANTA
CATARINA

Porto Alegre

RIO GRANDE
DO SUL

Brazilian Institute of Geography and Statistics
www.ibge.gov.br
WWW UN Commodity Trade Statistics
comtrade.un.org

Manufacturing industry

Manaus

Belém

Fortaleza

Maraba

Recife

Salvador

Brasília

Belo Horizonte

Rio de Janeiro

□ Iron and steel

□ Oil refinery

□ Shipbuilding

□ Aircraft

□ Mechanical engineering

○ Electronics

○ Publishing / Paper

○ Chemicals

○ Textiles / Clothing

○ Food processing

São Paulo

Curitiba

Porto Alegre

Service industry

◆ Banking and finance

◆ Tourism

● Major industrial centre

Scale 1 : 50 000 000

Main trading partners, 2016

Imports
% of total
Brazil imports

Exports
% of total
Brazil exports

USA
17.5%

China
19.0%

China
17.0%

USA
12.6%

Germany
6.6%

Argentina
7.2%

Argentina
6.6%

Netherlands
5.6%

South Korea
4.0%

Germany
2.6%

Italy
2.7%

Japan
2.5%

France
2.7%

Chile
2.2%

Brazil: Deforestation

Part of the Amazon rainforest in Rhôndonia, Brazil. The straight lines in the forest show where whole blocks of trees have been cut down.

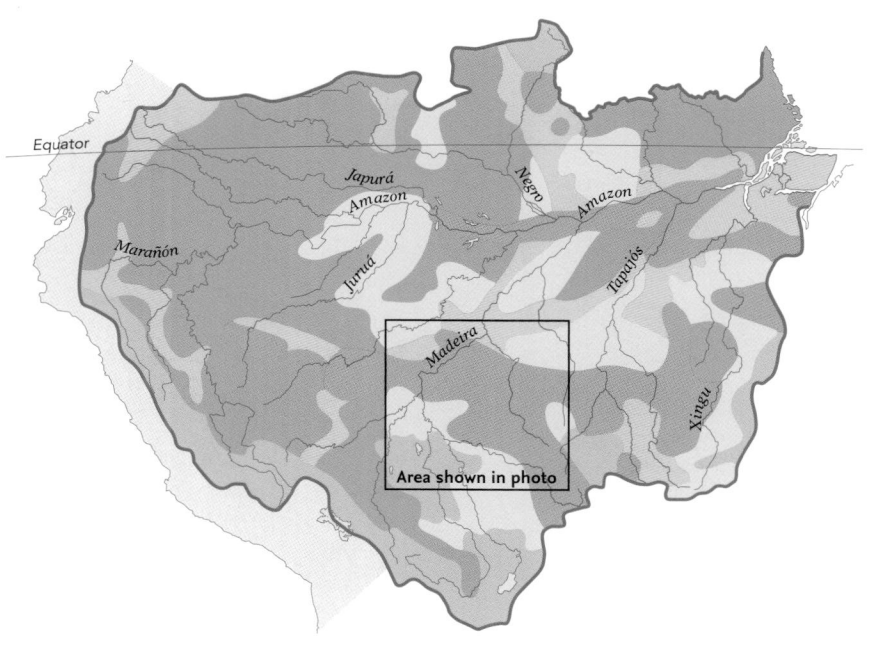

State of the Amazon rainforest

Rainforest

- Deforested by 2009
- High threat of deforestation
- Medium threat of deforestation
- Low threat of deforestation

Other vegetation

- Grassland or woodland
- No data

—— Boundary of Amazon Basin rainforest

Scale 1 : 35 000 000

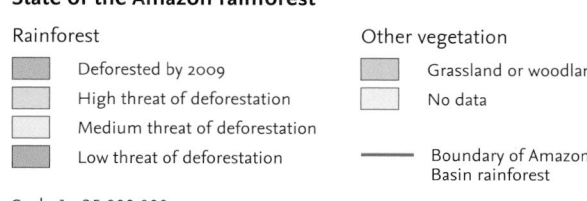

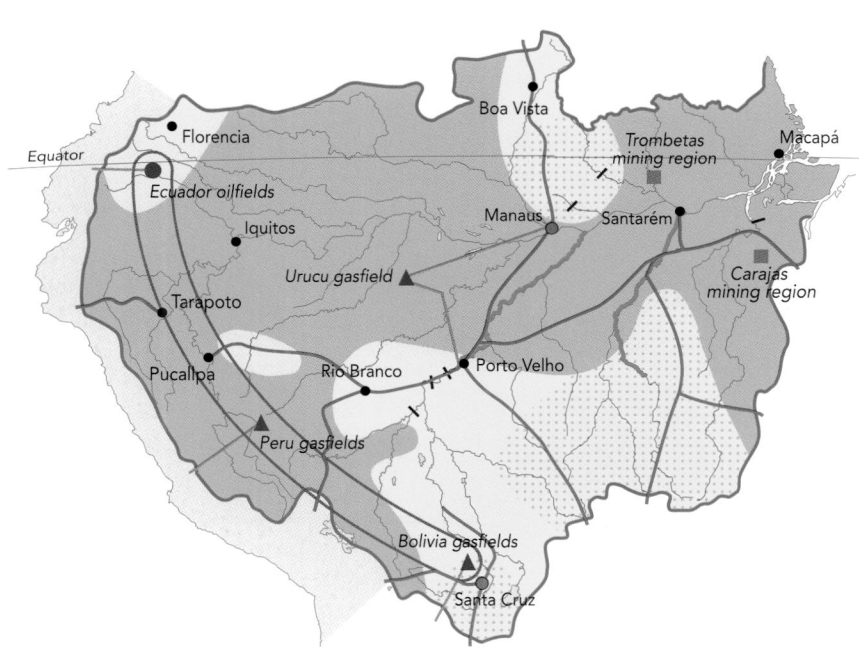

Threats to the Amazon rainforest

Extractive industry

- ● Oilfield
- ▲ Gasfield
- ▦ Mining region

—— Main highway
–⊢⊢ Major dam
—— Industrial waterway
—— Pipeline
—— Boundary of Western Amazon zone of oil and gas development

Main population centres

- ● over 1 000 000
- ● 100 000 – 500 000

Area of agricultural expansion

- Pasture for extensive cattle ranching
- Extensive cropping: for stock feed (soybeans, sorghum, maize), industrial crops (oil palm, sunflower, cotton) and biofuels (sugar cane, maize)

Scale 1 : 35 000 000

Africa: Relief

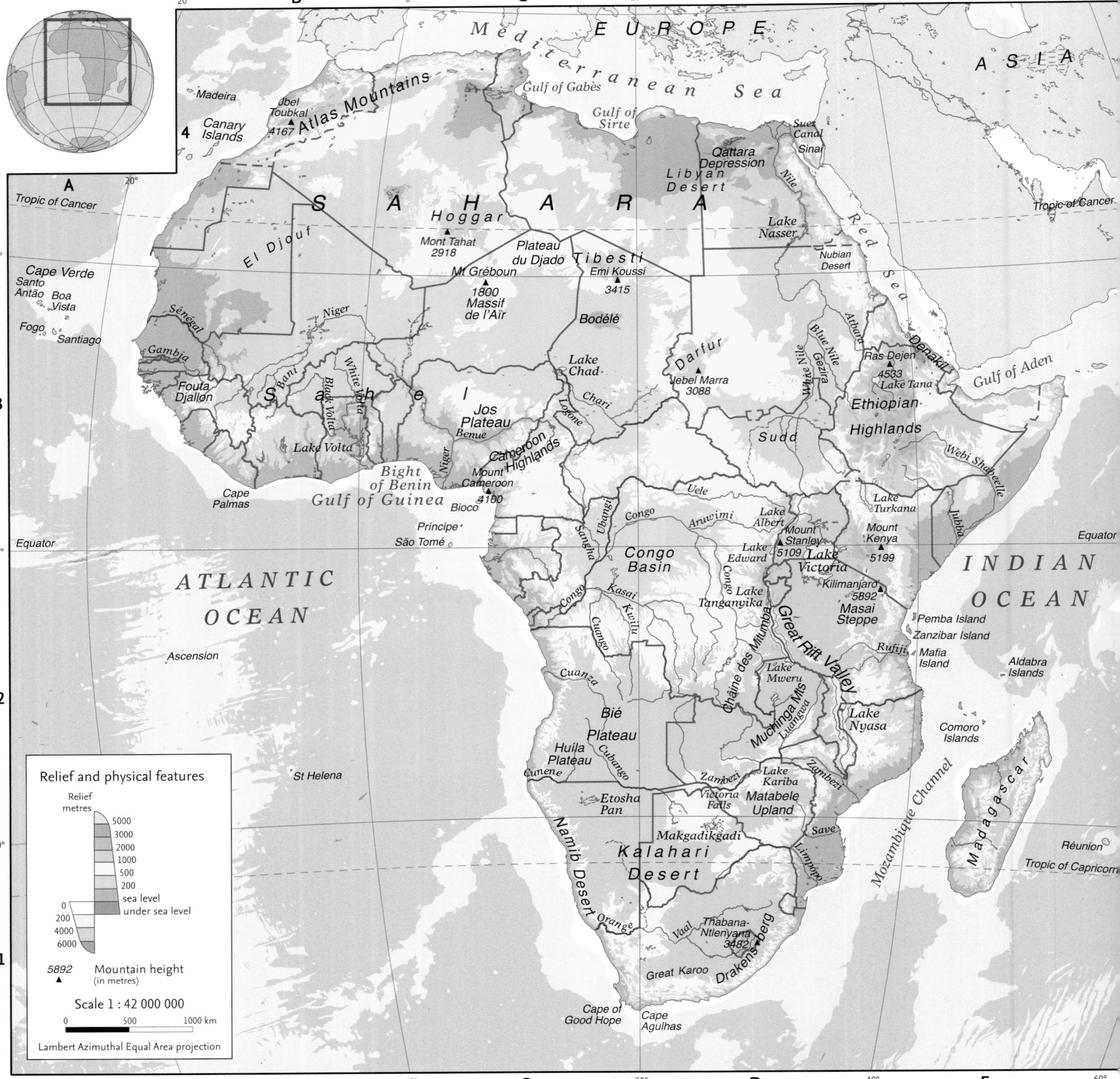

E U R O P E

A S I A

Mediterranean Sea

Madeira

Gulf of Gabès

Gulf of
Sirte

Suez
Canal
Sinai

Jbel
Toubkal
4167 *Atlas Mountains*

Canary
Islands

Qattara
Depression

*Libyan
Desert*

Nubian
Desert

Tropic of Cancer

Tropic of Cancer

S A H A R A

Hoggar

El Djouf

Mont Tahat
2918

Plateau
du Djado

T i b e s t i

Lake
Nasser

Red Sea

Cape Verde
Santo
Antão Boa
Vista

Fogo
Santiago

Sénégal

Niger

Mt Gréboun

1800
Massif
de l'Aïr

Emi Koussi
3415

Bodélé

Lake
Chad

Darfur

Jebel Marra
3088

Athara

Ras Dejen
4533
Lake Tana

Denakil

Gulf of Aden

Gambia

Fouta
Djallon

S a h e l

Bani

White Volta

Black Volta

Niger

Lake Volta

Benue

Jos
Plateau

Chari

Logone

Blue Nile
Gezira

White Nile

Niger

Sudd

*Ethiopian
Highlands*

Webi Shabeelle

Cape
Palmas

*Bight
of Benin*

Gulf of Guinea

Mount
Cameroon
4100

*Cameroon
Highlands*

Bioco

Uele

Ubangi

Congo

Aruwimi

Lake
Albert

Mount
Stanley
5109

Lake
Edward

Mount
Kenya
5199

Príncipe

São Tomé

Equator

Sangha

Lake
Victoria

Kilimanjaro
5892

*Masai
Steppe*

Equator

I N D I A N

O C E A N

A T L A N T I C

O C E A N

Ascension

*Congo
Basin*

Kasai

Congo

Lake
Tanganyika

Great Rift Valley

Chaîne des Mitumba

Rufiji

Pemba Island

Zanzibar Island

Mafia
Island

Aldabra
Islands

Kwilu

Cuango

Lake
Mweru

Muchinga Mts

Luangwa

Lake
Nyasa

Comoro
Islands

Cuanza

*Bié
Plateau*

Huíla
Plateau

Cubango

Cunene

Zambezi

Lake
Kariba

Zambezi

*Matabele
Upland*

Save

Limpopo

Madagascar

Réunion

Mozambique Channel

St Helena

Etosha
Pan

Victoria
Falls

Makgadikgadi

Namib Desert

**Kalahari
Desert**

Tropic of Capricorn

Orange

Vaal

Thabana-
Ntlenyana
3482

Drakensberg

Great Karoo

Cape of
Good Hope

Cape
Agulhas

Relief and physical features

Relief
metres

5000
3000
2000
1000
500
200
sea level
under sea level
0
200
4000
6000

5892 ▲ Mountain height
(in metres)

Scale 1 : 42 000 000

0   500   1000 km

Lambert Azimuthal Equal Area projection

Cross-section

line of cross-section

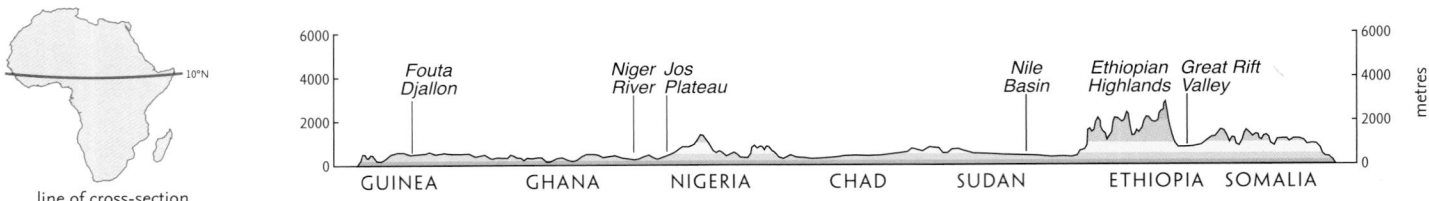

Fouta
Djallon	Niger
River	Jos
Plateau		Nile
Basin	Ethiopian
Highlands	Great Rift
Valley

6000
4000
2000

6000
4000
2000
metres

GUINEA   GHANA   NIGERIA   CHAD   SUDAN   ETHIOPIA   SOMALIA

A B C D E

20° 0° 20° 40° 60°

Azores (Portugal)

Madeira (Portugal)

EUROPE

Mediterranean Sea

Algiers
Tunis
TUNISIA
Tripoli
Benghazi
Alexandria
Cairo
Giza

ASIA

Rabat
Casablanca
MOROCCO

Canary Is (Spain)

Laayoune

WESTERN SAHARA

ALGERIA

LIBYA

EGYPT

Red Sea

Tropic of Cancer

4

MAURITANIA

Nouakchott

MALI

NIGER

CHAD

Lake Chad

Khartoum

SUDAN

ERITREA
Asmara

20°

CAPE VERDE

Praia

Dakar
SENEGAL

1
2

Bamako
BURKINA FASO
Niamey
Ouagadougou

NIGERIA

Ndjamena

DJIBOUTI
Djibouti

3

GUINEA

Conakry
Freetown
SIERRA LEONE
Monrovia
LIBERIA
Yamoussoukro
Abidjan
CÔTE D'IVOIRE
GHANA
Accra
3
BENIN
Lagos
Porto-Novo
Abuja

CAMEROON

Yaoundé

CENTRAL AFRICAN REPUBLIC

Bangui

SOUTH SUDAN

Juba

Addis Ababa

ETHIOPIA

SOMALIA

4

4
4
5

Libreville
GABON
CONGO
Brazzaville
Kinshasa

DEMOCRATIC REPUBLIC OF THE CONGO

UGANDA
Kampala

Lake Turkana

KENYA

Nairobi

Mogadishu

Equator

INDIAN OCEAN

0°

ATLANTIC OCEAN

Ascension Island (UK)

Luanda

Lake Victoria

6
7
Lake Tanganyika

Dodoma

TANZANIA

Mombasa
Dar es Salaam

Victoria
SEYCHELLES

Aldabra Is (Seychelles)

2

St Helena (UK)

ANGOLA

ZAMBIA
Lusaka

Lilongwe
MALAWI
Lake Nyasa

Moroni
COMOROS

Mayotte (France)

MADAGASCAR
Antananarivo

Port Louis

MOZAMBIQUE

Harare
ZIMBABWE
Beira

20°
MAURITIUS
Reunion (France)

NAMIBIA

Windhoek
Walvis Bay

BOTSWANA

Gaborone

Pretoria
Johannesburg

Maputo
ESWATINI (SWAZILAND)

Tropic of Capricorn

1

Bloemfontein
LESOTHO

SOUTH AFRICA

Cape Town

Legend
— International boundary
■ Capital city
○ Important city

1 THE GAMBIA
2 GUINEA-BISSAU
3 TOGO
4 EQUATORIAL GUINEA
5 SÃO TOMÉ & PRÍNCIPE
6 RWANDA
7 BURUNDI

Scale 1 : 42 000 000

0   500   1000 km

Lambert Azimuthal Equal Area projection

A B C D E

20° 0° 20° 40° 60°

Facts about Africa

Total land area	**30 343 578 sq. km**
Highest peak	**Kilimanjaro, 5892 m**
Longest river	**Nile, 6695 km**
Largest country	**Algeria, 2 381 741 sq. km**
Most populous country	**Nigeria, 182 202 000**

Population by country, 2015
top ten countries

Uganda 39 032
Algeria 39 667
Sudan 40 235
Kenya 46 050
Tanzania 53 470
South Africa 54 490
Dem. Rep. Congo 77 267
Egypt 91 508
Ethiopia 99 391
Nigeria 182 202

Population in thousands

GNI by country, 2015
top ten countries

Ethiopia 61 277
Tanzania 44 867
Kenya 62 953
Sudan 88 342
Angola 89 886
Morocco 98 706
Algeria 160 467
South Africa 306 706
Egypt 324 703
Nigeria 471 021

Gross National Income in US $ millions

Africa: Climate

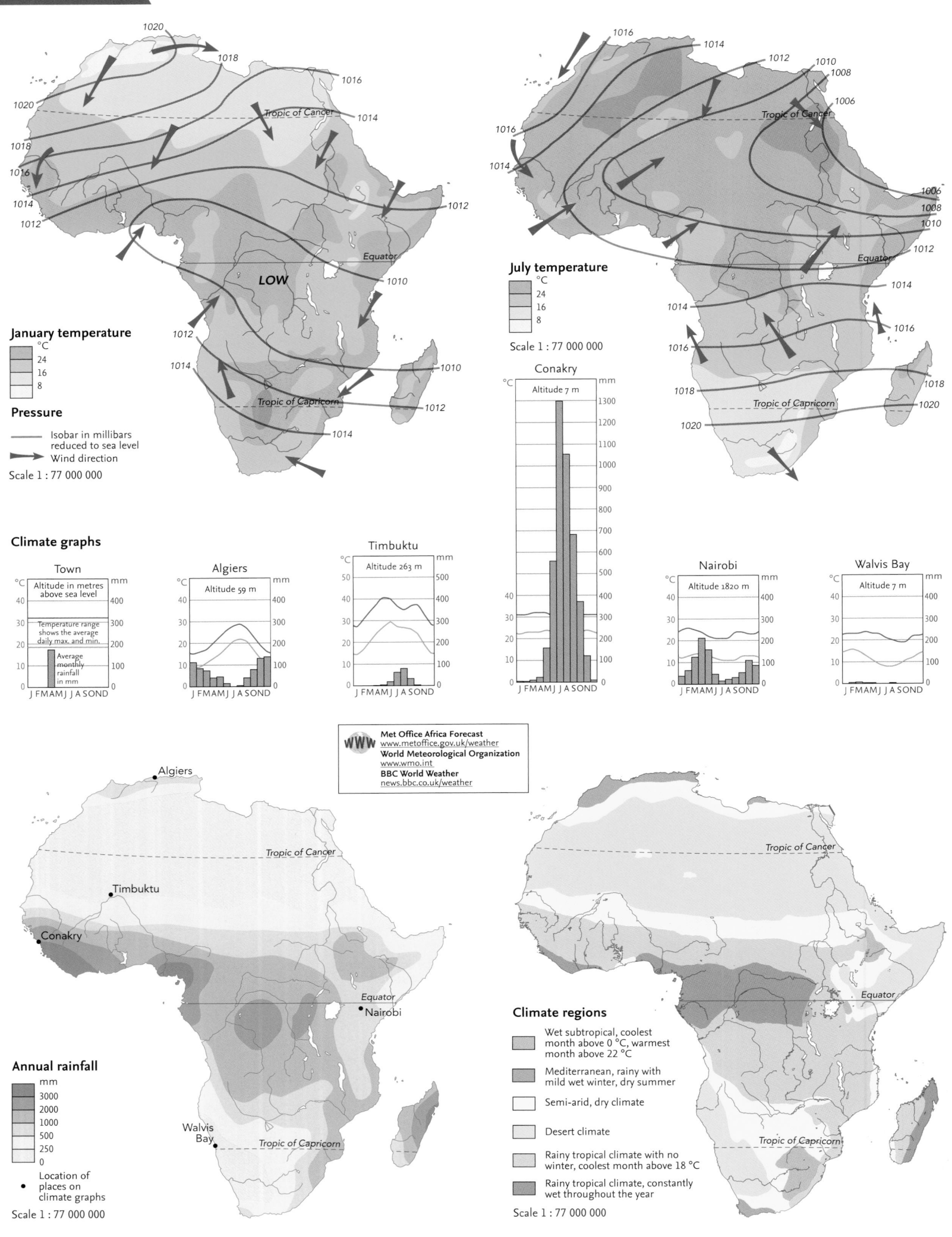

January temperature

°C
24
16
8

Pressure

— Isobar in millibars reduced to sea level

➤ Wind direction

Scale 1 : 77 000 000

July temperature

°C
24
16
8

Scale 1 : 77 000 000

Climate graphs

Town

°C | mm
Altitude in metres above sea level
Temperature range shows the average daily max. and min.
Average monthly rainfall in mm
J F M A M J J A S O N D

Algiers — Altitude 59 m

Timbuktu — Altitude 263 m

Conakry — Altitude 7 m

Nairobi — Altitude 1820 m

Walvis Bay — Altitude 7 m

WWW **Met Office Africa Forecast**
www.metoffice.gov.uk/weather
World Meteorological Organization
www.wmo.int
BBC World Weather
news.bbc.co.uk/weather

Annual rainfall

mm
3000
2000
1000
500
250
0

● Location of places on climate graphs

Scale 1 : 77 000 000

Climate regions

Wet subtropical, coolest month above 0 °C, warmest month above 22 °C

Mediterranean, rainy with mild wet winter, dry summer

Semi-arid, dry climate

Desert climate

Rainy tropical climate with no winter, coolest month above 18 °C

Rainy tropical climate, constantly wet throughout the year

Scale 1 : 77 000 000

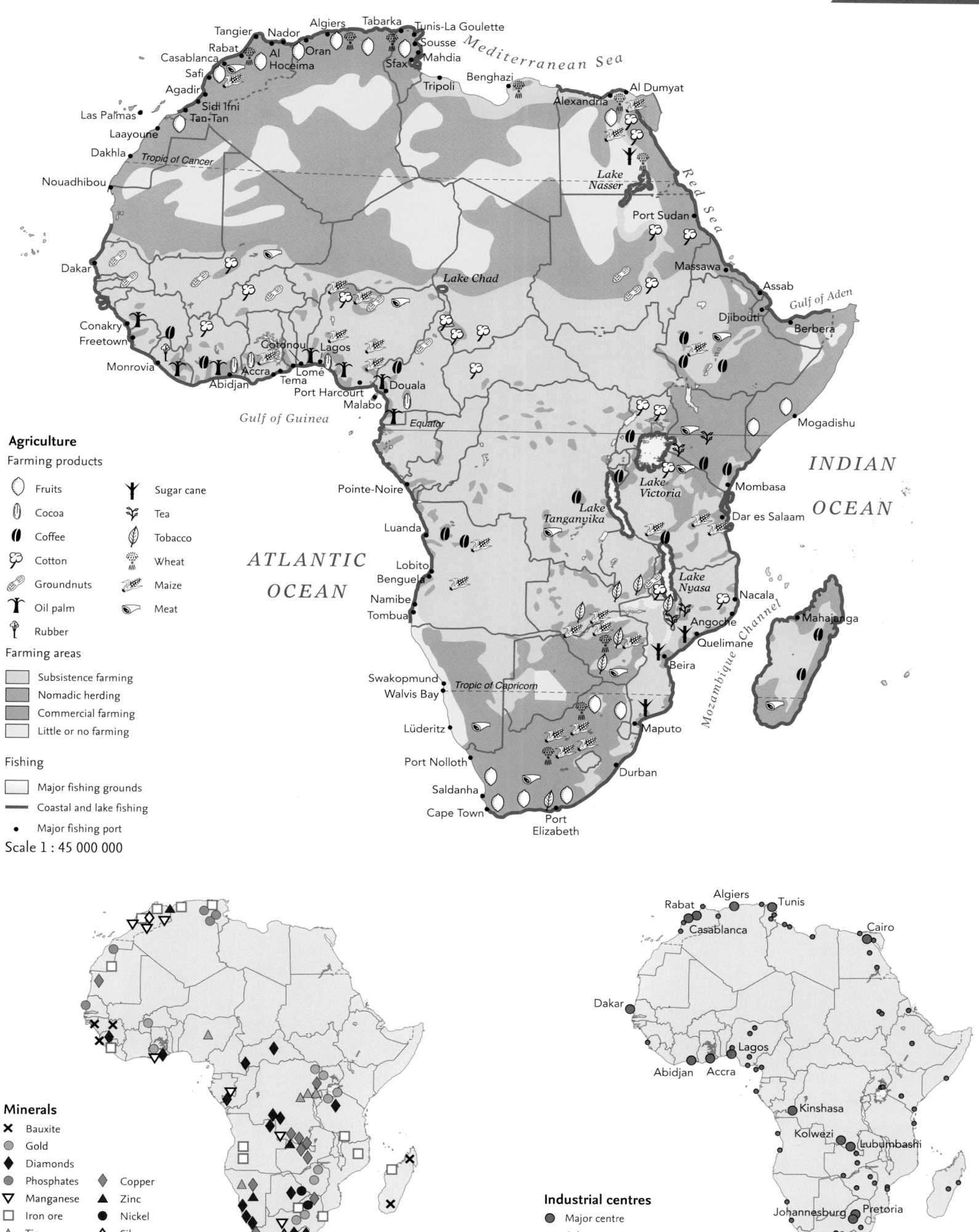

Agriculture

Farming products

- Fruits
- Cocoa
- Coffee
- Cotton
- Groundnuts
- Oil palm
- Rubber
- Sugar cane
- Tea
- Tobacco
- Wheat
- Maize
- Meat

Farming areas

- Subsistence farming
- Nomadic herding
- Commercial farming
- Little or no farming

Fishing

- Major fishing grounds
- Coastal and lake fishing
- Major fishing port

Scale 1 : 45 000 000

Minerals

- Bauxite
- Gold
- Diamonds
- Phosphates
- Manganese
- Iron ore
- Tin
- Copper
- Zinc
- Nickel
- Silver

Scale 1 : 100 000 000

Industrial centres

- Major centre
- Other centre

Scale 1 : 100 000 000

Africa: Population and Wealth

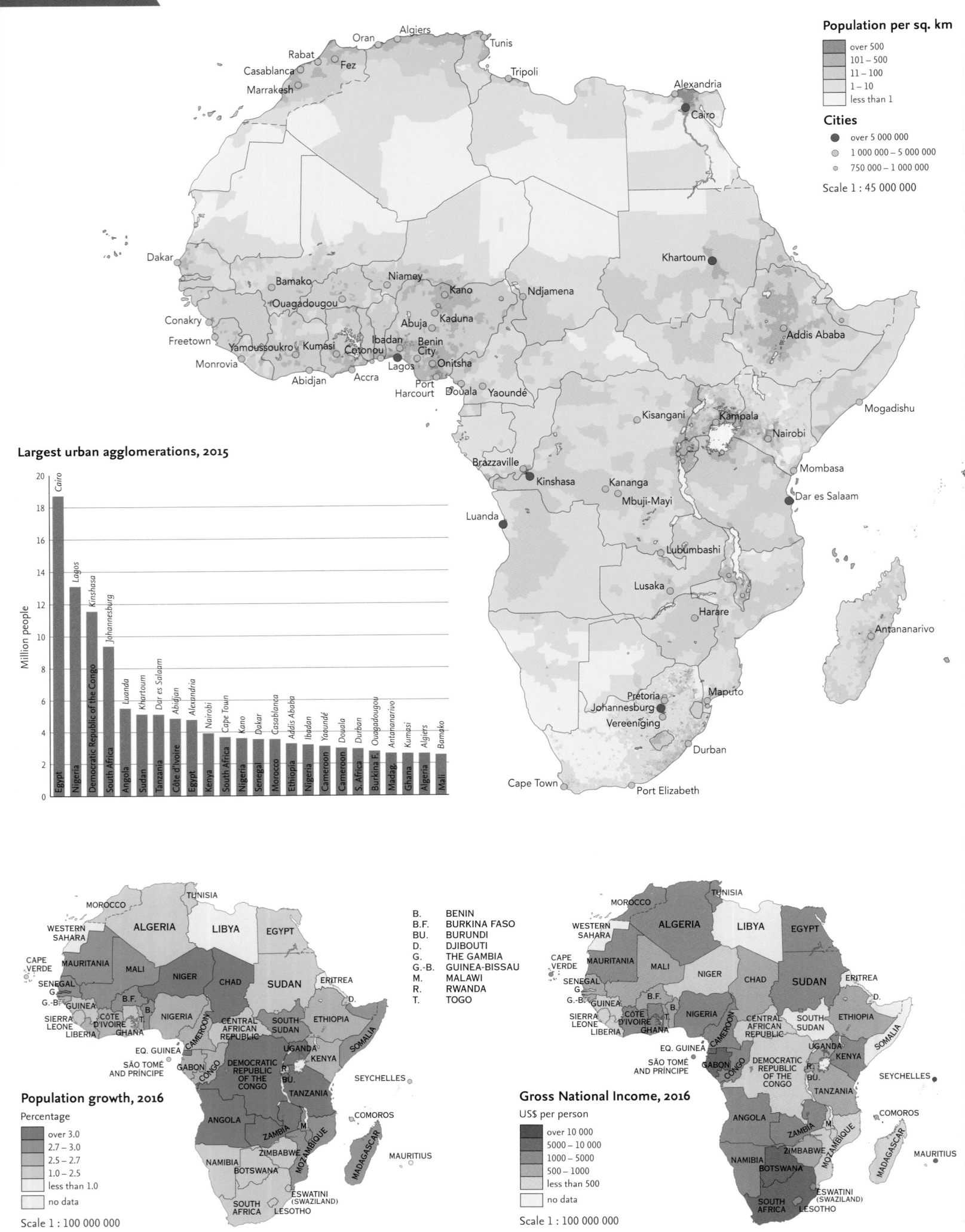

Population per sq. km
- over 500
- 101 – 500
- 11 – 100
- 1 – 10
- less than 1

Cities
- over 5 000 000
- 1 000 000 – 5 000 000
- 750 000 – 1 000 000

Scale 1 : 45 000 000

Largest urban agglomerations, 2015

Population growth, 2016

Percentage
- over 3.0
- 2.7 – 3.0
- 2.5 – 2.7
- 1.0 – 2.5
- less than 1.0
- no data

Scale 1 : 100 000 000

B.	BENIN
B.F.	BURKINA FASO
BU.	BURUNDI
D.	DJIBOUTI
G.	THE GAMBIA
G.-B.	GUINEA-BISSAU
M.	MALAWI
R.	RWANDA
T.	TOGO

Gross National Income, 2016

US$ per person
- over 10 000
- 5000 – 10 000
- 1000 – 5000
- 500 – 1000
- less than 500
- no data

Scale 1 : 100 000 000

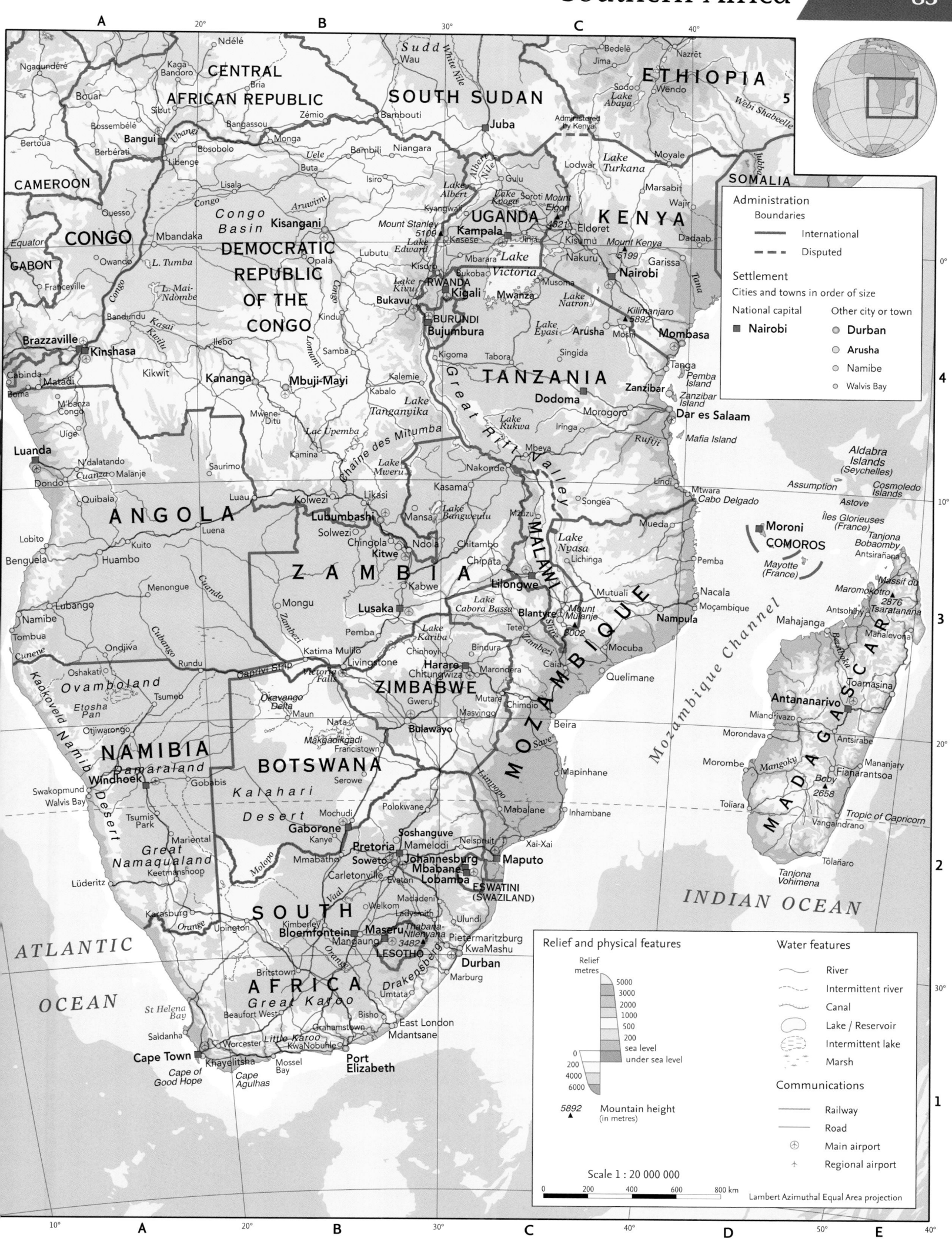

Administration

Boundaries

——— International

- - - Disputed

Settlement

Cities and towns in order of size

National capital

■ Nairobi

Other city or town

◉ Durban

◎ Arusha

○ Namibe

○ Walvis Bay

Relief and physical features

Relief metres

5000
3000
2000
1000
500
200
sea level
under sea level
200
4000
6000

▲ 5892 Mountain height (in metres)

Scale 1 : 20 000 000

0   200   400   600   800 km

Lambert Azimuthal Equal Area projection

Water features

~~~ River

~~~ Intermittent river

~~~ Canal

◯ Lake / Reservoir

◯ Intermittent lake

Marsh

Communications

——— Railway

——— Road

⊕ Main airport

✈ Regional airport

Relief and physical features

Relief metres
5000
3000
2000
1000
500
200
0 sea level
under sea level
200
4000
6000

5892 ▲ Mountain height (in metres)

Scale 1 : 20 000 000

0 200 400 600 800 km

Water features

~ River
~ Intermittent river
~ Canal
⬭ Lake / Reservoir
⬭ Intermittent lake
Marsh

Communications

Railway
Road
⊕ Main airport

Administration

Boundaries

—— International
- - - Disputed
······· Ceasefire line

Settlement

Cities and towns in order of size

National capital
■ Cairo

Other city or town
● Lagos
● Abidjan
○ Zaria
○ Luxor
○ Kankan

Lambert Azimuthal Equal Area projection

SPAIN
PORTUGAL
Lisbon
ITALY
MOROCCO
ALGERIA
SAHARA
TUNISIA
Tripoli
WESTERN SAHARA
Administered by Morocco
MAURITANIA
Azawad
NIGER
Massif de l'Aïr
MALI
CAPE VERDE
SENEGAL
THE GAMBIA
GUINEA-BISSAU
GUINEA
SIERRA LEONE
LIBERIA
CÔTE D'IVOIRE (IVORY COAST)
BURKINA FASO
GHANA
TOGO
BENIN
NIGERIA
CAMEROON
EQUATORIAL GUINEA
SÃO TOMÉ AND PRÍNCIPE
GABON
ANGOLA
ATLANTIC OCEAN
Gulf of Guinea
Bight of Benin
Tropic of Cancer
Ahaggar
Mt Tahat 2918
Plateau du Djado
Atlas Mountains
Haut Atlas Mountains
Jbel Toubkal 4167
Mont Cameroun 4100 ▲

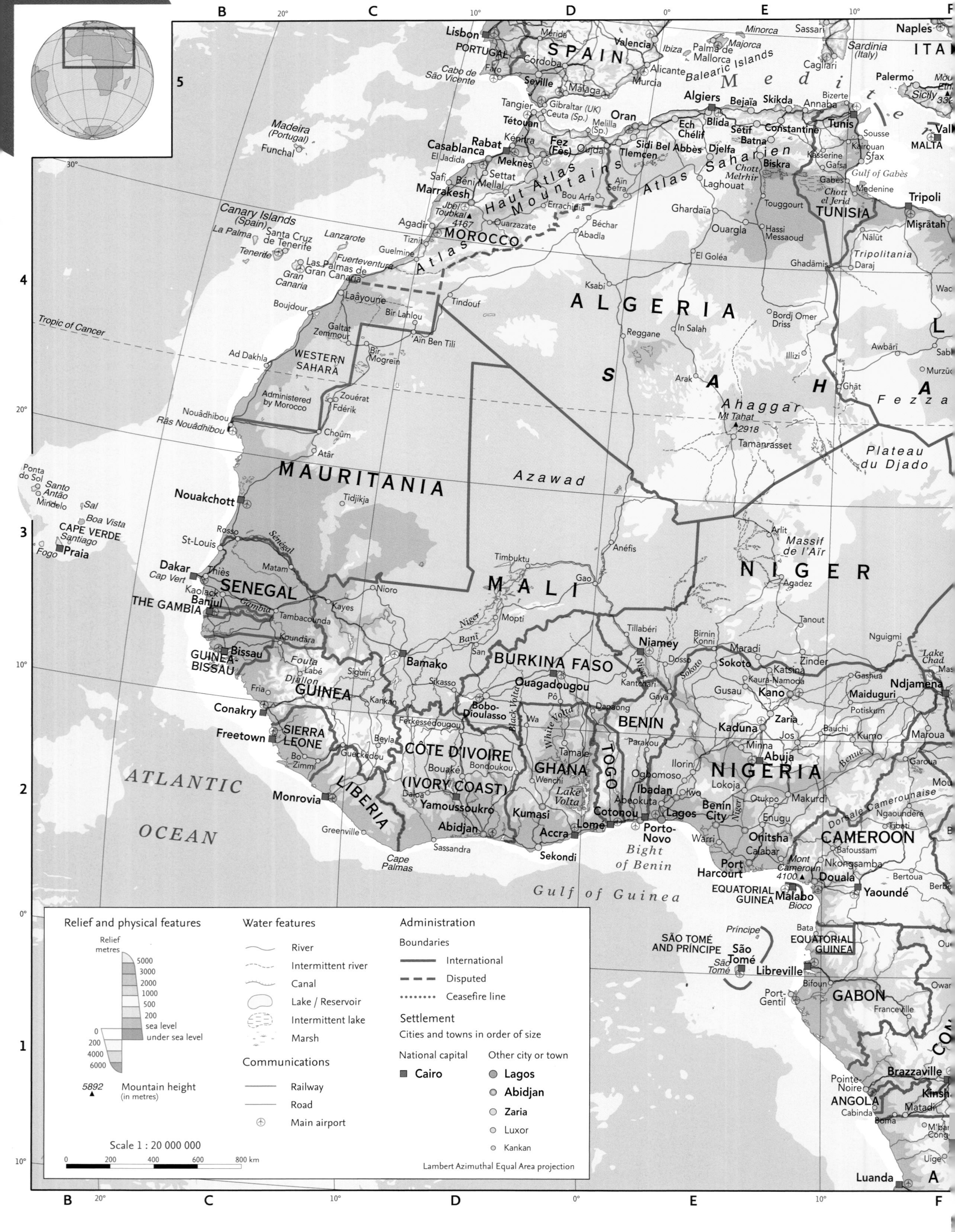

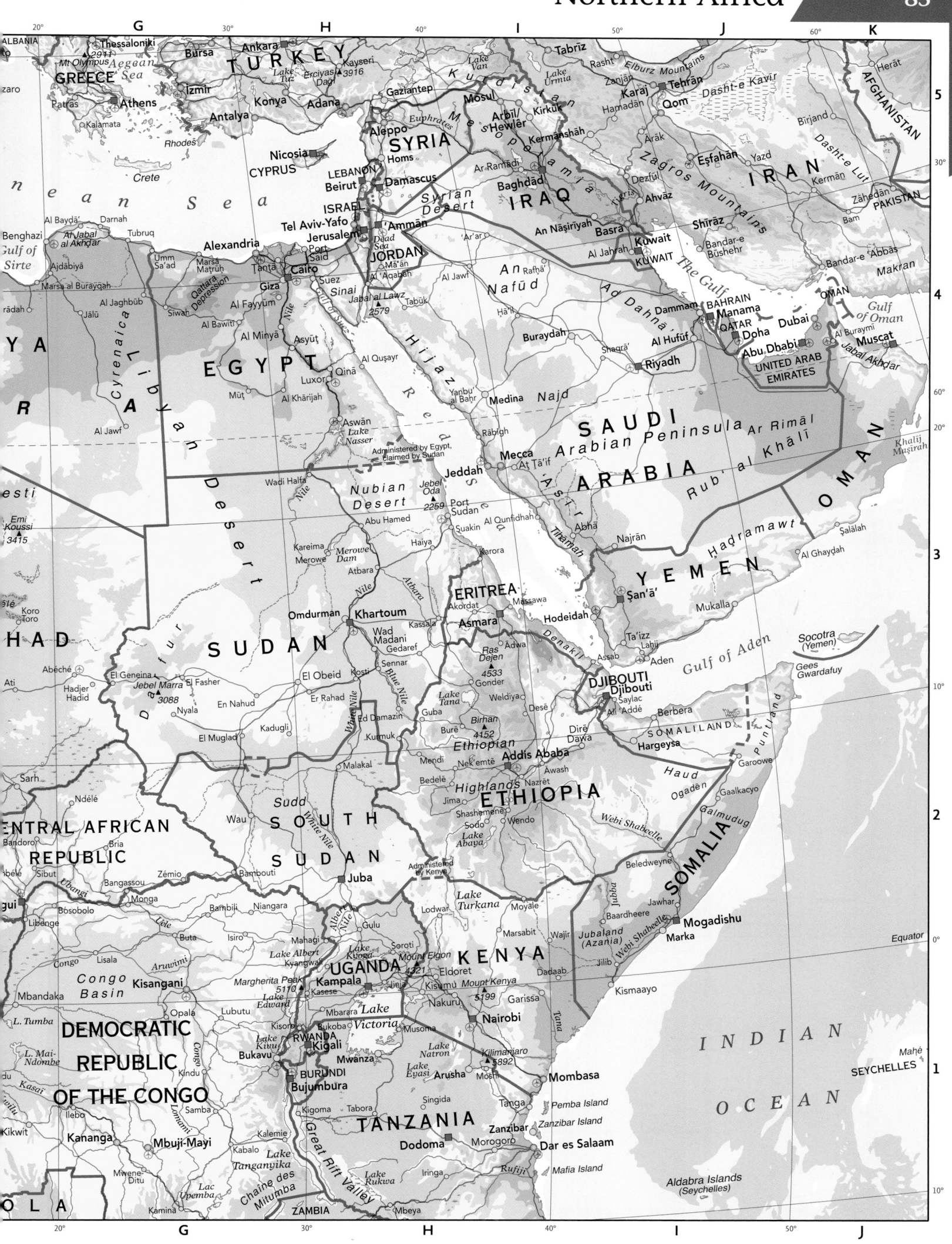

GREECE
Thessaloniki
Mt Olympus 2911
Patras
Athens
Aegean Sea
ALBANIA
Bursa
İzmir
Konya
Antalya
Rhodes
Crete
TURKEY
Ankara
Lake Tuz
Kayseri
Erciyas Dağı 3916
Adana
Gaziantep

Nicosia
CYPRUS
LEBANON
Beirut
ISRAEL
Tel Aviv-Yafo
Jerusalem
Alexandria
Al Baydā'
Darnah
Tubruq
Benghazi
Al Jabal al Akhdar
Gulf of Sirte
Ajdābiyā
Marsa al Burayqah
rādah
Jālū
Al Jaghbūb
Siwah
Umm Sa'ad
Marsa Matrūh
Tantā
Port Said
Cairo
Suez
Giza
Al Fayyūm

Aleppo
Homs
Damascus
SYRIA
Syrian Desert
Amman
Dead Sea
Ma'ān
Al 'Aqabah
JORDAN
'Ar'ar
Mosul
Arbīl/Hewlêr
Kirkūk
Kermanshah
Baghdad
IRAQ
An Nāşirīyah
Euphrates
Al Jawf
Rafhā'
An Nafūd
Hā'il
Tabrīz
Rasht
Zanjān
Elburz Mountains
Karaj
Qom
Tehrān
Hamadān
Dezfūl
Eşfahān
Ahvāz
Zagros Mountains
Basra
Shīrāz
Kuwait
KUWAIT
Al Jahrah
Dammam
Ad Dahnā'
Buraydah
AFGHANISTAN
Herāt
Dasht-e Kavir
Birjand
Yazd
Kermān
Zāhedān
Dasht-e Lut
Bam
IRAN
PAKISTAN
Bandar-e Būshehr
Bandar-e 'Abbās
Makran
BAHRAIN
Manama
QATAR
Doha
Dubai
Abu Dhabi
UNITED ARAB EMIRATES
Al Bur., aymi
OMAN
Gulf of Oman
Jabal Akhdar
Muscat
Khalīj Maşīrah

EGYPT
Al Jaghbūb
Cyrenaica
Libyan
Al Jawf
Al Bawiti
Al Minyā
Asyūţ
Al Khārijah
Al Qūşayr
Qinā
Luxor
Aswān
Lake Nasser
Mūţ
Jabal Lawz 2579
Tabūk
Sinai
Gulf of Aqaba
Hijaz
Red
Yanbu' al Bahr
Medina
Najd
Rābigh
Mecca
At Tā'if
Jeddah
Najrān
SAUDI
Arabian Peninsula
Ar Rimāl
Rub' al Khālī
ARABIA
Riyadh
Shaqrā'
Al Hufūf

LIBYA
Emi Koussi 3415
HAD
Abéché
Hadjer Hadid
Ati
Ndélé
Sarh
CENTRAL AFRICAN REPUBLIC
Bandoro
Bria
Sibut
gui
Bangassou
Zémio
Libenge
Bosobolo
DEMOCRATIC REPUBLIC OF THE CONGO
Mbandaka
L. Tumba
Lisala
Buta
Congo Basin
Kisangani
Opala
Aruwimi
Kindu
Lubutu
Kisoro
Bukavu
Lake Kivu
RWANDA
Kigali
Bukoba
BURUNDI
Bujumbura
Kigoma
L. Mai-Ndombe
Kananga
Mbuji-Mayi
Kalemie
Lake Tanganyika
ANGOLA
Mwene Ditu
Kamina
Lac Upemba
Chaîne des Mitumba
Great Rift Valley
ZAMBIA
Kasai
Kikwit
Ilebo
Samba
Lomami
Kabalo
Mweru

Administered by Egypt, claimed by Sudan
Wadi Halfa
Nubian Desert
Kareima
Merowe
Merowe Dam
Abu Hamed
Jebel Oda 2259
Port Sudan
Suakin
Al Qunfidhah
Haiya
Karora
Atbara
Haiya
SUDAN
Omdurman
Khartoum
Wad Madani
Kassala
Gedaref
Sennar
Darfur
El Geneina
Jebel Marra 3088
El Fasher
El Obeid
Kosti
En Nahud
Er Rahad
Nyala
Kadugli
El Muglad
Malakal
SOUTH SUDAN
Wau
Bambili
Niangara
Isiro
Bambouti
Juba
Gulu
Mahagi
Albert Nile
Lake Albert
Soroti
Kyangwali
UGANDA
Kampala
Jinja
Margherita Peak 5110
Kasese
Mbarara
Lake Edward
Lake Kyoga
Mount Elgon 4321
Eldoret
Kisumu
Mount Kenya 5199
Nakuru
KENYA
Lodwar
Lake Turkana
Moyale
Marsabit
Wajir
Dadaab
Nairobi
Garissa
Tana
White Nile
Sudd
Abara
Blue Nile
Kurmuk
Ed Damazin
Guba
Lake Tana
Bure
Birhan 4152
Gedo
Mendi
Nek'emte
Bedelē
ETHIOPIA
Highlands
Addis Ababa
Nazrēt
Āwash
Jima
Shashemenē
Sodo
Wendo
Lake Abaya
Dēsē
Weldiya
Dirē Dawa
SOMALILAND
Hargeysa
Haud
Ogadēn
Webi Shabeelle
Galmudug
SOMALIA
Beledweyne
Jubba
Baardheere
Jubaland (Azania)
Jilib
Webi Shabeelle
Mogadishu
Marka
Kismaayo

ERITREA
Akordat
Asmara
Massawa
Hodeidah
San'ā'
Ta'izz
Lahij
Aden
Ras Dejen 4533
Gonder
Ādwa
Denakil
Assab
Djibouti
DJIBOUTI
Saylac
Alī 'Addē
Berbera
Gulf of Aden
Socotra (Yemen)
Gees Gwardafuy
Puntland
Garoowe
Gaalkacyo
Jawhar
Dādaab
YEMEN
Hadramawt
Mukalla
Al Ghaydah
Şalālah
OMAN

TANZANIA
Kigoma
Tabora
Singida
Dodoma
Iringa
Lake Rukwa
Mbeya
Mafia Island
Morogoro
Dar es Salaam
Zanzibar
Zanzibar Island
Pemba Island
Tanga
Mombasa
Kilimanjaro 5892
Moshi
Arusha
Lake Eyasi
Lake Natron
Mwanza
Musoma
Lake Victoria
Rufiji
INDIAN OCEAN
Mahé
SEYCHELLES
Aldabra Islands (Seychelles)
Equator

Asia: Relief

5   60°   80°   **6**   80°   **5**   60°

A
B
C
D
E   F   G   H
K
J
I

ARCTIC OCEAN

Norwegian Sea

Arctic Circle

Barents Sea

Severnaya Zemlya

New Siberia Islands

Wrangel Island

Arctic Circle

Bering Sea

Aleutian Islands

Baltic Sea

Taymyr Peninsula

Laptev Sea

Khrebet Kolymskiy

Kamchatka Peninsula

Mys Lopatka

4

EUROPE

Ural Mountains

West Siberian Plain

Central Siberian Plateau

Nizhnyaya Tunguska

S   I   B   E   R   I   A

Verkhoyanskiy Khrebet

Lena

Sea of Okhotsk

Sakhalin

Kuril Islands

40°

Ob'

Yenisey

Angara

Stanovoy Khrebet

Khrebet Dzhugdzhur

Black Sea
Mount Elbrus 5642
Mount Ararat 5165

Caspian Sea

Aral Sea

Syr Darya

Lake Zaysan

Altai Mountains

Lake Baikal

Yablonovyy Khrebet

Selenga

Amur

Argun

Da Hinggan Ling

Amur

Sikhote-Alin

Hokkaido

PACIFIC OCEAN

3

Cyprus

Taurus Mts

Mediterranean Sea

Elburz Mts

Dasht-e Kavir

Zagros Mts

Iranian Plateau

Amu Darya

Irtysh

Tien Shan

Turpan Pendi

Lop Nur

Gobi

Manchuria

Huang He

Bo Hai

Sea of Japan (East Sea)

Honshū

Korea Strait

Kyūshū

Shikoku

An Nafud

Arabian Peninsula

Tropic of Cancer

The Gulf

Hindu Kush

Karakoram Ra.
K2 8611

Taklimakan Desert

Kunlun Shan

Plateau of Tibet

North China Plain

Chang Jiang

Gongga Shan 7514

Yellow Sea

East China Sea

Okinawa

Ryukyu Islands

Tropic of Cancer

Saipan
Guam

20°

Red Sea

Asir

Rub' al Khālī

Gulf of Oman

Makran

Sulaiman Range

Helmand

Indus

Sutlej

H i m a l a y a

Dhaulagiri 8167
Annapurna 8091
Mount Everest 8848

Ganges

Brahmaputra

Xi Jiang

Nan Ling

Chang Jiang

Taiwan

Luzon Strait

2

Gulf of Aden

AFRICA

Arabian Sea

Narmada

Godavari

Western Ghats

Deccan

Eastern Ghats

Yamuna

Thar Desert

Mouths of the Ganges

Arakan Yoma

Irrawaddy

Salween

Mekong

Bay of Bengal

Hainan Dao

Luzon

South China Sea

Philippines

Samar

Saipan
Guam

Laccadive Sea

Cape Comorin

Sri Lanka

Andaman Islands

Andaman Sea

Gulf of Thailand

Palawan

Sulu Sea

Mindanao

Celebes Sea

Halmahera

Equator

0°

INDIAN OCEAN

Nicobar Islands

Strait of Malacca

Peninsular Malaysia

Sumatra

Kepulauan Mentawai

Borneo

Celebes

Buru
Seram

Moluccas

New Guinea

OCEANIA

1

Java

Bali
Lombok

Java Sea

Flores

Flores Sea

Timor

Timor Sea

Banda Sea

Arafura Sea

Gulf of Carpentaria

Relief and physical features

Relief
metres

5000
3000
2000
1000
500
200
0   sea level
200   under sea level
4000
6000

▲ 8848   Mountain height (in metres)

Permanent ice (ice cap or glacier)

Scale 1 : 57 000 000

0   500   1000   1500 km

Lambert Azimuthal Equal Area projection

D   60°   **E**   80°   **F**   100°   **G**   120°   **H**   140°   **I**

Cross-section

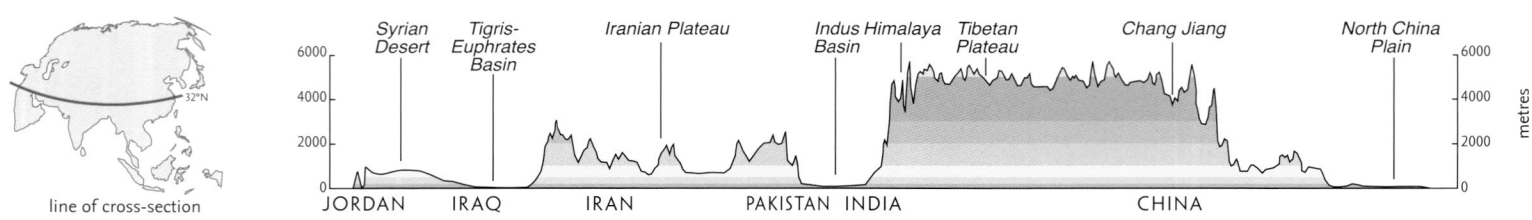

line of cross-section

32°N

Syrian Desert   Tigris-Euphrates Basin   Iranian Plateau   Indus Himalaya Basin   Tibetan Plateau   Chang Jiang   North China Plain

6000
4000
2000

metres

6000
4000
2000
0

JORDAN   IRAQ   IRAN   PAKISTAN   INDIA   CHINA

ATLANTIC OCEAN
EUROPE
Arctic Circle
Norwegian Sea
North Sea
Baltic Sea
Barents Sea
ARCTIC OCEAN
A B C D E F G H I J K
Bering Sea
Aleutian Islands
PACIFIC OCEAN

St Petersburg
Moscow
Perm
Chelyabinsk
Volgograd
Black Sea
TURKEY
Ankara
CYPRUS
LEBANON
ISRAEL
JORDAN
SYRIA
Mediterranean Sea
GEORGIA
ARMENIA
AZERBAIJAN
Caspian Sea
KAZAKHSTAN
Astana
Omsk
Novosibirsk
RUSSIA
Irkutsk
Yakutsk
Sea of Okhotsk
Sakhalin
Harbin
Sapporo

MONGOLIA
Ulan Bator
Almaty
Ürümqi
KYRGYZSTAN
TAJIKISTAN
Tashkent
UZBEKISTAN
TURKMENISTAN
Ashgabat
Baghdād
Tehrān
IRAQ
IRAN
KUWAIT
Kuwait
Riyadh
BAHRAIN
QATAR
UNITED ARAB EMIRATES
SAUDI ARABIA
YEMEN
Şan'ā'
Aden
Gulf of Aden
Socotra (Yemen)
Red Sea
Tropic of Cancer
AFGHANISTAN
Kābul
Islamabad
Lahore
PAKISTAN
Karachi
Muscat
OMAN
Delhi
New Delhi
NEPAL
BHUTAN
INDIA
Mumbai
Hyderabad
Chennai
Kolkata
Dhaka
BANGLADESH
MYANMAR (BURMA)
Nay Pyi Taw
Yangon
Lanzhou
Xi'an
Chongqing
CHINA
Shenyang
Beijing
Tianjin
P'yŏngyang
NORTH KOREA
Seoul
SOUTH KOREA
Nanjing
Shanghai
Wuhan
Guangzhou
Hong Kong
Kōbe
Ōsaka
Fukuoka
JAPAN
Tōkyō
Korea Strait
Japan (East Sea)
Sea of Japan (East Sea)
Yellow Sea
East China Sea
Taipei
TAIWAN
Luzon Strait
Luzon
Manila
PHILIPPINES
Yap
Guam
Northern Mariana Islands
Saipan
PALAU

Arabian Sea
Bay of Bengal
Andaman Is (India)
Nicobar Is (India)
Hanoi
Vientiane
THAILAND
Bangkok
CAMBODIA
Phnom Penh
Ho Chi Minh City
Gulf of Thailand
LAOS
VIETNAM
South China Sea
Sulu Sea
Mindanao
Davao
Celebes Sea
Halmahera
AFRICA
Sri Lanka
Jayewardenepura Kotte
Colombo
SRI LANKA
MALDIVES
INDIAN OCEAN
MALAYSIA
BRUNEI
Kuala Lumpur
Putrajaya
SINGAPORE
Borneo
Sumatra
INDONESIA
Celebes
Jakarta
Surabaya
Java
Java Sea
Flores Sea
Makassar
Banda Sea
Seram
Dili
EAST TIMOR
Arafura Sea
New Guinea
OCEANIA
Equator

International boundary
Capital city
Important city

Russia and Turkey straddle the continents of Europe and Asia

Scale 1 : 57 000 000

0 500 1000 1500 km

Lambert Azimuthal Equal Area projection

Facts about Asia

Total land area — **45 036 492 sq. km**

Highest peak — **Mt Everest, 8848 m**

Longest river — **Chang Jiang, 6380 km**

Largest country — **Russia, 17 075 400 sq. km** (including European Russia)

Most populous country — **China, 1 383 925 000**

Population by country, 2015 top ten countries

Philippines 100 699
Vietnam 93 448
Iran 79 109
Japan 126 573
Russia 143 457
Bangladesh 160 996
Pakistan 188 925
Indonesia 257 564
China 1 383 925
India 1 311 051

Population in thousands

GNI by country, 2015 top ten countries

Saudi Arabia 661 667
Iran 426 269
Thailand 375 320
Turkey 708 355
Indonesia 833 086
Russia 1 328 996
South Korea 1 384 259
India 2 064 436
Japan 4 548 953
China 10 961 623

Gross National Income in US $ millions

Asia: Climate

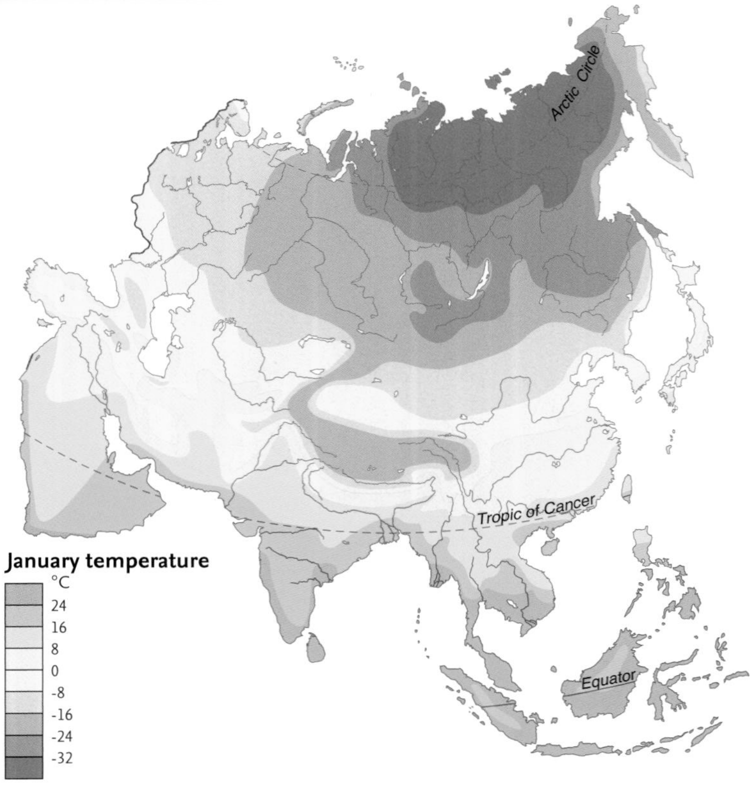

January temperature
°C
24
16
8
0
-8
-16
-24
-32

Scale 1 : 100 000 000

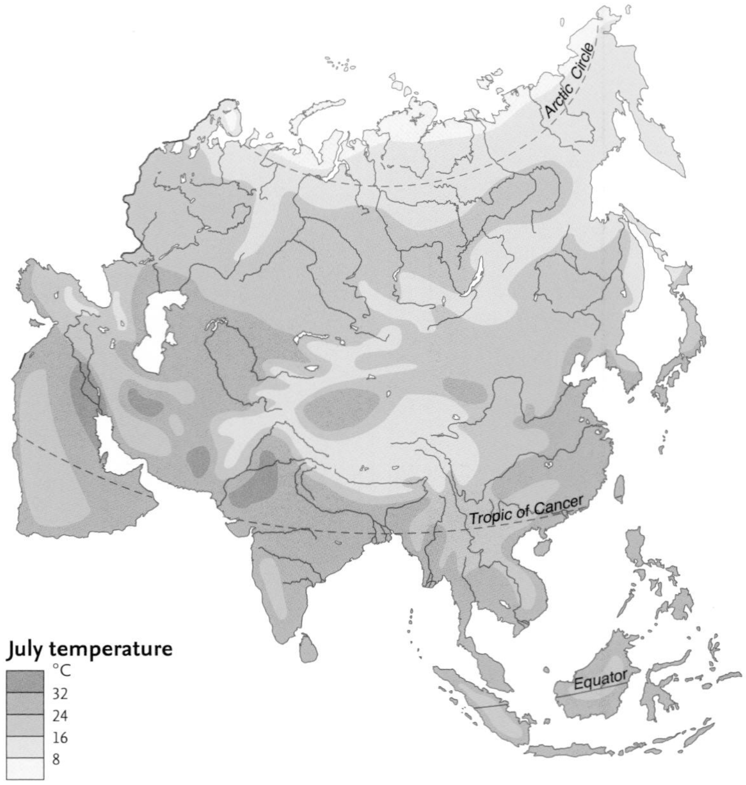

July temperature
°C
32
24
16
8

Scale 1 : 100 000 000

Arctic Circle

Tropic of Cancer

Equator

Climate graphs

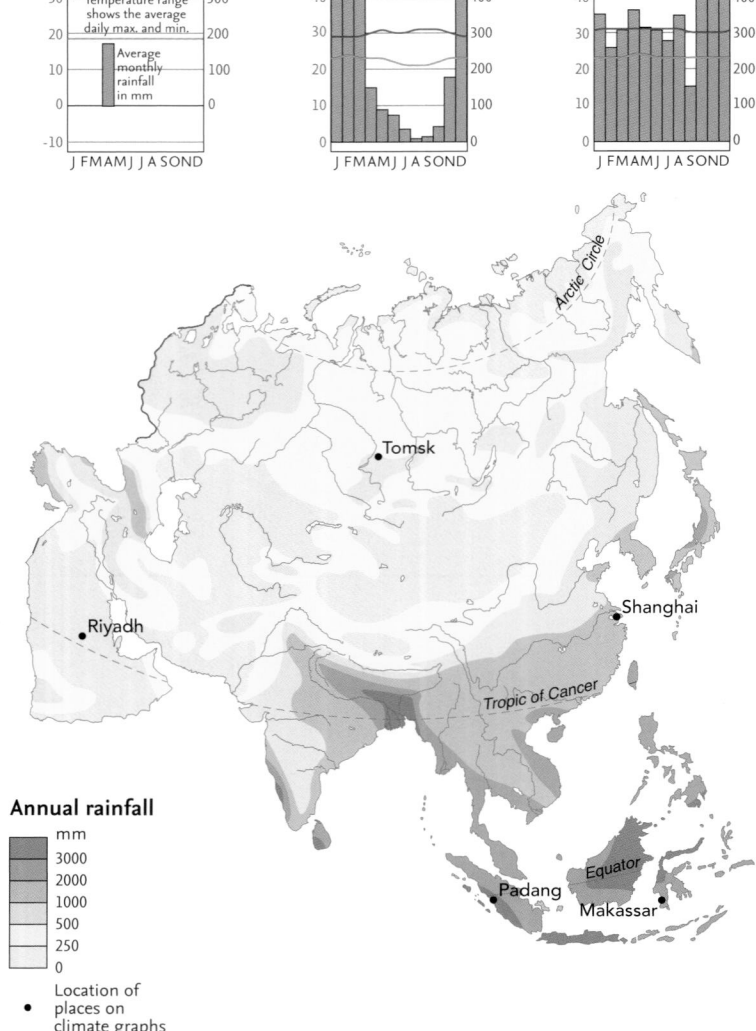

Town
°C
40
30
20
10
0
-10
mm
400
300
200
100
0

Altitude in metres above sea level

Temperature range shows the average daily max. and min.

Average monthly rainfall in mm

J F M A M J J A S O N D

Makassar
Altitude 2 m
°C
mm
700
600
500
400
300
200
100
0
J F M A M J J A S O N D

Padang
Altitude 7 m
°C
50
40
30
20
10
mm
500
400
300
200
100
0
J F M A M J J A S O N D

Riyadh
Altitude 590 m
°C
50
40
30
20
10
mm
500
400
300
200
100
0
J F M A M J J A S O N D

Shanghai
Altitude 7 m
°C
50
40
30
20
10
mm
500
400
300
200
100
0
J F M A M J J A S O N D

Tomsk
Altitude 122 m
°C
30
20
10
0
-10
-20
-30
mm
300
200
100
0
J F M A M J J A S O N D

Tomsk

Shanghai

Riyadh

Padang

Makassar

Tropic of Cancer

Equator

Arctic Circle

Annual rainfall
mm
3000
2000
1000
500
250
0

● Location of places on climate graphs

Scale 1 : 100 000 000

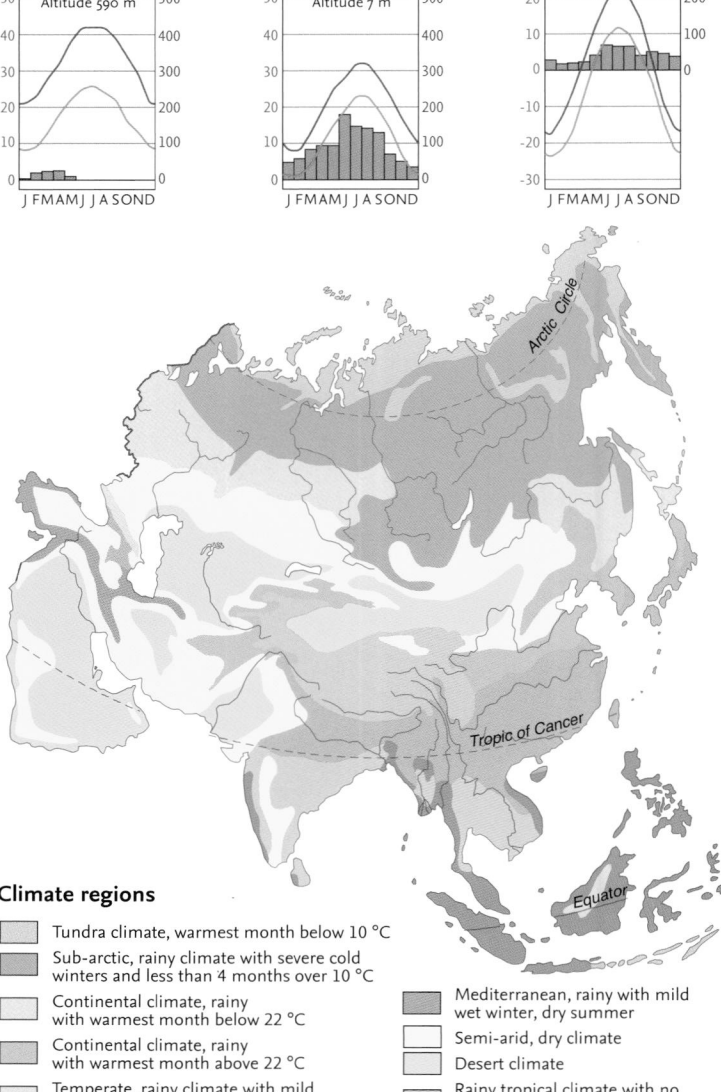

Arctic Circle

Tropic of Cancer

Equator

Climate regions

Tundra climate, warmest month below 10 °C

Sub-arctic, rainy climate with severe cold winters and less than 4 months over 10 °C

Continental climate, rainy with warmest month below 22 °C

Continental climate, rainy with warmest month above 22 °C

Temperate, rainy climate with mild winter, coolest month above 0 °C

Wet subtropical, coolest month above 0 °C, warmest month above 22 °C

Mediterranean, rainy with mild wet winter, dry summer

Semi-arid, dry climate

Desert climate

Rainy tropical climate with no winter, coolest month above 18 °C

Rainy tropical climate, constantly wet throughout the year

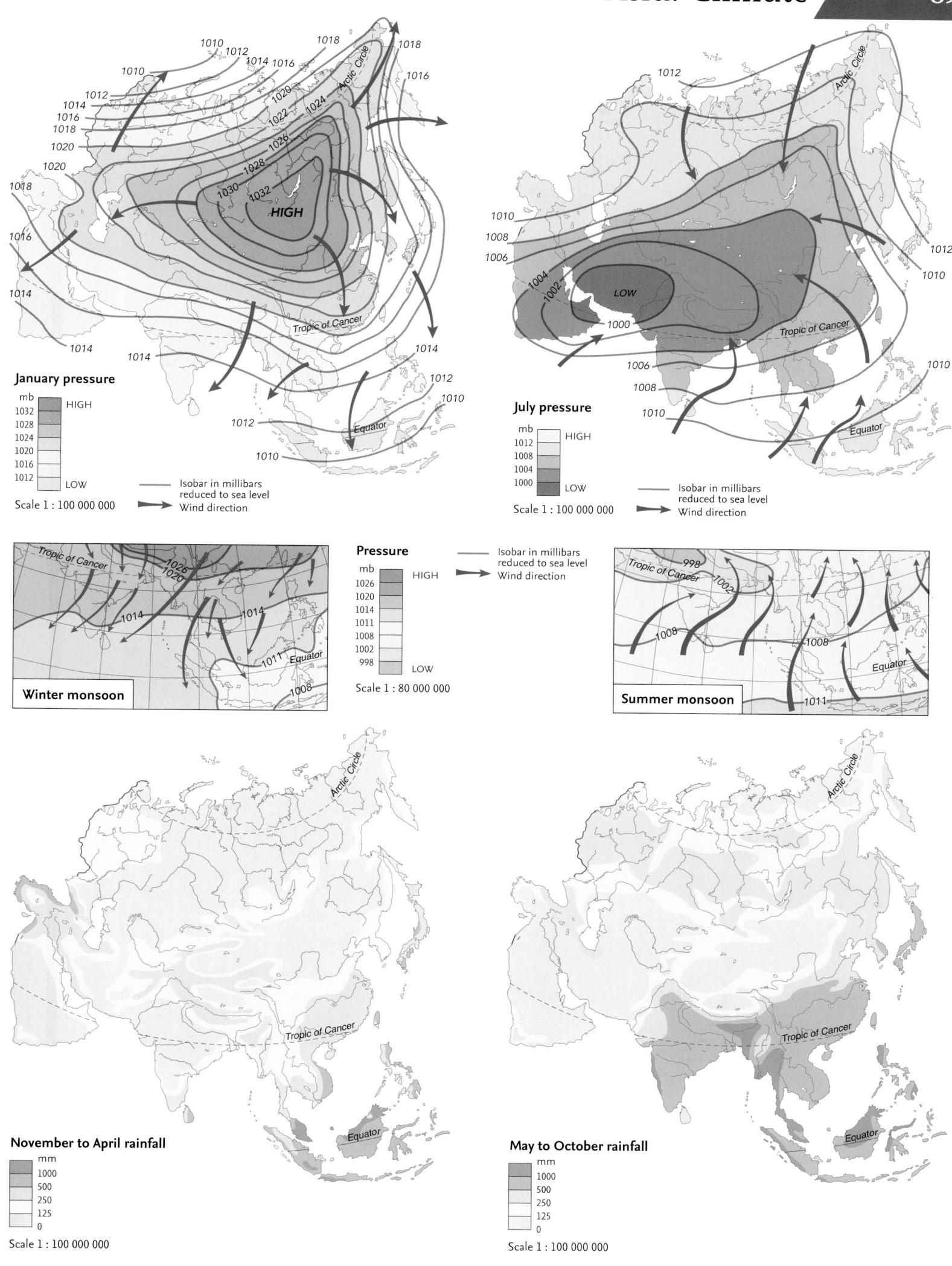

January pressure

mb
1032 HIGH
1028
1024
1020
1016
1012 LOW

Scale 1 : 100 000 000

— Isobar in millibars reduced to sea level
➤ Wind direction

July pressure

mb
1012 HIGH
1008
1004
1000 LOW

Scale 1 : 100 000 000

— Isobar in millibars reduced to sea level
➤ Wind direction

Winter monsoon

Pressure

mb
1026 HIGH
1020
1014
1011
1008
1002
998 LOW

Scale 1 : 80 000 000

— Isobar in millibars reduced to sea level
➤ Wind direction

Summer monsoon

November to April rainfall

mm
1000
500
250
125
0

Scale 1 : 100 000 000

May to October rainfall

mm
1000
500
250
125
0

Scale 1 : 100 000 000

Asia: Population and Cities

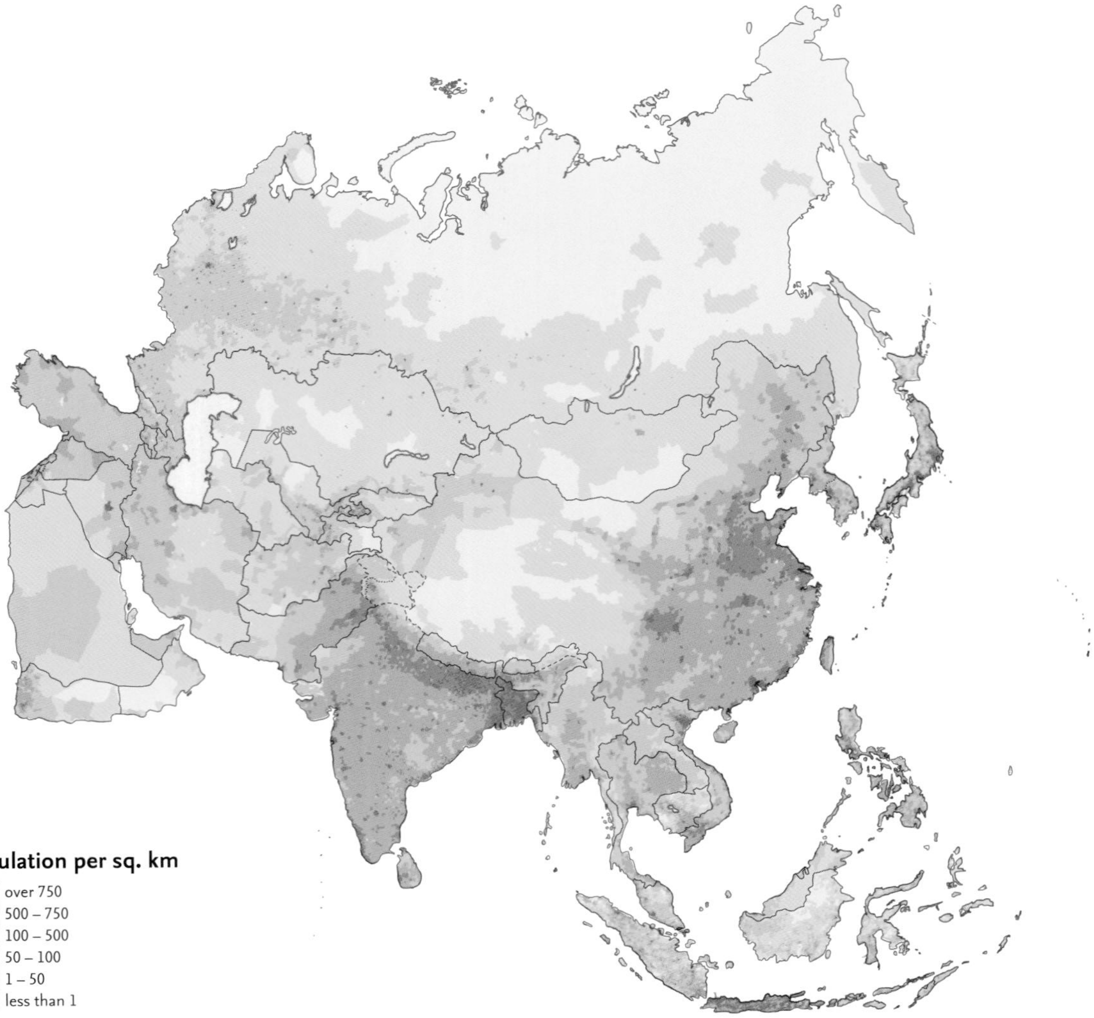

Top 10 densely populated countries, 2015

Country	Pop. per sq. km
Singapore	8770
Bahrain	1993
Maldives	1221
Bangladesh	1118
Taiwan	648
Lebanon	560
South Korea	507
India	414
Israel	365
Philippines	336

Population per sq. km

- over 750
- 500 – 750
- 100 – 500
- 50 – 100
- 1 – 50
- less than 1

Scale 1 : 75 000 000

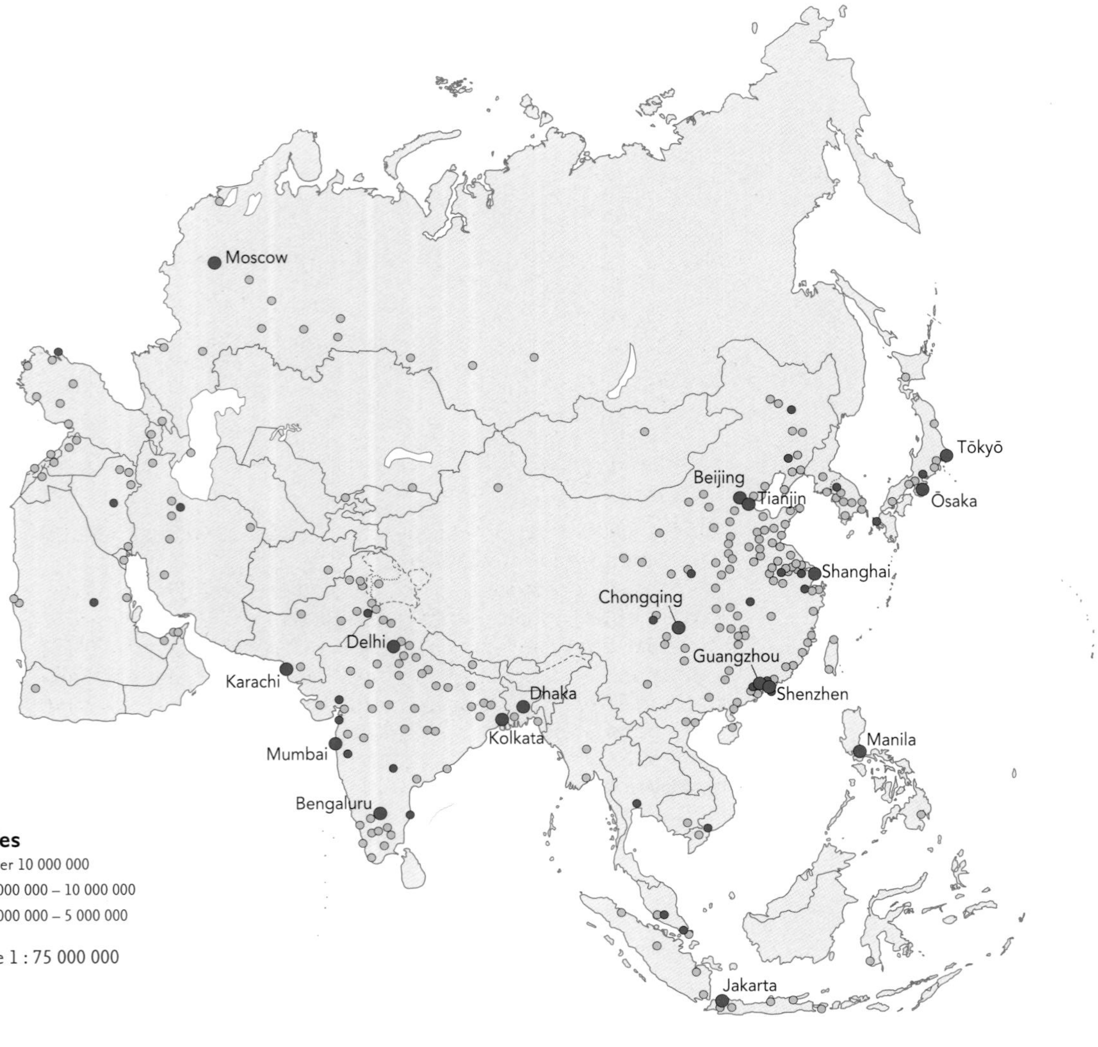

Population pyramids, 2015

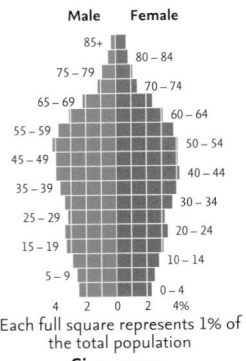

Each full square represents 1% of the total population

Singapore

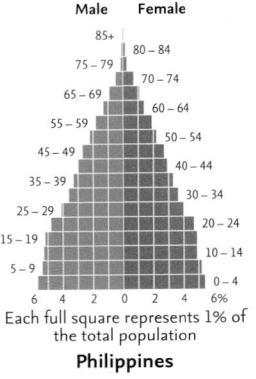

Each full square represents 1% of the total population

Philippines

Population growth, 1950 – 2050

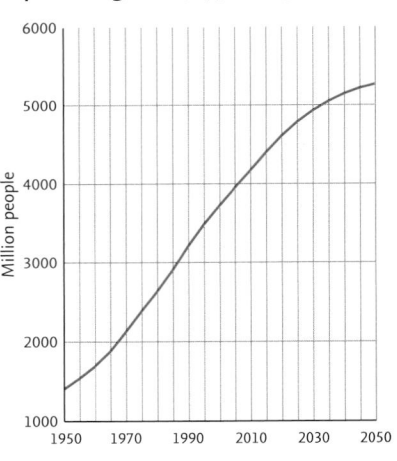

Cities

- ● over 10 000 000
- ● 5 000 000 – 10 000 000
- ○ 1 000 000 – 5 000 000

Scale 1 : 75 000 000

Top 5 largest urban agglomerations, 2015

Urban agglomeration	Population
Tōkyō (Japan)	38 001 018
Delhi (India)	25 703 168
Shanghai (China)	23 740 778
Mumbai (India)	21 042 538
Beijing (China)	20 383 994

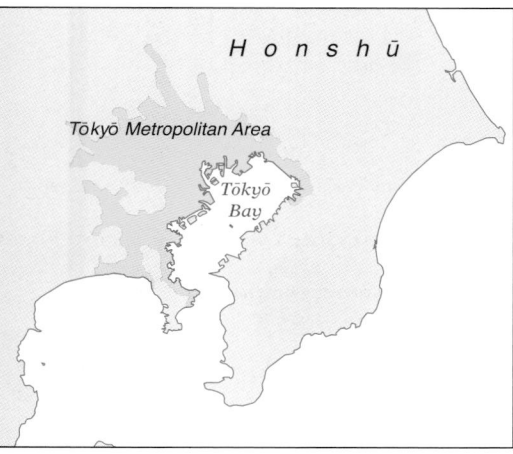

Tōkyō, the capital of Japan, has been the world's most populous metropolitan area since 1970.

This false-colour Landsat 7 image shows this vast conurbation, situated on the eastern shore of the Japanese island of Honshū. Tōkyō Bay dominates the centre of this scene. The greater Tōkyō area fans out in a crescent shape around the western, northern, and eastern shores of Tōkyō Bay. Pressure on the land has led to major land reclamation projects in the bay – obvious from the angular shape of the coastline. Tōkyō International airport is built entirely on reclaimed land.

Asia: Land Use

Urban

Cropland

Cropland and woodland

Grassland and grazing

Grassland and woodland

Temperate forest

Tropical forest

Coniferous forest

Scrubland or desert

Swamp and marsh

Tundra

Scale 1 : 50 000 000

Land use by region, 2014

Arable land

Permanent crops

Forest

Other

Russia

Central

Western   Eastern

Southern

Southeastern

Asia

15.5%   2.8%

62.6%   19.1%

Western Asia

1.2%
8.1%   4.1%

86.6%

Russia

7.5%   0.1%

42.6%   49.8%

Central Asia

0.2%
9.6%   3.0%

87.2%

Southern Asia

34.4%

48.1%

14.7%   2.8%

Eastern Asia

1.5%
9.9%

66.5%   22.1%

Southeastern Asia

16.0%

25.0%   10.3%

48.7%

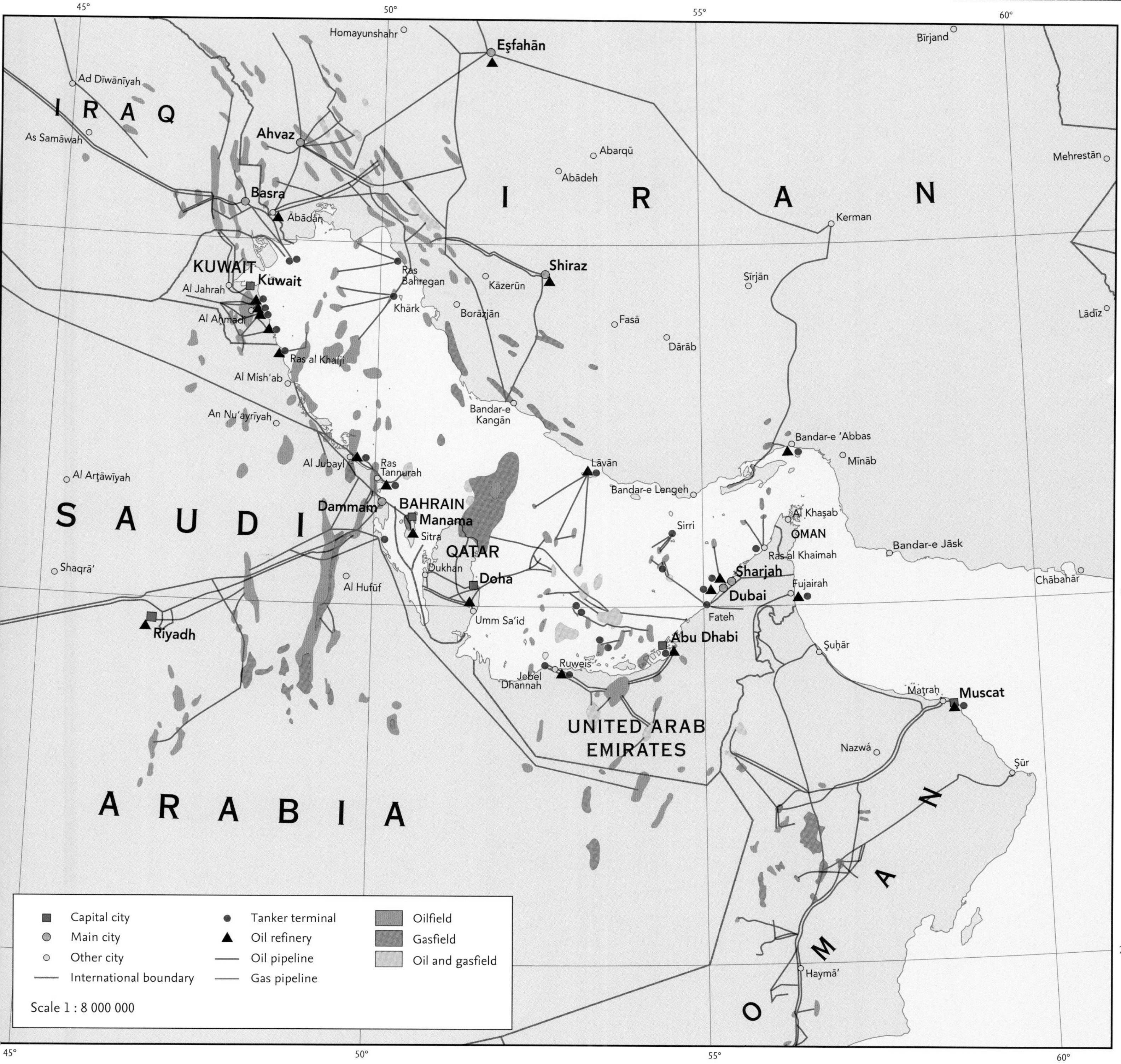

45° 50° 55° 60°

Homayunshahr
Eşfahān
Bīrjand

Ad Dīwānīyah
I R A Q
I R A N
Mehrestān

As Samāwah
Ahvaz
Abarqū
Abādeh
30°

Basra
Ābādān
Kerman

KUWAIT
Kuwait
Ras Bahregan
Kāzerūn
Shiraz
Sīrjān
Lādīz

Al Jahrah
Khārk
Borāzjān
Fasā

Al Aḥmadi
Dārāb

Ras al Khafji

Al Mish'ab

An Nu'ayrīyah
Bandar-e Kangān
Bandar-e 'Abbās
Mīnāb

Al Arṭāwīyah
Al Jubayl
Ras Tannurah
Lāvān
Bandar-e Lengeh
Bandar-e Jāsk
25°

S A U D I
Dammam
BAHRAIN
Manama
Sitra
Sirri
Al Khaṣab
OMAN
Ras al Khaimah

Shaqrā'
QATAR
Dukhan
Doha
Sharjah
Dubai
Fujairah
Chābahār

Al Hufūf
Umm Sa'id
Fateh
Ṣuḥār

Rīyadh
Abu Dhabi

Jebel Dhannah
Ruweis
Maṭraḥ
Muscat

A R A B I A
UNITED ARAB EMIRATES
Nazwá
Şūr

O M A N

Haymā'

Legend:
- ■ Capital city
- ◉ Main city
- ○ Other city
- — International boundary
- ● Tanker terminal
- ▲ Oil refinery
- — Oil pipeline
- — Gas pipeline
- ▨ Oilfield
- ▨ Gasfield
- ▨ Oil and gasfield

Scale 1 : 8 000 000

Oil and gas production

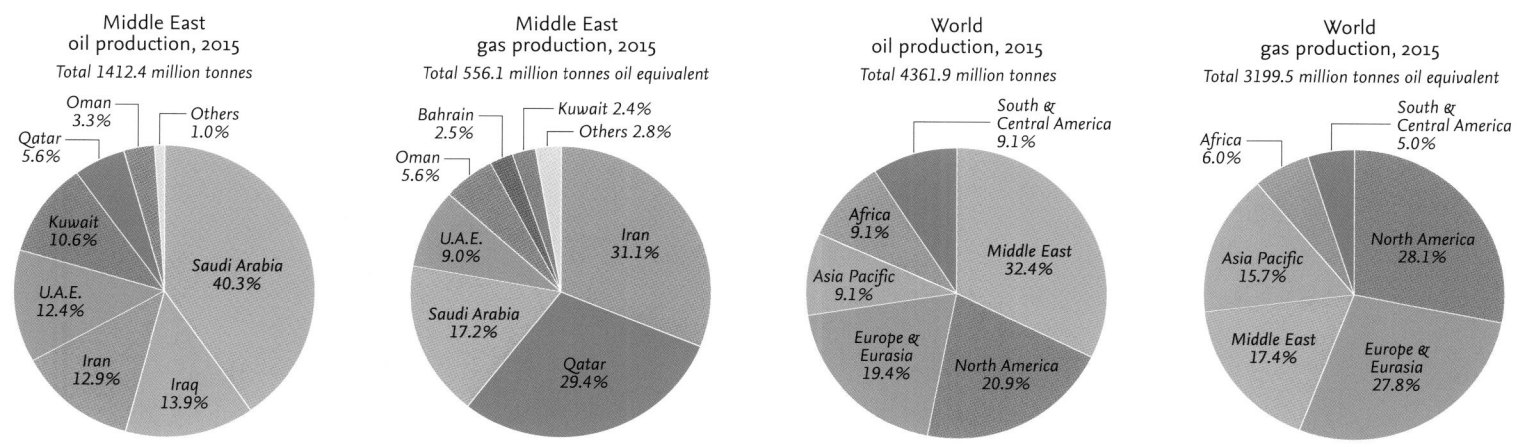

Middle East oil production, 2015
Total 1412.4 million tonnes

- Oman 3.3%
- Others 1.0%
- Qatar 5.6%
- Kuwait 10.6%
- U.A.E. 12.4%
- Iran 12.9%
- Iraq 13.9%
- Saudi Arabia 40.3%

Middle East gas production, 2015
Total 556.1 million tonnes oil equivalent

- Bahrain 2.5%
- Kuwait 2.4%
- Others 2.8%
- Oman 5.6%
- U.A.E. 9.0%
- Saudi Arabia 17.2%
- Qatar 29.4%
- Iran 31.1%

World oil production, 2015
Total 4361.9 million tonnes

- South & Central America 9.1%
- Africa 9.1%
- Asia Pacific 9.1%
- Europe & Eurasia 19.4%
- North America 20.9%
- Middle East 32.4%

World gas production, 2015
Total 3199.5 million tonnes oil equivalent

- South & Central America 5.0%
- Africa 6.0%
- Asia Pacific 15.7%
- Middle East 17.4%
- North America 28.1%
- Europe & Eurasia 27.8%

GREECE

Aegean Sea

TURKEY

Mediterranean Sea

CYPRUS

SYRIA

LEBANON

ISRAEL

JORDAN

EGYPT

LIBYA

Cyrenaica

Libyan Desert

Western Desert

Great Sand Sea

Calanscio Sand Sea

Rebiana Sand Sea

As Sarīr

Tropic of Cancer

CHAD

Erdi

Dépression du Mourdi

Massif Ennedi

Marra Plateau

SUDAN

Nubian Desert

Baiyuda Desert

Jebel Abyad Plateau

White Nile

Blue Nile

Nuba Mountains

ERITREA

ETHIOPIA

DJIBOUTI

SAUDI ARABIA

An Nafūd

Najd

Red Sea

Hijaz

Tihāmah

Sinai

Gulf of Suez

Gulf of Aqaba

Eastern Desert

Syrian Desert

Al Widyān

Al Hamad

IRAQ

Lake Nasser

Lake Nubia

Ankara • Yerevan • ARMENIA • Gyumri • Mt Ararat 5165

Athens • İzmir • Konya • Adana • Antalya • Aleppo • Mosul • Baghdad • Damascus • Beirut • Jerusalem • Amman • Cairo • Alexandria • Giza • Khartoum • Omdurman • Asmara • San'a • Djibouti • Mecca • Jeddah • Medina

AZERBAIJAN
TURKMENISTAN
UZBEKISTAN
TAJIKISTAN
Pamir
IRAN
AFGHANISTAN
PAKISTAN
INDIA
OMAN
UNITED ARAB EMIRATES
QATAR
BAHRAIN
KUWAIT
YEMEN

Caspian Sea
Karakum Desert
Gulf of Oman
Arabian Sea
Gulf of Aden
The Gulf
Strait of Hormuz

Baku, Xankändi, Qoris, van, Ahar, Tabrïz, Sarab, e Sahand, 3710, Marägheh, Miändoäb, häbad, Zänjän, Saqqez, Bijär, Sanandaj, n, häbäd-e Gharb, änshäh, Nahävand, Malayer, Borüjerd, Khorramäbäd, l 'Küt, Dezfül, Shüshtar, Susangerd, An Näsiriyah, Ahväz, Abadan, Basra, KUWAIT, Al Jahrah, Kuwait, Al Farwaniyah, Al Ahmadï, Al Mish'ab

Ardabïl, Bandar-e Anzalï, Rasht, Lähïjän, Qazvïn, Chalus, Ghaem Shahr, Amol, Sari, Karaj, Tehran, 5601, Qolleh-ye Damävand, Qom, Hamadän, Aräk, Golpäyegän, Khunsär, Homayunshahr, Najafäbäd, Esfahän, Shahr-e Kord, Shahreza, Käshän, Ardestän, Nä'ïn, Yazd, Bäfq, Abädeh, Abarqü, Eqlïd, Shïräz, Neyrïz, Fasä, Däräb, Jahrom, Lämerd, Firüzäbäd, Lämerd, Boräzjän, Bandar-e Büshehr, Farräshband, Käzerün, Masjed Soleymän, Ramhormoz, Kühe Dïnär 4432, 4074, Zarand, Rafsanjän, Kermän, Sïrjän, 4420, Bäft, Bäm, Kermän Desert

Turkmenbaşy, Nebitdag, Cheleken, Gumdag, Gyzylarbat, Bakharden, Ashgabat, Gonbad-e Kavus, Gorgän, Bojnürd, Qüchan, Mashhad, Neyshäbür, Sabzevär, Shährüd, Dämghän, Semnän, Mayamey, Ferdows, Torbat-e Jäm, Torbat-e Heydarïyeh, Käshmar, Herät, Tedzhen, Mary, Kerki, Andkhvoy, Sheberghän, Sar-e Pol, Meymaneh, Bala Morghäb, Chaghcharän, Hari Rüd, Faräh, Deläräm, Gereshk, Kandahär, Chaman, Mehrestän, Dasht-e Märgow, Dasht-e Arbu Lut, Gowd-e Zerah, Helmand

Dasht-e Kavïr, Kavïr-i-Namak, Qä'en, Bïrjand, Dasht-e Lut, Namakzär-e Shadad, Daryächeh-ye Sïstän, Zähedän, Lädïz, Khäsh, Nok Kundï, Dalbandïn, Raskoh, Chagai Hills, BALOCHISTAN, Hamun-i-Mashkel, Siahan Range, Saravän, Panjgür, Nagha, Kalat, Tump, Turbat, Gwadar, Pasni, Jiwani, Chäbahär, Makran, Bandar-e Jäsk, Iränshahr, Mïnäb, Hämün-e Jaz Müriän, Bandar-e 'Abbäs, Qeshm, Biaban, Bandar-e Lengeh, Al Khasab

Buxoro, Qarshi, Turkmenabat, Kelifskiy Uzboy, Termiz, Sho'rchi, Dushanbe, 4425, Külob, Khorugh, Feyzäbäd, Mazar-e Sharïf, Khanabad, Baghlän, Kholm, Bämïän, Kühe Bäbä, Kabul, Chärïkär, Jaläläbäd, Gardez, Khowst, Khyber Pass, Peshawar, Islamabad, Rawalpindi, Kohat, Banmi, Khänbäbäd, Barikot, Chitral, Drosh, Mongora, Gilgit, Mardan, Abbottäbäd, Nowshera, Talagang, Hindu Kush, Paropamisus, Kerki

HAZARAJAT, Ghaznï, Kälät, Zhob, Dera Ismä'ïl Khan, Lakki, Leiah, Tank, Mastung, Quetta, Nushki, Surab, Kalat, Jacobabad, Shikärpür, Jämpur, Rajanpur, Khanpur, Rahimyar Khan, Sukkur, Jacobabad, Sulaiman Range, Sibi, Loralai, Dera Ghazï Khan, Muzaffargarh, Multan, Bahawalpur, Ahmadpur East, Khanewal, Thal Desert, Faisalabad, Jhang, Sargodha, Daud Khel, Mianwali

Dahnä', Dammam, Dhahran, Abqaiq, Al Ghwaybiyah, Manama, BAHRAIN, QATAR, Dukhan, Doha, Al Hufüf, Ad, wiyah, Riyadh, Al Biyädh, Sulayyil, Rub' al Khälï, Ar Rimäl, Al Qa'ämïyät, Al Hïbak, Al Jubayl, Ras Tannurah, An Nu'ayrïyah, Sharjah, Dubai, Fujairah, Abu Dhabi, Al Buraymï, Al Khaburah, Sühär, Muscat, Matrah, Nazwä, Ibrä, Jabal Akhdar, Nu'aym, Sür, Ra's al Hadd, Jazïrat Masïrah, Khalïj Masïrah, Haymä', Jiddat al Haräsïs, Ra's Madrakah, Dawqah, Juzur al Halänïyät, Salälah, Mirbät, Jabal Mahrät, Al Ghaydah, Al Mahrah, Ra's Fartak, Sayhüt, Ash Shihr, Mukalla, Shibäm, Tarïm, Hadramawt, Habbän, N, MEN, Socotra (Yemen)

Scale 1 : 12 000 000

Relief and physical features

Relief metres: 5000, 3000, 2000, 1000, 500, 200, sea level, 0, 200, 4000, 6000, under sea level

5601 ▲ Mountain height (in metres)

Permanent ice (ice cap or glacier)

Water features

River
Intermittent river
Lake / Reservoir
Intermittent lake
Marsh

Communications

Railway
Road
⊕ Main airport

Administration

Boundaries
International
Disputed
Ceasefire line

Settlement

Cities and towns in order of size

National capital
■ Cairo

Other city or town
● Adana
● Medina
○ Port Sudan
· Kerma

0 150 300 450 km

Albers Conic Equal Area projection

Legend

Relief and physical features

Relief
metres
5000
3000
2000
1000
500
200
sea level
under sea level
0
200
4000
6000

8848 ▲ Mountain height
(in metres)

Permanent ice
(ice cap or glacier)

Water features

~ River
Intermittent river
Canal
Lake / Reservoir
Intermittent lake
Marsh

Communications

Railway
Road
⊕ Main airport

Administration

Boundaries

International
Disputed
Internal
Ceasefire line

Settlement

Cities and towns in order of size

National capital
■ Dhaka

Other city or town
● Mumbai
● Jaipur
● Ranchi
○ Jammu
○ Ghazni

Scale 1 : 15 000 000
0   150   300   450 km

Lambert Azimuthal Equal Area projection

Map labels

TURKMENISTAN
Mary
Kūlob
Dushanbe
TAJIKISTAN
Andkhvoy
Termiz
Khorugh
Qiemo
Mashhad
Neyshābūr
Sheberghan
Mazār-e Sharif
Taklimakan Desert
Meymaneh
Bala Morghab
XINJIANG UYGUR ZIZHIQU
Hotan
Herat
Hindu Kush
Chārīkār
Chitral
Gilgit
K2 8611
Karakoram Range
AKSAI CHIN
Administered by China
KUNLUN SHAN
Chaghcharan
Kābul
Administered by Pakistan Kashmir
Peshawar
Srinagar
JAMMU AND KASHMIR
Administered by India
AFGHANISTAN
HAZARAJAT
Ghaznī
Islamabad
Rawalpindi
Leh
Gar
Sutak
Dërub
Plateau of Tib
Farāh
Gereshk
Jammu
HIMACHAL
XIZANG ZIZHI
Sīl
Kermān
Bīrjand
Mehrestān
Dasht-e Mārgow
Dera Ismail Khan
Gujranwala
Lahore
Amritsar
PRADESH
Jalandhar
Ludhiana
Chandigarh
Dehra Dun
UTTARAKHAND
Yazd
Bafq
Helmand
Kandahār
Sargodha
Faisalabad
Dhaulagiri
Annapurna
8167 8091
Mount Everest
8848
Lhaze
IRAN
Dasht-e Lut
Chaman
Quetta
Dera Ghazi Khan
Multan
PUNJAB
HARYANA
Meerut
NEPAL
Kathmandu
Kangche
858
Sīrjān
Kermān Desert
Zāhedān
Lādīz
Chagai Hills
Mach
Jampur
Bahawalpur
Sutlej
Ahmadpur East
Delhi
Ghaziabad
Bareilly
UTTAR
Fatehgarh
Mathura
Gorakhpur
Darjiling
Hāmūn-e Jaz Mūriān
Khāsh
BALOCHISTAN
PAKISTAN
Khanpur
Rahimyar Khan
Bikaner
New Delhi
Faridabad
Agra
Lucknow
Bandar-e Abbās
Hamun-i-Mashkel
Shikarpur
Jacobabad
Wad
Sikar
PRADESH
Kanpur
Ghaghara
Darbhanga
Muzaffarpur
Al Khaşab
Trānshahr
Larkana
Sukkur
Jaisalmer
Jodhpur
Jaipur
Gwalior
Jhansi
Yamuna
Ganges
Allahabad
Varanasi
Patna
Munger
BIHAR
Bhagalpur
Gulf of Oman
Turbat
Bela
Nawabshah
Tando Adam
RAJASTHAN
Kota
Guna
Rewa
Mirzapur
Gaya
Rajshal
Asans
OMAN
Chābahār
Gwadar
Hyderabad
Mirpur Khas
Pali
Barmer
Udaipur
Sagar
Katni
JHARKHAND
Dhanbad
WES
BENG
Makran
Karachi
Mouths of the Indus
Indus
Bhuj
GUJARAT
Gandhinagar
Ahmadabad
MADHYA PRADESH
Bhopal
Jabalpur
Ranchi
Jamshedpur
Gulf of Kachchh
Gandhidham
Surendranagar
Indore
Khandwa
Gondia
Sambalpur
Bilaspur
Kharagpur
Okha
Jamnagar
Vadodara
Rajkot
Narmada
Satpura Range
CHHATTISGARH
Baleshwar
Porbandar
Bhavnagar
Tapti
Burhanpur
Nagpur
Raipur
ODISHA
Cuttack
Diu
Surat
INDIA
Jalgaon
Amravati
Kanker
Bhubaneswar
Daman
Dhule
Manmad
Jalna
Chandrapur
Jagdalpur
Puri
Nashik
Aurangabad
Godavari
Brahmapur
Mumbai
MAHARASHTRA
Deccan
Nizamabad
Pune
Solapur
TELANGANA
Warangal
Vizianagaram
Arabian Sea
Bidar
Bhima
Kalaburagi
Secunderabad
Rajahmundry
Vishakhapatnam
Kolhapur
Sangli
Vijayapura
Hyderabad
Eluru
Kakinada
Krishna
Vijayawada
Panaji
GOA
Raichur
Kurnool
Krishna
Guntur
Machilipatnam
Dharwad
Ballari
ANDHRA
Hubballi
PRADESH
Ongole
Davangere
Kadapa
Nellore
KARNATAKA
Chittradurga
Shivamogga
Tumakuru
Chittoor
Udupi
Mangaluru
Nilgiri Hills
Bengaluru
Vellore
Chennai
Kanchipuram
LAKSHADWEEP
Mysuru
Salem
Puducherry
Kozhikode
Erode
Cuddalore
Kumbakonam
Lakshadweep
Tiruppur
Tiruchchirappalli
Coimbatore
TAMIL NADU
Dindigul
Malabar Coast
KERALA
Kochi
Madurai
Jaffna
Alappuzha
Palk Strait
SRI LANKA
Trincomalee
Kollam
Thiruvananthapuram
Tuticorin
Puttalam
Batticaloa
Laccadive Sea
Nagercoil
Kurunegala
Kandy
Badulla
MALDIVES
Sri Jayewardenepura Kotte
Colombo
Adam's Peak 2243
Male
Galle
Matara
INDIA
B e
B a

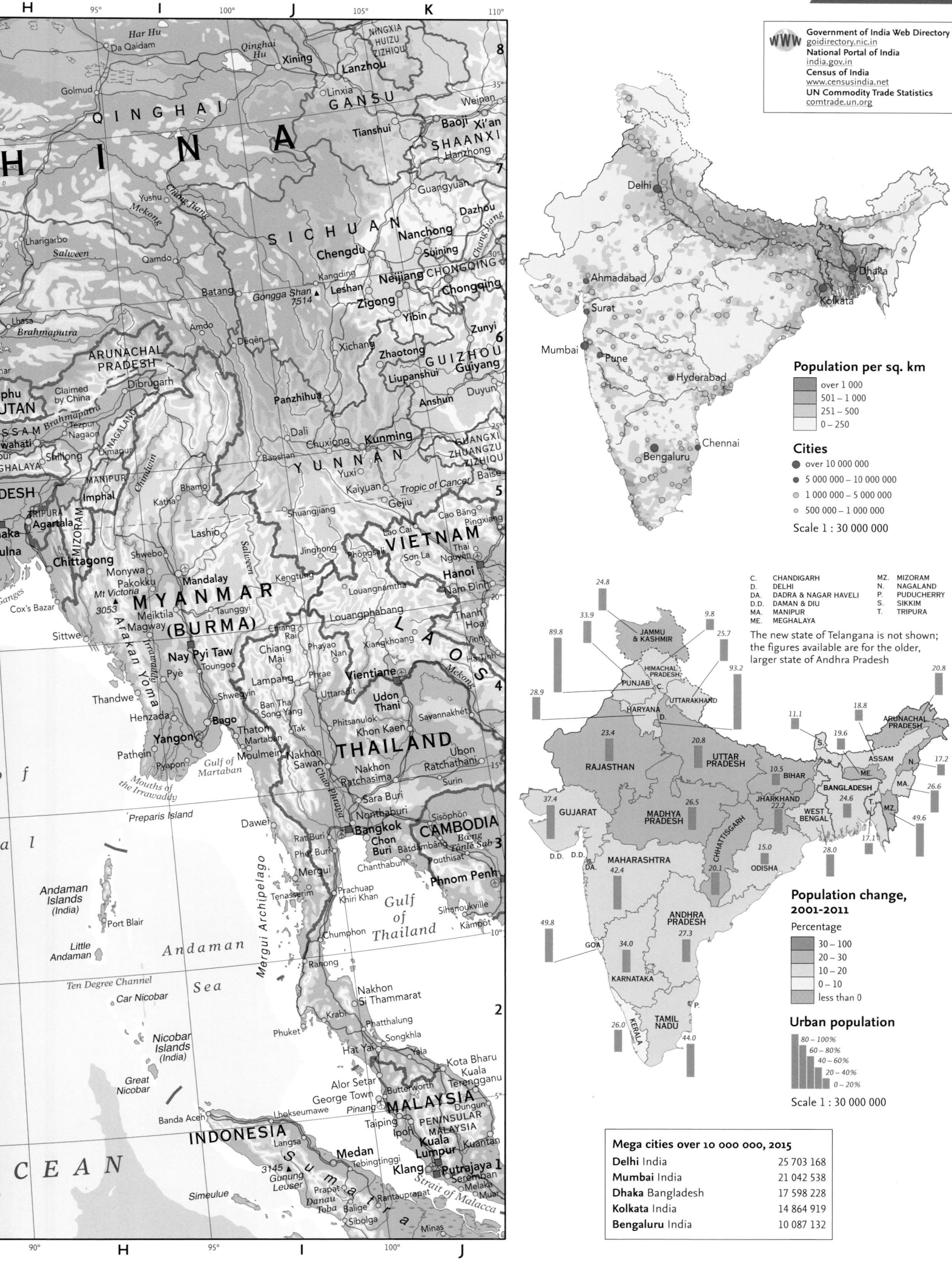

H 95° **I** 100° **J** 105° **K** 110°

Har Hu
Da Qaidam
Qinghai Hu
Golmud
Xining 8
Lanzhou
Golmud
Linxia GANSU
QINGHAI Baoji Xi'an 7
Tianshui SHAANXI
Hanzhong
Lharigarbo HINA Guangyuan
SICHUAN Dazhou
Yushu Nanchong
Mekong Chengdu Chang-Jiang
Chang Jiang Suining CHONGQING 30°
Lhasa Qamdo Gongga Shan Leshan Neijiang Chongqing
Brahmaputra Batang 7514 Zigong
Amdo Yibin Zunyi 6
ARUNACHAL Degen Xichang Zhaotong GUIZHOU
PRADESH Panzhihua Liupanshui Guiyang
phu Dibrugarh Anshun Duyun
Claimed Dali Duyun
UTAN by China Tezpur Baoshan Chuxiong Kunming GUANGXI 25°
Brahmaputra Nagaon ZHUANGZU
SSAM NAGALAND Yuxi ZHIQIU
wahati Shillong Dimapur YUNNAN Gejiu Cao Bang Baise
GHALAYA MANIPUR Bhamo Kaiyuan Tropic of Cancer Pingxiang
ESH Imphal Katha Shuangjiang Lao Cai VIETNAM
TRIPURA MIZORAM Lashio Jinghong Phongsali Son La Ngyuen 20°
ka Agartala Shwebo Kengtung Louangnamtha Hanoi
ulna Chittagong Monywa Mandalay Chiang Nam Dinh
Pakokku Mt Victoria Taunggyi Rai Louangphabang LAOS Thanh
Ganges 3053 Meiktila Phayao Xiangkhoang Hoa
Cox's Bazar Magway MYANMAR Chiang Nan Vinh
Sittwe (BURMA) Mai Vientiane 15°
Nay Pyi Taw Lampang Phrae
Pye Uttaradit
Thandwe Toungoo Phitsanulok Udon
Arakan Yoma Shwegyin Ban Tha Thani
Henzada Song Yang Tak Khon Kaen
Yangon Bago Thaton Savannakhet
Pathein Martaban THAILAND Ubon
Moulmein Nakhon Nakhon Ratchathani 15°
Gulf of Sawan Ratchasima Surin
Martaban Chao Phraya Sara Buri
Mouths of Nonthaburi Sisophon
the Irrawaddy Dawei Bangkok CAMBODIA
Preparis Island Rat Buri Chon Bang
Phet Buri Buri Batdambang Tonle Sap 3
Chanthaburi Pouthisat
Mergui Phnom Penh
Tenasserim Prachuap Sihanoukville
Andaman Khiri Khan Kampot
Islands Gulf
(India) of 10°
Port Blair Chumphon Thailand
Little Rahong
Andaman Nakhon
Ten Degree Channel Si Thammarat
Car Nicobar Sea Krabi
Phatthalung 2
Phuket Songkhla
Nicobar Hat Yai Yala
Islands Kota Bharu
(India) Kuala
Great Alor Setar Terengganu
Nicobar George Town Butterworth Dungun
Pinang MALAYSIA
Banda Aceh Taiping PENINSULAR
INDONESIA Ipoh MALAYSIA Kuantan 1
3145 Kuala
Gunung Klang Lumpur
Leuser Putrajaya
Simeulue Seremban
Danau Prapat Strait of Malacca
Toba Balige Muar
Sibolga
Minas

CEAN

H 90° **I** 95° **J** 100°

www Government of India Web Directory
goidirectory.nic.in
National Portal of India
india.gov.in
Census of India
www.censusindia.net
UN Commodity Trade Statistics
comtrade.un.org

Delhi
Ahmadabad
Surat Dhaka
Mumbai Kolkata
Pune
Hyderabad

Population per sq. km
- over 1 000
- 501 – 1 000
- 251 – 500
- 0 – 250

Bengaluru Chennai

Cities
- ● over 10 000 000
- ● 5 000 000 – 10 000 000
- ○ 1 000 000 – 5 000 000
- ○ 500 000 – 1 000 000

Scale 1 : 30 000 000

C.	CHANDIGARH	MZ.	MIZORAM
D.	DELHI	N.	NAGALAND
DA.	DADRA & NAGAR HAVELI	P.	PUDUCHERRY
D.D.	DAMAN & DIU	S.	SIKKIM
MA.	MANIPUR	T.	TRIPURA
ME.	MEGHALAYA		

The new state of Telangana is not shown;
the figures available are for the older,
larger state of Andhra Pradesh

24.8
33.9 9.8
89.8 JAMMU 25.7
& KASHMIR
HIMACHAL 93.2
28.9 PRADESH
PUNJAB C. UTTARAKHAND 20.8
HARYANA D. 11.1 18.8
23.4 20.8 ARUNACHAL
RAJASTHAN UTTAR 19.6 PRADESH
PRADESH S. 17.2
37.4 10.5 BIHAR ME. ASSAM N.
GUJARAT BANGLADESH MA. 26.6
26.5 JHARKHAND T.
D.D. D.D. MADHYA 22.2 WEST 49.6
DA. PRADESH BENGAL MZ.
15.0 24.6 17.1
MAHARASHTRA CHHATTISGARH 28.0
42.4 20.1 ODISHA
49.8 ANDHRA
GOA PRADESH
34.0 27.3
KARNATAKA
26.0 KERALA P.
TAMIL
44.0 NADU

Population change, 2001-2011

Percentage
- 30 – 100
- 20 – 30
- 10 – 20
- 0 – 10
- less than 0

Urban population
- 80 – 100%
- 60 – 80%
- 40 – 60%
- 20 – 40%
- 0 – 20%

Scale 1 : 30 000 000

Mega cities over 10 000 000, 2015	
Delhi India	25 703 168
Mumbai India	21 042 538
Dhaka Bangladesh	17 598 228
Kolkata India	14 864 919
Bengaluru India	10 087 132

Relief and physical features

Relief
metres
5000
3000
2000
1000
500
200
sea level
under sea level
200
4000
6000

▲ 8848 Mountain height
(in metres)

Permanent ice
(ice cap or glacier)

Water features

River

Intermittent river

Canal

Lake / Reservoir

Intermittent lake

Marsh

Communications

Railway

Road

⊕ Main airport

Administration

Boundaries

International

Disputed

Internal

Ceasefire line

Settlement

Cities and towns in order of size

National capital   Other city or town

■ Beijing   ● Mumbai
                    ● Yantai
                    ● Anshun
                    ○ Bikaner
                    ○ Lhasa

Scale 1 : 15 000 000

0   150   300   450 km

Conic Equidistant projection

MONGOLIA
GOLIA

Gobi

NEI MONGOL ZIZHIQU (INNER MONGOLIA)

Ulan Bator

Irkutsk · Slyudyanka · Angarsk · Zima · Kachug · Khorinsk · Ulan-Ude · Kyakhta · Darhan · Sretensk · Chita · Karymskoye · Borzya · Manzhouli · Choybalsan · Baruun Urt
Hövsgöl Nuur · Mörön · Bulgan · Tsetserleg · Bayanhongor · Arvayheer · Mandalgovi · Saynshand · Xilinhot · Hohhot · Baotou · Wuhai

Lake Baikal · Yablonovyy Khrebet · Da Hinggan Ling

MANCHURIA
HEILONGJIANG
Daqing · Qiqihar · Fuyu · Yichun · Hegang · Jiamusi · Jixi · Harbin · Mudanjiang · Songyuan · Baicheng · Taonan · Ullanhot · Nenjiang · Bei'an · Svobodnyy · Blagoveshchensk · Birobidzhan · Khabarovsk · Komsomol'sk-na-Amure · El'ban

JILIN
Changchun · Jilin · Yanji · Siping · Liaoyuan · Tonghua · Ch'ongjin · Ussuriysk · Vladivostok · Nakhodka · Lake Khanka

LIAONING
Shenyang · Fuxin · Fushun · Benxi · Anshan · Yingkou · Dandong · Chengde · Chifeng · Jinzhou · Lianshan · Qinhuangdao · Hamhŭng · Wŏnsan · Kimch'aek

NORTH KOREA
P'yŏngyang · Namp'o · Kaesŏng · Haeju · Chuncheon

SOUTH KOREA
Seoul · Incheon · Koyang · Daejeon · Jeonju · Gwangju · Daegu · Busan · Masan · Cheju-do

Sea of Japan (East Sea)

JAPAN
Honshū · Hiroshima · Okayama · Kōbe · Tottori · Matsuyama · Fukuoka · Kōchi · Shikoku · Kumamoto · Kyūshū · Kita-Kyūshū · Sasebo · Nagasaki · Kagoshima · Miyazaki · Oki-shotō · Tsushima · Korea Strait

HEBEI
Beijing · Tangshan · Tianjin · Baoding · Shijiazhuang · Zhangjiakou · Jining · Datong

Huang He · Yangquan · Taiyuan · Dezhou · Dongying · Yantai · Weihai
Bo Hai · Dalian · Korea Bay

SHANXI
Xingtai · Handan · Linqing · Changzhi · Linfen · Jiaozuo

SHANDONG
Jinan · Zibo · Weifang · Qingdao · Xintai · Rizhao · Jining · Heze · Zaozhuang · Lianyungang · Zhangshu · Yancheng

NINGXIA HUIZU ZIZHIQU · Yinchuan · Shizuishan · Wuhai
Qinghai Hu · Xining · Lanzhou · Linxia · Wuwei · Tianshui · Baoji

SHAANXI
Xi'an · Pingdingshan · Hanzhong · Weinan · Luoyang · Zhengzhou

HENAN
Nanyang · Zaoyang · Xinyang · Kaifeng · Shangqiu · Xinxiang · Anyang

Yellow Sea

JIANGSU
Xuzhou · Suqian · Huaibei · Suzhou · Yangzhou · Nantong · Zhangshu · Yancheng

HUBEI
Wuhan · Yichang · Jingzhou · Jingmen · Suizhou · Xiangyang · Dazhou · Enshi · Wanzhou

ANHUI
Hefei · Bengbu · Fuyang · Huainan · Lu'an · Tongling · Wuhu

East China Sea

ZHEJIANG
Hangzhou · Ningbo · Shaoxing · Jinhua · Quzhou · Taizhou · Wenzhou · Cixi

Shanghai · Suzhou · Wuxi · Changzhou · Zhenjiang · Nanjing · Jiaxing

SICHUAN
Chengdu · Nanchong · Suining · Neijiang · Leshan · Yibin · Zigong · Kangding · Gongga Shan 7514▲

CHONGQING · Chongqing

GUIZHOU
Guiyang · Anshun · Duyun · Zunyi · Zhaotong · Panzhihua · Liupanshui

HUNAN
Changsha · Zhuzhou · Xiangtan · Changde · Yiyang · Yueyang · Hengyang · Yongzhou · Shaoyang · Chenzhou · Pingxiang

JIANGXI
Nanchang · Jingdezhen · Jiujiang · Ji'an · Ganzhou · Nanping

Dongting Hu · Poyang Hu · Chang Jiang

FUJIAN
Fuzhou · Putian · Quanzhou · Xiamen · Sanming · Zhangping · Jinjiang · Meizhou · Jieyang · Matsu Tao

TAIWAN
Taipei · Keelung · Hsinchu · Taichung · Jiayi · Tainan · Kaohsiung · Tāitung

China claims Taiwan as its 23rd province

PACIFIC OCEAN
Ryukyu Islands · Okinawa · Naha

GUANGDONG
Guangzhou · Shenzhen · Foshan · Zhongshan · Jiangmen · Huizhou · Lufeng · Puning · Shantou · Hong Kong · Macao (Aomen)

GUANGXI ZHUANGZU ZIZHIQU
Nanning · Liuzhou · Guilin · Wuzhou · Yulin · Baise · Hechi · Qinzhou · Beihai · Pingxiang · Zhanjiang

YUNNAN
Kunming · Yuxi · Chuxiong · Dali · Kaiyuan · Gejiu · Jinghong · Shuangjiang

Xi Jiang · Nan Ling

HAINAN · Haikou · Qionghai · Dongfang

Gulf of Tongking · Leizhou Bandao

VIETNAM
Hanoi · Hai Phong · Nam Dinh · Thai Binh · Thanh Hoa · Vinh · Son La · Lao Cai · Cao Bằng · Thai Nguyen · Phongsali

LAOS
Louangphabang · Louangnamtha · Jinghong

PHILIPPINES
Luzon · Laoag · Aparri · Tuguegarao · San Fernando · Ilagan · Batan Islands · Babuyan Islands · Luzon Strait

China claims Taiwan as its 23rd province

China: Population

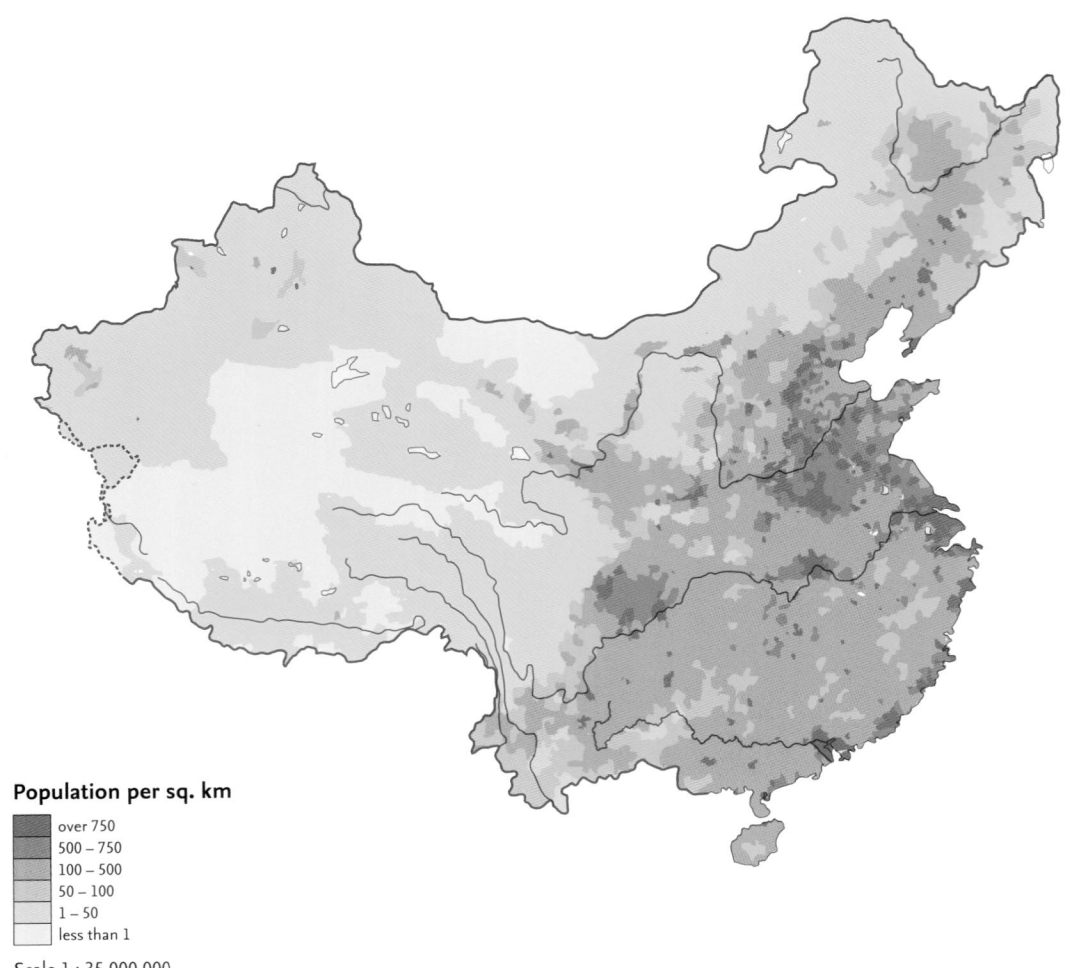

Population per sq. km

- over 750
- 500 – 750
- 100 – 500
- 50 – 100
- 1 – 50
- less than 1

Scale 1 : 35 000 000

Top 10 densely populated provinces

Province	Pop. per sq. km
Macao	21 593
Hong Kong	6634
Shanghai	3809
Beijing	1323
Tianjin	1298
Jiangsu	777
Shandong	627
Guangdong	603
Henan	568
Zhejiang	544

Population growth rates

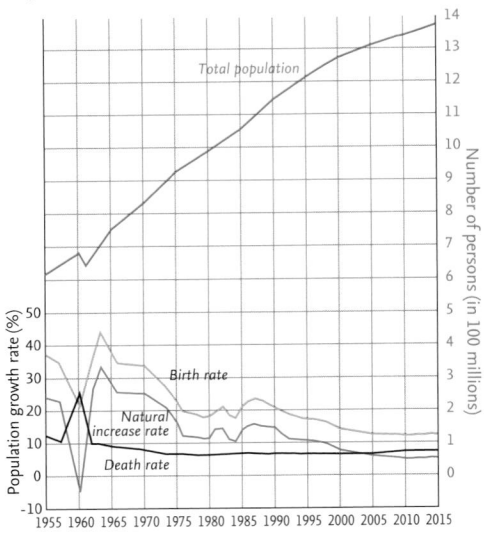

Population movement

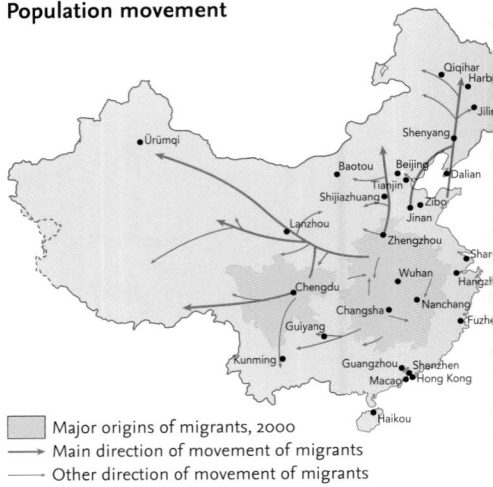

- Major origins of migrants, 2000
- → Main direction of movement of migrants
- → Other direction of movement of migrants

Scale 1 : 70 000 000

Cities

- ● over 10 000 000
- ● 5 000 000 – 10 000 000
- ● 1 000 000 – 5 000 000
- ● 500 000 – 1 000 000

Scale 1 : 35 000 000

Top 10 largest urban agglomerations, 2015

Urban agglomeration	Population
Shanghai	23 740 778
Beijing	20 383 994
Chongqing	13 331 579
Guangzhou	12 458 130
Tianjin	11 210 329
Shenzhen	10 749 473
Wuhan	7 905 572
Chengdu	7 555 705
Dongguan	7 434 935
Nanjing	7 369 157

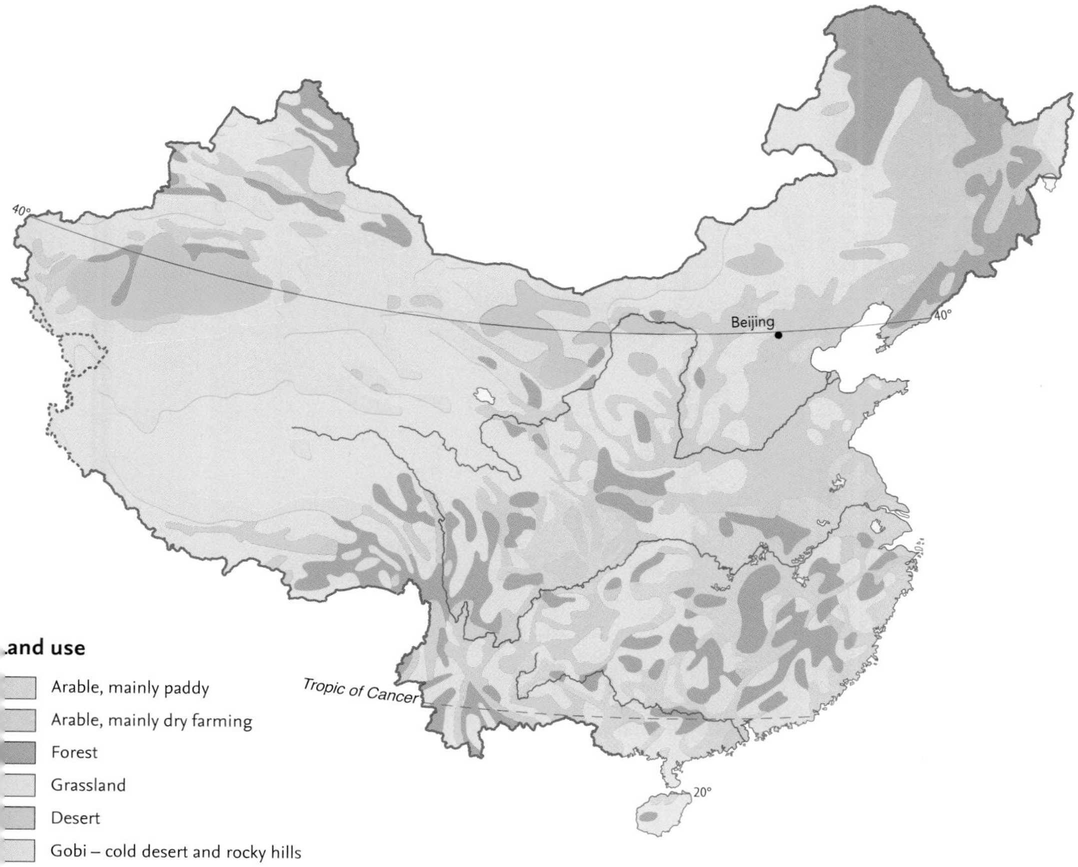

Land use

- Arable, mainly paddy
- Arable, mainly dry farming
- Forest
- Grassland
- Desert
- Gobi – cold desert and rocky hills

Scale 1 : 35 000 000

40°

Beijing

40°

Tropic of Cancer

20°

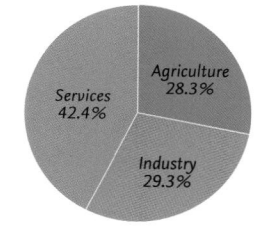

Manufacturing industry in east China

- □ Iron and steel
- □ Oil refining and petro-chemicals
- □ Shipbuilding
- □ Aircraft and aerospace
- □ Motor vehicles
- □ Engineering
- ○ Electronic and electrical goods
- ○ Chemicals
- ○ Textiles
- ● Major industrial centre

Scale 1 : 25 000 000

Shenyang Fushun
Liaoyang Benxi
Jinzhou Anshan
Huludao Yingkou Dandong
Tianjin Dalian
Yantai
Jinan Qingdao
Lianyungang
Nanjing Nantong
Shanghai
Hangzhou Ningbo
Wenzhou
Fuzhou
Guangzhou Xiamen
Shantou
Beihai Zhuhai Shenzhen
Zhanjiang
Hainan

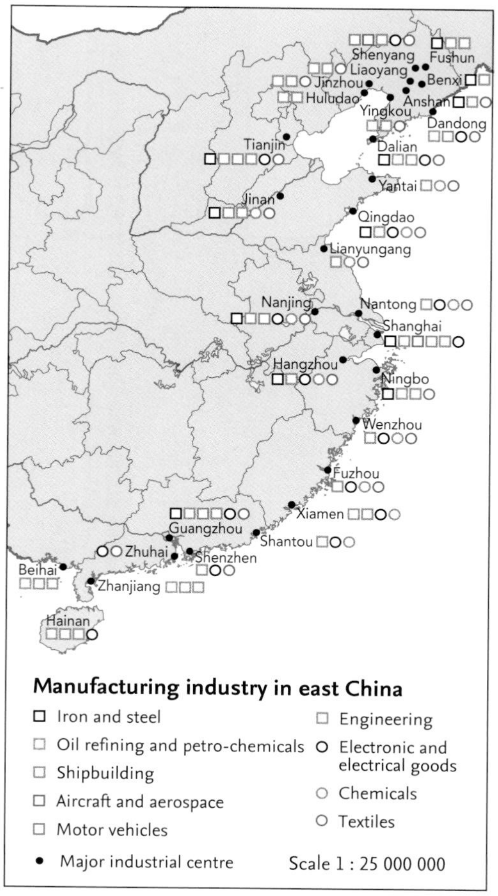

Employment by economic sector, 2015

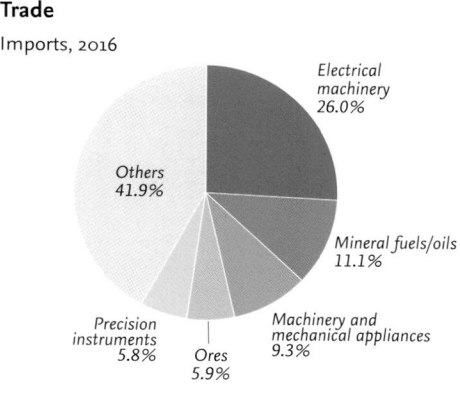

- Services 42.4%
- Agriculture 28.3%
- Industry 29.3%

Main trading partners

Imports
% of total
China* imports

- South Korea 10.0%
- Japan .2%
- USA .5%
- Germany .4%
- Australia 5%
- Malaysia 1%
- Brazil 9%
- Switzerland 5%
- Thailand 4%

Exports
% of total
China* exports

- USA 18.4%
- Hong Kong 13.7%
- Japan 6.2%
- South Korea 4.5%
- Germany 3.1%
- Vietnam 2.9%
- India 2.8%
- Netherlands 2.7%
- United Kingdom 2.7%
- Singapore 2.1%

*excluding Hong Kong and Macao

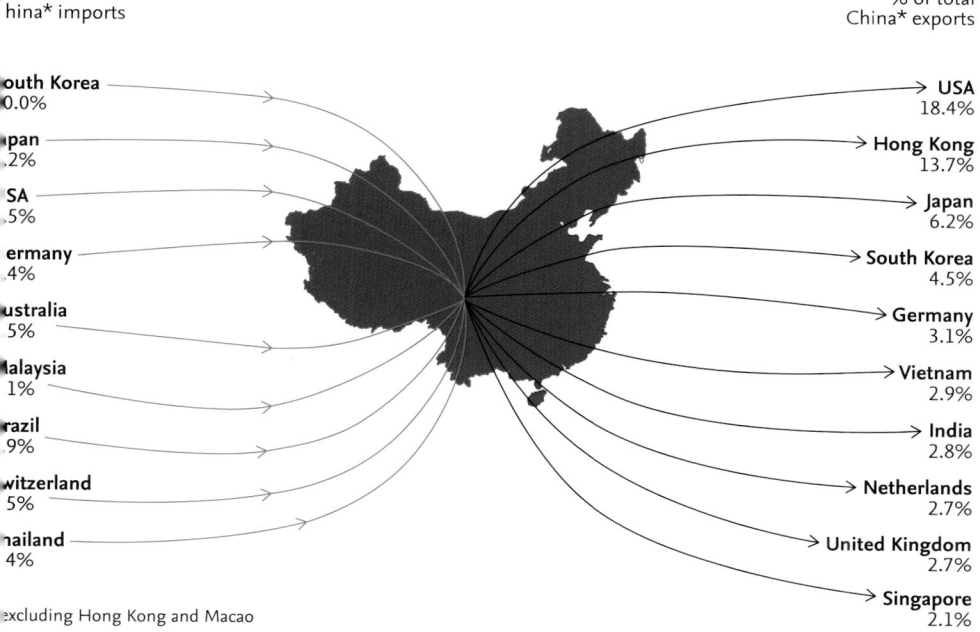

Trade

Imports, 2016

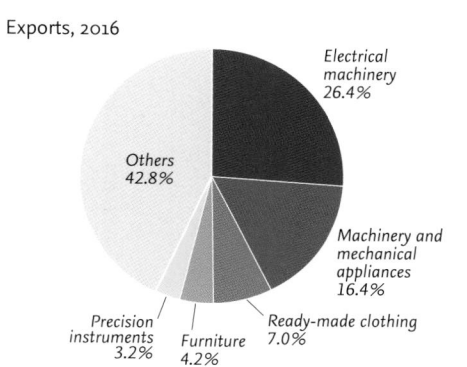

- Electrical machinery 26.0%
- Mineral fuels/oils 11.1%
- Machinery and mechanical appliances 9.3%
- Ores 5.9%
- Precision instruments 5.8%
- Others 41.9%

Exports, 2016

- Electrical machinery 26.4%
- Machinery and mechanical appliances 16.4%
- Ready-made clothing 7.0%
- Furniture 4.2%
- Precision instruments 3.2%
- Others 42.8%

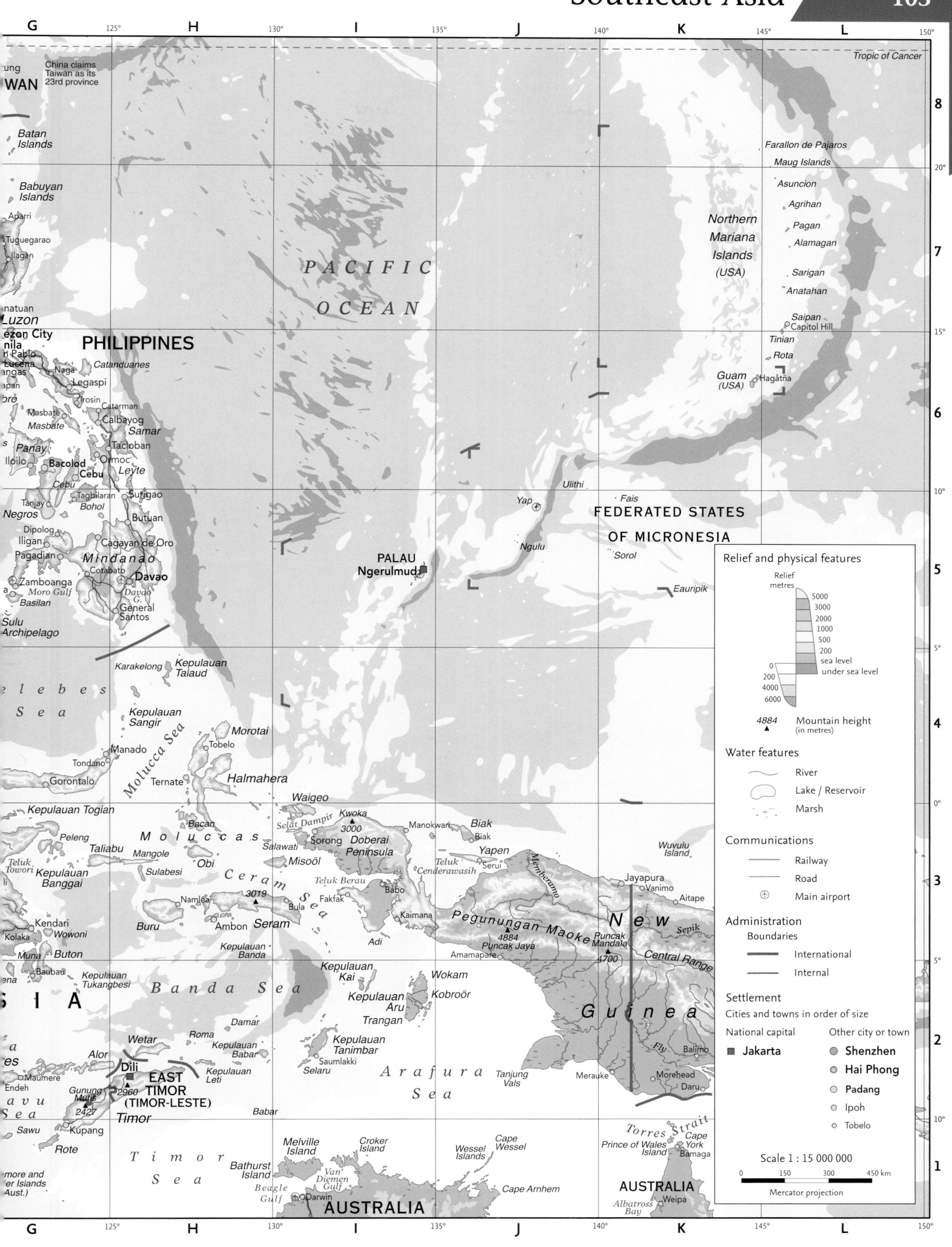

| G | | H | | I | | J | | K | | L | |

125°   130°   135°   140°   145°   150°

Tropic of Cancer

8

China claims
Taiwan as its
23rd province

WAN

*Batan
Islands*

Farallon de Pajaros

Maug Islands

20°

*Babuyan
Islands*

Asuncion

Agrihan

Pagan

Alamagan

7

Aparri

Tuguegarao

Ilagan

natuan

Luzon

Quezon City

Manila

an Pablo

Lucena

angas

apan

oro

PHILIPPINES

PACIFIC

OCEAN

Northern
Mariana
Islands
(USA)

Sarigan

Anatahan

15°

Saipan
Capitol Hill

Tinian

Catanduanes

Naga

Legaspi

Virosin

Catarman

Samar

Calbayog

Masbate

Masbate

Tacloban

Ormoc

Leyte

Panay

Iloilo

Bacolod

Cebu

Cebu

Tagbilaran

Bohol

Surigao

Butuan

Negros

Tanjay

Dipolog

Iligan

Pagadian

Cagayan de Oro

Cotabato

Mindanao

Davao

*Davao
G.*

Rota

Guam
(USA)

Hagåtña

6

Ulithi

Yap

Fais

FEDERATED STATES

OF MICRONESIA

10°

Ngulu

PALAU
Ngerulmud

Sorol

Eauripik

5

Moro Gulf

Basilan

Zamboanga

General
Santos

*Sulu
Archipelago*

Karakelong

*Kepulauan
Talaud*

*Celebes
Sea*

*Kepulauan
Sangir*

Manado

Tondano

Gorontalo

Kepulauan Togian

*Teluk
Towori*

*Kepulauan
Banggai*

Kendari

Kolaka

Wowoni

Muna

Buton

na

Baubau

*Kepulauan
Tukangbesi*

SIA

Molucca Sea

Ternate

Morotai

Tobelo

Halmahera

Waigeo

Bacan

Selat Dampir

Sorong

Salawati

Misoöl

Obi

Moluccas

*Ceram
Sea*

Namlea

Buru

Ambon

Seram

*Kepulauan
Banda*

Banda Sea

Kwoka
▲ 3000

Doberai
Peninsula

Teluk Berau

Babo

Fakfak

Bula

Manokwari

Biak

Biak

Yapen

Serui

*Teluk
Cenderawasih*

Kaimana

Adi

Amamapare

Jayapura

Vanimo

Aitape

*Wuvulu
Island*

New

5°

0°

▲ 3019

Pegunungan Maoke

4884 ▲
Puncak Jaya

Puncak
Mandala
▲ 4700

Memberamo

Sepik

Central Range

Guinea

5°

*Kepulauan
Kai*

Wokam

Kobroör

*Kepulauan
Aru*

Trangan

Damar

Roma

Wetar

Alor

Dili

EAST
TIMOR
(TIMOR-LESTE)

Gunung
Mutis
▲ 2960

2427

Timor

Kupang

Rote

*Kepulauan
Tanimbar*

Saumlakki

*Kepulauan
Babar*

*Kepulauan
Leti*

Selaru

Babar

*Arafura
Sea*

Tanjung
Vals

Merauke

Morehead

Daru

Fly

Balimo

Torres Strait

Prince of Wales
Island

Cape
York

Bamaga

10°

*Timor
Sea*

*Melville
Island*

*Croker
Island*

*Wessel
Islands*

*Cape
Wessel*

*Bathurst
Island*

*Van'
Diemen
Gulf*

*Beagle
Gulf*

Darwin

AUSTRALIA

Cape Arnhem

AUSTRALIA

Weipa

*Albatross
Bay*

2

1

Sawu

more and
er Islands
Aust.)

avu

Sea

Endeh

Maumere

Relief and physical features

Relief
metres

	5000
	3000
	2000
	1000
	500
	200
	sea level
	0
	under sea level
	200
	4000
	6000

4884 ▲   Mountain height
(in metres)

Water features

River

Lake / Reservoir

Marsh

Communications

Railway

Road

⊕   Main airport

Administration

Boundaries

International

Internal

Settlement

Cities and towns in order of size

National capital

■ Jakarta

Other city or town

● Shenzhen

◉ Hai Phong

◎ Padang

○ Ipoh

○ Tobelo

Scale 1 : 15 000 000

0   150   300   450 km

Mercator projection

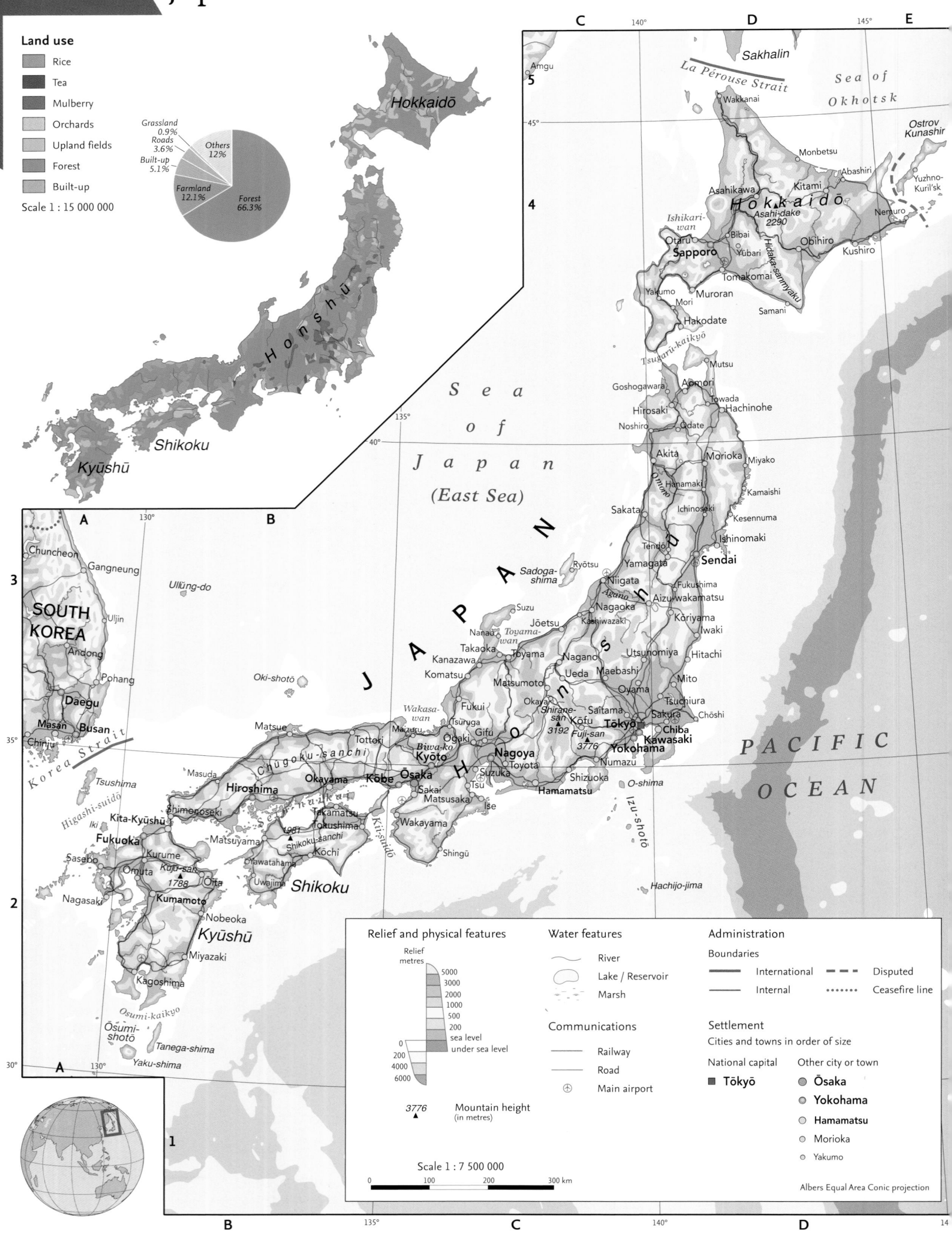

Land use

- Rice
- Tea
- Mulberry
- Orchards
- Upland fields
- Forest
- Built-up

Scale 1 : 15 000 000

Grassland 0.9%
Roads 3.6%
Built-up 5.1%
Others 12%
Farmland 12.1%
Forest 66.3%

Hokkaidō

Honshū

Shikoku

Kyūshū

Relief and physical features

Relief metres
5000
3000
2000
1000
500
200
sea level
0
under sea level
200
4000
6000

Water features

- River
- Lake / Reservoir
- Marsh

Communications

- Railway
- Road
- Main airport

3776 ▲ Mountain height (in metres)

Administration

Boundaries

- International
- Internal
- Disputed
- Ceasefire line

Settlement

Cities and towns in order of size

National capital
■ Tōkyō

Other city or town
- ◉ Ōsaka
- ◉ Yokohama
- ○ Hamamatsu
- ○ Morioka
- ○ Yakumo

Scale 1 : 7 500 000

0   100   200   300 km

Albers Equal Area Conic projection

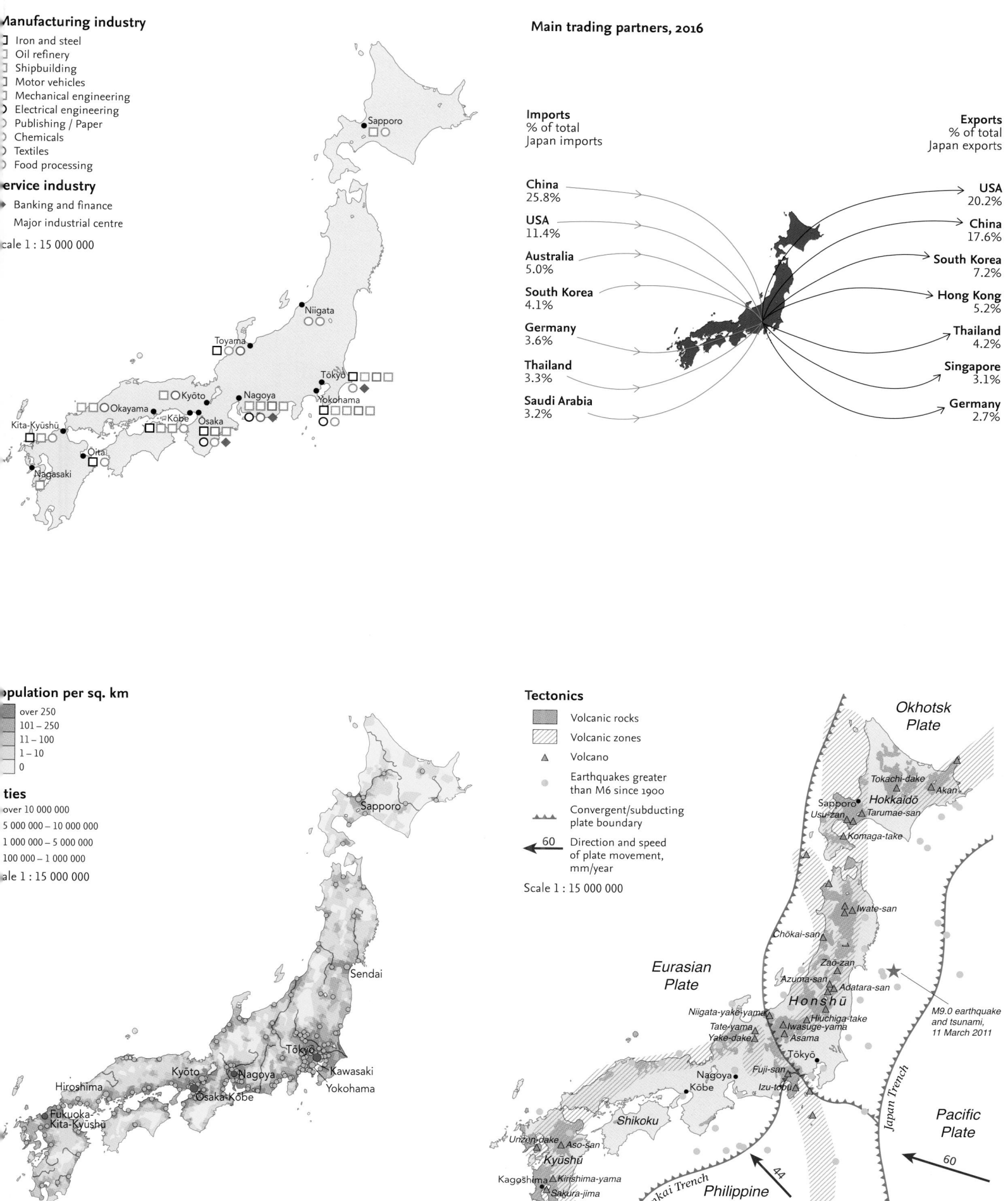

Manufacturing industry

- Iron and steel
- Oil refinery
- Shipbuilding
- Motor vehicles
- Mechanical engineering
- Electrical engineering
- Publishing / Paper
- Chemicals
- Textiles
- Food processing

Service industry

- Banking and finance
- Major industrial centre

Scale 1 : 15 000 000

Sapporo
Niigata
Toyama
Tōkyō
Kyōto
Nagoya
Yokohama
Okayama
Kōbe
Osaka
Kita-Kyūshū
Ōita
Nagasaki

Main trading partners, 2016

Imports
% of total
Japan imports

China 25.8%
USA 11.4%
Australia 5.0%
South Korea 4.1%
Germany 3.6%
Thailand 3.3%
Saudi Arabia 3.2%

Exports
% of total
Japan exports

USA 20.2%
China 17.6%
South Korea 7.2%
Hong Kong 5.2%
Thailand 4.2%
Singapore 3.1%
Germany 2.7%

Population per sq. km

- over 250
- 101 – 250
- 11 – 100
- 1 – 10
- 0

Cities

- over 10 000 000
- 5 000 000 – 10 000 000
- 1 000 000 – 5 000 000
- 100 000 – 1 000 000

Scale 1 : 15 000 000

Sapporo
Sendai
Tōkyō
Kawasaki
Yokohama
Kyōto
Nagoya
Osaka-Kōbe
Hiroshima
Fukuoka-Kita-Kyūshū

Tectonics

- Volcanic rocks
- Volcanic zones
- Volcano
- Earthquakes greater than M6 since 1900
- Convergent/subducting plate boundary
- 60 Direction and speed of plate movement, mm/year

Scale 1 : 15 000 000

Okhotsk Plate
Tokachi-dake
Akan
Sapporo
Usu-zan
Hokkaidō
Tarumae-san
Komaga-take
Iwate-san
Chōkai-san
Zaō-zan
Azuma-san
Adatara-san
Honshū
Eurasian Plate
M9.0 earthquake and tsunami, 11 March 2011
Niigata-yake-yama
Hiuchiga-take
Tate-yama
Iwasuge-yama
Yake-dake
Asama
Fuji-san
Nagoya
Izu-tōbu
Tōkyō
Kōbe
Japan Trench
Pacific Plate
60
Shikoku
Unzen-dake
Aso-san
Kyūshū
Kagoshima
Kirishima-yama
Sakura-jima
Nankai Trench
44
Philippine Sea Plate

C 120° D 140° E 160° F 180° G 16

4

Equator

Admiralty Islands

Nauru   *Gilbert Islands*   *Equator*

A S I A   *Puncak Jaya 4884▲*   *Mount Wilhelm 4509▲*   *Bismarck Sea*   *New Ireland*   *Bougainville Island*   *Solomon Islands*

New Guinea   *New Britain*   *Guadalcanal*   *Santa Cruz Islands*   **M E L A N E S I A**   *Samoa*

3   *Gulf of Papua*

Arafura Sea   *Torres Strait*   *Cape York*

Melville Island   *Arnhem Land*   *Gulf of Carpentaria*   *Cape York Peninsula*   *Coral Sea*   *Espirito Santo*   *Vanua Levu*

Timor Sea   *Fiji*   *Tomanivi 1323▲*   *Viti Levu*   *Niue*

I N D I A N   O C E A N   *Kimberley Plateau*   *Barkly Tableland*   *New Caledonia*   *Loyalty Islands*   *Tonga*

North West Cape   *Great Sandy Desert*   *MacDonnell Ranges*   *Tropic of Capricorn*

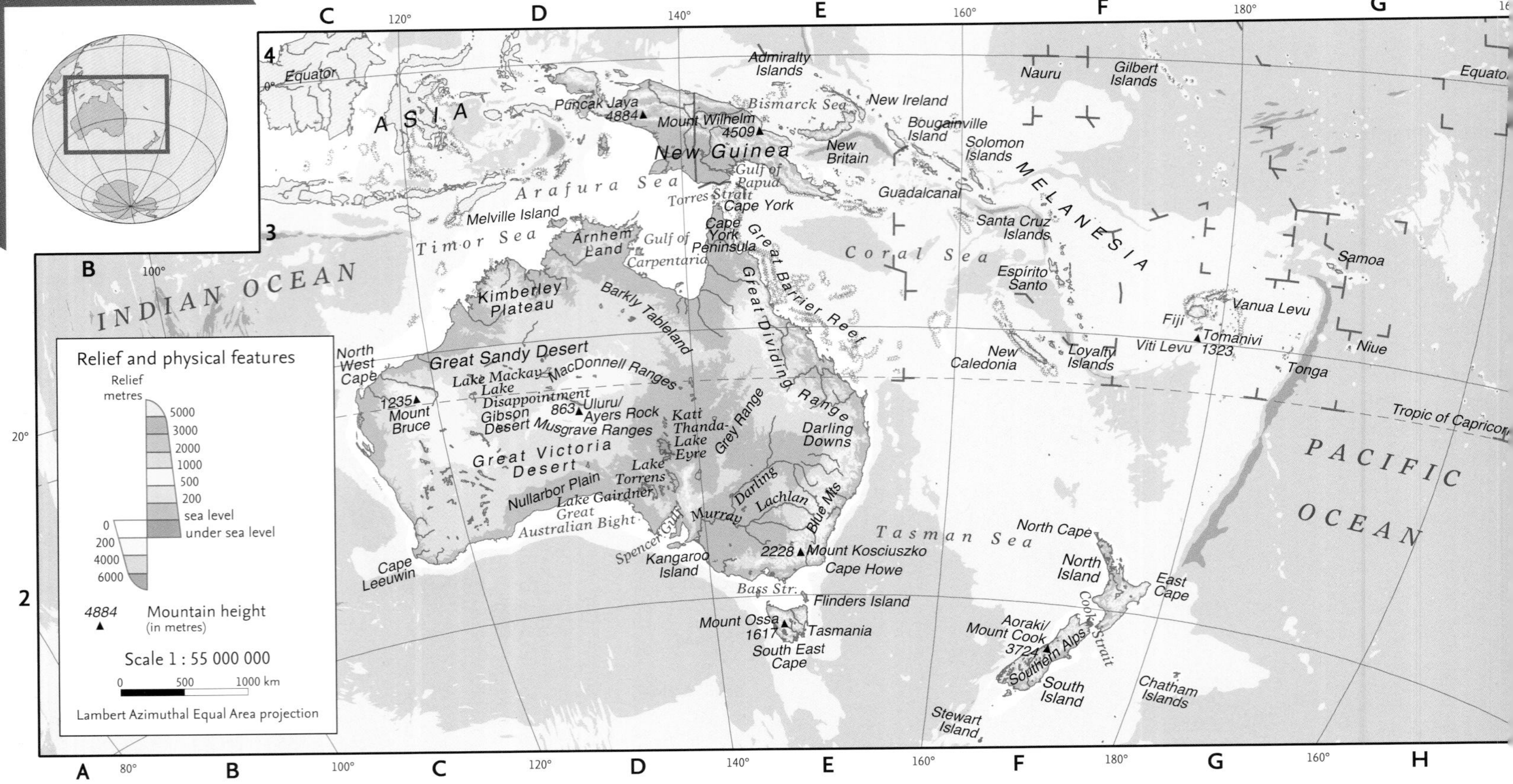

Relief and physical features
Relief metres

Lake Mackay   *Lake Disappointment*   *Uluru/ 863▲ Ayers Rock*   *Kati Thanda-Lake Eyre*   *Grey Range*   *Darling Downs*   **P A C I F I C**

20°   *1235▲ Mount Bruce*   *Gibson Desert*   *Musgrave Ranges*   *Darling*   *Lachlan*   **O C E A N**

Great Victoria Desert   *Lake Torrens*   *Blue Mts*

Nullarbor Plain   *Lake Gairdner*   *Murray*

Great Australian Bight   *Spencer Gulf*   *2228▲ Mount Kosciuszko*   *Cape Howe*

2   *Cape Leeuwin*   *Kangaroo Island*   *North Cape*   *East Cape*

4884 ▲	Mountain height (in metres)

Bass Str.   *Flinders Island*   *North Island*   *Southern Alps*

Scale 1 : 55 000 000   *Mount Ossa 1617▲*   *Tasmania*   *Aoraki/ Mount Cook 3724▲*

0   500   1000 km   *South East Cape*   *South Island*   *Chatham Islands*

Lambert Azimuthal Equal Area projection   *Stewart Island*

A 80° B 100° C 120° D 140° E 160° F 180° G 160° H

Cross-section

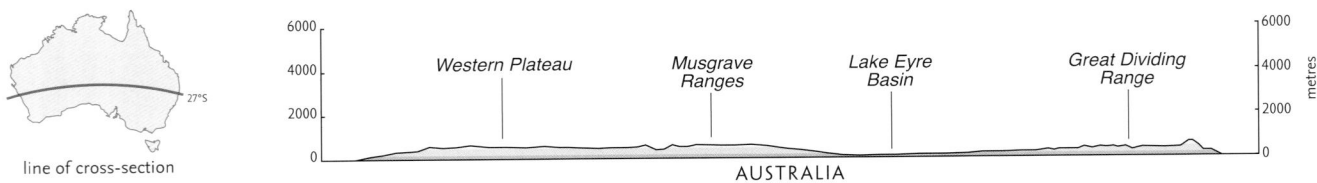

line of cross-section   27°S

Western Plateau   Musgrave Ranges   Lake Eyre Basin   Great Dividing Range   6000 4000 2000 metres

AUSTRALIA

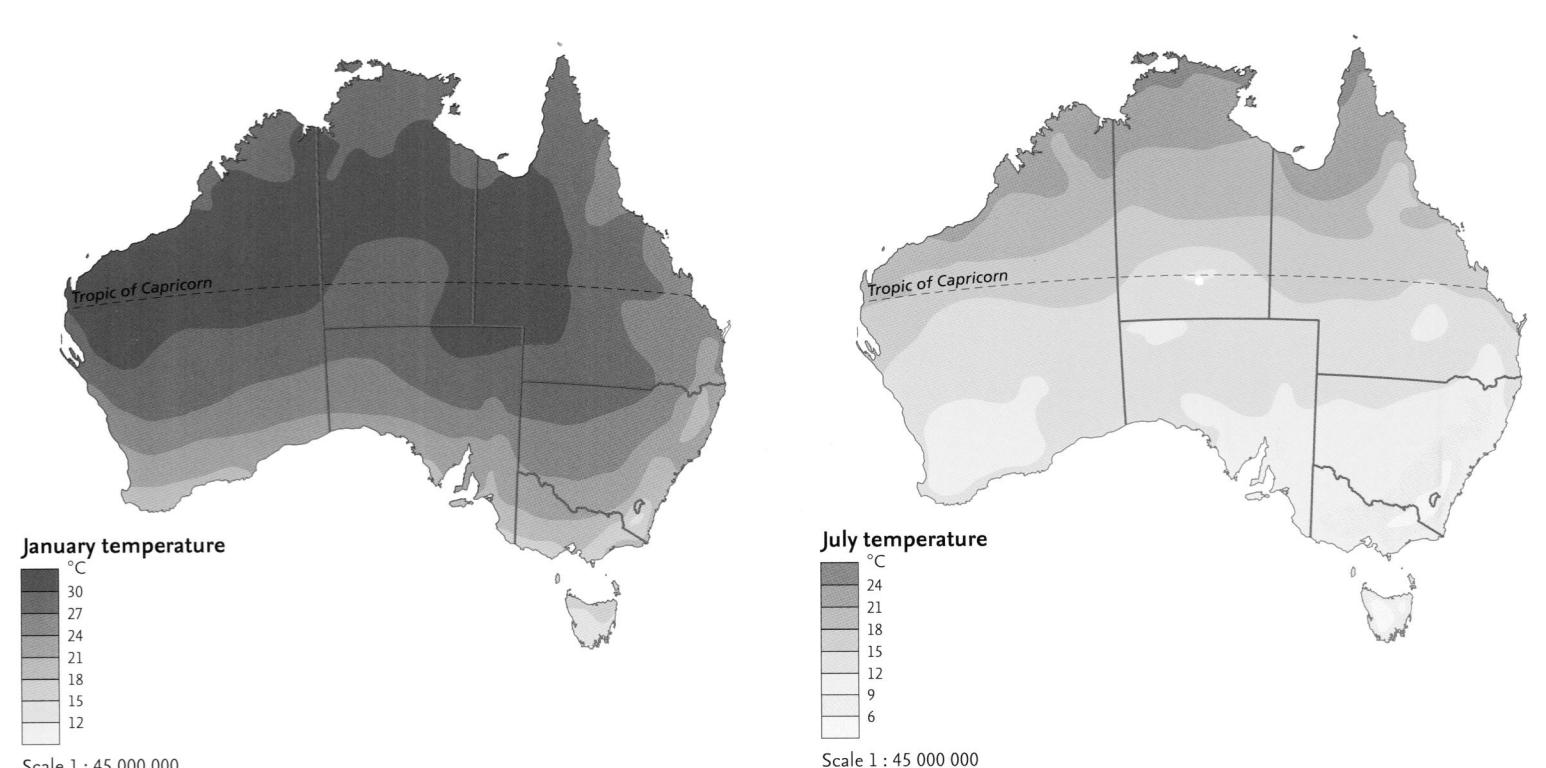

January temperature
°C
30
27
24
21
18
15
12

Scale 1 : 45 000 000

July temperature
°C
24
21
18
15
12
9
6

Scale 1 : 45 000 000

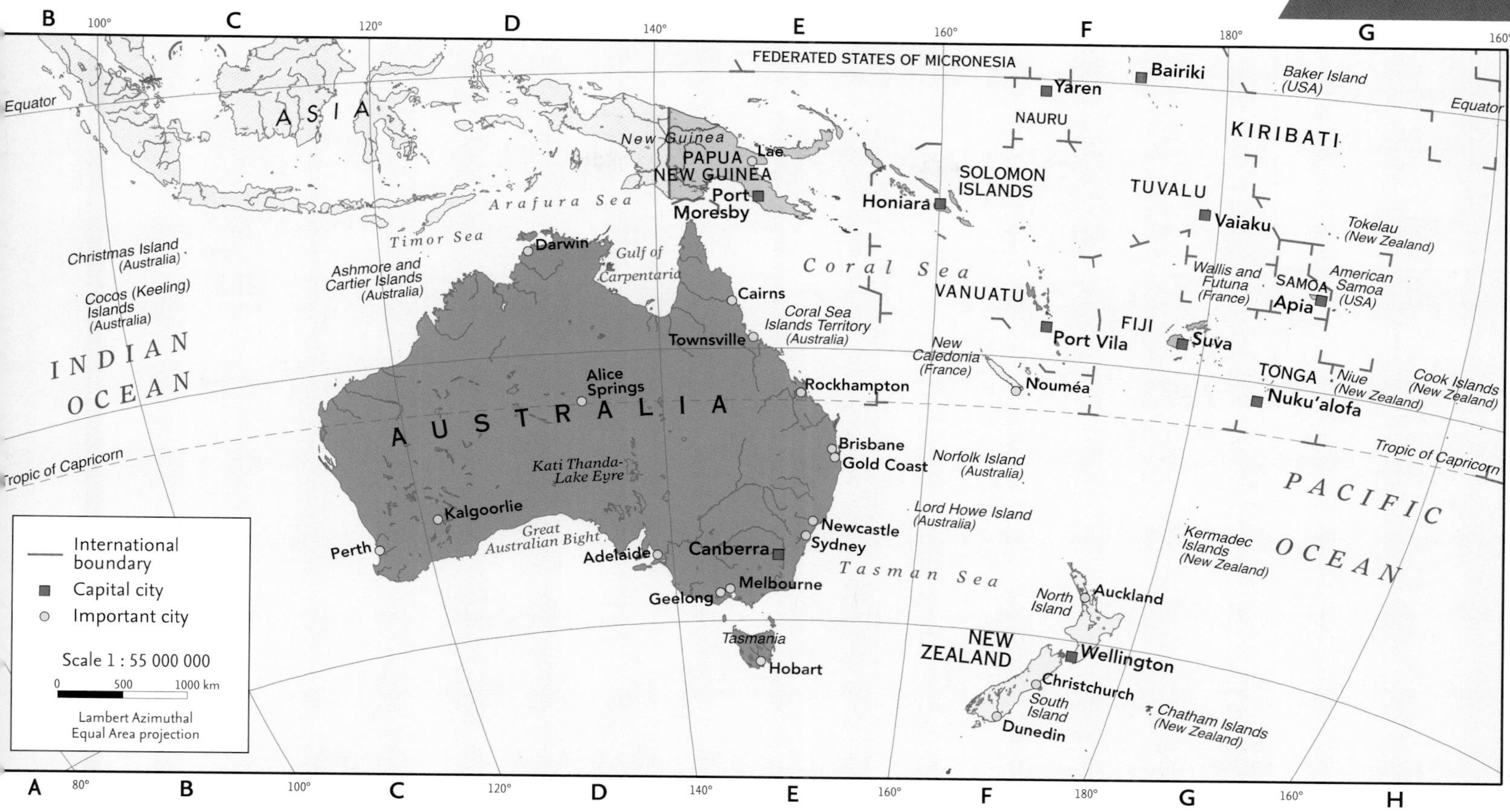

Map labels (political map):

FEDERATED STATES OF MICRONESIA

Equator

ASIA

New Guinea

PAPUA NEW GUINEA — Lae, Port Moresby

Arafura Sea

Timor Sea

Christmas Island (Australia)

Cocos (Keeling) Islands (Australia)

INDIAN OCEAN

Darwin

Gulf of Carpentaria

Ashmore and Cartier Islands (Australia)

Cairns

Townsville

Coral Sea

Coral Sea Islands Territory (Australia)

NAURU — Yaren

Bairiki

Baker Island (USA)

KIRIBATI

SOLOMON ISLANDS — Honiara

TUVALU — Vaiaku

Tokelau (New Zealand)

VANUATU — Port Vila

FIJI — Suva

Wallis and Futuna (France)

SAMOA — Apia

American Samoa (USA)

TONGA — Nuku'alofa

Niue (New Zealand)

Cook Islands (New Zealand)

Tropic of Capricorn

AUSTRALIA

Alice Springs

Kati Thanda-Lake Eyre

Rockhampton

Brisbane

Gold Coast

Norfolk Island (Australia)

Lord Howe Island (Australia)

New Caledonia (France) — Nouméa

PACIFIC OCEAN

Kermadec Islands (New Zealand)

Kalgoorlie

Perth

Great Australian Bight

Adelaide

Canberra

Newcastle

Sydney

Geelong

Melbourne

Tasman Sea

North Island

Auckland

Tasmania

Hobart

NEW ZEALAND — Wellington

Christchurch

South Island

Chatham Islands (New Zealand)

Dunedin

Legend:

— International boundary
■ Capital city
○ Important city

Scale 1 : 55 000 000

0   500   1000 km

Lambert Azimuthal Equal Area projection

Facts about Oceania

Total land area	**8 844 516 sq. km**
Highest peak	**Puncak Jaya, 4884 m**
Longest river	**Murray-Darling, 3672 km**
Largest country	**Australia, 7 692 024 sq. km**
Most populous country	**Australia, 23 969 000**

Population by country, 2015
top ten countries

Samoa 193 — Kiribati 112
Vanuatu 265 — Tonga 106
Solomon Islands 584 — F. S. Micronesia 104
Fiji 892

New Zealand 4529

Papua New Guinea 7619

Australia 23 969

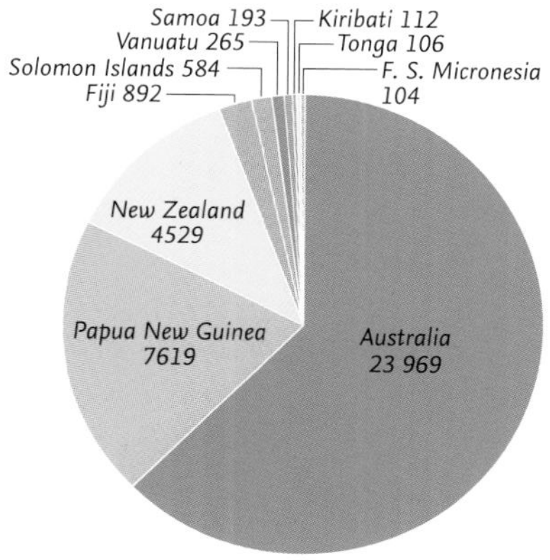

Population in thousands

GNI by country, 2015
top ten countries

Vanuatu 815 — Samoa 735
Solomon Islands 1121 — Tonga 440
Fiji 4203 — F. S. Micronesia 371
Papua New Guinea 16 527 — Kiribati 339

New Zealand 167 176

Australia 1 311 630

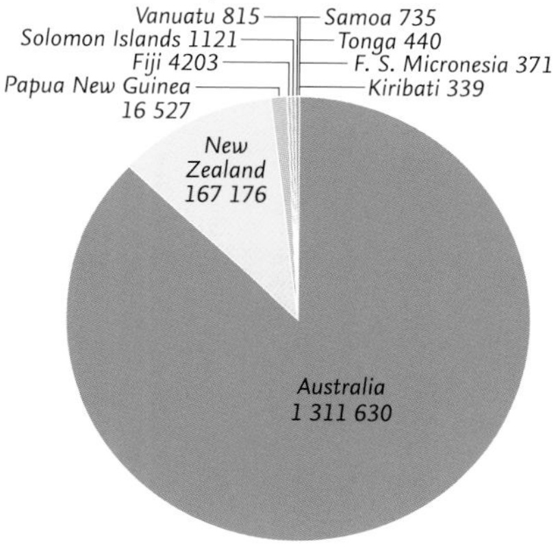

Gross National Income in US $ millions

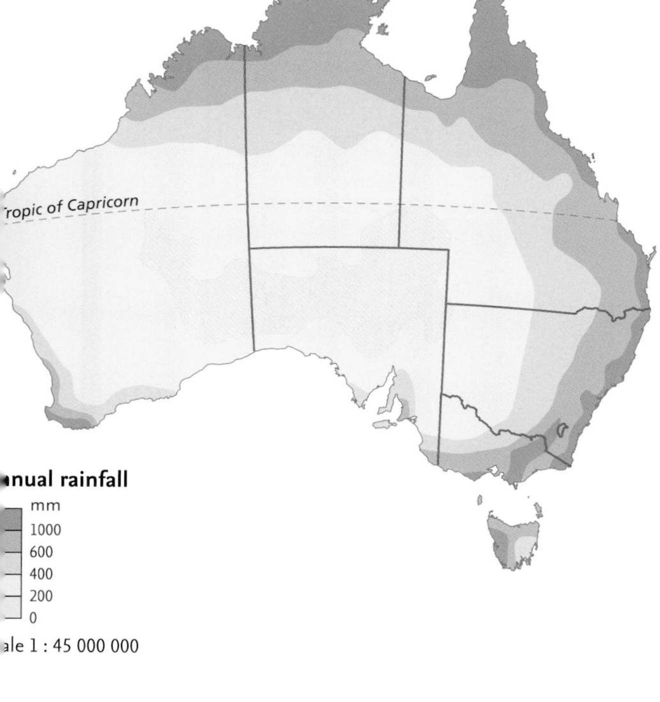

Annual rainfall

Tropic of Capricorn

mm
1000
600
400
200
0

Scale 1 : 45 000 000

Climate regions

Tropic of Capricorn

Tropical – wet summers
Summers hot to very hot, wet to very wet
Winters mild to warm, dry

Subtropical – wet summers
Summers hot, wet, humid
Winters mild, low rainfall

Temperate – uniform rainfall
Summers warm to hot, moderate rain
Winters cool to mild, moderate rain

Temperate – wet winters
Summers warm to hot, dry
Winters cool to mild, wet

Subtropical – arid
Summers hot to very hot, very dry
Winters mild to warm, dry

Subtropical/Warm Temperate – arid
Summers hot to very hot, very dry
Winters cool to mild, dry

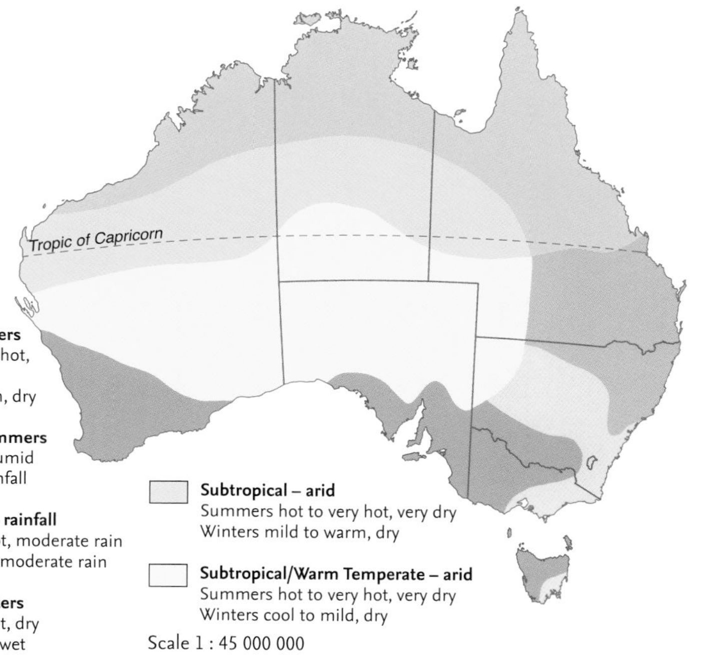

Scale 1 : 45 000 000

Relief and physical features

Relief metres

5000
3000
2000
1000
500
200
sea level
under sea level
0
200
4000
6000

▲ 4884 Mountain height (in metres)

Water features

～ River
～ Intermittent river
Lake / Reservoir
Intermittent lake
Marsh
Coral reef

Communications

Railway
Road
⊕ Main airport

Administration

Boundaries

International
Internal

Settlement

Cities and towns in order of size

National capital
■ Canberra

Other city or town
● Sydney
● Gold Coast
○ Newcastle
○ Darwin

Scale 1 : 20 000 000

0   200   400   600   800 km

Lambert Azimuthal Equal Area projection

NAURU

Kingsmill Group

Ontong Java Atoll

KIRIBATI

Phoenix Islands
Kanton
McKean
Rawaki
Nikumaroro
Orona
Manra

SOLOMON ISLANDS

Santa Isabel

TUVALU

Nui
Vaitupu

Nukufetau
Vaiaku
Funafuti

oniara
dalcanai

Malaita

Makira

Ndeni

Tokelau
(New Zealand)
Atafu
Nukunono

a Sound

Fakaofo

Rennell

Santa Cruz Islands

Swains Island

Pukapuka
(Danger Islands)

Nassau

Torres Islands

Rotuma
(Fiji)

Wallis and Futuna
(France)

Îles Wallis

SAMOA

American Samoa
(USA)

Suwarrow

VANUATU

Banks Islands

Matā'utu

Savai'i

Apia

Upolu

Manua Islands

Espíritu Santo

Îles de Hoorn

Tutuila

Rose Island

Malakula

Ambrym

Vanua Levu

▲ 210

Niuafo'ou

Tafahi
Niuatoputapu

Fagatogo

Éfaté

Port Vila

Yasawa Group

Tomanivi
▲ 1323

FIJI

Viti Levu

Suva

Lakeba
Kabara

Vava'u Group

Alofi

Niue
(New Zealand)

Palmerston

Erromango

Tanna

Kadavu

Vatoa
Tofua ▲ 500

Ha'apai Group

Cook Islands
(New Zealand)

New Caledonia
(France)

Îles Loyauté

Ono-i-Lau

TONGA

Nouméa

Nuku'alofa

Tongatapu Group

Ata

Tropic of Capricorn

P A C I F I C   O C E A N

Norfolk Island
(Australia)

Lord Howe Island
(Australia)

Raoul Island

Kermadec Islands
(New Zealand)

Cape Maria van Diemen
North Cape

North Island
(Te Ika-a-Māui)

Whangarei

A N   S E A

Auckland

Manukau

Bay of Plenty

East Cape

Hamilton

NEW

Lake Taupo

Gisborne

Mount Taranaki
(Mount Egmont) ▲ 2518

Hawke Bay

ZEALAND

Cape Farewell

Palmerston North

Napier

Nelson

Wellington

Aoraki/Mount Cook
▲ 3724

Southern Alps

Pegasus Bay

Cook Strait

Chatham Islands
(New Zealand)

South Island
(Te Waipounamu)

Christchurch

Cape Providence

Dunedin

Stewart Island
Invercargill

Bounty Islands
(New Zealand)

Antipodes Islands
(New Zealand)

Auckland Islands
(New Zealand)

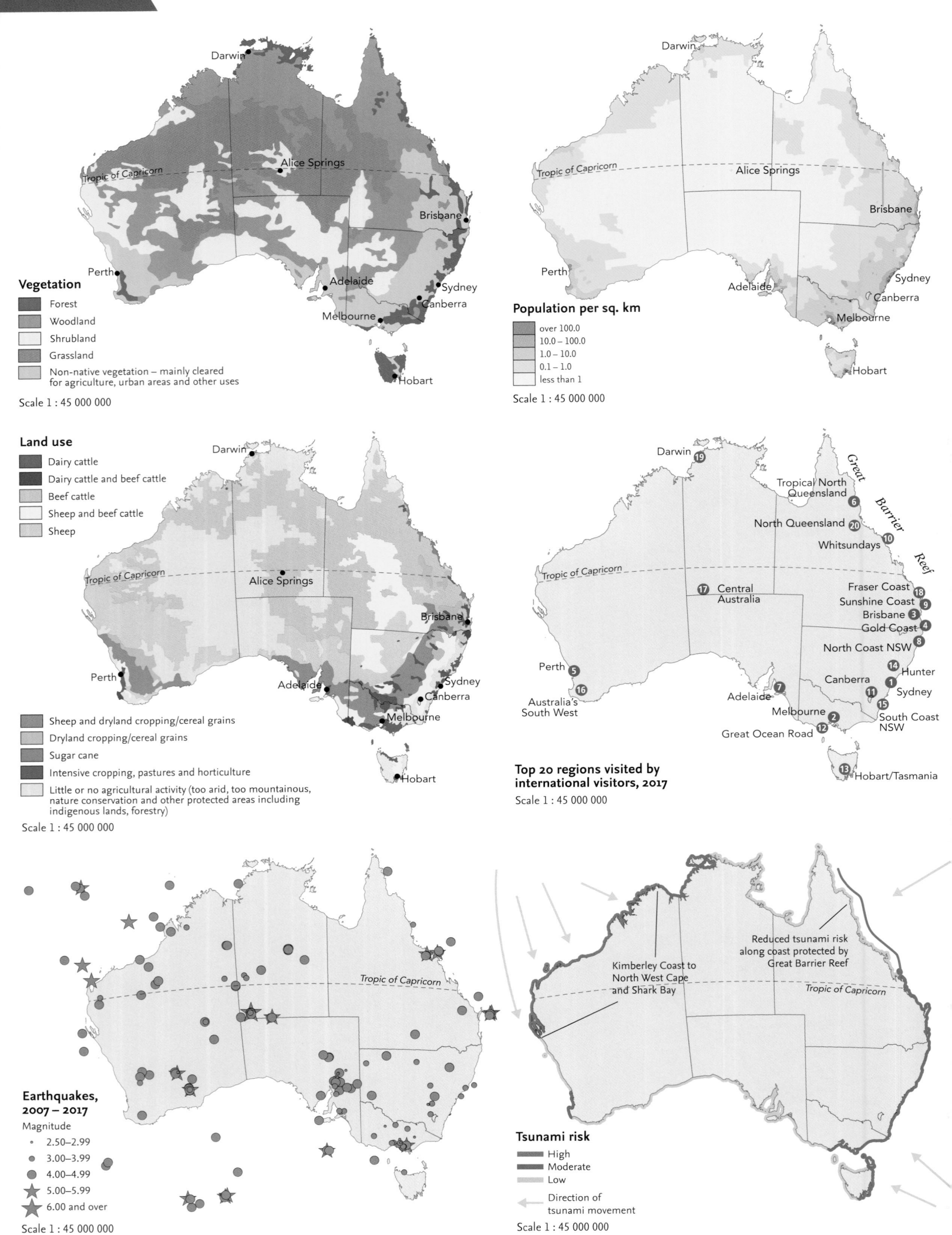

Vegetation

- Forest
- Woodland
- Shrubland
- Grassland
- Non-native vegetation – mainly cleared for agriculture, urban areas and other uses

Scale 1 : 45 000 000

Population per sq. km

- over 100.0
- 10.0 – 100.0
- 1.0 – 10.0
- 0.1 – 1.0
- less than 1

Scale 1 : 45 000 000

Land use

- Dairy cattle
- Dairy cattle and beef cattle
- Beef cattle
- Sheep and beef cattle
- Sheep
- Sheep and dryland cropping/cereal grains
- Dryland cropping/cereal grains
- Sugar cane
- Intensive cropping, pastures and horticulture
- Little or no agricultural activity (too arid, too mountainous, nature conservation and other protected areas including indigenous lands, forestry)

Scale 1 : 45 000 000

Top 20 regions visited by international visitors, 2017

Scale 1 : 45 000 000

Earthquakes, 2007 – 2017

Magnitude

- 2.50–2.99
- 3.00–3.99
- 4.00–4.99
- 5.00–5.99
- 6.00 and over

Scale 1 : 45 000 000

Tsunami risk

- High
- Moderate
- Low
- Direction of tsunami movement

Kimberley Coast to North West Cape and Shark Bay

Reduced tsunami risk along coast protected by Great Barrier Reef

Scale 1 : 45 000 000

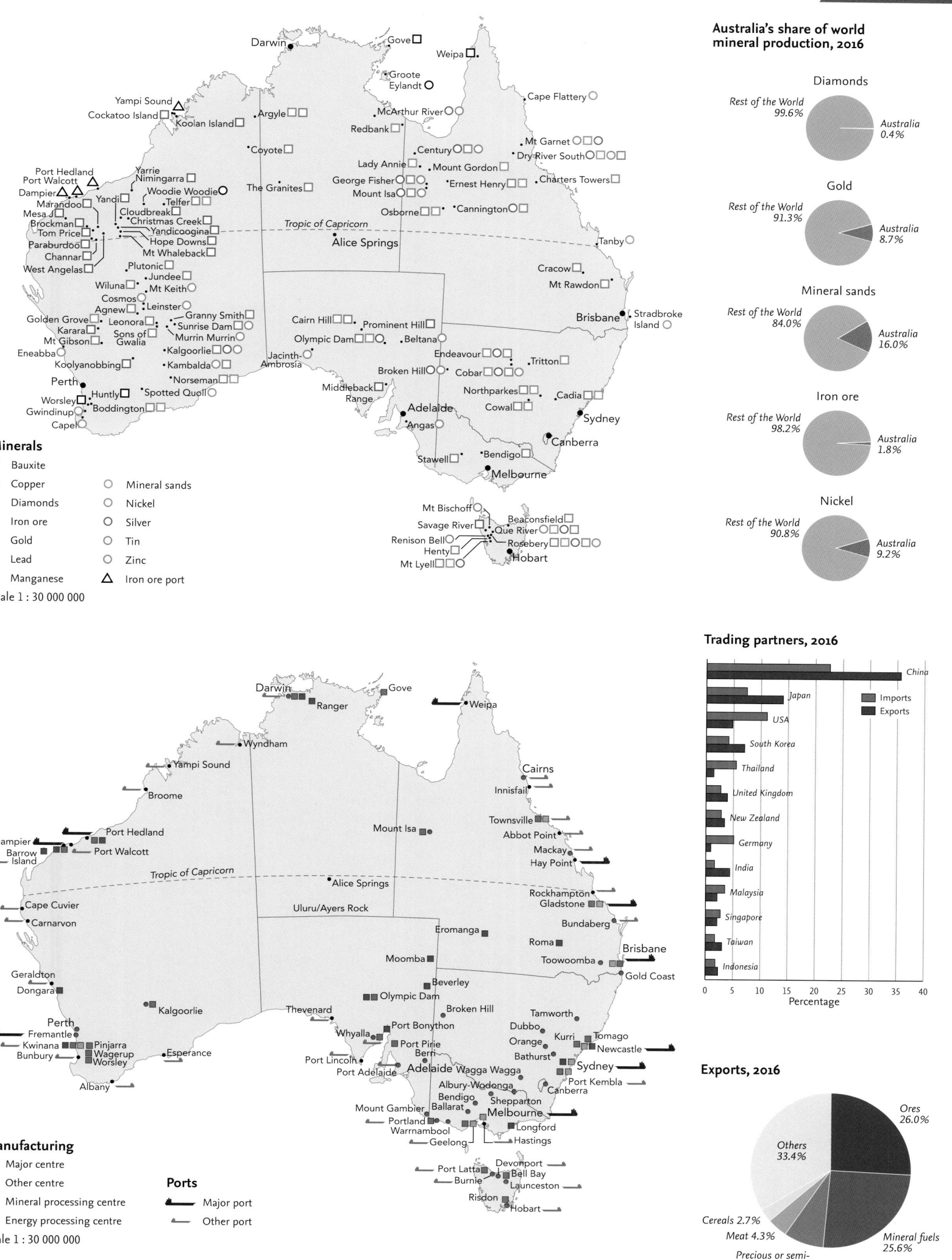

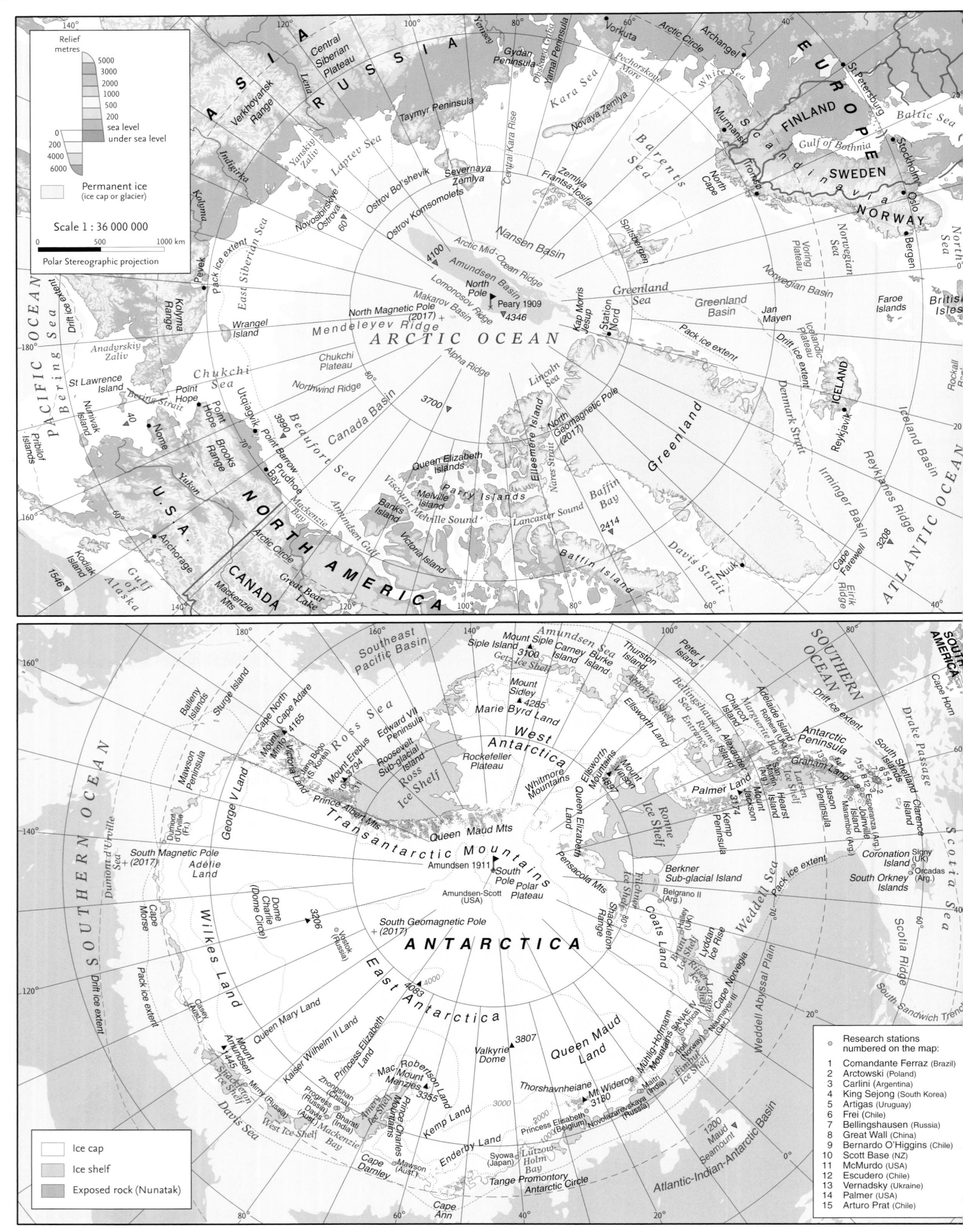

Relief
metres
5000
3000
2000
1000
500
200
0   sea level
200   under sea level
4000
6000

Permanent ice
(ice cap or glacier)

Scale 1 : 36 000 000

0   500   1000 km

Polar Stereographic projection

Ice cap

Ice shelf

Exposed rock (Nunatak)

Research stations
numbered on the map:
1 Comandante Ferraz (Brazil)
2 Arctowski (Poland)
3 Carlini (Argentina)
4 King Sejong (South Korea)
5 Artigas (Uruguay)
6 Frei (Chile)
7 Bellingshausen (Russia)
8 Great Wall (China)
9 Bernardo O'Higgins (Chile)
10 Scott Base (NZ)
11 McMurdo (USA)
12 Escudero (Chile)
13 Vernadsky (Ukraine)
14 Palmer (USA)
15 Arturo Prat (Chile)

United Nations factfile

Established:
24 October 1945

Headquarters:
New York, USA

Purpose:
Maintain international peace and security.
Develop friendly relations among nations.
Help to solve international, economic, social
cultural and humanitarian problems.
Help promote respect for human rights.
To be a centre for harmonizing the actions
of nations in attaining these ends.

Structure:
The 6 principal organs of the UN are:
General Assembly
Security Council
Economic and Social Council
Trusteeship Council (suspended since 1994)
International Court of Justice
Secretariat

Members:
There are 193 members.
Taiwan, Vatican City and Kosovo
are the only non-member countries.

Headquarters of UN agencies

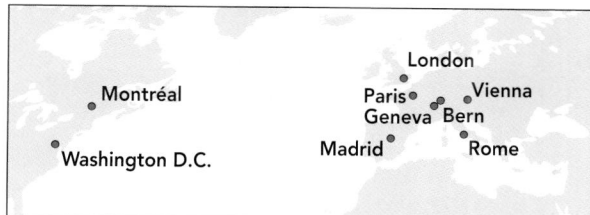

City	Organization
Rome, Italy	Food and Agricultural Organization
Washington D.C., USA	The World Bank
Montréal, Canada	International Civil Aviation Organization
Rome, Italy	International Fund for Agricultural Development
Geneva, Switzerland	International Labour Organization
London, UK	International Maritime Organization
Washington D.C., USA	International Monetary Fund
Geneva, Switzerland	International Telecommunication Union
Paris, France	UNESCO
Vienna, Austria	UN Industrial Development Organization
Bern, Switzerland	Universal Postal Union
Geneva, Switzerland	WHO
Geneva, Switzerland	World Intellectual Property Organization
Geneva, Switzerland	World Meteorological Organization
Madrid, Spain	World Tourism Organization

Structure of United Nations

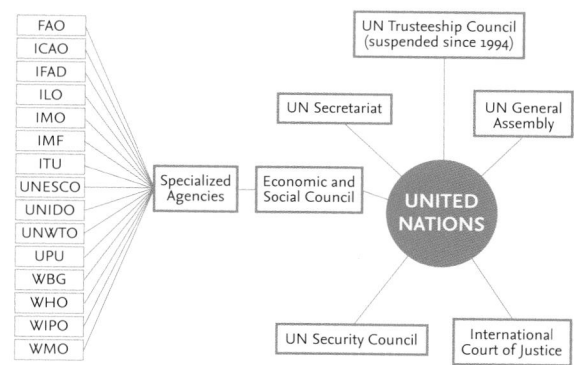

United Nations
www.un.org
Commonwealth
www.thecommonwealth.org

Commonwealth of Nations

NATO – North Atlantic Treaty Organization

Pacific Islands Forum

Arab League

ASEAN – Association of Southeast Asian Nations

Colombo Plan

ALADI (LAIA) – Latin American Integration Association

CARICOM – Caribbean Community

African Union

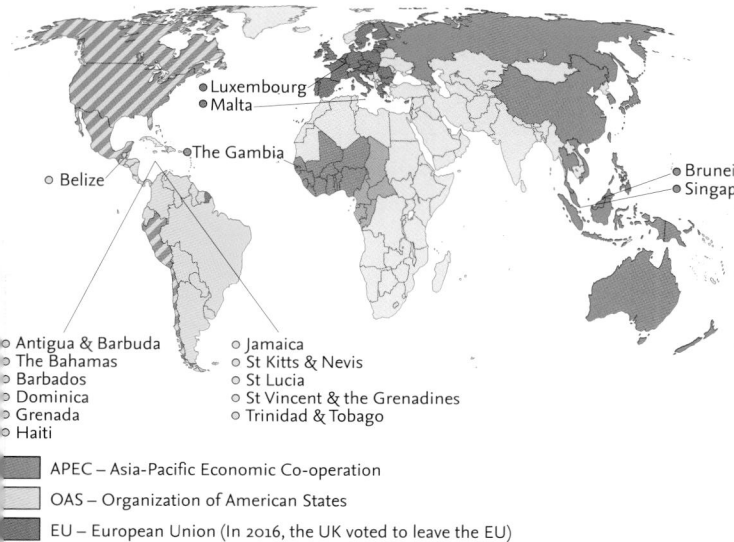

APEC – Asia-Pacific Economic Co-operation

OAS – Organization of American States

EU – European Union (In 2016, the UK voted to leave the EU)

ECOWAS – Economic Community of African States

CEMAC – Economic and Monetary Community of Central Africa

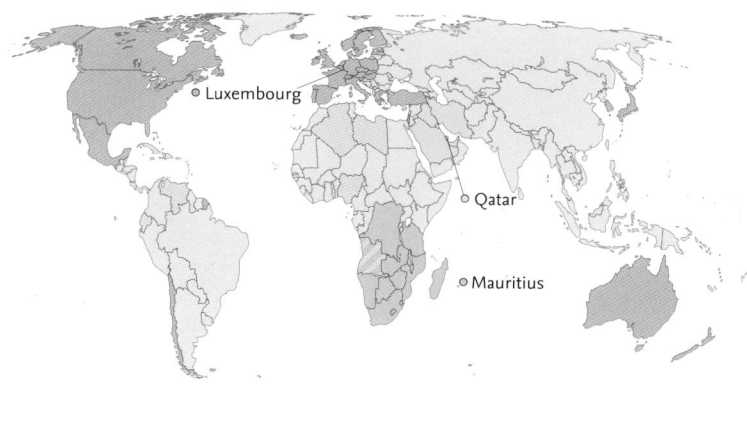

OECD – Organisation for Economic Co-operation and Development

SADC – Southern African Development Community

OPEC – Organization of Petroleum Exporting Countries

Scale 1 : 130 000 000

Countries shaded grey on all maps are not
members of the organizations listed

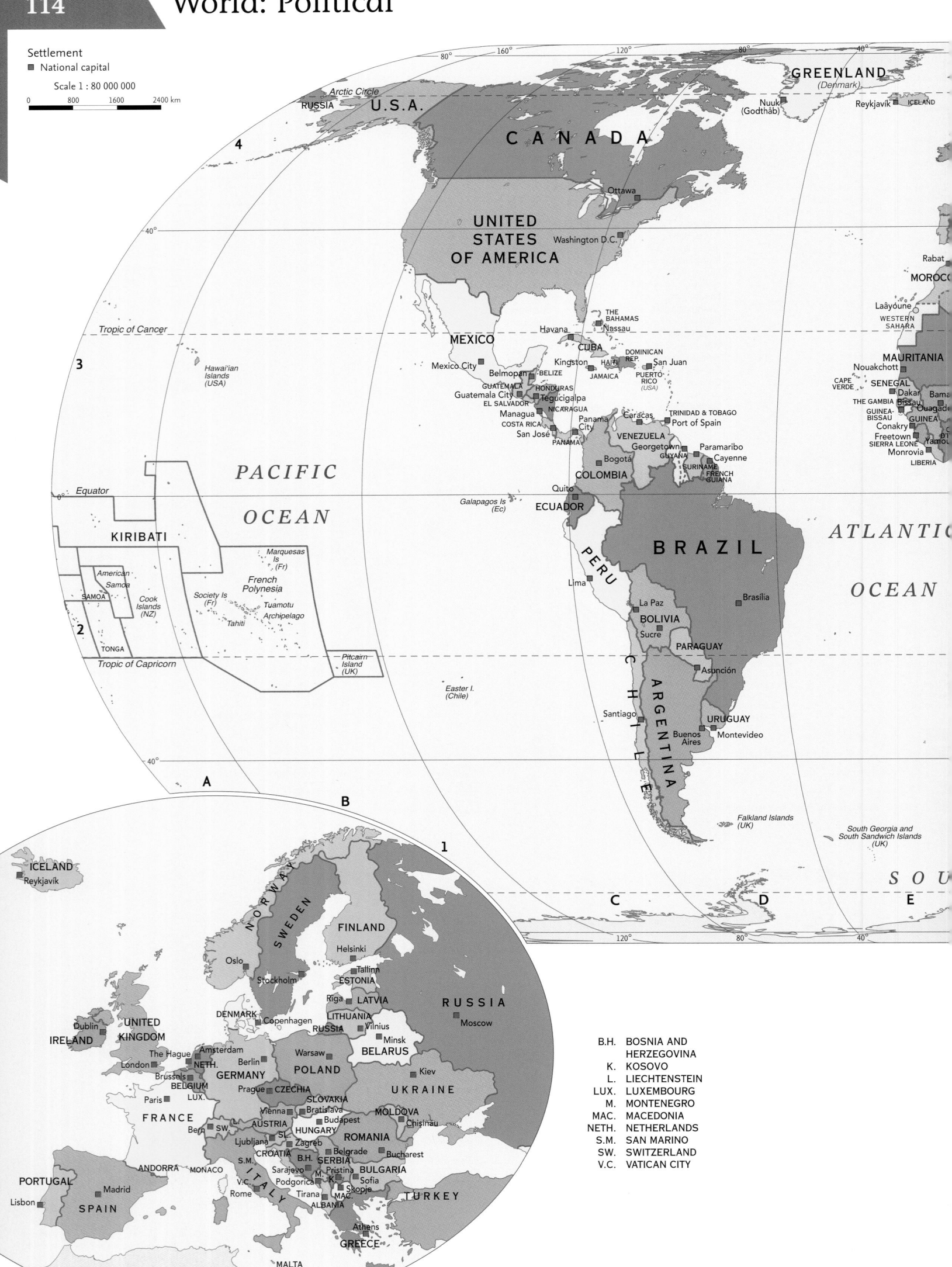

Settlement
■ National capital

Scale 1 : 80 000 000

0   800   1600   2400 km

GREENLAND
(Denmark)

Nuuk
(Godthåb)

Reykjavik · ICELAND

RUSSIA

U.S.A.

C A N A D A

Arctic Circle

Ottawa

UNITED
STATES
OF AMERICA

Washington D.C.

Rabat

MOROCCO

Laâyoune

WESTERN
SAHARA

Tropic of Cancer

MAURITANIA

Hawai'ian
Islands
(USA)

MEXICO

THE
BAHAMAS
Nassau

Havana

CUBA

Nouakchott

CAPE
VERDE

SENEGAL

Mexico City

Kingston

DOMINICAN
REP.
HAITI

San Juan

Dakar

THE GAMBIA Bissau

Bama

Belmopan · BELIZE

JAMAICA

PUERTO
RICO
(USA)

GUINEA-
BISSAU
GUINEA

Ouagade

GUATEMALA
Guatemala City
EL SALVADOR

HONDURAS
Tegucigalpa
NICARAGUA

Conakry
SIERRA LEONE
Freetown
Monrovia

Yamou

Managua
COSTA RICA

Caracas

TRINIDAD & TOBAGO
Port of Spain

LIBERIA

Panama
City

San José
PANAMA

VENEZUELA

Georgetown

Paramaribo

Cayenne

Bogotá

GUYANA
SURINAME
FRENCH
GUIANA

PACIFIC

COLOMBIA

Quito

Galapagos Is
(Ec)

ECUADOR

ATLANTIC

OCEAN

KIRIBATI

Marquesas
Is
(Fr)

French
Polynesia

PERU

B R A Z I L

OCEAN

American
Samoa

SAMOA

Cook
Islands
(NZ)

Society Is
(Fr)

Tuamotu
Archipelago

Lima

La Paz

Brasília

BOLIVIA

Tahiti

Sucre

PARAGUAY

TONGA

Tropic of Capricorn

Pitcairn
Island
(UK)

Easter I.
(Chile)

Asunción

C
H
I
L
E

A
R
G
E
N
T
I
N
A

URUGUAY

Santiago

Buenos
Aires

Montevideo

40°

A

B

1

Falkland Islands
(UK)

South Georgia and
South Sandwich Islands
(UK)

C

D

E

120°

80°

40°

S O U

ICELAND

Reykjavík

NORWAY

SWEDEN

FINLAND

Helsinki

Oslo

Tallinn

Stockholm

ESTONIA

RUSSIA

Riga

LATVIA

Moscow

Dublin

UNITED
KINGDOM

DENMARK

Copenhagen

LITHUANIA

Vilnius

IRELAND

The Hague

Amsterdam

NETH.

Berlin

RUSSIA

Minsk

London

Brussels

BELGIUM

GERMANY

Warsaw

POLAND

BELARUS

Kiev

Paris

LUX.

Prague

CZECHIA

UKRAINE

FRANCE

SLOVAKIA

Bern

SW.

AUSTRIA

Vienna

Bratislava

Budapest

MOLDOVA

Chisinau

SL.

HUNGARY

ROMANIA

Ljubljana

Zagreb

CROATIA

Belgrade

Bucharest

B.H.

SERBIA

PORTUGAL

ANDORRA

MONACO

S.M.

Sarajevo

M.

Pristina

BULGARIA

Podgorica

K.

Sofia

Madrid

V.C.

I T A L Y

Tirana

MAC.

Skopje

Lisbon

Rome

ALBANIA

TURKEY

SPAIN

Athens

GREECE

MALTA

B.H.   BOSNIA AND
        HERZEGOVINA
K.   KOSOVO
L.   LIECHTENSTEIN
LUX.   LUXEMBOURG
M.   MONTENEGRO
MAC.   MACEDONIA
NETH.   NETHERLANDS
S.M.   SAN MARINO
SW.   SWITZERLAND
V.C.   VATICAN CITY

International boundaries in the sea shown on this map indicate ownership of islands and island groups only. They do not infer the alignment of legal maritime boundaries.

Not all countries are named on the map.

ARCTIC OCEAN

RUSSIA

Arctic Circle

4

Moscow

INSET BOTTOM LEFT
R MORE DETAILED
MAP OF EUROPE

Astana

KAZAKHSTAN

Ulan Bator

MONGOLIA

NORTH
KOREA
P'yŏngyang
Seoul
SOUTH
KOREA

Bishkek
KYRGYZSTAN
Tashkent
TAJIKISTAN
Dushanbe

Beijing

JAPAN
Tōkyō

40°

PACIFIC
OCEAN

iers
Tunis
TUNISIA
Tripoli

GEORGIA Tbilisi
ARMENIA AZERBAIJAN
Ankara Yerevan Baku
TURKEY
CYPRUS SYRIA
LEBANON Damascus
ISRAEL JORDAN
Amman IRAQ
KUWAIT Kuwait
Baghdād

UZBEKISTAN
TURKMEN-
ISTAN
Ashgabat
Tehrān
Kābul
AFGHAN-
ISTAN
Islamabād
New
Delhi
PAKISTAN

CHINA

Taipei
TAIWAN

Tropic of Cancer

3

ERIA
LIBYA
EGYPT

Cairo

SAUDI
Riyadh
ARABIA

BAHRAIN QATAR
UNITED
ARAB
EMIRATES
Muscat

OMAN

NEPAL
Kathmandu

BHUTAN
Dhaka
BANGLA-
DESH

INDIA

Hanoi

MYANMAR
(BURMA)
Nay Pyi Taw
LAOS
Vientiane
VIETNAM

PHILIPPINES

Manila

Northern
Mariana
Islands
(USA)

MARSHALL
ISLANDS

NIGER
CHAD
mey
Ndjamena
NIGERIA
Abuja

Khartoum
ERITREA
Asmara
SUDAN

YEMEN
Şan'ā'

DJIBOUTI

THAILAND
Bangkok

CAMBODIA
Phnom
Penh

PALAU

FEDERATED STATES OF
MICRONESIA

rto Novo
CENTRAL
AFRICAN
REPUBLIC
Bangui
CAMEROON
Yaounde
TORIAL
GUINEA
eville
GABON

SOUTH
SUDAN
Juba
ETHIOPIA
Addis
Ababa

SOMALIA

SRI
LANKA

Sri Jayewardenepura Kotte

MALDIVES

Kuala Lumpur
MALAYSIA
BRUNEI
Putrajaya
SINGAPORE
Bandar Seri Begawan

Equator

NAURU

KIRIBATI

TUVALU

0°

CONGO
Brazzaville
Kinshasa

UGANDA
Kampala
RWANDA
Kigali
DEMOCRATIC
REPUBLIC
OF THE
CONGO
BURUNDI
Bujumbura

KENYA
Nairobi

Mogadishu

SEYCHELLES

INDONESIA

Jakarta

Dili
EAST
TIMOR

PAPUA
NEW
GUINEA
Port
Moresby

SOLOMON
ISLANDS
Honiara

Luanda

ANGOLA

ZAMBIA
Lusaka

TANZANIA
Dodoma

MALAWI
Lilongwe
Harare

COMOROS

INDIAN

OCEAN

VANUATU
Port-Vila

New
Caledonia
(Fr)

FIJI
Suva

2

NAMIBIA
Windhoek

ZIMBABWE
BOTS-
WANA
Gaborone
Pretoria
Maputo
ESWATINI
(SWAZILAND)

MOZAMBIQUE

MADAGASCAR
Antananarivo

MAURITIUS

Tropic of Capricorn

AUSTRALIA

Bloemfontein
LESOTHO
SOUTH Maseru
AFRICA

Cape Town

Canberra

NEW
ZEALAND
40°
Wellington

ERN OCEAN

40°

80°

120°

F

G

H

I

J

1

Îles
Kerguelen
(Fr)

ANTARCTICA

40°

80°

120°

The Continents

NORTH
AMERICA

60°N

EUROPE

ASIA

SOUTH
AMERICA

60°W

AFRICA

OCEANIA

60°E

60°S

ANTARCTICA

60°S

ANTARCTICA

Relief and physical features

Relief metres

5000
3000
2000
1000
500
200
0 sea level
200 under sea level
4000
6000

Permanent ice
(ice cap or glacier)

▲ 8848 Mountain height
(in metres)

▽ 11022 Ocean depth
(in metres)

Scale 1 : 80 000 000

0   800   1600   2400 km

Mountain heights	
	metres
Mt Everest (China/Nepal)	8848
K2 (China/Pakistan)	8611
Kangchenjunga (India/Nepal)	8586
Dhaulagiri I (Nepal)	8167
Annapurna I (Nepal)	8091
Cerro Aconcagua (Argentina)	6961
Nevado Ojos del Salado (Arg./Chile)	6908
Chimborazo (Ecuador)	6310
Denali (Mt McKinley) (USA)	6190
Mt Logan (Canada)	5959

Island areas	
	sq. km
Greenland	2 175 600
New Guinea	808 510
Borneo	745 561
Madagascar	587 040
Baffin Island	507 451
Sumatra	473 606
Honshū	227 414
Great Britain	218 476
Victoria Island	217 291
Ellesmere Island	196 236

Continents	
	sq. km
Asia	45 036 492
Africa	30 343 578
North America	24 680 331
South America	17 815 420
Antarctica	12 093 000
Europe	9 908 599
Oceania	8 844 516

Oceans

	sq. km
Pacific Ocean	166 241 000
Atlantic Ocean	86 557 000
Indian Ocean	73 427 000
Arctic Ocean	9 485 000

Lake areas

	sq. km
Caspian Sea	371 000
Lake Superior	82 100
Lake Victoria	68 870
Lake Huron	59 600
Lake Michigan	57 800
Lake Tanganyika	32 600
Great Bear Lake	31 328
Lake Baikal	30 500
Lake Nyasa	29 500

River lengths

	km
Nile (Africa)	6695
Amazon (S. America)	6516
Chang Jiang (Asia)	6380
Mississippi-Missouri (N. America)	5969
Ob'-Irtysh (Asia)	5568
Yenisey-Angara-Selenga (Asia)	5550
Huang He (Asia)	5464
Congo (Africa)	4667
Río de la Plata-Paraná (S. America)	4500
Irtysh (Asia)	4440

World: Tectonics

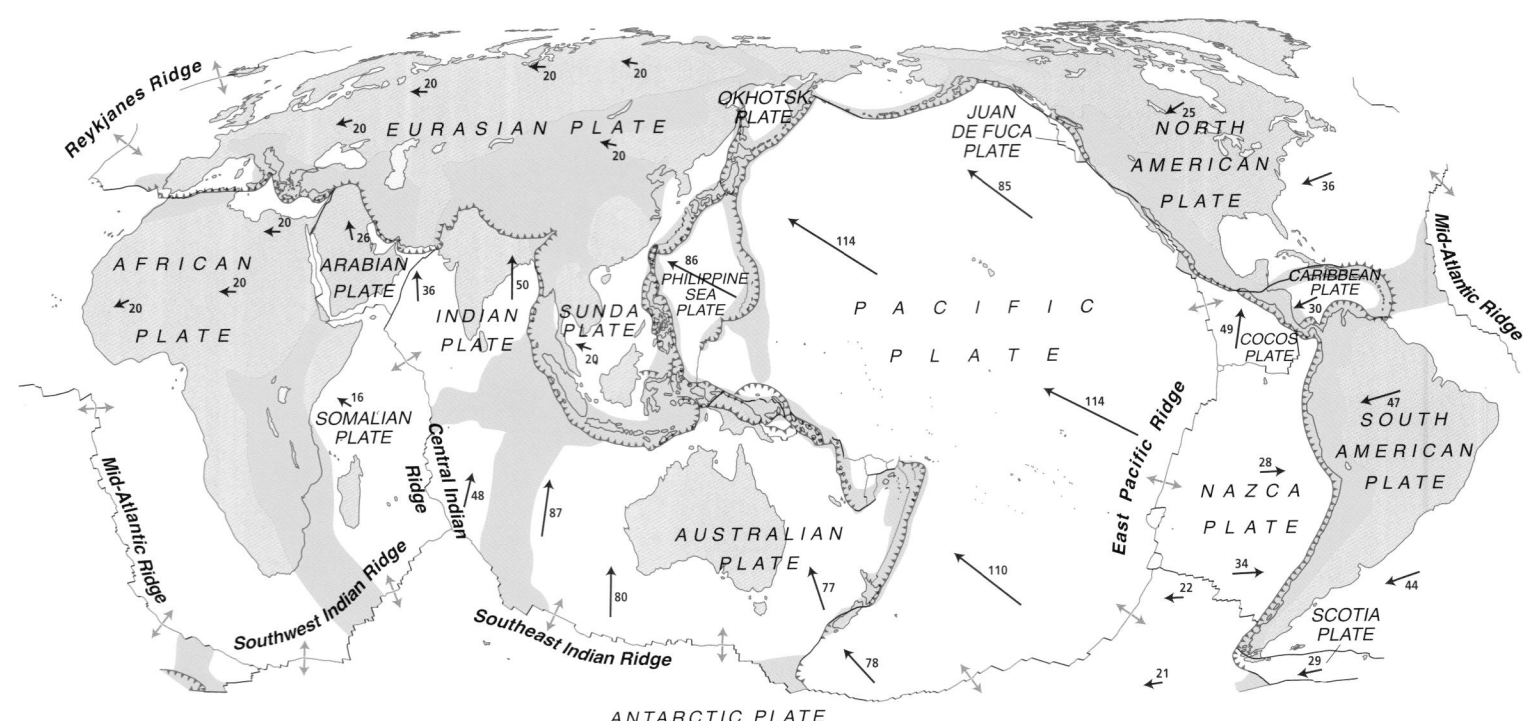

Tectonic plates

ﹸﹸﹸﹸﹸﹸ Convergent plate boundary –
where plates collide and one plate
is pulled down (subducted) into
the mantle and destroyed, or
plates thicken and fracture in
complex patterns

Scale 1 : 170 000 000

Divergent plate boundary –
where plates move away from each
other and new crust is created as
magma reaches the surface

Transform plate boundary –
where plates are dragged horizontally
past each other, creating great friction
and many faults

Diffuse boundary zone –
broad zone in which plate movement
and change to the Earth's surface
occur over a wide region, often in
complex patterns with many
micro-plates

⟵ 44 General direction of plate
movement and approximate
speed, mm/year

⟷ Movement at divergent plate
boundaries

Continental drift

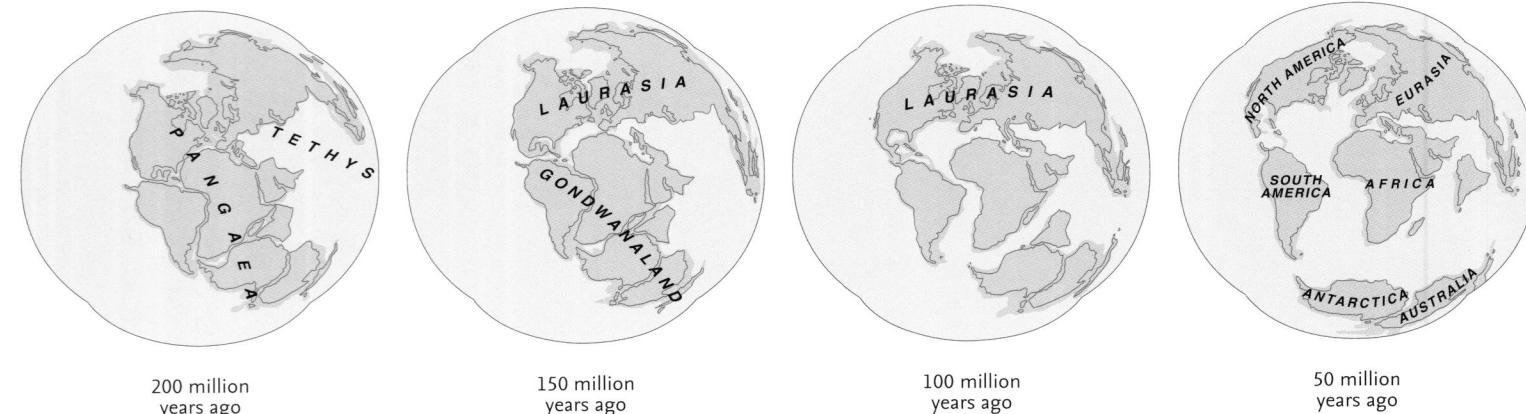

200 million
years ago

150 million
years ago

100 million
years ago

50 million
years ago

Major earthquakes since 1981

Year	Location	Magnitude	Deaths	Year	Location	Magnitude	Deaths	Year	Location	Magnitude	Deaths
1981	Kerman, Iran	7.3	2500	1991	Uttar Pradesh, India	6.1	1600	1999	Chi-Chi, Taiwan	7.7	2400
1982	Dhamar, Yemen	6.0	3000	1992	Flores, Indonesia	7.5	2500	2001	Gujarat, India	6.9	20 085
1983	Eastern Turkey	7.1	1500	1992	Erzincan, Turkey	6.8	500	2002	Hindu Kush, Afghanistan	6.0	1000
1985	Santiago, Chile	7.8	177	1992	Cairo, Egypt	5.9	550	2003	Boumerdes, Algeria	5.8	2266
1985	Michoacán, Mexico	8.1	20 000	1993	Northern Japan	7.8	185	2003	Bam, Iran	6.6	26 271
1986	El Salvador	7.5	1000	1993	Maharashtra, India	6.4	9748	2004	Sumatra, Indonesia	9.0	283 106
1987	Ecuador	7.0	2000	1994	Kuril Islands, Russia	8.3	10	2005	Sumatra, Indonesia	8.7	1313
1988	Yunnan, China	7.6	1000	1995	Kōbe, Japan	7.2	5502	2005	Muzzafarabad, Pakistan	7.6	80 361
1988	Spitak, Armenia	6.9	25 000	1995	Sakhalin, Russia	7.6	2500	2008	Sichuan Province, China	8.0	87 476
1988	Nepal / India	6.9	1000	1996	Yunnan, China	7.0	251	2010	Léogâne, Haiti	7.0	222 570
1990	Manjil, Iran	7.7	50 000	1998	Papua New Guinea	7.0	2183	2011	Tōhoku, Japan	9.0	14 500
1990	Luzon, Philippines	7.7	1600	1999	İzmit, Turkey	7.4	17 118	2015	Gorkha, Nepal	7.8	8831

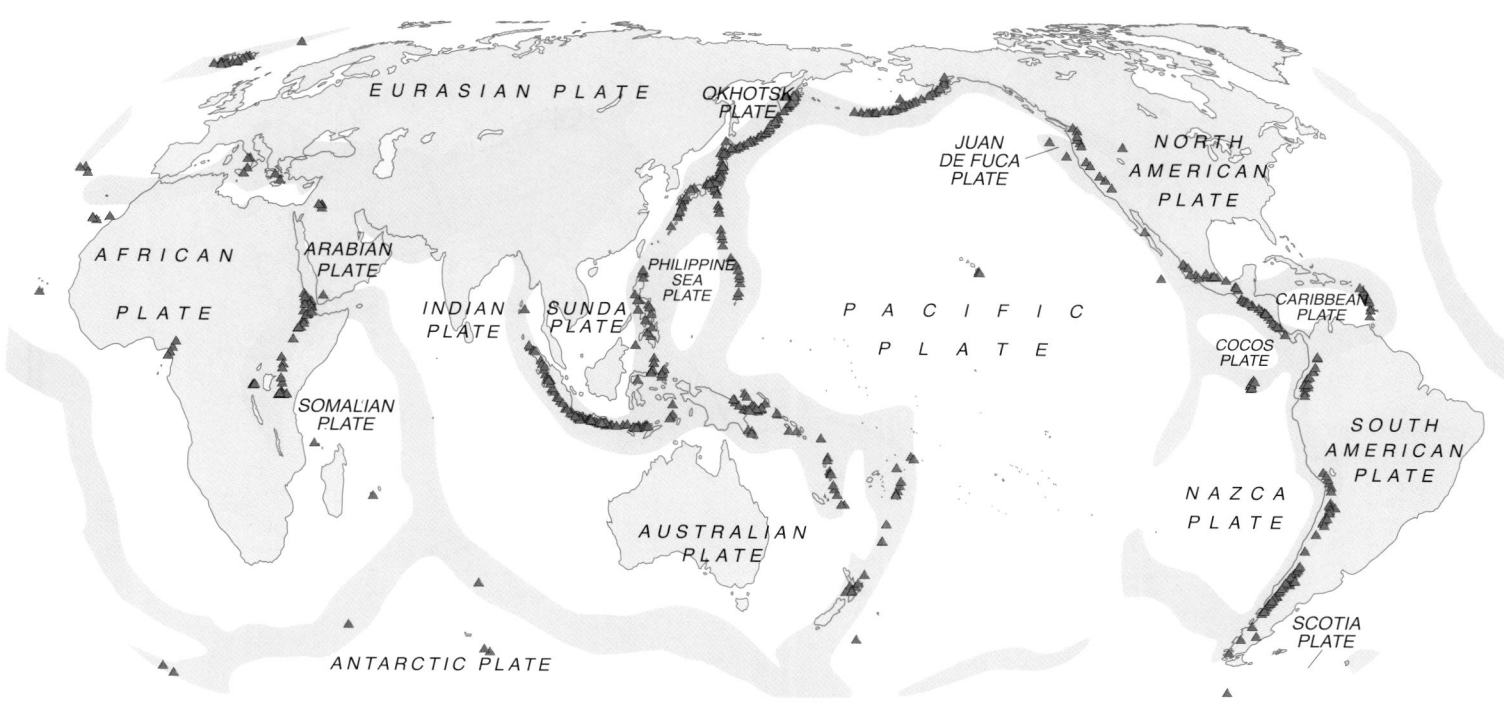

Volcanoes

▢ Earthquake and volcano zone	▲ Major volcanoes

Scale 1 : 170 000 000

Major volcanic eruptions since 1980

Year	Location	Year	Location
1980	Mount St Helens, USA	1993	Mayon, Philippines
1982	El Chichónal, Mexico	1993	Volcán Galeras, Colombia
1982	Gunung Galunggung, Indonesia	1994	Volcán Llaima, Chile
1983	Kilauea, Hawaii	1994	Rabaul, Papua New Guinea
1983	Ō-yama, Japan	1997	Soufrière Hills, Montserrat
1985	Nevado del Ruiz, Colombia	2000	Hekla, Iceland
1986	Lake Nyos, Cameroon	2001	Mount Etna, Italy
1991	Hekla, Iceland	2002	Nyiragongo, Dem. Rep. of the Congo
1991	Mount Pinatubo, Philippines	2010	Eyjafjallajökull, Iceland
1991	Unzen-dake, Japan		

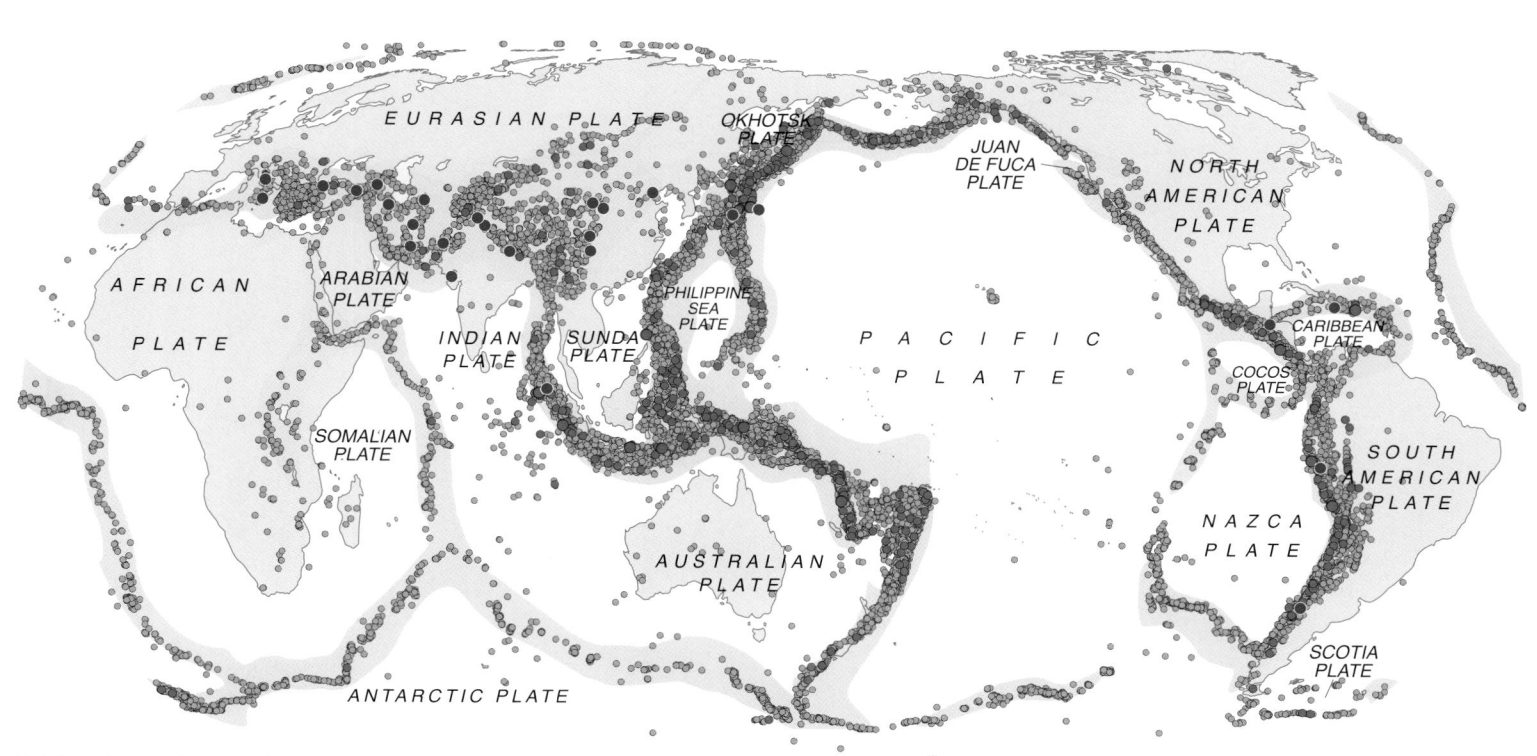

Earthquakes and tsunamis

▢ Earthquake and volcano zone

● Major tsunamis since 1990

Scale 1 : 170 000 000

Major earthquakes since 1900

● 'Deadliest' earthquakes
● Greater than 7.5 on the moment magnitude scale
● 5.5–7.5 on the moment magnitude scale

World: Climatic Systems

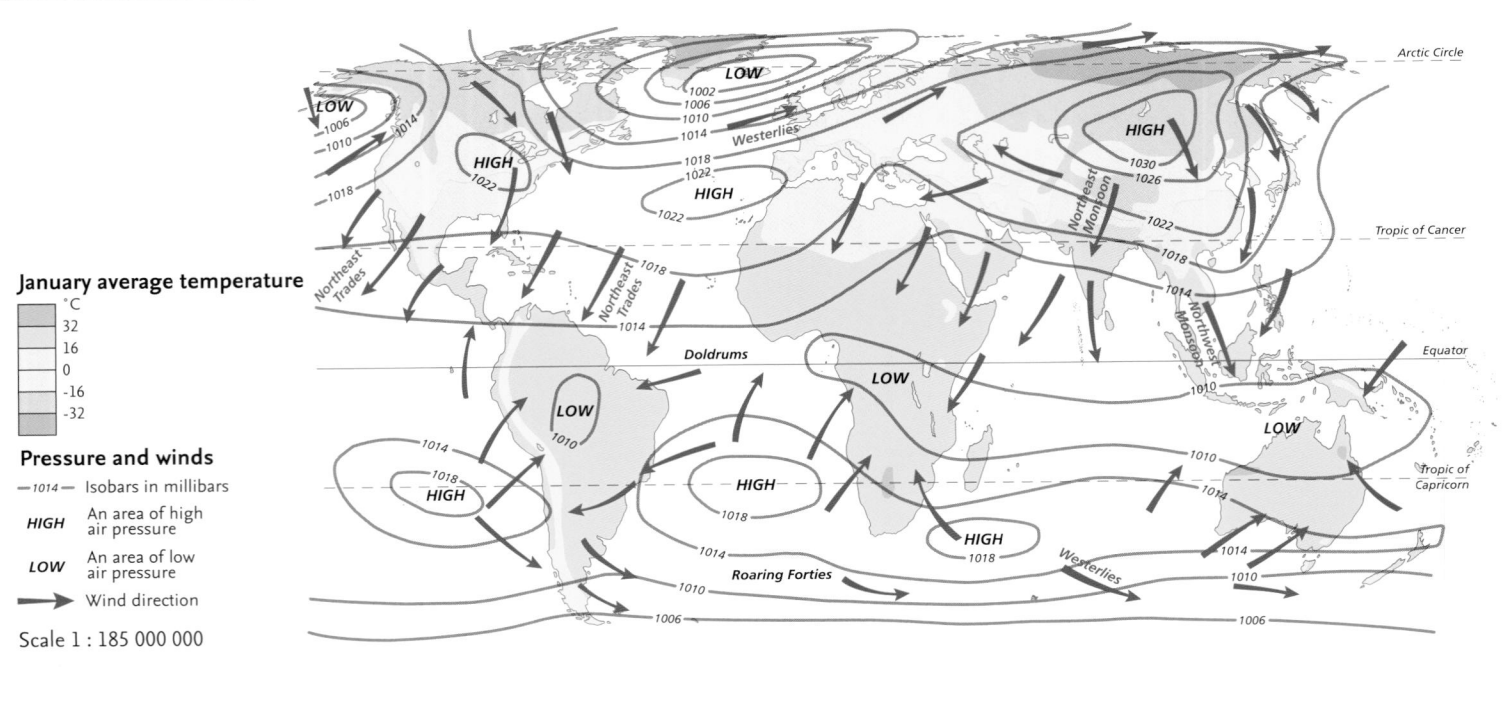

January average temperature

°C
32
16
0
-16
-32

Pressure and winds

—*1014*— Isobars in millibars

HIGH An area of high air pressure

LOW An area of low air pressure

→ Wind direction

Scale 1 : 185 000 000

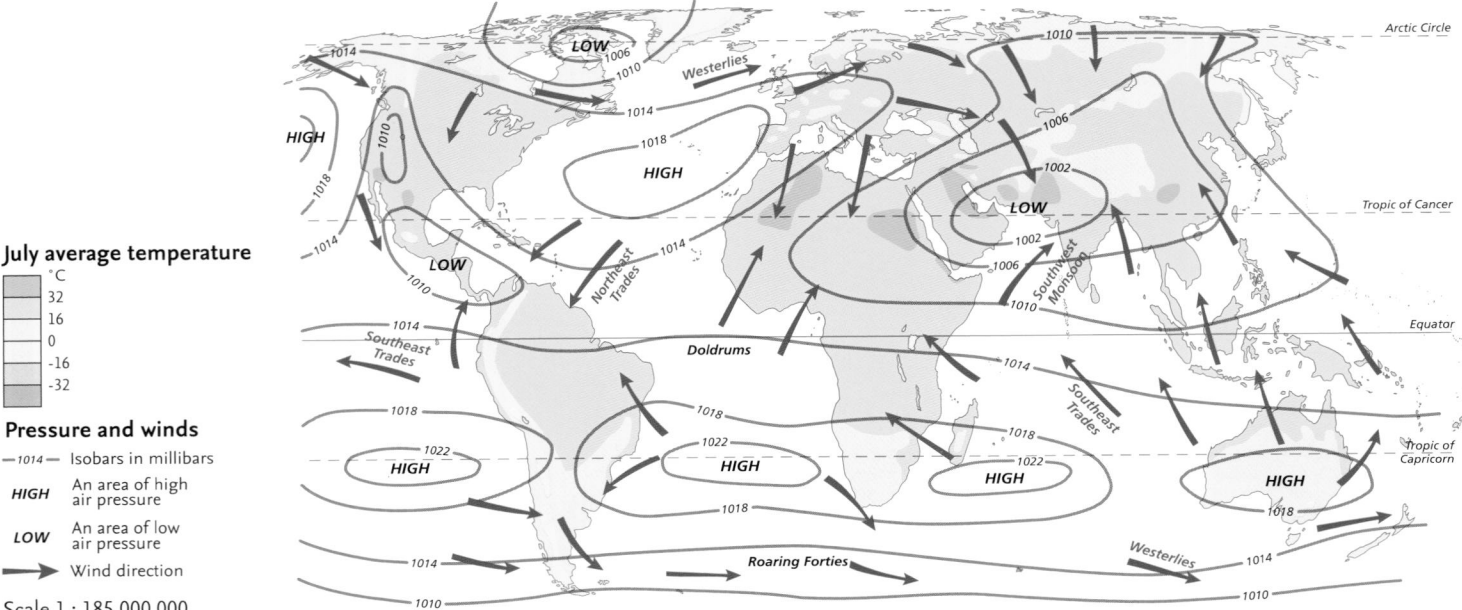

July average temperature

°C
32
16
0
-16
-32

Pressure and winds

—*1014*— Isobars in millibars

HIGH An area of high air pressure

LOW An area of low air pressure

→ Wind direction

Scale 1 : 185 000 000

Tropical storms

Main area of tornado activity

Tornado Alley – highest concentration of tornadoes

⑧ Likely number of severe tropical storms in 10 years

Arrows show typical storm paths

Scale 1 : 185 000 000

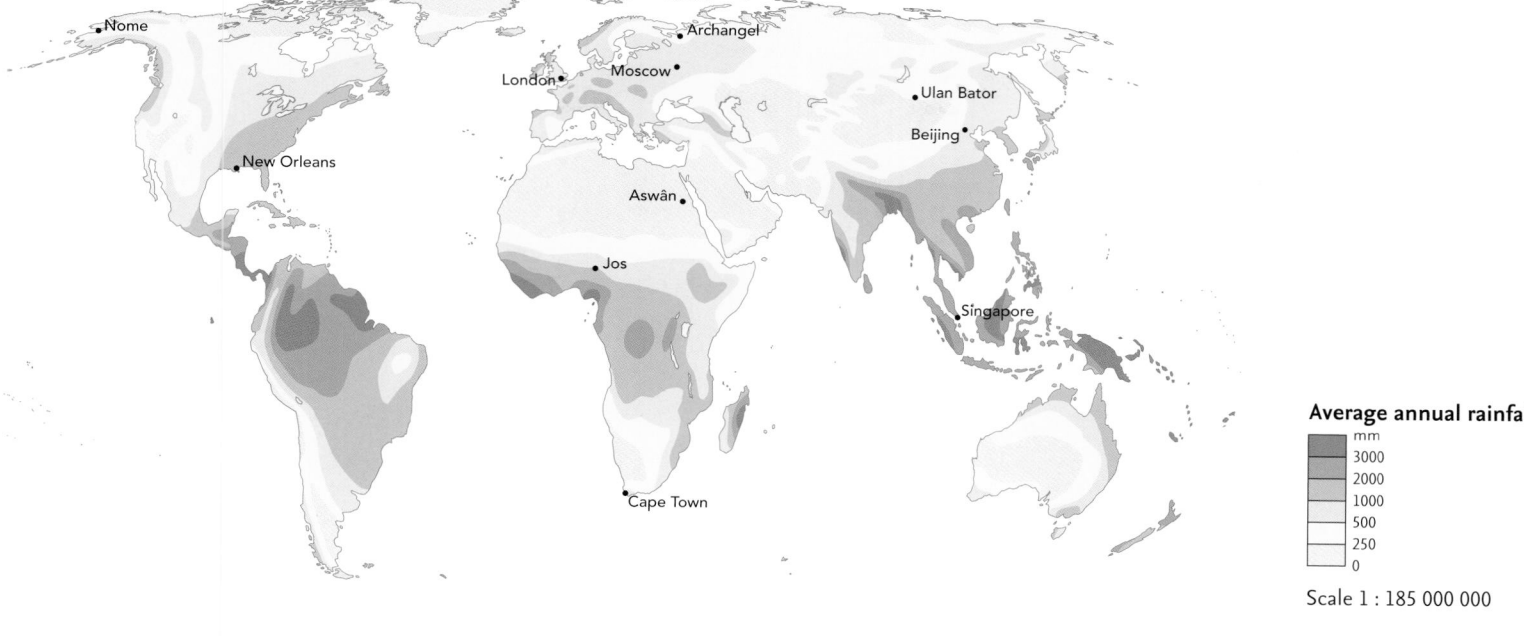

Average annual rainfall

mm
3000
2000
1000
500
250
0

Scale 1 : 185 000 000

Climate graphs

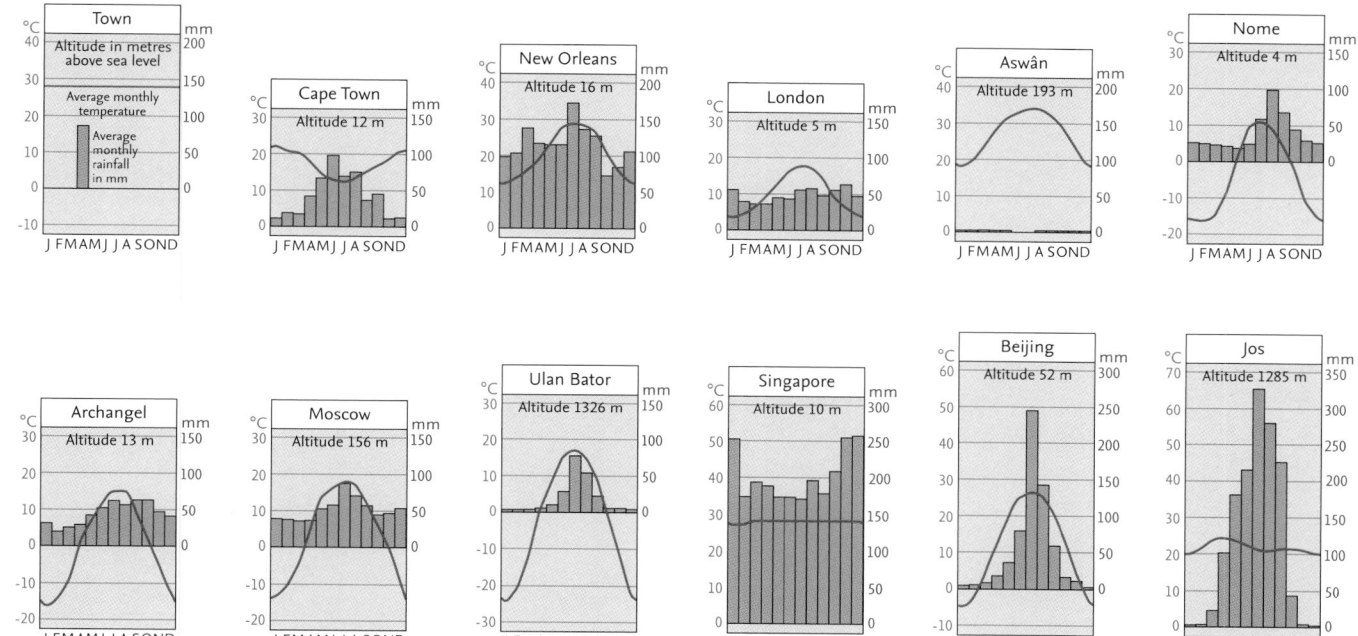

Major tropical storms since 2001

Year	Name	Location	Deaths
2001	Allison	Southern USA	41
2002	Rusa	South Korea	184
2003	Maemi	South Korea	130
2004	Ivan	Southern USA	52
2005	Katrina	Southern USA	1836
2006	Bilis	China	820
2007	Sidr	Bangladesh	4234
2008	Nargis	Myanmar	138 366
2009	Parma	Philippines	501
2010	Agatha	Guatemala	174
2011	Washi	Philippines	1439
2012	Sandy	Eastern USA	148
2013	Haiyan	Philippines	7986
2014	Hudhud	Eastern India/Nepal	109
2016	Matthew	Caribbean	546

World weather extremes

Hottest place	34.4 °C (annual mean)	Dalol, Ethiopia
Driest place	0.1 mm (annual mean)	Atacama Desert, Chile
Most sunshine	90% (4000 hours) (annual mean)	Yuma, Arizona, USA
Least sunshine	Nil for 182 days each year	South Pole
Coldest place	-56.6 °C (annual mean)	Plateau Station, Antarctica
Wettest place	11 873 mm (annual mean)	Meghalaya, India
Most rainy days	Up to 350 per year	Mount Waialeale, Hawaii, USA
Greatest snowfall	31 102 mm (19.2.1971 – 18.2.1972)	Mount Rainier, Washington, USA
Windiest place	322 km per hour in gales	Commonwealth Bay, Antarctica

World Meteorological Organization
www.wmo.int
Met Office
www.metoffice.gov.uk/weather

Ice cap

Tundra climate, warmest month below 10 °C

Sub-arctic, rainy climate with severe cold
winters and less than 4 months over 10 °C

Continental climate, rainy
with warmest month below 22 °C

Continental climate, rainy
with warmest month above 22 °C

Temperate, rainy climate with mild
winter, coolest month above 0 °C

Wet subtropical, coolest month
above 0 °C, warmest month above 22 °C

Mediterranean, rainy with mild
wet winter, dry summer

Semi-arid, dry climate

Desert climate

Rainy tropical climate with no
winter, coolest month above 18 °C

Rainy tropical climate, constantly
wet throughout the year

Ocean currents

⟶ Cold

⟶ Warm

⟶ Seasonal

Scale 1 : 90 000 000

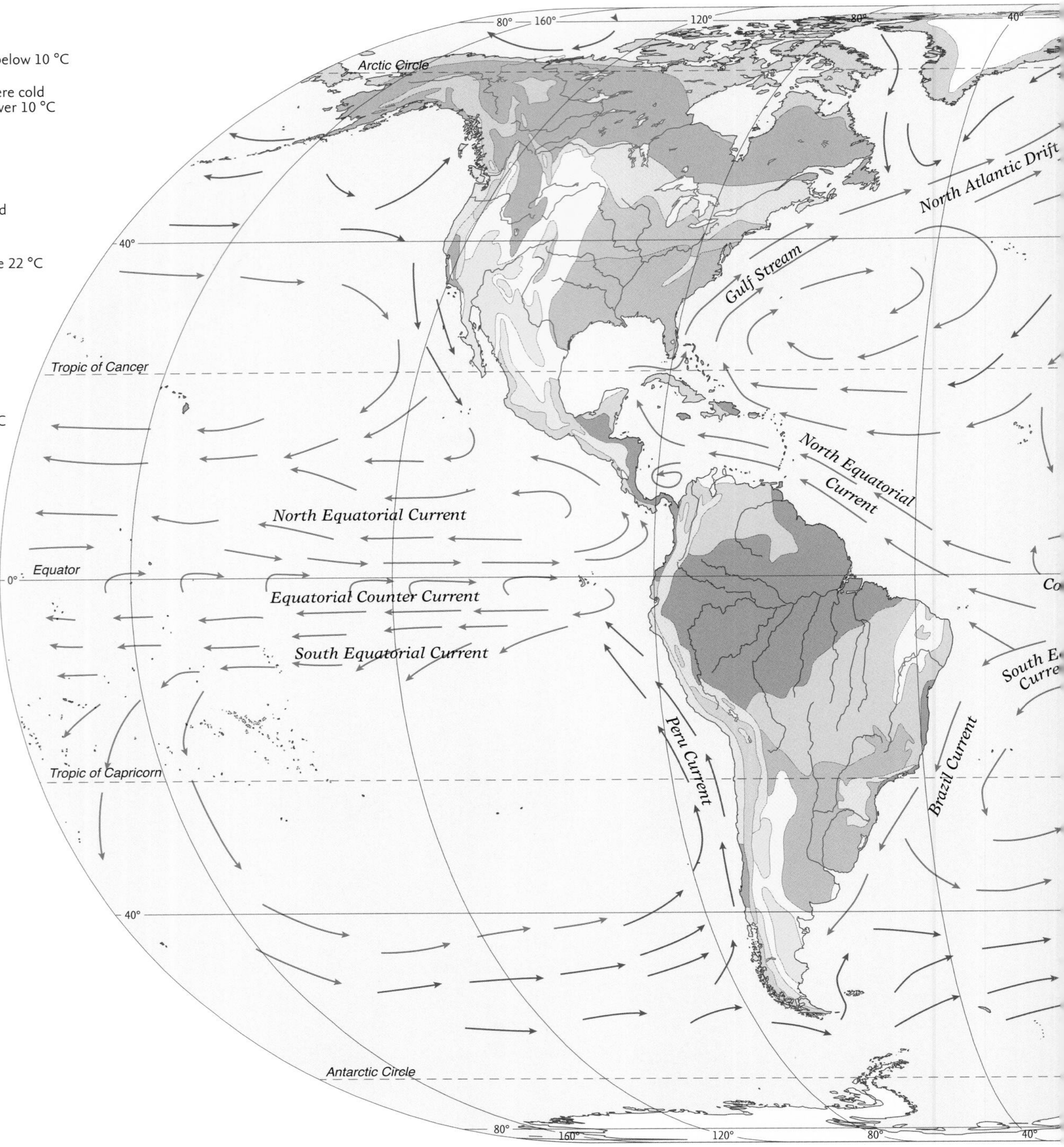

Arctic Circle

North Atlantic Drift

Gulf Stream

Tropic of Cancer

North Equatorial Current

North Equatorial Current

Equatorial Counter Current

South Equatorial Current

Co

South E
Curre

Peru Current

Brazil Current

0° Equator

Tropic of Capricorn

40°

Antarctic Circle

The impact of oceans on climate: air a

Normal circulation

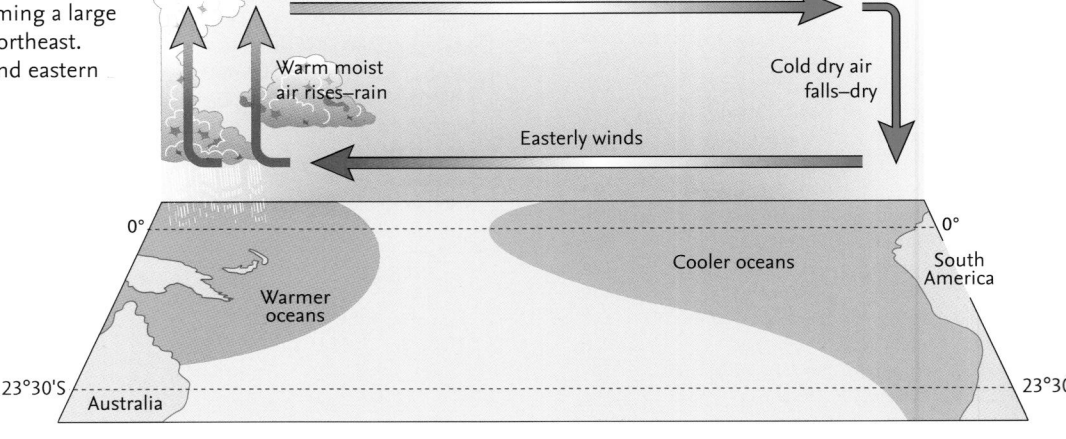

Warm moist
air rises–rain

Cold dry air
falls–dry

Easterly winds

0°   0°

Cooler oceans   South
America

Warmer
oceans

23°30'S   23°30

Australia

The oceans have a significant impact on
climate. Under normal conditions, easterly
winds push warm surface water across the
Pacific Ocean to Australia, forming a large
area of warmer water to the northeast.
This brings rain to northern and eastern
Australia.

World Meteorological Organization
www.wmo.int
Met Office
www.metoffice.gov.uk
United Nations Environment Programme
www.unep.org
World Conservation Monitoring Centre
www.unep-wcmc.org
World Resources Institute
www.wri.org

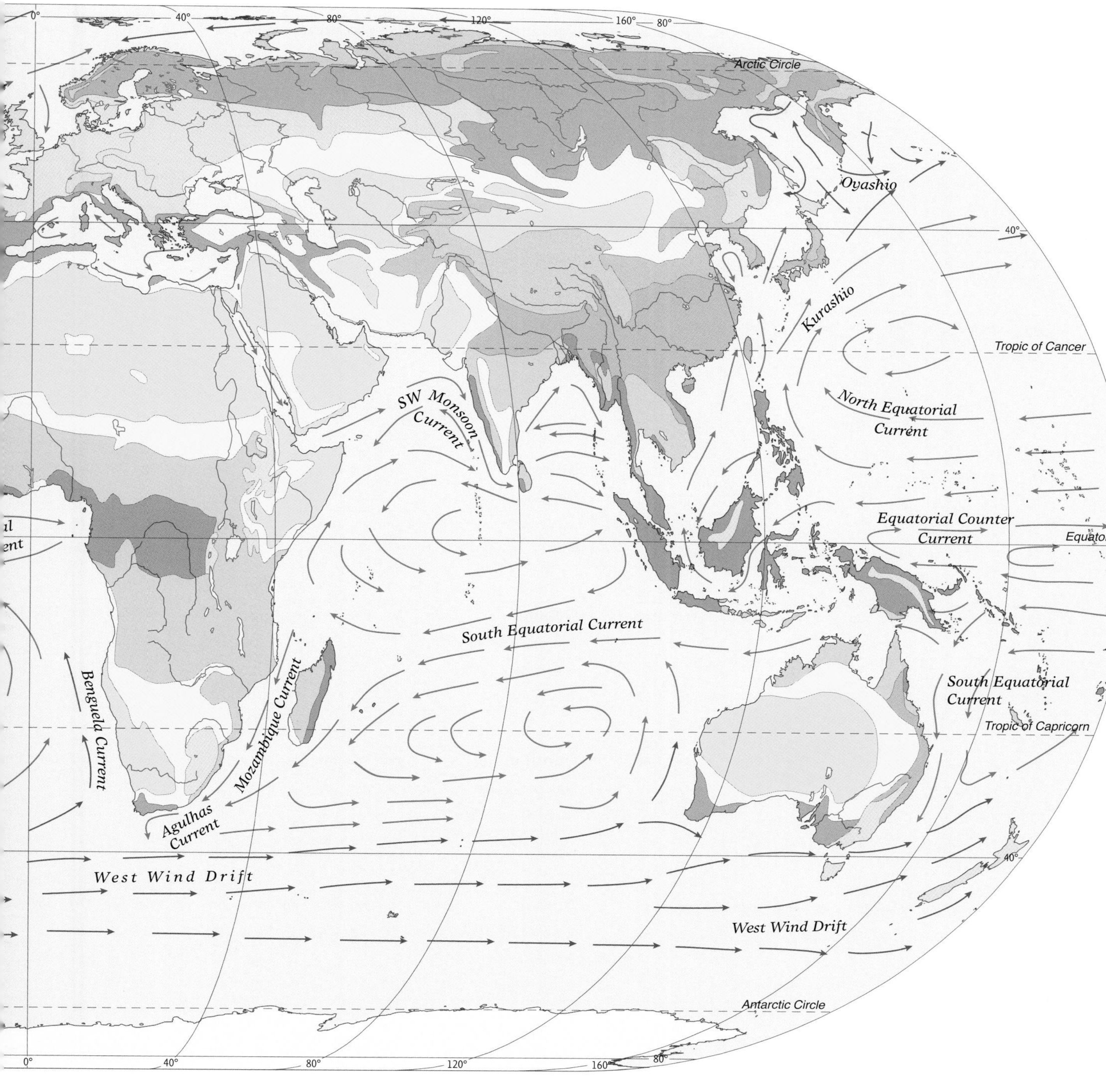

Arctic Circle

Oyashio

Kurashio

Tropic of Cancer

SW Monsoon
Current

North Equatorial
Current

Equatorial Counter
Current

Equator

0°

South Equatorial Current

South Equatorial
Current

Benguela Current

Mozambique Current

Tropic of Capricorn

40°

Agulhas
Current

West Wind Drift

West Wind Drift

Antarctic Circle

ter circulation in the Pacific Ocean

El Niño circulation

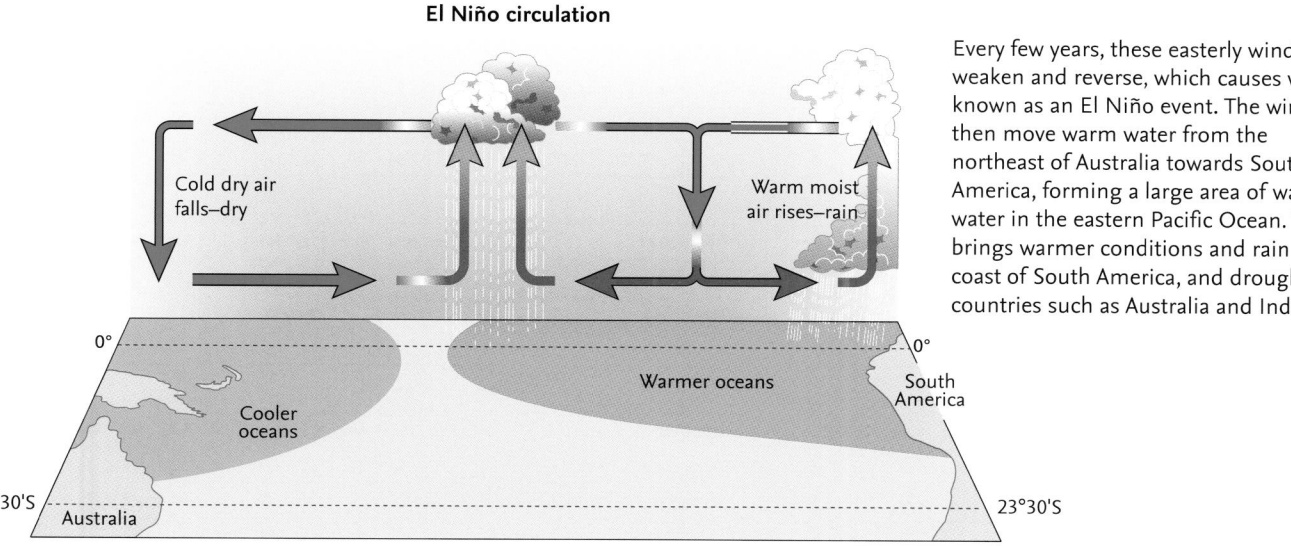

Cold dry air
falls—dry

Warm moist
air rises—rain

0°

Cooler
oceans

Warmer oceans

South
America

0°

°30'S

Australia

23°30'S

Every few years, these easterly winds weaken and reverse, which causes what is known as an El Niño event. The winds then move warm water from the northeast of Australia towards South America, forming a large area of warmer water in the eastern Pacific Ocean. This brings warmer conditions and rain to the coast of South America, and drought to countries such as Australia and Indonesia.

World: Climate Statistics

Aberystwyth — 52.25N 4.05W

	Jan	Feb	Mar	Apr	May	Jun	Jul	Aug	Sep	Oct	Nov	Dec
Temperature - max. (°C)	7	7	9	11	15	17	18	18	16	13	10	8
Temperature - min. (°C)	2	2	3	5	7	10	12	12	11	8	5	4
Rainfall - (mm)	97	72	60	56	65	76	99	93	108	118	111	96

Acapulco — 16.55N 99.52W

	Jan	Feb	Mar	Apr	May	Jun	Jul	Aug	Sep	Oct	Nov	Dec
Temperature - max. (°C)	31	31	31	32	32	33	32	33	32	32	32	31
Temperature - min. (°C)	22	22	22	23	25	25	25	25	24	24	23	22
Rainfall - (mm)	6	1	0	1	36	281	256	252	349	159	28	8

Algiers — 36.46N 3.04E

	Jan	Feb	Mar	Apr	May	Jun	Jul	Aug	Sep	Oct	Nov	Dec
Temperature - max. (°C)	15	16	17	20	23	26	28	29	27	23	19	16
Temperature - min. (°C)	9	9	11	13	15	18	21	22	21	17	13	11
Rainfall - (mm)	112	84	74	41	46	15	0	5	41	79	130	137

Auckland — 36.52S 174.46E

	Jan	Feb	Mar	Apr	May	Jun	Jul	Aug	Sep	Oct	Nov	Dec
Temperature - max. (°C)	23	24	22	20	17	15	15	15	16	18	20	22
Temperature - min. (°C)	15	16	15	12	10	8	7	8	9	11	12	14
Rainfall - (mm)	75	65	94	105	103	139	146	121	116	91	93	91

Belém — 1.26S 48.29W

	Jan	Feb	Mar	Apr	May	Jun	Jul	Aug	Sep	Oct	Nov	Dec
Temperature - max. (°C)	31	30	31	31	31	31	31	31	32	32	32	32
Temperature - min. (°C)	22	22	23	23	23	22	22	22	22	22	22	22
Rainfall - (mm)	318	358	358	320	259	170	150	112	89	84	66	155

Belfast — 54.36N 5.55W

	Jan	Feb	Mar	Apr	May	Jun	Jul	Aug	Sep	Oct	Nov	Dec
Temperature - max. (°C)	6	7	9	12	15	18	18	18	16	13	9	7
Temperature - min. (°C)	2	2	3	4	6	9	11	11	9	7	4	3
Rainfall - (mm)	80	52	50	48	52	68	94	77	80	83	72	90

Birmingham — 52.29N 1.53W

	Jan	Feb	Mar	Apr	May	Jun	Jul	Aug	Sep	Oct	Nov	Dec
Temperature - max. (°C)	5	6	9	12	16	19	20	20	17	13	9	6
Temperature - min. (°C)	2	2	3	5	7	10	12	12	10	7	5	3
Rainfall - (mm)	74	54	50	53	64	50	69	69	61	69	84	67

Blackpool — 53.49N 3.03W

	Jan	Feb	Mar	Apr	May	Jun	Jul	Aug	Sep	Oct	Nov	Dec
Temperature - max. (°C)	7	7	9	11	15	17	19	19	17	14	10	7
Temperature - min. (°C)	1	1	2	4	7	10	12	12	10	8	4	2
Rainfall - (mm)	78	54	64	51	53	59	61	78	86	93	89	87

Bourke — 30.07S 145.54E

	Jan	Feb	Mar	Apr	May	Jun	Jul	Aug	Sep	Oct	Nov	Dec
Temperature - max. (°C)	37	36	33	28	23	18	18	21	25	29	34	36
Temperature - min. (°C)	21	21	18	13	8	6	4	6	9	13	17	19
Rainfall - (mm)	36	38	28	28	25	28	23	20	20	23	31	36

Bucharest — 44.26N 26.06E

	Jan	Feb	Mar	Apr	May	Jun	Jul	Aug	Sep	Oct	Nov	Dec
Temperature - max. (°C)	1	4	10	18	23	27	30	30	25	18	10	4
Temperature - min. (°C)	-7	-5	-1	5	10	14	16	15	11	6	2	-3
Rainfall - (mm)	29	26	28	59	77	121	53	45	45	29	36	27

Charleston — 32.48N 79.58W

	Jan	Feb	Mar	Apr	May	Jun	Jul	Aug	Sep	Oct	Nov	Dec
Temperature - max. (°C)	14	15	19	23	27	30	31	31	28	24	19	15
Temperature - min. (°C)	6	7	10	14	19	23	24	24	22	16	11	7
Rainfall - (mm)	74	84	86	71	81	119	185	168	130	81	58	71

Clacton-on-Sea — 51.47N 1.0

	Jan	Feb	Mar	Apr	May	Jun	Jul	Aug	Sep	Oct	Nov	Dec
Temperature - max. (°C)	6	6	9	11	15	18	20	20	18	15	10	7
Temperature - min. (°C)	2	2	3	5	8	11	13	14	12	9	5	3
Rainfall - (mm)	49	31	43	40	40	45	43	43	48	48	55	50

Conakry — 9.31N 13.42

	Jan	Feb	Mar	Apr	May	Jun	Jul	Aug	Sep	Oct	Nov	Dec
Temperature - max. (°C)	31	31	32	32	32	30	28	28	29	31	31	31
Temperature - min. (°C)	22	23	23	23	24	23	22	22	23	23	24	23
Rainfall - (mm)	3	3	10	23	158	559	1298	1054	683	371	122	10

Darwin — 12.27S 130.5

	Jan	Feb	Mar	Apr	May	Jun	Jul	Aug	Sep	Oct	Nov	Dec
Temperature - max. (°C)	32	32	33	33	33	31	31	32	33	34	34	33
Temperature - min. (°C)	25	25	25	24	23	21	19	21	23	25	26	26
Rainfall - (mm)	386	312	254	97	15	3	0	3	13	51	119	23

Detroit — 42.19N 83.04

	Jan	Feb	Mar	Apr	May	Jun	Jul	Aug	Sep	Oct	Nov	Dec
Temperature - max. (°C)	-1	0	6	13	19	25	28	27	23	16	8	2
Temperature - min. (°C)	-7	-8	-3	3	9	14	17	17	13	7	1	-4
Rainfall - (mm)	53	53	64	64	84	91	84	69	71	51	61	58

Dublin — 53.20N 6.16

	Jan	Feb	Mar	Apr	May	Jun	Jul	Aug	Sep	Oct	Nov	Dec
Temperature - max. (°C)	8	8	10	13	15	18	20	19	17	14	10	8
Temperature - min. (°C)	1	2	3	4	6	9	11	11	9	6	4	3
Rainfall - (mm)	67	55	51	45	60	57	70	74	72	70	67	74

Dumfries — 55.04N 3.36

	Jan	Feb	Mar	Apr	May	Jun	Jul	Aug	Sep	Oct	Nov	Dec
Temperature - max. (°C)	6	6	8	11	14	17	19	18	16	13	9	7
Temperature - min. (°C)	1	1	2	3	6	9	11	10	9	6	3	1
Rainfall - (mm)	110	76	81	53	72	63	71	93	104	117	100	10

Durban — 29.51S 31.0

	Jan	Feb	Mar	Apr	May	Jun	Jul	Aug	Sep	Oct	Nov	Dec
Temperature – max. (°C)	28	28	28	26	24	23	23	23	23	24	25	27
Temperature – min. (°C)	21	21	20	17	14	11	10	12	15	16	18	20
Rainfall (mm)	119	126	132	84	56	34	35	49	73	110	118	12

Edinburgh — 55.57N 3.1

	Jan	Feb	Mar	Apr	May	Jun	Jul	Aug	Sep	Oct	Nov	Dec
Temperature - max. (°C)	6	7	9	11	14	17	18	18	16	13	9	7
Temperature - min. (°C)	1	1	2	4	6	9	11	11	9	7	3	2
Rainfall - (mm)	54	40	47	39	49	50	59	63	66	63	56	52

Glasgow — 55.52N 4.1

	Jan	Feb	Mar	Apr	May	Jun	Jul	Aug	Sep	Oct	Nov	Dec
Temperature - max. (°C)	6	7	9	12	15	18	19	19	16	13	9	7
Temperature - min. (°C)	0	0	2	3	6	9	10	10	9	6	2	1
Rainfall - (mm)	96	63	65	50	62	58	68	83	95	98	105	10

Helsinki — 60.10N 24.5

	Jan	Feb	Mar	Apr	May	Jun	Jul	Aug	Sep	Oct	Nov	Dec
Temperature - max. (°C)	-3	-4	0	6	14	19	22	20	15	8	3	-1
Temperature - min. (°C)	-9	-10	-7	-1	4	9	13	12	8	3	-1	-5
Rainfall - (mm)	56	42	36	44	41	51	51	68	71	73	68	6

Iguatu — 6.22S 39.1

	Jan	Feb	Mar	Apr	May	Jun	Jul	Aug	Sep	Oct	Nov	Dec
Temperature - max. (°C)	34	33	32	31	31	31	32	32	35	36	36	3
Temperature - min. (°C)	23	23	23	23	22	22	21	21	22	23	23	2
Rainfall - (mm)	89	173	185	160	61	61	36	5	18	18	10	3

Lerwick

60.09N 1.09W

	Jan	Feb	Mar	Apr	May	Jun	Jul	Aug	Sep	Oct	Nov	Dec
Temperature - max. (°C)	5	5	6	8	10	13	14	14	13	10	7	6
Temperature - min. (°C)	1	1	2	3	5	7	9	9	8	6	3	2
Rainfall - (mm)	127	93	93	72	64	64	67	78	113	119	140	147

London

51.30N 0.07W

	Jan	Feb	Mar	Apr	May	Jun	Jul	Aug	Sep	Oct	Nov	Dec
Temperature - max. (°C)	8	8	11	13	17	20	23	23	19	15	11	9
Temperature - min. (°C)	2	2	4	5	8	11	14	13	11	8	5	3
Rainfall - (mm)	52	34	42	45	47	53	38	47	57	62	52	54

Makassar

5.06S 119.27E

	Jan	Feb	Mar	Apr	May	Jun	Jul	Aug	Sep	Oct	Nov	Dec
Temperature - max. (°C)	29	29	29	30	31	30	30	31	31	31	30	29
Temperature - min. (°C)	23	24	23	23	23	22	21	21	21	22	23	23
Rainfall - (mm)	686	536	424	150	89	74	36	10	15	43	178	610

Manchester

53.29N 2.15W

	Jan	Feb	Mar	Apr	May	Jun	Jul	Aug	Sep	Oct	Nov	Dec
Temperature - max. (°C)	6	7	9	12	15	18	20	20	17	14	9	7
Temperature - min. (°C)	1	1	3	4	7	10	12	12	10	8	4	2
Rainfall - (mm)	69	50	61	51	61	67	65	79	74	77	78	78

Munich

48.08N 11.35E

	Jan	Feb	Mar	Apr	May	Jun	Jul	Aug	Sep	Oct	Nov	Dec
Temperature - max. (°C)	1	3	9	14	18	21	23	23	20	13	7	2
Temperature - min. (°C)	-5	-5	-1	3	7	11	13	12	9	4	0	-4
Rainfall - (mm)	59	53	48	62	109	125	139	107	85	66	57	47

Nairobi

1.17S 36.48E

	Jan	Feb	Mar	Apr	May	Jun	Jul	Aug	Sep	Oct	Nov	Dec
Temperature - max. (°C)	25	26	25	24	22	21	21	21	24	24	23	23
Temperature - min. (°C)	12	13	14	14	13	12	11	11	11	13	13	13
Rainfall - (mm)	38	64	125	211	158	46	15	23	31	53	109	86

Oban

56.25N 5.28W

	Jan	Feb	Mar	Apr	May	Jun	Jul	Aug	Sep	Oct	Nov	Dec
Temperature - max. (°C)	6	7	9	11	14	16	17	17	15	12	9	7
Temperature - min. (°C)	2	1	3	4	7	9	11	11	9	7	4	3
Rainfall - (mm)	146	109	83	90	72	87	120	116	141	169	146	172

Padang

0.58S 100.23E

	Jan	Feb	Mar	Apr	May	Jun	Jul	Aug	Sep	Oct	Nov	Dec
Temperature - max. (°C)	31	31	31	31	31	31	31	31	30	30	30	30
Temperature - min. (°C)	23	23	23	24	24	23	23	23	23	23	23	23
Rainfall - (mm)	351	259	307	363	315	307	277	348	152	495	518	480

Perth

31.56S 115.47E

	Jan	Feb	Mar	Apr	May	Jun	Jul	Aug	Sep	Oct	Nov	Dec
Temperature - max. (°C)	29	29	27	24	21	18	17	18	19	21	24	27
Temperature - min. (°C)	17	17	16	14	12	10	9	9	10	12	14	16
Rainfall - (mm)	8	10	20	43	130	180	170	145	86	56	20	13

Plymouth

50.22N 4.08W

	Jan	Feb	Mar	Apr	May	Jun	Jul	Aug	Sep	Oct	Nov	Dec
Temperature - max. (°C)	8	8	10	12	15	18	19	19	18	15	11	9
Temperature - min. (°C)	4	4	5	6	8	11	13	13	12	9	7	5
Rainfall - (mm)	99	74	69	53	63	53	70	77	78	91	113	110

Punta Arenas

53.09S 70.57W

	Jan	Feb	Mar	Apr	May	Jun	Jul	Aug	Sep	Oct	Nov	Dec
Temperature - max. (°C)	14	14	12	10	7	5	4	6	8	11	12	14
Temperature - min. (°C)	7	7	5	4	2	1	-1	1	2	3	4	6
Rainfall - (mm)	38	23	33	36	33	41	28	31	23	28	18	36

Quito

0.14S 78.30W

	Jan	Feb	Mar	Apr	May	Jun	Jul	Aug	Sep	Oct	Nov	Dec
Temperature - max. (°C)	22	22	22	21	21	22	22	23	23	22	22	22
Temperature - min. (°C)	8	8	8	8	8	7	7	7	7	8	7	8
Rainfall - (mm)	99	112	142	175	137	43	20	31	69	112	97	79

Riyadh

24.43N 46.41E

	Jan	Feb	Mar	Apr	May	Jun	Jul	Aug	Sep	Oct	Nov	Dec
Temperature - max. (°C)	21	23	28	32	38	42	42	42	39	34	29	21
Temperature - min. (°C)	8	9	13	18	22	25	26	24	22	16	13	9
Rainfall - (mm)	3	20	23	25	10	0	0	0	0	0	0	0

Santiago

33.28S 70.39W

	Jan	Feb	Mar	Apr	May	Jun	Jul	Aug	Sep	Oct	Nov	Dec
Temperature - max. (°C)	29	29	27	23	18	14	15	17	19	22	26	28
Temperature - min. (°C)	12	11	9	7	5	3	3	4	6	7	9	11
Rainfall - (mm)	3	3	5	13	64	84	76	56	31	15	8	5

Saskatoon

52.08N 106.39W

	Jan	Feb	Mar	Apr	May	Jun	Jul	Aug	Sep	Oct	Nov	Dec
Temperature - max. (°C)	-13	-11	-3	9	18	22	25	24	17	11	-1	-9
Temperature - min. (°C)	-24	-22	-14	-3	3	9	11	9	3	-3	-11	-19
Rainfall - (mm)	23	13	18	18	36	66	61	48	38	23	13	15

Seville

37.24N 5.58W

	Jan	Feb	Mar	Apr	May	Jun	Jul	Aug	Sep	Oct	Nov	Dec
Temperature - max. (°C)	15	17	20	24	27	32	36	36	32	26	20	16
Temperature - min. (°C)	6	7	9	11	13	17	20	20	18	14	10	7
Rainfall - (mm)	66	61	90	57	41	8	1	5	19	70	67	79

Shanghai

31.15N 121.29E

	Jan	Feb	Mar	Apr	May	Jun	Jul	Aug	Sep	Oct	Nov	Dec
Temperature - max. (°C)	8	8	13	19	25	28	32	32	28	23	17	12
Temperature - min. (°C)	1	1	4	10	15	19	23	23	19	14	7	2
Rainfall - (mm)	48	58	84	94	94	180	147	142	130	71	51	36

Timbuktu

16.46N 2.59W

	Jan	Feb	Mar	Apr	May	Jun	Jul	Aug	Sep	Oct	Nov	Dec
Temperature - max. (°C)	27	31	34	38	41	40	37	35	37	37	33	28
Temperature - min. (°C)	14	17	21	24	27	29	27	27	26	24	19	15
Rainfall - (mm)	0	0	0	0	4	19	62	79	33	3	0	0

Tomsk

56.30N 85.01E

	Jan	Feb	Mar	Apr	May	Jun	Jul	Aug	Sep	Oct	Nov	Dec
Temperature - max. (°C)	-18	-13	-6	3	12	19	23	20	14	3	-9	-16
Temperature - min. (°C)	-24	-22	-17	-7	3	9	12	10	4	-3	-14	-22
Rainfall - (mm)	28	18	20	23	41	69	66	66	41	51	46	38

Vancouver

49.16N 123.08W

	Jan	Feb	Mar	Apr	May	Jun	Jul	Aug	Sep	Oct	Nov	Dec
Temperature - max. (°C)	5	7	10	14	18	21	23	23	18	14	9	6
Temperature - min. (°C)	0	1	3	4	8	11	12	12	9	7	4	2
Rainfall - (mm)	218	147	127	84	71	64	31	43	91	147	211	224

Walvis Bay

22.58S 14.30E

	Jan	Feb	Mar	Apr	May	Jun	Jul	Aug	Sep	Oct	Nov	Dec
Temperature - max. (°C)	23	23	23	24	23	23	21	20	19	19	22	22
Temperature - min. (°C)	15	16	15	13	11	9	8	8	9	11	12	14
Rainfall - (mm)	0	5	8	3	3	0	0	3	0	0	0	0

York

53.58N 1.05W

	Jan	Feb	Mar	Apr	May	Jun	Jul	Aug	Sep	Oct	Nov	Dec
Temperature - max. (°C)	6	7	10	13	16	19	21	21	18	14	10	7
Temperature - min. (°C)	2	2	3	5	7	10	12	12	11	8	5	4
Rainfall - (mm)	59	46	37	41	50	50	62	68	55	56	65	50

World: Biomes, Soils and Soil Erosion

Ice cap and ice shelf
Extremely cold. No vegetation.

Mountain/Alpine
Very low night-time temperatures. Only a few dwarf trees and small leafed shrubs can grow.

Arctic tundra
Very cold climate. Simple vegetation such as mosses, lichens, grasses and flowering herbs.

Boreal/Taiga forest
Found between 50° and 70°N. Low temperatures. Vegetation consists of cold tolerant evergreen conifers.

Coniferous forest
Dense forests of pine, spruce and larch.

Mixed forest
Broadleaf and coniferous forests.

Mediterranean
Mild winters and dry summers. Vegetation is mixed shrubs and herbaceous plants.

Temperate grasslands
Grassland is the main vegetation. Summers are hot and winters cold.

Savanna grassland
Warm or hot climate. Tropical grasslands with scattered thorn bushtes or trees.

Tropical forest
Dense rainforest found in areas of high rainfall near the equator.

Monsoon forest
Areas which experience Monsoon rain. All trees are deciduous.

Dry tropical forest
Semi deciduous trees with low shrubs and bushes.

Sub tropical forest
Rainfall is seasonal. Vegetation is mainly hard leaf evergreen forest.

Desert
Hot with little rainfall. Very sparse vegetation except cacti and grasses adapted to the harsh conditions.

Scale 1 : 100 000 000

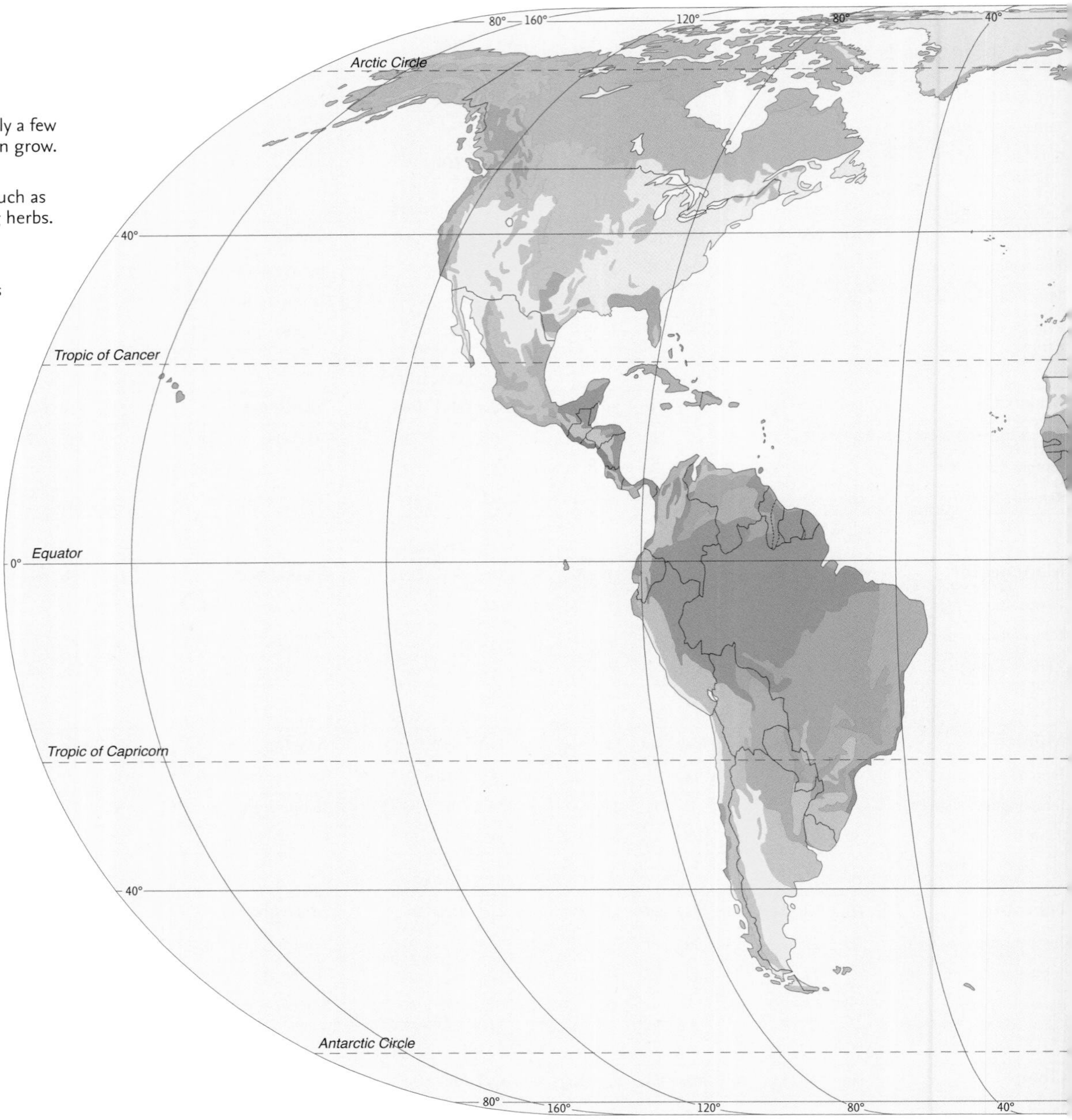

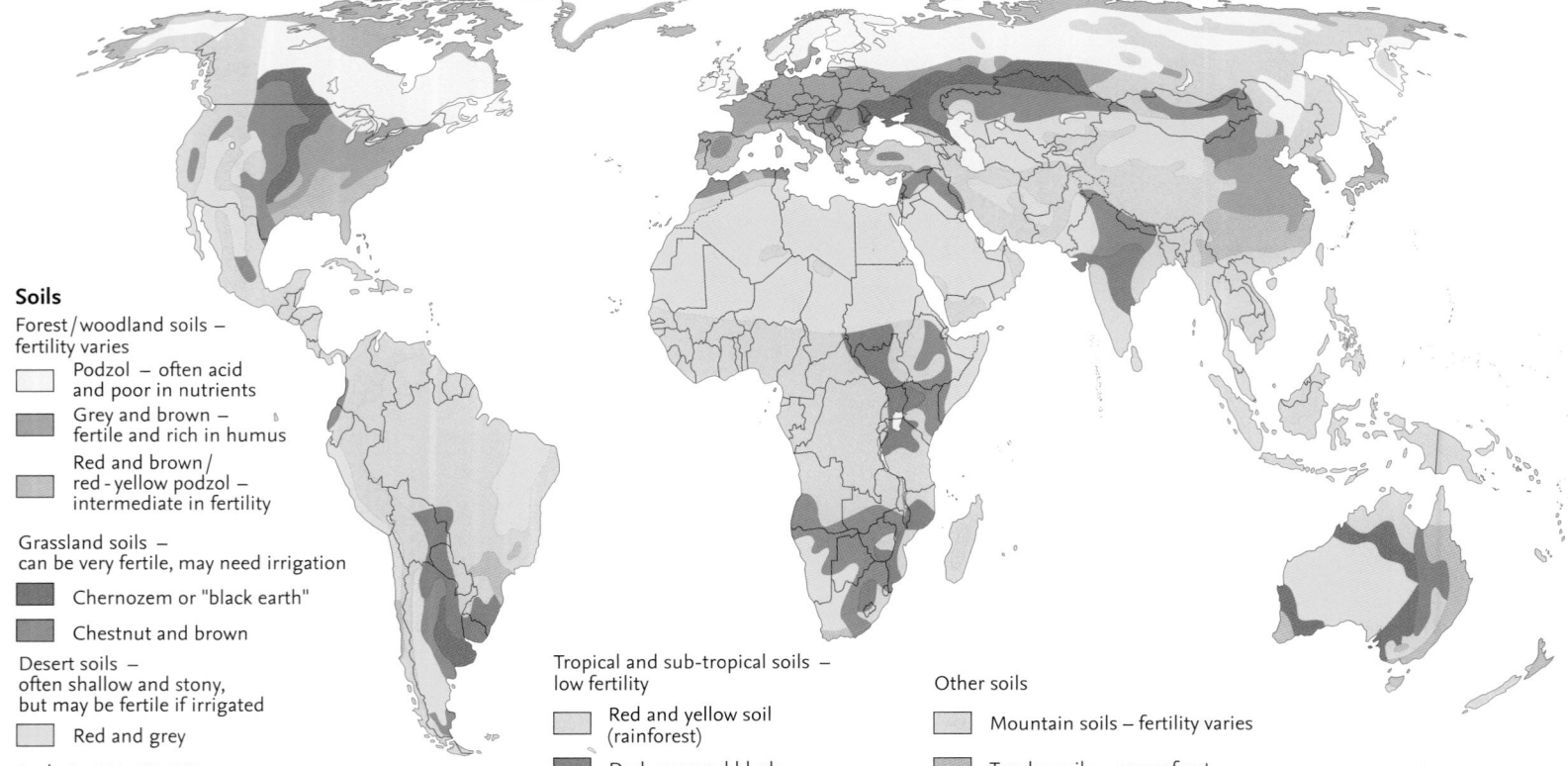

Soils

Forest/woodland soils –
fertility varies

Podzol – often acid and poor in nutrients

Grey and brown – fertile and rich in humus

Red and brown / red - yellow podzol – intermediate in fertility

Grassland soils –
can be very fertile, may need irrigation

Chernozem or "black earth"

Chestnut and brown

Desert soils –
often shallow and stony, but may be fertile if irrigated

Red and grey

Scale 1 : 140 000 000

Tropical and sub-tropical soils –
low fertility

Red and yellow soil (rainforest)

Dark grey and black

Other soils

Mountain soils – fertility varies

Tundra soils – permafrost

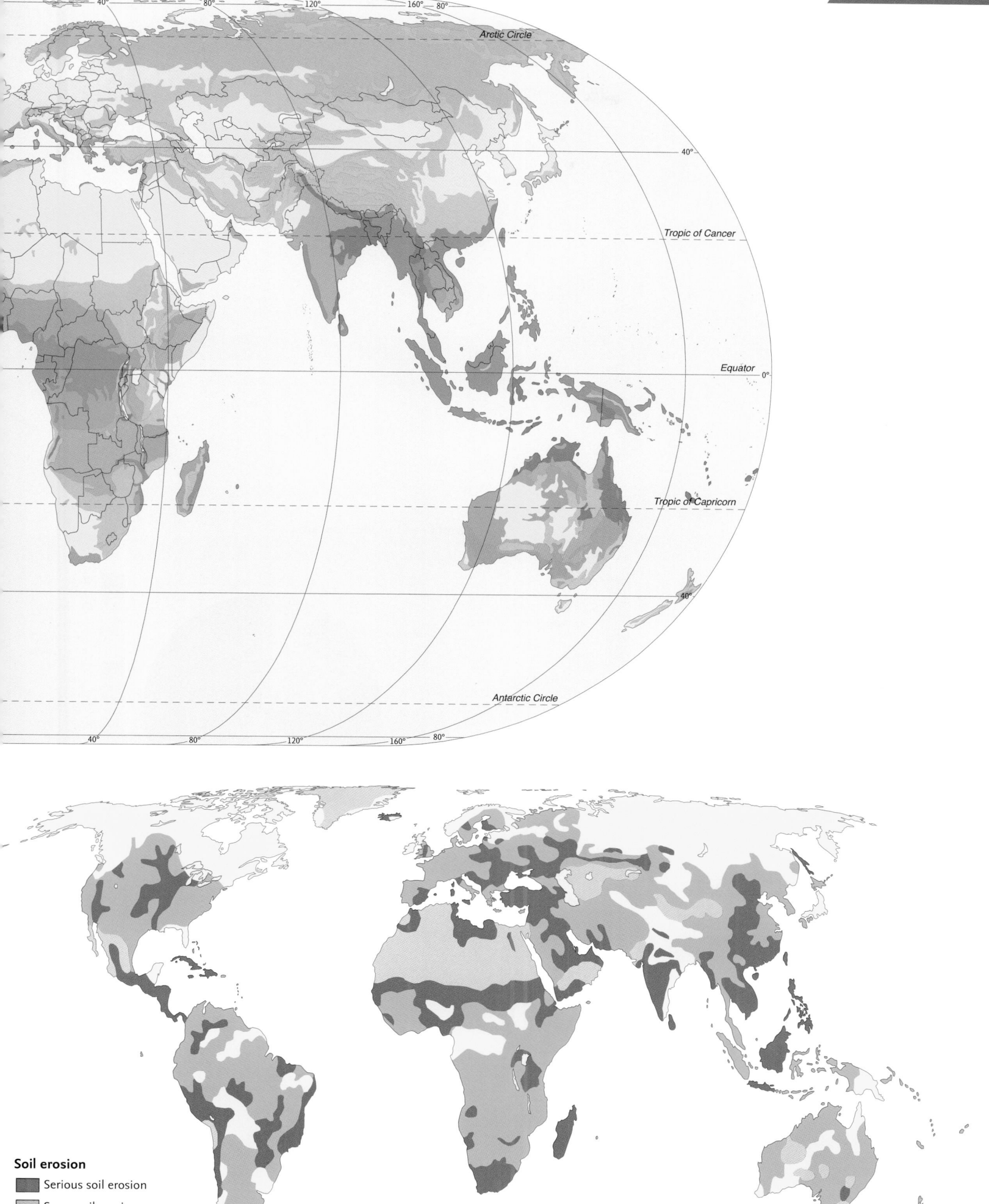

Soil erosion

- Serious soil erosion
- Some soil erosion
- No soil erosion
- No vegetation

Scale 1 : 140 000 000

World: Agriculture

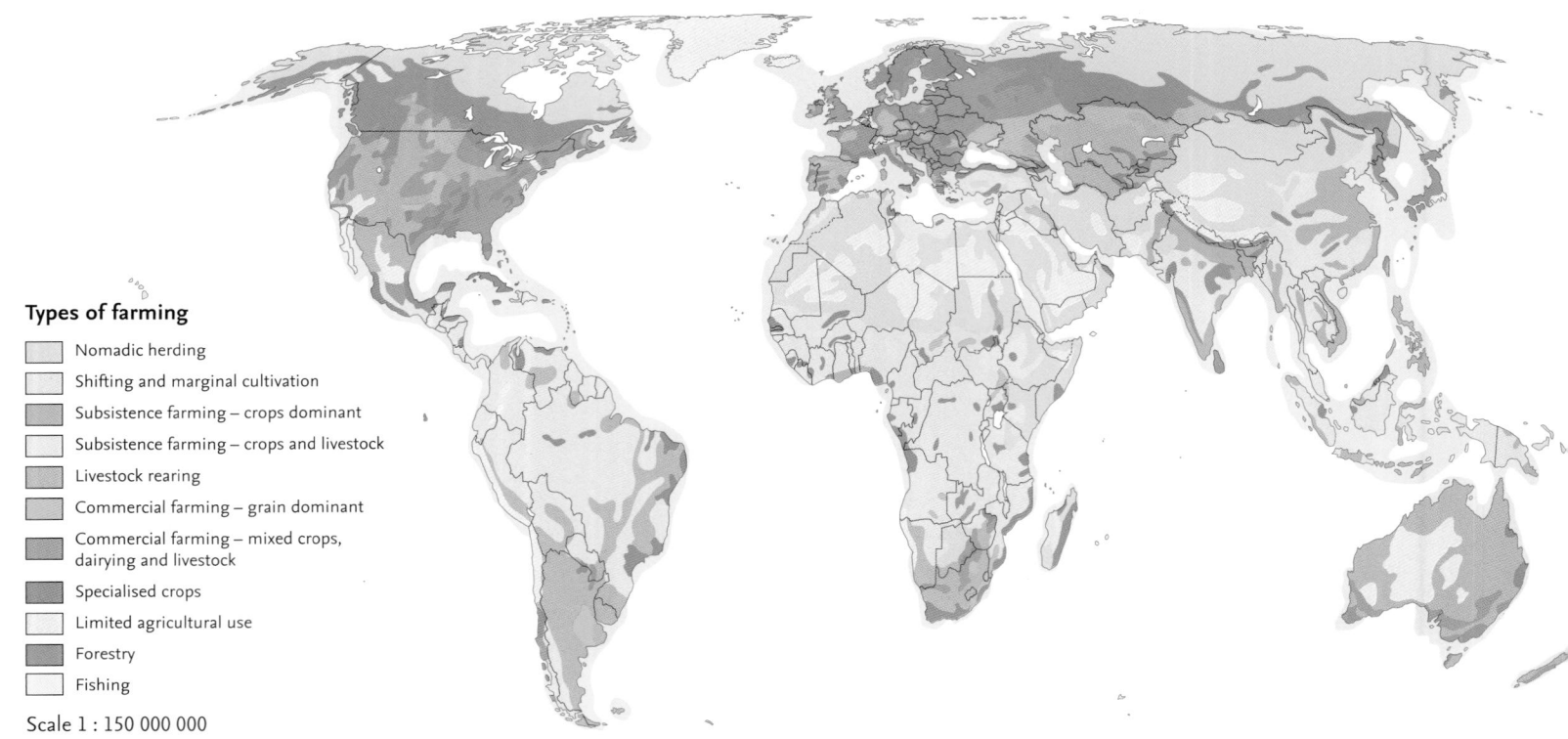

Types of farming

- Nomadic herding
- Shifting and marginal cultivation
- Subsistence farming – crops dominant
- Subsistence farming – crops and livestock
- Livestock rearing
- Commercial farming – grain dominant
- Commercial farming – mixed crops, dairying and livestock
- Specialised crops
- Limited agricultural use
- Forestry
- Fishing

Scale 1 : 150 000 000

World cereal production, 2014

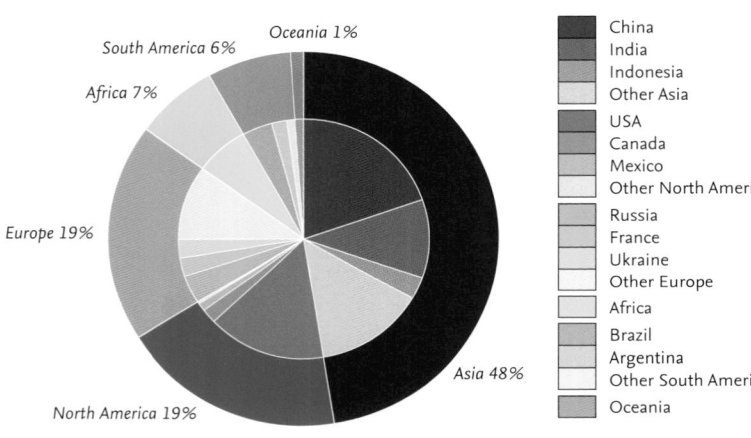

Oceania 1%
South America 6%
Africa 7%
Europe 19%
North America 19%
Asia 48%

- China
- India
- Indonesia
- Other Asia
- USA
- Canada
- Mexico
- Other North America
- Russia
- France
- Ukraine
- Other Europe
- Africa
- Brazil
- Argentina
- Other South America
- Oceania

World meat production, 2014

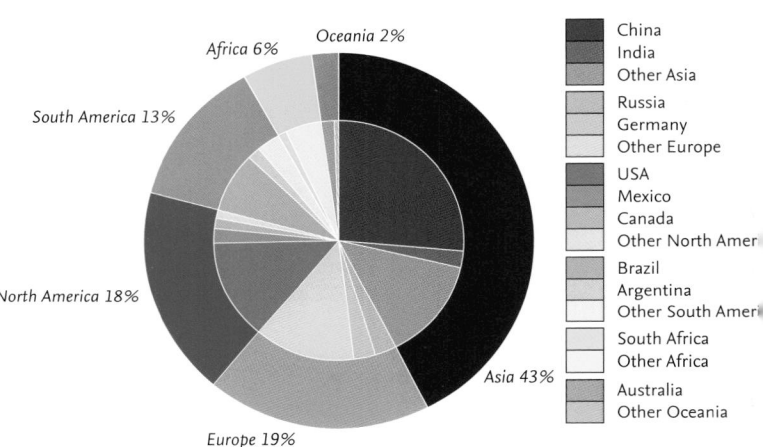

Africa 6%
Oceania 2%
South America 13%
North America 18%
Europe 19%
Asia 43%

- China
- India
- Other Asia
- Russia
- Germany
- Other Europe
- USA
- Mexico
- Canada
- Other North Ameri
- Brazil
- Argentina
- Other South Ameri
- South Africa
- Other Africa
- Australia
- Other Oceania

Projected population growth, 2006 – 2050

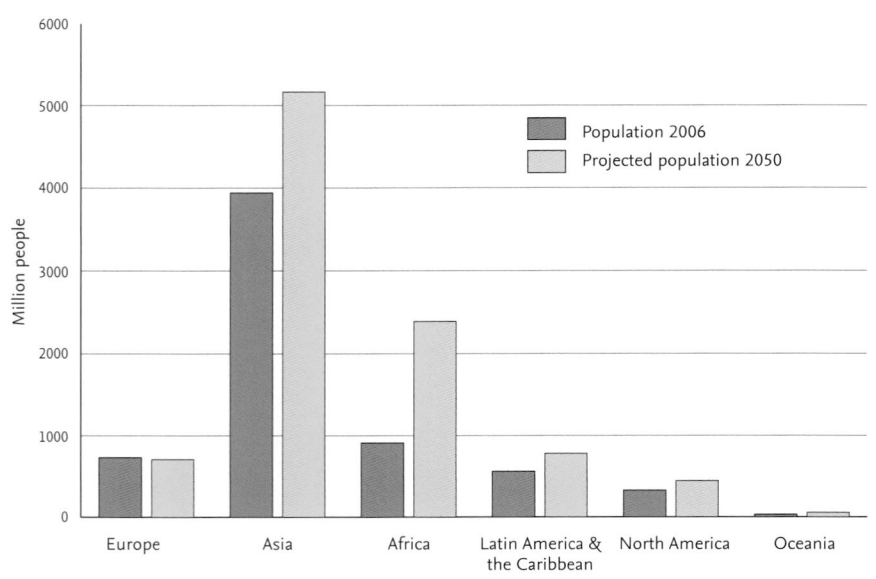

- Population 2006
- Projected population 2050

Million people

6000
5000
4000
3000
2000
1000
0

Europe | Asia | Africa | Latin America & the Caribbean | North America | Oceania

Closing the food gap

Required increase in food calories to feed 9.6 billion people in 2050.

69%

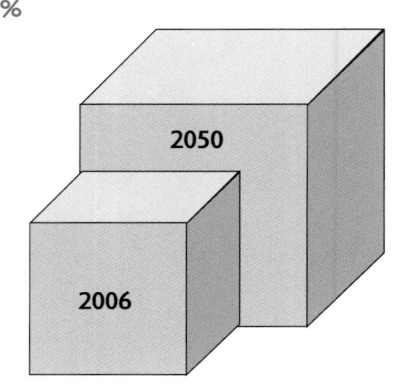

2050

2006

MEDCs and LEDCs

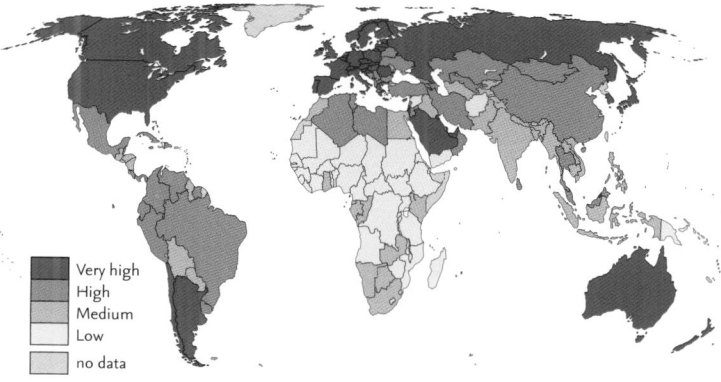

- MEDCs
- LEDCs
- no data

Scale 1 : 300 000 000

International organizations generally agree that countries can be categorized into more economically developed countries (MEDCs) and less economically developed countries (LEDCs). The group of MEDCs includes the following countries/regions: Canada; USA; Greenland; Chile; Uruguay; Europe as far east as the Baltic states, Poland, Slovakia, Hungary and Croatia; Greece; Cyprus; Israel; Saudi Arabia; Kuwait; Bahrain; Qatar; UAE; Oman; Seychelles; South Korea; Japan; Brunei; Singapore; Australia; New Zealand; several small Pacific and Caribbean islands.

Level of development

- Very high
- High
- Medium
- Low
- no data

This map categorizes countries by their stage of development: Very high; High; Medium; Low. Indicators, such as life expectancy as an index of population health and longevity, education as measured by adult literacy and school enrolment, and standards of living based on the GDP per capita, are used to measure the level of development. The development of regions, cities or villages can also be assessed using these indicators.

Low development

Burundi

Health

Under-5 mortality rate (per 1000 live births)	54
Life expectancy at birth	57

Education

Adult literacy	86%
School enrolment, primary	95%

Income

GDP per capita	$727
GNI per capita	$260
Poverty line (% of population)	78%

Medium development

India

Health

Under-5 mortality rate (per 1000 live births)	38
Life expectancy at birth	68

Education

Adult literacy	72%
School enrolment, primary	90%

Income

GDP per capita	$6105
GNI per capita	$1590
Poverty line (% of population)	21%

High development

Brazil

Health

Under-5 mortality rate (per 1000 live births)	15
Life expectancy at birth	75

Education

Adult literacy	93%
School enrolment, primary	92%

Income

GDP per capita	$15 474
GNI per capita	$9990
Poverty line (% of population)	4%

Very high development

Australia

Health

Under-5 mortality rate (per 1000 live births)	3
Life expectancy at birth	82

Education

Adult literacy	no data
School enrolment, primary	97

Income

GDP per capita	$46 271
GNI per capita	$60 050
Poverty line (% of population)	no data

GDP per capita, 1990 – 2015

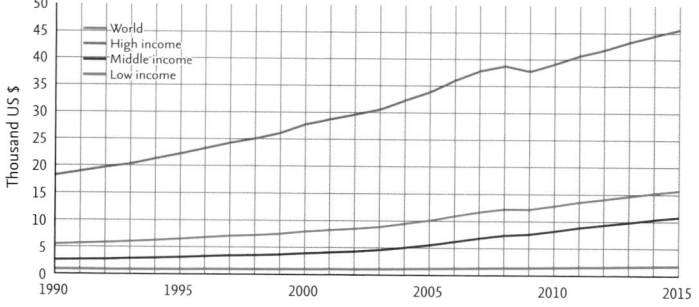

World; High income; Middle income; Low income

GNI per capita, 1980 – 2015

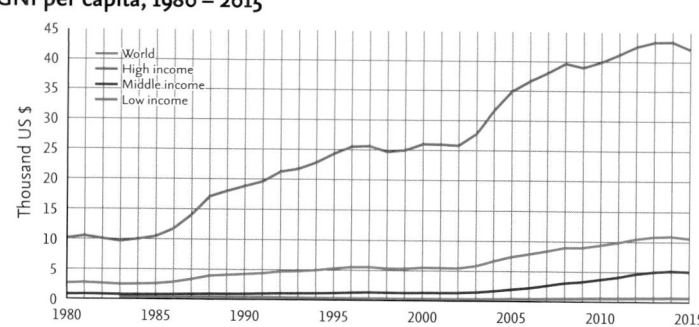

World; High income; Middle income; Low income

Primary school enrolment, 1980 – 2014

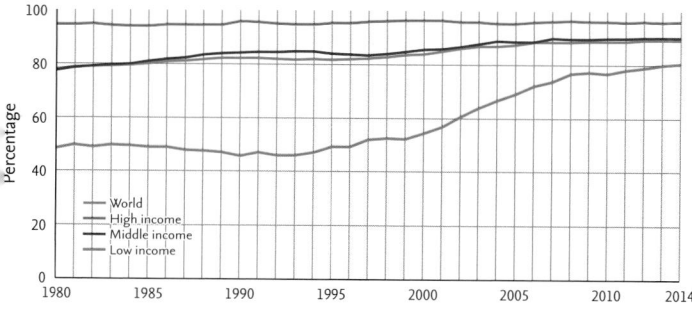

World; High income; Middle income; Low income

Life expectancy, 1980 – 2015

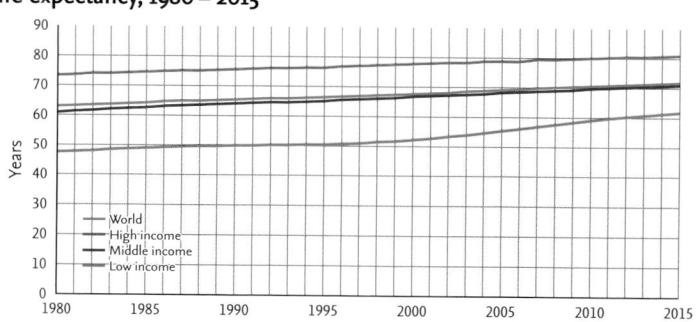

World; High income; Middle income; Low income

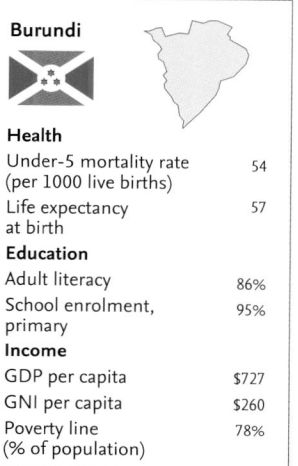

Population comparisons

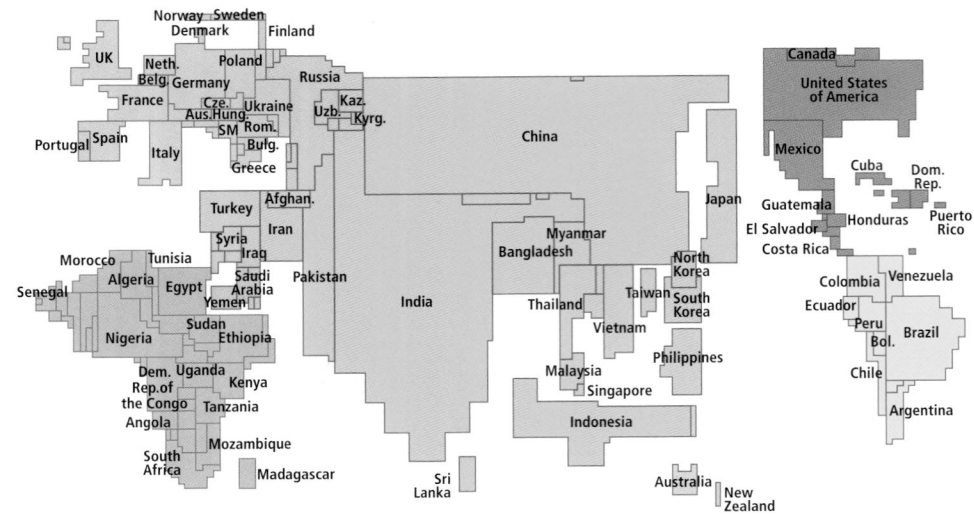

☐ 10 000 000 people

Population structure, 1950 – 2050
Each full square represents 1% of the total population

World

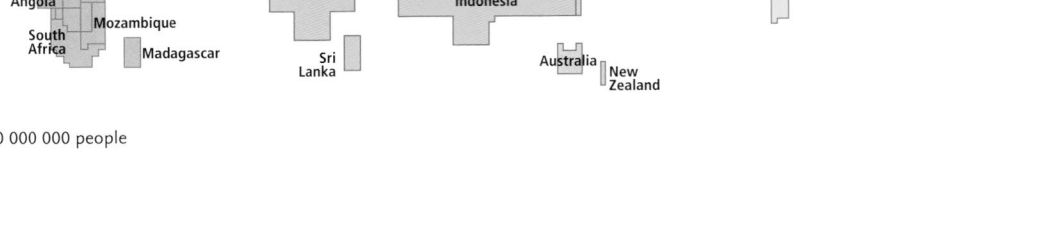

More developed regions

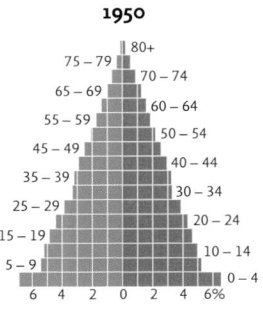
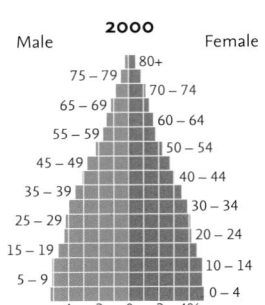
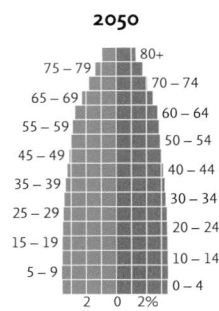

Least developed regions

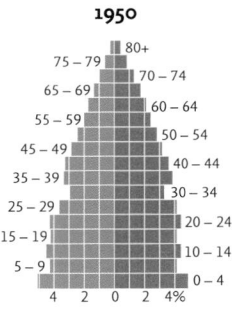
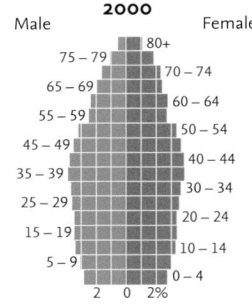
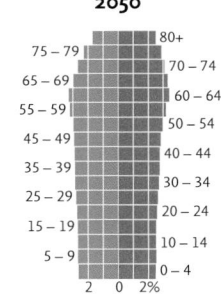

Largest countries by population, 2015

Country and continent	Population
China Asia	1 383 925 000
India Asia	1 311 051 000
United States of America N America	321 774 000
Indonesia Asia	257 564 000
Brazil S America	207 848 000
Pakistan Asia	188 925 000
Nigeria Africa	182 202 000
Bangladesh Asia	160 996 000
Russia Asia/Europe	143 457 000
Mexico N America	127 017 000
Japan Asia	126 573 000
Philippines Asia	100 699 000
Ethiopia Africa	99 391 000
Vietnam Asia	93 448 000
Egypt Africa	91 508 000
Germany Europe	80 689 000
Iran Asia	79 109 000
Turkey Asia	78 666 000
Dem. Rep. of the Congo Africa	77 267 000
Thailand Asia	67 959 000

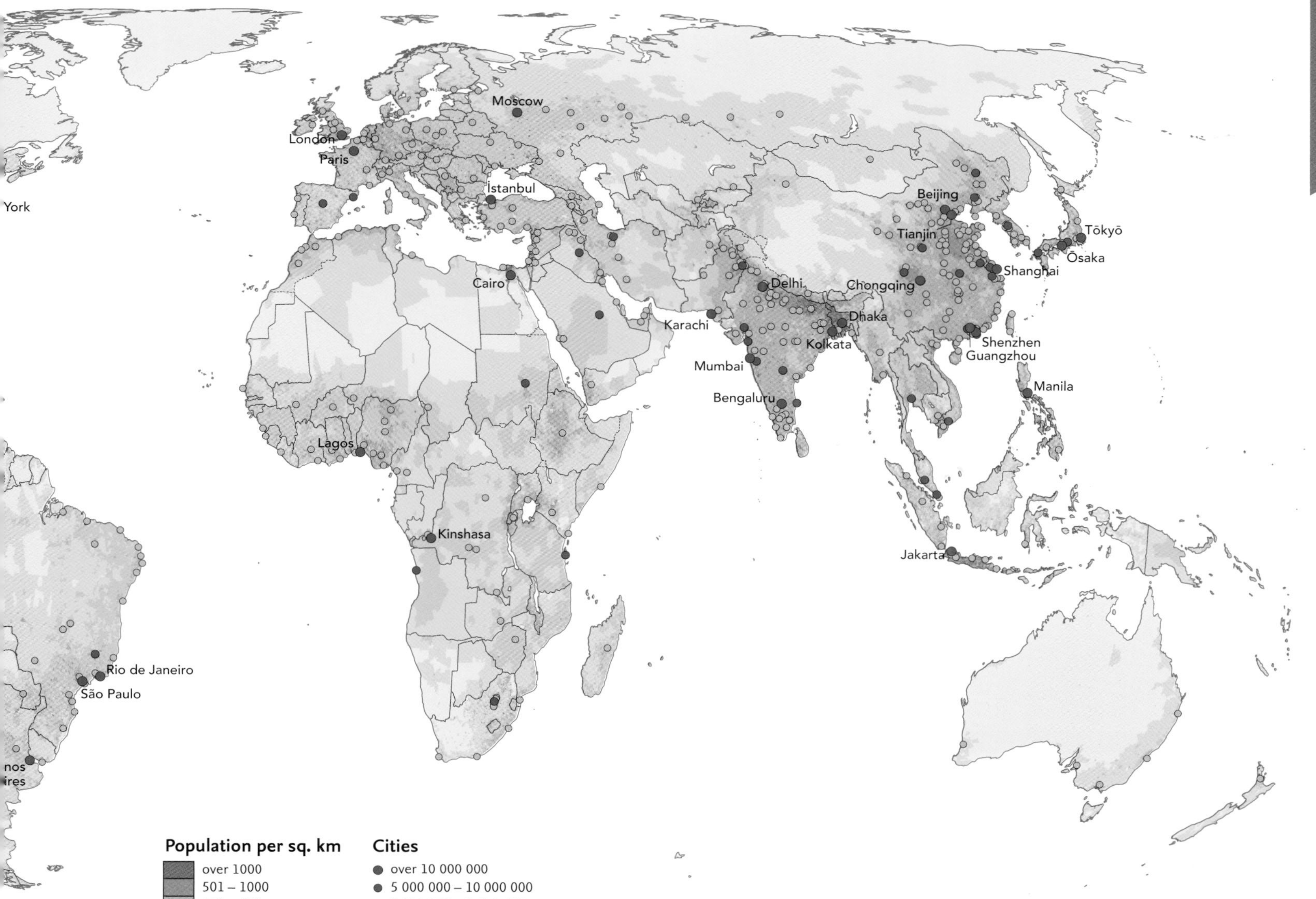

York

Moscow

London

Paris

İstanbul

Cairo

Lagos

Kinshasa

Karachi

Delhi

Mumbai

Bengaluru

Kolkata

Dhaka

Beijing

Tianjin

Chongqing

Shanghai

Shenzhen
Guangzhou

Tōkyō

Ōsaka

Manila

Jakarta

Rio de Janeiro

São Paulo

nos
ires

Population per sq. km

	over 1000
	501 – 1000
	101 – 500
	11 – 100
	1 – 10
	less than 1

Scale 1 : 100 000 000

Cities

- over 10 000 000
- 5 000 000 – 10 000 000
- 1 000 000 – 5 000 000

WWW United Nations Statistics Division
unstats.un.org
UN Population Information Network
www.un.org/popin
Population Reference Bureau
www.prb.org
World Bank
www.worldbank.org

World population growth, 1750 – 2050

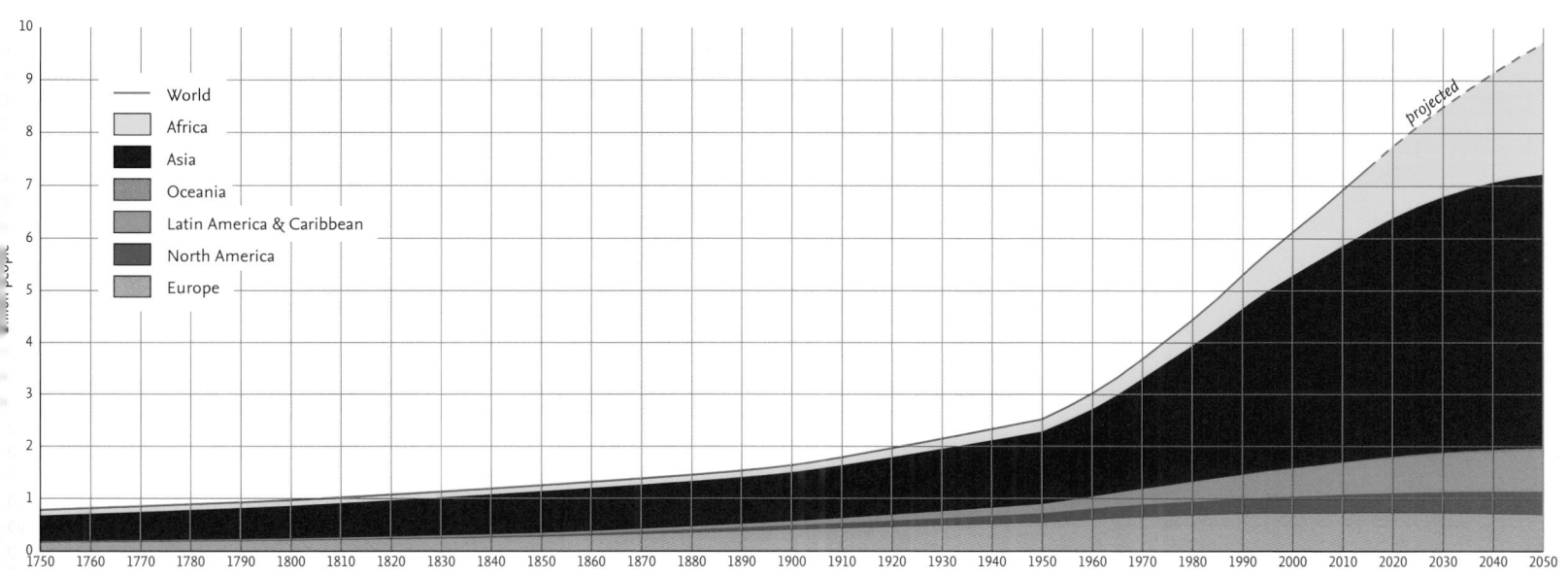

	World
	Africa
	Asia
	Oceania
	Latin America & Caribbean
	North America
	Europe

projected

1750 1760 1770 1780 1790 1800 1810 1820 1830 1840 1850 1860 1870 1880 1890 1900 1910 1920 1930 1940 1950 1960 1970 1980 1990 2000 2010 2020 2030 2040 2050

World: Urbanization

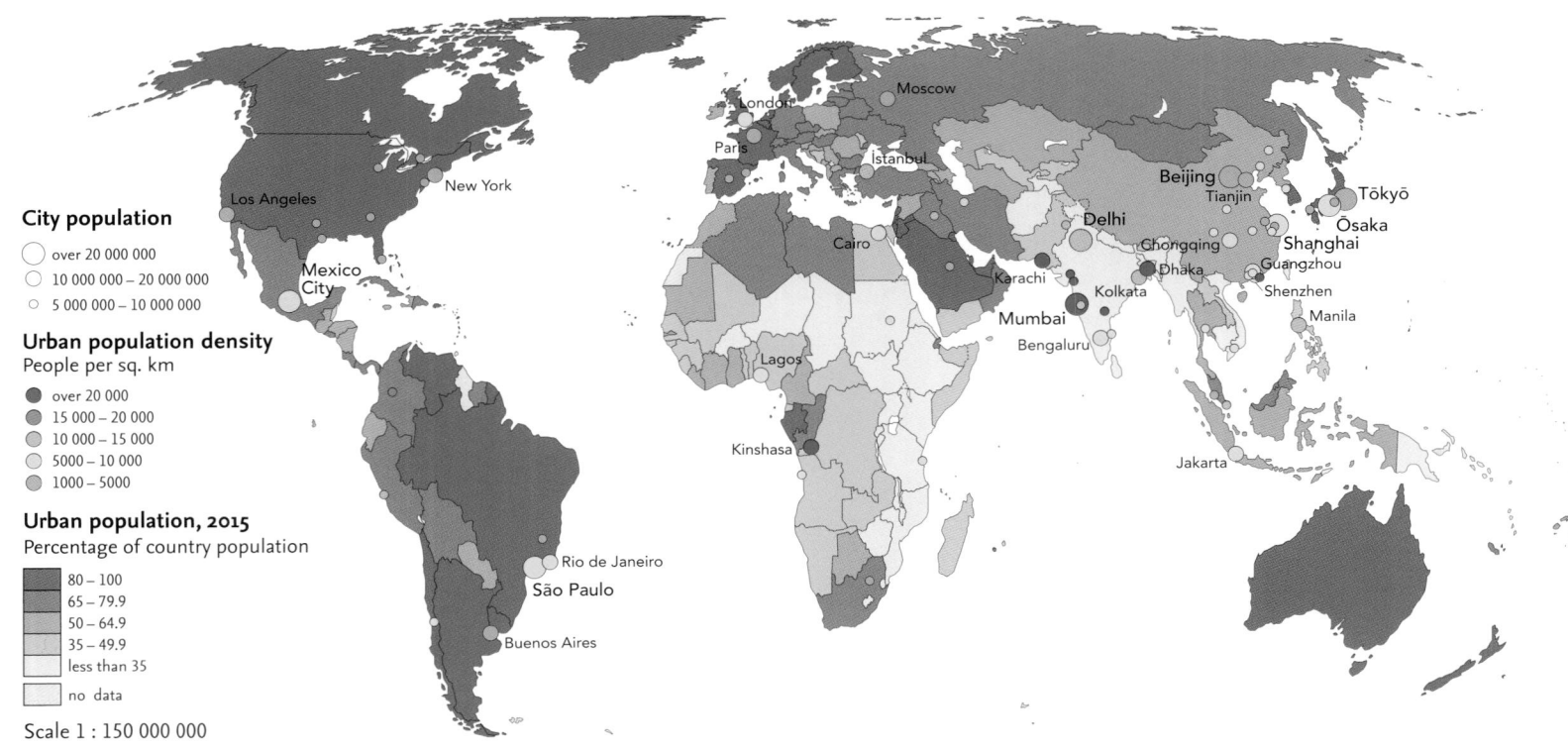

City population

◯ over 20 000 000
◯ 10 000 000 – 20 000 000
◯ 5 000 000 – 10 000 000

Urban population density
People per sq. km

● over 20 000
● 15 000 – 20 000
● 10 000 – 15 000
● 5000 – 10 000
● 1000 – 5000

Urban population, 2015
Percentage of country population

80 – 100
65 – 79.9
50 – 64.9
35 – 49.9
less than 35
no data

Scale 1 : 150 000 000

Largest urban agglomerations, 2015

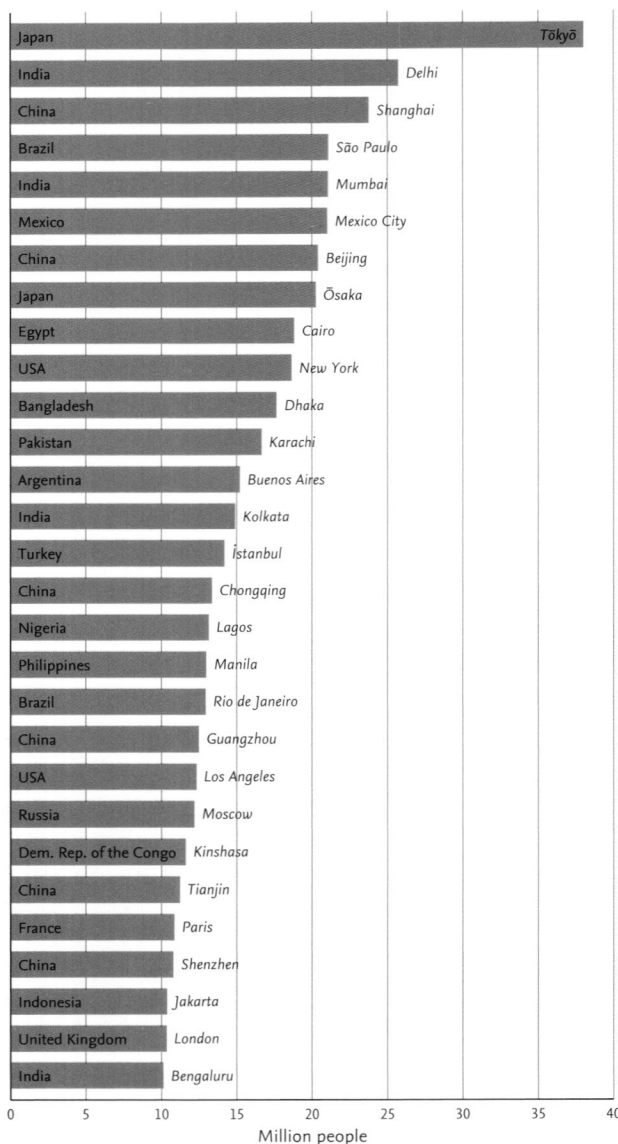

Country	City
Japan	Tōkyō
India	Delhi
China	Shanghai
Brazil	São Paulo
India	Mumbai
Mexico	Mexico City
China	Beijing
Japan	Ōsaka
Egypt	Cairo
USA	New York
Bangladesh	Dhaka
Pakistan	Karachi
Argentina	Buenos Aires
India	Kolkata
Turkey	İstanbul
China	Chongqing
Nigeria	Lagos
Philippines	Manila
Brazil	Rio de Janeiro
China	Guangzhou
USA	Los Angeles
Russia	Moscow
Dem. Rep. of the Congo	Kinshasa
China	Tianjin
France	Paris
China	Shenzhen
Indonesia	Jakarta
United Kingdom	London
India	Bengaluru

0   5   10   15   20   25   30   35   40
Million people

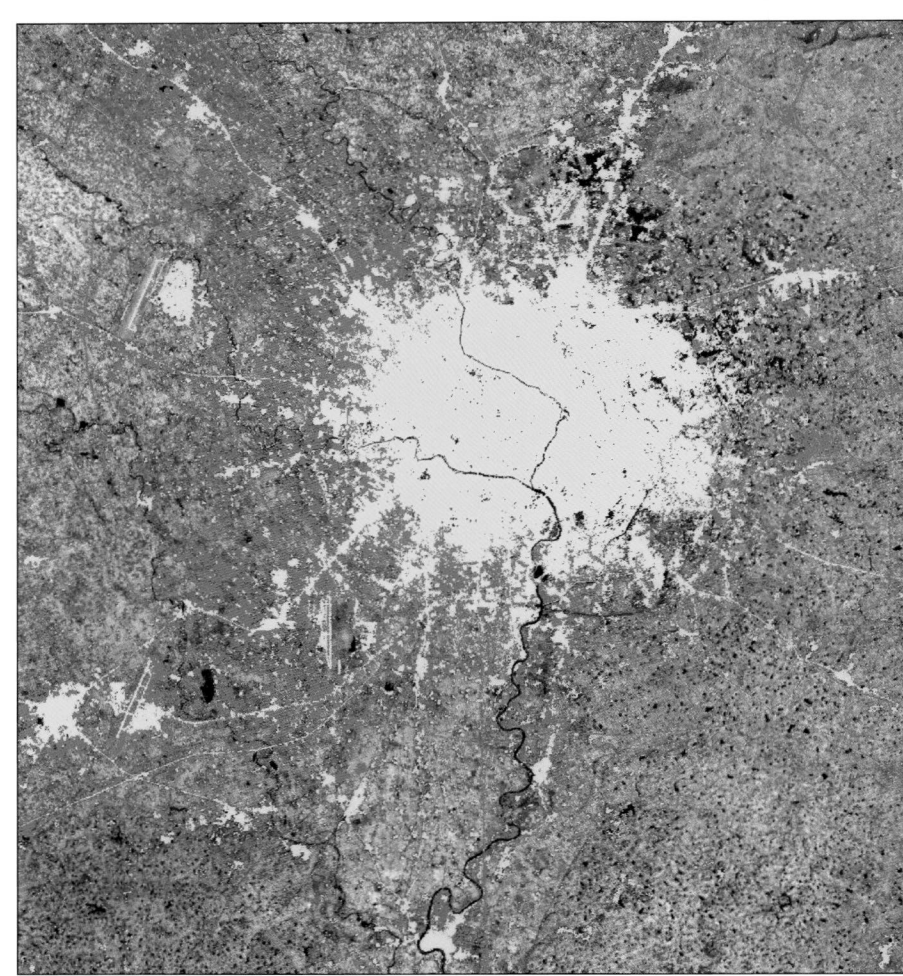

Chengdu urban growth

The city of Chengdu, located in Sichuan province, is one of the most important transportation, communication and economic centres in central China. This image shows the extent of its urban growth between 1990 and 2000.

Yellow areas show the extent of the urban area in 1990, while orange areas radiating out from the centre show what was built up in the 10 years after that. Today, the city has almost 8 million inhabitants.

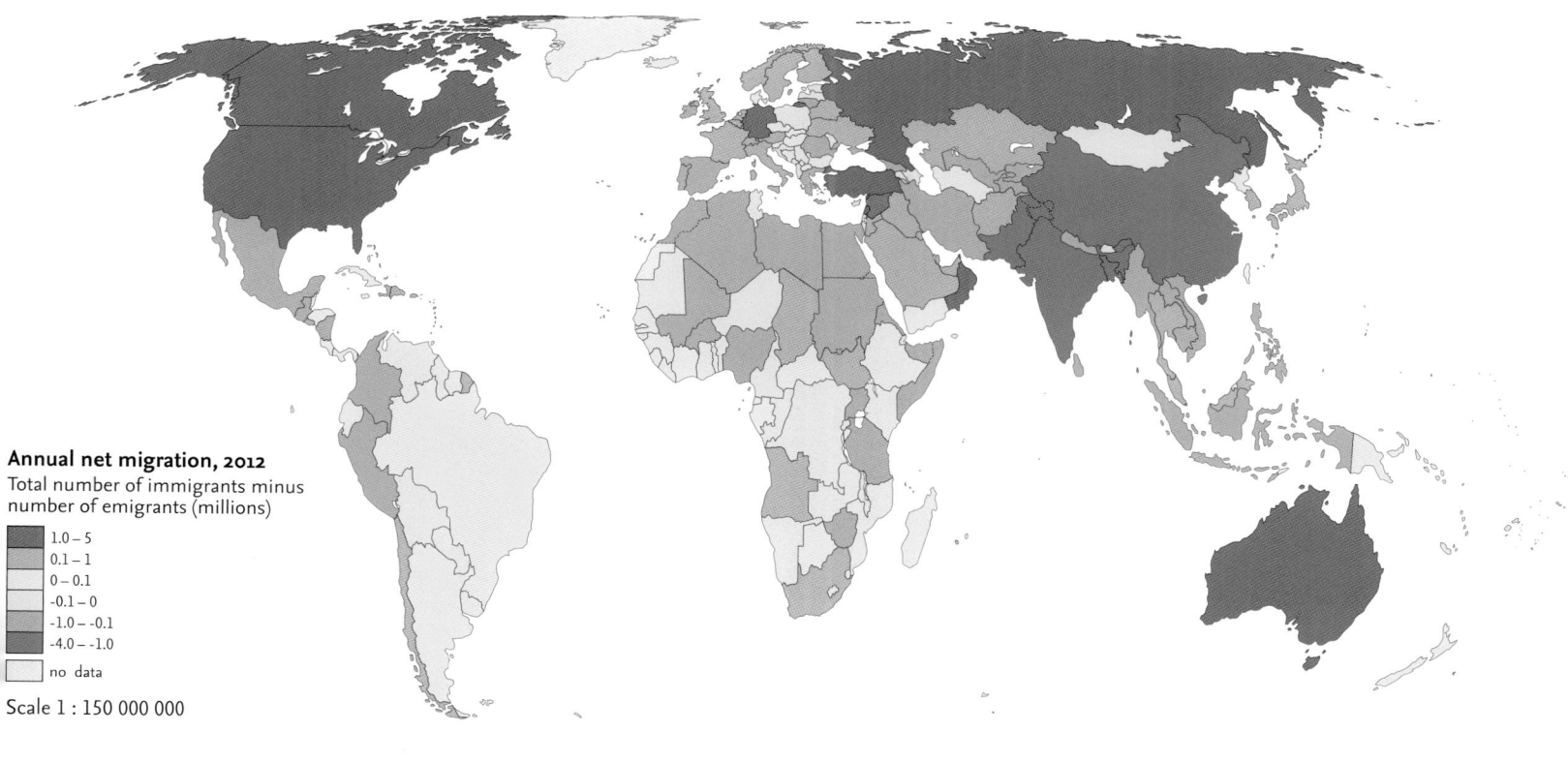

Annual net migration, 2012
Total number of immigrants minus
number of emigrants (millions)

- 1.0 – 5
- 0.1 – 1
- 0 – 0.1
- -0.1 – 0
- -1.0 – -0.1
- -4.0 – -1.0
- no data

Scale 1 : 150 000 000

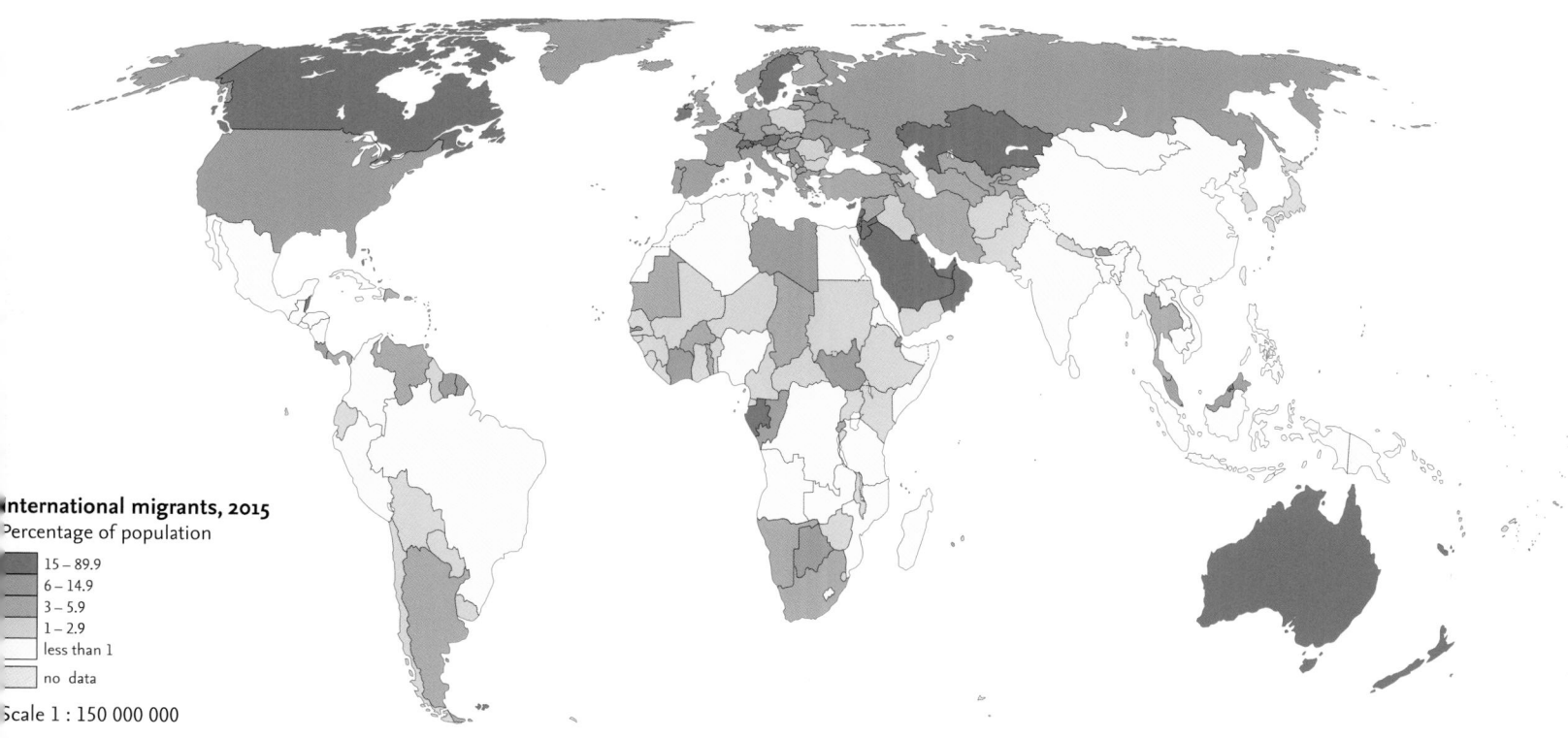

International migrants, 2015
Percentage of population

- 15 – 89.9
- 6 – 14.9
- 3 – 5.9
- 1 – 2.9
- less than 1
- no data

Scale 1 : 150 000 000

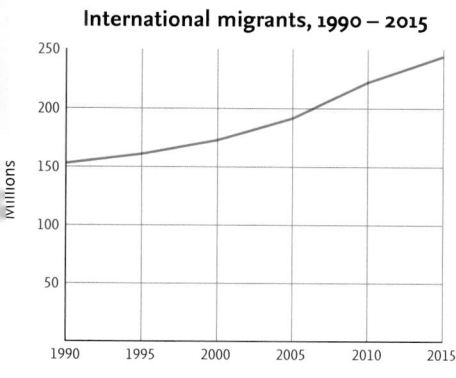

International migrants, 1990 – 2015

Millions

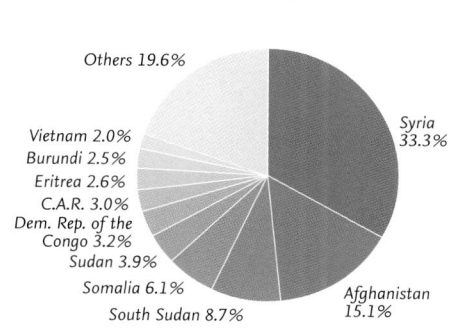

Origin of refugees, 2016

Others 19.6%
Vietnam 2.0%
Burundi 2.5%
Eritrea 2.6%
C.A.R. 3.0%
Dem. Rep. of the
Congo 3.2%
Sudan 3.9%
Somalia 6.1%
South Sudan 8.7%
Afghanistan 15.1%
Syria 33.3%

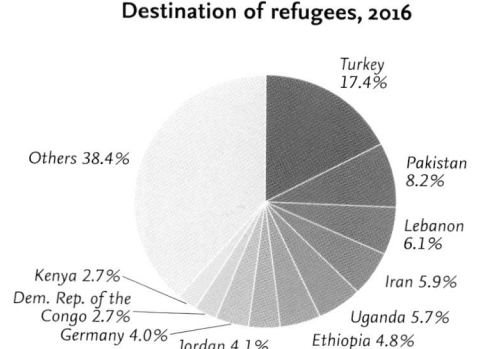

Destination of refugees, 2016

Turkey 17.4%
Pakistan 8.2%
Lebanon 6.1%
Iran 5.9%
Uganda 5.7%
Ethiopia 4.8%
Jordan 4.1%
Germany 4.0%
Dem. Rep. of the
Congo 2.7%
Kenya 2.7%
Others 38.4%

World: Birth and Death Rate, Infant Mortality Rate

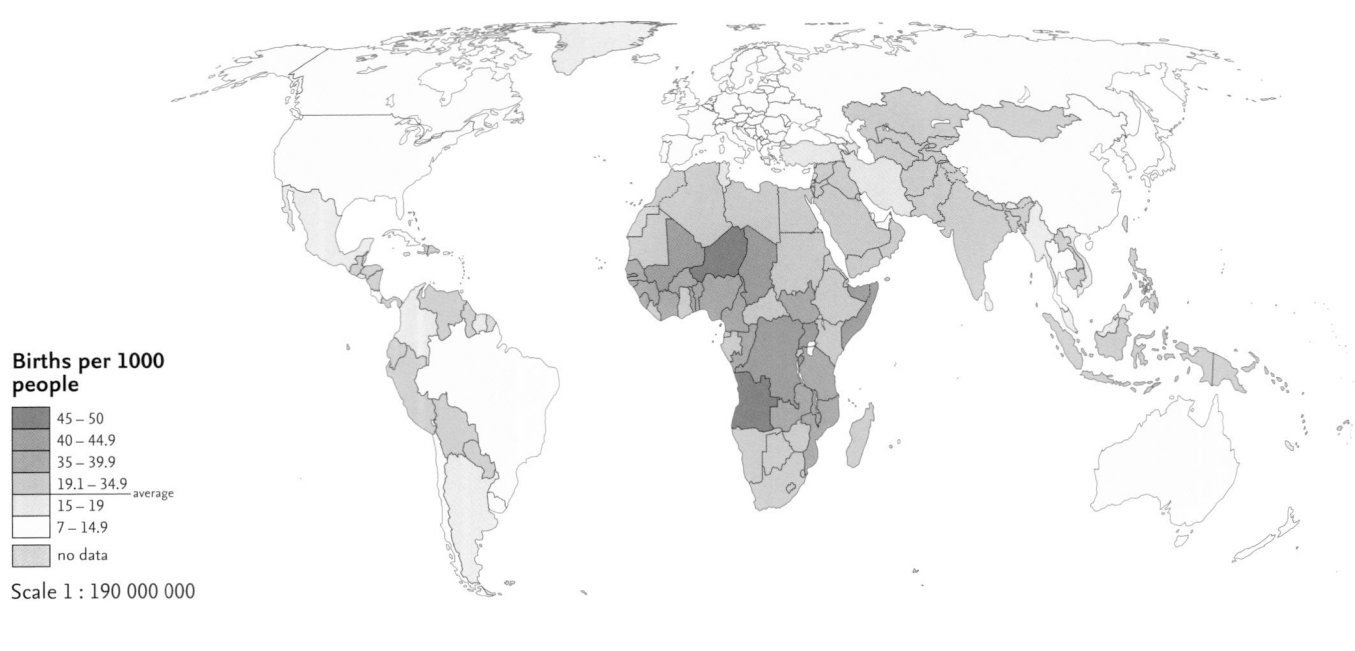

United Nations
Statistics Division
unstats.un.org
UN Population
Information Network
www.un.org/popin
Population Reference
Bureau
www.prb.org

Births per 1000 people

- 45 – 50
- 40 – 44.9
- 35 – 39.9
- 19.1 – 34.9 average
- 15 – 19
- 7 – 14.9
- no data

Scale 1 : 190 000 000

Birth rate
Birth rate is the number
births per thousand of t
population in one year.
World average 19.1.
Statistics are for 2015.

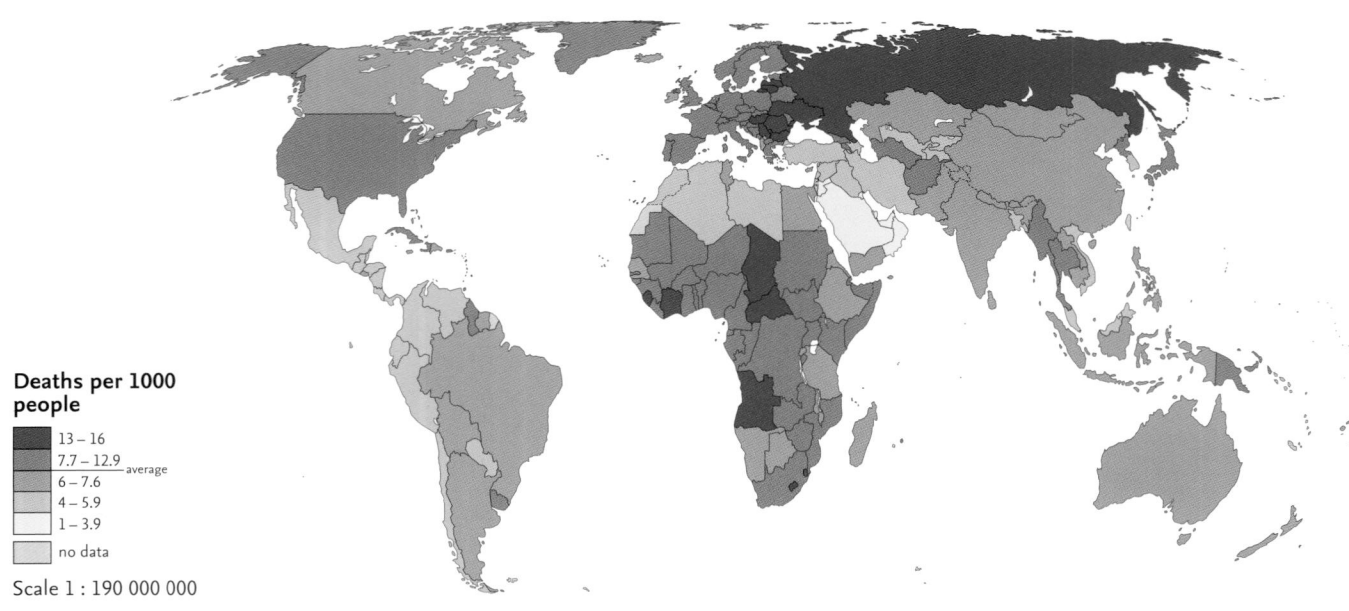

Deaths per 1000 people

- 13 – 16
- 7.7 – 12.9 average
- 6 – 7.6
- 4 – 5.9
- 1 – 3.9
- no data

Scale 1 : 190 000 000

Death rate
Death rate is the number
deaths per thousand of t
population in one year.
World average 7.7.
Statistics are for 2015.

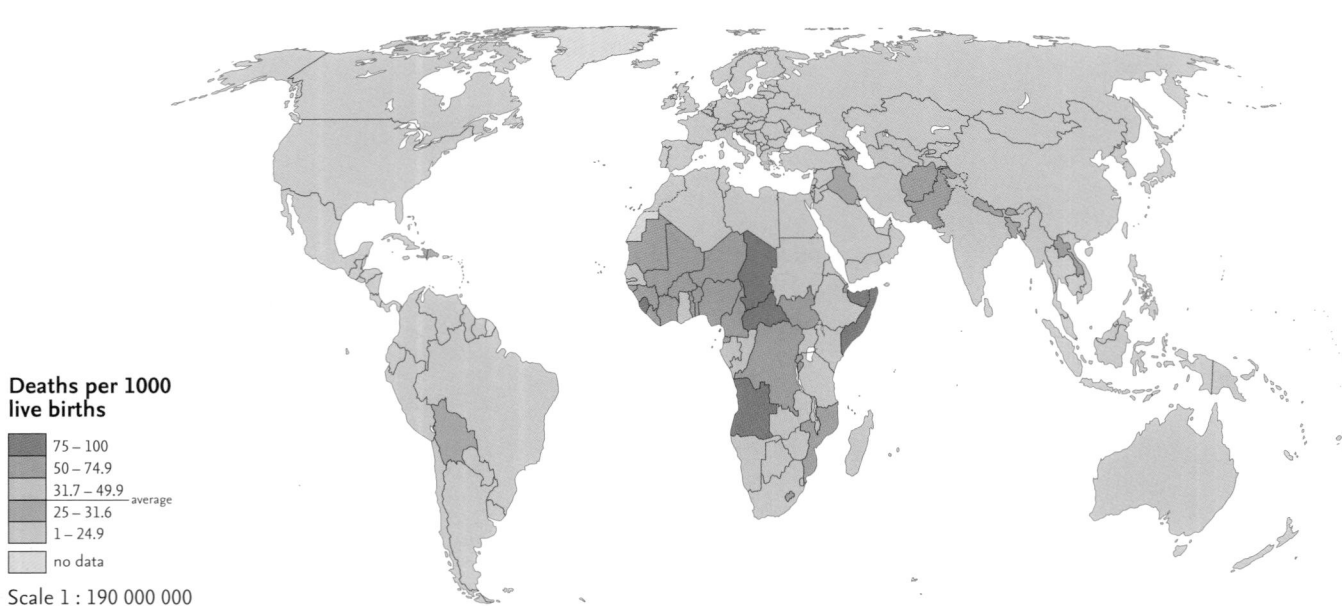

Deaths per 1000 live births

- 75 – 100
- 50 – 74.9
- 31.7 – 49.9 average
- 25 – 31.6
- 1 – 24.9
- no data

Scale 1 : 190 000 000

Infant mortality rat
Number of infants
dying before reachin
one year of age, per 10
live births in a given ye
World average 31.7.
Statistics are for 2015

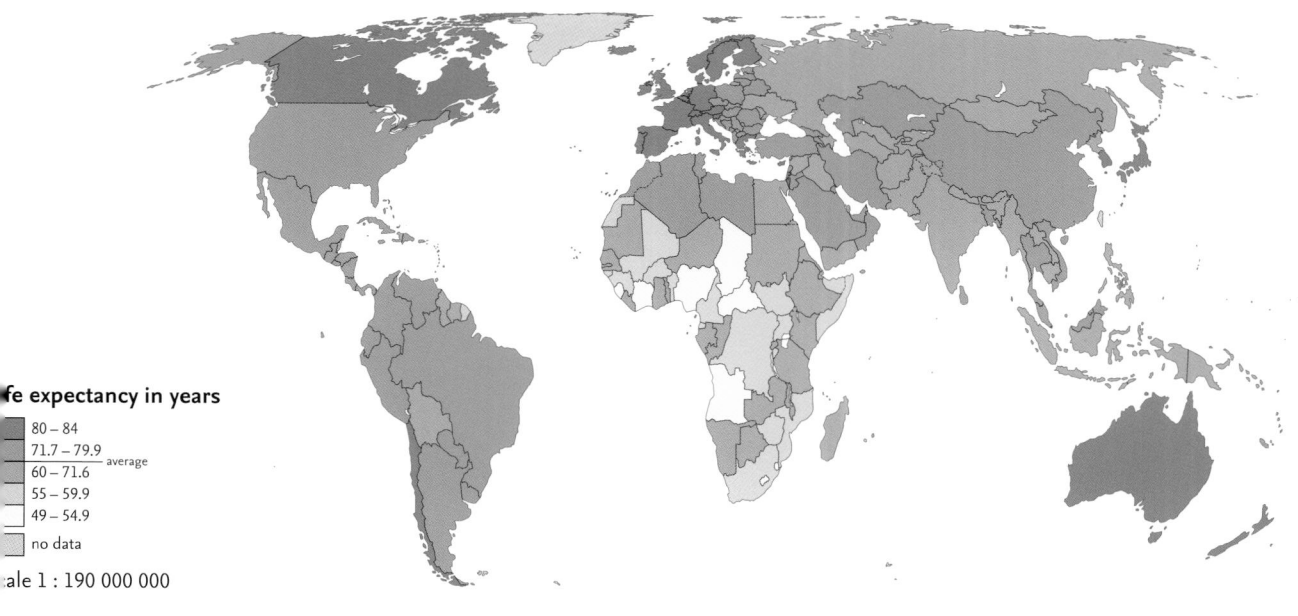

fe expectancy in years

	80 – 84
	71.7 – 79.9 — average
	60 – 71.6
	55 – 59.9
	49 – 54.9
	no data

ale 1 : 190 000 000

Life expectancy
Life expectancy is the average age a newborn infant would live to if patterns of mortality prevailing for all people at the time of its birth were to stay the same throughout its life. World average 71.7. Statistics are for 2015.

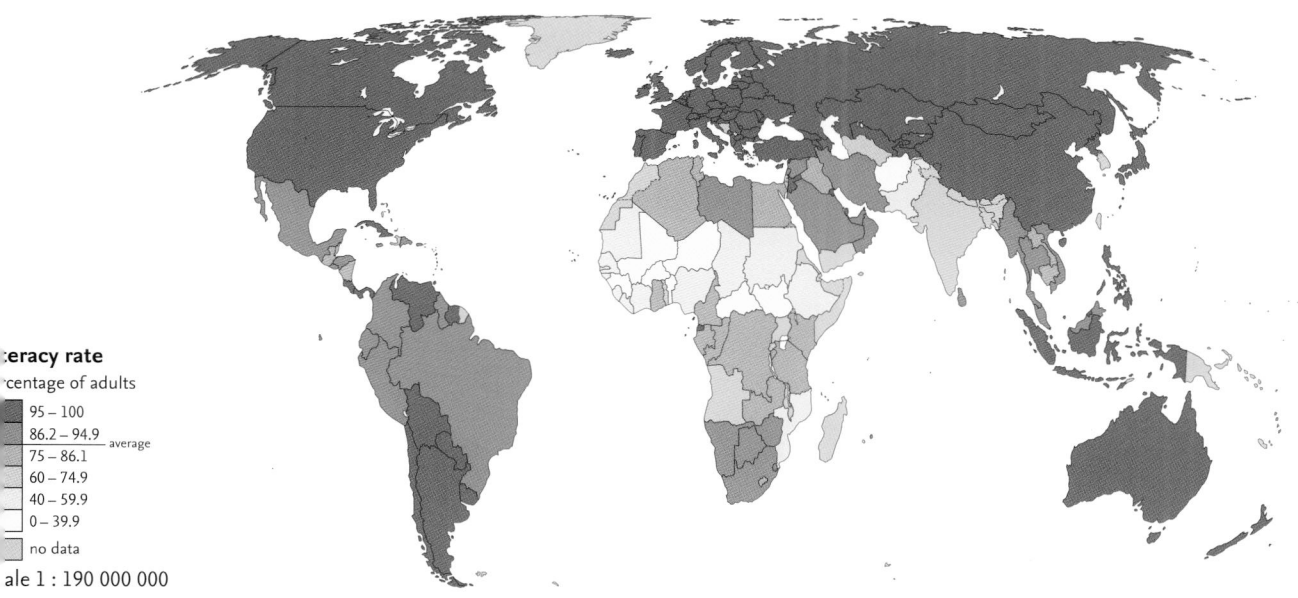

teracy rate

rcentage of adults

	95 – 100
	86.2 – 94.9 — average
	75 – 86.1
	60 – 74.9
	40 – 59.9
	0 – 39.9
	no data

ale 1 : 190 000 000

Literacy
The literacy rate shows the percentage of the population over 15 years old which is literate. The definition of 'literate' may vary greatly. World average 86.2%. Statistics are for 2015.

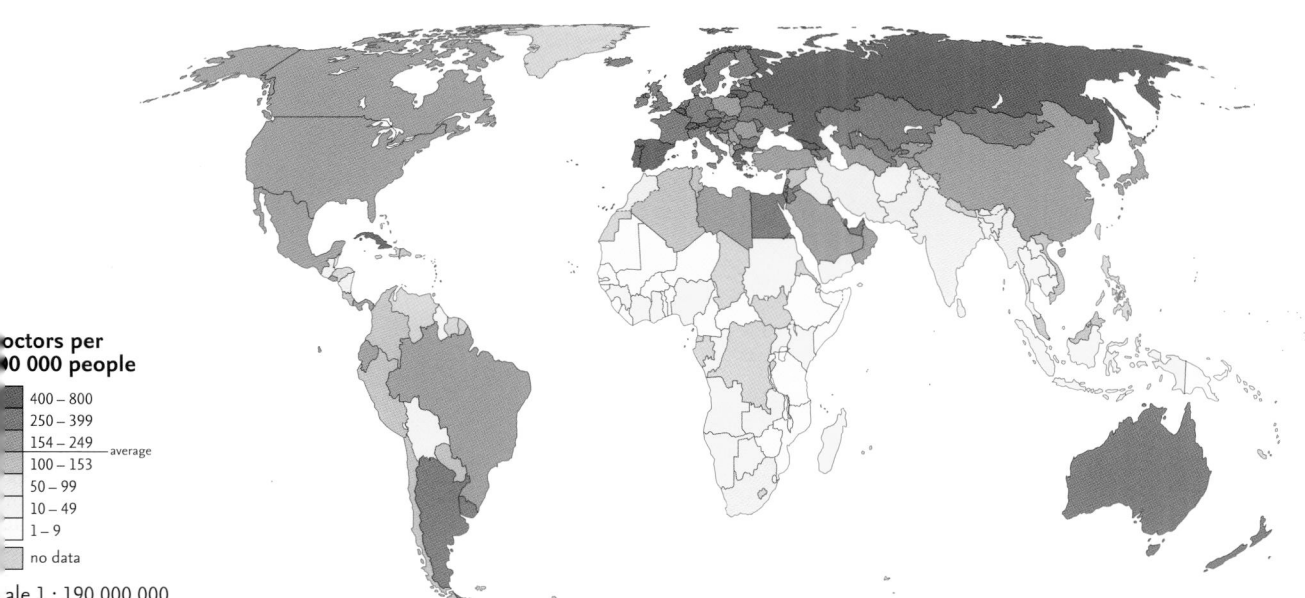

octors per
0 000 people

	400 – 800
	250 – 399
	154 – 249 — average
	100 – 153
	50 – 99
	10 – 49
	1 – 9
	no data

ale 1 : 190 000 000

Doctors
Number of physicians per thousand of the population. World average 154. Statistics are for 2009 – 2013.

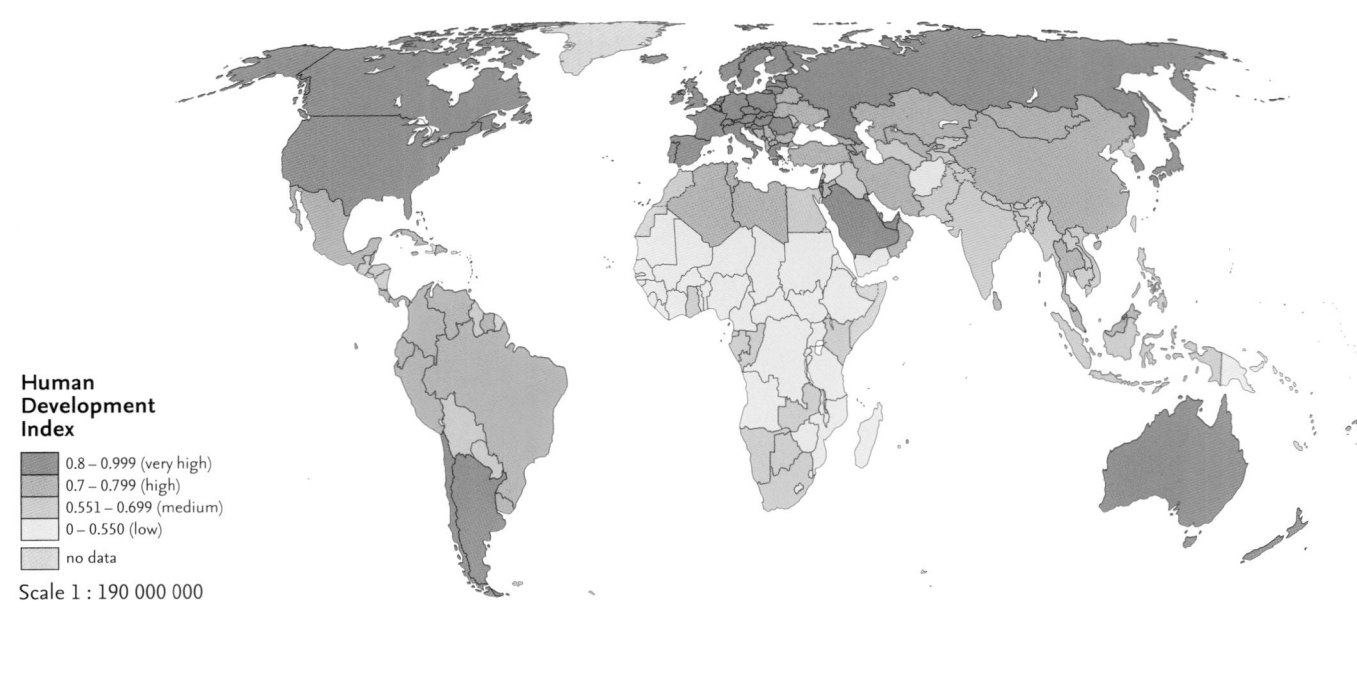

WWW

World Bank
www.worldbank.org
United Nations
Development Programme
www.undp.org
Millennium
Development Goals
millenniumindicators.un.or

Human Development Index

- 0.8 – 0.999 (very high)
- 0.7 – 0.799 (high)
- 0.551 – 0.699 (medium)
- 0 – 0.550 (low)
- no data

Scale 1 : 190 000 000

HDI
HDI measures the achievements of a count based on indicators of life expectancy, knowledg and standard of living. World average 0.717. Statistics are for 2015.

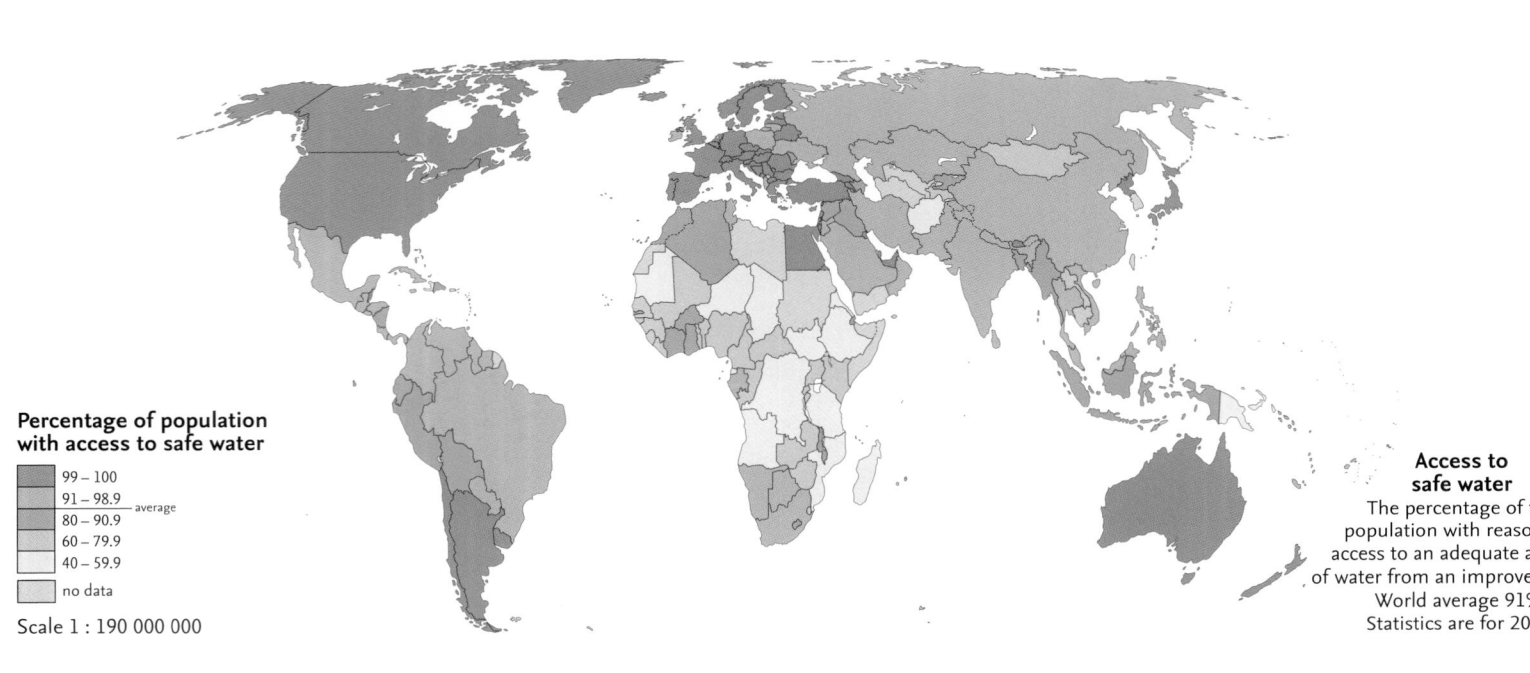

Percentage of population with access to safe water

- 99 – 100
- 91 – 98.9 average
- 80 – 90.9
- 60 – 79.9
- 40 – 59.9
- no data

Scale 1 : 190 000 000

Access to safe water
The percentage of the population with reasonable access to an adequate amount of water from an improved sourc World average 91%. Statistics are for 2015.

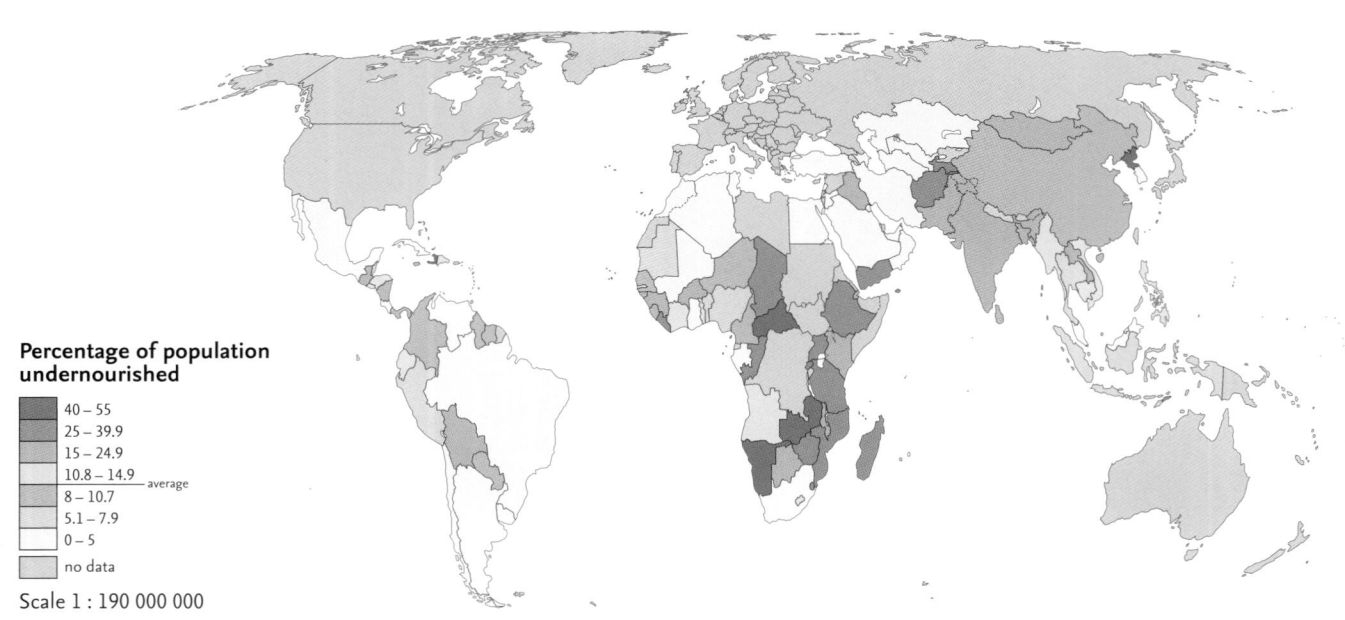

Percentage of population undernourished

- 40 – 55
- 25 – 39.9
- 15 – 24.9
- 10.8 – 14.9 average
- 8 – 10.7
- 5.1 – 7.9
- 0 – 5
- no data

Scale 1 : 190 000 000

Nutrition
Percentage of populatio undernourished in developing countries and countries in transitio World average 10.8%. Statistics are for 2015.

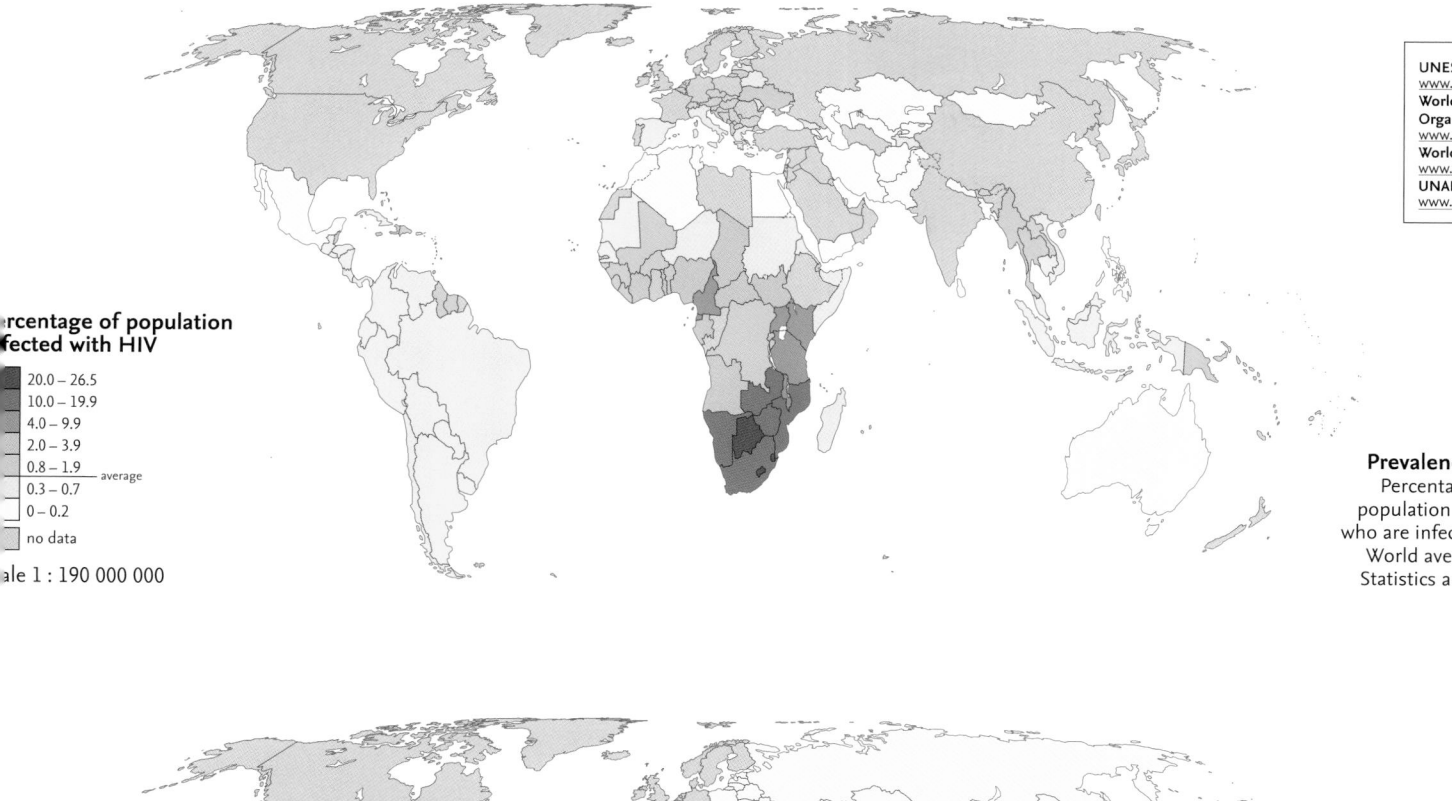

rcentage of population
fected with HIV

- 20.0 – 26.5
- 10.0 – 19.9
- 4.0 – 9.9
- 2.0 – 3.9
- 0.8 – 1.9 — average
- 0.3 – 0.7
- 0 – 0.2
- no data

ale 1 : 190 000 000

Prevalence of HIV
Percentage of the
population aged 15-49
who are infected with HIV.
World average 0.8%.
Statistics are for 2015.

UNESCO
www.unesco.org
**World Health
Organization**
www.who.ch
World Bank
www.worldbank.org
UNAIDS
www.unaids.org

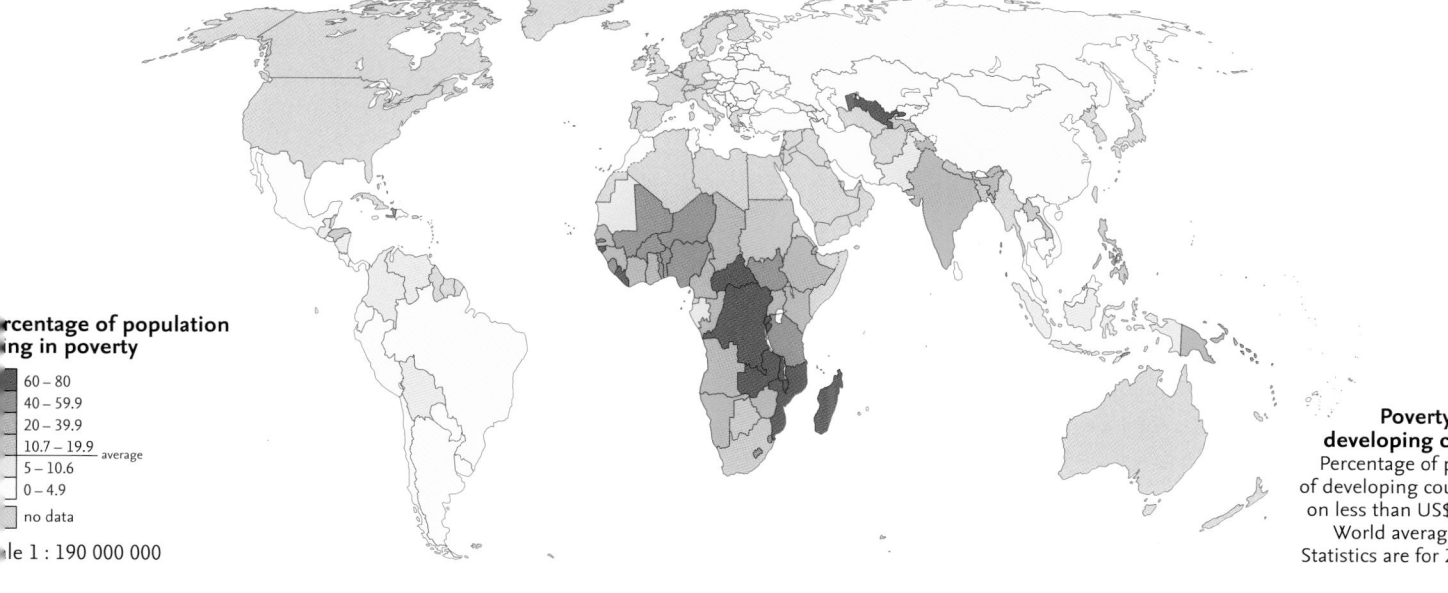

rcentage of population
ng in poverty

- 60 – 80
- 40 – 59.9
- 20 – 39.9
- 10.7 – 19.9 — average
- 5 – 10.6
- 0 – 4.9
- no data

le 1 : 190 000 000

**Poverty in
developing countries**
Percentage of population
of developing countries living
on less than US$ 1.90 a day.
World average 10.7%.
Statistics are for 2003 – 2014.

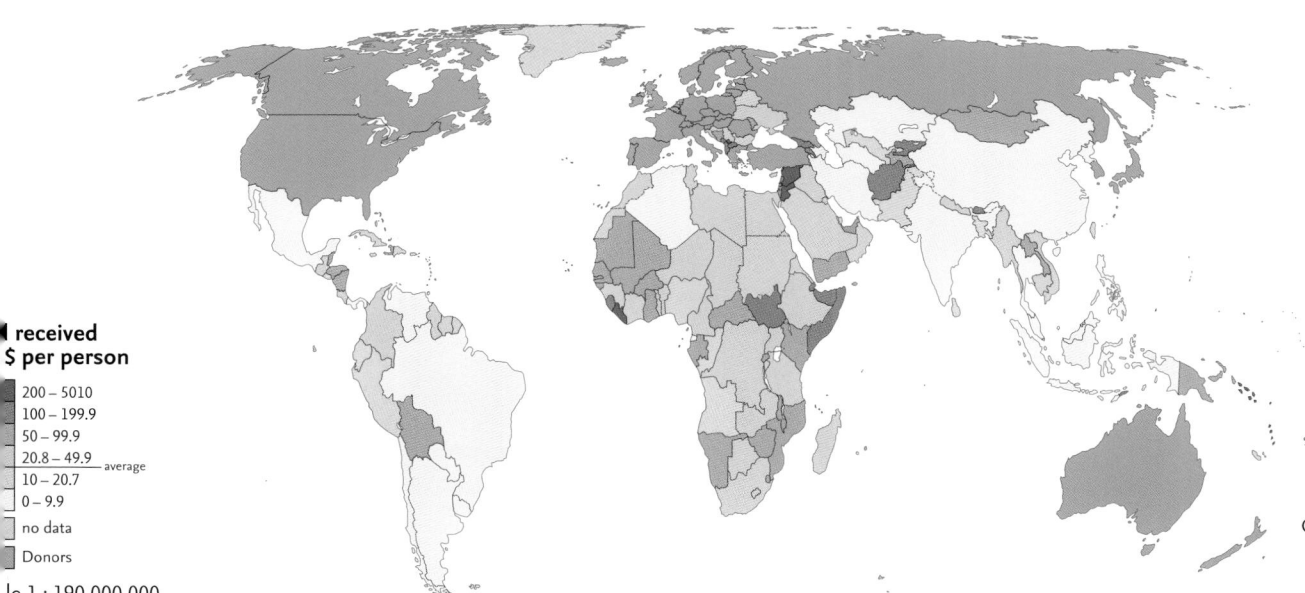

received
$ per person

- 200 – 5010
- 100 – 199.9
- 50 – 99.9
- 20.8 – 49.9 — average
- 10 – 20.7
- 0 – 9.9
- no data
- Donors

le 1 : 190 000 000

Aid received
Official development assistance
received in US$ per person.
World average US$ 20.8.
Statistics are for 2015.

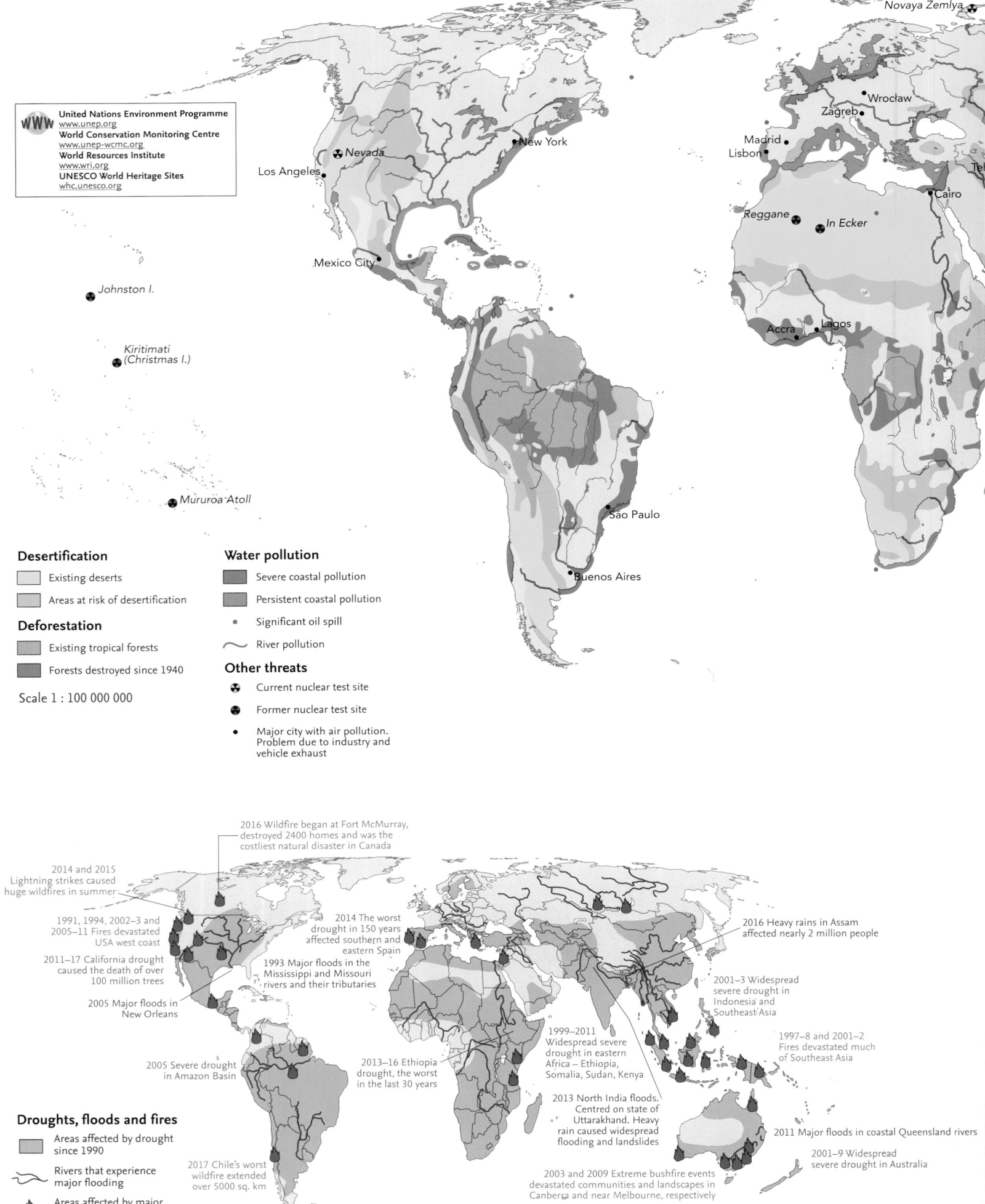

United Nations Environment Programme
www.unep.org
World Conservation Monitoring Centre
www.unep-wcmc.org
World Resources Institute
www.wri.org
UNESCO World Heritage Sites
whc.unesco.org

Novaya Zemlya

Wrocław
Zagreb
Madrid
Lisbon
Nevada
New York
Los Angeles
Reggane   In Ecker
Cairo
Tel
Mexico City
Accra   Lagos
Johnston I.
Kiritimati
(Christmas I.)
Mururoa Atoll
São Paulo
Buenos Aires

Desertification

Existing deserts

Areas at risk of desertification

Deforestation

Existing tropical forests

Forests destroyed since 1940

Scale 1 : 100 000 000

Water pollution

Severe coastal pollution

Persistent coastal pollution

• Significant oil spill

~ River pollution

Other threats

☢ Current nuclear test site

☢ Former nuclear test site

• Major city with air pollution. Problem due to industry and vehicle exhaust

2016 Wildfire began at Fort McMurray, destroyed 2400 homes and was the costliest natural disaster in Canada

2014 and 2015 Lightning strikes caused huge wildfires in summer

1991, 1994, 2002–3 and 2005–11 Fires devastated USA west coast

2011–17 California drought caused the death of over 100 million trees

2005 Major floods in New Orleans

2005 Severe drought in Amazon Basin

2017 Chile's worst wildfire extended over 5000 sq. km

2014 The worst drought in 150 years affected southern and eastern Spain

1993 Major floods in the Mississippi and Missouri rivers and their tributaries

2013–16 Ethiopia drought, the worst in the last 30 years

1999–2011 Widespread severe drought in eastern Africa – Ethiopia, Somalia, Sudan, Kenya

2013 North India floods. Centred on state of Uttarakhand. Heavy rain caused widespread flooding and landslides

2003 and 2009 Extreme bushfire events devastated communities and landscapes in Canberra and near Melbourne, respectively

2016 Heavy rains in Assam affected nearly 2 million people

2001–3 Widespread severe drought in Indonesia and Southeast Asia

1997–8 and 2001–2 Fires devastated much of Southeast Asia

2011 Major floods in coastal Queensland rivers

2001–9 Widespread severe drought in Australia

Droughts, floods and fires

Areas affected by drought since 1990

~ Rivers that experience major flooding

Areas affected by major forest fire since 1990

Scale 1 : 190 000 000

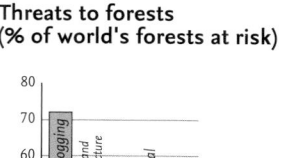

Threats to forests (% of world's forests at risk)

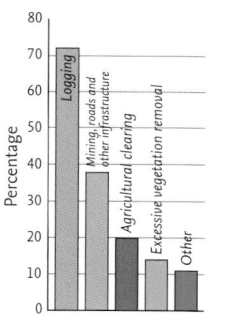

Number of threatened species, 2016

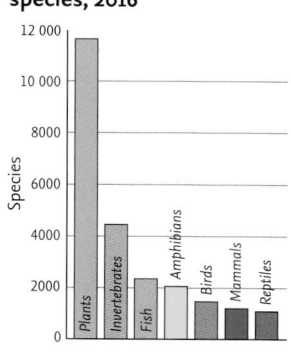

Countries with the most threatened plant species, 2016

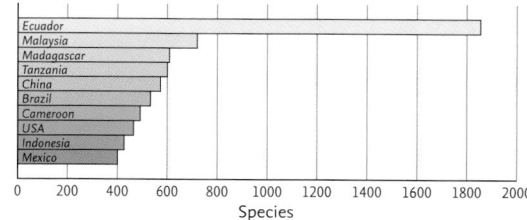

Total forest area, by region, 1990 – 2015

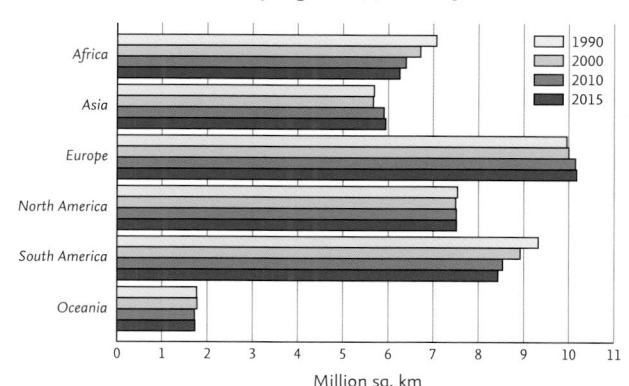

Forest area change, 2010 – 2015

World	-165 393 sq. km
South America	-101 226 sq. km
North America	3741 sq. km
Europe	19 105 sq. km
Africa	-141 795 sq. km
Asia	39 562 sq. km
Oceania	15 220 sq. km

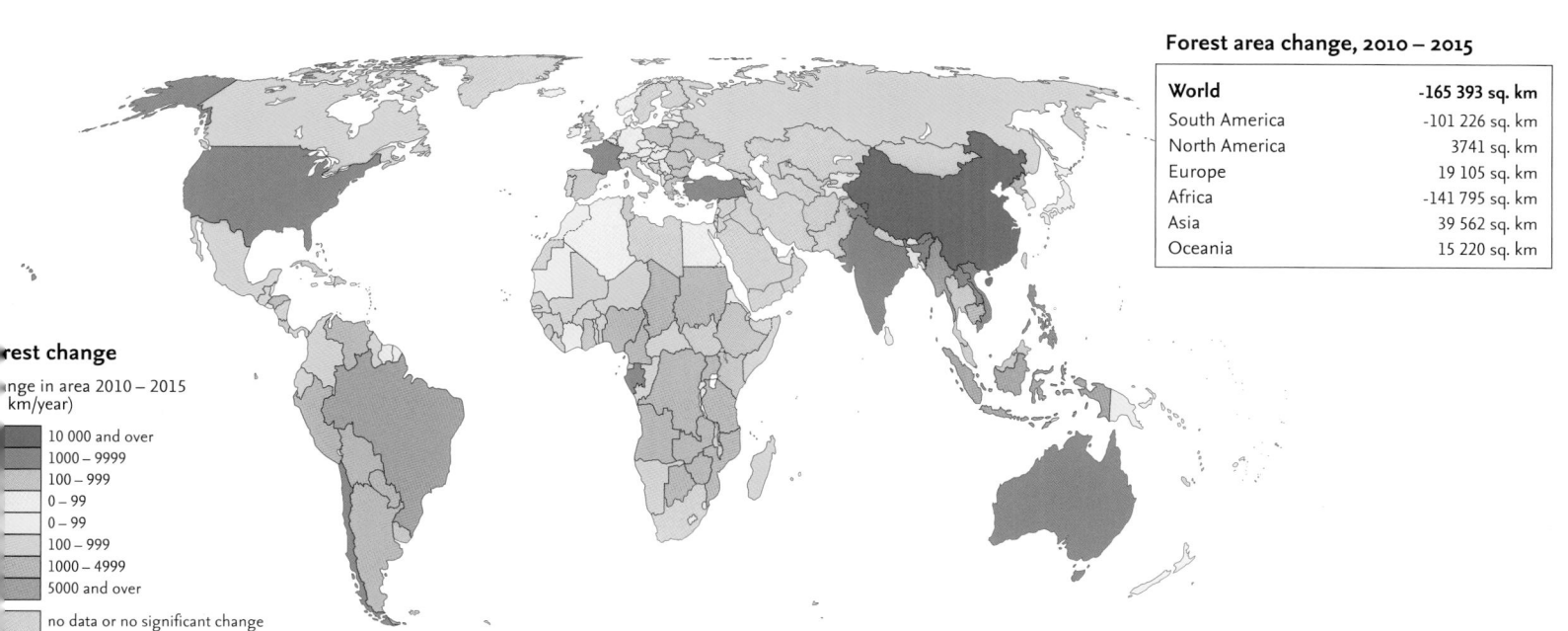

rest change

nge in area 2010 – 2015
km/year)

- 10 000 and over
- 1000 – 9999
- 100 – 999
- 0 – 99
- 0 – 99
- 100 – 999
- 1000 – 4999
- 5000 and over
- no data or no significant change

le 1 : 190 000 000

World: Climate Change

Global warming, 1910 – 2010

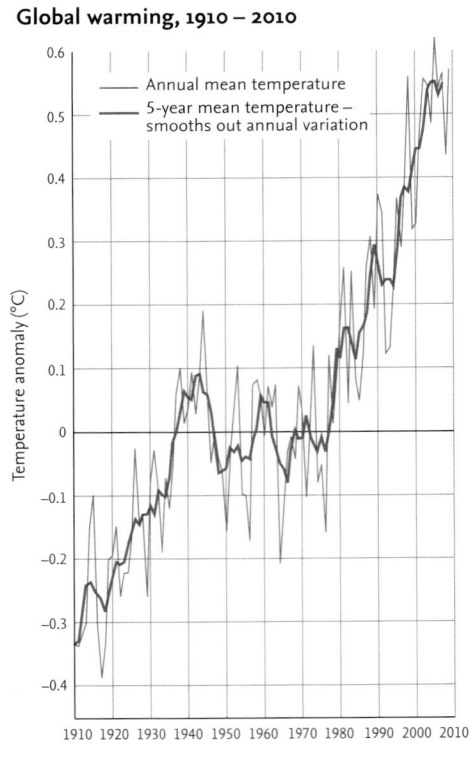

Annual mean temperature
5-year mean temperature – smooths out annual variation
Temperature anomaly (°C)
0.6
0.5
0.4
0.3
0.2
0.1
0
–0.1
–0.2
–0.3
–0.4
1910 1920 1930 1940 1950 1960 1970 1980 1990 2000 2010

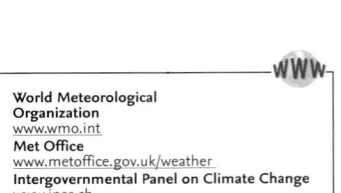

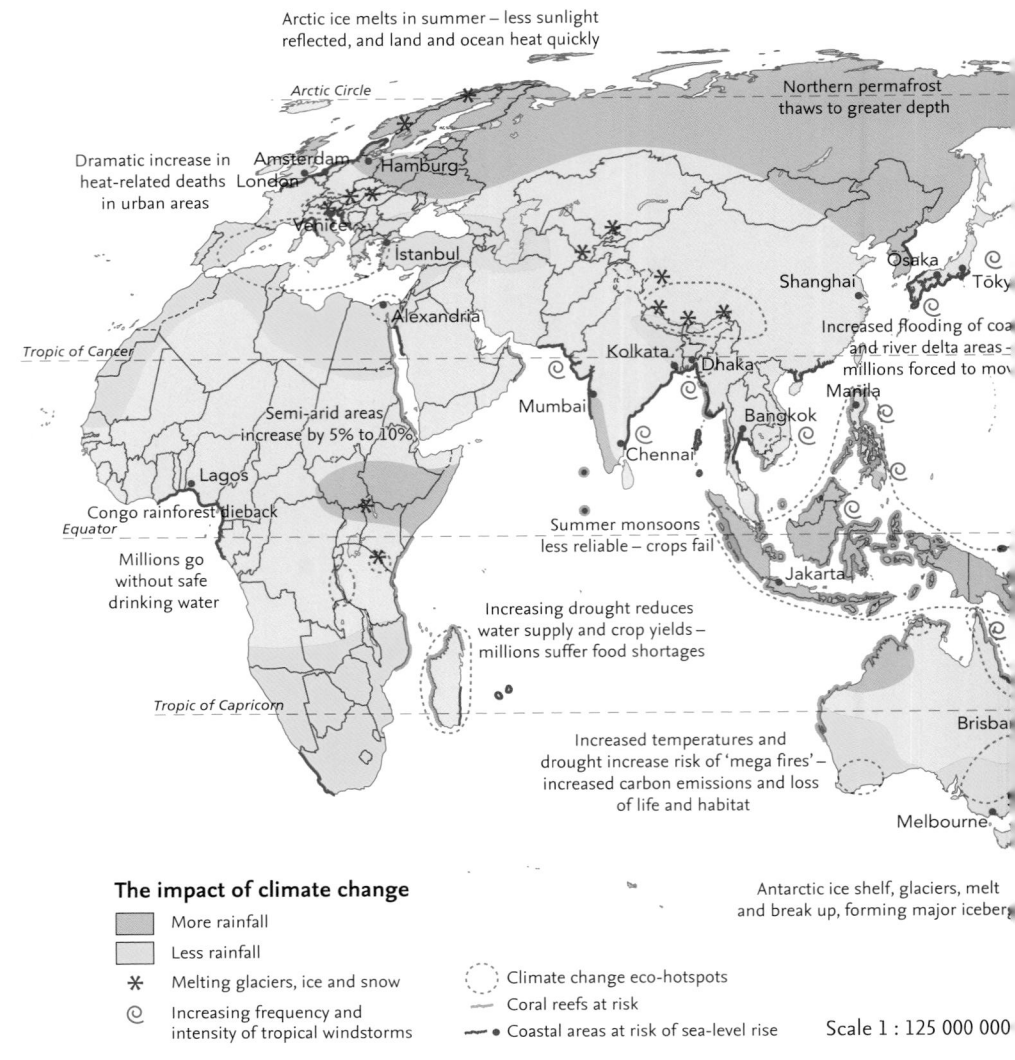

Arctic ice melts in summer – less sunlight reflected, and land and ocean heat quickly
Arctic Circle
Northern permafrost thaws to greater depth
Dramatic increase in heat-related deaths in urban areas
Amsterdam
London
Hamburg
Venice
Istanbul
Alexandria
Tropic of Cancer
Osaka
Tokyo
Shanghai
Increased flooding of coastal and river delta areas – millions forced to move
Kolkata
Dhaka
Mumbai
Manila
Bangkok
Chennai
Semi-arid areas increase by 5% to 10%
Lagos
Congo rainforest dieback
Equator
Summer monsoons less reliable – crops fail
Millions go without safe drinking water
Jakarta
Increasing drought reduces water supply and crop yields – millions suffer food shortages
Tropic of Capricorn
Brisbane
Increased temperatures and drought increase risk of 'mega fires' – increased carbon emissions and loss of life and habitat
Melbourne
Antarctic ice shelf, glaciers, melt and break up, forming major icebergs

WWW

World Meteorological Organization
www.wmo.int
Met Office
www.metoffice.gov.uk/weather
Intergovernmental Panel on Climate Change
www.ipcc.ch

The impact of climate change

- More rainfall
- Less rainfall
- Melting glaciers, ice and snow
- Increasing frequency and intensity of tropical windstorms
- Climate change eco-hotspots
- Coral reefs at risk
- Coastal areas at risk of sea-level rise

Scale 1 : 125 000 000

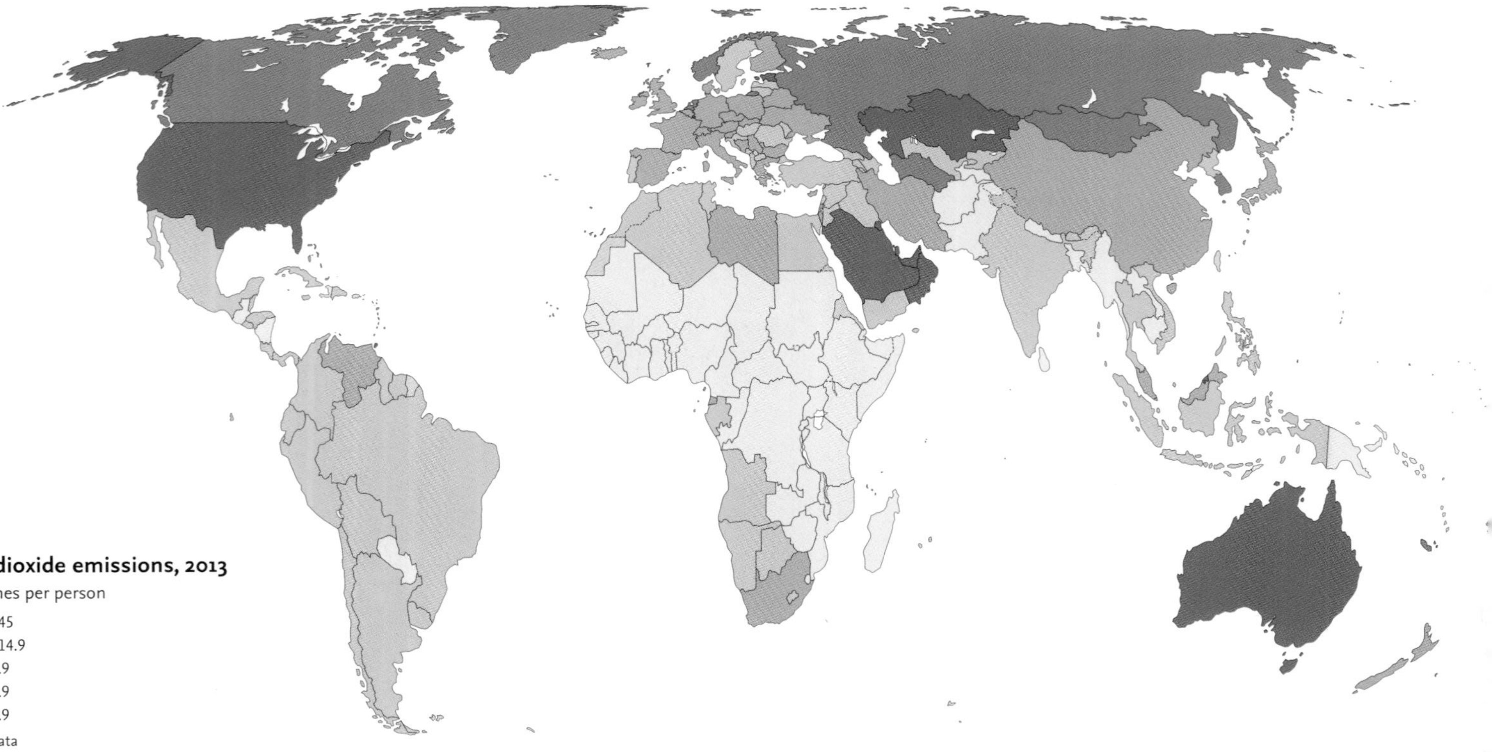

Carbon dioxide emissions, 2013

Metric tonnes per person

- 15 – 45
- 10 – 14.9
- 5 – 9.9
- 1 – 4.9
- 0 – 0.9
- no data

World average 5.

Scale 1 : 150 00 000

Decade 2001 – 10
warmest on record

Melt of Greenland ice sheet

Coniferous
forest dieback

All living things affected
by ecosystem change and habitat loss

Yields of most cereals crops decrease –
increased risk of world hunger
New York

Increase in diseases
carried by insects, e.g.
alaria and dengue fever

Los Angeles

New Orleans

Oceans warm and expand,
causing coastal flooding and
loss of land

Higher temperatures
increase urban pollution
and respiratory disease

ss of habitat –
nals and plants
ed to migrate
become extinct

eans warm and become
more acidic – all ocean
ecosystems affected

More violent tropical
windstorms increase
loss of life

Severe drought causes
dieback in Amazon
rainforest – increased
risk of fire and
loss of biodiversity

Equator

Many island groups
submerged – islanders
become environmental refugees

Mountain environments and
human activities affected
by loss of snow and ice

Rio de Janeiro

Oceans warm more slowly
than land – Southern Hemisphere
warms more slowly than
Northern Hemisphere

Buenos Aires

kland

Average sea level is predicted to increase
by between 18 and 59 cm by 2100, with
some forecasts as high as 1.5 m

Projected annual mean temperature change

These maps show projected change in annual mean surface air temperature given moderate growth in CO2 emissions, for three time periods, compared with the average temperature for 1980 – 99.

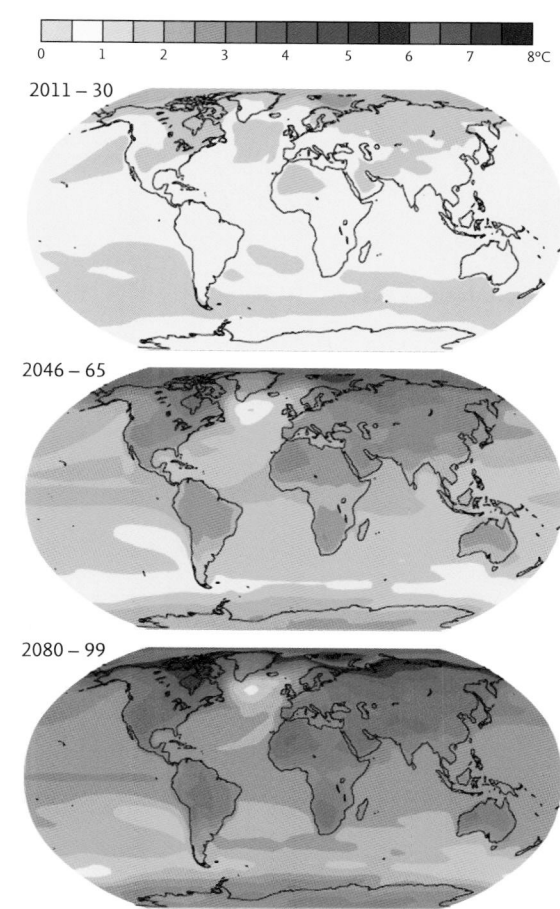

0 1 2 3 4 5 6 7 8°C

2011 – 30

2046 – 65

2080 – 99

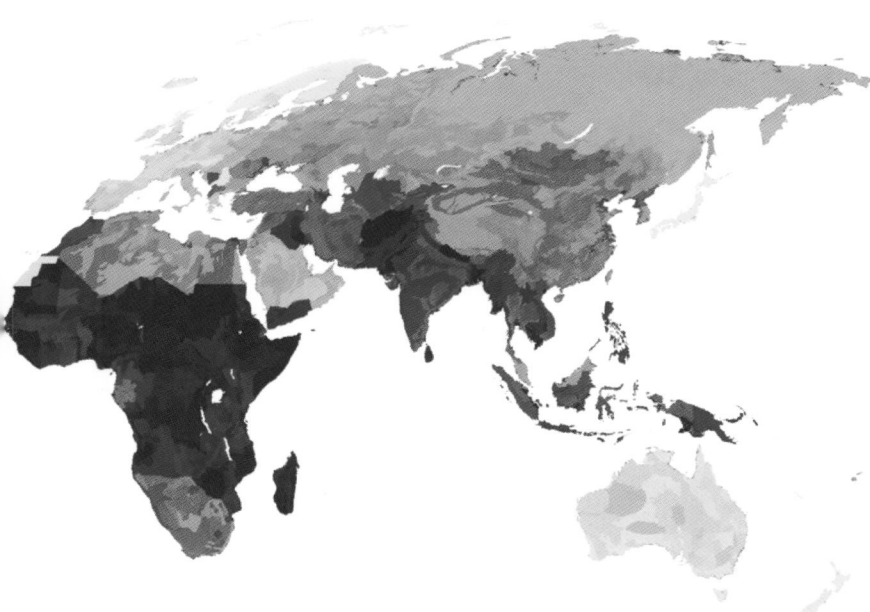

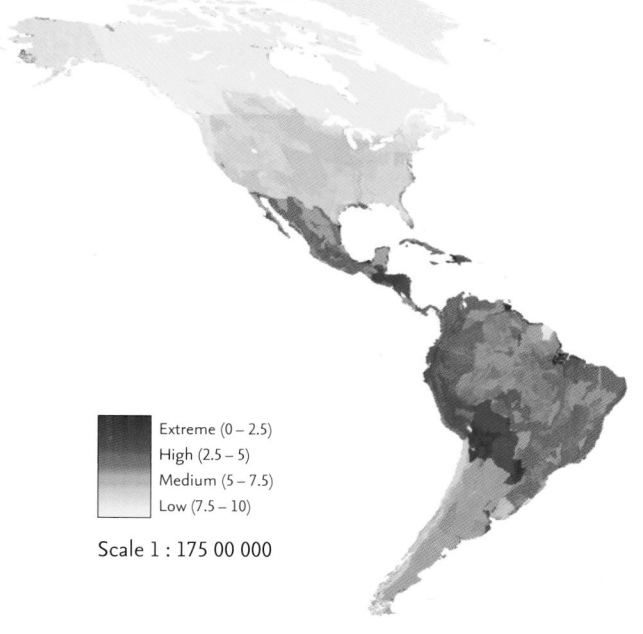

Extreme (0 – 2.5)
High (2.5 – 5)
Medium (5 – 7.5)
Low (7.5 – 10)

Scale 1 : 175 00 000

limate change vulnerability index, 2010

he climate change vulnerability index ranks how likely a country is to be harmed by
nanging patterns in climate, natural hazards and ecosystems caused by climate change,
nd how well prepared it is to combat the impacts of climate change. Norway is the
ountry best equipped to deal with climate change, with low population density, excellent
ealthcare and communication systems and high overall food, water and energy security.
 contrast Somalia, with scarce natural resources, low food security, political violence
nd human rights risk, is extremely vulnerable to the impacts of climate change.

Highest vulnerability

1 Somalia	5 Burundi	8 The Gambia
2 Haiti	6 Guinea	9 Chad
3 Afghanistan	7 Rwanda	10 Nigeria
4 Sierra Leone		

Of the 28 countries most at risk, 22 are in Africa.

World: Fuel Production and Energy

International Energy Agency
www.iea.org
BP Statistical Review of
World Energy
www.bp.com

Fuel production, 2015

Percentage of world production

>25%	11 – 25%	1 – 10%	
			Gas
			Oil
			Coal

Scale 1 : 190 000 000

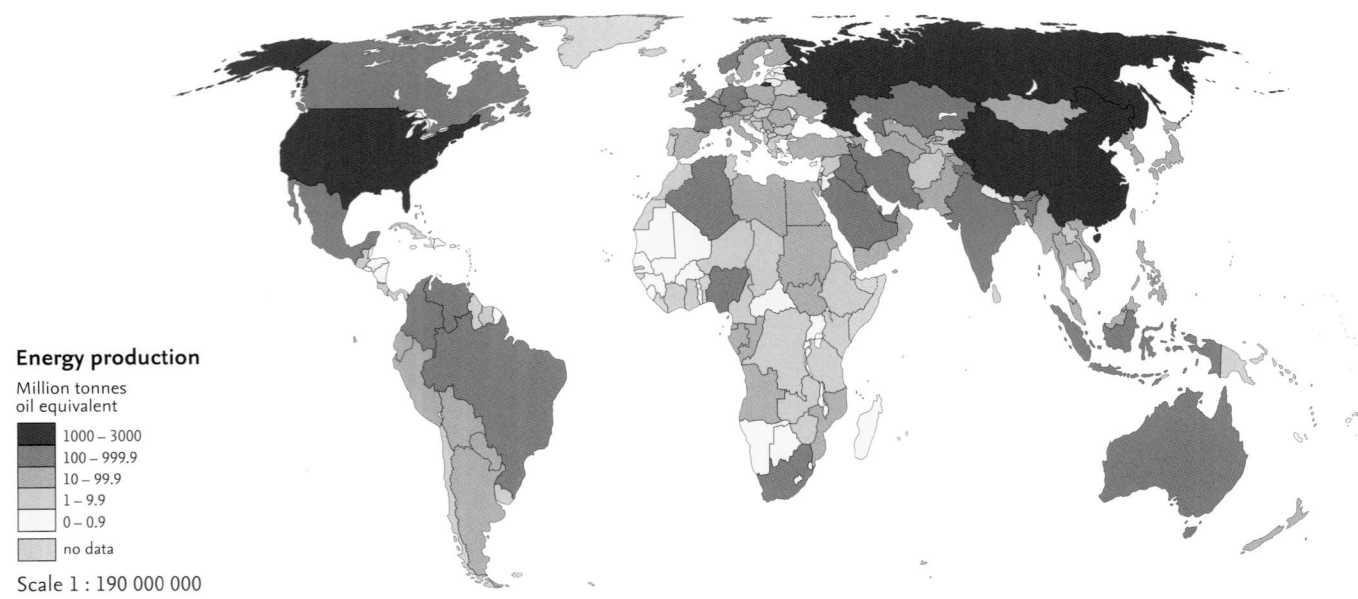

Energy production

Million tonnes
oil equivalent

	1000 – 3000
	100 – 999.9
	10 – 99.9
	1 – 9.9
	0 – 0.9
	no data

Scale 1 : 190 000 000

Energy production
Expressed as the number
of tonnes oil equivalent
produced in one year.
Statistics are for 2015

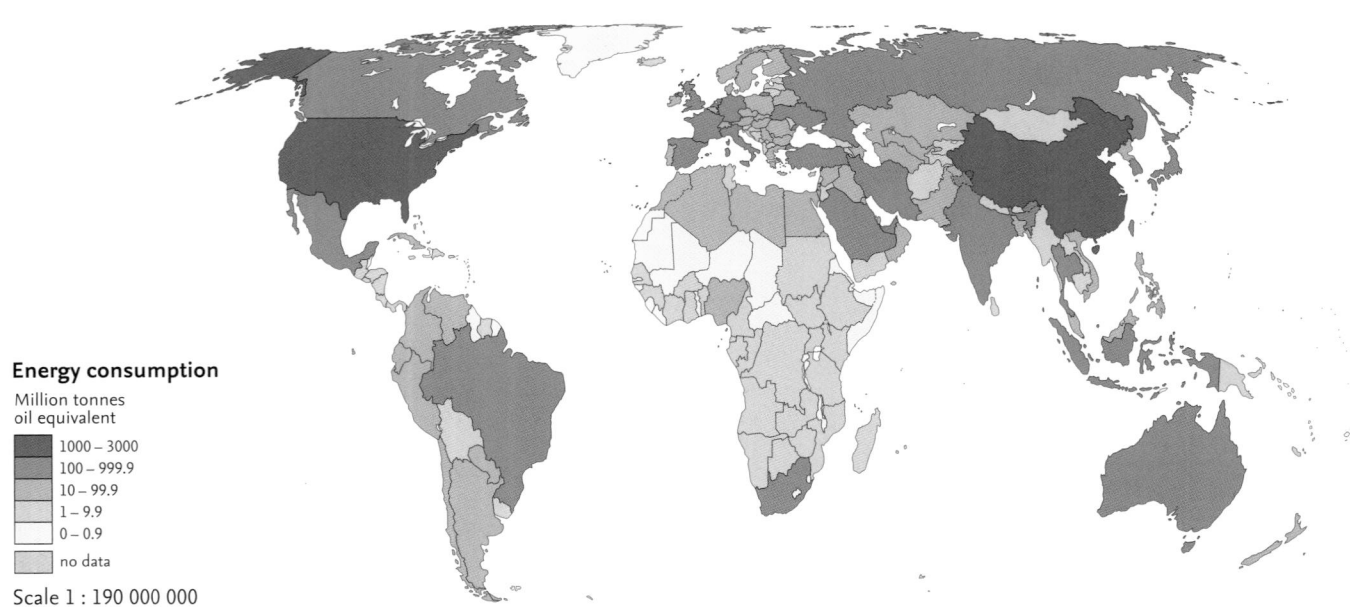

Energy consumption

Million tonnes
oil equivalent

	1000 – 3000
	100 – 999.9
	10 – 99.9
	1 – 9.9
	0 – 0.9
	no data

Scale 1 : 190 000 000

Energy consumption
Expressed as the number
of tonnes oil equivalent
used in one year.
Statistics are for 2013

Gross National Income

US$ per person

- 50 000 – 100 000
- 20 000 – 49 999
- 10 552 – 19 999 — average
- 3000 – 10 551
- 1000 – 2999
- 0 – 999
- no data

Scale 1 : 190 000 000

GNI
Gross National Income is the value of production of goods and services of each country measured in US$ per person in one year. World average US$ 10 552. Statistics are for 2015.

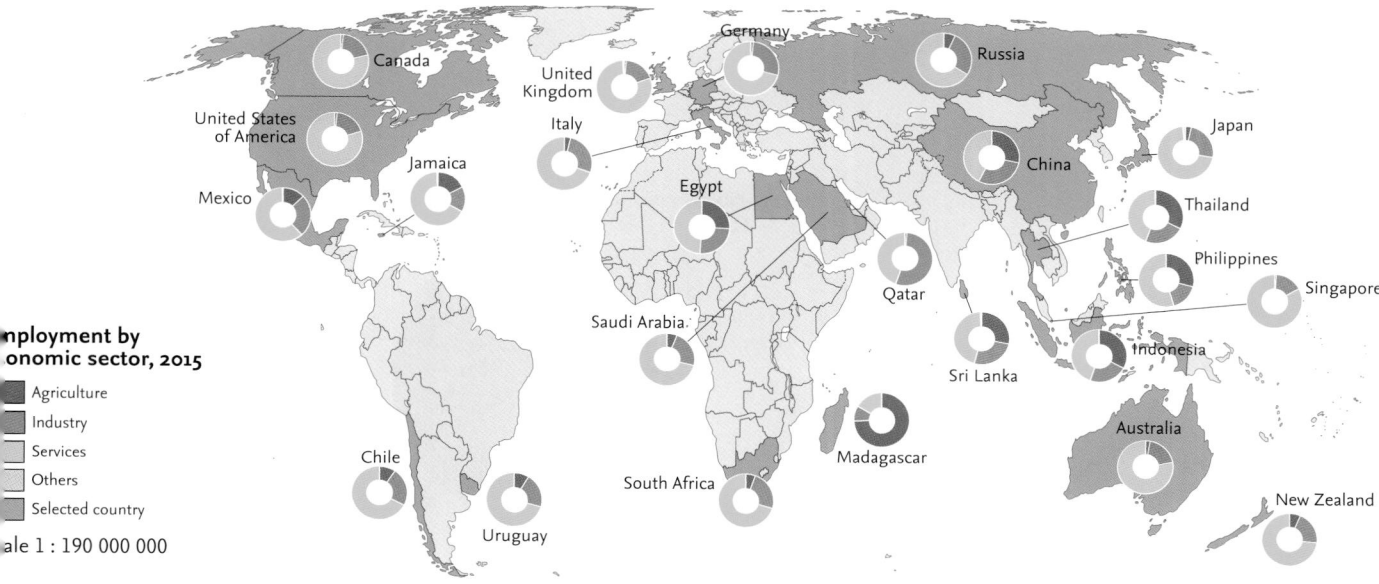

Employment by economic sector, 2015

- Agriculture
- Industry
- Services
- Others
- Selected country

Scale 1 : 190 000 000

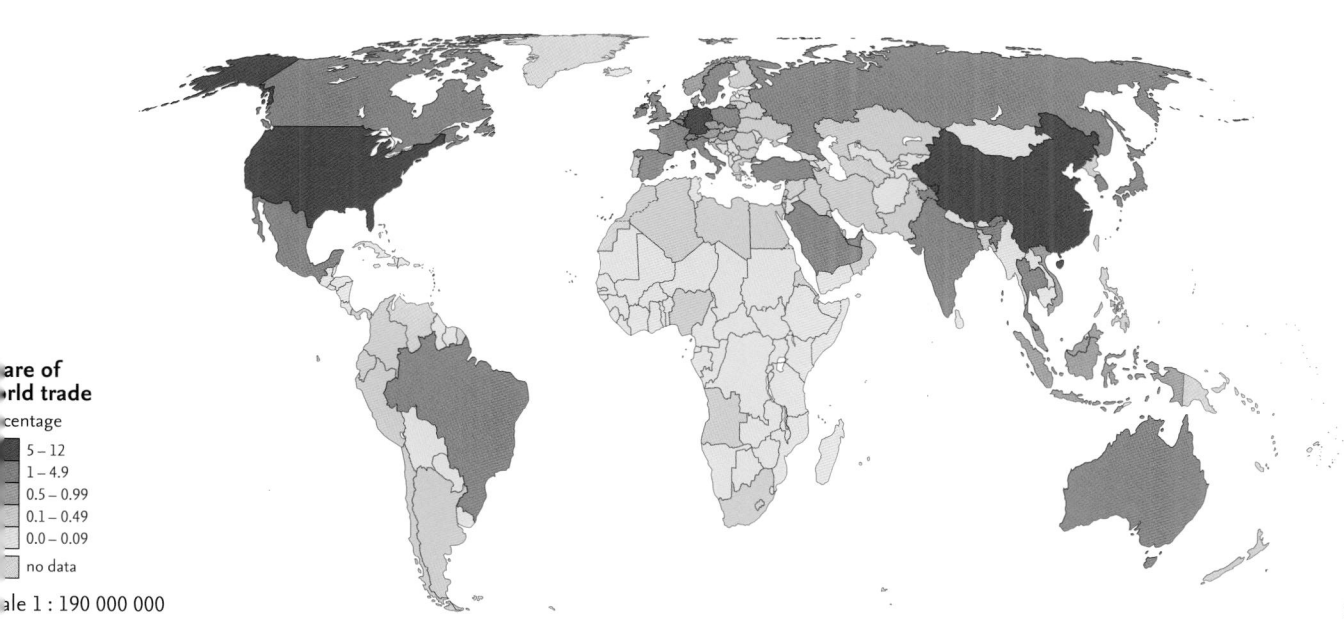

Share of world trade

percentage

- 5 – 12
- 1 – 4.9
- 0.5 – 0.99
- 0.1 – 0.49
- 0.0 – 0.09
- no data

Scale 1 : 190 000 000

Trade
Percentage of world trade (total of imports and exports divided by world total). Statistics are for 2014 – 2015.

World: Ecological Footprint

The Ecological Footprint measures the area of biologically productive land and water required to produce the resources an individual or a population consumes and to absorb the waste it generates. A country's Ecological Footprint is usually expressed in global hectares (gha) per person – the average area of land required to support each of that country's inhabitants.

Since 1961, when the data from which the Ecological Footprint is calculated first became available, there has been a marked increase in the contribution made by the carbon footprint – that is, the amount of forest land needed to absorb emissions of carbon dioxide (CO_2). Most CO_2 emissions come from the burning of fossil fuels.

Ecological Footprint is often compared with biocapacity, or the ability of the land to supply resources and absorb waste. A country's biocapacity, which can also be expressed in global hectares per person, is its total amount of biologically productive land divided by its population.

The demands of humanity, as measured by the Ecological Footprint, first exceeded the Earth's biocapacity in the 1970s. Since then, we have been using up biological resources faster than the Earth can regenerate them. Rapid steps could end this so-called 'overshoot' by the middle of the 21st century, lessen the risk of ecological collapse and create a biocapacity reserve.

World Ecological Footprint, 1961 – 2013

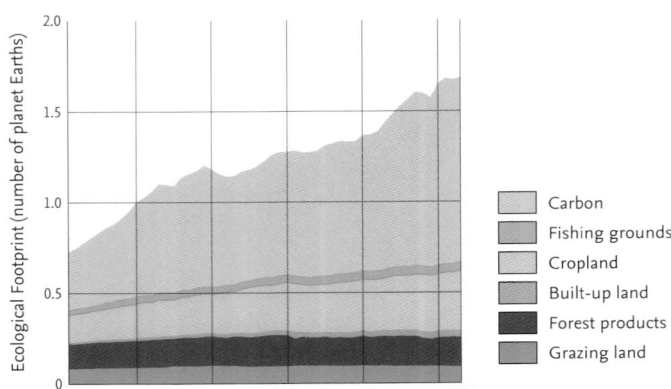

Return to sustainability

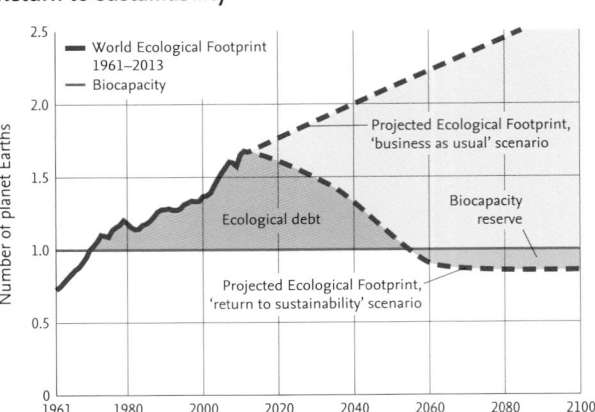

Ecological Footprint per country, per person, 2013

World average Ecological Footprint: 2.87 global hectares per person
World average biocapacity: 1.71 global hectares per person

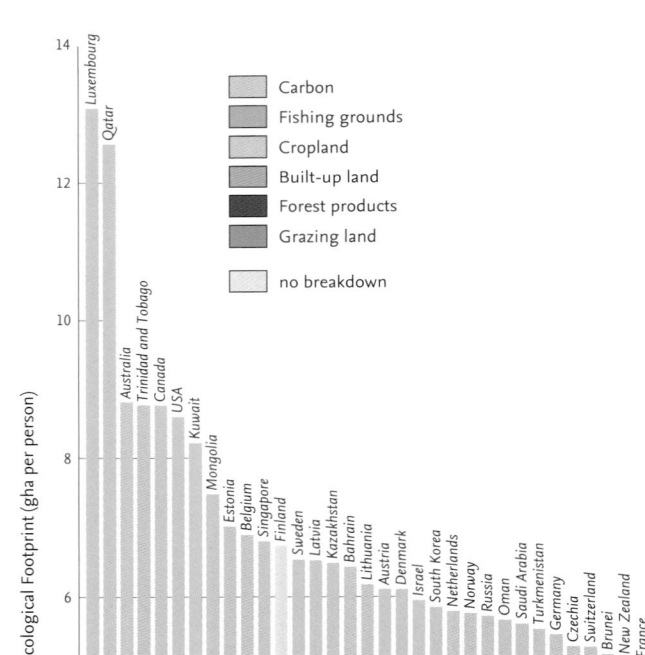

Biocapacity by country, 2013

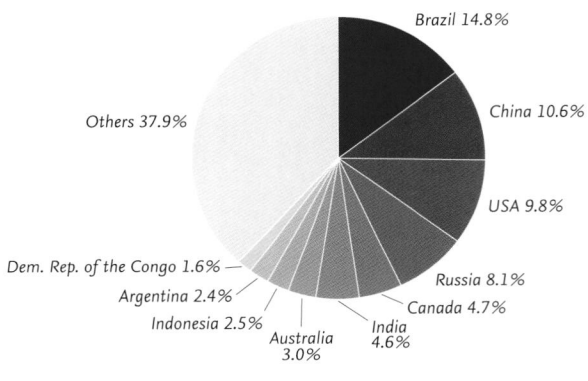

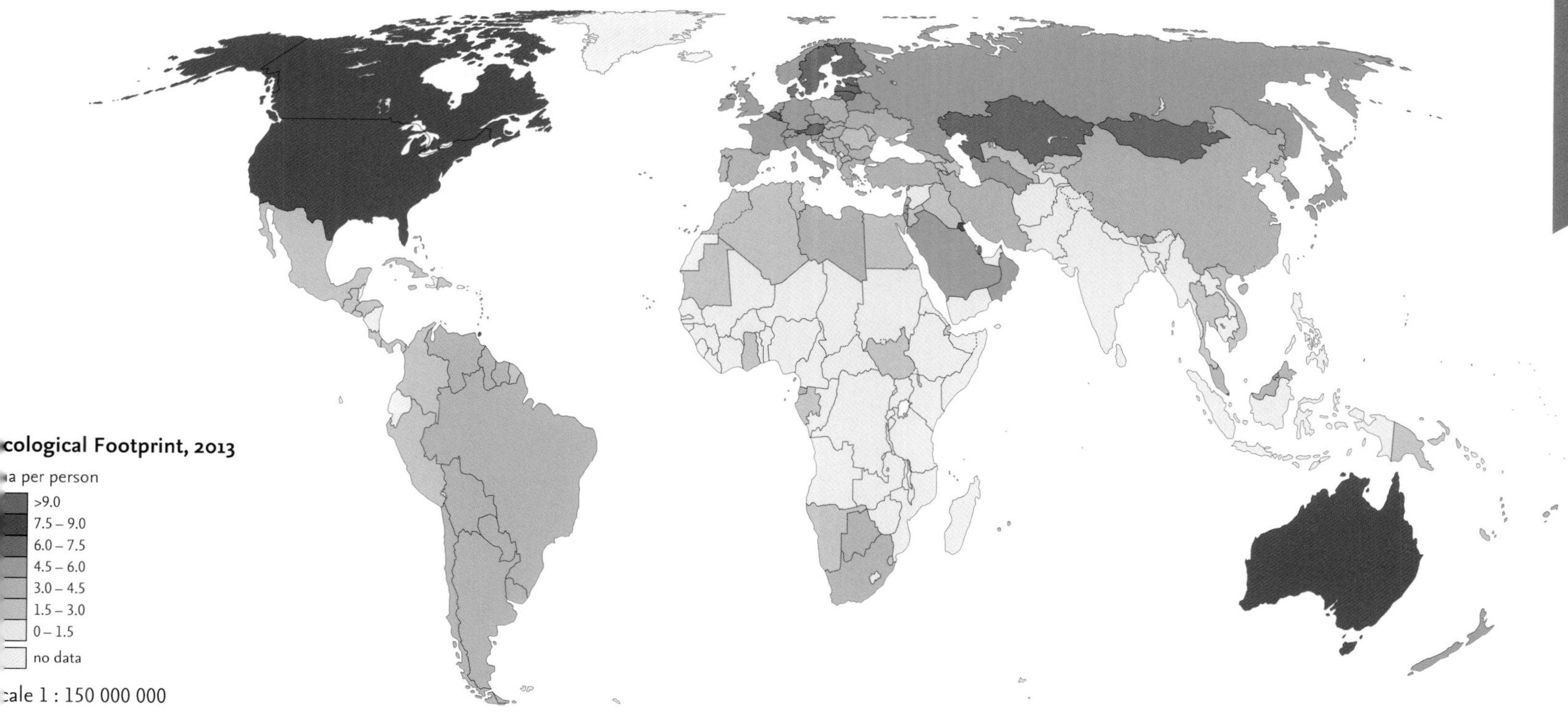

Ecological Footprint, 2013

a per person

- >9.0
- 7.5 – 9.0
- 6.0 – 7.5
- 4.5 – 6.0
- 3.0 – 4.5
- 1.5 – 3.0
- 0 – 1.5
- no data

cale 1 : 150 000 000

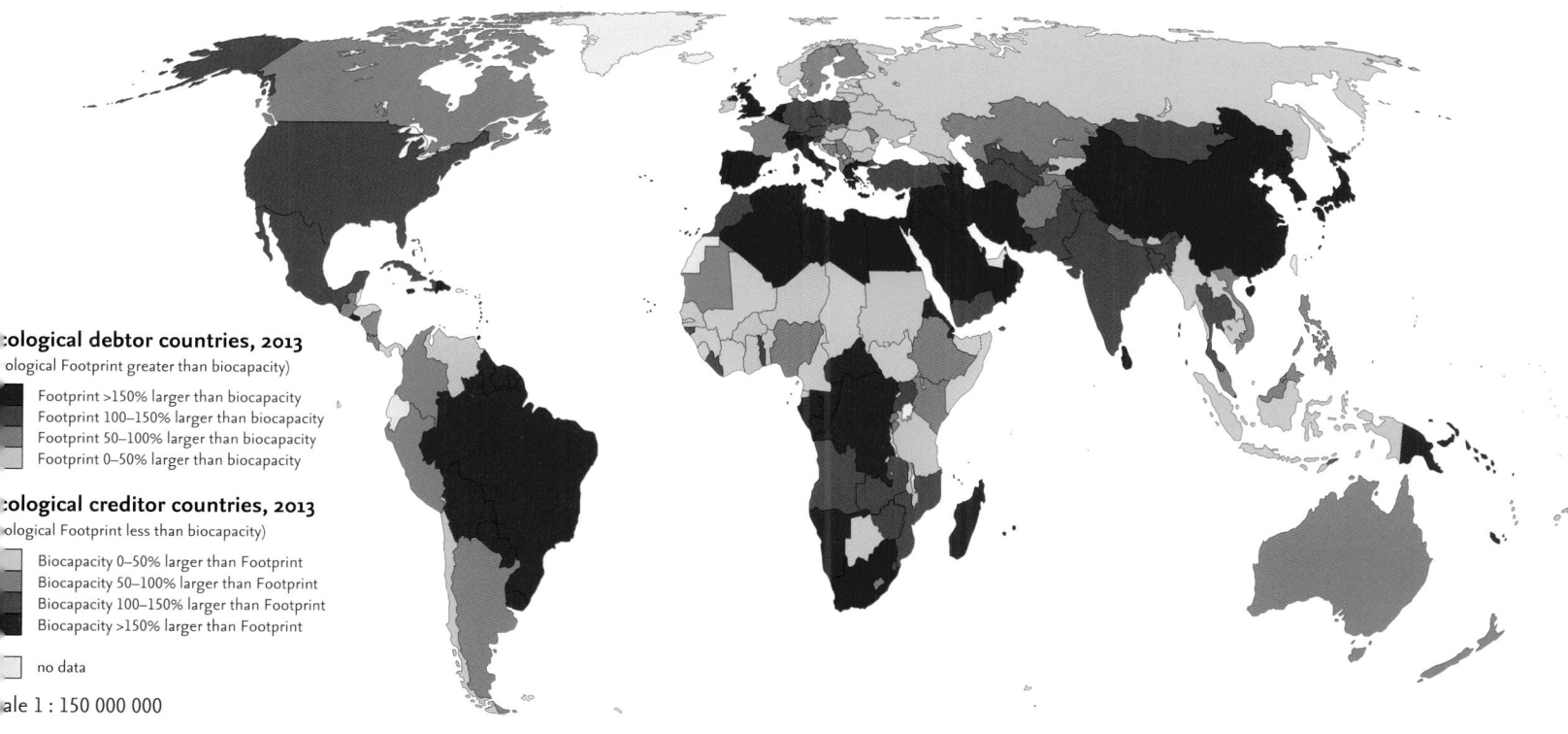

Ecological debtor countries, 2013

(ological Footprint greater than biocapacity)

- Footprint >150% larger than biocapacity
- Footprint 100–150% larger than biocapacity
- Footprint 50–100% larger than biocapacity
- Footprint 0–50% larger than biocapacity

Ecological creditor countries, 2013

(ological Footprint less than biocapacity)

- Biocapacity 0–50% larger than Footprint
- Biocapacity 50–100% larger than Footprint
- Biocapacity 100–150% larger than Footprint
- Biocapacity >150% larger than Footprint

- no data

ale 1 : 150 000 000

WWW Global Footprint Network
www.footprintnetwork.org
Footprint calculator
http://footprint.wwf.org.uk

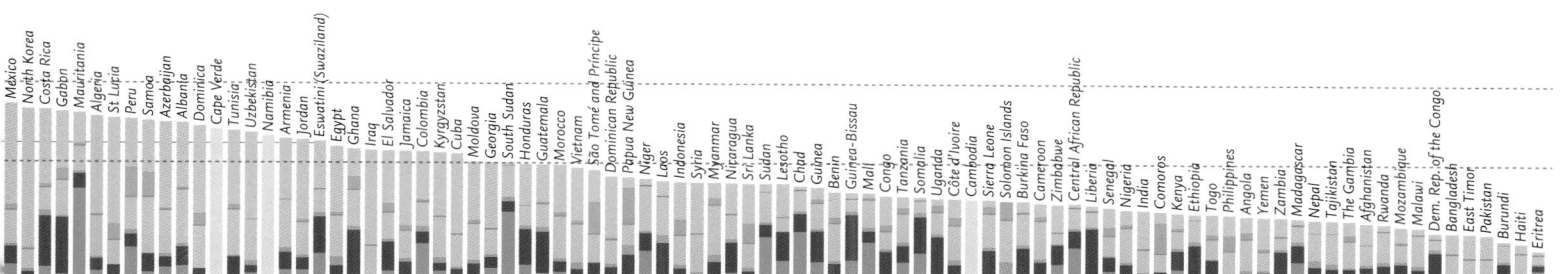

World: Tourism

WWW
World Tourism Organization
unwto.org
UNESCO World Heritage Sites
whc.unesco.org

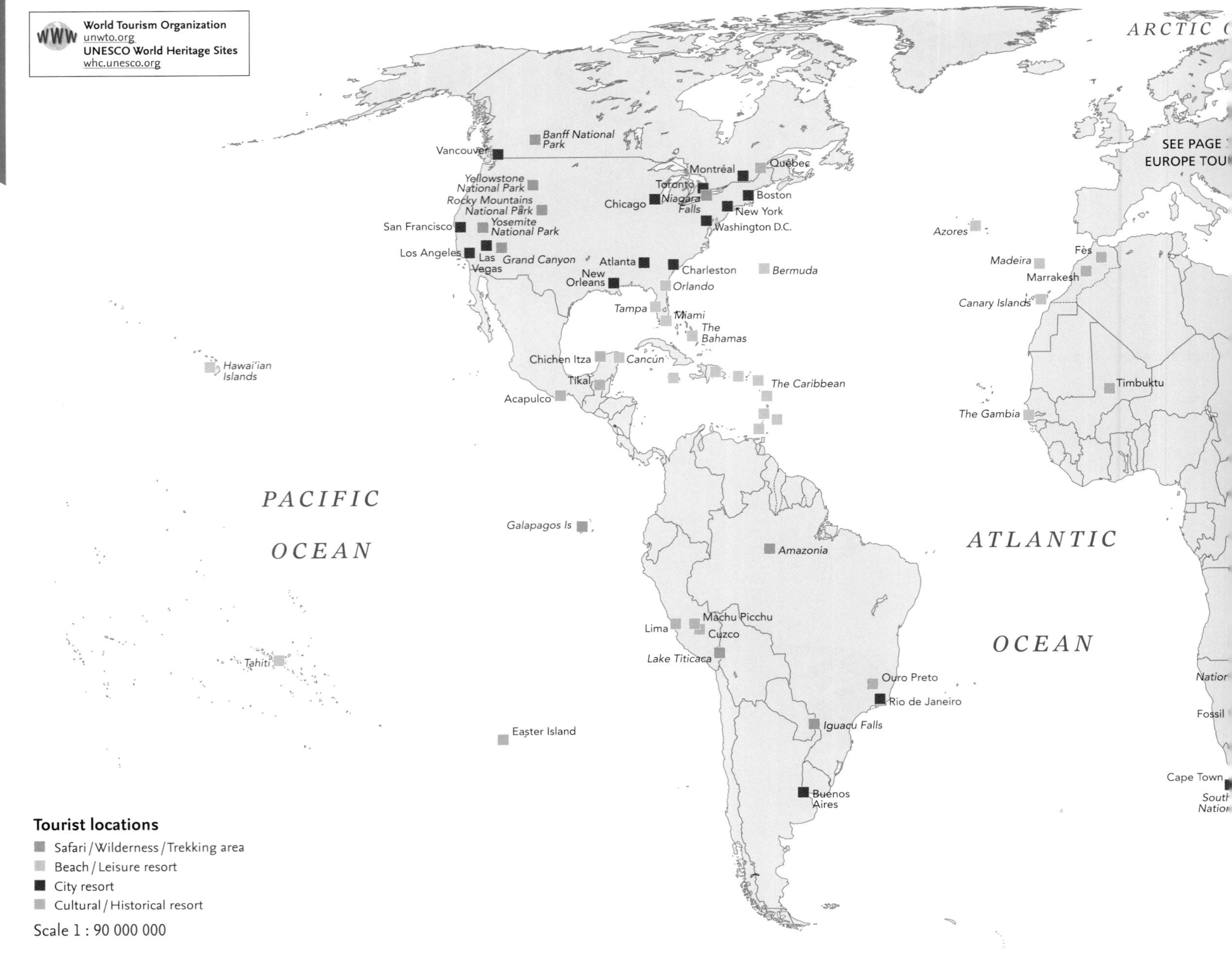

ARCTIC
SEE PAGE
EUROPE TOU
PACIFIC OCEAN
ATLANTIC OCEAN
Banff National Park
Vancouver
Yellowstone National Park
Rocky Mountains National Park
Yosemite National Park
San Francisco
Los Angeles
Las Vegas
Grand Canyon
Montréal
Québec
Toronto
Niagara Falls
Chicago
Boston
New York
Washington D.C.
Atlanta
Charleston
New Orleans
Orlando
Tampa
Miami
The Bahamas
Bermuda
Azores
Madeira
Fès
Marrakesh
Canary Islands
Timbuktu
The Gambia
Hawai'ian Islands
Chichen Itza
Cancún
Tikal
Acapulco
The Caribbean
Galapagos Is
Amazonia
Machu Picchu
Cuzco
Lima
Lake Titicaca
Tahiti
Easter Island
Ouro Preto
Rio de Janeiro
Iguaçu Falls
Buenos Aires
Natior
Fossil
Cape Town
South
Natior

Tourist locations

- Safari / Wilderness / Trekking area
- Beach / Leisure resort
- City resort
- Cultural / Historical resort

Scale 1 : 90 000 000

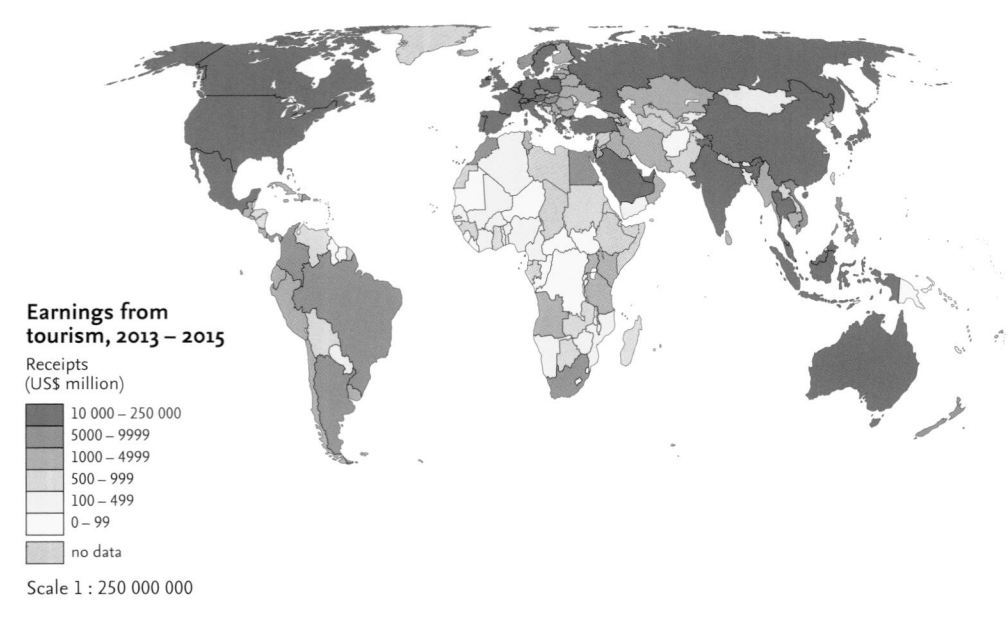

Earnings from tourism, 2013 – 2015

Receipts (US$ million)

- 10 000 – 250 000
- 5000 – 9999
- 1000 – 4999
- 500 – 999
- 100 – 499
- 0 – 99
- no data

Scale 1 : 250 000 000

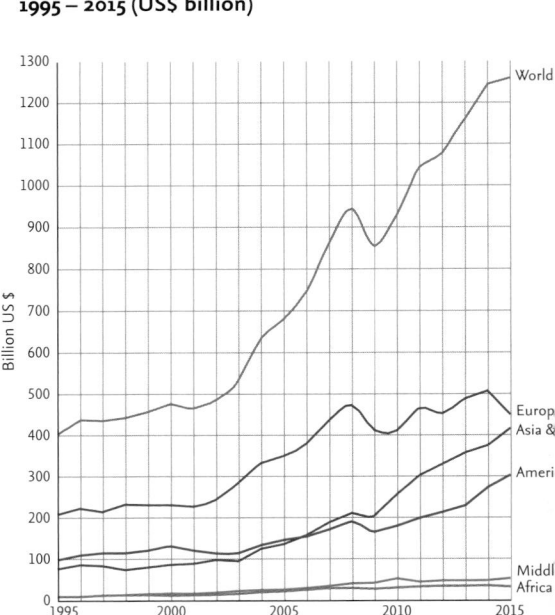

International tourism receipts, 1995 – 2015 (US$ billion)

1300
1200
1100
1000
900
800
700
600
500
400
300
200
100
0
Billion US $
1995
2000
2005
2010
2015
World
Europ
Asia &
Ameri
Middl
Africa

PACIFIC OCEAN

Moscow
Lake Baikal
Aleppo
Petra
iro/Pyramids
Red Sea
Abu Dhabi
Mecca
Goa
Maldives
East African
National Parks
Mombasa
Seychelles
Comoros
ake Kariba
ictoria Falls
ange
tional
k
Kruger
National Park
Durban
Mauritius
Reunion

Great Wall
Beijing
Xi'an
Kyōto
Tōkyō
Shanghai
Delhi
Lhasa
Agra/
Taj Mahal
Mt Everest
Jaipur
Sundarbans
Hong
Kong
Chiang Mai
Angkor
Bangkok
Koh Sumai
Sri
Lanka
Phuket
Mt Kinabalu
Singapore
Komodo
National Park
Bali

INDIAN OCEAN

Great Barrier Reef
Marine Park
Fiji
Uluru
Gold Coast
Blue Mountains
Sydney
Melbourne
North
Island
Auckland
South
Island

World's top tourist destinations, 2015

Tourist arrivals (million)	
France	84.5
United States of America	77.5
Spain	68.2
China	56.9
Italy	50.7
Turkey	39.5
Germany	35.0
United Kingdom	34.4
Mexico	32.1
Russia	31.3

Market share	%
France	7.12
United States of America	6.53
Spain	5.75
China	4.80
Italy	4.27
Turkey	3.33
Germany	2.95
United Kingdom	2.90
Mexico	2.71
Russia	2.64

International tourist arrivals by region, 1995 – 2015

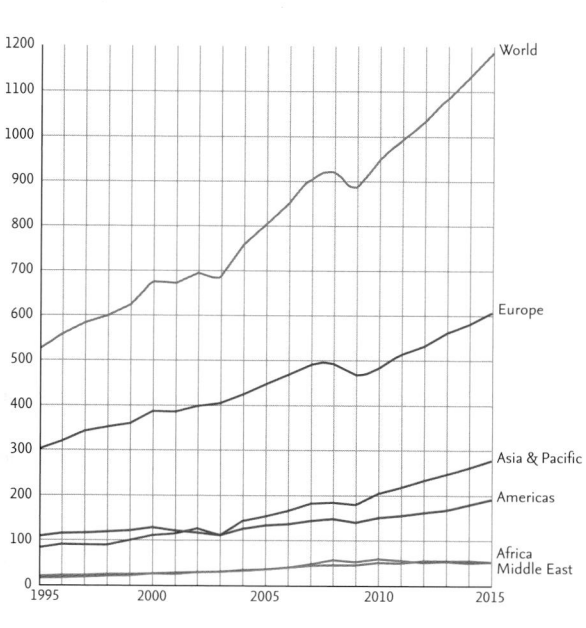

World
Europe
Asia & Pacific
Americas
Africa
Middle East

Tourist arrivals by region, 2015

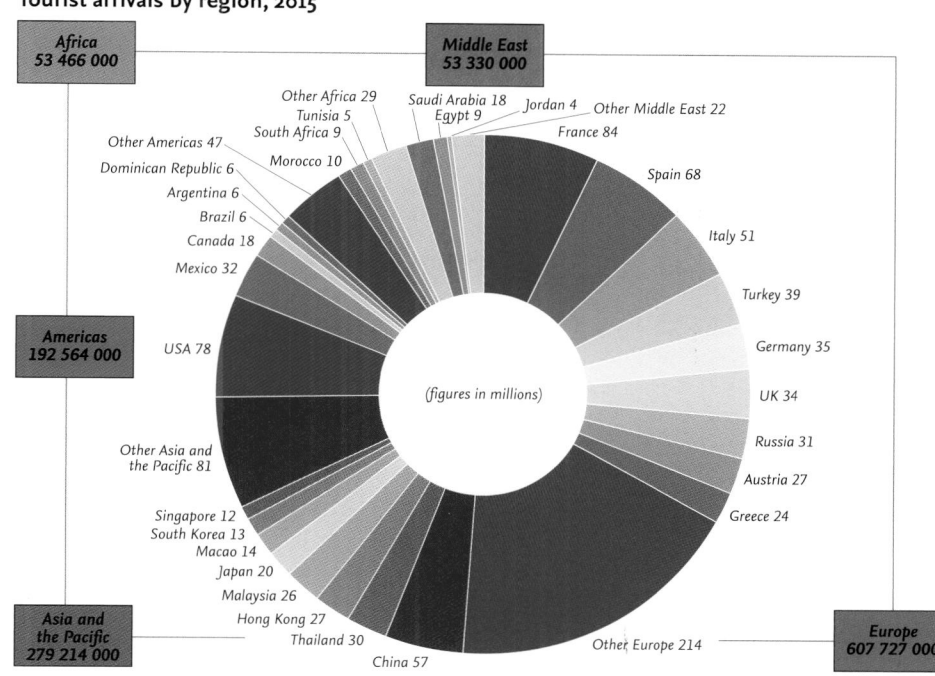

Africa
53 466 000

Middle East
53 330 000

Other Africa 29
Tunisia 5
South Africa 9
Morocco 10
Saudi Arabia 18
Egypt 9
Jordan 4
Other Middle East 22
France 84

Other Americas 47
Dominican Republic 6
Argentina 6
Brazil 6
Canada 18
Mexico 32

Spain 68
Italy 51
Turkey 39
Germany 35
UK 34
Russia 31
Austria 27
Greece 24

Americas
192 564 000

USA 78

Other Asia and
the Pacific 81

Singapore 12
South Korea 13
Macao 14
Japan 20
Malaysia 26
Hong Kong 27
Thailand 30
China 57

(figures in millions)

Asia and
the Pacific
279 214 000

Other Europe 214

Europe
607 727 000

World: Communications

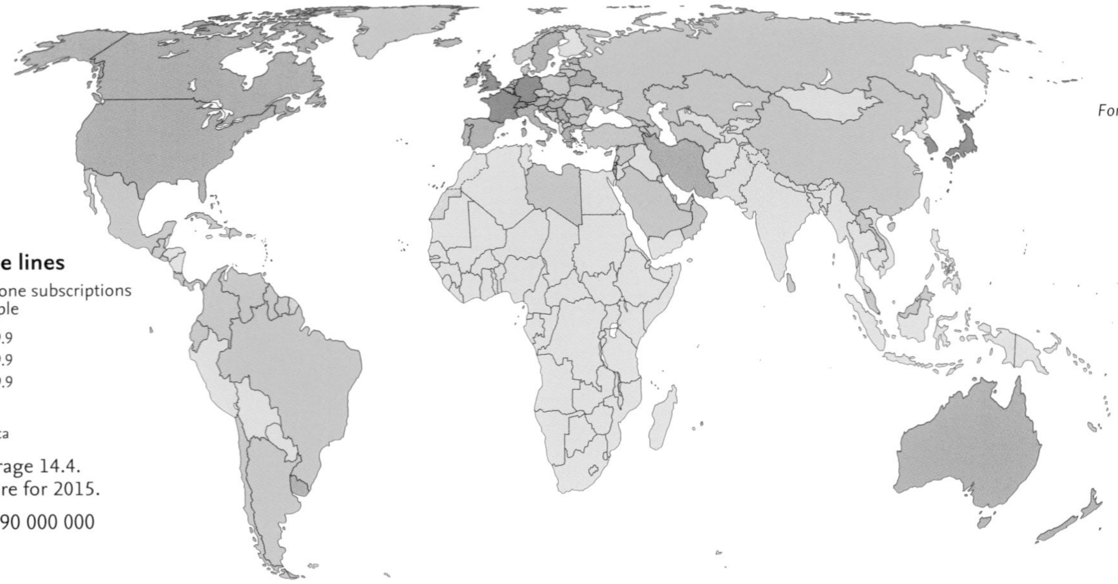

Telephone lines

Fixed telephone subscriptions per 100 people

- 50 – 79.9
- 30 – 49.9
- 10 – 29.9
- 0 – 9.9
- no data

World average 14.4.
Statistics are for 2015.

Scale 1 : 190 000 000

Fixed telephone lines, 2015

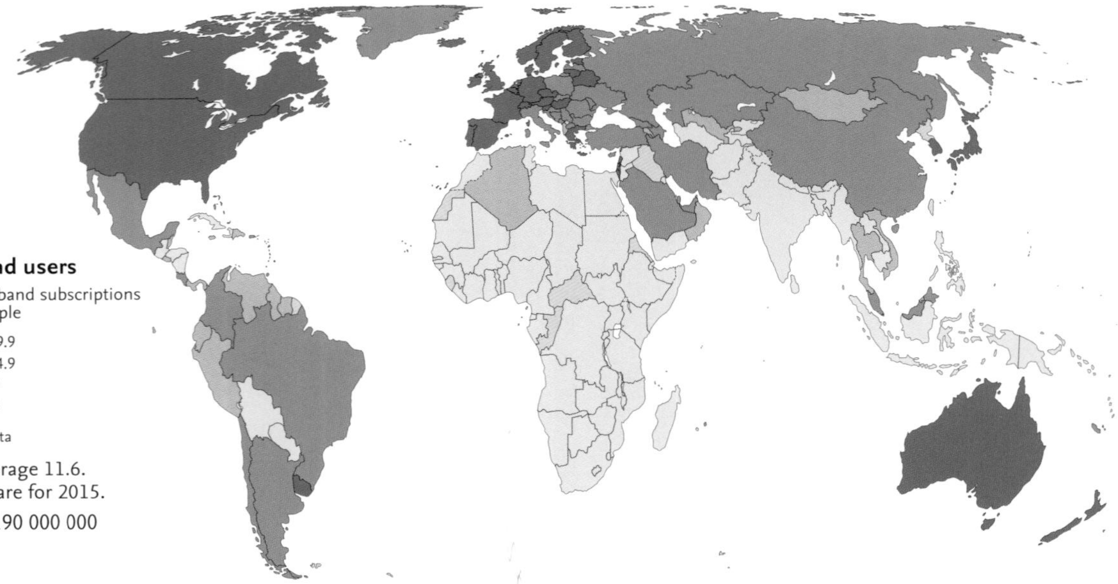

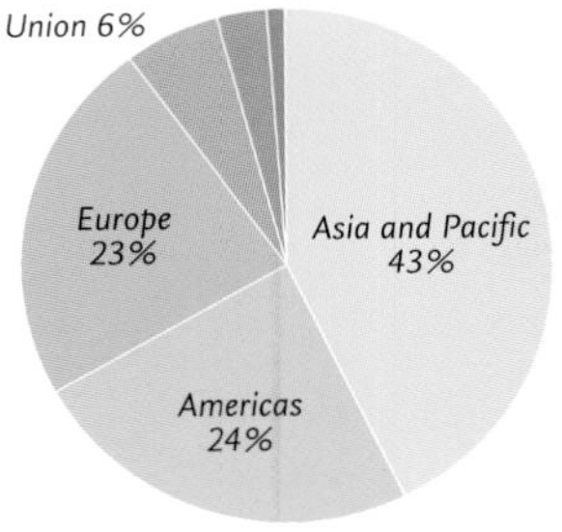

Arab states 3%
Africa 1%
Former Soviet Union 6%
Europe 23%
Asia and Pacific 43%
Americas 24%

World : 1 034 000 000

Broadband users

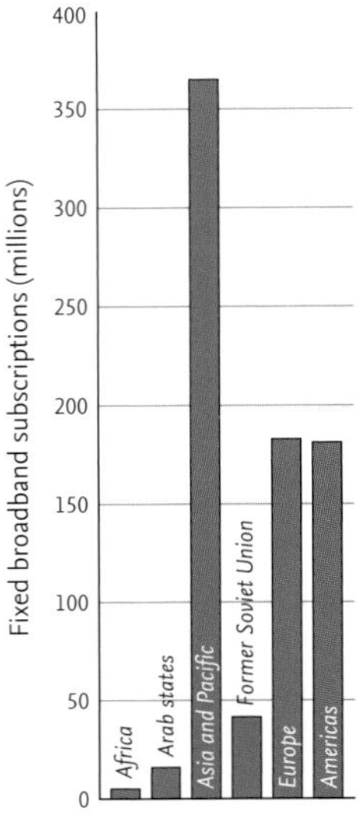

Fixed broadband subscriptions per 100 people

- 25 – 49.9
- 10 – 24.9
- 5 – 9.9
- 0 – 4.9
- no data

World average 11.6.
Statistics are for 2015.

Scale 1 : 190 000 000

Broadband users, 2015

400
350
300
250
200
150
100
50
0
Fixed broadband subscriptions (millions)
Africa
Arab states
Asia and Pacific
Former Soviet Union
Europe
Americas

World : 791 000 000

Mobile phone subscriptions, 2

Former Soviet Union 6%
Arab states 6%
Africa 10%
Europe 10%
Asia and Pacific 53%
Americas 15%

World : 7 178 000 000

Mobile phone subscriptions, 2015

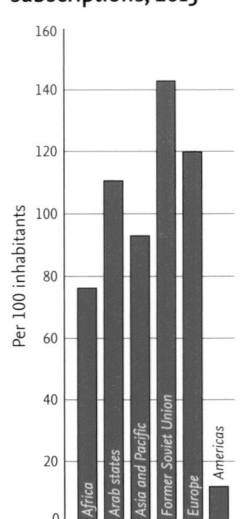

160
140
120
100
80
60
40
20
0
Per 100 inhabitants
Africa
Arab states
Asia and Pacific
Former Soviet Union
Europe
Americas

Growth in mobile phone subscriptions, 2010 – 2015

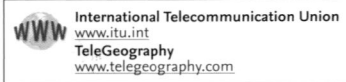

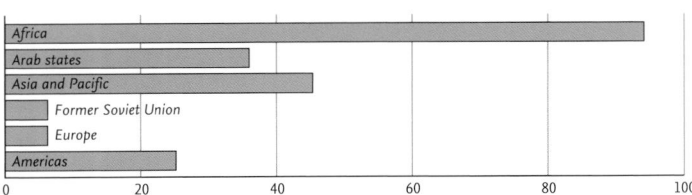

Africa
Arab states
Asia and Pacific
Former Soviet Union
Europe
Americas
0
20
40
60
80
100
Percentage increase

Mobile phone subscriptions

- Developed countries
- Developing countries

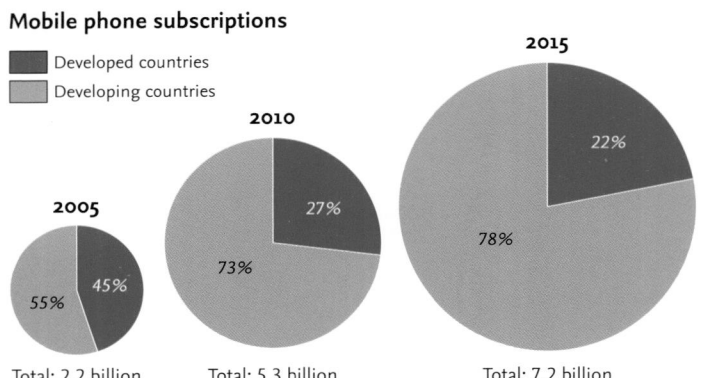

2005
55%
45%
Total: 2.2 billion
2010
27%
73%
Total: 5.3 billion
2015
22%
78%
Total: 7.2 billion

World communication equipment 2005 – 2015

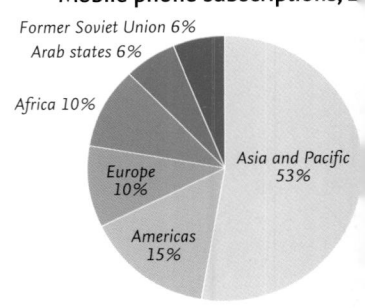

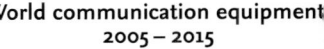

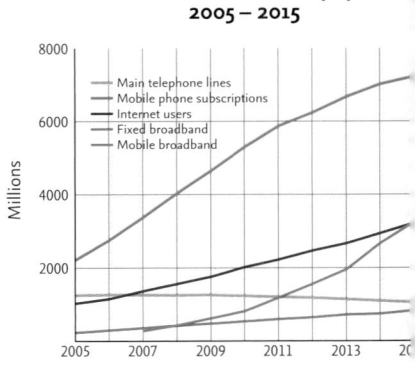

8000
6000
4000
2000
Millions
Main telephone lines
Mobile phone subscriptions
Internet users
Fixed broadband
Mobile broadband
2005
2007
2009
2011
2013
20

WWW
International Telecommunication Union
www.itu.int
TeleGeography
www.telegeography.com

World: Air Transport

Top 20 busiest airports, 2015

	Airport	Passengers carried
1	Atlanta	101 489 887
2	Beijing	89 938 628
3	Dubai	78 010 265
4	Chicago	76 942 493
5	Tōkyō	75 316 718
6	London Heathrow	74 989 914
7	Los Angeles	74 704 122
8	Hong Kong	68 342 785
9	Paris	65 771 288
0	Dallas/Fort Worth	64 072 468
1	İstanbul	61 836 781
2	Frankfurt	61 032 022
3	Shanghai	60 053 387
4	Amsterdam	58 284 848
5	New York (JFK)	56 845 250
6	Singapore	55 449 000
7	Guangzhou	55 201 915
8	Jakarta	54 053 905
9	Denver	54 014 903
0	Bangkok	52 808 013

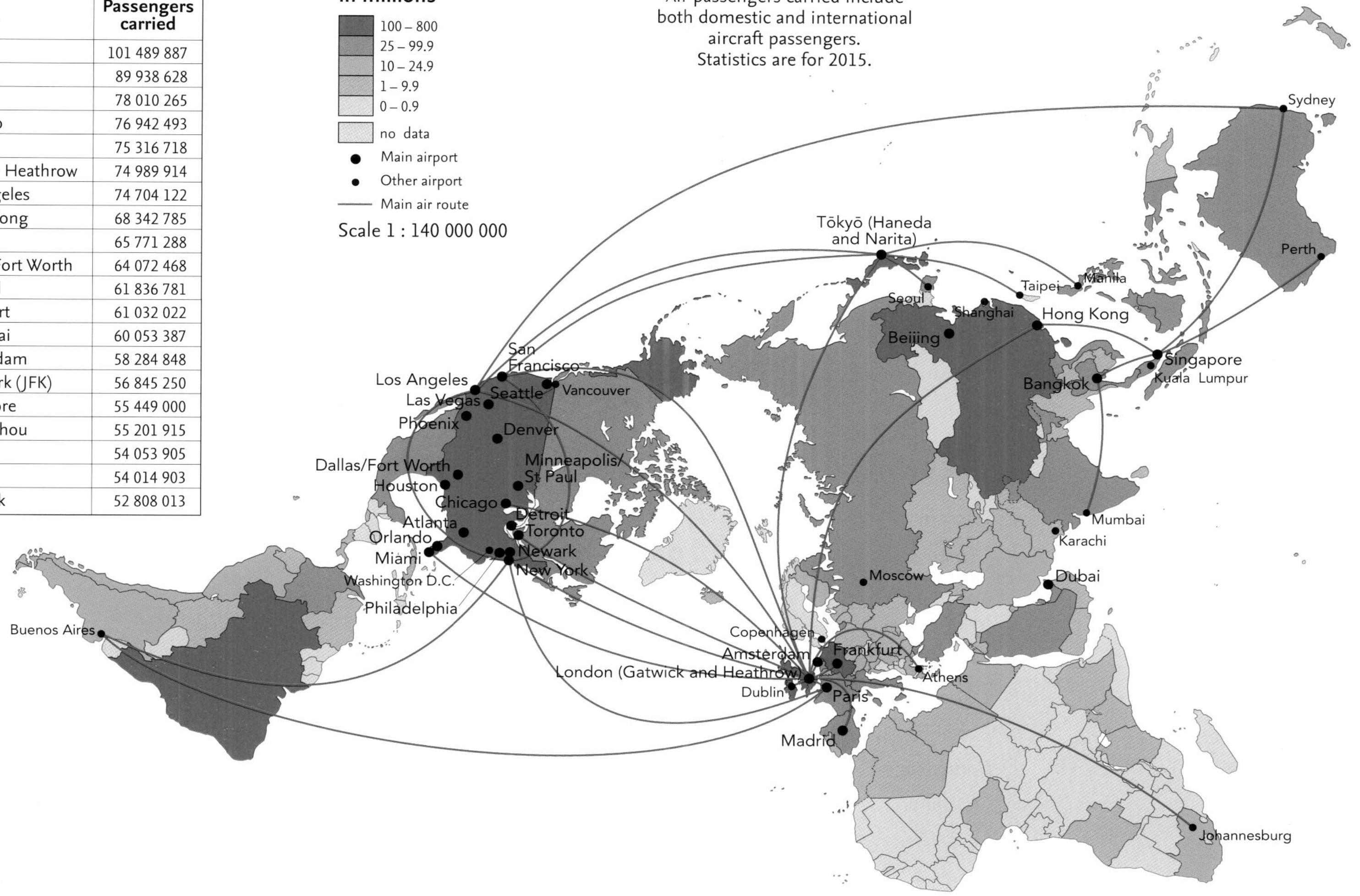

Air passengers carried in millions
100 – 800
25 – 99.9
10 – 24.9
1 – 9.9
0 – 0.9
no data
Main airport
Other airport
Main air route
Scale 1 : 140 000 000
Passengers carried
Air passengers carried include both domestic and international aircraft passengers. Statistics are for 2015.
Sydney
Perth
Tōkyō (Haneda and Narita)
Seoul
Taipei
Manila
Shanghai
Hong Kong
Beijing
Singapore
Kuala Lumpur
Bangkok
Mumbai
Karachi
Dubai
Moscow
Copenhagen
Amsterdam
Frankfurt
London (Gatwick and Heathrow)
Dublin
Paris
Athens
Madrid
Johannesburg
San Francisco
Los Angeles
Vancouver
Seattle
Las Vegas
Phoenix
Denver
Dallas/Fort Worth
Minneapolis/St Paul
Houston
Chicago
Detroit
Toronto
Atlanta
Orlando
Miami
Newark
New York
Washington D.C.
Philadelphia
Buenos Aires

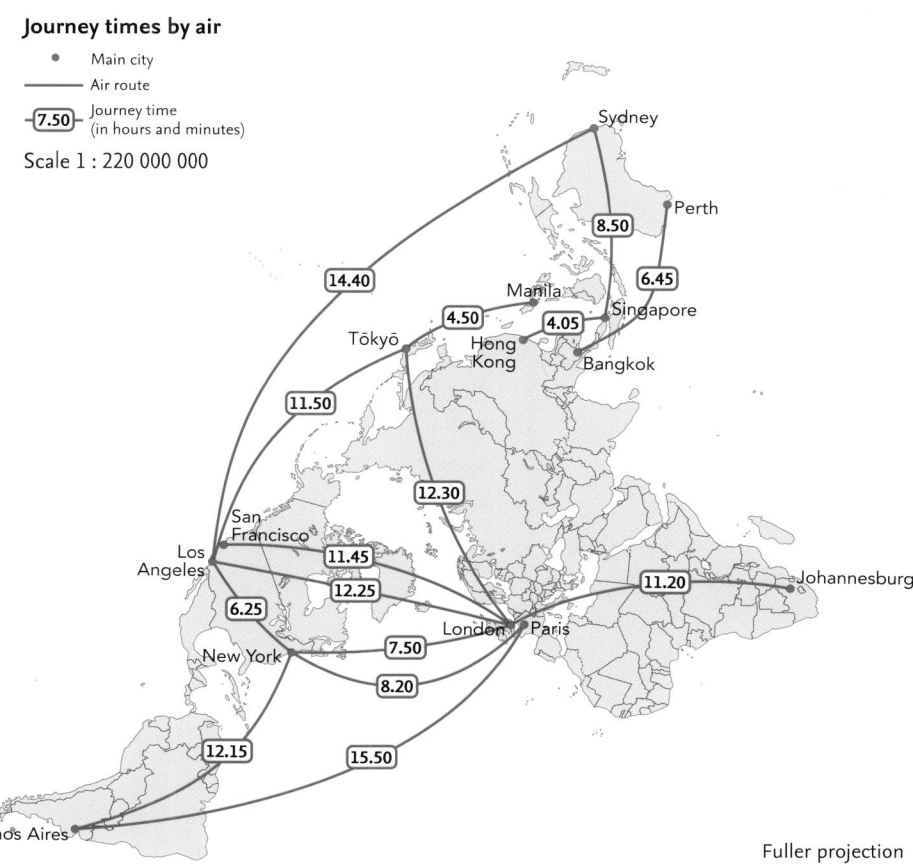

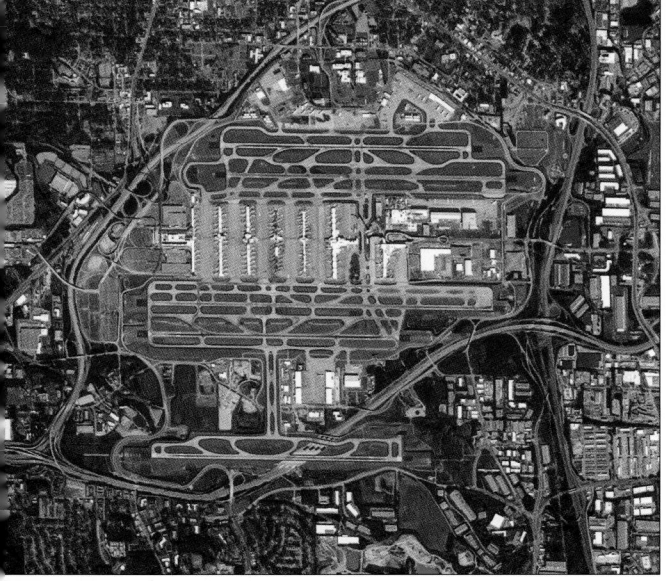

artsfield-Jackson Atlanta International Airport is the busiest in the orld, with over 100 million passengers passing through each year. age courtesy of the Earth Science and Remote Sensing Unit, ASA Johnson Space Center.

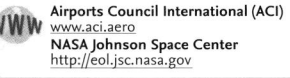

Journey times by air
Main city
Air route
7.50 Journey time (in hours and minutes)
Scale 1 : 220 000 000
Sydney
Perth
8.50
6.45
14.40
Manila
4.50
4.05
Singapore
Tōkyō
Hong Kong
Bangkok
11.50
12.30
San Francisco
Los Angeles
11.45
12.25
6.25
11.20
Johannesburg
London
Paris
New York
7.50
8.20
12.15
15.50
Buenos Aires
Fuller projection

WWW Airports Council International (ACI)
www.aci.aero
NASA Johnson Space Center
http://eol.jsc.nasa.gov

Flag	Country	Capital city	Population total 2015	Density persons per sq km 2015	Birth rate per 1000 population 2015	Death rate per 1000 population 2015	Life expectancy in years 2015	Population change % 2015	Urban population % 2015
	Afghanistan	Kābul	32 527 000	50	33	8	61	2.8	27
	Albania	Tirana	2 897 000	101	14	7	78	-0.2	57
	Algeria	Algiers	39 667 000	17	24	5	75	1.9	71
	Andorra	Andorra la Vella	70 000	151	..	..	..	-3.2	85
	Angola	Luanda	25 022 000	20	45	13	53	3.2	44
	Antigua and Barbuda	St John's	92 000	208	16	6	76	1.0	24
	Argentina	Buenos Aires	43 417 000	16	17	8	76	1.0	92
	Armenia	Yerevan	3 018 000	101	13	9	75	0.4	63
	Australia	Canberra	23 969 000	3	13	7	82	1.4	89
	Austria	Vienna	8 545 000	102	10	10	82	1.1	66
	Azerbaijan	Baku	9 754 000	113	17	6	71	1.2	55
	Bahamas, The	Nassau	388 000	28	15	6	75	1.3	83
	Bahrain	Manama	1 377 000	1 993	14	2	77	1.1	89
	Bangladesh	Dhaka	160 996 000	1 118	19	5	72	1.2	34
	Barbados	Bridgetown	284 000	660	12	11	76	0.3	31
	Belarus	Minsk	9 496 000	46	13	13	74	0.2	77
	Belgium	Brussels	11 299 000	370	11	10	81	0.2	98
	Belize	Belmopan	359 000	16	23	6	70	2.1	44
	Benin	Porto-Novo	10 880 000	97	36	9	60	2.6	44
	Bhutan	Thimphu	775 000	17	17	6	70	1.3	39
	Bolivia	La Paz/Sucre	10 725 000	10	24	7	69	1.5	69
	Bosnia and Herzegovina	Sarajevo	3 810 000	75	9	11	77	-0.2	40
	Botswana	Gaborone	2 262 000	4	25	8	64	1.9	57
	Brazil	Brasília	207 848 000	24	15	6	75	0.9	86
	Brunei	Bandar Seri Begawan	423 000	73	16	3	79	1.4	77
	Bulgaria	Sofia	7 150 000	64	9	15	74	-0.6	74
	Burkina Faso	Ouagadougou	18 106 000	66	40	9	59	2.9	30
	Burundi	Bujumbura	11 179 000	402	44	11	57	3.3	12
	Cambodia	Phnom Penh	15 578 000	86	24	6	69	1.6	21
	Cameroon	Yaoundé	23 344 000	49	36	11	56	2.5	54
	Canada	Ottawa	35 940 000	4	11	8	82	0.9	82
	Cape Verde	Praia	521 000	129	21	5	73	1.3	66
	Central African Republic	Bangui	4 900 000	8	33	14	51	2.0	40
	Chad	Ndjamena	14 037 000	11	45	14	52	3.3	22
	Chile	Santiago	17 948 000	24	13	5	82	1.0	90
	China	Beijing	1 383 925 000	144	12	7	76	0.5	56
	Colombia	Bogotá	48 229 000	42	15	6	74	0.9	76
	Comoros	Moroni	788 000	423	33	7	64	2.4	28
	Congo	Brazzaville	4 620 000	14	36	8	63	2.5	65
	Congo, Dem. Rep. of the	Kinshasa	77 267 000	33	42	10	59	3.1	42
	Costa Rica	San José	4 808 000	94	15	5	80	1.1	77
	Côte d'Ivoire	Yamoussoukro	22 702 000	70	37	13	52	2.4	54
	Croatia	Zagreb	4 240 000	75	9	13	77	-0.8	59
	Cuba	Havana	11 390 000	103	10	8	80	0.1	77
	Cyprus	Nicosia	1 165 000	126	11	7	80	1.0	67
	Czechia	Prague	10 543 000	134	11	11	79	0.2	73
	Denmark	Copenhagen	5 669 000	132	10	9	81	0.7	88
	Djibouti	Djibouti	888 000	38	25	9	62	1.3	77
	Dominica	Roseau	73 000	97	..	..	..	0.5	70

Land		Education and Health			Development			Communications			
Area sq km	Forest thousand sq km 2015	Adult literacy % 2015	Doctors per 100 000 population 2009-2013	Nutrition population under-nourished % 2015	Energy consumption million tonnes oil equivalent 2013	GNI per capita US$ 2015	HDI index 2015	Mobile phones subs per 100 population 2015	Broadband users subs per 100 population 2015	Country	Time Zones + or - GMT
652 225	14	38.2	27	26.8	7.6	610	0.479	61.6	0.3	Afghanistan	+4½
28 748	8	97.5	115	..	3.2	4 280	0.764	106.4	7.6	Albania	+1
2 381 741	20	79.6	121	<5	51.2	4 850	0.745	106.4	5.6	Algeria	+1
465	<1	>95	400	..	..	..	0.858	88.1	37.9	Andorra	+1
1 246 700	579	71.2	17	14.2	8.1	4 180	0.533	60.8	0.7	Angola	+1
442	<1	..	17	..	0.3	13 270	0.786	137.2	13.1	Antigua and Barbuda	-4
2 766 889	271	98.1	386	<5	93.6	12 450	0.827	146.7	16.3	Argentina	-3
29 800	3	99.8	270	5.8	3.7	3 880	0.743	115.9	9.6	Armenia	+4
7 692 024	1 248	>95	327	..	141.9	60 050	0.939	132.8	28.5	Australia	+8 to +10½
83 855	39	>95	483	..	36.8	47 260	0.893	157.4	28.7	Austria	+1
86 600	11	99.8	340	<5	15.3	6 560	0.759	111.3	19.8	Azerbaijan	+4
13 939	5	..	..	..	1.3	20 740	0.792	80.3	20.9	Bahamas, The	-5
691	<1	95.7	92	..	17.4	19 840	0.824	185.3	18.6	Bahrain	+3
143 998	14	61.5	36	16.4	27.9	1 190	0.579	81.9	3.1	Bangladesh	+6
430	<1	..	181	<5	0.6	14 510	0.795	116.5	27.2	Barbados	-4
207 600	86	99.7	392	..	30.0	6 470	0.796	123.6	31.4	Belarus	+2
30 520	7	>95	489	..	66.5	44 510	0.896	115.7	36.9	Belgium	+1
22 965	14	82.8	83	6.2	0.2	4 490	0.706	61.0	5.0	Belize	-6
112 620	43	38.5	6	7.5	2.1	840	0.485	85.6	0.7	Benin	+1
46 620	28	63.9	26	..	1.5	2 380	0.607	87.0	3.6	Bhutan	+6
1 098 581	548	95.1	47	15.9	7.5	3 000	0.674	92.2	1.6	Bolivia	-4
51 130	22	..	193	..	6.2	4 670	0.750	90.2	16.6	Bosnia and Herzegovina	+1
581 370	108	88.2	34	24.1	1.9	6 460	0.698	169.0	1.8	Botswana	+2
8 514 879	4 935	92.6	189	<5	318.7	9 990	0.754	126.6	12.3	Brazil	-2 to -5
5 765	4	96.7	144	<5	3.4	38 010	0.865	108.1	8.0	Brunei	+8
110 994	38	98.4	387	..	18.7	7 480	0.794	129.3	22.7	Bulgaria	+2
274 200	54	37.8	5	20.7	1.1	640	0.402	80.6	0.0	Burkina Faso	0
27 835	3	85.5	..	..	0.1	260	0.404	46.2	0.0	Burundi	+2
181 035	95	78.3	17	14.2	2.3	1 070	0.563	133.0	0.5	Cambodia	+7
475 442	188	75.0	8	9.9	3.5	1 320	0.518	71.8	0.1	Cameroon	+1
9 984 670	3 471	>95	207	..	363.5	47 250	0.920	83.0	36.3	Canada	-3½ to -8
4 033	<1	88.5	31	9.4	0.3	3 280	0.648	118.6	3.3	Cape Verde	-1
622 436	222	36.8	5	47.7	0.2	330	0.352	25.9	..	Central African Republic	+1
1 284 000	49	40.0	..	34.4	0.1	880	0.396	40.2	0.1	Chad	+1
756 945	177	96.6	103	<5	34.4	14 100	0.847	129.5	15.2	Chile	-3, -4 & -6
9 606 802	2 083	96.4	194	9.3	2 991.9	7 900	0.738	92.2	19.8	China	+8
1 141 748	585	94.6	147	8.8	40.3	7 140	0.727	115.7	11.2	Colombia	-5
1 862	<1	78.1	..	..	0.1	780	0.497	55.2	0.3	Comoros	+3
342 000	223	79.3	10	30.5	2.6	2 540	0.592	111.7	..	Congo	+1
2 345 410	1 526	77.2	..	..	3.3	410	0.435	53.0	..	Congo, Dem. Rep. of the	+1 & +2
51 100	28	97.7	111	<5	4.8	10 400	0.776	150.7	11.2	Costa Rica	-6
322 463	104	43.3	14	13.3	3.8	1 420	0.474	119.3	0.5	Côte d'Ivoire	0
56 538	19	99.3	300	..	9.2	12 760	0.827	103.8	23.2	Croatia	+1
110 860	32	99.7	672	<5	10.2	..	0.775	29.6	0.1	Cuba	-5
9 251	2	99.1	233	..	2.5	25 810	0.856	95.4	22.4	Cyprus	+2
78 864	27	>95	362	..	41.3	18 150	0.878	123.2	27.3	Czechia	+1
43 075	6	>95	348	..	18.7	60 270	0.925	128.3	42.5	Denmark	+1
23 200	<1	..	23	15.9	0.3	..	0.473	34.9	2.7	Djibouti	+3
750	<1	..	..	..	0.1	6 800	0.726	106.3	20.9	Dominica	-4

no data available

World: Country Statistics

Flag	Key Information		Population						
	Country	Capital city	Population total 2015	Density persons per sq km 2015	Birth rate per 1000 population 2015	Death rate per 1000 population 2015	Life expectancy in years 2015	Population change % 2015	Urban population % 2015
	Dominican Republic	Santo Domingo	10 528 000	217	21	6	74	1.2	79
	East Timor	Dili	1 185 000	80	37	7	69	2.3	33
	Ecuador	Quito	16 144 000	59	20	5	76	1.5	64
	Egypt	Cairo	91 508 000	91	27	6	71	2.1	43
	El Salvador	San Salvador	6 127 000	291	17	7	73	0.3	67
	Equatorial Guinea	Malabo	845 000	30	35	11	58	2.9	40
	Eritrea	Asmara	5 228 000	45	33	6	64	..	..
	Estonia	Tallinn	1 313 000	29	11	12	77	0.0	68
	Eswatini (Swaziland)	Lobamba/Mbabane	1 287 000	74	29	14	49	1.4	21
	Ethiopia	Addis Ababa	99 391 000	88	32	7	65	2.5	19
	Fiji	Suva	892 000	49	20	7	70	0.6	54
	Finland	Helsinki	5 503 000	16	10	10	81	0.3	84
	France	Paris	64 395 000	118	12	9	83	0.4	80
	Gabon	Libreville	1 725 000	6	30	8	65	2.2	87
	Gambia, The	Banjul	1 991 000	176	42	9	60	3.2	60
	Georgia	Tbilisi	4 000 000	57	13	12	75	-0.3	54
	Germany	Berlin	80 689 000	226	9	11	81	0.9	75
	Ghana	Accra	27 410 000	115	32	9	61	2.3	54
	Greece	Athens	10 955 000	83	9	11	82	-0.7	78
	Grenada	St George's	107 000	283	19	7	74	0.5	36
	Guatemala	Guatemala City	16 343 000	150	27	5	72	2.0	52
	Guinea	Conakry	12 609 000	51	36	10	59	2.7	37
	Guinea-Bissau	Bissau	1 844 000	51	37	12	55	2.4	49
	Guyana	Georgetown	767 000	4	19	8	67	0.4	29
	Haiti	Port-au-Prince	10 711 000	386	25	9	63	1.3	59
	Honduras	Tegucigalpa	8 075 000	72	21	5	73	1.4	55
	Hungary	Budapest	9 855 000	106	9	13	76	-0.2	71
	Iceland	Reykjavík	329 000	3	13	7	83	1.0	94
	India	New Delhi	1 311 051 000	414	20	7	68	1.2	33
	Indonesia	Jakarta	257 564 000	134	20	7	69	1.2	54
	Iran	Tehrān	79 109 000	48	17	5	76	1.2	73
	Iraq	Baghdād	36 423 000	83	34	5	70	3.2	69
	Ireland	Dublin	4 688 000	67	14	6	82	0.6	63
	Israel	Jerusalem[1]	8 064 000	365	21	5	82	2.0	92
	Italy	Rome	59 798 000	199	8	11	83	-0.1	69
	Jamaica	Kingston	2 793 000	254	17	7	76	0.4	55
	Japan	Tōkyō	126 573 000	335	8	10	84	-0.1	94
	Jordan	'Ammān	7 595 000	85	27	4	74	2.4	84
	Kazakhstan	Astana	17 625 000	6	23	7	72	1.5	53
	Kenya	Nairobi	46 050 000	79	34	8	62	2.6	26
	Kiribati	Bairiki	112 000	156	29	7	66	1.8	44
	Kosovo	Pristina	1 805 000	165	17	7	71	-1.1	..
	Kuwait	Kuwait	3 892 000	218	20	3	75	3.6	98
	Kyrgyzstan	Bishkek	5 940 000	30	27	6	71	2.1	36
	Laos	Vientiane	6 802 000	29	26	7	67	1.7	39
	Latvia	Rīga	1 971 000	31	11	14	74	-0.8	67
	Lebanon	Beirut	5 851 000	560	15	5	80	4.2	88
	Lesotho	Maseru	2 135 000	70	28	15	50	1.2	27
	Liberia	Monrovia	4 503 000	40	35	9	61	2.4	50

[1] Jerusalem - Disputed capital

| Land | | Education and Health | | | Development | | | Communications | | Country | Time Zones + or - GMT |
Area sq km	Forest thousand sq km 2015	Adult literacy % 2015	Doctors per 100 000 population 2009-2013	Nutrition population under-nourished % 2015	Energy consumption million tonnes oil equivalent 2013	GNI per capita US$ 2015	HDI index 2015	Mobile phones subs per 100 population 2015	Broadband users subs per 100 population 2015		
48 442	20	92.5	149	12.3	8.0	6 240	0.722	82.6	6.4	Dominican Republic	-4
14 874	7	64.1	7	26.9	0.2	2 290	0.605	117.4	0.1	East Timor	+9
272 045	125	94.5	172	10.9	17.2	6 030	0.739	79.8	9.7	Ecuador	-5
1 001 450	<1	75.8	283	<5	90.8	3 340	0.691	111.0	4.5	Egypt	+2
21 041	3	87.7	160	12.4	3.1	3 940	0.680	145.3	5.5	El Salvador	-6
28 051	16	95.2	..	..	1.6	12 820	0.592	66.7	0.5	Equatorial Guinea	+1
117 400	15	73.8	..	..	0.2	..	0.420	7.1	..	Eritrea	+3
45 200	22	99.8	324	..	2.3	18 320	0.865	148.7	30.0	Estonia	+2
17 364	6	87.5	17	26.8	0.5	3 280	0.541	73.2	0.5	Eswatini (Swaziland)	+2
1 133 880	125	49.0	2	32.0	5.3	590	0.448	42.8	0.5	Ethiopia	+3
18 330	10	..	43	<5	0.9	4 830	0.736	108.2	1.4	Fiji	+12
338 145	222	>95	290	..	29.9	46 560	0.895	135.4	31.7	Finland	+2
543 965	170	>95	319	..	267.8	40 710	0.897	102.6	41.3	France	+1
267 667	230	83.2	..	<5	1.6	9 200	0.697	161.1	0.6	Gabon	+1
11 295	5	55.6	4	5.3	0.2	..	0.452	137.8	0.2	Gambia, The	0
69 700	28	99.8	427	7.4	5.2	4 120	0.769	128.9	14.7	Georgia	+4
357 022	114	>95	389	..	340.1	45 790	0.926	116.7	37.2	Germany	+1
238 537	93	76.6	10	<5	6.6	1 480	0.579	129.7	0.3	Ghana	0
131 957	41	95.3	617	..	28.1	20 270	0.866	113.0	30.9	Greece	+2
378	<1	..	..	..	0.1	8 650	0.754	112.3	18.5	Grenada	-4
108 890	35	79.1	93	15.6	5.5	3 590	0.640	111.5	2.8	Guatemala	-6
245 857	64	30.5	10	16.4	1.0	470	0.414	87.2	0.0	Guinea	0
36 125	20	59.8	4	20.7	0.1	590	0.424	69.3	0.1	Guinea-Bissau	0
214 969	165	87.5	21	10.6	0.7	4 090	0.638	67.2	6.7	Guyana	-4
27 750	1	60.7	..	53.4	0.9	810	0.493	68.8	0.0	Haiti	-5
112 088	46	88.4	..	12.2	3.7	2 280	0.625	95.5	2.3	Honduras	-6
93 030	21	99.4	308	..	23.6	12 970	0.836	118.9	27.4	Hungary	+1
102 820	<1	>95	348	..	5.2	50 110	0.921	114.0	37.0	Iceland	0
3 166 620	707	72.2	70	15.2	593.0	1 590	0.624	78.1	1.3	India	+5½
1 919 445	910	95.4	20	7.6	175.4	3 440	0.689	132.3	1.1	Indonesia	+7 to +9
1 648 000	107	87.2	89	<5	256.2	..	0.774	93.4	10.9	Iran	+3½
438 317	8	79.7	61	22.8	45.0	5 820	0.649	93.8	..	Iraq	+3
70 282	8	>95	267	..	14.2	52 550	0.923	103.7	27.7	Ireland	0
22 072	2	..	334	..	22.4	35 770	0.899	133.5	27.4	Israel	+2
301 245	93	99.0	376	..	171.9	32 830	0.887	142.1	24.4	Italy	+1
10 991	3	88.5	..	8.1	2.9	4 930	0.730	111.5	8.1	Jamaica	-5
377 727	250	>95	230	..	493.2	38 840	0.903	126.5	30.7	Japan	+9
89 206	1	98.0	256	<5	8.5	4 680	0.741	179.4	4.2	Jordan	+2
2 717 300	33	99.8	362	<5	66.5	11 390	0.794	156.9	13.7	Kazakhstan	+5 & +6
582 646	44	78.0	20	21.2	6.2	1 340	0.555	80.7	0.3	Kenya	+3
717	<1	..	38	<5	0.0	3 390	0.588	38.8	0.1	Kiribati	+12 to +14
10 908	..	..	..	..	..	3 960	..	..	..	Kosovo	+1
17 818	<1	96.1	270	<5	41.0	42 150	0.800	231.8	1.5	Kuwait	+3
198 500	6	99.5	197	6.0	6.1	1 170	0.664	132.8	3.7	Kyrgyzstan	+6
236 800	188	79.9	18	18.5	2.9	1 740	0.586	53.1	0.5	Laos	+7
64 589	34	99.9	358	..	4.1	14 990	0.830	127.5	24.8	Latvia	+2
10 452	1	94.0	320	<5	7.6	7 710	0.763	92.2	25.4	Lebanon	+2
30 355	<1	79.4	..	11.2	0.4	1 280	0.497	100.9	0.1	Lesotho	+2
111 369	42	47.6	1	31.9	0.4	380	0.427	81.1	0.2	Liberia	0

.. no data available

	Key Information		Population						
Flag	Country	Capital city	Population total 2015	Density persons per sq km 2015	Birth rate per 1000 population 2015	Death rate per 1000 population 2015	Life expectancy in years 2015	Population change % 2015	Urban populatio % 2015
	Libya	Tripoli	6 278 000	4	20	5	72	0.3	79
	Liechtenstein	Vaduz	38 000	238	9	7	82	0.7	14
	Lithuania	Vilnius	2 878 000	44	11	14	75	-0.9	67
	Luxembourg	Luxembourg	567 000	219	11	7	82	2.4	90
	Macedonia (FYROM)[2]	Skopje	2 078 000	81	11	9	76	0.1	57
	Madagascar	Antananarivo	24 235 000	41	34	7	65	2.8	35
	Malawi	Lilongwe	17 215 000	145	39	7	64	3.1	16
	Malaysia	Kuala Lumpur/Putrajaya	30 331 000	91	17	5	75	1.4	75
	Maldives	Male	364 000	1 221	21	4	77	2.0	46
	Mali	Bamako	17 600 000	14	43	10	58	3.0	40
	Malta	Valletta	419 000	1 326	10	8	82	1.1	95
	Marshall Islands	Delap-Uliga-Djarrit	53 000	293	..	..	..	0.2	73
	Mauritania	Nouakchott	4 068 000	4	33	8	63	2.4	60
	Mauritius	Port Louis	1 273 000	624	10	8	74	0.1	40
	Mexico	Mexico City	127 017 000	64	18	5	77	1.3	79
	Micronesia, Fed. States of	Palikir	104 000	148	24	6	69	0.4	22
	Moldova	Chișinău	4 069 000	121	11	11	72	-0.1	45
	Monaco	Monaco-Ville	38 000	19 000	8	8	..	0.3	100
	Mongolia	Ulan Bator	2 959 000	2	23	6	70	1.7	72
	Montenegro	Podgorica	626 000	45	11	10	76	0.1	64
	Morocco	Rabat	34 378 000	77	20	6	74	1.3	60
	Mozambique	Maputo	27 978 000	35	39	11	55	2.8	32
	Myanmar (Burma)	Nay Pyi Taw	53 897 000	80	17	8	66	0.9	34
	Namibia	Windhoek	2 459 000	3	29	7	65	2.3	47
	Nauru	Yaren	10 000	476	..	..	..	5.1	100
	Nepal	Kathmandu	28 514 000	194	20	6	70	1.2	19
	Netherlands	Amsterdam/The Hague	16 925 000	408	10	9	82	0.4	91
	New Zealand	Wellington	4 529 000	17	13	7	81	1.9	86
	Nicaragua	Managua	6 082 000	47	20	5	75	1.1	59
	Niger	Niamey	19 899 000	16	49	9	62	4.0	19
	Nigeria	Abuja	182 202 000	197	39	13	53	2.6	48
	North Korea	P'yŏngyang	25 155 000	209	14	9	70	0.5	61
	Norway	Oslo	5 211 000	16	11	8	82	1.0	80
	Oman	Muscat	4 491 000	15	19	3	77	5.8	78
	Pakistan	Islamabad	188 925 000	214	29	7	66	2.1	39
	Palau	Ngerulmud	21 000	42	..	..	..	0.9	87
	Panama	Panama City	3 929 000	51	19	5	78	1.6	67
	Papua New Guinea	Port Moresby	7 619 000	16	28	8	63	2.1	13
	Paraguay	Asunción	6 639 000	16	21	6	73	1.3	60
	Peru	Lima	31 377 000	24	20	6	75	1.3	79
	Philippines	Manila	100 699 000	336	23	7	68	1.6	44
	Poland	Warsaw	38 612 000	123	10	10	78	-0.1	61
	Portugal	Lisbon	10 350 000	116	8	11	82	-0.4	63
	Qatar	Doha	2 235 000	195	12	1	79	2.9	99
	Romania	Bucharest	19 511 000	82	9	13	75	-0.5	55
	Russia	Moscow	143 457 000	8	13	13	71	0.2	74
	Rwanda	Kigali	11 610 000	441	31	7	65	2.3	29
	St Kitts and Nevis	Basseterre	56 000	215	..	..	..	1.1	32
	St Lucia	Castries	185 000	300	15	7	75	0.7	19

[2] FYROM - Former Yugoslav Republic of Macedonia

| Land | | Education and Health | | | Development | | | Communications | | | |
Area sq km	Forest thousand sq km 2015	Adult literacy % 2015	Doctors per 100 000 population 2009-2013	Nutrition population under-nourished % 2015	Energy consumption million tonnes oil equivalent 2013	GNI per capita US$ 2015	HDI index 2015	Mobile phones subs per 100 population 2015	Broadband users subs per 100 population 2015	Country	Time Zones + or - GMT
1 759 540	2	91.4	190	..	19.8	..	0.716	157.0	1.0	Libya	+1
160	<1	>95	..	..	..	..	0.912	109.3	41.9	Liechtenstein	+1
65 200	22	99.8	412	..	6.8	15 080	0.848	139.5	27.8	Lithuania	+2
2 586	<1	>95	290	..	4.6	77 480	0.898	148.5	36.0	Luxembourg	+1
25 713	10	97.8	263	..	2.8	5 140	0.748	98.8	17.2	Macedonia (FYROM)[2]	+1
587 041	125	64.7	16	33.0	1.3	420	0.512	44.1	0.1	Madagascar	+3
118 484	31	66.0	2	20.7	0.8	340	0.476	37.9	0.0	Malawi	+2
332 965	222	94.6	120	<5	81.6	10 570	0.789	143.9	10.0	Malaysia	+8
298	<1	99.3	142	5.2	0.6	6 950	0.701	206.7	6.5	Maldives	+5
1 240 140	47	33.1	8	<5	0.6	760	0.442	139.6	0.0	Mali	0
316	<1	94.1	349	..	2.2	23 900	0.856	129.3	37.9	Malta	+1
181	<1	98.3	44	..	..	4 770	..	29.3	1.9	Marshall Islands	+12
1 030 700	2	52.1	..	5.6	0.9	..	0.513	89.3	0.2	Mauritania	0
2 040	<1	90.6	106	<5	1.9	9 780	0.781	140.6	15.8	Mauritius	+4
1 972 545	660	94.5	210	<5	188.8	9 710	0.762	86.0	11.6	Mexico	-5 to -8
701	<1	..	18	..	..	3 560	0.638	21.5	3.1	Micronesia, F. S. of	+10 & +11
33 700	4	99.2	298	..	3.8	2 240	0.699	108.0	15.6	Moldova	+2
2	..	..	717	..	..	..	..	88.8	47.9	Monaco	+1
1 565 000	126	98.4	284	20.5	4.6	3 870	0.735	105.0	7.1	Mongolia	+7 & +8
13 812	8	98.7	211	..	1.2	7 220	0.807	162.2	18.1	Montenegro	+1
446 550	56	71.7	62	<5	19.0	3 030	0.647	126.9	3.4	Morocco	0
799 380	379	58.8	4	25.3	5.9	590	0.418	74.2	0.2	Mozambique	+2
676 577	290	93.1	61	14.2	8.9	1 160	0.556	75.7	0.1	Myanmar (Burma)	+6½
824 292	69	90.8	37	42.3	1.8	5 190	0.640	106.6	2.9	Namibia	+1
21	<1	..	71	..	0.0	11 850	..	..	..	Nauru	+12
147 181	36	64.7	..	7.8	2.4	730	0.558	96.8	1.1	Nepal	+5¾
41 526	4	>95	286	..	101.6	48 850	0.924	123.5	41.7	Netherlands	+1
270 534	102	>95	273	..	21.3	40 020	0.915	121.8	31.6	New Zealand	+12 & +12¾
130 000	31	82.5	90	16.6	2.1	1 940	0.645	116.1	1.9	Nicaragua	-6
1 267 000	11	19.1	2	9.5	0.9	390	0.353	46.5	0.1	Niger	+1
923 768	70	59.6	40	7.0	31.0	2 790	0.527	82.2	0.0	Nigeria	+1
120 538	50	100.0	..	41.6	14.1	..	..	12.9	..	North Korea	+8½
323 878	121	>95	428	..	46.8	93 530	0.949	111.1	39.7	Norway	+1
309 500	<1	94.0	243	<5	26.9	16 910	0.796	159.9	5.6	Oman	+4
881 888	15	56.4	83	22.0	66.4	1 440	0.550	66.9	1.0	Pakistan	+5
497	<1	99.5	138	..	..	12 180	0.788	111.5	5.8	Palau	+9
77 082	46	95.0	165	9.5	8.5	11 880	0.788	174.2	7.9	Panama	-5
462 840	336	63.4	6	..	2.5	..	0.516	46.6	0.2	Papua New Guinea	+10 & +11
406 752	153	95.5	123	10.4	12.1	4 190	0.693	105.4	3.1	Paraguay	-4
1 285 216	740	94.4	113	7.5	25.7	6 130	0.740	109.9	6.4	Peru	-5
300 000	80	96.6	..	13.5	33.6	3 550	0.682	115.8	4.8	Philippines	+8
312 683	94	99.8	222	..	98.1	13 310	0.855	142.7	19.0	Poland	+1
88 940	32	95.4	410	..	25.9	20 470	0.843	110.4	29.6	Portugal	0
11 437	<1	97.8	774	..	52.1	83 990	0.856	159.1	10.1	Qatar	+3
237 500	69	98.8	245	..	33.1	9 510	0.802	107.1	19.8	Romania	+2
7 075 400	8 149	99.7	431	..	765.0	11 450	0.804	159.9	18.9	Russia	+2 to +12
26 338	5	71.2	6	31.6	0.4	700	0.498	70.5	0.2	Rwanda	+2
261	<1	..	..	..	0.1	15 060	0.765	131.8	29.6	St Kitts and Nevis	-4
616	<1	..	11	..	0.2	7 350	0.735	101.5	15.4	St Lucia	-4

.. no data available

World: Country Statistics

Flag	Key Information		Population						
	Country	Capital city	Population total 2015	Density persons per sq km 2015	Birth rate per 1000 population 2015	Death rate per 1000 population 2015	Life expectancy in years 2015	Population change % 2015	Urban population % 2015
	St Vincent and the Grenadines	Kingstown	109 000	280	16	7	73	0.1	51
	Samoa	Apia	193 000	68	25	5	74	0.7	19
	San Marino	San Marino	32 000	525	8	7	..	0.6	94
	São Tomé and Príncipe	São Tomé	190 000	197	34	7	67	2.1	65
	Saudi Arabia	Riyadh	31 540 000	14	20	3	74	2.1	83
	Senegal	Dakar	15 129 000	77	38	6	67	3.1	44
	Serbia	Belgrade	7 046 000	91	9	15	75	-0.5	56
	Seychelles	Victoria	96 000	211	17	8	73	2.2	54
	Sierra Leone	Freetown	6 453 000	90	35	13	51	2.2	40
	Singapore	Singapore	5 604 000	8 770	10	5	83	1.2	100
	Slovakia	Bratislava	5 426 000	111	10	10	77	0.1	54
	Slovenia	Ljubljana	2 068 000	102	10	10	81	0.1	50
	Solomon Islands	Honiara	584 000	21	29	6	68	2.0	22
	Somalia	Mogadishu	10 787 000	17	43	12	56	2.5	40
	South Africa	Bloemfontein/Cape Town/Pretoria	54 490 000	45	20	12	57	1.6	65
	South Korea	Seoul	50 293 000	507	9	5	82	0.4	82
	South Sudan	Juba	12 340 000	19	36	11	56	3.5	19
	Spain	Madrid	46 122 000	91	9	9	83	-0.1	80
	Sri Lanka	Sri Jayewardenepura Kotte	20 715 000	316	16	7	75	0.9	18
	Sudan	Khartoum	40 235 000	22	33	8	64	2.2	34
	Suriname	Paramaribo	543 000	3	18	7	71	0.9	66
	Sweden	Stockholm	9 779 000	22	12	9	83	1.1	86
	Switzerland	Bern	8 299 000	201	10	8	83	1.1	74
	Syria	Damascus	18 502 000	101	23	6	70	-1.5	58
	Taiwan	Taipei	23 462 000	648	..	..	..	..	..
	Tajikistan	Dushanbe	8 482 000	59	30	6	70	2.2	27
	Tanzania	Dodoma	53 470 000	57	39	7	65	3.1	32
	Thailand	Bangkok	67 959 000	132	11	8	75	0.3	50
	Togo	Lomé	7 305 000	129	35	9	60	2.6	40
	Tonga	Nuku'alofa	106 000	142	24	6	73	0.6	24
	Trinidad and Tobago	Port of Spain	1 360 000	265	14	10	71	0.4	8
	Tunisia	Tunis	11 254 000	69	18	7	75	1.1	67
	Turkey	Ankara	78 666 000	101	16	6	75	1.5	73
	Turkmenistan	Ashgabat	5 374 000	11	21	8	66	1.2	50
	Tuvalu	Vaiaku	9 916	397	..	..	..	0.2	60
	Uganda	Kampala	39 032 000	162	43	9	59	3.3	16
	Ukraine	Kiev	44 824 000	74	11	15	71	-0.3	70
	United Arab Emirates	Abu Dhabi	9 157 000	118	11	2	78	0.8	86
	United Kingdom	London	64 716 000	266	12	9	82	0.8	83
	United States of America	Washington D.C.	321 774 000	33	12	8	79	0.8	82
	Uruguay	Montevideo	3 432 000	19	14	9	77	0.4	95
	Uzbekistan	Tashkent	29 893 000	67	24	5	68	1.7	36
	Vanuatu	Port Vila	265 000	22	26	5	72	2.2	26
	Vatican City	Vatican City	800	1600	..	..	..	..	..
	Venezuela	Caracas	31 108 000	34	19	6	174	1.3	89
	Vietnam	Hanoi	93 448 000	284	17	6	76	1.1	34
	Yemen	Şan'ā'	26 832 000	51	32	7	64	2.5	35
	Zambia	Lusaka	16 212 000	22	40	9	61	3.1	41
	Zimbabwe	Harare	15 603 000	40	35	9	59	2.3	32

Land		Education and Health			Development			Communications			
Area sq km	Forest thousand sq km 2015	Adult literacy % 2015	Doctors per 100 000 population 2009-2013	Nutrition population under-nourished % 2015	Energy consumption million tonnes oil equivalent 2013	GNI per capita US$ 2015	HDI index 2015	Mobile phones subs per 100 population 2015	Broadband users subs per 100 population 2015	Country	Time Zones + or - GMT
389	<1	..	..	6.2	0.1	6 630	0.722	103.7	15.5	St Vincent and the Grenadines	-4
2 831	2	99.0	48	<5	0.1	3 930	0.704	62.4	1.1	Samoa	+13
61	<1	..	510	..	..	..	..	115.2	36.6	San Marino	+1
964	<1	91.8	..	6.6	0.1	1 760	0.574	65.1	0.5	São Tomé and Príncipe	0
2 200 000	10	94.8	249	<5	248.7	23 550	0.847	176.6	11.9	Saudi Arabia	+3
196 720	83	55.6	6	10.0	2.5	980	0.494	100.0	0.7	Senegal	0
77 453	27	98.0	211		18.6	5 540	0.776	120.5	17.4	Serbia	+1
455	<1	95.3	107		0.3	14 680	0.782	158.1	14.3	Seychelles	+4
71 740	30	48.4	2	22.3	0.4	620	0.420	89.5	..	Sierra Leone	0
639	<1	96.8	195		79.3	52 090	0.925	146.5	26.4	Singapore	+8
49 035	19	>95	332		18.2	17 570	0.845	122.3	23.3	Slovakia	+1
20 251	12	99.7	252		7.0	22 250	0.890	113.2	27.6	Slovenia	+1
28 370	22	..	22	11.3	0.1	1 920	0.515	72.7	0.2	Solomon Islands	+11
637 657	64	..	4		0.3	..	..	52.5	0.7	Somalia	+3
1 219 090	92	94.6	78	<5	137.6	6 080	0.666	164.5	2.6	South Africa	+2
99 274	62	..	214	<5	277.6	27 450	0.901	118.5	40.3	South Korea	+9
644 329	72	32.0	..		7.4	790	0.418	23.9	..	South Sudan	+3
504 782	184	98.1	495		143.1	28 380	0.884	108.2	28.7	Spain	+1
65 610	21	92.6	68	22.0	7.1	3 800	0.766	110.6	2.9	Sri Lanka	+5½
1 861 484	192	58.6	28		7.4	1 920	0.490	70.5	0.1	Sudan	+3
163 820	153	95.5	..	8.0	1.2	9 360	0.725	136.8	9.6	Suriname	-3
449 964	281	>95	393		53.3	57 900	0.913	130.4	36.1	Sweden	+1
41 293	13	>95	405		32.8	84 550	0.939	136.5	45.1	Switzerland	+1
184 026	5	86.3	146		15.0		0.536	64.3	3.1	Syria	+2
36 179	..	..	..	..	110.9	..	..	..	..	Taiwan	+8
143 100	4	99.8	192	33.2	5.1	1 280	0.627	98.6	0.1	Tajikistan	+5
945 087	461	80.4	3	32.1	4.0	920	0.531	75.9	0.2	Tanzania	+3
513 115	164	94.0	39	7.4	128.6	5 720	0.740	152.7	9.2	Thailand	+7
56 785	2	66.5	5	11.4	0.8	540	0.487	67.7	0.9	Togo	0
748	<1	99.4	56		0.1	4 280	0.721	69.1	2.3	Tonga	+13
5 130	2	99.0	118	7.4	26.2	17 640	0.780	157.7	20.0	Trinidad and Tobago	-4
164 150	10	81.0	122	<5	8.5	3 930	0.725	129.9	4.3	Tunisia	+1
779 452	117	95.7	171	<5	130.2	9 950	0.767	96.0	12.4	Turkey	+3
488 100	41		239	<5	35.5	7 380	0.691	145.9	0.1	Turkmenistan	+5
25	<1	..	109		..	6 230	..	40.3	10.1	Tuvalu	+12
241 038	21	73.8	12	25.5	1.8	700	0.493	50.4	0.2	Uganda	+3
603 700	97	99.8	354		116.6	2 640	0.743	144.0	11.8	Ukraine	+2 & +4 (Crimea)
77 700	3	93.0	253	<5	100.6	43 090	0.840	187.3	12.9	United Arab Emirates	+4
243 609	31	>95	281		213.9	43 700	0.909	124.1	38.6	United Kingdom	0
9 826 635	3 101	>95	245		2 449.8	55 980	0.920	117.6	31.0	United States	-5 to -10
176 215	18	98.4	374	<5	5.3	15 720	0.795	160.2	26.3	Uruguay	-3
447 400	32	100.0	253	<5	49.0	2 160	0.701	73.3	6.0	Uzbekistan	+5
12 190	4	85.1	12	6.4	0.1	..	0.597	66.3	1.6	Vanuatu	+11
0.5	..	..	..	..	..	..	..	..	..	Vatican City	+1
912 050	467	95.4	..	<5	82.0	..	0.767	93.0	8.2	Venezuela	-4
329 565	148	94.5	119	11.0	52.9	1 990	0.683	130.6	8.1	Vietnam	+7
527 968	5	70.0	20	26.1	8.2	1 140	0.482	68.0	1.6	Yemen	+3
752 614	486	85.1	17	47.8	4.2	1 490	0.579	74.5	0.2	Zambia	+2
390 759	141	86.9	8	33.4	3.9	860	0.516	84.8	1.1	Zimbabwe	+2

.. no data available

Pages 158–163 show a variety of
demographic and economic indicators
by the world's seven regional groupings
(defined by the World Bank), as shown
on the right.

The colours on the maps below show
the average figures for each region.
The highest and lowest countries for
most indicators are also named.

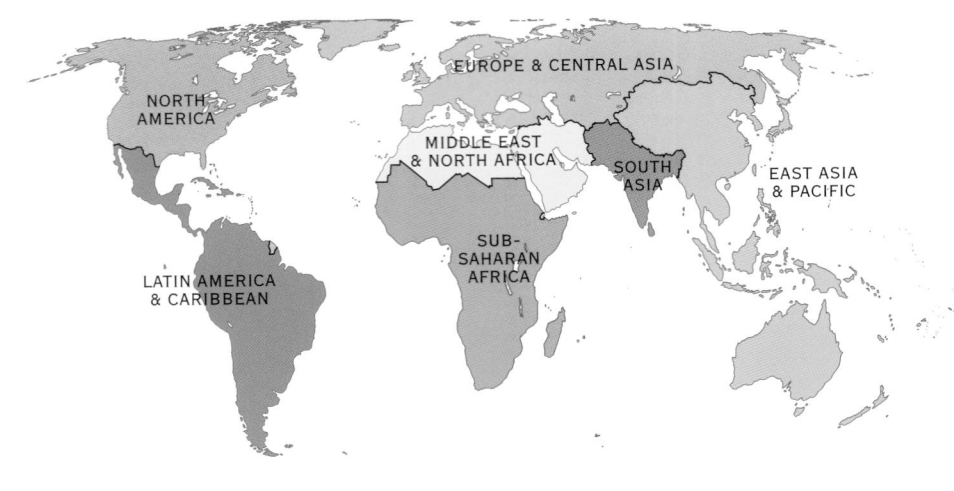

NORTH
AMERICA

EUROPE & CENTRAL ASIA

MIDDLE EAST
& NORTH AFRICA

SOUTH
ASIA

EAST ASIA
& PACIFIC

LATIN AMERICA
& CARIBBEAN

SUB-
SAHARAN
AFRICA

Scale 1 : 250 000 000

Birth rate
Number of births per 1000 people

	25 – 36.7
	20 – 24.9
	15 – 19.9
	10 – 14.9
	no data

World average 19.1
Statistics are for 2015

Scale 1 : 250 000 000

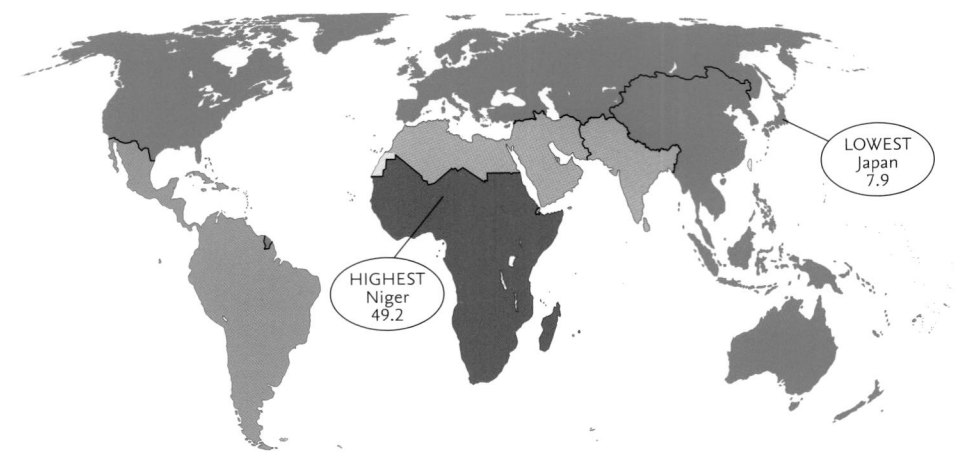

LOWEST
Japan
7.9

HIGHEST
Niger
49.2

Death rate
Number of deaths per 1000 people

	10 – 10.2
	8 – 9.9
	7 – 7.9
	5 – 6.9
	no data

World average 7.7
Statistics are for 2015

Scale 1 : 250 000 000

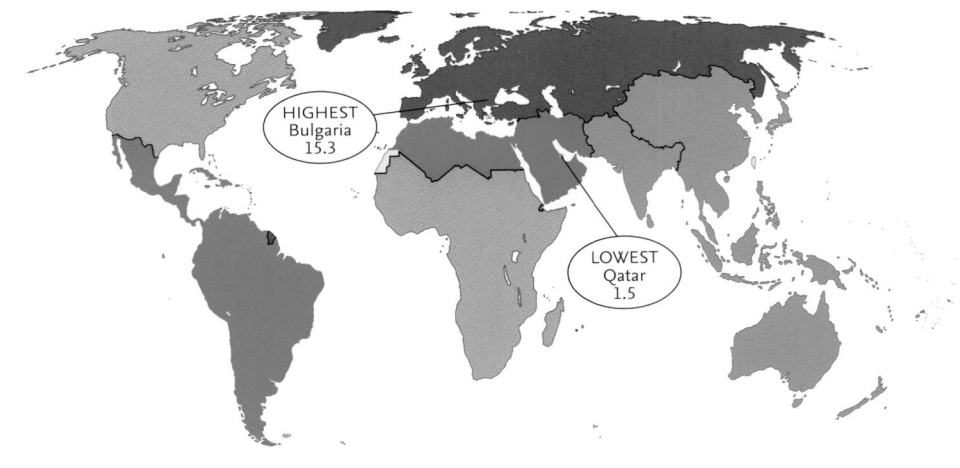

HIGHEST
Bulgaria
15.3

LOWEST
Qatar
1.5

Infant mortality rate
Number of infants dying before reaching
one year of age, per 1000 live births

	20 – 56.4
	15 – 19.9
	10 – 14.9
	5 – 9.9
	no data

World average 31.7
Statistics are for 2015

Scale 1 : 250 000 000

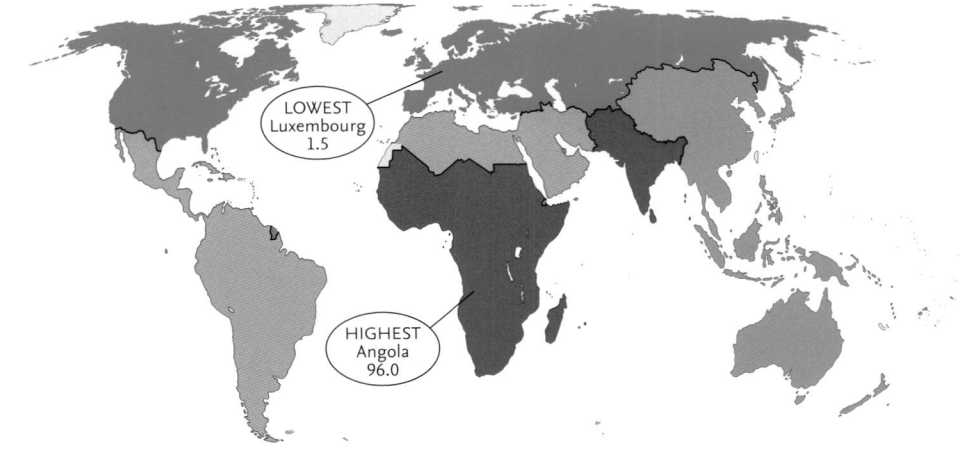

LOWEST
Luxembourg
1.5

HIGHEST
Angola
96.0

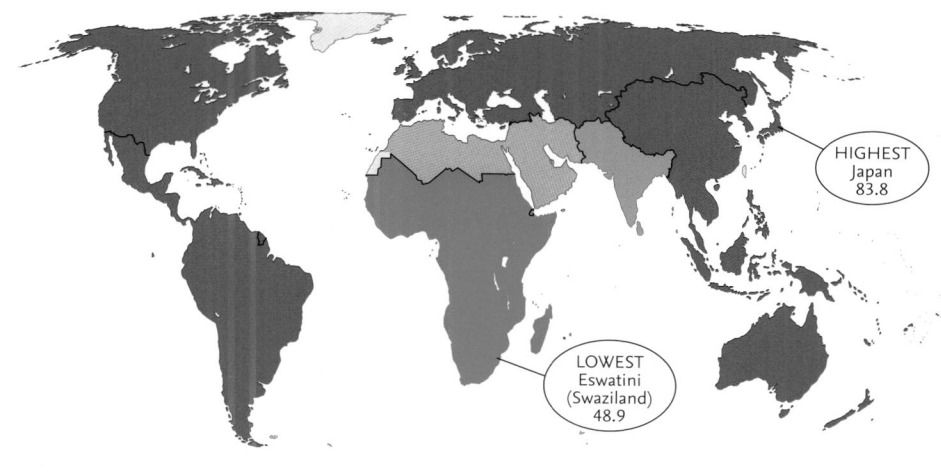

Life expectancy
Years

	75 – 79.1
	70 – 74.9
	65 – 69.9
	59 – 64.9
	no data

World average 71.7
Statistics are for 2015

Scale 1 : 250 000 000

HIGHEST
Japan
83.8

LOWEST
Eswatini
(Swaziland)
48.9

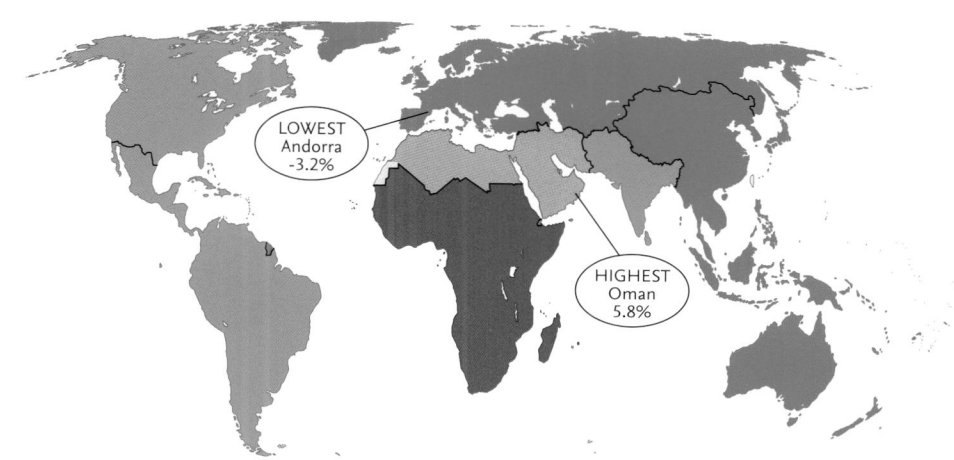

Population growth
Annual average growth, percentage

	2.2 – 2.8
	1.5 – 2.1
	0.8 – 1.4
	0.4 – 0.7
	no data

World average 1.2
Statistics are for 2006 – 2015

Scale 1 : 250 000 000

LOWEST
Andorra
-3.2%

HIGHEST
Oman
5.8%

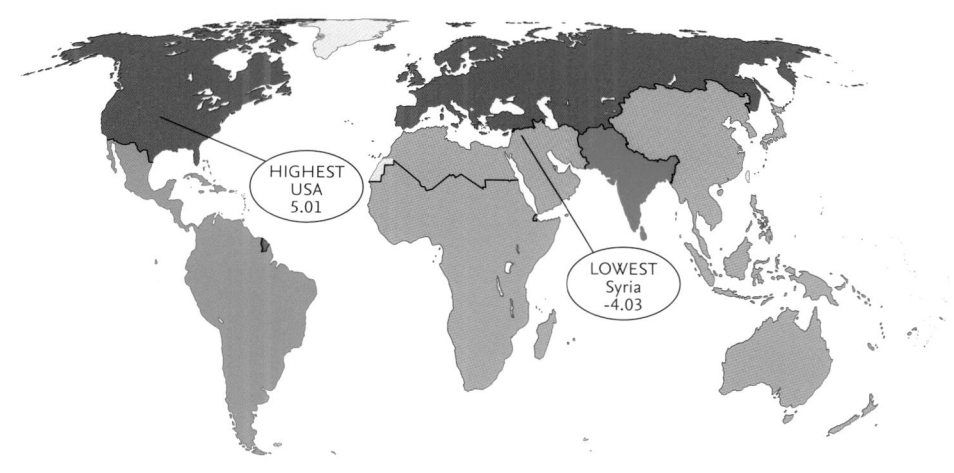

Migration
Annual net migration, millions

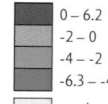

	0 – 6.2
	-2 – 0
	-4 – -2
	-6.3 – -4
	no data

Statistics are for 2012

Scale 1 : 250 000 000

HIGHEST
USA
5.01

LOWEST
Syria
-4.03

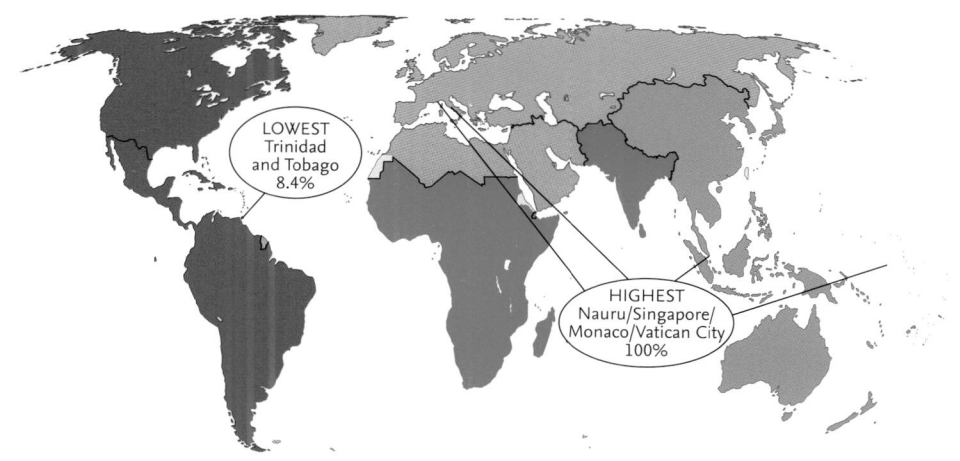

Urbanization
Urban population, percentage

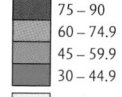

	75 – 90
	60 – 74.9
	45 – 59.9
	30 – 44.9
	no data

World average 53.9
Statistics are for 2015

Scale 1 : 250 000 000

LOWEST
Trinidad
and Tobago
8.4%

HIGHEST
Nauru/Singapore/
Monaco/Vatican City
100%

Human Development Index

HDI is based on life expectancy, knowledge and standard of living

- 0.8 – 0.999 (very high)
- 0.7 – 0.799 (high)
- 0.551 – 0.699 (medium)
- 0 – 0.550 (low)
- no data

World average 0.717
Statistics are for 2015

Scale 1 : 250 000 000

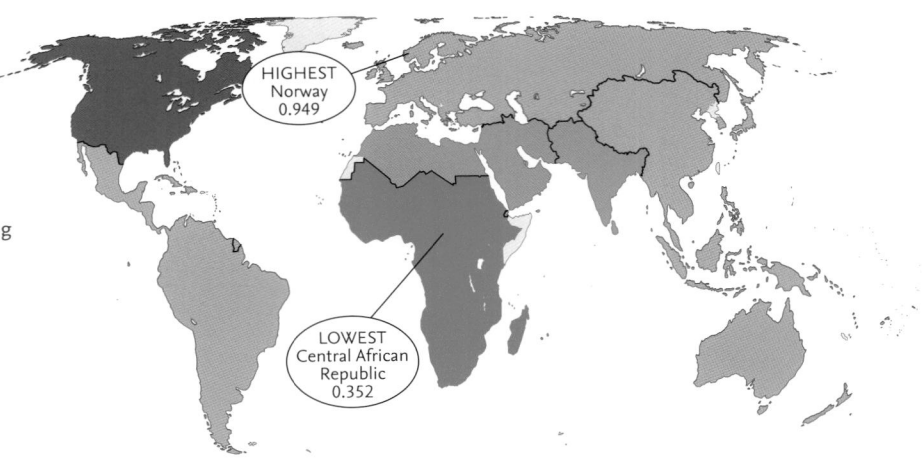

HIGHEST
Norway
0.949

LOWEST
Central African
Republic
0.352

Literacy rate

Percentage of adults

- 95 – 99.9
- 90 – 94.9
- 75 – 89.9
- 60 – 74.9
- no data

World average 86.2
Statistics are for 2015

Scale 1 : 250 000 000

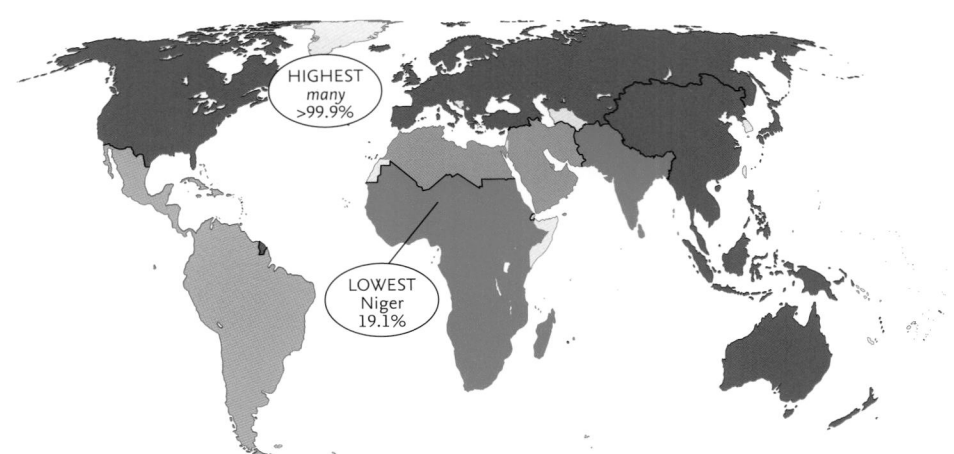

HIGHEST
many
>99.9%

LOWEST
Niger
19.1%

Nutrition

Percentage of population undernourished

- 10 – 19.9
- 9 – 9.9
- 8 – 8.9
- 7 – 7.9
- no data

World average 10.8
Statistics are for 2015

Scale 1 : 250 000 000

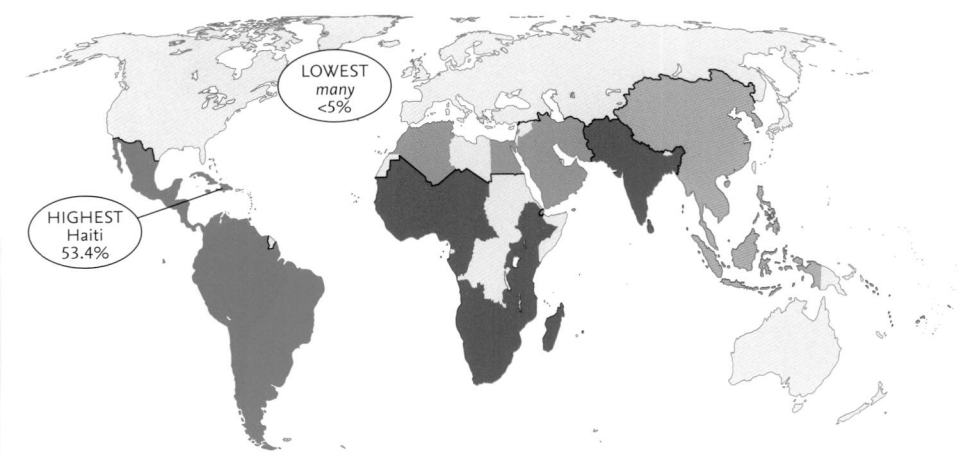

LOWEST
many
<5%

HIGHEST
Haiti
53.4%

Access to safe water

Percentage of population with access
to water from an improved source

- 98 – 100
- 94 – 97.9
- 90 – 93.9
- 60 – 89.9
- no data

World average 91
Statistics are for 2015

Scale 1 : 250 000 000

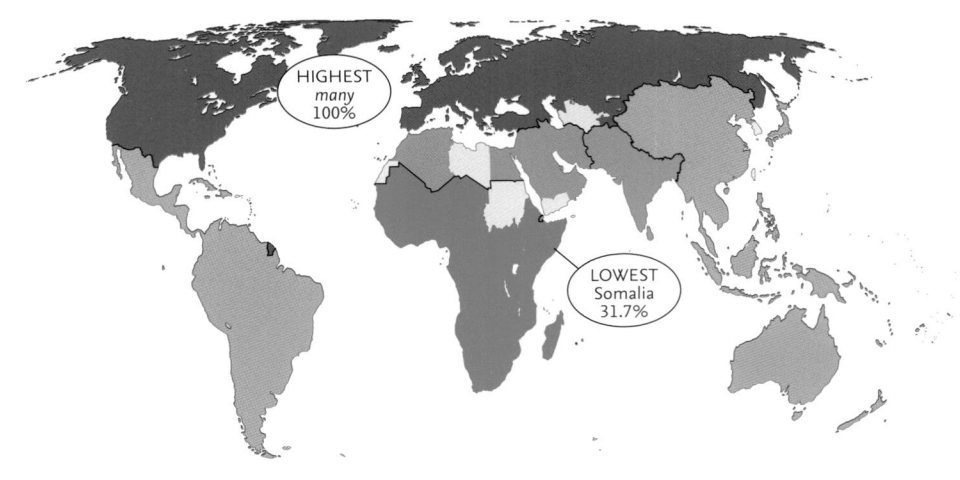

HIGHEST
many
100%

LOWEST
Somalia
31.7%

Doctors

Number of physicians per 100 000 people

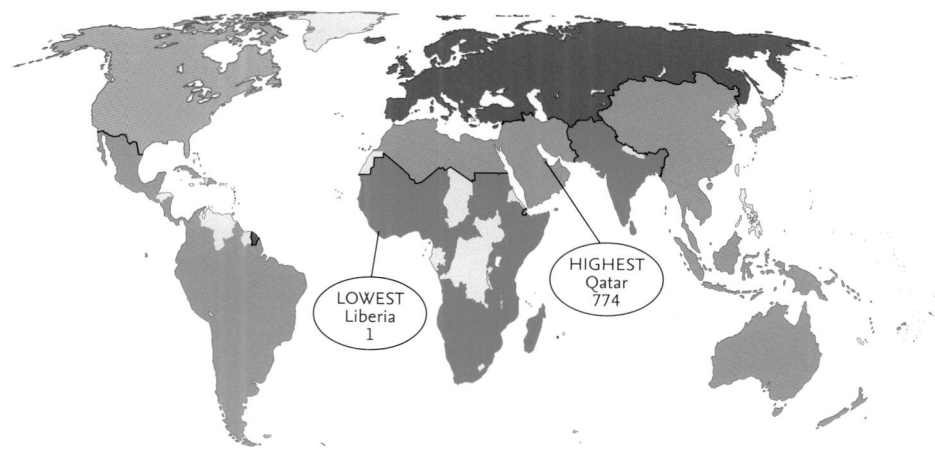

	300 – 399
	200 – 299
	100 – 199
	0 – 99
	no data

World average 154
Statistics are for 2009 – 2013

Scale 1 : 250 000 000

HIV

Percentage of population aged 15–49 infected with HIV

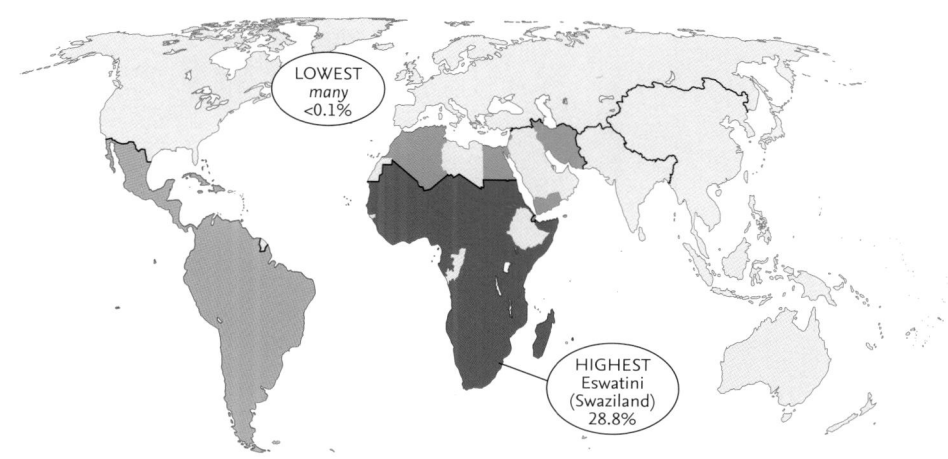

	0.6 – 5
	0.4 – 0.5
	0.1 – 0.3
	no data

World average 0.8
Statistics are for 2015

Scale 1 : 250 000 000

Poverty

Percentage of population living on less than US$ 1.90 a day

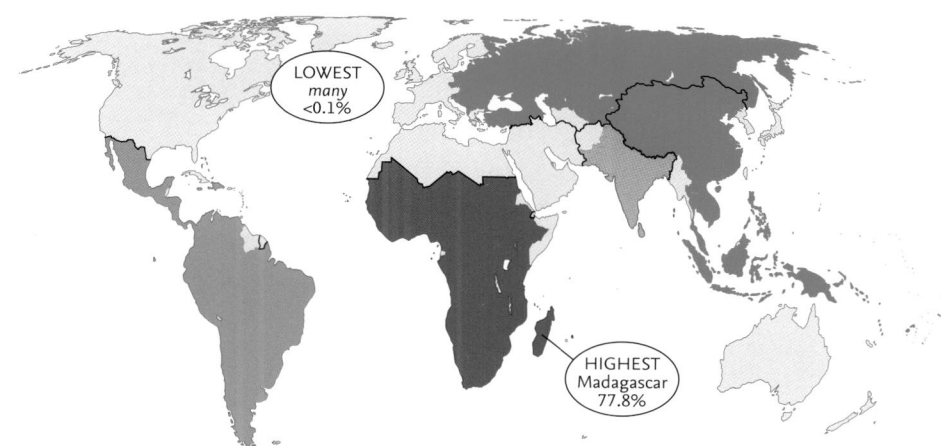

	20 – 41
	10 – 19.9
	5 – 9.9
	2 – 4.9
	no data

World average 10.7
Statistics are for 2003 – 2014

Scale 1 : 250 000 000

Aid

Official development assistance received, US$ per person

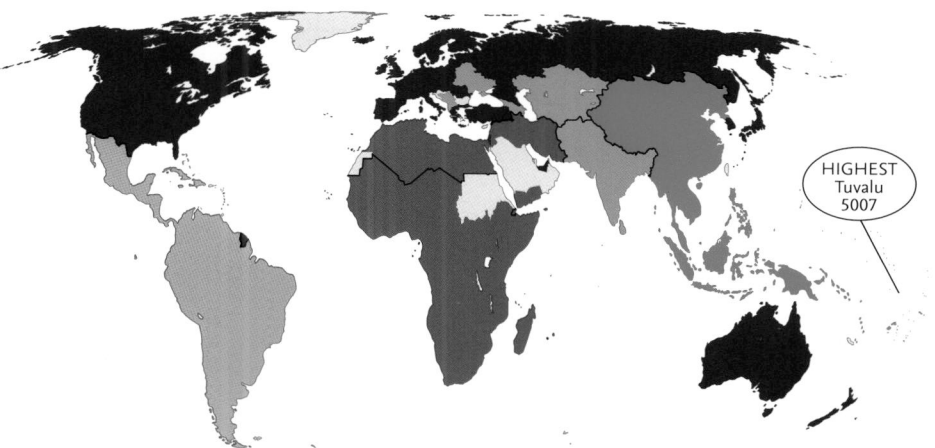

	20 – 57.1
	10 – 19.9
	5 – 9.9
	0 – 4.9
	no data
	Donors

World average 20.8
Statistics are for 2015

Scale 1 : 250 000 000

Gross National Income

GNI is the value of production of goods
and services of each country, US$ per person

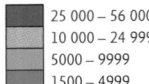

- 25 000 – 56 000
- 10 000 – 24 999
- 5000 – 9999
- 1500 – 4999
- no data

World average 10 552
Statistics are for 2015

Scale 1 : 250 000 000

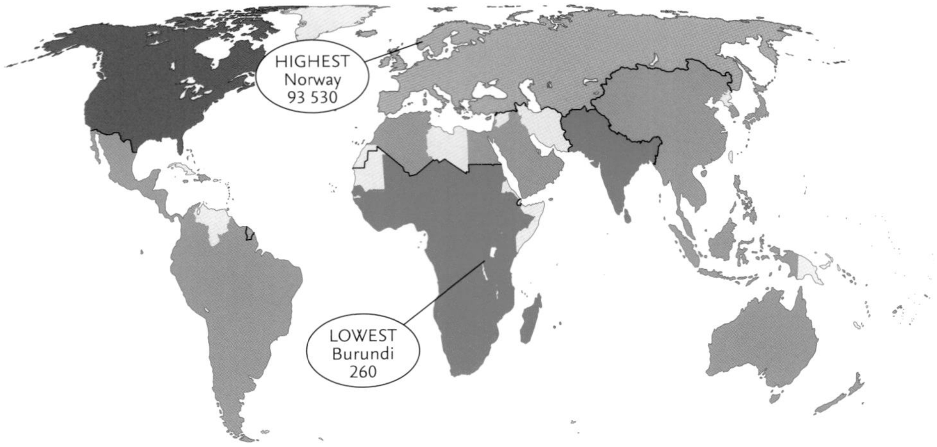

HIGHEST
Norway
93 530

LOWEST
Burundi
260

Trade

Percentage of world trade

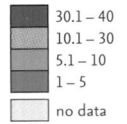

- 30.1 – 40
- 10.1 – 30
- 5.1 – 10
- 1 – 5
- no data

Statistics are for 2014 – 2015

Scale 1 : 250 000 000

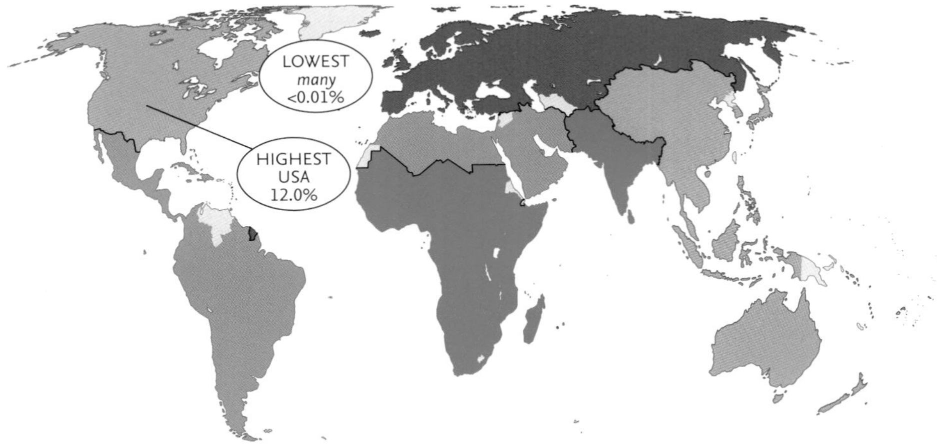

LOWEST
many
<0.01%

HIGHEST
USA
12.0%

Energy production

Million tonnes oil equivalent

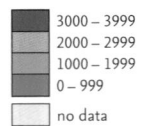

- 3000 – 3999
- 2000 – 2999
- 1000 – 1999
- 0 – 999
- no data

Statistics are for 2013

Scale 1 : 250 000 000

LOWEST
many
0

HIGHEST
China
2620.3

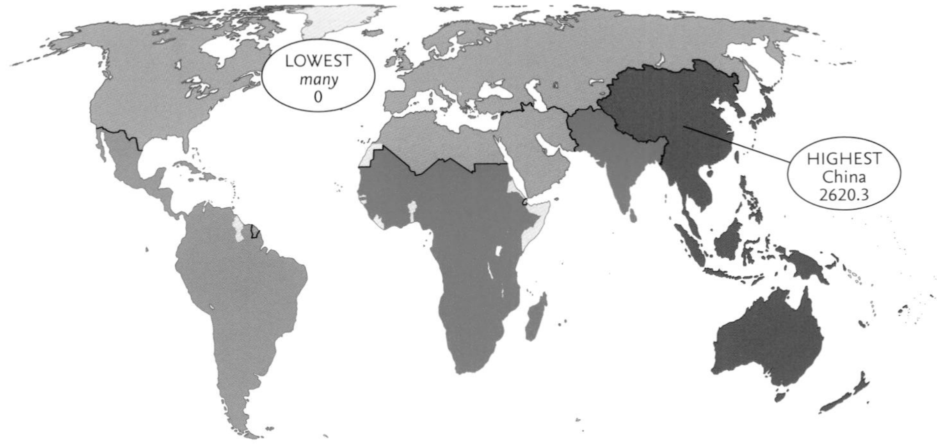

Energy consumption

Million tonnes oil equivalent

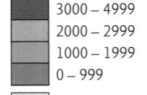

- 3000 – 4999
- 2000 – 2999
- 1000 – 1999
- 0 – 999
- no data

Statistics are for 2013

Scale 1 : 250 000 000

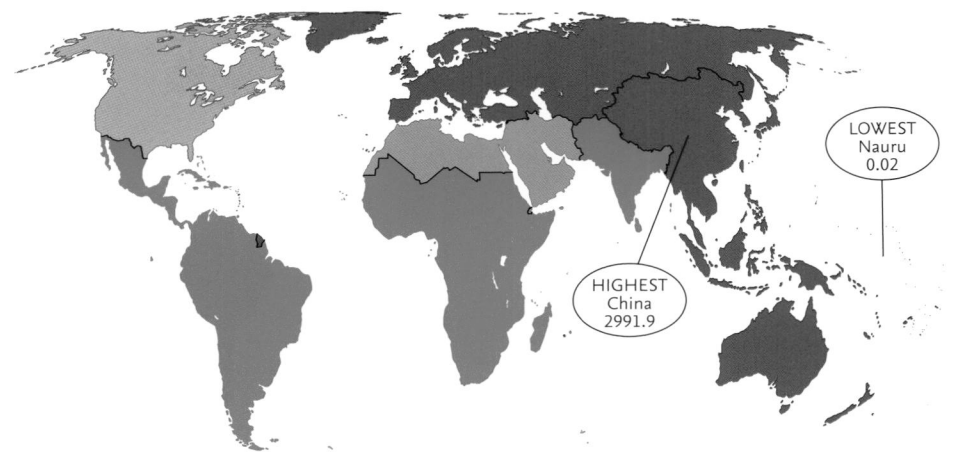

LOWEST
Nauru
0.02

HIGHEST
China
2991.9

Carbon dioxide emissions

Metric tonnes per person

- 9 – 16.1
- 6 – 8.9
- 3 – 5.9
- 0 – 2.9
- no data

World average 5.0
Statistics are for 2013

Scale 1 : 250 000 000

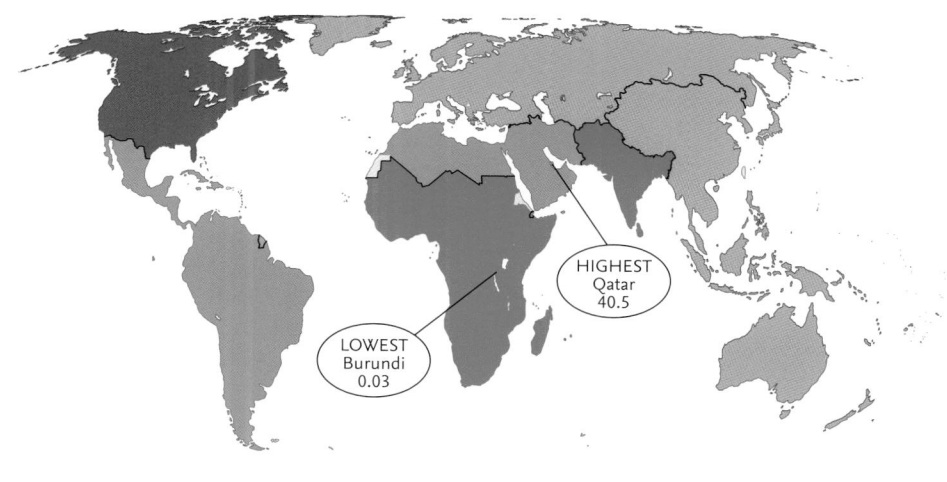

HIGHEST
Qatar
40.5

LOWEST
Burundi
0.03

Mobile phones

Subscriptions per 100 people

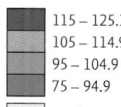

- 115 – 125.1
- 105 – 114.9
- 95 – 104.9
- 75 – 94.9
- no data

World average 98.3
Statistics are for 2015

Scale 1 : 250 000 000

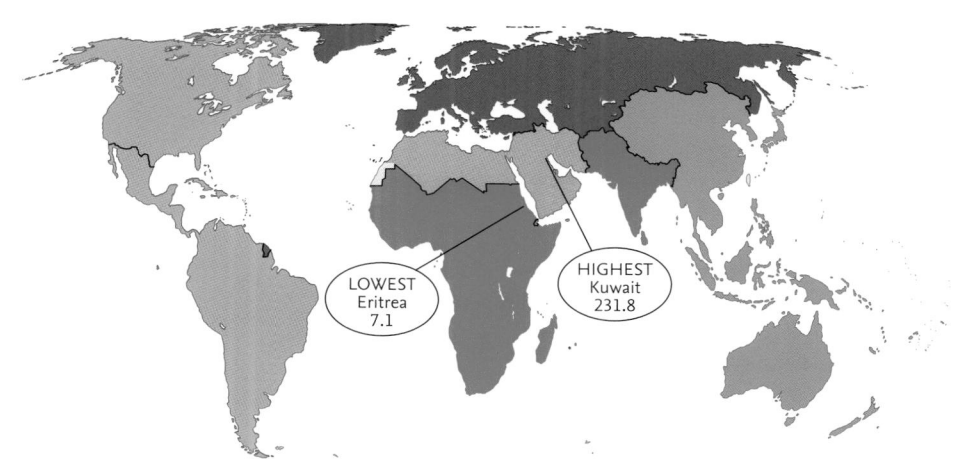

LOWEST
Eritrea
7.1

HIGHEST
Kuwait
231.8

Air passengers

Millions carried

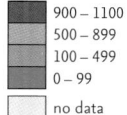

- 900 – 1100
- 500 – 899
- 100 – 499
- 0 – 99
- no data

Statistics are for 2015

Scale 1 : 250 000 000

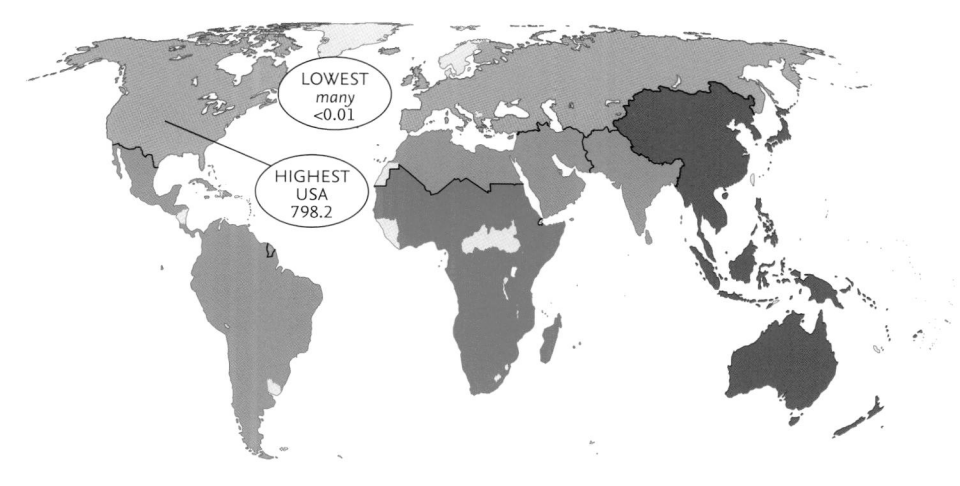

LOWEST
many
<0.01

HIGHEST
USA
798.2

Tourism

Earnings from international tourism, US$ billion

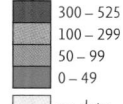

- 300 – 525
- 100 – 299
- 50 – 99
- 0 – 49
- no data

Statistics are for 2013 – 2015

Scale 1 : 250 000 000

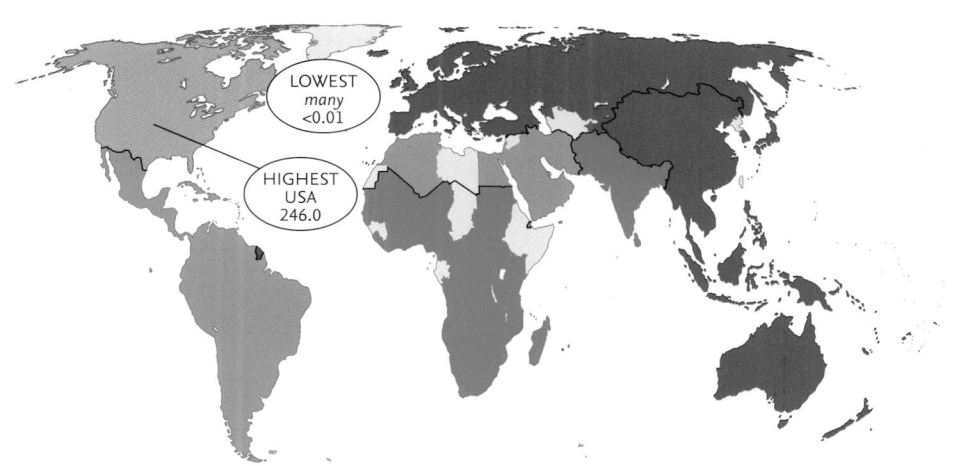

LOWEST
many
<0.01

HIGHEST
USA
246.0

Using the Dictionary

Geographical terms in the dictionary are arranged alphabetically.

Bold words in an entry identify key terms which are explained in greater detail within separate entries of their own.

Important terms which do not have separate entries are shown in *italic* and are explained in the entry in which they occur.

A

abrasion The wearing away of the landscape by rivers, **glaciers**, the sea or wind, caused by the load of debris that they carry. *See also* **corrasion**.

abrasion platform *See* **wave-cut platform**.

accuracy A measure of the degree of correctness.

acid rain Rain that contains a high concentration of pollutants, notably sulphur and nitrogen oxides. These pollutants are produced from factories, power stations burning **fossil fuels**, and car exhausts. Once in the **atmosphere**, the sulphur and nitrogen oxides combine with moisture to give sulphuric and nitric acids which fall as corrosive rain.

administrative region An area in which organizations carry out administrative functions; for example, the regions of local health authorities and water companies, and commercial sales regions.

adult literacy rate A percentage measure which shows the proportion of an adult population able to read. It is one of the measures used to assess the level of development of a country.

aerial photograph A photograph taken from above the ground. There are two types of aerial photograph – a vertical photograph (or 'bird's-eye view') and an oblique photograph where the camera is held at an angle. Aerial photographs are often taken from aircraft and provide useful information for map-making and surveys. *Compare* **satellite image**.

afforestation The conversion of open land to forest; especially, in Britain, the planting of coniferous trees in upland areas for commercial gain. *Compare* **deforestation**.

agglomerate A mass of coarse rock fragments or blocks of lava produced during a volcanic eruption.

agribusiness Modern **intensive farming** which uses machinery and artificial fertilizers to increase **yield** and output.
Thus agriculture resembles an industrial process in which the general running and managing of the farm could parallel that of large-scale industry.

agriculture Human management of the **environment** to produce food. The numerous forms of agriculture fall into three groups:

commercial agriculture, **subsistence agriculture** and **peasant agriculture**. *See also* **agribusiness**.

aid The provision of finance, personnel and equipment for furthering economic development and improving standards of living in the **Third World**. Most aid is organized by international institutions (e.g. the United Nations), by charities (e.g. Oxfam) (*see* **non-governmental organizations** (NGOs) or by national governments. Aid to a country from the international institutions is called *multilateral aid*. Aid from one country to another is called *bilateral aid*.

air mass A large body of air with generally the same temperature and moisture conditions throughout. Warm or cold and moist air masses usually develop over large bodies of water (**oceans**). Hot or cold and dry air masses develop over large land areas (**continents**).

alluvial fan A cone of **sediment** deposited at an abrupt change of slope; for example, where a post-glacial stream meets the flat floor of a **U-shaped valley**. Alluvial fans are also common in arid regions where streams flowing off **escarpments** may periodically carry large loads of sediment during **flash floods**.

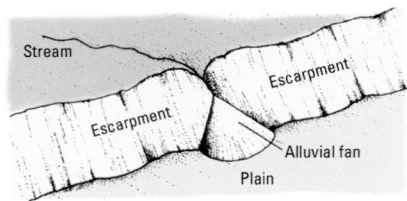

alluvial fan

alluvium Material deposited by a river in its middle and lower course. Alluvium comprises **silt**, sand and coarser debris eroded from the river's upper course and transported downstream. Alluvium is deposited in a graded sequence: coarsest first (heaviest) and finest last (lightest). Regular floods in the lower course create extensive layers of alluvium which can build up to a considerable depth on the **flood plain**.

alp A gentle slope above the steep sides of a glaciated valley, often used for summer grazing. *See also* **transhumance**.

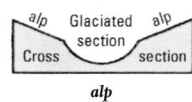

alp

analysis The examination of the constituent parts of a complex entity.

anemometer An instrument for measuring the velocity of the wind. An anemometer should be fixed on a post at least 5m above ground level. The wind blows the cups around and the speed is read off the dial in km/hr (or knots).

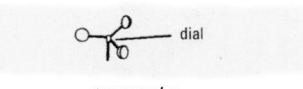

anemometer

annotation Labels in the form of text or graphics that can be individually selected, positioned or stored in a database.

antarctic circle Imaginary line that encircles the South Pole at **latitude** 66° 32'S.

anthracite A hard form of **coal** with a high carbon content and few impurities.

anticline An arch in folded **strata**; the opposite of **syncline**. *See* **fold**.

anticyclone An area of high atmospheric pressure with light winds, clear skies and settled **weather**. In summer, anticyclones are associated with warm and sunny conditions; in winter, they bring frost and fog as well as sunshine.

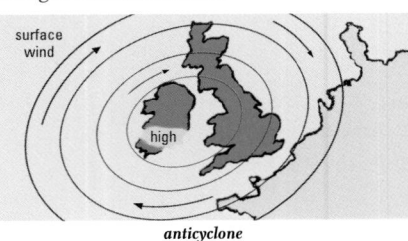

anticyclone

API (application programming interface) A set of interfaces, methods, procedures and tools used to build or customise a software program.

aquifer *See* **artesian basin**.

arable farming The production of cereal and root crops – as opposed to the keeping of livestock.

arc A coverage feature class representing lines and polygon boundaries.

archipelago A group or chain of islands.

arctic circle Imaginary line that encircles the North Pole at **latitude** 66° 32'N.

arête A knife-edged ridge separating two **corries** in a glaciated upland. The arête is formed by the progressive enlargement of corries by **weathering** and **erosion**. *See also* **pyramidal peak**.

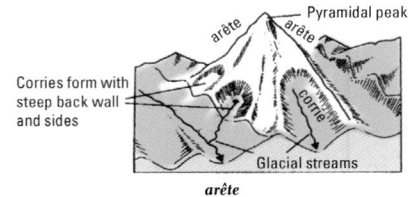

arête

artesian basin This consists of a shallow **syncline** with a layer of **permeable rock**, e.g. chalk, sandwiched between two impermeable layers, e.g. clay. Where the permeable rock is exposed at the surface, rainwater will enter the rock and the rock will become saturated. This is known as an *aquifer*. Boreholes can be sunk into the structure to tap the water in the aquifer.

asymmetrical fold Folded **strata** where the two limbs are at different angles to the horizontal.

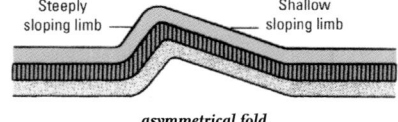

asymmetrical fold

atlas A collection of maps.

atmosphere The air which surrounds the Earth, and consists of three layers:
the *troposphere* (6 to 10km from the Earth's surface), the *stratosphere* (50km from the Earth's surface), and the *mesosphere* and *ionosphere*, an ionised region of rarefied gases (1000km from the Earth's surface). The atmosphere comprises oxygen (21%), nitrogen (78%), carbon dioxide, argon, helium and other gases in minute quantities.

attrition The process by which a river's load is

eroded through particles, such as pebbles and boulders, striking each other.

B

backwash The return movement of seawater off the beach after a wave has broken. *See also* **longshore drift** and **swash**.

bar graph A graph on which the values of a certain variable are shown by the length of shaded columns, which are numbered in sequence. *Compare* **histogram**.

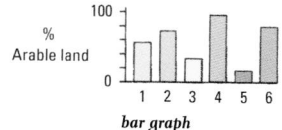

bar graph

barchan A type of crescent-shaped sand dune formed in desert regions where the wind direction is very constant. Wind blowing round the edges of the dune causes the crescent shape, while the dune may advance in a downwind direction as particles are blown over the crest.

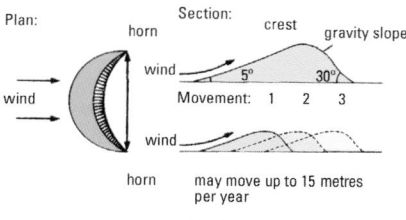

barchan

barograph An aneroid **barometer** connected to an arm and inked pen which records pressure changes continuously on a rotating drum. The drum usually takes a week to make one rotation.

barometer An instrument for measuring atmospheric pressure. There are two types, the *mercury barometer* and the *aneroid barometer*. The mercury barometer consists of a glass tube containing mercury which fluctuates in height as pressure varies. The aneroid barometer is a small metal box from which some of the air has been removed. The box expands and contracts as the air pressure changes. A series of levers joined to a pointer shows pressure on a dial.

barrage A type of dam built across a wide stretch of water, e.g. an estuary, for the purposes of water management. Such a dam may be intended to provide water supply, to harness wave energy or to control flooding, etc. There is a large barrage across Cardiff Bay in South Wales.

basalt A dark, fine-grained extrusive **igneous rock** formed when **magma** emerges onto the Earth's surface and cools rapidly. A succession of basalt **lava flows** may lead to the formation of a **lava plateau**.

base flow The water flowing in a stream which is fed only by **groundwater**. During dry periods it is only the base flow which passes through the stream channel.

base map Map on which thematic information can be placed.

batholith A large body of igneous material intruded into the Earth's **crust**. As the batholith slowly cools, large-grained **rocks** such as **granite** are formed.

Batholiths may eventually be exposed at the Earth's surface by the removal of overlying rocks through **weathering** and **erosion**.

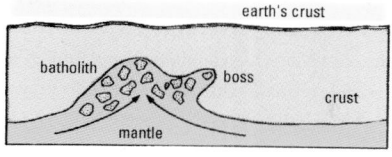

batholith

bay An indentation in the coastline with a **headland** on either side. Its formation is due to the more rapid **erosion** of softer rocks.

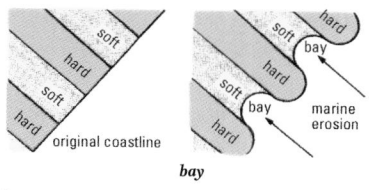

bay

beach A strip of land sloping gently towards the sea, usually recognized as the area lying between high and low tide marks.

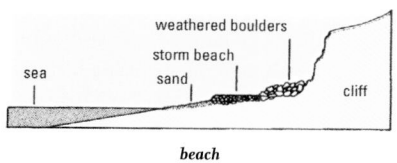

beach

bearing A compass reading between 0 and 360 degrees, indicating direction of one location from another.

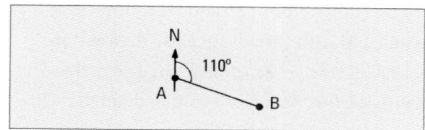

bearing The bearing from A to B is 110°.

Beaufort wind scale An international scale of wind velocities, ranging from 0 (calm) to 12 (hurricane).

bedrock The solid rock which usually lies beneath the soil.

bergschrund A large **crevasse** located at the rear of a **corrie** icefield in a glaciated region, formed by the weight of the ice in the corrie dragging away from the rear wall as the **glacier** moves downslope.

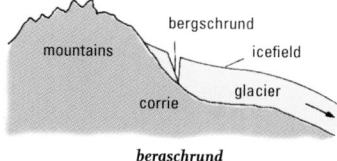

bergschrund

biodiversity The existence of a wide variety of plant and animal species in their natural environment.

biogas The production of methane and carbon dioxide, which can be obtained from plant or crop waste. Biogas is an example of a renewable source of energy (*see* **renewable resources, nonrenewable resources**).

biomass The total number of living organisms, both plant and animal, in a given area.

biome A complex community of plants and animals in a specific physical and climatic region. *See* **climate**.

biosphere The part of the Earth which contains living organisms. The biosphere contains a variety

of **habitats**, from the highest mountains to the deepest oceans.

birth rate The number of live births per 1000 people in a population per year.

bituminous coal Sometimes called house coal – a medium-quality **coal** with some impurities; the typical domestic coal. It is also the major fuel source for **thermal power stations**.

block mountain *or* **horst** A section of the Earth's **crust** uplifted by faulting. Mt Ruwenzori in the East African Rift System is an example of a block mountain.

blowhole A crevice, **joint** or **fault** in coastal rocks, enlarged by marine **erosion**. A blowhole often leads from the rear of a cave (formed by wave action at the foot of a **cliff**) up to the cliff top. As waves break in the cave they erode the roof at the point of weakness and eventually a hole is formed. Air and sometimes spray are forced up the blowhole to erupt at the surface.

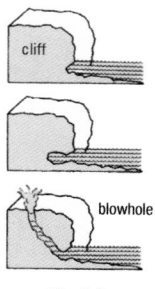

blowhole

bluff *See* **river cliff**.

boreal forest *See* **taiga**.

boulder clay *or* **till** The unsorted mass of debris dragged along by a **glacier** as *ground moraine* and dumped as the glacier melts. Boulder clay may be several metres thick and may comprise any combination of finely ground 'rock flour', sand, pebbles or boulders.

breakwater *or* **groyne** A wall built at right angles to a beach in order to prevent sand loss due to **longshore drift**.

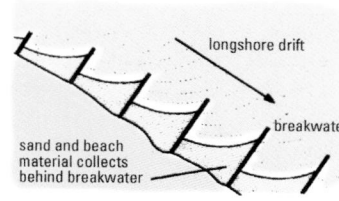

breakwater or groyne

breccia Rock fragments cemented together by a matrix of finer material; the fragments are angular and unsorted. An example of this is volcanic breccia, which is made up of coarse angular fragments of **lava** and **crust** rocks welded by finer material such as ash and **tuff**.

buffers Memory devices for temporarily storing data.

bush fallowing *or* **shifting cultivation** A system of **agriculture** in which there are no permanent fields. For example in the **tropical rainforest**, remote societies cultivate forest clearings for one year and then move on. The system functions successfully when forest **regeneration** occurs over a sufficiently long period to allow the soil to regain its fertility.

bushfire An uncontrolled fire in forests and grasslands.

business park An out-of-town site accommodating offices, high-technology companies and light industry. *Compare* **science park**.

butte An outlier of a **mesa** in arid regions.

C

cache A small high-speed memory that improves computer performance.

caldera A large crater formed by the collapse of the summit cone of a **volcano** during an eruption. The caldera may contain subsidiary cones built up by subsequent eruptions, or a crater lake if the volcano is extinct or dormant.

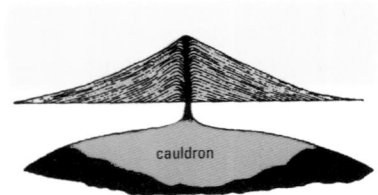

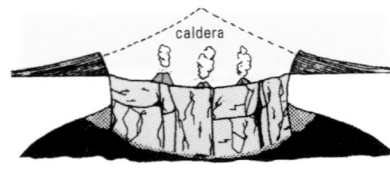

caldera

canal An artificial waterway, usually connecting existing **rivers**, **lakes** or **oceans**, constructed for navigation and transportation.

canyon A deep and steep-sided river valley occurring where rapid vertical **corrasion** takes place in arid regions. In such an **environment** the rate of **weathering** of the valley sides is slow. If the **rocks** of the region are relatively soft then the canyon profile becomes even more pronounced. The Grand Canyon of the Colorado River in the USA is the classic example.

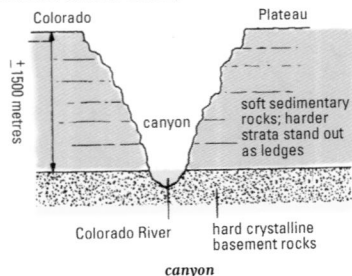

canyon

capital city Seat of government of a country or political unit.

cartogram A map showing statistical data in diagrammatic form.

cartography The technique of drawing maps or charts.

catchment 1. In **physical geography**, an alternative term to **river basin**.
2. In **human geography**, an area around a town or city – hence 'labour catchment' means the area from which an urban workforce is drawn.

cavern In **limestone** country, a large underground cave formed by the dissolving of limestone by subterranean streams.
See also **stalactite**, **stalagmite**.

cay A small low **island** or bank composed of sand and coral fragments. Commonly found in the Caribbean Sea.

CBD (Central Business District) This is the central zone of a town or city, and is characterized by high accessibility, high land values and limited space. The visible result of these factors is a concentration of high-rise buildings at the city centre. The CBD is dominated by retail and business functions, both of which require maximum accessibility.

CFCs (Chlorofluorocarbons) Chemicals used in the manufacture of some aerosols, the cooling systems of refrigerators and fast-food cartons. These chemicals are harmful to the **ozone** layer.

chalk A soft, whitish **sedimentary rock** formed by the accumulation of small fragments of skeletal matter from marine organisms; the rock may be almost pure calcium carbonate. Due to the **permeable** and soluble nature of the rock, there is little surface **drainage** in chalk landscapes.

channel *See* **strait**.

chernozem A deep, rich soil of the plains of southern Russia. The upper **horizons** are rich in lime and other plant nutrients; in the dry **climate** the predominant movement of **soil** moisture is upwards (*contrast* with **leaching**), and lime and other chemical nutrients therefore accumulate in the upper part of the **soil profile**.

choropleth A symbol or marked area on a map which denotes the distribution of some property.

choropleth map *See* **shading map**.

cirrus High, wispy or strand-like, thin **cloud** associated with the advance of a **depression**.

clay A soil composed of very small particles of **sediment**, less than 0.002 mm in diameter. Due to the dense packing of these minute particles, clay is almost totally impermeable, i.e. it does not allow water to drain through. Clay soils very rapidly waterlog in wet weather.

cliff A steep rockface between land and sea, the profile of which is determined largely by the nature of the coastal rocks. For example, resistant rocks such as **granite** (e.g. at Land's End, England) will produce steep and rugged cliffs.

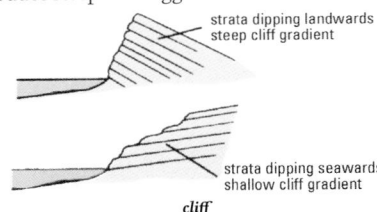

cliff

climate The average atmospheric conditions prevailing in a region, as distinct from its **weather**. A statement of climate is concerned with long-term trends. Thus the climate of, for example, the Amazon Basin is described as hot and wet all the year round; that of the Mediterranean Region as having hot dry summers and mild wet winters.
See **extreme climate**, **maritime climate**.

clint A block of **limestone**, especially when part of a **limestone pavement**, where the surface is composed of clints and **grykes**.

cloud A mass of small water drops or ice crystals formed by the **condensation** of water vapour in the **atmosphere**, usually at a considerable height above the Earth's surface. There are three main types of cloud: **cumulus**, **stratus** and **cirrus**, each of which has many variations.

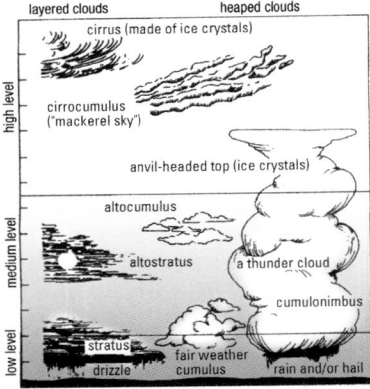

cloud

CMYK A colour model that combines cyan, magenta, yellow and black to create a range of colours in printing.

coal A **sedimentary rock** composed of decayed and compressed vegetative matter. Coal is usually classified according to a scale of hardness and purity ranging from **anthracite** (the hardest), through **bituminous coal** and **lignite** to **peat**.

cold front *See* **depression**.

commercial agriculture A system of **agriculture** in which food and materials are produced specifically for sale in the market, in contrast to **subsistence agriculture**. Commercial agriculture tends to be capital intensive. *See also* **agribusiness**.

Common Agricultural Policy (CAP) The policy of the European Union to support and subsidize certain crops and methods of animal husbandry.

common land Land which is not in the ownership of an individual or institution, but which is historically available to any member of the local community.

communications The contacts and linkages in an **environment**. For example, roads and railways are communications, as are telephone systems, newspapers, and radio and television.

commuter zone An area on or near to the outskirts of an urban area. Commuters are among the most affluent and mobile members of the urban community and can afford the greatest physical separation of home and work.

concordant coastline A coastline that is parallel to mountain ranges immediately inland. A rise in sea level or a sinking of the land cause the valleys to be flooded by the sea and the mountains to become a line of islands. *Compare* **discordant coastline**.

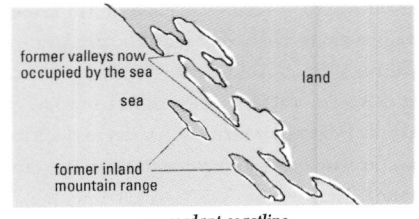

concordant coastline

condensation The process by which cooling vapour turns into a liquid. **Clouds**, for example, are formed by the condensation of water vapour in the **atmosphere**.

coniferous forest A forest of **evergreen** trees such as pine, spruce and fir. Natural coniferous forests occur considerably further north than forests of broad-leaved **deciduous** species, as coniferous trees are able to withstand harsher climatic conditions. The **taiga** areas of the northern hemisphere consist of coniferous forests.

conservation The preservation and management of the natural **environment**. In its strictest form, conservation may mean total protection of endangered species and habitats, as in nature reserves. In some cases, conservation of the man-made environment, e.g. ancient buildings, is undertaken.

continent One of the earth's large land masses. The world's continents are generally defined as Asia, Africa, North America, South America, Europe, Oceania and Antarctica.

continental climate The climate at the centre of large landmasses, typified by a large annual range in temperature, with precipitation most likely in the summer.

continental drift The theory that the Earth's continents move gradually over a layer of semi-molten rock underneath the Earth's **crust**. It is thought that the present-day continents once formed the supercontinent, **Pangaea**, which existed approximately 200 million years ago. *See also* **Gondwanaland**, **Laurasia** *and* **plate tectonics**.

continental shelf The seabed bordering the continents, which is covered by shallow water – usually of less than 200 metres. Along some coastlines the continental shelf is so narrow it is almost absent.

contour A line drawn on a map to join all places at the same height above sea level.

conurbation A continuous built-up urban area formed by the merging of several formerly separate towns or cities. Twentieth-century **urban sprawl** has led to the merging of towns.

coombe *See* **dry valley**.

cooperative A system whereby individuals pool their **resources** in order to optimize individual gains.

coordinates A set of numbers that defines the location of a point with reference to a system of axes.

core 1. In **physical geography**, the core is the innermost zone of the Earth. It is probably solid at the centre, and composed of iron and nickel.
2. In **human geography**, a central place or central region, usually the centre of economic and political activity in a region or nation.

corrasion The abrasive action of an agent of **erosion** (rivers, ice, the sea) caused by its load. For example the pebbles and boulders carried along by a river wear away the channel bed and the river bank. *Compare with* **hydraulic action**.

corrie, cirque *or* **cwm** A bowl-shaped hollow on a mountainside in a glaciated region; the area where a valley **glacier** originates. In glacial times the corrie contained an icefield, which in cross section appears as in diagram *a* above. The shape of the corrie is determined by the rotational erosive force of ice as the glacier moves downslope (diagram *b*).

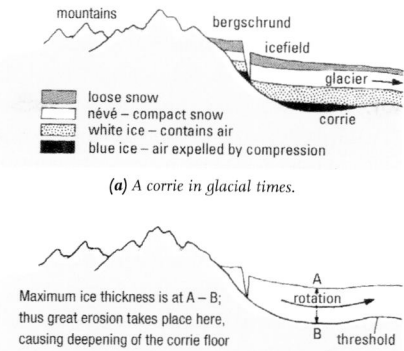

(a) A corrie in glacial times.

Maximum ice thickness is at A – B; thus great erosion takes place here, causing deepening of the corrie floor below the level of the threshold

(b) Erosion of a corrie.

corrosion **Erosion** by solution action, such as the dissolving of **limestone** by running water.

crag Rocky outcrop on a valley side formed, for example, when a **truncated spur** exists in a glaciated valley.

crag and tail A feature of lowland **glaciation**, where a resistant rock outcrop withstands **erosion** by a **glacier** and remains as a feature after the **Ice Age**. Rocks of volcanic or metamorphic origin are likely to produce such a feature. As the ice advances over the crag, material will be eroded from the face and sides and will be deposited as a mass of boulder clay and debris on the leeward side, thus producing a 'tail'.

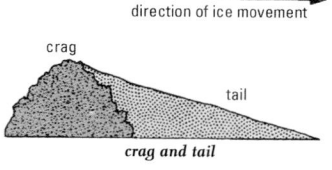

crag and tail

crevasse A crack or fissure in a **glacier** resulting from the stressing and fracturing of ice at a change in **gradient** or valley shape.

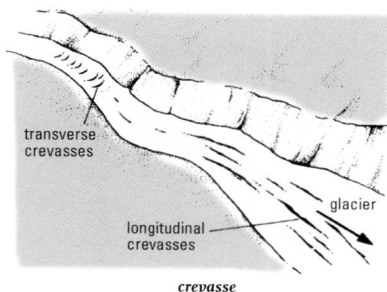

crevasse

cross section A drawing of a vertical section of a line of ground, deduced from a map. It depicts the **topography** of a system of **contours**.

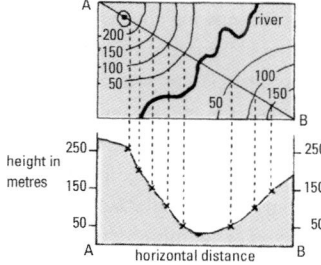

cross section Map and corresponding cross section.

crust The outermost layer of the Earth, representing only 0.1% of the Earth's total volume. It comprises continental crust and oceanic crust, which differ from each other in age as well as in physical and chemical characteristics. The crust, together with the uppermost layer of the **mantle**, is also known as the *lithosphere*.

culvert An artificial drainage channel for transporting water quickly from place to place.

cumulonimbus A heavy, dark **cloud** of great vertical height. It is the typical thunderstorm cloud, producing heavy showers of rain, snow or hail. Such clouds form where intense solar radiation causes vigorous convection.

cumulus A large **cloud** (smaller than a **cumulonimbus**) with a 'cauliflower' head and almost horizontal base. It is indicative of fair or, at worst, showery **weather** in generally sunny conditions.

cut-off *See* **oxbow lake**.

cyclone *See* **hurricane**.

D

dairying A **pastoral farming** system in which dairy cows produce milk that is used by itself or used to produce dairy products such as cheese, butter, cream and yoghurt.

dam A barrier built across a stream, river or **estuary** to create a body of water.

data A series of observations, measurements or facts which can be operated on by a computer programme.

data capture Any process for converting information into a form that can be handled by a computer.

database A large store of information. A GIS database includes data about spatial locations and shapes of geographical features.

datum A single piece of information.

death rate The number of deaths per 1000 people in a population per year.

deciduous woodland Trees which are generally of broad-leaved rather than **coniferous** habit, and which shed their leaves during the cold season.

deflation The removal of loose sand by wind **erosion** in desert regions. It often exposes a bare rock surface beneath.

deforestation The practice of clearing trees. Much deforestation is a result of development pressures, e.g. trees are cut down to provide land for agriculture and industry. *Compare* **afforestation**.

delta A fan-shaped mass consisting of the deposited load of a river where it enters the sea. A delta only forms where the river deposits material at a faster rate than can be removed by coastal currents. While deltas may take almost any shape and size, three types are generally recognized, as shown in the diagram overleaf.

DEM (Digital elevation model) Representation of the relief of a topographic surface.

denudation The wearing away of the Earth's surface by the processes of **weathering** and **erosion**.

depopulation A long-term decrease in the population of any given area, frequently caused by economic migration to other areas.

deposition The laying down of **sediments** resulting from **denudation**.

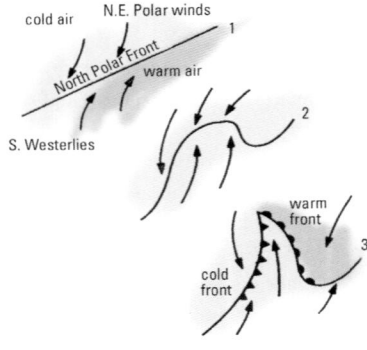

Arcuate delta, e.g. Nile. Note bifurcation of river into distributaries in delta

Bird's foot delta, e.g. Mississippi

Estuarine delta, e.g. Amazon

delta

depression An area of low atmospheric pressure occurring where warm and cold air masses come into contact. The passage of a depression is marked by thickening cloud, rain, a period of dull and drizzly weather and then clearing skies with showers. A depression develops as in the diagrams below.

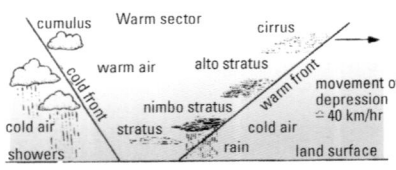

(a) The development of a depression.

(b) The passage of a depression.

desert An area where all forms of **precipitation** are so low that very little, if anything, can grow.
Deserts can be broadly divided into three types, depending upon average temperatures:
(a) *hot deserts*: occur in tropical latitudes in regions of high pressure where air is sinking and therefore making rainfall unlikely. *See* **cloud**.
(b) *temperate deserts*: occur in mid-latitudes in areas of high pressure. They are far inland, so moisture-bearing winds rarely deposit rainfall in these areas.
(c) *cold deserts*: occur in the northern latitudes, again in areas of high pressure. Very low temperatures throughout the year mean the air is unable to hold much moisture.

desertification The encroachment of **desert** conditions into areas which were once productive. Desertification can be due partly to climatic change, i.e. a move towards a drier climate in some parts of the world (possibly due to **global warming**), though human activity has also played a part through bad farming practices. The problem is particularly acute along the southern margins of the Sahara desert in the Sahel region between Mali and Mauritania in the west, and Ethiopia and Somalia in the east.

developing countries A collective term for those nations in Africa, Asia and Latin America which are undergoing the complex processes of modernization, **industrialization** and **urbanization**. *See also* **Third World**.

dew point The temperature at which the **atmosphere**, being cooled, becomes saturated with water vapour. This vapour is then deposited as drops of dew.

digitising Translating into a digital format for computer processing.

dip slope The gentler of the two slopes on either side of an escarpment crest; the dip slope inclines in the direction of the dipping **strata**; the steep slope in front of the crest is the **scarp slope**.

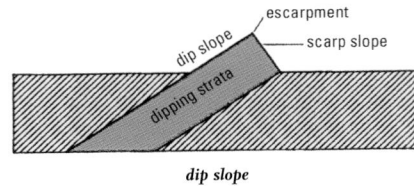

dip slope

discharge The volume of run-off in the channels of a **river basin**.

discordant coastline A coastline that is at right angles to the mountains and valleys immediately inland. A rise in sea level or a sinking of the land will cause the valleys to be flooded. A flooded river valley is known as a **ria**, whilst a flooded glaciated valley is known as a **fjord**. *Compare* **concordant coastline**.

discordant coastline

distributary An outlet stream which drains from a larger river or stream. Often found in a **delta** area. *Compare* **tributary**.

doldrums An equatorial belt of low atmospheric pressure where the **trade winds** converge. Winds are light and variable but the strong upward movement of air caused by this convergence produces frequent thunderstorms and heavy rains.

domain name That part of an internet address which identifies a group of computers by country or institution.

dormitory settlement A village located beyond the edge of a city but inhabited by residents who work in that city (*see* **commuter zone**).

drainage The removal of water from the land surface by processes such as streamflow and infiltration.

drainage basin *See* **river basin**.

drift Material transported and deposited by glacial action on the Earth's surface. *See also* **boulder clay**.

drought A prolonged period where rainfall falls below the requirement for a region.

dry valley *or* **coombe** A feature of **limestone** and **chalk** country, where valleys have been eroded in dry landscapes.

dune A mound or ridge of drifted sand, occurring on the sea coast and in deserts.

dyke **1.** An artificial **drainage** channel.
2. An artificial bank built to protect low-lying land from flooding.
3. A vertical or semi-vertical igneous intrusion occurring where a stream of **magma** has extended through a line of weakness in the surrounding **rock**. *See* **igneous rock**.

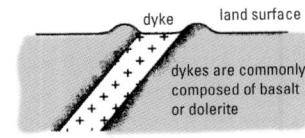

dyke Cross section of eroded dyke, showing how metamorphic margins, harder than dyke or surrounding rocks, resist erosion.

E

earthquake A movement or tremor of the Earth's crust. Earthquakes are associated with plate boundaries (*see* **plate tectonics**) and especially with subduction zones, where one plate plunges beneath another. Here the crust is subjected to tremendous stress. The rocks are forced to bend, and eventually the stress is so great that the rocks 'snap' along a **fault** line.

eastings The first element of a **grid reference**. *See* **northings**.

ecology The study of living things, their interrelationships and their relationships with the **environment**.

ecosystem A natural system comprising living organisms and their **environment**. The concept can be applied at the global scale or in the context of a smaller defined environment. The principle of the ecosystem is constant: all elements are intricately linked by flows of energy and nutrients.

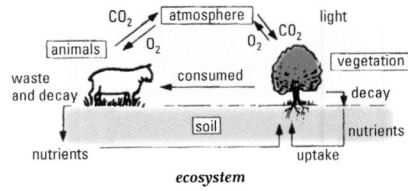

ecosystem

El Niño The occasional development of warm ocean surface waters along the coast of Ecuador and Peru. Where this warming occurs the tropical Pacific trade winds weaken and the usual up-welling of cold, deep ocean water is reduced. El Niño normally occurs late in the calendar year and lasts for a few weeks to a few months and can have a dramatic impact on weather patterns throughout the world.

emigration The movement of population out of a given area or country.

employment structure The distribution of the workforce between the **primary**, **secondary**, **tertiary**

and **quaternary sectors** of the economy. Primary employment is in **agriculture**, mining, forestry and fishing; secondary in manufacturing; tertiary in the retail, service and administration category; quaternary in information and expertise.

environment Physical surroundings: **soil**, vegetation, wildlife and the **atmosphere**.

equator The great circle of the Earth with a **latitude** of 0°, lying equidistant from the poles.

erosion The wearing away of the Earth's surface by running water (rivers and streams), moving ice (**glaciers**), the sea and the wind. These are called the *agents* of erosion.

erratic A boulder of a certain rock type resting on a surface of different geology. For example, blocks of **granite** resting on a surface of carboniferous **limestone** (e.g. deposited by a **glacier**).

escarpment A ridge of high ground as, for example, the **chalk** escarpments of southern England (the Downs and the Chilterns).

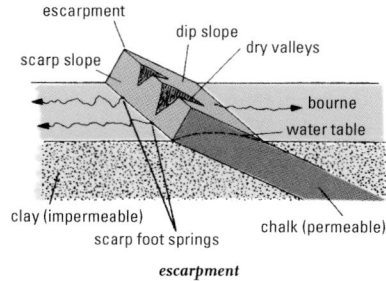

escarpment

esker A low, winding ridge of pebbles and finer **sediment** on a glaciated lowland.

estuary The broad mouth of a river where it enters the sea. An estuary forms where opposite conditions to those favourable for **delta** formation exist: deep water offshore, strong marine currents and a smaller **sediment** load.

ethnic group A group of people with a common identity such as culture, religion or skin colour.

evaporation The process whereby a substance changes from a liquid to a vapour. Heat from the sun evaporates water from seas, lakes, rivers, etc., and this process produces water vapour in the **atmosphere**.

evergreen A vegetation type in which leaves are continuously present. *Compare* **deciduous woodland**.

exfoliation A form of **weathering** whereby the outer layers of a **rock** or boulder shear off due to the alternate expansion and contraction produced by diurnal heating and cooling. Such a process is especially active in **desert** regions.

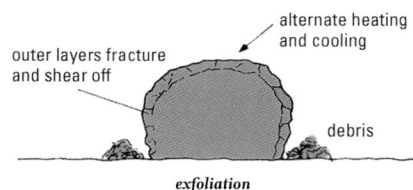

exfoliation

exports Goods and services sold to a foreign country (*compare* **imports**).

extensive farming A system of **agriculture** in which relatively small amounts of capital or labour investment are applied to relatively large areas of land. For example, sheep ranching is an extensive form of farming, and yields per unit area are low.

external processes Landscape-forming processes such as **weather** and **erosion**, in contrast to internal processes.

extreme climate A climate that is characterized by large ranges of temperature and sometimes of rainfall. *Compare* **temperate climate**, **maritime climate**.

F

fault A fracture in the Earth's crust on either side of which the **rocks** have been relatively displaced. Faulting occurs in response to stress in the Earth's crust; the release of this stress in fault movement is experienced as an **earthquake**. *See also* **rift valley**.

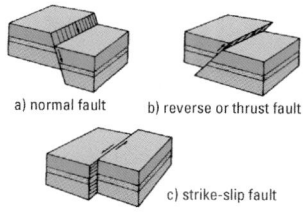

fault The main types.

feature class A collection of features with the same properties, attributes and spatial reference.

fell Upland rough grazing in a **hill farming** system, for example in the English Lake District.

fjord A deep, generally straight inlet of the sea along a glaciated coast. A fjord is a glaciated valley which has been submerged either by a post-glacial rise in sea level or a subsidence of the land.

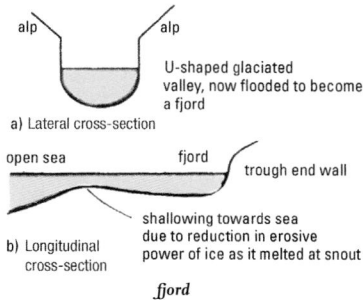

fjord

flash flood A sudden increase in river **discharge** and overland flow due to a violent rainstorm in the upper **river basin**.

flood plain The broad, flat valley floor of the lower course of a river, levelled by annual flooding and by the lateral and downstream movement of **meanders**.

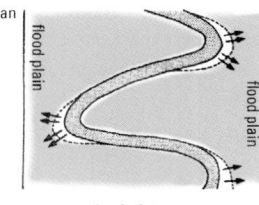

flood plain

flow line A diagram showing volumes of movement, e.g. of people, goods or information between places. The width of the flow line is proportional to the amount of movement, for example in portraying commuter flows into an urban centre from surrounding towns and villages.

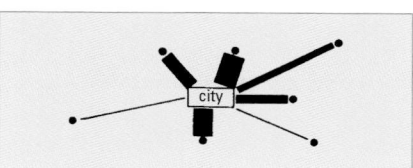

Flow line Commuter flows into a city.

fodder crop A crop grown for animal feed.

fold A bending or buckling of once horizontal rock **strata**. Many folds are the result of rocks being crumpled at plate boundaries (*see* **plate tectonics**), though **earthquakes** can also cause rocks to fold, as can igneous **intrusions**.

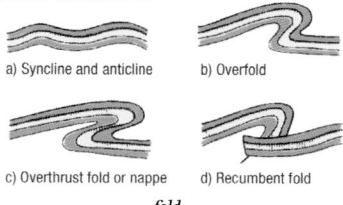

fold

fold mountains Mountains which have been formed by large-scale and complex folding. Studies of typical fold mountains (the Himalaya, Andes, Alps and Rockies) indicate that folding has taken place deep inside the Earth's **crust** and upper **mantle** as well as in the upper layers of the crust.

fossil fuel Any naturally occurring carbon or hydrocarbon fuel, notably coal, oil, peat and natural gas. These fuels have been formed by decomposed prehistoric organisms.

free trade The movement of goods and services between countries without any restrictions (such as quotas, tariffs or taxation) being imposed.

freeze-thaw A type of physical **weathering** whereby **rocks** are denuded by the freezing of water in cracks and crevices on the rock face. Water expands on freezing, and this process causes stress and fracture along any line of weakness in the rock. **Nivation** debris accumulates at the bottom of a rock face as **scree**.

front A boundary between two air masses. *See also* **depression**.

G

gazetteer A list of place names with their geographical coordinates.

GDP *See* **Gross Domestic Product**.

geosyncline A basin (a large **syncline**) in which thick marine sediments have accumulated.

geothermal energy A method of producing power from heat contained in the lower layers of the Earth's **crust**. New Zealand and Iceland both use superheated water or steam from geysers and volcanic **springs** to heat buildings and for hothouse cultivation and also to drive steam turbines to generate electricity. Geothermal energy is an example of a renewable resource of energy (*see* **renewable resources**, **nonrenewable resources**).

glaciation A period of cold **climate** during which time **ice sheets** and **glaciers** are the dominant forces of **denudation**.

glacier A body of ice occupying a valley and originating in a **corrie** or icefield. A glacier moves at a rate of several metres per day, the precise

speed depending upon climatic and **topographic**
conditions in the area in question.

global warming *or* **greenhouse effect**
The warming of the Earth's atmosphere caused
by an excess of carbon dioxide, which acts like a
blanket, preventing the natural escape of heat.
This situation has been developing over the last
150 years because of (a) the burning of **fossil fuels**,
which releases vast amounts of carbon dioxide
into the **atmosphere**, and (b) **deforestation**, which
results in fewer trees being available to take up
carbon dioxide (*see* **photosynthesis**).

globalization The process that enables financial
markets and companies to operate internationally
(as a result of deregulation and improved
communications). **Transnational corporations**
now locate their manufacturing in places that best
serve their global market at the lowest cost.

GNI (gross national income) *formerly* GNP
(gross national product) The total value of the
goods and services produced annually by a nation,
plus net property income from abroad.

Gondwanaland The southern-hemisphere
super-continent, consisting of the present South
America, Africa, India, Australasia and Antarctica,
which split from **Pangaea** *c*.200 million years ago.
Gondwanaland is part of the theory of **continental
drift**. *See also* **plate tectonics**.

GPS (global positioning system) A system of
earth-orbiting satellites, transmitting signals
continuously towards earth, which enable the
position of a receiving device on the earth's surface
to be accurately estimated from the difference in
arrival of the signals.

gradient 1. The measure of steepness of a line or
slope. In mapwork, the average gradient between
two points can be calculated as:

$$\frac{difference\ in\ altitude}{distance\ apart}$$

2. The measure of change in a property such as
density. In **human geography** gradients are found
in, for example, **population density**, land values
and **settlement** ranking.

granite An **igneous rock** having large crystals
due to slow cooling at depth in the Earth's **crust**.

green belt An area of land, usually around the
outskirts of a town or city on which building and
other developments are restricted by legislation.

greenfield site A development site for industry,
retailing or housing that has previously been used
only for agriculture or recreation. Such sites are
frequently in the **green belt**.

greenhouse effect *See* **global warming**.

Greenwich Meridian *See* **prime meridian**.

grid reference A method for specifying position
on a map. *See* **eastings** and **northings**.

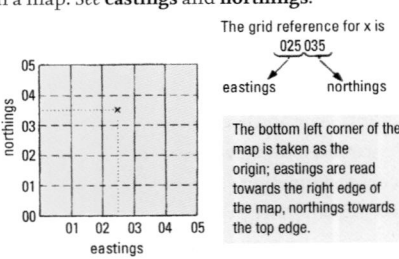

grid reference

Gross Domestic Product (GDP) The total value
of all goods and services produced domestically
by a nation during a year. It is equivalent to
Gross National Income (GNI) minus investment
incomes from foreign nations.

groundwater Water held in the bedrock of a
region, having percolated through the **soil** from
the surface. Such water is an important **resource** in
areas where **surface run-off** is limited or absent.

groyne *See* **breakwater**.

gryke An enlarged joint between blocks of **limestone**
(**clints**), especially in a **limestone pavement**.

gulf A large coastal indentation, similar to a **bay** but
larger in extent. Commonly formed as a result of
rising sea levels.

H

habitat A preferred location for particular species
of plants and animals to live and reproduce.

hanging valley A tributary valley entering a main
valley at a much higher level because of deepening
of the main valley, especially by glacial erosion.

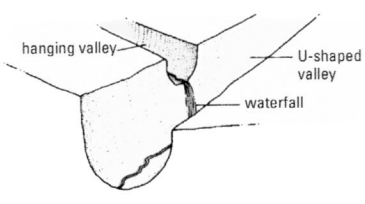

hanging valley

HDI (human development index)
A measurement of a country's achievements in
three areas: longevity, knowledge and standard of
living. Longevity is measured by life expectancy at
birth; knowledge is measured by a combination
of the adult literacy rate and the combined gross
primary, secondary and tertiary school enrolment
ratio; standard of living is measured by **GNI** per
capita.

headland A promontory of resistant **rock** along
the coastline. *See* **bay**.

hemisphere Any half of a globe or sphere.
The earth has traditionally been divided into
hemispheres by the **equator** (northern and
southern hemispheres) and by the **prime
meridian** and **International Date Line**
(eastern and western hemispheres).

hill farming A system of **agriculture** where sheep
(and to a lesser extent cattle) are grazed on upland
rough pasture.

hill shading Shadows drawn on a map to create a
3-dimensional effect and a sense of visual relief.

histogram A graph for showing values of classed
data as the areas of bars.

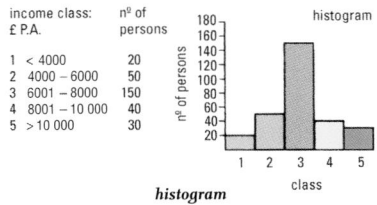

histogram

horizon The distinct layers found in the **soil
profile**. Usually three horizons are identified –
A, B and C, as in the diagram.

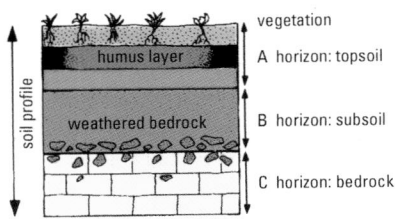

horizon A typical soil profile.

horst *See* **block mountain**.

horticulture The growing of plants and flowers for
commercial sale. It is now an international trade, for
example, orchids are grown in Southeast Asia for sale
in Europe.

human geography The study of people and their
activities in terms of patterns and processes of
population, **settlement**, economic activity and
communications. *Compare* **physical geography**.

hunter/gatherer economy A pre-agricultural
phase of development in which people survive
by hunting and gathering the animal and plant
resources of the natural **environment**. No
cultivation or herding is involved.

hurricane, cyclone *or* **typhoon** A wind of force
12 on the **Beaufort wind scale**, i.e. one having a
velocity of more than 118 km per hour. Hurricanes
can cause great damage by wind as well as from the
storm waves and floods that accompany them.

hydraulic action The erosive force of water alone,
as distinct from **corrasion**. A river or the sea will
erode partially by the sheer force of moving water
and this is termed 'hydraulic action'.

hydroelectric power The generation of
electricity by turbines driven by flowing water.
Hydroelectricity is most efficiently generated
in rugged **topography** where a head of water can
most easily be created, or on a large river where a
dam can create similar conditions. Whatever the
location, the principle remains the same – that
water descending via conduits from an upper
storage area passes through turbines and thus
creates electricity.

hydrological cycle The cycling of water through
sea, land and **atmosphere**.

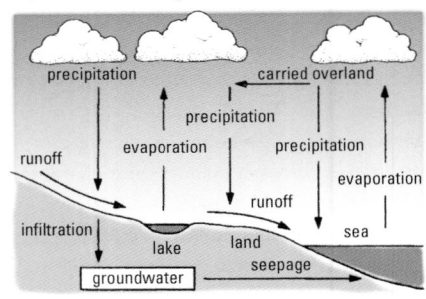

hydrological cycle

hydrosphere All the water on Earth, including that
present in the **atmosphere** as well as in oceans, seas,
ice sheets, etc.

hygrometer An instrument for measuring the
relative humidity of the **atmosphere**. It comprises
two thermometers, one of which is kept moist by
a wick inserted in a water reservoir. Evaporation
from the wick reduces the temperature of the 'wet
bulb' thermometer, and the difference between
the dry and the wet bulb temperatures is used to
calculate relative humidity from standard tables.

I

Ice Age A period of **glaciation** in which a cooling of **climate** leads to the development of **ice sheets, ice caps** and valley **glaciers**.

ice cap A covering of permanent ice over a relatively small land mass, e.g. Iceland.

ice sheet A covering of permanent ice over a substantial continental area such as Antarctica.

iceberg A large mass of ice which has broken off an **ice sheet** or **glacier** and left floating in the sea.

ID (Identifier) A unique value given to a particular object.

igneous rock A **rock** which originated as **magma** (molten rock) at depth in or below the Earth's **crust**. Igneous rocks are generally classified according to crystal size, colour and mineral composition. *See also* **plutonic rock**.

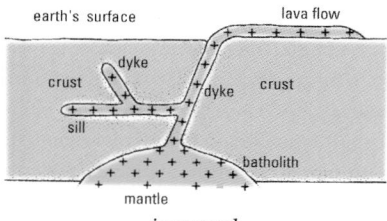

igneous rock

immigration The movement of people into a country or region from other countries or regions.

impermeable rock A rock that is non-porous and therefore incapable of taking in water or of allowing it to pass through between the grains. *Compare* **impervious rock**. *See also* **permeable rock**.

impervious rock A non-porous rock with no cracks or fissures through which water might pass.

imports Goods or services bought into one country from another (*compare* **exports**).

industrialization The development of industry on an extensive scale.

infiltration The gradual movement of water into the ground.

infrastructure The basic structure of an organization or system. The infrastructure of a city includes, for example, its roads and railways, schools, factories, power and water supplies.

inner city The ring of buildings around the **Central Business District (CBD)** of a town or city.

intensive farming A system of **agriculture** where relatively large amounts of capital and/or labour are invested on relatively small areas of land.

interglacial A warm period between two periods of **glaciation** and cold **climate**. The present interglacial began about 10,000 years ago.

interlocking spurs Obstacles of hard **rock** round which a river twists and turns in a V-shaped valley. **Erosion** is pronounced on the concave banks, and this ultimately causes the development of spurs which alternate on either side of the river and interlock as shown in the diagram.

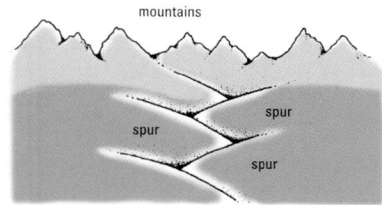

interlocking spurs A V-shaped valley with interlocking spurs.

International Date Line An imaginary line which approximately follows 180° **longitude**. The area of the world just east of the line is one day ahead of the area just west of the line.

international trade The exchange of goods and services between countries.

intrusion A body of **igneous rock** injected into the Earth's **crust** from the **mantle** below. *See* **dyke, sill, batholith**.

ionosphere *See* **atmosphere**.

irrigation A system of artificial watering of the land in order to grow crops. Irrigation is particularly important in areas of low or unreliable rainfall.

island A mass of land, smaller than a continent, which is completely surrounded by water.

isobar A line joining points of equal atmospheric pressure, as on the meteorological map below.

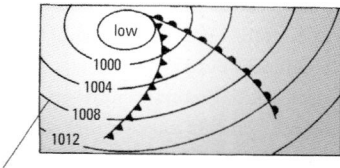

isobar, indicating atmospheric pressure in millibars

isobar

isohyet A line on a meteorological map joining places of equal rainfall.

isotherm A line on a meteorological map joining places of equal temperature.

J

joint A vertical or semi-vertical fissure in a **sedimentary rock**, contrasted with roughly horizontal bedding planes. In **igneous rocks** jointing may occur as a result of contraction on cooling from the molten state. Joints should be distinguished from **faults** in that they are on a much smaller scale and there is no relative displacement of the rocks on either side of the joint. Joints, being lines of weakness are exploited by **weathering**.

K

kame A short ridge of sand and gravel deposited from the water of a melted glacier.

karst topography An area of **limestone** scenery where **drainage** is predominantly subterranean.

kettle hole A small depression or hollow in a glacial outwash plain, formed when a block of ice embedded in the outwash deposits eventually melts, causing the **sediment** above to subside.

L

laccolith An igneous **intrusion**, domed and often of considerable dimensions, caused where a body of viscous **magma** has been intruded into the **strata** of the Earth's **crust**. These strata are buckled upwards over the laccolith.

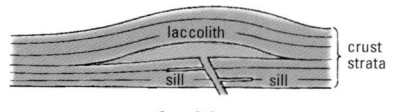

laccolith

lagoon 1. An area of sheltered coastal water behind a bay bar or **tombolo**.
2. The calm water behind a coral reef.

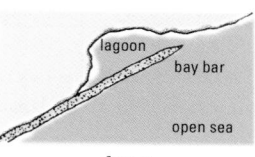

lagoon

lahar A landslide of volcanic debris mixed with water down the sides of a volcano, caused either by heavy rain or the heat of the volcano melting snow and ice.

lake A body of water completely surrounded by land.

land tenure A system of land ownership or allocation.

land use The function of an area of land. For example, the land use in rural areas could be farming or forestry, whereas urban land use could be housing or industry.

landform Any natural feature of the Earth's surface, such as mountains or valleys.

laterite A hard (literally 'brick-like') soil in tropical regions caused by the baking of the upper **horizons** by exposure to the sun.

latitude Distance north or south of the equator, as measured by degrees of the angle at the Earth's centre:

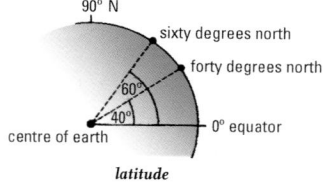

latitude

Laurasia The northern hemisphere supercontinent, consisting of the present North America, Europe and Asia (excluding India), which split from **Pangaea** *c.* 200 million years ago. Laurasia is part of the theory of **continental drift**. *See also* **plate tectonics**.

lava **Magma** extruded onto the Earth's surface via some form of volcanic eruption. Lava varies in viscosity (*see* **viscous lava**), colour and chemical composition. Acidic lavas tend to be viscous and flow slowly; basic lavas tend to be nonviscous and flow quickly. Commonly, **lava flows** comprise basaltic material, as for example in the process of sea-floor spreading (*see* **plate tectonics**).

lava flow A stream of **lava** issuing from some form of volcanic eruption. *See also* **viscous lava**.

lava plateau A relatively flat upland composed of layer upon layer of approximately horizontally bedded lavas. An example of this is the Deccan Plateau of India.

leaching The process by which soluble substances such as mineral salts are washed out of the upper soil layer into the lower layer by rain water.

levée The bank of a river, raised above the general level of the **flood plain** by **sediment** deposition during flooding. When the river bursts its banks, relatively coarse sediment is deposited first, and recurrent flooding builds up the river's banks accordingly. *See* diagram overleaf.

lignite A soft form of **coal**, harder than **peat** but softer than **bituminous coal**.

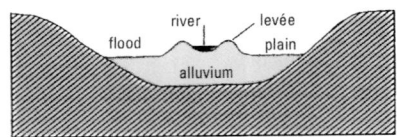

levée

limestone Calcium-rich **sedimentary rock** formed by the accumulation of the skeletal matter of marine organisms.

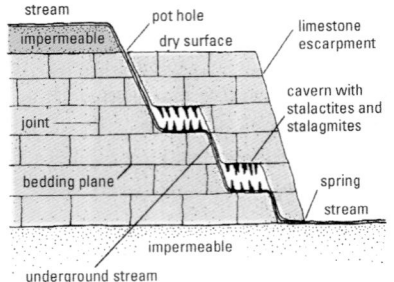

limestone

limestone pavement An exposed **limestone** surface on which the joints have been enlarged by the action of rainwater dissolving the limestone to form weak carbonic acid. These enlarged joints, or **grykes**, separate roughly rectangular blocks of limestone called **clints**.

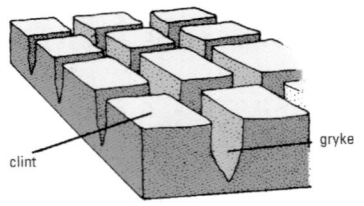

limestone pavement

location The position of population, settlement and economic activity in an area or areas. Location is a basic theme in **human geography**.

loess A very fine **silt** deposit, often of considerable thickness, transported by the wind prior to **deposition**. When irrigated, loess can be very fertile and, consequently, high **yields** can be obtained from crops grown on loess deposits.

longitude A measure of distance on the Earth's surface east or west of the Greenwich Meridian, an imaginary line running from pole to pole through Greenwich in London. Longitude, like **latitude**, is measured in degrees of an angle taken from the centre of the Earth.

The precise location of a place can be given by a **grid reference** comprising longitude and latitude. *See also* **map projection**, **prime meridian**.

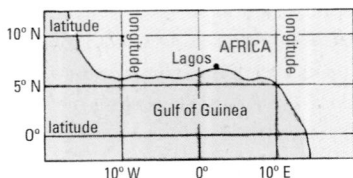

longitude *A grid showing the location of Lagos, Nigeria.*

longshore drift The net movement of material along a beach due to the oblique approach of waves to the shore. Beach deposits move in a zig-zag fashion, as shown in the diagram. Longshore drift is especially active on long, straight coastlines.

As waves approach, sand is carried up the beach by the **swash**, and retreats back down the beach with the **backwash**. Thus a single representative grain of sand will migrate in the pattern A, B, C, D, E, F in the diagram.

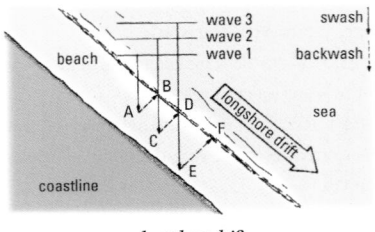

longshore drift

M

magma Molten rock originating in the Earth's **mantle**; it is the source of all **igneous rocks**.

malnutrition The condition of being poorly nourished, as contrasted with **undernutrition**, which is lack of a sufficient quantity of food. The diet of a malnourished person may be high in starchy foods but is invariably low in protein and essential minerals and vitamins.

mantle The largest of the concentric zones of the Earth's structure, overlying the **core** and surrounded in turn by the **crust**.

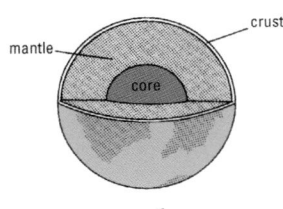

mantle

manufacturing industry The making of articles using physical labour or machinery, especially on a large scale. *See* **secondary sector**.

map Diagrammatic representation of an area – for example part of the earth's surface.

map projection A method by which the curved surface of the Earth is shown on a flat surface map. As it is not possible to show all the Earth's features accurately on a flat surface, some projections aim to show direction accurately at the expense of area, some the shape of the land and oceans, while others show correct area at the expense of accurate shape.

One of the projections most commonly used is the *Mercator projection*, devised in 1569, in which all lines of **latitude** are the same length as the equator. This results in increased distortion of area, moving from the equator towards the poles. This projection is suitable for navigation charts.

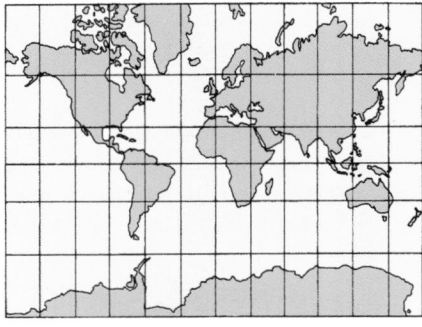

map projection *Mercator projection.*

The *Mollweide projection* shows the land masses the correct size in relation to each other but there is distortion of shape. As the Mollweide projection has no area distortion it is useful for showing distributions such as population distribution.

The only true representation of the Earth's surface is a globe.

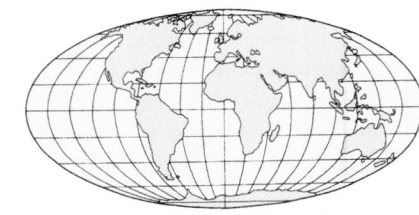

map projection *Mollweide projection.*

marble A whitish, crystalline **metamorphic rock** produced when **limestone** is subjected to great heat or pressure (or both) during Earth movements.

maritime climate A **temperate climate** that is affected by the closeness of the sea, giving a small annual range of temperatures – a coolish summer and a mild winter – and rainfall throughout the year. Britain has a maritime climate. *Compare* **extreme climate**.

market gardening An intensive type of **agriculture** traditionally located on the margins of urban areas to supply fresh produce on a daily basis to the city population. Typical market-garden produce includes salad crops, such as tomatoes, lettuce, cucumber, etc., cut flowers, fruit and some green vegetables.

mask A method of hiding features on a map to improve legibility.

maximum and minimum thermometer An instrument for recording the highest and lowest temperatures over a 24-hour period.

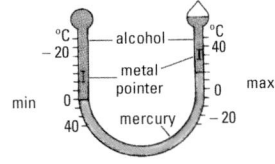

maximum and minimum thermometer

meander A large bend, especially in the middle or lower stages of a river's course. *See* **flood plain**. A meander is the result of lateral **corrasion**, which becomes dominant over vertical corrasion as the **gradient** of the river's course decreases. The characteristic features of a meander are summarized in the diagrams below. *See also* **oxbow lake**.

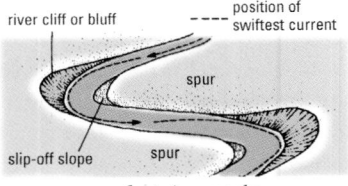

meander *A river meander.*

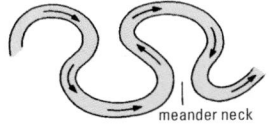

meander *Fully formed meanders.*

mesa A flat-topped, isolated hill in arid regions.

A mesa has a protective cap of hard **rock** underlain by softer, more readily eroded **sedimentary rock**. A **butte** is a relatively small outlier of a mesa.

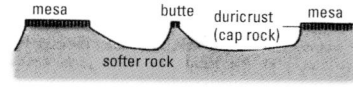

mesa

mesosphere *See* **atmosphere**.

metadata All Information used to describe content, quality, condition, origin and other characteristics of data.

metamorphic rock A **rock** which has been changed by intensive heat or pressure. Metamorphism implies an increase in hardness and resistance to **erosion**. Shale, for example, may be metamorphosed by pressure into **slate**; **sandstone** by heat into **quartzite**, **limestone** into **marble**. Metamorphism of pre-existing rocks is associated with the processes of **folding**, **faulting** and **vulcanicity**.

migration A permanent or semipermanent change of residence.

monoculture The growing of a single crop.

monsoon The term strictly means 'seasonal wind' and is used generally to describe a situation where there is a reversal of wind direction from one season to another. This is especially the case in South and Southeast Asia, where two monsoon winds occur, both related to the extreme pressure gradients created by the large land mass of the Asian continent.

moraine A collective term for debris deposited on or by **glaciers** and ice bodies in general. Several types of moraine are recognized: *lateral* moraine forms along the edges of a valley glacier where debris eroded from the valley sides, or weathered from the slopes above the glacier, collects; *medial* moraine forms where two lateral moraines meet at a glacier junction; *englacial* moraine is material which is trapped within the body of the glacier; and *ground* moraine is material eroded from the floor of the valley and used by the glacier as an abrasive tool. A *terminal* moraine is material bulldozed by the glacier during its advance and deposited at its maximum down-valley extent. *Recessional* moraines may be deposited at standstills during a period of general glacial retreat.

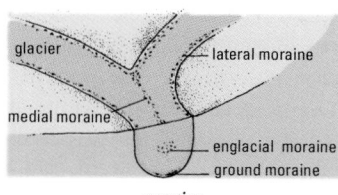

moraine

mortlake *See* **oxbow lake**.

mountain A natural upward projection of the Earth's surface, higher and steeper than a hill, and often having a rocky summit.

N

national park An area of scenic countryside protected by law from uncontrolled development. A national park has two main functions:
(a) to conserve the natural beauty of the landscape;
(b) to enable the public to visit and enjoy the countryside for leisure and recreation.

natural hazard A natural event which, in extreme cases, can lead to loss of life and destruction of property. Some natural hazards result from geological events, such as **earthquakes** and the eruption of **volcanoes**, whilst others are due to weather events such as **hurricanes**, floods and droughts.

natural increase The increase in population due to the difference between **birth rate** and **death rate**.

neap tides *See* **tides**.

névé Compact snow. In a **corrie** icefield, for example, four layers are recognized: blue and white ice at the bottom of the ice mass; névé overlying the ice and powder snow on the surface.

new town A new urban location created
(a) to provide overspill accommodation for a large city or **conurbation**;
(b) to provide a new focus for industrial development.

newly industrialized country (NIC)
A **developing country** which is becoming industrialized, for example Malaysia and Thailand. Some NICs have successfully used large-scale development to move into the industrialized world. Usually the capital for such developments comes from outside the country.

nivation The process of **weathering** by snow and ice, particularly through **freeze-thaw** action. Particularly active in cold **climates** and high altitudes – for example on exposed slopes above a **glacier**.

node A point representing the beginning or ending point of an edge or arc.

nomadic pastoralism A system of **agriculture** in dry grassland regions. People and stock (cattle, sheep, goats) are continually moving in search of pasture and water. The pastoralists subsist on meat, milk and other animal products.

non-governmental organizations (NGOs)
Independent organizations, such as charities (Oxfam, Water Aid) which provide aid and expertise to economically developing countries.

nonrenewable resources Resources of which there is a fixed supply, which will eventually be exhausted. Examples of these are metal ores and **fossil fuels**. *Compare* **renewable resources**.

North and South A way of dividing the industrialized nations, found predominantly in the North from those less developed nations in the South. The gap which exists between the rich 'North' and the poor 'South' is called the *development gap*.

northings The second element of a **grid reference**. *See* **eastings**.

nuclear power station An electricity-generating plant using nuclear fuel as an alternative to the conventional **fossil fuels** of **coal**, oil and gas.

nuée ardente A very hot and fast-moving cloud of gas, ash and rock that flows close to the ground after a violent ejection from a volcano. It is very destructive.

nunatak A mountain peak projecting above the general level of the ice near the edge of an **ice sheet**.

nutrient cycle The cycling of nutrients through the **environment**.

O

ocean A large area of sea. The world's oceans are the Pacific, Atlantic, Indian and Arctic. The Southern Ocean is made up of the areas of the Pacific, Atlantic and Indian Oceans south of latitude 60°S.

ocean current A movement of the surface water of an ocean.

opencast mining A type of mining where the mineral is extracted by direct excavation rather than by shaft or drift methods.

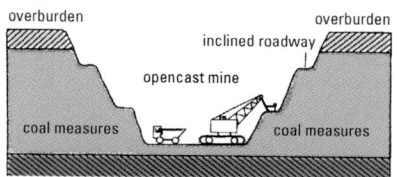

opencast mining

organic farming A system of farming that avoids the use of any artificial fertilizers or chemical pesticides, using only organic fertilizers and pesticides derived directly from animal or vegetable matter. Yields from organic farming are lower, but the products are sold at a premium price.

overfold *See* **fold**.

oxbow lake, mortlake *or* **cut-off**
A crescent-shaped lake originating in a **meander** that was abandoned when **erosion** breached the neck between bends, allowing the stream to flow straight on, bypassing the meander. The ends of the meander rapidly silt up and it becomes separated from the river.

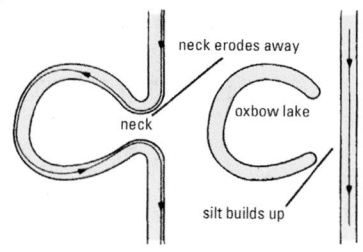

oxbow lake

ozone A form of oxygen found in a layer in the **stratosphere**, where it protects the Earth's surface from ultraviolet rays.

P

Pangaea The supercontinent or universal land mass in which all continents were joined together approximately 200 million years ago. *See* **continental drift**.

passage *See* **strait**.

pastoral farming A system of farming in which the raising of livestock is the dominant element. *See also* **nomadic pastoralism**.

peasant agriculture The growing of crops or raising of animals, partly for subsistence needs and partly for market sale. Peasant agriculture is thus an intermediate stage between subsistence and commercial farming.

peat Partially decayed and compressed vegetative

matter accumulating in areas of high rainfall and/or poor **drainage**.

peneplain A region that has been eroded until it is almost level. The more resistant rocks will stand above the general level of the land.

per capita income The **GNI** (gross national income) of a country divided by the size of its population. It gives the average income per head of the population if the national income were shared out equally. Per capita income comparisons are used as one indicator of levels of economic development.

periglacial features A periglacial landscape is one which has not been glaciated *per se*, but which has been affected by the severe **climate** prevailing around the ice margin.

permafrost The permanently frozen subsoil that is a feature of areas of **tundra**.

permeable rock Rock through which water can pass via a network of pores between the grains. *Compare* **pervious rock**. *See also* **impermeable rock**.

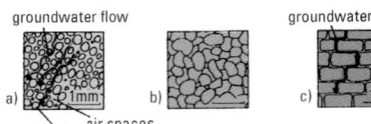

permeable rock (**a**) *Permeable rock*, (**b**) *impermeable rock*, (**c**) *pervious rock*.

pervious rock Rock which, even if non-porous, can allow water to pass through via interconnected joints, bedding planes and fissures. An example is **limestone**. *Compare* **permeable rock**. *See also* **impervious rock**.

photosynthesis The process by which green plants make carbohydrates from carbon dioxide and water, and give off oxygen. Photosynthesis balances **respiration**.

physical feature *See* **topography**.

physical geography The study of our **environment**, comprising such elements as geomorphology, hydrology, pedology, meteorology, climatology and biogeography.

pie chart A circular graph for displaying values as proportions:

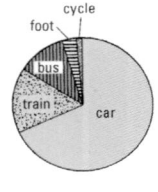

The journey to work: mode of transport.
(Sample of urban population)

Mode	No.	%	Sector° (% x 3.6)
Foot	25	3.2	11.5
Cycle	10	1.3	4.7
Bus	86	11.1	40.0
Train	123	15.9	57.2
Car	530	68.5	246.6
Total	774	100	360
		per cent	degrees

pie chart

plain A level or almost level area of land.

plantation agriculture A system of **agriculture** located in a tropical or semi-tropical **environment**, producing commodities for export to Europe, North America and other industrialized regions. Coffee, tea, bananas, rubber and sisal are examples of plantation crops.

plateau An upland area with a fairly flat surface and steep slopes. Rivers often dissect plateau surfaces.

plate tectonics The theory that the Earth's **crust** is divided into seven large, rigid plates, and several smaller ones, which are moving relative to each other over the upper layers of the Earth's **mantle**. *See* **continental drift**. **Earthquakes** and volcanic activity occur at the boundaries between the plates.

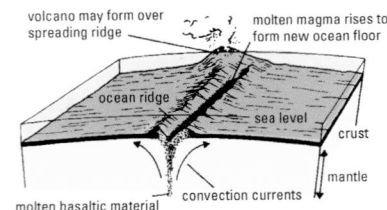

a) Constructive plate boundary

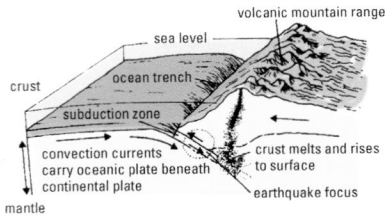

b) Destructive plate boundary

plate tectonics

plucking A process of glacial **erosion** whereby, during the passage of a valley **glacier** or other ice body, ice forming in cracks and fissures drags out material from a **rock** face. This is particularly the case with the backwall of a **corrie**.

plug The solidified material which seals the vent of a **volcano** after an eruption.

plutonic rock **Igneous rock** formed at depth in the Earth's **crust**; its crystals are large due to the slow rate of cooling. **Granite**, such as is found in **batholiths** and other deep-seated intrusions, is a common example.

podzol The characteristic **soil** of the **taiga** coniferous forests of Canada and northern Russia. Podzols are leached, greyish soils: iron and lime especially are leached out of the upper horizons, to be deposited as *hardpan* in the B **horizon**.

pollution Environmental damage caused by improper management of **resources**, or by careless human activity.

polygons Closed shapes defined by a connected sequences of coordinate pairs, where the first and last coordinate pair are the same.

polyline A series of connected segments which form a path to define a shape.

population change The increase of a population, the components of which are summarized in the following diagram.

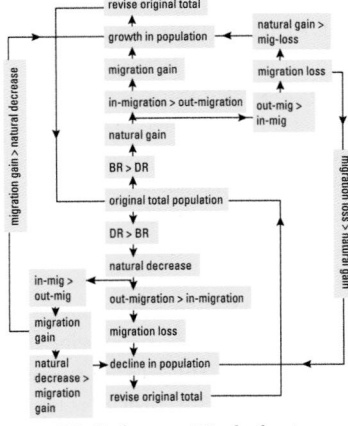

BR= birth rate   DR= death rate

population change

population density The number of people per unit area. Population densities are usually expressed per square kilometre.

population distribution The pattern of population location at a given **scale**.

population explosion On a global **scale**, the dramatic increase in population during the 20th century. The graph below shows world **population growth**.

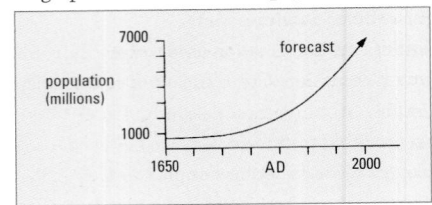

population explosion

population growth An increase in the population of a given region. This may be the result of natural increase (more births than deaths) or of in-migration, or both.

population pyramid A type of **bar graph** used to show population structure, i.e. the age and sex composition of the population for a given region or nation.

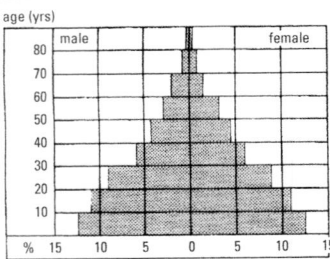

a) population pyramid Pyramid for India, showing high birth rates and death rates.

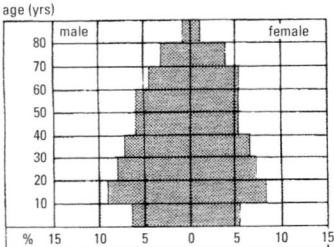

b) population pyramid Pyramid for England and Wales, showing low birth and death rates.

pothole **1.** A deep hole in limestone, caused by the enlargement of a **joint** through the dissolving effect of rainwater.

2. A hollow scoured in a river bed by the swirling of pebbles and small boulders in eddies.

precipitation Water deposited on the Earth's surface in the form of e.g. rain, snow, sleet, hail and dew.

prevailing wind The dominant wind direction of a region. Prevailing winds are named by the direction from which they blow.

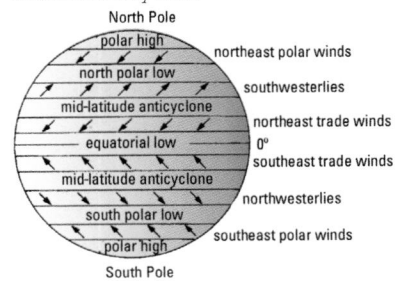

primary keys A set of properties in a database that uniquely identifies each record.

primary sector That sector of the national economy which deals with the production of primary materials: **agriculture**, mining, forestry and fishing. Primary products such as these have had no processing or manufacturing involvement. The total economy comprises the primary sector, the **secondary sector**, the **tertiary sector** and the **quaternary sector**.

primary source *See* **secondary source**.

prime meridian *or* **Greenwich Meridian** The line of 0° longitude passing through Greenwich in London.

pumped storage Water pumped back up to the storage lake of a **hydroelectric power** station, using surplus 'off-peak' electricity.

pyramidal peak A pointed mountain summit resulting from the headward extension of **corries** and **arêtes**. Under glacial conditions a given summit may develop corries on all sides, especially those facing north and east. As these erode into the summit, a formerly rounded profile may be changed into a pointed, steep-sided peak.

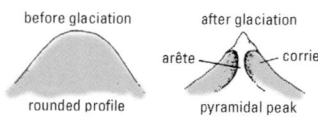

pyramidal peak

pyroclasts Rocky debris emitted during a volcanic eruption, usually following a previous emission of gases and prior to the outpouring of **lava** – although many eruptions do not reach the final lava stage.

Q

quality of life The level of wellbeing of a community and of the area in which the community lives.

quartz One of the commonest minerals found in the Earth's **crust**, and a form of silica (silicon+oxide). Most **sandstones** are composed predominantly of quartz.

quartzite A very hard and resistant **rock** formed by the metamorphism of **sandstone**.

quaternary sector That sector of the economy providing information and expertise. This includes the microchip and microelectronics industries. Highly developed economies are seeing an increasing number of their workforce employed in this sector. *Compare* **primary sector**, **secondary sector**, **tertiary sector**.

query A request to select features or records from a database.

R

rain gauge An instrument used to measure rainfall. Rain passes through a funnel into the jar below and

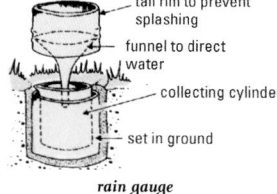

rain gauge

is then transferred to a measuring cylinder. The reading is in millimetres and indicates the depth of rain which has fallen over an area. *See* diagram.

raised beach *See* **wave-cut platform**.

range A long series or chain of mountains.

rapids An area of broken, turbulent water in a river channel, caused by a stratum of resistant **rock** that dips downstream. The softer rock immediately upstream and downstream erodes more quickly, leaving the resistant rock sticking up, obstructing the flow of the water. *Compare* **waterfall**.

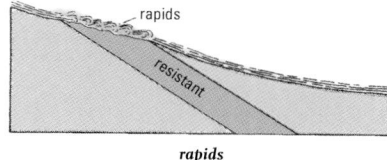

rapids

raster A pattern of closely spaced rows of dots that form an image.

raw materials The **resources** supplied to industries for subsequent manufacturing processes.

reef A ridge of rock, sand or coral whose top lies close to the sea's surface.

regeneration Renewed growth of, for example, forest after felling. Forest regeneration is crucial to the long-term stability of many **resource** systems, from **bush fallowing** to commercial forestry.

region An area of land which has marked boundaries or unifying internal characteristics. Geographers may identify regions according to physical, climatic, political, economic or other factors.

rejuvenation Renewed vertical **corrasion** by rivers in their middle and lower courses, caused by a fall in sea level, or a rise in the level of land relative to the sea.

relative humidity The relationship between the actual amount of water vapour in the air and the amount of vapour the air could hold at a particular temperature. This is usually expressed as a percentage. Relative humidity gives a measure of dampness in the **atmosphere**, and this can be determined by a **hygrometer**.

relief The differences in height between any parts of the Earth's surface. Hence a relief map will aim to show differences in the height of land by, for example, **contour** lines or by a colour key.

remote sensing The gathering of information by the use of electronic or other sensing devices in satellites.

renewable resources Resources that can be used repeatedly, given appropriate management and conservation. *Compare* **non-renewable resources**.

representative fraction The fraction of real size to which objects are reduced on a map; for example, on a 1:50 000 map, any object is shown at 1/50 000 of its real size.

reserves Resources which are available for future use.

reservoir A natural or artificial lake used for collecting or storing water, especially for water supply or **irrigation**.

resolution The smallest allowable separation between two coordinate values in a feature class.

resource Any aspect of the human and physical **environments** which people find useful in satisfying their needs.

respiration The release of energy from food in the cells of all living organisms (plants as well as animals). The process normally requires oxygen and releases carbon dioxide. It is balanced by **photosynthesis**.

revolution The passage of the Earth around the sun; one revolution is completed in 365.25 days. Due to the tilt of the Earth's axis ($23\frac{1}{2}$° from the vertical), revolution results in the sequence of seasons experienced on the Earth's surface.

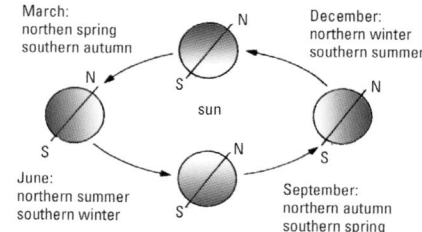

revolution The seasons of the year.

ria A submerged river valley, caused by a rise in sea level or a subsidence of the land relative to the sea.

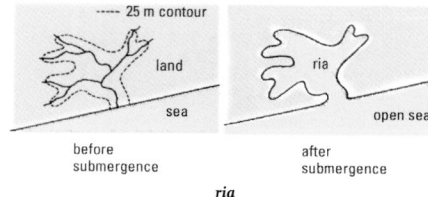

ria

ribbon lake A long, relatively narrow lake, usually occupying the floor of a U-shaped glaciated valley. A ribbon lake may be caused by the *overdeepening* of a section of the valley floor by glacial **abrasion**.

Richter scale A scale of **earthquake** measurement that describes the magnitude of an earthquake according to the amount of energy released, as recorded by **seismographs**.

rift valley A section of the Earth's **crust** which has been downfaulted. The **faults** bordering the rift valley are approximately parallel. There are two main theories related to the origin of rift valleys. The first states that tensional forces within the Earth's crust have caused a block of land to sink between parallel faults. The second theory states that compression within the Earth's crust has caused faulting in which two side blocks have risen up towards each other over a central block.

The most complex rift valley system in the world is that ranging from Syria in the Middle East to the river Zambezi in East Africa.

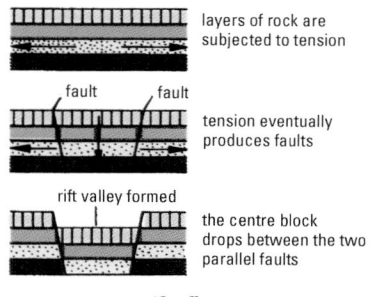

rift valley

river A large natural stream of fresh water flowing along a definite course, usually into the sea.

river basin The area drained by a river and its tributaries, sometimes referred to as a **catchment** area.

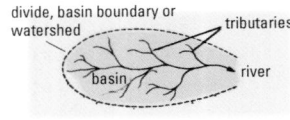

river basin

river cliff *or* **bluff** The outer bank of a **meander**. The cliff is kept steep by undercutting since river **erosion** is concentrated on the outer bank. *See* **meander** and **river's course**.

river's course The route taken by a river from its source to the sea. There are three major sections: the upper course, middle course and lower course.

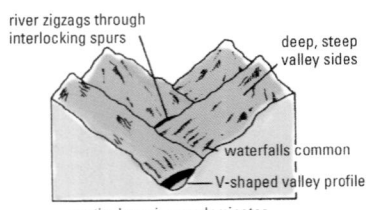

river's course Upper course.

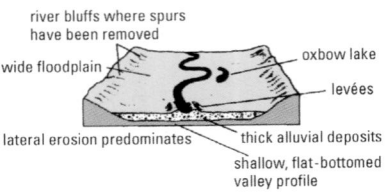

river's course Lower course.

river terrace A platform of land beside a river. This is produced when a river is **rejuvenated** in its middle or lower courses. The river cuts down into its **flood plain**, which then stands above the new general level of the river as paired terraces.

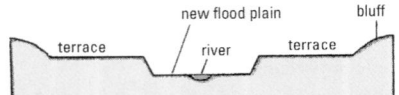

river terrace Paired river terraces above a flood plain.

roche moutonnée An outcrop of resistant **rock** sculpted by the passage of a **glacier**.

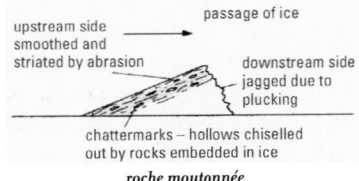

roche moutonnée

rock The solid material of the Earth's **crust**. *See* **igneous rock**, **sedimentary rock**, **metamorphic rock**.

rotation The movement of the Earth about its own axis. One rotation is completed in 24 hours. Due to the tilt of the Earth's axis, the length of day and night varies at different points on the Earth's surface. Days become longer with increasing latitude north; shorter with increasing latitude south. The situation is reversed during the northern midwinter (= the southern midsummer). *See* diagram.

rural depopulation The loss of population from the countryside as people move away from rural areas towards cities and **conurbations**.

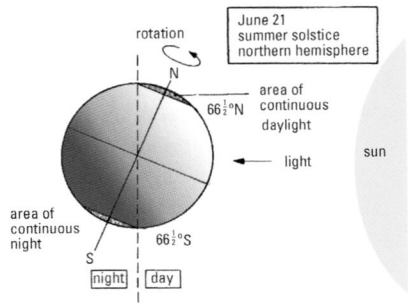

rotation The tilt of the Earth at the northern summer and southern winter solstice.

rural–urban migration The movement of people from rural to urban areas. *See* **migration** and **rural depopulation**.

S

saltpan A shallow basin, usually in a desert region, containing salt which has been deposited from an evaporated salt lake.

sandstone A common **sedimentary rock** deposited by either wind or water. Sandstones vary in texture from fine- to coarse- grained, but are invariably composed of grains of **quartz**, cemented by such substances as calcium carbonate or silica.

satellite image An image giving information about an area of the Earth or another planet, obtained from a satellite. Instruments on an Earth-orbiting satellite, such as Landsat, continually scan the Earth and sense the brightness of reflected light. When the information is sent back to Earth, computers turn it into *false-colour images* in which built-up areas appear in one colour (perhaps blue), vegetation in another (often red), bare ground in a third, and water in a fourth colour, making it easy to see their distribution and to monitor any changes. *Compare* **aerial photograph**.

savanna The grassland regions of Africa which lie between the **tropical rainforest** and the hot **deserts**. In South America, the *Llanos* and *Campos* regions are representative of the savanna type.

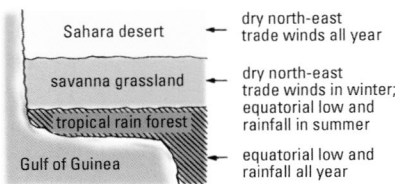

savanna The position of the savanna in West Africa.

scale The size ratio represented by a map; for example, on a map of scale 1:25 000, the real landscape is portrayed at 1/25 000 of its actual size.

scarp slope The steeper of the two slopes which comprise an **escarpment** of inclined **strata**. *Compare* **dip slope**.

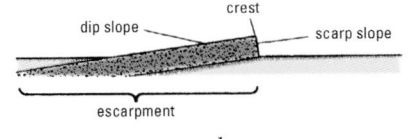

scarp slope

science park A site accommodating several companies involved in scientific work or research.

Science parks are linked to universities and tend to be located on **greenfield** and/or landscaped sites. *Compare* **business park**.

scree *or* **talus** The accumulated **weathering** debris below a **crag** or other exposed rock face. Larger boulders will accumulate at the base of the scree, carried there by greater momentum.

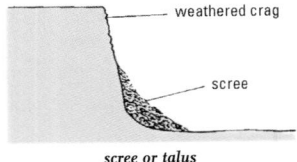

scree or talus

sea level The average height of the surface of the oceans and seas.

secondary sector The sector of the economy which comprises manufacturing and processing industries, in contrast with the **primary sector** which produces **raw materials**, the **tertiary sector** which provides **services**, and the **quaternary sector** which provides information.

secondary source A supply of information or data that has been researched or collected by an individual or group of people and made available for others to use; census data is an example of this. A *primary source* of data or information is one collected at first hand by the researcher who needs it; for example, a traffic count in an area, undertaken by a student for his or her own project.

sediment The material resulting from the **weathering** and **erosion** of the landscape, which has been deposited by water, ice or wind. It may be reconsolidated to form **sedimentary rock**.

sedimentary rock A rock which has been formed by the consolidation of **sediment** derived from pre-existing rocks. **Sandstone** is a common example of a rock formed in this way. **Chalk** and **limestone** are other types of sedimentary rock, derived from organic and chemical precipitations.

seif dune A linear sand dune, the ridge of sand lying parallel to the prevailing wind direction. The eddying movement of the wind keeps the sides of the dune steep.

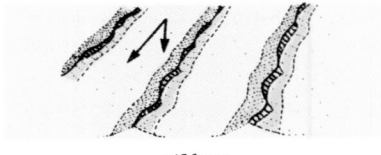

seif dunes

seismograph An instrument which measures and records the seismic waves which travel through the Earth during an **earthquake**.

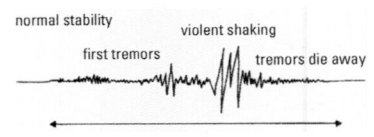

seismograph A typical seismograph trace.

seismology The study of **earthquakes**.

serac A pinnacle of ice formed by the tumbling and shearing of a **glacier** at an ice fall, i.e. the broken ice associated with a change in **gradient** of the valley floor.

service industry The people and organizations that provide a service to the public.

settlement Any location chosen by people as a permanent or semi-permanent dwelling place.

shading map or **choropleth map** A map in which shading of varying intensity is used. For example, the pattern of **population densities** in a region.

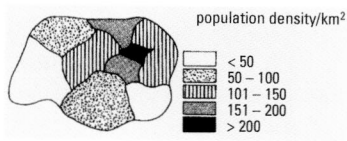

population density/km²
- < 50
- 50 – 100
- 101 – 150
- 151 – 200
- > 200

shading map

shanty town An area of unplanned, random, urban development often around the edge of a city. The shanty town is a major element of the structure of many **Third World** cities such as São Paulo, Mexico City, Nairobi, Kolkata and Lagos. The shanty town is characterized by high-density/low-quality dwellings, often constructed from the simplest materials such as scrap wood, corrugated iron and plastic sheeting – and by the lack of standard services such as sewerage and water supply, power supplies and refuse collection.

shape files A storage format for storing the location, shape and attributes of geographic features.

shifting cultivation *See* **bush fallowing**.

shoreface terrace A bank of **sediment** accumulating at the change of slope which marks the limit of a marine **wave-cut platform**.

Material removed from the retreating cliff base is transported by the undertow off the wave-cut platform to be deposited in deeper water offshore.

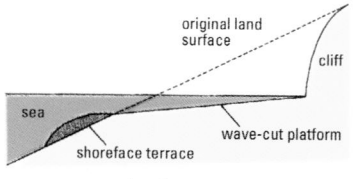

shoreface terrace

silage Any **fodder crop** harvested whilst still green. The crop is kept succulent by partial fermentation in a *silo*. It is used as animal feed during the winter.

sill 1. An igneous intrusion of roughly horizontal disposition. *See* **igneous rock**.
2. (Also called **threshold**) the lip of a **corrie**.

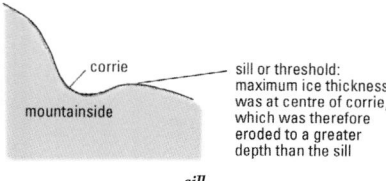

sill

silt Fine **sediment**, the component particles of which have a mean diameter of between 0.002 mm and 0.02 mm.

sinkhole *See* **pothole**.

slash and burn *See* **tropical rainforest**.

slate Metamorphosed shale or **clay**. Slate is a dense, fine-grained **rock** distinguished by the characteristic of *perfect cleavage*, i.e. it can be split along a perfectly smooth plane.

slip The amount of vertical displacement of **strata** at a **fault**.

smog A mixture of smoke and fog associated with urban and industrial areas, that creates an unhealthy **atmosphere**.

snow line The altitude above which permanent snow exists, and below which any snow that falls will not persist during the summer months.

socioeconomic group A group defined by particular social and economic characteristics, such as educational qualifications, type of job, and earnings.

soil The loose material which forms the uppermost layer of the Earth's surface, composed of the *inorganic fraction*, i.e. material derived from the **weathering** of bedrock, and the *organic fraction* – that is material derived from the decay of vegetable matter.

soil erosion The accelerated breakdown and removal of soil due to poor management. Soil erosion is particularly a problem in harsh **environments**.

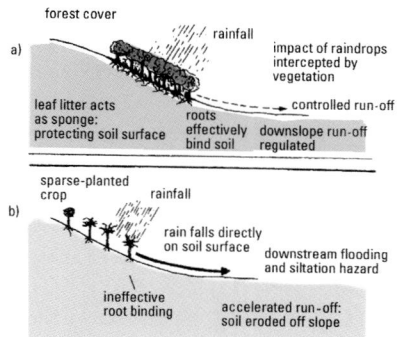

soil erosion a) Stable environment, b) unstable environment.

soil profile The sequence of layers or **horizons** usually seen in an exposed soil section.

solar power Heat radiation from the sun converted into electricity or used directly to provide heating. Solar power is an example of a renewable source of energy (*see* **renewable resources**).

solifluction A process whereby thawed surface soil creeps downslope over a permanently frozen **subsoil (permafrost)**.

spatial distribution The pattern of locations of, for example, population or **settlement** in a region.

spit A low, narrow bank of sand and shingle built out into an **estuary** by the process of **longshore drift**.

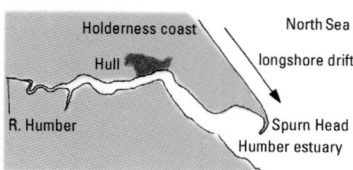

spit Spurn Head, a coastal spit.

spring The emergence of an underground stream at the surface, often occurring where **impermeable rock** underlies **permeable rock** or **pervious rock** or **strata**.

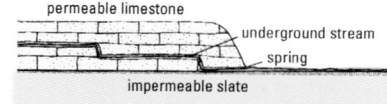

spring Rainwater enters through the fissures of the limestone and the stream springs out where the limestone meets slate.

spring tides *See* **tides**.

squatter settlement An area of peripheral urban settlement in which the residents occupy land to which they have no legal title. *See* **shanty town**.

stack A coastal feature resulting from the collapse of a natural arch. The stack remains after less resistant **strata** have been worn away by **weathering** and marine **erosion**.

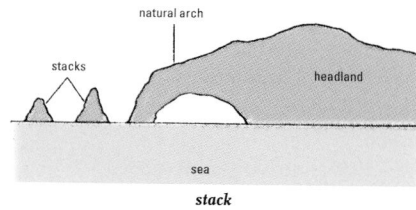

stack

stalactite A column of calcium carbonate hanging from the roof of a **limestone** cavern. As water passes through the limestone it dissolves a certain proportion, which is then precipitated by **evaporation** of water droplets dripping from the cavern roof. The drops splashing on the floor of a cavern further evaporate to precipitate more calcium carbonate as a **stalagmite**.

stalagmite A column of calcium carbonate growing upwards from a cavern floor. *Compare* **stalactite**. Stalactites and stalagmites may meet, forming a column or pillar.

staple diet The basic foodstuff which comprises the daily meals of a given people.

stereoplotter An instrument used for projecting an aerial photograph and converting locations of objects on the image to x-, y-, and z-coordinates. It plots these coordinates as a map.

Stevenson's screen A shelter used in weather stations, in which thermometers and other instruments may be hung.

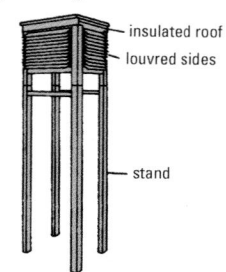

- insulated roof
- louvred sides
- stand

Stevenson's screen

strait, channel or **passage** A narrow body of water, between two land masses, which links two larger bodies of water.

strata Layers of **rock** superimposed one upon the other.

stratosphere The layer of the **atmosphere** which lies immediately above the troposphere and below the mesosphere and ionosphere. Within the stratosphere, temperature increases with altitude.

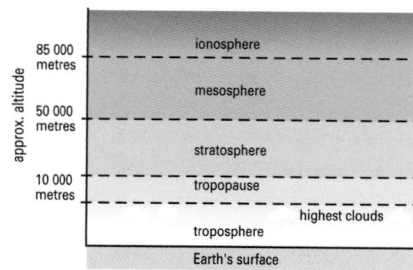

stratosphere

stratus Layer-cloud of uniform grey appearance, often associated with the warm sector of a **depression**. Stratus is a type of low **cloud** which may hang as mist over mountain tops.

striations The grooves and scratches left on bare **rock** surfaces by the passage of a **glacier**.

strip cropping A method of **soil** conservation whereby different crops are planted in a series of strips, often following **contours** around a hillside. The purpose of such a sequence of cultivation is to arrest the downslope movement of soil. *See* **soil erosion**.

subduction zone *See* **plate tectonics**.

subsistence agriculture A system of **agriculture** in which farmers produce exclusively for their own consumption, in contrast to **commercial agriculture** where farmers produce purely for sale at the market.

subsoil *See* **soil profile**.

suburbs The outer, and largest, parts of a town or city.

surface run-off That proportion of rainfall received at the Earth's surface which runs off either as channel flow or overland flow. It is distinguished from the rest of the rainfall, which either percolates into the soil or evaporates back into the **atmosphere**.

sustainable development The ability of a country to maintain a level of economic development, thus enabling the majority of the population to have a reasonable standard of living.

swallow hole *See* **pothole**.

swash The rush of water up the beach as a wave breaks. *See also* **backwash** and **longshore drift**.

syncline A trough in folded **strata**; the opposite of **anticline**. *See* **fold**.

T

taiga The extensive **coniferous forests** of Siberia and Canada, lying immediately south of the arctic **tundra**.

talus *See* **scree**.

tarn The postglacial lake which often occupies a **corrie**.

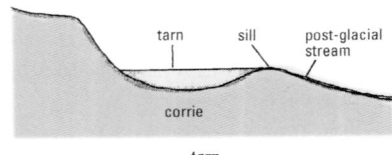
tarn

temperate climate A climate typical of mid-latitudes. Such a climate is intermediate between the extremes of hot (tropical) and cold (polar) climates. *Compare* **extreme climate**. *See also* **maritime climate**.

terminal moraine *See* **moraine**.

terracing A means of **soil** conservation and land utilization whereby steep hillsides are engineered into a series of flat ledges which can be used for **agriculture**, held in places by stone banks to prevent **soil erosion**.

terracing

tertiary sector That sector of the economy which provides **services** such as transport, finance and retailing, as opposed to the **primary sector** which provides **raw materials**, the **secondary sector** which processes and manufactures products, and the **quaternary sector** which provides information and expertise.

thermal power station An electricity-generating plant which burns **coal**, oil or natural gas to produce steam to drive turbines.

Third World A collective term for the poor nations of Africa, Asia and Latin America, as opposed to the 'first world' of capitalist, developed nations and the 'second world' of formerly communist, developed nations. The terminology is far from satisfactory as there are great social and political variations within the 'Third World'. Indeed, there are some countries where such extreme poverty prevails that these could be regarded as a fourth group. Alternative terminology includes '**developing countries**', 'economically developing countries' and 'less economically developed countries' (LEDC). **Newly industrialized countries** are those showing greatest economic development.

threshold *See* **sill** (sense 2).

tidal range The mean difference in water level between high and low tides at a given location. *See* **tides**.

tides The alternate rise and fall of the surface of the sea, approximately twice a day, caused by the gravitational pull of the moon and, to a lesser extent, of the sun.

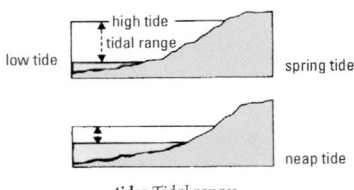
tides Tidal ranges.

till *See* **boulder clay**.

tombolo A **spit** which extends to join an island to the mainland.

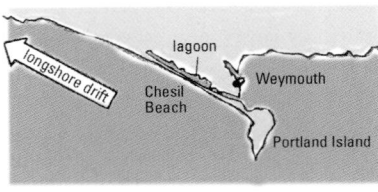
tombolo Chesil Beach, England.

topography The composition of the visible landscape, comprising both physical features and those made by people.

topsoil The uppermost layer of **soil**, more rich in organic matter than the underlying **subsoil**. *See* **horizon**, **soil profile**.

tornado A violent storm with winds circling around a small area of extremely low pressure. Characterized by a dark funnel-shaped cloud. Winds associated with tornadoes can reach speeds of over 480 km/h (300 mph).

trade winds Winds which blow from the subtropical belts of high pressure towards the equatorial belt of low pressure. In the northern hemisphere, the winds blow from the northeast and in the southern hemisphere from the southeast.

transhumance The practice whereby herds of farm animals are moved between regions of different climates. Pastoral farmers (*see* **pastoral farming**) take their herds from valley pastures in the winter to mountain pastures in the summer. *See also* **alp**.

transnational corporation (TNC) A company that has branches in many countries of the world, and often controls the production of the primary product and the sale of the finished article.

tributary A stream or river which feeds into a larger one. *Compare* **distributary**.

tropical rainforest The dense forest cover of the equatorial regions, reaching its greatest extent in the Amazon Basin of South America, the Congo Basin of Africa, and in parts of Southeast Asia and Indonesia. There has been much concern in recent years about the rate at which the world's rainforests are being cut down and burnt. The burning of large tracts of rainforest is thought to be contributing to **global warming**. Many governments and **conservation** bodies are now examining ways of protecting the remaining rainforests, which are unique **ecosystems** containing millions of plant and animal species.

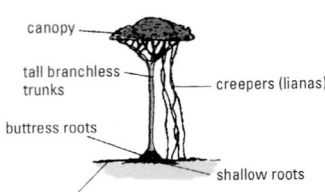

Intense bacterial activity breaks down fallen leaves, etc., to return nutrients to soil surface for immediate uptake by roots. Soils themselves are infertile: the nutrient cycle is concentrated in the vegetation and top few inches of soil.

a forest giant in the tropical rainforest

tropics The region of the Earth lying between the *tropics of Cancer* $(23\frac{1}{2}°\text{N})$ and *Capricorn* $(23\frac{1}{2}°\text{S})$. *See* **latitude**.

troposphere *See* **atmosphere**.

trough An area of low pressure, not sufficiently well-defined to be regarded as a **depression**.

truncated spur A spur of land that previously projected into a valley and has been completely or partially cut off by a moving **glacier**.

tsunami A very large, and often destructive, sea wave produced by a submarine **earthquake**. Tsunamis tend to occur along the coasts of Japan and parts of the Pacific Ocean, and can be the cause of large numbers of deaths.

tuff Volcanic ash or dust which has been consolidated into **rock**.

tundra The barren, often bare-rock plains of the far north of North America and Eurasia where subarctic conditions prevail and where, as a result, vegetation is restricted to low-growing, hardy shrubs and mosses and lichens.

typhoon *See* **hurricane**.

U

undernutrition A lack of a sufficient quantity of food, as distinct from **malnutrition** which is a consequence of an unbalanced diet.

urban decay The process of deterioration in the **infrastructure** of parts of the city. It is the result of

long-term shifts in patterns of economic activity, residential **location** and **infrastructure**.

urban sprawl The growth in extent of an urban area in response to improvements in transport and rising incomes, both of which allow a greater physical separation of home and work.

urbanization The process by which a national population becomes predominantly urban through a **migration** of people from the countryside to cities, and a shift from agricultural to industrial employment.

U-shaped valley A glaciated valley, characteristically straight in plan and U-shaped in **cross section**. *See* diagram. *Compare* **V-shaped valley**.

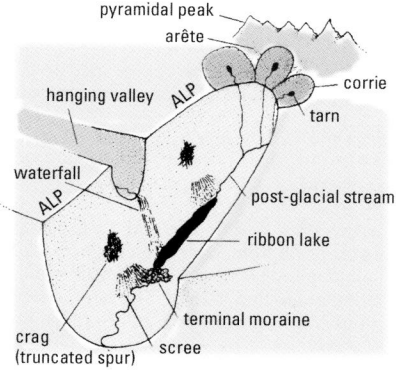

U-shaped valley

V

valley A long depression in the Earth's surface, usually containing a river, formed by **erosion** or by movements in the Earth's **crust**.

vector A quantity that has both magnitude and direction.

vegetation The plant life of a particular region.

viscous lava **Lava** that resists the tendency to flow. It is sticky, flows slowly and congeals rapidly. *Non-viscous* lava is very fluid, flows quickly and congeals slowly.

volcanic rock A category of **igneous rock** which comprises those rocks formed from **magma** which has reached the Earth's surface. **Basalt** is an example of a volcanic rock.

volcano A fissure in the Earth's **crust** through which **magma** reaches the Earth's surface. There are four main types of volcano:

(a) *Acid lava cone* – a very steep-sided cone composed entirely of acidic, **viscous lava** which flows slowly and congeals very quickly.

(b) *Composite volcano* – a single cone comprising alternate layers of ash (or other **pyroclasts**) and lava.

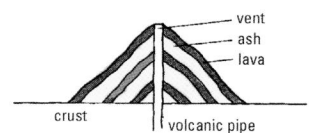

volcano Composite volcano.

(c) *Fissure volcano* – a volcano that erupts along a linear fracture in the crust, rather than from a single cone.

(d) *Shield volcano* – a volcano composed of very basic, non-viscous lava which flows quickly and

congeals slowly, producing a very gently sloping cone.

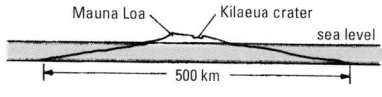

volcano Shield volcano.

V-shaped valley A narrow, steep-sided valley made by the rapid erosion of rock by streams and rivers. It is V-shaped in cross-section. *Compare* **U-shaped valley**.

vulcanicity A collective term for those processes which involve the intrusion of **magma** into the **crust**, or the extrusion of such molten material onto the Earth's surface.

W

wadi A dry watercourse in an arid region; occasional rainstorms in the desert may cause a temporary stream to appear in a wadi.

warm front *See* **depression**.

waterfall An irregularity in the long profile of a **river's course**, usually located in the upper course. *Compare* **rapids**.

waterfall

watershed The boundary, often a ridge of high ground, between two **river basins**.

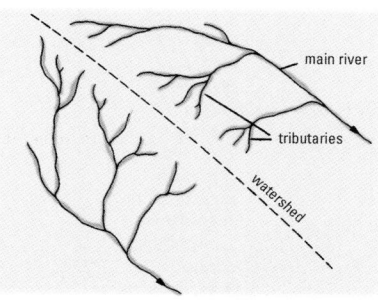

watershed

water table The level below which the ground is permanently saturated. The water table is thus the upper level of the **groundwater**. In areas where **permeable rock** predominates, the water table may be at some considerable depth.

wave-cut platform *or* **abrasion platform** A gently sloping surface eroded by the sea along a coastline.

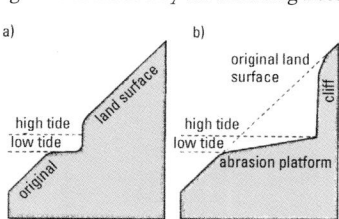

wave-cut platform a) Early in formation, b) later in formation.

weather The day-to-day conditions of e.g. rainfall, temperature and pressure, as experienced at a particular location.

weather chart A map or chart of an area giving

details of **weather** experienced at a particular time of day. Weather charts are sometimes called *synoptic charts*, as they give a synopsis of the weather at a particular time.

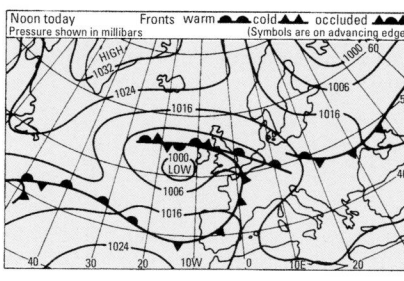

weather chart

weather station A place where all elements of the weather are measured and recorded. Each station will have a **Stevenson's screen** and a variety of instruments such as a **maximum and minimum thermometer**, a **hygrometer**, a **rain gauge**, a **wind vane** and an **anemometer**.

weathering The breakdown of rocks *in situ*; contrasted with **erosion** in that no large-scale transport of the denuded material is involved.

wet and dry bulb thermometer *See* **hygrometer**.

wind vane An instrument used to indicate wind direction. It consists of a rotating arm which always points in the direction from which the wind blows.

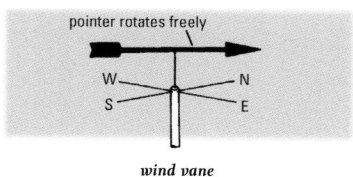

wind vane

Y

yardang Long, roughly parallel ridges of **rock** in arid and semi-arid regions. The ridges are undercut by wind **erosion** and the corridors between them are swept clear of sand by the wind. The ridges are oriented in the direction of the prevailing wind.

yield The productivity of land as measured by the weight or volume of produce per unit area.

Z

zeugen *Pedestal rocks* in arid regions; wind **erosion** is concentrated near the ground, where **corrasion** by wind-borne sand is most active. This leads to undercutting and the pedestal profile emerges.

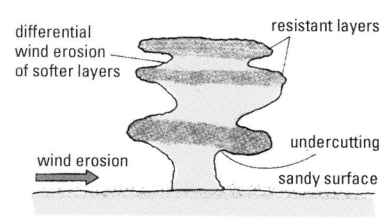

zeugen

How to use the Index

All the names on the maps in this atlas, except some of those on the special topic maps, are included in the index.

The names are arranged in **alphabetical order.** Where the name has more than one word the separate words are considered as one to decide the position of the name in the index:

Thetford
The Trossachs
The Wash
The Weald
Thiers
Thiès

Where there is more than one place with the same name, the country name is used to decide the order:

London Canada
London England

If both places are in the same country, the county or state name is also used:

Avon r. Brist. England
Avon r. Dor. England

Each entry in the index starts with the name of the place or feature, followed by the name of the country or region in which it is located. This is followed by the number of the most appropriate page on which the name appears, usually the largest scale map. Next comes the alphanumeric reference followed by the latitude and longitude.

Names of physical features such as rivers, capes, mountains etc are followed by a description. The descriptions are usually shortened to one or two letters – these abbreviations are keyed below. Town names are followed by a description only when the name may be confused with that of a physical feature:

Big Trout Lake town

To help to distinguish the different parts of each entry, different styles of type are used:

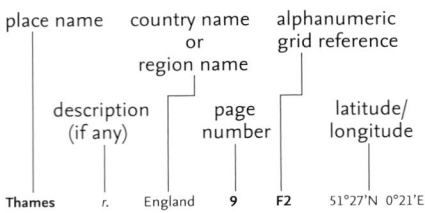

place name | country name or region name | alphanumeric grid reference
description (if any) | page number | latitude/longitude

Thames | r. | England | 9 | F2 | 51°27'N 0°21'E

To use the **alphanumeric grid reference** to find a feature on the map, first find the correct page and then look at the letters and numbers printed outside the frame along the top, bottom and sides of the map.

When you have found the correct letter and number follow the grid boxes up and along until you find the correct grid box in which the feature appears. You must then search the grid box until you find the name of the feature.

The **latitude and longitude reference** gives a more exact description of the position of the feature.

Page 1 of the atlas describes lines of latitude and lines of longitude, and explains how they are numbered and divided into degrees and minutes. Each name in the index has a different latitude and longitude reference, so the feature can be located accurately. The lines of latitude and lines of longitude shown on each map are numbered in degrees. These numbers are printed in black along the top, bottom and sides of the map frame.

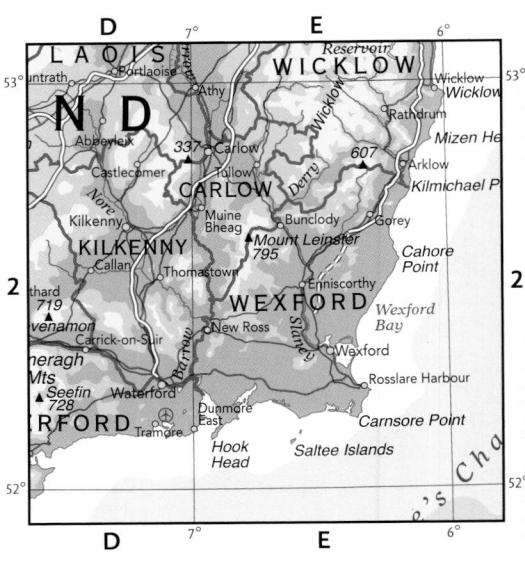

The drawing above shows part of the map on page 18 and the lines of latitude and lines of longitude.

The index entry for Wexford is given as follows:

Wexford Ireland **18 E2** .... 52°20'N 6°28'W

To locate Wexford, first find latitude 52°N and estimate 20 minutes north from 52 degrees to find 52°20'N, then find longitude 6°W and estimate 28 minutes west from 6 degrees to find 6°28'W. The symbol for the town of Wexford is where latitude 52°20'N and longitude 6°28'W meet.

On maps at a smaller scale than the map of Ireland, it is not possible to show every line of latitude and longitude. Only every 5 or 10 degrees of latitude and longitude may be shown. On these maps you must estimate the degrees and minutes to find the exact location of a feature.

Abbreviations

A. and B.	Argyll and Bute	i.	island	Oreg.	Oregon
Afgh.	Afghanistan	Ill.	Illinois	Orkn.	Orkney
Ala.	Alabama	I. o. W.	Isle of Wight	Oxon.	Oxfordshire
Ang.	Angus	is	islands	Pacific Oc.	Pacific Ocean
b.	bay	l.	lake	P. and K.	Perth and Kinross
Baja Calif.	Baja California	La.	Louisiana	P'boro.	Peterborough
Bangl.	Bangladesh	Lancs.	Lancashire	Pem.	Pembrokeshire
Bos. and Herz.	Bosnia and Herzegovina	Leics.	Leicestershire	pen.	peninsula
Brist.	Bristol	Lincs.	Lincolnshire	Phil.	Philippines
c.	cape	Lux.	Luxembourg	P.N.G.	Papua New Guinea
Cambs.	Cambridgeshire	Man.	Manitoba	pt	point
C.A.R.	Central African Republic	Mass.	Massachusetts	r.	river
Colo.	Colorado	Me.	Maine	r. mouth	river mouth
Corn.	Cornwall	Mich.	Michigan	resr	reservoir
Cumb.	Cumbria	Minn.	Minnesota	S. Africa	South Africa
d.	internal division e.g. county, state	Miss.	Mississippi	S. America	South America
Del.	Delaware	Mo.	Missouri	S. Atlantic Oc.	South Atlantic Ocean
Dem. Rep. Congo	Democratic Republic of the Congo	Mor.	Moray	S. C.	South Carolina
		mt.	mountain	S. China Sea	South China Sea
Derbys.	Derbyshire	mts	mountains	Shetl.	Shetland
des.	desert	N. Africa	North Africa	S. Korea	South Korea
Dev.	Devon	Na h-E. S.	Na h-Eileanan Siar	Som.	Somerset
Dom. Rep.	Dominican Republic	N. America	North America	S. Pacific Oc.	South Pacific Ocean
Don.	Donegal	N. Atlantic Oc.	North Atlantic Ocean	str.	strait
Dor.	Dorset	nature res.	nature reserve	Suff.	Suffolk
Dur.	Durham	N. C.	North Carolina	Switz.	Switzerland
Equat. Guinea	Equatorial Guinea	Neth.	Netherlands	T. and W.	Tyne and Wear
Ess.	Essex	Neth. Antilles	Netherlands Antilles	Tel. Wre.	Telford and Wrekin
est.	estuary	Nev.	Nevada	Tex.	Texas
E. Sussex	East Sussex	New.	Newport	Tipp.	Tipperary
E. Yorks.	East Riding of Yorkshire	Nfld. and Lab.	Newfoundland and Labrador	U.A.E.	United Arab Emirates
f.	physical feature, e.g. valley, plain, geographic area	N. Korea	North Korea	U.K.	United Kingdom
		N. M.	New Mexico	U.S.A.	United States of America
Falk.	Falkirk	N. Mariana Is	Northern Marianas Islands	Va.	Virginia
g.	gulf	Norf.	Norfolk	vol.	volcano
Ga.	Georgia	Northum.	Northumberland	Vt.	Vermont
Glos.	Gloucestershire	Notts.	Nottinghamshire	Water.	Waterford
Hants.	Hampshire	N. Pacific Oc.	North Pacific Ocean	Warwicks.	Warwickshire
High.	Highland	N. Y.	New York	Wick.	Wicklow
hd	headland	Oc.	Ocean	W. Va.	West Virginia
		Oh.	Ohio	Wyo.	Wyoming

A

Aa r. France 9 H2....51°00'N 2°07'E
Aabenraa Denmark 43 B1....55°02'N 9°25'E
Aachen Germany 46 B4....50°46'N 6°05'E
Aalborg Denmark 43 B2....57°03'N 9°55'E
Aalen Germany 46 D3....48°50'N 10°06'E
Aalst Belgium 42 D3....50°56'N 4°03'E
Aarhus Denmark 43 B2....56°09'N 10°12'E
Ābādān Iran 95 G6....30°20'N 48°15'E
Ābādeh Iran 95 H6....31°08'N 52°36'E
Abadla Algeria 84 D5....31°00'N 2°43'W
Abakan Russia 55 K3....53°42'N 91°25'E
Abarqū Iran 95 H6....31°06'N 53°13'E
Abashiri Japan 104 D4....44°01'N 144°15'E
Abaya, Lake Ethiopia 85 H2....6°19'N 37°53'E
Abaza Russia 98 G8....52°40'N 90°06'E
Abbeville France 44 D7....50°06'N 1°50'E
Abbeyfeale Ireland 18 B2....52°23'N 9°18'W
Abbey Head Scotland 15 F2....54°46'N 3°58'W
Abbeyleix Ireland 18 D2....52°55'N 7°21'W
Abbottabad Pakistan 95 L6....34°13'N 73°17'E
Abéché Chad 85 G3....13°50'N 20°49'E
Aberaeron Wales 10 C4....52°15'N 4°15'W
Aberchirder Scotland 17 G2....57°34'N 2°38'W
Aberdare Wales 10 D3....51°43'N 3°27'W
Aberdaron Wales 10 C4....52°48'N 4°43'W
Aberdeen Scotland 17 G2....57°09'N 2°06'W
Aberdeen d. Scotland 20 D5....57°10'N 2°11'W
Aberdeen U.S.A. 62 G6....45°28'N 98°31'W
Aberdeenshire d. Scotland 20 D5....57°21'N 2°32'W
Aberfeldy Scotland 17 F1....56°37'N 3°52'W
Aberford England 13 F2....53°50'N 1°21'W
Aberfoyle Scotland 14 E4....56°11'N 4°23'W
Abergavenny Wales 10 D3....51°49'N 3°01'W
Abergele Wales 10 D5....53°17'N 3°35'W
Aberlour Scotland 17 F2....57°29'N 3°13'W
Aberporth Wales 10 C4....52°08'N 4°33'W
Abersoch Wales 10 C4....52°50'N 4°30'W
Abertillery Wales 10 D3....51°44'N 3°08'W
Aberystwyth Wales 10 C4....52°25'N 4°05'W
Abhā Saudi Arabia 85 H2....18°14'N 42°27'E
Abidjan Côte d'Ivoire 84 D2....5°21'N 4°02'W
Abilene U.S.A. 62 G3....32°26'N 99°45'W
Abingdon England 8 D2....51°40'N 1°17'W
Abington Scotland 15 F3....55°30'N 3°41'W
Abitibi, Lake Canada 61 J6....48°55'N 80°01'W
Abkhazia d. Georgia 53 E2....43°15'N 40°45'E
Aboyne Scotland 17 G2....57°05'N 2°47'W
Abqaiq Saudi Arabia 95 G5....25°56'N 49°42'E
Abū 'Arīsh Saudi Arabia 94 F3....16°59'N 42°45'E
Abu Dhabi U.A.E. 95 H4....24°28'N 54°20'E
Abu Hamed Sudan 85 H3....19°30'N 33°24'E
Abuja Nigeria 84 E2....9°06'N 7°19'E
Abū Kamāl Syria 94 F6....34°26'N 40°56'E
Abū Nujaym Libya 49 H3....30°28'N 15°27'E
Abū Sunbul Egypt 94 D4....22°26'N 31°39'E
Abyad Sudan 94 C2....13°46'N 26°26'E
A Cañiza Spain 43 A5....42°13'N 8°16'W
Acaponeta Mexico 66 C5....22°30'N 105°25'W
Acapulco Mexico 66 C4....16°55'N 99°52'W
Acarigua Venezuela 72 C7....9°33'N 69°11'W
Accra Ghana 84 D2....5°35'N 0°14'W
Accrington England 12 E2....53°45'N 2°22'W
Acheloós r. Greece 50 D4....38°20'N 21°06'E
Achill Island Ireland 18 A3....53°56'N 10°00'W
Achinsk Russia 55 K3....56°17'N 90°34'E
A'Chralaig mt. Scotland 16 D2....57°11'N 5°09'W
Acklins Island Bahamas 67 J5....22°18'N 74°08'W
Acle England 9 G3....52°38'N 1°33'E
Aconcagua, Cerro mt. Argentina 73 B3....32°38'S 70°01'W
A Coruña Spain 45 A5....43°22'N 8°23'W
Adaja r. Spain 45 C4....41°33'N 4°51'W
Adam's Peak Sri Lanka 96 F2....6°49'N 80°28'E
Adana Turkey 51 K3....36°59'N 35°19'E
Adapazarı Turkey 51 I5....40°47'N 30°23'E
Ad Dahnā' des. Saudi Arabia 95 G5....20°40'N 46°52'E
Ad Dakhla Western Sahara 84 C4....23°42'N 15°56'W
Adderbury England 8 D3....52°01'N 1°19'W
Ad Dir'īyah Saudi Arabia 95 G4....24°45'N 46°34'E
Ad Dīwānīyah Iraq 94 F6....31°59'N 44°59'E
Adelaide Australia 108 C3....34°56'S 138°40'E
Aden Yemen 94 F2....12°49'N 44°59'E
Aden, Gulf of Somalia/Yemen 85 I3....11°44'N 45°16'E
Adi i. Indonesia 103 I3....4°15'S 133°27'E
Adi Ārk'ay Ethiopia 94 E2....13°24'N 38°03'E
Adigrat Ethiopia 94 E2....14°16'N 39°29'E
Adi Ugri Eritrea 94 E2....14°52'N 38°48'E
Adiyaman Turkey 51 M3....37°46'N 38°17'E
Admiralty Islands P.N.G. 108 D6....1°44'S 146°17'E
Adour r. France 44 C3....43°32'N 1°31'W
Adriatic Sea Europe 48 F5....44°19'N 13°24'E
Adwa Ethiopia 85 H3....14°09'N 38°52'E
Adwick le Street England 13 F2....53°34'N 1°12'W
Adycha r. Russia 55 O4....66°42'N 136°32'E
Aegean Sea Greece/Turkey 50 F4....39°00'N 24°51'E
Afghanistan Asia 95 K6....33°53'N 65°52'E
Africa 78
Afyonkarahisar Turkey 51 I4....38°46'N 30°33'E
Agadez Niger 84 E3....16°57'N 7°59'E
Agadir Morocco 84 D5....30°27'N 9°37'W
Agano r. Japan 104 C3....37°58'N 139°02'E
Agartala India 97 H5....23°50'N 91°16'E
Agde France 44 E3....43°18'N 3°28'E
Agen France 44 D4....44°12'N 0°38'E
Agios Dimitrios Greece 50 E3....37°49'N 23°51'E
Agios Efstratios i. Greece 50 F4....39°30'N 25°01'E
Agios Konstantinos Greece 50 E4....38°45'N 22°51'E
Agios Nikolaos Greece 50 F2....35°11'N 25°43'E
Agirwat Hills Sudan 94 E3....16°26'N 35°03'E
Agra India 96 E6....27°09'N 78°02'E
Ağrı Turkey 94 F7....39°43'N 43°04'E
Agrigento Italy 48 F4....37°18'N 13°35'E
Agrihan i. N. Mariana Is 103 L7....18°46'N 145°42'E
Aguadulce Panama 67 H2....8°12'N 80°33'W
Aguascalientes Mexico 66 D5....21°51'N 102°18'W
Aguascalientes d. Mexico 66 D5....21°57'N 102°11'W
Aguilar de Campóo Spain 45 C5....42°47'N 4°14'W
Águilas Spain 45 E2....37°25'N 1°35'W
Agulhas, Cape S. Africa 83 B1....34°50'S 20°03'E
Ahaggar f. Algeria 84 E4....23°10'N 4°23'E
Ahaus Germany 42 G5....52°05'N 7°01'E
Ahmadabad India 96 D5....23°03'N 72°37'E

Ahmadpur East Pakistan 96 D6....29°10'N 71°22'E
Ahvāz Iran 95 G6....31°15'N 48°40'E
Aigialousa Cyprus 51 K2....35°31'N 34°11'E
Aigina i. Greece 50 E3....37°41'N 23°31'E
Ailsa Craig i. Scotland 14 D3....55°15'N 5°06'W
'Aïn Beïda Algeria 48 E4....35°47'N 7°25'E
'Aïn Ben Tili Mauritania 84 D4....25°58'N 9°31'W
Aïn Sefra Algeria 84 D5....32°42'N 0°35'W
Aïr, Massif de l' mts Niger 84 E3....18°46'N 8°15'E
Airdrie Canada 60 G3....51°17'N 114°01'W
Airdrie Scotland 15 F3....55°52'N 3°58'W
Aisne r. France 44 E6....49°26'N 2°51'E
Aitape P.N.G. 103 K3....3°09'S 142°22'E
Aix-en-Provence France 44 F3....43°32'N 5°27'E
Aizkraukle Latvia 47 K7....56°36'N 25°15'E
Aizu-wakamatsu Japan 104 C3....37°29'N 139°56'E
Ajaccio France 44 H2....41°55'N 8°44'E
Ajdābiyā Libya 85 G5....30°45'N 20°13'E
Akbulak Russia 53 F3....50°59'N 55°36'E
Akçakale Turkey 51 M3....36°43'N 38°57'E
Akdağmadeni Turkey 51 L4....39°39'N 35°54'E
Akhalkalaki Georgia 53 E2....41°25'N 43°29'E
Akhdar, Al Jabal al mts Libya 49 H3....31°46'N 20°46'E
Akhdar, Jabal mts Oman 95 I4....23°22'N 57°00'E
Akhisar Turkey 51 G4....38°55'N 27°50'E
Akhtubinsk Russia 53 E2....48°20'N 46°05'E
Akimiski Island Canada 61 J3....53°08'N 81°17'W
Akita Japan 104 C3....39°43'N 140°07'E
Akkajaure l. Sweden 43 D4....67°41'N 17°29'E
Aknoul Morocco 45 D1....34°38'N 3°51'W
Akpatok Island Canada 61 L4....60°24'N 67°45'W
Akranes Iceland 43 X2....64°19'N 22°05'W
Akron U.S.A. 63 J5....41°07'N 81°33'W
Aksai Chin Asia 96 E8....35°08'N 79°11'E
Aksaray Turkey 51 K4....38°23'N 34°02'E
Aksarka Russia 52 G4....66°31'N 67°51'E
Akşehir Turkey 51 I4....38°21'N 31°24'E
Aksu China 98 E6....41°06'N 80°21'E
Āksum Ethiopia 94 E2....14°07'N 38°46'E
Aktau Kazakhstan 53 F2....43°39'N 51°12'E
Aktobe Kazakhstan 53 F3....50°13'N 57°10'E
Aktogay Kazakhstan 54 I2....47°06'N 79°42'E
Akureyri Iceland 43 Y2....65°41'N 18°07'W
Alabama d. U.S.A. 63 I3....32°41'N 86°42'W
Alabama r. U.S.A. 63 I3....31°09'N 87°57'W
Alagoinhas Brazil 72 F5....12°07'S 38°17'W
Al Ahmadī Kuwait 95 G5....29°04'N 48°02'E
Alakol', Ozero l. Kazakhstan 98 E7....46°03'N 81°30'E
Alakurtti Russia 43 G4....66°58'N 30°20'E
Alamagan i. N. Mariana Is 103 L7....17°35'N 145°52'E
Åland Islands Finland 43 D3....60°28'N 19°53'E
Alanya Turkey 51 J3....36°33'N 32°00'E
Alappuzha India 96 E2....9°30'N 76°21'E
Al 'Aqabah Jordan 94 E5....29°31'N 35°01'E
Al Artāwīyah Saudi Arabia 95 G5....26°30'N 45°21'E
Alaşehir Turkey 51 H4....38°21'N 28°30'E
Alaska d. U.S.A. 60 D4....63°41'N 143°45'W
Alaska, Gulf of U.S.A. 60 D3....58°10'N 147°57'W
Alaska Peninsula U.S.A. 60 C3....55°18'N 162°25'W
Alaska Range mts U.S.A. 60 D4....63°19'N 148°01'W
Alausí Ecuador 72 B6....2°10'S 78°52'W
Alavus Finland 43 E3....62°35'N 23°37'E
Alaw, Llyn resr Wales 10 C5....53°21'N 4°25'W
Albacete Spain 45 E3....39°00'N 1°50'W
Alba Iulia Romania 50 E8....46°05'N 23°36'E
Albania Europe 50 C5....41°56'N 19°34'E
Albany Australia 108 A3....34°58'S 117°54'E
Albany r. Canada 61 J3....52°08'N 81°59'W
Albany U.S.A. 63 L5....42°40'N 73°46'W
Albatross Bay Australia 103 K1....12°41'S 141°44'E
Al Bawītī Egypt 85 G4....28°21'N 28°50'E
Al Baydā' Libya 85 G5....32°44'N 21°44'E
Alberche r. Spain 45 C3....39°58'N 4°46'W
Albert France 42 B2....49°59'N 2°39'E
Albert, Lake Dem. Rep. Congo/Uganda 83 C5
....1°43'N 30°52'E
Alberta d. Canada 60 G3....52°45'N 113°59'W
Albert Lea U.S.A. 63 H5....43°39'N 93°22'W
Albert Nile r. South Sudan/Uganda 85 H2....3°36'N 32°02'E
Albi France 44 E3....43°56'N 2°08'E
Al Biyādh f. Saudi Arabia 95 G4....20°57'N 46°14'E
Alborán, Isla de i. Spain 45 D1....35°57'N 3°02'W
Albuquerque U.S.A. 62 E4....35°07'N 106°38'W
Al Buraymī Oman 95 I4....24°14'N 55°46'E
Albury Australia 108 D3....36°03'S 146°54'E
Alcalá de Henares Spain 45 D4....40°29'N 3°21'W
Alcalá la Real Spain 45 D2....37°28'N 3°55'W
Alcañiz Spain 45 E4....41°03'N 0°07'W
Alcázar de San Juan Spain 45 D3....39°23'N 3°11'W
Alcester England 8 D3....52°13'N 1°52'W
Alcoy-Alcoi Spain 45 E3....38°42'N 0°27'W
Alcúdia Spain 45 G3....39°52'N 3°08'E
Aldabra Islands Seychelles 85 I1....9°16'S 46°30'E
Aldan Russia 55 N3....58°36'N 125°25'E
Aldan r. Russia 55 N4....63°32'N 128°46'E
Aldbrough England 13 G2....53°50'N 0°07'W
Aldeburgh England 9 G3....52°09'N 1°36'E
Alderley Edge England 13 E2....53°18'N 2°14'W
Alderney i. Channel Is 11 Z9....49°42'N 2°15'W
Aldershot England 8 E2....51°15'N 0°45'W
Aldingham England 12 D3....54°08'N 3°06'W
Aldridge England 8 D3....52°36'N 1°55'W
Aleksandrovsk-Sakhalinskiy Russia 55 P3....51°08'N 142°21'E
Aleksin Russia 47 Q6....54°31'N 37°05'E
Alençon France 44 D6....48°26'N 0°06'E
Aleppo Syria 94 E7....36°12'N 37°09'E
Alès France 44 F4....44°08'N 4°05'E
Alessandria Italy 46 C1....44°54'N 8°38'E
Ålesund Norway 43 A3....62°28'N 6°12'E
Aleutian Islands U.S.A. 60 A3....53°03'N 176°15'W
Aleutian Range mts U.S.A. 60 C3....56°10'N 159°17'W
Alexander Archipelago is U.S.A. 60 E3....57°59'N 137°33'W
Alexandra, Cape S. Atlantic Oc. 73 F1....54°05'S 37°56'W
Alexandria Romania 50 F6....43°58'N 25°20'E
Alexandria Scotland 14 E3....55°59'N 4°35'W
Alexandria La. U.S.A. 63 H3....31°17'N 92°28'W
Alexandria Va. U.S.A. 63 K4....38°48'N 77°05'W
Alexandroupoli Greece 50 F5....40°51'N 25°53'E
Aleysk Russia 98 F8....52°30'N 82°51'E
Al Fayyūm Egypt 85 H4....29°18'N 30°51'E
Alford England 13 H2....53°16'N 0°11'E
Alfreton England 13 F2....53°06'N 1°23'W
Algarve f. Portugal 45 A2....37°16'N 8°07'W
Algeciras Spain 45 C2....36°07'N 5°27'W
Algeria Africa 84 E4....30°03'N 3°31'E

Al Ghardaqah Egypt 49 J2....27°12'N 33°48'E
Al Ghaydah Yemen 95 H3....16°14'N 52°13'E
Al Ghwaybiyah Saudi Arabia 95 G5....25°14'N 49°43'E
Algiers Algeria 84 E5....36°46'N 3°04'E
Algorta Spain 45 D5....43°21'N 2°59'W
Al Hasakah Syria 94 F7....36°30'N 40°44'E
Al Hibāk des. Saudi Arabia 95 H3....19°30'N 52°27'E
Al Hoceïma Morocco 48 C4....35°15'N 3°56'W
Al Hufūf Saudi Arabia 95 G5....25°22'N 49°35'E
Aliağa Turkey 50 G4....38°47'N 26°58'E
'Ali 'Addé Djibouti 85 I3....11°08'N 42°53'E
Aliakmonas r. Greece 50 E5....40°28'N 22°38'E
Äli Bayramlı Azerbaijan 95 G7....39°56'N 48°56'E
Alicante Spain 45 E3....38°21'N 0°28'W
Alice Springs town Australia 108 C4....23°42'S 133°52'E
Alingsås Sweden 43 C2....57°56'N 12°33'E
Al Ismā'īlīyah Egypt 49 J3....30°35'N 32°17'E
Al Jaghbūb Libya 85 G4....29°43'N 24°31'E
Al Jahrah Kuwait 95 G5....29°20'N 47°41'E
Al Jawf Libya 85 G4....24°14'N 23°24'E
Al Jawf Saudi Arabia 94 E5....29°47'N 39°55'E
Al Jawsh Libya 48 F3....32°01'N 11°42'E
Al Jubayl Saudi Arabia 95 G5....27°02'N 49°38'E
Aljustrel Portugal 45 A2....37°53'N 8°10'W
Al Karak Jordan 94 E6....31°10'N 35°42'E
Al Khābūrah Oman 95 I4....23°58'N 57°06'E
Al Khārijah Egypt 85 H4....25°24'N 30°33'E
Al Khasab Oman 95 I5....26°11'N 56°14'E
Al Khums Libya 48 F3....32°35'N 14°22'E
Alkmaar Neth. 42 D5....52°38'N 4°45'E
Al Kūt Iraq 95 G6....32°31'N 45°47'E
Allahabad India 96 F6....25°25'N 81°52'E
Allakh-Yun' Russia 55 O4....61°05'N 138°03'E
Allegheny r. U.S.A. 63 K5....40°27'N 79°59'W
Allegheny Mountains U.S.A. 63 J4....36°46'N 82°22'W
Allen, Lough l. Ireland 18 C4....54°09'N 8°03'W
Allendale Town England 13 E3....54°54'N 2°15'W
Allentown U.S.A. 63 K5....40°37'N 75°30'W
Aller r. Germany 46 C5....52°57'N 9°11'E
Al Līth Saudi Arabia 94 F4....20°10'N 40°16'E
Alloa Scotland 15 F4....56°07'N 3°47'W
Almansa Spain 45 E3....38°52'N 1°05'W
Al Mansūrah Egypt 49 J3....31°02'N 31°23'E
Almanzor mt. Spain 45 C4....40°15'N 5°18'W
Al Marj Libya 49 H3....32°29'N 20°50'E
Almaty Kazakhstan 54 I2....43°16'N 77°01'E
Almelo Neth. 42 F5....52°21'N 6°40'E
Almendra, Embalse de resr Spain 45 B4....41°17'N 6°14'W
Almería Spain 45 D2....36°50'N 2°27'W
Al'met'yevsk Russia 53 F3....54°51'N 52°23'E
Almina, Punta pt Spain 45 C1....35°54'N 5°16'W
Almodôvar Portugal 45 A2....37°31'N 8°04'W
Almond r. Scotland 17 F1....56°25'N 3°27'W
Al Mudawwara Jordan 94 E5....29°19'N 36°02'E
Almuñécar Spain 45 D2....36°44'N 3°41'W
Alnwick England 13 F4....55°25'N 1°42'W
Alofi Niue 109 I5....19°03'S 169°54'W
Alor i. Indonesia 103 G2....8°17'S 124°45'E
Alor Setar Malaysia 102 C4....6°08'N 100°22'E
Alpena U.S.A. 63 J6....45°03'N 83°27'W
Alpine U.S.A. 62 F3....30°18'N 103°35'W
Alps mts Europe 48 F6....46°00'N 7°30'E
Al Qa'āmīyāt f. Saudi Arabia 95 G3....17°59'N 47°47'E
Al Qaddāhīyah Libya 48 G3....31°22'N 15°12'E
Al Qāmishlī Syria 94 F7....37°03'N 41°13'E
Al Qaryatayn Syria 51 L2....34°13'N 37°14'E
Al Qunfidhah Saudi Arabia 94 F3....19°09'N 41°04'E
Al Qusayr Egypt 85 H4....26°07'N 34°13'E
Alsager England 13 E2....53°06'N 2°18'W
Alston England 13 E3....54°49'N 2°26'W
Altaelva r. Norway 43 E5....69°57'N 23°20'E
Altai Mountains Asia 98 F7....48°55'N 87°16'E
Altamira Brazil 72 D6....3°14'S 52°14'W
Altay China 98 F7....47°48'N 88°10'E
Altay Mongolia 98 H7....46°18'N 96°15'E
Altiplano f. Bolivia 72 C5....16°24'S 69°39'W
Altiplano Mexicano mts N. America 56 E3
....24°00'N 105°00'W
Alton England 8 E2....51°09'N 0°58'W
Altoona U.S.A. 63 K5....40°30'N 78°24'W
Altötting Germany 46 E3....48°14'N 12°41'E
Altrincham England 13 E2....53°23'N 2°21'W
Altun Shan mts China 98 F5....37°45'N 86°38'E
Alturas U.S.A. 62 B5....41°30'N 120°31'W
Al 'Uqaylah Libya 49 G3....30°13'N 19°12'E
Al 'Uwaynāt Libya 94 B4....21°46'N 24°51'E
Älvdalen Sweden 43 C3....61°13'N 14°04'E
Alveley England 8 C3....52°27'N 2°21'W
Älvsbyn Sweden 43 E4....65°40'N 21°00'E
Al Wajh Saudi Arabia 94 E5....26°17'N 36°25'E
Alwen Reservoir Wales 10 D5....53°05'N 3°35'W
Al Widyān f. Iraq/Saudi Arabia 94 F6....32°09'N 40°22'E
Alyth Scotland 17 F1....56°38'N 3°14'W
Alytus Lithuania 47 K6....54°23'N 24°03'E
Amadeus, Lake Australia 108 C4....24°50'S 131°09'E
Amadjuak Lake Canada 61 K4....64°57'N 71°09'W
Amadora Portugal 45 A3....38°46'N 9°14'W
Åmål Sweden 43 C2....59°03'N 12°44'E
Amamapare Indonesia 103 J3....4°54'S 136°58'E
Amapá Brazil 72 D7....2°02'N 50°50'W
Amarillo U.S.A. 62 F4....35°15'N 101°50'W
Amasya Turkey 51 K5....40°39'N 35°50'E
Amazon r. S. America 72 D7....0°01'N 50°37'W
Amazon, Mouths of the Brazil 72 E7....0°41'N 49°28'W
Ambarchik Russia 55 R4....69°35'N 162°13'E
Ambergate England 13 F2....53°04'N 1°29'W
Ambergris Cay i. Belize 66 G4....18°08'N 87°52'W
Amble England 13 F4....55°20'N 1°35'W
Ambleside England 12 E3....54°26'N 2°58'W
Ambon Indonesia 103 H3....3°43'S 128°11'E
Ambrym i. Vanuatu 109 F5....16°12'S 168°13'E
Ameland i. Neth. 42 E6....53°28'N 5°48'E
American Samoa is S. Pacific Oc. 109 I5....12°00'S 170°00'W
Amersfoort Neth. 42 E5....52°09'N 5°23'E
Amersham England 9 E2....51°41'N 0°36'W
Amesbury England 8 D2....51°10'N 1°47'W
Amfissa Greece 50 E4....38°32'N 22°22'E
Amgun' r. Russia 55 O3....53°01'N 139°38'E
Amiens France 44 E6....49°54'N 2°18'E
Amlwch Wales 10 C5....53°25'N 4°21'W
'Ammān Jordan 94 E6....31°57'N 35°56'E
Ammanford Wales 10 D3....51°48'N 3°59'W
Amol Iran 95 H7....36°27'N 52°20'E
Amorgos i. Greece 50 F3....36°49'N 25°54'E
Amos Canada 61 K2....48°34'N 78°08'W
Ampthill England 9 E3....52°02'N 0°30'W

Amravati India 96 E5....20°56'N 77°51'E
Amritsar India 96 D7....31°34'N 74°56'E
Amstelveen Neth. 42 D5....52°19'N 4°52'E
Amsterdam Neth. 42 D5....52°23'N 4°54'E
Amstetten Austria 46 F3....48°08'N 14°52'E
Amu Darya r. Asia 54 H2....43°50'N 59°00'E
Amund Ringnes Island Canada 61 I5....78°17'N 96°35'W
Amundsen Gulf Canada 60 F5....70°25'N 121°26'W
Amuntai Indonesia 102 F3....2°25'S 115°13'E
Amur r. Russia 55 P3....53°17'N 140°37'E
Anabar r. Russia 55 M5....73°13'N 113°31'E
Anadolu Dağları mts Turkey 51 L5....40°59'N 36°11'E
Anadyr' Russia 55 S4....64°44'N 177°20'E
Anadyrskiy Zaliv b. Russia 55 T4....63°56'N 177°42'W
Anambas, Kepulauan is Indonesia 102 D4....3°17'N 105°55'E
Anamur Turkey 51 J3....36°06'N 32°50'E
Anapa Russia 51 L7....44°54'N 37°20'E
Anápolis Brazil 72 E5....16°20'S 48°55'W
Anatahan i. N. Mariana Is 103 L7....16°21'N 145°42'E
Anatolia f. Turkey 51 J4....38°58'N 33°19'E
Anchorage U.S.A. 60 D4....61°12'N 149°52'W
Ancona Italy 48 F5....43°37'N 13°31'E
Åndalsnes Norway 43 A3....62°34'N 7°42'E
Andalusia f. Spain 45 C2....37°35'N 4°10'W
Andaman Islands India 97 H3....12°46'N 93°17'E
Andaman Sea Indian Oc. 97 I3....11°33'N 95°19'E
Anderlecht Belgium 42 D3....50°49'N 4°18'E
Andermatt Switz. 46 C2....46°38'N 8°36'E
Anderson r. Canada 60 F4....69°41'N 128°56'W
Anderson U.S.A. 63 I4....64°22'N 149°12'W
Andes mts S. America 73 B6....9°10'S 77°03'W
Andfjorden str. Norway 43 D5....68°53'N 16°04'E
Andhra Pradesh d. India 96 E4....16°03'N 79°11'E
Andkhvoy Afgh. 95 K7....36°59'N 65°08'E
Andong S. Korea 104 A3....36°33'N 128°43'E
Andorra Europe 45 F5....42°32'N 1°35'E
Andorra la Vella Andorra 45 F5....42°31'N 1°32'E
Andover England 8 D2....51°12'N 1°29'W
Andøya i. Norway 43 C5....69°11'N 15°48'E
Andreas Isle of Man 12 C3....54°22'N 4°27'W
Andria Italy 49 G5....41°14'N 16°18'E
Andros i. Bahamas 67 I5....24°25'N 78°09'W
Andros i. Greece 50 F3....37°53'N 24°57'E
Andújar Spain 45 C3....38°02'N 4°03'W
Anéfis Mali 84 E3....18°02'N 0°32'E
Anegada i. Virgin Is (U.K.) 67 L4....18°44'N 64°19'W
Aneto mt. Spain 45 F5....42°38'N 0°39'E
Angara r. Russia 55 K3....58°05'N 92°59'E
Angarsk Russia 99 I8....52°24'N 103°45'E
Ånge Sweden 43 C3....62°32'N 15°40'E
Ángel de la Guarda, Isla i. Mexico 66 B6
....29°25'N 113°24'W
Ängelholm Sweden 43 C2....56°15'N 12°52'E
Angers France 44 C5....47°28'N 0°33'W
Anglesey i. Wales 10 C5....53°18'N 4°23'W
Angola Africa 83 A3....11°40'S 17°34'E
Angola Basin f. Atlantic Oc. 117 F2....15°00'S 0°00'E
Angoulême France 44 D4....45°39'N 0°10'E
Angren Uzbekistan 98 C6....41°02'N 70°07'E
Anguilla i. Central America 67 L4....18°14'N 63°02'W
Angus d. Scotland 20 D5....56°43'N 2°55'E
Anhui d. China 99 L4....32°10'N 117°07'E
Ankara Turkey 51 J4....39°56'N 32°50'E
Anlaby England 13 G2....53°45'N 0°26'W
Annaba Algeria 84 E5....36°54'N 7°46'E
An Nabk Syria 51 L2....34°01'N 36°44'E
An Nafūd des. Saudi Arabia 94 F5....28°28'N 41°17'E
'Annah Iraq 94 F6....34°25'N 41°56'E
An Najaf Iraq 94 F6....31°59'N 44°20'E
Annalee r. Ireland 18 D4....54°02'N 7°23'W
Annalong Northern Ireland 14 D2....54°06'N 5°54'W
Annan Scotland 15 F2....54°59'N 3°15'W
Annan r. Scotland 15 F2....54°59'N 3°16'W
Annapolis U.S.A. 63 K4....38°58'N 76°30'W
Annapurna mt. Nepal 96 F6....28°34'N 83°49'E
Ann Arbor U.S.A. 63 J5....42°17'N 83°45'W
An Nāşirīyah Iraq 95 G6....31°01'N 46°14'E
An Nawfalīyah Libya 49 G3....30°51'N 17°52'E
Annecy France 44 G4....45°54'N 6°08'E
Anniston U.S.A. 63 I3....33°39'N 85°43'W
An Nu'ayrīyah Saudi Arabia 95 G5....27°29'N 48°26'E
An Nuşayrīyah, Jabal mts Syria 51 L2....35°15'N 36°05'E
Ansbach Germany 46 D3....49°18'N 10°36'E
Anshan China 99 M6....41°06'N 123°02'E
Anshun China 99 J3....26°15'N 105°57'E
Anstruther Scotland 15 G4....56°13'N 2°42'W
Antakya Turkey 51 L3....36°11'N 36°07'E
Antalya Turkey 51 I3....36°53'N 30°41'E
Antalya Körfezi g. Turkey 51 I3....36°40'N 30°58'E
Antananarivo Madagascar 83 D3....18°54'S 47°33'E
Antarctica 112
Antarctic Peninsula f. Antarctica 116 D1....65°00'S 64°00'W
An Teallach mt. Scotland 16 D2....57°48'N 5°16'W
Antequera Spain 45 C2....37°02'N 4°33'W
Antibes France 44 G3....43°35'N 7°07'E
Anticosti, Île d' i. Canada 61 L2....49°27'N 62°59'W
Antigua i. Antigua 67 L4....17°02'N 61°43'W
Antigua and Barbuda Central America 67 L4
....17°20'N 61°20'W
Antikythira i. Greece 50 E2....35°52'N 23°20'E
Antipodes Islands New Zealand 109 G1....49°39'S 178°44'E
Antofagasta Chile 73 B4....23°37'S 70°22'W
Antrim Northern Ireland 14 C2....54°43'N 6°12'W
Antrim f. Northern Ireland 18 E4....54°59'N 6°22'W
Antrim and Newtownabbey d. Northern Ireland 21 B4
....54°43'N 6°16'W
Antrim Hills Northern Ireland 14 C3....55°05'N 6°16'W
Antsirabe Madagascar 83 D3....19°53'S 47°03'E
Antsirañana Madagascar 83 D3....12°19'S 49°17'E
Antsohihy Madagascar 83 D3....14°53'S 47°59'E
Antwerp Belgium 42 D4....51°12'N 4°26'E
Antwerpen d. Belgium 42 D4....51°12'N 4°26'E
Anyang China 99 K5....36°04'N 114°22'E
Anzhero-Sudzhensk Russia 54 J3....56°08'N 86°01'E
Aomori Japan 104 D4....40°49'N 140°45'E
Aoraki/Mount Cook mt. New Zealand 109 G2
....43°37'S 170°08'E
Apalachee Bay U.S.A. 63 J2....29°59'N 84°06'W
Aparri Phil. 103 G7....18°21'N 121°40'E
Apatity Russia 43 H4....67°34'N 33°23'E
Apeldoorn Neth. 42 E5....52°12'N 5°58'E
Apennines mts Italy 48 F5....43°00'N 13°00'E
Apia Samoa 109 H5....13°50'S 171°44'W
Apostolos Andreas, Cape Cyprus 51 K2....35°41'N 34°35'E
Appalachian Mountains U.S.A. 63 J4....36°08'N 83°01'W
Appleby-in-Westmorland England 13 E3....54°35'N 2°29'W
Appledore England 11 C3....51°03'N 4°12'W

Aqaba, Gulf of Asia 94 D5 ....29°19'N 34°54'E
Arabian Peninsula Asia 85 I4 ....24°00'N 45°00'E
Arabian Sea Indian Oc. 86 E2 ....18°08'N 66°38'E
Aracaju Brazil 72 F5 ....10°52'S 37°03'W
Araçatuba Brazil 73 D4 ....21°12'S 50°22'W
Aracena, Sierra de hills Spain 45 B2 ....37°51'N 7°07'W
Arad Romania 50 D8 ....46°11'N 21°21'E
Arafura Sea Australia/Indonesia 108 C6 ....9°04'S 132°58'E
Aragón Spain 45 E4 ....41°20'N 0°50'W
Aragón r. Spain 45 E5 ....42°13'N 1°45'W
Araguaia r. Brazil 72 E6 ....5°24'S 48°41'W
Araguaína Brazil 72 E6 ....7°20'S 48°15'W
Araguari Brazil 72 E5 ....18°38'S 48°09'W
Arak Algeria 84 E4 ....25°18'N 3°39'E
Arāk Iran 95 G6 ....34°05'N 49°42'E
Arakan Yoma mts Myanmar 97 H5 ....20°18'N 94°07'E
Aral Sea Kazakhstan/Uzbekistan 54 H2 ....45°07'N 60°05'E
Aral'sk Kazakhstan 54 H2 ....46°46'N 61°43'E
Aranda de Duero Spain 45 D4 ....41°41'N 3°40'W
Aran Island Ireland 18 C4 ....54°59'N 8°35'W
Aran Islands Ireland 18 B3 ....53°07'N 9°44'W
Aranjuez Spain 45 D4 ....40°02'N 3°36'W
Arapgir Turkey 51 M4 ....39°02'N 38°29'E
Arapis, Akra pt Greece 50 F5 ....40°27'N 24°00'E
'Ar'ar Saudi Arabia 94 F6 ....30°58'N 40°58'E
Araraquara Brazil 73 E4 ....21°47'S 48°06'W
Ararat, Mount Turkey 53 E1 ....39°45'N 44°15'E
Arbīl/Hewlêr Iraq 94 F7 ....36°11'N 44°01'E
Arboga Sweden 43 C2 ....59°23'N 15°51'E
Arbroath Scotland 15 G4 ....56°34'N 2°35'W
Arbu Lut, Dasht-e des. Afgh. 95 J5 ....29°57'N 63°56'E
Arcachon France 44 C4 ....44°40'N 1°10'W
Archangel Russia 52 E4 ....64°33'N 40°33'E
Arctic Bay town Canada 61 J5 ....72°55'N 85°10'W
Arctic Ocean 112
Arctic Red r. Canada 60 E4 ....67°27'N 133°44'W
Ardabīl Iran 95 G7 ....38°14'N 48°15'E
Ardas r. Greece 50 G5 ....41°40'N 26°30'E
Ardèche r. France 44 F4 ....44°16'N 4°39'E
Ardennes f. Belgium 42 D2 ....49°56'N 4°52'E
Ardestān Iran 95 H6 ....33°20'N 52°21'E
Ardglass Northern Ireland 14 D2 ....54°15'N 5°36'W
Ardila r. Portugal 45 B3 ....38°10'N 7°28'W
Ardnamurchan, Point of Scotland 16 C1 ....56°43'N 6°13'W
Ardrishaig Scotland 14 D4 ....56°01'N 5°27'W
Ardrossan Scotland 14 E3 ....55°39'N 4°49'W
Ards and North Down d. Northern Ireland 21 C4 ....54°28'N 5°37'W
Ards Peninsula Northern Ireland 14 D2 ....54°30'N 5°25'W
Ardvasar Scotland 16 D2 ....57°03'N 5°55'W
Arena, Point U.S.A. 62 B4 ....38°57'N 123°44'W
Arendal Norway 43 B2 ....58°27'N 8°46'E
Arenig Fawr hill Wales 10 D4 ....52°55'N 3°45'W
Arequipa Peru 72 B5 ....16°23'S 71°32'W
Arganda Spain 45 D4 ....40°18'N 3°25'W
Argentan France 44 C6 ....48°45'N 0°01'W
Argentina S. America 73 C3 ....35°00'S 68°00'W
Argentino, Lago l. Argentina 73 B1 ....50°20'S 72°51'W
Argenton-sur-Creuse France 44 D5 ....46°36'N 1°31'E
Argeş r. Romania 50 G7 ....44°04'N 26°37'E
Argun' r. China/Russia 99 M8 ....53°18'N 121°20'E
Argyle, Lake Australia 108 B5 ....16°37'S 128°41'E
Argyll f. Scotland 14 C4 ....56°08'N 5°19'W
Argyll and Bute d. Scotland 20 C4 ....55°46'N 5°25'W
Arica Chile 72 B5 ....18°29'S 70°20'W
Arienas, Loch l. Scotland 16 D4 ....56°35'N 5°46'W
Arinos r. Brazil 72 D5 ....10°25'S 58°13'W
Ariquemes Brazil 72 C5 ....9°59'S 63°05'W
Arisaig Scotland 16 D1 ....56°55'N 5°50'W
Arisaig, Sound of str. Scotland 16 D1 ....56°51'N 5°56'W
Arizona d. U.S.A. 62 D3 ....34°11'N 111°37'W
Arkadelphia U.S.A. 63 H3 ....34°09'N 93°03'W
Arkaig, Loch l. Scotland 16 D1 ....56°58'N 5°13'W
Arkansas d. U.S.A. 63 H4 ....35°49'N 92°00'W
Arkansas r. U.S.A. 63 H3 ....33°49'N 91°08'W
Arkansas City U.S.A. 62 G4 ....37°04'N 97°03'W
Arklow Ireland 18 E2 ....52°48'N 6°10'W
Arkona, Kap c. Germany 46 E6 ....54°41'N 13°27'E
Arles France 44 F3 ....43°41'N 4°38'E
Arlit Niger 84 E3 ....18°42'N 7°21'E
Arlon Belgium 42 E2 ....49°41'N 5°49'E
Armagh Northern Ireland 14 C2 ....54°20'N 6°39'W
Armagh f. Northern Ireland 14 C2 ....54°18'N 6°39'W
Armagh City, Banbridge and Craigavon d. Northern Ireland 21 B4 ....54°19'N 6°39'W
Armant Egypt 49 J2 ....25°37'N 32°32'E
Armavir Russia 53 E2 ....45°01'N 41°06'E
Armenia Asia 53 E2 ....40°26'N 44°30'E
Armenia Colombia 72 B7 ....4°30'N 75°39'W
Armidale Australia 108 E3 ....30°32'S 151°41'E
Armyans'k Ukraine 51 J8 ....46°07'N 33°41'E
Arnhem Neth. 42 E4 ....51°59'N 5°53'E
Arnhem, Cape Australia 108 C5 ....12°19'S 136°58'E
Arnhem Land f. Australia 108 C5 ....13°26'S 133°57'E
Arnsberg Germany 46 C4 ....51°23'N 8°04'E
Ar Ramādī Iraq 94 F6 ....33°23'N 43°16'E
Arran i. Scotland 14 D3 ....55°35'N 5°20'W
Ar Raqqah Syria 94 E7 ....35°57'N 39°01'E
Arras France 44 E7 ....50°17'N 2°46'E
Arrecife Canary Islands 45 Z2 ....28°57'N 13°33'W
Arriagá Mexico 66 F4 ....16°16'N 93°52'W
Arrieta Canary Islands 45 Z2 ....29°08'N 13°28'W
Ar Rimāl f. Saudi Arabia 95 H4 ....21°43'N 52°53'E
Arrochar Scotland 14 E4 ....56°12'N 4°44'W
Ar Ruţbah Iraq 94 F6 ....33°01'N 40°11'E
Arta Greece 50 D4 ....39°10'N 20°59'E
Artesia U.S.A. 62 F3 ....32°52'N 104°25'W
Artois f. France 42 A3 ....50°40'N 1°55'E
Artois, Collines de l' hills France 9 G1 ....50°33'N 1°54'E
Artsyz Ukraine 51 H7 ....45°59'N 29°27'E
Aru, Kepulauan is Indonesia 103 I2 ....6°09'S 134°86'E
Arunachal Pradesh d. India 97 H6 ....27°28'N 92°48'E
Arundel England 9 E1 ....50°51'N 0°33'W
Arusha Tanzania 83 C4 ....3°22'S 36°37'E
Aruwimi r. Dem. Rep. Congo 83 B5 ....1°14'N 23°38'E
Arvayheer Mongolia 99 I7 ....46°08'N 102°47'E
Arviat Canada 61 I4 ....61°12'N 94°09'W
Arvidsjaur Sweden 43 D4 ....65°35'N 19°12'E
Arvika Sweden 43 C2 ....59°39'N 12°37'E
Arzamas Russia 52 E3 ....55°23'N 43°49'E
Asad, Buḩayrat al resr Syria 51 M3 ....36°05'N 38°03'E
Asahi-dake vol. Japan 104 D4 ....43°41'N 142°54'E
Asahikawa Japan 104 D4 ....43°46'N 142°22'E
Asansol India 96 G5 ....23°41'N 87°01'E
Ascension Island Atlantic Oc. 78 B2 ....8°00'S 14°00'W

Åsele Sweden 43 D4 ....64°10'N 17°22'E
Asenovgrad Bulgaria 50 F6 ....42°00'N 24°52'E
Asfordby England 8 E3 ....52°46'N 0°57'W
Ashbourne England 13 F2 ....53°01'N 1°44'W
Ashbourne Ireland 18 E3 ....53°31'N 6°23'W
Ashburton watercourse Australia 108 A4 ....21°43'S 114°54'E
Ashburton England 11 D2 ....50°31'N 3°45'W
Ashby de la Zouch England 8 D3 ....52°45'N 1°28'W
Ashford England 9 F2 ....51°09'N 0°53'E
Ashgabat Turkmenistan 54 G1 ....37°53'N 58°21'E
Ashington England 13 F4 ....55°11'N 1°34'W
Ashland U.S.A. 63 H6 ....46°35'N 90°53'W
Ashmore and Cartier Islands Australia 108 B5 ....12°38'S 122°40'E
Ash Shiḩr Yemen 95 G2 ....14°49'N 49°45'E
Ashton-under-Lyne England 13 E2 ....53°30'N 2°06'W
Asia 86
Asipovichy Belarus 47 M5 ....53°18'N 28°38'E
'Asīr f. Saudi Arabia 94 F4 ....20°53'N 40°14'E
Askern England 13 F2 ....53°37'N 1°09'W
Askim Norway 43 B2 ....59°35'N 11°10'E
Asmara Eritrea 85 H3 ....15°20'N 38°56'E
Asnen l. Sweden 43 C2 ....56°37'N 14°50'E
Aspang-Markt Austria 46 G2 ....47°33'N 16°05'E
Aspatria England 12 D3 ....54°46'N 3°20'W
Aspen U.S.A. 62 E4 ....39°11'N 106°49'W
Assab Eritrea 85 I3 ....12°59'N 42°43'E
As Samāwah Iraq 94 G6 ....31°15'N 45°19'E
As Sarīr f. Libya 49 H2 ....27°02'N 21°36'E
Assen Neth. 42 E5 ....53°00'N 6°33'E
As Sidrah Libya 49 G3 ....30°38'N 18°18'E
Assilah Morocco 45 B1 ....35°28'N 6°02'W
Assiniboine, Mount Canada 60 G3 ....50°57'N 115°34'W
As Sulaymānīyah/Slêmanî Iraq 95 G7 ....35°33'N 45°26'E
Assumption i. Seychelles 83 D4 ....9°30'S 47°20'E
As Sūq Saudi Arabia 94 F4 ....21°57'N 41°59'E
Assynt, Loch l. Scotland 16 D3 ....58°11'N 5°05'W
Astana Kazakhstan 54 I3 ....51°09'N 71°27'E
Astārā Iran 95 G7 ....38°27'N 48°52'E
Asti Italy 46 C1 ....44°54'N 8°13'E
Astorga Spain 45 B5 ....42°28'N 6°03'W
Astoria U.S.A. 62 B6 ....46°08'N 123°46'W
Astove i. Seychelles 83 D4 ....10°05'S 47°40'E
Astrakhan' Russia 53 E2 ....46°20'N 48°03'E
Asunción i. N. Mariana Is 103 L7 ....19°40'N 145°25'E
Asunción Paraguay 73 D4 ....25°16'S 57°39'W
Aswān Egypt 85 H4 ....24°02'N 32°56'E
Asyūţ Egypt 85 H4 ....27°07'N 31°08'E
Atacama Desert Chile 73 C4 ....26°13'S 69°39'W
Atafu i. Tokelau 109 H6 ....8°33'S 172°30'W
Atâr Mauritania 84 C3 ....20°32'N 13°03'W
Atasu Kazakhstan 54 I2 ....48°42'N 71°37'E
Atatürk Baraji resr Turkey 51 M3 ....37°28'N 38°26'E
Atbara Sudan 85 H3 ....17°43'N 33°55'E
Atbara r. Sudan 85 H3 ....17°40'N 33°58'E
Ath Belgium 42 C3 ....50°38'N 3°47'E
Athabasca r. Canada 60 G3 ....58°28'N 111°09'W
Athabasca, Lake Canada 60 H3 ....59°17'N 109°24'W
Athboy Ireland 18 E3 ....53°37'N 6°55'W
Athenry Ireland 18 C3 ....53°18'N 8°45'W
Athens Greece 50 E3 ....37°59'N 23°43'E
Atherstone England 8 D3 ....52°35'N 1°33'W
Atherton England 13 E2 ....53°31'N 2°29'W
Athlone Ireland 18 D3 ....53°25'N 7°57'W
Atholl, Forest of Scotland 17 E1 ....56°51'N 4°10'W
Athos mt. Greece 50 F5 ....40°10'N 24°19'E
Athy Ireland 18 E2 ....52°59'N 6°59'W
Ati Chad 85 F3 ....13°14'N 18°20'E
Atikokan Canada 63 H6 ....48°45'N 91°37'W
Atlanta U.S.A. 63 J3 ....33°46'N 84°22'W
Atlantic City U.S.A. 63 L4 ....39°21'N 74°26'W
Atlantic Ocean 116 D3
Atlas Mountains Africa 84 D5 ....30°13'N 7°41'W
Atlas Saharien mts Algeria 84 E5 ....32°41'N 0°20'E
Aţ Ţā'if Saudi Arabia 94 F4 ....21°15'N 40°20'E
Attleborough England 9 G3 ....52°31'N 1°01'E
Atyrau Kazakhstan 53 F2 ....47°08'N 51°56'E
Aube r. France 44 E6 ....48°34'N 3°43'E
Auchterarder Scotland 15 F4 ....56°18'N 3°42'W
Auchtermuchty Scotland 15 F4 ....56°18'N 3°14'W
Auckland New Zealand 109 G3 ....36°52'S 174°46'E
Auckland Islands New Zealand 109 F1 ....50°43'S 166°12'E
Auderville France 11 Z9 ....49°43'N 1°55'W
Audlem England 8 C3 ....52°59'N 2°31'W
Audruicq France 9 H1 ....50°52'N 2°05'E
Augher Northern Ireland 14 B2 ....54°25'N 7°08'W
Aughton England 13 F2 ....53°22'N 1°19'W
Augsburg Germany 46 D3 ....48°22'N 10°52'E
Augusta Australia 108 A3 ....34°19'S 115°09'E
Augusta Ga. U.S.A. 63 J3 ....33°28'N 82°02'W
Augusta Me. U.S.A. 63 M5 ....44°19'N 69°46'W
Aulnoye-Aymeries France 42 C3 ....50°12'N 3°51'E
Aurangabad India 96 E4 ....19°53'N 75°24'E
Aurich Germany 42 G6 ....53°28'N 7°30'E
Aurora U.S.A. 62 F4 ....39°43'N 104°53'W
Auskerry i. Scotland 17 G4 ....59°02'N 2°33'W
Austin U.S.A. 62 G3 ....30°16'N 97°42'W
Australia Oceania 108 B4 ....27°17'S 129°18'E
Australian Capital Territory d. Australia 108 D3 ....35°27'S 148°52'E
Austria Europe 46 E2 ....47°12'N 13°26'E
Authie r. France 9 G1 ....50°22'N 1°37'E
Auvergne, Monts d' mts France 44 E4 ....45°45'N 2°59'E
Auxerre France 44 E5 ....47°48'N 3°35'E
Avallon France 44 E5 ....47°30'N 3°54'E
Avanos Turkey 51 K4 ....38°43'N 34°51'E
Aveiro Portugal 45 A4 ....40°39'N 8°38'W
Avesta Sweden 43 D3 ....60°09'N 16°10'E
Aveyron r. France 44 D4 ....44°05'N 1°16'E
Aviemore Scotland 17 F2 ....57°12'N 3°49'W
Avignon France 44 F3 ....43°57'N 4°49'E
Ávila Spain 45 C4 ....40°40'N 4°41'W
Avilés Spain 45 C5 ....43°33'N 5°54'W
Avon r. Brist. England 8 C2 ....51°29'N 2°40'W
Avon r. Dor. England 8 D1 ....50°44'N 1°46'W
Avon r. Glos. England 8 C3 ....52°00'N 2°10'W
Avon r. Scotland 17 F2 ....57°25'N 3°22'W
Avonmore r. Ireland 10 A4 ....52°48'N 6°08'W
Avonmouth England 8 C2 ....51°30'N 2°42'W
Awash Ethiopia 85 I2 ....8°59'N 40°10'E
Awbārī Libya 84 F4 ....26°34'N 12°46'E
Awbārī, Idhān des. Libya 48 F2 ....27°23'N 10°25'E
Awe, Loch l. Scotland 14 D4 ....56°19'N 5°14'W
Axe r. England 11 D2 ....50°43'N 3°04'W
Axel Heiberg Island Canada 61 I5 ....79°47'N 91°17'W
Axminster England 8 C1 ....50°47'N 2°59'W
Ayacucho Peru 72 B5 ....13°10'S 74°13'W
Ayagoz Kazakhstan 54 J2 ....47°56'N 80°23'E

Ayan Russia 55 O3 ....56°26'N 138°12'E
Aydarko'l ko'li l. Uzbekistan 54 H2 ....41°02'N 66°33'E
Aydın Turkey 51 G3 ....37°50'N 27°49'E
Aylesbury England 8 E2 ....51°49'N 0°48'W
Aylesham England 9 G2 ....51°14'N 1°12'E
Aylsham England 9 G3 ....52°48'N 1°15'E
Ayr Scotland 14 E3 ....55°28'N 4°38'W
Ayr r. Scotland 14 E3 ....55°28'N 4°38'W
Ayre, Point of Isle of Man 12 C3 ....54°25'N 4°22'W
Ayvalık Turkey 50 G4 ....39°17'N 26°41'E
Azawad f. Mali 84 D4 ....20°20'N 3°00'W
Azerbaijan Asia 53 E2 ....40°23'N 48°09'E
Azopol'ye Russia 52 E4 ....65°18'N 45°11'E
Azores is Portugal 116 E3 ....37°45'N 25°40'W
Azov, Sea of Russia/Ukraine 53 D2 ....46°03'N 36°47'E
Azrou Morocco 48 B3 ....33°26'N 5°11'W
Azuero, Península de pen. Panama 67 H2 ....7°39'N 80°41'W
Azul, Cordillera mts Peru 72 B6 ....8°31'S 75°56'W
Az Zaqāzīq Egypt 49 J3 ....30°35'N 31°30'E
Az Zarqā' Jordan 94 E6 ....32°04'N 36°05'E

B

Baardheere Somalia 85 I2 ....2°19'N 42°18'E
Bābā, Kūh-e mts Afgh. 95 K6 ....34°48'N 68°27'E
Babadag Romania 51 H7 ....44°54'N 28°42'E
Babaeski Turkey 50 G5 ....41°26'N 27°06'E
Bāb al Mandab str. Africa/Asia 94 F2 ....12°21'N 43°26'E
Babar i. Indonesia 103 H2 ....7°57'S 129°51'E
Babbacombe Bay England 11 D2 ....50°31'N 3°28'W
Babia Góra mt. Poland 46 H3 ....49°35'N 19°32'E
Babo Indonesia 103 I3 ....2°35'S 133°21'E
Babruysk Belarus 47 M5 ....53°09'N 29°14'E
Bab-Termas hill Morocco 45 D1 ....34°29'N 3°53'W
Babuyan Islands Phil. 103 G7 ....19°13'N 121°59'E
Bacabal Brazil 72 E6 ....4°16'S 44°47'W
Bacan i. Indonesia 103 H3 ....0°44'S 127°35'E
Bacău Romania 47 L2 ....46°34'N 26°55'E
Back r. Canada 61 I4 ....66°32'N 95°51'W
Backwater Reservoir Scotland 17 F1 ....56°44'N 3°13'W
Bacolod Phil. 103 G6 ....10°37'N 122°57'E
Bac Liêu Vietnam 102 D5 ....9°15'N 105°45'E
Badajoz Spain 45 B3 ....38°53'N 6°57'W
Baden Austria 46 G3 ....48°00'N 16°15'E
Baden-Baden Germany 46 C3 ....48°45'N 8°15'E
Bad Neuenahr-Ahrweiler Germany 42 G3 ....50°33'N 7°07'E
Badulla Sri Lanka 96 F2 ....7°00'N 81°01'E
Baffin Bay sea Canada/Greenland 61 L5 ....72°51'N 66°20'W
Baffin Island Canada 61 L4 ....64°57'N 68°47'W
Bafoussam Cameroon 84 F2 ....5°28'N 10°26'E
Bāfq Iran 95 I6 ....31°34'N 55°21'E
Bafra Turkey 51 K5 ....41°34'N 35°55'E
Bāft Iran 95 I5 ....29°14'N 56°36'E
Bagé Brazil 73 D3 ....31°20'S 54°06'W
Baggy Point England 11 C3 ....51°08'N 4°16'W
Baghdād Iraq 94 F6 ....33°18'N 44°22'E
Baghlān Afgh. 95 K7 ....36°11'N 68°47'E
Bago Myanmar 97 I4 ....17°18'N 96°28'E
Bahariya Oasis Egypt 94 C5 ....27°56'N 28°51'E
Bahawalpur Pakistan 96 D6 ....29°23'N 71°45'E
Bahía, Islas de la i. Honduras 67 G4 ....16°13'N 86°56'W
Bahía Blanca Argentina 73 C3 ....38°43'S 62°18'W
Bahrain Asia 95 H5 ....26°29'N 50°51'E
Baia Mare Romania 47 J2 ....47°39'N 23°35'E
Baicheng China 99 M7 ....45°29'N 122°50'E
Baie-Comeau Canada 61 L2 ....49°13'N 68°10'W
Baikal, Lake Russia 55 L3 ....52°37'N 107°12'E
Bailieborough Ireland 18 E3 ....53°55'N 6°58'W
Bain r. England 13 G2 ....53°05'N 0°12'W
Bainbridge U.S.A. 63 J3 ....30°54'N 84°40'W
Bairnsdale Australia 108 D3 ....37°51'S 147°37'E
Baise China 99 J2 ....23°54'N 106°37'E
Baiyuda Desert Sudan 94 D3 ....18°03'N 32°59'E
Baja Hungary 46 H2 ....46°12'N 18°57'E
Baja California d. Mexico 66 B6 ....29°49'N 115°07'W
Baja California pen. Mexico 66 B6 ....30°40'N 115°41'W
Baja California Sur d. Mexico 66 B6 ....25°19'N 112°09'W
Baker, Mount vol. U.S.A. 62 B6 ....48°46'N 121°47'W
Baker Lake Canada 61 I4 ....64°09'N 95°23'W
Bakersfield U.S.A. 62 C4 ....35°22'N 118°59'W
Bakharden Turkmenistan 95 I7 ....38°27'N 57°24'E
Bakhtegan, Daryācheh-ye l. Iran 95 H5 ....29°18'N 53°52'E
Bakırköy Turkey 51 H5 ....40°58'N 28°51'E
Baku Azerbaijan 53 E2 ....40°22'N 49°50'E
Bala England 10 D4 ....52°55'N 3°36'W
Bala, Cerros de mts Bolivia 72 C5 ....13°49'S 68°25'W
Balabac Strait Malaysia/Phil. 102 F5 ....7°36'N 116°45'E
Balakovo Russia 53 E3 ....52°00'N 47°47'E
Bala Lake Wales 10 D4 ....52°52'N 3°39'W
Bālā Morghāb Afgh. 95 J7 ....35°35'N 63°21'E
Balashikha Russia 47 Q6 ....55°49'N 37°57'E
Balashov Russia 53 E3 ....51°32'N 43°09'E
Balaton, Lake Hungary 46 G2 ....46°46'N 17°32'E
Balbina, Represa de resr Brazil 72 D6 ....1°34'S 59°27'W
Balbriggan Ireland 18 E3 ....53°36'N 6°11'W
Baldock England 9 E2 ....51°59'N 0°11'W
Baldy Peak U.S.A. 62 E3 ....33°54'N 109°34'W
Balearic Islands Spain 45 F3 ....39°28'N 1°30'E
Balearic Sea Europe 45 F3 ....40°30'N 2°00'E
Baleine, Rivière à la r. Canada 61 L3 ....57°57'N 67°37'W
Baleshwar India 96 G5 ....21°30'N 86°56'E
Bali i. Indonesia 102 E2 ....8°41'S 114°55'E
Balige Indonesia 102 B4 ....2°20'N 99°03'E
Balıkesir Turkey 51 G4 ....39°38'N 27°52'E
Balīkh r. Syria/Turkey 51 M2 ....35°56'N 39°03'E
Balikpapan Indonesia 102 F3 ....1°12'S 116°49'E
Balimo P.N.G. 103 K2 ....7°59'S 142°57'E
Balintore Scotland 17 F2 ....57°45'N 3°54'W
Bali Sea Indonesia 102 E2 ....7°31'S 114°31'E
Balivanich Scotland 16 B2 ....57°28'N 7°22'W
Balkan Mountains Bulgaria/Serbia 50 E6 ....43°23'N 22°47'E
Balkhash Kazakhstan 54 I2 ....46°50'N 74°59'E
Balkhash, Lake Kazakhstan 54 I2 ....45°30'N 73°51'E
Ballaghan Point Ireland 14 C1 ....53°59'N 6°06'W
Ballantrae Scotland 14 D3 ....55°06'N 5°00'W
Ballarat Australia 108 D3 ....37°35'S 143°52'E
Ballari India 96 E4 ....15°10'N 76°53'E
Ballater Scotland 17 F2 ....57°03'N 3°02'W
Ballena, Punta pt Chile 73 B4 ....25°47'S 70°47'W
Ballina Ireland 18 C4 ....54°07'N 9°10'W
Ballinasloe Ireland 18 C3 ....53°20'N 8°13'W
Ballybay Ireland 14 C2 ....54°07'N 6°54'W
Ballybunnion Ireland 18 B2 ....52°31'N 9°40'W

Ballycastle Northern Ireland 14 C3 ....55°12'N 6°14'W
Ballyclare Northern Ireland 14 D2 ....54°45'N 5°59'W
Ballygawley Northern Ireland 14 B2 ....54°27'N 7°02'W
Ballyhaunis Ireland 18 C3 ....53°46'N 8°46'W
Ballymena Northern Ireland 14 C2 ....54°52'N 6°16'W
Ballymoney Northern Ireland 14 C3 ....55°04'N 6°31'W
Ballynahinch Northern Ireland 14 D2 ....54°24'N 5°53'W
Ballyquintin Point Northern Ireland 14 D2 ....54°19'N 5°29'W
Ballyshannon Ireland 18 C4 ....54°30'N 8°12'W
Balochistan f. Pakistan 96 B6 ....27°30'N 63°81'E
Balsas r. Mexico 66 D4 ....17°57'N 102°09'W
Balta Ukraine 47 M2 ....47°56'N 29°37'E
Baltasound Scotland 17 I5 ....60°46'N 0°52'W
Bălţi Moldova 49 I6 ....47°47'N 27°56'E
Baltic Sea g. Europe 43 D1 ....58°28'N 16°46'E
Baltimore U.S.A. 63 K4 ....39°17'N 76°37'W
Baltiysk Russia 46 H6 ....54°39'N 19°53'E
Balykshi Kazakhstan 53 F2 ....47°03'N 51°53'E
Bam Iran 95 I5 ....29°07'N 58°22'E
Bamaga Australia 108 D5 ....10°53'S 142°23'E
Bamako Mali 84 D3 ....12°38'N 7°59'W
Bamberg Germany 46 D3 ....49°54'N 10°53'E
Bambili Dem. Rep. Congo 83 B5 ....3°38'N 26°07'E
Bambouti C.A.R. 85 G2 ....5°22'N 27°12'E
Bāmiān Afgh. 95 K6 ....34°52'N 67°49'E
Bampton Dev. England 11 D2 ....50°59'N 3°29'W
Bampton Oxon. England 8 D2 ....51°43'N 1°33'W
Bañados del Izozog f. Bolivia 72 C5 ....18°20'S 61°45'W
Banagher Ireland 18 D3 ....53°11'N 7°59'W
Banaz Turkey 51 H4 ....38°44'N 29°44'E
Banbridge Northern Ireland 14 C2 ....54°21'N 6°16'W
Banbury England 8 D3 ....52°04'N 1°20'W
Banchory Scotland 17 G2 ....57°03'N 2°29'W
Banda, Kepulauan is Indonesia 103 H3 ....4°33'S 129°53'E
Banda Aceh Indonesia 102 B5 ....5°30'N 95°18'E
Bandar-e 'Abbās Iran 95 I5 ....27°11'N 56°18'E
Bandar-e Anzalī Iran 95 G7 ....37°28'N 49°26'E
Bandar-e Būshehr Iran 95 H5 ....28°58'N 50°51'E
Bandar-e Jāsk Iran 95 I5 ....25°40'N 57°47'E
Bandar-e Kangān Iran 95 H5 ....27°50'N 52°05'E
Bandar-e Lengeh Iran 95 H5 ....26°34'N 54°53'E
Bandar-e Torkeman Iran 95 H7 ....36°54'N 53°59'E
Bandar Lampung Indonesia 102 D2 ....5°27'S 105°17'E
Bandar Seri Begawan Brunei 102 E4 ....4°57'N 114°58'E
Banda Sea Indonesia 103 I2 ....5°40'S 130°07'E
Bandırma Turkey 51 G5 ....40°21'N 27°57'E
Bandon Ireland 18 C1 ....51°45'N 8°44'W
Bandon r. Ireland 18 C1 ....51°45'N 8°38'W
Bandundu Dem. Rep. Congo 83 A4 ....3°17'S 17°23'E
Bandung Indonesia 102 D2 ....6°56'S 107°35'E
Banff Canada 60 G3 ....51°11'N 115°35'W
Banff Scotland 17 G2 ....57°40'N 2°31'W
Bangassou C.A.R. 85 G2 ....4°44'N 22°50'E
Banggai, Kepulauan is Indonesia 103 G3 ....1°59'S 123°27'E
Bangka i. Indonesia 102 D3 ....2°07'S 106°17'E
Bangkok Thailand 102 C6 ....13°44'N 100°33'E
Bangladesh Asia 97 H5 ....23°47'N 89°49'E
Bangor Northern Ireland 14 D2 ....54°39'N 5°40'W
Bangor U.S.A. 63 M5 ....44°48'N 68°47'W
Bangor Wales 10 C5 ....53°14'N 4°08'W
Bangui C.A.R. 85 F2 ....4°20'N 18°33'E
Bangweulu, Lake Zambia 83 B3 ....11°13'S 29°39'E
Bani r. Mali 84 D3 ....14°30'N 4°13'E
Banī Mazār Egypt 49 J2 ....28°29'N 30°49'E
Banī Suwayf Egypt 49 J2 ....29°05'N 31°06'E
Banī Walīd Libya 48 F3 ....31°47'N 14°00'E
Bāniyās Syria 51 K2 ....35°11'N 35°57'E
Banja Luka Bos. and Herz. 50 B7 ....44°46'N 17°12'E
Banjarmasin Indonesia 102 E3 ....3°23'S 114°33'E
Banjul Gambia 84 C3 ....13°27'N 16°36'W
Banks Island Canada 60 F5 ....73°06'N 121°26'W
Banks Islands Vanuatu 109 F5 ....13°55'S 167°13'E
Banmi Pakistan 95 L6 ....33°00'N 70°40'E
Bann r. England 13 G2 ....52°33'N 6°33'W
Bann r. Northern Ireland 14 A4 ....55°09'N 6°42'W
Ban Tha Song Yang Thailand 102 B7 ....17°34'N 97°56'E
Bantry Ireland 18 B1 ....51°41'N 9°27'W
Bantry Bay Ireland 18 B1 ....51°34'N 9°53'W
Baoding China 99 L5 ....38°46'N 115°34'E
Baoji China 99 J4 ....34°21'N 107°08'E
Baoshan China 99 H3 ....25°07'N 99°05'E
Baotou China 99 K6 ....40°31'N 110°08'E
Ba'qūbah Iraq 94 F6 ....33°42'N 44°38'E
Bar Montenegro 50 C6 ....42°05'N 19°05'E
Bara Sudan 94 D2 ....13°40'N 30°21'E
Baracoa Cuba 67 J5 ....20°21'N 74°29'W
Baranavichy Belarus 47 L5 ....53°08'N 26°02'E
Baranīs Egypt 49 K1 ....23°53'N 35°27'E
Barbacena Brazil 73 E4 ....21°13'S 43°45'W
Barbados Central America 67 M3 ....13°09'N 59°25'W
Barbuda i. Antigua 67 L4 ....17°39'N 61°47'W
Barcaldine Australia 108 D4 ....23°32'S 145°19'E
Barcelona Spain 45 G4 ....41°25'N 2°12'E
Barcelona Venezuela 72 C8 ....10°06'N 64°41'W
Bárðarbunga mt. Iceland 43 Y2 ....64°38'N 17°32'W
Bardney England 13 G2 ....53°13'N 0°19'W
Bardsey Island Wales 10 C4 ....52°45'N 4°46'W
Bardsey Sound str. Wales 10 C4 ....52°47'N 4°48'W
Bareilly India 96 E6 ....28°22'N 79°27'E
Barentsburg Arctic Oc. 54 C5 ....77°49'N 14°20'E
Barents Sea Arctic Oc. 54 F5 ....75°18'N 42°14'E
Barham England 9 G2 ....51°12'N 1°10'E
Bari Italy 49 G5 ....41°07'N 16°52'E
Barinas Venezuela 72 B7 ....8°34'N 70°11'W
Barisan, Pegunungan mts Indonesia 102 C3 ....1°12'S 100°37'E
Barkly Tableland f. Australia 108 C5 ....18°06'S 135°52'E
Bârlad Romania 50 G8 ....46°13'N 27°39'E
Barlee, Lake Australia 108 A4 ....28°58'S 119°40'E
Barmer India 96 D6 ....25°44'N 71°26'E
Barmouth Wales 10 C4 ....52°43'N 4°03'W
Barmouth Bay Wales 10 C4 ....52°43'N 4°10'W
Barnard Castle England 13 F3 ....54°33'N 1°55'W
Barnaul Russia 54 J3 ....53°22'N 83°49'E
Barnet England 9 E2 ....51°39'N 0°12'W
Barnoldswick England 13 E2 ....53°55'N 2°11'W
Barnsley England 13 F2 ....53°34'N 1°28'W
Barnstaple England 11 C3 ....51°05'N 4°03'W
Barnstaple or Bideford Bay England 11 C3 ....51°05'N 4°23'W
Barquisimeto Venezuela 72 C8 ....10°03'N 69°15'W
Barra i. Scotland 16 B1 ....56°59'N 7°30'W
Barra, Sound of str. Scotland 16 B2 ....57°04'N 7°27'W
Barranquilla Colombia 72 B8 ....10°59'N 74°51'W
Barretos Brazil 73 E4 ....20°35'S 48°34'W
Barrhead Scotland 14 E3 ....55°48'N 4°24'W
Barrow r. Ireland 18 E2 ....52°23'N 6°57'W

arrow, Point U.S.A. 60 C5 ....71°23'N 156°22'W
arrow-in-Furness England 12 D3 ....54°07'N 3°13'W
arrow Island Australia 108 A4 ....20°49'S 115°22'E
arry Wales 11 B3 ....51°24'N 3°17'W
arstow U.S.A. 62 C3 ....34°54'N 117°01'W
artın Turkey 51 J5 ....41°38'N 32°21'E
arton-upon-Humber England 13 G2 ......53°41'N 0°27'W
artoszyce Poland 46 I6 ....54°15'N 20°49'E
aruun-Urt Mongolia 99 K7 ....46°31'N 113°22'E
arysaw Belarus 47 M6 ....54°14'N 28°31'E
aschurch England 8 C3 ....52°47'N 2°51'W
asel Switz. 46 B2 ....47°33'N 7°35'E
asilan i. Phil. 103 G5 ....6°32'N 121°52'E
asildon England 9 F2 ....51°35'N 0°29'E
asingstoke England 8 D2 ....51°16'N 1°06'W
asra Iraq 95 G6 ....30°29'N 47°48'E
assenthwaite Lake England 12 D3 ......54°40'N 3°14'W
asse-Terre Guadeloupe 67 L4 ....16°01'N 61°44'W
ass Rock i. Scotland 15 G4 ....56°05'N 2°38'W
ass Strait Australia 108 D3 ....39°43'S 146°11'E
astak Iran 95 H5 ....27°12'N 54°21'E
astia France 44 H3 ....42°42'N 9°27'E
astogne Belgium 42 E3 ....50°00'N 5°43'E
ata Equat. Guinea 84 E2 ....1°50'N 9°48'E
atabanó, Golfo de b. Cuba 67 H5 ......22°16'N 82°38'W
atang China 99 H4 ....30°01'N 99°08'E
atang Indonesia 102 C2 ....1°09'N 104°01'E
atang Indonesia 97 I6 ....6°57'S 109°43'E
atangas Phil. 103 G6 ....13°46'N 121°01'E
atan Islands Phil. 103 G8 ....20°46'N 122°05'E
atdâmbâng Cambodia 102 C6 ....13°06'N 103°14'E
ath and North East Somerset d. England 21 D2 ....51°21'N 2°28'W
athgate Scotland 15 F3 ....55°54'N 3°39'W
athurst Australia 108 D3 ....33°25'S 149°34'E
athurst Canada 61 L2 ....47°36'N 65°39'W
athurst Inlet Canada 60 H4 ....66°50'N 108°10'W
athurst Island Australia 108 C5 ......11°29'S 130°11'E
athurst Island Canada 61 I5 ....75°49'N 98°59'W
atley England 13 F2 ....53°43'N 1°38'W
atna Algeria 84 E5 ....35°32'N 6°13'E
aton Rouge U.S.A. 63 H3 ....30°27'N 91°11'W
atticaloa Sri Lanka 96 F2 ....7°42'N 81°39'E
attle England 9 F1 ....50°55'N 0°29'E
atu, Pulau-pulau is Indonesia 102 B3 ....0°14'S 98°16'E
ayamo Cuba 67 I5 ....20°22'N 76°38'W
ayanhongor Mongolia 99 I7 ....46°09'N 100°41'E
ayan-Uul Mongolia 99 K7 ....48°55'N 112°44'E
ayburt Turkey 51 N5 ....40°15'N 40°14'E
ay City Mich. U.S.A. 63 J5 ....43°35'N 83°53'W
ay City Tex. U.S.A. 63 G2 ....28°59'N 96°02'W
aydaratskaya Guba Russia 52 G4 ....69°29'N 66°01'E
aymak Russia 53 I3 ....52°31'N 58°15'E
ayonne France 44 C3 ....43°29'N 1°29'W
ayreuth Germany 46 D3 ....49°56'N 11°36'E
ayy al Kabīr, Wādī watercourse Libya 48 G3 ....31°11'N 15°53'E
aza Spain 45 D2 ....37°30'N 2°46'W
azardyuzyu, Gora mt. Azerbaijan 53 E2 ....41°12'N 47°52'E
eachy Head England 9 F1 ....50°44'N 0°15'E
eaconsfield England 8 E2 ....51°36'N 0°39'W
eagle Gulf Australia 103 H1 ....12°04'S 129°55'E
eaminster England 8 C1 ....50°49'N 2°45'W
eardmore Canada 63 I6 ....49°36'N 87°58'W
eata, Cabo c. Dom. Rep. 67 J4 ....17°38'N 71°23'W
eata, Isla i. Dom. Rep. 67 J4 ....17°36'N 71°30'W
eaufort Sea Canada/U.S.A. 60 F5 ......73°19'N 129°52'W
eaufort West S. Africa 83 B1 ....32°20'S 22°36'E
eauly Scotland 17 E2 ....57°29'N 4°28'W
eauly r. Scotland 17 E2 ....57°29'N 4°27'W
eauly Firth est. Scotland 17 E2 ......57°29'N 4°23'W
eaumaris Wales 10 C5 ....53°16'N 4°05'W
eaumont France 11 Z9 ....49°40'N 1°50'W
eaumont U.S.A. 63 H3 ....30°05'N 94°09'W
eaune France 44 F5 ....47°01'N 4°50'E
eauvais France 44 E6 ....49°26'N 2°05'E
eaver r. Canada 60 H3 ....55°22'N 107°45'W
eaver Creek town Canada 60 D4 ....62°23'N 140°49'W
ebington England 12 D2 ....53°21'N 3°00'W
eccles England 9 G3 ....52°28'N 1°34'E
ecerreá Spain 45 B5 ....42°51'N 7°09'W
echar Algeria 84 D5 ....31°36'N 2°13'W
eckingham England 13 G2 ....53°24'N 0°49'W
ckley U.S.A. 63 J4 ....37°47'N 81°11'W
dale England 13 F3 ....54°17'N 1°35'W
edelé Ethiopia 85 H2 ....8°28'N 36°21'E
edford England 9 E3 ....52°08'N 0°28'W
edford d. England 21 E3 ....52°10'N 0°28'W
edlington England 13 F4 ....55°08'N 1°36'W
edworth England 8 D3 ....52°29'N 1°28'W
ersheba Israel 49 J3 ....31°15'N 34°48'E
eville U.S.A. 62 G2 ....28°25'N 97°45'W
eg, Lough l. Northern Ireland 14 C2 ....54°47'N 6°27'W
i'an China 99 N7 ....48°11'N 126°31'E
ihai China 99 J2 ....21°27'N 109°08'E
ijing China 99 L5 ....39°52'N 116°27'E
inn an Oir hill Scotland 14 D3 ....55°54'N 5°59'W
inn Dearg mt. High. Scotland 16 E2 ...57°47'N 4°56'W
inn Dearg mt. P. and K. Scotland 17 F1 ....56°53'N 3°53'W
inn Heasgarnich mt. Scotland 14 E4 ...56°31'N 4°35'W
ira Mozambique 83 C3 ....19°50'S 34°52'E
ith Scotland 14 E3 ....55°45'N 4°38'W
ius Romania 47 J2 ....46°40'N 22°23'E
ja Portugal 45 B3 ....38°01'N 7°52'W
jaïa Algeria 84 E5 ....36°44'N 5°03'E
jar Spain 45 C4 ....40°24'N 5°46'W
késcsaba Hungary 46 I2 ....46°41'N 21°05'E
la Pakistan 96 C6 ....26°12'N 66°21'E
larus Europe 47 L5 ....54°01'N 28°39'E
laya r. Russia 55 N4 ....65°32'N 173°15'E
lchatów Poland 46 H4 ....51°22'N 19°22'E
lcher Islands Canada 61 K3 ....56°10'N 78°47'W
ledweyne Somalia 85 I2 ....4°44'N 45°13'E
lém Brazil 72 E6 ....1°28'S 48°29'W
lev Russia 47 Q5 ....53°48'N 36°10'E
lfast Northern Ireland 14 D2 ....54°36'N 5°55'W
lfast d. Northern Ireland 21 C4 ......54°36'N 5°55'W

Belfast Lough inlet Northern Ireland 14 D2 ....54°40'N 5°52'W
Belford England 13 F4 ....55°36'N 1°50'W
Belgium Europe 42 D3 ....50°55'N 4°14'E
Belgorod Russia 53 D3 ....50°35'N 36°37'E
Belgrade Serbia 50 D7 ....44°48'N 20°29'E
Belitung i. Indonesia 102 D3 ....2°47'S 108°14'E
Belize town Belize 66 G4 ....17°31'N 88°14'W
Belize Central America 66 G4 ....17°10'N 88°18'W
Bellac France 44 D5 ....46°08'N 1°03'E
Belle-Île i. France 44 B5 ....47°19'N 3°15'W
Belle Isle, Strait of Canada 61 M3 ...51°16'N 56°57'W
Bellingham England 13 E4 ....55°09'N 2°15'W
Bellingham U.S.A. 62 B6 ....48°45'N 122°28'W
Bellinzona Switz. 46 C2 ....46°12'N 9°01'E
Belluno Italy 46 E2 ....46°08'N 12°13'E
Belmopan Belize 66 G4 ....17°14'N 88°46'W
Belmullet Ireland 18 B4 ....54°14'N 9°59'W
Belo Horizonte Brazil 73 E5 ....19°55'S 43°56'W
Beloretsk Russia 53 F3 ....53°55'N 58°24'E
Beloye, Ozero Russia 52 D4 ....60°10'N 38°00'E
Belozersk Russia 52 D3 ....60°02'N 37°47'E
Belper England 13 F2 ....53°02'N 1°29'W
Belukha, Gora mt. Kazakhstan/Russia 54 J2 ....49°50'N 86°41'E
Belush'ye Russia 52 E4 ....66°55'N 47°36'E
Belyy Russia 47 O6 ....55°50'N 32°57'E
Bemidji U.S.A. 63 H6 ....47°27'N 94°52'W
Ben Alder mt. Scotland 17 E1 ....56°49'N 4°28'E
Benavente Spain 45 C5 ....42°00'N 5°40'W
Benbane Head Northern Ireland 14 C3 ..55°15'N 6°30'W
Benbecula i. Scotland 16 B2 ....57°27'N 7°23'W
Ben Cleuch hill Scotland 15 F4 ....56°11'N 3°46'W
Ben Cruachan mt. Scotland 14 D4 ......56°25'N 5°08'W
Bend U.S.A. 62 B5 ....44°04'N 121°17'W
Bender Moldova 49 N6 ....46°49'N 29°29'E
Bendigo Australia 108 D3 ....36°46'S 144°18'E
Benešov Czechia 46 F3 ....49°47'N 14°42'E
Bengal, Bay of sea Indian Oc. 96 G4 ..17°51'N 88°40'E
Bengaluru India 96 E3 ....12°57'N 77°34'E
Bengbu China 99 L4 ....32°54'N 117°23'E
Benghazi Libya 85 G5 ....32°06'N 20°04'E
Bengkulu Indonesia 102 C3 ....3°45'S 102°18'E
Benguela Angola 83 A3 ....12°36'S 13°21'E
Ben Hope hill Scotland 17 E3 ....58°25'N 4°36'W
Beni r. Bolivia 72 C5 ....11°01'S 66°07'W
Benidorm Spain 45 E3 ....38°32'N 0°08'W
Béni Mellal Morocco 84 D5 ....32°17'N 6°25'W
Benin Africa 84 E2 ....8°26'N 2°11'E
Benin, Bight of g. Africa 84 E2 ......5°17'N 3°27'E
Benin City Nigeria 84 E2 ....6°19'N 5°36'E
Beni-Saf Algeria 48 C4 ....35°20'N 1°21'W
Benjamim Constant Brazil 72 C6 ....4°23'S 69°58'W
Ben Klibreck mt. Scotland 17 E3 ......58°15'N 4°24'W
Ben Lawers mt. Scotland 14 E4 ....56°33'N 4°13'W
Ben Lomond hill Scotland 14 E4 ....56°11'N 4°38'W
Ben Loyal hill Scotland 17 E3 ....58°24'N 4°27'W
Ben Lui mt. Scotland 14 E4 ....56°24'N 4°49'W
Ben Macdui mt. Scotland 17 F2 ....57°05'N 3°40'W
Ben More hill Scotland 14 C4 ....56°25'N 6°00'W
Ben More mt. Scotland 14 E4 ....56°23'N 4°32'W
Ben More Assynt hill Scotland 16 E3 ..58°08'N 4°51'W
Ben Nevis mt. Scotland 16 D1 ....56°48'N 5°00'W
Bentley England 13 F2 ....53°33'N 1°09'W
Benue r. Nigeria 84 F2 ....7°49'N 6°48'E
Ben Vorlich hill Scotland 14 E4 ......56°21'N 4°13'W
Ben Wyvis mt. Scotland 17 E2 ....57°41'N 4°35'W
Benxi China 99 M6 ....41°16'N 123°45'E
Beoraid, Loch l. Scotland 16 D1 ......56°54'N 5°36'W
Berat Albania 50 C5 ....40°42'N 19°58'E
Berau, Teluk b. Indonesia 103 I3 .....2°28'S 132°36'E
Berber Sudan 94 D3 ....18°00'N 34°02'E
Berbera Somalia 85 I3 ....10°24'N 45°02'E
Berbérati C.A.R. 84 F2 ....4°14'N 15°47'E
Berck France 9 G1 ....50°25'N 1°35'E
Berdyans'k Ukraine 49 K6 ....46°46'N 36°48'E
Berdychiv Ukraine 47 M3 ....49°53'N 28°36'E
Berens River town Canada 60 I3 ....52°21'N 97°01'W
Berezivka Ukraine 47 N2 ....47°12'N 30°55'E
Berezniki Russia 52 F3 ....59°25'N 56°48'E
Berezovo Russia 52 G4 ....63°54'N 65°07'E
Bergama Turkey 50 G4 ....39°07'N 27°11'E
Bergamo Italy 46 C1 ....45°42'N 9°41'E
Bergen Norway 43 A3 ....60°23'N 5°22'E
Bergerac France 44 D4 ....44°51'N 0°29'E
Bergisch Gladbach Germany 46 B4 ......50°58'N 7°08'E
Bering Sea N. Pacific Oc. 56 B5 ......60°00'N 170°00'E
Bering Strait Russia/U.S.A. 55 U4 ....66°18'N 168°40'W
Berkel r. Neth. 42 F5 ....52°08'N 6°11'E
Berkeley England 8 C2 ....51°41'N 2°27'W
Berkshire Downs hills England 8 D2 ...51°30'N 1°20'W
Berlin Germany 46 E5 ....52°31'N 13°23'E
Bermuda i. N. Atlantic Oc. 67 L7 .....32°24'N 64°56'W
Bern Switz. 46 B2 ....46°57'N 7°27'E
Berneray i. Na h-E. Scotland 16 B1 ...56°47'N 7°38'W
Berneray i. Na h-E. Scotland 16 B2 ...57°44'N 7°18'W
Berry Head England 11 D2 ....50°24'N 3°29'W
Bertoua Cameroon 84 F2 ....4°35'N 13°41'E
Berwick-upon-Tweed England 13 E4 .....55°46'N 2°00'W
Besançon France 44 G5 ....47°15'N 6°01'E
Bessbrook Northern Ireland 14 C2 .....54°12'N 6°23'W
Betanzos Spain 45 A5 ....43°17'N 8°12'W
Beth, Oued r. Morocco 45 B1 ....34°25'N 6°26'W
Bethesda Wales 10 C5 ....53°11'N 4°03'W
Béthune France 42 B3 ....50°31'N 2°38'E
Betsiboka r. Madagascar 83 D3 ....15°58'S 46°27'E
Bettystown Ireland 10 A5 ....53°42'N 6°15'W
Betws-y-coed Wales 10 D5 ....53°05'N 3°48'W
Beult r. England 9 F2 ....51°13'N 0°25'E
Beverley England 13 G2 ....53°51'N 0°26'W
Bewdley England 8 C3 ....52°23'N 2°19'W
Bewl Water resr England 9 F2 ....51°04'N 0°23'E
Bexhill England 9 F1 ....50°50'N 0°29'E
Beykoz Turkey 51 H5 ....41°07'N 29°05'E
Beyla Guinea 84 D2 ....8°41'N 8°41'W
Beyneu Kazakhstan 53 F2 ....45°18'N 55°11'E
Beypazarı Turkey 51 I5 ....40°10'N 31°56'E
Beyşehir Turkey 51 I3 ....37°42'N 31°43'E
Beyşehir Gölü l. Turkey 51 I3 ....37°42'N 31°33'E
Béziers France 44 E3 ....43°21'N 3°13'E
Bhagalpur India 96 G6 ....25°15'N 86°56'E
Bhamo Myanmar 97 I5 ....24°18'N 97°17'E
Bhavnagar India 96 D5 ....21°46'N 72°14'E
Bhima r. India 96 E4 ....16°26'N 77°13'E
Bhopal India 96 E5 ....23°15'N 77°23'E
Bhubaneshwar India 96 G5 ....20°13'N 85°53'E

Bhuj India 96 C5 ....23°11'N 69°44'E
Bhutan Asia 97 H6 ....27°38'N 90°33'E
Biak Indonesia 103 J3 ....1°12'S 136°05'E
Biak i. Indonesia 103 J3 ....0°59'S 135°59'E
Biała Podlaska Poland 47 J5 ....52°02'N 23°07'E
Białystok Poland 47 J5 ....53°08'N 23°10'E
Biarritz France 44 C3 ....43°29'N 1°33'W
Bibai Japan 104 D4 ....43°18'N 141°52'E
Biberach an der Riß Germany 46 C3 ....48°06'N 9°47'E
Bicester England 8 D2 ....51°54'N 1°09'W
Bidar India 96 E4 ....17°54'N 77°34'E
Biddulph England 13 E2 ....53°07'N 2°10'W
Bidean nam Bian mt. Scotland 16 D1 ...56°39'N 5°02'W
Bideford England 11 C3 ....51°01'N 4°12'W
Biel/Bienne Switz. 46 B2 ....47°09'N 7°15'E
Bielefeld Germany 46 C5 ....52°01'N 8°32'E
Biella Italy 46 C1 ....45°34'N 8°04'E
Bielsko-Biała Poland 46 H3 ....49°49'N 19°03'E
Bifoun Gabon 84 F1 ....0°15'S 10°25'E
Biga Turkey 50 G5 ....40°13'N 27°13'E
Bigbury Bay England 11 D2 ....50°15'N 3°54'W
Biggar Scotland 15 F3 ....55°37'N 3°31'W
Biggleswade England 9 E3 ....52°05'N 0°16'W
Bighorn r. U.S.A. 62 E6 ....46°10'N 107°30'W
Bighorn Mountains U.S.A. 62 E5 ....44°06'N 106°55'W
Big Spring U.S.A. 62 F3 ....32°16'N 101°24'W
Big Trout Lake town Canada 61 J3 .....53°49'N 89°50'W
Bihać Bos. and Herz. 50 A7 ....44°49'N 15°53'E
Bihar d. India 96 G5 ....24°13'N 85°37'E
Bihor, Vârful mt. Romania 47 J2 ......46°27'N 22°44'E
Bijār Iran 95 G5 ....35°51'N 47°37'E
Bijeljina Bos. and Herz. 50 C7 ....44°46'N 19°14'E
Bijelo Polje Montenegro 50 C6 ....43°02'N 19°45'E
Bikaner India 96 D6 ....28°00'N 73°23'E
Bilaspur India 98 E2 ....22°05'N 82°09'E
Bila Tserkva Ukraine 47 N3 ....49°48'N 30°07'E
Bilbao Spain 45 D5 ....43°15'N 2°54'W
Bilecik Turkey 51 H5 ....40°09'N 29°57'E
Bilhorod-Dnistrovs'kyy Ukraine 49 J6 ....46°11'N 30°20'E
Billericay England 9 F2 ....51°38'N 0°25'E
Billingham England 13 F3 ....54°37'N 1°17'W
Billinghay England 13 G2 ....53°05'N 0°17'W
Billings U.S.A. 62 E6 ....45°48'N 108°27'W
Billingshurst England 9 E1 ....51°01'N 0°27'W
Bill of Portland hd England 8 C1 .....50°30'N 2°30'W
Bilopillya Ukraine 47 P4 ....51°09'N 34°20'E
Biloxi U.S.A. 63 I3 ....30°24'N 88°57'W
Bilston Scotland 15 F3 ....55°52'N 3°11'W
Bilton England 13 G2 ....53°47'N 0°15'W
Bimini Islands Bahamas 67 I6 ....25°46'N 79°14'W
Bindura Zimbabwe 83 C3 ....17°18'S 31°19'E
Bingham England 8 E3 ....52°57'N 0°57'W
Binghamton U.S.A. 63 K5 ....42°06'N 75°55'W
Bingley England 13 F2 ....53°51'N 1°50'W
Bintulu Malaysia 102 E4 ....3°12'N 113°03'E
Bioco i. Equat. Guinea 84 E2 ....3°16'N 8°31'E
Birāk Libya 48 F2 ....27°33'N 14°16'E
Birao C.A.R. 94 B2 ....10°15'N 22°48'E
Birecik Turkey 51 L3 ....37°01'N 37°59'E
Birhan mt. Ethiopia 85 H3 ....10°43'N 37°52'E
Birjand Iran 95 I6 ....32°53'N 59°08'E
Birkenhead England 12 D2 ....53°23'N 3°01'W
Birmingham England 8 D3 ....52°29'N 1°53'W
Birmingham U.S.A. 63 I3 ....33°32'N 86°47'W
Bîr Mogreïn Mauritania 84 C4 ....25°14'N 11°34'W
Birnin Konni Niger 84 E3 ....13°48'N 5°14'E
Birobidzhan Russia 99 O7 ....48°45'N 132°52'E
Birr Ireland 18 D3 ....53°06'N 7°55'W
Birsay Scotland 17 F4 ....59°08'N 3°18'W
Birstall England 8 D3 ....52°41'N 1°07'W
Biržai Lithuania 47 K7 ....56°12'N 24°45'E
Biscay, Bay of sea France/Spain 45 C6 ....45°40'N 5°07'W
Bischofshofen Austria 46 E2 ....47°25'N 13°13'E
Bishkek Kyrgyzstan 98 C6 ....42°54'N 74°32'E
Bisho S. Africa 83 B1 ....32°51'S 27°24'E
Bishop Auckland England 13 F3 ....54°40'N 1°41'W
Bishops Lydeard England 11 D3 ....51°04'N 3°11'W
Bishop's Stortford England 9 F2 ......51°52'N 0°10'E
Bishop's Waltham England 8 D1 ....50°57'N 1°13'W
Biskra Algeria 84 E5 ....34°49'N 5°44'E
Bismarck U.S.A. 62 F6 ....46°50'N 100°46'W
Bismarck Sea P.N.G. 108 D6 ....4°01'S 149°01'E
Bissau Guinea‚ÄîBissau 84 C3 ....11°53'N 15°38'W
Bistra mt. Serbia 50 D6 ....42°09'N 20°55'E
Bistrița Romania 47 K2 ....47°09'N 24°30'E
Bistrița r. Romania 47 L2 ....46°30'N 26°58'E
Bitburg Germany 42 F2 ....49°58'N 6°32'E
Bitola Macedonia 50 D5 ....41°01'N 21°20'E
Bitterroot Range mts U.S.A. 62 D6 ....47°16'N 115°41'W
Biwa-ko l. Japan 104 C3 ....35°09'N 135°59'E
Biysk Russia 54 J3 ....52°31'N 85°17'E
Bizerte Tunisia 48 F4 ....37°16'N 9°52'E
Bjørnøya i. Arctic Oc. 54 C5 ....74°24'N 19°07'E
Blackburn England 12 E2 ....53°45'N 2°29'W
Blackburn with Darwen d. England 21 D3 ....53°41'N 2°27'W
Black Combe hill England 12 D3 ....54°15'N 3°20'W
Blackfield England 8 D1 ....50°49'N 1°22'W
Black Forest mts Germany 46 C3 ....47°56'N 8°08'E
Black Head England 11 B2 ....50°00'N 5°07'W
Black Hill England 13 F2 ....53°32'N 1°53'W
Black Isle pen. Scotland 17 E2 ....57°35'N 4°19'W
Black Mountains hills Wales 10 D3 ....51°58'N 3°08'W
Blackpool England 12 D2 ....53°49'N 3°03'W
Blackpool d. England 21 D3 ....53°50'N 3°01'W
Black Sea Asia/Europe 51 M6 ....42°31'N 38°22'E
Blacksod Bay Ireland 18 A4 ....54°03'N 10°03'W
Black Volta r. Africa 84 D2 ....8°29'N 0°51'W
Blackwater r. England 9 F2 ....51°44'N 0°41'E
Blackwater r. Meath Ireland 18 E3 ....53°39'N 6°41'W
Blackwater r. Water. Ireland 18 D2 ...52°08'N 7°51'W
Blackwater r. Cork Ireland 18 C2 .....54°31'N 6°34'W
Blackwood Wales 10 D3 ....51°40'N 3°12'W
Blaenau Ffestiniog Wales 10 D4 ....52°59'N 3°57'W
Blaenau Gwent d. Wales 21 D2 ....51°46'N 3°12'W
Blaenavon Wales 10 D3 ....51°47'N 3°06'W
Blagdon England 8 C2 ....51°20'N 2°43'W
Blagoevgrad Bulgaria 50 E6 ....42°01'N 23°06'E
Blagoveshchensk Russia 55 N3 ....50°17'N 127°29'E
Blair Atholl Scotland 17 F1 ....56°46'N 3°50'W
Blairgowrie Scotland 15 F4 ....56°35'N 3°21'W
Blanc, Mont mt. France/Italy 44 G4 ...45°50'N 6°51'E
Blanca, Bahía b. Argentina 73 C3 .....39°08'S 61°47'W
Blanche, Lake Australia 108 C4 ....29°15'S 139°42'E
Blanc Nez, Cap c. France 9 G1 ....50°56'N 1°44'E
Blanco, Cape U.S.A. 62 B5 ....42°51'N 124°34'W
Blandford Forum England 8 C1 ....50°52'N 2°10'W

Blanquilla, Isla i. Venezuela 67 L3 ..11°51'N 64°35'W
Blantyre Malawi 83 C3 ....15°47'S 35°02'E
Blarney Ireland 18 C1 ....51°56'N 8°34'W
Bletchley England 8 E2 ....51°59'N 0°45'W
Blida Algeria 84 E5 ....36°33'N 2°55'E
Bloemfontein S. Africa 83 B2 ....29°07'S 26°13'E
Blois France 44 D5 ....47°35'N 1°20'E
Bloody Foreland pt Ireland 18 C5 .....55°10'N 8°18'W
Bloomington U.S.A. 63 I5 ....40°29'N 88°59'W
Blue Mountains U.S.A. 62 C6 ....45°27'N 118°38'W
Blue Nile r. Sudan 85 H3 ....15°38'N 32°30'E
Blue Stack hill Ireland 14 A2 ....54°45'N 8°05'W
Blue Stack Mountains hills Ireland 18 C4 ....54°42'N 8°14'W
Blyth Northum. England 13 F4 ....55°08'N 1°30'W
Blyth Notts. England 13 F2 ....53°22'N 1°04'W
Blytheville U.S.A. 63 I4 ....35°56'N 89°52'W
Bo Sierra Leone 84 C2 ....7°55'N 11°45'W
Boa Vista Brazil 72 C7 ....2°51'N 60°43'W
Boa Vista i. Cape Verde 84 B3 ....16°05'N 22°40'W
Bobaomby, Tanjona c. Madagascar 83 D3 ....11°57'S 49°15'E
Bobo-Dioulasso Burkina Faso 84 D3 ....11°11'N 4°18'W
Bóbr r. Poland 46 F4 ....52°03'N 15°04'E
Boby mt. Madagascar 83 D2 ....22°13'S 46°54'E
Bocholt Germany 46 B4 ....51°50'N 6°36'E
Boddam Scotland 17 H2 ....57°28'N 1°47'W
Bodélé f. Chad 85 F3 ....16°12'N 16°17'E
Boden Sweden 43 E4 ....65°49'N 21°41'E
Bodenham England 8 C3 ....52°09'N 2°41'W
Bodmin England 11 C2 ....50°28'N 4°43'W
Bodmin Moor f. England 11 C2 ....50°34'N 4°36'W
Bodø Norway 43 C4 ....67°17'N 14°23'E
Bodrum Turkey 50 G3 ....37°02'N 27°25'E
Boğazlıyan Turkey 51 K4 ....39°11'N 35°15'E
Boggeragh Mountains hills Ireland 18 B2 ....52°01'N 9°01'E
Bogie r. Scotland 17 G2 ....57°27'N 2°46'W
Bognor Regis England 8 E1 ....50°47'N 0°40'W
Bogor Indonesia 102 D2 ....6°35'S 106°45'E
Bogotá Colombia 72 B7 ....4°35'N 74°04'W
Bo Hai g. China 99 L5 ....38°32'N 119°14'E
Bohain-en-Vermandois France 42 C2 ....49°59'N 3°28'E
Bohemian Forest mts Germany 46 E3 ....49°42'N 12°27'E
Bohol i. Phil. 103 G5 ....9°55'N 124°16'E
Boise U.S.A. 62 C5 ....43°38'N 116°11'W
Bojnürd Iran 95 I7 ....37°27'N 57°19'E
Bolhrad Ukraine 49 I6 ....45°41'N 28°37'E
Bolívar, Pico mt. Venezuela 67 J2 ....8°33'N 70°59'W
Bolivia S. America 72 C5 ....16°23'S 64°00'W
Bollnäs Sweden 43 D3 ....61°21'N 16°24'E
Bolmen l. Sweden 43 C2 ....56°52'N 13°43'E
Bologna Italy 46 D1 ....44°29'N 11°22'E
Bol'shevik, Ostrov i. Russia 55 L5 ...78°39'N 102°16'E
Bol'shezemel'skaya Tundra f. Russia 52 F4 ....67°00'N 58°00'E
Bol'shoy Aluy r. Russia 55 Q4 ....66°29'N 159°26'E
Bol'shoy Lyakhovskiy, Ostrov i. Russia 55 P5 ....73°26'N 142°14'E
Bolsover England 13 F2 ....53°14'N 1°17'W
Bolt Head England 11 D2 ....50°12'N 3°47'W
Bolton England 13 E2 ....53°35'N 2°26'W
Bolu Turkey 51 I5 ....40°44'N 31°36'E
Bolus Head Ireland 18 A1 ....51°47'N 10°20'W
Bolzano Italy 46 D2 ....46°29'N 11°21'E
Boma Dem. Rep. Congo 83 A4 ....5°48'S 13°03'E
Bømlo i. Norway 43 A2 ....59°45'N 5°13'E
Bon, Cap c. Tunisia 48 F4 ....37°04'N 11°04'E
Bonaire i. Neth. Antilles 67 K3 ......12°12'N 68°12'W
Bonar Bridge Scotland 17 E2 ....57°54'N 4°21'W
Bonavista Canada 61 M2 ....48°33'N 52°43'W
Bondoukou Côte d'Ivoire 84 D2 ....8°03'N 2°48'W
Bo'ness Scotland 15 F4 ....56°01'N 3°36'W
Bonifacio France 44 H2 ....41°23'N 9°10'E
Bonifacio, Strait of France/Italy 44 H2 ....41°15'N 8°45'E
Bonn Germany 46 B4 ....50°44'N 7°04'E
Bonnyrigg Scotland 15 F3 ....55°52'N 3°06'W
Bontosunggu Indonesia 102 F2 ....5°41'S 119°43'E
Boothia, Gulf of Canada 61 J4 ....68°48'N 86°41'W
Boothia Peninsula Canada 61 I5 ....70°40'N 94°39'W
Bootle England 12 E2 ....53°27'N 2°59'W
Bor Turkey 51 K3 ....37°54'N 34°33'E
Borås Sweden 43 C2 ....57°44'N 12°57'E
Borāzjān Iran 95 H5 ....29°16'N 51°12'E
Bordeaux France 44 C4 ....44°51'N 0°34'W
Borden Island Canada 60 G5 ....78°31'N 111°01'W
Borden Peninsula Canada 61 J5 ....72°45'N 82°32'W
Bordj Messaouda Algeria 48 E3 ....30°10'N 9°25'E
Bordj Omer Driss Algeria 84 E4 ....28°11'N 6°47'E
Boreray i. Scotland 16 B2 ....57°42'N 7°16'W
Borgarnes Iceland 43 X2 ....64°32'N 21°55'W
Borken Germany 42 F4 ....51°50'N 6°51'E
Borkum i. Germany 42 F6 ....53°37'N 6°44'E
Borlänge Sweden 43 C3 ....60°29'N 15°26'E
Borneo i. Asia 102 E4 ....1°00'N 113°25'E
Bornholm i. Denmark 43 C1 ....55°09'N 14°38'E
Bornova Turkey 50 G4 ....38°27'N 27°11'E
Borodyanka Ukraine 47 M4 ....50°39'N 29°56'E
Borovichi Russia 52 D3 ....58°23'N 33°55'E
Borovskoy Kazakhstan 52 G3 ....53°47'N 64°12'E
Borüjerd Iran 95 G6 ....33°53'N 48°43'E
Boryspil' Ukraine 47 N4 ....50°21'N 30°58'E
Borzna Ukraine 47 O4 ....51°15'N 32°26'E
Borzya Russia 55 M3 ....50°11'N 116°31'E
Bosanska Dubica Bos. and Herz. 50 B7 ....45°11'N 16°48'E
Bosna r. Bos. and Herz. 50 C7 ....45°04'N 18°29'E
Bosnia and Herzegovina Europe 50 B7 ....44°23'N 17°40'E
Bosobolo Dem. Rep. Congo 83 A5 ....4°10'N 19°52'E
Bosporus str. Turkey 51 H5 ....41°20'N 29°06'E
Bossembélé C.A.R. 85 F2 ....5°15'N 17°38'E
Bosten Hu l. China 98 F6 ....41°53'N 87°24'E
Boston England 9 E3 ....52°58'N 0°01'W
Boston U.S.A. 63 L5 ....42°23'N 71°06'W
Boston Spa England 13 F2 ....53°54'N 1°20'W
Botevgrad Bulgaria 50 E6 ....42°54'N 23°47'E
Bothnia, Gulf of Finland/Sweden 43 D3 ....61°09'N 19°15'E
Botoşani Romania 47 L2 ....47°45'N 26°39'E
Botswana Africa 83 B2 ....22°55'S 22°47'E
Bottesford England 13 G2 ....53°33'N 0°38'W
Bouaké Côte d'Ivoire 84 D2 ....7°42'N 5°03'W
Bouar C.A.R. 84 F2 ....5°56'N 15°35'E
Bou Arfa Morocco 84 D5 ....32°34'N 1°56'W
Bougainville Island P.N.G. 108 E6 ....6°04'S 154°53'E
Bouillon Belgium 42 E2 ....49°48'N 5°06'E
Boujdour Western Sahara 84 C4 ....26°08'N 14°28'W
Boulder U.S.A. 62 E5 ....40°02'N 105°16'W
Boulogne-Billancourt France 44 E6 ....48°50'N 2°15'E
Boulogne-sur-Mer France 44 D7 ....50°43'N 1°37'E

Bounty Islands New Zealand 109 G2 ....47°40'S 179°02'E
Bourg-en-Bresse France 44 F5 ....46°12'N 5°14'E
Bourges France 44 E5 ....47°05'N 2°24'E
Bourke Australia 108 D3 ....30°07'S 145°54'E
Bourne England 9 E3 ....52°46'N 0°23'W
Bournemouth England 8 D1 ....50°43'N 1°53'W
Bournemouth d. England 21 E2 ....50°45'N 1°50'W
Bou Saâda Algeria 48 D4 ....35°13'N 4°11'E
Bow r. Canada 62 D6 ....49°58'N 111°41'W
Bowes England 13 E3 ....54°31'N 2°00'W
Bowland, Forest of England 12 E2 ....53°59'N 2°33'W
Boxtel Neth. 42 E4 ....51°35'N 5°20'E
Boyabat Turkey 51 K5 ....41°28'N 34°46'E
Boyle Ireland 18 C3 ....53°58'N 8°18'W
Boyne r. Ireland 18 E3 ....53°43'N 6°18'W
Bozeman U.S.A. 62 D6 ....45°42'N 111°02'W
Bozüyük Turkey 51 I4 ....39°55'N 30°01'E
Braan r. Scotland 15 F4 ....56°34'N 3°36'W
Brabant Wallon d. Belgium 42 D3 ....50°39'N 4°35'E
Brač i. Croatia 50 B6 ....43°17'N 16°31'E
Bracadale, Loch b. Scotland 16 C2 ......57°21'N 6°33'W
Bräcke Sweden 43 C3 ....62°46'N 15°26'E
Brackley England 8 D2 ....52°02'N 1°08'W
Bracknell England 8 E2 ....51°25'N 0°45'W
Bracknell Forest d. England 21 E2 .....51°24'N 0°45'W
Brad Romania 50 E8 ....46°07'N 22°48'E
Bradford England 13 F2 ....53°48'N 1°45'W
Bradford-on-Avon England 8 C2 ....51°21'N 2°15'W
Braemar Scotland 17 F2 ....57°00'N 3°24'W
Braga Portugal 45 A4 ....41°33'N 8°26'W
Bragança Brazil 72 E6 ....1°00'S 46°49'W
Bragança Portugal 45 B4 ....41°49'N 6°45'W
Brahmapur India 96 F4 ....19°21'N 84°52'E
Brahmaputra r. China/India 98 G2 ......23°36'N 90°31'E
Brăila Romania 51 G7 ....45°17'N 27°58'E
Braintree England 9 F2 ....51°53'N 0°33'E
Brämön i. Sweden 43 D3 ....62°13'N 17°45'E
Brampton England 12 E3 ....54°57'N 2°44'W
Branco r. Brazil 72 C7 ....1°18'S 61°52'W
Brandenburg an der Havel Germany 46 E5 ..52°25'N 12°34'E
Brandesburton England 13 G2 ....53°55'N 0°18'W
Brandon Canada 60 I3 ....49°51'N 99°57'W
Brandon England 9 F3 ....52°27'N 0°37'E
Brandon Head Ireland 18 A2 ....52°17'N 10°13'W
Brandon Mountain hill Ireland 18 A2 ...52°14'N 10°15'W
Bransgore England 8 D1 ....50°47'N 1°44'W
Brasília Brazil 72 E5 ....15°49'S 47°55'W
Braşov Romania 50 F7 ....45°40'N 25°36'E
Bratislava Slovakia 46 G3 ....48°09'N 17°06'E
Bratsk Russia 55 L3 ....56°16'N 101°41'E
Braunau am Inn Austria 46 E3 ....48°16'N 13°02'E
Braunschweig Germany 46 D5 ....52°17'N 10°32'E
Braunton England 11 C3 ....51°06'N 4°10'W
Brawley U.S.A. 62 C3 ....32°58'N 115°32'W
Bray Ireland 18 E3 ....53°12'N 6°07'W
Bray Head Ireland 18 A1 ....51°52'N 10°25'W
Brazil S. America 73 D6 ....9°00'S 54°33'W
Brazil Basin f. Atlantic Oc. 116 E2 ...15°00'S 30°00'W
Brazilian Highlands mts Brazil 72 E5 ..17°00'S 48°00'W
Brazos r. U.S.A. 62 G2 ....28°52'N 95°25'W
Brazzaville Congo 84 F1 ....4°17'S 15°11'E
Breamish r. England 13 E4 ....55°41'N 2°13'W
Brechin Scotland 17 G1 ....56°44'N 2°39'W
Breckland f. England 9 F3 ....52°28'N 0°39'E
Břeclav Czechia 46 G3 ....48°46'N 16°53'E
Brecon Wales 10 D3 ....51°57'N 3°24'W
Brecon Beacons f. Wales 10 D3 ....51°53'N 3°26'W
Breda Neth. 42 D4 ....51°35'N 4°46'E
Breiðafjörður b. Iceland 43 W2 ....65°03'N 24°07'W
Breiðdalsvík Iceland 43 Z2 ....64°48'N 14°02'W
Bremen Germany 46 C5 ....53°05'N 8°51'E
Bremerhaven Germany 46 C5 ....53°33'N 8°35'E
Brenner Pass Austria/Italy 46 D2 ......46°59'N 11°32'E
Brentwood England 9 F2 ....51°37'N 0°19'E
Brescia Italy 46 D1 ....45°32'N 10°13'E
Bressanone Italy 46 D2 ....46°43'N 11°40'E
Bressay i. Scotland 17 H5 ....60°16'N 1°18'W
Bressuire France 44 C5 ....46°50'N 0°30'W
Brest Belarus 47 J5 ....52°05'N 23°40'E
Brest France 44 A6 ....48°24'N 4°29'W
Bretton Wales 10 E5 ....53°10'N 2°58'W
Bria C.A.R. 85 G2 ....6°32'N 21°59'E
Briançon France 44 G4 ....44°54'N 6°38'E
Brianne, Llyn resr Wales 10 D4 ....52°08'N 3°45'W
Bride r. Ireland 18 D2 ....52°04'N 7°52'W
Bridgend Wales 11 D3 ....51°30'N 3°35'W
Bridgend d. Wales 21 D2 ....51°34'N 3°33'W
Bridgeport U.S.A. 63 L5 ....41°12'N 73°12'W
Bridgetown Barbados 67 M3 ....13°05'N 59°36'W
Bridgnorth England 8 C3 ....52°32'N 2°25'W
Bridgwater England 11 D3 ....51°08'N 3°00'W
Bridgwater Bay England 11 D3 ....51°16'N 3°19'W
Bridlington England 13 G3 ....54°05'N 0°12'W
Bridlington Bay England 13 G3 ....54°03'N 0°07'W
Bridport England 8 C1 ....50°44'N 2°45'W
Brig Switz. 46 B2 ....46°19'N 7°59'E
Brigg England 13 G2 ....53°33'N 0°29'W
Brighstone England 8 D1 ....50°39'N 1°23'W
Brightlingsea England 9 G2 ....51°49'N 1°01'E
Brighton England 8 E1 ....50°50'N 0°08'W
Brighton and Hove d. England 21 E2 ...50°51'N 0°08'W
Brindisi Italy 49 G5 ....40°38'N 17°56'E
Brisbane Australia 108 E4 ....27°33'S 153°03'E
Bristol England 8 C2 ....51°27'N 2°35'W
Bristol d. England 21 D2 ....51°28'N 2°36'W
Bristol U.S.A. 63 J4 ....36°36'N 82°10'W
Bristol Bay U.S.A. 60 B3 ....57°22'N 161°29'W
Bristol Channel est. England 8 B2 ....51°20'N 4°25'W
British Columbia d. Canada 60 F3 .....51°49'N 121°48'W
British Empire Range mts Canada 61 J6 ..82°22'N 80°08'W
British Isles Europe 116 E4 ....54°00'N 5°00'W
Briton Ferry Wales 10 D3 ....51°38'N 3°49'W
Britstown S. Africa 83 B1 ....30°35'S 23°30'E
Brittany f. France 44 B6 ....48°10'N 3°22'W
Brittas Bay Ireland 18 A4 ....52°26'N 6°03'W
Brive-la-Gaillarde France 44 D4 ......45°10'N 1°32'E
Brixham England 11 D2 ....50°24'N 3°31'W
Brno Czechia 46 G3 ....49°11'N 16°37'E
Broad r. U.S.A. 63 J3 ....34°00'N 81°04'W
Broadback r. Canada 63 K7 ....51°21'N 78°50'W
Broad Bay Scotland 16 C3 ....58°15'N 6°15'W
Broad Law hill Scotland 15 F3 ....55°30'N 3°21'W
Broadstairs England 9 G2 ....51°22'N 1°26'E
Broadway England 8 D3 ....52°02'N 1°51'W
Broadwey England 8 C1 ....50°39'N 2°28'W
Broadwindsor England 8 C1 ....50°49'N 2°48'W
Brockenhurst England 8 D1 ....50°49'N 1°34'W

Brock Island Canada 60 G5 ....77°53'N 114°21'W
Brodeur Peninsula Canada 61 J5 ......71°50'N 88°32'W
Brodick Scotland 14 D3 ....55°35'N 5°09'W
Brody Ukraine 47 K4 ....50°05'N 25°09'E
Broken Hill town Australia 108 D3 ....31°55'S 141°27'E
Bromley England 9 F2 ....51°24'N 0°01'E
Bromsgrove England 8 C3 ....52°20'N 2°04'W
Bromyard England 8 C3 ....52°11'N 2°30'W
Brønderslev Denmark 43 B2 ....57°17'N 9°58'E
Brønnøysund Norway 43 C4 ....65°28'N 12°12'E
Brooke England 9 G3 ....52°33'N 1°23'E
Brooke's Point town Phil. 102 F5 ....8°50'N 117°51'E
Brookings U.S.A. 62 G5 ....44°19'N 96°44'W
Brooks Canada 62 D7 ....50°35'N 111°54'W
Brooks Range mts U.S.A. 60 D4 ....69°18'N 144°41'W
Broom, Loch inlet Scotland 16 D2 ....57°56'N 5°19'W
Broome Australia 108 B5 ....17°55'S 122°14'E
Brora Scotland 17 F3 ....58°01'N 3°51'W
Brora r. Scotland 17 F3 ....58°01'N 3°52'W
Brosna r. Ireland 18 D3 ....53°13'N 7°57'W
Brotton England 13 G3 ....54°34'N 0°56'W
Brough Cumb. England 13 E3 ....54°32'N 2°19'W
Brough E. Yorks. England 13 G2 ......53°44'N 0°34'W
Brough Head Scotland 17 F4 ....59°08'N 3°21'W
Brough Ness pt Scotland 17 F3 ....58°44'N 2°58'W
Broughshane Northern Ireland 14 C2 ..54°54'N 6°12'W
Brownhills England 8 D3 ....52°39'N 1°56'W
Broxburn Scotland 15 F3 ....55°56'N 3°28'W
Bruay-la-Buissière France 42 B3 .....50°29'N 2°33'E
Brue r. England 8 C2 ....51°13'N 2°59'W
Brugge Belgium 42 C4 ....51°12'N 3°15'E
Brunei Asia 102 E4 ....5°06'N 114°18'E
Brunflo Sweden 43 C3 ....63°05'N 14°51'E
Brunswick U.S.A. 63 J3 ....31°09'N 81°30'W
Brussels Belgium 42 D3 ....50°50'N 4°21'E
Bruton England 8 C2 ....51°07'N 2°27'W
Bryansk Russia 53 D3 ....53°15'N 34°23'E
Bryher i. England 11 A1 ....49°57'N 6°23'W
Brynamman Wales 10 D3 ....51°49'N 3°52'W
Brynmawr Wales 10 D3 ....51°48'N 3°10'W
Buca Turkey 50 G4 ....38°22'N 27°11'E
Bucaramanga Colombia 72 B7 ....7°05'N 73°09'W
Bucharest Romania 50 G7 ....44°26'N 26°06'E
Buckfastleigh England 11 D2 ....50°29'N 3°46'W
Buckhaven Scotland 15 F4 ....56°11'N 3°02'W
Buckie Scotland 17 G2 ....57°41'N 2°58'W
Buckingham England 8 E2 ....51°59'N 0°59'W
Buckinghamshire d. England 21 E2 ...51°47'N 0°56'W
Buckley Wales 10 D5 ....53°10'N 3°05'W
Budapest Hungary 46 H3 ....47°30'N 19°04'E
Buddon Ness pt Scotland 15 G4 ......56°28'N 2°43'W
Bude England 11 C2 ....50°50'N 4°32'W
Bude Bay England 11 C2 ....50°50'N 4°38'W
Budennovsk Russia 53 E2 ....44°45'N 44°06'E
Buenaventura Colombia 72 B7 ....3°52'N 77°00'W
Buenos Aires Argentina 73 D3 ....34°36'S 58°24'W
Buenos Aires, Lago l. Argentina/Chile 73 B2
....46°31'S 72°13'W
Buffalo N. Y. U.S.A. 63 K5 ....42°53'N 78°52'W
Buffalo Wyo. U.S.A. 62 E5 ....44°20'N 106°41'W
Bug r. Poland 47 J5 ....51°30'N 23°39'E
Buguruslan Russia 53 F3 ....53°35'N 52°23'E
Builth Wells Wales 10 D4 ....52°09'N 3°24'W
Bujumbura Burundi 85 G1 ....3°24'S 29°22'E
Bukavu Dem. Rep. Congo 83 B4 ......2°30'S 28°49'E
Bukittinggi Indonesia 102 C3 ....0°15'S 100°20'E
Bukoba Tanzania 83 C4 ....1°18'S 31°48'E
Bula Indonesia 103 I3 ....3°06'S 130°28'E
Bulawayo Zimbabwe 83 B2 ....20°09'S 28°36'E
Bulgan Mongolia 99 I7 ....48°48'N 103°28'E
Bulgaria Europe 50 F6 ....42°51'N 25°15'E
Bulun Russia 55 N5 ....70°59'N 127°16'E
Bunbury Australia 108 A3 ....33°20'S 115°36'E
Bunclody Ireland 18 E2 ....52°39'N 6°39'W
Buncrana Ireland 18 D5 ....55°09'N 7°27'W
Bundaberg Australia 108 E4 ....24°52'S 152°22'E
Bundoran Ireland 18 C4 ....54°28'N 8°18'W
Bungay England 9 G3 ....52°27'N 1°27'E
Buôn Ma Thuột Vietnam 102 D6 ......12°38'N 108°05'E
Buraydah Saudi Arabia 94 F5 ....26°20'N 43°57'E
Burbage England 8 D2 ....52°21'N 1°40'W
Burdur Turkey 51 I3 ....37°43'N 30°17'E
Bure r. England 9 G3 ....52°37'N 1°43'E
Burë Ethiopia 85 H3 ....10°50'N 36°57'E
Burford England 8 D2 ....51°48'N 1°38'W
Burgas Bulgaria 50 G6 ....42°30'N 27°28'E
Burgess Hill town England 9 E1 .....50°57'N 0°08'W
Burghausen Germany 46 E3 ....48°10'N 12°50'E
Burghead Scotland 17 F2 ....57°42'N 3°29'W
Burgh le Marsh England 13 H2 ....53°10'N 0°14'E
Burgos Spain 45 D5 ....42°21'N 3°41'W
Burhanpur India 96 E5 ....21°18'N 76°14'E
Burkina Faso Africa 84 D3 ....11°39'N 1°18'W
Burlington Colo. U.S.A. 62 F4 ....39°19'N 102°17'W
Burlington Iowa U.S.A. 63 H5 ....40°49'N 91°06'W
Burlington Vt. U.S.A. 63 L5 ....44°28'N 73°13'W
Burma Asia 97 I5 ....22°37'N 95°02'E
Burnham England 8 E2 ....51°32'N 0°39'W
Burnham Market England 9 F3 ....52°57'N 0°44'E
Burnham-on-Crouch England 9 F2 ...51°38'N 0°49'E
Burnham-on-Sea England 8 C2 ....51°14'N 2°59'W
Burnie Australia 108 D2 ....41°03'S 145°57'E
Burniston England 13 G3 ....54°19'N 0°27'W
Burnley England 13 E2 ....53°47'N 2°15'W
Burns U.S.A. 62 C5 ....43°36'N 119°01'W
Burns Lake town Canada 60 F3 ....54°15'N 125°46'W
Burntisland Scotland 15 F4 ....56°04'N 3°14'W
Burntwood Green England 8 D3 ......52°41'N 1°54'W
Burra i. Scotland 17 H5 ....60°05'N 1°22'W
Burray i. Scotland 17 G3 ....58°51'N 2°53'W
Burro, Serranías del mts Mexico 66 D6 ..29°02'N 102°00'W
Burrow Head Scotland 14 E2 ....54°41'N 4°23'W
Burry Inlet Wales 10 C3 ....51°38'N 4°18'W
Burry Port Wales 10 C3 ....51°41'N 4°16'W
Bursa Turkey 51 H5 ....40°14'N 29°03'E
Būr Safājah Egypt 49 J2 ....26°45'N 33°55'E
Burscough Bridge England 12 E2 ....53°36'N 2°51'W
Burton-in-Kendal England 12 E3 ....54°11'N 2°43'W
Burton Latimer England 8 E3 ....52°22'N 0°41'W
Burton upon Trent England 8 D3 ....52°48'N 1°38'W
Buru i. Indonesia 103 H3 ....3°24'S 126°35'E
Burundi Africa 85 H1 ....3°36'S 30°03'E
Burwash Landing Canada 60 E4 .....61°21'N 138°52'W
Burwell England 9 F3 ....52°16'N 0°20'E
Burwick Scotland 17 G3 ....58°44'N 2°58'W
Bury England 13 E2 ....53°36'N 2°18'W
Bury St Edmunds England 9 F3 ......52°15'N 0°44'E
Busan S. Korea 99 N5 ....35°09'N 129°03'E

Bush r. Northern Ireland 14 C3 ......55°13'N 6°31'W
Bushmills Northern Ireland 14 C3 ...55°12'N 6°31'W
Buta Dem. Rep. Congo 83 B5 ....2°49'N 24°45'E
Bute i. Scotland 14 D3 ....55°49'N 5°06'W
Bute, Sound of str. Scotland 14 D3 ..55°44'N 5°19'W
Buton i. Indonesia 103 G3 ....4°57'S 123°00'E
Butte U.S.A. 62 D6 ....46°01'N 112°32'W
Butterworth Malaysia 102 C5 ....5°22'N 100°22'E
Buttevant Ireland 18 C2 ....52°14'N 8°40'W
Butt of Lewis hd Scotland 16 C3 .....58°32'N 6°17'W
Butuan Phil. 103 H5 ....8°56'N 125°32'E
Buxoro Uzbekistan 54 H1 ....39°46'N 64°25'E
Buxton England 13 F2 ....53°16'N 1°55'W
Buy Russia 52 E3 ....58°29'N 41°32'E
Buyr Nuur l. Mongolia 99 L7 ....47°47'N 117°53'E
Büyük Ağrı Dağı mt. Turkey 94 F7 ...39°44'N 44°15'E
Büyükmenderes r. Turkey 51 G3 .....37°28'N 27°11'E
Buzău Romania 50 G7 ....45°09'N 26°48'E
Buzuluk Russia 53 F3 ....52°45'N 52°09'E
Byarezina r. Belarus 47 L5 ....53°48'N 25°58'E
Byaroza Belarus 47 K5 ....52°32'N 24°59'E
Bydgoszcz Poland 46 H5 ....53°08'N 18°02'E
Byfield England 8 D3 ....52°11'N 1°14'W
Bylot Island Canada 61 K5 ....73°07'N 79°01'W
Byrranga, Gory mts Russia 55 K5 ....74°25'N 99°53'E
Bytom Poland 46 H4 ....50°21'N 18°55'E

C

Cabanatuan Phil. 103 G7 ....15°31'N 120°58'E
Caban Coch Reservoir Wales 10 D4 ..52°15'N 3°35'W
Cabimas Venezuela 72 B8 ....10°23'N 71°26'W
Cabinda Angola 84 F1 ....5°33'S 12°15'E
Cabo Frio Brazil 73 E4 ....22°51'S 42°02'W
Cabonga, Réservoir Canada 63 K6 ..47°20'N 76°32'W
Caborca Mexico 66 B7 ....30°44'N 112°09'W
Cabot Strait Canada 61 L2 ....47°39'N 60°16'W
Cabora Bassa, Lake resr Mozambique 83 C3
....15°46'S 31°11'E
Cabrera, Sierra de la mts Spain 45 B5 ..42°13'N 6°15'W
Cabriel r. Spain 45 E3 ....39°16'N 1°04'W
Cáceres Brazil 72 D5 ....16°03'S 57°41'W
Cáceres Spain 45 B3 ....39°29'N 6°21'W
Cachimbo, Serra do hills Brazil 72 D6 ..9°18'S 54°11'W
Cachoeiro de Itapemirim Brazil 73 E4 ..20°51'S 41°08'W
Cadillac U.S.A. 63 I5 ....44°14'N 85°23'W
Cádiz Spain 45 B2 ....36°32'N 6°17'W
Cádiz, Golfo de g. Spain 45 B2 ......36°44'N 7°14'W
Caen France 44 C6 ....49°11'N 0°21'W
Caerleon Wales 10 E3 ....51°37'N 2°57'W
Caernarfon Wales 10 C5 ....53°08'N 4°16'W
Caernarfon Bay Wales 10 C5 ....53°06'N 4°34'W
Caerphilly Wales 10 D3 ....51°35'N 3°13'W
Caerphilly d. Wales 21 D2 ....51°38'N 3°11'W
Caerwent Wales 10 E3 ....51°37'N 2°46'W
Cagayan de Oro Phil. 103 G5 ....8°29'N 124°39'E
Cagliari Italy 48 E4 ....39°13'N 9°08'E
Caha Mountains hills Ireland 18 B1 ..51°41'N 9°44'W
Cahirciveen Ireland 18 A1 ....51°57'N 10°13'W
Cahore Point Ireland 18 E2 ....52°33'N 6°11'W
Cahors France 44 D4 ....44°28'N 1°26'E
Cahul Moldova 51 H7 ....45°54'N 28°12'E
Caia Mozambique 83 C3 ....17°50'S 35°19'E
Caiabis, Serra dos hills Brazil 72 D5 ..11°46'S 56°21'W
Caicos Islands Turks and Caicos Is 67 J5 ..21°45'N 71°53'W
Caimodorro mt. Spain 45 E4 ....40°32'N 1°40'W
Cairn Gorm mt. Scotland 17 F2 .....57°07'N 3°39'W
Cairngorm Mountains Scotland 17 F2 ..57°08'N 3°45'W
Cairnryan Scotland 14 D2 ....54°58'N 5°02'W
Cairns Australia 108 D5 ....16°54'S 145°45'E
Cairn Toul mt. Scotland 17 F2 ....57°03'N 3°43'W
Cairo Egypt 85 H5 ....30°01'N 31°15'E
Caister-on-Sea England 9 G3 ....52°39'N 1°44'E
Caistor England 13 G2 ....53°30'N 0°19'W
Caithness f. Scotland 17 F3 ....58°24'N 3°22'W
Cajamarca Peru 72 B6 ....7°11'S 78°31'W
Calabar Nigeria 84 F2 ....4°59'N 8°19'E
Calafat Romania 50 E6 ....43°59'N 22°57'E
Calais France 44 D7 ....50°57'N 1°51'E
Calais U.S.A. 63 M6 ....45°10'N 67°18'W
Calama Chile 73 C4 ....22°29'S 68°56'W
Calamian Group is Phil. 102 F6 ......11°59'N 119°29'E
Calamocha Spain 45 E4 ....40°56'N 1°17'W
Calanscio Sand Sea des. Libya 49 H3 ..30°11'N 22°22'E
Calapan Phil. 103 G6 ....13°24'N 121°11'E
Călăraşi Romania 50 G7 ....44°12'N 27°19'E
Calatayud Spain 45 E4 ....41°22'N 1°37'W
Calbayog Phil. 103 G6 ....12°05'N 124°37'E
Caldas da Rainha Portugal 45 A3 ...39°24'N 9°08'W
Caldey Island Wales 10 C3 ....51°38'N 4°40'W
Calf of Man i. Isle of Man 12 C3 ....54°04'N 4°50'W
Calgary Canada 60 G3 ....51°02'N 114°04'W
Cali Colombia 72 B7 ....3°26'N 76°28'W
Caliente U.S.A. 62 D4 ....37°37'N 114°31'W
California d. U.S.A. 62 B5 ....38°15'N 122°50'W
California, Gulf of Mexico 66 B7 ....30°51'N 113°58'W
Callan Ireland 18 D2 ....52°32'N 7°24'W
Callander Scotland 14 E4 ....56°15'N 4°13'W
Callanish Scotland 16 C3 ....58°12'N 6°45'W
Callao Peru 72 B5 ....12°04'S 77°08'W
Callington England 11 C2 ....50°30'N 4°19'W
Calne England 8 C2 ....51°26'N 2°00'W
Caltanissetta Italy 48 F4 ....37°30'N 14°03'E
Calvi France 44 H4 ....42°34'N 8°45'E
Cam r. England 9 F3 ....52°21'N 0°16'E
Camagüey Cuba 67 I5 ....21°23'N 77°54'W
Camagüey, Archipiélago de is Cuba 67 I5
....22°44'N 78°34'W
Ca Mau, Mui c. Vietnam 102 C5 .....8°35'N 104°45'E
Camberley England 8 E2 ....51°20'N 0°44'W
Cambodia Asia 102 D6 ....13°05'N 105°10'E
Camborne England 11 B2 ....50°13'N 5°18'W
Cambrai France 42 C3 ....50°10'N 3°14'E
Cambrian Mountains Wales 10 D4 ..52°37'N 3°40'W
Cambridge England 9 F3 ....52°12'N 0°08'E
Cambridge Bay town Canada 60 H4 ..69°02'N 105°14'W
Cambridgeshire d. England 21 F3 ...52°25'N 0°02'E
Camden U.S.A. 63 L4 ....39°55'N 75°07'W
Camelford England 11 C2 ....50°37'N 4°41'W
Cameroon Africa 84 F2 ....5°45'N 12°41'E
Cameroon, Mont vol. Cameroon 84 E2 ..4°13'N 9°11'E
Cametá Brazil 72 E6 ....2°13'S 49°30'W
Campbell River town Canada 60 F3 ..50°01'N 125°14'W
Campbeltown Scotland 14 D3 ....55°25'N 5°36'W
Campeche Mexico 66 F4 ....19°51'N 90°30'W
Campeche d. Mexico 66 F4 ....18°53'N 90°28'W

Campeche, Bahía de g. Mexico 66 F4 ..19°30'N 93°30'W
Campina Grande Brazil 72 F6 ....7°14'S 35°49'W
Campinas Brazil 73 E4 ....22°55'S 47°04'W
Campo Grande Brazil 73 D4 ....20°24'S 54°34'W
Campos Brazil 73 E4 ....21°45'S 41°20'W
Câmpulung Moldovenesc Romania 47 K2 ..47°32'N 25°30'E
Camrose Wales 10 B3 ....51°50'N 5°01'W
Çan Turkey 50 G5 ....40°02'N 27°02'E
Canada N. America 60 F4 ....46°44'N 81°59'W
Canadian r. U.S.A. 62 G4 ....35°11'N 95°52'W
Canadian Shield f. N. America 56 F4 ..50°00'N 80°00'W
Çanakkale Turkey 50 G5 ....40°08'N 26°23'E
Canarreos, Archipiélago de los is Cuba 67 H5
....21°44'N 82°12'W
Canary Islands N. Atlantic Oc. 45 X2 ..30°08'N 18°27'W
Canaveral, Cape U.S.A. 63 J2 ....28°26'N 80°36'W
Canberra Australia 108 D3 ....35°19'S 149°09'E
Cancún Mexico 66 G5 ....21°10'N 86°50'W
Caniapiscau r. Canada 61 L3 ....57°39'N 69°25'W
Caniapiscau, Lac l. Canada 61 K3 ..54°21'N 70°31'W
Canisp hill Scotland 16 D3 ....58°07'N 5°03'W
Çankaya Turkey 51 J4 ....39°53'N 32°49'E
Çankırı Turkey 51 J5 ....40°36'N 33°36'E
Canna i. Scotland 16 C2 ....57°04'N 6°34'W
Cannes France 44 G3 ....43°33'N 7°01'E
Cannock England 8 C3 ....52°41'N 2°02'W
Canora Canada 62 F7 ....51°39'N 102°25'W
Cantabrian Mountains Spain 45 C5 ..43°07'N 4°13'W
Canterbury England 9 G2 ....51°17'N 1°05'E
Cân Thơ Vietnam 102 D6 ....10°01'N 105°46'E
Cao Băng Vietnam 102 D8 ....22°41'N 106°17'E
Capbreton France 44 C3 ....43°39'N 1°26'W
Cape Breton Island Canada 61 L2 ...46°45'N 60°24'W
Capel St Mary England 9 G3 ....52°00'N 1°04'E
Cape Town S. Africa 83 A1 ....33°57'S 18°28'E
Cape Verde N. Atlantic Oc. 84 B3 ...15°47'N 24°31'W
Cape York Peninsula Australia 108 D5 ..12°33'S 142°33'E
Cap-Haïtien Haiti 67 J4 ....19°46'N 72°15'W
Capitol Hill town N. Mariana Is 103 L7 ..15°12'N 145°45'E
Capraia, Isola di i. Italy 48 E5 ......43°04'N 9°48'E
Capricorn Channel Australia 108 E4 ..22°20'S 151°46'E
Caprivi Strip f. Namibia 83 B3 ......18°11'S 21°44'E
Caquetá r. Colombia 72 C6 ....1°27'S 69°25'W
Caracal Romania 50 F7 ....44°07'N 24°21'E
Caracas Venezuela 72 C8 ....10°28'N 66°59'W
Caransebeş Romania 50 E7 ....45°25'N 22°14'E
Caratasca, Laguna de lagoon Honduras 67 H4
....15°20'N 83°57'W
Caratinga Brazil 73 E5 ....19°45'S 42°04'W
Caravaca de la Cruz Spain 45 E3 ...38°07'N 1°51'W
Carbonara, Capo c. Italy 48 E4 .....39°06'N 9°32'E
Carcassonne France 44 E3 ....43°13'N 2°22'E
Cardiff Wales 10 D3 ....51°29'N 3°11'W
Cardiff d. Wales 21 D2 ....51°30'N 3°12'W
Cardigan Wales 10 C4 ....52°05'N 4°40'W
Cardigan Bay Wales 10 C4 ....52°33'N 4°32'W
Carei Romania 47 J2 ....47°41'N 22°28'E
Carey, Lake Australia 108 B4 ....28°57'S 122°21'E
Caribbean Sea N. Atlantic Oc. 67 H4 ..19°03'N 83°05'W
Caribou Mountains Canada 60 G3 ...59°02'N 115°22'W
Cark Mountain hill Ireland 14 B2 ...54°53'N 7°52'W
Carletonville S. Africa 83 B2 ....26°21'S 27°24'E
Carlingford Lough inlet Ireland/U.K. 18 E4 ..54°05'N 6°14'W
Carlisle England 12 E3 ....54°54'N 2°56'W
Carlow Ireland 18 E2 ....52°50'N 6°56'W
Carlow d. Ireland 18 E2 ....52°47'N 6°52'W
Carluke Scotland 15 F3 ....55°44'N 3°50'W
Carmacks Canada 60 E4 ....62°05'N 136°17'W
Carmarthen Wales 10 C3 ....51°51'N 4°19'W
Carmarthen Bay Wales 10 C3 ....51°38'N 4°32'W
Carmarthenshire d. Wales 21 C2 ....51°57'N 4°19'W
Carmel Head Wales 10 C5 ....53°25'N 4°34'W
Carmen, Isla i. Mexico 66 B6 ....25°59'N 111°09'W
Carnac France 44 B5 ....47°35'N 3°04'W
Carn Dearg hill Scotland 17 E2 .....57°06'N 4°16'W
Carndonagh Ireland 14 B3 ....55°15'N 7°15'W
Carnedd Llywelyn mt. Wales 10 D5 ..53°10'N 3°58'W
Carnedd y Filiast hill Wales 10 D4 ..52°59'N 3°41'W
Carnegie, Lake Australia 108 B4 ....26°10'S 122°54'E
Carn Eighe mt. Scotland 16 D2 .....57°17'N 5°07'W
Carnforth England 12 E3 ....54°08'N 2°46'W
Carnic Alps mts Italy 46 E2 ....46°40'N 12°48'E
Carnlough Northern Ireland 14 D2 ..54°59'N 5°59'W
Carn Mòr hill Scotland 17 F2 ....57°15'N 3°13'W
Carn nan Gabhar mt. Scotland 17 F1 ..56°50'N 3°41'W
Carnot, Cape Australia 108 C3 ......34°55'S 135°37'E
Carnoustie Scotland 15 G4 ....56°30'N 2°42'W
Carnsore Point Ireland 18 E2 ....52°10'N 6°22'W
Caroline Islands N. Pacific Oc. 117 I3 ..6°35'N 144°24'E
Carpathian Mountains Europe 47 J3 ..48°45'N 23°45'E
Carpentaria, Gulf of Australia 108 C5 ..14°06'S 139°04'E
Carpentras France 44 F4 ....44°04'N 5°03'E
Carra, Lough l. Ireland 18 B3 ....53°44'N 9°14'W
Carrantuohill mt. Ireland 18 B1 .....51°59'N 9°44'W
Carrara Italy 46 D1 ....44°04'N 10°06'E
Carrickfergus Northern Ireland 14 D2 ..54°43'N 5°48'W
Carrickmacross Ireland 18 E3 ....53°59'N 6°43'W
Carrick-on-Shannon Ireland 18 C3 ..53°56'N 8°05'W
Carrick-on-Suir Ireland 18 D2 ......52°21'N 7°25'W
Carron r. Falk. Scotland 15 F4 ......56°02'N 3°44'W
Carron r. High. Scotland 16 E2 .....57°53'N 4°22'W
Carrowmore Lake Ireland 18 B4 .....54°11'N 9°47'W
Carson City U.S.A. 62 C4 ....39°10'N 119°46'W
Carsphairn Scotland 14 E3 ....55°13'N 4°16'W
Cartagena Colombia 72 B8 ....10°23'N 75°33'W
Cartagena Spain 45 E2 ....37°36'N 0°59'W
Carteret France 11 Z9 ....49°23'N 1°47'W
Carteret, Cap de c. France 11 Z9 ...49°22'N 1°48'W
Carterton England 8 D2 ....51°46'N 1°36'W
Cartmel England 12 E3 ....54°12'N 2°57'W
Caruaru Brazil 72 F6 ....8°13'S 35°52'W
Carvin France 42 B3 ....50°29'N 2°57'E
Casablanca Morocco 84 D5 ....33°35'N 7°34'W
Casa Grande U.S.A. 62 D3 ....32°53'N 111°45'W
Cascade Range mts Canada/U.S.A. 62 F7
....41°49'N 122°21'E
Cascavel Brazil 73 D4 ....24°55'S 53°28'W
Cashel Ireland 18 D2 ....52°31'N 7°53'W
Casper U.S.A. 62 E5 ....42°52'N 106°20'W
Caspian Lowland f. Kazakhstan/Russia 53 E2
....44°15'N 45°42'E
Caspian Sea l. Asia/Europe 53 F2 ..42°00'N 51°00'E
Cassiar Mountains Canada 60 E3 ...59°40'N 130°31'W
Cassley r. Scotland 16 E2 ....57°58'N 4°34'W
Castanhal Brazil 72 E6 ....1°18'S 47°55'W

Castelló de la Plana Spain 45 E3 ....39°59'N 0°02'W
Castlebar Ireland 18 B3 ....53°51'N 9°17'W
Castlebay Scotland 16 B1 ....56°57'N 7°29'W
Castleblayney Ireland 18 E4 ....54°07'N 6°43'W
Castle Cary England 8 C2 ....51°05'N 2°31'W
Castlecomer Ireland 18 D2 ....52°48'N 7°13'W
Castleconnell Ireland 18 C2 ....52°43'N 8°30'W
Castlederg Northern Ireland 14 B2 ....54°42'N 7°35'W
Castle Donington England 8 D3 ....52°50'N 1°20'W
Castle Douglas Scotland 15 F2 ....54°56'N 3°56'W
Castleford England 13 F2 ....53°43'N 1°21'W
Castleisland Ireland 18 B2 ....52°14'N 9°27'W
Castletown Isle of Man 12 C3 ....54°05'N 4°39'W
Castres France 44 E3 ....43°36'N 2°14'E
Castries St Lucia 67 L3 ....14°00'N 60°59'W
Castro Verde Portugal 45 A2 ....37°42'N 8°05'W
Catalonia d. Spain 45 F4 ....41°50'N 1°30'E
Catamarca Argentina 73 C4 ....28°26'S 65°45'W
Catanduanes i. Phil. 103 G6 ....13°46'N 124°14'E
Catania Italy 48 G4 ....37°30'N 15°05'E
Catanzaro Italy 49 G4 ....38°55'N 16°36'E
Catarman Phil. 103 G6 ....12°29'N 124°38'E
Caterham England 9 E2 ....51°17'N 0°05'W
Cat Island Bahamas 67 I5 ....24°28'N 75°30'W
Catoche, Cabo c. Mexico 66 G5 ....21°37'N 87°06'W
Catterick England 13 F3 ....54°23'N 1°38'W
Cauca r. Colombia 67 J2 ....8°54'N 74°29'W
Caucaia Brazil 72 F6 ....3°42'S 38°42'W
Caucasus mts Asia/Europe 53 E2 ....43°53'N 40°00'E
Caudry France 42 C3 ....50°07'N 3°25'E
Causeway Coast and Glens d. Northern Ireland 20 B4 ....54°58'N 6°28'W
Cavan Ireland 18 D3 ....53°59'N 7°22'W
Cavan d. Ireland 18 D3 ....53°57'N 7°15'W
Cawston England 9 G3 ....52°46'N 1°10'E
Caxias Brazil 72 E6 ....4°54'S 43°19'W
Caxias do Sul Brazil 73 D4 ....29°13'S 51°11'W
Cayenne French Guiana 72 D7 ....4°53'N 52°21'W
Cayman Brac i. Cayman Is 67 I4 ....19°43'N 79°48'W
Cayman Islands Central America 67 H4 ....19°31'N 81°15'W
Cebu Phil. 103 G6 ....10°17'N 123°55'E
Cebu i. Phil. 103 G6 ....10°26'N 123°53'E
Cedar r. U.S.A. 63 J5 ....43°40'N 84°23'W
Cedar City U.S.A. 62 D4 ....37°41'N 113°04'W
Cedar Rapids town U.S.A. 63 H5 ....41°59'N 91°40'W
Cedros, Isla i. Mexico 66 A6 ....28°11'N 115°20'W
Cegléd Hungary 46 H2 ....47°10'N 19°48'E
Celebes i. Indonesia 102 G3 ....2°01'S 120°29'E
Celebes Sea Indonesia/Phil. 102 G4 ....3°03'N 121°10'E
Celje Slovenia 46 F2 ....46°14'N 15°15'E
Celle Germany 46 D5 ....52°38'N 10°05'E
Celtic Sea Ireland/U.K. 11 A2 ....50°54'N 6°33'W
Cemlyn, Llyn l. Wales 10 B4 ....52°57'N 3°43'W
Cenderawasih, Teluk b. Indonesia 103 J3 ....2°05'S 135°33'E
Central, Cordillera mts Colombia 72 B7 ....1°38'N 76°51'W
Central, Cordillera mts Peru 72 B6 ....10°02'S 76°25'W
Central African Republic Africa 85 G2 ....6°25'N 20°12'E
Central Bedfordshire d. England 21 E3 ....51°59'N 0°30'W
Central Range mts P.N.G. 103 K3 ....4°57'S 142°36'E
Central Russian Upland Russia 53 D3 ....53°00'N 38°00'E
Central Siberian Plateau f. Russia 55 M4 ....67°03'N 110°35'E
Cephalonia i. Greece 50 D4 ....38°14'N 20°21'E
Ceram Sea Indonesia 103 I3 ....2°33'S 130°11'E
Ceredigion d. Wales 21 D3 ....52°19'N 3°58'W
Cernavodă Romania 51 H7 ....44°21'N 28°02'E
Cerro de Pasco Peru 72 B5 ....10°42'S 76°14'W
Cervo r. Spain 45 B5 ....43°41'N 7°26'W
České Budějovice Czechia 46 F3 ....48°59'N 14°29'E
Cetinje Montenegro 50 C6 ....42°23'N 18°55'E
Ceuta N. Africa 48 B4 ....35°53'N 5°20'W
Cévennes mts France 44 E3 ....43°50'N 3°17'E
Ceyhan Turkey 51 K3 ....37°01'N 35°47'E
Ceyhan r. Turkey 51 K3 ....36°42'N 35°37'E
Chābahār Iran 95 J5 ....25°18'N 60°38'E
Chad Africa 85 F3 ....15°07'N 18°13'E
Chad, Lake Africa 84 F3 ....13°27'N 14°24'E
Chadron U.S.A. 62 F5 ....42°50'N 102°57'W
Chagai Hills Afgh./Pakistan 96 B6 ....29°17'N 63°23'E
Chaghcharān Afgh. 95 K6 ....34°28'N 65°03'E
Chagos Archipelago is Indian Oc. 117 G2 ....6°00'S 72°00'E
Chale England 8 D1 ....50°36'N 1°19'W
Chalkida Greece 50 E4 ....38°27'N 23°37'E
Challenger Deep f. N. Pacific Oc. 117 I3 ....11°17'N 142°30'E
Châlons-en-Champagne France 44 F6 ....48°58'N 4°22'E
Chalon-sur-Saône France 44 F5 ....46°48'N 4°51'E
Chālūs Iran 95 H7 ....36°37'N 51°26'E
Chaman Pakistan 96 C7 ....30°55'N 66°28'E
Chambéry France 44 F4 ....45°34'N 5°55'E
Champaign U.S.A. 63 I5 ....40°06'N 88°17'W
Champlain, Lake Canada/U.S.A. 63 L5 ....44°23'N 73°22'W
Chandalar r. U.S.A. 60 D4 ....66°36'N 145°51'W
Chandigarh d. India 98 D4 ....30°42'N 76°48'E
Chandrapur India 96 E4 ....19°57'N 79°21'E
Changchun China 99 N6 ....43°53'N 125°20'E
Changde China 99 K3 ....29°03'N 111°42'E
Chang Jiang r. China 99 M4 ....31°24'N 121°48'E
Changsha China 99 K3 ....28°10'N 112°59'E
Changzhi China 99 K5 ....36°06'N 113°09'E
Changzhou China 99 L4 ....31°47'N 119°59'E
Chania Greece 50 F2 ....35°30'N 24°02'E
Channel Islands English Channel 11 Z9 ....49°20'N 2°37'W
Channel Islands U.S.A. 62 C3 ....33°41'N 119°26'W
Channel-Port-aux-Basques Canada 61 M2 ....47°33'N 59°01'W
Channel Tunnel France/U.K. 9 G2 ....51°04'N 1°24'E
Chanthaburi Thailand 102 C6 ....12°37'N 102°08'E
Chao Phraya r. Thailand 102 C6 ....13°40'N 100°36'E
Chaouèn Morocco 48 B4 ....35°11'N 5°16'W
Chapala, Laguna de l. Mexico 66 D5 ....20°15'N 103°00'W
Chapayevo Kazakhstan 53 F3 ....50°12'N 51°10'E
Chapel-en-le-Frith England 13 F2 ....53°20'N 1°54'W
Chapeltown England 13 F2 ....53°28'N 1°28'W
Chapleau Canada 61 J2 ....47°51'N 83°24'W
Chard England 8 C1 ....50°52'N 2°58'W
Chārīkār Afgh. 95 K7 ....35°02'N 69°15'E
Charkayuvom Russia 52 F4 ....65°49'N 54°51'E
Charlbury England 8 D2 ....51°52'N 1°29'W
Charleroi Belgium 42 D3 ....50°24'N 4°27'E
Charles, Cape U.S.A. 63 K4 ....37°10'N 75°58'W
Charleston S. C. U.S.A. 63 K3 ....32°48'N 79°58'W
Charleston W. Va. U.S.A. 63 J4 ....38°21'N 81°39'W
Charlestown Ireland 18 C3 ....53°57'N 8°47'W
Charleville-Mézières France 44 F6 ....49°46'N 4°44'E
Charlotte U.S.A. 63 J4 ....35°14'N 80°50'W

Charlottesville U.S.A. 63 K4 ....38°02'N 78°30'W
Charlottetown Canada 61 L2 ....46°16'N 63°09'W
Chartres France 44 D6 ....48°27'N 1°30'E
Chassiron, Pointe de pt France 44 C5 ....46°03'N 1°24'W
Châteaubriant France 44 C5 ....47°43'N 1°22'W
Châteaudun France 44 D6 ....48°04'N 1°20'E
Châteauroux France 44 D5 ....46°48'N 1°41'E
Château-Thierry France 44 E6 ....49°03'N 3°25'E
Châtellerault France 44 D5 ....46°49'N 0°33'E
Chatham England 9 F2 ....51°23'N 0°31'E
Chatham Islands New Zealand 109 H2 ....43°24'S 176°11'W
Chattahoochee r. U.S.A. 63 J3 ....30°55'N 84°58'W
Chattanooga U.S.A. 63 I4 ....35°02'N 85°21'W
Chatteris England 9 F3 ....52°27'N 0°03'E
Chaumont France 44 F6 ....48°07'N 5°08'E
Cheadle England 8 D3 ....52°59'N 1°59'W
Cheb Czechia 46 E4 ....50°05'N 12°23'E
Cheboksary Russia 52 E3 ....56°09'N 47°13'E
Cheboygan U.S.A. 63 J6 ....45°39'N 84°28'W
Cheddar England 8 C2 ....51°17'N 2°47'W
Cheju-do i. S. Korea 99 N4 ....33°34'N 126°43'E
Chekhov Russia 47 Q6 ....55°09'N 37°28'E
Cheleken Turkmenistan 95 H7 ....39°25'N 53°01'E
Chełm Poland 47 K4 ....51°08'N 23°29'E
Chelmer r. England 9 F2 ....51°45'N 0°40'E
Chelmsford England 9 F2 ....51°44'N 0°29'E
Cheltenham England 8 C2 ....51°54'N 2°04'W
Chelyabinsk Russia 52 G3 ....55°11'N 61°24'E
Chemnitz Germany 46 E4 ....50°50'N 12°56'E
Chengde China 99 L6 ....40°52'N 117°58'E
Chengdu China 99 I4 ....30°43'N 104°04'E
Chennai India 96 F3 ....13°06'N 80°16'E
Chenzhou China 99 K3 ....25°44'N 113°00'E
Chepstow Wales 10 E3 ....51°38'N 2°40'W
Cher r. France 44 D5 ....47°20'N 0°29'E
Cherbourg-Octeville France 44 C6 ....49°38'N 1°37'W
Cherepovets Russia 52 D3 ....59°08'N 37°55'E
Chergui, Chott ech l. Algeria 48 D3 ....34°03'N 0°16'W
Cherkasy Ukraine 47 O3 ....49°26'N 32°05'E
Cherkessk Russia 53 E2 ....44°13'N 42°03'E
Chernihiv Ukraine 47 N4 ....51°29'N 31°19'E
Chernivtsi Ukraine 47 K3 ....48°19'N 25°56'E
Chernyakhovsk Russia 47 I6 ....54°38'N 21°49'E
Chernyshevskiy Russia 55 M4 ....62°56'N 112°36'E
Cherskogo, Khrebet mts Russia 55 P4 ....63°42'N 146°57'E
Chervonohrad Ukraine 47 K4 ....50°23'N 24°14'E
Cherwell r. England 8 D2 ....51°44'N 1°15'W
Chesapeake Bay U.S.A. 63 K4 ....38°05'N 76°14'W
Chesham England 9 E2 ....51°43'N 0°37'W
Cheshire East d. England 21 D3 ....53°09'N 2°18'W
Cheshire West and Chester d. England 21 D3 ....53°11'N 2°46'W
Cheshskaya Guba b. Russia 52 E4 ....67°20'N 46°30'E
Cheshunt England 9 E2 ....51°42'N 0°02'W
Chesil Beach f. England 8 C1 ....50°38'N 2°36'W
Chester England 12 E2 ....53°12'N 2°54'W
Chesterfield England 13 F2 ....53°14'N 1°25'W
Chester-le-Street England 13 F3 ....54°52'N 1°34'W
Chetumal Mexico 66 G4 ....18°30'N 88°18'W
Cheviot Hills England 13 E4 ....55°12'N 2°39'W
Chew Magna England 8 C2 ....51°22'N 2°37'W
Chew Valley Lake resr England 8 C2 ....51°20'N 2°38'W
Cheyenne U.S.A. 62 F5 ....41°09'N 104°49'W
Cheyenne r. U.S.A. 62 F5 ....44°44'N 101°09'W
Chhattisgarh d. India 96 F5 ....21°29'N 81°46'E
Chiang Mai Thailand 102 B7 ....18°47'N 98°59'E
Chiang Rai Thailand 102 B7 ....19°55'N 99°53'E
Chiapas d. Mexico 66 F4 ....16°23'N 92°17'W
Chiba Japan 104 D3 ....35°37'N 140°07'E
Chibougamau Canada 61 K2 ....49°55'N 74°22'W
Chicago U.S.A. 63 I5 ....41°55'N 87°38'W
Chichester England 8 E1 ....50°50'N 0°46'W
Chiclayo Peru 72 B6 ....6°44'S 79°51'W
Chicoutimi Canada 61 K2 ....48°26'N 71°03'W
Chidley, Cape Canada 61 L4 ....60°26'N 64°20'W
Chiemsee l. Germany 46 E2 ....47°52'N 12°28'E
Chifeng China 99 L6 ....42°11'N 119°02'E
Chiganak Kazakhstan 54 I2 ....45°10'N 73°57'E
Chihuahua Mexico 66 C6 ....28°38'N 106°07'W
Chihuahua d. Mexico 66 C6 ....29°10'N 106°11'W
Chile S. America 73 B3 ....34°06'S 71°23'W
Chilham England 9 F2 ....51°15'N 0°58'E
Chillán Chile 73 B3 ....36°37'S 72°07'W
Chiloé, Isla de i. Chile 73 B2 ....42°26'S 74°29'W
Chilpancingo Mexico 66 E4 ....17°33'N 99°30'W
Chiltern Hills England 8 E2 ....51°39'N 0°50'W
Chimborazo mt. Ecuador 72 B6 ....1°27'S 78°50'W
Chimbote Peru 72 B6 ....9°03'S 78°35'W
Chimboy Uzbekistan 53 F2 ....42°56'N 59°47'E
Chimoio Mozambique 83 C3 ....19°07'S 33°28'E
China Asia 98 H3 ....38°39'N 78°40'E
Chindwin r. Myanmar 97 I5 ....21°27'N 95°15'E
Chingola Zambia 83 B3 ....12°33'S 27°54'E
Chinhoyi Zimbabwe 83 C3 ....17°21'S 30°11'E
Chinju S. Korea 104 A3 ....35°10'N 128°05'E
Chioggia Italy 46 E1 ....45°12'N 12°16'E
Chios Greece 50 G4 ....38°22'N 26°08'E
Chios i. Greece 50 F4 ....38°24'N 25°58'E
Chipata Zambia 83 C3 ....13°37'S 32°38'E
Chippenham England 8 C2 ....51°27'N 2°07'W
Chipping Campden England 8 D3 ....52°03'N 1°47'W
Chipping Norton England 8 D2 ....51°57'N 1°32'W
Chipping Ongar England 9 F2 ....51°42'N 0°15'E
Chipping Sodbury England 8 C2 ....51°32'N 2°23'W
Chiriquí, Golfo de b. Panama 67 H2 ....8°02'N 82°04'W
Chirk Wales 10 D4 ....52°56'N 3°03'W
Chirnside Scotland 15 G3 ....55°48'N 2°12'W
Chirripo mt. Costa Rica 67 H2 ....9°30'N 83°30'W
Chisasibi Canada 61 K3 ....53°49'N 78°59'W
Chișinău Moldova 49 I6 ....47°02'N 28°50'E
Chistopol' Russia 52 F3 ....55°21'N 50°36'E
Chita Russia 55 M3 ....52°03'N 113°31'E
Chitambo Zambia 83 C3 ....12°54'S 30°37'E
Chitradurga India 96 E3 ....14°14'N 76°22'E
Chitral Pakistan 96 D8 ....35°53'N 71°47'E
Chittagong Bangl. 97 H5 ....22°20'N 91°49'E
Chittoor India 96 E3 ....13°12'N 79°05'E
Chitungwiza Zimbabwe 83 C3 ....18°01'S 31°04'E
Chojnice Poland 46 G5 ....53°42'N 17°34'E
Cholet France 44 C5 ....47°04'N 0°53'W
Chomutov Czechia 46 E4 ....50°28'N 13°24'E
Chon Buri Thailand 102 C6 ....13°22'N 101°02'E
Chŏngjin N. Korea 99 N6 ....41°46'N 129°45'E
Chongqing China 99 J3 ....29°34'N 106°32'E
Chongqing d. China 99 J4 ....30°04'N 107°39'E
Chonos, Archipiélago de los is Chile 73 B2 ....44°59'S 75°31'W

Chorley England 12 E2 ....53°39'N 2°38'W
Chornobyl' Ukraine 47 N4 ....51°16'N 30°14'E
Chornomors'ke Ukraine 51 J7 ....45°30'N 32°43'E
Chortkiv Ukraine 47 K3 ....49°01'N 25°47'E
Chōshi Japan 104 D3 ....35°44'N 140°49'E
Choûm Mauritania 84 C4 ....21°20'N 12°59'W
Choybalsan Mongolia 99 K7 ....47°57'N 114°34'E
Christchurch England 8 D1 ....50°44'N 1°47'W
Christchurch New Zealand 109 G2 ....43°31'S 172°37'E
Christmas Island Indian Oc. 102 D1 ....10°30'S 105°44'E
Chūgoku-sanchi mts Japan 104 B2 ....34°45'N 132°19'E
Chukchi Sea Russia/U.S.A. 55 T4 ....69°12'N 171°31'W
Chukotskiy Poluostrov pen. Russia 55 T4 ....65°58'N 175°16'W
Chulmleigh England 11 D2 ....50°55'N 3°52'W
Chumphon Thailand 102 B6 ....10°31'N 99°13'E
Chuncheon S. Korea 99 N5 ....37°52'N 127°46'E
Chunya r. Russia 55 K4 ....61°36'N 96°31'E
Chur Switz. 46 C2 ....46°51'N 9°32'E
Churchill Canada 61 I3 ....58°44'N 94°05'W
Churchill r. Man. Canada 61 I3 ....58°11'N 94°23'W
Churchill r. Nfld. and Lab. Canada 61 L3 ....53°16'N 60°14'W
Churchill, Cape Canada 61 I3 ....58°45'N 93°16'W
Church Stretton England 8 C3 ....52°32'N 2°48'W
Chusovoy Russia 52 F3 ....58°18'N 57°48'E
Chuxiong China 99 I3 ....25°02'N 101°32'E
Ciechanów Poland 46 I5 ....52°53'N 20°38'E
Ciego de Ávila Cuba 67 I5 ....21°50'N 78°45'W
Cienfuegos Cuba 67 H5 ....22°10'N 80°25'W
Cigüela r. Spain 45 D3 ....39°08'N 3°43'W
Cihanbeyli Turkey 51 J4 ....38°40'N 32°56'E
Cilacap Indonesia 102 D2 ....7°41'S 109°00'E
Cimone, Monte mt. Italy 46 D1 ....44°11'N 10°42'E
Cinca r. Spain 45 F4 ....41°26'N 0°21'E
Cincinnati U.S.A. 63 J4 ....39°06'N 84°32'W
Cinderford England 8 C2 ....51°49'N 2°30'W
Ciney Belgium 42 E3 ....50°18'N 5°06'E
Cirebon Indonesia 102 D2 ....6°45'S 108°34'E
Cirencester England 8 D2 ....51°43'N 1°58'W
City of Kingston upon Hull d. England 21 E3 ....53°46'N 0°19'W
Ciudad Bolívar Venezuela 72 C7 ....8°01'N 63°35'W
Ciudad del Carmen Mexico 66 F4 ....18°39'N 91°51'W
Ciudad Delicias Mexico 66 C6 ....28°10'N 105°30'W
Ciudad de Valles Mexico 66 E5 ....21°59'N 99°00'W
Ciudad Guayana Venezuela 72 C7 ....8°20'N 62°37'W
Ciudad Ixtepec Mexico 66 E4 ....16°35'N 95°06'W
Ciudad Juárez Mexico 66 C7 ....31°44'N 106°28'W
Ciudad Madero Mexico 66 E5 ....22°19'N 97°51'W
Ciudad Obregón Mexico 66 C6 ....27°28'N 109°57'W
Ciudad Real Spain 45 D3 ....38°59'N 3°54'W
Ciudad Rodrigo Spain 45 B4 ....40°36'N 6°31'W
Ciudad Victoria Mexico 66 E5 ....23°45'N 99°08'W
Ciutadella de Menorca Spain 45 G4 ....40°00'N 3°52'E
Civitavecchia Italy 48 F5 ....42°05'N 11°48'E
Çivril Turkey 51 H4 ....38°18'N 29°43'E
Cixi China 99 M4 ....30°10'N 121°14'E
Clackmannanshire d. Scotland 20 D5 ....56°09'N 3°45'W
Clacton-on-Sea England 9 G2 ....51°47'N 1°09'E
Claonaig Scotland 14 D3 ....55°45'N 5°24'W
Clara Ireland 18 D3 ....53°20'N 7°37'W
Clare d. Ireland 18 C2 ....52°53'N 8°50'W
Clare r. Ireland 18 B3 ....53°19'N 9°03'W
Clare Island Ireland 18 A3 ....53°49'N 10°01'W
Claremorris Ireland 18 C3 ....53°43'N 8°59'W
Clarksville U.S.A. 63 I4 ....36°32'N 87°20'W
Clay Cross England 13 F2 ....53°10'N 1°25'W
Claydon England 9 G3 ....52°06'N 1°07'E
Clay Head Isle of Man 12 C3 ....54°12'N 4°23'W
Clayton U.S.A. 62 F4 ....36°28'N 103°12'W
Clear, Cape Ireland 18 B1 ....51°25'N 9°31'W
Clear Island Ireland 18 B1 ....51°26'N 9°28'W
Cleator Moor England 12 D3 ....54°31'N 3°31'W
Cleethorpes England 13 G2 ....53°33'N 0°02'W
Cleobury Mortimer England 8 C3 ....52°23'N 2°29'W
Clermont-Ferrand France 44 E4 ....45°46'N 3°05'E
Clevedon England 8 C2 ....51°26'N 2°51'W
Cleveland U.S.A. 63 J5 ....41°30'N 81°41'W
Cleveland Hills England 13 F3 ....54°22'N 1°13'W
Cleveleys England 12 D2 ....53°53'N 3°02'W
Clew Bay Ireland 18 B3 ....53°48'N 9°47'W
Cliffe England 9 F2 ....51°28'N 0°30'E
Clinton U.S.A. 62 G4 ....35°32'N 98°58'W
Clipperton, Île N. Pacific Oc. 56 ....10°21'N 109°19'W
Clisham hill Scotland 16 C2 ....57°58'N 6°49'W
Clitheroe England 13 E2 ....53°52'N 2°23'W
Clogher Head Ireland 18 E3 ....53°48'N 6°13'W
Clonakilty Ireland 18 C1 ....51°37'N 8°53'W
Clones Ireland 18 D4 ....54°10'N 7°13'W
Clonmel Ireland 18 D2 ....52°21'N 7°43'W
Cloud Peak U.S.A. 62 E5 ....44°24'N 107°01'W
Clovis U.S.A. 62 F3 ....34°27'N 103°12'W
Cluanie, Loch l. Scotland 16 D2 ....57°09'N 5°07'W
Cluj-Napoca Romania 47 J2 ....46°46'N 23°36'E
Clun England 8 B3 ....52°25'N 3°02'W
Clydach Wales 10 D3 ....51°42'N 3°54'W
Clyde r. Scotland 15 E3 ....55°55'N 4°29'W
Clyde, Firth of est. Scotland 14 E3 ....55°25'N 4°59'W
Clydebank Scotland 14 E3 ....55°54'N 4°24'W
Clyde River town Canada 61 L5 ....70°23'N 68°31'W
Coahuila d. Mexico 66 D6 ....27°30'N 102°24'W
Coalville England 8 D3 ....52°43'N 1°22'W
Coastal Plain f. U.S.A. 63 H3 ....30°25'N 94°23'W
Coast Mountains Canada 60 E3 ....56°20'N 127°48'W
Coast Ranges mts U.S.A. 62 B5 ....40°40'N 123°59'W
Coatbridge Scotland 15 E3 ....55°52'N 4°01'W
Coats Island Canada 61 J4 ....62°41'N 82°53'W
Coatzacoalcos Mexico 66 F4 ....18°08'N 94°26'W
Cobh Ireland 18 C1 ....51°51'N 8°18'W
Cochabamba Bolivia 72 C5 ....17°25'S 66°11'W
Cochrane Canada 63 J6 ....49°04'N 81°03'W
Cockburnspath Scotland 15 G3 ....55°56'N 2°22'W
Cockermouth England 12 D3 ....54°40'N 3°22'W
Coco r. Honduras/Nicaragua 67 H3 ....14°59'N 83°15'W
Coco, Isla de i. N. Pacific Oc. 68 B4 ....5°32'N 87°04'W
Cocos Islands Indian Oc. 102 B1 ....11°56'S 96°56'E
Cocuy, Sierra Nevada del mt. Colombia 67 J2 ....6°28'N 72°19'W
Cod, Cape U.S.A. 63 L5 ....41°58'N 70°01'W
Coddington England 13 G2 ....53°05'N 0°45'W
Codó Brazil 72 E6 ....4°28'S 43°50'W
Codsall England 8 C3 ....52°38'N 2°11'W
Coeur d'Alene U.S.A. 62 C6 ....47°41'N 116°47'W
Coffs Harbour Australia 108 E3 ....30°19'S 153°06'E
Coggeshall England 9 F2 ....51°52'N 0°42'E
Coiba, Isla de i. Panama 67 H2 ....7°27'N 81°51'W

Coigeach, Rubha pt Scotland 16 D3 ....58°06'N 5°28'W
Coimbatore India 96 E3 ....10°59'N 76°57'E
Coimbra Portugal 45 A4 ....40°13'N 8°25'W
Colchester England 9 F2 ....51°53'N 0°54'E
Coldstream Scotland 15 G3 ....55°39'N 2°15'W
Coleford England 8 C2 ....51°48'N 2°37'W
Coleraine Northern Ireland 14 C3 ....55°08'N 6°40'W
Colima Mexico 66 D4 ....19°14'N 103°45'W
Colima d. Mexico 66 D4 ....19°03'N 103°59'W
Colima, Nevado de vol. Mexico 66 D4 ....19°33'N 103°37'W
Coll i. Scotland 14 C4 ....56°36'N 6°36'W
Collier Bay Australia 108 B5 ....16°15'S 124°15'E
Colmar France 44 G6 ....48°05'N 7°21'E
Colne England 13 E2 ....53°51'N 2°11'W
Colne r. England 9 F2 ....51°51'N 0°02'E
Cologne Germany 46 B4 ....50°56'N 6°57'E
Colombia S. America 72 B7 ....3°45'N 72°22'W
Colombo Sri Lanka 96 E2 ....6°56'N 79°50'E
Colón Panama 67 I2 ....9°22'N 79°55'W
Colonsay i. Scotland 14 C4 ....56°05'N 6°15'W
Colorado r. Argentina 73 C3 ....39°42'S 62°07'W
Colorado r. Mexico/U.S.A. 62 D3 ....31°56'N 115°01'W
Colorado d. U.S.A. 62 E4 ....39°02'N 105°31'W
Colorado r. U.S.A. 62 G2 ....28°40'N 96°01'W
Colorado Plateau f. U.S.A. 62 E4 ....37°27'N 109°54'W
Colorado Springs town U.S.A. 62 F4 ....38°52'N 104°47'W
Coltishall England 9 G3 ....52°44'N 1°22'E
Columbia U.S.A. 63 J3 ....33°59'N 81°01'W
Columbia r. U.S.A. 62 B6 ....46°11'N 123°23'W
Columbia, Mount Canada 60 G3 ....52°08'N 117°25'W
Columbus Ga. U.S.A. 63 J3 ....32°32'N 84°59'W
Columbus Miss. U.S.A. 63 I3 ....33°33'N 88°25'W
Columbus Oh. U.S.A. 63 J4 ....39°58'N 83°00'W
Colville r. U.S.A. 60 C5 ....70°20'N 150°32'W
Colwyn Bay town Wales 10 D5 ....53°18'N 3°43'W
Comacchio Italy 46 E1 ....44°41'N 12°11'E
Combe Martin England 11 C3 ....51°12'N 4°01'W
Comber Northern Ireland 14 D2 ....54°33'N 5°44'W
Comeragh Mountains Ireland 18 D2 ....52°18'N 7°39'W
Como Italy 46 C1 ....45°48'N 9°05'E
Como, Lake Italy 46 C1 ....45°57'N 9°11'E
Comodoro Rivadavia Argentina 73 C2 ....45°56'S 67°30'W
Comorin, Cape India 86 ....8°04'N 77°35'E
Comoros Africa 83 D3 ....11°50'S 44°17'E
Comrat Moldova 51 H8 ....46°18'N 28°40'E
Comrie Scotland 15 F4 ....56°23'N 3°59'W
Conakry Guinea 84 C2 ....9°31'N 13°42'W
Concarneau France 44 B5 ....47°53'N 3°55'W
Concepción Chile 73 B3 ....36°50'S 73°04'W
Conception, Point U.S.A. 62 B3 ....34°27'N 120°26'W
Conchos r. Mexico 66 D6 ....29°35'N 104°29'W
Concord U.S.A. 63 L5 ....43°12'N 71°33'W
Concordia Argentina 73 D3 ....31°23'S 57°59'W
Congleton England 13 E2 ....53°10'N 2°13'E
Congo Africa 84 F1 ....2°24'S 15°10'E
Congo r. Congo/Dem. Rep. Congo 83 A4 ....6°05'S 12°26'E
Congo, Democratic Republic of the Africa 83 B4 ....3°43'S 22°17'E
Congo Basin f. Africa 84 F1 ....1°00'S 20°00'E
Coningsby England 13 G2 ....53°06'N 0°10'W
Coniston England 12 D3 ....54°22'N 3°05'W
Coniston Water l. England 12 D3 ....54°19'N 3°04'W
Conn, Lough l. Ireland 18 B4 ....54°01'N 9°16'W
Connah's Quay Wales 10 D5 ....53°13'N 3°04'W
Connecticut d. U.S.A. 63 L5 ....41°41'N 72°36'W
Connecticut r. U.S.A. 63 L5 ....41°16'N 72°22'W
Connemara f. Ireland 18 B3 ....53°28'N 9°52'W
Conon Bridge Scotland 17 E2 ....57°34'N 4°26'W
Consett England 13 F3 ....54°51'N 1°50'W
Con Son i. Vietnam 102 D5 ....8°42'N 106°40'E
Constance, Lake Germany/Switz. 46 C2 ....47°40'N 9°17'E
Constanța Romania 51 H7 ....44°11'N 28°37'E
Constantine Algeria 84 E5 ....36°23'N 6°38'E
Conwy Wales 10 D5 ....53°17'N 3°50'W
Conwy d. Wales 21 D3 ....53°10'N 3°37'W
Conwy r. Wales 10 D5 ....53°14'N 3°48'W
Conwy Bay Wales 10 C5 ....53°16'N 4°02'W
Cook Islands S. Pacific Oc. 109 I5 ....20°05'S 160°06'W
Cookstown Northern Ireland 14 C2 ....54°38'N 6°44'W
Cook Strait New Zealand 109 G2 ....40°32'S 174°07'E
Cooktown Australia 108 D5 ....15°28'S 145°17'E
Coolangatta Australia 108 E4 ....28°10'S 153°31'E
Cooper Creek watercourse Australia 108 C4 ....28°29'S 137°43'E
Coos Bay town U.S.A. 62 B5 ....43°21'N 124°12'W
Copenhagen Denmark 43 C1 ....55°40'N 12°34'E
Copiapó Chile 73 B4 ....27°18'S 70°23'W
Copinsay i. Scotland 17 G3 ....58°54'N 2°40'W
Corabia Romania 50 F6 ....43°47'N 24°29'E
Coral Harbour Canada 61 J4 ....64°12'N 83°18'W
Coral Sea S. Pacific Oc. 108 E5 ....13°27'S 151°06'E
Coral Sea Islands Territory Australia 108 E5 ....15°01'S 150°43'E
Corbie France 42 B2 ....49°55'N 2°31'E
Corbridge England 13 E3 ....54°58'N 2°01'W
Corby England 8 E3 ....52°29'N 0°41'W
Córdoba Argentina 73 C3 ....31°24'S 64°11'W
Córdoba Mexico 66 E4 ....18°55'N 96°53'W
Córdoba Spain 45 C2 ....37°53'N 4°46'W
Córdoba, Sierras de mts Argentina 73 C3 ....32°55'S 64°22'W
Corfe Castle England 8 C1 ....50°38'N 2°03'W
Corfu i. Greece 50 C4 ....39°36'N 19°47'E
Corinth Greece 50 E3 ....37°56'N 22°55'E
Corixa Grande r. Bolivia/Brazil 72 D5 ....17°30'S 57°56'W
Cork Ireland 18 C1 ....51°54'N 8°28'W
Cork d. Ireland 18 C2 ....52°01'N 8°39'W
Cork City d. Ireland 18 C2 ....51°54'N 8°28'W
Çorlu Turkey 51 G5 ....41°09'N 27°48'E
Corner Brook Canada 61 M2 ....48°54'N 57°47'W
Cornwall d. England 21 C2 ....50°30'N 4°33'W
Cornwall, Cape England 11 B2 ....50°08'N 5°47'W
Cornwallis Island Canada 61 I5 ....75°08'N 94°56'W
Coro Venezuela 72 C8 ....11°23'N 69°40'W
Coronado, Bahía de b. Costa Rica 67 H2 ....8°55'N 83°48'W
Coronation Gulf Canada 60 G4 ....68°08'N 112°32'W
Corpus Christi U.S.A. 62 G2 ....27°44'N 97°27'W
Corral de Cantos mt. Spain 45 C3 ....39°44'N 4°24'W
Corrib, Lough l. Ireland 18 B3 ....53°27'N 9°19'W
Corrientes Argentina 73 D4 ....27°27'S 58°48'W
Corrientes, Cabo c. Mexico 66 C5 ....20°26'N 105°42'W
Corse, Cap c. France 44 H3 ....43°02'N 9°22'E
Corserine hill Scotland 14 E3 ....55°09'N 4°21'W
Corsham England 8 C2 ....51°26'N 2°11'W
Corsica i. France 44 H3 ....42°00'N 8°29'E
Corte France 44 H3 ....42°18'N 9°09'E
Cortegana Spain 45 B2 ....37°55'N 6°49'W
Cortina d'Ampezzo Italy 46 E2 ....46°32'N 12°09'E

Corton England 9 G3....................52°31'N 1°45'E
Çorum Turkey 51 K5..................40°33'N 34°57'E
Corumbá Brazil 72 D5.............19°00'S 57°37'W
Corwen Wales 10 D4...............52°59'N 3°22'W
Cosenza Italy 49 G4................39°18'N 16°15'E
Cosmoledo Islands Seychelles 83 D4.....9°30'S 49°00'E
Cosne-Cours-sur-Loire France 44 E5.....47°25'N 2°56'E
Costa Blanca f. Spain 45 E3............38°03'N 0°20'W
Costa Brava f. Spain 45 G4...........41°28'N 3°05'E
Costa del Sol f. Spain 45 C2.........36°25'N 5°06'W
Costa de Mosquitos f. Nicaragua 67 H3....12°08'N 83°52'W
Costa Rica Central America 67 H3......10°08'N 84°19'W
Cotabato Phil. 103 G5.................7°13'N 124°14'E
Côte d'Azur f. France 44 G3.........43°33'N 7°13'E
Côte d'Ivoire Africa 84 D2............7°35'N 4°22'W
Cothi r. Wales 10 C3................51°52'N 4°10'W
Cotonou Benin 84 E2.................6°21'N 2°27'E
Cotopaxi, Volcán vol. Ecuador 72 B6.....0°39'S 78°26'W
Cotswold Hills England 8 C2..........51°36'N 2°15'W
Cottbus Germany 46 F4...............51°45'N 14°21'E
Cottenham England 9 F3.............52°17'N 0°08'E
Cottesmore England 8 E3............52°43'N 0°40'W
Coulogne France 42 A3..............50°55'N 1°53'E
Coupar Angus Scotland 15 F4........56°33'N 3°16'W
Courland Lagoon b. Lithuania/Russia 43 E1
                                    55°16'N 21°06'E
Coutances France 44 C6.............49°03'N 1°27'W
Coventry England 8 D3..............52°24'N 1°31'W
Covilhã Portugal 45 B4.............40°17'N 7°29'W
Cowan, Lake Australia 108 B3.......31°45'S 121°59'E
Cowbridge Wales 11 D3.............51°28'N 3°27'W
Cowdenbeath Scotland 15 F4........56°07'N 3°20'W
Cowes England 8 D1................50°46'N 1°18'W
Cowfold England 9 E1...............50°59'N 0°16'W
Cow Green Reservoir England 13 E3.....54°40'N 2°20'W
Coxhaique Chile 73 B2.............45°36'S 72°05'W
Cox's Bazar Bangl. 97 H5..........21°27'N 91°59'E
Cozumel, Isla de i. Mexico 66 G5....20°22'N 86°53'W
Craig U.S.A. 62 E5.................40°31'N 107°32'W
Craigavon Northern Ireland 14 C2....54°26'N 6°21'W
Craig Goch Reservoir Wales 10 D4....52°19'N 3°37'W
Craignure Scotland 14 D4..........56°28'N 5°43'W
Crail Scotland 15 G4..............56°16'N 2°38'W
Craiova Romania 50 F7.............44°19'N 23°48'E
Cramlington England 13 F4.........55°05'N 1°35'W
Cranbrook Canada 60 G2...........49°32'N 115°45'W
Cranleigh England 9 E2............51°08'N 0°29'W
Crawley England 9 E2..............51°07'N 0°11'W
Creag Meagaidh mt. Scotland 17 E1....56°57'N 4°36'W
Credenhill England 8 C3...........52°05'N 2°48'W
Crediton England 11 D2............50°48'N 3°39'W
Cree Lake Canada 60 H3...........57°31'N 106°29'W
Cremona Italy 46 D1...............45°08'N 10°01'E
Cres i. Croatia 50 A7.............44°51'N 14°28'E
Crescent City U.S.A. 62 B5........41°47'N 124°09'W
Creston U.S.A. 63 H5..............41°03'N 94°22'W
Creswell England 13 F2...........53°16'N 1°13'W
Crete i. Greece 50 F2............35°28'N 24°41'E
Creuse r. France 44 D5............47°00'N 0°34'E
Crewe England 13 E2..............53°06'N 2°26'W
Crewkerne England 8 C1...........50°53'N 2°48'W
Crianlarich Scotland 14 E4........56°24'N 4°37'W
Criccieth Wales 10 C4.............52°55'N 4°14'W
Criciúma Brazil 73 E4.............28°45'S 49°25'W
Crickhowell Wales 10 D3...........51°51'N 3°08'W
Crieff Scotland 15 F4.............56°23'N 3°50'W
Criffel hill Scotland 15 F2.......54°57'N 3°38'W
Crimea pen. Ukraine 49 J6.........45°20'N 34°05'E
Crimond Scotland 17 H2...........57°36'N 1°55'W
Croatia Europe 50 B7.............45°02'N 15°14'E
Croisilles France 9 H1...........50°12'N 2°53'E
Croker Island Australia 103 I1....11°04'S 132°38'E
Cromarty Scotland 17 E2..........57°41'N 4°02'W
Cromarty Firth est. Scotland 17 E2.....57°38'N 4°19'W
Cromdale, Hills of Scotland 17 F2....57°19'N 3°31'W
Cromer England 9 G3..............52°56'N 1°18'E
Cronamuck Mountain hill Ireland 14 B2....54°54'N 7°51'W
Crook England 13 F3..............54°43'N 1°45'W
Crooked Island Bahamas 67 J5......22°48'N 74°14'W
Crooked Island Passage str. Bahamas 67 J5
                                    22°29'N 74°55'W
Croom Ireland 18 C2..............52°31'N 8°43'W
Crosby England 12 D2.............53°29'N 3°02'W
Cross Fell hill England 13 E3.....54°42'N 2°29'W
Crossgar Northern Ireland 14 D2...54°24'N 5°45'W
Crossmaglen Northern Ireland 14 C2....54°04'N 6°36'W
Crotone Italy 49 G4..............39°05'N 17°08'E
Crouch r. England 9 F2...........51°38'N 0°56'E
Crowborough England 9 F2.........51°04'N 0°10'E
Crowland England 9 E3............52°41'N 0°10'W
Crowle England 13 G2.............53°37'N 0°50'W
Crowthorne England 8 E2..........51°22'N 0°48'W
Croyde England 11 C3.............51°08'N 4°13'W
Croydon England 9 E2.............51°23'N 0°06'W
Crozet Islands Indian Oc. 117 G1....47°00'S 52°00'E
Cruden Bay town Scotland 17 H2.....57°25'N 1°51'W
Crumlin Northern Ireland 14 C2....54°38'N 6°13'W
Cruz, Cabo c. Cuba 67 I4.........19°51'N 77°43'W
Cruzeiro do Sul Brazil 72 B6......7°41'S 72°40'W
Cuando r. Angola/Zambia 83 B3....17°39'S 23°24'E
Cuanza r. Angola 83 A4...........9°21'S 13°08'E
Cuauhtémoc Mexico 66 C6..........28°24'N 106°53'W
Cuba Central America 67 H5........21°18'N 80°06'W
Cubango r. Angola/Namibia 83 B3....18°01'S 21°26'E
Cuckfield England 9 E2...........51°00'N 0°09'W
Cúcuta Colombia 72 B7............7°53'N 72°31'W
Cuddalore India 96 E3............11°42'N 79°43'E
Cuenca Ecuador 72 B6.............2°53'S 79°00'W
Cuenca Spain 45 D4...............40°04'N 2°08'W
Cuenca, Serranía de mts Spain 45 D4....40°38'N 2°08'W
Cuernavaca Mexico 66 E4..........18°56'N 99°11'W
Cuiabá Brazil 72 D5..............15°33'S 56°04'W
Cuilcagh hill Ireland/U.K. 14 B2....54°12'N 7°49'W
Cuillin Sound str. Scotland 16 C2....57°08'N 6°21'W
Culiacán Mexico 66 C5............24°47'N 107°27'W
Cullen Scotland 17 G2............57°41'N 2°49'W
Cullera Spain 45 E3..............39°10'N 0°13'W
Cullompton England 11 D2.........50°51'N 3°23'W
Cullybackey Northern Ireland 14 C2....54°53'N 6°21'W
Cul Mòr hill Scotland 16 D3.......58°03'N 5°07'W
Culuene r. Brazil 72 D5..........11°11'S 53°09'W
Culzean Bay Scotland 14 D3........55°22'N 4°49'W
Cumaná Venezuela 72 C8...........10°24'N 64°09'W
Cumberland U.S.A. 63 K4..........39°38'N 78°47'W
Cumberland Sound str. Canada 61 L4....64°08'N 63°14'W
Cumbernauld Scotland 15 F3........55°57'N 3°59'W
Cumbria d. England 21 D4.........54°35'N 3°17'W

Cumnock Scotland 14 E3...........55°27'N 4°16'W
Cunene r. Angola 83 A3...........17°15'S 11°46'E
Cuneo Italy 48 E5................44°24'N 7°33'E
Cupar Scotland 15 F4.............56°19'N 3°01'W
Cupica, Golfo de b. Colombia 67 I2....6°25'N 77°46'W
Curaçao i. Neth. Antilles 67 K3....12°12'N 69°04'W
Curitiba Brazil 73 E4............25°28'S 49°17'W
Cusco Peru 72 B5................13°31'S 71°59'W
Cushendall Northern Ireland 14 C3....55°05'N 6°04'W
Cuttack India 96 G5.............20°27'N 85°55'E
Cuxhaven Germany 46 C5..........53°52'N 8°42'E
Cuyo Islands Phil. 103 G6........11°11'N 121°10'E
Cwmbrân Wales 10 D3.............51°39'N 3°02'W
Cyclades is Greece 50 F3.........37°14'N 24°37'E
Cyprus Asia 51 J2...............35°38'N 33°17'E
Cyrenaica f. Libya 49 H2.........26°00'N 22°24'E
Czechia Europe 46 F3............49°38'N 15°37'E
Częstochowa Poland 46 H4.........50°48'N 19°07'E

D

Dąbrowa Górnicza Poland 46 H4....50°21'N 19°15'E
Dachau Germany 46 D3............48°15'N 11°27'E
Dadaab Kenya 85 I2..............0°07'N 40°19'E
Daegu S. Korea 99 N5.............35°52'N 128°35'E
Daejeon S. Korea 99 N5..........36°22'N 127°24'E
Dagupan Phil. 102 G7............16°04'N 120°21'E
Da Hinggan Ling mts China 99 L6....43°33'N 117°52'E
Dahlak Archipelago is Eritrea 94 F3....15°58'N 40°04'E
Dahm, Ramlat des. Saudi Arabia/Yemen 94 G3
                                    17°09'N 45°00'E
Dailly Scotland 14 E3...........55°17'N 4°43'W
Dakar Senegal 84 C3.............14°43'N 17°28'W
Dakhla Oasis Egypt 94 C4.........25°25'N 28°53'E
Dakol'ka r. Belarus 47 M5........52°08'N 28°52'E
Dalaman Turkey 51 H3............36°47'N 28°48'E
Đa Lat Vietnam 102 D6...........11°56'N 108°30'E
Dalbandin Pakistan 95 J5........28°56'N 64°30'E
Dalbeattie Scotland 15 F2.......54°56'N 3°49'W
Dali China 99 I3...............25°33'N 100°13'E
Dalian China 99 M5.............38°51'N 121°37'E
Dalkeith Scotland 15 F3.........55°54'N 3°04'W
Dallas U.S.A. 62 G3.............32°46'N 96°48'W
Dalmally Scotland 14 E4.........56°24'N 4°58'W
Dalmatia f. Bos. and Herz./Croatia 50 A7....44°01'N 15°30'E
Dalmellington Scotland 14 E3.....55°19'N 4°24'W
Dalry Scotland 14 E3............55°43'N 4°43'W
Dalrymple Scotland 14 E3........55°24'N 4°35'W
Dalrymple, Mount Australia 108 D4....20°59'S 148°37'E
Dalton U.S.A. 63 J3.............34°49'N 84°56'W
Dalton-in-Furness England 12 D3....54°09'N 3°11'W
Daly r. Australia 108 C5........13°31'S 130°28'E
Daman India 96 D5..............20°24'N 72°58'E
Damanhûr Egypt 49 J3...........31°02'N 30°28'E
Damar i. Indonesia 103 H2.......7°08'S 128°37'E
Damaraland f. Namibia 83 A2.....21°58'S 17°06'E
Damascus Syria 94 E6............33°30'N 36°20'E
Damāvand, Qolleh-ye mt. Iran 95 H7....35°58'N 52°07'E
Damghan Iran 95 H7.............36°09'N 54°19'E
Dammam Saudi Arabia 95 H5.......26°24'N 50°10'E
Dampier Australia 108 A4........20°41'S 116°47'E
Dampir, Selat str. Indonesia 103 I3....0°40'S 130°43'E
Đa Nẵng Vietnam 102 D7.........16°01'N 108°12'E
Dandong China 99 M6............40°06'N 124°22'E
Dane r. England 13 E2..........53°15'N 2°31'W
Danube r. Bulgaria/Croatia/Serbia 49 I6....45°26'N 29°38'E
Danube Delta Romania/Ukraine 51 H7....45°11'N 29°13'E
Danville U.S.A. 63 K4...........36°35'N 79°24'W
Dapaong Togo 84 E3.............10°53'N 0°15'E
Da Qaidam China 98 H5..........37°49'N 95°18'E
Daqing China 99 N7.............46°28'N 125°01'E
Dar'ā Syria 94 E6..............32°38'N 36°07'E
Dārāb Iran 95 H5...............28°45'N 54°32'E
Darabani Romania 47 L3.........48°11'N 26°36'E
Daraj Libya 84 F5..............30°10'N 10°29'E
Darbhanga India 96 G6..........26°10'N 85°57'E
Dardanelles str. Turkey 50 G5....40°12'N 26°25'E
Dar es Salaam Tanzania 83 C4....6°48'S 39°16'E
Darhan Mongolia 99 J7..........49°23'N 105°49'E
Darién, Golfo del g. Colombia 72 B7....8°56'N 77°01'W
Darjiling India 96 G6..........27°03'N 88°16'E
Darling r. Australia 108 D3.....34°05'S 141°56'E
Darling Downs hills Australia 108 D4....27°58'S 149°54'E
Darlington England 13 F3........54°31'N 1°33'W
Darlington d. England 21 E4.....54°33'N 1°34'W
Darmstadt Germany 44 H6.........49°52'N 8°38'E
Darnah Libya 85 G5.............32°42'N 22°40'E
Dart r. England 11 D2..........50°25'N 3°39'W
Dartford England 9 F2..........51°27'N 0°13'E
Dartmoor hills England 11 C2....50°36'N 4°01'W
Dartmouth Canada 63 N5.........44°41'N 63°35'W
Dartmouth England 11 D2........50°21'N 3°35'W
Darton England 13 F2...........53°35'N 1°31'W
Darwen England 13 E2...........53°42'N 2°28'W
Darwin Australia 108 C5........12°27'S 130°51'E
Datong China 99 K6.............40°03'N 113°20'E
Daud Khel Pakistan 95 L6.........32°51'N 71°37'E
Daugava r. Latvia 43 F1.........57°03'N 24°04'E
Daugavpils Latvia 43 F1.........55°53'N 26°31'E
Davao Phil. 103 H5.............7°05'N 125°34'E
Davao Gulf Phil. 103 H5.........6°22'N 125°49'E
Davenport U.S.A. 63 H5..........41°32'N 90°33'W
Daventry England 8 D3..........52°15'N 1°10'W
David Panama 67 H2.............8°27'N 82°25'W
Davis Strait Canada/Greenland 61 M4....66°43'N 56°19'W
Davos Switz. 46 C2.............46°48'N 9°49'E
Dawei Myanmar 97 I3............14°06'N 98°13'E
Dawlish England 11 D2..........50°35'N 3°28'W
Dawqah Oman 95 H3..............18°37'N 54°04'E
Dawson Canada 60 E4............64°04'N 139°24'W
Dawson Creek town Canada 60 F3....55°46'N 120°17'W
Daxian China 99 J4.............31°05'N 107°26'E
Dayr az Zawr Syria 94 F7........35°19'N 40°06'E
Dayton U.S.A. 63 J4............39°45'N 84°11'W
Daytona Beach town U.S.A. 63 J2....29°13'N 81°01'W
Dazhou China 99 J4.............31°12'N 107°28'E
Dead Sea l. Asia 94 E6.........31°18'N 35°27'E
Deal England 9 G2..............51°13'N 1°24'E
Dean, Forest of England 8 C2....51°48'N 2°32'W
Dearne r. England 13 F2........53°29'N 1°14'W

Death Valley f. U.S.A. 62 C4....36°34'N 117°01'W
Debak Malaysia 102 E4..........1°31'N 111°29'E
Debar Macedonia 50 D5..........41°31'N 20°31'E
Debenham England 9 G3..........52°14'N 1°11'E
Debrecen Hungary 47 I2.........47°32'N 21°37'E
Debre Zeyit Ethiopia 83 C5......8°45'N 38°57'E
Decatur U.S.A. 63 I3...........34°37'N 86°59'W
Deccan f. India 96 E4..........18°40'N 77°05'E
Děčín Czechia 46 F4............50°47'N 14°13'E
Dee r. Scotland 17 G2..........57°09'N 2°05'W
Dee est. Wales 10 D5............53°18'N 3°09'W
Dee r. Wales 10 D5.............53°13'N 3°01'W
Deele r. Ireland 18 B2.........54°51'N 7°28'W
Dehra Dun India 96 E7..........30°20'N 78°05'E
Dej Romania 47 J2..............47°09'N 23°53'E
Delano Peak U.S.A. 62 D4.......38°23'N 112°21'W
Delārām Afgh. 95 J6............32°11'N 63°28'E
Delaware d. U.S.A. 63 K4.........38°58'N 75°28'W
Delft Neth. 42 D5..............52°01'N 4°21'E
Delfzijl Neth. 42 F6...........53°20'N 6°55'E
Delgado, Cabo c. Mozambique 83 D3....10°41'S 40°36'E
Delhi India 96 E6..............28°38'N 77°17'E
Delhi d. India 98 D3...........28°38'N 77°08'E
Delice r. Turkey 51 K5.........40°31'N 34°13'E
Del Rio U.S.A. 62 F2...........29°21'N 100°54'W
Demanda, Sierra de la mts Spain 45 D5....42°13'N 3°27'W
Deming U.S.A. 62 E3............32°16'N 107°45'W
Demirci Turkey 51 H4...........39°02'N 28°39'E
Demirkazık Tepe mt. Turkey 51 K3....37°48'N 35°09'E
Dempo, Gunung vol. Indonesia 102 C3....4°02'S 103°06'E
Denakil f. Africa 85 I3.........14°27'N 40°44'E
Denali U.S.A. 60 C4............63°05'N 150°20'W
Denbigh Wales 10 D5............53°11'N 3°25'W
Denbighshire d. Wales 21 D3......53°06'N 3°20'W
Den Burg Neth. 42 D6...........53°03'N 4°49'E
Dendermonde Belgium 42 D4......51°01'N 4°07'E
Den Helder Neth. 42 D5.........52°58'N 4°46'E
Denizli Turkey 51 H3...........37°46'N 29°05'E
Denmark Europe 43 B2...........56°13'N 10°09'E
Denmark Strait Greenland/Iceland 61 P4....66°11'N 28°09'W
Denny Scotland 15 F4...........56°01'N 3°54'W
Denpasar Indonesia 102 F2......8°41'S 115°10'E
Denton U.S.A. 62 G3............33°15'N 97°08'W
D'Entrecasteaux Islands P.N.G. 108 E6....9°38'S 151°02'E
Denver U.S.A. 62 E4............39°45'N 105°02'W
Dêqên China 99 H3.............28°26'N 98°50'E
Dera Ghazi Khan Pakistan 96 D7....30°05'N 70°44'E
Dera Ismail Khan Pakistan 96 D7....31°51'N 70°56'E
Derbent Russia 53 E2...........42°04'N 48°17'E
Derby Australia 108 B5.........17°19'S 123°38'E
Derby England 8 D3.............52°55'N 1°28'W
Derby d. England 21 E3.........52°55'N 1°28'W
Derbyshire d. England 21 E3.....53°11'N 1°36'W
Dereham England 9 F3...........52°41'N 0°56'E
Derg r. Ireland/U.K. 18 D4......54°44'N 7°26'W
Derg, Lough l. Don. Ireland 18 D4....54°37'N 7°51'W
Derg, Lough l. Tipp. Ireland 18 C3....52°54'N 8°28'W
Derry r. Ireland 18 E2.........52°41'N 6°40'W
Derry Northern Ireland 14 B2....54°59'N 7°20'W
Derry and Strabane d. Northern Ireland 20 B4
                                    54°56'N 7°10'W
Derryveagh Mountains Ireland 18 C4....54°56'N 8°14'W
Dersingham England 9 F3........52°51'N 0°31'E
Derudeb Sudan 94 E3............17°38'N 36°05'E
Derwent r. England 13 G2........53°45'N 0°58'W
Derwent Reservoir Derbys. England 13 F2....53°25'N 1°44'W
Derwent Reservoir Dur. England 13 F3....54°52'N 1°58'W
Derwent Water l. England 12 D3....54°34'N 3°10'W
Desaguadero r. Argentina 73 C3....34°03'S 66°43'W
Des Moines U.S.A. 63 H5.........41°36'N 93°37'W
Des Moines r. U.S.A. 63 H5......40°23'N 91°28'W
Desna r. Russia 47 P5..........50°32'N 30°33'E
Desna r. Russia/Ukraine 47 N4....50°32'N 30°33'E
Dessau-Roßlau Germany 46 E4......51°50'N 12°15'E
Desventuradas, Islas is Chile 68 B2....26°30'S 80°00'W
Detroit U.S.A. 63 J5...........42°19'N 83°04'W
Deva r. Scotland 17 G2.........57°40'N 2°13'W
Deventer Neth. 42 F5...........52°15'N 6°10'E
Deveron r. Scotland 17 G2......57°40'N 2°31'W
Devil's Bit Mountain hill Ireland 18 D2....52°49'N 7°55'W
Devil's Bridge Wales 10 D4......52°23'N 3°51'W
Devil's Lake town U.S.A. 62 G6....48°02'N 98°46'W
Devizes England 8 D2...........51°21'N 1°59'W
Devon d. England 21 D2.........50°32'N 3°51'W
Devon r. England 13 G2.........53°04'N 0°50'W
Devon r. Scotland 15 F4........56°07'N 3°51'W
Devon Island Canada 61 I5......75°20'N 91°06'W
Devonport Australia 108 D2......41°11'S 146°20'E
Devrez r. Turkey 51 K5.........41°27'N 35°01'E
Dewsbury England 13 F2.........53°41'N 1°38'W
Dezfūl Iran 95 G6.............32°22'N 48°24'E
Dezhou China 99 L5.............37°25'N 116°19'E
Dhahran Saudi Arabia 95 H5......26°19'N 50°07'E
Dhaka Bangl. 97 H5.............23°43'N 90°24'E
Dhamār Yemen 94 F2.............14°34'N 44°26'E
Dhanbad India 96 G5............23°47'N 86°25'E
Dharwad India 96 E4............15°27'N 75°04'E
Dhaulagiri mt. Nepal 96 F6......28°40'N 83°29'E
Dhule India 96 D5.............20°53'N 74°46'E
Diablo, Picacho del mt. Mexico 66 A7....30°59'N 115°24'W
Diamantina watercourse Australia 108 C4....26°30'S 139°22'E
Diamantina, Chapada f. Brazil 72 E5....14°21'S 43°09'W
Dibrugarh India 97 H6..........27°30'N 94°55'E
Dickinson U.S.A. 62 F6.........46°53'N 102°48'W
Didcot England 8 D2...........51°36'N 1°15'W
Dieppe France 44 D6............49°55'N 1°05'E
Diest Belgium 42 E3............50°59'N 5°03'E
Digne-les-Bains France 44 G4....44°06'N 6°15'E
Dijon France 44 F5.............47°20'N 5°03'E
Diksmuide Belgium 42 B4........51°02'N 2°52'E
Dili East Timor 103 H2.........8°35'S 125°36'E
Dillon U.S.A. 62 D6............45°13'N 112°37'W
Dimapur India 97 H6............25°54'N 93°47'E
Dimitrovgrad Bulgaria 50 F6.....42°03'N 25°35'E
Dimitrovgrad Russia 53 E3.......54°13'N 49°35'E
Dinan France 44 B6.............48°27'N 2°03'W
Dinant Belgium 42 D3...........50°16'N 4°56'E
Dinar Turkey 51 I4.............38°04'N 30°10'E
Dīnār, Kūh-e mt. Iran 95 H6.....30°49'N 51°32'E
Dinard France 44 B6............48°38'N 2°04'W
Dinaric Alps mts Bos. and Herz./Croatia 50 B7
                                    44°18'N 16°16'E
Dindigul India 96 E3...........10°22'N 77°59'E
Dingle Ireland 18 A2...........52°08'N 10°16'W

Dingle Bay Ireland 18 A2........52°00'N 10°22'W
Dingwall Canada 17 E2..........46°54'N 60°29'W
Dipolog Phil. 103 G5...........8°39'N 123°26'E
Dir Pakistan 95 L7.............35°12'N 71°57'E
Dirē Dawa Ethiopia 85 I2........9°34'N 41°53'E
Dirranbandi Australia 108 D4....28°35'S 148°14'E
Disappointment, Cape S. Atlantic Oc. 73 F1
                                    54°51'S 36°07'W
Disappointment, Lake Australia 108 B4....23°30'S 122°40'E
Disko I. Greenland 61 M4.......69°44'N 53°37'E
Diss England 9 G3.............52°23'N 1°07'E
Distington England 12 D3.......54°36'N 3°32'W
Distrito Federal d. Mexico 66 E4....19°15'N 99°08'W
Diu India 96 D5...............20°40'N 71°03'E
Divnoye Russia 49 L6...........45°55'N 43°20'E
Divriği Turkey 51 M4...........39°22'N 38°06'E
Dixon Entrance str. Canada/U.S.A. 60 E3
                                    54°18'N 133°23'E
Diyarbakır Turkey 51 L4........37°55'N 40°14'E
Djado Niger 84 F4.............21°00'N 12°18'E
Djado, Plateau du f. Niger 84 F4....21°30'N 12°00'E
Djelfa Algeria 84 E5...........34°38'N 3°16'E
Djibouti Africa 85 I3.........11°34'N 42°55'E
Djibouti town Djibouti 85 I3....11°32'N 43°09'E
Djouce Mountain hill Ireland 10 A5....53°08'N 6°15'W
Dnieper r. Belarus 47 N4.......51°16'N 30°34'E
Dnieper r. Ukraine 47 O2.......46°30'N 32°19'E
Dniester r. Moldova 47 N2......46°25'N 30°11'E
Dniester r. Ukraine 47 M3......48°06'N 28°30'E
Dnipro r. Ukraine 47 P3........48°30'N 35°05'E
Dniprodzerzhyns'k Ukraine 47 P3....48°30'N 34°39'E
Dniprorudne Ukraine 47 P2......47°23'N 34°58'E
Doba Chad 85 F2...............8°40'N 16°51'E
Doberai Peninsula Indonesia 103 I3....1°19'S 132°27'E
Doboj Bos. and Herz. 50 C7......44°45'N 18°06'E
Dobrich Bulgaria 51 G6.........43°33'N 27°49'E
Dochart r. Scotland 14 E4......56°28'N 4°18'W
Docking England 9 F3...........52°54'N 0°38'E
Dodecanese is Greece 50 G2......35°57'N 27°47'E
Dodge City U.S.A. 62 F4........37°46'N 100°03'W
Dodman Point England 11 C2......50°13'N 4°48'W
Dodoma Tanzania 83 C4..........6°10'S 35°45'E
Doetinchem Neth. 42 F4.........51°58'N 6°17'E
Doha Qatar 95 H5..............25°17'N 51°33'E
Dokkum Neth. 42 E6............53°19'N 5°59'E
Dolbenmaen Wales 10 C4.........52°58'N 4°14'W
Dole France 44 F5.............47°06'N 5°30'E
Dolgellau Wales 10 D4..........52°45'N 3°53'W
Dolomites mts Italy 46 D1......46°42'N 11°37'E
Dolyna Ukraine 47 J3...........48°58'N 23°59'E
Dolyns'ka Ukraine 47 O3........48°07'N 32°46'E
Dominica Central America 67 L4....15°18'N 61°15'W
Dominican Republic Central America 67 J4
                                    18°57'N 70°23'W
Don r. Russia 54 F2............47°06'N 39°16'E
Don r. Scotland 17 G2..........57°10'N 2°05'W
Donaghadee Northern Ireland 14 D2....54°38'N 5°32'W
Don Benito Spain 45 C3.........38°58'N 5°51'W
Doncaster England 13 F2........53°31'N 1°08'W
Dondo Angola 83 A4............9°41'S 14°27'E
Donegal Ireland 18 C4..........54°39'N 8°07'W
Donegal d. Ireland 18 C4.......54°56'N 8°07'W
Donegal Bay Ireland 18 C4......54°31'N 8°21'W
Donegal Point Ireland 18 B2....52°43'N 9°38'W
Donets'k Ukraine 49 K6.........47°59'N 37°47'E
Dongara Australia 108 A4.......29°17'S 114°54'E
Dongfang China 99 J1..........19°03'N 108°39'E
Đông Hơi Vietnam 102 D7........17°26'N 106°36'E
Dongting Hu l. China 99 K3......29°20'N 112°57'E
Dongying China 99 L5..........37°25'N 118°41'E
Donostia Spain 45 D5...........43°19'N 1°59'W
Doon r. Scotland 14 E3.........55°26'N 4°39'W
Doon, Loch l. Scotland 14 E3....55°15'N 4°24'W
Dorchester England 8 C1........50°43'N 2°26'W
Dordogne r. France 44 C4.......45°00'N 0°29'W
Dordrecht Neth. 42 D4.........51°48'N 4°41'E
Dörgön Nuur l. Mongolia 98 G7....47°33'N 93°37'E
Dorking England 9 E2...........51°14'N 0°20'W
Dornbirn Austria 46 C2.........47°26'N 9°45'E
Dornoch Scotland 17 E2.........57°53'N 4°02'W
Dornoch Firth est. Scotland 17 E2....57°53'N 4°04'W
Dorsale Camerounaise f. Cameroon/Nigeria 84 F2
                                    5°59'N 10°49'E
Dorset d. England 21 D2........50°53'N 2°18'W
Dortmund Germany 46 B4.........51°30'N 7°27'E
Dos Bahías, Cabo c. Argentina 73 C2....44°56'S 65°32'W
Dosso Niger 84 E3.............13°03'N 3°12'E
Dōshi Afgh. 95 K7.............35°38'N 68°46'E
Dothan U.S.A. 63 I3............31°14'N 85°24'W
Douai France 44 E7............50°22'N 3°05'E
Douala Cameroon 84 E2..........4°03'N 9°42'E
Douglas Isle of Man 12 C3......54°09'N 4°29'W
Douglas Scotland 15 F3.........55°33'N 3°51'W
Douglas U.S.A. 62 E3...........31°20'N 109°33'W
Doullens France 42 B3.........50°09'N 2°21'E
Doune Scotland 15 E4...........56°11'N 4°03'W
Dounreay Scotland 17 F3........58°35'N 3°45'W
Dourados Brazil 73 D4..........22°13'S 54°49'W
Douro r. Portugal 45 A4........41°09'N 8°34'W
Dove r. Derbys. England 8 D4....52°50'N 1°35'W
Dove r. Suff. England 9 G3......52°21'N 1°11'E
Dover England 9 G2............51°08'N 1°19'E
Dover U.S.A. 63 K4............39°09'N 75°32'W
Dover, Strait of France/U.K. 9 G1....50°53'N 1°23'E
Down d. Northern Ireland 18 F4....54°20'N 5°55'W
Downham Market England 9 F3....52°36'N 0°23'E
Downpatrick Northern Ireland 14 D2....54°19'N 5°42'W
Downpatrick Head Ireland 18 B4....54°20'N 9°21'W
Downton England 8 D1..........50°59'N 1°45'W
Drâa, Hammada du f. Algeria 48 B2....28°29'N 8°17'W
Drachten Neth. 42 F6..........53°06'N 6°06'E
Draguignan France 44 G3........43°32'N 6°28'E
Drahichyn Belarus 47 K5........52°11'N 25°10'E
Drakensberg mts Lesotho/S. Africa 83 B2....29°59'S 28°56'E
Drama Greece 50 F5.............41°09'N 24°08'E
Drammen Norway 43 B2...........59°45'N 10°12'E
Draperstown Northern Ireland 14 C2....54°48'N 6°46'W
Drau r. Austria 46 F2.........46°38'N 14°57'E
Drava r. Europe 50 C7.........45°33'N 18°56'E
Drenthe d. Neth. 42 F5.........52°53'N 6°43'E
Dresden Germany 46 E4..........51°03'N 13°45'E
Dreux France 44 D6............48°44'N 1°23'E
Driffield England 13 G2........54°00'N 0°27'W
Drina r. Bos. and Herz./Serbia 50 C7....44°55'N 19°22'E
Drobeta-Turnu Severin Romania 50 E7....44°37'N 22°40'E
Drogheda Ireland 18 E3.........53°43'N 6°21'W
Drohobych Ukraine 47 J3........49°22'N 23°32'E
Droitwich Spa England 8 C3.....52°16'N 2°09'W

Dromore Northern Ireland 14 C2 ....54°25'N 6°08'W
Dronfield England 13 F2 ....53°18'N 1°28'W
Drosh Pakistan 95 L7 ....35°33'N 71°50'E
Drumheller Canada 60 G3 ....51°27'N 112°42'W
Drummore Scotland 14 E2 ....54°41'N 4°54'W
Druskininkai Lithuania 47 K5 ....53°59'N 24°01'E
Druts' r. Belarus 47 N5 ....53°03'N 30°03'E
Drygarn Fawr hill Wales 10 D4 ....52°13'N 3°40'W
Drymen Scotland 14 E4 ....56°04'N 4°27'W
Duarte, Pico mt. Dom. Rep. 67 J4 ....19°03'N 70°58'W
Ḑubā Saudi Arabia 95 H5 ....27°20'N 35°45'E
Dubai U.A.E. 95 I5 ....25°14'N 55°17'E
Dubawnt Lake Canada 60 H4 ....63°05'N 101°38'W
Dubbo Australia 108 D3 ....32°16'S 148°39'E
Dublin Ireland 18 E3 ....53°20'N 6°16'W
Dublin Bay Ireland 18 E3 ....53°21'N 6°10'W
Dublin City d. Ireland 18 E3 ....53°24'N 6°18'W
Dubno Ukraine 47 K4 ....50°25'N 25°43'E
Dubrovnik Croatia 50 C6 ....42°39'N 18°06'E
Dubrovytsya Ukraine 47 L4 ....51°34'N 26°34'E
Dudinka Russia 55 J4 ....69°22'N 86°11'E
Dudley England 8 C3 ....52°31'N 2°05'W
Duero r. Spain 45 B4 ....41°02'N 6°56'W
Dufftown Scotland 17 F2 ....57°27'N 3°08'W
Dufourspitze mt. Italy/Switz. 46 B1 ....45°57'N 7°53'E
Dugi Otok i. Croatia 50 A7 ....44°01'N 15°01'E
Duisburg Germany 46 B4 ....51°28'N 6°47'E
Dukhān Qatar 95 H5 ....25°25'N 50°47'E
Duluth U.S.A. 63 H6 ....46°45'N 92°07'W
Dulverton England 11 D3 ....51°02'N 3°33'W
Dumas U.S.A. 62 F4 ....35°53'N 101°59'W
Dumbarton Scotland 14 E3 ....55°57'N 4°34'W
Dumfries Scotland 15 F3 ....55°04'N 3°36'W
Dumfries and Galloway d. Scotland 20 D4 ..55°09'N 3°46'W
Dumyāṭ Egypt 49 J3 ....31°25'N 31°49'E
Dunaff Head Ireland 14 B3 ....55°18'N 7°31'W
Dunany Point Ireland 18 E3 ....53°52'N 6°14'W
Dunaújváros Hungary 46 H2 ....46°59'N 18°56'E
Dunbar Scotland 15 G4 ....56°00'N 2°31'W
Dunblane Scotland 15 F4 ....56°11'N 3°58'W
Duncansby Head Scotland 17 F3 ....58°39'N 3°01'W
Dunchurch England 8 D3 ....52°20'N 1°17'W
Dundalk Ireland 18 E4 ....54°00'N 6°24'W
Dundalk Bay Ireland 18 E3 ....53°57'N 6°13'W
Dundee Scotland 15 G4 ....56°28'N 2°58'W
Dundee d. Scotland 20 D5 ....56°29'N 2°59'W
Dundonald Northern Ireland 14 D2 ....54°36'N 5°48'W
Dundrum Bay Northern Ireland 14 D2 ......54°13'N 5°46'W
Dunedin New Zealand 109 G2 ....45°53'S 170°30'E
Dunfermline Scotland 15 F4 ....56°04'N 3°27'W
Dungannon Northern Ireland 14 C2 ....54°30'N 6°46'W
Dungarvan Ireland 18 D2 ....52°05'N 7°38'W
Dungeness hd England 9 F1 ....50°55'N 0°59'E
Dungiven Northern Ireland 14 C2 ....54°55'N 6°55'W
Dungun Malaysia 102 C4 ....4°46'N 103°23'E
Dungunab Sudan 94 E4 ....21°04'N 37°04'E
Dunholme England 13 G2 ....53°18'N 0°28'W
Dunhuang China 98 G6 ....40°07'N 94°40'E
Dunkerque France 44 E7 ....51°02'N 2°22'E
Dunkery Beacon hill England 11 D3 ....51°10'N 3°35'W
Dunkirk France 44 E7 ....51°02'N 2°22'E
Dún Laoghaire Ireland 18 E3 ....53°17'N 6°08'W
Dún Laoghaire-Rathdown d. Ireland 18 E3..53°17'N 6°12'W
Dunleer Ireland 18 E3 ....53°50'N 6°23'W
Dunloy Northern Ireland 14 C3 ....55°00'N 6°24'W
Dunmore East Ireland 18 E2 ....52°09'N 6°59'W
Dunmurry Northern Ireland 14 D2 ....54°33'N 5°59'W
Dunnet Bay Scotland 17 F3 ....58°37'N 3°24'W
Dunnet Head Scotland 17 F3 ....58°41'N 3°23'W
Dunoon Scotland 14 E3 ....55°57'N 4°56'W
Duns Scotland 15 G3 ....55°47'N 2°21'W
Dunstable England 9 E2 ....51°53'N 0°31'W
Dunvegan, Loch b. Scotland 16 C2 ....57°31'N 6°41'W
Durance r. France 44 F3 ....43°55'N 4°45'E
Durango Mexico 66 D5 ....24°02'N 104°43'W
Durango d. Mexico 66 D5 ....24°44'N 104°59'W
Durango U.S.A. 62 E4 ....37°16'N 107°52'W
Durban S. Africa 83 C2 ....29°51'S 31°02'E
Düren Germany 42 F3 ....50°48'N 6°29'E
Durham England 13 F3 ....54°47'N 1°35'W
Durham d. England 21 D4 ....54°42'N 2°09'W
Durham U.S.A. 63 K4 ....35°59'N 78°54'W
Durmitor mt. Montenegro 50 C6 ....43°07'N 19°03'E
Durness Scotland 16 E3 ....58°34'N 4°45'W
Durness, Kyle of inlet Scotland 16 E3 ......58°34'N 4°49'W
Durrës Albania 50 C5 ....41°19'N 19°27'E
Dursey Head Ireland 18 A1 ....51°34'N 10°13'W
Dursley England 8 C2 ....51°41'N 2°21'W
Dushanbe Tajikistan 96 C8 ....38°38'N 68°51'E
Düsseldorf Germany 46 B4 ....51°14'N 6°47'E
Duyun China 99 J3 ....26°13'N 107°32'E
Düzce Turkey 51 I5 ....40°50'N 31°09'E
Dyat'kovo Russia 47 P5 ....53°36'N 34°21'E
Dyce Scotland 17 G2 ....57°12'N 2°11'W
Dyer, Cape Canada 61 L4 ....66°39'N 61°16'W
Dyfi r. Wales 10 D4 ....52°33'N 3°56'W
Dymchurch England 9 F2 ....51°01'N 0°59'E
Dymock England 8 C2 ....51°59'N 2°26'W
Dzerzhinsk Russia 52 E3 ....56°14'N 43°28'E
Dzhankoy Ukraine 49 J6 ....45°43'N 34°24'E
Dzhugdzhur, Khrebet mts Russia 55 O3 ..55°53'N 135°07'E
Dzisna r. Belarus 47 M6 ....55°33'N 28°13'E

[Ea]ling England 9 E2 ....51°31'N 0°18'W
[Ea]rlston Scotland 15 G3 ....55°38'N 2°41'W
[Ea]rn r. Scotland 15 F4 ....56°20'N 3°20'W
[Ea]rn, Loch l. Scotland 14 E4 ....56°23'N 4°15'W
[Ea]singwold England 13 F3 ....54°07'N 1°11'W
[Ea]st Anglian Heights hills England 9 F3 ..52°03'N 0°15'E
[Ea]st Ayrshire d. Scotland 20 C4 ....55°29'N 4°15'W
[Ea]stbourne England 9 F1 ....50°46'N 0°18'E
[Ea]st Cape New Zealand 109 G3 ....37°40'S 178°33'E
[Ea]st China Sea N. Pacific Oc. 99 N4 ......31°00'N 127°22'E
[Ea]st Dunbartonshire d. Scotland 20 C4 ..55°56'N 4°11'W
[Ea]ster Island S. Pacific Oc. 116 C4 ....27°05'S 109°17'W
[Ea]stern Desert Egypt 49 J2 ....26°39'N 32°52'E
[Ea]stern Ghats mts India 96 E3 ....11°54'N 77°22'E
[Ea]ster Ross f. Scotland 16 E2 ....57°49'N 4°24'W
[Ea]st Falkland i. Falkland Is 73 D1 ....52°11'S 57°55'W
[Ea]st Fen f. England 13 H2 ....53°05'N 0°04'E
[Ea]stfield England 13 G3 ....54°15'N 0°24'W
[Ea]st Frisian Islands Germany 46 B5 ......53°45'N 7°00'E

East Grinstead England 9 E2 ....51°08'N 0°01'W
East Kilbride Scotland 14 E3 ....55°46'N 4°10'W
Eastleigh England 8 D1 ....50°58'N 1°22'W
East Linton Scotland 15 G3 ....55°59'N 2°39'W
East Loch Tarbert inlet Scotland 16 C2 ..57°51'N 6°46'W
East London S. Africa 83 B1 ....33°01'S 27°56'E
East Looe England 11 C2 ....50°21'N 4°27'W
East Lothian d. Scotland 20 D4 ....55°57'N 2°45'W
Eastmain Canada 61 K3 ....52°14'N 78°30'W
Eastmain r. Canada 61 K3 ....52°14'N 78°24'W
Easton England 8 C1 ....50°33'N 2°26'W
East Renfrewshire d. Scotland 20 C4 ......55°46'N 4°21'W
East Riding of Yorkshire d. England 21 E3 ..53°55'N 0°19'W
Eastry England 9 G2 ....51°15'N 1°18'E
East Sea N. Pacific Oc. 104 B3 ....39°13'N 133°37'E
East Sussex d. England 21 F2 ....50°53'N 0°17'E
East Timor Asia 103 H2 ....8°57'S 125°59'E
Eastwood England 13 F2 ....53°01'N 1°18'W
Eaton Socon England 9 E3 ....52°13'N 0°17'W
Eau Claire U.S.A. 63 H5 ....44°49'N 91°30'W
Eau Claire, Lac à l' l. Canada 61 K3 ......56°13'N 74°07'W
Eauripik atoll Micronesia 103 K5 ....6°43'N 143°04'E
Ebbw Vale Wales 10 D3 ....51°47'N 3°12'W
Eberswalde Germany 46 F5 ....52°50'N 13°49'E
Ebinur Hu l. China 98 E6 ....44°46'N 82°51'E
Ebro r. Spain 45 F4 ....40°43'N 0°51'E
Ecclefechan Scotland 15 F3 ....55°04'N 3°16'W
Eccleshall England 8 C3 ....52°52'N 2°15'W
Ech Chélif Algeria 84 E5 ....36°09'N 1°17'E
Écija Spain 45 C2 ....37°33'N 5°04'W
Eck, Loch l. Scotland 14 E4 ....56°04'N 4°59'W
Eckington England 8 C3 ....52°04'N 2°07'W
Ecuador S. America 72 B6 ....1°08'S 78°05'W
Eday i. Scotland 17 G4 ....59°11'N 2°50'W
Ed Da'ein Sudan 94 C2 ....11°27'N 26°09'E
Ed Damazin Sudan 85 H3 ....11°47'N 34°20'E
Ed Damer Sudan 94 D3 ....17°26'N 33°58'E
Ed Debba Sudan 94 D3 ....18°00'N 30°55'E
Ed Dueim Sudan 94 D2 ....13°57'N 32°17'E
Eden r. England 12 D3 ....54°57'N 3°01'W
Edessa Greece 50 E5 ....40°48'N 22°04'E
Edgeøya i. Arctic Oc. 54 D5 ....77°32'N 22°45'E
Edinburgh Scotland 15 F3 ....55°57'N 3°11'W
Edinburgh d. Scotland 20 D4 ....55°56'N 3°17'W
Edirne Turkey 50 G5 ....41°39'N 26°34'E
Edmonton Canada 60 G3 ....53°33'N 113°33'W
Edmundston Canada 61 L2 ....47°23'N 68°20'W
Edremit Turkey 50 G4 ....39°35'N 27°00'E
Edson Canada 60 G3 ....53°35'N 116°25'W
Edward, Lake Dem. Rep. Congo/Uganda 83 B4
 ....0°17'S 29°40'E
Edwards Plateau f. U.S.A. 62 F3 ....30°28'N 100°22'W
Éfaté i. Vanuatu 109 F5 ....17°38'S 168°30'E
Effingham U.S.A. 63 I4 ....39°07'N 88°33'W
Eger Hungary 46 I2 ....47°54'N 20°22'E
Egilsay i. Scotland 17 G4 ....59°09'N 2°55'W
Egilsstaðir Iceland 43 Z2 ....65°16'N 14°25'W
Eğirdir Turkey 51 I3 ....37°51'N 30°51'E
Eğirdir Gölü l. Turkey 51 I3 ....37°59'N 30°53'E
Eglinton Northern Ireland 14 B3 ....55°02'N 7°11'W
Egremont England 12 D3 ....54°29'N 3°32'W
Egvekinot Russia 55 T4 ....66°20'N 179°07'W
Egypt Africa 85 G4 ....29°53'N 31°16'E
Eifel hills Germany 46 B4 ....50°10'N 6°39'E
Eigg i. Scotland 14 C4 ....56°54'N 6°10'W
Eighty Mile Beach f. Australia 108 B5 ......19°54'S 120°10'E
Eilat Israel 49 J3 ....29°33'N 34°56'E
Eilean Siar d. Scotland 20 B6 ....58°15'N 6°33'W
Eindhoven Neth. 42 E4 ....51°26'N 5°29'E
Eisenhüttenstadt Germany 46 F5 ....52°09'N 14°38'E
Eishort, Loch inlet Scotland 16 D2 ....57°09'N 5°59'W
Ekibastuz Kazakhstan 98 D1 ....51°46'N 75°27'E
Ekostrovskaya Imandra, Ozero l. Russia 43 H4
 ....67°29'N 32°23'E
Eksjö Sweden 43 C2 ....57°40'N 14°59'E
Elazığ Turkey 51 M4 ....38°39'N 39°15'E
Elba, Isola d' i. Italy 48 F5 ....42°50'N 10°16'E
El'ban Russia 99 P8 ....50°03'N 136°26'E
Elbasan Albania 50 D5 ....41°07'N 20°05'E
Elbe r. Germany 46 C5 ....53°53'N 9°05'E
Elbert, Mount U.S.A. 62 E4 ....39°05'N 106°25'W
Elbistan Turkey 51 L4 ....38°12'N 37°11'E
Elblag Poland 46 H6 ....54°10'N 19°24'E
El'brus mt. Russia 53 E2 ....43°22'N 42°25'E
Elburz Mountains Iran 95 G7 ....36°52'N 49°43'E
El Callao Venezuela 67 L2 ....7°17'N 61°47'W
Elche-Elx Spain 45 E3 ....38°16'N 0°41'W
Elda Spain 45 E3 ....38°29'N 0°47'W
El Dorado U.S.A. 63 H3 ....33°13'N 92°36'W
Eldoret Kenya 85 H2 ....0°31'N 35°15'E
El Eulma Algeria 48 E4 ....36°07'N 5°48'E
Eleuthera i. Bahamas 67 I6 ....25°21'N 76°22'W
El Fasher Sudan 85 G3 ....13°36'N 25°20'E
El Geneina Sudan 85 G3 ....13°26'N 22°26'E
Elgin Scotland 17 F2 ....57°39'N 3°19'W
El'ginskiy Russia 55 P4 ....64°32'N 141°40'E
El Goléa Algeria 84 E5 ....30°34'N 2°58'E
Elgon, Mount Kenya/Uganda 85 H2 ......1°08'N 34°34'E
El Hierro i. Canary Islands 45 X1 ....27°40'N 17°56'W
Elhovo Bulgaria 50 G6 ....42°11'N 26°34'E
Elista Russia 53 E2 ....46°19'N 44°16'E
El Jadida Morocco 84 D5 ....33°12'N 8°27'W
Ełk Poland 47 J5 ....53°50'N 22°22'E
Elko U.S.A. 62 D5 ....40°51'N 115°46'W
Ellef Ringnes Island Canada 61 H5 ......78°38'N 101°56'W
Ellensburg U.S.A. 62 B6 ....46°59'N 120°32'W
Ellesmere England 8 C3 ....52°54'N 2°54'W
Ellesmere Island Canada 61 J5 ....77°10'N 83°03'W
Ellesmere Port England 12 E2 ....53°17'N 2°54'W
Ellice r. Canada 60 H4 ....67°56'N 103°59'W
Ellon Scotland 17 G2 ....57°22'N 2°04'W
Elmalı Turkey 51 H3 ....36°44'N 29°55'E
El Meghaïer Algeria 48 E4 ....33°56'N 5°56'E
El Muglad Sudan 85 G3 ....11°01'N 27°44'E
El Obeid Sudan 85 H3 ....13°10'N 30°11'E
El Oued Algeria 48 E4 ....33°21'N 6°54'E
El Paso U.S.A. 62 E3 ....31°46'N 106°24'W
El Puerto de Santa María Spain 45 B2 ......36°36'N 6°13'W
El Salvador Central America 66 G3 ....13°22'N 88°59'W
El Tigre Venezuela 67 L2 ....8°52'N 64°16'W
Eluru India 96 F4 ....16°44'N 81°09'E
Elvas Portugal 45 B3 ....38°53'N 7°10'W
Elverum Norway 43 B3 ....60°53'N 11°33'E
Ely England 9 F3 ....52°24'N 0°15'E
Ely U.S.A. 62 D4 ....39°15'N 114°53'W

Ely, Isle of f. England 9 F3 ....52°27'N 0°14'E
Emba Kazakhstan 53 F2 ....48°47'N 58°07'E
Emden Germany 46 B5 ....53°22'N 7°13'E
Emerson Canada 62 G6 ....49°02'N 97°11'W
Emi Koussi mt. Chad 85 F3 ....19°46'N 18°34'E
Emirdağ Turkey 51 I4 ....39°01'N 31°09'E
Emmeloord Neth. 42 E5 ....52°43'N 5°45'E
Emmen Neth. 42 F5 ....52°47'N 6°54'E
Emory Peak U.S.A. 62 F2 ....29°15'N 103°18'W
Ems r. Germany 46 B5 ....53°18'N 7°22'E
Endeh Indonesia 103 G2 ....8°47'S 121°38'E
Endicott Mountains U.S.A. 60 C4 ......67°50'N 152°33'W
Enfield England 9 E2 ....51°39'N 0°05'W
Engel's Russia 53 E3 ....51°29'N 46°06'E
Enggano i. Indonesia 102 C2 ....5°25'S 102°20'E
England d. U.K. 21 E3 ....52°48'N 1°24'W
English Channel France/U.K. 9 E1 ....49°59'N 1°24'W
Enköping Sweden 43 D2 ....59°38'N 17°06'E
En Nahud Sudan 85 G3 ....12°42'N 28°25'E
Ennedi, Massif mts Chad 94 B3 ....16°59'N 22°58'E
Ennerdale Water l. England 12 D3 ....54°30'N 3°22'W
Ennis Ireland 18 C2 ....52°51'N 8°59'W
Enniscorthy Ireland 18 E2 ....52°30'N 6°34'W
Enniskerry Ireland 10 A5 ....53°11'N 6°10'W
Enniskillen Northern Ireland 14 B2 ......54°20'N 7°37'W
Ennistymon Ireland 18 B2 ....52°56'N 9°17'W
Enns r. Austria 46 F3 ....48°14'N 14°31'E
Enschede Neth. 42 F5 ....52°13'N 6°54'E
Ensenada Mexico 66 A7 ....31°52'N 116°37'W
Enshi China 99 J4 ....30°13'N 109°28'E
Enugu Nigeria 84 E2 ....6°24'N 7°31'E
Envira r. Brazil 72 B6 ....7°31'S 70°14'W
Epping England 9 F2 ....51°42'N 0°07'E
Eppynt, Mynydd hills Wales 10 D4 ....52°05'N 3°28'W
Epsom England 9 E2 ....51°20'N 0°16'W
Epworth England 13 G2 ....53°32'N 0°49'W
Eqlīd Iran 95 H6 ....30°53'N 52°42'E
Equatorial Guinea Africa 84 E2 ....3°00'N 8°36'E
Équeurdreville-Hainneville France 11 Z9 ..49°39'N 1°39'W
Erbeskopf hill Germany 42 G2 ....49°43'N 7°04'E
Erciyes Dağı mt. Turkey 51 K4 ....38°32'N 35°27'E
Erdemli Turkey 51 K3 ....36°36'N 34°19'E
Erdi f. Chad 94 B3 ....19°02'N 21°36'E
Ereğli Konya Turkey 51 K3 ....37°30'N 34°03'E
Ereğli Zonguldak Turkey 51 I5 ....41°17'N 31°25'E
Erfurt Germany 46 D4 ....50°59'N 11°02'E
Ergani Turkey 51 M4 ....38°15'N 39°46'E
Ergene r. Turkey 50 G5 ....40°59'N 26°22'E
Ericht r. Scotland 17 F1 ....56°34'N 3°15'W
Ericht, Loch l. Scotland 17 E1 ....56°48'N 4°25'W
Erie U.S.A. 63 J5 ....42°07'N 80°06'W
Erie, Lake Canada/U.S.A. 61 J2 ....42°14'N 80°53'W
Eriskay i. Scotland 16 B2 ....57°04'N 7°16'W
Eritrea Africa 85 H3 ....15°57'N 37°33'E
Erlangen Germany 46 D3 ....49°35'N 11°01'E
Ermenek Turkey 51 J3 ....36°37'N 32°54'E
Ermoupoli Greece 50 F3 ....37°26'N 24°56'E
Erode India 96 E3 ....11°21'N 77°43'E
Errachidia Morocco 84 D5 ....31°54'N 4°29'W
Er Rahad Sudan 85 H3 ....12°44'N 30°38'E
Errigal hill Ireland 18 C5 ....55°02'N 8°07'W
Erris Head Ireland 18 A4 ....54°19'N 10°01'W
Errochty, Loch l. Scotland 17 E1 ....56°45'N 4°11'W
Erromango i. Vanuatu 109 F5 ....18°49'S 168°58'E
Erzgebirge mts Czechia/Germany 46 E4 ..50°33'N 13°07'E
Erzincan Turkey 51 M4 ....39°45'N 39°29'E
Erzurum Turkey 51 N4 ....39°55'N 41°17'E
Esbjerg Denmark 43 B1 ....55°28'N 8°27'E
Escanaba U.S.A. 63 I6 ....45°45'N 87°03'W
Escárcega Mexico 66 F4 ....18°39'N 90°43'W
Esch-sur-Alzette Lux. 42 E2 ....49°30'N 5°59'E
Eschweiler Germany 42 F3 ....50°49'N 6°18'E
Eşfahān Iran 95 H6 ....32°41'N 51°39'E
Esha Ness hd Scotland 17 H5 ....60°30'N 1°37'W
Esk r. Scotland 15 F3 ....55°56'N 3°04'W
Eske, Lough l. Ireland 14 A2 ....54°42'N 8°04'W
Eski Gediz Turkey 51 H4 ....39°03'N 29°25'E
Eskilstuna Sweden 43 D2 ....59°22'N 16°32'E
Eskişehir Turkey 51 I4 ....39°47'N 30°31'E
Esla r. Spain 45 B4 ....41°30'N 6°01'W
Eslāmābād-e Gharb Iran 95 G6 ....34°06'N 46°31'E
Esperance Australia 108 B3 ....33°49'S 121°52'E
Espigüete mt. Spain 45 C5 ....42°57'N 4°47'W
Espírito Santo i. Vanuatu 109 F5 ....15°16'S 166°35'E
Espoo Finland 43 F3 ....60°12'N 24°40'E
Esquel Argentina 73 B2 ....42°55'S 71°20'W
Essen Germany 46 B4 ....51°28'N 7°03'E
Essequibo r. Guyana 72 D7 ....6°23'N 58°36'W
Essex d. England 21 F2 ....51°50'N 0°42'E
Estados, Isla de los i. Argentina 73 C1 ..54°44'S 64°16'W
Estats, Pic d' mt. France/Spain 45 F5 ......42°40'N 1°24'E
Estevan Canada 60 H2 ....49°08'N 102°59'W
Estonia Europe 43 F2 ....58°44'N 25°26'E
Estrela, Serra da mts Portugal 45 B4 ......40°11'N 7°57'W
Estrella mt. Spain 45 D3 ....38°24'N 3°36'W
Eswatini Africa 83 C2 ....26°29'S 31°30'E
Étaples France 44 D7 ....50°31'N 1°39'E
Ethiopia Africa 85 H2 ....6°30'N 39°41'E
Ethiopian Highlands f. Ethiopia 85 H2 ......8°49'N 36°39'E
Etimesğut Turkey 51 J4 ....39°56'N 32°39'E
Etive, Loch inlet Scotland 14 D4 ....56°27'N 5°07'W
Etna, Mount vol. Italy 48 G4 ....37°45'N 15°00'E
Etosha Pan f. Namibia 83 A3 ....18°52'S 16°19'E
Ettelbruck Lux. 42 F2 ....49°51'N 6°06'E
Ettrick Forest Scotland 15 F3 ....55°31'N 3°05'W
Ettrick Water r. Scotland 15 G3 ....55°31'N 2°49'W
Etwall England 8 D3 ....52°53'N 1°36'W
Eugene U.S.A. 62 B5 ....44°04'N 123°05'W
Eugenia, Punta pt Mexico 66 A6 ....27°51'N 115°04'W
Euphrates r. Asia 94 F6 ....30°59'N 47°24'E
Eureka U.S.A. 62 B5 ....40°48'N 124°09'W
Europa, Picos de mts Spain 45 C5 ....43°07'N 5°01'W
Europe 34
Evans, Lac l. Canada 61 K3 ....50°49'N 77°07'W
Evanston U.S.A. 62 D5 ....41°17'N 110°56'W
Evansville U.S.A. 63 I4 ....37°59'N 87°32'W
Evaton S. Africa 83 B2 ....26°32'S 27°49'E
Everest, Mount China/Nepal 98 F3 ......27°59'N 86°55'E
Everglades f. U.S.A. 63 J2 ....26°15'N 81°02'W
Evesham England 8 D3 ....52°06'N 1°57'W
Evesham, Vale of f. England 8 D3 ....52°05'N 1°57'W
Évora Portugal 45 B3 ....38°34'N 7°54'W
Évreux France 44 D6 ....49°01'N 1°09'E
Evvoia i. Greece 50 F4 ....38°19'N 24°14'E
Ewe, Loch b. Scotland 16 D2 ....57°50'N 5°40'W
Exe r. England 11 D2 ....50°41'N 3°29'W

Exeter England 11 D2 ....50°43'N 3°32'W
Exminster England 11 D2 ....50°41'N 3°30'W
Exmoor hills England 11 D3 ....51°10'N 3°46'W
Exmouth England 11 D2 ....50°37'N 3°25'W
Exuma Cays is Bahamas 67 I5 ....24°35'N 76°34'W
Exuma Sound str. Bahamas 67 I5 ....24°17'N 75°59'W
Eyasi, Lake Tanzania 83 C1 ....3°38'S 35°05'E
Eye P'boro. England 9 E3 ....52°37'N 0°11'W
Eye Suff. England 9 G3 ....52°19'N 1°09'E
Eyemouth Scotland 15 G3 ....55°52'N 2°05'W
Eye Peninsula Scotland 16 C3 ....58°14'N 6°14'W
Ezhva Russia 52 F4 ....61°48'N 50°45'E
Ezine Turkey 50 G4 ....39°46'N 26°19'E

F

Faenza Italy 46 D1 ....44°17'N 11°53'E
Făgăraş Romania 50 F7 ....45°51'N 24°59'E
Fagatogo American Samoa 109 H5 ....14°17'S 170°41'W
Fagersta Sweden 43 C2 ....59°59'N 15°49'E
Fairbanks U.S.A. 60 D4 ....64°50'N 147°47'W
Fair Head Northern Ireland 14 C3 ....55°14'N 6°08'W
Fair Isle i. Scotland 17 H4 ....59°34'N 1°38'W
Fairmont U.S.A. 63 H5 ....43°39'N 94°28'W
Fairweather, Mount Canada/U.S.A. 60 E3
 ....58°54'N 137°29'W
Fais i. Micronesia 103 K5 ....9°45'N 140°33'E
Faisalabad Pakistan 96 D7 ....31°24'N 73°09'E
Fakaofo atoll Tokelau 109 H6 ....9°23'S 171°08'W
Fakenham England 9 F3 ....52°50'N 0°51'E
Fakfak Indonesia 103 I3 ....2°55'S 132°17'E
Fal r. England 11 C2 ....50°14'N 4°58'W
Falcon Lake Mexico/U.S.A. 66 E6 ....26°53'N 99°20'W
Falkenberg Sweden 43 C2 ....56°55'N 12°31'E
Falkirk Scotland 15 F4 ....56°00'N 3°47'W
Falkirk d. Scotland 20 D4 ....55°59'N 3°48'W
Falkland Islands S. Atlantic Oc. 73 D1 ..50°55'S 59°36'W
Falköping Sweden 43 C2 ....58°10'N 13°33'E
Falmouth England 11 B2 ....50°09'N 5°04'W
Falmouth Bay England 11 B2 ....50°08'N 5°04'W
Falso, Cabo c. Mexico 66 C5 ....22°53'N 109°59'W
Falster i. Denmark 43 B1 ....54°49'N 11°58'E
Falun Sweden 43 C3 ....60°36'N 15°38'E
Famagusta Cyprus 51 J2 ....35°06'N 33°57'E
Fanad Head Ireland 14 B3 ....55°17'N 7°38'W
Fane r. Ireland 18 E3 ....53°57'N 6°22'W
Fannich, Loch l. Scotland 16 D2 ....57°39'N 5°03'W
Farafra Oasis Egypt 94 C5 ....26°43'N 28°09'E
Farāh Afgh. 95 J6 ....32°23'N 62°07'E
Farallon de Pajaros vol. N. Mariana Is 103 K8
 ....20°32'N 144°55'E
Farasān, Jazā'ir is Saudi Arabia 94 F3 ..16°48'N 41°41'E
Fareham England 8 D1 ....50°51'N 1°11'W
Farewell, Cape New Zealand 109 G2 ....40°29'S 172°40'E
Fargo U.S.A. 62 G6 ....46°52'N 96°49'W
Faridabad India 96 E6 ....28°25'N 77°19'E
Farnborough England 8 E2 ....51°17'N 0°45'W
Farndon England 12 E2 ....53°05'N 2°53'W
Farne Islands England 13 F4 ....55°38'N 1°37'W
Farnham England 8 E2 ....51°13'N 0°48'W
Faro Portugal 45 B2 ....37°01'N 7°56'W
Fårö i. Sweden 43 D2 ....57°58'N 19°22'E
Faroe Islands Europe 34 D5 ....62°00'N 7°00'W
Farrāshband Iran 95 H5 ....28°52'N 52°05'E
Fasā Iran 95 H5 ....28°56'N 53°38'E
Fastiv Ukraine 47 M4 ....50°04'N 29°55'E
Fatehgarh India 96 E6 ....27°22'N 79°36'E
Faulquemont France 42 F2 ....49°03'N 6°36'E
Faversham England 9 F2 ....51°19'N 0°53'E
Faxaflói b. Iceland 43 X2 ....64°27'N 22°58'W
Fayetteville U.S.A. 63 K4 ....35°02'N 78°53'W
Fdérik Mauritania 84 C4 ....22°42'N 12°44'W
Feale r. Ireland 18 B2 ....52°28'N 9°38'W
Fear, Cape U.S.A. 63 K3 ....33°51'N 77°58'W
Fehmarn i. Germany 46 D6 ....54°29'N 11°07'E
Feira de Santana Brazil 72 F5 ....12°12'S 38°57'W
Feldkirch Austria 46 C2 ....47°15'N 9°36'E
Felixstowe England 9 G2 ....51°58'N 1°21'E
Femunden l. Norway 43 B3 ....62°05'N 11°48'E
Feniton England 11 D2 ....50°47'N 3°16'W
Feodosiya Ukraine 49 K6 ....45°02'N 35°22'E
Ferdows Iran 95 I6 ....33°59'N 58°10'E
Fergus Falls U.S.A. 62 G6 ....46°17'N 96°07'W
Ferkessédougou Côte d'Ivoire 84 D2 ......9°35'N 5°13'W
Fermanagh f. Northern Ireland 18 D4 ......54°16'N 7°35'W
Fermanagh and Omagh d. Northern Ireland 21 B4
 ....54°29'N 7°45'W
Fermoy Ireland 18 C2 ....52°08'N 8°17'W
Ferndown England 8 D1 ....50°48'N 1°54'W
Ferrara Italy 46 D1 ....44°50'N 11°38'E
Ferrol Spain 45 A5 ....43°29'N 8°13'W
Ferryhill England 13 F3 ....54°41'N 1°33'W
Fès Morocco 84 D5 ....34°04'N 4°57'W
Fethaland, Point of Scotland 17 H5 ....60°39'N 1°18'W
Fethard Ireland 18 D2 ....52°28'N 7°42'W
Fethiye Turkey 51 H3 ....36°37'N 29°06'E
Fetlar i. Scotland 17 I5 ....60°38'N 0°49'W
Feuilles, Rivière aux r. Canada 61 K3 ..58°46'N 70°13'W
Feyẓābād Afgh. 95 L7 ....37°05'N 70°41'E
Fez Morocco 84 D5 ....34°04'N 4°57'W
Fezzan f. Libya 84 F4 ....25°00'N 14°00'E
Ffestiniog Wales 10 D4 ....52°58'N 3°56'W
Fianarantsoa Madagascar 83 D2 ....21°27'S 47°07'E
Fife d. Scotland 20 D5 ....56°16'N 2°58'W
Fife Ness pt Scotland 15 G4 ....56°16'N 2°35'W
Figeac France 44 E4 ....44°37'N 2°01'E
Figueira da Foz Portugal 45 A4 ....40°10'N 8°51'W
Figueres Spain 45 G5 ....42°16'N 2°58'E
Figuig Morocco 48 C3 ....32°09'N 1°17'W
Fiji S. Pacific Oc. 109 G5 ....17°51'S 177°08'E
Filadelfia Paraguay 73 C4 ....22°22'S 60°03'W
Filey England 13 G3 ....54°13'N 0°18'W
Filton England 8 C2 ....51°30'N 2°35'W
Findhorn r. Scotland 17 F2 ....57°38'N 3°38'W
Fingal Ireland 10 A5 ....53°30'N 6°15'W
Finisterre, Cape Spain 45 A5 ....42°53'N 9°15'W
Finland Europe 43 F3 ....63°43'N 26°54'E
Finland, Gulf of Europe 43 E2 ....59°31'N 22°42'E
Finlay r. Canada 60 F3 ....56°41'N 124°49'W
Finn r. Ireland 14 B2 ....54°50'N 7°28'W
Finspång Sweden 43 C2 ....58°42'N 15°46'E
Finstown Scotland 17 F4 ....59°00'N 3°07'W
Fintona Northern Ireland 14 B2 ....54°29'N 7°19'W
Fionn Loch l. Scotland 16 D2 ....57°46'N 5°28'W
Fionnphort Scotland 14 C4 ....56°19'N 6°22'W

Fisher Strait Canada 61 J4..............................63°14'N 83°06'W
Fishguard Wales 10 C3...................................51°59'N 4°58'W
Fishguard Bay Wales 10 C4..............................52°01'N 4°58'W
Five Barrows Hill England 11 D3........................51°07'N 3°49'W
Flagstaff U.S.A. 62 D4.................................35°12'N 111°39'W
Flamborough England 13 G3.............................54°07'N 0°07'W
Flamborough Head England 13 G3........................54°07'N 0°03'W
Flannan Isles Scotland 16 B3..........................58°18'N 7°39'W
Flåsjön l. Sweden 43 C4................................64°06'N 15°53'E
Flathead Lake U.S.A. 62 D6............................47°52'N 114°03'W
Flat Holm i. Wales 11 D3..............................51°23'N 3°07'W
Fleet England 8 E2.....................................51°17'N 0°50'W
Fleetwood England 12 D2...............................53°55'N 3°02'W
Flensburg Germany 46 C6...............................54°47'N 9°25'E
Flevoland d. Neth. 42 E5..............................52°17'N 5°07'E
Flinders r. Australia 108 D5..........................17°37'S 140°35'E
Flinders Island Australia 108 D3......................39°56'S 148°04'E
Flinders Ranges mts Australia 108 C3..................31°24'S 138°40'E
Flin Flon Canada 60 H3................................54°46'N 101°51'W
Flint U.S.A. 63 J5....................................43°01'N 83°42'W
Flint Wales 10 D5.....................................53°15'N 3°08'W
Flintshire d. Wales 21 D3.............................53°11'N 3°07'W
Florence Italy 48 F5..................................43°46'N 11°15'E
Florence U.S.A. 63 K3.................................34°11'N 79°45'W
Florencia Colombia 72 B7..............................1°36'N 75°36'W
Flores i. Indonesia 103 G2............................8°29'S 121°14'E
Flores Sea Indonesia 102 F2...........................7°41'S 119°59'E
Floresta Brazil 72 F6.................................8°31'S 38°32'W
Florianópolis Brazil 73 E4............................27°32'S 48°32'W
Florida d. U.S.A. 63 J3...............................30°12'N 83°09'W
Florida, Straits of Bahamas/U.S.A. 67 H5..............23°59'N 81°35'W
Florida Keys is U.S.A. 63 J1..........................24°41'N 81°38'W
Florina Greece 50 D5..................................40°46'N 21°24'E
Florø Norway 43 A3....................................61°36'N 5°01'E
Flotta i. Scotland 17 F3..............................58°50'N 3°07'W
Fly r. P.N.G. 103 K2..................................8°18'S 142°36'E
Foča Bos. and Herz. 50 C6.............................43°29'N 18°45'E
Fochabers Scotland 17 F2..............................57°37'N 3°06'W
Foggia Italy 49 G5....................................41°28'N 15°33'E
Fogo i. Cape Verde 84 B3..............................14°59'N 24°18'W
Foinaven hill Scotland 16 E3..........................58°25'N 4°53'W
Foix France 44 D3.....................................42°58'N 1°36'E
Folkestone England 9 G2...............................51°05'N 1°10'E
Fonseca, Golfo de b. Central America 66 G3
....13°03'N 88°12'W
Fontainebleau France 44 E6............................48°25'N 2°43'E
Fontur pt Iceland 43 Z2...............................66°23'N 14°32'W
Førde Norway 43 A3....................................61°27'N 5°52'E
Fordingbridge England 8 D1............................50°56'N 1°47'W
Foreland hd England 8 D1..............................50°41'N 1°04'W
Foreland Point England 11 D3..........................51°15'N 3°47'W
Forfar Scotland 17 G1.................................56°39'N 2°53'W
Forli Italy 46 E1.....................................44°14'N 12°02'E
Formby England 12 D2..................................53°34'N 3°04'W
Formentera i. Spain 45 F3.............................38°40'N 1°24'E
Formosa Argentina 73 D4...............................26°07'S 58°12'W
Forres Scotland 17 F2.................................57°37'N 3°37'W
Forssa Finland 43 E3..................................60°49'N 23°39'E
Fort Albany Canada 61 J3..............................52°13'N 81°41'W
Fortaleza Brazil 72 F6................................3°43'S 38°32'W
Fort Augustus Scotland 16 E2..........................57°09'N 4°41'W
Fort Chipewyan Canada 60 G3...........................58°42'N 111°07'W
Fort Collins U.S.A. 62 E5.............................40°35'N 105°05'W
Fort-de-France Martinique 67 L3.......................14°37'N 61°05'W
Fortescue r. Australia 108 A4.........................21°02'S 116°06'E
Fort Frances Canada 61 I2.............................48°37'N 93°24'W
Fort Good Hope Canada 60 F4...........................66°16'N 128°39'W
Forth r. Scotland 14 F5...............................56°07'N 3°52'W
Forth, Firth of est. Scotland 15 F4...................56°01'N 3°13'W
Fort Lauderdale U.S.A. 63 J2..........................26°04'N 80°11'W
Fort Liard Canada 60 F4...............................60°14'N 123°24'W
Fort McMurray Canada 60 G3............................56°43'N 111°21'W
Fort McPherson Canada 60 E4...........................67°33'N 134°44'W
Fort Nelson Canada 60 F3..............................58°45'N 122°39'W
Fort Peck Reservoir l. U.S.A. 62 E6...................47°47'N 106°55'W
Fort Pierce U.S.A. 63 J2..............................27°18'N 80°24'W
Fortrose Scotland 17 E2...............................57°35'N 4°08'W
Fort St John Canada 60 F3.............................56°15'N 120°49'W
Fort Severn Canada 61 J3..............................56°00'N 87°39'W
Fort-Shevchenko Kazakhstan 53 F2......................44°29'N 50°17'E
Fort Simpson Canada 60 F4.............................61°52'N 121°22'W
Fort Smith Canada 60 G4...............................60°00'N 112°13'W
Fort Smith U.S.A. 63 H4...............................35°26'N 94°24'W
Fortuneswell England 8 C1.............................50°34'N 2°27'W
Fort Wayne U.S.A. 63 I5...............................41°04'N 85°08'W
Fort William Scotland 16 D1...........................56°49'N 5°06'W
Fort Worth U.S.A. 63 G3...............................32°46'N 97°19'W
Fort Yukon U.S.A. 60 D4...............................66°35'N 145°13'W
Foshan China 99 K2....................................23°03'N 113°06'E
Fossano Italy 46 B1...................................44°33'N 7°43'E
Fougères France 44 C6.................................48°21'N 1°12'W
Foula i. Scotland 17 G5...............................60°10'N 2°10'W
Foulness Point England 9 F2...........................51°37'N 0°57'E
Fouta Djallon f. Guinea 84 C3.........................11°26'N 12°34'W
Fowey r. England 11 C2................................50°26'N 4°41'W
Foxe Basin g. Canada 61 K4............................66°53'N 78°58'W
Foxe Channel Canada 61 J4.............................64°53'N 81°03'W
Foxe Peninsula Canada 61 K4...........................64°48'N 77°03'W
Foxford Ireland 18 B3.................................53°58'N 9°07'W
Fox Islands U.S.A. 60 B3..............................52°45'N 168°53'W
Foyle r. U.K. 18 D5...................................54°53'N 7°26'W
Foyle, Lough inlet Ireland/U.K. 18 D5.................55°07'N 7°07'W
Foz do Iguaçu Brazil 73 D4............................25°30'S 54°32'W
Framlingham England 9 G3..............................52°13'N 1°21'E
France Europe 44 E5...................................46°57'N 2°11'E
Franceville Gabon 84 F1...............................1°37'S 13°37'E
Francistown Botswana 83 B2............................21°10'S 27°29'E
Frankfort U.S.A. 63 J4................................38°12'N 84°53'W
Frankfurt am Main Germany 46 C4.......................50°07'N 8°41'E
Frankfurt (Oder) Germany 46 F5........................52°21'N 14°33'E
Franklin D. Roosevelt Lake resr U.S.A. 62 C6
....48°16'N 118°09'W
Frantsa-Iosifa, Zemlya is Russia 54 G5................79°40'N 58°29'E
Fraser r. Canada 60 F3................................49°19'N 121°38'W
Fraserburgh Scotland 17 G2............................57°42'N 2°01'W
Fraser Island Australia 108 E4........................25°12'S 153°11'E
Freckleton England 12 E2..............................53°45'N 2°52'W
Fredericia Denmark 43 B1..............................55°34'N 9°45'E
Fredericton Canada 61 L2..............................45°57'N 66°39'W
Fredrikstad Norway 43 B2..............................59°13'N 10°56'E
Freeport Bahamas 67 I6................................26°30'N 78°45'W
Freetown Sierra Leone 84 C2...........................8°28'N 13°12'W
Freiburg im Breisgau Germany 46 B3....................48°00'N 7°50'E
Fréjus France 44 G3...................................43°26'N 6°45'E
Fremantle Australia 108 A3............................32°05'S 115°42'E

French Guiana S. America 72 D7........................3°56'N 53°03'W
French Polynesia is S. Pacific Oc. 114 B2
....18°43'S 147°32'W
Freshwater England 8 D1...............................50°41'N 1°31'W
Fresno U.S.A. 62 C4...................................36°46'N 119°46'W
Frévent France 9 H1...................................50°16'N 2°17'E
Freyming-Merlebach France 42 F2.......................49°09'N 6°48'E
Fria Guinea 84 C3.....................................10°24'N 13°35'W
Friedrichshafen Germany 46 C2.........................47°39'N 9°31'E
Friesland d. Neth. 42 E6..............................53°08'N 5°48'E
Frinton-on-Sea England 9 G2...........................51°50'N 1°15'E
Frisa, Loch l. Scotland 14 C4.........................56°34'N 6°06'W
Frisian Islands Europe 34 E4..........................54°00'N 7°00'E
Frizington England 12 D3..............................54°32'N 3°30'W
Frobisher Bay Canada 61 L4............................63°18'N 67°31'W
Frodsham England 12 E2................................53°18'N 2°44'W
Frohavet b. Norway 43 B3..............................63°52'N 9°12'E
Frome England 8 C2....................................51°14'N 2°19'W
Frome r. England 8 C1.................................50°41'N 2°05'W
Frome, Lake Australia 108 C3..........................30°43'S 139°48'E
Frøya i. Norway 43 B3.................................63°41'N 8°39'E
Fruges France 9 H1....................................50°31'N 2°08'E
Frýdek-Místek Czechia 46 H3...........................49°41'N 18°21'E
Fuenlabrada Spain 45 D4...............................40°17'N 3°47'W
Fuerteventura i. Canary Islands 45 Y2.................28°36'N 14°04'W
Fujairah U.A.E. 95 I5.................................25°06'N 56°21'E
Fujian d. China 99 L3.................................25°52'N 117°59'E
Fuji-san vol. Japan 104 C3............................35°22'N 138°43'E
Fukui Japan 104 C3....................................36°04'N 136°13'E
Fukuoka Japan 104 B2..................................33°35'N 130°24'E
Fukushima Japan 104 D3................................37°45'N 140°28'E
Fulda Germany 46 C4...................................50°33'N 9°41'E
Fulford England 13 F2.................................53°56'N 1°04'W
Fulham England 9 E2...................................51°29'N 0°13'W
Fumay France 42 D2....................................49°59'N 4°42'E
Funabashi Japan 104 D3................................35°42'N 139°59'E
Funafuti atoll Tuvalu 109 G6..........................8°25'S 179°13'E
Funchal Atlantic Oc. 84 B5............................32°39'N 16°54'W
Fundy, Bay of Canada 61 L2............................44°06'N 67°03'W
Fürth Germany 46 D3...................................49°29'N 10°57'E
Fushun China 99 M6....................................41°51'N 123°50'E
Fuxian China 99 M6....................................42°02'N 121°41'E
Fuyang China 99 L4....................................32°51'N 115°50'E
Fuyu China 99 M7......................................47°44'N 124°26'E
Fuzhou Fujian China 99 L3.............................26°07'N 119°21'E
Fuzhou Jiangxi China 99 L3............................27°58'N 116°17'E
Fyn i. Denmark 43 B1..................................55°38'N 10°17'E

G

Gaalkacyo Somalia 85 I2...............................6°46'N 47°25'E
Gabès Tunisia 48 F3...................................33°53'N 10°07'E
Gabès, Golfe de g. Tunisia 48 F3......................34°08'N 10°40'E
Gabon Africa 84 F1....................................0°56'S 11°32'E
Gaborone Botswana 83 B2...............................24°38'S 25°56'E
Gabrovo Bulgaria 50 F6................................42°53'N 25°20'E
Gadsden U.S.A. 63 I3..................................34°03'N 86°04'W
Gaer Wales 10 D3......................................51°53'N 3°12'W
Gafsa Tunisia 48 E3...................................34°26'N 8°51'E
Gagarin Russia 47 P6..................................55°33'N 35°01'E
Gagnon Canada 61 L3...................................51°52'N 68°07'W
Gagra Georgia 51 N6...................................43°18'N 40°16'E
Gainesville U.S.A. 63 J2..............................29°36'N 82°20'W
Gainsborough England 13 G2............................53°24'N 0°46'W
Gairdner, Lake Australia 108 C3.......................31°17'S 135°38'E
Gairloch Scotland 16 D2...............................57°44'N 5°42'W
Gair Loch b. Scotland 16 D2...........................57°43'N 5°44'W
Galapagos Islands Ecuador 68 B3.......................0°03'S 89°05'W
Galashiels Scotland 15 G3.............................55°37'N 2°49'W
Galați Romania 51 H7..................................45°27'N 28°03'E
Gala Water r. Scotland 15 G3..........................55°36'N 2°47'W
Galdhøpiggen mt. Norway 43 B3.........................61°38'N 8°19'E
Galich Russia 52 E3...................................58°22'N 42°20'E
Galilee, Sea of l. Israel 49 K3.......................32°49'N 35°37'E
Gallabat Sudan 94 E2..................................12°57'N 36°06'E
Galle Sri Lanka 96 F2.................................6°04'N 80°09'E
Galley Head Ireland 18 C1.............................51°32'N 8°57'W
Gallinas, Punta pt Colombia 67 J3.....................12°27'N 71°42'W
Gallipoli Italy 49 G5.................................40°03'N 18°00'E
Gallipoli Turkey 50 G5................................40°25'N 26°39'E
Gällivare Sweden 43 E4................................67°08'N 20°40'E
Gallup U.S.A. 62 E4...................................35°32'N 108°45'W
Galston Scotland 14 E3................................55°36'N 4°23'W
Galtat Zemmour Western Sahara 84 C4...................25°08'N 12°24'W
Galtee Mountains hills Ireland 18 C2..................52°19'N 8°16'W
Galveston U.S.A. 63 H2................................29°15'N 94°54'W
Galveston Bay U.S.A. 63 H2............................29°40'N 94°46'W
Galway Ireland 18 B3..................................53°16'N 9°03'W
Galway d. Ireland 18 B3...............................53°22'N 9°16'W
Galway Bay Ireland 18 B3..............................53°12'N 9°16'W
Galway City d. Ireland 18 B3..........................53°16'N 9°03'W
Gambia r. Gambia 84 C3................................13°28'N 16°35'W
Gambia Africa 84 C3...................................13°28'N 16°35'W
Gäncä Azerbaijan 53 E2................................40°41'N 46°22'E
Gandadiwata, Bukit mt. Indonesia 102 F3...............2°43'S 119°25'E
Gander Canada 61 M2...................................48°54'N 54°17'W
Gandhidham India 96 D5................................23°06'N 70°08'E
Gandhinagar India 96 D5...............................23°14'N 72°44'E
Gandía Spain 45 E3....................................38°58'N 0°10'W
Ganges r. Bangl./India 96 G5..........................23°30'N 90°08'E
Ganges, Mouths of the Bangl./India 96 G5
....21°17'N 88°23'E
Gangneung S. Korea 104 A3.............................37°46'N 128°52'E
Gannett Peak U.S.A. 62 E5.............................43°12'N 109°39'W
Gansu d. China 98 H6..................................40°01'N 97°56'E
Ganzhou China 99 K3...................................25°50'N 114°53'E
Gao Mali 84 D3..16°16'N 0°02'W
Gar China 98 E4.......................................32°33'N 80°05'E
Gara, Lough l. Ireland 18 C3..........................53°57'N 8°28'W
Garabogaz Turkmenistan 53 F2..........................41°33'N 52°34'E
Garabogazköl Aylagy b. Turkmenistan 53 F2
....41°24'N 53°32'E
Garanhuns Brazil 72 F6................................8°52'S 36°22'W
Garcia Sola, Embalse de resr Spain 45 C3..............39°14'N 5°02'W
Gard r. France 44 F3..................................43°51'N 4°37'E
Garda, Lake Italy 46 D1...............................45°28'N 10°33'E
Garden City U.S.A. 62 F4..............................37°59'N 100°53'W
Gardēz Afgh. 95 K6....................................33°38'N 69°09'E
Garelochhead Scotland 14 E4...........................56°05'N 4°50'W
Garforth England 13 F2................................53°48'N 1°23'W
Garissa Kenya 85 H1...................................0°25'S 39°40'E
Garmisch-Partenkirchen Germany 46 D2..................47°30'N 11°06'E
Garonne r. France 44 C4...............................44°53'N 0°32'W
Garoowe Somalia 85 I2.................................8°23'N 48°28'E

Garoua Cameroon 84 F2.................................9°19'N 13°23'E
Garron Point Northern Ireland 14 D3...................55°03'N 5°57'W
Garry r. Scotland 16 E2...............................57°04'N 4°46'W
Garry, Loch l. Scotland 17 E1.........................56°48'N 4°15'W
Garstang England 12 E2................................53°54'N 2°46'W
Garvagh Northern Ireland 14 C2........................54°59'N 6°41'W
Gary U.S.A. 63 I5.....................................41°35'N 87°20'W
Gascony, Gulf of France 44 B3.........................43°43'N 2°00'W
Gascoyne r. Australia 108 A4..........................24°44'S 114°03'E
Gashua Nigeria 84 F3..................................12°51'N 11°04'E
Gaspé Canada 61 L2....................................48°48'N 64°32'W
Gaspé, Péninsule de pen. Canada 61 L2.................48°35'N 65°31'W
Gastonia U.S.A. 63 J4.................................35°17'N 81°13'W
Gata, Cabo de c. Spain 45 D2..........................36°43'N 2°11'W
Gatehouse of Fleet Scotland 14 E2.....................54°53'N 4°11'W
Gateshead England 13 F3...............................54°57'N 1°36'W
Gatineau r. Canada 63 K6..............................45°27'N 75°42'W
Gävle Sweden 43 D3....................................60°41'N 17°08'E
Gaya India 96 G5......................................24°48'N 85°00'E
Gaya Niger 84 E3......................................11°54'N 3°27'E
Gaza town Gaza 94 D6..................................31°31'N 34°30'E
Gaza Asia 49 J3.......................................31°22'N 34°19'E
Gaziantep Turkey 51 L3................................37°03'N 37°21'E
Gdańsk Poland 46 H6...................................54°21'N 18°39'E
Gdańsk, Gulf of Poland/Russia 46 H6...................54°31'N 19°12'E
Gdynia Poland 46 H6...................................54°31'N 18°33'E
Geal Charn hill Scotland 17 E2........................57°12'N 3°30'W
Gedaref Sudan 85 H3...................................14°02'N 35°23'E
Gediz r. Turkey 51 G4.................................38°35'N 26°48'E
Geel Belgium 42 E4....................................51°09'N 5°00'E
Geelong Australia 108 D3..............................38°08'S 144°21'E
Gejiu China 99 I2.....................................23°22'N 103°09'E
Gela Italy 48 F4......................................37°04'N 14°15'E
Gelderland d. Neth. 42 F5.............................52°03'N 6°08'E
Gelibolu Turkey 51 H5.................................38°03'N 30°42'E
Gelligaer Wales 10 D3.................................51°40'N 3°15'W
Gelsenkirchen Germany 46 B4...........................51°33'N 7°06'E
Gemlik Turkey 51 H5...................................40°25'N 29°09'E
General Santos Phil. 103 H5...........................6°08'N 125°15'E
Geneva Switz. 48 E6...................................46°13'N 6°09'E
Geneva, Lake France/Switz. 44 G5......................46°22'N 6°16'E
Genil r. Spain 45 C2..................................37°42'N 5°18'W
Genk Belgium 42 E3....................................50°57'N 5°31'E
Genoa Italy 46 C1.....................................44°25'N 8°56'E
Genoa, Gulf of Italy 48 E5............................44°08'N 8°57'E
George r. Canada 61 L3................................58°19'N 65°55'W
Georgetown Guyana 72 D7...............................6°49'N 58°09'W
George Town Malaysia 102 C5...........................5°26'N 100°17'E
Georgia Asia 53 E2....................................41°49'N 43°59'E
Georgia d. U.S.A. 63 J3...............................32°35'N 83°28'W
Georgian Bay Canada 61 J2.............................45°17'N 80°51'W
Georgina watercourse Australia 108 C4.................24°54'S 139°35'E
Georgiyevka Kazakhstan 98 E7..........................49°16'N 81°34'E
Georgiyevsk Russia 53 E2..............................44°09'N 43°29'E
Gera Germany 46 E4....................................50°53'N 12°06'E
Geraldton Australia 108 A4............................28°46'S 114°37'E
Gerede Turkey 51 J5...................................40°48'N 32°12'E
Gereshk Afgh. 95 J6...................................31°51'N 64°37'E
Gerlachovský štít mt. Slovakia 46 I3..................49°11'N 20°09'E
Germany Europe 46 D4..................................51°18'N 10°22'E
Gevgelija Macedonia 50 E5.............................41°09'N 22°30'E
Geyik Dağ mt. Turkey 51 J3............................36°52'N 32°11'E
Geyve Turkey 51 I5....................................40°30'N 30°15'E
Ghadāmis Libya 84 E5..................................30°05'N 9°34'E
Ghaem Shahr Iran 95 H7................................36°32'N 52°39'E
Ghaghara r. India 96 F6...............................25°42'N 84°51'E
Ghana Africa 84 D2....................................8°23'N 0°47'W
Ghardaïa Algeria 84 E5................................32°20'N 3°49'E
Gharyān Libya 48 F3...................................32°11'N 13°01'E
Ghāt Libya 84 F4......................................25°10'N 10°13'E
Ghazaouet Algeria 48 C4...............................35°06'N 1°51'W
Ghaziabad India 96 E6.................................28°40'N 77°25'E
Ghazni Afgh. 95 K6....................................33°33'N 68°27'E
Ghent Belgium 42 C4...................................51°03'N 3°43'E
Giant's Causeway f. Northern Ireland 14 C3
....55°14'N 6°31'W
Gibraltar Gibraltar 45 C2.............................36°08'N 5°21'W
Gibraltar, Strait of Morocco/Spain 45 B1..............35°50'N 6°05'W
Gibson Desert Australia 108 B4........................24°46'S 123°25'E
Gien France 44 E5.....................................47°41'N 2°38'E
Gießen Germany 46 C4..................................50°35'N 8°41'E
Gifu Japan 104 C3.....................................35°25'N 136°46'E
Gigha i. Scotland 14 D3...............................55°41'N 5°46'W
Gijón/Xixón Spain 45 C5...............................43°32'N 5°39'W
Gila r. U.S.A. 62 D3..................................32°45'N 114°31'W
Gilgit Pakistan 96 D8.................................35°54'N 74°21'E
Gill, Lough l. Ireland 18 C4..........................54°15'N 8°25'W
Gillette U.S.A. 62 E5.................................44°18'N 105°29'W
Gillingham Dor. England 8 C2..........................51°02'N 2°17'W
Gillingham Medway England 9 F2........................51°23'N 0°33'E
Gilwern Wales 10 D3...................................51°49'N 3°06'W
Gimbala, Jebel mt. Sudan 94 B2........................13°00'N 24°20'E
Giresun Turkey 51 M5..................................40°55'N 38°23'E
Girona Spain 45 G4....................................41°58'N 2°49'E
Gironde est. France 44 C4.............................45°31'N 0°59'W
Girvan Scotland 14 E3.................................55°15'N 4°51'W
Gisborne New Zealand 109 H3...........................38°39'S 178°01'E
Giurgiu Romania 50 F6.................................43°54'N 25°57'E
Giza Egypt 85 H4......................................29°59'N 31°12'E
Gizhiga Russia 55 R4..................................62°01'N 160°28'E
Gjirokastër Albania 50 D5.............................40°04'N 20°09'E
Gjøvik Norway 43 B3...................................60°48'N 10°41'E
Gladstone Australia 108 E4............................23°51'S 151°18'E
Glan r. Germany 42 G2.................................49°47'N 7°42'E
Glanton England 13 F4.................................55°25'N 1°53'W
Glasgow Scotland 14 E3................................55°52'N 4°15'W
Glasgow d. Scotland 20 C4.............................55°52'N 4°15'W
Glasgow U.S.A. 62 E6..................................48°10'N 106°34'W
Glass, Loch l. Scotland 17 E2.........................57°44'N 4°31'W
Glastonbury England 8 C2..............................51°09'N 2°43'W
Glazov Russia 52 F3...................................58°09'N 52°41'E
Glenarm Northern Ireland 14 D2........................54°58'N 5°56'W
Glen Coe f. Scotland 16 D1............................56°41'N 5°05'W
Glendale U.S.A. 62 D3.................................33°32'N 112°12'W
Glengad Head Ireland 18 D5............................55°20'N 7°10'W
Glen Garry f. Scotland 16 D2..........................57°03'N 5°05'W
Glenluce Scotland 14 E2...............................54°53'N 4°49'W
Glen More f. Scotland 17 E2...........................57°09'N 4°44'W
Glen Moriston f. Scotland 16 E2.......................57°09'N 4°52'W
Glennallen U.S.A. 60 D4...............................62°09'N 145°32'W
Glenrothes Scotland 15 F4.............................56°12'N 3°10'W
Glen Shee f. Scotland 17 F1...........................56°48'N 3°29'W
Glinton England 9 E3..................................52°38'N 0°18'W
Gliwice Poland 46 H4..................................50°18'N 18°40'E
Głogów Poland 46 G4...................................51°40'N 16°05'E
Glomfjord Norway 43 C4................................66°49'N 13°57'E
Glorieuses, Îles is Indian Oc. 83 D3..................11°34'S 47°18'E

Glossop England 13 F2.................................53°27'N 1°57'W
Gloucester England 8 C2...............................51°52'N 2°14'W
Gloucestershire d. England 21 D2......................51°49'N 2°11'W
Glusburn England 13 F2................................53°54'N 1°59'W
Glyder Fawr hill Wales 10 C5..........................53°06'N 4°02'W
Glynneath Wales 10 D3.................................51°45'N 3°37'W
Gmünd Austria 46 F3...................................48°47'N 14°59'E
Gniezno Poland 46 G5..................................52°32'N 17°36'E
Goa d. India 96 D4....................................15°24'N 74°11'E
Goat Fell hill Scotland 14 D3.........................55°37'N 5°11'W
Gobabis Namibia 83 A2.................................22°27'S 18°58'E
Gobi des. China/Mongolia 99 J6........................44°59'N 107°19'E
Gobowen England 8 B3..................................52°54'N 3°02'W
Goch Germany 42 F4....................................51°40'N 6°09'E
Godalming England 9 E2................................51°11'N 0°37'W
Godavari r. India 96 F4...............................16°57'N 81°49'E
Godmanchester England 9 E3............................52°19'N 0°10'W
Goes Neth. 42 C4......................................51°30'N 3°54'E
Goiânia Brazil 72 E5..................................16°41'S 49°16'W
Gökçeada i. Turkey 50 F5..............................40°10'N 25°48'E
Göksun Turkey 51 L4...................................38°02'N 36°30'E
Gölcük Turkey 51 H5...................................40°43'N 29°49'E
Gold Coast town Australia 108 E4......................28°03'S 153°26'E
Golmud China 98 G5....................................36°21'N 94°50'E
Golpäyegän Iran 95 H6.................................33°23'N 50°13'E
Golspie Scotland 17 F2................................57°58'N 3°59'W
Gómez Palacio Mexico 66 D6............................25°35'N 103°32'W
Gonaïves Haiti 67 J4..................................19°27'N 72°42'W
Gonbad-e Kavus Iran 95 I7.............................37°14'N 55°07'E
Gonder Ethiopia 85 H3.................................12°39'N 37°28'E
Gondiya India 96 F5...................................21°28'N 80°12'E
Gongga Shan mt. China 99 I3...........................29°57'N 101°55'E
Good Hope, Cape of S. Africa 83 A1....................34°22'S 18°29'E
Goodwick Wales 10 C4..................................52°00'N 4°59'W
Goole England 13 G2...................................53°42'N 0°53'W
Göppingen Germany 46 C3...............................48°43'N 9°39'E
Gora mt. Russia 54 H4.................................64°59'N 60°03'E
Gorakhpur India 96 F6.................................26°45'N 83°25'E
Gorebridge Scotland 15 F3.............................55°50'N 3°03'W
Gorey Ireland 18 E2...................................52°40'N 6°18'W
Gorgān Iran 95 H7.....................................36°50'N 54°24'E
Gori Georgia 53 E2....................................41°59'N 44°07'E
Goris Armenia 95 G7...................................39°30'N 46°20'E
Gorizia Italy 46 E1...................................45°57'N 13°36'E
Görlitz Germany 46 F4.................................51°09'N 14°59'E
Gornji Vakuf Bos. and Herz. 50 B6.....................43°55'N 17°36'E
Gorno-Altaysk Russia 98 F8............................51°59'N 85°53'E
Gornyak Russia 98 E8..................................50°59'N 81°28'E
Gorontalo Indonesia 103 G4............................0°34'N 123°01'E
Gort Ireland 18 C3....................................53°04'N 8°49'W
Gorzów Wielkopolski Poland 46 F5......................52°44'N 15°14'E
Gosberton England 9 E3................................52°52'N 0°10'W
Gosford Australia 108 E3..............................33°25'S 151°20'E
Gosforth Cumb. England 12 D3..........................54°25'N 3°27'W
Gosforth T. and W. England 13 F4......................55°00'N 1°37'W
Goshogawara Japan 104 D4..............................40°48'N 140°26'E
Gospić Croatia 50 A7..................................44°33'N 15°23'E
Gosport England 8 D1..................................50°48'N 1°08'W
Gostivar Macedonia 50 D5..............................41°47'N 20°54'E
Gotha Germany 46 D4...................................50°57'N 10°42'E
Gothenburg Sweden 43 B2...............................57°43'N 11°58'E
Gotland i. Sweden 43 D2...............................57°36'N 18°52'E
Göttingen Germany 46 C4...............................51°32'N 9°56'E
Gouda Neth. 42 D5.....................................52°00'N 4°42'E
Gouin, Réservoir resr Canada 61 K2....................48°39'N 74°39'W
Goulburn Australia 108 D3.............................34°47'S 149°45'E
Gourdon France 44 D4..................................44°45'N 1°23'E
Governador Valadares Brazil 72 E5.....................18°49'S 41°57'W
Gower pen. Wales 10 C3................................51°36'N 4°15'W
Gowna, Lough l. Ireland 18 D3.........................53°53'N 7°35'W
Göynük Turkey 51 I5...................................40°24'N 30°46'E
Grafham Water resr England 9 E3.......................52°18'N 0°19'W
Grafton Australia 108 E4..............................29°41'S 152°57'E
Grafton U.S.A. 62 G6..................................48°24'N 97°26'W
Grahamstown S. Africa 83 B1...........................33°19'S 26°32'E
Grain England 9 F2....................................51°27'N 0°43'E
Grampian Mountains Scotland 17 E1.....................56°47'N 4°37'W
Granada Spain 45 D2...................................37°11'N 3°36'W
Gran Canaria i. Canary Islands 45 Y1..................27°47'N 15°23'W
Gran Chaco f. Argentina/Paraguay 73 C4................22°08'S 62°24'W
Grand Bahama i. Bahamas 67 I6.........................26°34'N 78°29'W
Grand Canyon f. U.S.A. 62 D4..........................36°03'N 112°09'W
Grand Canyon town U.S.A. 62 D4........................36°03'N 112°09'W
Grand Cayman i. Cayman Is 67 H4.......................19°23'N 81°06'W
Grande, Bahía b. Argentina 73 C1......................50°45'S 68°18'W
Grande Prairie Canada 60 G3...........................55°11'N 118°47'W
Grandes, Salinas f. Argentina 73 C3...................30°24'S 65°31'W
Grand Est d. France 42 E4.............................49°10'N 5°30'E
Grand Falls - Windsor Canada 61 M2....................48°53'N 55°25'W
Grand Forks U.S.A. 62 G6..............................47°55'N 97°06'W
Grand Island U.S.A. 62 G5.............................40°56'N 98°23'W
Grand Junction U.S.A. 62 E4...........................39°04'N 108°33'W
Grand Rapids town U.S.A. 63 I5........................42°57'N 85°40'W
Grand Turk Turks and Caicos Is 67 J5..................21°28'N 71°08'W
Grangemouth Scotland 15 F4............................56°01'N 3°43'W
Grange-over-Sands England 12 E3.......................54°11'N 2°55'W
Gran Tarajal Canary Islands 45 Y2.....................28°12'N 14°01'W
Grantham England 8 E3.................................52°55'N 0°39'W
Grantown-on-Spey Scotland 17 F2.......................57°20'N 3°36'W
Grants Pass U.S.A. 62 B5..............................42°29'N 123°19'W
Grasse France 44 G3...................................43°39'N 6°55'E
Grassington England 13 F3.............................54°04'N 1°59'W
Grave, Pointe de pt France 44 C4......................45°35'N 1°04'W
Gravelines France 9 H1................................50°59'N 2°08'E
Gravesend England 9 F2................................51°26'N 0°22'E
Grays England 9 F2....................................51°28'N 0°20'E
Graz Austria 46 F2....................................47°04'N 15°27'E
Great Abaco i. Bahamas 67 I6..........................26°08'N 77°12'W
Great Australian Bight g. Australia 108 B3
....33°06'S 129°50'E
Great Baddow England 9 F2.............................51°43'N 0°30'E
Great Barrier Reef Australia 108 D5...................11°25'S 144°09'E
Great Basin U.S.A. 62 C4..............................39°35'N 116°09'W
Great Bear Lake Canada 60 G4..........................66°03'N 119°59'W
Great Belt str. Denmark 46 D6.........................55°34'N 10°52'E
Great Bend U.S.A. 62 G4...............................38°23'N 98°47'W
Great Bernera i. Scotland 16 C3.......................58°14'N 6°52'W
Great Blasket Island Ireland 18 A2....................52°06'N 10°32'W
Great Clifton England 12 D3...........................54°39'N 3°29'W
Great Cumbrae i. Scotland 14 E3.......................55°47'N 4°58'W
Great Dividing Range mts Australia 108 D3
....37°30'S 144°27'E
Great Dunmow England 9 F2.............................51°52'N 0°22'E
Greater Antilles is Caribbean Sea 67 H5...............21°05'N 81°40'W
Greater London d. England 21 E2.......................51°30'N 0°11'W
Greater Manchester d. England 21 D3...................53°31'N 2°22'W

Great Exuma i. Bahamas 67 I5 ....23°35'N 75°54'W
Great Falls town U.S.A. 62 D6 ....47°30'N 111°17'W
Great Gonerby England 8 E3 ....52°56'N 0°40'W
Greatham England 13 F3 ....54°38'N 1°14'W
Great Harwood England 12 E2 ....53°47'N 2°24'W
Great Inagua i. Bahamas 67 J5 ....21°13'N 73°26'W
Great Karoo f. S. Africa 83 B1 ....32°29'S 23°21'E
Great Linford England 8 E3 ....52°04'N 0°46'W
Great Malvern England 8 C3 ....52°07'N 2°19'W
Great Namaqualand f. Namibia 83 A2 ....26°29'S 16°25'E
Great Nicobar i. India 97 H2 ....7°06'N 94°08'E
Great Ormes Head Wales 10 D5 ....53°21'N 3°52'W
Great Ouse r. England 9 F3 ....52°46'N 0°23'E
Great Plains f. N. America 56 E4 ....45°00'N 100°00'W
Great Rhos hill Wales 10 D4 ....52°16'N 3°12'W
Great Rift Valley f. Africa 83 C4 ....7°00'S 33°00'E
Great Salt Lake U.S.A. 62 D5 ....40°58'N 112°26'W
Great Sand Sea des. Egypt/Libya 49 H2 ....28°55'N 24°22'E
Great Sandy Desert Australia 108 B4 ....20°35'S 123°36'E
Great Shelford England 9 F3 ....52°09'N 0°08'E
Great Slave Lake Canada 60 G4 ....61°26'N 114°35'W
Great Stour r. England 9 G2 ....51°20'N 1°14'E
Great Torrington England 11 C2 ....50°57'N 4°08'W
Great Victoria Desert Australia 108 B4 ....28°43'S 128°38'E
Great Whernside hill England 13 F3 ....54°10'N 1°59'W
Great Yarmouth England 9 G3 ....52°36'N 1°44'E
Gredos, Sierra de mts Spain 45 C4 ....40°08'N 5°43'W
Greece Europe 50 D4 ....39°03'N 21°56'E
Greeley U.S.A. 62 F5 ....40°25'N 104°41'W
Green r. U.S.A. 62 E4 ....38°12'N 109°53'W
Green Bay town U.S.A. 63 I5 ....44°30'N 88°02'W
Greenland i. N. America 61 N5 ....72°21'N 41°01'W
Greenlaw Scotland 15 G3 ....55°42'N 2°28'W
Greenock Scotland 14 E3 ....55°57'N 4°46'W
Greenore Point Ireland 10 A4 ....52°14'N 6°18'W
Green River town U.S.A. 62 E5 ....41°36'N 109°29'W
Greensboro U.S.A. 63 K4 ....36°04'N 79°48'W
Greenstone Point Scotland 16 D2 ....57°56'N 5°40'W
Greenville Liberia 84 D2 ....5°01'N 9°02'W
Greenville Miss. U.S.A. 63 H3 ....33°22'N 91°01'W
Greenville S. C. U.S.A. 63 J3 ....34°50'N 82°27'W
Greenwich England 9 E2 ....51°29'N 0°00'W
Greifswald Germany 46 E6 ....54°05'N 13°24'E
Grená Denmark 43 B2 ....56°24'N 10°54'E
Grenada Central America 67 L3 ....12°03'N 61°38'W
Grenade France 44 D3 ....43°46'N 1°18'E
Grenoble France 44 F4 ....45°11'N 5°44'E
Greta r. England 13 E3 ....54°09'N 2°37'W
Gretna Scotland 15 F2 ....54°59'N 3°04'W
Greven Germany 42 G5 ....52°06'N 7°38'E
Grevena Greece 50 D5 ....40°05'N 21°25'E
Grey Range hills Australia 108 D4 ....28°13'S 142°35'E
Grimsby England 13 G2 ....53°34'N 0°04'W
Grímsey i. Iceland 43 Y2 ....66°32'N 17°59'W
Gris Nez, Cap c. France 9 G1 ....50°52'N 1°36'E
Gritley Scotland 17 G3 ....58°56'N 2°45'W
Grodzisk Wielkopolski Poland 46 G5 ....52°13'N 16°22'E
Groningen Neth. 42 F6 ....53°13'N 6°34'E
Groningen d. Neth. 42 F6 ....53°16'N 6°40'E
Groote Eylandt i. Australia 108 C5 ....13°58'S 137°09'E
Grosser Speikkogel mt. Austria 46 F2 ....46°48'N 14°58'E
Großglockner mt. Austria 46 E2 ....47°05'N 12°41'E
Groundhog r. Canada 61 J2 ....49°40'N 81°56'W
Groznyy Russia 53 E2 ....43°19'N 45°42'E
Grudziądz Poland 46 H5 ....53°30'N 18°45'E
Gruinard Bay Scotland 16 D2 ....57°53'N 5°32'W
Guacanayabo, Golfo de b. Cuba 67 I5 ....20°31'N 77°38'W
Guadajoz r. Spain 45 C2 ....37°35'N 4°51'W
Guadalajara Mexico 66 D5 ....20°40'N 103°24'W
Guadalajara Spain 45 D4 ....40°38'N 3°09'W
Guadalcanal i. Solomon Is 109 F6 ....9°38'S 160°05'E
Guadalete r. Spain 45 B2 ....36°32'N 6°14'W
Guadalope r. Spain 45 E4 ....41°15'N 0°02'W
Guadalquivir r. Spain 45 B2 ....36°48'N 6°21'W
Guadalupe r. U.S.A. 62 G2 ....29°09'N 118°23'W
Guadalupe, Sierra de mts Spain 45 C3 ....39°20'N 5°49'W
Guadarrama, Sierra de mts Spain 45 C4 ....40°40'N 4°10'W
Guadeloupe i. Central America 67 L4 ....16°30'N 61°29'W
Guadiana r. Portugal/Spain 45 B2 ....37°11'N 7°24'W
Guadix Spain 45 D2 ....37°18'N 3°07'W
Guajira, Península de la pen. Colombia 72 B8 ....11°59'N 71°45'W
Guam i. N. Pacific Oc. 103 K6 ....13°29'N 144°58'E
Guanajuato Mexico 66 D5 ....21°01'N 101°15'W
Guanajuato d. Mexico 66 D5 ....21°00'N 101°00'W
Guanare Venezuela 67 K2 ....9°03'N 69°44'W
Guane Cuba 67 H5 ....22°13'N 84°05'W
Guangdong d. China 99 K2 ....23°49'N 114°45'E
Guangxi Zhuangzu Zizhiqu d. China 99 J2 ....23°52'N 108°27'E
Guangyuan China 99 J4 ....32°24'N 105°51'E
Guangzhou China 99 K2 ....23°09'N 113°21'E
Guanipa r. Venezuela 67 L2 ....9°53'N 62°26'W
Guantánamo Cuba 67 I5 ....20°07'N 75°13'W
Guaporé r. Bolivia/Brazil 72 C5 ....11°57'S 65°04'W
Guara, Sierra de mts Spain 45 E5 ....42°15'N 0°20'W
Guarda Portugal 45 B4 ....40°33'N 7°16'W
Guasave Mexico 66 C6 ....25°33'N 108°30'W
Guatemala Central America 66 F4 ....15°43'N 90°16'W
Guatemala City Guatemala 66 F3 ....14°37'N 90°31'W
Guaviare r. Colombia 72 C7 ....4°02'N 67°45'W
Guayaquil Ecuador 72 B6 ....2°10'S 79°56'W
Guayaquil, Golfo de g. Ecuador 68 B3 ....3°10'S 80°53'W
Guaymas Mexico 66 B6 ....27°57'N 110°53'W
Guazhou China 98 H6 ....40°27'N 95°48'E
Guba Ethiopia 85 H3 ....11°16'N 35°17'E
Guba Dolgaya Russia 52 F5 ....70°18'N 58°37'E
Gudbrandsdalen f. Norway 43 B3 ....61°58'N 9°20'E
Guéckédou Guinea 84 C2 ....8°33'N 10°11'W
Guelma Algeria 48 E4 ....36°27'N 7°29'E
Guelmine Morocco 84 C4 ....28°59'N 10°02'W
Guéret France 44 D5 ....46°10'N 1°52'E
Guernsey i. Channel Is 11 Y9 ....49°29'N 2°36'W
Guerrero d. Mexico 66 D4 ....17°41'N 100°48'W
Guiana Highlands mts Guyana/Venezuela 72 C7 ....6°18'N 63°41'W
Guildford England 9 E2 ....51°14'N 0°34'W
Guilin China 99 K3 ....25°17'N 110°19'E
Guinea Africa 84 C3 ....10°50'N 11°28'E
Guinea, Gulf of Africa 84 E2 ....2°31'N 4°26'E
Guinea-Bissau Africa 84 C3 ....11°54'N 14°45'W
Guînes France 42 A3 ....50°52'N 1°52'E
Güiria Venezuela 67 L3 ....10°33'N 62°19'W
Guisborough England 13 F3 ....54°32'N 1°03'W
Guise France 42 C3 ....49°54'N 3°38'E
Guiyang China 99 J3 ....26°33'N 106°39'E
Guizhou d. China 99 J3 ....26°59'N 106°45'E

Gujarat d. India 96 D5 ....22°51'N 72°32'E
Gujranwala Pakistan 96 D7 ....32°07'N 74°13'E
Gullane Scotland 15 G4 ....56°02'N 2°50'W
Gulu Uganda 85 H2 ....2°44'N 32°17'E
Gumdag Turkmenistan 95 H7 ....39°11'N 54°29'E
Gümüşhane Turkey 51 M5 ....40°29'N 39°28'E
Guna India 96 E5 ....24°39'N 77°19'E
Guntur India 96 F4 ....16°19'N 80°26'E
Guri, Embalse de resr Venezuela 67 L2 ....7°38'N 62°47'W
Gusau Nigeria 84 E3 ....12°15'N 6°37'E
Gushgy Turkmenistan 95 J7 ....35°15'N 62°17'E
Güstrow Germany 46 E5 ....53°48'N 12°11'E
Guwahati India 97 H6 ....26°09'N 91°46'E
Guyana S. America 72 D7 ....5°59'N 59°59'W
Gwadar Pakistan 96 B6 ....25°09'N 62°23'E
Gwalior India 96 E6 ....26°15'N 78°10'E
Gwangju S. Korea 99 N5 ....35°09'N 126°54'E
Gwardafuy, Gees c. Somalia 85 J3 ....11°49'N 51°16'E
Gweebarra Bay Ireland 18 C4 ....54°53'N 8°30'W
Gweru Zimbabwe 83 B3 ....19°27'S 29°50'E
Gwynedd d. Wales 21 C3 ....53°00'N 4°02'W
Gydan Peninsula Russia 54 I5 ....70°08'N 77°30'E
Gyöngyös Hungary 46 H2 ....47°46'N 19°56'E
Győr Hungary 46 G2 ....47°41'N 17°39'E
Gypsumville Canada 60 I3 ....51°47'N 98°37'W
Gyumri Armenia 94 F8 ....40°47'N 43°51'E
Gyzylarbat Turkmenistan 54 G1 ....38°59'N 56°17'E

H

Haapajärvi Finland 43 F3 ....63°45'N 25°20'E
Haapsalu Estonia 43 E2 ....58°56'N 23°33'E
Haarlem Neth. 42 D5 ....52°22'N 4°38'E
Habbān Yemen 95 G2 ....14°20'N 47°05'E
Hachijo-jima i. Japan 104 C2 ....33°07'N 139°50'E
Hachinohe Japan 104 D4 ....40°32'N 141°31'E
Hadd, Ra's al pt Oman 95 I4 ....22°30'N 59°50'E
Haddington Scotland 15 G3 ....55°58'N 2°46'W
Haderslev Denmark 43 B1 ....55°15'N 9°29'E
Hadjer Hadid Chad 85 G3 ....13°23'N 21°20'E
Had Kourt Morocco 45 C1 ....34°31'N 5°48'W
Hadleigh England 9 F3 ....52°03'N 0°57'E
Hadramawt f. Yemen 95 G2 ....15°07'N 47°48'E
Hadyach Ukraine 47 O4 ....50°22'N 33°59'E
Haeju N. Korea 99 N5 ....38°02'N 125°45'E
Hagar Nish Plateau f. Eritrea 94 E3 ....17°03'N 37°58'E
Hagåtña Guam 103 K6 ....13°29'n 144°45'E
Hagen Germany 46 B4 ....51°22'N 7°28'E
Hag's Head Ireland 18 B2 ....52°56'N 9°29'W
Hague, Cap de la c. France 11 Z9 ....49°44'N 1°55'W
Haida Gwaii is Canada 60 E3 ....53°59'N 133°20'W
Haifa Israel 49 J3 ....32°50'N 34°58'E
Haikou China 99 K2 ....20°01'N 110°18'E
Hā'il Saudi Arabia 94 F5 ....27°33'N 41°41'E
Hailsham England 9 F1 ....50°52'N 0°15'E
Hainan d. China 99 J1 ....19°09'N 109°33'E
Hainan i. China 99 J1 ....18°51'N 110°29'E
Hainaut d. Belgium 42 D3 ....50°29'N 4°00'E
Haines U.S.A. 60 E3 ....59°13'N 135°25'W
Hai Phong Vietnam 102 D8 ....20°48'N 106°43'E
Haiti Central America 67 J4 ....19°19'N 73°30'W
Haiya Sudan 85 H3 ....18°20'N 36°23'E
Hakodate Japan 104 D4 ....41°47'N 140°44'E
Halabjah/Helebce Iraq 95 G6 ....35°11'N 45°56'E
Halāniyāt, Juzur al is Oman 95 I3 ....17°30'N 56°11'E
Halden Norway 43 B2 ....59°07'N 11°25'E
Halesowen England 8 C3 ....52°27'N 2°03'W
Halesworth England 9 G3 ....52°21'N 1°30'E
Halifax Canada 61 L2 ....44°39'N 63°36'W
Halifax England 13 F2 ....53°44'N 1°51'W
Halkirk Scotland 17 F3 ....58°31'N 3°29'W
Halladale r. Scotland 17 F3 ....58°33'N 3°54'W
Hall Beach town Canada 61 J4 ....68°42'N 81°17'W
Halle Belgium 42 D3 ....50°44'N 4°14'E
Halle Germany 46 D4 ....51°29'N 11°59'E
Halls Creek town Australia 108 B5 ....18°17'S 127°40'E
Halmahera i. Indonesia 103 H4 ....1°06'N 128°32'E
Halmstad Sweden 43 C2 ....56°40'N 12°52'E
Halstead England 9 F2 ....51°57'N 0°39'E
Halton d. England 21 D3 ....53°20'N 2°43'W
Haltwhistle England 13 E3 ....54°58'N 2°27'W
Hamadān Iran 95 G6 ....34°46'N 48°30'E
Ḩamāh Syria 94 E7 ....35°08'N 36°45'E
Hamamatsu Japan 104 C2 ....34°42'N 137°44'E
Hamar Norway 43 B3 ....60°48'N 11°05'E
Hambleton Hills England 13 F3 ....54°19'N 1°14'W
Hamburg Germany 46 C5 ....53°34'N 9°59'E
Hämeenlinna Finland 43 F3 ....60°59'N 24°27'E
Hamersley Range mts Australia 108 A4 ....22°11'S 116°31'E
Hamhŭng N. Korea 99 N5 ....39°55'N 127°33'E
Hami China 98 G6 ....42°48'N 93°27'E
Hamilton Bermuda 67 L7 ....32°18'N 64°46'W
Hamilton Canada 61 K2 ....43°15'N 79°51'W
Hamilton New Zealand 109 G3 ....37°48'S 175°16'E
Hamilton Scotland 15 E3 ....55°47'N 4°03'W
Hamīm, Wādī al watercourse Libya 49 H3 ....30°04'N 21°35'E
Hamina Finland 43 F3 ....60°34'N 27°12'E
Hamm Germany 46 B4 ....51°41'N 7°49'E
Hammamet, Golfe de g. Tunisia 48 F4 ....36°09'N 10°50'E
Hammerdal Sweden 43 C3 ....63°35'N 15°21'E
Hammerfest Norway 43 E5 ....70°40'N 23°40'E
Hampshire d. England 21 E2 ....51°10'N 1°13'W
Hampshire Downs hills England 8 D2 ....51°20'N 1°35'W
Hamstreet England 9 F2 ....51°04'N 0°52'E
Hanamaki Japan 104 D3 ....39°23'N 141°07'E
Hancock U.S.A. 63 H6 ....47°08'N 88°36'W
Handa Island Scotland 16 D3 ....58°23'N 5°13'W
Handan China 99 K5 ....36°35'N 114°32'E
Hangzhou China 99 M4 ....30°15'N 120°10'E
Hanna Canada 62 D7 ....51°38'N 111°56'W
Hannover Germany 46 C5 ....52°23'N 9°44'E
Hanöbukten b. Sweden 46 F6 ....55°48'N 14°37'E
Hanoi Vietnam 102 D8 ....21°01'N 105°51'E
Hantsavichy Belarus 47 L5 ....52°46'N 26°27'E
Hanzhong China 99 J4 ....33°04'N 107°03'E
Haparanda Sweden 43 F4 ....65°50'N 24°08'E
Happy Valley-Goose Bay town Canada 61 L3 ....53°19'N 60°07'W
Harare Zimbabwe 83 C3 ....17°49'S 31°04'E
Ḩarāsīs, Jiddat al des. Oman 95 I3 ....18°59'N 55°09'E
Harbin China 99 N7 ....45°40'N 126°37'E
Harderwijk Neth. 42 E5 ....52°21'N 5°37'E
Haren Germany 42 G5 ....52°48'N 7°15'E
Hargeysa Somalia 85 I2 ....9°32'N 44°05'E
Har Hu l. China 98 H5 ....38°18'N 97°23'E

Hari Rūd r. Afgh./Iran 95 J7 ....36°50'N 60°58'E
Harlech Wales 10 C4 ....52°52'N 4°06'W
Harleston England 9 G3 ....52°24'N 1°18'E
Harlingen Neth. 42 E6 ....53°10'N 5°25'E
Harlow England 9 F2 ....51°46'N 0°05'E
Harney Basin U.S.A. 62 C5 ....43°23'N 119°55'W
Härnösand Sweden 43 D3 ....62°38'N 17°56'E
Har Nuur l. Mongolia 98 G7 ....48°02'N 93°23'E
Harpenden England 9 E2 ....51°49'N 0°21'W
Harray, Loch of l. Scotland 17 F4 ....59°01'N 3°13'W
Harricanaw r. Canada 61 K3 ....50°58'N 79°33'W
Harris, Sound of str. Scotland 16 B2 ....57°46'N 7°10'W
Harrisburg U.S.A. 63 K5 ....40°17'N 76°54'W
Harrogate England 13 F2 ....53°59'N 1°32'W
Hârşova Romania 51 G7 ....44°41'N 27°57'E
Harstad Norway 43 D5 ....68°47'N 16°32'E
Harteigan mt. Norway 43 A3 ....60°12'N 7°05'E
Harter Fell hill England 12 E3 ....54°29'N 2°52'W
Hart Fell hill Scotland 15 F3 ....55°24'N 3°24'W
Hartford U.S.A. 63 L5 ....41°46'N 72°42'W
Hartland England 11 C2 ....50°59'N 4°29'W
Hartland Point England 11 C3 ....51°01'N 4°33'W
Hartlepool England 13 F3 ....54°41'N 1°13'W
Hartlepool d. England 21 E4 ....54°40'N 1°15'W
Har Us Nuur l. Mongolia 98 G7 ....47°53'N 92°19'E
Harwich England 9 G2 ....51°56'N 1°16'E
Haryana d. India 96 E6 ....29°11'N 76°12'E
Haskovo Bulgaria 50 F5 ....41°56'N 25°32'E
Haslemere England 8 E2 ....51°05'N 0°43'W
Hasselt Belgium 42 E3 ....50°56'N 5°20'E
Hassi Messaoud Algeria 84 E5 ....31°41'N 6°10'E
Hässleholm Sweden 43 C2 ....56°10'N 13°46'E
Hastings England 9 F1 ....50°51'N 0°35'E
Hatfield England 13 G2 ....53°35'N 0°59'W
Ha Tinh Vietnam 102 D7 ....18°18'N 105°55'E
Hatteras, Cape U.S.A. 63 K4 ....35°14'N 75°34'W
Hattiesburg U.S.A. 63 I3 ....31°23'N 89°19'W
Hat Yai Thailand 102 C5 ....7°01'N 100°26'E
Haud f. Ethiopia 85 I2 ....8°37'N 44°15'E
Haugesund Norway 43 A2 ....59°24'N 5°18'E
Haukivesi l. Finland 43 G3 ....62°06'N 28°28'E
Haut f. Ethiopia 85 I2 ....?
Haut Atlas mts Morocco 84 D5 ....30°51'N 8°03'W
Haut-Folin hill France 44 F5 ....46°59'N 4°01'E
Hauts-de-France d. France 42 B3 ....50°14'N 2°43'E
Hauts Plateaux f. Algeria 48 C3 ....33°42'N 0°42'W
Havant England 8 E1 ....50°52'N 0°59'W
Haverfordwest Wales 10 C3 ....51°48'N 4°58'W
Haverhill England 9 F3 ....52°05'N 0°26'E
Havre U.S.A. 62 E6 ....48°32'N 109°41'W
Havre-St-Pierre Canada 61 L3 ....50°14'N 63°28'W
Hawaii i. U.S.A. 116 B3 ....20°02'N 155°17'W
Hawaiian Islands N. Pacific Oc. 116 A3 ....28°26'N 174°25'W
Hawarden Wales 10 D5 ....53°11'N 3°02'W
Hawes England 13 E3 ....54°18'N 2°12'W
Haweswater Reservoir England 12 E3 ....54°30'N 2°48'W
Hawick Scotland 15 G3 ....55°26'N 2°47'W
Hawke Bay New Zealand 109 G3 ....39°24'S 177°23'E
Hawkhurst England 9 F2 ....51°03'N 0°31'E
Haxby England 13 F3 ....54°01'N 1°04'W
Hay Australia 108 D3 ....34°31'S 144°48'E
Hay r. Canada 60 G4 ....60°48'N 117°00'W
Haydarābād Iran 94 G7 ....37°04'N 45°05'E
Haydon Bridge England 13 E3 ....54°59'N 2°15'W
Hayle England 11 B2 ....50°11'N 5°25'W
Haymā' Oman 95 I3 ....19°54'N 56°13'E
Hay-on-Wye Wales 10 D4 ....52°05'N 3°07'W
Hay River town Canada 60 G4 ....60°51'N 115°40'W
Hayshah, Sabkhat al f. Libya 49 G3 ....31°55'N 15°19'E
Haywards Heath England 9 E1 ....50°59'N 0°06'W
Hazarajat f. Afgh. 95 K6 ....32°29'N 65°07'E
Hazebrouck France 42 B3 ....50°43'N 2°32'E
Heacham England 9 F3 ....52°54'N 0°30'E
Headcorn England 9 F2 ....51°10'N 0°38'E
Heanor England 13 F2 ....53°01'N 1°21'W
Hearst Canada 63 J6 ....49°41'N 83°41'W
Heathfield England 9 F1 ....50°58'N 0°16'E
Hebei d. China 99 L5 ....38°33'N 115°49'E
Hebron West Bank 49 J3 ....31°53'N 34°49'E
Hecate Strait Canada 60 E3 ....52°36'N 130°27'W
Hechi China 99 J2 ....24°38'N 108°04'E
Heckington England 9 E3 ....52°59'N 0°18'W
Hede Sweden 43 C3 ....62°25'N 13°32'E
Heerenveen Neth. 42 E5 ....52°58'N 5°56'E
Heerlen Neth. 42 E3 ....50°53'N 5°59'E
Hefei China 99 L4 ....31°51'N 117°19'E
Hegang China 99 O7 ....47°13'N 130°13'E
Heidelberg Germany 46 C3 ....49°24'N 8°41'E
Heighington England 13 G2 ....53°13'N 0°27'W
Heilbronn Germany 46 C3 ....49°08'N 9°12'E
Heilen, Loch l. Scotland 17 F3 ....58°36'N 3°17'W
Heilongjiang d. China 99 N7 ....46°55'N 128°30'E
Heilong Jiang r. China 99 O7 ....48°25'N 134°59'E
Heinola Finland 43 F3 ....61°12'N 26°02'E
Hekla vol. Iceland 43 Y1 ....63°59'N 19°41'W
Helena U.S.A. 62 D6 ....46°36'N 112°01'W
Helensburgh Scotland 14 E4 ....56°00'N 4°44'W
Helgoländer Bucht g. Germany 46 C6 ....54°10'N 8°14'E
Hellín Spain 45 E3 ....38°31'N 1°41'W
Helmand r. Afgh. 95 J6 ....31°13'N 61°35'E
Helmond Neth. 42 E4 ....51°28'N 5°40'E
Helmsdale Scotland 17 F3 ....58°07'N 3°39'W
Helmsdale r. Scotland 17 F3 ....58°07'N 3°38'W
Helmsley England 13 F3 ....54°15'N 1°04'W
Helsingborg Sweden 43 C2 ....56°03'N 12°42'E
Helsinger Denmark 46 E7 ....56°02'N 12°37'E
Helsinki Finland 43 F3 ....60°10'N 24°57'E
Helston England 11 B2 ....50°06'N 5°16'W
Helvellyn hill England 12 D3 ....54°32'N 3°01'W
Hemel Hempstead England 9 E2 ....51°45'N 0°27'W
Henan d. China 99 K4 ....33°38'N 112°54'E
Henares r. Spain 45 D4 ....40°25'N 3°29'W
Hendon England 9 E2 ....51°34'N 0°13'W
Henfield England 9 E1 ....50°56'N 0°16'W
Hengelo Neth. 42 F5 ....52°16'N 6°48'E
Hengoed Wales 10 D3 ....51°39'N 3°14'W
Hengyang China 99 K3 ....26°53'N 112°32'E
Heniches'k Ukraine 49 J6 ....46°10'N 34°48'E
Henley-on-Thames England 8 E2 ....51°32'N 0°54'W
Hennef Germany 42 G3 ....50°47'N 7°18'E
Henrietta Maria, Cape Canada 61 J3 ....55°21'N 82°13'W
Henzada Myanmar 97 I4 ....17°36'N 95°26'E
Herāt Afgh. 95 J6 ....34°22'N 62°11'E
Hereford England 8 C3 ....52°04'N 2°43'W
Herefordshire d. England 21 D3 ....52°07'N 2°40'W
Herm i. Channel Is 11 Y9 ....49°28'N 2°26'W

Herma Ness hd Scotland 17 I5 ....60°51'N 0°54'W
Hermosillo Mexico 66 B6 ....29°04'N 110°58'W
Herne Germany 42 G4 ....51°32'N 7°13'E
Herne Bay town England 9 G2 ....51°22'N 1°08'E
Herning Denmark 43 B2 ....56°08'N 8°58'E
Hertford England 9 E2 ....51°48'N 0°05'W
Hertfordshire d. England 21 F2 ....51°55'N 0°09'E
Hesdin France 9 H1 ....50°22'N 2°03'E
Heswall England 12 D2 ....53°20'N 3°06'W
Hetton England 13 E3 ....54°01'N 2°03'W
Hexham England 13 E3 ....54°58'N 2°07'W
Heysham England 12 E3 ....54°02'N 2°54'W
Heywood England 13 E2 ....53°36'N 2°13'W
Heze China 99 L5 ....35°17'N 115°32'E
Hidaka-sanmyaku mts Japan 104 D4 ....42°49'N 142°38'E
Hidalgo d. Mexico 66 E5 ....20°35'N 99°07'W
Hidalgo del Parral Mexico 66 C6 ....26°56'N 105°41'W
Higashi-suidō str. Japan 104 A2 ....33°55'N 129°23'E
Higham Ferrers England 9 E3 ....52°18'N 0°36'W
Highbridge England 8 C2 ....51°13'N 2°59'W
Highclere England 8 D2 ....51°20'N 1°22'W
Highland d. Scotland 20 C5 ....57°23'N 4°59'W
High Peak hills England 13 F2 ....53°23'N 1°54'W
High Seat hill England 13 E3 ....54°24'N 2°18'W
Highworth England 8 D2 ....51°38'N 1°43'W
High Wycombe England 8 E2 ....51°38'N 0°45'W
Hiiumaa i. Estonia 43 E2 ....58°50'N 22°24'E
Hijaz f. Saudi Arabia 94 E5 ....26°08'N 37°01'E
Hilāl, Ra's al pt Libya 49 H3 ....32°54'N 22°09'E
Hildesheim Germany 46 C5 ....52°09'N 9°57'E
Hillah Iraq 94 F6 ....32°27'N 44°24'E
Hillerød Denmark 43 C1 ....55°56'N 12°18'E
Hillside Scotland 17 G1 ....56°45'N 2°29'W
Hillswick Scotland 17 H5 ....60°29'N 1°29'W
Hilpsford Point England 12 D3 ....54°02'N 3°12'W
Hilversum Neth. 42 E5 ....52°13'N 5°11'E
Himachal Pradesh d. India 96 E7 ....31°59'N 77°23'E
Himalaya mts Asia 96 F6 ....33°06'N 76°46'E
Hinckley England 8 D3 ....52°33'N 1°23'W
Hinderwell England 13 G3 ....54°32'N 0°46'W
Hindhead England 8 E2 ....51°07'N 0°44'W
Hindley England 12 E2 ....53°32'N 2°35'W
Hindu Kush mts Afgh./Pakistan 95 K6 ....34°58'N 67°52'E
Hinnøya i. Norway 43 D5 ....68°37'N 15°58'E
Hirosaki Japan 104 D4 ....40°36'N 140°28'E
Hiroshima Japan 104 B2 ....34°22'N 132°27'E
Hirson France 42 D3 ....49°55'N 4°05'E
Hirwaun Wales 10 D3 ....51°44'N 3°31'W
Hispaniola i. Caribbean Sea 67 J5 ....20°18'N 72°57'W
Hitachi Japan 104 D3 ....36°35'N 140°39'E
Hitchin England 9 E2 ....51°57'N 0°17'W
Hitra i. Norway 43 B3 ....63°31'N 8°49'E
Hjälmaren l. Sweden 43 C2 ....59°14'N 15°51'E
Hjørring Denmark 43 B2 ....57°28'N 10°01'E
Hlybokaye Belarus 47 L6 ....55°08'N 27°40'E
Hobart Australia 108 D2 ....42°52'S 147°19'E
Hobro Denmark 43 B2 ....56°38'N 9°48'E
Ho Chi Minh City Vietnam 102 D6 ....10°45'N 106°42'E
Hochschwab mt. Austria 46 F2 ....47°38'N 15°09'E
Hoddesdon England 9 E2 ....51°46'N 0°01'W
Hodeidah Yemen 94 F2 ....14°50'N 42°54'E
Hódmezővásárhely Hungary 46 I2 ....46°25'N 20°21'E
Hodna, Chott el f. Algeria 48 D4 ....35°27'N 4°55'E
Hodnet England 8 C3 ....52°51'N 2°35'W
Hoek van Holland Neth. 42 D4 ....51°58'N 4°08'E
Hof Germany 46 D4 ....50°19'N 11°55'E
Höfn Iceland 43 Z2 ....64°16'N 15°13'W
Hofsjökull ice cap Iceland 43 Y2 ....64°49'N 18°52'W
Hohhot China 99 K6 ....40°43'N 111°44'E
Hokkaidō i. Japan 104 D4 ....43°33'N 143°27'E
Holbæk Denmark 43 B1 ....55°43'N 11°44'E
Holbeach England 9 F3 ....52°48'N 0°01'E
Holbeach Marsh England 9 F3 ....52°51'N 0°02'E
Holderness pen. England 13 G2 ....53°52'N 0°18'W
Holguín Cuba 67 I5 ....20°54'N 76°14'W
Hollabrunn Austria 46 G3 ....48°34'N 16°05'E
Holland Fen f. England 9 E3 ....52°59'N 0°11'W
Hollesley Bay England 9 G3 ....52°02'N 1°28'E
Hollington England 9 F1 ....50°53'N 0°33'E
Hollingworth England 13 F2 ....53°28'N 1°59'W
Holme-on-Spalding-Moor England 13 G2 ....53°50'N 0°47'W
Holmfirth England 13 F2 ....53°34'N 1°47'W
Holstebro Denmark 43 B2 ....56°21'N 8°37'E
Holsworthy England 11 C2 ....50°49'N 4°21'W
Holt England 9 G3 ....52°55'N 1°05'E
Holyhead Wales 10 C5 ....53°19'N 4°38'W
Holyhead Bay Wales 10 C5 ....53°22'N 4°40'W
Holy Island England 13 F4 ....55°41'N 1°47'W
Holy Island Wales 10 C5 ....53°15'N 4°41'W
Holywell Wales 10 D5 ....53°17'N 3°13'W
Homāyunshahr Iran 95 H6 ....32°59'N 50°23'E
Homburg Germany 42 G2 ....49°19'N 7°20'E
Home Bay Canada 61 L4 ....68°52'N 67°23'W
Homs Syria 94 E6 ....34°44'N 36°44'E
Homyel' Belarus 47 N5 ....52°25'N 31°01'E
Honduras Central America 66 G3 ....14°47'N 86°43'W
Honduras, Gulf of Belize/Honduras 66 G4 ....16°20'N 87°30'W
Hønefoss Norway 43 B3 ....60°10'N 10°14'E
Hong Kong China 99 K2 ....22°16'N 114°11'E
Hong Kong d. China 99 K2 ....22°21'N 114°19'E
Honiara Solomon Is 109 E6 ....9°26'S 159°57'E
Honiton England 11 D2 ....50°48'N 3°11'W
Honley England 13 F2 ....53°36'N 1°48'W
Honshū i. Japan 104 D3 ....35°42'N 133°20'E
Hood, Mount vol. U.S.A. 62 B6 ....45°23'N 121°42'W
Hood Point Australia 108 A3 ....34°19'S 119°33'E
Hoogeveen Neth. 42 F5 ....52°43'N 6°30'E
Hook England 8 E2 ....51°17'N 0°58'W
Hook Head Ireland 18 E2 ....52°07'N 6°56'W
Hoorn Neth. 42 E5 ....52°39'N 5°04'E
Hope, Loch l. Scotland 17 E3 ....58°28'N 4°38'W
Hope, Point U.S.A. 60 B4 ....68°21'N 166°49'W
Hopedale Canada 61 L3 ....55°27'N 60°00'W
Hörby Sweden 46 E6 ....55°51'N 13°40'E
Horley England 9 E2 ....51°10'N 0°10'W
Hormuz, Strait of Iran/Oman 95 I5 ....26°35'N 56°59'E
Horn c. Iceland 43 X2 ....66°28'N 22°29'W
Horn, Cape Chile 73 C1 ....56°05'S 67°17'W
Hornavan l. Sweden 43 D4 ....66°11'N 17°44'E
Horncastle England 13 G2 ....53°12'N 0°07'W
Hornepayne Canada 63 J6 ....49°13'N 84°47'W
Hornsea England 13 G2 ....53°55'N 0°10'W
Horodnya Ukraine 47 N4 ....51°53'N 31°36'E
Horodok Ukraine 47 J3 ....49°47'N 23°39'E
Horrabridge England 11 C2 ....50°31'N 4°06'W
Horsens Denmark 43 B1 ....55°52'N 9°51'E

Horsham Australia 108 D3......36°43'S 142°13'E
Horsham England 9 E2......51°04'N 0°19'W
Horten Norway 43 B2......59°25'N 10°28'E
Horwich England 12 E2......53°36'N 2°33'W
Hotan China 98 E5......37°07'N 80°02'E
Houffalize Belgium 42 E3......50°08'N 5°48'E
Houghton le Spring England 13 F3......54°50'N 1°28'W
Houghton Regis England 9 E2......51°54'N 0°31'W
Hourn, Loch inlet Scotland 16 D2......57°08'N 5°42'W
Houston U.S.A. 63 G2......29°43'N 95°19'W
Hovd Mongolia 98 G2......47°59'N 91°41'E
Hove England 9 E1......50°50'N 0°10'W
Hoveton England 9 G3......52°43'N 1°25'E
Hövsgöl Nuur l. Mongolia 99 I8......50°59'N 100°42'E
Howden England 13 G2......53°45'N 0°52'W
Hoy i. Scotland 17 F3......58°50'N 3°16'W
Høyanger Norway 43 A3......61°13'N 6°04'E
Hoyerswerda Germany 46 F4......51°27'N 14°16'E
Höytiäinen l. Finland 43 G3......62°46'N 29°43'E
Hradec Králové Czechia 46 F4......50°13'N 15°50'E
Hrebinka Ukraine 47 O4......50°06'N 32°26'E
Hrodna Belarus 47 J5......53°41'N 23°49'E
Hsinchu Taiwan 99 M2......24°48'N 120°58'E
Huaibei China 99 L4......33°57'N 116°51'E
Huainan China 99 L4......32°36'N 117°02'E
Huambo Angola 83 A3......12°46'S 15°44'E
Huancayo Peru 72 B5......12°03'S 75°11'W
Huang He r. China 99 L5......37°46'N 118°57'E
Huangshi China 99 L4......30°10'N 115°08'E
Huascarán, Nevado de mt. Peru 72 B6......9°09'S 77°36'W
Hubballi India 96 E4......15°18'N 75°15'E
Hubei d. China 99 K4......31°09'N 111°36'E
Hucknall England 13 F2......53°02'N 1°12'W
Huddersfield England 13 F2......53°39'N 1°47'W
Hudiksvall Sweden 43 D3......61°43'N 17°06'E
Hudson r. U.S.A. 63 L5......40°54'N 73°56'W
Hudson Bay sea Canada 61 J3......58°50'N 86°00'W
Hudson Strait Canada 61 K4......63°31'N 74°25'W
Huê Vietnam 102 D7......16°26'N 107°33'E
Huelva Spain 45 B2......37°16'N 6°55'W
Huércal-Overa Spain 45 E2......37°23'N 1°55'W
Huesca Spain 45 E5......42°08'N 0°25'W
Huizhou China 99 K2......23°05'N 114°25'E
Hull Canada 63 K6......45°27'N 75°45'W
Hulun Buir China 99 L7......49°04'N 119°46'E
Hulun Nur l. China 99 L7......48°32'N 117°11'E
Hulwän Egypt 49 J2......29°55'N 31°18'E
Humber, Mouth of the England 13 H2......53°33'N 0°06'E
Humboldt r. U.S.A. 62 C5......40°04'N 118°36'W
Humphreys Peak U.S.A. 62 D4......35°21'N 111°40'W
Húnaflói b. Iceland 43 X2......65°46'N 20°50'W
Hunan d. China 99 K3......27°26'N 111°22'E
Hungarian Plain f. Hungary 49 G6......46°30'N 19°00'E
Hungary Europe 46 H2......47°01'N 18°59'E
Hungerford England 8 D2......51°25'N 1°31'W
Hunish, Rubha pt Scotland 16 C2......57°42'N 6°24'W
Hunmanby England 13 G3......54°11'N 0°19'W
Hunsrück hills Germany 46 B3......49°47'N 7°00'E
Hunstanton England 9 F3......52°56'N 0°30'E
Huntingdon England 9 E3......52°20'N 0°11'W
Huntington U.S.A. 63 J4......38°25'N 82°18'W
Huntly Scotland 17 G2......57°27'N 2°47'W
Huntsville Ala. U.S.A. 63 I3......34°46'N 86°34'W
Huntsville Tex. U.S.A. 63 G3......30°42'N 95°34'W
Huron U.S.A. 62 G5......44°23'N 98°13'W
Huron, Lake Canada/U.S.A. 61 J2......44°39'N 82°23'W
Hurstpierpoint England 9 E1......50°56'N 0°11'W
Husum Germany 46 C6......54°29'N 9°04'E
Hutton Rudby England 13 F3......54°27'N 1°17'W
Huzhou China 99 M4......30°50'N 120°08'E
Hvannadalshnúkur vol. Iceland 43 Y2......64°01'N 16°41'W
Hvar i. Croatia 50 B6......43°08'N 16°33'E
Hyargas Nuur l. Mongolia 98 G7......49°02'N 93°18'E
Hyderabad India 96 E4......17°21'N 78°25'E
Hyderabad Pakistan 96 C6......25°21'N 68°23'E
Hyères France 44 G3......43°07'N 6°08'E
Hyrynsalmi Finland 43 G4......64°40'N 28°29'E
Hythe Hants. England 8 D1......50°52'N 1°24'W
Hythe Kent England 9 G2......51°04'N 1°05'E
Hyvinkää Finland 43 F3......60°38'N 24°51'E

I

Ialomiţa r. Romania 50 G7......44°43'N 27°51'E
Iar Connaught f. Ireland 18 B3......53°21'N 9°19'W
Iaşi Romania 49 I6......47°10'N 27°35'E
Ibadan Nigeria 84 E2......7°24'N 3°55'E
Ibagué Colombia 72 B7......4°24'N 75°13'W
Ibar r. Kosovo/Serbia 50 D6......43°43'N 20°45'E
Ibb Yemen 94 F2......14°03'N 44°09'E
Ibiza Spain 45 F3......38°54'N 1°27'E
Ibiza i. Spain 45 F3......39°10'N 1°39'E
Ibrā' Oman 95 I4......22°41'N 58°33'E
Ibstock England 8 D3......52°42'N 1°24'W
Ica Peru 72 B5......14°04'S 75°43'W
Iceland Europe 43 X2......64°42'N 18°19'W
Ichinoseki Japan 104 D3......38°55'N 141°07'E
Icklesham England 9 F1......50°55'N 0°40'E
Idaho d. U.S.A. 62 D5......44°08'N 114°08'W
Idaho Falls town U.S.A. 62 D5......43°32'N 112°01'W
Idar-Oberstein Germany 42 G2......49°42'N 7°18'E
Idfū Egypt 49 J1......24°55'N 32°49'E
Idi mt. Greece 50 F2......35°13'N 24°47'E
Idlib Syria 51 L2......35°56'N 36°38'E
Ieper Belgium 42 B3......50°51'N 2°53'E
Iešjávri l. Norway 43 F5......69°39'N 24°28'E
Igan Malaysia 102 E4......2°51'N 111°44'E
Iggesund Sweden 43 D3......61°39'N 17°05'E
Iğneada Burnu pt Turkey 51 H5......41°53'N 28°03'E
Igoumenitsa Greece 50 D4......39°30'N 20°17'E
Iguaçu r. Brazil 73 D4......25°36'S 54°35'W
Iisalmi Finland 43 F3......63°34'N 27°11'E
IJmuiden Neth. 42 D5......52°27'N 4°37'E
IJssel r. Neth. 42 E5......52°35'N 5°50'E
IJsselmeer l. Neth. 42 E5......52°46'N 5°26'E
IJzer r. Belgium 42 B3......51°09'N 2°44'E
Ikaahuk Canada 60 F5......71°55'N 125°00'W
Ikaria i. Greece 50 G3......37°35'N 26°13'E
Iki i. Japan 104 A2......33°45'N 129°39'E
Ilagan Phil. 103 G7......17°06'N 121°53'E
Ilchester England 8 C2......51°00'N 2°41'W
Ilebo Dem. Rep. Congo 83 B4......4°21'S 20°36'E
Île-de-France d. France 42 B1......48°39'N 2°36'E
Ilford England 9 F2......51°33'N 0°05'E
Ilfracombe England 11 C3......51°12'N 4°07'W

Ilhéus Brazil 72 F5......14°46'S 39°02'W
Iligan Phil. 103 G5......8°13'N 124°15'E
Ilkeston England 8 D3......52°58'N 1°18'W
Ilkley England 13 F2......53°56'N 1°49'W
Illinois d. U.S.A. 63 I4......39°52'N 89°07'W
Illinois r. U.S.A. 63 H4......38°56'N 90°33'W
Illizi Algeria 84 E4......26°29'N 8°30'E
Ilminster England 8 C1......50°56'N 2°54'W
Iloilo Phil. 103 G6......10°41'N 122°32'E
Ilorin Nigeria 84 E2......8°30'N 4°34'E
Ilovlya Russia 53 E2......49°19'N 43°59'E
Imatra Finland 43 G3......61°11'N 28°47'E
Immingham England 13 G2......53°37'N 0°13'W
Imola Italy 46 D1......44°21'N 11°42'E
Imperatriz Brazil 72 E6......5°33'S 47°26'W
Imphal India 97 H5......24°46'N 93°56'E
Imroz Turkey 50 F5......40°10'N 25°55'E
Inarijärvi l. Finland 43 F5......68°57'N 27°37'E
Inchard, Loch b. Scotland 16 D3......58°27'N 5°04'W
Incheon S. Korea 99 N5......37°28'N 126°39'E
Inchkeith i. Scotland 15 F4......56°02'N 3°08'W
Indalsälven r. Sweden 43 D3......62°32'N 17°24'E
Independence U.S.A. 63 H4......39°07'N 94°26'W
Inderbor Kazakhstan 53 F2......48°33'N 51°44'E
India Asia 96 E5......22°00'N 79°00'E
Indiana d. U.S.A. 63 I5......40°09'N 86°01'W
Indianapolis U.S.A. 63 I4......39°46'N 86°10'W
Indian Ocean 117 G2
Indigirka r. Russia 55 P5......71°28'N 149°53'E
Indonesia Asia 102 E2......4°12'S 112°02'E
Indore India 96 E5......22°40'N 75°53'E
Indre r. France 44 D5......47°14'N 0°12'E
Indus r. China/Pakistan 96 C5......23°56'N 67°38'E
Indus, Mouths of the Pakistan 96 C5......24°36'N 66°36'E
İnebolu Turkey 51 J5......41°58'N 33°45'E
İnegöl Turkey 51 H5......40°04'N 29°30'E
Infiernillo, Presa resr Mexico 66 D4......18°41'N 101°57'W
Infiesto Spain 45 C5......43°21'N 5°20'W
Ingatestone England 9 F2......51°40'N 0°23'E
Ingleborough hill England 13 E3......54°10'N 2°24'W
Ingleton England 13 E3......54°09'N 2°28'W
Ingoldmells England 13 H2......53°12'N 0°20'E
Ingolstadt Germany 46 D3......48°46'N 11°27'E
Inhambane Mozambique 83 C2......23°47'S 35°31'E
Inhul r. Ukraine 47 N2......46°58'N 31°58'E
Inhulets' r. Ukraine 47 N2......46°41'N 32°49'E
Inishbofin i. Ireland 18 A3......53°38'N 10°14'W
Inisheer i. Ireland 18 B3......53°04'N 9°30'W
Inishmaan i. Ireland 18 B3......53°05'N 9°33'W
Inishmore i. Ireland 18 B3......53°09'N 9°47'W
Inishmurray i. Ireland 18 C4......54°26'N 8°40'W
Inishowen pen. Ireland 18 D5......55°13'N 7°17'W
Inishowen Head Ireland 14 C3......55°14'N 6°55'W
Inishtrahull i. Ireland 18 D5......55°28'N 7°13'W
Inishtrahull Sound str. Ireland 14 B3......55°27'N 7°28'W
Inishturk i. Ireland 18 A3......53°42'N 10°08'W
Inn r. Europe 46 D2......46°55'N 10°29'E
Inner Mongolia d. China 99 I6......40°12'N 103°26'E
Inner Sound str. Scotland 16 D2......57°21'N 5°57'W
Innsbruck Austria 46 D2......47°16'N 11°24'E
Inny r. Ireland 18 D3......53°33'N 7°50'W
Inowrocław Poland 46 H5......52°48'N 18°16'E
In Salah Algeria 84 E4......27°13'N 2°25'E
Insch Scotland 17 G2......57°20'N 2°37'W
Inta Russia 52 F4......65°59'N 60°00'E
International Falls town U.S.A. 63 H6......48°36'N 93°25'W
Inukjuak Canada 61 K3......58°28'N 78°04'W
Inuvialuit f. Canada 60 F4......69°10'N 128°00'W
Inuvik Canada 60 E4......68°24'N 133°43'W
Inveraray Scotland 14 D4......56°14'N 5°04'W
Inverbervie Scotland 17 G1......56°51'N 2°17'W
Invercargill New Zealand 109 F2......46°25'S 168°22'E
Inverclyde d. Scotland 20 C2......55°54'N 4°44'W
Invergordon Scotland 17 E2......57°42'N 4°10'W
Inverkeithing Scotland 15 F4......56°02'N 3°24'W
Inverness Scotland 17 E2......57°29'N 4°13'W
Inverurie Scotland 17 G2......57°17'N 2°22'W
Ioannina Greece 50 D4......39°40'N 20°51'E
Iona i. Scotland 14 C4......56°19'N 6°25'W
Ionian Islands Greece 50 C4......39°26'N 19°33'E
Ionian Sea Greece/Italy 50 C4......38°11'N 18°29'E
Ios i. Greece 50 F3......36°44'N 25°22'E
Iowa d. U.S.A. 63 H5......42°12'N 92°47'W
Iowa City U.S.A. 63 H5......41°40'N 91°32'W
Ipoh Malaysia 102 C4......4°40'N 101°04'E
Ipswich England 9 G3......52°03'N 1°09'E
Iput' r. Russia 47 N5......52°30'N 31°37'E
Iputs' r. Belarus 47 N5......52°26'N 31°04'E
Iqaluit Canada 61 L4......63°45'N 68°36'W
Iquique Chile 73 B4......20°14'S 70°07'W
Iquitos Peru 72 B6......3°50'S 73°13'W
Iraklion Greece 50 F2......35°19'N 25°08'E
Iran Asia 95 H6......31°28'N 55°05'E
Iran, Pegunungan mts Indonesia 102 E4......1°47'N 114°46'E
Iranian Plateau f. Iran 86 D3......32°00'N 55°00'E
Īrānshahr Iran 95 J5......27°13'N 60°42'E
Irapuato Mexico 66 D5......20°41'N 101°23'W
Iraq Asia 94 F6......32°50'N 42°21'E
Irbid Jordan 94 E6......32°34'N 35°51'E
Ireland Europe 18 D3......53°33'N 7°43'W
Ireland's Eye i. Ireland 18 E3......53°24'N 6°03'W
Iringa Tanzania 83 C4......7°48'S 35°43'E
Iriri r. Brazil 72 D6......3°52'S 52°37'W
Irish Sea Ireland/U.K. 18 F3......53°40'N 5°11'W
Irkutsk Russia 55 L3......52°11'N 104°09'E
Iron Mountain U.S.A. 63 I6......45°49'N 88°04'W
Ironwood U.S.A. 63 H6......46°27'N 90°09'W
Irosin Phil. 103 G6......12°42'N 124°00'E
Irrawaddy r. Myanmar 97 I4......15°48'N 95°05'E
Irrawaddy, Mouths of the Myanmar 97 H4......15°35'N 94°02'E
Irsha r. Ukraine 47 M4......50°46'N 29°35'E
Irthing r. England 12 E3......54°55'N 2°49'W
Irtysh r. Kazakhstan/Russia 54 H4......61°07'N 68°50'E
Irún Spain 45 E5......43°20'N 1°48'W
Irvine Scotland 14 E3......55°37'N 4°40'W
Irvinestown Northern Ireland 14 B2......54°28'N 7°37'W
Isabela Phil. 103 G5......6°40'N 121°59'E
Isabelia, Cordillera mts Nicaragua 67 G3......13°15'N 85°59'W
Ísafjörður Iceland 43 X2......66°05'N 23°10'W
Isar r. Germany 46 E3......48°49'N 12°59'E
Isbister Scotland 17 H5......60°36'N 1°19'W
Ise Japan 104 C2......34°29'N 136°43'E
Isère, Pointe pt French Guiana 72 D7......5°47'N 53°57'W
Ishikari-wan b. Japan 104 D4......43°17'N 140°58'E
Ishim r. Kazakhstan/Russia 54 I3......57°43'N 71°13'E
Ishinomaki Japan 104 D3......38°25'N 141°17'E

Isiro Dem. Rep. Congo 83 B5......2°46'N 27°36'E
İskenderun Turkey 51 L3......36°34'N 36°08'E
İskenderun Körfezi b. Turkey 51 K3......36°38'N 35°54'E
Iskūr r. Bulgaria 50 F6......43°44'N 24°27'E
Isla r. Ang. Scotland 17 F1......56°32'N 3°22'W
Isla r. Mor. Scotland 17 G2......57°31'N 2°47'W
Islamabad Pakistan 96 D7......33°42'N 73°08'E
Islandmagee pen. Northern Ireland 14 D2......54°50'N 5°41'W
Islas Malvinas is S. Atlantic Oc. 73 D1......50°55'S 59°36'W
Islay i. Scotland 14 C3......55°48'N 6°20'W
Isle of Anglesey d. Wales 21 C3......53°18'N 4°23'W
Isle of Wight d. England 21 E2......50°41'N 1°18'W
Isles of Scilly d. England 21 B1......49°55'N 6°17'W
Isnā Egypt 49 J2......25°16'N 32°30'E
Isparta Turkey 51 I3......37°46'N 30°32'E
Israel Asia 49 J3......32°12'N 34°48'E
Istanbul Turkey 51 H5......41°07'N 28°58'E
Istria pen. Croatia 46 E1......45°12'N 13°53'E
Itabuna Brazil 72 F5......14°47'S 39°17'W
Itaituba Brazil 72 D6......4°16'S 56°00'W
Itajaí Brazil 73 E4......26°52'S 48°41'W
Italy Europe 48 F5......41°46'N 14°35'E
Itambé, Pico de mt. Brazil 72 E5......18°23'S 43°20'W
Itapetininga Brazil 73 E4......23°36'S 48°03'W
Itiquira r. Brazil 72 D5......17°18'S 56°20'W
Iul'tin Russia 55 T4......67°51'N 178°47'W
Ivalo Finland 43 F5......68°39'N 27°32'E
Ivano-Frankivs'k Ukraine 47 K3......48°55'N 24°43'E
Ivanovo Russia 52 E3......56°59'N 40°59'E
Ivatsevichy Belarus 47 K5......52°43'N 25°21'E
Ivdel' Russia 52 G4......60°39'N 60°26'E
Ivittuut Greenland 61 N4......61°13'N 48°10'W
Ivory Coast Africa 84 D2......7°35'N 4°22'W
Ivybridge England 11 D2......50°23'N 3°55'W
Iwaki Japan 104 D3......37°03'N 140°53'E
Iwo Nigeria 84 E2......7°38'N 4°10'E
Ixworth England 9 F3......52°18'N 0°50'E
Izabal, Lago de l. Guatemala 66 G4......15°30'N 89°08'W
Izhevsk Russia 52 F3......56°48'N 53°10'E
Izhma r. Russia 52 F4......65°01'N 53°56'E
Izmayil Ukraine 49 I6......45°21'N 28°51'E
İzmir Turkey 50 G4......38°24'N 27°10'E
İzmir Körfezi g. Turkey 50 G4......38°30'N 26°44'E
İzmit Turkey 51 H5......40°46'N 29°56'E
Izu-shotō is Japan 104 C2......34°24'N 139°14'E
Izyum Ukraine 53 D2......49°13'N 37°16'E

J

Jabalón r. Spain 45 C3......38°53'N 4°05'W
Jabalpur India 96 E5......23°10'N 79°57'E
Jablah Syria 51 K2......35°21'N 35°56'E
Jaca Spain 45 E5......42°34'N 0°34'W
Jackson U.S.A. 63 H3......32°19'N 90°12'W
Jacksonville U.S.A. 63 J3......30°18'N 81°42'W
Jacmel Haiti 67 J4......18°16'N 72°32'W
Jacobabad Pakistan 96 C6......28°15'N 68°29'E
Jādū Libya 48 F3......31°58'N 12°04'E
Jaén Spain 45 D2......37°46'N 3°47'W
Jaffna Sri Lanka 96 F2......9°41'N 79°59'E
Jagdalpur India 96 F4......19°04'N 82°07'E
Jahrom Iran 95 H5......28°31'N 53°33'E
Jaipur India 96 E6......26°51'N 75°50'E
Jaisalmer India 96 D6......26°52'N 70°56'E
Jajce Bos. and Herz. 50 B7......44°21'N 17°16'E
Jakarta Indonesia 102 D2......6°07'S 106°48'E
Jakobstad Finland 43 E3......63°40'N 22°42'E
Jalālābād Afgh. 95 L6......34°26'N 70°28'E
Jalandhar India 96 E7......31°18'N 75°40'E
Jalgaon India 96 E5......21°01'N 75°41'E
Jalna India 96 E4......19°49'N 75°57'E
Jalón r. Spain 45 E4......41°47'N 1°02'W
Jālū Libya 85 G4......29°03'N 21°33'E
Jamaica Central America 67 I4......17°30'N 77°19'W
Jamaica Channel Haiti/Jamaica 67 I4......18°29'N 75°24'W
Jambi Indonesia 102 C3......1°37'S 103°37'E
James r. U.S.A. 62 G5......42°53'N 97°18'W
James Bay Canada 61 J3......53°23'N 80°25'W
James Shoal S. China Sea 102 E4......3°58'N 112°21'E
Jamestown U.S.A. 62 G6......46°53'N 98°43'W
Jammu India 96 E7......32°42'N 74°56'E
Jammu and Kashmir Asia 96 E7......34°06'N 76°59'E
Jamnagar India 96 D5......22°29'N 70°06'E
Jampur Pakistan 96 D6......29°37'N 70°41'E
Jämsänkoski Finland 43 F3......61°56'N 25°11'E
Jamshedpur India 96 G5......22°46'N 86°12'E
Jandiá hill Canary Islands 45 Y2......28°06'N 14°21'W
Jan Mayen i. Arctic Oc. 34 D6......72°00'N 8°00'W
Japan Asia 104 C3......36°48'N 133°17'E
Japan, Sea of N. Pacific Oc. 104 B3......39°13'N 133°37'E
Japurá r. Brazil 72 C6......3°06'S 64°45'W
Jardines de la Reina, Archipiélago de los is Cuba 67 I5......20°50'N 79°01'W
Järpen Sweden 43 C3......63°22'N 13°28'E
Järvenpää Finland 43 F3......60°29'N 25°06'E
Jasper Canada 60 G3......52°53'N 118°05'W
Jastrzębie-Zdrój Poland 46 H3......49°57'N 18°35'E
Java i. Indonesia 102 D2......8°12'S 107°16'E
Java Sea Indonesia 102 E3......4°56'S 110°49'E
Jawhar Somalia 85 I2......2°46'N 45°31'E
Jaya, Puncak mt. Indonesia 103 J3......4°03'S 137°12'E
Jayapura Indonesia 103 K3......2°34'S 140°42'E
Jāzān Saudi Arabia 94 F3......16°56'N 42°32'E
Jaz Mūrīān, Hāmūn-e l. Iran 95 I5......27°32'N 58°47'E
Jebel Abyad Plateau f. Sudan 94 C3......19°25'N 28°59'E
Jedburgh Scotland 15 G3......55°29'N 2°33'W
Jeddah Saudi Arabia 94 E4......21°30'N 39°08'E
Jefferson City U.S.A. 63 H4......38°37'N 92°11'W
Jelenia Góra Poland 46 F4......50°55'N 15°44'E
Jelgava Latvia 43 E2......56°39'N 23°44'E
Jember Indonesia 102 E2......8°05'S 113°45'E
Jena Germany 46 D4......50°56'N 11°36'E
Jendouba Tunisia 48 E4......36°28'N 8°47'E
Jeonju S. Korea 99 N5......35°51'N 127°09'E
Jequié Brazil 72 E5......13°51'S 40°05'W
Jequitinhonha r. Brazil 72 E5......15°51'S 38°52'W
Jérémie Haiti 67 J4......18°38'N 74°09'W
Jerez de la Frontera Spain 45 B2......36°41'N 6°08'W
Jerid, Chott el f. Tunisia 48 E3......33°38'N 8°28'E
Jersey i. Channel Is 11 Z8......49°13'N 2°07'W
Jerusalem Israel/West Bank 49 K3......31°47'N 35°13'E
Jesup U.S.A. 63 J3......31°34'N 81°59'W
Jhang Pakistan 95 L6......31°17'N 72°23'E

Jhansi India 96 E6......25°27'N 78°37'E
Jharkhand d. India 96 G5......23°36'N 85°06'E
Jiamusi China 99 O7......46°47'N 130°15'E
Ji'an China 99 K3......27°09'N 114°56'E
Jiangmen China 99 K2......22°35'N 113°06'E
Jiangsu d. China 99 L4......33°10'N 119°42'E
Jiangxi d. China 99 L3......27°21'N 115°22'E
Jiaozuo China 99 K5......35°12'N 113°15'E
Jiaxing China 99 M4......30°46'N 120°49'E
Jiayi Taiwan 99 M2......23°29'N 120°27'E
Jiehkkevárri mt. Norway 43 D5......69°28'N 19°51'E
Jieyang China 99 L2......23°34'N 116°19'E
Jihlava Czechia 46 F3......49°24'N 15°36'E
Jilf al Kabīr, Haḍabat al f. Egypt 94 C4......23°12'N 25°56'E
Jilib Somalia 85 I2......0°30'N 42°47'E
Jilin China 99 N6......43°53'N 126°33'E
Jilin d. China 99 N6......43°33'N 125°10'E
Jima Ethiopia 85 H2......7°40'N 36°49'E
Jiménez Mexico 66 D6......27°08'N 104°57'W
Jinan China 99 L5......36°38'N 117°01'E
Jingdezhen China 99 L3......29°21'N 117°21'E
Jinghong China 99 I2......21°57'N 100°52'E
Jingmen China 99 K4......30°58'N 112°10'E
Jingzhou China 99 K4......30°21'N 112°10'E
Jinhua China 99 L3......29°10'N 119°41'E
Jining Nei Mongol China 99 K6......40°54'N 113°06'E
Jining Shandong China 99 L5......35°22'N 116°29'E
Jinja Uganda 85 H2......0°28'N 33°14'E
Jinjiang China 99 L2......24°46'N 118°33'E
Jinzhou China 99 M6......41°02'N 121°10'E
Jiparaná r. Brazil 72 C5......8°09'S 62°50'W
Jiu r. Romania 50 E6......43°47'N 23°48'E
Jiujiang China 99 L3......29°43'N 116°00'E
Jiwani Pakistan 95 J5......25°07'N 61°48'E
Jixi China 99 O7......45°13'N 130°53'E
João Pessoa Brazil 72 F6......7°05'S 34°50'W
Jodhpur India 96 D6......26°16'N 73°07'E
Joensuu Finland 43 G3......62°36'N 29°46'E
Jõetsu Japan 104 C3......37°10'N 138°14'E
Johannesburg S. Africa 83 B2......26°09'S 27°59'E
John o'Groats Scotland 17 F3......58°38'N 3°04'W
Johnston Wales 10 C3......51°45'N 4°59'W
Johnstone Scotland 14 E3......55°50'N 4°31'W
Johor Bahru Malaysia 102 C4......1°29'N 103°46'E
Jokkmokk Sweden 43 D4......66°37'N 19°49'E
Jolo i. Phil. 103 G5......5°57'N 121°06'E
Jones Sound str. Canada 61 J5......75°58'N 88°58'W
Jönköping Sweden 43 C2......57°46'N 14°09'E
Jonquière Canada 61 K2......48°25'N 71°14'W
Joplin U.S.A. 63 H4......37°12'N 94°31'W
Jordan Asia 94 E6......31°17'N 36°26'E
Jörn Sweden 43 E4......65°03'N 20°03'E
Jos Nigeria 84 E2......9°55'N 8°53'E
Joseph Bonaparte Gulf Australia 108 B5......14°08'S 128°39'E
Juan Fernández, Archipiélago is S. Pacific Oc. 68 B2......33°24'S 80°00'W
Juàzeiro do Norte Brazil 72 F6......7°11'S 39°14'W
Juba South Sudan 85 H2......4°53'N 31°38'E
Jubaland Somalia 85 I2......0°45'N 39°45'E
Jubba r. Somalia 85 I1......0°15'S 42°37'E
Júcar r. Spain 45 E3......39°09'N 0°13'W
Juchitán Mexico 66 E4......16°29'N 95°02'W
Judenburg Austria 46 F2......47°11'N 14°41'E
Juist i. Germany 42 G6......53°40'N 7°01'E
Juliaca Peru 72 B5......15°28'S 70°11'W
Junction City U.S.A. 62 G4......39°03'N 96°50'W
Juneau U.S.A. 60 E3......58°19'N 134°23'W
Jungfrau mt. Switz. 46 B2......46°33'N 7°58'E
Junggar Pendi basin China 98 F7......45°02'N 87°38'E
Jura mts France/Switz. 44 F4......45°38'N 5°26'E
Jura i. Scotland 14 C4......56°00'N 5°56'W
Jura, Sound of str. Scotland 14 D3......55°51'N 5°49'W
Jurbarkas Lithuania 47 J6......55°05'N 22°46'E
Jūrmala Latvia 47 J7......56°57'N 23°40'E
Juruá r. Brazil 72 C6......2°39'S 65°48'W
Juruena r. Brazil 72 D5......7°21'S 58°08'W
Jutaí r. Brazil 72 C6......2°45'S 66°58'W
Jutland pen. Denmark 43 B2......56°13'N 9°08'E
Juventud, Isla de la i. Cuba 67 H5......21°27'N 82°50'W
Jyväskylä Finland 43 F3......62°14'N 25°44'E

K

K2 mt. China/Pakistan 98 D5......35°52'N 76°34'E
Kabaena i. Indonesia 103 G2......5°15'S 121°50'E
Kabalo Dem. Rep. Congo 83 B4......6°02'S 26°57'E
Kābul Afgh. 95 K6......34°30'N 69°11'E
Kabwe Zambia 83 B3......14°27'S 28°26'E
Kachchh, Gulf of India 96 C5......22°35'N 68°57'E
Kachug Russia 55 L3......53°54'N 105°47'E
Kadapa India 96 E3......14°29'N 78°48'E
Kadavu i. Fiji 109 G5......19°00'S 178°10'E
Kadıköy Turkey 51 H5......40°59'N 29°01'E
Kadirli Turkey 51 L3......37°22'N 36°05'E
Kadugli Sudan 85 G3......11°01'N 29°42'E
Kaduna Nigeria 84 E3......10°30'N 7°25'E
Kadzherom Russia 52 F4......64°42'N 55°55'E
Kaesŏng N. Korea 99 N5......37°58'N 126°33'E
Kafireas, Akra pt Greece 50 F4......38°10'N 24°35'E
Kaga Bandoro C.A.R. 85 F2......6°57'N 19°11'E
Kagoshima Japan 104 B2......31°34'N 130°33'E
Kahramanmaraş Turkey 51 L3......37°35'N 36°55'E
Kai, Kepulauan is Indonesia 103 I2......5°26'S 132°59'E
Kaifeng China 99 K4......34°43'N 114°24'E
Kaimana Indonesia 103 I3......3°45'S 133°49'E
Kairouan Tunisia 48 F4......35°41'N 10°06'E
Kaiserslautern Germany 46 B3......49°27'N 7°46'E
Kaiyuan China 99 I2......23°40'N 103°14'E
Kajaani Finland 43 F4......64°13'N 27°43'E
Kakhovs'ke Vodoskhovyshche resr Ukraine 47 O2......47°30'N 33°42'E
Kakinada India 96 F4......16°59'N 82°18'E
Kaktovik U.S.A. 60 D5......70°04'N 143°44'W
Kalaburagi India 96 E4......17°20'N 76°47'E
Kalach-na-Donu Russia 53 E2......48°42'N 43°31'E
Kalahari Desert Africa 83 B2......23°28'S 22°18'E
Kalajoki Finland 43 E4......64°15'N 23°57'E
Kalamaria Greece 50 E5......40°36'N 22°57'E
Kalamata Greece 50 E3......37°02'N 22°07'E
Kalāt Afgh. 95 K6......32°05'N 66°58'E
Kalecik Turkey 51 J5......40°05'N 33°26'E
Kalemie Dem. Rep. Congo 83 B4......5°56'S 29°08'E
Kalgoorlie Australia 108 B3......30°50'S 121°30'E
Kaliakra, Nos pt Bulgaria 51 H6......43°22'N 28°28'E
Kalimantan f. Indonesia 102 E3......2°10'S 111°35'E

Kaliningrad Russia 46 I6 .... 54°42'N 20°31'E
Kalinkavichy Belarus 47 M5 .... 52°08'N 29°15'E
Kalispell U.S.A. 62 D6 .... 48°11'N 114°19'W
Kalisz Poland 46 H4 .... 51°46'N 18°05'E
Kalixälven r. Sweden 43 E4 .... 65°51'N 23°08'E
Kallavesi l. Finland 43 F3 .... 62°47'N 27°47'E
Kallsjön l. Sweden 43 C3 .... 63°37'N 13°00'E
Kalmar Sweden 43 D2 .... 56°40'N 16°22'E
Kaltag U.S.A. 60 C4 .... 64°20'N 158°52'W
Kaluga Russia 53 D3 .... 54°31'N 36°16'E
Kalundborg Denmark 43 B1 .... 55°41'N 11°06'E
Kalush Ukraine 47 K3 .... 49°02'N 24°22'E
Kama r. Russia 52 F3 .... 56°01'N 53°46'E
Kamaishi Japan 104 D3 .... 39°16'N 141°53'E
Kaman Turkey 51 J4 .... 39°22'N 33°43'E
Kamchatka Peninsula Russia 55 Q3 .... 56°10'N 159°12'E
Kamen', Gory mts Russia 55 K4 .... 69°06'N 95°00'E
Kamenskoye Russia 55 R4 .... 62°33'N 166°10'E
Kamensk-Ural'skiy Russia 52 G3 .... 56°28'N 61°48'E
Kamina Dem. Rep. Congo 83 B4 .... 8°44'S 24°57'E
Kamin'-Kashyrs'kyy Ukraine 47 K4 .... 51°37'N 24°58'E
Kamloops Canada 60 F3 .... 50°41'N 120°21'W
Kampala Uganda 85 H2 .... 0°20'N 32°34'E
Kampen Neth. 42 E5 .... 52°33'N 5°55'E
Kâmpóng Cham Cambodia 102 D6 .... 11°59'N 105°26'E
Kâmpôt Cambodia 102 C6 .... 10°36'N 104°12'E
Kam''yanets'-Podil's'kyy Ukraine 47 L3 .... 48°41'N 26°35'E
Kamyshin Russia 53 E3 .... 50°06'N 45°25'E
Kananga Dem. Rep. Congo 83 B4 .... 5°51'S 22°22'E
Kanash Russia 52 E3 .... 55°30'N 47°28'E
Kanazawa Japan 104 C3 .... 36°34'N 136°39'E
Kanchipuram India 96 E3 .... 12°51'N 79°43'E
Kandahär Afgh. 95 K6 .... 31°37'N 65°47'E
Kandalaksha Russia 43 H4 .... 67°10'N 32°23'E
Kandalakshskiy Zaliv g. Russia 43 H4 .... 66°38'N 33°25'E
Kandıra Turkey 51 I5 .... 41°04'N 30°08'E
Kandy Sri Lanka 96 F2 .... 7°19'N 80°34'E
Kandyagash Kazakhstan 53 F2 .... 49°27'N 57°21'E
Kangal Turkey 51 L4 .... 39°14'N 37°23'E
Kangaroo Island Australia 108 C3 .... 35°48'S 137°11'E
Kangävar Iran 95 G6 .... 34°29'N 47°51'E
Kangchenjunga mt. India/Nepal 96 G6 .... 27°41'N 88°12'E
Kangding China 97 J7 .... 30°03'N 101°56'E
Kangean, Kepulauan is Indonesia 102 F2 .... 6°56'S 115°13'E
Kangertittivaq str. Greenland 61 P5 .... 70°31'N 24°44'W
Kangiqsualujjuaq Canada 61 L3 .... 58°35'N 65°45'W
Kangiqsujuaq Canada 61 K4 .... 61°34'N 71°56'W
Kangmar China 96 F6 .... 28°30'N 89°33'E
Kanin, Poluostrov pen. Russia 52 E4 .... 66°50'N 44°50'E
Kanin Nos, Mys c. Russia 52 E4 .... 68°00'N 43°00'E
Kankaanpää Finland 43 E3 .... 61°49'N 22°25'E
Kankakee U.S.A. 63 I5 .... 41°07'N 87°51'W
Kankan Guinea 84 D3 .... 10°23'N 9°19'W
Kanker India 96 F5 .... 20°16'N 81°32'E
Kano Nigeria 84 E3 .... 12°01'N 8°31'E
Kanpur India 96 F6 .... 26°27'N 80°24'E
Kansas d. U.S.A. 62 G4 .... 38°35'N 98°34'W
Kansas r. U.S.A. 62 G4 .... 39°07'N 94°40'W
Kansas City U.S.A. 63 H4 .... 39°11'N 94°45'W
Kansk Russia 55 K3 .... 56°10'N 95°43'E
Kantchari Burkina Faso 84 E3 .... 12°29'N 1°30'E
Kanton atoll Kiribati 109 H6 .... 2°44'S 171°42'W
Kanye Botswana 83 B2 .... 24°58'S 25°21'E
Kaohsiung Taiwan 99 M2 .... 22°39'N 120°20'E
Kaokoveld f. Namibia 83 A3 .... 14°41'S 12°33'E
Kaolack Senegal 84 C3 .... 14°09'N 16°04'W
Kaposvár Hungary 46 G2 .... 46°22'N 17°48'E
Kapuskasing Canada 61 J2 .... 49°26'N 82°26'W
Karabük Turkey 51 J5 .... 41°11'N 32°38'E
Karabutak Kazakhstan 54 H2 .... 49°55'N 60°09'E
Karaganda Kazakhstan 54 I2 .... 49°52'N 73°04'E
Karaginskiy Zaliv b. Russia 55 R3 .... 59°32'N 164°48'E
Karaj Iran 95 H7 .... 35°45'N 50°58'E
Karakelong i. Indonesia 103 H4 .... 4°22'N 126°43'E
Karakoram Range mts Asia 96 D8 .... 36°18'N 74°54'E
Karakum Desert Turkmenistan 54 G2 .... 38°58'N 60°05'E
Karaman Turkey 51 J3 .... 37°11'N 33°13'E
Karamay China 98 E7 .... 45°31'N 84°54'E
Karand Iran 95 G6 .... 34°14'N 46°16'E
Karapınar Turkey 51 J3 .... 37°43'N 33°33'E
Karasburg Namibia 83 A2 .... 28°01'S 18°45'E
Kara Sea Russia 54 I5 .... 74°13'N 71°44'E
Karasuk Russia 54 I3 .... 53°43'N 78°03'E
Karbalā' Iraq 94 F6 .... 32°36'N 44°01'E
Karcag Hungary 46 I2 .... 47°19'N 20°55'E
Karditsa Greece 50 D4 .... 39°21'N 21°55'E
Kärdla Estonia 43 E2 .... 58°59'N 22°45'E
Kardzhali Bulgaria 50 F5 .... 41°39'N 25°22'E
Kareima Sudan 85 H3 .... 18°31'N 31°49'E
Kariba, Lake resr Zambia/Zimbabwe 83 B3 .... 17°37'S 27°17'E
Karimata, Selat str. Indonesia 102 D3 .... 1°50'S 108°40'E
Karkinits'ka Zatoka g. Ukraine 49 J6 .... 45°27'N 32°11'E
Karlovac Croatia 50 A7 .... 45°29'N 15°33'E
Karlovo Bulgaria 50 F6 .... 42°39'N 24°48'E
Karlovy Vary Czechia 46 E4 .... 50°14'N 12°53'E
Karlshamn Sweden 43 C2 .... 56°11'N 14°52'E
Karlskoga Sweden 43 C2 .... 59°20'N 14°33'E
Karlskrona Sweden 43 C2 .... 56°12'N 15°38'E
Karlsruhe Germany 46 C3 .... 49°01'N 8°24'E
Karlstad Sweden 43 C2 .... 59°23'N 13°31'E
Karmøy i. Norway 43 A2 .... 59°11'N 5°15'E
Karnataka d. India 96 E4 .... 15°37'N 75°29'E
Karnobat Bulgaria 50 G6 .... 42°38'N 26°59'E
Karora Eritrea 85 H3 .... 17°41'N 38°23'E
Karpathos i. Greece 50 G2 .... 35°36'N 27°10'E
Karpenisi Greece 50 D4 .... 38°55'N 21°48'E
Karpogory Russia 52 E4 .... 64°01'N 44°25'E
Kärsava Latvia 47 L7 .... 56°47'N 27°41'E
Karşıyaka Turkey 50 G4 .... 38°27'N 27°06'E
Karstula Finland 43 F3 .... 62°53'N 24°48'E
Kartal Turkey 51 H5 .... 40°54'N 29°11'E
Kartaly Russia 55 M3 .... 51°30'N 114°25'E
Kaş Turkey 51 H3 .... 36°12'N 29°37'E
Kasaï r. Dem. Rep. Congo 83 A4 .... 3°02'S 16°58'E
Kasama Zambia 83 C3 .... 10°12'S 31°12'E
Kasese Uganda 85 H2 .... 0°10'N 30°05'E
Kāshān Iran 95 H6 .... 33°58'N 51°30'E
Kashi China 98 D5 .... 39°29'N 76°03'E
Kashiwazaki Japan 104 C3 .... 37°22'N 138°33'E
Kāshmar Iran 95 I6 .... 35°10'N 58°22'E
Kasimov Russia 53 D3 .... 54°56'N 41°24'E
Kasos i. Greece 50 G2 .... 35°23'N 26°52'E
Kassala Sudan 85 H3 .... 15°24'N 36°22'E
Kassel Germany 46 C4 .... 51°19'N 9°30'E
Kasserine Tunisia 48 E4 .... 35°11'N 8°50'E

Kastamonu Turkey 51 J5 .... 41°22'N 33°46'E
Kastelli Greece 50 E2 .... 35°30'N 23°38'E
Kastoria Greece 50 D5 .... 40°31'N 21°16'E
Kastsyukovichy Belarus 47 O5 .... 53°21'N 32°09'E
Katerini Greece 50 E5 .... 40°16'N 22°31'E
Kate's Needle mt. Canada/U.S.A. 60 E3 .... 57°02'N 132°02'W
Katha Myanmar 97 I5 .... 24°11'N 96°20'E
Katherine Australia 108 C5 .... 14°28'S 132°18'E
Kathmandu Nepal 96 G6 .... 27°42'N 85°18'E
Katima Mulilo Namibia 83 B3 .... 17°32'S 24°15'E
Kati Thanda-Lake Eyre (North) Australia 108 C4 .... 28°24'S 137°16'E
Kati Thanda-Lake Eyre (South) Australia 108 C4 .... 28°30'S 137°25'E
Katni India 96 F5 .... 23°50'N 80°23'E
Katowice Poland 46 H4 .... 50°16'N 19°01'E
Kātrīna, Jabal mt. Egypt 49 J2 .... 28°31'N 33°58'E
Katrine, Loch l. Scotland 14 E4 .... 56°15'N 4°34'W
Katrineholm Sweden 43 D2 .... 58°59'N 16°14'E
Katsina Nigeria 84 E3 .... 12°59'N 7°36'E
Kattegat str. Denmark/Sweden 43 B2 .... 56°49'N 11°21'E
Kauhajoki Finland 43 E3 .... 62°25'N 22°11'E
Kaunas Lithuania 43 E1 .... 54°54'N 23°55'E
Kaura-Namoda Nigeria 84 E3 .... 12°37'N 6°35'E
Kavala Greece 50 F5 .... 40°56'N 24°23'E
Kavarna Bulgaria 51 H6 .... 43°26'N 28°19'E
Kavīr, Dasht-e des. Iran 95 H6 .... 34°36'N 54°41'E
Kawasaki Japan 104 C2 .... 35°32'N 139°43'E
Kawm Umbū Egypt 49 J1 .... 24°28'N 32°55'E
Kayes Mali 84 C3 .... 14°26'N 11°27'W
Kayseri Turkey 51 K4 .... 38°43'N 35°29'E
Kazach'ye Russia 55 O5 .... 70°45'N 136°09'E
Kazakhstan Asia 54 H2 .... 49°18'N 82°53'E
Kazan' Russia 52 E3 .... 55°47'N 49°07'E
Kazanlak Bulgaria 50 F6 .... 42°37'N 25°23'E
Kazbek mt. Georgia/Russia 53 E2 .... 42°45'N 44°34'E
Kāzerūn Iran 95 H5 .... 29°37'N 51°39'E
Kazym-Mys Russia 52 G4 .... 64°43'N 65°36'E
Kea i. Greece 50 F3 .... 37°38'N 24°24'E
Keady Northern Ireland 14 C2 .... 54°15'N 6°42'W
Kearney U.S.A. 62 G5 .... 40°43'N 99°05'W
Keban Baraji resr Turkey 51 M4 .... 38°53'N 38°55'E
Kebkabiya Sudan 94 B2 .... 13°37'N 24°06'E
Kebnekaise mt. Sweden 43 D4 .... 67°55'N 18°31'E
Kebock Head Scotland 16 C3 .... 58°03'N 6°21'W
Keçiören Turkey 51 J5 .... 40°00'N 32°50'E
Kecskemét Hungary 46 H2 .... 46°55'N 19°42'E
Kėdainiai Lithuania 43 E1 .... 55°17'N 23°59'E
Keelung Taiwan 99 M3 .... 25°07'N 121°43'E
Keen, Mount hill Scotland 17 G1 .... 56°58'N 2°59'W
Keetmanshoop Namibia 83 A2 .... 26°35'S 18°09'E
Keewatin Canada 63 H6 .... 49°46'N 94°34'W
Keflavík Iceland 43 X2 .... 64°00'N 22°34'W
Kegworth England 8 D3 .... 52°50'N 1°17'W
Keighley England 13 F2 .... 53°52'N 1°55'W
Keitele l. Finland 43 F3 .... 62°52'N 26°00'E
Keith Scotland 17 G2 .... 57°33'N 2°57'W
Kelifskiy Uzboy f. Turkmenistan 95 J7 .... 38°07'N 63°33'E
Kelkit r. Turkey 51 L5 .... 40°51'N 36°26'E
Kellett, Cape Canada 60 F5 .... 71°59'N 125°59'W
Kells Ireland 18 E3 .... 53°44'N 6°52'W
Kelmė Lithuania 47 J6 .... 55°38'N 22°56'E
Kelo Chad 84 F2 .... 9°18'N 15°49'E
Kelowna Canada 60 G2 .... 49°53'N 119°29'W
Kelso Scotland 15 G3 .... 55°36'N 2°26'W
Keluang Malaysia 102 C4 .... 1°59'N 103°19'E
Kelvedon England 9 F2 .... 51°50'N 0°42'E
Kem' Russia 52 D4 .... 64°57'N 34°34'E
Kemerovo Russia 54 J3 .... 55°23'N 86°01'E
Kemi Finland 43 F4 .... 65°46'N 24°33'E
Kemijärvi Finland 43 F4 .... 66°43'N 27°23'E
Kemijärvi l. Finland 43 F4 .... 66°35'N 27°25'E
Kemijoki r. Finland 43 F4 .... 65°47'N 24°32'E
Kemnay Scotland 17 G2 .... 57°14'N 2°27'W
Kempston England 9 E3 .... 52°07'N 0°30'W
Kempten Germany 46 D2 .... 47°43'N 10°18'E
Kenai U.S.A. 60 C4 .... 60°35'N 151°16'W
Kendal England 12 E3 .... 54°20'N 2°45'W
Kendari Indonesia 103 G3 .... 3°59'S 122°35'E
Kendawangan Indonesia 102 E3 .... 2°30'S 110°14'E
Kengtung Myanmar 97 I5 .... 21°18'N 99°38'E
Kenilworth England 8 D3 .... 52°21'N 1°35'W
Kenmare Ireland 18 B1 .... 51°53'N 9°35'W
Kenmare River inlet Ireland 18 A1 .... 51°43'N 10°03'W
Kennet r. England 8 E2 .... 51°27'N 0°57'W
Kenora Canada 61 I2 .... 49°47'N 94°30'W
Kent d. England 21 F2 .... 51°12'N 0°37'E
Kent r. England 12 E3 .... 54°15'N 2°48'W
Kentucky d. U.S.A. 63 J4 .... 37°24'N 84°54'W
Kentucky r. U.S.A. 63 I4 .... 38°41'N 85°10'W
Kenya Africa 85 H2 .... 0°59'N 37°32'E
Kerala d. India 96 E3 .... 11°31'N 75°51'E
Kerch Ukraine 49 K6 .... 45°22'N 36°29'E
Kerema P.N.G. 108 D6 .... 7°56'S 145°48'E
Keren Eritrea 94 E3 .... 15°46'N 38°28'E
Kerinci, Gunung vol. Indonesia 102 C3 .... 1°42'S 101°15'E
Kerki Turkmenistan 95 K7 .... 37°51'N 65°13'E
Kerkyra Greece 50 C4 .... 39°37'N 19°55'E
Kerma Sudan 94 D3 .... 19°37'N 30°26'E
Kermadec Islands S. Pacific Oc. 109 H3 .... 30°19'S 178°19'W
Kermān Iran 95 I6 .... 30°17'N 57°04'E
Kermān Desert Iran 95 I5 .... 28°27'N 59°19'E
Kermānshāh Iran 95 G6 .... 34°19'N 47°02'E
Kerry d. Ireland 18 B2 .... 52°09'N 9°28'W
Kerry Head Ireland 18 B2 .... 52°25'N 9°57'W
Keşan Turkey 50 G5 .... 40°51'N 26°37'E
Kesennuma Japan 104 D3 .... 38°54'N 141°33'E
Kessingland England 9 G3 .... 52°25'N 1°43'E
Keswick England 12 D3 .... 54°36'N 3°07'W
Ketapang Indonesia 102 E3 .... 1°50'S 110°00'E
Ketchikan U.S.A. 60 E3 .... 55°20'N 131°38'W
Kettering England 8 E3 .... 52°24'N 0°44'W
Keweenaw Bay U.S.A. 63 I6 .... 46°52'N 88°26'W
Key, Lough l. Ireland 18 C4 .... 54°01'N 8°15'W
Keynsham England 8 C2 .... 51°25'N 2°30'W
Khabarovsk Russia 55 O2 .... 48°30'N 135°08'E
Khadyzhensk Russia 51 M7 .... 44°25'N 39°32'E
Khambhat, Gulf of India 96 D4 .... 19°59'N 71°29'E
Khānābād Afgh. 95 K7 .... 36°42'N 69°09'E
Khandwa India 96 E5 .... 21°49'N 76°21'E
Khanewal Pakistan 96 D6 .... 30°18'N 71°58'E
Khanka, Lake China/Russia 99 O6 .... 44°54'N 132°45'E
Khanpur Pakistan 96 D6 .... 28°37'N 70°41'E
Khantayskoye, Ozero l. Russia 55 K4 .... 68°25'N 91°57'E
Khanty-Mansiysk Russia 52 G4 .... 61°05'N 69°01'E

Kharagpur India 96 G5 .... 22°20'N 87°20'E
Kharkiv Ukraine 47 Q3 .... 49°59'N 36°16'E
Khartoum Sudan 85 H3 .... 15°32'N 32°32'E
Khasavyurt Russia 53 E2 .... 43°14'N 46°35'E
Khāsh Iran 95 J5 .... 28°12'N 61°14'E
Khashm el Girba Sudan 94 E3 .... 14°56'N 35°51'E
Khatanga Russia 55 L5 .... 71°57'N 102°24'E
Khatangskiy Zaliv b. Russia 55 L5 .... 73°19'N 107°17'E
Khayelitsha S. Africa 83 A1 .... 34°05'S 18°39'E
Khenchela Algeria 48 E4 .... 35°26'N 7°10'E
Khenifra Morocco 48 B3 .... 32°58'N 5°37'W
Kherson Ukraine 49 J6 .... 46°39'N 32°37'E
Kheta r. Russia 55 L5 .... 71°55'N 102°04'E
Khimki Russia 47 Q6 .... 55°53'N 37°26'E
Khmel'nyts'kyy Ukraine 47 L3 .... 49°25'N 26°59'E
Khon Kaen Thailand 102 C7 .... 16°27'N 102°52'E
Khorinsk Russia 99 J8 .... 52°09'N 109°48'E
Khorramābād Iran 95 G6 .... 33°27'N 48°19'E
Khorugh Tajikistan 95 L7 .... 37°29'N 71°35'E
Khoshgort Russia 52 G4 .... 65°22'N 65°43'E
Khouribga Morocco 48 B3 .... 32°53'N 6°55'W
Khowst Afgh. 95 K6 .... 33°21'N 69°59'E
Khromtau Kazakhstan 53 F3 .... 50°10'N 58°22'E
Khŭjand Tajikistan 98 B6 .... 40°15'N 69°38'E
Khulna Bangl. 97 G5 .... 22°50'N 89°33'E
Khunsar Iran 95 H6 .... 33°10'N 50°17'E
Khust Ukraine 47 J3 .... 48°10'N 23°18'E
Khvoy Iran 94 F7 .... 38°33'N 44°58'E
Khyber Pass Afgh./Pakistan 95 L6 .... 34°08'N 71°12'E
Kiantajärvi l. Finland 43 F4 .... 64°58'N 29°06'E
Kičevo Macedonia 50 D5 .... 41°30'N 20°58'E
Kidderminster England 8 C3 .... 52°23'N 2°15'W
Kidsgrove England 13 E2 .... 53°05'N 2°14'W
Kidwelly Wales 10 C3 .... 51°44'N 4°18'W
Kiel Germany 46 D6 .... 54°19'N 10°08'E
Kiel Canal Germany 43 B1 .... 54°10'N 9°27'E
Kielce Poland 46 I4 .... 50°51'N 20°37'E
Kielder Water resr England 13 E4 .... 55°12'N 2°34'W
Kieler Bucht b. Germany 46 D6 .... 54°27'N 10°41'E
Kiev Ukraine 47 N4 .... 50°26'N 30°34'E
Kigali Rwanda 85 H1 .... 1°59'S 30°05'E
Kigoma Tanzania 83 B4 .... 4°51'S 29°40'E
Kii-suidō str. Japan 104 B2 .... 33°57'N 134°49'E
Kikinda Serbia 50 D7 .... 45°50'N 20°28'E
Kikori r. P.N.G. 108 D6 .... 7°22'S 144°14'E
Kikwit Dem. Rep. Congo 83 A4 .... 5°03'S 18°50'E
Kilbrannan Sound str. Scotland 14 D3 .... 55°25'N 5°27'W
Kilcoole Ireland 10 A5 .... 53°06'N 6°03'W
Kilcormac Ireland 18 D3 .... 53°10'N 7°44'W
Kilcullen Ireland 18 E3 .... 53°08'N 6°45'W
Kildare Ireland 18 E3 .... 53°10'N 6°55'W
Kildare d. Ireland 18 E3 .... 53°17'N 6°47'W
Kilimanjaro mt. Tanzania 83 C4 .... 3°03'S 37°21'E
Kilis Turkey 51 L3 .... 36°43'N 37°07'E
Kilkee Ireland 18 B2 .... 52°41'N 9°38'W
Kilkeel Northern Ireland 14 D2 .... 54°04'N 5°59'W
Kilkenny Ireland 18 D2 .... 52°39'N 7°15'W
Kilkenny d. Ireland 18 D2 .... 52°34'N 7°14'W
Kilkis Greece 50 E5 .... 40°59'N 22°52'E
Killala Bay Ireland 18 B4 .... 54°16'N 9°08'W
Killarney Ireland 18 B2 .... 52°03'N 9°30'W
Killeen U.S.A. 62 G3 .... 31°08'N 97°44'W
Killin Scotland 14 E4 .... 56°28'N 4°19'W
Killorglin Ireland 18 B2 .... 52°06'N 9°47'W
Killybegs Ireland 18 C4 .... 54°38'N 8°27'W
Kilmallock Ireland 18 C2 .... 52°24'N 8°35'W
Kilmarnock Scotland 14 E3 .... 55°37'N 4°30'W
Kilmelford Scotland 14 D4 .... 56°16'N 5°28'W
Kilmichael Point Ireland 18 E2 .... 52°44'N 6°08'W
Kilrea Northern Ireland 14 C2 .... 54°57'N 6°33'W
Kilrush Ireland 18 B2 .... 52°38'N 9°29'W
Kilsyth Scotland 15 E3 .... 55°59'N 4°03'W
Kilwinning Scotland 14 E3 .... 55°39'N 4°42'W
Kimberley S. Africa 83 B2 .... 28°44'S 24°46'E
Kimberley Plateau f. Australia 108 B5 .... 17°26'S 127°05'E
Kimch'aek N. Korea 99 N6 .... 40°41'N 129°12'E
Kinabalu, Gunung mt. Malaysia 102 F5 .... 6°04'N 116°33'E
Kinder Scout hill England 13 F2 .... 53°23'N 1°52'W
Kindersley Canada 62 F7 .... 51°28'N 109°10'W
Kindu Dem. Rep. Congo 83 B4 .... 2°57'S 25°53'E
Kineshma Russia 52 E3 .... 57°27'N 42°07'E
King Island Australia 108 D3 .... 39°50'S 143°58'E
Kingman U.S.A. 62 D4 .... 35°14'N 114°02'W
Kingsbridge England 11 D2 .... 50°17'N 3°47'W
Kingsclere England 8 D2 .... 51°19'N 1°14'W
Kingscourt Ireland 18 E3 .... 53°54'N 6°48'W
King's Lynn England 9 F3 .... 52°45'N 0°24'E
Kingsnorth England 9 F2 .... 51°07'N 0°52'E
Kings Peak U.S.A. 62 D5 .... 40°45'N 110°23'W
Kingston Canada 61 K2 .... 44°14'N 76°30'W
Kingston Jamaica 67 I4 .... 18°00'N 76°47'W
Kingston upon Hull England 13 G2 .... 53°45'N 0°20'W
Kingston upon Thames England 9 E2 .... 51°25'N 0°18'W
Kingstown St Vincent 67 L3 .... 13°10'N 61°15'W
Kingsville U.S.A. 62 G2 .... 27°27'N 97°47'W
Kingswood England 8 C2 .... 51°28'N 2°30'W
Kings Worthy England 8 D2 .... 51°06'N 1°18'W
Kington England 8 B3 .... 52°12'N 3°02'W
Kingussie Scotland 17 E2 .... 57°05'N 4°03'W
King William Island Canada 61 I4 .... 69°10'N 97°45'W
Kinlochbervie Scotland 16 D3 .... 58°28'N 5°03'W
Kinlochleven Scotland 16 E1 .... 56°43'N 4°58'W
Kinloss Scotland 17 F2 .... 57°38'N 3°33'W
Kinna Sweden 43 C2 .... 57°31'N 12°40'E
Kinnegad Ireland 18 D3 .... 53°27'N 7°06'W
Kinross Scotland 15 F4 .... 56°12'N 3°25'W
Kinsale Ireland 18 C1 .... 51°42'N 8°31'W
Kinshasa Dem. Rep. Congo 83 A4 .... 4°22'S 15°23'E
Kintore Scotland 17 G2 .... 57°14'N 2°21'W
Kintyre pen. Scotland 14 D3 .... 55°30'N 5°39'W
Kircubbin Northern Ireland 14 D2 .... 54°29'N 5°31'W
Kiribati Pacific Oc. 109 H6 .... 6°00'S 164°59'W
Kırıkhan Turkey 51 L3 .... 36°29'N 36°22'E
Kırıkkale Turkey 51 J4 .... 39°50'N 33°30'E
Kirkbean Scotland 15 F2 .... 54°53'N 3°36'W
Kirkby England 12 E2 .... 53°29'N 2°53'W
Kirkby in Ashfield England 13 F2 .... 53°06'N 1°16'W
Kirkby Lonsdale England 12 E3 .... 54°12'N 2°36'W
Kirkby Stephen England 12 E3 .... 54°29'N 2°21'W
Kirkcaldy Scotland 15 F4 .... 56°07'N 3°09'W
Kirkcolm Scotland 14 D2 .... 54°58'N 5°05'W
Kirkconnel Scotland 15 E3 .... 55°23'N 4°00'W
Kirkcudbright Scotland 15 E2 .... 54°50'N 4°03'W
Kirkenes Norway 43 G5 .... 69°43'N 30°01'E
Kirkham England 12 E2 .... 53°47'N 2°52'W

Kirkintilloch Scotland 14 E3 .... 55°56'N 4°09'W
Kirkkonummi Finland 43 F3 .... 60°07'N 24°27'E
Kirkland Lake town Canada 61 J2 .... 48°10'N 80°02'W
Kırklareli Turkey 50 G5 .... 41°44'N 27°13'E
Kirk Michael Isle of Man 12 C3 .... 54°17'N 4°35'W
Kirkūk Iraq 94 F6 .... 35°24'N 44°24'E
Kirkwall Scotland 17 G3 .... 58°59'N 2°58'W
Kirov Russia 47 P6 .... 54°04'N 34°20'E
Kirov Russia 52 E3 .... 59°52'N 30°59'E
Kirovsk Russia 43 H4 .... 67°37'N 33°40'E
Kirriemuir Scotland 17 F1 .... 56°41'N 3°00'W
Kirs Russia 52 F3 .... 59°20'N 52°13'E
Kırşehir Turkey 51 K4 .... 39°09'N 34°09'E
Kirtlington England 8 D2 .... 51°52'N 1°16'W
Kirton in Lindsey England 13 G2 .... 53°29'N 0°35'W
Kiruna Sweden 43 E4 .... 67°51'N 20°14'E
Kisangani Dem. Rep. Congo 83 B5 .... 0°34'N 25°11'E
Kislovodsk Russia 49 L5 .... 43°55'N 42°44'E
Kismaayo Somalia 85 I1 .... 0°19'S 42°31'E
Kisoro Uganda 85 G1 .... 1°17'S 29°45'E
Kisumu Kenya 85 H2 .... 0°04'S 34°47'E
Kita-Kyūshū Japan 104 B2 .... 33°52'N 130°50'E
Kitami Japan 104 D4 .... 43°49'N 143°53'E
Kitimat Canada 60 F3 .... 54°03'N 128°39'W
Kittilä Finland 43 F4 .... 67°38'N 24°54'E
Kitwe Zambia 83 B3 .... 12°48'S 28°12'E
Kiurvesi Finland 43 F3 .... 62°59'N 26°38'E
Kivu, Lake Dem. Rep. Congo/Rwanda 83 B4 .... 1°55'S 29°09'E
Kizel Russia 52 F3 .... 59°03'N 57°39'E
Kızıl Dağı mt. Turkey 51 M4 .... 39°57'N 38°12'E
Kızılırmak r. Turkey 51 K5 .... 41°49'N 35°54'E
Kladno Czechia 46 F4 .... 50°09'N 14°08'E
Klagenfurt am Wörthersee Austria 46 F2 .... 46°38'N 14°19'E
Klaipėda Lithuania 43 E1 .... 55°43'N 21°09'E
Klamath r. U.S.A. 62 B5 .... 41°27'N 124°02'W
Klamath Falls town U.S.A. 62 B5 .... 42°15'N 121°46'W
Klang Malaysia 102 C4 .... 3°02'N 101°25'E
Klazienaveen Neth. 42 F5 .... 52°44'N 6°59'E
Kleve Germany 42 F4 .... 51°47'N 6°08'E
Klimovo Russia 47 O5 .... 52°23'N 32°12'E
Klin Russia 52 D3 .... 56°20'N 36°43'E
Klintsy Russia 47 O5 .... 52°45'N 32°15'E
Kłodzko Poland 46 G4 .... 50°26'N 16°39'E
Klyuchevskaya, Sopka vol. Russia 55 R3 .... 56°01'N 160°41'E
Knaresborough England 13 F3 .... 54°01'N 1°28'W
Knighton Wales 10 D4 .... 52°20'N 3°03'W
Knin Croatia 50 B7 .... 44°03'N 16°12'E
Knockaboy hill Ireland 18 B1 .... 51°48'N 9°26'W
Knockadoon Head Ireland 18 D1 .... 51°53'N 7°52'W
Knockalongy hill Ireland 18 C4 .... 54°12'N 8°46'W
Knock Hill Scotland 17 G2 .... 57°35'N 2°46'W
Knocklayd hill Northern Ireland 14 C3 .... 55°10'N 6°15'W
Knockmealdown Mountains hills Ireland 18 C2 .... 52°14'N 8°04'W
Knottingley England 13 F2 .... 53°42'N 1°15'W
Knowle England 8 D3 .... 52°23'N 1°44'W
Knoxville U.S.A. 63 J4 .... 35°59'N 83°56'W
Knutsford England 12 E2 .... 53°18'N 2°22'W
Kōbe Japan 104 C2 .... 34°41'N 135°11'E
Koblenz Germany 46 B4 .... 50°21'N 7°35'E
Kobroör i. Indonesia 103 I2 .... 6°07'S 134°30'E
Kobryn Belarus 47 K5 .... 52°12'N 24°20'E
Kočani Macedonia 50 E5 .... 41°55'N 22°23'E
Kochi India 96 E2 .... 9°55'N 76°14'E
Kōchi Japan 104 B2 .... 33°33'N 133°32'E
Kochubey Russia 53 E2 .... 44°29'N 46°38'E
Kodiak U.S.A. 60 C3 .... 57°46'N 152°30'W
Kodiak Island U.S.A. 60 C3 .... 57°26'N 153°20'W
Kōfu Japan 104 C3 .... 35°39'N 138°34'E
Køge Denmark 43 C1 .... 55°27'N 12°11'E
Kohat Pakistan 95 L6 .... 33°37'N 71°30'E
Kokand Uzbekistan 98 C6 .... 40°31'N 70°57'E
Kokkola Finland 43 E3 .... 63°51'N 23°08'E
Kokpekti Kazakhstan 98 F7 .... 48°46'N 82°21'E
Kokshetau Kazakhstan 54 H3 .... 53°17'N 69°23'E
Kola Russia 43 H5 .... 68°52'N 33°03'E
Kolaka Indonesia 103 G3 .... 4°03'S 121°38'E
Kola Peninsula Russia 52 D4 .... 67°29'N 34°49'E
Kolding Denmark 43 B1 .... 55°30'N 9°28'E
Kolguyev, Ostrov i. Russia 52 E4 .... 69°07'N 49°03'E
Kolhapur India 96 D4 .... 16°40'N 74°19'E
Kolkata India 96 G5 .... 22°33'N 88°21'E
Kollam India 96 E2 .... 8°53'N 76°36'E
Kołobrzeg Poland 46 F6 .... 54°11'N 15°34'E
Kolomna Russia 53 D3 .... 55°05'N 38°47'E
Kolomyya Ukraine 47 K3 .... 48°32'N 25°02'E
Koluli Eritrea 94 F2 .... 14°24'N 40°20'E
Kolvitskoye, Ozero l. Russia 43 H4 .... 67°04'N 33°36'E
Kolwezi Dem. Rep. Congo 83 B3 .... 10°42'S 25°28'E
Kolyma r. Russia 55 R4 .... 69°22'N 161°24'E
Kolymskiy, Khrebet mts Russia 55 R4 .... 66°50'N 167°12'E
Komatsu Japan 104 C3 .... 36°23'N 136°28'E
Komotini Greece 50 F5 .... 41°07'N 25°24'E
Komsomolets, Ostrov i. Russia 55 K6 .... 80°42'N 94°20'E
Komsomol'sk Ukraine 47 O3 .... 49°01'N 33°39'E
Komsomol'sk-na-Amure Russia 55 O3 .... 50°36'N 136°55'E
Kong Christian IX Land f. Greenland 61 O4 .... 66°49'N 37°44'W
Kongsberg Norway 43 B2 .... 59°40'N 9°39'E
Kongsvinger Norway 43 C3 .... 60°12'N 12°01'E
Konin Poland 46 H5 .... 52°13'N 18°16'E
Konosha Russia 52 E4 .... 60°58'N 40°16'E
Konotop Ukraine 47 O4 .... 51°14'N 33°12'E
Konstanz Germany 46 C2 .... 47°40'N 9°10'E
Konya Turkey 51 J4 .... 37°52'N 32°29'E
Konzhakovskiy Kamen', Gora mt. Russia 52 F3 .... 59°37'N 59°08'E
Köping Sweden 43 D2 .... 59°31'N 16°00'E
Koprivnica Croatia 46 G2 .... 46°10'N 16°50'E
Korçë Albania 50 D5 .... 40°37'N 20°47'E
Korčula i. Croatia 50 B6 .... 42°54'N 16°56'E
Korea Bay China/N. Korea 99 M5 .... 39°05'N 124°20'E
Korea Strait Japan/S. Korea 104 A2 .... 34°12'N 128°41'E
Körfez Turkey 51 H5 .... 40°47'N 29°42'E
Korinthiakos Kolpos str. Greece 50 E4 .... 38°16'N 22°34'E
Kōriyama Japan 104 D3 .... 37°24'N 140°22'E
Korkuteli Turkey 51 I3 .... 37°04'N 30°11'E
Korla China 98 F6 .... 41°39'N 86°08'E
Köröğlu Tepesi mt. Turkey 51 J5 .... 40°30'N 32°01'E
Korosten' Ukraine 47 M4 .... 50°57'N 28°39'E
Koro Toro Chad 85 F3 .... 16°05'N 18°30'E
Korsakov Russia 55 P2 .... 46°38'N 142°45'E
Kortrijk Belgium 42 C3 .... 50°49'N 3°16'E
Koryakskiy Khrebet mts Russia 55 S4 .... 62°59'N 177°49'E
Koryazhma Russia 52 E4 .... 61°19'N 47°12'E
Kos i. Greece 50 G3 .... 36°46'N 27°07'E

Kościerzyna Poland 46 G6 ....54°07'N 17°59'E
Kosciuszko, Mount Australia 108 D3 ....36°28'S 148°15'E
Košice Slovakia 46 I3 ....48°43'N 21°16'E
Kosovo Europe 50 D6 ....42°35'N 21°00'E
Kosovska Mitrovica Kosovo 50 D6 ....42°52'N 20°52'E
Kostanay Kazakhstan 54 H3 ....53°12'N 63°40'E
Kosti Sudan 85 H3 ....13°09'N 32°38'E
Kostomuksha Russia 52 D4 ....64°34'N 30°33'E
Kostroma Russia 52 E3 ....57°46'N 40°58'E
Kostrzyn nad Odrą Poland 46 F5 ....52°35'N 14°37'E
Koszalin Poland 46 G6 ....54°11'N 16°11'E
Kota India 96 E6 ....25°10'N 75°57'E
Kota Bharu Malaysia 102 C5 ....6°08'N 102°16'E
Kotabumi Indonesia 102 C3 ....4°51'S 104°55'E
Kota Kinabalu Malaysia 102 F5 ....5°58'N 116°05'E
Kotel'nich Russia 52 E3 ....58°18'N 48°20'E
Kotel'nyy Russia 55 O5 ....76°00'N 137°59'E
Kotel'nyy, Ostrov i. Russia 55 O5 ....75°07'N 139°31'E
Kotlas Russia 52 E4 ....61°16'N 46°38'E
Kötlutangi pt Iceland 43 Y1 ....63°24'N 18°45'W
Kotuy r. Russia 55 L5 ....71°55'N 102°06'E
Kotzebue U.S.A. 60 B4 ....66°53'N 162°32'W
Kotzebue Sound str. U.S.A. 60 B4 ....66°33'N 163°11'W
Koundâra Guinea 84 C3 ....12°30'N 13°19'W
Kouvola Finland 43 F3 ....60°52'N 26°42'E
Kovel' Ukraine 47 K4 ....51°13'N 24°43'E
Kovrov Russia 52 E3 ....56°22'N 41°19'E
Kowloon China 102 E8 ....22°20'N 114°13'E
Koyang S. Korea 99 N5 ....37°38'N 126°49'E
Kozan Turkey 51 K3 ....37°28'N 35°48'E
Kozani Greece 50 D5 ....40°18'N 21°48'E
Kozelets' Ukraine 47 N4 ....50°55'N 31°07'E
Kozhikode India 96 E3 ....11°15'N 75°45'E
Kozyatyn Ukraine 47 M3 ....49°42'N 28°49'E
Krabi Thailand 102 B5 ....8°05'N 98°56'E
Krâchéh Cambodia 102 D6 ....12°27'N 106°03'E
Kragujevac Serbia 50 D7 ....44°01'N 20°55'E
Kraków Poland 46 H4 ....50°03'N 19°56'E
Kraljevo Serbia 49 H5 ....43°43'N 20°41'E
Kramfors Sweden 43 D3 ....62°56'N 17°46'E
Kranj Slovenia 46 F2 ....46°15'N 14°21'E
Krasino Russia 52 F4 ....70°44'N 54°28'E
Krasnoborsk Russia 52 E4 ....61°33'N 45°56'E
Krasnodar Russia 53 D2 ....45°02'N 38°59'E
Krasnohrad Ukraine 47 P3 ....49°22'N 35°28'E
Krasnokamsk Russia 52 F3 ....58°05'N 55°45'E
Krasnoperekops'k Ukraine 51 J7 ....45°57'N 33°49'E
Krasnotur'insk Russia 52 G3 ....59°47'N 60°13'E
Krasnoufimsk Russia 52 F3 ....56°36'N 57°46'E
Krasnoyarsk Russia 55 K3 ....56°03'N 92°50'E
Krasnyy Luch Ukraine 53 D2 ....48°08'N 38°55'E
Krefeld Germany 46 B4 ....51°20'N 6°33'E
Kremenchuk Ukraine 47 O3 ....49°04'N 33°25'E
Kremenchuts'ka Vodoskhovyshche resr Ukraine 47 O3
....49°18'N 32°42'E
Kretinga Lithuania 46 I6 ....55°53'N 21°14'E
Krishna r. India 96 F4 ....16°01'N 80°53'E
Kristiansand Norway 43 A2 ....58°08'N 7°59'E
Kristianstad Sweden 43 C2 ....56°02'N 14°10'E
Kristiansund Norway 43 A3 ....63°07'N 7°45'E
Kristinehamn Sweden 43 C2 ....59°19'N 14°07'E
Krk i. Croatia 50 A7 ....45°02'N 14°47'E
Kropotkin Russia 53 E2 ....45°26'N 40°34'E
Kropyvnyts'kyy Ukraine 47 O3 ....48°30'N 32°16'E
Krosno Poland 47 I3 ....49°41'N 21°46'E
Kruševac Serbia 50 D6 ....43°35'N 21°19'E
Krychaw Belarus 47 N5 ....53°44'N 31°43'E
Krymsk Russia 51 L7 ....44°55'N 37°59'E
Krytiko Pelagos sea Greece 50 F3 ....36°11'N 25°24'E
Kryvyy Rih Ukraine 47 O2 ....47°54'N 33°21'E
Ksabi Algeria 84 D4 ....28°54'N 0°47'W
Ksar el Boukhari Algeria 48 D4 ....35°52'N 2°45'E
Ksar el Kebir Morocco 48 B4 ....35°01'N 5°54'W
Kuala Lumpur Malaysia 102 C4 ....3°06'N 101°42'E
Kuala Terengganu Malaysia 102 C5 ....5°19'N 103°07'E
Kuantan Malaysia 102 C4 ....3°50'N 103°21'E
Kuban' r. Russia 51 L7 ....45°19'N 37°22'E
Kuching Malaysia 102 E4 ....1°32'N 110°20'E
Kugluktuk Canada 60 G4 ....67°46'N 115°07'W
Kuhmo Finland 43 G4 ....64°07'N 29°30'E
Kuito Angola 83 A3 ....12°23'S 16°57'E
Kujū-san vol. Japan 104 B2 ....33°05'N 131°16'E
Kūl r. Iran 95 I5 ....27°04'N 55°44'E
Kulandy Kazakhstan 53 F2 ....46°03'N 59°32'E
Kuldīga Latvia 43 E2 ....56°58'N 21°59'E
Kŭlob Tajikistan 95 K7 ....37°54'N 69°51'E
Kul'sary Kazakhstan 53 F2 ....46°56'N 54°00'E
Kulunda Russia 98 D5 ....52°33'N 78°56'E
Kulundinskoye, Ozero l. Russia 98 D8 ...53°08'N 79°46'E
Kumamoto Japan 104 B2 ....32°47'N 130°43'E
Kumanovo Macedonia 50 D6 ....42°08'N 21°43'E
Kumasi Ghana 84 D2 ....6°42'N 1°38'W
Kumbakonam India 96 E3 ....10°58'N 79°23'E
Kumertau Russia 53 F3 ....52°44'N 55°46'E
Kumla Sweden 43 C2 ....59°07'N 15°10'E
Kumo Nigeria 84 F3 ....10°06'N 11°11'E
Kunashir, Ostrov i. Russia 104 E4 ....44°13'N 146°23'E
Kungur Russia 52 F3 ....57°24'N 56°56'E
Kunlun Shan mts China 98 D5 ....36°11'N 78°10'E
Kunming China 99 I3 ....25°02'N 102°44'E
Kuohijärvi l. Finland 43 F3 ....61°12'N 24°59'E
Kuopio Finland 43 F3 ....62°53'N 27°41'E
Kupa r. Croatia/Slovenia 50 B7 ....45°28'N 16°25'E
Kupang Indonesia 103 G1 ....10°12'S 123°35'E
Kupiškis Lithuania 43 F1 ....55°49'N 24°59'E
Kup"yans'k Ukraine 53 D2 ....49°42'N 37°37'E
Kuqa China 98 E6 ....41°38'N 83°01'E
Kurdistan f. Asia 94 F7 ....37°00'N 42°00'E
Kuressaare Estonia 43 E2 ....58°16'N 22°29'E
Kurgan Russia 54 H3 ....55°28'N 65°23'E
Kurikka Finland 43 E3 ....62°37'N 22°25'E
Kuril Islands Russia 55 P2 ....46°04'N 148°33'E
Kuril'sk Russia 55 P2 ....45°13'N 147°57'E
Kuril Trench f. N. Pacific Oc. 117 I4 ......41°44'N 146°33'E
Kurmuk Sudan 85 H3 ....10°31'N 34°16'E
Kurnool India 96 E4 ....15°49'N 77°59'E
Kursk Russia 53 D3 ....51°45'N 36°12'E
Kurşumlija Serbia 50 D6 ....43°08'N 21°17'E
Kurume Japan 104 B2 ....33°18'N 130°31'E
Kurunegala Sri Lanka 96 F2 ....7°30'N 80°19'E
Kuşadası Turkey 50 G3 ....37°51'N 27°15'E
Kushiro Japan 104 D4 ....42°59'N 144°23'E
Kuskokwim Mountains U.S.A. 60 C4 ....64°24'N 155°17'W
Kütahya Turkey 51 H4 ....39°25'N 29°59'E
Kutaisi Georgia 53 E2 ....42°16'N 42°43'E
Kutno Poland 46 H5 ....52°14'N 19°22'E
Kuujjuaq Canada 61 L3 ....58°10'N 68°13'W

Kuusamo Finland 43 G4 ....65°58'N 29°09'E
Kuwait Asia 95 G5 ....29°22'N 47°08'E
Kuwait town Kuwait 95 G5 ....29°18'N 47°55'E
Kuybyshevskoye Vodokhranilische resr Russia 53 E3
....54°55'N 49°00'E
Kuytun China 98 E6 ....44°20'N 84°53'E
Kuznetsk Russia 53 E3 ....53°07'N 46°37'E
Kvaløya i. Norway 43 D5 ....69°38'N 18°30'E
KwaMashu S. Africa 83 C2 ....29°44'S 30°59'E
KwaNobuhle S. Africa 83 B1 ....33°48'S 25°24'E
Kwilu r. Angola/Dem. Rep. Congo 83 A4 ...3°23'S 17°22'E
Kwoka mt. Indonesia 103 I3 ....0°38'S 132°28'E
Kyakhta Russia 55 L3 ....50°21'N 106°30'E
Kyangwali Uganda 85 H2 ....1°15'N 30°45'E
Kyle of Lochalsh Scotland 16 D2 ....57°17'N 5°43'W
Kyle of Tongue inlet Scotland 17 E3 ......58°28'N 4°27'W
Kyllini mt. Greece 50 E3 ....37°56'N 22°24'E
Kyoga, Lake Uganda 85 H2 ....1°28'N 32°53'E
Kyōto Japan 104 C3 ....34°59'N 135°46'E
Kyparissia Greece 50 D3 ....37°15'N 21°41'E
Kypshak, Ozero l. Kazakhstan 54 H3 ......50°09'N 68°23'E
Kyrenia Cyprus 51 J2 ....35°20'N 33°19'E
Kyrgyzstan Asia 98 C6 ....41°47'N 74°37'E
Kyrta Russia 52 F4 ....64°04'N 57°40'E
Kythira i. Greece 50 E3 ....36°16'N 22°55'E
Kythnos i. Greece 50 F3 ....37°26'N 24°27'E
Kyūshū i. Japan 104 B2 ....31°30'N 131°45'E
Kyustendil Bulgaria 50 E6 ....42°17'N 22°41'E
Kyyivs'ke Vodoskhovyshche resr Ukraine 47 N4
....50°54'N 30°30'E
Kyzyl Russia 55 K3 ....51°43'N 94°24'E
Kyzylorda Kazakhstan 54 H2 ....44°51'N 65°30'E

L

Laâyoune Western Sahara 84 C4 ....27°09'N 13°12'W
Labé Guinea 84 C3 ....11°20'N 12°18'W
Labrador f. Canada 61 L3 ....54°04'N 62°29'W
Labrador City Canada 61 L3 ....52°59'N 66°54'W
Labrador Sea Canada/Greenland 61 M4 ...60°07'N 56°06'W
Labytnangi Russia 52 G4 ....66°42'N 66°18'E
Laccadive Sea Asia 96 D2 ....10°00'N 73°00'E
Laceby England 13 G2 ....53°32'N 0°10'W
Lachlan r. Australia 108 D3 ....34°21'S 143°57'E
La Crosse U.S.A. 63 H5 ....43°48'N 91°12'W
Ladhar Bheinn mt. Scotland 16 D2 ....57°05'N 5°35'W
Lādīz Iran 95 J5 ....28°55'N 61°18'E
Ladoga, Lake Russia 54 E4 ....60°48'N 31°37'E
Ladybank Scotland 15 F4 ....56°17'N 3°08'W
Ladybower Reservoir England 13 F2 ....53°23'N 1°45'W
Ladysmith S. Africa 83 B2 ....28°34'S 29°47'E
Lae P.N.G. 108 D6 ....6°43'S 147°00'E
Læsø i. Denmark 43 B2 ....57°15'N 11°05'E
Lafayette U.S.A. 63 H3 ....30°14'N 92°03'W
Lagan r. Northern Ireland 14 D2 ....54°37'N 5°54'W
Lagan' Russia 53 E2 ....45°25'N 47°18'E
Laggan, Loch l. Scotland 17 E1 ....56°56'N 4°31'W
Laghouat Algeria 84 E5 ....33°42'N 2°53'E
La Gomera i. Canary Islands 45 X2 ....28°14'N 17°18'W
Lagos Nigeria 84 E2 ....6°26'N 3°20'E
Lagos Portugal 45 A2 ....37°06'N 8°41'W
La Grande U.S.A. 62 C6 ....45°19'N 118°02'W
La Grande 2, Réservoir Canada 61 K3 ....53°52'N 76°54'W
La Grande 3, Réservoir Canada 61 K3 ....53°36'N 75°18'W
La Grande 4, Réservoir Canada 61 K3 ....54°13'N 73°17'W
La Gran Sabana f. Venezuela 67 L2 ....5°13'N 61°40'W
Lahad Datu Malaysia 102 F5 ....5°02'N 118°20'E
Lahat Indonesia 102 C3 ....3°46'S 103°34'E
Lahij Yemen 94 F2 ....13°02'N 44°52'E
Lāhījān Iran 95 G7 ....37°11'N 49°56'E
Lahore Pakistan 96 D7 ....31°33'N 74°23'E
Lahti Finland 43 F3 ....60°59'N 25°41'E
Laidon, Loch l. Scotland 17 E1 ....56°39'N 4°39'W
Laihia Finland 43 E3 ....62°58'N 22°01'E
Lainioälven r. Sweden 43 E4 ....67°22'N 22°39'E
Lairg Scotland 17 E3 ....58°01'N 4°24'W
Lake City U.S.A. 63 J3 ....30°10'N 82°39'W
Lake District f. England 12 D3 ....54°30'N 3°10'W
Lakeland U.S.A. 63 J2 ....27°59'N 81°58'W
Lakki Pakistan 95 L6 ....32°35'N 70°58'E
Lakonikos Kolpos b. Greece 50 E3 ....36°32'N 22°42'E
Laksefjorden str. Norway 43 F5 ....70°52'N 27°00'E
Lakshadweep d. India 96 D3 ....10°35'N 73°13'E
Lakshadweep is India 96 D3 ....10°59'N 72°11'E
La Línea de la Concepción Spain 45 C2 ...36°10'N 5°21'W
La Louvière Belgium 42 D3 ....50°28'N 4°11'E
La Mancha f. Spain 45 D3 ....39°15'N 2°58'W
Lamar U.S.A. 62 F4 ....38°06'N 102°38'W
La Martre, Lac l. Canada 60 G4 ....63°19'N 118°02'W
Lambay Island Ireland 18 F3 ....53°29'N 5°59'W
Lambourn England 8 D2 ....51°30'N 1°32'W
Lambourn Downs hills England 8 D2 .....51°32'N 1°32'W
Lamego Portugal 45 B4 ....41°06'N 7°48'W
Lāmerd Iran 95 H5 ....27°22'N 53°08'E
Lamia Greece 50 E4 ....38°54'N 22°25'E
Lamlash Scotland 14 D3 ....55°32'N 5°08'W
Lammermuir Hills Scotland 15 G3 ....55°49'N 2°50'W
Lampang Thailand 102 B7 ....18°16'N 99°32'E
Lampeter Wales 10 C4 ....52°07'N 4°05'W
Lanark Scotland 15 F3 ....55°40'N 3°47'W
Lancashire d. England 21 D3 ....53°57'N 2°51'W
Lancaster England 12 E3 ....54°03'N 2°48'W
Lancaster Canal England 12 E2 ....53°59'N 2°48'W
Lancaster Sound str. Canada 61 J5 ....74°15'N 89°18'W
Landeck Austria 46 D2 ....47°08'N 10°34'E
Lander U.S.A. 62 E5 ....42°50'N 108°42'W
Landes f. France 44 C4 ....44°48'N 0°55'W
Landguard Point England 9 G2 ....51°56'N 1°19'E
Land's End pt England 11 B2 ....50°03'N 5°45'W
Landshut Germany 46 E3 ....48°33'N 12°10'E
Landskrona Sweden 46 E6 ....55°52'N 12°50'E
Lanesborough Ireland 18 D3 ....53°40'N 7°59'W
Langavat, Loch l. Na h-E. S. Scotland 16 C2
....57°48'N 6°59'W
Langavat, Loch l. Na h-E. S. Scotland 16 C3
....58°02'N 6°49'W
Langeland i. Denmark 43 B1 ....54°50'N 10°55'E
Langeoog i. Germany 42 G6 ....53°46'N 7°36'E
Langholm Scotland 15 G3 ....55°09'N 2°59'W
Langøya i. Norway 43 C5 ....68°44'N 14°27'E
Langport England 8 C2 ....51°02'N 2°50'W
Langres France 44 F5 ....47°52'N 5°20'E
Langsa Indonesia 102 B4 ....4°25'N 97°57'E
Langstrothdale Chase hills England 13 E3 ...54°13'N 2°18'W
Languedoc f. France 44 D3 ....43°10'N 1°57'E

Lanivet England 11 C2 ....50°26'N 4°46'W
Länkäran Azerbaijan 95 G7 ....38°45'N 48°51'E
Lannion France 44 B6 ....48°44'N 3°27'W
Lansing U.S.A. 63 J5 ....42°44'N 84°33'W
Lanzarote i. Canary Islands 45 Z2 ....29°09'N 13°35'W
Lanzhou China 99 I5 ....36°04'N 103°43'E
Laoag Phil. 102 G7 ....18°14'N 120°36'E
Lao Cai Vietnam 102 C8 ....22°26'N 103°59'E
Laois d. Ireland 18 D2 ....52°57'N 7°23'W
Laojunmiao China 98 H5 ....39°46'N 97°33'E
Laon France 44 E6 ....49°34'N 3°38'E
Laos Asia 102 C7 ....19°30'N 103°01'E
La Palma i. Canary Islands 45 X2 ....28°33'N 17°44'W
La Palma Panama 67 I2 ....8°21'N 78°11'W
La Palma del Condado Spain 45 B2 ......37°23'N 6°33'W
La Paragua Venezuela 67 L2 ....6°50'N 63°19'W
La Paz Bolivia 72 C5 ....16°30'S 68°10'W
La Paz Mexico 66 B5 ....24°08'N 110°17'W
La Pérouse Strait Japan/Russia 104 D5 ...45°35'N 141°33'E
La Plata Argentina 73 D3 ....34°55'S 57°58'W
La Plata, Río de str. Argentina/Uruguay 73 D3
....34°39'S 57°53'W
Lappajärvi l. Finland 43 E3 ....63°07'N 23°41'E
Lappeenranta Finland 43 G3 ....61°03'N 28°11'E
Lappland f. Europe 43 D4 ....67°12'N 18°37'E
Laptev Sea Russia 55 N5 ....76°05'N 125°40'E
Lapua Finland 43 E3 ....62°58'N 23°00'E
Larache Morocco 48 B4 ....35°12'N 6°09'W
Laramie U.S.A. 62 E5 ....41°20'N 105°36'W
Laredo U.S.A. 62 G2 ....27°30'N 99°30'W
La Rioja Argentina 73 C4 ....29°25'S 66°51'W
Larisa Greece 50 E4 ....39°38'N 22°25'E
Larkana Pakistan 96 C6 ....27°31'N 68°13'E
Larnaca Cyprus 51 J2 ....34°55'N 33°38'E
Larne Northern Ireland 14 D2 ....54°51'N 5°49'W
Larne Lough inlet Northern Ireland 14 D2 ...54°49'N 5°47'W
La Rochelle France 44 C5 ....46°10'N 1°09'W
La Roche-sur-Yon France 44 C5 ....46°40'N 1°27'W
La Ronge Canada 60 H3 ....55°06'N 105°17'W
Larvik Norway 43 B2 ....59°03'N 10°05'E
La Sagra f. Spain 45 D4 ....38°03'N 3°56'W
La Sagra mt. Spain 45 D2 ....37°58'N 2°35'W
Las Cruces U.S.A. 62 E3 ....32°19'N 106°47'W
La Serena Chile 73 B4 ....29°53'S 71°16'W
Lashio Myanmar 97 I5 ....22°57'N 97°44'E
Las Marismas marsh Spain 45 B2 ....37°07'N 6°35'W
Las Palmas de Gran Canaria Canary Islands 45 Y2
....28°06'N 15°26'W
La Spezia Italy 46 C1 ....44°07'N 9°49'E
Las Tórtolas, Cerro mt. Chile 73 C4 ....29°56'S 69°52'W
Las Tunas Cuba 67 I5 ....20°57'N 76°57'W
Las Vegas U.S.A. 62 C4 ....36°10'N 115°09'W
Las Villuercas mt. Spain 45 C3 ....39°29'N 5°23'W
Latakia Syria 94 E7 ....35°31'N 35°47'E
Latheron Scotland 17 F3 ....58°17'N 3°22'W
Latina Italy 48 F5 ....41°28'N 12°54'E
La Tortuga, Isla i. Venezuela 67 K3 ....10°58'N 65°17'W
La Tuque Canada 63 L6 ....47°27'N 72°47'W
Latvia Europe 43 E2 ....56°47'N 23°49'E
Lauchhammer Germany 46 E4 ....51°30'N 13°46'E
Launceston Australia 108 D2 ....41°27'S 147°09'E
Launceston England 11 C2 ....50°38'N 4°21'W
Laurencekirk Scotland 17 G1 ....56°50'N 2°28'W
Lausanne Switz. 48 E6 ....46°32'N 6°39'E
Laut i. Indonesia 102 F3 ....3°39'S 116°18'E
Laval France 44 C6 ....48°04'N 0°46'W
Lavenham England 9 F3 ....52°06'N 0°48'E
Lawton U.S.A. 62 G3 ....34°37'N 98°24'W
Lawz, Jabal al mt. Saudi Arabia 49 K2 ...28°39'N 35°18'E
Laxey Isle of Man 12 C3 ....54°14'N 4°24'W
Laxford, Loch inlet Scotland 16 D3 ....58°25'N 5°06'W
Lázaro Cárdenas Baja Calif. Mexico 66 A7
....30°30'N 115°56'W
Lázaro Cárdenas Michoacán Mexico 66 D4
....17°57'N 102°12'W
Leader Water r. Scotland 15 G3 ....55°36'N 2°40'W
Leane, Lough l. Ireland 18 B2 ....52°02'N 9°34'W
Leatherhead England 9 E2 ....51°17'N 0°19'W
Lebanon Asia 49 K3 ....33°17'N 35°20'E
Łebork Poland 46 G6 ....54°32'N 17°45'E
Lecce Italy 49 G5 ....40°20'N 18°11'E
Lech r. Austria/Germany 46 D2 ....47°36'N 10°40'E
Lechlade-on-Thames England 8 D2 ....51°42'N 1°41'W
Le Creusot France 9 G1 ....50°13'N 1°38'E
Ledbury England 8 C3 ....52°02'N 2°25'W
Lee r. Ireland 18 C1 ....51°54'N 8°25'W
Leeds England 13 F2 ....53°48'N 1°33'W
Leek England 13 E2 ....53°07'N 2°01'W
Leeming England 13 F3 ....54°18'N 1°33'W
Lee Moor England 11 C2 ....50°26'N 4°01'W
Leer Germany 42 G6 ....53°15'N 7°28'E
Leeuwarden Neth. 42 E6 ....53°12'N 5°48'E
Leeuwin, Cape Australia 108 A3 ....34°23'S 115°09'E
Leeward Islands Caribbean Sea 67 L4 ....16°49'N 64°04'W
Lefkada i. Greece 50 D4 ....38°45'N 20°35'E
Legaspi Phil. 103 G6 ....13°08'N 123°44'E
Legnica Poland 46 G4 ....51°13'N 16°10'E
Leh India 96 E7 ....34°09'N 77°36'E
Le Havre France 44 D6 ....49°30'N 0°08'E
Leiah Pakistan 95 L6 ....30°58'N 70°58'E
Leicester England 8 D3 ....52°38'N 1°08'W
Leicester d. England 21 E3 ....52°39'N 1°07'W
Leicestershire d. England 21 E3 ....52°39'N 1°09'W
Leichhardt r. Australia 108 C5 ....17°35'S 139°44'E
Leiden Neth. 42 D5 ....52°10'N 4°30'E
Leigh England 12 E2 ....53°30'N 2°31'W
Leighton Buzzard England 8 E2 ....51°55'N 0°40'W
Leinster f. Ireland 18 E2 ....52°37'N 6°47'W
Leinster, Mount hill Ireland 18 E2 ....52°37'N 6°47'W
Leipzig Germany 46 E4 ....51°21'N 12°23'E
Leiston England 9 G3 ....52°13'N 1°35'E
Leith Scotland 15 F3 ....55°59'N 3°10'W
Leith Hill England 9 E2 ....51°11'N 0°22'W
Leitrim d. Ireland 18 C4 ....54°19'N 8°13'W
Leixlip Ireland 18 E3 ....53°22'N 6°29'W
Leizhou Bandao pen. China 99 J2 ....21°03'N 109°41'E
Lek r. Neth. 42 D4 ....51°54'N 4°34'E
Leka Norway 43 B4 ....65°05'N 11°44'E
Leksozero, Ozero l. Russia 43 G3 ....63°51'N 30°48'E
Lelystad Neth. 42 E5 ....52°32'N 5°29'E
Le Mans France 44 D6 ....48°00'N 0°12'E
Lena r. Russia 55 N5 ....72°20'N 126°37'E
Lens France 44 E7 ....50°26'N 2°50'E
Lensk Russia 55 M4 ....60°44'N 114°53'E
Leoben Austria 46 F2 ....47°23'N 15°06'E
Leominster England 8 C3 ....52°14'N 2°44'W
León Mexico 66 D5 ....21°07'N 101°44'W

León Spain 45 C5 ....42°36'N 5°34'W
Le Puy-en-Velay France 44 E4 ....45°03'N 3°53'E
Lerum Sweden 43 C2 ....57°46'N 12°17'E
Lerwick Scotland 17 H5 ....60°09'N 1°09'W
Lesbos i. Greece 50 F4 ....39°08'N 25°56'E
Les Cayes Haiti 67 J4 ....18°14'N 73°47'W
Leshan China 99 I3 ....29°37'N 103°44'E
Leskovac Serbia 50 D6 ....42°59'N 21°56'E
Lesotho Africa 83 B2 ....29°38'S 28°26'E
Les Pieux France 11 Z9 ....49°31'N 1°48'W
Les Sables-d'Olonne France 44 C5 ....46°30'N 1°46'W
Lesser Antilles is Caribbean Sea 67 K3 ...12°28'N 67°56'W
Lesser Slave Lake Canada 60 G3 ....55°28'N 115°09'W
Lestijärvi l. Finland 43 F3 ....63°30'N 24°47'E
Leszno Poland 46 G4 ....51°51'N 16°35'E
Letchworth Garden City England 9 E2 ...51°59'N 0°13'W
Lethbridge Canada 60 G2 ....49°41'N 112°49'W
Leti, Kepulauan is Indonesia 103 H2 .....8°18'S 127°58'E
Letterkenny Ireland 18 D4 ....54°57'N 7°43'W
Leuchars Scotland 15 G4 ....56°23'N 2°53'W
Leuser, Gunung mt. Indonesia 102 B4 ...3°46'N 97°11'E
Leuven Belgium 42 D3 ....50°52'N 4°43'E
Levadeia Greece 50 E4 ....38°26'N 22°53'E
Leven England 13 G2 ....53°54'N 0°18'W
Leven Scotland 15 G4 ....56°12'N 2°59'W
Leven, Loch inlet Scotland 16 D1 ....56°41'N 5°06'W
Leven, Loch l. Scotland 15 F4 ....56°12'N 3°23'W
Levens England 12 E3 ....54°16'N 2°47'W
Leverkusen Germany 46 B4 ....51°03'N 6°59'E
Lewes England 9 F1 ....50°52'N 0°01'E
Lewis, Isle of i. Scotland 16 C3 ....58°09'N 6°59'W
Lexington U.S.A. 63 J4 ....38°02'N 84°31'W
Leyburn England 13 F3 ....54°19'N 1°50'W
Leyland England 12 E2 ....53°42'N 2°42'W
Leyte i. Phil. 103 G6 ....11°05'N 124°31'E
Lezhë Albania 50 C5 ....41°46'N 19°39'E
L'gov Russia 53 D3 ....51°39'N 35°16'E
Lharigarbo China 98 G4 ....32°15'N 91°43'E
Lhasa China 98 G3 ....29°39'N 91°05'E
Lhazê China 98 F3 ....29°08'N 87°36'E
Lhokseumawe Indonesia 102 B5 ....5°09'N 97°08'E
L'Hospitalet de Llobregat Spain 45 G4 ...41°22'N 2°10'E
Lianshan China 99 M6 ....40°41'N 120°55'E
Lianyungang China 99 L4 ....34°37'N 119°11'E
Liaoning d. China 99 M6 ....41°30'N 122°45'E
Liaoyuan China 99 N6 ....42°54'N 125°08'E
Liard r. Canada 60 F4 ....61°51'N 121°17'W
Libenge Dem. Rep. Congo 83 A5 ....3°37'N 18°42'E
Liberal U.S.A. 62 F4 ....37°03'N 100°57'W
Liberec Czechia 46 F4 ....50°45'N 15°03'E
Liberia Africa 84 D2 ....6°52'N 9°55'W
Libin Belgium 42 E2 ....49°59'N 5°16'E
Libourne France 44 C4 ....44°55'N 0°14'E
Libreville Gabon 84 E2 ....0°28'N 9°27'E
Libya Africa 84 F4 ....26°07'N 17°09'E
Libyan Desert Egypt/Libya 85 G4 ....24°51'N 25°00'E
Libyan Plateau f. Egypt/Libya 49 I3 ......30°59'N 25°49'E
Lichfield England 8 D3 ....52°41'N 1°50'W
Lichinga Mozambique 83 C3 ....13°17'S 35°14'E
Lida Belarus 47 K5 ....53°53'N 25°19'E
Liddel r. Scotland 15 G3 ....55°04'N 2°57'W
Liechtenstein Europe 44 H5 ....47°07'N 9°36'E
Liège Belgium 42 E3 ....50°38'N 5°35'E
Liège d. Belgium 42 E3 ....50°29'N 5°42'E
Lieksa Finland 43 G3 ....63°19'N 30°02'E
Lienz Austria 46 E2 ....46°50'N 12°46'E
Liepāja Latvia 43 E2 ....56°31'N 21°01'E
Liévin France 42 B3 ....50°25'N 2°47'E
Liffey r. Ireland 18 E3 ....53°21'N 6°14'W
Lifford Ireland 18 D4 ....54°50'N 7°29'W
Ligurian Sea France/Italy 44 H3 ....43°30'N 8°50'E
Likasi Dem. Rep. Congo 83 B3 ....10°58'S 26°47'E
Lilla Edet Sweden 43 C2 ....58°08'N 12°08'E
Lille France 44 E7 ....50°38'N 3°04'E
Lillehammer Norway 43 B3 ....61°06'N 10°29'E
Lilleshall England 8 C3 ....52°44'N 2°24'W
Lillestrøm Norway 43 B2 ....59°59'N 11°02'E
Lilongwe Malawi 83 C3 ....13°57'S 33°47'E
Lima Peru 72 B5 ....12°04'S 77°03'W
Limassol Cyprus 51 J2 ....34°41'N 33°02'E
Limavady Northern Ireland 14 C3 ....55°03'N 6°57'W
Limburg d. Belgium 42 E4 ....51°04'N 5°27'E
Limburg d. Neth. 42 E4 ....51°15'N 5°54'E
Limerick Ireland 18 C2 ....52°40'N 8°37'W
Limerick d. Ireland 18 C2 ....52°29'N 8°50'W
Limingen l. Norway 43 C4 ....64°48'N 13°33'E
Limnos i. Greece 50 F4 ....39°51'N 25°21'E
Limoges France 44 D4 ....45°50'N 1°15'E
Limousin f. France 44 D4 ....45°34'N 1°17'E
Limoux France 44 E3 ....43°04'N 2°13'E
Limpopo r. S. Africa/Zimbabwe 83 C2 ...25°13'S 33°32'E
Linares Spain 45 D3 ....38°06'N 3°37'W
Lincoln England 13 G2 ....53°14'N 0°32'W
Lincoln U.S.A. 62 G5 ....40°51'N 96°40'W
Lincolnshire d. England 21 E3 ....53°07'N 0°14'W
Lincolnshire Wolds hills England 13 G2 ...53°30'N 0°19'W
Lindesnes c. Norway 43 A2 ....58°00'N 7°06'E
Lindfield England 9 E2 ....51°01'N 0°05'W
Lindi Tanzania 83 C4 ....9°59'S 39°40'E
Lindos Greece 51 H3 ....36°05'N 28°05'E
Line Islands Kiribati 116 B3 ....5°19'N 161°36'W
Linfen China 99 K5 ....36°05'N 111°32'E
Lingen Germany 46 B5 ....52°32'N 7°19'E
Lingfield England 9 E2 ....51°11'N 0°01'W
Lingga, Kepulauan is Indonesia 102 D3 ...0°02'S 105°19'E
Linhares Brazil 73 E5 ....19°27'S 40°08'W
Linköping Sweden 43 C2 ....58°25'N 15°38'E
Linlithgow Scotland 15 F3 ....55°58'N 3°36'W
Linney Head Wales 10 B3 ....51°37'N 5°05'W
Linnhe, Loch inlet Scotland 14 D4 ....56°31'N 5°33'W
Linqing China 99 L5 ....36°49'N 115°40'E
Linxia China 99 I5 ....35°31'N 103°04'E
Linz Austria 46 F3 ....48°19'N 14°18'E
Lions, Gulf of France 44 E3 ....43°00'N 3°31'E
Lipari, Isole is Italy 48 F4 ....38°39'N 14°43'E
Lipetsk Russia 53 D3 ....52°37'N 39°36'E
Liphook England 8 E2 ....51°04'N 0°48'W
Lipova Romania 50 D8 ....46°05'N 21°43'E
Lippe r. Germany 42 F4 ....51°39'N 6°36'E
Lisakovsk Kazakhstan 53 G3 ....52°28'N 62°30'E
Lisala Dem. Rep. Congo 83 B5 ....2°10'N 21°32'E
Lisbon Portugal 45 A3 ....38°44'N 9°08'W
Lisburn Northern Ireland 14 C2 ....54°31'N 6°02'W
Lisburn and Castlereagh d. Northern Ireland 21 B4
....54°31'N 6°01'W

Liscannor Bay Ireland 18 B2 .... 52°55'N 9°26'W
Liskeard England 11 C2 .... 50°27'N 4°28'W
Lismore Australia 108 E4 .... 28°47'S 153°19'E
Lismore Ireland 18 D2 .... 52°08'N 7°56'W
Lisnaskea Northern Ireland 14 B2 .... 54°15'N 7°26'W
Liss England 8 E2 .... 51°03'N 0°53'W
Listowel Ireland 18 B2 .... 52°26'N 9°29'W
Lithuania Europe 47 J6 .... 55°29'N 23°45'E
Little Abaco i. Bahamas 67 I6 .... 26°54'N 77°50'W
Little Andaman i. India 97 H3 .... 10°38'N 92°31'E
Little Belt str. Denmark 43 B1 .... 55°15'N 9°47'E
Littleborough England 12 E2 .... 53°39'N 2°06'W
Little Cayman i. Cayman Is 67 H4 .... 19°42'N 80°04'W
Littlehampton England 9 E1 .... 50°49'N 0°33'W
Little Inagua Island Bahamas 67 J5 .... 21°31'N 72°59'W
Little Karoo f. S. Africa 83 B1 .... 33°43'S 20°46'E
Little Minch str. Scotland 16 B2 .... 57°32'N 7°00'W
Little Ouse r. England 9 F3 .... 52°30'N 0°22'E
Littleport England 9 F3 .... 52°27'N 0°19'E
Little Rock town U.S.A. 63 H3 .... 34°46'N 92°18'W
Liupanshui China 99 I3 .... 26°40'N 104°48'E
Liuzhou China 99 J2 .... 24°21'N 109°22'E
Liverpool Canada 63 N5 .... 44°02'N 64°43'W
Liverpool England 12 E2 .... 53°25'N 2°59'W
Livingston Scotland 15 F3 .... 55°54'N 3°31'W
Livingstone Zambia 83 B3 .... 17°52'S 25°52'E
Livorno Italy 48 F5 .... 43°32'N 10°19'E
Lizard England 11 B1 .... 49°58'N 5°12'W
Lizard Point England 11 B1 .... 49°57'N 5°17'W
Ljubljana Slovenia 46 F2 .... 46°03'N 14°30'E
Ljungan r. Sweden 43 D3 .... 62°18'N 17°23'E
Ljungby Sweden 43 C2 .... 56°51'N 13°59'E
Ljusdal Sweden 43 D3 .... 61°50'N 16°06'E
Llanarth Wales 10 C4 .... 52°12'N 4°18'W
Llanbadarn Fawr Wales 10 C4 .... 52°24'N 4°04'W
Llanberis Wales 10 C5 .... 53°07'N 4°08'W
Llandeilo Wales 10 D3 .... 51°53'N 3°59'W
Llandovery Wales 10 D3 .... 51°59'N 3°48'W
Llandrindod Wells Wales 10 D4 .... 52°14'N 3°23'W
Llandudno Wales 10 C5 .... 53°19'N 3°50'W
Llandwrog Wales 10 C5 .... 53°05'N 4°19'W
Llandysul Wales 10 C4 .... 52°03'N 4°18'W
Llanegwad Wales 10 C3 .... 51°52'N 4°09'W
Llanelli Wales 10 C3 .... 51°41'N 4°10'W
Llanes Spain 45 C5 .... 43°25'N 4°44'W
Llanfair Caereinion Wales 10 D4 .... 52°39'N 3°20'W
Llanfairfechan Wales 10 D5 .... 53°15'N 3°58'W
Llanfairpwllgwyngyll Wales 10 C5 .... 53°13'N 4°12'W
Llanfair-yn-neubwll Wales 10 C5 .... 53°16'N 4°32'W
Llanfyllin Wales 10 D4 .... 52°46'N 3°16'W
Llangadog Wales 10 D3 .... 51°56'N 3°53'W
Llangefni Wales 10 C5 .... 53°15'N 4°19'W
Llangeler Wales 10 C4 .... 52°02'N 4°22'W
Llangelynin Wales 10 C4 .... 52°39'N 4°07'W
Llangoed Wales 10 D5 .... 53°18'N 4°05'W
Llangollen Wales 10 D4 .... 52°58'N 3°10'W
Llangurig Wales 10 D4 .... 52°24'N 3°36'W
Llanidloes Wales 10 D4 .... 52°27'N 3°32'W
Llanllwchaiarn Wales 10 D4 .... 52°32'N 3°17'W
Llanllyfni Wales 10 C5 .... 53°03'N 4°17'W
Llanos f. Col./Venez. 72 C7 .... 5°54'N 69°50'W
Llanrumney Wales 11 D3 .... 51°31'N 3°07'W
Llanrwst Wales 10 D5 .... 53°08'N 3°48'W
Llansannan Wales 10 D5 .... 53°11'N 3°36'W
Llantrisant Wales 10 D3 .... 51°33'N 3°22'W
Llantwit Major Wales 11 D3 .... 51°25'N 3°29'W
Llanwnda Wales 10 C5 .... 53°05'N 4°17'W
Llanwnog Wales 10 D4 .... 52°32'N 3°27'W
Llanybydder Wales 10 C4 .... 52°04'N 4°09'W
Llay Wales 10 D5 .... 53°06'N 3°00'W
Lleida Spain 45 F4 .... 41°36'N 0°38'E
Llerena Spain 45 B3 .... 38°15'N 6°01'W
Lleyn Peninsula Wales 10 C4 .... 52°51'N 4°34'W
Lloyd George, Mount Canada 60 F3 .... 57°50'N 124°57'W
Lloydminster Canada 60 G3 .... 53°17'N 110°00'W
Llullaillaco, Volcán vol. Chile 73 C4 .... 24°42'S 68°33'W
Lobamba Swaziland 83 C2 .... 26°26'S 31°12'E
Lobito Angola 83 A3 .... 12°24'S 13°32'E
Lochaline Scotland 14 D4 .... 56°32'N 5°47'W
Lochboisdale Scotland 16 B2 .... 57°09'N 7°19'W
Lochgelly Scotland 15 F4 .... 56°08'N 3°18'W
Lochgilphead Scotland 14 D4 .... 56°02'N 5°26'W
Lochinver Scotland 16 D3 .... 58°09'N 5°14'W
Lochmaben Scotland 15 F3 .... 55°08'N 3°26'W
Lochmaddy Scotland 16 B2 .... 57°36'N 7°10'W
Lochnagar mt. Scotland 17 F1 .... 56°58'N 3°15'W
Lochranza Scotland 14 D3 .... 55°42'N 5°17'W
Lochy, Loch l. Scotland 16 E1 .... 56°56'N 4°58'W
Lockerbie Scotland 15 F3 .... 55°07'N 3°21'W
Loddon England 9 G3 .... 52°32'N 1°29'E
Lodeynoye Pole Russia 52 D4 .... 60°44'N 33°34'E
Lodwar Kenya 85 H2 .... 3°06'N 35°34'E
Łódź Poland 46 H4 .... 51°46'N 19°27'E
Lofoten is Norway 43 C5 .... 68°06'N 12°44'E
Logan, Mount Canada 60 D4 .... 60°40'N 140°02'W
Loggerheads England 8 C3 .... 52°55'N 2°23'W
Logroño Spain 45 D5 .... 42°28'N 2°26'W
Loire r. France 44 B5 .... 47°17'N 2°07'W
Loja Ecuador 72 B6 .... 4°00'S 79°14'W
Lokan tekojärvi resr Finland 43 F4 .... 67°56'N 27°35'E
Lokeren Belgium 42 D4 .... 51°06'N 4°00'E
Løkken Norway 43 B3 .... 63°07'N 9°42'E
Lokoja Nigeria 84 E2 .... 7°49'N 6°44'E
Lolland i. Denmark 43 B1 .... 54°47'N 11°21'E
Lom Bulgaria 50 E6 .... 43°49'N 23°14'E
Lomami r. Dem. Rep. Congo 83 B5 .... 0°47'N 24°17'E
Lombok i. Indonesia 102 F2 .... 9°07'S 116°13'E
Lomé Togo 84 E2 .... 6°09'N 1°13'E
Lommel Belgium 42 E4 .... 51°14'N 5°19'E
Lomond, Loch l. Scotland 14 E4 .... 56°04'N 4°37'W
Łomża Poland 47 J5 .... 53°11'N 22°05'E
London Canada 61 J2 .... 42°59'N 81°14'W
London England 9 E2 .... 51°30'N 0°07'W
Londonderry Northern Ireland 14 B2 ...... 54°59'N 7°20'W
Londonderry, Cape Australia 108 B5 ...... 13°47'S 126°53'E
Long, Loch inlet Scotland 14 E4 .... 56°06'N 4°51'W
Longa, Proliv str. Russia 55 S5 .... 70°10'N 178°17'E
Long Ashton England 8 C2 .... 51°25'N 2°41'W
Long Beach town U.S.A. 62 C3 .... 33°47'N 118°20'W
Long Bennington England 8 E3 .... 52°59'N 0°46'W
Long Eaton England 8 D3 .... 52°54'N 1°16'W
Longford Ireland 18 D3 .... 53°44'N 7°48'W
Longford England 13 F4 .... 53°45'N 2°07'W
Longhorsley England 13 F4 .... 55°15'N 1°46'W
Longhoughton England 13 F4 .... 55°26'N 1°37'W
Long Island Bahamas 67 I5 .... 23°18'N 75°06'W

Long Island U.S.A. 63 L5 .... 40°49'N 72°36'W
Longlac Canada 61 J2 .... 49°47'N 86°33'W
Longridge England 12 E2 .... 53°50'N 2°36'W
Long Stratton England 9 G3 .... 52°29'N 1°14'E
Longton England 12 E2 .... 53°44'N 2°48'W
Longtown England 12 E4 .... 55°00'N 2°58'W
Longuyon France 42 E2 .... 49°27'N 5°37'E
Long Xuyên Vietnam 102 D6 .... 10°20'N 105°25'E
Longyearbyen Arctic Oc. 54 C5 .... 77°59'N 15°44'E
Lons-le-Saunier France 44 F5 .... 46°41'N 5°33'E
Lookout, Cape U.S.A. 63 K3 .... 34°37'N 76°33'W
Loop Head Ireland 18 B2 .... 52°33'N 9°56'W
Lop Nur f. China 98 G6 .... 40°28'N 90°20'E
Lopphavet b. Norway 43 E5 .... 70°21'N 21°03'E
Loralai Pakistan 95 K6 .... 30°21'N 68°43'E
Lorca Spain 45 E2 .... 37°41'N 1°41'W
Lord Howe Island Australia 109 E3 .... 31°26'S 158°57'E
Lorn, Firth of est. Scotland 14 D4 .... 56°15'N 5°54'W
Los Ángeles Chile 73 B3 .... 37°28'S 72°21'W
Los Angeles U.S.A. 62 C3 .... 34°01'N 118°15'W
Los Mochis Mexico 66 C6 .... 25°48'N 108°59'W
Los Roques, Islas is Venezuela 67 K3 .... 11°55'N 66°39'W
Lossie r. Scotland 17 F2 .... 57°43'N 3°17'W
Lossiemouth Scotland 17 F2 .... 57°43'N 3°17'W
Lostwithiel England 11 C2 .... 50°24'N 4°40'W
Lot r. France 44 D4 .... 44°19'N 0°20'E
Loth Scotland 17 G4 .... 59°12'N 2°41'W
Lotta r. Finland/Russia 43 G5 .... 68°40'N 30°14'E
Louangnamtha Laos 102 C8 .... 21°03'N 101°29'E
Louangphabang Laos 102 C7 .... 19°54'N 102°10'E
Loughborough England 8 D3 .... 52°46'N 1°12'W
Loughor r. Wales 10 C3 .... 51°42'N 4°03'W
Loughrea Ireland 18 C3 .... 53°12'N 8°35'W
Loughton England 9 F2 .... 51°39'N 0°04'E
Louisiana d. U.S.A. 63 H3 .... 30°40'N 91°56'W
Louisville U.S.A. 63 I4 .... 38°15'N 85°46'W
Loukhi Russia 43 H4 .... 66°04'N 33°03'E
Lourdes France 44 C3 .... 43°06'N 0°02'W
Louth England 13 G2 .... 53°22'N 0°01'W
Louth d. Ireland 18 E3 .... 53°53'N 6°31'W
Lovech Bulgaria 50 F6 .... 43°09'N 24°42'E
Lovozero Russia 52 D4 .... 68°01'N 34°59'E
Lowell U.S.A. 63 L5 .... 42°39'N 71°19'W
Lower Lough Erne l. Northern Ireland 14 B2
.... 54°29'N 7°51'W
Lowestoft England 9 G3 .... 52°29'N 1°45'E
Loyal, Loch l. Scotland 16 E3 .... 58°25'N 4°22'W
Loyauté, Îles is New Caledonia 109 F4 .. 20°23'S 167°17'E
Loyne, Loch l. Scotland 16 D2 .... 57°06'N 5°05'W
Loznica Serbia 50 C7 .... 44°33'N 19°15'E
Lozova Ukraine 53 D2 .... 49°26'N 35°56'E
Lu'an China 99 L4 .... 31°45'N 116°32'E
Luanda Angola 83 A4 .... 8°50'S 13°14'E
Luarca Spain 45 B5 .... 43°32'N 6°31'W
Luau Angola 83 B3 .... 10°42'S 22°15'E
Lubango Angola 83 A3 .... 14°55'S 13°30'E
Lubartów Poland 47 J4 .... 51°28'N 22°37'E
Lubbock U.S.A. 62 F3 .... 33°38'N 101°51'W
Lübeck Germany 46 D6 .... 53°52'N 10°42'E
Lübecker Bucht b. Germany 46 D6 ...... 54°03'N 10°47'E
Lubin Poland 46 G4 .... 51°24'N 16°13'E
Lublin Poland 47 J4 .... 51°14'N 22°35'E
Lubnaig, Loch l. Scotland 14 E4 .... 56°18'N 4°19'W
Lubny Ukraine 47 O4 .... 50°01'N 33°00'E
Lubuklinggau Indonesia 102 C3 .... 3°23'S 102°56'E
Lubumbashi Dem. Rep. Congo 83 B3 .. 11°40'S 27°29'E
Lubutu Dem. Rep. Congo 83 B4 .... 0°44'S 26°35'E
Lucan Ireland 10 A5 .... 53°21'N 6°27'W
Luce Bay Scotland 14 E2 .... 54°47'N 4°52'W
Lucena Phil. 103 G6 .... 13°56'N 121°36'E
Lucena Spain 45 C2 .... 37°25'N 4°29'W
Lučenec Slovakia 46 H3 .... 48°21'N 19°41'E
Lucerne Switz. 46 C2 .... 47°03'N 8°18'E
Lucknow India 96 F5 .... 26°51'N 80°58'E
Lüderitz Namibia 83 A2 .... 26°40'S 15°09'E
Ludgershall England 8 D2 .... 51°15'N 1°37'W
Ludhiana India 96 E7 .... 30°54'N 75°53'E
Ludlow England 8 C3 .... 52°22'N 2°43'W
Ludvika Sweden 43 C3 .... 60°09'N 15°12'E
Ludwigsburg Germany 46 C3 .... 48°54'N 9°12'E
Ludwigshafen am Rhein Germany 46 C3
.... 49°28'N 8°26'E
Ludwigslust Germany 46 D5 .... 53°20'N 11°30'E
Luena Angola 83 A3 .... 11°47'S 19°54'E
Lufeng China 99 L2 .... 22°58'N 115°41'E
Lufkin U.S.A. 63 H3 .... 31°21'N 94°44'W
Luga Russia 43 G2 .... 58°43'N 29°51'E
Luga r. Russia 43 G2 .... 59°40'N 28°18'E
Lugano Switz. 46 C2 .... 46°01'N 8°57'E
Lugg r. Wales 10 E4 .... 52°02'N 2°38'W
Lugo Spain 45 B5 .... 43°01'N 7°33'W
Lugoj Romania 50 D7 .... 45°42'N 21°55'E
Luhans'k Ukraine 53 D2 .... 48°33'N 39°19'E
Luichart, Loch l. Scotland 16 E2 .... 57°37'N 4°48'W
Luing i. Scotland 14 D4 .... 56°14'N 5°39'W
Łuków Poland 47 J4 .... 51°56'N 22°24'E
Luleå Sweden 43 E4 .... 65°35'N 22°10'E
Luleälven r. Sweden 43 E4 .... 65°35'N 22°03'E
Lüleburgaz Turkey 50 G5 .... 41°25'N 27°21'E
Lumberton U.S.A. 63 K3 .... 34°36'N 79°05'W
Lunan Bay Scotland 17 G1 .... 56°39'N 2°30'W
Lund Sweden 43 C1 .... 55°42'N 13°12'E
Lundy i. England 11 C3 .... 51°11'N 4°39'W
Lune r. England 12 E3 .... 54°03'N 2°49'W
Lüneburg Germany 46 D5 .... 53°15'N 10°25'E
Lunéville France 44 G6 .... 48°36'N 6°30'E
Luninyets Belarus 47 L5 .... 52°14'N 26°48'E
Luoyang China 99 K4 .... 34°38'N 112°27'E
Lure France 44 G5 .... 47°41'N 6°30'E
Lurgainn, Loch l. Scotland 16 D3 ...... 58°02'N 5°14'W
Lurgan Northern Ireland 14 C2 .... 54°27'N 6°19'W
Lusaka Zambia 83 B3 .... 15°23'S 28°16'E
Lushnjë Albania 50 C5 .... 40°57'N 19°42'E
Lut, Dasht-e des. Iran 95 I6 .... 30°47'N 58°45'E
Lutherstadt Wittenberg Germany 46 E4 51°53'N 12°39'E
Luton England 9 E2 .... 51°53'N 0°25'W
Luton d. England 21 E2 .... 51°54'N 0°25'W
Luts'k Ukraine 47 K4 .... 50°45'N 25°21'E
Lutterworth England 8 D3 .... 52°27'N 1°12'W
Luxembourg Europe 42 E2 .... 49°49'N 6°01'E
Luxembourg town Lux. 42 F2 .... 49°36'N 6°08'E
Luxor Egypt 85 H4 .... 25°43'N 32°38'E
Luza Russia 52 E4 .... 60°38'N 47°16'E
Luziânia Brazil 72 E5 .... 16°17'S 47°53'W
Luzon i. Phil. 103 G7 .... 15°24'N 122°02'E

Luzon Strait Phil. 102 G8 .... 20°19'N 121°07'E
L'viv Ukraine 47 K3 .... 49°50'N 24°02'E
Lycksele Sweden 43 D4 .... 64°36'N 18°41'E
Lydd England 9 F1 .... 50°57'N 0°55'E
Lydford England 11 C2 .... 50°39'N 4°06'W
Lydney England 8 C2 .... 51°44'N 2°32'W
Lyme Bay England 8 C1 .... 50°39'N 2°59'W
Lyme Regis England 8 C1 .... 50°43'N 2°56'W
Lymington England 8 D1 .... 50°45'N 1°33'W
Lynchburg U.S.A. 63 K4 .... 37°24'N 79°09'W
Lyndhurst England 8 D1 .... 50°52'N 1°35'W
Lynmouth England 11 D3 .... 51°14'N 3°50'W
Lynn Lake town Canada 60 H3 .... 56°51'N 101°03'W
Lynton England 11 D3 .... 51°14'N 3°50'W
Lyon France 44 F4 .... 45°45'N 4°52'E
Lyon r. Scotland 17 F1 .... 56°37'N 3°58'W
Lys'va Russia 52 F3 .... 58°08'N 57°48'E
Lysychans'k Ukraine 53 D2 .... 48°55'N 38°26'E
Lysyye Gory Russia 53 E3 .... 51°31'N 44°49'E
Lytchett Minster England 8 C1 .... 50°44'N 2°03'W
Lytham St Anne's England 12 D2 .... 53°45'N 3°02'W

M

Ma'ān Jordan 94 E6 .... 30°12'N 35°43'E
Ma'arrat an Nu'mān Syria 51 L2 .... 35°39'N 36°40'E
Maas r. Neth. 42 D4 .... 51°43'N 4°53'E
Maaseik Belgium 42 E4 .... 51°05'N 5°48'E
Maastricht Neth. 42 E3 .... 50°51'N 5°41'E
Mabalane Mozambique 83 C2 .... 23°50'S 32°37'E
Mablethorpe England 13 H2 .... 53°20'N 0°16'E
Macao China 99 K2 .... 22°15'N 113°34'E
Macassar Strait Indonesia 102 F3 ...... 3°55'S 117°24'E
Macclesfield England 12 E2 .... 53°16'N 2°07'W
MacDonnell Ranges mts Australia 108 C4 23°33'S 131°18'E
Macduff Scotland 17 G2 .... 57°40'N 2°30'W
Macedo de Cavaleiros Portugal 45 B4 . 41°32'N 6°57'W
Macedonia Europe 50 D5 .... 41°31'N 21°46'E
Maceió Brazil 72 F6 .... 9°36'S 35°40'W
Macgillycuddy's Reeks mts Ireland 18 B1 51°57'N 9°52'W
Mach Pakistan 96 C6 .... 29°52'N 67°28'E
Machala Ecuador 72 B6 .... 3°17'S 79°57'W
Machilipatnam India 96 F4 .... 16°11'N 81°10'E
Machrihanish Scotland 14 D3 .... 55°25'N 5°44'W
Machynlleth Wales 10 D4 .... 52°35'N 3°51'W
Mackay Australia 108 D4 .... 21°10'S 149°11'E
Mackay, Lake Australia 108 B4 .... 22°36'S 128°28'E
Mackenzie r. Canada 60 E4 .... 69°15'N 134°11'W
Mackenzie King Island Canada 60 G5 . 77°42'N 111°56'W
Mackenzie Mountains Canada 60 E4 ... 65°04'N 133°03'W
MacLeod, Lake Australia 108 A4 .... 24°08'S 113°43'E
Mâcon France 44 F5 .... 46°19'N 4°50'E
Macon U.S.A. 63 J3 .... 32°53'N 83°37'W
Macroom Ireland 18 C1 .... 51°54'N 8°58'W
Madadeni S. Africa 83 C2 .... 27°45'S 30°02'E
Madagascar Africa 83 D3 .... 19°57'S 46°27'E
Madeira r. Brazil 72 C6 .... 3°23'S 58°47'W
Madeira is N. Atlantic Oc. 84 C5 .... 33°15'N 16°57'W
Madeley England 8 C3 .... 52°38'N 2°26'W
Madera Mexico 66 C6 .... 29°11'N 108°11'W
Madhya Pradesh d. India 96 E5 .... 23°32'N 78°56'E
Madison U.S.A. 63 I5 .... 43°04'N 89°23'W
Madona Latvia 47 L7 .... 56°51'N 26°13'E
Madrakah, Ra's c. Oman 95 I3 .... 19°01'N 57°51'E
Madre, Laguna lagoon Mexico 66 E6 .. 25°06'N 97°37'W
Madre, Sierra mts C. America 56 F2 ... 15°00'N 90°00'W
Madre de Dios r. Peru 72 C5 .... 10°59'S 66°07'W
Madre del Sur, Sierra mts Mexico 66 D4 18°07'N 101°24'W
Madre Occidental, Sierra mts Mexico 66 C6
.... 28°46'N 108°51'W
Madre Oriental, Sierra mts Mexico 66 D6
.... 26°41'N 101°44'W
Madrid Spain 45 D4 .... 40°26'N 3°40'W
Madura i. Indonesia 102 E2 .... 7°02'S 113°11'E
Madurai India 96 E2 .... 9°55'N 78°07'E
Maebashi Japan 104 C3 .... 36°23'N 139°04'E
Maesteg Wales 10 D3 .... 51°36'N 3°40'W
Maestra, Sierra mts Cuba 67 I4 .... 19°54'N 77°33'W
Mafia Island Tanzania 83 C4 .... 7°48'S 39°52'E
Mafraq Jordan 94 E6 .... 32°20'N 36°13'E
Magadan Russia 55 Q3 .... 59°38'N 151°00'E
Magdalena r. Colombia 72 B8 .... 11°06'N 74°52'W
Magdalena Mexico 66 B7 .... 30°38'N 110°59'W
Magdeburg Germany 46 D5 .... 52°07'N 11°38'E
Magellan, Strait of Chile 73 B1 .... 53°42'S 71°59'W
Magerøya i. Norway 43 F5 .... 70°59'N 25°50'E
Maggiorasca, Monte mt. Italy 46 C1 .. 44°33'N 9°30'E
Maggiore, Lake Italy 46 C1 .... 45°56'N 8°36'E
Maghera Northern Ireland 14 C2 ...... 54°50'N 6°40'W
Magherafelt Northern Ireland 14 C2 .. 54°45'N 6°36'W
Maghull England 12 E2 .... 53°31'N 2°57'W
Magilligan Point Northern Ireland 14 C3 55°12'N 6°56'W
Magnitogorsk Russia 53 F3 .... 53°24'N 59°08'E
Magway Myanmar 97 H5 .... 20°09'N 94°56'E
Mahābād Iran 95 G7 .... 36°44'N 45°41'E
Mahajanga Madagascar 83 D3 .... 15°41'S 46°21'E
Mahalevona Madagascar 83 D3 .... 15°24'S 49°53'E
Maharashtra d. India 96 E4 .... 19°24'N 75°18'E
Mahé i. Seychelles 85 J1 .... 4°38'S 55°24'E
Mahilyow Belarus 47 N5 .... 53°55'N 30°20'E
Mahón Spain 45 H4 .... 39°53'N 4°17'E
Mahrāt, Jabal mt. Yemen 95 H3 .... 17°07'N 51°07'E
Maicao Colombia 67 J3 .... 11°25'N 72°23'W
Maidenhead England 9 E2 .... 51°31'N 0°43'W
Maidstone England 9 F2 .... 51°16'N 0°31'E
Maiduguri Nigeria 84 F3 .... 11°50'N 13°08'E
Main r. Northern Ireland 14 C2 .... 54°43'N 6°18'W
Mai-Ndombe, Lac l. Dem. Rep. Congo 83 A4
.... 2°15'S 18°22'E
Maine d. U.S.A. 63 M6 .... 45°20'N 69°21'W
Mainland i. Orkn. Scotland 17 F4 ..... 59°04'N 3°15'W
Mainland i. Shetl. Scotland 17 H5 .... 60°21'N 1°17'W
Mainz Germany 46 C4 .... 50°00'N 8°16'E
Maiquetía Venezuela 67 K3 .... 10°32'N 66°56'W
Maíz, Islas del is Nicaragua 67 H3 .... 12°10'N 83°02'W
Maizuru Japan 104 C3 .... 35°28'N 135°24'E
Maja Jezercë mt. Albania 50 C6 ...... 42°26'N 19°50'E
Major, Puig mt. Spain 45 G3 .... 39°48'N 2°49'E
Majorca i. Spain 45 G3 .... 39°57'N 2°43'E
Makale Indonesia 102 F3 .... 3°06'S 119°52'E

Makarska Croatia 50 B6 .... 43°18'N 17°02'E
Makassar Indonesia 102 F2 .... 5°06'S 119°27'E
Makat Kazakhstan 53 F2 .... 47°37'N 53°14'E
Makgadikgadi f. Botswana 83 B2 ...... 20°45'S 25°35'E
Makira i. Solomon Is 109 F5 .... 10°38'S 161°38'E
Makran f. Iran/Pakistan 95 J5 .... 26°29'N 60°27'E
Makurdi Nigeria 84 E2 .... 7°43'N 8°33'E
Mala, Punta pt Panama 67 H2 .... 7°27'N 80°00'W
Malabar Coast f. India 96 D3 .... 12°16'N 74°30'E
Malabo Equat. Guinea 84 E2 .... 3°45'N 8°46'E
Malacca, Strait of Indonesia/Malaysia 102 B5
.... 5°41'N 98°38'E
Maladzyechna Belarus 47 L6 .... 54°18'N 26°52'E
Málaga Spain 45 C2 .... 36°43'N 4°25'W
Malahide Ireland 18 E3 .... 53°27'N 6°09'W
Malaita i. Solomon Is 109 F6 .... 8°58'S 161°09'E
Malakal South Sudan 85 H2 .... 9°30'N 31°40'E
Malakula i. Vanuatu 109 F5 .... 16°16'S 167°19'E
Malang Indonesia 102 E2 .... 7°56'S 112°46'E
Malanje Angola 83 A4 .... 9°33'S 16°23'E
Mälaren l. Sweden 43 D2 .... 59°27'N 17°13'E
Malatya Turkey 51 M4 .... 38°20'N 38°20'E
Malawi Africa 83 C3 .... 11°32'S 33°43'E
Malåyer Iran 95 G6 .... 34°17'N 48°48'E
Malaysia Asia 102 C4/E4 .... 3°39'N 108°45'E
Malbork Poland 46 H6 .... 54°02'N 19°02'E
Maldives Indian Oc. 96 D2 .... 6°09'N 72°23'E
Maldon England 9 F2 .... 51°44'N 0°40'E
Male Maldives 96 D1 .... 4°18'N 73°29'E
Maleas, Akra pt Greece 50 E3 .... 36°26'N 23°12'E
Malgomaj l. Sweden 43 D4 .... 64°44'N 16°15'E
Mali Africa 84 D3 .... 13°54'N 5°34'W
Malili Indonesia 103 G3 .... 2°37'S 121°07'E
Malin Head Ireland 18 D5 .... 55°23'N 7°24'W
Mallaig Scotland 16 D2 .... 57°00'N 5°50'W
Mallawī Egypt 51 M4 .... 27°43'N 30°50'E
Mallow Ireland 18 C2 .... 52°08'N 8°39'W
Malmedy Belgium 42 F3 .... 50°26'N 6°02'E
Malmesbury England 8 C2 .... 51°35'N 2°06'W
Malmö Sweden 43 C1 .... 55°36'N 13°01'E
Måløy Norway 43 A3 .... 61°56'N 5°07'E
Malozemel'skaya Tundra f. Russia 52 F4 67°50'N 50°00'E
Malpas England 8 C3 .... 53°01'N 2°46'W
Malpaso mt. Canary Islands 45 W1 ... 27°44'N 18°01'W
Malpelo, Isla de i. N. Pacific Oc. 68 B4 3°59'N 81°34'W
Malta Europe 48 F4 .... 35°49'N 14°18'E
Maltby England 13 F2 .... 53°25'N 1°12'W
Malton England 13 G3 .... 54°08'N 0°48'W
Malvern Hills England 8 C3 .... 52°04'N 2°20'W
Malyy Anyuy r. Russia 55 R4 .... 68°27'N 161°01'E
Mama r. Russia 55 P4 .... 66°28'N 143°13'E
Mamelodi S. Africa 83 C2 .... 25°42'S 28°23'E
Mamuju Indonesia 102 F3 .... 2°40'S 118°51'E
Man, Isle of i. Irish Sea 14 E2 .... 54°16'N 4°41'W
Manacor Spain 45 G3 .... 39°34'N 3°14'E
Manado Indonesia 103 G4 .... 1°34'N 124°52'E
Managua Nicaragua 67 G3 .... 12°07'N 86°17'W
Manama Bahrain 95 H5 .... 26°12'N 50°35'E
Mananjary Madagascar 83 D2 .... 21°14'S 48°20'E
Manaus Brazil 72 D6 .... 3°04'S 60°00'W
Manavgat Turkey 51 I3 .... 36°48'N 31°26'E
Manchester England 13 E2 .... 53°29'N 2°15'W
Manchuria f. China 99 M7 .... 46°27'N 123°48'E
Mand r. India 95 H5 .... 21°42'N 83°15'E
Mandala, Puncak mt. Indonesia 103 K3 4°43'S 140°21'E
Mandalay Myanmar 97 I5 .... 21°59'N 96°06'E
Mandalgovĭ Mongolia 99 J7 .... 45°42'N 106°19'E
Mangalia Romania 51 H6 .... 43°49'N 28°34'E
Mangaluru India 96 D3 .... 12°53'N 74°51'E
Manguang S. Africa 83 B2 .... 29°09'S 26°16'E
Mangoky r. Madagascar 83 D2 .... 23°25'S 45°25'E
Mangole i. Indonesia 103 H3 .... 1°51'S 125°49'E
Mangotsfield England 8 C2 .... 51°29'N 2°31'W
Manicouagan, Réservoir Canada 61 L3 51°18'N 68°18'W
Maniitsoq Greenland 61 M4 .... 65°26'N 52°55'W
Manila Phil. 103 G6 .... 14°34'N 120°59'E
Manipur d. India 97 H5 .... 24°53'N 93°56'E
Manisa Turkey 50 G4 .... 38°36'N 27°25'E
Manitoba d. Canada 60 I3 .... 53°40'N 98°06'W
Manitoba, Lake Canada 60 I3 .... 51°34'N 99°04'W
Manizales Colombia 72 B7 .... 5°00'N 75°30'W
Manmad India 96 D5 .... 20°15'N 74°30'E
Mannheim Germany 46 C3 .... 49°29'N 8°28'E
Manningtree England 9 G2 .... 51°57'N 1°04'E
Manokwari Indonesia 103 I3 .... 0°52'S 134°06'E
Manorbier Wales 10 C3 .... 51°39'N 4°48'W
Manorhamilton Ireland 18 C4 .... 54°18'N 8°11'W
Manra i. Kiribati 109 H6 .... 4°26'S 171°13'W
Manresa Spain 45 F4 .... 41°43'N 1°50'E
Mansa Zambia 83 B3 .... 11°11'S 28°53'E
Mansel Island Canada 61 K4 .... 62°05'N 79°35'W
Mansfield England 13 F2 .... 53°09'N 1°12'W
Mansfield U.S.A. 63 J5 .... 40°45'N 82°32'W
Manston England 8 C1 .... 50°56'N 2°16'W
Mantua Italy 46 D1 .... 45°09'N 10°47'E
Manukau New Zealand 109 G3 ...... 36°58'S 174°50'E
Manzanares Spain 45 D3 .... 39°00'N 3°21'W
Manzhouli China 99 L7 .... 49°20'N 117°29'E
Maoke, Pegunungan mts Indonesia 103 J3 3°34'S 135°25'E
Mapinhane Mozambique 83 C2 ...... 22°17'S 35°06'E
Maputo Mozambique 83 C2 .... 25°56'S 32°34'E
Maraba Brazil 72 E6 .... 5°23'S 49°08'W
Maracaibo Venezuela 72 B8 .... 10°40'N 71°38'W
Maracaibo, Lake inlet Venezuela 72 B7 9°45'N 71°36'W
Maracaju, Serra de hills Brazil 73 D4 . 21°59'S 55°53'W
Maracay Venezuela 72 C8 .... 10°16'N 67°35'W
Marādah Libya 85 F4 .... 29°12'N 19°12'E
Maradi Niger 84 E3 .... 13°31'N 7°07'E
Marāgheh Iran 95 G7 .... 37°23'N 46°14'E
Marajó, Ilha de i. Brazil 72 E6 ...... 0°45'S 50°38'W
Marand Iran 95 G7 .... 38°26'N 45°46'E
Marañón r. Peru 72 B6 .... 4°27'S 73°30'W
Marathon Canada 63 I6 .... 48°43'N 86°23'W
Marathonas Greece 50 E4 .... 38°09'N 23°58'E
Marazion England 11 B2 .... 50°07'N 5°28'W
Marbella Spain 45 C2 .... 36°31'N 4°52'W
Marburg Germany 46 C4 .... 50°48'N 8°46'E
Marburg S. Africa 83 C1 .... 30°43'S 30°26'E
March England 9 F3 .... 52°33'N 0°05'E
Marche-en-Famenne Belgium 42 E3 50°14'N 5°21'E
Marchtrenk Austria 46 F3 .... 48°12'N 14°07'E
Mardan Pakistan 95 L6 .... 34°14'N 72°04'E
Mar del Plata Argentina 73 D3 ..... 37°59'S 57°35'W
Mardın Turkey 94 F7 .... 37°18'N 40°46'E
Maree, Loch l. Scotland 16 D2 ...... 57°38'N 5°21'W
Maresfield England 9 F1 .... 50°59'N 0°05'E

Margarita, Isla de i. Venezuela 72 C8 ....11°06'N 63°53'W
Margate England 9 G2 ....51°23'N 1°23'E
Margery Hill England 13 F2 ....53°28'N 1°43'W
Märgow, Dasht-e des. Afgh. 95 J6 ....30°27'N 62°22'E
Marhanets' Ukraine 47 P2 ....47°40'N 34°37'E
Marías, Islas is Mexico 66 C5 ....21°25'N 106°33'W
Maria van Diemen, Cape New Zealand 109 G3
.........34°29'S 172°38'E
Ma'rib Yemen 95 G3 ....15°23'N 45°26'E
Maribor Slovenia 46 F2 ....46°32'N 15°40'E
Marie-Galante i. Guadeloupe 67 L4 ....15°56'N 61°14'W
Mariental Namibia 83 A2 ....24°39'S 17°58'E
Mariestad Sweden 43 C2 ....58°43'N 13°50'E
Marijampolė Lithuania 47 J6 ....54°33'N 23°22'E
Marília Brazil 73 E4 ....22°13'S 49°57'W
Mar"ina Horka Belarus 47 M5 ....53°31'N 28°08'E
Maringá Brazil 73 D4 ....23°27'S 51°59'W
Maritime Alps mts France/Italy 44 G4 ....44°16'N 6°56'E
Maritsa r. Bulgaria 50 G5 ....41°43'N 26°20'E
Mariupol' Ukraine 49 K6 ....47°06'N 37°33'E
Marka Somalia 85 I2 ....1°43'N 44°44'E
Markermeer l. Neth. 42 E5 ....52°34'N 5°14'E
Market Deeping England 9 E3 ....52°41'N 0°19'W
Market Drayton England 8 C3 ....52°54'N 2°29'W
Market Harborough England 8 E3 ....52°29'N 0°55'W
Markethill Northern Ireland 14 C2 ....54°17'N 6°31'W
Market Rasen England 13 G2 ....53°23'N 0°20'W
Market Warsop England 13 F2 ....53°12'N 1°09'W
Market Weighton England 13 G2 ....53°52'N 0°40'W
Markha r. Russia 55 M4 ....63°29'N 118°52'E
Marlborough England 8 D2 ....51°25'N 1°44'W
Marlborough Downs hills England 8 D2 ....51°29'N 1°48'W
Marlow England 8 E2 ....51°34'N 0°46'W
Marmande France 44 D4 ....44°31'N 0°10'E
Marmara, Sea of g. Turkey 51 H5 ....40°43'N 28°26'E
Marmaris Turkey 51 H3 ....36°50'N 28°15'E
Marne r. France 44 E6 ....48°49'N 2°25'E
Marne-la-Vallée France 44 E6 ....48°51'N 2°36'E
Maromokotro mt. Madagascar 83 D3 ....14°01'S 48°58'E
Marondera Zimbabwe 83 C3 ....18°13'S 31°34'E
Maroni r. French Guiana 72 D7 ....5°44'N 54°01'W
Maroua Cameroon 84 F3 ....10°37'N 14°19'E
Marple England 13 E2 ....53°24'N 2°04'W
Marquesas Islands French Polynesia 114 B2
.........8°39'S 139°15'W
Marquette U.S.A. 63 I6 ....46°32'N 87°25'W
Marra, Jebel mt. Sudan 85 G3 ....12°54'N 24°11'E
Marrakesh Morocco 84 D5 ....31°39'N 7°58'W
Marra Plateau f. Sudan 94 C4 ....13°24'N 24°25'E
Marsá al 'Alam Egypt 49 J2 ....25°04'N 34°50'E
Marsa al Burayqah Libya 85 F5 ....30°22'N 19°35'E
Marsabit Kenya 85 H1 ....2°20'N 37°59'E
Marsala Italy 48 H4 ....37°48'N 12°26'E
Marsá Maţrūḥ Egypt 85 G5 ....31°20'N 27°16'E
Marseille France 44 F3 ....43°18'N 5°23'E
Marsfjället mt. Sweden 43 C4 ....65°06'N 15°23'E
Märsta Sweden 43 D2 ....59°37'N 17°53'E
Martaban Myanmar 97 I4 ....16°34'N 97°34'E
Martaban, Gulf of Myanmar 97 I4 ....16°20'N 96°57'E
Martapura Indonesia 102 C3 ....4°20'S 104°21'E
Martin Slovakia 46 H3 ....49°04'N 18°55'E
Martinique i. Central America 67 L3 ....14°36'N 60°56'W
Martin Vaz, Islas is S. Atlantic Ocean 68 E2
.........20°30'S 28°51'W
Martock England 8 C1 ....50°58'N 2°46'W
Martok Kazakhstan 53 F3 ....50°43'N 56°28'E
Mary Turkmenistan 95 J7 ....37°34'N 61°52'E
Maryborough Australia 108 E4 ....25°32'S 152°41'E
Maryland d. U.S.A. 63 K4 ....38°39'N 76°30'W
Maryport England 12 D3 ....54°43'N 3°30'W
Masan S. Korea 99 N5 ....35°14'N 128°36'E
Masbate Phil. 103 G6 ....12°20'N 123°37'E
Masbate i. Phil. 103 G6 ....12°20'N 123°36'E
Mascara Algeria 48 D4 ....35°23'N 0°08'E
Maseru Lesotho 83 B2 ....29°19'S 27°29'E
Mashhad Iran 95 I7 ....36°18'N 59°35'E
Mashkel, Hamun-i- f. Pakistan 96 B6 ....28°15'N 63°02'E
Maşīrah, Jazīrat i. Oman 95 I4 ....20°16'N 58°58'E
Maşīrah, Khalīj b. Oman 95 I3 ....19°47'N 58°22'E
Masjed Soleymān Iran 95 G6 ....31°57'N 49°17'E
Mask, Lough l. Ireland 18 B3 ....53°37'N 9°21'W
Mason City U.S.A. 63 H5 ....43°09'N 93°12'W
Massachusetts d. U.S.A. 63 L5 ....42°23'N 72°18'W
Massachusetts Bay U.S.A. 63 L5 ....42°25'N 70°51'W
Massakory Chad 84 F3 ....12°59'N 15°43'E
Massawa Eritrea 85 H3 ....15°36'N 39°27'E
Massif Central mts France 44 E4 ....45°16'N 3°25'E
Mastung Pakistan 95 K5 ....29°45'N 66°56'E
Masuda Japan 104 B2 ....34°40'N 131°50'E
Masvingo Zimbabwe 83 C2 ....20°04'S 30°48'E
Matadi Dem. Rep. Congo 83 A4 ....5°49'S 13°29'E
Matagami Canada 63 K6 ....49°46'N 77°38'W
Matam Senegal 84 C3 ....15°40'N 13°16'W
Matamoros Mexico 66 E6 ....25°53'N 97°34'W
Matanzas Cuba 67 H5 ....23°04'N 81°34'W
Matara Sri Lanka 96 F2 ....5°58'N 80°29'E
Mataram Indonesia 102 F2 ....8°35'S 116°10'E
Mataró Spain 45 G4 ....41°33'N 2°26'E
Matā'utu Wallis and Futuna Is 109 H5 ....13°17'S 176°09'W
Matehuala Mexico 62 F1 ....23°40'N 100°38'W
Mathura India 96 E6 ....27°26'N 77°43'E
Matlock England 13 F2 ....53°08'N 1°33'W
Maţraḥ Oman 95 I4 ....23°37'N 58°32'E
Matsue Japan 104 B3 ....35°28'N 133°03'E
Matsumoto Japan 104 C3 ....36°15'N 137°58'E
Matsusaka Japan 104 C2 ....34°34'N 136°33'E
Matsu Tao i. Taiwan 99 M3 ....26°13'N 120°03'E
Matsuyama Japan 104 B2 ....33°49'N 132°46'E
Matterhorn mt. Italy/Switz. 46 B1 ....45°59'N 7°40'E
Maturín Venezuela 72 C7 ....9°44'N 63°09'W
Maubeuge France 42 C3 ....50°17'N 3°58'E
Mauchline Scotland 14 E3 ....55°31'N 4°23'W
Maughold Head Isle of Man 12 C3 ....54°18'N 4°18'W
Maug Islands N. Mariana Is 103 L8 ....20°02'N 145°16'E
Maumere Indonesia 103 G2 ....8°40'S 122°13'E
Maun Botswana 83 B3 ....19°57'S 23°25'E
Mauritania Africa 84 C3 ....19°51'N 11°35'W
Mauritius country Indian Oc. 79 E1 ....20°10'S 58°00'E
May, Isle of i. Scotland 15 G4 ....56°11'N 2°33'W
Maya r. Russia 55 O4 ....60°26'N 134°33'E
Mayaguana i. Bahamas 67 J5 ....22°23'N 72°56'W
Mayagüez Puerto Rico 67 K4 ....18°12'N 67°08'W
Mayamey Iran 95 I7 ....36°27'N 55°40'E
Mayar hill Scotland 17 F1 ....56°51'N 3°15'W
Maybole Scotland 14 E3 ....55°21'N 4°41'W
Mayen Germany 42 G3 ....50°20'N 7°13'E

Mayenne r. France 44 C5 ....47°30'N 0°32'W
Maykop Russia 53 E2 ....44°36'N 40°07'E
Mayo Canada 60 E4 ....63°37'N 135°54'W
Mayo d. Ireland 18 B3 ....53°46'N 9°13'W
Mayotte i. Africa 83 D3 ....12°59'S 45°09'E
Mazār-e Sharīf Afgh. 95 K7 ....36°43'N 67°07'E
Mazatlán Mexico 66 C5 ....23°14'N 106°27'W
Mažeikiai Lithuania 43 E2 ....56°18'N 22°22'E
Mazyr Belarus 47 M5 ....52°03'N 29°15'E
Mbabane Swaziland 83 C2 ....26°20'S 31°09'E
Mbandaka Dem. Rep. Congo 83 A4 ....0°03'N 18°17'E
M'banza Congo Angola 83 A4 ....6°14'S 14°15'E
Mbarara Uganda 85 H1 ....0°35'S 30°37'E
Mbeya Tanzania 83 C4 ....8°53'S 33°26'E
Mbuji-Mayi Dem. Rep. Congo 83 B4 ....6°06'S 23°36'E
McClintock Channel Canada 60 H5 ....71°10'N 101°39'W
McClure Strait Canada 60 G5 ....74°09'N 114°57'W
McCook U.S.A. 62 F5 ....40°14'N 100°39'W
McGrath U.S.A. 60 C4 ....62°52'N 155°37'W
McKinley, Mount U.S.A. 60 C4 ....63°05'N 150°20'W
Mdantsane S. Africa 83 B1 ....32°58'S 27°48'E
Mead, Lake resr U.S.A. 62 D4 ....36°12'N 114°24'W
Mealasta Island Scotland 16 B3 ....58°05'N 7°10'W
Meall a' Bhuiridh mt. Scotland 16 E1 ....56°37'N 4°51'W
Meath d. Ireland 18 E3 ....53°41'N 6°35'W
Meaux France 44 E6 ....48°58'N 2°53'E
Mecca Saudi Arabia 94 E4 ....21°25'N 39°47'E
Mechelen Belgium 42 D4 ....51°01'N 4°29'E
Mecheria Algeria 48 C3 ....33°33'N 0°19'W
Meckenheim Germany 42 G3 ....50°37'N 7°02'E
Medan Indonesia 102 B4 ....3°38'N 98°40'E
Medellín Colombia 72 B7 ....6°13'N 75°35'W
Meden r. England 13 G2 ....53°25'N 0°59'W
Medenine Tunisia 48 F3 ....33°21'N 10°31'E
Medetsiz Tepe mt. Turkey 51 K3 ....37°24'N 34°37'E
Medicine Hat Canada 60 G3 ....50°03'N 110°41'W
Medina Saudi Arabia 94 E4 ....24°31'N 39°32'E
Medina del Campo Spain 45 C4 ....41°19'N 4°54'W
Mediterranean Sea World 98 D4 ....33°25'N 22°48'E
Mednogorsk Russia 53 F3 ....51°19'N 57°35'E
Medvezh'yegorsk Russia 52 D4 ....62°55'N 34°29'E
Medway r. England 21 F2 ....51°22'N 0°34'E
Medway d. England 9 F2 ....51°21'N 0°27'E
Meerut India 96 E6 ....29°02'N 77°45'E
Megara Greece 50 E4 ....38°00'N 23°21'E
Meghalaya d. India 97 H6 ....25°36'N 91°22'E
Mehrān Iran 95 J6 ....30°59'N 61°31'E
Meiktila Myanmar 97 I5 ....20°50'N 95°53'E
Meiningen Germany 46 D4 ....50°34'N 10°25'E
Meißen Germany 46 E4 ....51°10'N 13°28'E
Meizhou China 99 L2 ....24°17'N 116°09'E
Mek'elē Ethiopia 94 F2 ....13°31'N 39°28'E
Meknès Morocco 84 D5 ....33°53'N 5°30'W
Mekong r. Asia 97 K3 ....10°53'N 105°14'E
Mekong, Mouths of the Vietnam 102 D5 ....9°03'N 106°31'E
Melaka Malaysia 102 C4 ....2°09'N 102°17'E
Melanesia is Pacific Oc. 106 F3 ....10°00'S 165°00'E
Melbourn England 9 F3 ....52°05'N 0°02'E
Melbourne Australia 108 D3 ....37°49'S 144°59'E
Melbourne U.S.A. 63 J2 ....28°01'N 80°43'W
Melby Scotland 17 H5 ....60°18'N 1°40'W
Melilla N. Africa 48 C4 ....35°18'N 2°57'W
Melitopol' Ukraine 47 P2 ....46°51'N 35°22'E
Melksham England 8 C2 ....51°22'N 2°08'W
Melrhir, Chott f. Algeria 84 E5 ....34°15'N 6°23'E
Melrose Scotland 15 G3 ....55°36'N 2°43'W
Meltham England 13 F2 ....53°36'N 1°51'W
Melton Mowbray England 8 E3 ....52°46'N 0°53'W
Melun France 44 E6 ....48°32'N 2°39'E
Melvich Scotland 17 F3 ....58°33'N 3°55'W
Melville Canada 60 H3 ....50°56'N 102°49'W
Melville Bay Greenland 61 L4 ....76°00'N 64°00'W
Melville Island Australia 108 C5 ....11°37'S 130°55'E
Melville Island Canada 60 H5 ....75°14'N 109°26'W
Melville Peninsula Canada 61 J4 ....68°00'N 84°12'W
Melvin, Lough l. Ireland/U.K. 18 C4 ....54°25'N 8°09'W
Memberamo r. Indonesia 103 J3 ....1°32'S 137°52'E
Memmingen Germany 46 D2 ....47°59'N 10°11'E
Memphis U.S.A. 63 H4 ....35°09'N 90°04'W
Mena Ukraine 47 O4 ....51°31'N 32°14'E
Menai Bridge Wales 10 C5 ....53°13'N 4°10'W
Menai Strait Wales 10 C5 ....53°09'N 4°17'W
Mende France 44 E4 ....44°31'N 3°30'E
Mendī Ethiopia 85 H2 ....9°49'N 35°03'E
Mendip Hills England 8 C2 ....51°19'N 2°46'W
Mendoza Argentina 73 C3 ....32°53'S 68°50'W
Menongue Angola 83 A3 ....14°38'S 17°41'E
Mentok Indonesia 102 C3 ....2°01'S 105°12'E
Menzel Bourguiba Tunisia 48 E4 ....37°09'N 9°46'E
Meppel Neth. 42 F5 ....52°42'N 6°11'E
Meppen Germany 42 G5 ....52°41'N 7°18'E
Merano Italy 46 D2 ....46°41'N 11°10'E
Merauke Indonesia 103 K2 ....8°31'S 140°25'E
Mere England 8 C2 ....51°05'N 2°16'W
Merefa Ukraine 47 Q3 ....49°49'N 36°04'E
Mergui Myanmar 97 I3 ....12°27'N 98°37'E
Mergui Archipelago is Myanmar 97 I3 ....11°38'N 97°41'E
Mérida Mexico 66 G5 ....20°59'N 89°37'W
Mérida Spain 45 B3 ....38°56'N 6°20'W
Mérida Venezuela 72 B7 ....8°36'N 71°07'W
Mérida, Cordillera de mts Venezuela 67 J2
.........7°59'N 71°35'W
Meridian U.S.A. 63 I3 ....32°23'N 88°40'W
Merowe Sudan 85 H3 ....18°27'N 31°51'E
Merowe Dam resr. Sudan D3 ....18°30'N 31°55'E
Merrick hill Scotland 14 E3 ....55°08'N 4°28'W
Mersch Lux. 42 F2 ....49°45'N 6°07'E
Mersey est. England 12 E2 ....53°21'N 2°56'W
Merseyside d. England 21 D3 ....53°32'N 3°06'W
Mersin Turkey 51 K3 ....36°49'N 34°37'E
Merthyr Tydfil Wales 10 D3 ....51°45'N 3°23'W
Merthyr Tydfil d. Wales 21 D2 ....51°44'N 3°20'W
Mértola Portugal 45 B2 ....37°38'N 7°39'W
Merzifon Turkey 51 K5 ....40°52'N 35°27'E
Merzig Germany 42 F2 ....49°27'N 6°38'E
Mesolongi Greece 50 D4 ....38°22'N 21°26'E
Mesopotamia f. Iraq 85 I5 ....34°23'N 42°19'E
Messina Italy 48 G4 ....38°11'N 15°33'E
Messiniakos Kolpos b. Greece 50 E3 ....36°51'N 22°03'E
Mesta r. Bulgaria 50 F5 ....41°26'N 24°02'E
Meta r. Col./Venez. 72 C7 ....6°10'N 67°24'W
Metheringham England 13 G2 ....53°08'N 0°23'W
Methwold England 9 F3 ....52°31'N 0°33'E
Metković Croatia 50 B6 ....43°03'N 17°40'E
Metlika Slovenia 46 F1 ....45°39'N 15°19'E

Metz France 44 G6 ....49°07'N 6°11'E
Meuse r. Belgium/France 42 E4 ....51°08'N 5°51'E
Mevagissey England 11 C2 ....50°16'N 4°47'W
Mexborough England 13 F2 ....53°30'N 1°17'W
Mexicali Mexico 66 A7 ....32°39'N 115°28'W
Mexico Central America 66 C5 ....31°47'N 114°01'W
México d. Mexico 66 C4 ....19°38'N 99°46'W
Mexico, Gulf of Mexico/U.S.A. 66 F5 ....22°09'N 95°51'W
Mexico City Mexico 66 E4 ....19°24'N 99°12'W
Meymaneh Afgh. 95 J7 ....35°56'N 64°45'E
Mezen' Russia 52 E4 ....65°50'N 44°18'E
Mezen' r. Russia 52 E4 ....65°50'N 44°18'E
Mezha r. Russia 47 N6 ....55°43'N 31°30'E
Mezquital r. Mexico 66 D5 ....21°52'N 105°29'W
Miami U.S.A. 63 J2 ....25°41'N 80°18'W
Miāndoāb Iran 95 G7 ....36°58'N 46°07'E
Miandrivazo Madagascar 83 D3 ....19°30'S 45°29'E
Mīāneh Iran 95 G7 ....37°24'N 47°40'E
Mianwali Pakistan 95 L6 ....32°32'N 71°34'E
Miass Russia 52 G3 ....54°58'N 60°05'E
Michigan d. U.S.A. 63 I6 ....46°12'N 88°00'W
Michigan, Lake U.S.A. 63 I5 ....43°02'N 87°18'W
Michipicoten Island Canada 63 I6 ....47°41'N 85°48'W
Michipicoten River town Canada 63 J6 ....47°57'N 84°50'W
Michoacán d. Mexico 66 D4 ....18°21'N 102°59'W
Michurinsk Russia 53 E3 ....52°55'N 40°30'E
Micronesia is Pacific Oc. 117 I3 ....11°40'N 147°31'E
Micronesia, Federated States of N. Pacific Oc. 103 K5
.........3°37'N 153°49'E
Mid and East Antrim d. Northern Ireland 20 B4
.........54°53'N 6°14'W
Middlesbrough England 13 F3 ....54°34'N 1°14'W
Middlesbrough d. England 21 E4 ....54°33'N 1°14'W
Middleton England 13 E2 ....53°33'N 2°12'W
Middleton in Teesdale England 13 E3 ....54°38'N 2°05'W
Middleton St George England 13 F3 ....54°31'N 1°28'W
Middlewich England 13 E2 ....53°12'N 2°27'W
Midhurst England 8 E1 ....50°59'N 0°44'W
Midi, Canal du France 44 E3 ....43°14'N 2°32'E
Midland U.S.A. 62 F3 ....32°01'N 101°58'W
Midleton Ireland 18 C1 ....51°55'N 8°10'W
Midlothian d. Scotland 20 D4 ....55°50'N 3°06'W
Mid Ulster d. Northern Ireland 21 B4 ....54°39'N 6°44'W
Miekojärvi l. Finland 43 F4 ....66°34'N 24°25'E
Mielec Poland 47 I4 ....50°17'N 21°26'E
Miercurea Ciuc Romania 50 F8 ....46°22'N 25°48'E
Mikhaylovka Russia 53 E3 ....50°04'N 43°15'E
Mikhaylovskiy Russia 98 D8 ....51°40'N 79°45'E
Mikkeli Finland 43 F3 ....61°41'N 27°17'E
Mikun' Russia 52 F4 ....62°22'N 50°05'E
Milan Italy 46 C1 ....45°28'N 9°11'E
Milas Turkey 51 G3 ....37°18'N 27°46'E
Milborne Port England 8 C1 ....50°58'N 2°28'W
Mildenhall England 9 F3 ....52°21'N 0°31'E
Mildura Australia 108 D3 ....34°12'S 142°11'E
Miles City U.S.A. 62 E6 ....46°25'N 105°47'W
Milford Haven Wales 10 B3 ....51°43'N 5°02'W
Milk r. U.S.A. 62 E6 ....48°03'N 106°19'W
Millárs r. Spain 45 E3 ....39°57'N 0°04'W
Millau France 44 E4 ....44°06'N 3°05'E
Mille Lacs lakes U.S.A. 63 H6 ....46°14'N 93°39'W
Milleur Point Scotland 14 D3 ....55°01'N 5°07'W
Millom England 12 D3 ....54°13'N 3°16'W
Millport Scotland 14 E3 ....55°45'N 4°56'W
Milnthorpe England 12 E3 ....54°14'N 2°46'W
Milos i. Greece 50 F3 ....36°39'N 24°25'E
Milton Keynes England 8 E3 ....52°01'N 0°44'W
Milton Keynes d. England 21 E3 ....52°05'N 0°44'W
Milwaukee U.S.A. 63 I5 ....43°01'N 87°55'W
Mimizan France 44 C4 ....44°12'N 1°14'W
Mīnāb Iran 95 I5 ....27°09'N 57°04'E
Minas Indonesia 97 J1 ....0°52'N 101°30'E
Minatitlán Mexico 66 F4 ....18°01'N 94°33'W
Mindanao i. Phil. 103 H5 ....7°48'N 125°06'E
Mindelo Cape Verde 84 B3 ....16°52'N 24°59'W
Mindoro i. Phil. 103 G6 ....13°05'N 120°52'E
Mindoro Strait Phil. 102 F6 ....12°47'N 119°59'E
Minehead England 11 D3 ....51°12'N 3°29'W
Mingäçevir Azerbaijan 53 E2 ....40°46'N 47°03'E
Mingulay i. Scotland 16 B1 ....56°49'N 7°37'W
Minna Nigeria 84 E2 ....9°38'N 6°32'E
Minneapolis U.S.A. 63 H5 ....44°55'N 93°18'W
Minnesota d. U.S.A. 63 H6 ....47°08'N 92°44'W
Minnesota r. U.S.A. 63 H5 ....44°55'N 93°11'W
Miño r. Portugal/Spain 45 A4 ....41°56'N 8°45'W
Minorca i. Spain 45 G4 ....40°06'N 3°51'E
Minot U.S.A. 62 F6 ....48°13'N 101°18'W
Minsk Belarus 47 M5 ....53°53'N 27°34'E
Minsterley England 8 C3 ....52°38'N 2°55'W
Mintlaw Scotland 17 H2 ....57°31'N 1°59'W
Miranda de Ebro Spain 45 D5 ....42°42'N 2°56'W
Mirandela Portugal 45 B4 ....41°29'N 7°10'W
Mirbāţ Oman 95 H3 ....17°02'N 54°43'E
Miri Malaysia 102 E4 ....4°27'N 114°01'E
Mirim, Lagoa l. Brazil/Uruguay 73 D3 ....32°40'S 52°59'W
Mirnyy Russia 55 M4 ....62°25'N 114°10'E
Mirpur Khas Pakistan 96 C6 ....25°32'N 69°04'E
Mirzapur India 96 F6 ....25°06'N 82°39'E
Miskitos, Cayos is Nicaragua 67 H3 ....14°24'N 82°44'W
Miskolc Hungary 46 I3 ....48°06'N 20°48'E
Misoöl i. Indonesia 103 I3 ....1°53'S 130°06'E
Mişrātah Libya 48 F3 ....32°23'N 15°04'E
Missinaibi r. Canada 61 J3 ....50°45'N 81°31'W
Mississippi d. U.S.A. 63 I3 ....32°33'N 89°45'W
Mississippi r. U.S.A. 63 H2 ....29°07'N 89°17'W
Mississippi Delta U.S.A. 63 I2 ....29°05'N 89°06'W
Missoula U.S.A. 62 D6 ....46°53'N 113°58'W
Missouri d. U.S.A. 63 H4 ....38°27'N 92°10'W
Missouri r. U.S.A. 63 H4 ....38°50'N 90°09'W
Mistassini, Lac l. Canada 61 K3 ....50°11'N 73°34'W
Mistelbach Canada 61 K3 ....50°13'N 73°48'W
Mitchell r. Australia 108 D5 ....15°14'S 141°37'E
Mitchell U.S.A. 62 G5 ....43°42'N 98°02'W
Mitchell, Mount U.S.A. 63 J4 ....35°51'N 82°20'W
Mitchelstown Ireland 18 C2 ....52°16'N 8°16'W
Mito Japan 104 D3 ....36°23'N 140°28'E
Mittimatalik Canada 108 C3 ....72°42'N 78°00'W
Mitumba, Chaîne des mts Dem. Rep. Congo 83 B3
.........11°46'S 26°06'E
Miyako Japan 104 D3 ....39°38'N 141°57'E
Miyazaki Japan 104 B2 ....31°54'N 131°25'E
Mizdah Libya 48 F3 ....31°26'N 12°59'E
Mizen Head Cork Ireland 18 B1 ....51°26'N 9°49'W
Mizen Head Wick. Ireland 18 E2 ....52°51'N 6°03'W
Mizoram d. India 97 H5 ....23°27'N 92°50'E
Mjölby Sweden 43 C2 ....58°20'N 15°08'E
Mława Poland 46 I5 ....53°07'N 20°23'E

Mljet i. Croatia 50 B6 ....42°44'N 17°27'E
Mmabatho S. Africa 83 B2 ....25°47'S 25°37'E
Mobile U.S.A. 63 I3 ....30°40'N 88°04'W
Mobile Bay U.S.A. 63 I3 ....30°24'N 88°01'W
Mobridge U.S.A. 62 F6 ....45°32'N 100°25'W
Moçambique Mozambique 83 D3 ....15°05'S 40°41'E
Mocha Yemen 94 F2 ....13°20'N 43°12'E
Mochudi Botswana 83 B2 ....24°25'S 26°08'E
Mocuba Mozambique 83 C3 ....16°53'S 36°58'E
Modbury England 11 D2 ....50°21'N 3°53'W
Modena Italy 46 D1 ....44°39'N 10°56'E
Moelfre Wales 10 C5 ....53°21'N 4°14'W
Moel Sych hill Wales 10 D4 ....52°53'N 3°23'W
Moffat Scotland 15 F3 ....55°20'N 3°26'W
Mogadishu Somalia 85 I2 ....2°04'N 45°20'E
Mohawk r. U.S.A. 63 L5 ....42°46'N 73°44'W
Mohyliv Podil's'kyy Ukraine 47 L3 ....48°27'N 27°48'E
Mo i Rana Norway 43 C4 ....66°19'N 14°10'E
Mold Wales 10 D5 ....53°10'N 3°08'W
Molde Norway 43 A3 ....62°44'N 7°10'E
Moldova Europe 49 I6 ....46°59'N 28°55'E
Moldoveanu, Vârful mt. Romania 50 F7 ....45°36'N 24°45'E
Molopo watercourse Botswana/S. Africa 83 B2
.........28°32'S 20°13'E
Moluccas is Indonesia 103 H3 ....0°30'S 127°26'E
Molucca Sea Indonesia 103 H3 ....1°08'S 125°11'E
Mombasa Kenya 85 H1 ....3°59'S 39°40'E
Møn i. Denmark 43 C1 ....55°00'N 12°22'E
Mona, Isla i. Puerto Rico 67 K4 ....18°04'N 67°52'W
Monach, Sound of str. Scotland 16 B2 ....57°33'N 7°39'W
Monach Islands Scotland 16 B2 ....57°32'N 7°41'W
Monaco Europe 44 G3 ....43°44'N 7°26'E
Monadhliath Mountains Scotland 17 E2 ....57°04'N 4°31'W
Monaghan Ireland 18 E4 ....54°15'N 6°57'W
Monaghan d. Ireland 18 E4 ....54°10'N 6°59'W
Mona Passage str. Dom. Rep./Puerto Rico 67 K4
.........18°01'N 68°06'W
Monar, Loch l. Scotland 16 D2 ....57°25'N 5°08'W
Monbetsu Japan 104 D4 ....44°21'N 143°21'E
Monchegorsk Russia 43 H4 ....67°57'N 32°56'E
Mönchengladbach Germany 42 F4 ....51°12'N 6°25'E
Monclova Mexico 66 D6 ....26°53'N 101°30'W
Moncton Canada 61 L2 ....46°04'N 64°47'W
Mondego r. Portugal 45 A4 ....40°10'N 8°39'W
Mondovì Italy 46 B1 ....44°23'N 7°49'E
Moneymore Northern Ireland 14 C2 ....54°41'N 6°40'W
Monforte de Lemos Spain 45 B5 ....42°32'N 7°30'W
Monga Dem. Rep. Congo 83 B5 ....4°11'N 22°50'E
Mongolia Asia 99 I7 ....46°59'N 103°48'E
Mongora Pakistan 95 L6 ....34°46'N 72°30'E
Mongu Zambia 83 B3 ....15°15'S 23°08'E
Moniaive Scotland 15 F3 ....55°12'N 3°55'V
Monmouth Wales 10 E3 ....51°49'N 2°43'W
Monmouthshire d. Wales 21 D2 ....51°47'N 2°58'W
Monnow r. U.K. 8 C2 ....51°49'N 2°43'W
Monroe U.S.A. 63 H3 ....32°30'N 92°06'W
Monrovia Liberia 84 C2 ....6°20'N 10°46'W
Mons Belgium 42 C3 ....50°27'N 3°57'E
Montana Bulgaria 50 E6 ....43°25'N 23°13'E
Montana d. U.S.A. 62 E6 ....46°44'N 109°17'W
Montargis France 44 E5 ....47°59'N 2°44'E
Montauban France 44 D4 ....44°01'N 1°21'E
Montbéliard France 44 G5 ....47°30'N 6°49'E
Mont-de-Marsan France 44 C3 ....43°53'N 0°30'W
Monte-Carlo Monaco 44 G3 ....43°44'N 7°25'E
Montego Bay town Jamaica 67 I4 ....18°28'N 77°54'W
Montélimar France 44 F4 ....44°33'N 4°45'E
Montemorelos Mexico 66 E6 ....25°11'N 99°49'W
Montenegro Europe 50 C6 ....43°01'N 19°05'E
Montería Colombia 72 B7 ....8°43'N 75°53'W
Monterrey Mexico 66 D6 ....25°42'N 100°18'W
Montes Claros Brazil 72 E5 ....16°42'S 43°49'W
Montevideo Uruguay 73 D3 ....34°52'S 56°13'W
Monte Vista U.S.A. 62 E4 ....37°36'N 106°09'W
Montgomery U.S.A. 63 I3 ....32°23'N 86°19'W
Montgomery Wales 10 D4 ....52°34'N 3°09'W
Mont-Joli Canada 63 M6 ....48°35'N 68°12'W
Montluçon France 44 E5 ....46°21'N 2°36'E
Montmagny Canada 63 L6 ....46°59'N 70°34'W
Montpelier U.S.A. 63 L5 ....44°16'N 72°35'W
Montpellier France 44 E3 ....43°37'N 3°53'E
Montréal Canada 61 K2 ....45°32'N 73°39'W
Montreuil France 9 G1 ....50°28'N 1°46'E
Montrose Scotland 17 G1 ....56°42'N 2°28'W
Montserrat i. Central America 67 L4 ....16°44'N 62°12'W
Monywa Myanmar 97 I5 ....22°05'N 95°13'E
Monza Italy 46 C1 ....45°35'N 9°17'E
Monzón Spain 45 F4 ....41°55'N 0°11'E
Moore, Lake Australia 108 A4 ....29°43'S 117°28'E
Moose r. Canada 61 J3 ....52°20'N 80°31'W
Moose Jaw Canada 60 H3 ....50°26'N 105°33'W
Moosomin Canada 62 F7 ....50°09'N 101°41'W
Moosonee Canada 61 J3 ....51°16'N 80°40'W
Mopti Mali 84 D3 ....14°30'N 4°11'W
Mora Sweden 43 C3 ....61°00'N 14°32'E
Morar, Loch l. Scotland 16 D1 ....56°57'N 5°43'W
Moray d. Scotland 20 D5 ....57°30'N 3°16'W
Moray Firth b. Scotland 17 E2 ....57°31'N 4°11'W
Morbach Germany 42 G2 ....49°48'N 7°06'E
Morden Canada 62 G6 ....49°12'N 98°07'W
More, Loch l. Scotland 16 E3 ....58°18'N 4°53'W
Morecambe England 12 E3 ....54°04'N 2°52'W
Morecambe Bay England 12 D3 ....54°07'N 3°04'W
Moree Australia 108 D4 ....29°28'S 149°52'E
Morehead P.N.G. 103 K2 ....8°44'S 141°39'E
Morelia Mexico 66 D4 ....19°39'N 101°12'W
Morelos d. Mexico 66 E4 ....18°47'N 98°59'W
Morena, Sierra mts Spain 45 B2 ....37°57'N 6°06'W
Moretonhampstead England 11 D2 ....50°40'N 3°46'W
Morgan City U.S.A. 63 H2 ....29°43'N 91°25'W
Mori Japan 104 D4 ....42°06'N 140°34'E
Morioka Japan 104 D3 ....39°42'N 141°08'E
Moriston r. Scotland 16 E2 ....57°13'N 4°36'W
Morlaix France 44 B6 ....48°35'N 3°50'W
Morley England 13 F2 ....53°45'N 1°36'W
Morocco Africa 84 D5 ....31°57'N 5°40'W
Morogoro Tanzania 83 C4 ....6°47'S 37°40'E
Moro Gulf Phil. 103 G5 ....6°59'N 123°21'E
Morombe Madagascar 83 D2 ....21°46'S 43°21'E
Mörön Mongolia 99 I7 ....49°28'N 100°08'E
Morondava Madagascar 83 D2 ....20°18'S 44°17'E
Morón de la Frontera Spain 45 C2 ....37°08'N 5°27'W
Moroni Comoros 83 D3 ....11°39'S 43°14'E
Morotai i. Indonesia 103 H4 ....2°23'N 128°35'E
Morpeth England 13 F4 ....55°10'N 1°41'W
Morriston Wales 10 D3 ....51°40'N 3°56'W
Morro, Punta pt Chile 73 B4 ....27°07'S 70°59'W

Morrosquillo, Golfo de b. Colombia 67 I2.....9°33'N 75°39'W
Morshansk Russia 52 E3..........................53°27'N 41°49'E
Morte Bay England 11 C3..........................51°10'N 4°14'W
Mortehoe England 11 C3..........................51°11'N 4°12'W
Morvern f. Scotland 16 D1.......................56°36'N 5°53'W
Mosborough England 8 F2.........................53°20'N 1°22'W
Moscow Russia 52 D3...............................55°45'N 37°38'E
Moscow U.S.A. 62 C6.............................46°44'N 116°58'W
Mosel r. Germany 42 G3...........................50°22'N 7°36'E
Moselle r. France 44 G4..........................49°27'N 6°22'E
Moshi Tanzania 83 C4...............................3°23'S 37°20'E
Mosjøen Norway 43 C4.............................65°51'N 13°12'E
Mosquitos, Golfo de los b. Panama 67 H2
                                                 8°56'N 81°17'W
Moss Norway 43 B2.................................59°26'N 10°39'E
Mossel Bay town S. Africa 83 B1.................34°11'S 22°08'E
Mossoró Brazil 72 F6................................5°08'S 37°15'W
Mostaganem Algeria 48 D4.......................35°55'N 0°06'E
Mostar Bos. and Herz. 50 B6...................43°20'N 17°49'E
Mosul Iraq 94 F7...................................36°18'N 43°05'E
Møsvatnet l. Norway 43 B2......................59°51'N 8°06'E
Motala Sweden 43 C2.............................58°32'N 15°02'E
Motherwell Scotland 15 F3......................55°48'N 3°59'W
Motril Spain 45 D2.................................36°45'N 3°31'W
Moulins France 44 E5.............................46°34'N 3°20'E
Moulmein Myanmar 97 I4........................16°30'N 97°40'E
Moundou Chad 84 F2...............................8°36'N 16°05'E
Mount Gambier town Australia 108 D3....37°52'S 140°48'E
Mount Isa town Australia 108 C4...........20°45'S 139°29'E
Mountmellick Ireland 18 D3...................53°07'N 7°20'W
Mountrath Ireland 18 D3.......................53°00'N 7°28'W
Mount's Bay England 11 B2....................50°05'N 5°29'W
Mountsorrel England 8 D3......................52°44'N 1°08'W
Mourdi, Dépression du f. Chad 94 B3.....18°01'N 21°06'E
Mourne r. Northern Ireland 14 B2..........54°50'N 7°28'W
Mourne Mountains Northern Ireland 14 C2
                                                 54°06'N 6°11'W
Mousa i. Scotland 17 H5..........................60°00'N 1°11'W
Mouscron Belgium 42 C3.........................50°44'N 3°13'E
Mouzon France 42 E2.............................49°37'N 5°05'E
Moy r. Ireland 18 B4...............................54°07'N 9°08'W
Moyale Ethiopia 85 H2............................3°32'N 39°03'E
Moyen Atlas mts Morocco 48 B3.............32°25'N 5°37'W
Mo'ynoq Uzbekistan 53 F2.....................43°45'N 58°58'E
Mozambique Africa 83 C2......................20°09'S 34°14'E
Mozambique Channel Africa 83 D2........20°15'S 40°16'E
M'Saken Tunisia 48 F4...........................35°43'N 10°35'E
Mtsensk Russia 47 Q5............................53°17'N 36°36'E
Mtwara Tanzania 83 D3...........................10°19'S 40°09'E
Muar Malaysia 102 C4.............................2°02'N 102°34'E
Muarabungo Indonesia 102 C3.............1°27'S 102°08'E
Much Wenlock England 8 C3..................52°36'N 2°33'W
Muck i. Scotland 16 C1..........................56°50'N 6°14'W
Muckish Mountain hill Ireland 14 A3.....55°06'N 8°00'W
Muckle Roe i. Scotland 17 H5................60°21'N 1°25'W
Mudanjiang China 99 N6.......................44°32'N 129°34'E
Mudurnu Turkey 51 I5...........................40°27'N 31°13'E
Mueda Mozambique 83 C3....................11°38'S 39°34'E
Muğla Turkey 51 H3.............................37°12'N 28°21'E
Muhammad Qol Sudan 94 E4................20°54'N 37°07'E
Mühlhausen/Thüringen Germany 46 D4..51°13'N 10°27'E
Muhos Finland 43 F4............................64°48'N 25°58'E
Muine Bheag Ireland 18 E2...................52°42'N 6°58'W
Muirkirk Scotland 15 E3.......................55°31'N 4°04'W
Muirneag hill Scotland 16 C3...............58°22'N 6°18'W
Mukacheve Ukraine 47 J3......................48°27'N 22°43'E
Mukalla Yemen 95 G2...........................14°34'N 49°06'E
Mulanje, Mount Malawi 83 C3.............15°54'S 35°35'E
Mulde r. Germany 46 E4.......................51°52'N 12°15'E
Mulhacén mt. Spain 45 D2...................37°02'N 3°18'W
Mulhouse France 44 G5........................47°45'N 7°20'E
Mull i. Scotland 14 D4.........................56°27'N 5°58'W
Mull, Sound of str. Scotland 14 C4.......56°37'N 6°01'W
Mullaghareirk Mountains Ireland 18 B3..52°22'N 9°17'W
Mullaghcleevaun hill Ireland 10 A5.......53°06'N 6°24'W
Mull Head Scotland 17 G4....................59°23'N 2°53'W
Mullingar Ireland 18 D3......................53°31'N 7°20'W
Mull of Galloway c. Scotland 14 E2......54°38'N 4°52'W
Mull of Kintyre hd Scotland 14 D3.......55°17'N 5°50'W
Mull of Oa hd Scotland 14 C3...............55°35'N 6°20'W
Multan Pakistan 96 D7.........................30°12'N 71°35'E
Mumbai India 96 D4............................18°56'N 72°51'E
Muna i. Indonesia 103 G2.....................5°02'S 122°30'E
Muna r. Russia 55 N4..........................67°51'N 123°04'E
Mundesley England 9 G3......................52°53'N 1°26'E
Mundford England 9 F3.......................52°31'N 0°39'E
Munger India 96 G6............................25°22'N 86°28'E
Munich Germany 46 D3.......................48°08'N 11°35'E
Münster Germany 46 B4.....................51°57'N 7°38'E
Muojärvi l. Finland 43 G4...................65°55'N 29°38'E
Muonio Finland 43 E4........................67°57'N 23°40'E
Muonioälven r. Finland/Sweden 43 E4....67°10'N 23°33'E
Murallón, Cerro mt. Chile 73 B2...........49°50'S 73°27'W
Murashi Russia 52 E3..........................59°24'N 48°58'E
Murchison watercourse Australia 108 A4..27°39'S 114°09'E
Murcia Spain 45 E2............................37°59'N 1°06'W
Mureşul r. Romania 50 D8....................46°11'N 20°29'E
Muret France 44 D3............................43°28'N 1°20'E
Müritz l. Germany 46 E5.....................53°25'N 12°43'E
Murmansk Russia 52 D4.....................68°57'N 33°07'E
Murmanskiy Bereg f. Russia 52 D4.....67°00'N 38°00'E
Murom Russia 52 E3...........................55°34'N 42°04'E
Muroran Japan 104 D4........................42°19'N 140°58'E
Murray r. Australia 108 C3...................35°22'S 139°18'E
Murray Bridge Australia 108 C3..........35°07'S 139°17'E
Murrumbidgee r. Australia 108 D3.......34°42'S 143°13'E
Murzūq Libya 84 F4...........................25°54'N 13°55'E
Mürzzuschlag Austria 46 F2...............47°37'N 15°41'E
Musala mt. Bulgaria 50 E6..................42°11'N 23°35'E
Muscat Oman 95 I4.............................23°36'N 58°35'E
Musgrave Ranges mts Australia 108 C4..26°17'S 131°30'E
Muskogee U.S.A. 63 G4.......................35°47'N 95°23'W
Musmar Sudan 94 E3...........................18°13'N 36°40'E
Musoma Tanzania 83 C4.......................1°32'S 33°47'E
Musselburgh Scotland 15 F3..................55°57'N 3°03'W
Mustafakemalpaşa Turkey 51 H5.........40°02'N 28°23'E
Mūṭ Egypt 85 G4...............................25°28'N 28°58'E
Mut Turkey 51 J3...............................36°39'N 33°26'E
Mutare Zimbabwe 83 C3.....................18°58'S 32°39'E
Mutis, Gunung mt. Indonesia 103 G2...9°35'S 124°14'E
Mutsu Japan 104 D4..........................41°17'N 141°10'E
Mutuali Mozambique 83 C3................14°52'S 37°01'E
Muyezerskiy Russia 52 D4..................63°57'N 32°01'E
Muzaffargarh Pakistan 95 L6..............30°03'N 71°14'E
Muzaffarpur India 96 G6...................26°05'N 85°28'E
Mwanza Tanzania 83 C4.......................2°30'S 32°56'E
Mwene-Ditu Dem. Rep. Congo 83 B4....7°01'S 23°27'E

Mweru, Lake Dem. Rep. Congo/Zambia 83 B4
                                                 8°57'S 28°46'E
Myanmar Asia 97 I5...........................22°37'N 95°02'E
Mykolayiv Ukraine 49 J6....................46°57'N 32°02'E
Myla Russia 52 F4.............................65°27'N 50°52'E
Myronivka Ukraine 47 N3....................49°39'N 30°59'E
Myrtle Beach town U.S.A. 63 K3..........33°43'N 78°54'W
Mysuru India 96 E3...........................12°16'N 76°36'E
My Tho Vietnam 102 D6.....................10°20'N 106°23'E
Mytilini Greece 50 G4.......................39°07'N 26°33'E
Mzuzu Malawi 83 C3.........................11°27'S 34°00'E

N

Naas Ireland 18 E3............................53°13'N 6°40'W
Naberezhnyye Chelny Russia 52 F3....55°42'N 52°21'E
Nabeul Tunisia 48 F4.......................36°29'N 10°45'E
Nacala Mozambique 83 D3................14°34'S 40°40'E
Nador Morocco 48 C4......................35°11'N 2°56'W
Nadvoitsy Russia 52 D4...................63°54'N 34°17'E
Nadym Russia 54 I4.........................65°29'N 72°34'E
Næstved Denmark 43 B1..................55°14'N 11°46'E
Nafplio Greece 50 E3.......................37°34'N 22°49'E
Naga Phil. 103 G6...........................13°35'N 123°11'E
Nagaland d. India 97 H6..................26°03'N 94°37'E
Nagano Japan 104 C3......................36°38'N 138°11'E
Nagaoka Japan 104 C3....................37°26'N 138°51'E
Nagaon India 97 H6........................26°19'N 92°42'E
Nagasaki Japan 104 A2....................32°46'N 129°52'E
Nagercoil India 96 E2.......................8°10'N 77°28'E
Nagha Kalat Pakistan 95 K5..............27°23'N 65°13'E
Nagorno-Karabakh d. Azerbaijan 53 E2..40°00'N 46°30'E
Nagoya Japan 104 C3.......................35°10'N 136°53'E
Nagpur India 96 E5..........................21°09'N 79°05'E
Nagurskoye Russia 54 F6.................80°31'N 47°57'E
Nagykanizsa Hungary 46 G2.............46°28'N 16°59'E
Naha Japan 99 N3............................26°12'N 127°39'E
Nahāvand Iran 95 G6.......................34°12'N 48°22'E
Na h-Eileanan Siar d. Scotland 20 B5..57°54'N 6°48'W
Nailsworth England 8 C2................51°42'N 2°13'W
Nain Canada 61 L3...........................56°31'N 61°31'W
Na'īn Iran 95 H6.............................32°50'N 53°03'E
Nairn Scotland 17 F2.......................57°35'N 3°52'W
Nairn r. Scotland 17 F2...................57°35'N 3°52'W
Nairobi Kenya 85 H1........................1°17'S 36°48'E
Najafābād Iran 95 H6......................32°37'N 51°20'E
Najd f. Saudi Arabia 94 F5................26°14'N 40°21'E
Najrān Saudi Arabia 94 F3...............17°34'N 44°17'E
Nakhodka Russia 55 O2...................42°48'N 132°54'E
Nakhon Ratchasima Thailand 102 C6..14°57'N 102°08'E
Nakhon Sawan Thailand 102 C7........15°40'N 100°06'E
Nakhon Si Thammarat Thailand 102 B5..8°25'N 99°58'E
Nakina Canada 63 I7........................50°10'N 86°43'W
Nakonde Zambia 83 C4......................9°21'S 32°42'E
Nakskov Denmark 43 B1...................54°49'N 11°09'E
Nakuru Kenya 85 H1.........................0°16'S 36°05'E
Nal'chik Russia 53 E2.....................43°29'N 43°38'E
Nālūt Libya 84 F5............................31°49'N 10°57'E
Namak, Kavīr-e f. Iran 95 I6............34°26'N 57°32'E
Namakzar-e Shadad f. Iran 95 I6......30°44'N 58°01'E
Namangan Uzbekistan 98 C6.............40°59'N 71°38'E
Nam Co l. China 98 G4....................30°42'N 90°35'E
Nam Đinh Vietnam 102 D8...............20°22'N 106°11'E
Namib Desert Namibia 83 A2............25°21'S 15°06'E
Namibe Angola 83 A3.......................15°11'S 12°10'E
Namibia Africa 83 A2......................23°22'S 15°55'E
Namlea Indonesia 103 H3..................3°14'S 127°05'E
Namp'o N. Korea 99 N5...................38°43'N 125°23'E
Nampula Mozambique 83 C3..............15°10'S 39°13'E
Namsos Norway 43 B4.....................64°28'N 11°31'E
Namur Belgium 42 D3......................50°28'N 4°52'E
Namur d. Belgium 42 D3..................50°16'N 4°53'E
Nan Thailand 102 C7.......................18°47'N 100°47'E
Nanaimo Canada 62 B6....................49°10'N 123°56'W
Nanao Japan 104 C3........................37°03'N 136°58'E
Nanchang China 99 L3....................28°42'N 115°58'E
Nanchong China 99 J4.....................30°46'N 106°04'E
Nancy France 44 G6........................48°42'N 6°11'E
Nanjing China 99 L4.......................32°04'N 118°50'E
Nan Ling mts China 99 K2...............24°59'N 111°08'E
Nanning China 99 J2........................22°49'N 108°24'E
Nanortalik Greenland 61 N4............60°09'N 45°15'W
Nanping China 99 L3......................26°41'N 118°09'E
Nantes France 44 C5........................47°13'N 1°33'W
Nantes à Brest, Canal de France 44 B5..47°42'N 2°07'W
Nantong China 99 M4.....................31°59'N 120°56'E
Nantucket Island U.S.A. 63 M5........41°17'N 69°59'W
Nantwich England 13 E2.................53°04'N 2°31'W
Nant-y-moch Reservoir Wales 10 D4..52°28'N 3°54'W
Nanyang China 99 K4.....................33°01'N 112°35'E
Nao, Cabo de la c. Spain 45 F3.........38°44'N 0°15'E
Napaimiut U.S.A. 60 C4..................61°38'N 158°24'W
Napier New Zealand 109 G3.............39°30'S 176°53'E
Naples Italy 48 F5............................40°51'N 14°15'E
Narberth Wales 10 C3.....................51°48'N 4°45'W
Narbonne France 44 E3....................43°11'N 3°01'E
Narborough Leics. England 8 D3.....52°34'N 1°13'W
Narborough Norf. England 9 F3.......52°41'N 0°35'E
Nares Strait Canada/Greenland 61 K5..79°12'N 71°28'W
Narmada r. India 96 D5...................21°43'N 73°06'E
Narodnaya, Gora mt. Russia 52 F4...65°01'N 60°06'E
Naro-Fominsk Russia 47 Q6............55°22'N 36°45'E
Närpes Finland 43 E3.......................62°29'N 21°21'E
Narva Estonia 43 G2.......................59°22'N 28°11'E
Narvik Norway 43 D5......................68°26'N 17°25'E
Nar'yan-Mar Russia 52 F4...............67°40'N 53°10'E
Naryn Kyrgyzstan 98 D6..................41°19'N 75°56'E
Nashik India 96 D5........................20°00'N 73°52'E
Nashville U.S.A. 63 I4.....................36°11'N 86°46'W
Näsijärvi l. Finland 43 E3...............61°35'N 23°44'E
Nassau Bahamas 67 I6....................25°05'N 77°23'W
Nassau i. Cook Is 109 I5.................11°32'S 165°22'W
Nasser, Lake resr Egypt 85 H4.........23°09'N 33°02'E
Nässjö Sweden 43 C2.....................57°39'N 14°43'E
Nata Botswana 83 B2.....................20°12'S 26°10'E
Natal Brazil 72 F6..........................5°44'S 35°10'W
Natchez U.S.A. 63 H3....................31°35'N 91°24'W
Natron, Lake Tanzania 83 C4.........2°18'S 36°02'E
Natuna, Kepulauan is Indonesia 102 D4..4°12'N 107°23'E
Natuna Besar i. Indonesia 102 D4.....4°04'N 108°28'E
Nauru S. Pacific Oc. 109 F6............0°35'S 166°56'E
Navalmoral de la Mata Spain 45 C3..39°53'N 5°32'W
Navan Ireland 18 E3........................53°39'N 6°41'W
Navapolatsk Belarus 47 M6.............55°32'N 28°40'E
Naver, Loch l. Scotland 17 E3.........58°17'N 4°24'W
Naver r. Scotland 17 E3.................58°31'N 4°13'W

Naver, Loch l. Scotland 17 E3.........58°17'N 4°24'W
Navlya Russia 47 P5........................52°49'N 34°31'E
Navojoa Mexico 66 C6.....................27°04'N 109°32'W
Nawabshah Pakistan 96 C6..............26°13'N 68°25'E
Naxçıvan Azerbaijan 95 G7...............39°13'N 45°24'E
Naxos i. Greece 50 F3......................37°02'N 25°35'E
Nayarit d. Mexico 66 D5...................22°07'N 104°45'W
Nay Pyi Taw Myanmar 97 I4.............19°44'N 96°13'E
Nazareth Israel 49 K3.....................32°40'N 35°18'E
Nazas r. Mexico 66 D6....................25°34'N 104°55'W
Nazilli Turkey 51 H3.......................37°55'N 28°19'E
Nazrēt Ethiopia 85 H2....................8°32'N 39°15'E
Nazwá Oman 95 I4.........................22°56'N 57°31'E
N'dalatando Angola 83 A4..............9°18'S 14°56'E
Ndélé C.A.R. 85 F2..........................8°25'N 20°38'E
Ndeni i. Solomon Is 109 F5.............10°41'S 166°07'E
Ndjamena Chad 84 F3....................12°08'N 15°03'E
Ndola Zambia 83 B3........................12°57'S 28°39'E
Neagh, Lough l. Northern Ireland 14 C2..54°40'N 6°24'W
Nea Liosia Greece 50 E4.................38°04'N 23°42'E
Neapoli Greece 50 E3......................36°31'N 23°04'E
Neath Wales 10 D3.........................51°39'N 3°48'W
Neath r. Wales 10 D3.....................51°39'N 3°49'W
Neath Port Talbot d. Wales 21 D2...51°43'N 3°49'W
Nebitdag Turkmenistan 95 H7.........39°27'N 54°17'E
Neblina, Pico da mt. Brazil 72 C7.....0°49'N 66°13'W
Nebraska d. U.S.A. 62 F5.................41°30'N 100°06'W
Neckar r. Germany 44 H6.................49°31'N 8°27'E
Needham Market England 9 G3........52°09'N 1°03'E
Needles U.S.A. 62 D3......................34°50'N 114°36'W
Nefteyugansk Russia 52 F3..............56°06'N 54°14'E
Nefyn Wales 10 C4.........................52°56'N 4°31'W
Negotin Serbia 50 E7.....................44°13'N 22°33'E
Negra, Punta pt Peru 68 B3.............6°05'S 81°21'W
Negro r. Argentina 73 C2................41°01'S 62°48'W
Negro r. Brazil 72 C6......................3°08'S 59°57'W
Negro, Cabo c. Morocco 45 C1.........35°41'N 5°17'W
Negros i. Phil. 103 G5.....................9°43'N 122°50'E
Neijiang China 99 I3.......................29°35'N 105°04'E
Nei Mongol Zizhiqu d. China 99 I6..40°12'N 103°26'E
Neiße r. Germany/Poland 46 F5........52°04'N 14°46'E
Neiva Colombia 72 B7.....................2°55'N 75°15'W
Nek'emtē Ethiopia 85 H2.................9°06'N 36°32'E
Neksø Denmark 46 F6.....................55°03'N 15°08'E
Nelidovo Russia 47 O7...................56°14'N 32°47'E
Nellore India 96 E3.........................14°29'N 79°59'E
Nelson Canada 60 G2.....................49°29'N 117°17'W
Nelson r. Canada 61 I3....................56°58'N 92°45'W
Nelson England 13 E2.....................53°50'N 2°13'W
Nelson New Zealand 109 G2............41°17'S 173°15'E
Nelspruit S. Africa 83 C2.................25°28'S 30°59'E
Neman r. Russia 47 J6.....................55°02'N 22°02'E
Neman r. Russia 47 J6.....................55°03'N 22°14'E
Nementcha, Monts des mts Algeria 48 E3..34°48'N 6°23'E
Nemuro Japan 104 E4.....................43°17'N 145°30'E
Nenagh Ireland 18 C2....................52°52'N 8°12'W
Nene r. England 9 F3......................52°49'N 0°13'E
Nenjiang China 99 N7.....................49°04'N 125°12'E
Nepal Asia 96 F6............................28°59'N 82°06'E
Nephin hill Ireland 18 B4................54°01'N 9°22'W
Neris r. Lithuania 43 F1..................54°55'N 23°53'E
Ness r. Scotland 17 E2....................57°29'N 4°14'W
Ness, Loch l. Scotland 17 E2...........57°10'N 4°37'W
Neston England 12 D2....................53°17'N 3°04'W
Nestos r. Greece 50 F5....................40°51'N 24°48'E
Netherlands Europe 42 E5...............52°35'N 5°33'E
Netley Abbey England 8 D1............50°52'N 1°19'W
Nettilling Lake Canada 61 K4..........66°30'N 70°39'W
Neubrandenburg Germany 46 E5.....53°33'N 13°15'E
Neufchâteau Belgium 42 E2............49°51'N 5°27'E
Neumünster Germany 46 C6............54°05'N 9°59'E
Neunkirchen Germany 42 G2..........49°21'N 7°10'E
Neuquén Argentina 73 C3...............38°57'S 68°03'W
Neuruppin Germany 46 E5.............52°56'N 12°48'E
Neustrelitz Germany 46 E5.............53°22'N 13°04'E
Neuwied Germany 46 B4................50°26'N 7°28'E
Nevada d. U.S.A. 62 C4..................39°03'N 117°06'W
Nevada, Sierra mts Spain 45 D2.......37°04'N 3°20'W
Nevada, Sierra mts U.S.A. 62 B5......40°07'N 121°00'W
Nevel' Russia 47 M7........................56°01'N 29°55'E
Nevers France 44 E5.......................47°00'N 3°09'E
Nevinnomyssk Russia 49 L5............44°38'N 41°56'E
Nevis, Loch inlet Scotland 16 D2......57°00'N 5°42'W
Nevşehir Turkey 51 K4...................38°37'N 34°43'E
New Addington England 9 E2..........51°21'N 0°01'W
New Alresford England 8 D2...........51°05'N 1°10'W
Newark U.S.A. 63 L5.......................40°44'N 74°24'W
Newark-on-Trent England 13 G2.....53°04'N 0°48'W
New Bern U.S.A. 63 K4...................35°05'N 77°03'W
Newbiggin-by-the-Sea England 13 F4..55°11'N 1°31'W
Newbridge Ireland 18 E3...............53°11'N 6°48'W
Newbridge Wales 10 D3.................51°40'N 3°09'W
New Britain i. P.N.G. 108 D6..........5°42'S 148°56'E
New Brunswick d. Canada 61 L2......46°41'N 66°28'W
Newburgh Scotland 15 F4...............56°21'N 3°14'W
Newbury England 8 D2..................51°24'N 1°19'W
New Caledonia is S. Pacific Oc. 109 F4..21°41'S 167°07'E
Newcastle Australia 108 E3...........32°56'S 151°44'E
Newcastle Northern Ireland 14 D2..54°13'N 5°53'W
Newcastle Emlyn Wales 10 C4........52°02'N 4°28'W
Newcastleton Scotland 15 G3.........55°11'N 2°49'W
Newcastle-under-Lyme England 13 E2..53°01'N 2°13'W
Newcastle West Ireland 18 B2........52°27'N 9°03'W
Newcastle upon Tyne England 13 F3..54°59'N 1°37'W
New Cumnock Scotland 14 E3........55°23'N 4°11'W
New Delhi India 96 E6...................28°36'N 77°17'E
Newent England 8 C2.....................51°56'N 2°24'W
New Forest nature res. England 8 D1..50°52'N 1°37'W
Newfoundland i. Canada 61 M2.......48°30'N 56°04'W
Newfoundland and Labrador d. Canada 61 M3
                                                 55°44'N 56°53'W
New Galloway Scotland 14 E3.........55°05'N 4°08'W
New Georgia Sound str. Solomon Is 108 E6
                                                 7°21'S 156°36'E
New Glasgow Canada 63 N6...........45°35'N 62°35'W
New Guinea i. Indonesia/P.N.G. 103 K2..5°26'S 140°49'E
New Hampshire d. U.S.A. 63 L5.......44°02'N 71°34'W
Newhaven England 9 F1.................50°48'N 0°03'E
New Haven U.S.A. 63 L5.................41°18'N 72°56'W
New Jersey d. U.S.A. 63 L4.............39°57'N 74°26'W
New Ireland i. P.N.G. 108 E6...........3°33'S 152°14'E
New Liskeard Canada 63 K6............47°31'N 79°41'W
Newmarket England 9 F3................52°15'N 0°25'E
Newmarket-on-Fergus Ireland 18 C2..52°46'N 8°53'W
New Mexico d. U.S.A. 62 E3............34°32'N 105°55'W
New Milton England 8 D1...............50°45'N 1°40'W
Newnham England 8 C2..................51°48'N 2°27'W

New Orleans U.S.A. 63 H2...............29°58'N 90°03'W
New Pitsligo Scotland 17 G2............57°36'N 2°12'W
Newport Ess. England 9 F2.............51°59'N 0°13'E
Newport I. o. W. England 8 D1........50°42'N 1°17'W
Newport New. Wales 10 E3.............51°35'N 2°59'W
Newport Pem. Wales 10 C4............52°01'N 4°50'W
Newport Tel. Wre. England 8 C3.....52°46'N 2°22'W
Newport d. Wales 21 D2................51°35'N 2°59'W
Newport Bay Wales 10 C4..............52°02'N 4°53'W
Newport News U.S.A. 63 K4...........37°00'N 76°26'W
Newport Pagnell England 8 E3........52°05'N 0°43'W
New Providence i. Bahamas 67 I6.....25°03'N 77°25'W
Newquay England 11 B2.................50°25'N 5°04'W
New Quay Wales 10 C4..................52°13'N 4°22'W
New Romney England 9 F1.............50°59'N 0°56'E
New Ross Ireland 18 E2..................52°23'N 6°56'W
Newry Northern Ireland 14 C2.........54°10'N 6°19'W
Newry Canal Northern Ireland 14 C2..54°16'N 6°21'E
Newry, Mourne and Down d. Northern Ireland 21 B4
                                                 54°10'N 6°18'W
New Siberia Islands Russia 55 P5.....76°08'N 149°21'E
New South Wales d. Australia 108 D3..32°42'S 146°24'E
Newton Abbot England 11 D2..........50°32'N 3°37'W
Newton Aycliffe England 13 F3........54°37'N 1°34'W
Newtonbutler Northern Ireland 14 B2..54°10'N 7°21'W
Newtonhill Scotland 17 G2..............57°02'N 2°09'W
Newton-le-Willows England 12 E2....53°27'N 2°38'W
Newton Mearns Scotland 14 E3.......55°46'N 4°20'W
Newtonmore Scotland 17 E2............57°04'N 4°07'W
Newton St Cyres England 11 D2......50°46'N 3°35'W
Newton Stewart Scotland 14 E2.......54°58'N 4°29'W
Newtown Wales 10 D4...................52°31'N 3°19'W
Newtownabbey Northern Ireland 14 D2..54°39'N 5°54'W
Newtownards Northern Ireland 14 D2..54°35'N 5°41'W
Newtown St Boswells Scotland 15 G3..55°35'N 2°40'W
Newtownstewart Northern Ireland 14 B2..54°43'N 7°22'W
New York U.S.A. 63 L5...................40°41'N 73°59'W
New York d. U.S.A. 63 K5...............42°43'N 75°14'W
New Zealand Oceania 109 G2..........42°54'S 174°10'E
Neyrīz Iran 95 H5...........................29°12'N 54°19'E
Neyshābūr Iran 95 I7......................36°12'N 58°46'E
Ngaoundéré Cameroon 84 F2..........7°19'N 13°34'E
Ngerulmud Palau 103 I5.................7°30'N 134°39'E
Nguigmi Niger 84 F3.....................14°14'N 13°05'E
Ngulu atoll Micronesia 103 J5..........8°28'N 137°37'E
Nha Trang Vietnam 102 D6............12°11'N 109°11'E
Niamey Niger 84 E3.......................13°31'N 2°07'E
Niangara Dem. Rep. Congo 83 B5....3°40'N 27°52'E
Nias i. Indonesia 102 B4.................1°11'N 97°04'E
Nicaragua Central America 67 G3.....13°13'N 85°57'W
Nicaragua, Lake Nicaragua 67 G3....11°31'N 85°17'W
Nice France 44 G3.........................43°42'N 7°17'E
Nicobar Islands India 97 H2...........8°00'N 93°59'E
Nicosia Cyprus 51 J2......................35°10'N 33°22'E
Nicoya, Golfo de b. Costa Rica 67 H2..9°42'N 84°48'W
Nidd r. England 13 F3....................54°01'N 1°13'W
Nidzica Poland 46 I5......................53°22'N 20°26'E
Niedersachsen d. Germany 42 G5....52°43'N 8°53'E
Nienburg Germany 46 C5...............52°38'N 9°13'E
Niers r. Germany 42 E4..................51°42'N 5°57'E
Nieuwpoort Belgium 42 B4............51°08'N 2°45'E
Nieves, Pico de las mt. Canary Islands 45 Y1
                                                 27°57'N 15°34'W
Niğde Turkey 51 K3.......................37°59'N 34°41'E
Niger Africa 84 E3..........................17°03'N 10°05'E
Niger r. Africa 84 E2.......................4°17'N 6°05'E
Nigeria Africa 84 E2.......................9°09'N 7°54'E
Nigg Bay Scotland 17 E2................57°43'N 4°05'W
Niigata Japan 104 C3.....................37°55'N 139°03'E
Nijmegen Neth. 42 E4....................51°50'N 5°52'E
Nikel' Russia 43 G5.......................69°24'N 30°13'E
Nikol'sk Russia 52 E3....................59°32'N 45°27'E
Nikopol' Ukraine 47 P2..................47°34'N 34°24'E
Niksar Turkey 51 L5.......................40°35'N 36°57'E
Nikšić Montenegro 50 C6...............42°46'N 18°56'E
Nikumaroro atoll Kiribati 109 H6.....4°43'S 174°31'W
Nile r. Africa 85 H5........................30°11'N 31°06'E
Nile Delta Egypt 94 D6..................30°50'N 31°00'E
Nilgiri Hills India 96 E3.................11°08'N 76°28'E
Nîmes France 44 F3........................43°50'N 4°21'E
Ningbo China 99 M3......................29°54'N 121°34'E
Ningxia Huizu Zizhiqu d. China 99 J5..37°11'N 105°28'E
Niobrara r. U.S.A. 62 G5................42°46'N 98°02'W
Nioro Mali 84 D3...........................15°14'N 9°36'W
Niort France 44 C5.........................46°20'N 0°28'W
Nipigon Canada 61 J2....................49°00'N 88°17'W
Nipigon, Lake Canada 61 J2............49°43'N 88°33'W
Nipissing, Lake Canada 63 K6.........46°15'N 79°39'W
Niš Serbia 50 D6...........................43°19'N 21°54'E
Nith r. Scotland 15 F3...................55°02'N 3°36'W
Nitra Slovakia 46 H3......................48°19'N 18°05'E
Niue i. S. Pacific Oc. 109 I5............19°03'S 169°45'W
Nivelles Belgium 42 D3.................50°36'N 4°20'E
Nizamabad India 96 E4..................18°40'N 78°07'E
Nizhnekamsk Russia 52 F3.............55°38'N 51°55'E
Nizhneudinsk Russia 55 K3............54°55'N 98°58'E
Nizhnevartovsk Russia 54 I4...........60°56'N 76°38'E
Nizhniy Tagil Russia 52 F3..............57°56'N 59°56'E
Nizhniy Novgorod Russia 52 E3......56°17'N 43°54'E
Nizhnyaya Tura Russia 52 F3..........58°37'N 59°48'E
Nizhnyaya Tunguska r. Russia 55 J4..65°47'N 87°59'E
Nizhyn Ukraine 47 N4...................51°02'N 31°53'E
Nizip Turkey 51 L3........................36°59'N 37°48'E
Nkongsamba Cameroon 84 E2........4°58'N 9°57'E
Nobeoka Japan 104 B2...................32°34'N 131°41'E
Nogales Mexico 66 B7....................31°19'N 110°57'W
Nogent-le-Rotrou France 44 D6......48°19'N 0°49'E
Nohfelden Germany 42 G2.............49°35'N 7°08'E
Noirmoutier, Île de i. France 44 B5..46°58'N 2°16'W
Nok Kundi Pakistan 95 J5..............28°49'N 62°50'E
Nolinsk Russia 52 F3......................57°33'N 49°57'E
Nome U.S.A. 60 B4........................64°32'N 165°28'W
Nonthaburi Thailand 102 C6...........13°51'N 100°32'E
Noord-Brabant d. Neth. 42 E4........51°32'N 5°01'E
Noord-Holland d. Neth. 42 D5........52°46'N 4°54'E
Nordaustlandet i. Arctic Oc. 54 D5..79°36'N 22°37'E
Norden Germany 42 G6..................53°36'N 7°12'E
Norderney i. Germany 42 G6..........53°44'N 7°19'E
Norderstedt Germany 46 D5...........53°44'N 10°00'E
Nordhorn Germany 42 G5..............52°26'N 7°05'E
Nordhausen Germany 46 D4..........51°30'N 10°47'E
Nordrhein-Westfalen d. Germany 42 G4..51°04'N 7°25'E
Nore r. Ireland 18 E2.....................52°26'N 6°58'W
Norfolk d. England 21 F3................52°44'N 0°59'E
Norfolk U.S.A. 63 K4.....................36°53'N 76°16'W
Norfolk Broads f. England 9 G3.......52°43'N 1°28'E
Norfolk Island S. Pacific Oc. 109 F4..28°59'S 167°59'E

Noril'sk Russia 55 J4 ....69°19'N 88°08'E
Normandy f. France 44 C6 ....48°53'N 0°32'W
Normanton Australia 108 D5 ....17°41'S 141°05'E
Norra Storfjället mts Sweden 43 C4 ....65°53'N 15°07'E
Norrköping Sweden 43 D2 ....58°36'N 16°12'E
Norrtälje Sweden 43 D2 ....59°45'N 18°41'E
Norseman Australia 108 B3 ....32°14'S 121°47'E
Northallerton England 13 F3 ....54°20'N 1°26'W
North America 56
North American Basin f. Atlantic Oc. 116 D3
.........................30°00'N 60°00'W
Northampton England 8 E3 ....52°14'N 0°54'W
Northamptonshire d. England 21 E3 ....52°12'N 0°55'W
North Ayrshire d. Scotland 20 C4 ....55°44'N 4°44'W
North Battleford Canada 60 H3 ....52°46'N 108°17'W
North Bay town Canada 61 K2 ....46°19'N 79°28'W
North Berwick Scotland 15 G4 ....56°04'N 2°43'W
North Cape New Zealand 109 G3 ....34°25'S 173°03'E
North Cape Norway 43 F5 ....71°10'N 25°47'E
North Carolina d. U.S.A. 63 K4 ....36°13'N 79°52'W
North Cave England 13 G2 ....53°47'N 0°39'W
North Channel U.K. 14 C3 ....55°23'N 6°51'W
North China Plain f. China 86 G3 ....34°30'N 117°00'E
North Dakota d. U.S.A. 62 F6 ....47°19'N 100°24'W
North Dorset Downs hills England 8 C1 .....50°46'N 2°32'W
North Downs hills England 9 E2 ....51°14'N 0°58'W
North East Lincolnshire d. England 21 E3 ...53°37'N 0°12'W
Northern Dvina r. Russia 52 E4 ....64°31'N 40°33'E
Northern Ireland d. U.K. 21 B4 ....54°38'N 6°49'W
Northern Mariana Islands N. Pacific Oc. 103 K7
.........................17°15'N 143°32'E
Northern Territory d. Australia 108 C5 ....17°40'S 133°30'E
North Esk r. Scotland 17 G1 ....56°45'N 2°26'W
North European Plain f. Europe 34 G4 ......56°00'N 27°00'E
North Foreland c. England 9 G2 ....51°23'N 1°27'E
North Frisian Islands Germany 46 C6 ....54°52'N 8°02'E
North Harris f. Scotland 16 C2 ....57°59'N 6°48'W
North Hykeham England 13 G2 ....53°11'N 0°35'W
North Island New Zealand 109 G3 ....38°11'S 173°23'E
North Korea Asia 99 N6 ....40°01'N 126°39'E
North Lanarkshire d. Scotland 20 D4 ....55°53'N 3°57'W
North Lincolnshire d. England 21 E3 ....53°37'N 0°35'W
North Platte U.S.A. 62 F5 ....41°09'N 100°46'W
North Platte r. U.S.A. 62 F5 ....41°10'N 100°48'W
North Ronaldsay i. Scotland 17 G4 ....59°24'N 2°26'W
North Ronaldsay Firth str. Scotland 17 G4 ...59°20'N 2°29'W
North Saskatchewan r. Canada 60 H3 ......53°13'N 105°11'W
North Sea Europe 34 E4 ....56°00'N 4°00'E
North Shields England 13 F4 ....55°01'N 1°27'W
North Siberian Lowland f. Russia 55 L5 .....73°26'N 103°17'E
North Somercotes England 13 H2 ....53°27'N 0°09'E
North Somerset d. England 21 D2 ....51°24'N 2°48'W
North Sunderland England 13 F4 ....55°35'N 1°39'W
North Tidworth England 8 D2 ....51°14'N 1°40'W
North Tyne r. England 13 E3 ....54°59'N 2°08'W
North Ugie r. Scotland 17 H2 ....57°32'N 1°55'W
North Uist i. Scotland 16 B2 ....57°37'N 7°26'W
Northumberland d. England 20 D4 ....55°09'N 2°35'W
Northumberland Strait Canada 63 N6 ....46°50'N 64°23'W
North Walsham England 9 G3 ....52°49'N 1°23'E
North West Cape Australia 108 A4 ....21°49'S 114°12'E
Northwest Territories d. Canada 60 H4 .....63°48'N 105°17'W
Northwich England 13 E2 ....53°16'N 2°31'W
North York Moors f. England 13 G3 ....54°23'N 0°50'W
North Yorkshire d. England 21 E4 ....54°12'N 1°59'W
Norton England 13 G3 ....54°08'N 0°47'W
Norton Fitzwarren England 11 D3 ....51°02'N 3°08'W
Norton Sound str. U.S.A. 60 B4 ....63°58'N 163°01'W
Norway Europe 43 B3 ....62°46'N 10°30'E
Norway House Canada 60 I3 ....53°56'N 97°52'W
Norwegian Sea N. Atlantic Oc. 34 D5 ......66°00'N 2°00'E
Norwich England 9 G3 ....52°38'N 1°18'E
Noshiro Japan 104 D4 ....40°12'N 140°01'E
Nosovaya Russia 52 F4 ....68°15'N 54°35'E
Noss, Isle of i. Scotland 17 H5 ....60°09'N 1°00'W
Nottingham England 8 D3 ....52°57'N 1°09'W
Nottingham d. England 21 E3 ....52°58'N 1°10'W
Nottinghamshire d. England 21 E3 ....53°03'N 0°59'W
Nouâdhibou Mauritania 84 C4 ....21°04'N 17°00'W
Nouâdhibou, Râs c. Mauritania 84 C4 ......20°51'N 17°04'W
Nouakchott Mauritania 84 C3 ....18°06'N 15°58'W
Nouméa New Caledonia 109 F4 ....22°18'S 166°26'E
Noup Head Scotland 17 F4 ....59°20'N 3°04'W
Nova Gradiška Croatia 50 B7 ....45°16'N 17°23'E
Novara Italy 46 C1 ....45°27'N 8°37'E
Nova Scotia d. Canada 61 L2 ....45°53'N 65°45'W
Novaya Sibir', Ostrov i. Russia 55 P5 ....75°04'N 148°22'E
Novaya Zemlya is Russia 54 G5 ....71°41'N 55°45'E
Nové Zámky Slovakia 46 H2 ....47°59'N 18°09'E
Novi Pazar Serbia 50 D6 ....43°08'N 20°30'E
Novi Sad Serbia 50 C7 ....45°16'N 19°51'E
Novoanninskiy Russia 53 E3 ....50°32'N 42°41'E
Novodvinsk Russia 52 E4 ....64°25'N 40°50'E
Novo Hamburgo Brazil 73 D4 ....29°40'S 51°09'W
Novohrad-Volyns'kyy Ukraine 47 L4 ....50°36'N 27°37'E
Novokuznetsk Russia 54 J3 ....53°45'N 87°09'E
Novo Mesto Slovenia 46 F1 ....45°48'N 15°10'E
Novomoskovsk Russia 53 D3 ....54°01'N 38°19'E
Novomoskovs'k Ukraine 47 P3 ....48°38'N 35°14'E
Novooleksiyivka Ukraine 51 K8 ....46°14'N 34°39'E
Novorossiysk Russia 53 D2 ....44°43'N 37°47'E
Novosibirsk Russia 54 J3 ....55°03'N 83°02'E
Novovolyns'k Ukraine 47 K4 ....50°43'N 24°11'E
Novyy Port Russia 54 I4 ....68°13'N 73°02'E
Nowshera Pakistan 95 L6 ....34°00'N 72°01'E
Nowy Sącz Poland 46 I3 ....49°38'N 20°42'E
Noyabr'sk Russia 54 I4 ....63°13'N 75°32'E
Nu'aym f. Oman 95 I4 ....23°14'N 55°59'E
Nuba Mountains Sudan 94 D2 ....11°28'N 30°33'E
Nubian Desert Sudan 85 H4 ....20°25'N 34°58'E
Nudo Coropuna mt. Peru 72 B5 ....15°29'S 72°43'W
Nuevo Casas Grandes Mexico 66 C7 ....30°23'N 107°56'W
Nuevo Laredo Mexico 66 E6 ....27°29'N 99°31'W
Nuevo León d. Mexico 66 E6 ....25°51'N 99°56'W
Nui atoll Tuvalu 109 G6 ....7°12'S 177°12'E
Nuku'alofa Tonga 109 H4 ....21°07'S 175°12'W
Nukufetau atoll Tuvalu 109 G6 ....8°03'S 178°25'E
Nukunonu atoll Tokelau 109 H6 ....9°05'S 171°50'W
Nukus Uzbekistan 54 G2 ....42°27'N 59°36'E
Nullarbor Plain f. Australia 108 B3 ....31°01'S 129°03'E
Numazu Japan 104 C3 ....35°05'N 138°52'E
Nunavut d. Canada 61 I4 ....66°30'N 89°54'W
Nuneaton England 8 D3 ....52°31'N 1°28'W
Nunivak Island U.S.A. 60 B3 ....59°58'N 166°18'W
Nuoro Italy 48 E5 ....40°19'N 9°20'E
Nuqrah Saudi Arabia 94 F5 ....25°36'N 41°26'E
Nuremberg Germany 46 D3 ....49°27'N 11°06'E

Nurmes Finland 43 G3 ....63°33'N 29°07'E
Nushki Pakistan 95 K5 ....29°34'N 66°02'E
Nuuk Greenland 61 M4 ....64°11'N 51°45'W
Nyagan' Russia 52 G4 ....62°09'N 65°24'E
Nyala Sudan 85 G3 ....12°03'N 24°55'E
Nyasa, Lake Africa 83 C4 ....9°59'S 34°05'E
Nyborg Denmark 43 B1 ....55°19'N 10°47'E
Nybro Sweden 43 C2 ....56°44'N 15°55'E
Nyíregyháza Hungary 47 I2 ....47°57'N 21°43'E
Nykarleby Finland 43 E3 ....63°31'N 22°32'E
Nykøbing Falster Denmark 43 B1 ....54°46'N 11°53'E
Nyköping Sweden 43 D2 ....58°45'N 17°01'E
Nynäshamn Sweden 43 D2 ....58°54'N 17°57'E
Nyrob Russia 52 F4 ....60°43'N 56°42'E
Nyurba Russia 55 M4 ....63°17'N 118°17'E
Nyzhn'ohirs'kyy Ukraine 51 K7 ....45°27'N 34°45'E

O

Oadby England 8 D3 ....52°36'N 1°05'W
Oahe, Lake U.S.A. 62 F5 ....44°49'N 100°32'W
Oakengates England 8 C3 ....52°42'N 2°26'W
Oakham England 8 E3 ....52°40'N 0°44'W
Oakland U.S.A. 62 B4 ....37°50'N 122°15'W
Oaxaca Mexico 66 E4 ....17°05'N 96°40'W
Oaxaca d. Mexico 66 E4 ....17°22'N 96°20'W
Ob' r. Russia 52 G4 ....66°47'N 69°08'E
Oban Scotland 14 D4 ....56°25'N 5°28'W
Obi i. Indonesia 103 H3 ....1°33'S 127°41'E
Obihiro Japan 104 D4 ....42°55'N 143°12'E
Obninsk Russia 52 D3 ....55°04'N 36°38'E
Oboyan' Russia 47 Q4 ....51°13'N 36°16'E
Obozerskiy Russia 52 E4 ....63°28'N 40°19'E
Obshchiy Syrt f. Russia 53 F3 ....51°20'N 52°00'E
Obskaya Guba str. Russia 54 I4 ....67°13'N 72°49'E
Ob"yachevo Russia 52 E4 ....60°20'N 49°37'E
Occidental, Cordillera mts Colombia 72 B7
.........................1°36'N 77°47'W
Occidental, Cordillera mts Peru 72 B5 ......16°07'S 71°46'W
Ocean Falls town Canada 60 F3 ....52°21'N 127°41'W
Oceania 106
Oceanside U.S.A. 62 C3 ....33°12'N 117°23'W
Ocher Russia 52 F3 ....57°55'N 54°44'E
Ochil Hills Scotland 15 F4 ....56°12'N 3°49'W
Oda, Jebel mt. Sudan 85 H4 ....20°20'N 36°39'E
Ódáðahraun f. Iceland 43 Y2 ....64°48'N 17°37'W
Ödate Japan 104 D4 ....40°16'N 140°34'E
Ödemiş Turkey 51 G4 ....38°13'N 27°58'E
Odense Denmark 43 B1 ....55°24'N 10°23'E
Oder r. Germany 46 C4 ....51°43'N 9°56'E
Odesa Ukraine 49 J6 ....46°28'N 30°39'E
Odessa U.S.A. 62 F3 ....31°50'N 102°20'W
Odintsovo Russia 47 Q6 ....55°40'N 37°18'E
Odisha d. India 96 F5 ....20°57'N 84°15'E
Odra r. Germany/Poland 46 H3 ....49°54'N 18°19'E
Offaly d. Ireland 18 D3 ....53°15'N 7°35'W
Offenbach am Main Germany 46 C4 ....50°06'N 8°46'E
Offenburg Germany 46 B3 ....48°29'N 7°57'E
Ogaden f. Ethiopia 85 I2 ....7°09'N 45°27'E
Ögaki Japan 104 C3 ....35°21'N 136°37'E
Ogbomoso Nigeria 84 E2 ....8°08'N 4°14'E
Ogden U.S.A. 62 D5 ....41°14'N 111°57'W
Ogilvie r. Canada 60 E4 ....65°50'N 137°13'W
Oglio r. Italy 46 D1 ....45°01'N 10°40'E
Ogoki r. Canada 61 I7 ....51°40'N 85°58'W
Ogulin Croatia 50 A7 ....45°16'N 15°14'E
Ohio d. U.S.A. 63 J5 ....40°27'N 82°28'W
Ohio r. U.S.A. 63 I4 ....37°05'N 89°12'W
Ohrid Macedonia 50 D5 ....41°07'N 20°49'E
Ohrid, Lake Albania/Macedonia 50 D5 .....41°02'N 20°43'E
Oich r. Scotland 16 E2 ....57°09'N 4°40'W
Oich, Loch l. Scotland 16 E2 ....57°04'N 4°46'W
Oise r. France 44 E6 ....48°59'N 2°04'E
Öita Japan 104 B2 ....33°13'N 131°37'E
Oiti mt. Greece 50 E4 ....38°48'N 22°16'E
Ojinaga Mexico 66 D6 ....29°33'N 104°25'W
Ojos del Salado, Nevado mt. Argentina/Chile 73 C4
.........................27°06'S 68°35'W
Oka r. Russia 47 Q5 ....56°20'N 43°59'E
Okanogan r. U.S.A. 62 C6 ....48°06'N 119°41'W
Okavango Delta f. Botswana 83 B3 ....19°42'S 23°02'E
Okaya Japan 104 C3 ....36°03'N 138°04'E
Okayama Japan 104 B2 ....34°39'N 133°55'E
Okeechobee, Lake U.S.A. 63 J2 ....26°56'N 81°00'W
Okehampton England 11 C2 ....50°44'N 4°00'W
Okha India 96 C5 ....22°26'N 69°08'E
Okha Russia 55 P3 ....53°33'N 143°01'E
Okhotsk Russia 55 P3 ....59°22'N 143°22'E
Okhotsk, Sea of Japan/Russia 104 D4 ......44°58'N 144°06'E
Okhtyrka Ukraine 47 P4 ....50°19'N 34°54'E
Okinawa i. Japan 99 N3 ....26°27'N 127°58'E
Oki-shotō is Japan 104 B3 ....36°07'N 133°26'E
Oklahoma d. U.S.A. 62 G4 ....35°41'N 97°24'W
Oklahoma City U.S.A. 62 G4 ....35°31'N 97°31'W
Okovskiy Les f. Russia 52 D3 ....56°10'N 34°20'E
Oksskolten mt. Norway 43 C4 ....66°01'N 14°20'E
Oktyabr'skiy Russia 52 F3 ....61°05'N 43°07'E
Oktyabr'skiy Russia 53 F3 ....54°28'N 53°31'E
Oktyabr'skoye Russia 52 G4 ....62°27'N 66°22'E
Oktyabr'skoy Revolyutsii, Ostrov i. Russia 55 K5
.........................79°00'N 96°42'E
Öland i. Sweden 43 D2 ....56°57'N 17°02'E
Olbia Italy 48 E5 ....40°55'N 9°30'E
Old Crow Canada 60 E4 ....67°36'N 139°54'W
Oldenburg Germany 46 C5 ....53°09'N 8°14'E
Oldenzaal Neth. 42 F5 ....52°19'N 6°56'E
Oldham England 13 E2 ....53°33'N 2°07'W
Old Head of Kinsale Ireland 18 C1 ....51°36'N 8°31'W
Old Leake England 13 H2 ....53°02'N 0°06'E
Oldmeldrum Scotland 17 G2 ....57°20'N 2°19'W
Olean U.S.A. 63 K5 ....42°05'N 78°26'W
Olekma r. Russia 55 N4 ....60°05'N 120°27'E
Olekminsk Russia 55 N4 ....60°24'N 120°21'E
Oleksandriya Ukraine 47 O3 ....48°41'N 33°07'E
Olenek r. Russia 55 M4 ....68°28'N 112°35'E
Olenek r. Russia 55 M5 ....72°58'N 119°45'E
Oleněkskiy Zaliv b. Russia 55 N5 ....73°22'N 121°09'E
Oléron, Île d' i. France 44 C4 ....45°55'N 1°20'W
Olevs'k Ukraine 47 L4 ....51°13'N 27°39'E
Olney England 8 E3 ....52°09'N 0°42'W
Olomouc Czechia 46 G3 ....49°36'N 17°16'E
Olonets Russia 52 D4 ....60°58'N 32°59'E
Oloron-Ste-Marie France 44 C3 ....43°12'N 0°36'W
Olsztyn Poland 46 I5 ....53°47'N 20°29'E
Olt r. Romania 50 F7 ....44°22'N 24°47'E

Olympia U.S.A. 62 B6 ....47°02'N 122°53'W
Olympos Cyprus 51 J2 ....34°56'N 32°51'E
Olympus, Mount Greece 50 E5 ....40°05'N 22°21'E
Olympus, Mount U.S.A. 62 B6 ....47°45'N 123°47'W
Olyutorskiy Zaliv b. Russia 55 R3 ....59°51'N 168°08'E
Omagh Northern Ireland 14 B2 ....54°36'N 7°17'W
Omaha U.S.A. 62 G5 ....41°17'N 95°58'W
Oman Asia 95 H3 ....18°15'N 53°34'E
Oman, Gulf of Asia 95 I5 ....25°37'N 56°49'E
Ombersley England 8 C3 ....52°16'N 2°14'W
Omdurman Sudan 85 H3 ....15°38'N 32°28'E
Ommen Neth. 42 F5 ....52°32'N 6°25'E
Omolon r. Russia 55 Q4 ....68°44'N 158°43'E
Omono r. Japan 104 D3 ....39°41'N 140°04'E
Omsk Russia 54 I3 ....55°00'N 73°22'E
Omsukchan Russia 55 Q4 ....62°25'N 155°43'E
Omulew r. Poland 46 I5 ....53°04'N 21°33'E
Ōmuta Japan 104 B2 ....33°02'N 130°28'E
Onchan Isle of Man 12 C3 ....54°11'N 4°27'W
Ondjiva Angola 83 A3 ....17°04'S 15°44'E
Onega Russia 52 D4 ....63°55'N 38°02'E
Onega r. Russia 52 D4 ....63°55'N 38°07'E
Onega, Lake Russia 52 D4 ....62°05'N 35°21'E
Oneşti Romania 50 G8 ....46°16'N 26°46'E
Ongole India 96 F4 ....15°32'N 80°02'E
Onitsha Nigeria 84 E2 ....6°08'N 6°48'E
Ono-i-Lau i. Fiji 109 H4 ....20°39'S 178°45'W
Ontario d. Canada 61 I3 ....51°51'N 91°22'W
Ontario, Lake Canada/U.S.A. 61 K2 ....43°31'N 77°57'W
Ontong Java Atoll Solomon Is 109 E6 ....5°24'S 159°34'E
Oosterschelde est. Neth. 42 C4 ....51°38'N 3°35'E
Oost-Vlaanderen d. Belgium 42 C3 ....50°56'N 3°44'E
Opala Dem. Rep. Congo 83 B4 ....0°36'S 24°22'E
Opava Czechia 46 G3 ....49°56'N 17°54'E
Opochka Russia 43 G2 ....56°43'N 28°41'E
Opole Poland 46 G4 ....50°40'N 17°56'E
Oporto Portugal 45 A4 ....41°11'N 8°36'W
Oradea Romania 47 I2 ....47°04'N 21°57'E
Oran Algeria 84 D5 ....35°42'N 0°38'W
Orange France 44 F4 ....44°09'N 4°49'E
Orange r. Namibia/S. Africa 83 A2 ....28°36'S 16°28'E
Orange, Cabo c. Brazil 72 D7 ....4°22'N 51°17'W
Oranmore Ireland 18 C3 ....53°16'N 8°55'W
Orchila, Isla i. Venezuela 67 K3 ....11°45'N 66°09'W
Orchy r. Scotland 14 D4 ....56°24'N 5°01'W
Ord, Mount hill Australia 108 B5 ....17°19'S 125°29'E
Ordu Turkey 51 L5 ....40°59'N 37°53'E
Örebro Sweden 43 C2 ....59°16'N 15°14'E
Oregon d. U.S.A. 62 B5 ....43°43'N 120°32'W
Orël Russia 53 D3 ....52°58'N 36°05'E
Orenburg Russia 53 F3 ....51°46'N 55°05'E
Orford Ness hd England 9 G3 ....52°05'N 1°35'E
Orhei Moldova 47 M2 ....47°22'N 28°50'E
Oriental, Cordillera mts Bolivia 72 C5 ....16°47'S 66°35'W
Oriental, Cordillera mts Colombia 72 B7 ..7°42'N 72°45'W
Oriental, Cordillera mts Peru 72 B5 ....10°29'S 74°41'W
Orillia Canada 63 K5 ....44°36'N 79°25'W
Orinoco r. Col./Venez. 72 C7 ....8°35'N 61°50'W
Orinoco Delta Venezuela 72 C7 ....9°22'N 60°44'W
Oristano Italy 48 E4 ....39°55'N 8°35'E
Orivesi l. Finland 43 G3 ....62°14'N 29°27'E
Orizaba Mexico 66 E4 ....18°53'N 97°06'W
Örkelljunga Sweden 43 C2 ....56°17'N 13°17'E
Orkney d. Scotland 20 D6 ....58°59'N 2°42'W
Orkney Islands Scotland 17 F4 ....59°06'N 3°20'W
Orlando U.S.A. 63 J2 ....28°31'N 81°21'W
Orléans France 44 D5 ....47°55'N 1°54'E
Ormoc Phil. 103 G6 ....11°00'N 124°37'E
Ormskirk England 12 E2 ....53°34'N 2°53'W
Orne r. France 44 C6 ....49°16'N 0°14'W
Örnsköldsvik Sweden 43 D3 ....63°18'N 18°43'E
Oronsay i. Scotland 14 C4 ....56°01'N 6°12'W
Orrin r. Scotland 17 E2 ....57°33'N 4°29'W
Orrin Reservoir Scotland 16 E2 ....57°30'N 4°45'W
Orsha Belarus 47 N6 ....54°30'N 30°26'E
Orsk Russia 53 F3 ....51°07'N 58°33'E
Orşova Romania 50 E7 ....44°42'N 22°25'E
Oruro Bolivia 72 C5 ....17°59'S 67°09'W
Osa, Península de pen. Costa Rica 67 H2 ...8°34'N 83°32'W
Ōsaka Japan 104 C2 ....34°42'N 135°30'E
Oshakati Namibia 83 A3 ....17°45'S 15°43'E
Oshawa Canada 61 K2 ....43°54'N 78°51'W
O-shima i. Japan 104 C2 ....34°44'N 139°28'E
Osijek Croatia 50 C7 ....45°35'N 18°42'E
Ösjön l. Sweden 43 C3 ....63°04'N 15°26'E
Oskarshamn Sweden 43 D2 ....57°16'N 16°26'E
Oslo Norway 43 B2 ....59°55'N 10°46'E
Osmancık Turkey 51 K5 ....40°58'N 34°48'E
Osmaniye Turkey 51 L3 ....37°04'N 36°15'E
Osnabrück Germany 46 C5 ....52°17'N 8°04'E
Osorno Chile 73 B2 ....40°35'S 73°09'W
Osorno Spain 45 C5 ....42°25'N 4°21'W
Oss Neth. 42 E4 ....51°45'N 5°32'E
Ossa mt. Greece 50 E4 ....39°48'N 22°41'E
Ossa, Mount Australia 108 D2 ....41°56'S 146°12'E
Ostend Belgium 42 B4 ....51°13'N 2°55'E
Österdalälven r. Sweden 43 C3 ....61°40'N 13°15'E
Österdalen f. Norway 43 B3 ....62°05'N 10°36'E
Östersund Sweden 43 C3 ....63°11'N 14°39'E
Ostrava Czechia 46 H3 ....49°51'N 18°17'E
Ostróda Poland 46 H5 ....53°42'N 19°58'E
Ostrov Russia 52 D3 ....57°21'N 28°21'E
Ostrowiec Świętokrzyski Poland 47 I4 ......50°56'N 21°24'E
Ostrów Mazowiecka Poland 47 I5 ....52°48'N 21°53'E
Ostrów Wielkopolski Poland 46 G4 ....51°39'N 17°49'E
Ostrzeszów Poland 46 G4 ....51°25'N 17°56'E
Osŭm r. Bulgaria 50 F6 ....43°42'N 24°50'E
Osumi-kaikyo str. Japan 104 B2 ....30°50'N 130°52'E
Ösumi-shotō is Japan 104 B2 ....30°30'N 130°36'E
Osuna Spain 45 C2 ....37°14'N 5°06'W
Oswestry England 8 B3 ....52°51'N 3°03'W
Otaru Japan 104 D4 ....43°12'N 140°59'E
Otjiwarongo Namibia 83 A2 ....20°28'S 16°40'E
Otley England 13 F2 ....53°54'N 1°41'W
Otranto Italy 50 C5 ....40°09'N 18°30'E
Otranto, Strait of Albania/Italy 50 C5 ....40°36'N 18°42'E
Otta Norway 43 B3 ....61°46'N 9°31'E
Ottawa Canada 61 K2 ....45°25'N 75°40'W
Ottawa r. Canada 61 K2 ....45°24'N 74°16'W
Ottawa Islands Canada 61 J3 ....59°57'N 80°09'W
Otter r. England 11 D2 ....50°38'N 3°18'W
Otterburn England 13 E4 ....55°14'N 2°11'W
Ottery r. England 11 C2 ....50°39'N 4°20'W
Ottignies Belgium 42 D3 ....50°39'N 4°34'E
Otukpo Nigeria 84 E2 ....7°13'N 8°05'E
Ouachita r. U.S.A. 63 H3 ....31°50'N 91°49'W
Ouagadougou Burkina Faso 84 D3 ....12°22'N 1°31'W

Ouargla Algeria 84 E5 ....31°59'N 5°22'E
Ouarzazate Morocco 84 D5 ....30°56'N 6°54'W
Oudenaarde Belgium 42 C3 ....50°51'N 3°36'E
Ouesso Congo 84 F2 ....1°36'N 16°04'E
Ouezzane Morocco 48 B3 ....34°46'N 5°32'W
Oughter, Lough l. Ireland 18 D4 ....54°01'N 7°28'W
Ouistreham France 44 C6 ....49°17'N 0°16'W
Oujda Morocco 84 D5 ....34°44'N 1°54'W
Oulainen Finland 43 F4 ....64°16'N 24°49'E
Oulton England 9 G3 ....52°30'N 1°43'E
Oulu Finland 43 F4 ....65°01'N 25°30'E
Oulujärvi l. Finland 43 F4 ....64°17'N 27°15'E
Oundle England 9 E3 ....52°29'N 0°28'W
Oupeye Belgium 42 E3 ....50°42'N 5°39'E
Ourense Spain 45 B5 ....42°21'N 7°51'W
Ouse r. E. Sussex England 9 F1 ....50°48'N 0°03'E
Ouse r. E. Yorks. England 13 G2 ....53°44'N 0°54'E
Outer Hebrides is Scotland 16 B2 ....57°53'N 7°21'W
Outokumpu Finland 43 G3 ....62°43'N 29°01'E
Out Skerries is Scotland 17 I5 ....60°26'N 0°47'W
Ovamboland f. Namibia 83 A3 ....17°50'S 15°41'E
Overijssel d. Neth. 42 F5 ....52°25'N 6°32'E
Overton Wales 10 E4 ....52°58'N 2°56'W
Övertorneå Sweden 43 E4 ....66°24'N 23°37'E
Oviedo Spain 45 C5 ....43°22'N 5°50'W
Ovruch Ukraine 47 M4 ....51°20'N 28°49'E
Owando Congo 84 F1 ....0°29'S 15°55'E
Owen Stanley Range mts P.N.G. 108 D6 ...8°59'S 147°57'E
Owyhee r. U.S.A. 62 C5 ....43°48'N 117°04'W
Öxarfjörður b. Iceland 43 Y2 ....66°12'N 16°47'W
Oxelösund Sweden 43 D2 ....58°40'N 17°05'E
Oxford England 8 D2 ....51°45'N 1°15'W
Oxfordshire d. England 21 E2 ....51°54'N 1°27'W
Oxnard U.S.A. 62 C3 ....34°12'N 119°12'W
Oxted England 9 F2 ....51°16'N 0°01'E
Oyama Japan 104 C3 ....36°18'N 139°48'E
Oykel r. Scotland 16 E2 ....57°55'N 4°24'W
Ozark Plateau f. U.S.A. 63 H4 ....36°58'N 93°31'W
Ozarks, Lake of the U.S.A. 63 H4 ....38°14'N 93°08'W
Ózd Hungary 46 I3 ....48°13'N 20°19'E
Ozernovskiy Russia 55 Q3 ....51°30'N 156°35'E

P

Paamiut Greenland 61 N4 ....62°01'N 49°40'W
Pabbay i. Na h-E. S. Scotland 16 B1 ....56°51'N 7°34'W
Pabbay i. Na h-E. S. Scotland 16 B2 ....57°46'N 7°18'W
Pabianice Poland 46 H4 ....51°40'N 19°22'E
Pachuca Mexico 66 E5 ....20°09'N 98°44'W
Pacific Ocean 116 B3
Padang Indonesia 102 C3 ....0°58'S 100°23'E
Paderborn Germany 46 C4 ....51°43'N 8°45'E
Padiham England 13 E2 ....53°48'N 2°19'W
Padre Island U.S.A. 62 G2 ....26°57'N 97°22'W
Padstow England 11 C2 ....50°32'N 4°56'W
Padua Italy 46 D1 ....45°24'N 11°53'E
Pag i. Croatia 50 A7 ....44°31'N 14°53'E
Pagadian Phil. 103 G5 ....7°50'N 123°29'E
Pagai Selatan i. Indonesia 102 C3 ....2°58'S 100°24'E
Pagai Utara i. Indonesia 102 C3 ....2°36'S 100°04'E
Pagan i. N. Mariana Is 103 L7 ....18°08'N 145°49'E
Page U.S.A. 62 D4 ....36°55'N 111°28'W
Paget, Mount S. Atlantic Oc. 73 F1 ....54°23'S 36°44'W
Paignton England 11 D2 ....50°26'N 3°34'W
Päijänne l. Finland 43 F3 ....61°30'N 25°26'E
Painswick England 8 C2 ....51°47'N 2°12'W
Paisley Scotland 14 E3 ....55°51'N 4°26'W
Pakanbaru Indonesia 102 C4 ....0°34'N 101°30'E
Pakaraima Mountains S. America 67 L1 ....3°47'N 63°40'W
Pakistan Asia 96 C6 ....28°01'N 64°37'E
Pakokku Myanmar 97 I5 ....21°21'N 95°07'E
Pakxé Laos 102 D7 ....15°04'N 105°50'E
Palana Russia 55 Q4 ....59°05'N 159°52'E
Palangkaraya Indonesia 102 E3 ....2°18'S 113°55'E
Palatka Russia 55 Q4 ....60°08'N 150°56'E
Palau N. Pacific Oc. 103 I5 ....7°23'N 134°07'E
Palawan i. Phil. 102 F5 ....8°50'N 117°43'E
Palembang Indonesia 102 C3 ....2°56'S 104°46'E
Palencia Spain 45 C5 ....42°01'N 4°31'W
Palermo Italy 48 F4 ....38°07'N 13°21'E
Pali India 96 D6 ....25°46'N 73°26'E
Palk Strait India/Sri Lanka 96 E2 ....9°36'N 79°18'E
Palma de Mallorca Spain 45 G3 ....39°35'N 2°40'E
Palmas, Cape Liberia 84 D2 ....4°22'N 7°32'W
Palmerston atoll Cook Is 109 I5 ....18°01'S 163°03'W
Palmerston North New Zealand 109 G2 ...40°22'S 175°37'E
Palmira Colombia 72 B7 ....3°31'N 76°16'W
Palopo Indonesia 102 G3 ....3°01'S 120°11'E
Palos, Cabo de c. Spain 45 E2 ....37°37'N 0°41'W
Palu Indonesia 102 F3 ....0°54'S 119°54'E
Pamiers France 44 D3 ....43°07'N 1°37'E
Pamir mts Asia 95 L7 ....38°39'N 72°48'E
Pampas f. Argentina 73 C3 ....36°23'S 64°07'W
Pamplona Spain 45 E5 ....42°49'N 1°39'W
Panagyurishte Bulgaria 50 F6 ....42°30'N 24°10'E
Panaji India 96 D4 ....15°30'N 73°50'E
Panama Central America 67 H2 ....8°22'N 81°33'W
Panama, Gulf of Panama 67 I2 ....7°38'N 79°21'W
Panama, Isthmus of f. C. America 56 F2 ...9°00'N 80°00'W
Panama Canal Panama 67 I2 ....9°07'N 79°45'W
Panamá City Panama 67 I2 ....8°56'N 79°36'W
Panay i. Phil. 103 G6 ....11°10'N 122°30'E
Pančevo Serbia 50 D7 ....44°52'N 20°39'E
Panevėžys Lithuania 43 F1 ....55°44'N 24°23'E
Pangkalanbuun Indonesia 102 E3 ....2°40'S 111°38'E
Pangkalpinang Indonesia 102 D3 ....2°08'S 106°06'E
Pangnirtung Canada 61 L4 ....66°03'N 65°48'W
Panjgur Pakistan 95 J5 ....26°58'N 64°07'E
Pantelleria, Isola di i. Italy 48 F3 ....36°47'N 12°04'E
Panzhihua China 99 I3 ....26°35'N 101°43'E
Papa Stour i. Scotland 17 H5 ....60°21'N 1°42'W
Papa Westray i. Scotland 17 G4 ....59°22'N 2°52'W
Papenburg Germany 42 G6 ....53°05'N 7°24'E
Paphos Cyprus 51 J2 ....34°47'N 32°25'E
Papua, Gulf of P.N.G. 108 D6 ....8°34'S 144°45'E
Papua New Guinea Oceania 108 D6 ....6°05'S 146°34'E
Par England 11 C2 ....50°21'N 4°42'W
Paracel Islands S. China Sea 102 E7 ....16°46'N 112°39'E
Paraguai r. Brazil 72 D5 ....22°06'S 57°57'W
Paraguay S. America 73 D4 ....23°27'S 58°39'W
Paraguay r. Argentina 73 D4 ....22°45'S 58°44'W
Parakou Benin 84 E2 ....9°22'N 2°36'E
Paramaribo Suriname 72 D7 ....5°51'N 55°17'W
Paraná Argentina 73 C3 ....31°44'S 60°31'W

Paraná r. S. America 73 D3............................33°52'S 59°12'W
Paranaguá Brazil 73 E4...............................25°32'S 48°33'W
Paranaíba r. Brazil 72 D5.............................20°04'S 51°00'W
Parângul Mare, Vârful mt. Romania 50 E7...45°21'N 23°33'E
Pardubice Czechia 46 F4..............................50°03'N 15°47'E
Parecis, Serra dos hills Brazil 72 C5.............11°28'S 63°12'W
Parepare Indonesia 102 F3............................4°01'S 119°40'E
Paria, Península de pen. Venezuela 67 L3 ...10°43'N 62°58'W
Parima, Serra mts Brazil 67 L1.....................2°57'N 64°15'W
Paris France 44 E6..48°52'N 2°21'E
Parma Italy 46 D1..44°48'N 10°19'E
Parnaíba Brazil 72 E6...................................2°56'S 41°45'W
Parnaíba r. Brazil 72 E6................................3°02'S 41°51'W
Parnassos mt. Greece 50 E4.........................38°32'N 22°38'E
Pärnu Estonia 43 F2....................................58°23'N 24°30'E
Paropamisus mts Afgh. 95 J7.......................35°06'N 61°20'E
Paros i. Greece 50 E3...................................37°06'N 25°08'E
Parrett r. England 11 D3..............................51°08'N 3°00'W
Parry, Cape Canada 61 F5............................70°12'N 124°31'W
Parry Islands Canada 60 G5.........................76°50'N 111°03'W
Parseta r. Poland 46 F5................................54°11'N 15°34'E
Parthenay France 44 C5...............................46°39'N 0°15'W
Partry Mountains hills Ireland 18 B3...........53°36'N 9°39'W
Pasadena U.S.A. 62 C3................................34°11'N 118°08'W
Pașcani Romania 47 L2................................47°15'N 26°44'E
Pasni Pakistan 95 J5....................................25°13'N 63°31'E
Passau Germany 46 E3................................48°34'N 13°25'E
Passo Fundo Brazil 73 D4............................28°18'S 52°24'W
Pastavy Belarus 47 L6.................................55°07'N 26°50'E
Pasto Colombia 72 B7..................................1°11'N 77°17'W
Patagonia f. Argentina 73 B1........................51°44'S 71°19'W
Patchway England 8 C2................................51°32'N 2°34'W
Paterson U.S.A. 63 L5..................................40°54'N 74°09'W
Pathein Myanmar 97 H4...............................16°45'N 94°44'E
Patna India 96 G6..25°35'N 85°16'E
Patos Albania 50 C5.....................................40°40'N 19°39'E
Patos, Lagoa dos l. Brazil 73 D3..................30°39'S 50°58'W
Patos de Minas Brazil 72 E5........................18°36'S 46°30'W
Patraïkos Kolpos b. Greece 50 D4................38°15'N 21°26'E
Patras Greece 50 D4....................................38°14'N 21°45'E
Patrington England 13 G2............................53°41'N 0°01'W
Patos Greece 50 D4.....................................38°14'N 21°45'E
Pau France 44 C3..43°18'N 0°22'W
Paulo Afonso Brazil 72 F6............................9°20'S 38°13'W
Pavia Italy 46 C1...45°11'N 9°09'E
Pavlodar Kazakhstan 54 I3...........................52°18'N 77°02'E
Pavlohrad Ukraine 47 P3..............................48°31'N 35°53'E
Pavlovskaya Russia 49 K6............................46°09'N 39°47'E
Payapon Myanmar 97 I4...............................16°16'N 95°41'E
Pay-Khoy, Khrebet hills Russia 52 G4..........69°17'N 62°53'E
Paysandú Uruguay 73 D3.............................32°19'S 58°05'W
Pazardzhik Bulgaria 50 F6............................42°12'N 24°20'E
Peace r. Canada 60 G3.................................58°54'N 111°50'W
Peacehaven England 9 E1............................50°48'N 0°00'W
Peace River town Canada 60 G3...................56°15'N 117°17'W
Peak, Mount U.S.A. 62 E4...........................38°26'N 109°12'W
Pearl r. U.S.A. 63 I3......................................30°10'N 89°37'W
Peć Kosovo 50 C6..42°39'N 20°17'E
Pechora Russia 52 F4...................................65°09'N 53°54'E
Pechora r. Russia 52 F4................................68°13'N 53°54'E
Pechorskoye More sea Russia 52 F4.............69°00'N 55°00'E
Pecos U.S.A. 62 F3......................................31°23'N 103°30'W
Pecos r. U.S.A. 62 F2...................................29°50'N 101°28'W
Pécs Hungary 46 H2....................................46°05'N 18°13'E
Pedro Juan Caballero Paraguay 73 D4.........22°29'S 55°44'W
Peebles Scotland 15 F3.................................55°39'N 3°12'W
Peel r. Canada 60 E4....................................68°03'N 134°26'W
Peel Isle of Man 12 C3.................................54°13'N 4°41'W
Pegasus Bay New Zealand 109 G2..............43°20'S 172°49'E
Peipus, Lake Estonia/Russia 43 F2...............58°38'N 27°28'E
Pekalongan Indonesia 102 D2......................6°54'S 109°38'E
Pelat, Mont mt. France 44 G4......................44°16'N 6°43'E
Peleng i. Indonesia 103 G3...........................1°15'S 123°29'E
Pello Finland 43 E4......................................66°47'N 23°59'E
Pelotas Brazil 73 D3....................................31°46'S 52°19'W
Pelotas, Rio das r. Brazil 73 D4...................27°35'S 51°24'W
Pemba Mozambique 83 D3.........................12°59'S 40°32'E
Pemba Zambia 83 C3..................................16°33'S 27°22'E
Pemba Island Tanzania 83 C4......................5°25'S 39°46'E
Pembrey Wales 10 C3.................................51°41'N 4°17'W
Pembroke Canada 63 K6..............................45°49'N 77°06'W
Pembroke Wales 10 C3................................51°40'N 4°55'W
Pembroke Dock Wales 10 C3.......................51°41'N 4°57'W
Pembrokeshire d. Wales 21 C2.....................51°55'N 4°48'W
Pembury England 9 F2.................................51°09'N 0°19'E
Peñalara mt. Spain 45 D4.............................40°51'N 3°56'W
Peña Nevada, Cerro mt. Mexico 66 E5.........23°46'N 99°50'W
Peñaranda de Bracamonte Spain 45 C4........40°55'N 5°11'W
Penarth Wales 11 D3...................................51°26'N 3°10'W
Penas, Golfo de g. Chile 73 B2.....................47°18'S 75°35'W
Pendine Wales 10 C3..................................51°45'N 4°34'W
Pendlebury England 13 E2...........................53°30'N 2°19'W
Pendle Hill England 13 E2...........................53°52'N 2°18'W
Pendleton U.S.A. 62 C6...............................45°39'N 118°48'W
Penicuik Scotland 15 F3...............................55°50'N 3°13'W
Peninsular Malaysia Malaysia 102 C4...........3°59'N 102°43'E
Penkridge England 8 C3..............................52°43'N 2°07'W
Pennines hills England 13 E3.......................54°23'N 2°18'W
Pennsylvania d. U.S.A. 63 K5.......................41°18'N 78°00'W
Penny Icecap Canada 61 L4.........................67°10'N 66°02'W
Penrhyn Mawr pt Wales 10 C4.....................52°51'N 4°43'W
Penrith England 12 E3.................................54°40'N 2°45'W
Penryn England 11 B2..................................50°10'N 5°06'W
Pensacola U.S.A. 63 I3.................................30°27'N 87°13'W
Penticton Canada 62 C6..............................49°30'N 119°35'W
Pentland Firth str. Scotland 17 F3................58°43'N 3°16'W
Pentland Hills Scotland 15 F3......................55°43'N 3°30'W
Pentland Skerries is Scotland 17 G3.............58°41'N 2°54'W
Penygadair hill Wales 10 D4.........................52°42'N 3°55'W
Pen-y-Ghent hill England 13 E3....................54°10'N 2°15'W
Penza Russia 53 E3......................................53°12'N 45°01'E
Penzance England 11 B2..............................50°07'N 5°32'W
Penzhinskaya Guba b. Russia 55 R4.............62°33'N 163°30'E
Peoria U.S.A. 63 I5......................................40°41'N 89°37'W
Peregrebnoye Russia 52 G4..........................62°59'N 65°11'E
Pereira Colombia 72 B7...............................4°45'N 75°41'W
Périgueux France 44 D4...............................45°11'N 0°43'E
Perija, Sierra de mts Venezuela 67 J2...........9°09'N 73°12'W
Perito Moreno Argentina 73 B2.....................46°36'S 71°02'W
Perlas, Punta de pt Nicaragua 67 H3............12°24'N 83°31'W
Perm' Russia 52 F3......................................58°01'N 56°14'E
Pernik Bulgaria 50 E6..................................42°36'N 23°02'E
Péronne France 42 C2.................................49°56'N 2°56'E
Perpignan France 44 E3...............................42°42'N 2°54'E
Perranporth England 11 B2..........................50°21'N 5°09'W
Pershore England 8 C3................................52°07'N 2°04'W

Perth Australia 108 A3.................................31°56'S 115°47'E
Perth Scotland 15 F4...................................56°24'N 3°26'W
Perth and Kinross d. Scotland 20 C5............56°37'N 4°07'W
Peru S. America 72 B5.................................5°50'S 77°14'W
Perugia Italy 48 F5......................................43°07'N 12°23'E
Pervomays'k Ukraine 47 N3.........................48°03'N 30°51'E
Pescara Italy 48 F5......................................42°27'N 14°12'E
Pesebre, Punta pt Canary Islands 45 Y2.......28°07'N 14°29'W
Peshawar Pakistan 96 D7.............................34°01'N 71°40'E
Peshkopi Albania 50 D5...............................41°41'N 20°26'E
Peterborough Canada 61 K2.........................44°18'N 78°20'W
Peterborough England 9 E3..........................52°34'N 0°14'W
Peterborough d. England 21 E3....................52°36'N 0°16'W
Peterhead Scotland 17 H2............................57°31'N 1°47'W
Peterlee England 13 F3................................54°46'N 1°20'W
Petersfield England 8 E2..............................51°00'N 0°56'W
Petersville U.S.A. 60 C4...............................62°33'N 150°50'W
Petit Mécatina r. Canada 61 M3...................50°40'N 59°25'W
Petrich Bulgaria 50 E5..................................41°24'N 23°12'E
Petrolina Brazil 72 E6..................................9°22'S 40°25'W
Petropavlovsk Kazakhstan 54 H3.................54°51'N 69°06'E
Petropavlovsk-Kamchatskiy Russia 55 Q3
....53°01'N 158°44'E
Petroșani Romania 50 E7..............................45°25'N 23°23'E
Petrozavodsk Russia 52 D4..........................61°48'N 34°19'E
Petworth England 9 E1.................................50°59'N 0°36'W
Pevensey England 9 F1................................50°49'N 0°21'E
Pewsey England 8 D2..................................51°20'N 1°46'W
Pforzheim Germany 46 C3...........................48°53'N 8°42'E
Phan Thiêt Vietnam 102 D6.........................10°55'N 108°06'E
Phatthalung Thailand 102 C5.......................7°39'N 100°06'E
Phayao Thailand 102 B7..............................19°10'N 99°57'E
Phet Buri Thailand 102 B6...........................13°06'N 99°56'E
Philadelphia U.S.A. 63 K4............................39°57'N 75°10'W
Philippeville Belgium 42 D4..........................50°12'N 4°33'E
Philippines Asia 103 G6...............................15°36'N 122°55'E
Phitsanulok Thailand 102 C7........................16°50'N 100°18'E
Phnom Penh Cambodia 102 C6....................11°33'N 104°57'E
Phoenix U.S.A. 62 D3..................................33°31'N 112°07'W
Phoenix Islands Kiribati 109 H6....................2°43'S 173°22'W
Phôngsali Laos 102 C8.................................21°41'N 102°08'E
Phrae Thailand 102 C7................................18°07'N 100°12'E
Phuket Thailand 102 B5...............................7°53'N 98°23'E
Piacenza Italy 46 C1....................................45°03'N 9°42'E
Piatra Neamț Romania 47 L2........................46°56'N 26°22'E
Piave r. Italy 46 F1......................................45°32'N 12°44'E
Picardy f. France 44 D6...............................49°47'N 1°35'E
Pickering England 13 G3..............................54°15'N 0°47'W
Pickering, Vale of f. England 13 G3..............54°13'N 0°45'W
Piedras Negras Mexico 66 D3......................28°40'N 100°34'W
Pieksämäki Finland 43 F3.............................62°18'N 27°10'E
Pielinen l. Finland 43 G3..............................63°14'N 29°41'E
Pierre U.S.A. 62 F5.....................................44°23'N 100°23'W
Pietermaritzburg S. Africa 83 C2.................29°36'S 30°23'E
Pietrosa mt. Romania 47 K2..........................47°34'N 24°41'E
Pihlajavesi l. Finland 43 G3..........................61°45'N 28°46'E
Pijijiapan Mexico 66 F4................................15°46'N 93°14'W
Piła Poland 46 G5.......................................53°09'N 16°45'E
Pilbara f. Australia 108 A4............................22°45'S 117°00'E
Pimperne England 8 C1...............................50°53'N 2°08'W
Pinang i. Malaysia 102 C5............................5°21'N 100°11'E
Pınarbaşı Turkey 51 L4................................38°44'N 36°25'E
Pinar del Río Cuba 67 H5.............................22°25'N 83°43'W
Pindus Mountains Greece 50 D4...................39°56'N 20°56'E
Pine Bluff U.S.A. 63 H3...............................34°16'N 92°02'W
Pinega Russia 52 E4....................................64°41'N 43°24'E
Pineios r. Greece 50 E4................................39°53'N 22°43'E
Pingdingshan China 99 K4...........................33°45'N 113°18'E
Pingxiang Guangxi China 99 J2.....................22°03'N 106°50'E
Pingxiang Jiangxi China 99 K3......................27°42'N 113°52'E
Pinsk Belarus 47 L5.....................................52°08'N 26°06'E
Pionerskiy Russia 52 G4...............................61°08'N 62°51'E
Piotrków Trybunalski Poland 46 H4..............51°25'N 19°41'E
Pipmuacan, Réservoir Canada 63 L6............49°37'N 70°33'W
Piraeus Greece 50 E3..................................37°56'N 23°38'E
Pirot Serbia 50 E6.......................................43°09'N 22°43'E
Pisa Italy 48 F5...43°42'N 10°24'E
Písek Czechia 46 F3....................................49°19'N 14°10'E
Pisuerga r. Spain 45 C4...............................41°34'N 4°50'W
Pisz Poland 47 I5..53°38'N 21°48'E
Pitcairn Island S. Pacific Oc. 116 B2.............25°03'S 130°06'W
Pitcairn Islands S. Pacific Oc. 116 B2...........23°35'S 126°31'W
Piteå Sweden 43 E4....................................65°19'N 21°30'E
Pitești Romania 50 F7.................................44°52'N 24°53'E
Pitlochry Scotland 15 F4..............................56°42'N 3°44'W
Pittsburgh U.S.A. 63 K5...............................40°26'N 79°59'W
Piz Bernina mt. Italy/Switz. 46 C2................46°23'N 9°54'E
Placentia Spain 45 B4..................................40°02'N 6°05'W
Platinum U.S.A. 60 B3.................................58°59'N 161°48'W
Platte r. U.S.A. 62 G5..................................41°04'N 95°53'W
Plauen Germany 46 E4................................50°30'N 12°08'E
Plavsk Russia 47 Q5....................................53°42'N 37°18'E
Playa Blanca Canary Islands 45 Z2..............28°52'N 13°50'W
Plenty, Bay of g. New Zealand 109 G3.........37°37'S 176°59'E
Plesetsk Russia 52 E4..................................62°43'N 40°18'E
Pleven Bulgaria 50 F6..................................43°25'N 24°37'E
Płock Poland 46 H5.....................................52°33'N 19°43'E
Pločno mt. Bos. and Herz. 50 B6..................43°36'N 17°35'E
Ploiești Romania 50 G7...............................44°56'N 26°02'E
Plomb du Cantal mt. France 44 E4...............45°03'N 2°46'E
Plovdiv Bulgaria 50 F6.................................42°10'N 24°44'E
Plungė Lithuania 43 E1................................55°55'N 21°51'E
Plymouth England 11 C2.............................50°22'N 4°08'W
Plymouth d. England 21 C2..........................50°23'N 4°03'W
Plympton England 11 C2.............................50°23'N 4°03'W
Plymstock England 11 C2............................50°21'N 4°06'W
Plynlimon hill Wales 10 D4..........................52°28'N 3°46'W
Plzeň Czechia 46 E3....................................49°45'N 13°23'E
Pô Burkina Faso 84 D3................................11°12'N 1°08'W
Po r. Italy 46 E1..45°02'N 12°11'E
Pobeda, Gora mt. Russia 55 P4...................65°12'N 145°54'E
Pocatello U.S.A. 62 D5................................42°54'N 112°25'W
Pochep Russia 47 O5..................................52°56'N 33°27'E
Pocklington England 13 G2..........................53°56'N 0°47'W
Poços de Caldas Brazil 73 E4.......................21°48'S 46°31'W
Podgorica Montenegro 50 C6......................42°27'N 19°17'E
Podkamennaya Tunguska r. Russia 55 K4....61°36'N 90°08'E
Podol'sk Russia 52 D3.................................55°25'N 37°34'E
Pohang S. Korea 104 A3..............................36°01'N 129°22'E
Pointe-à-Pitre Guadeloupe 72 C8.................16°15'N 61°32'W
Pointe-Noire Congo 84 F1...........................4°44'S 11°53'E
Poitiers France 44 D5..................................46°35'N 0°20'E
Pokaran India 96 D6....................................26°53'N 71°57'E
Pokrovs'k Ukraine 49 K6.............................48°17'N 37°10'E
Poland Europe 46 H4...................................52°07'N 19°27'E
Polatlı Turkey 51 J4.....................................39°35'N 32°08'E
Polatsk Belarus 47 M6.................................55°29'N 28°47'E

Polegate England 9 F1.................................50°49'N 0°15'E
Pol-e Khomrī Afgh. 95 K7............................35°56'N 68°46'E
Polis Cyprus 51 J2.......................................35°01'N 32°25'E
Pollaphuca Reservoir Ireland 18 E3.............53°08'N 6°30'W
Polokwane S. Africa 83 B2...........................23°54'S 29°27'E
Polperro England 11 C2...............................50°20'N 4°31'W
Poltava Ukraine 47 P3.................................49°36'N 34°34'E
Polygyros Greece 50 E5................................40°23'N 23°27'E
Polykastro Greece 50 E5...............................40°59'N 22°34'E
Polynesia is Pacific Oc. 116 B2......................8°00'S 170°00'E
Pombal Portugal 45 B3................................39°55'N 8°37'W
Ponce Puerto Rico 67 K4.............................18°00'N 66°37'W
Ponferrada Spain 45 B5................................42°33'N 6°36'W
Ponta do Sol Cape Verde 84 B3...................17°10'N 25°05'W
Ponta Grossa Brazil 73 D4...........................25°03'S 50°07'W
Pont-à-Mousson France 42 F1......................48°54'N 6°03'E
Pontardawe Wales 10 D3.............................51°43'N 3°51'W
Pontefract England 13 F2.............................53°41'N 1°18'W
Ponteland England 13 F4.............................55°03'N 1°44'W
Pontevedra Spain 45 A5...............................42°27'N 8°37'W
Pontianak Indonesia 102 D3........................0°03'S 109°18'E
Pontoise France 44 E6.................................49°03'N 2°06'E
Pontycymer Wales 10 D3.............................51°37'N 3°35'W
Pontypool Wales 10 D3...............................51°42'N 3°02'W
Pontypridd Wales 10 D3..............................51°36'N 3°20'W
Poole England 8 D1.....................................50°43'N 1°59'W
Poole d. England 21 E2................................50°44'N 1°57'W
Poole Bay England 8 D1...............................50°40'N 1°55'W
Pooley Bridge England 12 E3........................54°37'N 2°49'W
Poopó, Lago de l. Bolivia 72 C5...................18°50'S 67°05'W
Popigay r. Russia 55 L5................................72°56'N 106°10'E
Poplar Bluff U.S.A. 63 H4.............................36°47'N 90°23'W
Popocatépetl, Volcán vol. Mexico 66 E4......19°02'N 98°38'W
Poprad Slovakia 46 I3..................................49°04'N 20°18'E
Porbandar India 96 C5.................................21°39'N 69°40'E
Pori Finland 43 E3.......................................61°29'N 21°48'E
Porlock England 11 D3.................................51°13'N 3°36'W
Poronaysk Russia 55 P2...............................49°16'N 143°03'E
Porsangerfjorden str. Norway 43 F5............70°19'N 25°18'E
Porsangerhalvøya pen. Norway 43 F5...........70°45'N 25°01'E
Porsgrunn Norway 43 B2.............................59°08'N 9°39'E
Porsuk r. Turkey 51 I4..................................39°41'N 31°58'E
Portadown Northern Ireland 14 C2...............54°25'N 6°26'W
Portaferry Northern Ireland 14 D2................54°23'N 5°32'W
Portage la Prairie Canada 60 I2....................49°58'N 98°19'W
Portalegre Portugal 45 B3............................39°18'N 7°25'W
Port Angeles U.S.A. 62 B6...........................48°06'N 123°25'W
Port Arthur U.S.A. 63 H2.............................29°51'N 93°58'W
Port Askaig Scotland 14 C3..........................55°51'N 6°06'W
Port Augusta Australia 108 C3......................32°29'S 137°45'E
Port-au-Prince Haiti 67 J4............................18°33'N 72°19'W
Portavogie Northern Ireland 14 D2...............54°27'N 5°26'W
Port Blair India 97 H3..................................11°41'N 92°42'E
Port-de-Paix Haiti 67 J4...............................19°57'N 72°50'W
Port Elizabeth S. Africa 83 B1......................33°57'S 25°37'E
Port Ellen Scotland 14 C3.............................55°38'N 6°11'W
Port Erin Isle of Man 12 C3..........................54°05'N 4°45'W
Port-Gentil Gabon 84 E1..............................0°46'S 8°49'E
Port Glasgow Scotland 14 E3........................55°56'N 4°41'W
Port Harcourt Nigeria 84 E1.........................4°46'N 7°01'E
Porthcawl Wales 11 D3................................51°29'N 3°42'W
Port Hedland Australia 108 A4.....................20°23'S 118°37'E
Porthleven England 11 B2............................50°05'N 5°19'W
Port Hope Simpson Canada 61 M3...............52°31'N 55°47'W
Portimão Portugal 45 A2..............................37°08'N 8°32'W
Port Isaac Bay England 11 C2.......................50°36'N 4°49'W
Portishead England 8 C2..............................51°29'N 2°46'W
Portknockie Scotland 17 G2..........................57°42'N 2°51'W
Portland Australia 108 D3.............................38°21'S 141°34'E
Portland Me. U.S.A. 63 L5............................43°41'N 70°17'W
Portland Oreg. U.S.A. 62 B6.........................45°29'N 122°38'W
Portland, Isle of pen. England 8 C1...............50°33'N 2°25'W
Portlaoise Ireland 18 D3...............................53°02'N 7°18'W
Portlethen Scotland 17 G2...........................57°04'N 2°08'W
Port Lincoln Australia 108 C3........................34°43'S 135°49'E
Port Louis Mauritius 79 E1...........................20°10'S 57°30'E
Port Macquarie Australia 108 E3...................31°25'S 152°53'E
Port Moresby P.N.G. 108 D6........................9°28'S 147°13'E
Portnahaven Scotland 14 C3.........................55°41'N 6°30'W
Porto Alegre Brazil 73 D3.............................30°03'S 51°11'W
Porto Esperidião Brazil 72 D5........................15°50'S 58°32'W
Port of Ness Scotland 16 C3.........................58°30'N 6°14'W
Port of Spain Trinidad and Tobago 67 L3 ....10°37'N 61°30'W
Portogruaro Italy 46 E1................................45°46'N 12°50'E
Porto-Novo Benin 84 E2..............................6°30'N 2°40'E
Porto Santana Brazil 72 D6..........................0°01'S 51°09'W
Porto-Vecchio France 44 H2.........................41°35'N 9°16'E
Porto Velho Brazil 72 C6..............................8°47'S 63°54'W
Portoviejo Ecuador 72 A6............................1°06'S 80°28'W
Portpatrick Scotland 14 D2...........................54°51'N 5°07'W
Port Pirie Australia 108 C3...........................33°10'S 138°02'E
Portree Scotland 16 C2................................57°25'N 6°12'W
Portrush Northern Ireland 14 C3...................55°12'N 6°39'W
Port Said Egypt 85 H5.................................31°16'N 32°18'E
Portsmouth England 8 D1............................50°48'N 1°06'W
Portsmouth d. England 21 E2.......................50°50'N 1°04'W
Portsmouth U.S.A. 63 J4..............................38°44'N 82°59'W
Portsoy Scotland 17 G2...............................57°41'N 2°41'W
Portstewart Northern Ireland 14 C3.............55°11'N 6°43'W
Port Sudan Sudan 85 H3.............................19°36'N 37°12'E
Port Talbot Wales 10 D3..............................51°36'N 3°48'W
Portugal Europe 45 B3.................................39°41'N 7°57'W
Portumna Ireland 18 C3...............................53°06'N 8°13'W
Port Vila Vanuatu 109 F5.............................17°44'S 168°17'E
Port William Scotland 14 E2.........................54°46'N 4°35'W
Posadas Argentina 73 D4.............................27°25'S 55°50'W
Poso Indonesia 103 G3................................1°24'S 120°47'E
Potenza Italy 49 F5......................................40°38'N 15°48'E
Poti Georgia 53 E2......................................42°09'N 41°40'E
Potiskum Nigeria 84 F3................................11°42'N 11°04'E
Potosí Bolivia 72 C5.....................................19°36'S 65°47'W
Potsdam Germany 46 E5..............................52°24'N 13°04'E
Poulton-le-Fylde England 12 E2...................53°51'N 2°59'W
Poûthĭsăt Cambodia 102 C6.........................12°32'N 103°57'E
Powell, Lake resr U.S.A. 62 D4.....................37°34'N 110°37'W
Powick England 8 C3...................................52°10'N 2°15'W
Powys d. Wales 21 D3..................................52°23'N 3°25'W
Poyang Hu l. China 99 L3.............................29°05'N 116°22'E
Požarevac Serbia 50 D7...............................44°37'N 21°11'E
Poza Rica Mexico 66 E5................................20°35'N 97°26'W
Poznań Poland 46 G5...................................52°25'N 16°56'E
Pozoblanco Spain 45 C3...............................38°23'N 4°50'W
Prabumulih Indonesia 102 C2.......................3°26'S 104°13'E
Prachuap Khiri Khan Thailand 102 B6............11°49'N 99°49'E
Prague Czechia 46 F4...................................50°04'N 14°26'E
Praia Cape Verde 84 B3...............................14°55'N 23°29'W

Polegate England 9 F1.................................50°49'N 0°15'E
Pol-e Khomrī Afgh. 95 K7............................35°56'N 68°46'E
Polis Cyprus 51 J2.......................................35°01'N 32°25'E
Prapat Indonesia 102 B4..............................2°41'N 98°57'E
Prawle Point England 11 D2.........................50°12'N 3°44'W
Preparis Island Cocos Is 97 H3....................14°51'N 93°39'E
Přerov Czechia 46 G3..................................49°27'N 17°27'E
Presidente Prudente Brazil 73 D4.................22°10'S 51°23'W
Prešov Slovakia 46 I3...................................48°59'N 21°16'E
Prespa, Lake Europe 50 D5...........................40°52'N 21°03'E
Presque Isle town U.S.A. 63 M6...................46°41'N 68°01'W
Prestatyn Wales 10 D5.................................53°20'N 3°24'W
Presteigne Wales 10 D4...............................52°16'N 3°00'W
Preston Dor. England 8 C1...........................50°39'N 2°25'W
Preston Lancs. England 12 E2......................53°46'N 2°42'W
Prestonpans Scotland 15 G3........................55°58'N 2°59'W
Prestwick Scotland 14 E3.............................55°30'N 4°37'W
Pretoria S. Africa 83 B2................................25°44'S 28°13'E
Preveza Greece 50 D4..................................38°57'N 20°45'E
Prievidza Slovakia 46 H3..............................48°47'N 18°38'E
Prijedor Bos. and Herz. 50 B7......................44°59'N 16°43'E
Prijepolje Serbia 50 C6.................................43°23'N 19°39'E
Prilep Macedonia 50 D5...............................41°21'N 21°33'E
Primorsko-Akhtarsk Russia 51 M8...............46°03'N 38°10'E
Prince Albert Canada 60 H3.........................53°12'N 105°44'W
Prince Alfred, Cape Canada 60 F5................74°20'N 124°47'W
Prince Charles Island Canada 61 K4.............67°48'N 76°12'W
Prince Edward Island d. Canada 61 L2..........46°41'N 63°09'W
Prince Edward Islands Indian Oc. 117 F1.....47°00'S 37°00'E
Prince George Canada 60 F3.......................53°55'N 122°46'W
Prince of Wales Island Australia 108 D5.......10°43'S 142°09'E
Prince of Wales Island Canada 61 I5.............72°27'N 99°08'W
Prince of Wales Island U.S.A. 60 E3.............55°38'N 132°45'W
Prince Patrick Island Canada 60 G5.............76°57'N 118°47'W
Prince Rupert Canada 60 E3.........................54°19'N 130°19'W
Princes Risborough England 8 E2.................51°43'N 0°50'W
Príncipe i. São Tomé and Príncipe 84 E2......1°39'N 7°22'E
Pripet r. Ukraine 47 N4................................51°16'N 30°16'E
Pripet Marshes Belarus/Ukraine 47 K4........51°39'N 24°34'E
Pristina Kosovo 50 D6.................................42°40'N 21°10'E
Privas France 44 F4......................................44°44'N 4°36'E
Prizren Kosovo 50 D6..................................42°13'N 20°43'E
Probolinggo Indonesia 102 E2......................7°47'S 113°13'E
Probus England 11 C2.................................50°18'N 4°57'W
Providence U.S.A. 63 L5...............................41°50'N 71°25'W
Providence, Cape New Zealand 109 F2.........46°01'S 166°28'E
Providencia, Isla de i. Caribbean Sea 67 H3
....13°21'N 81°20'W
Provins France 44 E6...................................48°34'N 3°18'E
Provo U.S.A. 62 D5.....................................40°17'N 111°41'W
Prudhoe Bay town U.S.A. 60 D5...................70°18'N 148°10'W
Prüm Germany 42 F3..................................50°13'N 6°25'E
Pruszków Poland 46 I5................................52°10'N 20°49'E
Prut r. Europe 47 M1...................................45°28'N 28°12'E
Pryluky Ukraine 47 O4.................................50°35'N 32°24'E
Przemyśl Poland 47 J3.................................49°47'N 22°46'E
Psara i. Greece 50 F4..................................38°37'N 25°35'E
Psebay Russia 51 N7...................................44°07'N 40°47'E
Psel r. Russia/Ukraine 47 P4........................51°05'N 35°15'E
Pskov Russia 43 G2.....................................57°49'N 28°19'E
Pskov, Lake Estonia/Russia 43 F2................58°02'N 27°56'E
Pucallpa Peru 72 B6....................................8°22'S 74°35'W
Pudozh Russia 52 D4..................................61°49'N 36°22'E
Pudsey England 13 F2.................................53°48'N 1°40'W
Puducherry India 96 E3...............................11°57'N 79°48'E
Puebla Mexico 66 E4...................................19°02'N 98°12'W
Puebla d. Mexico 66 E4...............................18°04'N 98°39'W
Pueblo U.S.A. 62 F4....................................38°17'N 104°38'W
Puente-Genil Spain 45 C2............................37°23'N 4°46'W
Puerto de la Estaca Canary Islands 45 X1....27°47'N 17°54'W
Puerto del Rosario Canary Islands 45 Z2.....28°30'N 13°52'W
Puerto Deseado Argentina 73 C2................47°45'S 65°55'W
Puertollano Spain 45 C3..............................38°41'N 4°06'W
Puerto Montt Chile 73 B2............................41°27'S 72°58'W
Puerto Natales Chile 73 B1..........................51°35'S 72°24'W
Puerto Peñasco Mexico 66 B7......................31°19'N 113°32'W
Puerto Princesa Phil. 102 F5.........................9°45'N 118°45'E
Puerto Rico i. Central America 67 K4............17°45'N 66°34'W
Puerto Vallarta Mexico 66 C5.......................20°40'N 105°14'W
Pula Croatia 46 E1.......................................44°53'N 13°51'E
Pulborough England 9 E1.............................50°57'N 0°30'W
Puttusk Poland 46 I5...................................52°42'N 21°05'E
Pune India 96 D4..18°32'N 73°57'E
Puning China 99 L2......................................23°17'N 116°09'E
Punjab d. India 96 E7..................................31°00'N 75°18'E
Punta Arenas Chile 73 B1.............................53°09'S 70°57'W
Punta Gorda Nicaragua 67 H3......................11°32'N 83°46'W
Punto Fijo Venezuela 67 J3..........................11°39'N 70°11'W
Pur r. Russia 54 I4.......................................67°33'N 77°53'E
Purari r. P.N.G. 108 D6................................7°46'S 144°54'E
Purbeck, Isle of pen. England 8 C1...............50°39'N 2°01'W
Puri India 96 G4..19°48'N 85°55'E
Purmerend Neth. 42 D5...............................52°31'N 4°57'E
Purus r. Brazil/Peru 72 C6............................3°42'S 61°28'W
Pustoshka Russia 47 M7..............................56°20'N 29°22'E
Putian China 99 L3......................................25°26'N 119°00'E
Puting, Tanjung pt Indonesia 102 E3............3°35'S 111°50'E
Putrajaya Malaysia 102 C4...........................2°55'N 101°39'E
Puttalam Sri Lanka 96 E2.............................8°01'N 79°50'E
Putumayo r. Colombia 72 B6........................2°43'S 70°03'W
Puvurnituq Canada 61 K4............................60°02'N 77°17'W
Puy de Dôme mt. France 44 E4....................45°46'N 2°58'E
Puy de Sancy mt. France 44 E4....................45°31'N 2°49'E
Pwllheli Wales 10 C4...................................52°53'N 4°25'W
Pyaozero, Ozero l. Russia 43 G4..................66°11'N 30°47'E
Pyasina r. Russia 55 J5................................73°35'N 86°19'E
Pyatigorsk Russia 53 E2...............................44°03'N 43°04'E
Pyè Myanmar 97 I4......................................18°48'N 95°13'E
Pyhäjoki Finland 43 F4................................64°28'N 24°15'E
Pyhäselkä l. Finland 43 G3...........................62°31'N 29°41'E
Pyinmana Myanmar 97 I4............................19°44'N 96°13'E
Pyle Wales 11 D3..51°32'N 3°42'W
Pylos Greece 50 D3.....................................36°55'N 21°42'E
P'yŏngyang N. Korea 99 N5.........................39°01'N 125°45'E
Pyramid Lake U.S.A. 62 C5..........................40°09'N 119°37'W
Pyrenees mts Europe 45 G5.........................42°30'N 2°00'E
Pyrgos Greece 50 D3...................................37°40'N 21°27'E
Pyryatyn Ukraine 47 O4..............................50°14'N 32°30'E

Q

Qâ'en Iran 95 I6...33°42'N 59°05'E
Qamanittuaq Canada 61 I4..........................64°17'N 95°43'W
Qamdo China 98 H4....................................31°13'N 97°08'E
Qarshi Uzbekistan 95 K7..............................38°52'N 65°48'E
Qasigiannguit Greenland 61 M4....................68°48'N 51°11'W
Qatar Asia 95 H5...25°25'N 51°57'E

Qattara Depression f. Egypt 85 G4..............29°48'N 27°06'E
Qazax Azerbaijan 53 E2..............41°06'N 45°21'E
Qazvīn Iran 95 G7..............36°17'N 49°58'E
Qeshm Iran 95 I5..............26°57'N 56°15'E
Qiemo China 98 F5..............38°05'N 85°33'E
Qijiaojing China 98 G6..............43°25'N 91°38'E
Qilian Shan mts China 98 H5..............39°21'N 97°06'E
Qinā Egypt 85 H4..............26°08'N 32°45'E
Qingdao China 99 M5..............36°05'N 120°24'E
Qinghai d. China 98 H5..............36°07'N 96°31'E
Qinghai Hu l. China 99 I5..............36°49'N 100°06'E
Qinhuangdao China 99 L5..............39°56'N 119°38'E
Qinzhou China 99 J2..............21°57'N 108°31'E
Qionghai China 99 K1..............19°13'N 110°29'E
Qiqihar China 99 M7..............47°13'N 123°58'E
Qom Iran 95 H6..............34°38'N 50°51'E
Qo'ng'irot Uzbekistan 53 F2..............43°04'N 58°51'E
Qornet es Saouda mt. Lebanon 51 L2..............34°18'N 36°06'E
Quang Ngai Vietnam 102 D7..............15°04'N 108°50'E
Quantock Hills England 11 D3..............51°10'N 3°15'W
Quanzhou China 99 K3..............25°57'N 111°05'E
Quba Azerbaijan 53 E2..............41°22'N 48°31'E
Quchan Iran 95 I7..............36°59'N 58°29'E
Québec Canada 61 K2..............46°48'N 71°15'W
Québec d. Canada 61 K3..............54°45'N 74°31'W
Queenborough England 9 F2..............51°25'N 0°45'E
Queen Charlotte Islands Canada 60 E3..............53°59'N 133°20'W
Queen Charlotte Sound str. Canada 60 F3
..............51°24'N 129°09'W
Queen Elizabeth Islands Canada 61 I4..............76°31'N 107°31'W
Queen Maud Gulf Canada 60 H4..............68°13'N 102°08'W
Queensland d. Australia 108 D4..............22°37'S 144°17'E
Quelimane Mozambique 83 C3..............17°53'S 36°53'E
Querétaro Mexico 66 D5..............20°37'N 100°22'W
Querétaro d. Mexico 66 E5..............20°51'N 99°50'W
Quetta Pakistan 96 C7..............30°14'N 67°03'E
Quetzaltenango Guatemala 66 F3..............14°50'N 91°30'W
Quezon City Phil. 103 G6..............14°36'N 121°01'E
Quibala Angola 83 A3..............10°44'S 14°59'E
Quibdó Colombia 72 B7..............5°39'N 76°38'W
Quimper France 44 A5..............47°59'N 4°06'W
Quintana Roo d. Mexico 66 G4..............18°44'N 88°47'W
Quito Ecuador 72 B6..............0°14'S 78°30'W
Quoich, Loch l. Scotland 16 D2..............57°03'N 5°18'W
Quoile r. Northern Ireland 14 D2..............54°21'N 5°42'W
Quy Nhơn Vietnam 102 D6..............13°44'N 109°13'E
Quzhou China 99 L3..............28°57'N 118°52'E

R

Raahe Finland 43 F4..............64°41'N 24°29'E
Raalte Neth. 42 F5..............52°23'N 6°17'E
Raasay i. Scotland 16 C2..............57°23'N 6°02'W
Raasay, Sound of str. Scotland 16 C2..............57°26'N 6°06'W
Raba Indonesia 102 F2..............8°32'S 118°46'E
Rabat Morocco 84 D5..............34°01'N 6°47'W
Rābigh Saudi Arabia 94 E4..............22°50'N 39°00'E
Race, Cape Canada 61 M2..............46°38'N 53°09'W
Rach Gia Vietnam 102 D5..............9°59'N 105°06'E
Radom Poland 46 I4..............51°24'N 21°09'E
Radomsko Poland 46 H4..............51°04'N 19°27'E
Radstock England 8 C2..............51°17'N 2°27'W
Rafha' Saudi Arabia 94 F5..............29°33'N 43°25'E
Rafsanjān Iran 95 I6..............30°24'N 55°59'E
Raglan Wales 10 D3..............51°46'N 2°51'W
Ragusa Italy 48 F4..............36°55'N 14°44'E
Rahachow Belarus 47 N5..............53°05'N 30°03'E
Rahimyar Khan Pakistan 96 D6..............28°22'N 70°19'E
Raichur India 96 E4..............16°13'N 77°18'E
Rainier, Mount vol. U.S.A. 62 B6..............46°54'N 121°44'W
Raipur India 96 F5..............21°14'N 81°39'E
Rajahmundry India 96 F4..............17°00'N 81°52'E
Rajanpur Pakistan 95 L5..............29°05'N 70°24'E
Rajasthan d. India 96 D6..............26°40'N 73°31'E
Rajkot India 96 D5..............22°14'N 70°53'E
Rajshahi Bangl. 96 G5..............24°22'N 88°36'E
Rakhiv Ukraine 47 K3..............48°03'N 24°12'E
Rakitnoye Russia 47 P4..............50°50'N 35°50'E
Rakvere Estonia 43 F2..............59°21'N 26°22'E
Raleigh U.S.A. 63 K4..............35°47'N 78°37'W
Rame Head England 11 C2..............50°19'N 4°15'W
Rāmhormoz Iran 95 G6..............31°10'N 49°35'E
Râmnicu Vâlcea Romania 50 F7..............45°07'N 24°22'E
Ramsbottom England 13 E2..............53°39'N 2°19'W
Ramsey England 9 E3..............52°27'N 0°06'W
Ramsey Isle of Man 12 C3..............54°19'N 4°23'W
Ramsey Bay Isle of Man 12 C3..............54°20'N 4°22'W
Ramsey Island Wales 10 B3..............51°51'N 5°22'W
Ramsgate England 9 G2..............51°20'N 1°25'E
Rancagua Chile 73 B3..............34°11'S 70°44'W
Ranchi India 96 G5..............23°22'N 85°22'E
Randers Denmark 43 B2..............56°27'N 10°03'E
Rangoon Myanmar 97 I4..............16°49'N 96°08'E
Rangpur Bangl. 97 G6..............25°46'N 89°16'E
Rankin Inlet Canada 61 I4..............62°52'N 92°03'W
Rannoch, Loch l. Scotland 17 E1..............56°41'N 4°23'W
Rannoch Moor f. Scotland 16 E1..............56°38'N 4°46'W
Ranong Thailand 102 B5..............9°57'N 98°38'E
Rantauprapat Indonesia 102 B4..............2°06'N 99°47'E
Raoul Island Indian Oc. 109 H4..............29°15'S 177°57'W
Rapallo Italy 46 C1..............44°21'N 9°14'E
Raphoe Ireland 14 B2..............54°52'N 7°35'W
Rapid City U.S.A. 62 F5..............44°04'N 103°14'W
Ras Dejen mt. Ethiopia 85 H3..............13°12'N 38°23'E
Rasht Iran 95 G7..............37°16'N 49°34'E
Raskoh mts Pakistan 95 K5..............28°54'N 65°26'E
Ras Tannūrah Saudi Arabia 95 H5..............26°38'N 50°10'E
Rat Buri Thailand 102 B6..............13°31'N 99°50'E
Rathdrum Ireland 18 E2..............52°56'N 6°14'W
Rathenow Germany 46 E5..............52°37'N 12°20'E
Rathfriland Northern Ireland 14 C2..............54°14'N 6°09'W
Rathkeale Ireland 18 C2..............52°31'N 8°56'W
Rathlin Island Northern Ireland 14 C3..............55°17'N 6°10'W
Rathluirc Ireland 18 C2..............52°21'N 8°41'W
Ratne Ukraine 47 K4..............51°40'N 24°32'E
Rättvik Sweden 43 C3..............60°53'N 15°08'E
Rauma Finland 43 E3..............61°08'N 21°31'E
Raunds England 9 E3..............52°20'N 0°32'W
Ravenna Italy 46 E1..............44°25'N 12°13'E
Ravensthorpe Australia 108 B3..............33°34'S 120°01'E
Rawaki i. Kiribati Oc. 116 A6..............3°42'S 170°40'W
Rawalpindi Pakistan 96 D7..............33°38'N 73°08'E
Rawicz Poland 46 G4..............51°37'N 16°51'E
Rawlins U.S.A. 62 E5..............41°48'N 107°13'W

Rawson Argentina 73 C2..............43°15'S 65°06'W
Rawtenstall England 13 E2..............53°42'N 2°17'W
Rayleigh England 9 F2..............51°35'N 0°36'E
Razgrad Bulgaria 50 G6..............43°32'N 26°30'E
Ré, Île de i. France 44 C5..............46°10'N 1°22'W
Reading England 8 E2..............51°27'N 0°58'W
Reading d. England 21 E2..............51°27'N 0°59'W
Rebiana Sand Sea des. Libya 94 B4..............24°42'N 21°18'E
Reboly Russia 43 G3..............63°50'N 30°48'E
Rechytsa Belarus 47 N5..............52°22'N 30°26'E
Recife Brazil 72 F6..............8°02'S 34°48'W
Red r. U.S.A. 63 H3..............31°05'N 91°44'W
Red Bluff U.S.A. 62 B5..............40°11'N 122°14'W
Redcar England 13 F3..............54°37'N 1°03'W
Redcar and Cleveland d. England 21 E4..............54°33'N 1°02'W
Red Deer Canada 60 G3..............52°16'N 113°49'W
Redding U.S.A. 62 B5..............40°36'N 122°29'W
Redditch England 8 D3..............52°19'N 1°56'W
Redhill England 9 E2..............51°14'N 0°10'W
Redruth England 11 B2..............50°14'N 5°14'W
Red Lakes Canada 61 I3..............51°01'N 93°50'W
Red Lakes U.S.A. 63 H6..............48°03'N 94°44'W
Red Sea Africa/Asia 94 E4..............26°30'N 34°42'E
Red Wharf Bay Wales 10 C5..............53°19'N 4°11'W
Ree, Lough l. Ireland 18 D3..............53°32'N 7°59'W
Regensburg Germany 46 E3..............49°01'N 12°06'E
Reggane Algeria 84 E4..............26°46'N 0°09'E
Reggio di Calabria Italy 49 G4..............38°06'N 15°39'E
Reggio nell'Emilia Italy 46 D1..............44°41'N 10°38'E
Regina Canada 60 H3..............50°27'N 104°37'W
Reidh, Rubha pt Scotland 16 D2..............57°52'N 5°51'W
Reigate England 9 E2..............51°14'N 0°12'W
Reims France 44 F6..............49°15'N 4°03'E
Reindeer Lake Canada 60 H4..............57°24'N 102°23'W
Reinosa Spain 45 C5..............42°59'N 4°07'W
Reiphólsfjöll hill Iceland 43 X2..............65°41'N 22°20'W
Reliance Canada 60 H4..............62°43'N 109°06'W
Relizane Algeria 48 D4..............35°44'N 0°40'E
Rena Norway 43 B3..............61°08'N 11°22'E
Renfrewshire d. Scotland 20 C4..............55°52'N 4°31'W
Reni Ukraine 51 H7..............45°27'N 28°18'E
Rennell i. Solomon Is 109 F5..............11°40'S 160°18'E
Rennes France 44 C6..............48°07'N 1°41'W
Reno r. Italy 46 E1..............44°35'N 12°17'E
Reno U.S.A. 62 C4..............39°32'N 119°48'W
Republican r. U.S.A. 62 G4..............39°06'N 96°52'W
Repulse Bay town Canada 61 J4..............66°32'N 86°08'W
Resistencia Argentina 73 D4..............27°24'S 58°59'W
Reşiţa Romania 50 D7..............45°18'N 21°53'E
Resolute Canada 61 I5..............74°41'N 94°46'W
Resolution Island Canada 61 L4..............61°34'N 64°52'W
Retford England 13 G2..............53°19'N 0°57'W
Rethel France 42 D2..............49°31'N 4°23'E
Rethymno Greece 50 F2..............35°21'N 24°28'E
Réunion i. Indian Oc. 117 G2..............20°00'S 55°00'E
Reus Spain 45 F4..............41°09'N 1°06'E
Reutlingen Germany 46 C3..............48°30'N 9°12'E
Rewa India 96 F5..............24°32'N 81°18'E
Reykjavík Iceland 43 X2..............64°08'N 21°55'W
Reynosa Mexico 66 E6..............26°04'N 98°17'W
Rēzekne Latvia 43 F2..............56°31'N 27°20'E
Rhayader Wales 10 D4..............52°18'N 3°31'W
Rheine Germany 42 G5..............52°17'N 7°28'E
Rheinland-Pfalz d. Germany 42 G2..............49°46'N 7°27'E
Rhine r. Europe 46 B4..............51°53'N 6°03'E
Rhins of Galloway, The pen. Scotland 14 D2
..............54°55'N 5°07'W
Rhode Island d. U.S.A. 63 L5..............41°40'N 71°35'W
Rhodes Greece 51 H3..............36°26'N 28°13'E
Rhodes i. Greece 51 H3..............36°15'N 28°10'E
Rhodope Mountains Bulgaria/Greece 50 E5
..............41°52'N 23°41'E
Rhondda f. Wales 10 D3..............51°38'N 3°25'W
Rhondda Cynon Taff d. Wales 21 D2..............51°36'N 3°23'W
Rhône r. France/Switz. 44 F3..............43°37'N 4°40'E
Rhyl Wales 10 D5..............53°19'N 3°29'W
Riau, Kepulauan is Indonesia 102 C4..............0°34'N 104°11'E
Ribble r. England 13 E2..............53°45'N 2°45'W
Ribe Denmark 43 B1..............55°20'N 8°46'E
Ribeirão Preto Brazil 73 E4..............21°12'S 47°48'W
Ribnița Moldova 47 M2..............47°46'N 29°00'E
Richfield U.S.A. 62 D4..............38°46'N 112°05'W
Richland U.S.A. 62 C6..............46°19'N 119°17'W
Richmond England 13 F3..............54°24'N 1°44'W
Richmond U.S.A. 63 K4..............37°34'N 77°28'W
Riesa Germany 46 E4..............51°19'N 13°17'E
Rifstangi pt Iceland 43 Y2..............66°33'N 16°13'W
Riga Latvia 43 F2..............56°56'N 24°07'E
Riga, Gulf of Estonia/Latvia 43 E2..............57°24'N 23°45'E
Rigside Scotland 15 F3..............55°36'N 3°47'W
Riihimäki Finland 43 F3..............60°44'N 24°47'E
Rijeka Croatia 50 A7..............45°19'N 14°26'E
Rimini Italy 48 F5..............44°04'N 12°34'E
Rimouski Canada 61 L2..............48°27'N 68°32'W
Rimsdale, Loch l. Scotland 17 E3..............58°17'N 4°10'W
Ringkøbing Denmark 43 B2..............56°05'N 8°15'E
Ringvassøya i. Norway 43 D5..............69°55'N 18°56'E
Ringwood England 8 D1..............50°51'N 1°47'W
Riobamba Ecuador 72 B6..............1°41'S 78°42'W
Rio Branco Brazil 72 C5..............10°01'S 67°48'W
Río Cuarto Argentina 73 C3..............33°08'S 64°21'W
Rio de Janeiro Brazil 73 E4..............22°53'S 43°17'W
Río Gallegos Argentina 73 C1..............51°39'S 69°15'W
Rio Grande town Brazil 73 D3..............32°04'S 52°08'W
Rio Grande r. Mexico/U.S.A. 67 E6..............25°57'N 97°10'W
Riohacha Colombia 72 B8..............11°32'N 72°58'W
Rio Verde Brazil 72 D5..............17°48'S 50°55'W
Ripley England 13 F2..............53°03'N 1°24'W
Ripon England 13 F3..............54°08'N 1°32'W
Risca Wales 10 D3..............51°36'N 3°06'W
Rishton England 13 E2..............53°46'N 2°25'W
Riva del Garda Italy 46 D1..............45°53'N 10°50'E
Riverside U.S.A. 62 C3..............33°57'N 117°24'W
Rivière-du-Loup Canada 61 L2..............47°50'N 69°32'W
Rivne Ukraine 47 L4..............50°37'N 26°14'E
Riyadh Saudi Arabia 95 G4..............24°43'N 46°41'E
Rize Turkey 51 N5..............41°02'N 40°32'E
Rizhao China 99 L5..............35°19'N 119°33'E
Rjukan Norway 43 B2..............59°53'N 8°34'E
Rjuvbrokkene mt. Norway 43 A2..............59°11'N 7°10'E
Roadford Reservoir England 11 C2..............50°42'N 4°13'W
Roanne France 44 F5..............46°03'N 4°05'E
Roanoke U.S.A. 63 K4..............37°16'N 79°58'W
Roanoke r. U.S.A. 63 K4..............36°02'N 76°22'W
Robertsfors Sweden 43 E4..............64°11'N 20°52'E
Roberval Canada 61 K2..............48°31'N 72°14'W
Robson, Mount Canada 60 G3..............53°07'N 119°06'W
Roca, Cabo da c. Portugal 45 A3..............38°47'N 9°29'W

Rocha Uruguay 73 D3..............34°30'S 54°19'W
Rochdale England 13 E2..............53°37'N 2°10'W
Rochefort Belgium 42 E3..............50°10'N 5°13'E
Rochefort France 44 C4..............45°57'N 0°58'W
Rochester England 9 F2..............51°23'N 0°30'E
Rochester Minn. U.S.A. 63 H5..............44°02'N 92°27'W
Rochester N. Y. U.S.A. 63 K5..............43°09'N 77°38'W
Rochford England 9 F2..............51°35'N 0°42'E
Rockford U.S.A. 63 I5..............42°17'N 89°04'W
Rockhampton Australia 108 E4..............23°23'S 150°34'E
Rockingham Forest England 9 E3..............52°31'N 0°32'W
Rocky Mountains Canada/U.S.A. 60 F3..............40°57'N 107°58'W
Rodel Scotland 16 C2..............57°45'N 6°58'W
Rodez France 44 E4..............44°22'N 2°34'E
Roe r. Northern Ireland 14 C3..............55°06'N 6°58'W
Roermond Neth. 42 E4..............51°12'N 5°59'E
Roeselare Belgium 42 C3..............50°57'N 3°08'E
Rokiškis Lithuania 43 F1..............55°57'N 25°35'E
Rolla U.S.A. 63 H4..............37°56'N 91°46'W
Roma i. Indonesia 103 H2..............7°31'S 127°25'E
Romain, Cape U.S.A. 63 K3..............32°59'N 79°22'W
Roman Romania 47 L2..............46°55'N 26°55'E
Romania Europe 49 H6..............46°07'N 24°36'E
Romanzof, Cape U.S.A. 60 B4..............61°49'N 166°06'W
Rombas France 42 F2..............49°15'N 6°05'E
Rome Italy 48 F5..............41°54'N 12°30'E
Romford England 9 F2..............51°35'N 0°11'E
Romney Marsh f. England 9 F2..............51°03'N 0°54'E
Romny Ukraine 47 O4..............50°45'N 33°28'E
Romsey England 8 D1..............50°59'N 1°30'W
Rona i. Scotland 16 C2..............57°33'N 5°57'W
Rona i. Scotland 16 D4..............59°07'N 5°49'W
Ronas Hill Scotland 17 H5..............60°32'N 1°27'W
Ronda Spain 45 C2..............36°44'N 5°10'W
Rondonópolis Brazil 72 D5..............16°29'S 54°38'W
Rønne Denmark 43 C1..............55°06'N 14°43'E
Ronse Belgium 42 C3..............50°45'N 3°36'E
Roosendaal Neth. 42 D4..............51°31'N 4°28'E
Roque de los Muchachos vol. Canary Islands 45 X2
..............28°45'N 17°51'W
Roquefort France 44 C4..............44°02'N 0°19'W
Roraima, Mount Guyana 72 C7..............5°15'N 60°44'W
Røros Norway 43 B3..............62°34'N 11°23'E
Rosario Argentina 73 C3..............32°56'S 60°41'W
Roscoff France 44 B6..............48°43'N 3°59'W
Roscommon Ireland 18 C3..............53°38'N 8°11'W
Roscommon d. Ireland 18 C3..............53°49'N 8°16'W
Roscrea Ireland 18 D2..............52°57'N 7°48'W
Roseau Dominica 67 L4..............15°17'N 61°23'W
Roseburg U.S.A. 62 B5..............43°13'N 123°21'W
Roseires Reservoir Sudan 94 D2..............11°33'N 34°31'E
Rosenheim Germany 46 E2..............47°51'N 12°08'E
Roşiori de Vede Romania 50 F7..............44°07'N 25°00'E
Roslavl' Russia 47 O5..............53°57'N 32°51'E
Rossan Point Ireland 18 C4..............54°42'N 8°48'W
Rossel Island P.N.G. 108 E5..............11°24'S 154°10'E
Rossington England 13 F2..............53°29'N 1°03'W
Rosslare Harbour Ireland 18 E2..............52°15'N 6°20'W
Rosso Mauritania 84 C3..............16°29'N 15°47'W
Ross of Mull pen. Scotland 14 C4..............56°18'N 6°19'W
Ross-on-Wye England 8 C2..............51°55'N 2°35'W
Rossosh' Russia 53 D3..............50°12'N 39°33'E
Røssvatnet l. Norway 43 C4..............65°46'N 14°19'E
Rostock Germany 46 E6..............54°05'N 12°07'E
Rostov-na-Donu Russia 53 D2..............47°13'N 39°44'E
Roswell U.S.A. 62 F3..............33°21'N 104°30'W
Rota i. N. Mariana Is 103 L6..............14°09'N 145°17'E
Rote i. Indonesia 103 G1..............10°29'S 123°24'E
Rothbury England 13 F4..............55°19'N 1°54'W
Rother r. England 8 E1..............50°57'N 0°32'E
Rotherham England 13 F2..............53°26'N 1°21'W
Rothes Scotland 17 F2..............57°32'N 3°12'W
Rothesay Scotland 14 D3..............55°50'N 5°03'W
Rothwell England 8 E3..............52°25'N 0°48'W
Rotterdam Neth. 42 D4..............51°55'N 4°30'E
Rotuma i. Fiji 109 G5..............12°29'S 177°05'E
Roubaix France 44 E7..............50°42'N 3°10'E
Rouen France 44 D6..............49°26'N 1°06'E
Round Hill England 13 F3..............54°24'N 1°59'W
Round Mountain Australia 108 E3..............30°24'S 152°15'E
Rousay i. Scotland 17 F4..............59°11'N 3°08'W
Rouyn-Noranda Canada 63 K6..............48°14'N 79°02'W
Rovaniemi Finland 43 F4..............66°29'N 25°42'E
Rovigo Italy 46 D1..............45°04'N 11°47'E
Rovinj Croatia 46 E1..............45°05'N 13°38'E
Royale, Isle i. U.S.A. 63 I6..............48°02'N 88°38'W
Royal Leamington Spa England 8 D3..............52°17'N 1°32'W
Royal Tunbridge Wells England 9 F2..............51°08'N 0°16'E
Royan France 44 C4..............45°38'N 1°01'W
Royston England 9 E3..............52°03'N 0°01'W
Royton England 12 E2..............53°34'N 2°07'W
Ruabon Wales 10 D4..............52°59'N 3°02'W
Rub' al Khālī des. Saudi Arabia 95 G3..............19°01'N 46°30'E
Rubtsovsk Russia 54 J3..............51°33'N 81°09'E
Rudnya Russia 47 N6..............54°57'N 31°06'E
Rudnyy Kazakhstan 54 H3..............52°57'N 63°07'E
Rufiji r. Tanzania 83 C4..............8°02'S 39°17'E
Rugby England 8 D3..............52°22'N 1°16'W
Rugby U.S.A. 62 F6..............48°20'N 100°01'W
Rugeley England 8 D3..............52°46'N 1°56'W
Rügen i. Germany 46 E6..............54°23'N 13°27'E
Ruhr r. Germany 42 F4..............51°26'N 6°43'E
Rukwa, Lake Tanzania 83 C4..............8°09'S 32°25'E
Rum i. Scotland 16 C1..............56°59'N 6°22'W
Ruma Serbia 50 C7..............45°01'N 19°50'E
Rum Cay i. Bahamas 67 J5..............23°42'N 74°48'W
Runcorn England 12 E2..............53°20'N 2°42'W
Rundu Namibia 83 A3..............17°54'S 19°47'E
Ruoqiang China 98 F5..............38°58'N 88°08'E
Ruse Bulgaria 50 F6..............43°49'N 25°57'E
Rushden England 8 E3..............52°17'N 0°36'W
Russia Asia/Europe 54 I4..............57°12'N 40°44'E
Ruteng Indonesia 102 G2..............8°33'S 120°25'E
Ruthin Wales 10 D5..............53°07'N 3°19'W
Rutland d. England 21 E3..............52°42'N 0°38'W
Rutland Water resr England 8 E3..............52°39'N 0°40'W
Ruza Russia 47 Q6..............55°42'N 36°13'E
Ruzayevka Russia 53 E3..............54°03'N 44°58'E
Ružomberok Slovakia 46 H3..............49°05'N 19°17'E
Rwanda Africa 85 G1..............2°16'S 29°58'E
Ryan, Loch b. Scotland 14 D3..............55°01'N 5°05'W
Ryazan' Russia 53 D3..............54°37'N 39°44'E
Rybachiy, Poluostrov f. Russia 52 D4..............69°40'N 32°32'E
Rybinsk Russia 52 D3..............58°03'N 38°51'E
Rybinskoye Vodokhranilishche resr Russia 52 D3
..............58°21'N 38°27'E

Rybnik Poland 46 H4..............50°06'N 18°33'E
Ryde England 8 D1..............50°44'N 1°10'W
Rye England 9 F1..............50°57'N 0°44'E
Rye r. England 13 G3..............54°10'N 0°44'W
Rye Bay England 9 F1..............50°54'N 0°45'E
Ryōtsu Japan 104 C3..............38°04'N 138°25'E
Ryukyu Islands Japan 99 M2..............24°13'N 124°52'E
Rzeszów Poland 47 J4..............50°02'N 22°01'E
Rzhev Russia 52 D3..............56°16'N 34°20'E

S

Saale r. Germany 46 D4..............51°57'N 11°56'E
Saarbrücken Germany 46 B3..............49°15'N 6°58'E
Saaremaa i. Estonia 43 E2..............58°14'N 22°46'E
Saarland d. Germany 42 F2..............49°28'N 6°53'E
Saarlouis Germany 42 F2..............49°20'N 6°46'E
Sab' Ābār Syria 51 L1..............33°42'N 37°47'E
Šabac Serbia 50 C7..............44°46'N 19°42'E
Sabadell Spain 45 G4..............41°33'N 2°05'E
Sabah d. Malaysia 102 F5..............5°27'N 116°59'E
Sabana, Archipiélago de is Cuba 67 H5..............23°18'N 80°46'W
Sabhā Libya 84 F4..............26°55'N 14°28'E
Sabinas Mexico 66 D6..............27°52'N 101°07'W
Sable, Cape Canada 61 L2..............43°25'N 65°39'W
Sable, Cape U.S.A. 63 J2..............25°08'N 81°10'W
Sable Island Canada 61 M2..............43°57'N 59°55'W
Şabyā Saudi Arabia 94 F2..............17°07'N 42°35'E
Sabzevār Iran 95 I7..............36°12'N 57°37'E
Sacramento U.S.A. 62 B4..............38°34'N 121°25'W
Sacramento Mountains U.S.A. 62 E3..............34°23'N 106°04'W
Sado r. Portugal 45 A3..............38°25'N 8°36'W
Sadoga-shima i. Japan 104 C3..............37°56'N 138°33'E
Säffle Sweden 43 C2..............59°08'N 12°56'E
Saffron Walden England 9 F3..............52°02'N 0°15'E
Safi Morocco 84 D5..............32°22'N 9°15'W
Safonovo Russia 47 O6..............55°07'N 33°14'E
Safonovo Russia 52 E4..............65°41'N 48°08'E
Sagar India 96 E5..............23°50'N 78°45'E
Sagres Portugal 45 A2..............37°01'N 8°57'W
Sahand, Kūh-e mt. Iran 95 G7..............37°38'N 46°28'E
Sahara des. Africa 84 E4..............19°01'N 4°03'E
Saidpur Bangl. 96 G6..............25°46'N 88°58'E
Saimaa l. Finland 43 G3..............61°15'N 28°21'E
St Abb's Head Scotland 15 G3..............55°55'N 2°09'W
St Agnes England 11 B2..............50°19'N 5°12'W
St Agnes i. England 11 A1..............49°53'N 6°21'W
St Albans England 9 E2..............51°45'N 0°20'W
St Aldhelm's Head England 8 C1..............50°35'N 2°03'W
St-Amand-les-Eaux France 42 C3..............50°26'N 3°25'E
St-Amand-Montrond France 44 E5..............46°44'N 2°30'E
St Andrews Scotland 15 G4..............56°20'N 2°48'W
St Anne Channel Is 11 Z9..............49°43'N 2°12'W
St Ann's Head Wales 10 B3..............51°41'N 5°12'W
St Anthony Canada 61 M3..............51°20'N 55°23'W
St Asaph Wales 10 D5..............53°15'N 3°27'W
St Austell England 11 C2..............50°20'N 4°47'W
St Austell Bay England 11 C2..............50°19'N 4°45'W
St-Barthélemy i. Central America 67 L4..............17°54'N 62°49'W
St Bees England 12 D3..............54°30'N 3°35'W
St Bees Head England 12 D3..............54°31'N 3°38'W
St Brelade Channel Is 11 Z8..............49°11'N 2°12'W
St Bride's Bay Wales 10 B3..............51°48'N 5°18'W
St-Brieuc France 44 B6..............48°31'N 2°45'W
St Catherine's Point England 8 D1..............50°34'N 1°17'W
St Clears Wales 10 C3..............51°49'N 4°30'W
St Cloud U.S.A. 63 H6..............45°34'N 94°10'W
St Columb Major England 11 C2..............50°26'N 4°56'W
St David's Wales 10 B3..............51°53'N 5°16'W
St David's Head Wales 10 B3..............51°54'N 5°20'W
St-Dié France 44 G6..............48°17'N 6°57'E
St-Dizier France 44 F6..............48°39'N 4°57'E
Saintes France 44 C4..............45°45'N 0°37'W
St-Étienne France 44 F4..............45°26'N 4°24'E
Saintfield Northern Ireland 14 D2..............54°27'N 5°49'W
St Gallen Switz. 46 C2..............47°26'N 9°23'E
St George's Grenada 67 L3..............12°03'N 61°45'W
St George's Channel Ireland/U.K. 18 E1..............51°58'N 6°08'W
St Germans England 11 C2..............50°24'N 4°19'W
St Govan's Head Wales 10 C3..............51°36'N 4°55'W
St Helena i. Atlantic Oc. 78 B2..............16°00'S 6°00'W
St Helena Bay S. Africa 83 A1..............32°43'S 18°07'E
St Helens England 12 E2..............53°27'N 2°44'W
St Helens, Mount vol. U.S.A. 62 B6..............46°08'N 122°13'W
St Helier Channel Is 11 Z8..............49°11'N 2°06'W
St Ives Cambs. England 9 E3..............52°20'N 0°04'W
St Ives Corn. England 11 B2..............50°13'N 5°28'W
St Ives Bay England 11 B2..............50°13'N 5°28'W
St-Jean, Lac l. Canada 63 L6..............48°37'N 72°07'W
St Joe r. U.S.A. 62 C6..............47°25'N 116°45'W
Saint John Canada 61 L2..............45°16'N 66°04'W
St John Channel Is 11 Z8..............49°15'N 2°08'W
St John r. U.S.A. 63 M6..............45°46'N 66°12'W
St John's Antigua 67 L4..............17°05'N 61°51'W
St John's Canada 61 M2..............47°28'N 52°18'W
St John's Point Northern Ireland 14 D2..............54°13'N 5°39'W
St John's Town of Dalry Scotland 14 E3..............55°06'N 4°10'W
St Joseph U.S.A. 63 H4..............39°48'N 94°51'W
St Joseph, Lake Canada 63 H7..............50°59'N 90°57'W
St Just England 11 B2..............50°08'N 5°41'W
St Keverne England 11 B2..............50°03'N 5°05'W
St Kilda i. Scotland 16 A2..............57°49'N 8°33'W
St Kitts and Nevis Central America 67 L4..............17°17'N 62°35'W
St Lawrence inlet Canada 61 L2..............48°18'N 69°30'W
St Lawrence, Gulf of Canada 61 L2..............48°20'N 61°29'W
St Lawrence U.S.A. 60 B4..............63°05'N 169°50'W
St-Lô France 44 C6..............49°07'N 1°05'W
St-Louis Senegal 84 C3..............16°00'N 16°29'W
St Louis U.S.A. 63 H4..............38°43'N 90°14'W
St Lucia Central America 67 L3..............13°57'N 60°53'W
St Magnus Bay Scotland 17 H5..............60°24'N 1°36'W
St-Malo France 44 B6..............48°39'N 2°00'W
St-Malo, Golfe de g. France 44 B6..............48°48'N 2°16'W
St Margaret's Hope Scotland 17 G3..............58°49'N 2°57'W
St Martin Channel Is 11 Y9..............49°26'N 2°33'W
St-Martin i. Central America 67 L4..............18°08'N 62°59'W
St Martin's i. England 11 A1..............49°58'N 6°17'W
St Mary's i. England 11 A1..............49°56'N 6°16'W
St Matthew Island U.S.A. 60 A4..............60°27'N 172°49'W
St-Maurice r. Canada 63 L6..............46°21'N 72°32'W
St Mawes England 11 B2..............50°09'N 5°01'W
St Moritz Switz. 46 C2..............46°30'N 9°53'E
St-Nazaire France 44 B5..............47°17'N 2°13'W

St Neots England 9 E3 .... 52°14′N 0°16′W
St-Niklaas Belgium 42 D4 ....51°10′N 4°10′E
St-Omer France 42 B3 ....50°45′N 2°16′E
St Ouen Channel Is 11 Z8 ....49°14′N 2°12′W
St Paul U.S.A. 63 H5 ....44°57′N 93°05′W
St Peter Port Channel Is 11 Y9 ....49°28′N 2°32′W
St Petersburg Russia 54 E3 ....59°56′N 30°18′E
St Petersburg U.S.A. 63 J2 ....27°45′N 82°42′W
St Pierre and Miquelon is N. America 61 M2
....46°42′N 56°29′W
St-Pol-sur-Ternoise France 9 H1 ......50°23′N 2°20′E
St Pölten Austria 46 F3 ....48°12′N 15°38′E
St-Quentin France 44 E6 ....49°51′N 3°17′E
St Sampson Channel Is 11 Y9 ....49°29′N 2°31′W
St Vincent and the Grenadines Central America 67 L3
....12°50′N 60°52′W
St-Vith Belgium 42 F3 ....50°17′N 6°07′E
St Wendel Germany 42 G2 ....49°28′N 7°09′E
Saipan i. N. Mariana Is 103 L7 ....15°15′N 145°49′E
Saitama Japan 104 C3 ....35°51′N 139°39′E
Saittanulkki hill Finland 43 F4 ....66°57′N 25°48′E
Sajama, Nevado mt. Bolivia 72 C5 ...18°09′S 68°52′W
Saka Morocco 45 D1 ....34°37′N 3°23′W
Sakai Japan 104 C2........................34°34′N 135°29′E
Sakākā Saudi Arabia 94 F5 ....29°56′N 40°05′E
Sakakawea, Lake U.S.A. 62 F6........47°45′N 102°15′W
Sakarya r. Turkey 51 I5 ....41°07′N 30°38′E
Sakata Japan 104 C3 ....38°54′N 139°49′E
Sakhalin i. Russia 55 P2 ....48°10′N 142°40′E
Şäki Azerbaijan 53 E2.....................41°12′N 47°11′E
Sakura Japan 104 D3 ....35°44′N 140°13′E
Sal i. Cape Verde 84 B3 ....16°49′N 22°59′W
Sala Sweden 43 D2.........................59°55′N 16°36′E
Salado r. Argentina 73 C3...............32°27′S 60°49′W
Salado r. Mexico 66 E6 ....26°45′N 99°26′W
Şalālah Oman 95 H3 ....17°02′N 54°10′E
Salamanca Spain 45 C4 ....40°58′N 5°39′W
Salavat i. Indonesia 103 I3 ....1°05′S 130°53′E
Salayar i. Indonesia 102 G2 ....6°08′S 120°30′E
Šalčininkai Lithuania 47 K6 ....54°18′N 25°23′E
Salcombe England 11 D2.................50°14′N 3°46′W
Saldanha S. Africa 83 A1 ....33°01′S 17°57′E
Sale Australia 108 D4 ....38°06′S 147°06′E
Sale England 12 E2........................53°26′N 2°19′W
Salehurst England 9 F1 ....50°59′N 0°30′E
Salekhard Russia 52 G4..................66°31′N 66°43′E
Salem India 96 E3 ....11°37′N 78°08′E
Salem U.S.A. 62 B5 ....44°54′N 122°58′W
Salerno Italy 48 F5 ....40°40′N 14°47′E
Salerno, Golfo di g. Italy 48 F5 ......40°25′N 14°43′E
Salford England 13 E2....................53°29′N 2°18′W
Salihli Turkey 51 H4.......................38°29′N 28°08′E
Salihorsk Belarus 47 L5 ....52°47′N 27°32′E
Salinas U.S.A. 62 B4......................36°41′N 121°39′W
Salisbury England 8 D2 ....51°04′N 1°48′W
Salisbury r. U.S.A. 63 K4 ....38°22′N 75°36′W
Salisbury Plain f. England 8 C2 ......51°15′N 2°03′W
Salluit Canada 61 K4......................62°11′N 75°42′W
Salmon r. U.S.A. 62 C6 ....45°52′N 116°45′W
Salmon Arm Canada 62 C7.............50°42′N 119°17′W
Salmon River Mountains U.S.A. 62 C5...44°46′N 115°01′W
Salo Finland 43 E3 ....60°23′N 23°08′E
Sal'sk Russia 53 E2........................46°28′N 41°33′E
Salt r. U.S.A. 62 D3 ....33°22′N 112°17′W
Salta Argentina 73 C4 ....24°45′S 65°25′W
Saltash England 11 C2 ....50°24′N 4°13′W
Saltcoats Scotland 14 E3 ....55°38′N 4°47′W
Saltee Islands Ireland 18 E2............52°07′N 6°36′W
Saltillo Mexico 66 D6 ....25°25′N 101°01′W
Salt Lake City U.S.A. 62 D5............40°42′N 111°54′W
Salton Sea l. U.S.A. 62 C3.............33°28′N 115°58′W
Salvador Brazil 72 F5.....................12°57′S 38°25′W
Salween r. China/Myanmar 97 I5.....24°06′N 98°35′E
Salyan Azerbaijan 53 E1 ....39°35′N 48°58′E
Salzburg Austria 46 E2...................47°48′N 13°03′E
Salzgitter Germany 46 D5...............52°10′N 10°24′E
Samandağ Turkey 51 K3 ....36°04′N 35°58′E
Samani Japan 104 D4....................42°08′N 142°54′E
Samar i. Phil. 103 H6 ....11°54′N 125°43′E
Samara Russia 53 F3.....................53°11′N 50°09′E
Samarinda Indonesia 102 F3 ....0°29′S 117°11′E
Sāmarrā' Iraq 94 F6.......................34°12′N 43°54′E
Samba Dem. Rep. Congo 83 B4......4°38′S 26°20′E
Sambalpur India 96 F5 ....21°27′N 83°59′E
Sambas Indonesia 102 D4..............1°22′N 109°19′E
Sambir Ukraine 47 J3.....................49°31′N 23°12′E
Samer France 9 G1.......................50°38′N 1°45′E
Samoa S. Pacific Oc. 109 H5..........13°58′S 173°23′W
Samos i. Greece 50 G3 ....37°49′N 26°44′E
Samothraki i. Greece 50 G4 ....40°24′N 25°34′E
Sampit Indonesia 102 E3................2°34′S 112°55′E
Samsun Turkey 51 L5.....................41°17′N 36°19′E
San Mali 84 D3 ....13°18′N 4°54′W
Şan'ā' Yemen 94 F3 ....15°23′N 44°11′E
Sanandaj Iran 95 G7 ....35°16′N 46°58′E
San Andrés, Isla de i. Caribbean Sea 67 H3
....12°33′N 81°41′W
San Angelo U.S.A. 62 F3................31°28′N 100°23′W
San Antonio U.S.A. 62 G2...............29°22′N 98°27′W
San Antonio, Cabo c. Cuba 67 H5...21°51′N 84°55′W
San Benedicto, Isla i. Mexico 66 B4...19°19′N 110°47′W
San Cristóbal Venezuela 72 B7........7°45′N 72°15′W
San Cristóbal de la Laguna Canary Islands 45 X2
....28°28′N 16°19′W
Sancti Spíritus Cuba 67 I5..............21°56′N 79°26′W
Sanda Island Scotland 14 D3 ....55°16′N 5°35′W
Sandakan Malaysia 102 F5 ....5°51′N 118°05′E
Sandane Norway 43 A3..................61°47′N 6°14′E
Sandanski Bulgaria 50 E5...............41°34′N 23°16′E
Sanday i. Scotland 17 G4 ....59°15′N 2°29′W
Sanday Sound str. Scotland 17 G4...59°12′N 2°34′W
Sandbach England 13 E2 ....53°09′N 2°22′W
Sandhurst England 8 E2.................51°21′N 0°48′W
San Diego U.S.A. 62 C3..................32°43′N 117°05′W
Sandıklı Turkey 51 I4......................38°28′N 30°16′E
Sandnes Norway 43 A2..................58°51′N 5°44′E
Sandnessjøen Norway 43 C4...........66°01′N 12°39′E
Sandoway Myanmar 97 H4..............18°27′N 94°22′E
Sandown England 8 D1..................50°40′N 1°09′W
Sandpoint U.S.A. 62 C6..................48°16′N 116°33′W
Sandray i. Scotland 16 B1...............56°54′N 7°30′W
Sandviken Sweden 43 D3 ....60°37′N 16°46′E
Sandwich England 9 G2.................51°16′N 1°20′E
Sandy England 9 E3.......................52°08′N 0°18′W
Sandy Cape Australia 108 E4...........24°42′S 153°15′E
Sandy Lake town Canada 61 I3........53°03′N 93°18′W

San Felipe Mexico 66 B7 ....31°02′N 114°50′W
San Fernando Phil. 102 G7 ....16°38′N 120°18′E
San Fernando Spain 45 B2 ....36°28′N 6°11′W
San Fernando de Apure Venezuela 72 C7.....7°49′N 67°28′W
San Francisco U.S.A. 62 B4............37°45′N 122°25′W
San Francisco de Paula, Cabo c. Argentina 73 C2
....49°42′S 67°40′W
Sangir, Kepulauan is Indonesia 103 G4...2°15′N 124°57′E
Sangkulirang Indonesia 102 F3.......0°55′N 117°58′E
Sangli India 96 D4 ....16°53′N 74°38′E
Sangre de Cristo Range mts India 96 E4..38°19′N 106°01′W
San Jorge, Golfo de g. Argentina 73 C2...45°57′S 65°55′W
San José Costa Rica 67 H2.............9°57′N 84°02′W
San Jose U.S.A. 62 B4 ....37°18′N 121°57′W
San José, Isla i. Mexico 66 B5.........24°54′N 110°33′W
San José del Cabo Mexico 66 C5......23°04′N 109°44′W
San Juan Argentina 73 C3 ....31°33′S 68°31′W
San Juan r. Costa Rica/Nicaragua 67 H3......10°57′N 83°44′W
San Juan Puerto Rico 67 K4 ....18°26′N 66°04′W
San Juan r. U.S.A. 62 D4 ....37°15′N 110°30′W
San Juan Mountains U.S.A. 62 E4...37°35′N 107°17′W
Şanlıurfa Turkey 51 M3 ....37°09′N 38°49′E
San Lorenzo Spain 45 D5 ....42°14′N 2°58′W
Sanlúcar de Barrameda Spain 45 B2...36°46′N 6°21′W
San Luis Obispo U.S.A. 62 B4 ....35°18′N 120°40′W
San Luis Potosí Mexico 66 D5.........22°10′N 100°57′W
San Luis Potosí d. Mexico 66 D5......22°51′N 100°48′W
San Marcos U.S.A. 62 G2...............29°51′N 97°56′W
San Marino Europe 48 F5...............43°58′N 12°27′E
San Marino San Marino 48 F5.........43°57′N 12°27′E
San Matías, Golfo g. Argentina 73 C2...41°20′S 64°35′W
San Miguel r. Bolivia 72 C5.............13°52′S 63°54′W
San Miguel El Salvador 66 G3 ....13°32′N 88°08′W
San Miguel de Tucumán Argentina 73 C4...26°48′S 65°16′W
Sanming China 99 L3 ....26°11′N 117°39′E
San Pablo Phil. 103 G6 ....14°04′N 121°18′E
San Pedro de Ycumandyyú Paraguay 73 D4
....24°08′S 57°08′W
San Pedro, Sierra de mts Spain 45 B3...39°31′N 7°15′W
San Pedro Sula Honduras 66 G4.....15°28′N 88°01′W
Sanquhar Scotland 15 F3 ....55°22′N 3°56′W
San Quintín, Cabo c. Mexico 62 C3...30°23′N 116°01′W
Sanremo Italy 44 G3 ....43°49′N 7°47′E
San Salvador i. Bahamas 67 J5.......24°07′N 74°27′W
San Salvador El Salvador 66 G3......13°43′N 89°11′W
San Salvador de Jujuy Argentina 73 C4...24°10′S 65°20′W
San Sebastián Spain 45 D5 ....43°19′N 1°59′W
San Sebastián de la Gomera Canary Islands 45 X2
....28°05′N 17°06′W
Santa Ana El Salvador 66 G3...........14°00′N 89°31′W
Santa Ana U.S.A. 62 C3.................33°45′N 117°56′W
Santa Barbara U.S.A. 62 C3............34°27′N 119°43′W
Santa Clara Cuba 67 I5 ....22°24′N 79°56′W
Santa Cruz Bolivia 72 C5................17°47′S 63°12′W
Santa Cruz de la Palma Canary Islands 45 X2
....28°41′N 17°46′W
Santa Cruz de Tenerife Canary Islands 45 X2
....28°27′N 16°15′W
Santa Cruz Islands Solomon Is 109 F5.......10°46′S 167°21′E
Santa Fé Argentina 73 C3...............31°37′S 60°42′W
Santa Fe U.S.A. 62 E4 ....35°42′N 105°57′W
Santa Isabel i. Solomon Is 109 E6....7°54′S 159°11′E
Santa Margarita, Isla i. Mexico 66 B5...24°25′N 111°50′W
Santa Maria Brazil 73 D4................29°41′S 53°48′W
Santa Maria U.S.A. 62 B3...............34°58′N 120°26′W
Santa Maria di Leuca, Capo c. Italy 50 C4...39°47′N 18°21′E
Santa Marta Colombia 72 B8...........11°16′N 74°12′W
Santander Spain 45 D5...................43°28′N 3°48′W
Santarém Brazil 72 D6 ....2°27′S 54°43′W
Santarém Portugal 45 A3 ....39°15′N 8°41′W
Santa Rosa Argentina 73 C3 ....36°37′S 64°17′W
Santa Rosalía Mexico 66 B6............27°21′N 112°18′W
Santiago i. Cape Verde 84 B3 ....15°19′N 23°45′W
Santiago Chile 73 B3 ....33°28′S 70°39′W
Santiago Dom. Rep. 67 J4 ....19°29′N 70°41′W
Santiago de Compostela Spain 45 A5...42°53′N 8°32′W
Santiago de Cuba Cuba 67 I5 ....20°00′N 75°49′W
Sant Jordi, Golf de g. Spain 45 F4....40°49′N 0°56′E
Santo André Brazil 73 E4 ....23°38′S 46°30′W
Santo Antão i. Cape Verde 84 B3 ....17°01′N 25°21′W
Santo Domingo Dom. Rep. 67 K4.....18°31′N 69°52′W
Santoña Spain 45 D5 ....43°27′N 3°27′W
Santos Brazil 73 E4 ....23°58′S 46°20′W
San Valentín, Cerro mt. Chile 73 B2...46°35′S 73°27′W
São Francisco r. Brazil 72 E5...........10°19′S 36°31′W
São José do Rio Preto Brazil 73 E4...20°49′S 49°22′W
São Luís Brazil 72 E6 ....2°35′S 44°18′W
Saône r. France 44 F4....................45°44′N 4°49′E
São Paulo Brazil 73 E4 ....23°35′S 46°43′W
São Tomé São Tomé and Príncipe 84 E2...0°19′N 6°44′E
São Tomé i. São Tomé and Príncipe 84 E2...0°21′N 6°35′E
São Tomé, Cabo de c. Brazil 73 E4...22°00′S 40°59′W
São Tomé and Príncipe Africa 84 E2...1°00′N 7°04′E
São Vicente, Cabo de c. Portugal 45 A2...37°01′N 8°59′W
Sapporo Japan 104 D4...................43°04′N 141°20′E
Sapri Italy 49 G5 ....40°04′N 15°38′E
Saqqaq Greenland 61 M5...............70°01′N 51°56′W
Saqqez Iran 95 G7.........................36°12′N 46°15′E
Sarāb Iran 95 G7...........................37°55′N 47°31′E
Sara Buri Thailand 102 C6..............14°29′N 100°57′E
Sarajevo Bos. and Herz. 50 C6........43°51′N 18°25′E
Sarandë Albania 50 D4...................39°53′N 20°01′E
Saransk Russia 53 E3 ....54°11′N 45°12′E
Sarapul Russia 52 F3.....................56°30′N 53°48′E
Sarasota U.S.A. 63 J2....................27°19′N 82°33′W
Saratov Russia 53 E3.....................51°34′N 45°59′E
Saravan Iran 95 J5.........................27°20′N 62°25′E
Saray Turkey 51 G5 ....41°26′N 27°55′E
Sardinia i. Italy 48 E5.....................40°16′N 8°40′E
Sarektjåkkå mt. Sweden 43 D4........67°27′N 17°43′E
Sar-e Pol Afghn. 95 K7...................36°15′N 65°57′E
Sargodha Pakistan 96 D7................32°01′N 72°41′E
Sarh Chad 85 F2............................9°07′N 18°23′E
Sārī Iran 95 H7 ....36°33′N 53°03′E
Sarigan i. N. Mariana Is 103 L7 ......16°42′N 145°48′E
Sariyer Turkey 51 H5.....................41°10′N 29°03′E
Sark i. Channel Is 11 Y9 ....49°24′N 2°24′W
Şarkışla Turkey 51 L4 ....39°21′N 36°25′E
Şarköy Turkey 51 G5......................40°37′N 27°06′E
Särna Sweden 43 C3......................61°42′N 13°08′E
Sarny Ukraine 47 L4.......................51°20′N 26°37′E
Saros Körfezi b. Turkey 50 G5..........40°34′N 26°36′E
Sarov Russia 53 E3........................54°56′N 43°20′E
Sarpsborg Norway 43 B2................59°17′N 11°08′E
Sarreboug France 44 G6 ....48°44′N 7°03′E
Sarreguemines France 42 G2 ....49°07′N 7°04′E

Sarria Spain 45 B5.........................42°47′N 7°24′W
Sarthe r. France 44 C5 ....47°34′N 0°31′W
Sasebo Japan 104 A2....................33°09′N 129°44′E
Saskatchewan d. Canada 60 H3......53°08′N 106°03′W
Saskatchewan r. Canada 60 H3 ......53°40′N 100°27′W
Saskatoon Canada 60 H3................52°08′N 106°39′W
Sassandra Côte d'Ivoire 84 D2........4°57′N 6°05′W
Sassari Italy 48 E5 ....40°43′N 8°34′E
Sassnitz Germany 46 E6.................54°31′N 13°38′E
Satka Russia 52 F3........................55°04′N 58°58′E
Satpura Range mts India 96 D5.......21°47′N 74°23′E
Satu Mare Romania 47 J3...............47°47′N 22°53′E
Sauðárkrókur Iceland 43 Y2............65°45′N 19°40′W
Saudi Arabia Asia 94 F4 ....23°41′N 44°13′E
Sault Sainte Marie Canada 61 J2.....46°31′N 84°20′W
Saumlakki Indonesia 103 I2.............8°00′S 131°20′E
Saurimo Angola 83 B4...................9°39′S 20°25′E
Sava r. Europe 50 D7.....................44°50′N 20°28′E
Savai'i i. Samoa 109 H5 ....13°25′S 172°39′W
Savannah U.S.A. 63 J3...................32°04′N 81°07′W
Savannah r. U.S.A. 63 J3................32°02′N 80°53′W
Savannakhét Laos 102 C7...............16°32′N 104°46′E
Save r. Mozambique/Zimbabwe 83 C2...20°56′S 35°03′E
Savinskiy Russia 52 E4...................62°56′N 40°09′E
Savona Italy 46 C1.........................44°19′N 8°29′E
Savu Sea Indonesia 103 G2............9°51′S 121°22′E
Sawel Mountain hill Northern Ireland 14 B2
....54°49′N 7°02′W
Sawhāj Egypt 49 J2 ....26°31′N 31°38′E
Sawston England 9 F3....................52°07′N 0°10′E
Sawtry England 9 E3......................52°26′N 0°17′W
Sawu i. Indonesia 103 G1...............10°32′S 121°58′E
Saxilby England 13 G2 ....53°16′N 0°40′W
Saxmundham England 9 G3...........52°13′N 1°29′E
Sayhūt Yemen 95 H3 ....15°15′N 51°19′E
Saylac Somalia 85 I3 ....11°17′N 43°28′E
Saynshand Mongolia 99 K6............44°46′N 110°12′E
Scafell Pike hill England 12 D3........54°27′N 3°13′W
Scalasaig Scotland 14 C4...............56°04′N 6°11′W
Scalby England 13 G3....................54°18′N 0°27′W
Scalloway Scotland 17 H5 ....60°08′N 1°17′W
Scalp hill Ireland 18 C2..................52°59′N 8°29′W
Scalpay i. High. Scotland 16 D2......57°18′N 5°59′W
Scalpay i. Na h-E. S. Scotland 16 C2...57°52′N 6°39′W
Scalp Mountain hill Ireland 14 B3....55°06′N 7°22′W
Scampton England 13 G2...............53°18′N 0°33′W
Scandinavia f. Europe 34 F5...........65°00′N 18°00′E
Scapa Flow inlet Scotland 17 F3......58°54′N 3°08′W
Scarba i. Scotland 14 D4................56°10′N 5°45′W
Scarborough England 13 G3 ....54°17′N 0°24′W
Scarp i. Scotland 16 B3..................58°01′N 7°11′W
Schaffhausen Switz. 46 C2..............47°42′N 8°38′E
Schagen Neth. 42 D5.....................52°47′N 4°48′E
Schefferville Canada 61 L3..............54°47′N 66°48′W
Scheldt r. Belgium 42 D4................51°21′N 4°15′E
Schiehallion mt. Scotland 17 E1.......56°40′N 4°06′W
Schiermonnikoog i. Neth. 42 F6.......53°31′N 6°17′E
Schleswig Germany 46 C6..............54°31′N 9°33′E
Schwäbische Alb mts Germany 46 C2...47°59′N 8°43′E
Schwaner, Pegunungan mts Indonesia 102 E3
....0°46′S 112°26′E
Schwarzer Mann hill Germany 42 F3...50°15′N 6°21′E
Schwedt/Oder Germany 46 F5.........53°04′N 14°18′E
Schweinfurt Germany 46 D4............50°03′N 10°13′E
Schwerin Germany 46 D5...............53°38′N 11°25′E
Scilly, Isles of England 11 A1..........49°53′N 6°17′W
Scioto r. U.S.A. 63 J4....................38°44′N 82°59′W
Scole England 9 G3 ....52°22′N 1°09′E
Scone Scotland 15 F4 ....56°25′N 3°24′W
Scotland d. U.K. 20 D5 ....57°01′N 3°53′W
Scottish Borders d. Scotland 20 D4...55°40′N 2°44′W
Scottsbluff U.S.A. 62 F5.................41°54′N 103°41′W
Scourie Scotland 16 D3..................58°21′N 5°09′W
Scranton U.S.A. 63 K5...................41°25′N 75°39′W
Scridain, Loch inlet Scotland 14 C4...56°21′N 6°11′W
Scunthorpe England 13 G2 ....53°35′N 0°39′W
Scuol Switz. 46 D2.........................46°48′N 10°18′E
Scutari, Lake Albania/Montenegro 50 C6...42°14′N 19°12′E
Seaford England 9 F1.....................50°46′N 0°06′E
Seaham England 13 F3...................54°50′N 1°20′W
Seamer England 13 G3...................54°14′N 0°26′W
Seascale England 12 D3.................54°24′N 3°29′W
Seaton Cumb. England 12 D3..........54°40′N 3°31′W
Seaton Dev. England 11 D2.............50°42′N 3°04′W
Seaton Delaval England 13 F4..........55°04′N 1°31′W
Seattle U.S.A. 62 B6......................47°36′N 122°20′W
Sebastián Vizcaíno, Bahía b. Mexico 66 B6
....28°08′N 114°45′W
Sebeş Romania 50 E7 ....45°58′N 23°34′E
Şebinkarahisar Turkey 51 M5 ....40°17′N 38°25′E
Secunderabad India 96 E4 ....17°25′N 78°27′E
Sedan France 44 F6.......................49°42′N 4°57′E
Sedbergh England 13 E3.................54°19′N 2°31′W
Seefin hill Ireland 18 D2..................52°14′N 7°36′W
Segezha Russia 52 D4...................63°45′N 34°19′E
Segorbe Spain 45 E3......................39°51′N 0°28′W
Segovia Spain 45 C4 ....40°57′N 4°06′W
Segura r. Spain 45 E3 ....38°06′N 0°38′W
Segura, Sierra de mts Spain 45 D2...37°59′N 2°46′W
Seiland i. Norway 43 E5..................70°28′N 23°18′E
Seinäjoki Finland 43 E3..................62°47′N 22°51′E
Seine r. France 44 E6.....................49°26′N 0°15′E
Seine, Baie de b. France 44 C6........49°29′N 0°32′W
Sekondi Ghana 84 D2....................4°58′N 1°43′W
Selaru i. Indonesia 103 I2...............8°13′S 130°55′E
Selatan, Tanjung pt Indonesia 102 E3...4°09′S 114°38′E
Selattyn England 8 C3 ....52°53′N 3°05′W
Selawik U.S.A. 60 B4.....................66°36′N 160°16′W
Selby England 13 F2 ....53°47′N 1°04′W
Selkirk Canada 60 I3 ....50°09′N 96°53′W
Selkirk Scotland 15 G3...................55°33′N 2°50′W
Sellindge England 9 F2 ....51°06′N 0°59′E
Selsey England 8 E1......................50°44′N 0°47′W
Selsey Bill hd England 8 E1............50°43′N 0°49′W
Selvas f. Brazil 72 B6.....................6°29′S 71°47′W
Selwyn Mountains Canada 60 E4.....64°16′N 131°38′W
Selwyn Range hills Australia 108 C4...21°14′S 139°54′E
Semarang Indonesia 102 E2...........6°55′S 110°29′E
Semenivka Ukraine 47 O5...............52°10′N 32°35′E
Seminoe Reservoir U.S.A. 62 E5......42°06′N 106°51′W
Semipalatinsk Kazakhstan 54 J3......50°25′N 80°19′E
Semnān Iran 95 H7........................35°30′N 53°21′E
Semois r. Belgium/France 42 D2......49°53′N 4°45′E
Sendai Japan 104 D3.....................38°15′N 140°53′E
Senegal Africa 84 C3.....................14°29′N 14°41′W
Sénégal r. Mauritania 84 C3 ....16°00′N 16°31′W

Senja i. Norway 43 D5....................69°20′N 17°14′E
Sennar Sudan 85 H3......................13°31′N 33°36′E
Sens France 44 E6 ....48°12′N 3°17′E
Seoul S. Korea 99 N5.....................37°32′N 127°00′E
Sepik r. P.N.G. 103 K3 ....3°53′S 144°33′E
Sept-Îles Canada 61 L3..................50°13′N 66°23′W
Seram i. Indonesia 103 H3..............3°03′S 129°24′E
Serang Indonesia 102 D2...............6°04′S 106°09′E
Serbia Europe 50 D6......................44°01′N 20°55′E
Şereflikoçhisar Turkey 51 J4...........38°56′N 33°33′E
Seremban Malaysia 102 C4.............2°41′N 101°54′E
Seret r. Ukraine 47 K3...................48°36′N 25°51′E
Sergino Russia 52 G4.....................62°33′N 65°39′E
Sergiyev Posad Russia 52 D3..........56°19′N 38°08′E
Serik Turkey 51 I3..........................36°57′N 31°07′E
Serov Russia 52 G3........................59°38′N 60°34′E
Serowe Botswana 83 B2.................22°24′S 26°42′E
Serpukhov Russia 53 D3.................54°55′N 37°25′E
Serra da Mesa, Represa resr Brazil 72 E5...14°17′S 48°30′W
Serres Greece 50 E5......................41°06′N 23°33′E
Serui Indonesia 103 J3...................1°52′S 136°17′E
Sestroretsk Russia 43 G3 ....60°05′N 29°57′E
Sète France 44 E3.........................43°24′N 3°42′E
Sete Lagoas Brazil 72 E5................19°28′S 44°13′W
Setesdal f. Norway 43 A2................59°15′N 7°23′E
Sétif Algeria 84 E5.........................36°11′N 5°25′E
Seto-naikai sea Japan 104 B2..........33°38′N 132°17′E
Settat Morocco 84 D5....................32°58′N 7°36′W
Settle England 13 E3 ....54°04′N 2°17′W
Setúbal Portugal 45 A3...................38°32′N 8°53′W
Setúbal, Baía de b. Portugal 45 A3...38°20′N 9°02′W
Seul, Lac l. Canada 63 H7...............50°21′N 92°29′W
Sevan Armenia 53 E2 ....40°33′N 44°58′E
Sevastopol' Ukraine 49 J5...............44°36′N 33°31′E
Seven Heads Ireland 18 C1.............51°34′N 8°42′W
Sevenoaks England 9 F2 ....51°16′N 0°12′E
Severn r. Canada 61 J3..................55°59′N 87°36′W
Severn r. U.K. 8 C2........................51°51′N 2°21′W
Severnaya Zemlya is Russia 55 L6...80°09′N 103°23′E
Severnyy Russia 52 G4..................67°36′N 64°13′E
Severnyy, Ostrov i. Russia 54 G5.....75°00′N 58°00′E
Severo-Kuril'sk Russia 55 Q3...........50°40′N 156°06′E
Sevier Lake U.S.A. 62 D4................38°56′N 113°09′W
Seville Spain 45 C2........................37°24′N 5°58′W
Seward U.S.A. 60 D4......................60°09′N 149°24′W
Seward Peninsula U.S.A. 60 B4........65°29′N 164°05′W
Seychelles Indian Oc. 79 E2............4°40′S 55°43′E
Seydişehir Turkey 51 I3..................37°25′N 31°52′E
Seyðisfjörður Iceland 43 Z2.............65°16′N 14°02′W
Seyhan r. Turkey 51 K3..................36°44′N 34°54′E
Seym r. Russia/Ukraine 47 P4..........51°16′N 34°16′E
Seymchan Russia 55 Q4.................62°50′N 152°20′E
Sfântu Gheorghe Romania 50 F7.....45°52′N 25°48′E
Sfax Tunisia 48 F3.........................34°45′N 10°45′E
Sgurr Alasdair hill Scotland 16 C2...57°12′N 6°13′W
Sgurr Dhomhnuill hill Scotland 16 D1...56°45′N 5°27′W
Sgurr Mòr mt. Scotland 16 D2.........57°42′N 5°01′W
Shaanxi d. China 99 J4..................34°43′N 108°13′E
Shadrinsk Russia 52 G3.................56°07′N 63°37′E
Shaftesbury England 8 C2..............51°00′N 2°12′W
Shahr-e Kord Iran 95 H6................32°19′N 50°49′E
Shahrezā Iran 95 H6......................32°00′N 51°52′E
Shāhrūd Iran 95 H7........................36°24′N 54°56′E
Shakhovskaya Russia 47 P7............56°02′N 35°30′E
Shakhty Russia 53 E2....................47°42′N 40°12′E
Shakhun'ya Russia 52 E3 ....57°40′N 46°36′E
Shalkar Kazakhstan 53 F2..............47°47′N 59°39′E
Shandong d. China 99 L5................36°22′N 117°45′E
Shandong Bandao pen. China 99 M5...37°05′N 121°02′E
Shanghai China 99 M4...................31°15′N 121°29′E
Shangqiu China 99 L4 ....34°24′N 115°38′E
Shanklin England 8 D1...................50°38′N 1°10′W
Shannon r. Ireland 18 C2...............52°40′N 8°38′W
Shannon, Mouth of the Ireland 18 B2...52°31′N 9°51′W
Shantarskiye Ostrova is Russia 55 O3...55°20′N 137°22′E
Shantou China 99 L2.....................23°24′N 116°42′E
Shanxi d. China 99 K5....................38°03′N 111°48′E
Shaoguan China 99 K3..................24°48′N 113°37′E
Shaoxing China 99 M4...................30°01′N 120°38′E
Shaoyang China 99 K3...................27°14′N 111°30′E
Shap England 12 E3.......................54°32′N 2°41′W
Shapinsay i. Scotland 17 G4............59°02′N 2°48′W
Shaqrā' Saudi Arabia 94 G5............25°15′N 45°16′E
Sharjah U.A.E. 95 I5......................25°21′N 55°23′E
Shark Bay Australia 108 A4..............25°17′S 113°32′E
Shashemené Ethiopia 85 H2............7°12′N 38°36′E
Shchigry Russia 47 Q4...................51°52′N 36°56′E
Sheberghān Afghn. 95 K7...............36°42′N 65°45′E
Sheboygan U.S.A. 63 I5.................43°45′N 87°43′W
Sheelin, Lough l. Ireland 18 D3........53°49′N 7°19′W
Sheep Haven b. Ireland 14 B3.........55°12′N 7°55′W
Sheerness England 9 F2.................51°26′N 0°46′E
Sheffield England 13 F2..................53°23′N 1°28′W
Shelby U.S.A. 62 D6......................48°29′N 111°48′W
Shelikhova, Zaliv g. Russia 55 Q4....60°40′N 157°23′E
Shelikof Strait U.S.A. 60 C3............57°27′N 155°17′W
Shenyang China 99 M6..................41°46′N 123°24′E
Shenzhen China 99 K2...................22°33′N 114°09′E
Shepetivka Ukraine 47 L4...............50°11′N 27°04′E
Sheppey, Isle of i. England 9 F2.......51°24′N 0°46′E
Shepshed England 8 D3.................52°46′N 1°18′W
Shepton Mallet England 8 C2..........51°11′N 2°33′W
Sherborne England 8 C1.................50°57′N 2°31′W
Sherbrooke Canada 61 K2..............45°24′N 71°54′W
Shereiq Sudan 94 D3....................18°42′N 33°40′E
Sheridan U.S.A. 62 E5...................44°48′N 106°55′W
Sheringham England 9 G3..............52°57′N 1°13′E
Sherwood Forest England 13 F2......53°04′N 1°07′W
's-Hertogenbosch Neth. 42 E4.........51°41′N 5°19′E
Shetland d. Scotland 20 E7............60°14′N 0°57′W
Shetland Islands Scotland 17 I5.......60°36′N 0°47′W
Shetpe Kazakhstan 53 F2...............44°09′N 52°17′E
Sheyenne r. U.S.A. 62 G6...............47°03′N 96°50′W
Shiant Islands Scotland 16 C2.........57°53′N 6°25′W
Shibām Yemen 95 G3.....................15°59′N 48°57′E
Shiel, Loch l. Scotland 16 D1...........56°47′N 5°34′W
Shieldaig Scotland 16 D2................57°31′N 5°39′W
Shifnal England 8 C3 ....52°40′N 2°22′W
Shihezi China 98 F6.......................44°14′N 86°03′E
Shijiazhuang China 99 K5...............38°00′N 114°30′E
Shikarpur India 96 E3 ....14°14′N 75°18′E
Shikarpur Pakistan 95 K5...............27°56′N 68°42′E
Shikoku i. Japan 104 B2.................33°08′N 133°49′E
Shikoku-sanchi mts Japan 104 B2...33°26′N 132°53′E
Shildon England 13 F3...................54°38′N 1°39′W
Shilega Russia 52 E4.....................64°04′N 44°06′E

Shillong India 97 H6.....................................25°33'N 91°53'E
Shimonoseki Japan 104 B2..............33°57'N 130°57'E
Shin, Loch l. Scotland 17 E3..............58°09'N 4°38'W
Shingū Japan 104 C2..........................33°43'N 136°00'E
Shining Tor hill England 13 E2...........53°16'N 2°00'W
Shipley England 13 F2..........................53°50'N 1°47'W
Shipston on Stour England 8 D3.........52°04'N 1°37'W
Shirane-san mt. Japan 104 C3..........35°40'N 138°13'E
Shīrāz Iran 95 H5.................................29°37'N 52°31'E
Shire r. Malawi 83 C3..........................17°41'S 35°19'E
Shivamogga India 96 E3.....................13°54'N 75°31'E
Shizuishan China 99 J5........................38°58'N 106°27'E
Shizuoka Japan 104 C2......................34°58'N 138°23'E
Shklow Belarus 47 N6...........................54°13'N 30°17'E
Shkodër Albania 50 C6.........................42°04'N 19°31'E
Shona, Eilean i. Scotland 16 D1........56°48'N 5°53'W
Sho'rchi Uzbekistan 95 K7..................37°59'N 67°46'E
Shostka Ukraine 47 O4.........................51°51'N 33°28'E
Shpola Ukraine 47 N3............................49°01'N 31°23'E
Shreveport U.S.A. 63 H3.....................32°29'N 93°46'W
Shrewsbury England 8 C3....................52°42'N 2°45'W
Shropshire d. England 21 D3.............52°45'N 2°38'W
Shuangjiang China 99 H4...................23°28'N 99°49'E
Shubarkudyk Kazakhstan 53 F2........49°05'N 56°28'E
Shumagin Islands U.S.A. 60 C3........55°09'N 161°00'W
Shumen Bulgaria 50 G6........................43°16'N 26°56'E
Shuqrah Yemen 95 G2...........................13°24'N 45°40'E
Shūshtar Iran 95 G6..............................32°01'N 48°49'E
Shwebo Myanmar 97 I5.......................22°34'N 95°43'E
Shwegyin Myanmar 97 I4....................17°56'N 96°52'E
Shymkent Kazakhstan 54 H2.............42°19'N 69°38'E
Siahan Range mts Pakistan 95 J5.....27°13'N 63°38'E
Šiauliai Lithuania 43 E1........................55°56'N 23°19'E
Šibenik Croatia 50 A6............................43°44'N 15°54'E
Siberia f. Russia 55 M4.........................65°18'N 115°57'E
Siberut i. Indonesia 102 B3...................1°23'S 98°41'E
Sibi Pakistan 95 J5.................................29°30'N 67°55'E
Sibiu Romania 50 F7.............................45°48'N 24°10'E
Sibolga Indonesia 102 B4......................1°40'N 98°48'E
Sibsey England 13 H2...........................53°02'N 0°01'E
Sibu Malaysia 102 E4...........................2°17'N 111°51'E
Sibut C.A.R. 85 F2..................................5°44'N 19°05'E
Sichuan d. China 99 I4.........................30°05'N 103°11'E
Sicily i. Italy 48 F4...............................38°21'N 14°09'E
Sidi Bel Abbès Algeria 84 D5..............35°12'N 0°38'W
Sidi Kacem Morocco 48 B3..................34°12'N 5°39'W
Sidlaw Hills Scotland 15 F4.................56°26'N 3°21'W
Sidmouth England 11 D2.....................50°41'N 3°14'W
Sidney U.S.A. 62 F5............................41°12'N 103°00'W
Sidon Lebanon 49 K3...........................33°33'N 35°23'E
Siedlce Poland 47 J5..............................52°10'N 22°17'E
Siegen Germany 46 C4.........................50°52'N 8°01'E
Sierra Leone Africa 84 C2.....................8°35'N 11°58'W
Sighetu Marmaţiei Romania 47 J6.....47°56'N 23°54'E
Sighișoara Romania 50 F8...................46°14'N 24°47'E
Siglufjörður Iceland 43 Y2....................66°08'N 18°52'W
Sigüenza Spain 45 D4...........................41°05'N 2°37'W
Siguiri Guinea 84 D3...........................11°28'N 9°10'W
Sihanoukville Cambodia 102 C6.......10°38'N 103°34'E
Siilinjärvi Finland 43 F3.......................63°05'N 27°40'E
Siirt Turkey 94 F7.................................37°55'N 41°58'E
Sikar India 96 E6..................................27°31'N 75°13'E
Sikasso Mali 84 D3..............................11°19'N 5°40'W
Sikeston U.S.A. 63 I4............................36°51'N 89°34'W
Sikhote-Alin' mts Russia 55 O2..........43°58'N 133°53'E
Sikkim d. India 96 G6...........................27°31'N 88°27'E
Sil r. Spain 45 B5..................................42°28'N 7°42'W
Siletiteniz, Ozero l. Kazakhstan 98 C8...53°11'N 72°53'E
Silifke Turkey 51 J3................................36°22'N 33°56'E
Siling Co l. China 98 F4.......................31°47'N 88°41'E
Silistra Bulgaria 50 G7.........................44°07'N 27°16'E
Silivri Turkey 51 H5...............................41°04'N 28°16'E
Siljan l. Sweden 43 C3..........................60°53'N 14°44'E
Šilutė Lithuania 43 I6............................55°21'N 21°28'E
Silver City U.S.A. 62 E3......................32°45'N 108°19'W
Silverstone England 8 D3.....................52°05'N 1°02'W
Silverton England 11 D2.......................50°49'N 3°29'W
Simav Turkey 51 H4..............................39°05'N 28°58'E
Simēn mts Ethiopia 94 E3...................13°16'N 37°50'E
Simeulue i. Indonesia 102 B4................2°41'N 96°08'E
Simferopol' Ukraine 49 J5.....................44°57'N 34°07'E
Simojärvi l. Finland 43 F4.....................66°01'N 27°15'E
Simpson Desert Australia 108 C4........24°59'S 136°50'E
Simrishamn Sweden 46 F6...................55°33'N 14°21'E
Sinai pen. Egypt 85 H4.........................29°03'N 33°51'E
Sinaloa d. Mexico 66 C6......................25°42'N 108°11'W
Sincelejo Colombia 72 B7......................9°17'N 75°24'W
Sinclair's Bay Scotland 17 F3..............58°30'N 3°07'W
Sindor Russia 52 F4..............................62°52'N 51°54'E
Sines Portugal 45 A2.............................37°58'N 8°52'W
Singa Sudan 94 D2................................13°09'N 33°54'E
Singapore Asia 102 C4..........................1°27'N 104°32'E
Singapore town Singapore 102 C4......1°19'N 103°51'E
Singaraja Indonesia 102 F2...................8°06'S 115°06'E
Singida Tanzania 83 C4.........................4°50'S 34°45'E
Singkawang Indonesia 102 D4...............0°57'N 108°59'E
Sinj Croatia 50 B6..................................43°42'N 16°38'E
Sinkat Sudan 94 E3...............................18°45'N 36°49'E
Sinop Turkey 51 K6................................42°02'N 35°08'E
Sint Maarten i. Neth. Antilles 67 L4...18°02'N 63°04'W
Sion Mills Northern Ireland 14 B2.......54°47'N 7°28'W
Sioux City U.S.A. 62 G5......................42°32'N 96°23'W
Sioux Falls town U.S.A. 62 G5............43°32'N 96°43'W
Sioux Lookout Canada 61 I3................50°06'N 91°56'W
Sipacate Guatemala 66 F3...................13°59'N 91°08'W
Siping China 99 M6..............................43°04'N 124°24'E
Sipura i. Indonesia 102 B3...................2°12'S 99°42'E
Sira r. Norway 43 A2.............................58°16'N 6°24'E
Siret r. Romania 50 H7.........................45°25'N 28°02'E
Sīrjān Iran 95 I5......................................29°27'N 55°40'E
Sirte Libya 85 F5....................................31°09'N 16°40'E
Sirte, Gulf of Libya 85 F5.....................31°11'N 18°03'E
Širvan Azerbaijan 53 E1.......................39°56'N 48°56'E
Sisak Croatia 50 B7...............................45°29'N 16°23'E
Sisimiut Greenland 61 M4....................66°56'N 53°40'W
Sisophon Cambodia 102 C6................13°34'N 102°59'E
Sīstān, Daryācheh-ye marsh Afgh./Iran 95 J6
....31°33'N 61°10'E
Sisteron France 44 F4...........................44°12'N 5°57'E
Siteia Greece 50 G2..............................35°12'N 26°06'E
Sitka U.S.A. 60 E3...............................57°03'N 135°18'W
Sittard Neth. 42 E3................................50°59'N 5°51'E
Sittingbourne England 9 F2................51°20'N 0°44'E
Sittwe Myanmar 97 H5.......................20°08'N 92°54'E
Sivas Turkey 51 L4................................39°43'N 37°00'E
Siverek Turkey 51 M3...........................37°44'N 39°21'E
Sivrihisar Turkey 51 I4..........................39°27'N 31°32'E

Sīwah Egypt 85 G4................................29°09'N 25°30'E
Skadovs'k Ukraine 51 J8.......................46°07'N 32°54'E
Skaftárós r. mouth Iceland 43 Y1.......63°41'N 17°47'W
Skagen Denmark 43 B2.......................57°43'N 10°35'E
Skagerrak str. Denmark/Norway 43 B2...57°27'N 8°13'E
Skagway U.S.A. 60 E3.......................59°29'N 135°18'W
Skara Sweden 43 C2.............................58°23'N 13°26'E
Skarzysko-Kamienna Poland 46 I4.....51°07'N 20°53'E
Skegness England 13 H2.....................53°09'N 0°20'E
Skellefteå Sweden 43 E4......................64°45'N 20°58'E
Skellefteälven r. Sweden 43 E4...........64°42'N 21°07'E
Skelmersdale England 12 E2..............53°33'N 2°46'W
Skerries Ireland 18 E3..........................53°35'N 6°06'W
Ski Norway 43 B2..................................59°43'N 10°50'E
Skibbereen Ireland 18 B1....................51°33'N 9°16'W
Skiddaw hill England 12 D3................54°39'N 3°09'W
Skien Norway 43 B2..............................59°12'N 9°36'E
Skikda Algeria 84 E5............................36°54'N 6°57'E
Skipton England 13 E2.........................53°58'N 2°01'W
Skive Denmark 43 B2............................56°34'N 9°02'E
Skokholm Island Wales 10 B3............51°41'N 5°16'W
Skomer Island Wales 10 B3................51°44'N 5°20'W
Skopje Macedonia 50 D5.....................41°59'N 21°27'E
Skövde Sweden 43 C2...........................58°23'N 13°51'E
Skovorodino Russia 55 N3..................54°05'N 123°52'E
Skye i. Scotland 16 C2..........................57°21'N 6°20'W
Skyros i. Greece 50 F4.........................38°53'N 24°35'E
Slagelse Denmark 43 B1......................55°24'N 11°22'E
Slamet vol. Indonesia 102 D2...............7°14'S 109°10'E
Slaney r. Ireland 18 E2.........................52°25'N 6°34'W
Slatina Romania 50 F7.........................44°26'N 24°22'E
Slave r. Canada 60 G4..........................61°17'N 113°31'W
Slave Lake town Canada 60 G4..........55°17'N 114°47'W
Slavonski Brod Croatia 50 C7.............45°10'N 18°01'E
Slavyansk-na-Kubani Russia 51 M7...45°16'N 38°08'E
Slawharad Belarus 47 N5....................53°27'N 31°00'E
Sleaford England 13 G2.......................53°00'N 0°24'W
Sleat, Sound of str. Scotland 16 D2...57°02'N 5°53'W
Sleights England 13 G3........................54°27'N 0°40'W
Slieve Anierin hill Ireland 14 B2.........54°05'N 7°59'W
Slieve Beagh hill Ireland/U.K. 14 B2...54°20'N 7°12'W
Slievecallan hill Ireland 18 B2............52°51'N 9°16'W
Slieve Car hill Ireland 18 B4...............54°04'N 9°40'W
Slieve Donard hill Northern Ireland 14 D2...54°11'N 5°55'W
Slievenamon hill Ireland 18 D2..........52°26'N 7°34'W
Slieve Snaght hill Ireland 18 D5.........55°12'N 7°20'W
Sligo Ireland 18 C4...............................54°17'N 8°28'W
Sligo d. Ireland 18 C4...........................54°07'N 8°30'W
Sligo Bay Ireland 18 C4.......................54°18'N 8°55'W
Sliven Bulgaria 50 G6...........................42°41'N 26°19'E
Slobozia Romania 50 G7.....................44°34'N 27°23'E
Slonim Belarus 47 K5............................53°05'N 25°19'E
Slough England 9 E2.............................51°31'N 0°36'W
Slough d. England 21 E2.....................51°30'N 0°35'W
Slovakia Europe 46 H3.........................48°45'N 19°35'E
Slovenia Europe 46 F1..........................46°09'N 14°37'E
Slov''yans'k Ukraine 53 D2.................48°51'N 37°37'E
Slovyechna r. Belarus 47 M4...............51°39'N 29°43'E
Sluch r. Ukraine 47 L4.........................51°37'N 26°39'E
Słupsk Poland 46 G6.............................54°27'N 17°02'E
Slutsk Belarus 47 L5..............................53°01'N 27°32'E
Slyne Head Ireland 18 A3....................53°24'N 10°14'W
Slyudyanka Russia 99 I8.....................51°28'N 103°36'E
Smallwood Reservoir Canada 61 L3...54°01'N 64°50'W
Smarhon' Belarus 47 L6.......................54°29'N 26°25'E
Smila Ukraine 47 N3.............................49°12'N 31°54'E
Smoky r. Canada 60 G3........................56°08'N 117°20'W
Smøla i. Norway 43 A3..........................63°23'N 7°59'E
Smolensk Russia 53 D3........................54°47'N 32°04'E
Smolikas mt. Greece 50 D5..................40°05'N 20°56'E
Smolyan Bulgaria 50 F5.......................41°35'N 24°41'E
Snæfell mt. Iceland 43 Z2.....................64°48'N 15°35'W
Snaefell hill Isle of Man 12 C3.............54°16'N 4°28'W
Snaith England 13 F2............................53°41'N 1°01'W
Snåsa Norway 43 C4............................64°15'N 12°23'E
Sneek Neth. 42 E6.................................53°02'N 5°40'E
Snettisham England 9 F3......................52°53'N 0°30'E
Snežnik mt. Slovenia 46 F1.................45°35'N 14°26'E
Śniardwy, Jezioro l. Poland 47 I5.......53°46'N 21°42'E
Snizort, Loch b. Scotland 16 C2.........57°33'N 6°28'W
Snøtinden mt. Norway 43 C4...............66°38'N 13°57'E
Snov r. Ukraine 47 N4..........................51°32'N 31°32'E
Snowdon mt. Wales 10 C5...................53°04'N 4°04'W
Soay i. Scotland 16 C2..........................57°09'N 6°15'W
Sobradinho, Barragem de resr Brazil 72 E5
....10°14'S 42°24'W
Sobral Brazil 72 E6.................................3°41'S 40°19'W
Sochi Russia 53 D2..............................43°36'N 39°44'E
Society Islands is French Polynesia 116 B2
....17°22'S 152°28'W
Socorro, Isla i. Mexico 66 B4..............18°51'N 110°58'W
Socotra i. Yemen 95 H2......................12°34'N 54°30'E
Sodankylä Finland 43 F4......................67°25'N 26°34'E
Söderhamn Sweden 43 D3...................61°18'N 17°04'E
Södertälje Sweden 43 D2.....................59°12'N 17°38'E
Sodo Ethiopia 85 H2...............................6°49'N 37°42'E
Södra Kvarken str. Finland/Sweden 43 D3...60°19'N 19°02'E
Sofia Bulgaria 50 E6.............................42°41'N 23°19'E
Sognefjorden inlet Norway 43 A3.......61°05'N 5°33'E
Soham England 9 F3.............................52°20'N 0°20'E
Soignies Belgium 42 D3........................50°35'N 4°04'E
Soissons France 44 E6..........................49°23'N 3°20'E
Söke Turkey 50 G3................................37°45'N 27°23'E
Sokhumi Georgia 53 E2........................43°00'N 41°02'E
Sokoto Nigeria 84 E3............................13°05'N 5°15'E
Sokoto r. Nigeria 84 E3.........................11°23'N 4°09'E
Solapur India 96 E4..............................17°41'N 75°55'E
Solihull England 8 D3...........................52°25'N 1°47'W
Solikamsk Russia 52 F3.......................59°42'N 56°44'E
Sol'-Iletsk Russia 53 F3.........................51°06'N 54°58'E
Sollefteå Sweden 43 D3.......................63°10'N 17°17'E
Solomon Islands S. Pacific Oc. 109 F6...7°13'S 157°49'E
Solomon Sea S. Pacific Oc. 108 E6.....7°01'S 152°18'E
Solway Firth est. Scotland 15 F2.........54°41'N 3°38'W
Solwezi Zambia 83 B3.........................12°10'S 26°26'E
Soma Turkey 50 G4..............................39°10'N 27°36'E
Somalia Africa 85 I2..............................3°56'N 46°23'E
Sombor Serbia 50 C7............................45°47'N 19°07'E
Somerset d. England 21 D2................51°04'N 2°56'W
Somerset Island Canada 61 I5............73°19'N 93°22'W
Somerton England 8 C2......................51°03'N 2°44'W
Sommen l. Sweden 43 C2.....................58°00'N 15°17'E
Sønderborg Denmark 46 C6................54°55'N 9°48'E
Sondrio Italy 46 C2...............................46°10'N 9°52'E
Songea Tanzania 83 C3......................10°39'S 35°38'E
Songkhla Thailand 102 C5....................7°10'N 100°35'E

Songyuan China 99 M7......................45°05'N 124°53'E
Sơn La Vietnam 102 C8.......................21°20'N 103°57'E
Sonora d. Mexico 66 B6......................29°42'N 110°36'W
Sonora r. Mexico 66 B6......................28°47'N 111°54'W
Soria Spain 45 D4.................................41°47'N 2°26'W
Soroca Moldova 49 I6..........................48°09'N 28°17'E
Sorochinsk Russia 53 F3......................52°21'N 52°59'E
Sorol atoll Micronesia 103 K5...............8°10'N 140°22'E
Sorong Indonesia 103 I3........................0°54'S 131°17'E
Soroti Uganda 85 H2.............................1°42'N 33°37'E
Søroya i. Norway 43 E5........................70°34'N 22°32'E
Sorraia r. Portugal 45 A3.....................39°02'N 8°50'W
Sorsele Sweden 43 D4..........................65°31'N 17°33'E
Sortavala Russia 43 G3.......................61°42'N 30°41'E
Soshanguve S. Africa 83 B2...............25°31'S 28°06'E
Sosna r. Russia 47 R5...........................52°41'N 38°54'E
Sosneado mt. Argentina 73 C3............34°44'S 69°59'W
Sosnogorsk Russia 52 F4.....................63°36'N 53°53'E
Sosnovka Russia 52 E4........................66°30'N 40°34'E
Sosnowiec Poland 46 H4......................50°17'N 19°08'E
Sos'va Russia 52 G3.............................59°08'N 61°48'E
Souk Ahras Algeria 48 E4....................36°17'N 7°59'E
Souk el Arbaâ du Rharb Morocco 45 C1...34°40'N 5°58'W
Souris r. Canada 62 G6.......................49°41'N 99°40'W
Sousse Tunisia 48 F4...........................35°47'N 10°39'E
Soustons France 44 C3.........................43°45'N 1°20'W
South Africa Africa 83 B1....................30°06'S 24°04'E
Southam England 8 D3.......................52°15'N 1°23'W
South America 72
Southampton England 8 D1...............50°55'N 1°24'W
Southampton d. England 21 E2..........50°56'N 1°24'W
Southampton Island Canada 61 J4.....64°31'N 85°04'W
South Anston England 13 F2...............53°21'N 1°13'W
South Australia d. Australia 108 C3....30°27'S 132°43'E
South Ayrshire d. Scotland 20 C4........55°09'N 4°47'W
South Bank England 13 F3.................54°35'N 1°10'W
South Bend U.S.A. 63 I5....................41°40'N 86°13'W
Southborough England 9 F2...............51°09'N 0°16'E
South Carolina d. U.S.A. 63 J3...........34°02'N 80°47'W
South Cave England 13 G2.................53°46'N 0°36'W
South China Sea N. Pacific Oc. 102 F6...12°00'N 117°49'E
South Dakota d. U.S.A. 62 F5.............44°27'N 100°14'W
South Dorset Downs hills England 8 C1...50°42'N 2°37'W
South Downs hills England 8 E1.........50°53'N 0°28'W
South Dublin d. Ireland 18 E3.............53°16'N 6°24'W
South East Cape Australia 108 D2......43°38'S 146°55'E
Southend-on-Sea England 9 F2..........51°32'N 0°43'E
Southend-on-Sea d. England 21 F2....51°33'N 0°42'E
Southern Alps mts New Zealand 109 G2...43°26'S 170°28'E
Southern Ocean 116 E1
Southern Uplands hills Scotland 14 E3...55°14'N 4°32'W
Southery England 9 F3.........................52°32'N 0°24'E
South Esk r. Scotland 17 G1...............56°43'N 2°33'W
South Georgia and South Sandwich Islands S. Atlantic Oc.
73 F1 53°50'S 36°30'W
South Gloucestershire d. England 21 D2...51°33'N 2°27'W
South Harris pen. Scotland 16 B2........57°49'N 7°03'W
South Island New Zealand 109 G2.....44°24'S 172°31'E
South Kirkby England 13 F2................53°36'N 1°19'W
South Korea Asia 99 N5......................35°32'N 128°04'E
South Lanarkshire d. Scotland 20 D4...55°38'N 3°49'W
Southminster England 9 F2................51°40'N 0°50'E
South Molton England 11 D3.............51°01'N 3°50'W
South Nahanni r. Canada 60 F4.........61°03'N 123°18'W
South Ockendon England 9 F2...........51°31'N 0°18'E
South Ossetia d. Georgia 53 E2..........42°00'N 44°06'E
South Platte r. U.S.A. 62 F5...............41°08'N 100°47'W
Southport Australia 108 E4.................27°56'S 153°23'E
Southport England 12 D2...................53°39'N 3°00'W
South Ronaldsay i. Scotland 17 G3....58°47'N 2°54'W
South Saskatchewan r. Canada 60 H3...53°09'N 105°08'W
South Shields England 13 F3..............54°59'N 1°26'W
South Sudan Africa 85 G2..................7°01'N 30°00'E
South Tyne r. England 13 E3..............54°59'N 2°08'W
South Uist i. Scotland 16 B2...............57°17'N 7°22'W
South Walls pen. Scotland 17 F3.........58°47'N 3°08'W
Southwell England 13 G2...................53°05'N 0°58'W
Southwold England 9 G3....................52°19'N 1°41'E
South Woodham Ferrers England 9 F2...51°39'N 0°37'E
South Wootton England 9 F3.............52°46'N 0°26'E
South Yorkshire d. England 21 E3......53°28'N 1°16'W
Sovetsk Russia 47 I6............................55°05'N 21°53'E
Sovetskiy Russia 52 G4.......................61°26'N 63°30'E
Soweto S. Africa 83 B2........................26°15'S 27°50'E
Sozh r. Europe 47 N4...........................51°57'N 30°49'E
Spain Europe 45 D4.............................40°26'N 3°48'W
Spalding England 9 E3.........................52°47'N 0°09'W
Sparks U.S.A. 62 C4..........................39°32'N 119°46'W
Sparti Greece 50 E3.............................37°04'N 22°26'E
Spartivento, Capo c. Italy 48 E4..........37°56'N 16°05'E
Spatha, Akra pt Greece 50 E2.............35°41'N 23°44'E
Spencer Gulf est. Australia 108 C3......34°54'S 136°27'E
Spennymoor England 13 F3...............54°42'N 1°35'W
Sperrin Mountains hills Northern Ireland 14 B2
54°47'N 7°09'W
Spey r. Scotland 17 F2.........................57°39'N 3°06'W
Speyer Germany 44 H6........................49°19'N 8°24'E
Spijkenisse Neth. 42 D4......................51°50'N 4°19'E
Spilsby England 13 H2.........................53°10'N 0°06'E
Spitsbergen i. Arctic Oc. 54 C5............78°37'N 16°06'E
Split Croatia 50 B6...............................43°31'N 16°27'E
Spofforth England 13 F2......................53°57'N 1°27'W
Spokane U.S.A. 62 C6......................47°38'N 117°22'W
Spratly Islands S. China Sea 102 E6...10°01'N 114°21'E
Spree r. Germany 46 E5........................52°32'N 13°13'E
Springfield U.S.A. 63 I4......................39°48'N 89°39'W
Springfield Mass. U.S.A. 63 L5...........42°05'N 72°35'W
Springfield Mo. U.S.A. 63 H4.............37°16'N 93°18'W
Sprowston England 9 G3.....................52°39'N 1°19'E
Spurn Head England 13 H2................53°34'N 0°05'E
Srebrenica Bos. and Herz. 50 C7.........44°07'N 19°19'E
Srednekolymsk Russia 55 Q4.............67°32'N 153°38'E
Sretensk Russia 55 M3........................52°08'N 117°41'E
Sri Aman Malaysia 102 E4...................1°12'N 111°30'E
Sri Jayewardenepura Kotte Sri Lanka 96 E2...6°56'N 79°54'E
Sri Lanka Asia 96 F2............................7°29'N 80°42'E
Srinagar India 96 D7...........................34°08'N 74°51'E
Stadskanaal Neth. 42 F5......................52°59'N 6°59'E
Staffa i. Scotland 14 C4.......................56°26'N 6°20'W
Stafford England 8 C3.........................52°48'N 2°07'W
Staffordshire d. England 21 D3...........52°52'N 2°04'W
Staines-upon-Thames England 9 E2...51°26'N 0°31'W
Stalbridge England 8 C1......................50°57'N 2°23'W
Stalham England 9 G3.........................52°46'N 1°31'E
Stalowa Wola Poland 47 J4.................50°34'N 22°03'E
Stamford England 9 E3........................52°39'N 0°29'W

Stamford Bridge England 13 G2.........53°59'N 0°55'W
Standish England 12 E2.......................53°35'N 2°40'W
Stanley England 13 F3..........................53°53'N 1°42'W
Stanley Falkland Is 73 D1....................51°43'S 57°52'W
Stanley, Mount Dem. Rep. Congo/Uganda 83 B5
0°25'N 29°56'E
Stannington England 13 F4.................55°06'N 1°40'W
Stanovoy Khrebet mts Russia 55 N3...57°21'N 120°44'E
Stansted Mountfitchet England 9 F2...51°54'N 0°12'E
Stanton England 9 F3...........................52°19'N 0°53'E
Staraya Russa Russia 52 D3...............57°59'N 31°22'E
Stara Zagora Bulgaria 50 F6...............42°26'N 25°38'E
Stargard Szczeciński Poland 46 F5......53°20'N 15°03'E
Starogard Gdański Poland 46 H5........53°58'N 18°31'E
Starokostyantyniv Ukraine 47 L3........49°45'N 27°13'E
Start Bay England 11 D2......................50°18'N 3°37'W
Start Point England 11 D2....................50°13'N 3°38'W
Staryya Darohi Belarus 47 M5............53°02'N 28°17'E
Staryy Oskol Russia 53 D3..................51°18'N 37°51'E
Stavanger Norway 43 A2......................58°58'N 5°44'E
Staveley England 13 F2........................53°16'N 1°21'W
Stavropol' Russia 53 E2........................45°03'N 41°59'E
Stavropol'skaya Vozvyshennost' hills Russia 53 E2
45°05'N 42°35'E
Steenwijk Neth. 42 F5..........................52°47'N 6°07'E
Steep Holm i. England 8 B2................51°20'N 3°06'W
Stefansson Island Canada 60 H5........73°21'N 105°54'W
Steinfurt Germany 42 G5.....................52°09'N 7°21'E
Steinkjer Norway 43 B4.......................64°01'N 11°30'E
Stenness, Loch of l. Scotland 17 F4....59°00'N 3°16'W
Sterling U.S.A. 62 F5..........................40°39'N 103°09'W
Sterlitamak Russia 53 F3.....................53°36'N 55°53'E
Stevenage England 9 E2......................51°54'N 0°12'W
Stewart Canada 60 F3.........................55°57'N 129°59'W
Stewart r. Canada 60 E4......................63°18'N 139°26'W
Stewart Island New Zealand 109 F2...47°09'S 167°55'E
Stewarton Scotland 14 E3...................55°41'N 4°31'W
Steyning England 9 E1.........................50°53'N 0°20'W
Steyr Austria 46 F3...............................48°02'N 14°25'E
Stikine r. Canada 60 E3.......................56°41'N 132°19'W
Stilton England 9 E3.............................52°29'N 0°17'W
Stinchar r. Scotland 14 D3...................55°06'N 5°01'W
Stirling Scotland 15 F4........................56°07'N 3°56'W
Stirling d. Scotland 20 D4...................56°17'N 4°23'W
Stjørdalshalsen Norway 43 B3............63°28'N 10°55'E
Stob Choire Claurigh mt. Scotland 16 E1...56°50'N 4°51'W
Stockholm Sweden 43 D2...................59°20'N 18°04'E
Stockport England 13 E2.....................53°24'N 2°09'W
Stockton U.S.A. 62 B4.......................37°57'N 121°17'W
Stockton-on-Tees England 13 F3.........54°34'N 1°19'W
Stockton-on-Tees d. England 21 E4....54°34'N 1°21'W
Stœ̌ng Trêng Cambodia 102 D6.........13°28'N 105°59'E
Stoer, Point of Scotland 16 D3............58°16'N 5°23'W
Stoke-on-Trent England 13 E2............53°00'N 2°11'W
Stoke-on-Trent d. England 21 D3.........53°01'N 2°10'W
Stokesay England 8 C3.........................52°26'N 2°50'W
Stokesley England 13 F3......................54°28'N 1°11'W
Stolin Belarus 47 L4.............................51°53'N 26°50'E
Stone England 8 C3..............................52°54'N 2°09'W
Stonehaven Scotland 17 G1...............56°58'N 2°12'W
Stony Rapids town Canada 60 H3.......59°15'N 105°59'W
Stora Lulevatten l. Sweden 43 D4.......67°09'N 19°28'E
Storavan l. Sweden 43 D4....................65°40'N 18°16'E
Støren Norway 43 B3...........................63°02'N 10°17'E
Stornoway Scotland 16 C3...................58°13'N 6°23'W
Storrington England 9 E1.....................50°55'N 0°27'W
Storsjön l. Sweden 43 C3.....................63°13'N 14°16'E
Storskrymten mt. Norway 43 B3.........62°22'N 9°03'E
Storuman Sweden 43 D4.....................65°05'N 17°09'E
Storuman l. Sweden 43 D4..................65°11'N 16°54'E
Stotfold England 9 E3...........................52°01'N 0°14'W
Stour r. Dor. England 8 D1...................50°44'N 1°46'W
Stour r. Kent England 9 G2..................51°18'N 1°21'E
Stour r. Warwicks. England 8 D3.........52°11'N 1°44'W
Stourbridge England 8 C3...................52°27'N 2°09'W
Stourport-on-Severn England 8 C3......52°20'N 2°17'W
Stowbtsy Belarus 47 L5........................53°28'N 26°44'E
Stowmarket England 9 F3....................52°11'N 0°59'E
Stow-on-the-Wold England 8 D2........51°56'N 1°43'W
Strabane Northern Ireland 14 B2.........54°50'N 7°27'W
Stradbroke England 9 G3....................52°19'N 1°16'E
Stralsund Germany 46 E6....................54°18'N 13°05'E
Stranda Norway 43 A3.........................62°18'N 6°57'E
Strangford Lough inlet Northern Ireland 14 D2
54°28'N 5°35'W
Stranraer Scotland 14 D2.....................54°54'N 5°02'W
Strasbourg France 44 G6.....................48°35'N 7°44'E
Stratford-upon-Avon England 8 D3......52°11'N 1°43'W
Strathaven Scotland 15 E3..................55°41'N 4°04'W
Strathbeg, Loch of l. Scotland 17 H2...57°37'N 1°54'W
Strathbogie f. Scotland 17 G2.............57°26'N 2°53'W
Strathmore r. Scotland 16 E3.............58°25'N 4°39'W
Strathspey f. Scotland 17 F2...............57°11'N 3°47'W
Strathy Point Scotland 17 E3..............58°36'N 4°01'W
Stratton England 11 C2.......................50°50'N 4°31'W
Stratton St Margaret England 8 D2....51°35'N 1°45'W
Straubing Germany 46 E3....................48°54'N 12°35'E
Straumnes pt Iceland 43 X2................66°26'N 23°10'W
Streatley England 8 D2........................51°32'N 1°09'W
Street England 8 C2.............................51°08'N 2°44'W
Strelka Russia 55 Q4............................61°52'N 152°11'E
Stretham England 9 F3........................52°21'N 0°13'E
Strimonas r. Greece 50 E5...................40°48'N 23°51'E
Stroma, Island of Scotland 17 F3........58°42'N 3°08'W
Stromboli, Isola i. Italy 48 G4.............38°45'N 15°14'E
Stromness Scotland 17 F3...................58°58'N 3°18'W
Strömsund Sweden 43 C3....................63°52'N 15°34'E
Stronsay i. Scotland 17 G4..................59°08'N 2°33'W
Stronsay Firth str. Scotland 17 G4......59°06'N 2°50'W
Stroud England 8 C2............................51°45'N 2°13'W
Struer Denmark 43 B2.........................56°29'N 8°36'E
Strule r. Northern Ireland 14 B2..........54°43'N 7°21'W
Struma r. Bulgaria 50 E5......................41°23'N 23°20'E
Strumble Head Wales 10 B4...............52°02'N 5°08'W
Strumica Macedonia 50 E5..................41°26'N 22°38'E
Stryy Ukraine 47 J3..............................49°15'N 23°51'E
Studley England 8 D3..........................52°16'N 1°54'W
Stupino Russia 47 R6...........................54°54'N 38°05'E
Sturry England 9 G2.............................51°18'N 1°07'E
Sturt Stony Desert Australia 108 D4...28°20'S 141°15'E
Stuttgart Germany 46 C3......................48°47'N 9°10'E
Styr r. Belarus/Ukraine 47 L5...............52°08'N 26°35'E
Suakin Sudan 85 H3............................19°06'N 37°18'E
Subotica Serbia 50 C8..........................46°06'N 19°41'E
Suceava Romania 47 L2.......................47°40'N 26°16'E
Suck r. Ireland 18 C3...........................53°16'N 8°03'W
Sucre Bolivia 72 C5.............................19°06'S 65°18'W

Sudak Ukraine 51 K7............44°51'N 34°59'E
Sudan Africa 85 G3............13°34'N 30°02'E
Sudbury Canada 61 J2............46°29'N 80°59'W
Sudbury England 9 F3............52°03'N 0°44'E
Sudd f. South Sudan 85 G2............7°43'N 29°41'E
Sudety mts Czechia/Poland 46 F4............50°46'N 15°50'E
Suez Egypt 85 H4............29°58'N 32°33'E
Suez, Gulf of Egypt 85 H4............28°03'N 33°33'E
Suez Canal Egypt 49 J3............30°47'N 32°19'E
Suffolk d. England 21 F3............52°10'N 0°52'E
Suhār Oman 95 I4............24°22'N 56°44'E
Suhl Germany 46 D4............50°36'N 10°42'E
Suining China 99 J4............30°29'N 105°33'E
Suizhou China 99 K4............31°42'N 113°20'E
Sukabumi Indonesia 102 D2............6°58'S 106°53'E
Sukadana Indonesia 102 D3............1°12'S 109°59'E
Sukhinichi Russia 47 P6............54°07'N 35°22'E
Sukkur Pakistan 96 C6............27°42'N 68°55'E
Sula i. Norway 43 A3............61°09'N 4°55'E
Sulawesi i. Indonesia 103 H3............2°12'S 125°58'E
Sulina Romania 51 H7............45°09'N 29°39'E
Sullana Peru 72 A6............4°56'S 80°41'W
Sulu Archipelago is Phil. 103 G5............6°55'N 123°10'E
Sulu Sea N. Pacific Oc. 102 F5............8°20'N 119°46'E
Sumatra i. Indonesia 102 B4............3°05'N 98°12'E
Sumba i. Indonesia 102 G2............9°49'S 120°11'E
Sumbawa i. Indonesia 102 F2............8°54'S 118°45'E
Sumburgh Scotland 17 H4............59°52'N 1°17'W
Sumburgh Head Scotland 17 H4............59°51'N 1°16'W
Summer Isles Scotland 18 D3............58°01'N 5°30'W
Sumqayıt Azerbaijan 53 E2............40°35'N 49°40'E
Sumy Ukraine 47 P4............50°55'N 34°48'E
Sunart, Loch inlet Scotland 16 D1............56°40'N 5°51'W
Sunda, Selat str. Indonesia 102 C2............6°32'S 104°55'E
Sunderland England 13 F3............54°54'N 1°23'W
Sundsvall Sweden 43 D3............62°24'N 17°17'E
Sungurlu Turkey 51 K5............40°11'N 34°22'E
Suolijärvet l. Finland 43 G4............66°14'N 28°04'E
Suomenjoki Finland 43 F3............62°37'N 27°07'E
Suoyarvi Russia 52 E4............62°06'N 32°22'E
Superior U.S.A. 63 H6............46°41'N 92°01'W
Superior, Lake Canada/U.S.A. 61 J2............47°46'N 87°14'W
Sūq ash Shuyūkh Iraq 95 G6............30°51'N 46°20'E
Suqian China 99 L4............33°55'N 118°18'E
Sūr Oman 95 I4............22°34'N 59°31'E
Surab Pakistan 95 K5............28°29'N 66°19'E
Surabaya Indonesia 102 E2............7°13'S 112°45'E
Surakarta Indonesia 102 E2............7°31'S 110°52'E
Surat India 96 D5............21°11'N 72°53'E
Surendranagar India 96 D5............22°42'N 71°41'E
Surgut Russia 54 I4............61°13'N 73°22'E
Surigao Phil. 103 H5............9°48'N 125°29'E
Surin Thailand 102 C6............14°52'N 103°32'E
Suriname S. America 72 D7............4°05'N 56°22'W
Surrey d. England 21 E2............51°15'N 0°29'W
Surtsey i. Iceland 43 X1............63°18'N 20°36'W
Süsangerd Iran 95 G6............31°37'N 48°04'E
Suşehri Turkey 51 M5............40°10'N 38°04'E
Susuman Russia 55 P4............62°47'N 148°02'E
Susurluk Turkey 51 H4............39°55'N 28°09'E
Sutak India 96 E7............33°07'N 77°34'E
Sutherland f. Scotland 17 E3............58°16'N 4°24'W
Sutlej r. India/Pakistan 96 D6............29°24'N 71°08'E
Sutterton England 9 E3............52°54'N 0°06'W
Sutton England 9 F3............52°23'N 0°07'E
Sutton Bridge England 9 F3............52°46'N 0°11'E
Sutton Coldfield England 8 D3............52°34'N 1°49'W
Sutton in Ashfield England 13 F2............53°08'N 1°16'W
Suva Fiji 109 G5............18°07'S 178°28'E
Suvorov Russia 47 Q6............54°07'N 36°31'E
Suwałki Poland 46 I6............54°06'N 22°56'E
Suwarrow atoll Cook Is 109 I5............13°11'S 162°57'W
Suzhou Anhui China 99 L4............33°34'N 116°59'E
Suzhou Jiangsu China 99 M4............31°18'N 120°40'E
Suzu Japan 104 C3............37°26'N 137°15'E
Suzuka Japan 104 C2............34°53'N 136°35'E
Svalbard is Arctic Oc. 54 C5............79°47'N 16°13'E
Svapa r. Russia 47 P4............51°44'N 34°57'E
Sveg Sweden 43 C3............62°02'N 14°23'E
Svendborg Denmark 43 B1............55°04'N 10°37'E
Svetlograd Russia 49 L6............45°20'N 42°51'E
Svetogorsk Russia 43 G3............61°07'N 28°51'E
Sviahnúkar vol. Iceland 43 Y2............64°25'N 17°09'W
Svitavy Czechia 46 G3............49°45'N 16°28'E
Svitlovods'k Ukraine 47 O3............49°03'N 33°15'E
Svobodnyy Russia 55 N3............51°23'N 128°04'E
Svyetlahorsk Belarus 47 M5............52°38'N 29°46'E
Swadlincote England 8 D3............52°46'N 1°33'W
Swaffham England 9 F3............52°39'N 0°41'E
Swains Island atoll American Samoa 109 H5............11°01'S 171°03'W
Swakopmund Namibia 83 A2............22°41'S 14°32'E
Swale r. England 13 F3............54°05'N 1°21'W
Swanage England 8 D1............50°36'N 1°58'W
Swanley England 9 F2............51°24'N 0°11'E
Swan River town Canada 62 F7............52°06'N 101°16'W
Swansea Wales 10 D3............51°37'N 3°57'W
Swansea d. Wales 21 D2............51°39'N 3°57'W
Swansea Bay Wales 10 D3............51°34'N 3°54'W
Swaziland Africa 83 C2............26°29'S 31°30'E
Sweden Europe 43 C3............61°48'N 15°08'E
Sweetwater r. U.S.A. 62 E5............42°27'N 106°55'W
Świdnica Poland 46 G4............50°50'N 16°29'E
Świdwin Poland 46 F5............53°47'N 15°47'E
Swift Current Canada 60 H3............50°17'N 107°47'W
Swilly, Lough inlet Ireland 18 D5............55°15'N 7°34'W
Swindon England 8 D2............51°33'N 1°47'W
Swindon d. England 21 E2............51°35'N 1°45'W
Switzerland Europe 48 E6............46°44'N 8°18'E
Swords Ireland 18 E3............53°27'N 6°13'W
Sybil Point Ireland 18 A2............52°11'N 10°28'W
Sydney Australia 108 E3............33°55'S 151°11'E
Sydney Canada 61 L2............46°06'N 60°08'W
Syktyvkar Russia 52 F4............61°41'N 50°48'E
Sylarna mt. Norway/Sweden 43 C3............63°01'N 12°12'E
Sylt i. Germany 43 B1............54°49'N 8°15'E
Syracuse U.S.A. 63 K5............43°04'N 76°11'W
Syr Darya r. Asia 98 A7............46°05'N 60°55'E
Syria Asia 94 E6............35°25'N 39°22'E
Syrian Desert Asia 94 E6............32°02'N 39°22'E
Syros i. Greece 50 F3............37°27'N 24°53'E
Syzran' Russia 53 E3............53°10'N 48°29'E

Szczecin Poland 46 F5............53°26'N 14°34'E
Szczecinek Poland 46 G5............53°42'N 16°42'E
Szczytno Poland 46 I5............53°34'N 20°59'E
Szeged Hungary 46 I2............46°15'N 20°09'E
Székesfehérvár Hungary 46 H2............47°12'N 18°25'E
Szekszárd Hungary 46 H2............46°22'N 18°42'E
Szolnok Hungary 46 I2............47°10'N 20°12'E
Szombathely Hungary 46 G2............47°15'N 16°38'E

T

Ţabas Iran 95 I6............33°35'N 56°52'E
Tabasco d. Mexico 66 F4............18°03'N 92°59'W
Tábor Czechia 46 F3............49°24'N 14°42'E
Tabora Tanzania 83 C4............5°00'S 32°47'E
Tabrīz Iran 95 G7............38°04'N 46°17'E
Tabūk Saudi Arabia 94 E5............28°22'N 36°38'E
Täby Sweden 43 D2............59°27'N 18°04'E
Tacheng China 98 E7............46°43'N 83°01'E
Tacloban Phil. 103 H6............11°12'N 125°01'E
Tacna Peru 72 B5............18°01'S 70°15'W
Tacoma U.S.A. 62 B6............47°15'N 122°27'W
Tacuarembó Uruguay 73 D3............31°42'S 55°59'W
Tadcaster England 13 F2............53°53'N 1°16'W
Tadjoura Djibouti 94 F2............11°46'N 42°48'E
Tadmur Syria 94 E6............34°34'N 38°17'E
Taf r. Wales 10 C3............51°47'N 4°27'W
Taganrog Russia 49 K6............47°14'N 38°55'E
Taganrog, Gulf of Russia/Ukraine 49 K6............47°00'N 38°31'E
Tagbilaran Phil. 103 G5............9°38'N 123°53'E
Tagula Island P.N.G. 108 E5............11°33'S 153°23'E
Tagus r. Portugal 45 A3............38°59'N 8°56'W
Tahat, Mont mt. Algeria 84 E4............23°18'N 5°37'E
Tahiti i. French Polynesia 114 B2............17°49'S 149°15'W
Taichung Taiwan 99 M2............24°09'N 120°42'E
Tain Scotland 17 E2............57°49'N 4°03'W
Tainan Taiwan 99 M2............23°01'N 120°13'E
Tainaro, Akra pt Greece 50 E3............36°23'N 22°29'E
Taipei Taiwan 99 M3............25°04'N 121°33'E
Taiping Malaysia 102 C4............4°55'N 100°42'E
Taitung Taiwan 99 M2............22°45'N 121°08'E
Taivalkoski Finland 43 G4............65°34'N 28°14'E
Taivaskero hill Finland 43 F4............68°04'N 24°02'E
Taiwan Asia 99 M2............23°34'N 121°32'E
Taiwan Strait China/Taiwan 99 L2............23°49'N 119°16'E
Taiyuan China 99 K5............37°48'N 112°38'E
Taizhou China 99 M3............28°39'N 121°32'E
Ta'izz Yemen 94 F2............13°35'N 43°59'E
Tajikistan Asia 87 E3............38°54'N 71°08'E
Tak Thailand 102 B7............16°51'N 99°08'E
Takamatsu Japan 104 B2............34°19'N 134°03'E
Takaoka Japan 104 C3............36°45'N 137°01'E
Taklimakan Desert China 98 E5............38°25'N 80°50'E
Talagang Pakistan 95 L6............32°55'N 72°29'E
Talaud, Kepulauan is Indonesia 103 H4............4°05'N 127°24'E
Talavera de la Reina Spain 45 C3............39°58'N 4°49'W
Talca Chile 73 B3............35°26'S 71°39'W
Talcahuano Chile 73 B3............36°44'S 73°07'W
Taldykorgan Kazakhstan 54 I2............44°59'N 78°22'E
Talgarth Wales 10 D3............51°59'N 3°14'W
Taliabu i. Indonesia 103 G3............1°47'S 124°43'E
Tallahassee U.S.A. 63 J3............30°26'N 84°17'W
Tallinn Estonia 43 F2............59°27'N 24°45'E
Taloyoak Canada 61 I4............69°27'N 93°22'W
Talsi Latvia 43 E2............57°15'N 22°35'E
Taltson r. Canada 60 G4............61°24'N 112°43'W
Tamale Ghana 84 D2............9°25'N 0°51'W
Tamanrasset Algeria 84 E4............22°48'N 5°33'E
Tamar r. England 11 C2............50°29'N 4°13'W
Tamaulipas d. Mexico 66 E5............22°41'N 99°13'W
Tambacounda Senegal 84 C3............13°47'N 13°40'W
Tambelan, Kepulauan is Indonesia 102 D4............1°03'N 107°03'E
Tambov Russia 53 E3............52°43'N 41°26'E
Tambre r. Spain 45 A5............42°49'N 8°51'W
Tâmega r. Portugal 45 A4............41°05'N 8°17'W
Tamiahua, Laguna de lagoon Mexico 66 E5............21°39'N 97°36'W
Tamil Nadu d. India 96 E3............11°11'N 78°08'E
Tamiš r. Serbia 50 D7............44°50'N 20°39'E
Tampa U.S.A. 63 J2............27°57'N 82°29'W
Tampere Finland 43 E3............61°30'N 23°48'E
Tampico Mexico 66 E5............22°16'N 97°52'W
Tamsweg Austria 46 E2............47°08'N 13°47'E
Tamworth Australia 108 E3............31°06'S 150°56'E
Tamworth England 8 D3............52°38'N 1°41'W
Tana r. Kenya 85 I1............2°31'S 40°30'E
Tana, Lake Ethiopia 85 H3............11°55'N 37°16'E
Tanafjorden inlet Norway 43 G5............70°32'N 28°13'E
Tanami Desert Australia 108 C5............19°26'S 131°26'E
Tanana U.S.A. 60 C4............65°12'N 152°04'W
Tanaro r. Italy 46 C1............45°01'N 8°47'E
Tando Adam Pakistan 96 C5............25°43'N 68°40'E
Tandragee Northern Ireland 14 C2............54°21'N 6°24'W
Tanega-shima i. Japan 104 B1............30°28'N 130°58'E
Tanga Tanzania 83 C4............5°06'S 39°05'E
Tanganyika, Lake Africa 83 B4............5°00'S 29°26'E
Tangier Morocco 84 D5............35°47'N 5°49'W
Tangshan China 99 L5............39°34'N 118°13'E
Tanimbar, Kepulauan is Indonesia 103 I2............7°29'S 131°40'E
Tanjay Phil. 103 G5............9°29'N 123°09'E
Tanjungpandan Indonesia 102 D3............2°46'S 107°37'E
Tanjungredeb Indonesia 102 F4............2°09'N 117°27'E
Tank Pakistan 95 L6............32°14'N 70°29'E
Tanna i. Vanuatu 109 F5............19°32'S 169°14'E
Tanout Niger 84 E3............14°56'N 8°53'E
Ţanţa Egypt 85 H5............30°47'N 31°00'E
Tanzania Africa 83 C4............6°14'S 34°03'E
Taonan China 99 M7............45°12'N 122°48'E
Taourirt Morocco 48 C3............34°25'N 2°55'W
Tapachula Mexico 66 F3............14°56'N 92°15'W
Tapajós r. Brazil 72 D6............2°23'S 54°48'W
Tapi r. India 96 D5............21°13'N 72°58'E
Taquarí r. Brazil 72 D5............19°05'S 57°22'W
Tar r. Ireland 18 D2............52°17'N 7°50'W
Tara r. Bos. and Herz./Montenegro 50 C6............43°20'N 18°53'E
Tarakan Indonesia 102 F4............3°20'N 117°37'E
Taranaki, Mount vol. New Zealand 109 G3............39°18'S 174°03'E
Tarancón Spain 45 D4............40°01'N 3°00'W
Taransay i. Scotland 16 B2............57°55'N 7°02'W
Taranto Italy 49 G5............40°28'N 17°14'E
Taranto, Gulf of Italy 49 G5............40°07'N 17°20'E
Tarbat Ness pt Scotland 17 F2............57°52'N 3°46'W
Tarbert A. and B. Scotland 14 D3............55°58'N 5°50'W
Tarbert A. and B. Scotland 14 D3............55°52'N 5°25'W

Tarbert Na h-E. S. Scotland 16 C2............57°54'N 6°48'W
Tarbes France 44 D3............43°14'N 0°05'E
Târgoviște Romania 50 F7............44°56'N 25°27'E
Târgu Jiu Romania 50 E7............45°03'N 23°17'E
Târgu Mureș Romania 47 K2............46°32'N 24°34'E
Târgu Secuiesc Romania 50 G8............46°00'N 26°08'E
Tarija Bolivia 73 C4............21°36'S 64°47'W
Tarim Yemen 95 G3............16°08'N 49°23'E
Tarim Basin China 98 E5............39°41'N 80°53'E
Tarleton England 12 E2............53°41'N 2°50'W
Tarn r. France 44 D4............44°05'N 1°03'E
Tarnica mt. Poland 47 J3............49°05'N 22°46'E
Tarnobrzeg Poland 47 I4............50°35'N 21°40'E
Tarnów Poland 46 I4............50°01'N 20°59'E
Tarragona Spain 45 F4............41°07'N 1°15'E
Tarsus Turkey 51 K3............36°54'N 34°53'E
Tartu Estonia 43 F2............58°23'N 26°43'E
Ţarţūs Syria 51 K2............34°54'N 35°53'E
Tashk, Daryācheh-ye l. Iran 95 H5............29°42'N 53°29'E
Tashkent Uzbekistan 54 H2............41°16'N 69°15'E
Tasiilaq Greenland 61 O4............65°37'N 37°42'W
Tasikmalaya Indonesia 102 D2............7°19'S 108°17'E
Tasmania d. Australia 108 D2............42°27'S 145°20'E
Tasman Sea S. Pacific Oc. 108 G2............40°31'S 170°54'E
Tatabánya Hungary 46 H2............47°34'N 18°26'E
Tatarbunary Ukraine 51 H7............45°50'N 29°37'E
Tatarsk Russia 54 I3............55°13'N 75°59'E
Tatarskiy Proliv str. Russia 55 P3............50°29'N 141°05'E
Tatvan Turkey 94 F7............38°29'N 42°17'E
Taunggyi Myanmar 97 I5............20°49'N 97°05'E
Taunton England 11 D2............51°01'N 3°06'W
Taunus hills Germany 46 B4............50°10'N 7°59'E
Taupo, Lake New Zealand 109 G3............38°48'S 175°55'E
Tauragė Lithuania 47 J6............55°15'N 22°17'E
Taurus Mountains Turkey 51 J3............37°30'N 32°09'E
Tavda Russia 52 G3............58°05'N 65°19'E
Taverham England 9 G3............52°41'N 1°12'E
Tavira Portugal 45 B2............37°08'N 7°38'W
Tavistock England 11 C2............50°33'N 4°08'W
Tavşanlı Turkey 51 H4............39°32'N 29°28'E
Tavy r. England 11 C2............50°27'N 4°09'W
Taw r. England 11 D3............51°04'N 4°03'W
Tawau Malaysia 102 F4............4°16'N 117°54'E
Tawe r. Wales 10 D3............51°37'N 3°55'W
Tawitawi i. Phil. 102 F5............5°14'N 119°57'E
Tay r. Scotland 15 F4............56°23'N 3°24'W
Tay, Firth of est. Scotland 15 F4............56°25'N 3°07'W
Tay, Loch l. Scotland 14 E4............56°30'N 4°11'W
Taymā' Saudi Arabia 94 E5............27°39'N 38°28'E
Taymura r. Russia 55 K4............63°43'N 98°05'E
Taymyr, Ozero l. Russia 55 L5............74°20'N 101°51'E
Taymyr Peninsula Russia 55 J5............73°54'N 89°12'E
Tây Ninh Vietnam 102 D6............11°17'N 106°07'E
Tayport Scotland 15 G4............56°27'N 2°53'W
Taytay Phil. 102 F6............10°49'N 119°30'E
Taz r. Russia 54 I4............67°34'N 78°36'E
Taza Morocco 48 C3............34°16'N 3°56'W
Tbilisi Georgia 53 E2............41°42'N 44°48'E
Tczew Poland 46 H6............54°06'N 18°48'E
Te Anau, Lake New Zealand 109 F2............45°18'S 167°48'E
Tébessa Algeria 48 E4............35°23'N 8°12'E
Tebingtinggi Indonesia 102 B4............3°19'N 99°08'E
Tecuci Romania 50 G7............45°51'N 27°26'E
Tedzhen Turkmenistan 95 J7............37°22'N 60°25'E
Tees r. England 13 F3............54°35'N 1°15'W
Tees Bay England 13 F3............54°41'N 1°09'W
Tegal Indonesia 102 D2............6°51'S 109°07'E
Tegucigalpa Honduras 66 G3............14°05'N 87°12'W
Tehrān Iran 95 H7............35°39'N 51°23'E
Tehuantepec, Gulf of Mexico 66 F4............15°47'N 94°53'W
Teide, Pico del vol. Canary Islands 45 X2............28°16'N 16°37'W
Teifi r. Wales 10 C4............52°05'N 4°40'W
Teign r. England 11 D2............50°32'N 3°35'W
Teignmouth England 11 D2............50°33'N 3°30'W
Te Ike-a-Māui i. New Zealand 109 G3............38°11'S 173°23'E
Teith r. Scotland 14 E4............56°09'N 3°59'W
Tekirdağ Turkey 50 G5............40°59'N 27°30'E
Telangana d. India 96 E4............18°00'N 79°00'E
Tel Aviv-Yafo Israel 49 J3............32°04'N 34°46'E
Teles Pires r. Brazil 72 D6............7°20'S 58°03'W
Telford England 8 C3............52°41'N 2°27'W
Telford and Wrekin d. England 21 D3............52°43'N 2°29'W
Telpoziz, Gora mt. Russia 52 F4............63°54'N 59°09'E
Tembenchi r. Russia 55 K4............64°35'N 99°49'E
Teme r. England 8 C3............52°10'N 2°13'W
Temirtau Kazakhstan 54 I3............50°03'N 72°57'E
Temple Ewell England 9 G2............51°09'N 1°16'E
Templemore Ireland 18 D2............52°48'N 7°50'W
Temryuk Russia 51 L7............45°17'N 37°23'E
Temuco Chile 73 B3............38°44'S 72°35'W
Tenali India 96 E4............16°15'N 80°38'E
Tenasserim Myanmar 97 I3............12°02'N 98°58'E
Tenbury Wells England 8 C3............52°18'N 2°36'W
Tenby Wales 10 C3............51°40'N 4°42'W
Ten Degree Channel India 97 H2............9°57'N 92°51'E
Tendō Japan 104 D3............38°21'N 140°22'E
Tenerife i. Canary Islands 45 X2............28°28'N 16°39'W
Tennessee d. U.S.A. 63 I4............36°12'N 85°01'W
Tennessee r. U.S.A. 63 I4............37°08'N 88°25'W
Tenterden England 9 F2............51°04'N 0°41'E
Tentudia mt. Spain 45 B3............38°03'N 6°19'W
Teófilo Otôni Brazil 72 E5............17°52'S 41°31'W
Tepic Mexico 66 D5............21°31'N 104°55'W
Teplice Czechia 46 E4............50°38'N 13°50'E
Terebovlya Ukraine 47 K3............49°18'N 25°42'E
Teresina Brazil 72 E6............5°06'S 42°48'W
Terme Turkey 51 L5............41°12'N 36°59'E
Términos, Laguna de lagoon Mexico 66 F4............18°30'N 91°37'W
Termiz Uzbekistan 95 K7............37°15'N 67°17'E
Tern r. England 8 C3............52°40'N 2°40'W
Ternate Indonesia 103 H4............0°49'N 127°20'E
Terneuzen Neth. 42 C4............51°19'N 3°50'E
Terni Italy 48 F5............42°33'N 12°39'E
Ternopil' Ukraine 47 K3............49°33'N 25°36'E
Terrace Canada 60 F3............54°32'N 128°37'W
Terrassa Spain 45 G4............41°34'N 2°00'E
Terre Haute U.S.A. 63 I4............39°28'N 87°24'W
Terschelling i. Neth. 42 E6............53°27'N 5°28'E
Teseney Eritrea 94 E3............15°07'N 36°39'E
Teslin Canada 60 E4............60°12'N 132°39'W
Test r. England 8 D2............50°56'N 1°29'W
Tetas, Punta pt Chile 73 B4............23°28'S 70°34'W
Tetbury England 8 C2............51°38'N 2°09'W
Tete Mozambique 83 C3............16°10'S 33°36'E
Tetney England 13 G2............53°29'N 0°01'W
Tétouan Morocco 84 D5............35°34'N 5°23'W

Tetovo Macedonia 50 D6............42°00'N 20°58'E
Teuco r. Argentina 73 C4............25°39'S 60°11'W
Teviot r. Scotland 15 G3............55°36'N 2°26'W
Teviothead Scotland 15 G3............55°20'N 2°56'W
Te Waipounamu i. New Zealand 109 G2............44°24'S 172°31'E
Tewkesbury England 8 C2............51°59'N 2°09'W
Texarkana U.S.A. 63 H3............33°25'N 94°08'W
Texas d. U.S.A. 62 G3............31°58'N 99°13'W
Texel i. Neth. 42 D6............53°09'N 4°46'E
Texoma, Lake U.S.A. 62 G3............33°59'N 96°53'W
Tezpur India 97 H6............26°36'N 92°42'E
Thabana-Ntlenyana mt. Lesotho 83 B2............29°29'S 29°16'E
Thai Binh Vietnam 102 D8............20°24'N 106°19'E
Thailand Asia 102 C7............16°14'N 101°59'E
Thailand, Gulf of Asia 102 C6............11°08'N 101°16'E
Thai Nguyên Vietnam 102 D8............21°31'N 105°52'E
Thal Desert Pakistan 95 L6............31°25'N 71°33'E
Thame England 8 E2............51°45'N 0°58'W
Thame r. England 8 D2............51°38'N 1°10'W
Thames est. England 9 F2............51°30'N 0°31'E
Thames r. England 9 F2............51°27'N 0°21'E
Thandwe Myanmar 97 H4............18°27'N 94°22'E
Thanet, Isle of pen. England 9 G2............51°22'N 1°17'E
Thanh Hoa Vietnam 102 D7............19°47'N 105°49'E
Thar Desert India/Pakistan 96 C6............25°48'N 69°50'E
Thasos i. Greece 50 F5............40°40'N 24°31'E
Thatcham England 8 D2............51°24'N 1°16'W
Thaton Myanmar 97 I4............16°54'N 97°23'E
Thaxted England 9 F2............51°57'N 0°21'E
The Bahamas Central America 67 I6............24°55'N 77°44'W
The Calf hill England 13 E3............54°22'N 2°31'W
The Cheviot hill England 13 E4............55°29'N 2°09'W
The Cuillin hills Scotland 16 C2............57°14'N 6°17'W
The Fens f. England 9 E3............52°42'N 0°08'W
The Gambia Africa 84 C3............13°22'N 16°25'W
The Great Oasis Egypt 94 D4............24°52'N 30°42'E
The Gulf Asia 95 H5............28°03'N 50°06'E
The Hague Neth. 42 D5............52°04'N 4°18'E
Thelon r. Canada 60 I4............64°17'N 96°18'W
The Marsh England 9 F3............52°50'N 0°10'E
The Minch str. Scotland 16 C3............58°02'N 6°02'W
The Mullet b. Ireland 18 A4............54°10'N 10°07'W
The Mumbles Wales 10 D3............51°34'N 4°00'W
The Naze pt England 9 G2............51°52'N 1°17'E
The Needles f. England 8 D1............50°40'N 1°37'W
The North Sound str. Scotland 17 G4............59°17'N 2°43'W
Theodore Roosevelt r. Brazil 72 C6............7°35'S 60°21'W
The Old Man of Coniston hill England 12 D3............54°22'N 3°07'W
The Pas Canada 60 H3............53°49'N 101°16'W
Thermaïkos Kolpos g. Greece 50 E5............40°11'N 22°54'E
The Solent str. England 8 D1............50°45'N 1°23'W
The Sound est. England 11 C2............50°21'N 4°09'W
Thessaloniki Greece 50 E5............40°38'N 22°57'E
The Storr hill Scotland 16 C2............57°31'N 6°11'W
Thet r. England 9 F3............52°24'N 0°45'E
Thetford England 9 F3............52°25'N 0°45'E
The Trossachs hills Scotland 14 E4............56°13'N 4°26'W
The Wash b. England 9 F3............52°55'N 0°11'E
The Weald f. England 9 F2............51°05'N 0°18'E
Thiers France 44 E4............45°51'N 3°33'E
Thiès Senegal 84 C3............14°48'N 16°56'W
Thimphu Bhutan 97 G6............27°29'N 89°42'E
Thionville France 44 G6............49°22'N 6°10'E
Thira i. Greece 50 F3............36°27'N 25°27'E
Thirlmere resr England 12 D3............54°33'N 3°04'W
Thirsk England 13 F3............54°14'N 1°20'W
Thiruvananthapuram India 96 E2............8°30'N 76°57'E
Thisted Denmark 43 B2............56°57'N 8°41'E
Thomastown Ireland 18 D2............52°31'N 7°07'W
Thompson Canada 60 I3............55°48'N 97°55'W
Thornaby-on-Tees England 13 F3............54°34'N 1°17'W
Thornbury England 8 C2............51°36'N 2°31'W
Thorne England 13 G2............53°37'N 0°58'W
Thornhill Scotland 15 F3............55°15'N 3°46'W
Thornton England 12 D2............53°52'N 3°00'W
Thrakiko Pelagos sea Greece 50 F5............40°22'N 24°46'E
Thrapston England 9 E3............52°24'N 0°32'W
Thuin Belgium 42 D3............50°20'N 4°17'E
Thule Greenland 61 L5............77°28'N 69°11'W
Thunder Bay town Canada 61 J2............48°26'N 89°15'W
Thurles Ireland 18 D2............52°41'N 7°49'W
Thurrock d. England 21 F2............51°31'N 0°22'E
Thursby England 12 D3............54°51'N 3°03'W
Thurso Scotland 17 F3............58°36'N 3°31'W
Thurso r. Scotland 17 F3............58°36'N 3°31'W
Thurso Bay Scotland 17 F3............58°38'N 3°32'W
Tianjin China 99 L5............39°04'N 117°15'E
Tianshui China 99 J4............34°30'N 105°37'E
Tiaret Algeria 48 D4............35°20'N 1°19'E
Tibati Cameroon 84 F2............6°26'N 12°35'E
Tibesti mts Chad 85 F4............20°53'N 17°03'E
Tibet, Plateau of f. China 98 E4............33°48'N 84°16'E
Tiburón, Isla i. Mexico 66 B6............29°08'N 112°29'W
Ticehurst England 9 F2............51°03'N 0°25'E
Tidjikja Mauritania 84 C3............18°31'N 11°26'W
Tiel Neth. 42 E4............51°52'N 5°25'E
Tielt Belgium 42 C3............50°59'N 3°20'E
Tienen Belgium 42 D3............50°48'N 4°56'E
Tien Shan mts China/Kyrgyzstan 98 D6............40°48'N 76°25'E
Tierra del Fuego, Isla Grande de i. Argentina/Chile 73 C1............54°11'S 68°48'W
Tiétar r. Spain 45 C3............39°56'N 5°54'W
Tigre r. Venezuela 72 C7............9°26'N 62°25'W
Tigris r. Iraq/Syria 95 G6............30°59'N 47°25'E
Tihāmah f. Saudi Arabia 85 I3............17°18'N 42°25'E
Tijuana Mexico 66 A7............32°29'N 117°02'W
Tikhoretsk Russia 53 E2............45°50'N 40°06'E
Tikhvin Russia 52 D3............59°39'N 33°32'E
Tikrīt Iraq 94 F6............34°33'N 43°37'E
Tiksi Russia 55 N5............71°38'N 128°36'E
Tilburg Neth. 42 E4............51°33'N 5°05'E
Tilbury England 9 F2............51°28'N 0°22'E
Tilehurst England 8 D2............51°27'N 1°02'W
Tillabéri Niger 84 E3............14°13'N 1°29'E
Tillicoultry Scotland 15 F4............56°09'N 3°44'W
Til'tim Russia 52 G4............65°12'N 63°13'E
Ţīmā Egypt 49 J2............26°53'N 31°25'E
Timanskiy Kryazh f. Russia 52 F4............65°00'N 50°00'E
Timashëvsk Russia 53 E2............45°37'N 38°56'E
Timbuktu Mali 84 D3............16°46'N 2°59'W
Timiş r. Romania 50 D7............45°27'N 20°52'E
Timișoara Romania 50 D7............45°46'N 21°14'E
Timmins Canada 61 J2............48°29'N 81°21'W
Timor i. East Timor/Indonesia 103 H2............8°49'S 126°02'E
Timor-Leste Asia 103 H2............8°57'S 125°59'E
Timor Sea Australia/Indonesia 108 B5............11°23'S 126°22'E

Timrå Sweden 43 D3....................................62°30'N 17°20'E
Tindouf Algeria 84 D4................................27°42'N 8°07'W
Tinian i. N. Mariana Is 103 L6...........14°58'N 145°41'E
Tinos i. Greece 50 F3..................................37°40'N 25°12'E
Tintagel England 11 C2.............................50°40'N 4°45'W
Tinto hill Scotland 15 F3.........................55°36'N 3°40'W
Tipperary Ireland 18 C2...........................52°28'N 8°10'W
Tipperary d. Ireland 18 D2.....................52°43'N 7°54'W
Tiptree England 9 F2.................................51°49'N 0°45'E
Tirana Albania 50 C4..................................41°19'N 19°49'E
Tiraspol Moldova 49 I6.............................46°51'N 29°37'E
Tiree i. Scotland 14 C4..............................56°30'N 6°57'W
Tirga Mòr hill Scotland 16 C2...............57°59'N 6°59'W
Tiruchirappalli India 96 E3.....................10°49'N 78°41'E
Tiruppur India 96 E3.................................11°06'N 77°18'E
Tisa r. Serbia 50 D7..................................45°08'N 20°17'E
Tisza r. Hungary 47 I2..............................46°09'N 20°04'E
Titicaca, Lake Bolivia/Peru 72 C5......15°49'S 69°40'W
Tiverton England 11 D2............................50°54'N 3°29'W
Tizi Ouzou Algeria 48 D4.........................36°41'N 4°05'E
Tiznit Morocco 84 D4...............................29°41'N 9°43'W
Tiztoutine Morocco 45 D1.......................34°58'N 3°09'W
Tlaxcala Mexico 66 E4...............................19°21'N 98°13'W
Tlaxcala d. Mexico 66 E4..........................19°35'N 98°20'W
Tlemcen Algeria 84 E5................................34°54'N 1°19'W
Toamasina Madagascar 83 D3................18°09'S 49°22'E
Toba, Danau l. Indonesia 102 B4............2°32'N 98°50'E
Tobago i. Trinidad and Tobago 67 L3....11°17'N 60°38'W
Tobelo Indonesia 103 H4..........................1°44'N 127°57'E
Tobermory Scotland 16 C1........................56°38'N 6°04'W
Toboali Indonesia 102 D3..........................2°59'S 106°30'E
Tobol r. Kazakhstan/Russia 54 H3........58°10'N 68°13'E
Tobol'sk Russia 54 H3................................58°14'N 68°16'E
Tocantins r. Brazil 72 E6.........................1°49'S 49°13'W
Todmorden England 13 E2......................53°43'N 2°06'W
Toft Scotland 17 H5...................................60°28'N 1°13'W
Togian, Kepulauan is Indonesia 103 G3...0°06'S 121°53'E
Togo Africa 84 E2.......................................8°27'N 1°11'E
Tok U.S.A. 60 D4...63°21'N 143°01'W
Tokat Turkey 51 L5....................................40°19'N 36°32'E
Tokelau is S. Pacific Oc. 109 H6...........8°30'S 171°28'W
Tokushima Japan 104 B2..........................34°04'N 134°34'E
Tōkyō Japan 104 C3...................................35°40'N 139°46'E
Tōkyō d. Japan 104 C3...............................35°22'N 139°03'E
Tôlañaro Madagascar 83 D2....................25°02'S 46°58'E
Toledo Spain 45 C3.....................................39°52'N 4°01'W
Toledo U.S.A. 63 J5....................................41°39'N 83°33'W
Toledo, Montes de mts Spain 45 C3......39°39'N 4°54'W
Toledo Bend Reservoir U.S.A. 63 H3....31°38'N 93°43'W
Toliara Madagascar 83 D2.......................23°22'S 43°39'E
Tolitoli Indonesia 103 G4.........................1°05'N 120°50'E
Tollesbury England 9 F2............................51°45'N 0°50'E
Tolsta Head Scotland 16 C3.....................58°21'N 6°10'W
Toluca Mexico 66 E4..................................19°18'N 99°39'W
Tol'yatti Russia 53 E3................................53°31'N 49°26'E
Tomakomai Japan 104 D4.........................42°38'N 141°36'E
Tomanivi mt. Fiji 109 G5.........................17°37'S 178°00'E
Tomaszów Lubelski Poland 47 J4..........50°28'N 23°25'E
Tomaszów Mazowiecki Poland 46 I4.....51°32'N 20°01'E
Tombigbee r. U.S.A. 63 I3........................31°11'N 87°57'W
Tombua Angola 83 A3.................................15°50'S 11°50'E
Tomelloso Spain 45 D3..............................39°09'N 3°00'W
Tomini, Teluk b. Indonesia 102 G3.......0°21'S 120°54'E
Tomsk Russia 54 J3....................................56°30'N 85°01'E
Tomtabacken hill Sweden 43 C2............57°30'N 14°29'E
Tonbridge England 9 F2...........................51°12'N 0°17'E
Tondano Indonesia 103 G4......................1°21'N 124°56'E
Tønder Denmark 46 C6..............................54°57'N 8°52'E
Tone r. England 8 C2..................................51°04'N 2°56'W
Tonelagee hill Ireland 10 A5..................53°03'N 6°23'W
Tonga S. Pacific Oc. 109 H4.....................20°05'S 173°48'W
Tongatapu Group is Tonga 109 H4.......21°07'S 174°45'W
Tongeren Belgium 42 E3...........................50°47'N 5°28'E
Tonghua China 99 N6.................................41°43'N 125°57'E
Tongking, Gulf of China/Vietnam 99 J2...20°29'N 108°15'E
Tongliao China 99 M6................................43°31'N 122°14'E
Tongling China 99 L4..................................30°55'N 117°52'E
Tongue Scotland 17 E3...............................58°29'N 4°25'W
Tônlé Sab, Bœng l. Cambodia 102 C6....13°04'N 103°51'E
Tonopah U.S.A. 62 C4................................38°04'N 117°14'W
Tønsberg Norway 43 B2............................59°17'N 10°23'E
Toowoomba Australia 108 E4...................27°33'S 151°58'E
Topeka U.S.A. 63 G4...................................39°04'N 95°36'W
Topozero, Ozero l. Russia 43 H4...........65°42'N 32°00'E
Topsham England 11 D2............................50°41'N 3°28'W
Torbat-e Heydarīyeh Iran 95 I7.............35°13'N 59°06'E
Torbat-e Jām Iran 95 J7............................35°15'N 60°34'E
Torbay d. England 21 D2.........................50°26'N 3°34'W
Tor Bay England 11 D2..............................50°25'N 3°32'W
Tordesillas Spain 45 C4.............................41°31'N 4°59'W
Torenberg hill Neth. 42 E5......................52°14'N 5°52'E
Torfaen d. Wales 21 D2.............................51°44'N 3°05'W
Tormes r. Spain 45 B4................................41°18'N 6°27'W
Torneälven r. Sweden 43 F4....................65°49'N 24°09'E
Torneträsk l. Sweden 43 D5.....................68°23'N 18°56'E
Tornio Finland 43 F4..................................65°50'N 24°11'E
Toronto Canada 61 K2...............................43°40'N 79°23'W
Toropets Russia 47 N7..............................56°30'N 31°38'E
Torpoint England 11 C2.............................50°22'N 4°12'W
Torquay England 11 D2.............................50°28'N 3°31'W
Torrecerredo mt. Spain 45 C5................43°12'N 4°49'W
Torre mt. Portugal 45 B4..........................40°20'N 7°35'W
Torremolinos Spain 45 C2.......................36°36'N 4°30'W
Torrens, Lake Australia 108 C3...............30°32'S 137°28'E
Torreón Mexico 66 D6...............................25°31'N 103°27'W
Torres Islands Vanuatu 109 F5...............13°08'S 166°17'E
Torres Strait Australia 108 D6................9°50'S 142°11'E
Torres Vedras Portugal 45 A3.................39°06'N 9°15'W
Torrevieja Spain 45 E2...............................37°59'N 0°40'W
Torridge r. England 11 C2........................50°59'N 4°11'W
Torridon Scotland 16 D2...........................57°33'N 5°31'W
Torridon, Loch b. Scotland 16 D2..........57°37'N 5°50'W
Tortosa Spain 45 F4...................................40°50'N 0°32'E
Toruń Poland 46 H5...................................53°01'N 18°37'E
Tory Island Ireland 18 C5.........................55°16'N 8°13'W
Torzhok Russia 52 D3................................57°02'N 34°57'E
Tosno Russia 43 G2....................................59°33'N 30°54'E
Tosya Turkey 51 K5....................................40°59'N 34°04'E
Totland England 8 D1................................50°41'N 1°32'W
Tot'ma Russia 52 E3..................................59°59'N 42°46'E
Totnes England 11 D2................................50°26'N 3°41'W
Totton England 8 D1.................................50°55'N 1°29'W
Tottori Japan 104 B3..................................35°29'N 134°14'E
Toubkal, Jbel mt. Morocco 84 D5........31°03'N 7°57'W
Touggourt Algeria 84 F5...........................33°06'N 6°04'E
Toulon France 44 F3...................................43°08'N 5°56'E
Toulouse France 44 D3...............................43°37'N 1°26'E

Toungoo Myanmar 97 I4..........................18°55'N 96°25'E
Touraine f. France 44 D5...........................47°14'N 0°21'E
Tournai Belgium 42 C3..............................50°36'N 3°24'E
Tournon-sur-Rhône France 44 F4.........45°04'N 4°50'E
Tours France 44 D5....................................47°23'N 0°42'E
Tove r. England 8 E3...................................52°05'N 0°50'W
Towada Japan 104 D4.................................40°36'N 141°12'E
Towcester England 8 E3.............................52°08'N 0°59'W
Towori, Teluk b. Indonesia 103 G3........2°02'S 121°57'E
Toyama Japan 104 C3.................................36°41'N 137°13'E
Toyama-wan b. Japan 104 C3..................36°54'N 137°14'E
Toyota Japan 104 C3..................................35°05'N 137°10'E
Tozeur Tunisia 48 E3.................................33°55'N 8°07'E
Trabzon Turkey 51 M5...............................40°59'N 39°44'E
Trafalgar, Cabo c. Spain 45 B2...............36°11'N 6°02'W
Tralee Ireland 18 B2...................................52°16'N 9°42'W
Tralee Bay Ireland 18 B2...........................52°18'N 9°57'W
Tranås Sweden 43 C2.................................58°02'N 14°59'E
Trangan i. Indonesia 103 I2......................6°35'S 134°16'E
Transnistria Europe 47 M2......................47°45'N 29°03'E
Transylvanian Alps mts Romania 47 J1...45°35'N 24°40'E
Trapani Italy 48 F4....................................38°01'N 12°31'E
Traunsee l. Austria 46 E2..........................47°54'N 13°47'E
Traverse City U.S.A. 63 I5.........................44°46'N 85°37'W
Travnik Bos. and Herz. 50 B7..................44°14'N 17°40'E
Trawsfynydd, Llyn resr Wales 10 D4....52°55'N 3°59'W
Trebišov Slovakia 47 I3..............................48°39'N 21°44'E
Tredegar Wales 10 D3...............................51°46'N 3°15'W
Tregaron Wales 10 D4...............................52°13'N 3°56'W
Treig, Loch l. Scotland 16 E1...................56°48'N 4°44'W
Trelleborg Sweden 43 C1...........................55°22'N 13°10'E
Tremadog Bay Wales 10 C4.....................52°52'N 4°16'W
Trenčín Slovakia 46 H3.............................48°53'N 18°02'E
Trent r. England 13 G2...............................53°38'N 0°43'W
Trento Italy 46 D2......................................46°04'N 11°08'E
Trenton U.S.A. 63 L5..................................40°13'N 74°47'W
Treorchy Wales 10 D3................................51°39'N 3°30'W
Tresco i. England 11 A1..............................49°57'N 6°19'W
Tres Puntas, Cabo c. Argentina 73 C2....47°08'S 65°53'W
Treviso Italy 46 E1......................................45°40'N 12°15'E
Trevose Head England 11 B2...................50°33'N 5°06'W
Trier Germany 46 B3..................................49°45'N 6°38'E
Trieste Italy 46 E1......................................45°39'N 13°46'E
Trikala Greece 50 D4.................................39°33'N 21°46'E
Trim Ireland 18 E3......................................53°33'N 6°47'W
Trincomalee Sri Lanka 96 F2...................8°37'N 81°13'E
Trindade, Ilha da i. S. Atlantic Ocean 68 E2
....20°31'S 29°19'W
Tring England 8 E2.....................................51°48'N 0°39'W
Trinidad i. Trinidad and Tobago 67 L3....10°27'N 61°13'W
Trinidad U.S.A. 62 F4................................37°11'N 104°30'W
Trinidad and Tobago Central America 67 L3
....10°49'N 61°00'W
Tripoli Greece 50 E3..................................37°31'N 22°23'E
Tripoli Lebanon 49 K3..............................34°26'N 35°52'E
Tripoli Libya 84 F5......................................32°52'N 13°08'E
Tripolitania f. Libya 48 F3........................30°39'N 13°17'E
Tripura d. India 97 H5................................23°36'N 91°35'E
Tristan da Cunha i. Atlantic Oc. 116 E2....38°00'S 12°00'W
Trnava Slovakia 46 G3..............................48°22'N 17°36'E
Trobriand Islands P.N.G. 108 E6.............8°33'S 151°09'E
Troisdorf Germany 42 G3.........................50°49'N 7°09'E
Trois-Rivières Canada 61 K2...................46°21'N 72°35'W
Troitsk Russia 53 G3..................................54°08'N 61°36'E
Trollhättan Sweden 43 C2........................58°16'N 12°18'E
Tromsø Norway 43 D5...............................69°39'N 18°57'E
Trondheim Norway 43 B3.........................63°25'N 10°22'E
Troon Scotland 14 E3.................................55°32'N 4°40'W
Trostan hill Northern Ireland 14 C3......55°03'N 6°09'W
Troup Head Scotland 17 G2.....................57°42'N 2°18'W
Trout Lake Canada 63 H7.........................51°15'N 93°06'W
Trowbridge England 8 C2.........................51°19'N 2°12'W
Troyes France 44 F6...................................48°18'N 4°05'E
Trubchevsk Russia 47 O5.........................52°35'N 33°47'E
Trujillo Peru 72 B6.....................................8°07'S 79°02'W
Truro Canada 61 L2...................................45°22'N 63°13'W
Truro England 11 B2.................................50°16'N 5°03'W
Tsaratanana, Massif du mts Madagascar 83 D3
....13°44'S 48°59'E
Tsetserleg Mongolia 99 I7........................47°19'N 101°29'E
Tschikskoye Vodokhranilishche resr Russia 51 M7
....45°07'N 39°28'E
Tsimlyanskoye Vodokhranilishche resr Russia 53 E2
....48°00'N 43°00'E
Tsna r. Belarus 47 L5.................................52°09'N 27°01'E
Tsu Japan 104 C2.......................................34°43'N 136°31'E
Tsuchiura Japan 104 D3............................36°04'N 140°12'E
Tsugarū-kaikyō str. Japan 104 D4.........41°16'N 140°21'E
Tsumeb Namibia 83 A3.............................19°14'S 17°43'E
Tsumis Park Namibia 83 A2....................23°47'S 17°31'E
Tsuruga Japan 104 C3...............................35°38'N 136°04'E
Tsushima is Japan 104 A2.........................34°24'N 129°23'E
Tuam Ireland 18 C3...................................53°31'N 8°51'W
Tuamotu Archipelago is French Polynesia 116 B2
....14°29'S 142°50'W
Tuapse Russia 53 D2.................................44°06'N 39°04'E
Tuban Indonesia 102 E2...........................6°55'S 112°02'E
Tubbercurry Ireland 18 C4......................54°03'N 8°43'W
Tübingen Germany 46 C3.........................48°31'N 9°04'E
Tubruq Libya 85 G5...................................32°04'N 23°57'E
Tucson U.S.A. 62 D3.................................32°14'N 110°54'W
Tucumcari U.S.A. 62 F4............................35°12'N 103°44'W
Tucuruí Brazil 72 E6..................................3°42'S 49°44'W
Tucuruí, Represa resr Brazil 72 E6.........4°26'S 49°07'W
Tudela Spain 45 E5.....................................42°03'N 1°36'W
Tuela r. Portugal 45 B4..............................41°38'N 7°08'W
Tuguegarao Phil. 103 G7..........................17°37'N 121°43'E
Tui Spain 45 A5..42°03'N 8°38'W
Tukangbesi, Kepulauan is Indonesia 103 G2
....5°40'S 123°55'E
Tukums Latvia 43 E2.................................56°58'N 23°10'E
Tula Russia 53 D3.......................................54°12'N 37°37'E
Tulcea Romania 51 H7...............................45°10'N 28°48'E
Tul'chyn Ukraine 47 M3...........................48°41'N 28°50'E
Tulit'a Canada 60 F4..................................64°55'N 125°31'W
Tullamore Ireland 18 D3...........................53°17'N 7°30'W
Tulle France 44 D4.....................................45°16'N 1°46'E
Tullow Ireland 18 E2.................................52°48'N 6°44'W
Tullybrack hill Northern Ireland 14 B2....54°23'N 7°52'W
Tulsa U.S.A. 62 G4.....................................36°09'N 95°58'W
Tumaco Colombia 72 B7...........................1°48'N 78°49'W
Tumakuru India 96 E3...............................13°19'N 77°06'E
Tumba, Lac l. Dem. Rep. Congo 83 A4....0°52'S 18°05'E
Tummel r. Scotland 17 F1..........................56°39'N 3°40'W
Tummel, Loch l. Scotland 17 F1...............56°42'N 3°58'W

Tump Pakistan 95 J5..................................26°06'N 62°26'E
Tumucumaque, Serra hills Brazil 72 D7....1°59'N 56°09'W
Tunceli Turkey 51 M4................................39°06'N 39°33'E
Tundzha r. Bulgaria 50 G5.......................41°39'N 26°33'E
Tunis Tunisia 84 F5...................................36°46'N 10°16'E
Tunisia Africa 48 E3...................................34°52'N 9°24'E
Tunja Colombia 72 B7...............................5°30'N 73°22'W
Tunnsjøen l. Norway 43 C4......................64°42'N 13°24'E
Tuolumne r. U.S.A. 62 B4.........................37°36'N 121°10'W
Tura Russia 55 L4..64°16'N 100°15'E
Turabah Saudi Arabia 94 F4....................21°14'N 41°37'E
Turbat Pakistan 96 B6...............................26°01'N 63°07'E
Turbo Colombia 67 I2................................8°05'N 76°43'W
Turda Romania 47 J2.................................46°34'N 23°47'E
Turgutlu Turkey 51 G4..............................38°29'N 27°42'E
Turhal Turkey 51 L5..................................40°23'N 36°04'E
Turia r. Spain 45 E3...................................39°26'N 0°18'W
Turin Italy 46 B1...45°04'N 7°41'E
Turinsk Russia 52 G3.................................58°04'N 63°42'E
Turkana, Lake Ethiopia/Kenya 85 H2....3°59'N 35°57'E
Turkey Asia/Europe 51 I4.........................39°19'N 34°21'E
Turkmenabat Turkmenistan 54 H1.........39°05'N 63°34'E
Turkmenbaşy Turkmenistan 53 F2........40°02'N 52°59'E
Turkmenistan Asia 87 D4.........................40°00'N 60°00'E
Turks and Caicos Islands Central America 67 J5
....21°59'N 71°36'W
Turks Islands Turks and Caicos Is 67 J5....21°25'N 71°09'W
Turku Finland 43 E3....................................60°27'N 22°15'E
Turnhout Belgium 42 D4...........................51°19'N 4°57'E
Turnu Măgurele Romania 50 F6.............43°45'N 24°51'E
Turpan China 98 F6...................................42°52'N 89°12'E
Turquino, Pico mt. Cuba 67 I5................20°00'N 76°51'W
Turriff Scotland 17 G2................................57°32'N 2°28'W
Tuscaloosa U.S.A. 63 I3............................33°11'N 87°30'W
Tutbury England 8 D3................................52°51'N 1°41'W
Tuticorin India 96 E2................................8°48'N 78°08'E
Tuttlingen Germany 46 C2........................47°59'N 8°49'E
Tutuila i. American Samoa 109 H5.........14°16'S 170°33'W
Tuvalu S. Pacific Oc. 109 G6....................7°24'S 178°20'E
Tuxford England 13 G2..............................53°14'N 0°54'W
Tuxpan Mexico 66 E5.................................20°58'N 97°22'W
Tuxtla Gutiérrez Mexico 66 F4...............16°46'N 93°08'W
Tuz, Lake Turkey 51 J4..............................38°42'N 33°24'E
Tuzla Bos. and Herz. 50 C7.......................44°33'N 18°42'E
Tver' Russia 52 D3.....................................56°50'N 35°54'E
Tweed r. U.K. 13 E4....................................55°45'N 2°06'W
Twin Falls town U.S.A. 62 D5..................42°35'N 114°27'W
Twyford England 8 E2................................51°29'N 0°52'W
Tyler U.S.A. 63 G3......................................32°22'N 95°18'W
Tynda Russia 55 N3....................................55°07'N 124°44'E
Tyne r. Scotland 15 G4..............................56°00'N 2°36'W
Tyne and Wear d. England 20 E4............54°56'N 1°16'W
Tynemouth England 13 F4........................55°01'N 1°25'W
Tynset Norway 43 B3..................................62°16'N 10°47'E
Tyre Lebanon 49 K3...................................33°15'N 35°14'E
Tyrrhenian Sea France/Italy 48 F5..........40°13'N 10°15'E
Tyumen' Russia 54 H3...............................57°09'N 65°28'E
Tywi r. Wales 10 C3....................................51°48'N 4°20'W

U

Uaupés Brazil 72 C6...................................0°06'S 67°02'W
Ubangi r. C.A.R./Dem. Rep. Congo 85 F1....0°25'S 17°44'E
Úbeda Spain 45 D3.....................................38°01'N 3°22'W
Uberaba Brazil 73 E4.................................19°46'S 47°53'W
Uberlândia Brazil 72 E5.............................18°56'S 48°14'W
Ubon Ratchathani Thailand 102 C7.......15°14'N 104°53'E
Ucayali r. Peru 72 B6.................................4°28'S 73°29'W
Uchur r. Russia 55 O3.................................57°19'N 131°17'E
Uckfield England 9 F1................................50°58'N 0°06'E
Uda r. Russia 55 O3....................................54°41'N 135°18'E
Udaipur India 96 D5...................................24°35'N 73°47'E
Uddevalla Sweden 43 B2...........................58°21'N 11°57'E
Uddjaure l. Sweden 43 D4........................65°56'N 17°52'E
Udine Italy 46 E2..46°04'N 13°14'E
Udon Thani Thailand 102 C7...................17°22'N 102°50'E
Udupi India 96 D3......................................13°20'N 74°46'E
Ueda Japan 104 C3.....................................36°24'N 138°15'E
Uele r. Dem. Rep. Congo 83 B5................3°32'N 25°16'E
Uelzen Germany 46 D5..............................52°58'N 10°34'E
Ufa Russia 53 F3..54°44'N 55°58'E
Uganda Africa 85 H2.................................2°34'N 32°37'E
Uglegorsk Russia 55 P2.............................49°02'N 142°02'E
Uig Scotland 16 C2.....................................57°35'N 6°21'W
Uíge Angola 83 A4......................................7°36'S 15°05'E
Uinta Mountains U.S.A. 62 D5...............40°36'N 110°59'W
Ukhta Russia 52 F4....................................63°33'N 53°46'E
Ukiah U.S.A. 62 B4....................................39°09'N 123°13'W
Ukmergė Lithuania 47 K6.........................55°15'N 24°46'E
Ukraine Europe 47 N3...............................49°23'N 31°18'E
Ulaangom Mongolia 98 G7......................49°57'N 92°09'E
Ulan Bator Mongolia 99 J7.......................47°48'N 106°58'E
Ulanhot China 99 M7................................46°04'N 122°03'E
Ulan-Khol Russia 53 E2.............................45°26'N 46°51'E
Ulan-Ude Russia 55 L3..............................51°49'N 107°38'E
Uliastay Mongolia 98 H7...........................47°36'N 96°48'E
Ulithi atoll Micronesia 103 J6..................10°07'N 139°40'E
Uljin S. Korea 104 A3................................36°59'N 129°23'E
Ullapool Scotland 16 D2...........................57°54'N 5°10'W
Ullswater l. England 12 E3.......................54°34'N 2°54'W
Ullŭng-do i. S. Korea 104 B3...................37°30'N 130°55'E
Ulm Germany 46 C3...................................48°25'N 9°59'E
Ulster Canal Ireland/U.K. 14 B2.............54°14'N 7°01'W
Uludağ mt. Turkey 51 H5.........................40°06'N 29°17'E
Ulundi S. Africa 83 C2...............................28°19'S 31°25'E
Uluru/Ayers Rock hill Australia 108 C4....25°20'S 131°05'E
Ulva i. Scotland 14 C4...............................56°28'N 6°13'W
Ulverston England 12 D3...........................54°12'N 3°05'W
Ul'yanovsk Russia 53 E3............................54°18'N 48°23'E
Uman' Ukraine 47 N3................................48°45'N 30°14'E
Umba Russia 52 D4....................................66°41'N 34°23'E
Umboi i. P.N.G. 108 D6.............................5°42'S 147°50'E
Umeå Sweden 43 E3...................................63°50'N 20°17'E
Umeälven r. Sweden 43 D4.......................63°46'N 20°19'E
Umm Keddada Sudan 94 D2....................13°35'N 26°42'E
Umm Ruwaba Sudan 85 H3.....................12°52'N 31°10'E
Umm Sa'ad Libya 85 G5............................31°34'N 25°03'E
Umtata S. Africa 83 B1..............................31°35'S 28°47'E
Umuarama Brazil 73 D4.............................23°46'S 53°19'W
Una r. Bos. and Herz./Croatia 50 B7......45°16'N 16°56'E
Unecha Russia 47 O5.................................52°50'N 32°41'E
Ungava, Péninsule d' pen. Canada 61 K4....60°46'N 74°25'W
Ungava Bay Canada 61 L3........................59°16'N 67°29'W
Unimak Island U.S.A. 60 B3....................54°58'N 164°02'W

United Arab Emirates Asia 95 H4...........23°30'N 52°20'E
United Kingdom Europe 20........................54°35'N 1°53'W
United States of America N. America 62 G4
....38°59'N 99°57'W
Unst i. Scotland 17 I5..................................60°46'N 0°53'W
Upa r. Russia 47 Q6....................................54°01'N 36°20'E
Upavon England 8 D2.................................51°18'N 1°48'W
Upemba, Lac l. Dem. Rep. Congo 83 B4....8°39'S 26°29'E
Upernavik Greenland 61 M5...................72°48'N 56°09'W
Upington S. Africa 83 B2...........................28°28'S 21°15'E
Upolu i. Samoa 109 H5.............................14°04'S 171°39'W
Upper Klamath Lake U.S.A. 62 B5.........42°22'N 121°53'W
Upper Lough Erne l. Northern Ireland 14 B2
....54°15'N 7°34'W
Upper Tean England 8 D3.........................52°57'N 1°59'W
Uppingham England 8 E3.........................52°35'N 0°43'W
Uppsala Sweden 43 D2..............................59°51'N 17°38'E
Upton upon Severn England 8 C3..........52°04'N 2°13'W
Ural r. Kazakhstan/Russia 53 F2............46°55'N 51°46'E
Ural Mountains Russia 54 H4..................66°50'N 63°48'E
Uranium City Canada 60 H3....................59°31'N 108°43'W
Ure r. England 13 F3..................................54°05'N 1°20'W
Urengoy Russia 54 I4..................................65°55'N 78°13'E
Urganch Uzbekistan 54 H2......................41°32'N 60°39'E
Urie r. Scotland 17 G2................................57°16'N 2°22'W
Urla Turkey 50 G4......................................38°17'N 26°46'E
Urmia, Lake Iran 94 G7.............................37°57'N 45°17'E
Uruapan Mexico 66 D4..............................19°25'N 102°04'W
Urubamba r. Peru 72 B5............................10°46'S 73°47'W
Uruguaiana Brazil 73 D4...........................29°45'S 57°03'W
Uruguay r. Argentina/Brazil/Uruguay 73 D4
....33°52'S 58°25'W
Uruguay S. America 73 D3........................32°45'S 55°56'W
Ürümqi China 98 F6...................................43°44'N 87°34'E
Urziceni Romania 50 G7...........................44°43'N 26°37'E
Usa r. Russia 52 F4....................................66°00'N 57°36'E
Uşak Turkey 51 H4.....................................38°40'N 29°24'E
Ushuaia Argentina 73 C1..........................54°46'S 68°19'W
Usinsk Russia 52 F4...................................66°01'N 57°36'E
Usk Wales 10 D3...51°42'N 2°54'W
Usk r. Wales 10 E3......................................51°34'N 2°59'W
Usk Reservoir Wales 10 D3.......................51°56'N 3°44'W
Usogorsk Russia 52 E4...............................63°26'N 48°41'E
Usol'ye-Sibirskoye Russia 55 L3.............52°40'N 103°30'E
Ussuriysk Russia 55 O2..............................43°48'N 131°57'E
Ust'-Ilimsk Russia 55 L3............................58°02'N 102°42'E
Ust'-Ilych Russia 52 F4..............................62°33'N 56°43'E
Ústí nad Labem Czechia 46 F4................50°40'N 14°03'E
Ust'-Kamchatsk Russia 55 R3..................56°15'N 162°32'E
Ust'-Kamenogorsk Kazakhstan 54 J2.....49°52'N 82°46'E
Ust'-Kara Russia 52 G4..............................69°13'N 64°59'E
Ust'-Kulom Russia 52 F4...........................61°41'N 53°42'E
Ust'-Kut Russia 55 L3.................................56°45'N 105°42'E
Ust'-Maya Russia 55 O4.............................60°27'N 134°31'E
Ust'-Olenek Russia 55 M5.........................72°55'N 119°44'E
Ust'-Tsil'ma Russia 52 F4..........................65°26'N 52°10'E
Ustyurt Plateau f. Kazakhstan/Uzbekistan 53 F2
....43°29'N 56°11'E
Utah d. U.S.A. 62 D4.................................39°34'N 111°34'W
Utena Lithuania 47 K6..............................55°30'N 25°36'E
Utica U.S.A. 63 K5.....................................43°06'N 75°15'W
Utiel Spain 45 E3..39°34'N 1°12'W
Utqiagvik U.S.A. 60 C5.............................71°18'N 156°43'W
Utrecht Neth. 42 E5...................................52°05'N 5°07'E
Utrecht d. Neth. 42 E5..............................52°07'N 5°12'E
Utrera Spain 45 C2.....................................37°11'N 5°46'W
Utsunomiya Japan 104 C3........................36°34'N 139°54'E
Utta Russia 53 E2.......................................46°26'N 46°02'E
Uttaradit Thailand 102 C7.......................17°37'N 100°04'E
Uttarakhand d. India 96 E7.....................30°11'N 79°08'E
Uttar Pradesh d. India 96 E6...................27°37'N 79°17'E
Uttoxeter England 8 D3............................52°54'N 1°52'W
Uusikaupunki Finland 43 E3....................60°48'N 21°25'E
Uvs Nuur l. Mongolia 98 G8....................50°20'N 92°39'E
Uwajima Japan 104 B2..............................33°13'N 132°34'E
Uxbridge England 9 E2..............................51°33'N 0°29'W
Uyuni, Salar de f. Bolivia 73 C4..............20°13'S 67°36'W
Uzbekistan Asia 87 E4...............................40°00'N 60°00'E
Uzhhorod Ukraine 47 J3...........................48°37'N 22°17'E
Užice Serbia 50 C6......................................43°51'N 19°51'E
Uzlovaya Russia 53 D3...............................53°59'N 38°11'E
Uzunköprü Turkey 50 G5..........................41°15'N 26°41'E

V

Vaal r. S. Africa 83 B2.................................29°05'S 23°39'E
Vaasa Finland 43 E3...................................63°06'N 21°38'E
Vác Hungary 46 H2....................................47°47'N 19°09'E
Vadodara India 96 D5................................22°16'N 73°14'E
Vadsø Norway 43 G5..................................70°05'N 29°44'E
Vaduz Liechtenstein 46 C2.......................47°08'N 9°32'E
Værøy i. Norway 43 C4..............................67°39'N 12°36'E
Vaganski Vrh mt. Croatia 50 A7..............44°22'N 15°30'E
Váh r. Slovakia 46 H2.................................47°46'N 18°08'E
Vaiaku Tuvalu 109 G6...............................8°28'S 179°10'E
Vaitupu i. Tuvalu 109 G6..........................7°27'S 178°43'E
Valdai Hills Russia 34 H4..........................57°10'N 33°00'E
Valdepeñas Spain 45 D3............................38°46'N 3°22'W
Valdés, Península pen. Argentina 73 C2....42°35'S 63°25'W
Valdez U.S.A. 60 D4...................................61°07'N 146°16'W
Valdivia Chile 73 B3...................................39°50'S 73°13'W
Val-d'Or Canada 61 K2..............................48°06'N 77°47'W
Valdosta U.S.A. 63 J3.................................30°51'N 83°18'W
Valdres f. Norway 43 B3.............................60°55'N 9°07'E
Valence France 44 F4..................................44°56'N 4°54'E
Valencia Spain 45 E3..................................39°29'N 0°23'W
Valencia d. Spain 45 E3..............................39°17'N 0°57'W
Valencia, Golfo de g. Spain 45 F3............39°28'N 0°02'E
Valencia Venezuela 72 C8.........................10°10'N 67°59'W
Valencia de Alcántara Spain 45 B3.........39°25'N 7°14'W
Valenciennes France 44 E7........................50°21'N 3°32'E
Valer, Mont mt. France 44 D3.................42°48'N 1°05'E
Valinco, Golfe de g. France 44 H2...........41°40'N 8°50'E
Valjevo Serbia 50 C7..................................44°17'N 19°55'E
Valka Latvia 43 F2.....................................57°46'N 26°00'E
Valkeakoski Finland 43 F3........................61°15'N 24°03'E
Valkenswaard Neth. 42 E4........................51°21'N 5°27'E
Valladolid Spain 45 C4..............................41°39'N 4°43'W
Valle de la Pascua Venezuela 67 K2........9°10'N 65°57'W
Valledupar Colombia 72 B8......................10°30'N 73°16'W
Valletta Malta 48 F4..................................35°54'N 14°30'E
Valley Wales 10 C5.....................................53°17'N 4°34'W
Valparaíso Chile 73 B3...............................33°03'S 71°36'W

Vals, Tanjung c. Indonesia 103 J2 ....8°26'S 137°40'E
Vammala Finland 43 E3 ....61°20'N 22°56'E
Van Turkey 94 F7 ....38°30'N 43°22'E
Van, Lake Turkey 94 F7 ....38°37'N 42°47'E
Vanadzor Armenia 53 E2 ....40°49'N 44°28'E
Vancouver Canada 60 F2 ....49°16'N 123°08'W
Vancouver Island Canada 60 F2 ....49°28'N 125°39'W
Vänern l. Sweden 43 C2 ....59°05'N 13°36'E
Vänersborg Sweden 43 C2 ....58°23'N 12°20'E
Vangaindrano Madagascar 83 D2 ....23°22'S 47°34'E
Vanimo P.N.G. 103 K3 ....2°42'S 141°20'E
Vännäs Sweden 43 D3 ....63°55'N 19°46'E
Vannes France 44 B5 ....47°39'N 2°45'W
Vantaa Finland 43 F3 ....60°18'N 24°57'E
Vanua Levu i. Fiji 109 G5 ....16°10'S 179°40'E
Vanuatu S. Pacific Oc. 109 F5 ....16°05'S 167°04'E
Van Diemen Gulf Australia 103 I1 ....11°54'S 132°00'E
Varanasi India 96 F6 ....25°20'N 83°04'E
Varangerfjorden str. Norway 43 G5 ....70°04'N 29°07'E
Varaždin Croatia 46 G2 ....46°19'N 16°22'E
Varberg Sweden 43 C2 ....57°07'N 12°16'E
Vardar r. Macedonia 50 E5 ....41°07'N 22°32'E
Varėna Lithuania 47 K6 ....54°13'N 24°35'E
Varese Italy 46 C1 ....45°49'N 8°50'E
Varkaus Finland 43 F3 ....62°19'N 27°54'E
Varna Bulgaria 51 G6 ....43°12'N 27°54'E
Varnamo Sweden 43 C2 ....57°11'N 14°03'E
Várpalota Hungary 46 H2 ....47°12'N 18°08'E
Västerås Sweden 43 D2 ....59°37'N 16°33'E
Västervik Sweden 43 D2 ....57°45'N 16°39'E
Vasyl'kiv Ukraine 47 N4 ....50°11'N 30°19'E
Vatersay i. Scotland 16 B1 ....56°56'N 7°38'W
Vatican City Europe 35 F3 ....41°54'N 12°27'E
Vatnajökull ice cap Iceland 43 Y2 ....64°28'N 16°37'W
Vättern l. Sweden 43 C2 ....58°05'N 14°21'E
Vava'u Group is Tonga 109 H5 ....18°24'S 174°21'W
Vawkavysk Belarus 47 K5 ....53°09'N 24°27'E
Växjö Sweden 43 C2 ....56°53'N 14°49'E
Vechte r. Germany 42 F5 ....52°37'N 6°43'E
Veendam Neth. 42 F6 ....53°06'N 6°53'E
Veenendaal Neth. 42 E5 ....52°01'N 5°33'E
Vega i. Norway 43 B4 ....65°39'N 11°53'E
Vejle Denmark 43 B1 ....55°43'N 9°32'E
Velen Germany 42 F4 ....51°53'N 6°59'E
Veles Macedonia 50 D5 ....41°42'N 21°47'E
Vélez-Málaga Spain 45 C2 ....36°47'N 4°06'W
Velhas r. Brazil 72 E5 ....17°13'S 44°49'W
Velika Morava canal Serbia 50 D7 ....44°43'N 21°03'E
Velikaya r. Russia 47 M7 ....57°50'N 28°15'E
Velikaya r. Russia 55 S4 ....64°32'N 176°06'E
Velikiye Luki Russia 52 D3 ....56°20'N 30°31'E
Velikiy Novgorod Russia 52 D3 ....58°33'N 31°16'E
Velikiy Ustyug Russia 52 E4 ....60°46'N 46°18'E
Veliko Tarnovo Bulgaria 50 F6 ....43°05'N 25°39'E
Velizh Russia 47 N6 ....55°36'N 31°12'E
Vellore India 96 E3 ....12°56'N 79°07'E
Vel'sk Russia 52 E4 ....61°03'N 42°05'E
Vendôme France 44 D5 ....47°48'N 1°04'E
Venezuela S. America 67 K2 ....7°35'N 66°30'W
Venezuela, Golfo de g. Venezuela 72 B8 ....11°32'N 71°03'W
Venice Italy 46 E1 ....45°26'N 12°20'E
Venice, Gulf of Europe 46 E1 ....45°19'N 12°43'E
Venray Neth. 42 E4 ....51°31'N 5°58'E
Venta r. Latvia/Lithuania 43 E2 ....56°24'N 22°14'E
Ventnor England 8 D1 ....50°36'N 1°12'W
Ventspils Latvia 43 E2 ....57°23'N 21°36'E
Vera Spain 45 E2 ....37°15'N 1°52'W
Veracruz Mexico 66 E4 ....19°11'N 96°09'W
Veracruz d. Mexico 66 E5 ....20°54'N 97°46'W
Vercelli Italy 46 C1 ....45°19'N 8°26'E
Verdalsøra Norway 43 B3 ....63°47'N 11°29'E
Verde r. Brazil 72 D5 ....21°10'S 51°58'W
Verde r. U.S.A. 62 D3 ....33°33'N 111°39'W
Verdun France 44 F6 ....49°10'N 5°24'E
Verín Spain 45 B4 ....41°56'N 7°25'W
Verkhnevilyuysk Russia 55 N4 ....63°26'N 120°12'E
Verkhoyansk Russia 55 O4 ....67°32'N 133°27'E
Verkhoyanskiy Khrebet mts Russia 55 N5 ....70°07'N 128°50'E
Vermont d. U.S.A. 63 L5 ....44°03'N 72°42'W
Veroia Greece 50 E5 ....40°32'N 22°13'E
Verona Italy 46 D1 ....45°26'N 10°59'E
Versailles France 44 E6 ....48°48'N 2°08'E
Vert, Cap c. Senegal 84 C3 ....14°44'N 17°31'W
Verviers Belgium 42 E3 ....50°35'N 5°52'E
Verwood England 8 D1 ....50°53'N 1°52'W
Veselaya, Gora mt. Russia 53 F3 ....54°34'N 57°59'E
Vesoul France 44 G5 ....47°38'N 6°09'E
Vesterålen is Norway 43 C5 ....68°43'N 13°59'E
Vestfjorden str. Norway 43 C4 ....67°40'N 13°54'E
Vestmannaeyjar is Iceland 43 X1 ....63°24'N 20°13'W
Vesturhorn hd Iceland 43 Z2 ....64°17'N 14°59'W
Vesuvius vol. Italy 48 F5 ....40°50'N 14°26'E
Veszprém Hungary 46 G2 ....47°06'N 17°54'E
Vetluga Russia 52 E3 ....57°52'N 45°48'E
Veurne Belgium 42 B4 ....51°04'N 2°40'E
Vézère r. France 44 D4 ....44°53'N 0°53'E
Vezirköprü Turkey 51 K5 ....41°09'N 35°28'E
Viana do Castelo Portugal 45 A4 ....41°42'N 8°49'W
Viborg Denmark 43 B2 ....56°27'N 9°24'E
Vic Spain 45 G4 ....41°56'N 2°15'E
Vicenza Italy 46 D1 ....45°33'N 11°33'E
Vichy France 44 E5 ....46°08'N 3°26'E
Victoria d. Australia 108 D3 ....36°56'S 144°52'E
Victoria r. Australia 108 C5 ....15°23'S 130°17'E
Victoria Canada 60 F2 ....48°25'N 123°22'W
Victoria Seychelles 79 E2 ....4°38'S 55°28'E
Victoria, Lake Africa 83 C4 ....0°59'S 32°51'E
Victoria, Mount Myanmar 97 H5 ....21°11'N 93°56'E
Victoria, Mount P.N.G. 108 D6 ....8°49'S 147°30'E
Victoria Falls Zambia/Zimbabwe 83 B3 ....17°49'S 25°42'E
Victoria Island Canada 60 H5 ....70°42'N 106°38'W
Vidma Argentina 73 C2 ....40°50'S 63°00'W
Vidma, Lago l. Argentina 73 B2 ....49°35'S 72°49'W
Vienna Austria 46 G3 ....48°12'N 16°23'E
Vienne France 44 F4 ....45°31'N 4°53'E
Vienne r. France 44 D5 ....47°13'N 0°05'E
Vientiane Laos 102 C7 ....17°58'N 102°37'E
Vierzon France 44 E5 ....47°14'N 2°04'E
Vieste Italy 50 B5 ....41°53'N 16°11'E
Vietnam Asia 102 D7 ....19°20'N 104°48'E
Vignemale mt. France 44 C3 ....42°47'N 0°09'W
Vigo Spain 45 A5 ....42°14'N 8°43'W
Vijayapura India 96 E4 ....16°49'N 75°48'E
Vijayawada India 96 F4 ....16°33'N 80°39'E

Vík Iceland 43 Y1 ....63°26'N 19°02'W
Vikna i. Norway 43 B4 ....64°53'N 10°50'E
Vilagarcía Spain 45 A5 ....42°36'N 8°45'W
Vilaine r. France 44 B5 ....47°35'N 2°16'W
Vila Real Portugal 45 B4 ....41°18'N 7°44'W
Vilcabamba, Cordillera mts Peru 72 B5 ....12°30'S 73°27'W
Vilhelmina Sweden 43 D4 ....64°37'N 16°41'E
Vilhena Brazil 72 C5 ....12°42'S 60°07'W
Viljandi Estonia 43 F2 ....58°22'N 25°35'E
Vilkaviškis Lithuania 43 E1 ....54°39'N 23°03'E
Vil'kitskogo, Proliv str. Russia 55 K5 ....77°30'N 98°42'E
Villach Austria 46 E2 ....46°37'N 13°50'E
Villahermosa Mexico 66 F4 ....18°00'N 92°53'W
Villa Insurgentes Mexico 66 B6 ....25°16'N 111°47'W
Villarrobledo Spain 45 D3 ....39°16'N 2°36'W
Villavicencio Colombia 72 B7 ....4°07'N 73°36'W
Villefranche-sur-Saône France 44 F4 ....45°59'N 4°44'E
Villena Spain 45 E3 ....38°38'N 0°51'W
Villeneuve-sur-Lot France 44 D4 ....44°25'N 0°42'E
Villeurbanne France 44 F4 ....45°46'N 4°54'E
Vilnius Lithuania 43 F1 ....54°40'N 25°16'E
Vilvoorde Belgium 42 D3 ....50°55'N 4°27'E
Vilyuy r. Russia 55 N4 ....64°24'N 126°28'E
Vindelälven r. Sweden 43 D3 ....63°56'N 19°51'E
Vinh Vietnam 102 D7 ....18°38'N 105°42'E
Vinkovci Croatia 50 C7 ....45°17'N 18°49'E
Vinnytsya Ukraine 47 M3 ....49°14'N 28°30'E
Viranşehir Turkey 51 M3 ....37°13'N 39°47'E
Virden Canada 62 F6 ....49°51'N 100°56'W
Vire France 44 C6 ....48°50'N 0°53'W
Virginia d. U.S.A. 63 K4 ....37°47'N 78°19'W
Virgin Islands (U.K.) Central America 67 L4 ....18°37'N 64°37'W
Virgin Islands (U.S.A.) Central America 67 L4 ....18°14'N 64°53'W
Virovitica Croatia 50 B7 ....45°50'N 17°23'E
Virton Belgium 42 E2 ....49°34'N 5°33'E
Vis i. Croatia 50 B6 ....43°05'N 16°06'E
Visaginas Lithuania 47 L6 ....55°36'N 26°26'E
Visby Sweden 43 D2 ....57°38'N 18°18'E
Viscount Melville Sound str. Canada 60 G5 ....73°50'N 112°57'W
Viseu Portugal 45 B4 ....40°40'N 7°55'W
Vishakhapatnam India 96 F4 ....17°42'N 83°22'E
Viterbo Italy 48 F5 ....42°24'N 12°07'E
Viti Levu i. Fiji 109 G5 ....18°05'S 177°19'E
Vitim r. Russia 55 M3 ....59°26'N 112°35'E
Vitória Brazil 73 E4 ....20°19'S 40°21'W
Vitória da Conquista Brazil 72 E5 ....14°50'S 40°47'W
Vitoria-Gasteiz Spain 45 D5 ....42°51'N 2°39'W
Vitsyebsk Belarus 47 N6 ....55°12'N 30°10'E
Vittel France 44 F6 ....48°12'N 5°57'E
Vizianagaram India 96 F4 ....18°08'N 83°31'E
Vlaams-Brabant d. Belgium 42 D3 ....50°56'N 4°36'E
Vlaardingen Neth. 42 D4 ....51°54'N 4°21'E
Vlădeasa, Vârful mt. Romania 47 J2 ....46°45'N 22°50'E
Vladikavkaz Russia 53 E2 ....43°02'N 44°41'E
Vladimir Russia 52 E3 ....56°08'N 40°24'E
Vladivostok Russia 55 O2 ....43°07'N 131°56'E
Vlieland i. Neth. 42 D6 ....53°16'N 4°57'E
Vlissingen Neth. 42 C4 ....51°27'N 3°34'E
Vlorë Albania 50 C5 ....40°28'N 19°30'E
Vltava r. Czechia 46 F3 ....50°19'N 14°29'E
Voe Scotland 17 H5 ....60°21'N 1°16'W
Vohimena, Tanjona c. Madagascar 83 D2 ....25°36'S 45°12'E
Volda Norway 43 A3 ....62°08'N 6°05'E
Volga r. Russia 53 E2 ....45°47'N 47°34'E
Volga Uplands hills Russia 34 I4 ....53°15'N 45°45'E
Volgodonsk Russia 53 E2 ....47°32'N 42°08'E
Volgograd Russia 53 E2 ....48°44'N 44°30'E
Völklingen Germany 42 F2 ....49°15'N 6°51'E
Volodymyr-Volyns'kyy Ukraine 47 K4 ....50°51'N 24°20'E
Vologda Russia 52 D3 ....59°13'N 39°54'E
Volos Greece 50 E4 ....39°22'N 22°57'E
Vol'sk Russia 53 E3 ....52°02'N 47°22'E
Volta, Lake resr Ghana 84 D2 ....6°23'N 0°05'E
Volta Redonda Brazil 73 E4 ....22°30'S 44°07'W
Volzhskiy Russia 53 E2 ....53°24'N 50°05'E
Voreioi Sporades is Greece 50 E4 ....39°15'N 23°27'E
Vorkuta Russia 52 G4 ....67°29'N 64°05'E
Voronezh Russia 53 D3 ....51°38'N 39°12'E
Vorskla r. Russia 47 P3 ....48°55'N 34°08'E
Vosges mts France 44 G5 ....47°46'N 6°41'E
Voss Norway 43 A3 ....60°38'N 6°27'E
Vostochnyy Sayan mts Russia 55 K3 ....54°43'N 94°48'E
Votkinsk Russia 52 F3 ....57°03'N 53°58'E
Vouziers France 42 D2 ....49°24'N 4°42'E
Voznesens'k Ukraine 47 N2 ....47°33'N 31°21'E
Vranje Serbia 50 D6 ....42°33'N 21°54'E
Vratsa Bulgaria 50 E6 ....43°12'N 23°33'E
Vrbas r. Bos. and Herz. 50 B7 ....45°07'N 17°31'E
Vršac Serbia 50 D7 ....45°07'N 21°17'E
Vuktyl Russia 52 F4 ....63°52'N 57°19'E
Vung Tau Vietnam 102 D6 ....10°22'N 107°05'E
Vuollerim Sweden 43 E4 ....66°26'N 20°37'E
Vyaz'ma Russia 47 P6 ....55°13'N 34°18'E
Vyborg Russia 43 G3 ....60°42'N 28°46'E
Vychegda r. Russia 52 D4 ....64°40'N 35°00'E
Vygozero, Ozero l. Russia 52 D4 ....63°31'N 34°33'E
Vyrnwy, Lake Wales 10 D4 ....52°46'N 3°29'W
Vyshniy-Volochek Russia 52 D3 ....57°35'N 34°33'E
Vytegra Russia 52 D4 ....61°00'N 36°26'E

W

Wa Ghana 84 D3 ....10°04'N 2°30'W
Wabasca r. Canada 60 G3 ....58°18'N 115°23'W
Wabash r. U.S.A. 63 I4 ....37°50'N 88°01'W
Wabush Canada 61 L3 ....52°55'N 66°49'W
Waco U.S.A. 62 G3 ....31°34'N 97°08'W
Wad Pakistan 96 C6 ....27°20'N 66°30'E
Waddān Libya 84 F4 ....29°09'N 16°09'E
Waddenzee str. Neth. 42 D5 ....52°51'N 4°51'E
Waddington England 13 G2 ....53°10'N 0°32'W
Waddington, Mount Canada 60 F3 ....51°21'N 125°18'W
Wadebridge England 11 C2 ....50°31'N 4°50'W
Wadhurst England 9 F2 ....51°04'N 0°20'E
Wadi Halfa Sudan 85 H4 ....21°48'N 31°20'E
Wad Madani Sudan 85 H3 ....14°22'N 33°30'E
Wagga Wagga Australia 108 D3 ....35°08'S 147°23'E
Wāḥāt Jālū Libya 85 G4 ....29°14'N 21°04'E
Wahpeton U.S.A. 62 G6 ....46°15'N 96°50'W
Waigeo i. Indonesia 103 I3 ....0°11'S 130°59'E
Wainfleet All Saints England 13 H2 ....53°06'N 0°14'E

Waingapu Indonesia 102 G2 ....9°38'S 120°15'E
Waini Point Guyana 72 D7 ....8°22'N 59°44'W
Wainwright U.S.A. 60 C5 ....70°39'N 159°51'W
Wakasa-wan b. Japan 104 C3 ....35°45'N 135°36'E
Wakayama Japan 104 C2 ....34°13'N 135°10'E
Wakefield England 13 F2 ....53°41'N 1°30'W
Wakkanai Japan 104 D5 ....45°24'N 141°40'E
Wałbrzych Poland 46 G4 ....50°46'N 16°18'E
Wałcz Poland 46 G5 ....53°17'N 16°29'E
Wales d. U.K. 21 D3 ....52°04'N 3°41'W
Wallasey England 12 D2 ....53°26'N 3°04'W
Wallingford England 8 D2 ....51°36'N 1°08'W
Wallis and Futuna is S. Pacific Oc. 109 H5 ....13°24'S 177°57'W
Walls Scotland 17 H5 ....60°14'N 1°33'W
Walney, Isle of i. England 12 D3 ....54°04'N 3°16'W
Walsall England 8 D3 ....52°35'N 1°59'W
Waltham on the Wolds England 8 E3 ....52°49'N 0°49'W
Walton-on-Thames England 9 E2 ....51°23'N 0°25'W
Walvis Bay town Namibia 83 A2 ....22°58'S 14°30'E
Wandsworth England 9 E2 ....51°27'N 0°12'W
Wantage England 8 D2 ....51°35'N 1°25'W
Wanzhou China 99 J4 ....30°47'N 108°22'E
Warangal India 96 E4 ....17°59'N 79°35'E
Warboys England 9 E3 ....52°24'N 0°05'W
Warburton watercourse Australia 108 C4 ....27°54'S 137°19'E
Ward Hill Scotland 17 F3 ....58°54'N 3°22'W
Ward's Stone hill England 12 E3 ....54°02'N 2°38'W
Wareham England 8 C1 ....50°41'N 2°07'W
Waremme Belgium 42 E3 ....50°42'N 5°15'E
Warminster England 8 C2 ....51°12'N 2°11'W
Warrego r. Australia 108 D3 ....30°24'S 145°21'E
Warrenpoint Northern Ireland 14 C2 ....54°06'N 6°15'W
Warri Nigeria 84 E2 ....5°35'N 5°45'E
Warrington England 12 E2 ....53°23'N 2°36'W
Warrington d. England 21 D3 ....53°24'N 2°33'W
Warsaw Poland 46 I5 ....52°15'N 21°01'E
Warta r. Poland 46 F5 ....52°35'N 14°37'E
Warwick England 8 D3 ....52°17'N 1°35'W
Warwickshire d. England 21 E3 ....52°19'N 1°32'W
Washington England 13 F3 ....54°54'N 1°31'W
Washington U.S.A. 63 K4 ....38°54'N 77°01'W
Washington d. U.S.A. 62 B6 ....47°36'N 120°19'W
Washington, Mount U.S.A. 63 L5 ....44°18'N 71°18'W
Waskaganish Canada 61 K3 ....51°28'N 78°46'W
Wast Water l. England 12 D3 ....54°26'N 3°18'W
Watampone Indonesia 102 G3 ....4°31'S 120°21'E
Watchet England 11 D3 ....51°11'N 3°20'W
Waterford Ireland 18 D2 ....52°15'N 7°07'W
Waterford d. Ireland 18 D2 ....52°10'N 7°53'W
Watergate Bay England 11 B2 ....50°27'N 5°05'W
Waterlooville England 8 D1 ....50°53'N 1°02'W
Water of Saughs r. Scotland 17 G1 ....56°47'N 2°37'W
Watertown U.S.A. 62 G5 ....44°53'N 97°07'W
Watford England 9 E2 ....51°39'N 0°23'W
Watlington England 8 D2 ....51°39'N 1°01'W
Watson Lake town Canada 60 F4 ....60°05'N 128°42'W
Watten, Loch l. Scotland 17 F3 ....58°29'N 3°21'W
Watton England 9 F3 ....52°34'N 0°50'E
Wau South Sudan 85 G2 ....7°40'N 27°59'E
Wausau U.S.A. 63 I5 ....44°58'N 89°37'W
Waveney r. England 9 G3 ....52°29'N 1°41'E
Wear r. England 13 F3 ....54°54'N 1°22'W
Webi Shabeelle r. Somalia 85 I2 ....0°10'N 42°46'E
Wedmore England 8 C2 ....51°14'N 2°49'W
Weener Germany 42 G6 ....53°10'N 7°21'E
Weert Neth. 42 E4 ....51°15'N 5°43'E
Weifang China 99 L5 ....36°42'N 119°03'E
Weihai China 99 M5 ....37°30'N 122°07'E
Weinan China 99 J4 ....34°27'N 109°33'E
Weipa Australia 103 K1 ....12°37'S 141°55'E
Weldiya Ethiopia 85 H3 ....11°49'N 39°36'E
Welkom S. Africa 83 B2 ....27°59'S 26°44'E
Welland Canada 63 K5 ....52°52'N 0°03'E
Welland r. England 9 E3 ....52°52'N 0°03'E
Wellesley Islands Australia 108 C5 ....16°18'S 139°33'E
Wellingborough England 8 E3 ....52°18'N 0°42'W
Wellington New Zealand 109 G2 ....41°18'S 174°46'E
Wellington Som. England 11 D2 ....50°59'N 3°13'W
Wellington Tel. Wre. England 8 C3 ....52°42'N 2°31'W
Wells England 8 C2 ....51°13'N 2°39'W
Wells, Lake Australia 108 B4 ....26°40'S 123°16'E
Wells-next-the-Sea England 9 F3 ....52°57'N 0°51'E
Wels Austria 46 F3 ....48°10'N 14°01'E
Welshpool Wales 10 D4 ....52°40'N 3°09'W
Welwyn Garden City England 9 E2 ....51°48'N 0°12'W
Wem England 8 C3 ....52°51'N 2°44'W
Wembley England 9 E2 ....51°33'N 0°18'W
Wemyss Bay town Scotland 14 E3 ....55°53'N 4°53'W
Wenchi Ghana 84 D2 ....7°45'N 2°07'W
Wendo Ethiopia 85 H2 ....6°35'N 38°25'E
Wendover England 8 E2 ....51°46'N 0°44'W
Wenlock Edge f. England 8 C3 ....52°27'N 2°49'W
Wensleydale f. England 13 E3 ....54°09'N 2°02'W
Wensum r. England 9 G3 ....52°37'N 1°20'E
Wenzhou China 99 M3 ....27°59'N 120°41'E
Wesel Germany 42 F4 ....51°40'N 6°38'E
Weser r. Germany 46 C5 ....53°15'N 8°29'E
Wessel, Cape Australia 108 C5 ....11°03'S 136°46'E
Wessel Islands Australia 108 C5 ....11°19'S 136°26'E
West Australian Basin f. Indian Oc. 117 H2 ....17°42'S 102°36'E
West Bank Asia 49 K3 ....31°52'N 35°19'E
West Bengal d. India 96 G5 ....22°34'N 87°20'E
West Berkshire d. England 21 E2 ....51°28'N 1°20'W
West Bridgford England 8 D3 ....52°56'N 1°08'W
West Bromwich England 8 D3 ....52°31'N 1°59'W
Westbury England 8 C2 ....51°15'N 2°11'W
West Calder Scotland 15 F3 ....55°51'N 3°34'W
West Dunbartonshire d. Scotland 20 C4 ....55°59'N 4°31'W
Western Australia d. Australia 108 B4 ....24°24'S 121°53'E
Western Desert Egypt 49 I2 ....26°42'N 29°45'E
Western Dvina r. Europe 47 N6 ....55°28'N 30°54'E
Western Ghats mts India 96 D3 ....14°19'N 74°54'E
Western Sahara Africa 84 C4 ....22°14'N 15°05'W
Wester Ross f. Scotland 16 D2 ....57°39'N 5°20'W
Westerschelde est. Neth. 42 C4 ....51°27'N 3°25'E
West Falkland i. Falkland Is 73 C1 ....51°16'S 61°32'W
West Fen f. Cambs. England 9 F3 ....52°32'N 0°05'E
West Fen f. Lincs. England 13 G2 ....53°04'N 0°05'E
West Frisian Islands Neth. 42 D6 ....53°11'N 4°37'E
Westhill Scotland 17 G2 ....57°09'N 2°17'W
West Kirby England 12 D2 ....53°22'N 3°11'W
West Lavington England 8 D2 ....51°17'N 1°59'W
West Linton Scotland 15 F3 ....55°45'N 3°21'W
West Loch Roag b. Scotland 16 C3 ....58°15'N 6°57'W
West Lothian d. Scotland 20 D4 ....55°54'N 3°31'W

West Malling England 9 F2 ....51°18'N 0°25'E
Westmeath d. Ireland 18 D3 ....53°34'N 7°24'W
West Mersea England 9 F2 ....51°47'N 0°56'E
West Midlands d. England 21 E3 ....52°28'N 1°49'W
Weston-super-Mare England 8 C2 ....51°21'N 2°59'W
West Palm Beach town U.S.A. 63 J2 ....26°40'N 80°09'W
Westport Ireland 18 B3 ....53°48'N 9°31'W
Westray i. Scotland 17 F4 ....59°18'N 3°02'W
Westray Firth str. Scotland 17 F4 ....59°16'N 3°07'W
West Siberian Plain f. Russia 54 J4 ....62°39'N 80°21'E
West Sussex d. England 21 E2 ....51°00'N 0°18'W
West Virginia d. U.S.A. 63 J4 ....38°45'N 80°28'W
West-Vlaanderen d. Belgium 42 B3 ....50°59'N 2°56'E
Westward Ho! England 11 C3 ....51°02'N 4°14'W
West Yorkshire d. England 21 D3 ....53°46'N 2°04'W
Wetar i. Indonesia 103 H2 ....7°49'S 126°13'E
Wetherby England 13 F2 ....53°56'N 1°23'W
Wetzlar Germany 44 H7 ....50°34'N 8°30'E
Wexford Ireland 18 E2 ....52°20'N 6°28'W
Wexford d. Ireland 18 E2 ....52°37'N 6°32'W
Wexford Bay Ireland 18 E2 ....52°25'N 6°19'W
Weybridge England 9 E2 ....51°22'N 0°27'W
Weymouth England 8 C1 ....50°37'N 2°27'W
Whalsay i. Scotland 17 I5 ....60°21'N 0°57'W
Whangarei New Zealand 109 G3 ....35°43'S 174°19'E
Wharfe r. England 13 F2 ....53°50'N 1°08'W
Wheeler Peak Nev. U.S.A. 62 D4 ....38°57'N 114°17'W
Wheeler Peak N. M. U.S.A. 62 E4 ....36°33'N 105°24'W
Whernside hill England 13 E3 ....54°14'N 2°24'W
Whitburn Scotland 15 F3 ....55°52'N 3°41'W
Whitby England 13 G3 ....54°29'N 0°37'W
Whitchurch England 8 C3 ....52°58'N 2°41'W
Whitchurch Wales 11 D3 ....51°31'N 3°13'W
White r. U.S.A. 63 H3 ....33°59'N 91°09'W
White, Lake Australia 108 B4 ....21°03'S 129°07'E
Whitecourt Canada 60 G3 ....54°08'N 115°43'W
Whitehaven England 12 D3 ....54°33'N 3°35'W
Whitehead Northern Ireland 14 D2 ....54°45'N 5°42'W
Whitehill England 8 E2 ....51°06'N 0°52'W
Whitehorse Canada 60 E4 ....60°44'N 135°06'W
White Nile r. Sudan/South Sudan/Uganda 85 H3 ....15°38'N 32°30'E
White Sea Russia 52 D4 ....65°51'N 36°58'E
White Volta r. Burkina Faso/Ghana 84 D2 ....9°07'N 1°10'W
Whitfield England 9 G2 ....51°09'N 1°17'E
Whitland Wales 10 C3 ....51°49'N 4°37'W
Whitley Bay town England 13 F4 ....55°03'N 1°27'W
Whitney, Mount U.S.A. 62 C4 ....36°35'N 118°16'W
Whitsand Bay England 11 C2 ....50°20'N 4°20'W
Whitstable England 9 G2 ....51°22'N 1°01'E
Whittlesey England 9 E3 ....52°34'N 0°08'W
Whyalla Australia 108 C3 ....33°03'S 137°31'E
Wichita U.S.A. 62 G4 ....37°42'N 97°20'W
Wichita Falls town U.S.A. 62 G3 ....33°55'N 98°29'W
Wick Scotland 17 F3 ....58°26'N 3°06'W
Wick r. Scotland 17 F3 ....58°26'N 3°05'W
Wickford England 9 F2 ....51°37'N 0°31'E
Wickham England 8 D1 ....50°54'N 1°11'W
Wickham Market England 9 G3 ....52°09'N 1°22'E
Wicklow Ireland 18 E2 ....52°59'N 6°02'W
Wicklow d. Ireland 18 E3 ....53°02'N 6°27'W
Wicklow Head Ireland 18 E2 ....52°58'N 5°59'W
Wicklow Mountains Ireland 18 E3 ....52°53'N 6°34'W
Widecombe in the Moor England 11 D2 ....50°34'N 3°49'W
Wide Firth str. Scotland 17 F4 ....59°01'N 3°02'W
Widnes England 12 E2 ....53°21'N 2°44'W
Wieluń Poland 46 H4 ....51°13'N 18°34'E
Wiener Neustadt Austria 46 G2 ....47°49'N 16°15'E
Wiesbaden Germany 46 C4 ....50°05'N 8°14'E
Wiesmoor Germany 42 G6 ....53°25'N 7°45'E
Wigan England 12 E2 ....53°33'N 2°38'W
Wight, Isle of i. England 8 D1 ....50°39'N 1°07'W
Wigston England 8 D3 ....52°35'N 1°06'W
Wigton England 12 D3 ....54°50'N 3°10'W
Wigtown Scotland 14 E2 ....54°52'N 4°27'W
Wigtown Bay Scotland 14 E2 ....54°48'N 4°19'W
Wijchen Neth. 42 E4 ....51°48'N 5°43'E
Wildhorn mt. Switz. 46 B2 ....46°22'N 7°22'E
Wilhelm, Mount P.N.G. 108 D6 ....5°46'S 144°52'E
Wilhelmshaven Germany 46 C5 ....53°32'N 8°08'E
Willebroek Belgium 42 D4 ....51°04'N 4°22'E
William, Mount Australia 108 D3 ....37°19'S 142°35'E
Williams Lake town Canada 60 F3 ....52°08'N 122°09'W
Willingdon England 9 F1 ....50°48'N 0°15'E
Williston U.S.A. 62 F6 ....48°10'N 103°37'W
Williston Lake Canada 60 F3 ....55°51'N 123°43'W
Williton England 11 D3 ....51°09'N 3°19'W
Wills, Lake Australia 108 B4 ....21°20'S 128°37'E
Wilmington Del. U.S.A. 63 K4 ....39°43'N 75°38'W
Wilmington N. C. U.S.A. 63 K3 ....34°13'N 77°58'W
Wilmslow England 13 E2 ....53°20'N 2°14'W
Wilson's Promontory pen. Australia 108 D3 ....38°55'S 146°27'E
Wilton England 8 D2 ....51°05'N 1°52'W
Wiltshire d. England 21 E2 ....51°24'N 1°53'W
Wiltz Lux. 42 E2 ....49°58'N 5°56'E
Wimblington England 9 F3 ....52°31'N 0°05'E
Wimborne Minster England 8 D1 ....50°48'N 1°59'W
Wimereux France 9 G1 ....50°46'N 1°37'E
Wincanton England 8 C2 ....51°03'N 2°25'W
Winchester England 8 D2 ....51°04'N 1°19'W
Windermere England 12 E3 ....54°23'N 2°54'W
Windermere l. England 12 E3 ....54°18'N 2°57'W
Windhoek Namibia 83 A2 ....22°34'S 17°04'E
Windrush r. England 8 D2 ....51°43'N 1°25'W
Windsor Canada 63 J5 ....42°18'N 83°01'W
Windsor England 9 E2 ....51°29'N 0°37'W
Windsor and Maidenhead d. England 21 E2 ....51°28'N 0°40'W
Windward Islands Caribbean Sea 67 L4 ....15°42'N 60°03'W
Windward Passage str. Cuba/Haiti 67 J4 ....19°40'N 74°11'W
Wingate England 13 F3 ....54°44'N 1°23'W
Winisk r. Canada 61 J3 ....55°01'N 85°22'W
Winkleigh England 11 D2 ....50°51'N 3°56'W
Winnebago, Lake U.S.A. 63 I5 ....44°00'N 88°28'W
Winnemucca U.S.A. 62 C5 ....40°59'N 117°44'W
Winnipeg Canada 60 I2 ....49°53'N 97°10'W
Winnipeg, Lake Canada 60 I3 ....51°31'N 96°40'W
Winnipegosis, Lake Canada 60 H3 ....53°05'N 100°40'W
Winsford England 13 E2 ....53°12'N 2°31'W
Winslow England 8 E2 ....51°57'N 0°53'W
Winslow U.S.A. 62 D4 ....35°02'N 110°42'W
Winston-Salem U.S.A. 63 J4 ....36°07'N 80°17'W
Winterswijk Neth. 42 F4 ....51°58'N 6°42'E

Winterthur Switz. 46 C2................47°30'N 8°43'E
Winterton England 13 G2.........53°39'N 0°36'W
Wirksworth England 13 F2........53°05'N 1°34'W
Wirral pen. England 12 D2........53°22'N 3°07'W
Wisbech England 9 F3.............52°40'N 0°10'E
Wisconsin d. U.S.A. 63 I5........44°30'N 89°32'W
Wishaw Scotland 15 F3............55°46'N 3°55'W
Wismar Germany 46 D5............53°53'N 11°28'E
Witham England 9 F2..............51°48'N 0°38'E
Witham r. England 9 F3...........52°56'N 0°05'E
Witheridge England 11 D2.........50°55'N 3°42'W
Withernsea England 13 H2........53°44'N 0°02'E
Witney England 8 D2.............51°47'N 1°29'W
Wittenberge Germany 46 D5.......52°59'N 11°45'E
Wittlich Germany 42 F2...........49°59'N 6°53'E
Wittmund Germany 42 G6..........53°35'N 7°47'E
Wiveliscombe England 11 D3......51°03'N 3°19'W
Wivenhoe England 9 F2...........51°51'N 0°58'E
Wkra r. Poland 46 I5.............52°27'N 20°45'E
Władysławowo Poland 46 H6.......54°47'N 18°25'E
Włocławek Poland 46 H5..........52°39'N 19°05'E
Wokam i. Indonesia 103 I2.........5°45'S 134°31'E
Woking England 9 E2.............51°19'N 0°34'W
Wokingham England 8 E2.........51°25'N 0°50'W
Wokingham d. England 21 E2......51°24'N 0°53'W
Wolfsberg Austria 46 F2..........46°50'N 14°51'E
Wolfsburg Germany 46 D5.........52°25'N 10°48'E
Wollaston Lake Canada 60 H3.....58°16'N 103°22'W
Wollongong Australia 108 E3......34°25'S 150°51'E
Wolsingham England 13 F3........54°44'N 1°53'W
Wolvega Neth. 42 F5.............52°53'N 6°00'E
Wolverhampton England 8 C3.....52°35'N 2°08'W
Wombwell England 13 F2..........53°31'N 1°24'W
Wŏnsan N. Korea 99 N5...........39°09'N 127°27'E
Woodbridge England 9 G3........52°06'N 1°19'E
Woodcote England 8 D2...........51°32'N 1°04'W
Woodhall Spa England 13 G2......53°09'N 0°13'W
Woodlark Island P.N.G. 108 E6.....8°58'S 152°47'E
Woods, Lake of the Canada/U.S.A. 61 I2...49°22'N 94°50'W
Woodstock England 8 D2.........51°51'N 1°21'W
Wooler England 13 E4...........55°33'N 2°01'W
Worcester England 8 C3..........52°12'N 2°13'W
Worcester S. Africa 83 A1.........33°38'S 19°27'E
Worcester U.S.A. 63 L5...........42°16'N 71°48'W
Worcestershire d. England 21 D3...52°12'N 2°12'W
Wörgl Austria 46 E2.............47°29'N 12°05'E
Workington England 12 D3........54°39'N 3°32'W
Worksop England 13 F2...........53°19'N 1°07'W
Worms Germany 44 H6............49°38'N 8°21'E
Worms Head Wales 10 C3.........51°34'N 4°21'W
Worth England 9 E2..............51°07'N 0°09'W
Worthing England 9 E1...........50°49'N 0°22'W
Wowoni i. Indonesia 103 G3.......4°09'S 123°13'E
Wragby England 13 G2...........53°17'N 0°18'W
Wrangel Island Russia 55 T5......71°07'N 178°56'W
Wrangell U.S.A. 60 E3...........56°28'N 132°22'W
Wrangle England 13 H2..........53°02'N 0°07'E
Wrath, Cape Scotland 16 D3.......58°38'N 5°00'W
Wreake r. England 8 D3..........52°42'N 1°06'W
Wrexham Wales 10 E5............53°03'N 2°59'W
Wrexham d. Wales 21 D3.........53°01'N 2°59'W
Wrigley Canada 60 F4............63°12'N 123°24'W
Wrocław Poland 46 G4............51°06'N 17°02'E
Wuhai China 99 J5..............39°36'N 106°53'E
Wuhan China 99 K4..............30°37'N 114°18'E
Wuhu China 99 L4...............31°21'N 118°25'E
Wuppertal Germany 42 G4........51°16'N 7°09'E
Würzburg Germany 44 C3.........49°48'N 9°55'E
Wuvulu Island P.N.G. 103 K3.......1°43'S 142°50'E
Wuwei China 99 I5..............37°52'N 102°38'E
Wuxi China 99 M4..............31°31'N 120°18'E
Wuzhou China 99 K2.............23°28'N 111°22'E
Wye r. England 8 C2.............51°11'N 0°56'E
Wye r. Wales 10 E3.............51°37'N 2°40'W
Wylye r. England 8 D2...........51°04'N 1°48'W
Wymondham England 9 G3........52°34'N 1°07'E
Wyndham Australia 108 B5.......15°29'S 128°05'E
Wynyard Canada 62 F7...........51°46'N 104°12'W
Wyoming d. U.S.A. 62 E5.........42°57'N 107°30'W
Wythall England 8 D3...........52°23'N 1°53'W

X

Xai-Xai Mozambique 83 C2........25°02'S 33°41'E
Xankändi Azerbaijan 53 E2........39°49'N 46°46'E

Xanthi Greece 50 F5..............41°09'N 24°53'E
Xiamen China 99 L2.............24°29'N 118°11'E
Xi'an China 99 J4..............34°12'N 108°59'E
Xiangkhoang Laos 102 C7.........19°21'N 103°25'E
Xiangtan China 99 K3............27°52'N 112°47'E
Xiangyang China 99 K4...........32°03'N 112°07'E
Xichang China 99 I3.............27°55'N 102°11'E
Xigazê China 98 F3.............29°17'N 88°45'E
Xi Jiang r. China 99 K2.........22°23'N 113°20'E
Xilinhot China 99 L6............43°54'N 116°08'E
Xingtai China 99 K5............37°01'N 114°33'E
Xingu r. Brazil 72 D6............1°37'S 52°12'W
Xining China 99 I5..............36°35'N 101°40'E
Xinjiang Uygur Zizhiqu d. China 98 D6...40°15'N 78°50'E
Xintai China 99 L5.............35°55'N 117°45'E
Xinxiang China 99 K5............35°14'N 113°54'E
Xinyang China 99 K4............32°08'N 114°04'E
Xixón Spain 45 C5..............43°32'N 5°39'W
Xizang Zizhiqu d. China 98 F4.....31°26'N 88°12'E
Xun Jiang r. China 99 K2........23°27'N 111°25'E
Xuwen China 102 E8............20°18'N 110°09'E
Xuzhou China 99 L4............34°12'N 117°14'E

Y

Yablonovyy Khrebet mts Russia 55 L3...50°48'N 108°47'E
Yakima U.S.A. 62 B6.............46°36'N 120°29'W
Yakumo Japan 104 D4............42°15'N 140°15'E
Yaku-shima i. Japan 104 B2.......30°15'N 130°36'E
Yakutsk Russia 55 N4............61°59'N 129°40'E
Yala Thailand 102 C5.............6°32'N 101°17'E
Yalova Turkey 51 H5............40°39'N 29°17'E
Yalta Ukraine 51 K7............44°30'N 34°11'E
Yamagata Japan 104 D3..........38°15'N 140°20'E
Yamal Peninsula Russia 54 H5.....70°40'N 69°23'E
Yambol Bulgaria 50 G6..........42°29'N 26°30'E
Yamoussoukro Côte d'Ivoire 84 D2...6°48'N 5°15'W
Yamuna r. India 96 F6...........25°26'N 81°57'E
Yana r. Russia 55 O5............71°09'N 135°57'E
Yanbu' al Bahr Saudi Arabia 94 E4...24°05'N 38°06'E
Yancheng China 99 M4...........33°22'N 120°09'E
Yangon Myanmar 97 I4...........16°49'N 96°08'E
Yangquan China 99 K5...........37°52'N 113°33'E
Yangzhou China 99 L4...........32°23'N 119°25'E
Yanji China 99 N6.............42°54'N 129°31'E
Yanskiy Zaliv g. Russia 55 O5....71°55'N 135°13'E
Yantai China 99 M5............37°30'N 121°21'E
Yaoundé Cameroon 84 F2.........3°51'N 11°30'E
Yap i. Micronesia 103 J5.........9°30'N 138°12'E
Yapen i. Indonesia 103 J3........1°46'S 136°12'E
Yaqui r. Mexico 66 B6...........27°36'N 110°36'W
Yare r. England 9 G3............52°35'N 1°28'E
Yarm England 13 F3.............54°30'N 1°21'W
Yarmouth Canada 61 L2..........43°50'N 66°07'W
Yarmouth England 8 D1.........50°42'N 1°30'W
Yarono Russia 52 G4............68°11'N 69°23'E
Yaroslavl' Russia 52 D3.........57°37'N 39°53'E
Yartsevo Russia 47 O6...........55°04'N 32°41'E
Yasawa Group is Fiji 109 G5......16°56'S 177°18'E
Yasyel'da r. Belarus 47 L5.......52°08'N 26°27'E
Yatağan Turkey 51 H3...........37°20'N 28°09'E
Yate England 8 C2.............51°32'N 2°25'W
Yatton England 8 C2............51°23'N 2°49'W
Yavari r. Brazil/Peru 72 B6.......4°18'S 69°59'W
Yaví, Cerro mt. Venezuela 72 C7...5°32'N 65°58'W
Yawatahama Japan 104 B2........33°27'N 132°26'E
Yazd Iran 95 H6...............31°53'N 54°21'E
Yealmpton England 11 D2........50°21'N 3°59'W
Yekaterinburg Russia 52 G3......56°53'N 60°35'E
Yelets Russia 53 D3............52°36'N 38°29'E
Yell i. Scotland 17 H5..........60°35'N 1°06'W
Yellowknife Canada 60 G4.......62°29'N 114°19'W
Yellow Sea N. Pacific Oc. 99 N5...35°28'N 125°29'E
Yellowstone r. U.S.A. 62 F6......47°59'N 103°59'W
Yell Sound str. Scotland 17 H5....60°37'N 1°15'W
Yemen Asia 94 G2.............14°48'N 45°46'E
Yenisey r. Russia 55 J5..........70°22'N 82°59'E
Yeniseysk Russia 55 K3..........58°27'N 92°13'E
Yeovil England 8 C1............50°56'N 2°38'W
Yerevan Armenia 53 E2..........40°11'N 44°32'E
Yereymentau Kazakhstan 98 C8....51°36'N 73°08'E
Yershov Russia 53 E3...........51°20'N 48°18'E
Yeşilırmak r. Turkey 51 L5.......41°27'N 36°36'E
Yes Tor hill England 11 C2.......50°41'N 4°01'W
Yevpatoriya Ukraine 49 J6.......45°12'N 33°22'E

Yeysk Russia 53 D2............46°43'N 38°17'E
Yibin China 99 I3.............28°46'N 104°36'E
Yichang China 99 K4...........30°41'N 111°19'E
Yichun China 99 N7............47°37'N 128°52'E
Yinchuan China 99 J5...........38°26'N 106°18'E
Yingkou China 99 M6...........40°40'N 122°15'E
Yining China 98 E6............43°54'N 81°22'E
Yiyang China 99 K3............28°37'N 112°16'E
Yli-Kitka l. Finland 43 G4.......66°10'N 28°46'E
Ylitornio Finland 43 E4.........66°20'N 23°41'E
Y Llethr hill Wales 10 D4........52°49'N 3°59'W
Ylöjärvi Finland 43 E3..........61°34'N 23°36'E
Yogyakarta Indonesia 102 E2......7°47'S 110°23'E
Yokohama Japan 104 C3.........35°26'N 139°37'E
Yongzhou China 99 K3..........26°25'N 111°35'E
Yonne r. France 44 E6..........48°23'N 2°58'E
York England 13 F2............53°58'N 1°05'W
York d. England 21 E3..........53°57'N 1°04'W
York, Cape Australia 108 D5......10°41'S 142°36'E
York, Cape Canada 61 J5........73°47'N 87°15'W
York, Vale of f. England 13 F3....54°13'N 1°32'W
Yorkshire Wolds hills England 13 G2...53°53'N 0°35'W
Yorkton Canada 60 H3..........51°12'N 102°27'W
Yoshkar-Ola Russia 52 E3.......56°38'N 47°54'E
Youghal Ireland 18 D1..........51°58'N 7°51'W
Yozgat Turkey 51 K4...........39°49'N 34°47'E
Ygrgyz Kazakhstan 54 H2........48°36'N 61°18'E
Yser r. France 9 H1............50°54'N 2°37'E
Ystad Sweden 43 C1............55°26'N 13°49'E
Ystalyfera Wales 10 D3.........51°46'N 3°47'W
Ystwyth r. Wales 10 C4.........52°24'N 4°05'W
Ysyk-Köl l. Kyrgyzstan 98 D6.....42°25'N 77°12'E
Ythan r. Scotland 17 G2.........57°22'N 1°57'W
Yūbari Japan 104 D4............43°04'N 141°59'E
Yucatán d. Mexico 66 G5........20°35'N 89°05'W
Yucatán pen. Mexico 66 F4.......19°17'N 90°15'W
Yucatan Channel Cuba/Mexico 67 G5...22°16'N 86°46'W
Yueyang China 99 K3...........29°23'N 113°07'E
Yukon d. Canada 60 E4..........63°23'N 135°52'W
Yukon r. Canada/U.S.A. 60 B4.....62°44'N 164°41'W
Yulin China 99 K2.............22°37'N 110°12'E
Yuma U.S.A. 62 D3.............32°43'N 114°38'W
Yunak Turkey 51 I4............38°48'N 31°44'E
Yungas f. Bolivia 72 C5.........16°51'S 65°20'W
Yunnan d. China 99 I2..........24°45'N 101°07'E
Yushu China 98 H4.............32°59'N 96°59'E
Yuxi China 99 I2..............24°20'N 102°33'E
Yuzhno-Kuril'sk Russia 104 E4....44°04'N 145°49'E
Yuzhno-Sakhalinsk Russia 55 P2...46°57'N 142°39'E
Yuzhnoukrayinsk Ukraine 47 N2...47°50'N 31°11'E
Yuzhnyy, Ostrov i. Russia 54 G5...72°00'N 54°00'E

Z

Zaandam Neth. 42 D5............52°26'N 4°51'E
Zabīd Yemen 94 F2.............14°11'N 43°15'E
Zacatecas Mexico 66 D5..........22°46'N 102°38'W
Zacatecas d. Mexico 66 D5........23°56'N 102°42'W
Zadar Croatia 50 A7............44°07'N 15°14'E
Zafra Spain 45 B3.............38°26'N 6°25'W
Zagreb Croatia 50 A7...........45°48'N 15°58'E
Zagros Mountains Iran 95 G6......34°02'N 47°10'E
Zāhedān Iran 95 J6............29°30'N 60°52'E
Zahlé Lebanon 49 K3...........33°50'N 35°55'E
Zaječar Serbia 50 E6...........43°54'N 22°16'E
Zākhū/Zaxo Iraq 94 F7..........37°08'N 42°42'E
Zakynthos Greece 50 D3.........37°47'N 20°54'E
Zakynthos i. Greece 50 D3.......37°45'N 20°42'E
Zalaegerszeg Hungary 46 G2......46°51'N 16°53'E
Zalău Romania 47 J2...........47°11'N 23°04'E
Zambezi r. Africa 83 C3.........15°41'S 30°25'E
Zambia Africa 83 B3...........14°13'S 27°30'E
Zamboanga Phil. 103 G5.........6°56'N 122°05'E
Zamora Spain 45 C4............41°31'N 5°44'W
Zamość Poland 47 J4...........50°43'N 23°16'E
Zanjān Iran 95 G7.............36°40'N 48°27'E
Zanzibar Tanzania 83 C4.........6°08'S 39°14'E
Zanzibar Island Tanzania 83 C4....6°17'S 39°32'E
Zaoyang China 99 K4...........32°10'N 112°46'E
Zaozhuang China 99 L4..........34°52'N 117°34'E
Zapadnaya Dvina Russia 47 O7....56°16'N 32°06'E
Zapadnyy Sayan f. Russia 55 J3...51°41'N 88°08'E
Zapolyarnyy Russia 43 G5.......69°26'N 30°50'E
Zaporizhzhya Ukraine 47 P2......47°50'N 35°10'E

Zara Turkey 51 L4.............39°54'N 37°45'E
Zaragoza Spain 45 E4...........41°40'N 0°51'W
Zarand Iran 95 I6.............30°49'N 56°34'E
Zaraza Venezuela 67 K2..........9°21'N 65°18'W
Zaria Nigeria 84 E3............11°07'N 7°43'E
Zarzis Tunisia 48 F3...........33°30'N 11°05'E
Zawiercie Poland 46 H4.........50°29'N 19°26'E
Zawilah Libya 48 G2...........26°08'N 15°08'E
Zaysan Kazakhstan 98 E7.........47°27'N 84°55'E
Zaysan, Lake Kazakhstan 54 J2....48°05'N 83°34'E
Zealand i. Denmark 43 B1........55°23'N 11°42'E
Zeebrugge Belgium 42 C4........51°20'N 3°16'E
Zeeland d. Neth. 42 C4.........51°31'N 3°49'E
Zeil, Mount Australia 108 C4.....23°24'S 132°24'E
Zelenodol'sk Russia 52 E3.......55°49'N 48°32'E
Zelenograd Russia 47 Q7........56°00'N 37°12'E
Zémio C.A.R. 85 G2............5°00'N 25°05'E
Zenica Bos. and Herz. 50 B7......44°11'N 17°55'E
Zerah, Gowd-e f. Afgh. 95 J5......29°50'N 62°27'E
Zeya Russia 55 N3............53°47'N 126°54'E
Zêzere r. Portugal 45 A3........39°28'N 8°20'W
Zgierz Poland 46 H4...........51°51'N 19°24'E
Zhalpaktal Kazakhstan 53 E2......49°40'N 49°28'E
Zhambyl Kazakhstan 98 C6........42°50'N 71°25'E
Zhanaozen Kazakhstan 53 F2......43°18'N 52°53'E
Zhangjiakou China 99 K6........40°41'N 114°55'E
Zhangping China 99 L3..........25°21'N 117°28'E
Zhangshu China 99 L3..........28°04'N 115°30'E
Zhanjiang China 99 K2..........21°10'N 110°22'E
Zhaotong China 99 I3...........27°22'N 103°41'E
Zhashkiv Ukraine 47 N3.........49°15'N 30°08'E
Zhejiang d. China 99 M3.........29°21'N 120°06'E
Zheleznogorsk Russia 47 P5......52°19'N 35°23'E
Zhengzhou China 99 K4..........34°41'N 113°41'E
Zhenjiang China 99 L4..........32°10'N 119°25'E
Zheshart Russia 52 E4..........62°04'N 49°34'E
Zhezkazgan Kazakhstan 54 H2.....47°45'N 67°44'E
Zhitikara Kazakhstan 53 G3.......52°08'N 62°09'E
Zhlobin Belarus 47 N5..........52°54'N 30°02'E
Zhmerynka Ukraine 47 M3........49°03'N 28°06'E
Zhob Pakistan 95 K6...........31°21'N 69°32'E
Zhongshan China 99 K2.........22°31'N 113°26'E
Zhotvi Vody Ukraine 47 O3.......48°21'N 33°30'E
Zhukovskiy Russia 47 R6.........55°35'N 38°08'E
Zhuzhou China 99 K3...........27°49'N 113°07'E
Zhytkavichy Belarus 47 L5.......52°13'N 27°52'E
Zhytomyr Ukraine 47 M4........50°15'N 28°40'E
Zibo China 99 L5.............36°47'N 118°06'E
Zielona Góra Poland 46 F4.......51°57'N 15°30'E
Zighan Libya 49 H2...........25°27'N 22°07'E
Zigong China 99 I3............29°24'N 104°49'E
Žilina Slovakia 46 H3..........49°14'N 18°44'E
Zillah Libya 49 G2............28°32'N 17°33'E
Zima Russia 99 I8............53°54'N 101°59'E
Zimbabwe Africa 83 B3.........22°06'S 30°59'E
Zimmi Sierra Leone 84 C2........7°16'N 11°17'W
Zimnicea Romania 50 F6.........43°40'N 25°22'E
Zinder Niger 84 E3............13°48'N 8°59'E
Zlatoust Russia 52 F3..........55°10'N 59°35'E
Zlín Czechia 46 G3............49°13'N 17°41'E
Zmiyevka Russia 47 Q5..........52°40'N 36°23'E
Znam"yanka Ukraine 47 O3.......48°43'N 32°41'E
Znojmo Czechia 46 G3..........48°51'N 16°04'E
Zolochiv Ukraine 47 K3.........49°48'N 24°54'E
Zolotonosha Ukraine 47 O3.......49°42'N 32°02'E
Zonguldak Turkey 51 I5.........41°27'N 31°46'E
Zouar Chad 85 F4.............20°27'N 16°35'E
Zouérat Mauritania 84 C4........22°46'N 12°29'W
Zrenjanin Serbia 50 D7.........45°23'N 20°25'E
Zugdidi Georgia 53 E2..........42°30'N 41°52'E
Zugspitze mt. Austria/Germany 46 D2...47°26'N 10°59'E
Zuid-Holland d. Neth. 42 D4......51°57'N 4°28'E
Zújar r. Spain 45 C3...........39°01'N 5°46'W
Zülpich Germany 42 F3..........50°41'N 6°40'E
Zunyi China 99 J3.............27°40'N 106°54'E
Zürich Switz. 46 C2...........47°23'N 8°32'E
Zutphen Neth. 42 F5...........52°09'N 6°12'E
Zuwārah Libya 48 F3...........32°56'N 12°05'E
Zvolen Slovakia 46 H3..........48°35'N 19°08'E
Zvornik Bos. and Herz. 50 C7.....44°24'N 19°07'E
Zwickau Germany 46 E4.........50°43'N 12°30'E
Zwolle Neth. 42 F5............52°30'N 6°06'E
Zyryanovsk Kazakhstan 98 E7.....49°46'N 84°21'E